ITALIAN-ENGLISH
ENGLISH-
THE IDEAL COM
ALL LEARNERS OF ITALIAN

ITALIAN

453 BBC

067009

WITHDRAWN

067009

LEARNER'S DICTIONARY

#53

poordo

© Larousse-Bordas, 1997

ISBN 0-563-40084-6

Published by BBC Books, a division of BBC Worldwide Ltd,
Woodlands, 80 Wood Lane, London W12 0TT
First published 1997

Printed and bound in Great Britain by Mackays of Chatham
Cover printed by Belmont Press Ltd, Northampton

Introduction

The BBC *Italian Learner's Dictionary* is the result of a collaboration between the BBC and the Larousse Language Reference team. It is aimed at all learners of Italian and can be used either independently or alongside the BBC's best-selling *Italianissimo* course.

Containing over 42,000 translations, the dictionary provides thorough coverage of everyday Italian and detailed coverage of GCSE word lists. There are also handy cultural notes throughout, giving a useful insight into the country and its language and traditions.

Whether you are reading, writing, listening or speaking, the dictionary makes communication simpler as each word is clearly divided, where appropriate, into its different meanings and parts of speech, while there is essential guidance on Italian pronunciation.

Up-to-date and easy to use, this dictionary is the ideal companion for all learners, whether at school, at home or travelling abroad.

Abbreviations

abbreviation	*abbr*
adjective	*adj*
adverb	*adv*
adjective	*agg*
American English	Am
anatomy	ANAT
article	*art*
auxiliary	*aus*
automobile, cars	AUT(O)
auxiliary	*aux*
adverb	*avv*
British English	Br
commerce, business	COMM
comparative	*compar*
computers	COMPUT
conjunction	*conj/cong*
continuous	*cont*
culinary, cooking	CULIN
before	*dav*

– *dav* s indicates that the translation is always used directly before the noun which it modifies

juridical, legal	DIR
exclamation	*excl/esclam*
feminine	*f*
informal	*fam*
figurative	*fig*
finance, financial	FIN
formal	*fml/form*
inseparable	*fus*

– shows that a phrasal verb is 'fused', i.e. inseparable, e.g. **look after** where the object cannot come between the verb and the particle, e.g. I *looked after him* but not *I *looked him after*

generally	*gen*
geography	GEOG
gerund	*ger*
grammar	GRAMM
informal	*inf*
computers	INFORM
interrogative	*interr*
invariable	*inv*

Abbreviazioni

abbreviazione
aggettivo
avverbio
aggettivo
inglese americano
anatomia
articolo
ausiliare
automobile
ausiliare
avverbio
inglese britannico
commercio
comparativo
informatica
congiunzione
forma progressiva
cucina, culinaria
davanti a

– *dav* s indica che la traduzione viene sempre usata davanti al sostantivo del quale è attributo

diritto
esclamazione
femminile
familiare
figurato
finanza
formale
non separabile

– indica che un 'phrasal verb' (verbo + preposizione o avverbio) non può essere separato dalla sua particella. Ad esempio, con **look after**, il complemento oggetto non può essere frapposto al verbo e alla preposizione; si dice cioè I *looked after him* ma non si può dire *I *looked him after*

generalmente
geografia
gerundio
grammatica
familiare
informatica
interrogativo
invariabile

juridical, legal	JUR	diritto
masculine	*m*	maschile
mathematics	MAT(H)	matematica
medicine	MED	medicina
military	MIL	militare
music	MUS	musica
noun	*n*	sostantivo
nautical, maritime	NAUT	nautica
numeral	*num*	numerale
oneself	*o.s.*	
pejorative	*pej*	spregiativo
plural	*pl*	plurale
politics	POL	politica
past participle	*pp*	participio passato
preposition	*prep*	preposizione
pronoun	*pron*	pronome
past tense	*pt*	passato
	qc	qualcosa
	qn	qualcuno
registered trademark	®	marchio registrato
religion	RELIG	religione
noun	*s*	sostantivo
someone, somebody	*sb*	
school	SCH/SCOL	scuola
Scottish English	*Scot*	scozzese
separable	*sep*	separabile
– shows that a phrasal verb is separable, e.g. **let in**, **help out** where the object can come between the verb and the particle, e.g. I *let her in, he helped me out*		– indica che un 'phrasal verb' (verbo + preposizione o avverbio) può essere separato dalla sua particella. Ad esempio **let in**, **help out**, per i quali il complemento oggetto si situa tra il verbo e la particella: I *let her in, he helped me out*
singular	*sg*	singolare
subject	*sog*	soggetto
pejorative	*spreg*	spregiativo
something	*sthg*	
subject	*subj*	soggetto
superlative	*superl*	superlativo
technology	TECH/TECNOL	tecnica, tecnologia
verb	*v/vb*	verbo
intransitive verb	*vi*	verbo intransitivo
impersonal verb	*v impers*	verbo impersonale
vulgar	*volg*	volgare
reflexive verb	*vr*	verbo riflessivo
transitive verb	*vt*	verbo transitivo
vulgar	*vulg*	volgare
cultural equivalent	≃	equivalenza culturale

English compounds

A compound is a word or expression which has a single meaning but is made up of more than one word, e.g. **point of view**, **kiss of life**, **virtual reality** and **West Indies**. It is a feature of this dictionary that English compounds appear in the A–Z list in strict alphabetical order. The compound **blood test** will therefore come after **bloodshot** which itself follows **blood pressure**.

Composti inglesi

In inglese si definiscono composti quelle espressioni che, pur essendo formate da più di una parola, costituiscono un'unica unità di significato, come ad es. **point of view**, **kiss of life**, **virtual reality** e **West Indies**. In questo dizionario i composti inglesi seguono l'ordine alfabetico generale. Il composto **blood test** figura perciò dopo **bloodshot** che, a sua volta, segue **blood pressure**.

Trademarks

Words considered to be trademarks have been designated in this dictionary by the symbol ®. However, neither the presence nor the absence of such designation should be regarded as affecting the legal status of any trademark.

Marchi registrati

Le parole considerate marchi registrati sono contrassegnate in questo dizionario con il simbolo ®. In ogni caso, né la presenza né l'assenza di tale simbolo implica alcuna valutazione del reale stato giuridico di un marchio.

Phonetic Transcription

English vowels

[ɪ] pit, big, rid
[e] pet, tend
[æ] pat, bag, mad
[ʌ] run, cut
[ɒ] pot, log
[ʊ] put, full
[ə] mother, suppose
[iː] bean, weed
[ɑː] barn, car, laugh
[ɔː] born, lawn
[uː] loop, loose
[ɜː] burn, learn, bird

English diphthongs

[eɪ] bay, late, great
[aɪ] buy, light, aisle
[ɔɪ] boy, foil
[əʊ] no, road, blow
[aʊ] now, shout, town
[ɪə] peer, fierce, idea
[eə] pair, bear, share
[ʊə] poor, sure, tour

Semi-vowels

you, spaniel   [j]
wet, why, twin   [w]

Consonants

pop, people	[p]	porta, sapore
bottle, bib	[b]	barca, libro
train, tip	[t]	torre, patata
dog, did	[d]	dare, odore
come, kitchen	[k]	cane, chiesa
gag, great	[g]	gara, ghiro
chain, wretched	[tʃ]	cena, ciao
jet, fridge	[dʒ]	gente, gioco
fib, physical	[f]	fine, afa
vine, livid	[v]	vero, ovvio
think, fifth	[θ]	
this, with	[ð]	
seal, peace	[s]	stella, casa
zip, his	[z]	sdraio, rosa
sheep, machine	[ʃ]	scimmia, ascia
usual, measure	[ʒ]	
how, perhaps	[h]	
metal, comb	[m]	mamma, amico
night, dinner	[n]	notte, anno
sung, parking	[ŋ]	
	[ɲ]	gnocchi, ogni

Trascrizione Fonetica

Vocali italiane

[a] pane, casa
[e] verde, entrare
[ɛ] letto, pezzo
[i] vino, isola
[o] monte, pozzo
[ɔ] corpo, sciocco
[u] una, cultura

Semivocali

ieri, viola
fuori, guasto

Consonanti

little, **help**	[l]	**l**ana, po**ll**o
	[ʎ]	**gli**, fi**gli**o
right, **carry**	[r]	**r**e, do**r**ato

The symbol ['] indicates that the following syllable carries primary stress and the symbol [ˌ] that the following syllable carries secondary stress.

I simboli ['] e [ˌ] indicano rispettivamente un accento primario e uno secondario nella sillaba seguente.

The symbol [ʳ] in English phonetics indicates that the final 'r' is pronounced only when followed by a word beginning with a vowel. Note that it is nearly always pronounced in American English.

Il simbolo [ʳ] nella trascrizione fonetica dell'inglese indica che la 'r' in fine di parola viene pronunciata soltanto se seguita da una parola che comincia per vocale. Da notare che nell'inglese americano la 'r' viene quasi sempre pronunciata.

The position of the tonic stress in Italian is indicated by a dot immediately beneath the accented vowel on Italian headwords (**camera**, **valigia**). No dot is given on those words which end in an accented vowel, as Italian spelling allows for a written accent in these cases (**città**, **perché**). Full phonetics have been provided for words of foreign origin which do not follow Italian pronunciation rules (**cracker** ['krɛker], **brioche** [bri'ɔʃ]).

L'accento nelle voci italiane è segnalato da un punto sotto la vocale accentata (**camera**, **valigia**), con l'eccezione delle parole con l'accento sull'ultima sillaba, per le quali l'ortografia italiana prevede l'accento grafico (**città**, **perché**). Le parole di origine straniera sono seguite dalla trascrizione fonetica nei casi in cui la pronuncia generalmente adottata non rispetta le regole fonetiche dell'italiano (**cracker** ['krɛker], **brioche** [bri'ɔʃ]).

Italian Verbs

Key: *pr ind* = present indicative, *imperf* = imperfect, *fut* = future, *cond* = conditional, *pr subj* = present subjunctive, *imperat* = imperative, *ger* = gerund, *pp* = past participle

AMARE: *pr ind* amo, ami, ama, amiamo, amate, amano, *imperf* amavo, amavi, amava, amavamo, amavate, amavano, *fut* amerò, amerai, amerà, ameremo, amerete, ameranno, *cond* amerei, ameresti, amerebbe, ameremmo, amereste, amerebbero, *pr subj* ami, ami, ami, amiamo, amiate, amino, *imperat* ama, ami, amate, *ger* amando, *pp* amato

andare: *pr ind* vado, vai, va, andiamo, andate, vanno, *fut* andrò, *cond* andrei, *pr subj* vada, vada, vada, andiamo, andiate, vadano, *imperat* va', vada, andate, *ger* andando, *pp* andato

aprire: *pr ind* apro, *pr subj* apra, *pp* aperto

avere: *pr ind* ho, hai, ha, abbiamo, avete, hanno, *imperf* avevo, *fut* avrò, *cond* avrei, *pr subj* abbia, *imperat* abbi, abbia, abbiate, *ger* avendo, *pp* avuto

bere: *pr ind* bevo, *imperf* bevevo, *fut* berrò, *cond* berrei, *pr subj* beva, *imperat* bevi, beva, bevete, *ger* bevendo, *pp* bevuto

cadere: *fut* cadrò

correre: *pp* corso

cuocere: *pr ind* cuocio, cuoci, cuoce, cociamo, cocete, cuociono, *pp* cotto

dare: *pr ind* do, dai, dà, diamo, date, danno, *fut* darò, *pr subj* dia, *imperat* da', dia, date

dire: *pr ind* dico, dici, dice, diciamo, dite, dicono, *imperf* dicevo, *fut* dirò, *pr subj* dica, dica, dica, diciamo, diciate, dicano, *imperat* di', dica, dite, *ger* dicendo, *pp* detto

dovere: *pr ind* devo, devi, deve, dobbiamo, dovete, devono, *fut* dovrò, *cond* dovrei, *pr subj* deva, deva, deva, dobbiamo, dobbiate, devano

essere: *pr ind* sono, sei, è, siamo, siete, sono, *imperf* ero, eri, era, eravamo, eravate, erano, *fut* sarò, *cond* sarei, *pr subj* sia, *imperat* sii, sia, siate, *ger* essendo, *pp* stato

fare: *pr ind* faccio, fai, fa, facciamo, fate, fanno, *imperf* facevo, *pr subj* faccia, *imperat* fai, faccia, fate, *ger* facendo, *pp* fatto

FINIRE: *pr ind* finisco, finisci, finisce, finiamo, finite, finiscono, *imperf* finivo, finivi, finiva, finivamo, finivate, finivano, *fut* finirò, finirai, finirà, finiremo, finirete, finiranno, *cond* finirei, finiresti, finirebbe, finiremmo, finireste, finirebbero, *pr subj* finisca, finisca, finisca, finiamo, finiate, finiscano, *imperat* finisci, finisca, finite, *ger* finendo, *pp* finito

giungere: *pp* giunto

leggere: *pp* letto

mettere: *pp* messo

morire: *pr ind* muoio, muori, muore, moriamo, morite, muoiono, *fut* morirò, *pr subj* muoia, *imperat* muori, muoia, morite, *pp* morto

muovere: *pp* mosso

nascere: *pp* nato

piacere: *pr ind* piaccio, piaci, piace, piacciamo, piacete, piacciono, *pr subj* piaccia, *pp* piaciuto

porre: *pr ind* pongo, poni, pone, poniamo, ponete, pongono, *imperf* ponevo, *fut* porrò, *cond* porrei, *pr subj* ponga, *imperat* poni, ponga, ponete, *ger* ponendo, *pp* posto

potere: *pr ind* posso, puoi, può, possiamo, potete, possono, *fut* potrò, *pr subj* possa

prendere: *pp* preso

ridurre: *pr ind* riduco, *imperf* riducevo, *fut* ridurrò, *pr subj* riduca, *ger* riducendo, *pp* ridotto

riempire: *pr ind* riempio, riempi, riempie, riempiamo, riempite, riempiono, *ger* riempiendo

rimanere: *pr ind* rimango, rimani, rimane, rimaniamo, rimanete, rimangono, *fut* rimarrò, *pr subj* rimanga, *pp* rimasto

rispondere: *pp* risposto

salire: *pr ind* salgo, sali, sale, saliamo, salite, salgono, *pr subj* salga

sapere: *pr ind* so, sai, sa, sappiamo, sapete, sanno, *fut* saprò, *pr subj* sappia, *imperat* sappi, sappia, sappiate

scegliere: *pr ind* scelgo, scegli, sceglie, scegliamo, scegliete, scelgono, *pr subj* scelga, *imperat* scegli, scelga, scegliete, *pp* scelto

sciogliere: *pr ind* sciolgo, sciogli, scioglie, sciogliamo, sciogliete, sciolgono, *pr subj* sciolga, *imperat* sciogli, sciolga, sciogliete, *pp* sciolto

scrivere: *pp* scritto

sedere: *pr ind* siedo, siedi, siede, sediamo, sedete, siedono, *pr subj* sieda

SERVIRE: *pr ind* servo, servi, serve, serviamo, servite, servono, *imperf* servivo, servivi, serviva, servivamo, servivate, servivano, *fut* servirò, servirai, servirà, serviremo, servirete, serviranno, *cond* servirei, serviresti, servirebbe, serviremmo, servireste, servirebbero, *pr subj* serva, serva, serva, serviamo, serviate, servano, *imperat* servi, serva, servite, *ger* servendo, *pp* servito

spegnere: *pr ind* spengo, spegni, spegne, spegniamo, spegnete, spengono, *pr subj* spenga, *pp* spento

stare: *pr ind* sto, stai, sta, stiamo, state, stanno, *fut* starò, *pr subj* stia, *imperat* sta, stia, state, *pp* stato

tacere: *pr ind* taccio, taci, tace, tacciamo, tacete, tacciono, *pr subj* taccia, *pp* taciuto

TEMERE: *pr ind* temo, temi, teme, temiamo, temete, temono, *imperf* temevo, temevi, temeva, temevamo, temevate, temevano, *fut* temerò, temerai, temerà, temeremo, temerete, temeranno, *cond* temerei, temeresti, temerebbe, temeremmo, temereste, temerebbero, *pr subj* tema, tema, tema, temiamo, temiate, temano, *imperat* temi, tema, temete, *ger* temendo, *pp* temuto

tenere: *pr ind* tengo, tieni, tiene, teniamo, tenete, tengono, *fut* terrò, *pr subj* tenga

togliere: *pr ind* tolgo, togli, toglie, togliamo, togliete, tolgono, *pr subj* tolga, *imperat* togli, tolga, togliete, *pp* tolto

trarre: *pr ind* traggo, trai, trae, traiamo, traete, traggono, *fut* trarrò, *pr subj* tragga, *imperat* trai, tragga, traete, *ger* traendo, *pp* tratto

uscire: *pr ind* esco, esci, esce, usciamo, uscite, escono, *pr subj* esca

vedere: *fut* vedrò, *pp* visto

venire: *pr ind* vengo, vieni, viene, veniamo, venite, vengono, *fut* verrò, *pr subj* venga, *pp* venuto

vivere: *pp* vissuto

volere: *pr ind* voglio, vuoi, vuole, vogliamo, volete, vogliono, *fut* vorrò, *cond* vorrei, *pr subj* voglia

Numbers

Cardinal numbers are used for counting. The most important ones are:

0 zero	15 quindici	30 trenta
1 uno (ƒ una)	16 sedici	40 quaranta
2 due	17 diciassette	50 cinquanta
3 tre	18 diciotto	60 sessanta
4 quattro	19 diciannove	70 settanta
5 cinque	20 venti	80 ottanta
6 sei	21 ventuno	90 novanta
7 sette	22 ventidue	100 cento
8 otto	23 ventitrè	101 centouno
9 nove	24 ventiquattro	102 centodue
10 dieci	25 venticinque	110 centodieci
11 undici	26 ventisei	200 duecento
12 dodici	27 ventisette	201 duecentouno
13 tredici	28 ventotto	300 trecento
14 quattordici	29 ventinove	900 novecento

1 000	mille	1 000 000		un milione
1 001	milleuno	2 000 000		due milioni
1 002	milledue	1 000 000 000		un miliardo
1 100	millecento	2 000 000 000		due miliardi
2 000	duemila			
10 000	diecimila			

NOTES:
- when **tre** is added to the end of another number it is written with an accent: **cinquantatrè**.
- the plural of **mille** is **mila**.
- before **uno** and **otto** the vowel at the end of **venti**, **trenta** etc. is dropped (**ventuno**, **sessantotto**), but before **mille** and **mila** the vowel at the end of the word is retained (**milleuno**).
- both **milione** and **miliardo** have a plural form (**milioni**, **miliardi**) which is used after a plural number: **quattro milioni**, **nove miliardi**. They are followed by **di** if used with another noun: **due milioni di disoccupati**, **tre miliardi di lire**.
- the numeral **uno** has several different forms: **un**, **una** and **un'**. These are used in just the same way as the indefinite article (see dictionary entry for **uno**).
- all other numbers, including **cento**, are invariable: **seicento abitanti**, **dieci settimane**.

Contrary to English usage, Italian uses a comma to mark the decimal part of a number: **6,5** (**sei virgola cinque** = 6 point 5). Numbers of four digits and above (**2.000**, **10.321**) are normally written with a full stop before the last three digits.

Ordinal numbers are used for putting things in order. From 1 to 10 they are:

1st	primo(a)	5th	quinto(a)	8th	ottavo(a)
2nd	secondo(a)	6th	sesto(a)	9th	nono(a)
3rd	terzo(a)	7th	settimo(a)	10th	decimo(a)
4th	quarto(a)				

From **undici** onwards, the final vowel of the cardinal number is dropped and the ending **-esimo** is added: **undici** → **undic-** → **undicesimo**, **cinquanta** → **cinquant-** → **cinquantesimo**.

The ordinal numbers behave like adjectives and always agree with the noun they precede: **la prima volta**, **il quarto uomo**.

For more information on numbers, look at the entries for **sei** and **sesto** on the Italian-English side of your dictionary, and at the entries for **six** and **sixth** on the English-Italian side.

Dates

The most usual ways of asking the date are: **che data è (oggi)?** or **quanti ne abbiamo oggi?** The reply will follow the pattern **è il cinque luglio** or **(ne abbiamo) cinque**.

Remember that the cardinal numbers are used in dates in Italian: **il dieci gennaio**, **il venticinque febbraio**. The first of the month is the exception to this rule: **il primo marzo**.

To say the year in Italian: 1997, for example, is **il millenovecentonovantasette**.

The days of the week are:

Monday	**lunedì**
Tuesday	**martedì**
Wednesday	**mercoledì**
Thursday	**giovedì**
Friday	**venerdì**
Saturday	**sabato**
Sunday	**domenica**

The months of the year are:

January	**gennaio**
February	**febbraio**
March	**marzo**
April	**aprile**
May	**maggio**
June	**giugno**
July	**luglio**
August	**agosto**
September	**settembre**
October	**ottobre**
November	**novembre**
December	**dicembre**

Note that the days of the week and the months of the year start with a small letter in Italian.

For more information on days and months, look at the entries for **sabato** and **settembre** on the Italian-English side of your dictionary, and at **Saturday** and **September** on the English-Italian side.

The Time

The most usual ways of asking the time are: **che ora è?** or **che ore sono?**
Here are some possible answers:

sono le cinque (del mattino/di sera)

sono le cinque e cinque

**sono le cinque e un quarto/
e quindici**

sono le cinque e mezza or
mezzo/e trenta

**sono le sei meno venticinque/
le cinque e trentacinque**

**sono le sei meno un quarto/
le cinque e quarantacinque**

è l'una (del pomeriggio/di notte)

è mezzogiorno (= midday)**/
è mezzanotte** (= midnight)

In Italian you may find times expressed using the 24-hour clock: **il treno
delle quattordici e venti**, for example, would leave at 2.20 p.m.

A

a (ad + vocale) prep **1.** (complemento di termine) to; **dare qc a qn** to give sthg to sb, to give sb sthg; **chiedere qc a qn** to ask sb sthg.
2. (stato in luogo) at; **abito a Torino** I live in Turin; **stiamo a casa** let's stay (at) home; **la piscina è a due chilometri da qui** the swimming pool is two kilometres from here.
3. (moto a luogo) to; **andiamo a letto** let's go to bed; **torno a Roma** I'm going back to Rome; **mi porti allo stadio?** can you take me to the stadium?
4. (temporale) at; **c'è un volo alle 8.30** there's a flight at 8.30; **a domani!** see you tomorrow!; **al mattino** in the morning; **alla sera** in the evening.
5. (modo, mezzo): **alla milanese** in the Milanese style, the Milanese way; **riscaldamento a gas** gas heating; **a piedi** on foot; **vestire alla moda** to dress fashionably; **scrivere a matita** to write in pencil.
6. (con prezzi) at; **comprare qc a metà prezzo** to buy sthg half-price.
7. (per caratteristica): **camicia a maniche corte** short-sleeved shirt; **finestra a doppi vetri** double-glazed window.
8. (per rapporto) per, a; **50 chilometri all'ora** 50 kilometres per o an hour; **pagato a ore** paid by the hour.

A abbr = **autostrada**.
abbacchio sm spring lamb; **~ alla romana** lamb cooked slowly with white wine or vinegar, rosemary, anchovies and garlic.
abbaglianti smpl: **accendere gli ~** to put one's headlights on full beam (Br) o high beam (Am).
abbagliare vt (accecare) to dazzle.
abbaiare vi to bark.
abbandonare vt (persona, luogo) to abandon, to leave; (ricerche) to abandon, to give up.
abbandono sm (di persona, luogo) neglect; (rinuncia) abandonment.
abbassare vt to lower; (volume, radio, tv) to turn down.
▶ **abbassarsi** vr (persona) to bend down; (livello) to drop; **abbassarsi a fare qc** to lower o.s. by doing sthg.
abbasso esclam: **~ la scuola!** down with school!
abbastanza avv (a sufficienza) enough; (piuttosto) rather, quite; **averne ~ di** to have had enough of.
abbattere vt (muro) to knock down; (albero) to cut down; (cavallo) to destroy; (aereo) to shoot down; (sconfiggere) to defeat.
▶ **abbattersi** vr to lose heart.
abbattuto, -a agg (depresso) depressed.
abbazia sf abbey.

abbeverare vt (animali) to water.
▶ **abbeverarsi** vr to drink.

abbia → **avere**.

abbiente agg well-off.

abbigliamento sm clothes (pl); ~ **donna** women's wear; ~ **sportivo** sportswear; ~ **uomo** menswear.

abbinare vt: ~ **qc (a qc)** to link sthg (to sthg).

abboccare vi to bite.

abboccato, -a agg sweetish.

abbonamento sm (a giornale) subscription; (a autobus, teatro) season ticket; **fare l'~ (a qc)** (a giornale) to take out a subscription (to sthg); (a autobus, teatro) to buy a season ticket (for sthg).

abbonarsi vr: ~ **(a qc)** (a autobus, teatro) to buy a season ticket (for sthg); (a giornale) to subscribe (to sthg).

abbonato, -a sm, f (a giornale) subscriber; (a autobus, teatro) season ticket holder; (a telefono) subscriber; (TV) licence holder.

abbondante agg abundant.

abbondanza sf abundance.

abbordabile agg (prezzo) reasonable.

abbottonare vt to button up.
▶ **abbottonarsi** vr: **abbottonarsi il cappotto** to button up one's coat.

abbottonatura sf buttons (pl).

abbozzare vt (disegno) to sketch; ~ **un sorriso** to smile faintly.

abbozzo sm sketch.

abbracciare vt to embrace, to hug; (fede) to embrace; (professione) to take up.
▶ **abbracciarsi** vr to embrace, to hug one another.

abbraccio sm embrace, hug.

abbreviare vt to shorten.

abbreviazione sf abbreviation.

abbronzante ◆ agg suntan (dav s) ◆ sm suntan cream.

abbronzare vt to tan.
▶ **abbronzarsi** vr to get a tan.

abbronzato, -a agg tanned.

abbronzatura sf suntan.

abbrustolire vt (pane) to toast; (caffè) to roast.

abdicare vi to abdicate.

abete sm fir tree.

abile agg (bravo) capable; (mossa, manovra) skilful; (idoneo): ~ **(a qc)** fit (for sthg).

abilità sf (bravura) ability; (astuzia) cleverness.

abilmente avv (con bravura) skilfully; (con astuzia) cleverly.

abisso sm abyss.

abitacolo sm (di auto) inside; (di aereo) cockpit, cabin; (di camion) cab.

abitante smf (di paese) inhabitant; (di casa) occupant.

abitare ◆ vi to live ◆ vt to live in; **dove abita?** where do you live?; **abito a Roma** I live in Rome; **abito in Italia** I live in Italy.

abitato, -a ◆ agg (casa) occupied; (paese) inhabited ◆ sm built-up area.

abito sm (da donna) dress; (da uomo) suit; ~ **da sera** evening dress.
▶ **abiti** smpl clothes.

abituale agg usual.

abitualmente avv usually.

abituare vt to accustom; ~ **qn a fare qc** to accustom sb to doing sthg.
▶ **abituarsi** vr (adattarsi): **abituarsi a qc** to get used to sthg; **abituarsi a fare qc** to get used to doing sthg.

abitudine sf habit; **aver l'~ di fare qc** to be in the habit of doing sthg; **per ~** out of habit.

abolire vt (tassa) to abolish; (legge) to repeal; (eliminare) to eliminate.

aborigeno, -a sm, f aborigine.

abortire vi (accidentalmente) to miscarry; (volontariamente) to have an abortion.

aborto sm (volontario) abortion; ~ **(spontaneo)** miscarriage.

abrogare vt (legge) to repeal.

Abruzzo sm: l'~ the Abruzzo (region of central Italy).

abside sf apse.

abusare : abusare di v + prep (posizione, potere) to take advantage of; (persona) to rape; ~ **dell'alcool** to drink too much.

abusivo, -a agg unauthorized, unlawful.

abuso sm (eccesso) overindulgence; (uso illecito) abuse.

a.C. (abbr di avanti Cristo) BC.

accademia sf academy, school; ~ **di belle arti** fine arts academy.

accadere vi to happen.

accaduto sm: raccontare l'~ to describe what happened.

accalcarsi vr to crowd.

accampamento sm camp.

accampare vt (truppe) to encamp; (richieste) to make; (diritti) to assert.

► **accamparsi** vr (in tende) to camp; (fig: in alloggio) to camp (out).

accanimento sm (tenacia) tenacity; (odio) fury.

accanito, -a agg (odio) fierce; (lavoratore) assiduous; **fumatore** ~ chain smoker.

accanto ◆ avv nearby ◆ agg inv next door ◆ prep: ~ **a** beside.

accaparrare vt (fare incetta) to buy up; (voti, favore) to secure, to gain; **accaparrarsi qc** to secure sthg for o.s.

accappatoio sm bathrobe.

accarezzare vt (persona, animale) to caress, to stroke; (fig: idea) to toy with.

accattone, -a sm, f beggar.

accavallare vt (gambe) to cross.

► **accavallarsi** vr (eventi) to overlap.

accecare vt (rendere cieco) to blind; (abbagliare) to dazzle.

accedere vi: ~ **a qc** to gain access to sthg.

accelerare ◆ vi to accelerate ◆ vt to speed up.

accelerato, -a ◆ agg quick ◆ sm stopping train.

acceleratore sm accelerator.

accendere vt (fuoco, sigaretta) to light; (radio, luce, fornello, motore) to turn on; (speranza, odio) to arouse; **scusi, ha da ~?** excuse me, have you got a light?

► **accendersi** vr (prendere fuoco) to catch fire; (entrare in funzione) to start up.

accendigas sm inv lighter for gas ring.

accendino sm (cigarette) lighter.

accennare vt (menzionare) to mention; (indicare) to point to; ~ **un sorriso** to half-smile.

► **accennare a** v + prep (menzionare) to mention; (alludere a) to hint at; (dare segno di) to show signs of.

accensione sf ignition.

accentare vt (parola, sillaba) to stress.

accento sm accent; **mettere l'~ su qc** to stress sthg.

accentuare vt (differenze, difetto, pregio) to emphasize.

► **accentuarsi** vr to become more marked.

accerchiare vt to encircle, to surround.

accertamento sm check.

accertare vt to check.

► **accertarsi di** vr + prep to make sure of.

acceso, -a ◆ pp → **accendere** ◆ agg (fuoco, sigaretta) lighted; (radio, luce, motore) on; (colore) bright.

accessibile agg (luogo) accessible; (prezzo) affordable.

accesso sm (entrata) access; (MED) fit; (fig: impeto) outburst.

accessori smpl accessories.

accettare vt to accept; (proposta) to agree to; ~ **di fare qc** to agree to do sthg; **'si accettano carte di credito'** 'credit cards welcome'.

accettazione sf (locale) reception; **'~ bagagli'** 'check-in'.

acchiappare *vt* to catch.

acciacco, -chi *sm* ailment.

acciaio *sm* steel; **~ inossidabile** stainless steel.

accidentale *agg* accidental.

accidentalmente *avv* accidentally.

accidentato, -a *agg* uneven.

accidenti *esclam* (*con rabbia*) blast!, damn!; (*con stupore*) good heavens!

acciuffare *vt* to catch.

acciuga, -ghe *sf* anchovy; **acciughe al limone** *fresh anchovies marinated in lemon juice and dressed with oil.*

acclamare *vt* (*applaudire*) to cheer, to applaud; (*eleggere*) to acclaim.

accludere *vt* to enclose.

accogliente *agg* cosy.

accoglienza *sf* welcome.

accogliere *vt* to receive; (*dare il benvenuto*) to welcome.

accoltellare *vt* to knife.

accomodare *vt* to repair.

▶ **accomodarsi** *vr* (*sedersi*) to sit down; (*venire avanti*) to come in; **s'accomodi!** (*si sieda*) take a seat!; (*venga avanti*) come in!

accompagnamento *sm* accompaniment.

accompagnare *vt* (*persona*) to go/come with, to accompany; (*piatto, abito*) to go with; (*con musica*) to accompany.

accompagnatore, -trice *sm, f* companion; **~ turistico** tourist guide.

acconsentire *vi*: **~ (a qc)** to agree (to sthg).

accontentare *vt* to satisfy, to keep happy.

▶ **accontentarsi: accontentarsi di** *vr + prep* to be satisfied with.

acconto *sm* down payment; **dare un ~** to pay a deposit; **in ~** on account.

accorciare *vt* to shorten.

accordare *vt* (*strumento*) to tune; (*concedere*) to grant; (*colori*) to match.

▶ **accordarsi** *vr* (*mettersi d'accordo*) to agree.

accordo *sm* (*patto*) agreement; (*armonia*) harmony; **d'~!** all right!; **andare d'~ con qn** to get on well with sb; **essere d'~ con** to agree with; **mettersi d'~ con qn** (*trovare un accordo*) to reach an agreement with sb; (*per appuntamento*) to make an arrangement with sb.

accorgersi : accorgersi di *v + prep* to notice.

accorrere *vi* (*in aiuto*) to rush up; (*verso un luogo*) to rush.

accorto, -a ♦ *pp* → **accorgersi** ♦ *agg* shrewd.

accostare ♦ *vt* (*persona*) to approach; (*porta*) to leave ajar; (*avvicinare*): **~ qc a qc** to move sthg near sthg ♦ *vi* to pull in; (*nave*) to come alongside; (*cambiare rotta*) to change course; (*in auto*) to draw up.

accreditare *vt* (*fatto, notizia*) to confirm; (*denaro*) to credit.

accrescere *vt* to increase.

▶ **accrescersi** *vr* to grow.

accucciarsi *vr* (*cane*) to lie down.

accudire *vt* (*malato, bambino*) to look after.

▶ **accudire a** *v + prep* (*casa, faccende*) to attend to.

accumulare *vt* to accumulate; (*denaro*) to save; (*accatastare*) to pile up.

accurato, -a *agg* (*lavoro*) careful; (*persona*) thorough.

accusa *sf* (*di una colpa*) accusation; (DIR) charge.

accusare *vt*: **~ qn (di qc)** (*incolpare*) to accuse sb of sthg; (DIR) to charge.

acerbo, -a *agg* unripe.

acero *sm* maple.

aceto *sm* vinegar.

acetone *sm* (*per unghie*) nail varnish remover.

ACI *sm* (*abbr di Automobile Club d'Italia*) ≃ AA (Br), ≃ AAA (Am).

acidità *sf*: **~ di stomaco** heartburn.

acido, -a ♦ *agg* (*sapore*) sour; (*commento, persona*) sharp ♦ *sm* acid.

acino *sm* grape.

acne sf acne.

acqua sf water; **sott'~** underwater; **~ corrente** running water; **~ cotta** Tuscan soup made from stale bread, onions and tomatoes; **~ dolce** fresh water; **~ minerale (gassata/naturale)** (carbonated/still) mineral water; **~ ossigenata** hydrogen peroxide; **~ del rubinetto** tap water; **~ salata** salt water; **~ tonica** tonic water; **acque termali** hot springs; **~ in bocca!** keep it to yourself!; **'~ non potabile'** 'not drinking water'.

acquaforte (pl **acqueforti**) sf etching.

acquaio sm sink.

acquamarina (pl **acquemarine**) sf aquamarine.

acquaragia sf turpentine.

acquario sm aquarium.

▶ **Acquario** sm Aquarius.

acquasanta sf holy water.

acquatico, -a, -ci, -che agg (pianta, animale) aquatic; (SPORT) water (dav s).

acquavite sf brandy.

acquazzone sm cloudburst.

acquedotto sm aqueduct.

acqueo agg m → **vapore**.

acquerello sm watercolour.

acquirente smf buyer.

acquisire vt (ottenere) to acquire.

acquistare vt (comperare) to buy; (ottenere) to acquire.

acquisto sm purchase; **fare acquisti** to shop.

acquolina sf: **far venire l'~ in bocca a qn** to make sb's mouth water.

acquoso, -a agg watery.

acrilico, -a, -ci, -che agg & sm acrylic.

acrobata, -i, -e smf acrobat.

acrobazia sf (di acrobata) acrobatic feat; (di aereo) stunt.

acropoli sf inv acropolis.

aculeo sm (di vespa) sting; (di riccio) spine; (di pianta) prickle.

acume sm acumen.

acustico, -a, -ci, -che agg acoustic.

acuto, -a agg (voce, suono) high-pitched; (intenso) intense; (appuntito) pointed; (intelligente) sharp; (MAT) acute.

ad → **a**.

adagio avv slowly; **'entrare/uscire ~'** sign warning drivers to enter or leave side roads etc slowly.

adattamento sm (adeguamento, di opera) adaptation; (modifica) adjustment.

adattare vt to adapt.

▶ **adattarsi** vr: **adattarsi (a qc)** (adeguarsi) to adapt (to sthg).

adatto, -a agg: **~ (a)** suitable (for); **~ a fare qc** suitable to do sthg.

addebitare vt: **~ una spesa a qn** to charge an expense to sb; **~ una somma in conto a qn** to debit a sum from sb's account.

addestramento sm training.

addestrare vt to train.

addetto, -a ◆ agg (persona) responsible ◆ sm, f person responsible; **~ stampa** press attaché; **gli addetti ai lavori** (fig) the experts.

addio esclam goodbye!

addirittura ◆ avv (perfino) even; (direttamente) directly ◆ esclam really?

addirsi : addirsi a vr + prep to be suitable for.

additivo sm additive.

addizionale agg additional.

addizione sf addition.

addobbo sm decoration; **addobbi natalizi** Christmas decorations.

addolcire vt to sweeten.

addolorare vt to sadden.

▶ **addolorarsi** vr to upset o.s.

addome sm abdomen.

addomesticare vt to house-train.

addormentare vt to send to sleep.

▶ **addormentarsi** vr to fall asleep.

addossare vt (al muro) to lean; (attribuire) to lay.

addosso ♦ avv (sulla persona) on ♦ prep: ~ a (su) on; (contro) against; **mettersi qc** ~ to put sthg on; **dare** ~ **a** (criticare) to attack; **eravamo uno** ~ **all'altro** we were right next to each other.

adeguare vt: ~ qc a qc to adjust sthg to sthg.

▶ **adeguarsi** vr: **adeguarsi a qc** to adapt to sthg.

adeguato, -a agg adequate.

adempiere vt (compiere) to carry out; (esaudire) to grant.

adenoidi sfpl adenoids.

aderente agg (attillato) close-fitting; (adesivo) adhesive.

aderire vi: ~ a qc (attaccarsi) to stick to sthg; (partito) to join sthg; (proposta) to support sthg; (richiesta) to agree to sthg.

adesivo, -a agg ♦ agg adhesive ♦ sm (etichetta) sticky label.

adesso avv (ora) now; (tra poco) any moment now; (poco fa) just now.

adiacente agg adjacent.

adibire vt: ~ qc a qc to use sthg as sthg.

Adige sm: l'~ the River Adige.

adirarsi vr to get angry.

adocchiare vt (scorgere) to glimpse; (guardare) to eye.

adolescente smf adolescent.

adolescenza sf adolescence.

adoperare vt to use.

adorabile agg adorable.

adorare vt (persona, cosa) to adore; (divinità) to worship.

adottare vt (bambino) to adopt; (misure, decisione) to take.

adottivo, -a agg (figlio, patria) adopted; (genitori) adoptive.

adozione sf adoption.

adriatico, -a, -ci, -che agg Adriatic.

▶ **Adriatico** sm: l'**Adriatico** the Adriatic (Sea).

adulterio sm adultery.

adulto, -a agg & sm, f (di età) adult.

aerare vt to air.

aereo, -a ♦ agg air (dav s) ♦ sm (aero)plane, aircraft; ~ **da turismo** light aircraft.

aerobico, -a, -ci, -che agg aerobic.

aeronautica sf (aviazione) airforce.

aeroplano sm (aero)plane (Br), airplane (Am).

aeroporto sm airport.

aerosol sm aerosol.

A.F. (abbr di alta frequenza) HF.

afa sf closeness.

affabile agg affable.

affacciarsi vr (mostrarsi) to show o.s.

▶ **affacciarsi su** vr + prep to show o.s. at.

affamato, -a agg starving.

affannarsi vr (stancarsi) to tire o.s.; (agitarsi) to worry.

affanno sm (di respiro) breathlessness; (ansia) worry.

affare sm business; (faccenda) business, affair; (occasione) bargain; (fam: cosa) thing; **è un ~!** it's a bargain!; **affari** business (sg); **per affari** on business; **fare affari con** to do business with; **Affari Esteri** Foreign Affairs.

affascinante agg fascinating.

affascinare vt to charm, to fascinate.

affaticarsi vr to get tired.

affatto avv completely; **non ... ~** not ... at all; **niente ~** not at all.

affermare vt to affirm.

▶ **affermarsi** vr to make a name for o.s.

affermativo, -a agg affirmative.

affermazione sf (dichiarazione) affirmation; (successo) success.

afferrare vt (prendere) to seize; (capire) to grasp.

▶ **afferrarsi a** vr + prep to grasp at.

affettare vt to slice.

affettato, -a ♦ agg (a fette) sliced;

(*artificioso*) affected ◆ *sm* sliced cold meat.

affetto, -a ◆ *sm* (*attaccamento*) affection ◆ *agg*: **essere ~ da** (*malattia*) to suffer from.

affettuoso, -a *agg* affectionate.

affezionarsi *vr*: **~ a** to become fond of.

affezionato, -a *agg* fond.

affidamento *sm* (DIR) custody; (*fiducia*): **fare ~ su** to rely on.

affidare *vt* to entrust; **~ qn/qc a qn** to entrust sb/sthg to sb.

affiggere *vt* (*cartello, poster*) to stick up.

affilare *vt* to sharpen.

affilato, -a *agg* (*lama, punta*) sharp.

affinché *cong* in order that, so that.

affinità *sf inv* affinity.

affissione *sf*: '**divieto di ~**' 'post no bills'.

affisso, -a ◆ *pp* → **affiggere** ◆ *sm* poster.

affittare *vt* (*dare in affitto*) to let, to rent (out); (*prendere in affitto*) to rent; '**affittasi**' 'to let'.

affitto *sm* rent; **dare in ~** to let, to rent (out); **prendere in ~** to rent.

affliggere *vt* to torment.

▶ **affliggersi** *vr* to torment o.s.

afflitto, -a ◆ *pp* → **affliggere** ◆ *agg* afflicted.

affluente *sm* tributary.

affluire *vi* (*fiume*) to flow; (*gente, merce*) to pour in.

affogare *vi & vt* to drown.

affogato *sm* (*gelato*) ice cream or '*semifreddo*' with coffee, whisky or a liqueur poured over it.

affollato, -a *agg* crowded.

affondare *vi & vt* to sink.

affrancare *vt* to stamp.

affrancatura *sf* postage.

affresco, -schi *sm* fresco.

affrettare *vt* to hurry.

▶ **affrettarsi** *vr* to hurry.

affrontare *vt* (*nemico*) to confront; (*spesa*) to meet; (*argomento*) to tackle.

affronto *sm* insult.

affumicato, -a *agg* (*cibo*) smoked; (*vetro*) tinted; (*annerito*) blackened.

afoso, -a *agg* close.

Africa *sf*: **l'~** Africa.

africano, -a *agg & sm, f* African.

afta *sf* mouth ulcer.

agenda *sf* diary.

agente *sm* agent; **~ di polizia** policeman (*f* policewoman); **gli agenti atmosferici** the elements.

agenzia *sf* (*impresa*) agency; (*succursale*) branch; **~ di cambio** bureau de change; **~ immobiliare** estate agent's (Br), real-estate office (Am); **~ di viaggi** travel agency.

agevolare *vt* (*facilitare*) to facilitate; (*aiutare*) to help.

agevolazione *sf*: **~ di pagamento** easy (payment) terms (*pl*).

aggeggio *sm* thing.

aggettivo *sm* adjective.

agghiacciante *agg* terrible.

aggiornare *vt* (*persona, opera*) to bring up-to-date; (*seduta*) to postpone.

▶ **aggiornarsi** *vr* to bring o.s. up-to-date.

aggiornato, -a *agg* up-to-date.

aggirare *vt* to get round.

▶ **aggirarsi** *vr* to wander.

▶ **aggirarsi su** *vr + prep* to be about.

aggiudicare *vt* to award.

▶ **aggiudicarsi** *vr* to gain.

aggiungere *vt* to add.

aggiunta *sf*: **in ~** in addition.

aggiunto, -a *pp* → **aggiungere**.

aggiustare *vt* to mend.

▶ **aggiustarsi** *vr* to come to an agreement.

agglomerato *sm*: **~ urbano** built-up area.

aggrapparsi *vr* to cling on; **~ a** to cling to.

aggravare *vt* to make worse.

▶ **aggravarsi** *vr* to get worse.

aggredire *vt* to attack.

aggressione *sf* attack.

aggressivo, -a *agg* aggressive.

agguato *sm* ambush.

agiato, -a *.agg (persona)* well-off; *(vita)* comfortable.

agile *agg* agile, nimble.

agio *sm*: **essere a proprio ~** to feel at ease; **mettersi a proprio ~** to make o.s. at home.

agire *vi (comportarsi)* to act; **~ da** *(fare da)* to act as.

agitare *vt* to shake; *(mano)* to wave; *(coda)* to wag; *(turbare)* to upset; **'~ prima dell'uso'** 'shake before use'.

▶ **agitarsi** *vr (turbarsi)* to get worked up; *(muoversi)* to writhe; *(mare)* to get rough; **agitarsi nel letto** to toss and turn in bed.

agitato, -a *agg (inquieto)* worried; *(mare)* rough.

agitazione *sf (inquietudine)* agitation; *(subbuglio)* turmoil.

agli = **a** + **gli**, → **a**.

aglio *sm* garlic.

agnello *sm* lamb; **~ alla norcina** *leg of lamb larded with ham, garlic, parsley and marjoram.*

agnolotti *smpl ravioli stuffed with pork, salami, Parmesan cheese and spinach.*

ago *(pl aghi) sm* needle.

agonia *sf* agony.

agopuntura *sf* acupuncture.

agosto *sm* August, → **settembre**.

agricolo, -a *agg* agricultural.

agricoltore *sm (contadino)* farm worker; *(imprenditore)* farmer.

agricoltura *sf* agriculture.

agriturismo *sm* farm holidays *(pl).*

AGRITURISMO

A form of tourism popular in Italy, 'agriturismo' offers people the opportunity to spend their summer holiday on traditional farms in the Italian countryside. This type of holiday is particularly popular with those who enjoy the outdoors lifestyle, good home cooking and healthy exercise in beautiful rural surroundings. As well as participating in a range of sports such as horseriding, walking, tennis and bowls, holidaymakers also have the opportunity to help on the farm.

---

agro, -a *agg* sour.

agrodolce *sm*: **in ~** in a sweet and sour sauce.

agrume *sm* citrus fruit.

aguzzare *vt* to sharpen; **~ le orecchie** to prick up one's ears.

aguzzo, -a *agg* sharp.

ahi *esclam* ouch!

ai = **a** + **i**, → **a**.

Aia *sf*: **l'~** The Hague.

AIDS *sm o sf* AIDS.

A.I.G. *(abbr di Associazione Italiana Alberghi per la Gioventù)* = YHA.

air-terminal ['ɜr 'tɛrminal] *sm inv* air terminal.

aiuola *sf* flower bed.

aiutante *smf* assistant.

aiutare *vt* to help; **~ qn (a fare qc)** to help sb (to do sthg).

aiuto *sm* help, assistance; *(assistente)* assistant; **~!** help!; **chiedere ~** to ask for help; **essere di ~ a qn** to be of help to sb; **venire in ~ di qn** to come to sb's aid.

al = **a** + **il**, → **a**.

ala *(pl ali) sf* wing; *(giocatore)* winger.

alano *sm* Great Dane.

alba *sf* dawn; **all'~** at dawn.

albanese *agg & smf* Albanian.

Albania *sf*: **l'~** Albania.

albergatore, -trice *sm, f* hotelier.

albergo, -ghi *sm* hotel; **~ diurno** *public toilets where people can also wash, have a haircut, get their clothes ironed etc.*; **~ per la gioventù** youth hostel.

albero *sm* tree; *(di nave)* mast; *(di macchina)* shaft; **~ genealogico** family tree; **~ di Natale** Christmas tree.

albese *sf* thin slices of raw beef served with oil, lemon and mushrooms or Parmesan cheese.

albicocca, -che *sf* apricot.

albino, -a *agg & sm, f* albino.

album *sm inv* album; ~ **da disegno** sketch book.

albume *sm* egg white.

alcol = **alcool**.

alcolico, -a, -ci, -che ◆ *agg* alcoholic ◆ *sm* alcoholic drink.

alcolizzato, -a *sm, f* alcoholic.

alcool *sm* alcohol.

alcuno, -a *agg s*: **non ... ~** *(nessuno)* no, not any.

▶ **alcuni, -e** ◆ *agg pl* some, a few ◆ *pron pl* some; **alcuni di** some of, a few of.

aldilà *sm*: **l'~** the next life.

alfabeto *sm* alphabet.

alfiere *sm (portabandiera)* standard bearer; *(negli scacchi)* bishop.

alga, -ghe *sf (di mare)* seaweed.

algebra *sf* algebra.

Algeria *sf*: **l'~** Algeria.

aliante *sm* glider.

alibi *sm inv* alibi.

alice *sf* anchovy; **alici areganate** anchovies cooked in oil, vinegar, garlic, parsley and oregano.

alienazione *sf (pazzia)* insanity; (DIR) transfer.

alieno, -a *sm, f* alien.

alimentare ◆ *agg* food *(dav s)* ◆ *vt (nutrire)* to feed; *(fig: rafforzare)* to strengthen; *(rifornire)* to supply.

▶ **alimentari** *smpl (cibi)* foodstuffs; **negozio di alimentari** grocer's.

alimentazione *sf (nutrimento)* nutrition; *(rifornimento)* supply.

alimento *sm* food.

▶ **alimenti** *smpl* alimony *(sg)*.

aliscafo *sm* hydrofoil.

alito *sm* breath.

all' = **a + l'**, → **a**.

alla = **a + la**, → **a**.

allacciare *vt (scarpe)* to tie up; *(cintura, vestito)* to fasten; *(telefono, gas)* to connect.

▶ **allacciarsi** *vr* to fasten.

allagare *vt* to flood.

▶ **allagarsi** *vr* to flood.

allargare *vt (ampliare)* to widen; *(aprire)* to open.

▶ **allargarsi** *vr* to widen.

allarmare *vt* to alarm.

allarme *sm* alarm; ~ **d'incendio** fire alarm; **dare l'~** to give the alarm.

allattare *vt (al seno)* to breast-feed; *(artificialmente)* to bottle-feed.

alle = **a + le**, → **a**.

alleanza *sf* alliance.

allearsi *vr* to form an alliance.

allegare *vt* to enclose.

alleggerire *vt* to lighten.

allegria *sf* cheerfulness.

allegro, -a ◆ *agg (contento)* cheerful; *(colore)* bright; *(vivace)* lively ◆ *sm* (MUS) allegro.

allenamento *sm* training; **tenersi in ~** to keep in training.

allenare *vt* to train.

▶ **allenarsi** *vr* to train.

allenatore, -trice *sm, f* trainer, coach.

allentare *vt (vite, nodo)* to loosen; *(sorveglianza, disciplina)* to relax.

▶ **allentarsi** *vr* to work loose.

allergia *sf* allergy.

allergico, -a, -ci, -che *agg* allergic; **essere ~ a qc** to be allergic to sthg.

allestire *vt (mostra, spettacolo)* to get ready.

allevamento *sm (attività)* breeding, rearing; *(animali)* stock.

allevare *vt (animale)* to breed; *(bambino)* to bring up.

allibratore *sm* bookmaker.

allievo, -a *sm, f* pupil, student.

alligatore *sm* alligator.

allineare *vt* to align.

▶ **allinearsi** *vr (mettersi in fila)* to line up.

allo = **a + lo**, → **a**.

allodola *sf* skylark.

alloggiare *vi* to stay.

alloggio *sm* accommodation.

allontanare *vt* (*mandare via*) to send away; (*pericolo*) to avert.

▶ **allontanarsi** *vr* to go away.

allora ♦ *avv* then ♦ *cong* (*in tal caso*) then; (*ebbene*) well then, so; **da ~** since then.

alloro *sm* laurel.

alluce *sm* big toe.

allucinante *agg* (*spaventoso*) terrifying; (*incredibile*) incredible.

allucinazione *sf* hallucination.

alludere : **alludere a** *v + prep* to allude to.

alluminio *sm* aluminium.

allungare *vt* (*accrescere*) to lengthen; (*gambe*) to stretch; (*diluire*) to water down.

▶ **allungarsi** *vr* (*accrescersi*) to lengthen; (*distendersi*) to stretch out.

allusione *sf* allusion; **fare allusioni** to drop hints.

alluso *pp* → **alludere**.

alluvione *sf* flood.

almeno *avv* at least.

Alpi *sfpl*: **le ~** the Alps.

alpinismo *sm* climbing.

alpinista, -i, -e *smf* climber.

alpino, -a *agg* alpine.

alquanto *avv* somewhat.

alt *esclam* halt!

altalena *sf* (*con funi*) swing; (*su asse*) see-saw (Br), teeter-totter (Am).

altare *sm* altar.

alterare *vt* to affect.

▶ **alterarsi** *vr* (*merce*) to be affected; (*irritarsi*) to get angry.

alternare *vt*: **~ qn/qc a** to alternate sb/sthg with.

▶ **alternarsi** *vr* to alternate.

alternativa *sf* alternative.

alternato, -a *agg* alternate; (*corrente*) alternating.

alterno, -a *agg* alternate.

altezza *sf* (*statura, di cosa*) height; (*di acqua*) depth; (*altitudine*) altitude.

altezzoso, -a *agg* haughty.

altipiano = **altopiano**.

altitudine *sf* altitude.

altro, -a *agg* 1. (*diverso*) other; **ha un ~ modello?** have you got another o a different model?

2. (*supplementare*) other; **un ~ caffè?** another coffee?; **vorrei altre due bottiglie** I'd like two more bottles.

3. (*rimanente*) other; **gli altri passeggeri sono pregati di restare al loro posto** would all remaining passengers please stay in their seats.

4. (*nel tempo*) other; **l'~ giorno** the other day; **l'altr'anno** last year; **l'~ ieri** the day before yesterday; **domani l'~** the day after tomorrow.

5. (*in espressioni*): **è tutt'~ che bello** it's far from being beautiful; **d'altra parte** on the other hand.

♦ *pron*: **l'~** the other (one); **un ~** another (one); **gli altri** (*il prossimo*) others, other people; (**desidera**) **~?** (do you want) anything else?; **l'uno o l'~** one or the other; **se non ~** at least; **senz'~** of course; **tra l'~** among other things.

altroché *esclam* and how!

altronde : **d'altronde** *avv* on the other hand.

altrove *avv* elsewhere.

altrui *agg inv* other people's.

altruista, -i, -e *agg* altruistic.

altura *sf* high ground.

alunno, -a *sm, f* pupil.

alveare *sm* beehive.

alzare *vt* (*oggetto*) to lift; (*prezzi, volume, voce*) to raise.

▶ **alzarsi** *vr* (*dal letto, dalla sedia*) to get up; (*aumentare*) to rise; (*vento*) to get up.

amaca, -che *sf* hammock.

amalgamare *vt* to combine.

▶ **amalgamarsi** *vr* to combine.

amante ♦ *smf* lover ♦ *agg*: **~ di qc** fond of sthg.

amare *vt* (*persona*) to love; (*cosa*) to be fond of.

amareggiato, -a *agg* embittered.

amarena *sf* sour black cherry.

amaretto *sm* (*biscotto*) macaroon; (*liquore*) a liqueur made with almonds.

amarezza *sf* bitterness.

amaro, -a ♦ *agg* (*sapore*) bitter; (*spiacevole*) nasty ♦ *sm* bitter after-dinner liqueur.

amatriciana *sf* → **bucatini**.

ambasciata *sf* embassy.

ambasciatore, -trice *sm, f* ambassador.

ambedue *agg inv & pron* both.

ambientale *agg* environmental.

ambientare *vt* (*film*) to set.

▶ **ambientarsi** *vr* to get used to a place.

ambiente *sm* (*natura*) environment; (*cerchia*) surroundings (*pl*).

ambiguo, -a *agg* (*parola, testo*) ambiguous; (*comportamento, persona*) dubious.

ambizione *sf* ambition.

ambizioso, -a *agg* ambitious.

ambra *sf* amber.

ambulante *agg* itinerant.

ambulanza *sf* ambulance.

ambulatorio *sm* surgery.

America *sf*: l'~ America; l'~ **latina** Latin America.

americano, -a *agg & sm, f* American.

amianto *sm* asbestos.

amichevole *agg* friendly.

amicizia *sf* friendship; **fare ~ (con qn)** to make friends (with sb).

amico, -a, -ci, -che *sm, f* friend; **~ del cuore** best friend.

amido *sm* starch.

ammaccare *vt* to dent.

ammaccatura *sf* (*su metallo*) dent; (*su gamba*) bruise.

ammaestrare *vt* to train.

ammainare *vt* to lower.

ammalarsi *vr* to fall ill.

ammalato, -a ♦ *agg* ill ♦ *sm, f* patient.

ammassare *vt* to amass, to pile up.

ammazzare *vt* to kill.

▶ **ammazzarsi** *vr* to kill o.s.

ammenda *sf* fine.

ammesso, -a *pp* → **ammettere**.

ammettere *vt* (*riconoscere*) to admit; (*permettere*) to allow; (*a esame, scuola*) to accept; (*supporre*) to suppose, to assume.

amministrare *vt* to run, to manage.

amministratore *sm* (*di condominio*) manager; **~ delegato** managing director.

ammirare *vt* to admire.

ammiratore, -trice *sm, f* admirer.

ammirazione *sf* admiration.

ammissione *sf* (*a esame*) admittance.

ammobiliato, -a *agg* furnished; **non ~** unfurnished.

ammollo *sm* soaking; **lasciare qc in ~** to leave sthg to soak.

ammoniaca *sf* ammonia.

ammonire *vt* (*rimproverare*) to warn; (SPORT) to book.

ammonizione *sf* (*rimprovero*) warning; (SPORT) booking.

ammontare : ammontare a *v + prep* to amount to.

ammorbidente *sm* fabric softener.

ammorbidire *vt* (*rendere morbido*) to soften.

ammortizzatore *sm* shock absorber.

ammucchiare *vt* to pile up.

ammuffito, -a *agg* mouldy.

ammutinamento *sm* mutiny.

amnistia *sf* amnesty.

amo *sm* bait.

amore *sm* love; **fare l'~ (con qn)** to make love (with sb); **amor proprio** self-esteem.

ampio, -a *agg* (*vasto*) wide; (*spazioso*) spacious; (*abbondante*) abundant.

ampliare *vt* to widen.

amplificatore *sm* amplifier.

amputare *vt* to amputate.

amuleto *sm* amulet.

anabbaglianti *smpl* dipped headlights (Br), dimmed headlights (Am).

anagrafe *sf* (*ufficio*) registry office (Br), office of vital statistics (Am).

analcolico, -a, -ci, -che ♦ *agg* non-alcoholic ♦ *sm* soft drink.

analfabeta, -i, -e *agg* & *smf* illiterate.

analisi *sf inv* (*studio*) analysis; (MED) test; ~ **del sangue** blood test.

analista, -i, -e *smf* analyst.

analizzare *vt* to analyse.

analogo, -a, -ghi, -ghe *agg* similar.

ananas *sm inv* pineapple.

anarchia *sf* anarchy.

ANAS *sf* (*abbr di Azienda Nazionale Autonoma delle Strade*) *national road board.*

anatomia *sf* anatomy.

anatomico, -a, -ci, -che *agg* (*sedile*) contoured.

anatra *sf* duck.

anca, -che *sf* hip.

anche *cong* (*pure*) also, too; (*persino*) even.

ancora¹ *sf* anchor.

ancora² *avv* (*tuttora*) still; (*persino*) even; (*di nuovo*) again; (*di più*) more, still; ~ **più bello** even more beautiful; ~ **un po'** a bit more; ~ **una volta** once more; **non** ~ not yet.

andare *vi* **1.** (*muoversi*) to go; **scusi, per ~ alla stazione?** could you tell me the way to the station, please?; ~ **a Napoli** to go to Naples; ~ **avanti/indietro** to go forwards/backwards; ~ **in vacanza** to go on holiday (Br), to go on vacation (Am).

2. (*strada*) to go.

3. (*indica uno stato*): **come va?** (*persona*) how are you?; (*situazione*) how are things?, how's it going?; ~ **bene/male** (*situazione*) to go well/badly; **c'è qualcosa che non va?** is something wrong?

4. (*piacere*): **il suo modo di fare non mi va** I don't like the way he behaves; **non mi va di mangiare** I don't feel like eating.

5. (*funzionare*) to work.

6. (*con participio passato*): **dove va messa la chiave?** where does the key go?; ~ **perso** (*essere smarrito*) to get lost.

7. (*in espressioni*): ~ **bene a qn** (*come misura*) to fit sb; **queste scarpe mi vanno bene** these shoes fit (me); **ti va bene andare al cinema?** do you feel like going to the cinema?; ~ **via** (*partire*) to leave; (*macchia*) to come out.

♦ *sm*: **a lungo** ~ in time.

▶ **andarsene** *vr* to go away.

andata *sf*: **all'**~ on the way there; ~ **e ritorno** return (ticket) (Br), round-trip ticket (Am).

andatura *sf* walk.

andirivieni *sm inv* coming and going.

anello *sm* (*da dito*) ring; (*di catena*) link; ~ **di fidanzamento** engagement ring.

anemia *sf* anaemia.

anestesia *sf* anaesthesia.

anestetico *sm* anaesthetic.

anfiteatro *sm* amphitheatre.

anfora *sf* amphora.

angelo *sm* angel.

angina *sf* tonsillitis; ~ **pectoris** angina.

anglicano, -a *agg* Anglican.

angolo *sm* corner; ~ **cottura** kitchen area; **all'**~ on the corner.

angora *sf*: **d'**~ angora (*dav s*).

angoscia *sf* anguish.

anguilla *sf* eel.

anguria *sf* watermelon.

anice *sm* aniseed.

anidride *sf*: ~ **carbonica** carbon dioxide.

anima *sf* soul.

animale *agg* & *sm* animal; ~ **domestico** pet.

animato, -a agg (discussione) lively, animated.

animatore, -trice sm, f: ~ turistico entertainment organizer (in holiday village).

animazione sf liveliness; (di strada) bustle.

animo sm (mente) mind; (cuore) heart; (coraggio): **perdersi d'~** to lose heart.

anitra = **anatra**.

annaffiare vt to water.

annaffiatoio sm watering can.

annata sf year; (di vino) vintage.

annegare vt & vi to drown.

▶ **annegarsi** vr to drown o.s.

anniversario sm anniversary.

anno sm year; **buon ~!** Happy New Year!; **quanti anni hai?** how old are you?; **ho 21 anni** I'm 21; **un bambino di tre anni** a three-year-old; **~ accademico** academic year; **~ bisestile** leap year; **~ scolastico** school year.

annodare vt to tie.

annoiare vt to bore.

▶ **annoiarsi** vr to get bored.

annotare vt (prendere nota) to note down; (commentare) to annotate.

annuale agg annual.

annuario sm yearbook.

annuire vi (con la testa) to nod.

annullare vt (partita, riunione, francobollo) to cancel; (matrimonio) to annul; (rendere vano) to destroy.

annunciare vt to announce; (indicare) to indicate.

annunciatore, -trice sm, f announcer.

Annunciazione sf: **l'~** the Annunciation.

annuncio sm announcement; **~ pubblicitario** advertisement; **annunci economici** classified ads.

annuo, -a agg annual, yearly.

annusare vt to smell.

annuvolamento sm clouding over.

ano sm anus.

anomalo, -a agg anomalous.

anonimo, -a agg anonymous.

anoressia sf anorexia.

anormale ♦ agg abnormal ♦ smf abnormal person.

ANSA sf (abbr di Agenzia Nazionale Stampa Associata) national press agency.

ansia sf anxiety.

ansimare vi to pant.

ansioso, -a agg (inquieto) anxious; (impaziente): **~ di fare qc** eager to do sthg.

anta sf (di finestra) shutter; (di armadio) door.

antagonista, -i, -e smf rival.

antartico, -a, -ci, -che agg Antarctic.

Antartide sf: **l'~** Antarctica.

anteguerra sm prewar period.

antenato, -a sm, f ancestor.

antenna sf aerial.

anteprima sf preview; **presentare qc in ~** to preview sthg.

anteriore agg (sedili, ruote) front (dav s); (nel tempo) previous.

antiabbaglianti = **anabbaglianti**.

antibiotico sm antibiotic.

anticamera sf anteroom.

antichità sf inv (passato) antiquity; (oggetto) antique.

anticipare vt (partenza) to bring forward; (denaro) to pay in advance.

anticipo sm (di denaro) advance; (di tempo): **il treno ha 10 minuti d'~** the train is 10 minutes early; **essere/arrivare in ~** to be/arrive early.

antico, -a, -chi, -che agg (mobilio) antique; (dell'antichità) ancient.

anticoncezionale agg & sm contraceptive.

anticonformista, -i, -e agg & smf nonconformist.

anticorpo sm antibody.

antidoto sm antidote.

antifascista, -i, -e agg & smf antifascist.

antifurto ♦ *agg inv* antitheft (*dav s*) ♦ *sm* antitheft device.

antigelo *sm inv* antifreeze.

Antille *sfpl*: **le ~** the West Indies.

antimafia *agg inv* anti-Mafia.

antincendio *agg inv* fire (*dav s*).

antinebbia ♦ *agg inv* fog (*dav s*) ♦ *sm inv* fog lamp.

antiorario *agg m* → **senso**.

antipasto *sm* hors d'œuvre; **~ di mare** mixed seafood hors d'œuvre; **~ a scelta** *hors d'œuvres chosen from a buffet of grilled or baked vegetables, pickled foods, cold meats etc.*

antipatia *sf* antipathy.

antipatico, -a, -ci, -che *agg* unpleasant.

antiquariato *sm* (*commercio*) antique trade; **oggetti d'~** antiques.

antiquario, -a *sm, f* antique dealer.

antiquato, -a *agg* old-fashioned.

antiruggine *agg inv* rustproof.

antirughe *agg inv* antiwrinkle (*dav s*).

antisettico, -a, -ci, -che *agg & sm* antiseptic.

antitetanica *sf* antitetanus injection.

antivipera *sm inv* antiviper serum.

antivivisezione *sf* antivivisection.

antologia *sf* anthology.

anulare ♦ *agg* ring (*dav s*) ♦ *sm* ring finger.

anzi *cong* (*al contrario*) on the contrary; (*o meglio*) or rather.

anziano, -a ♦ *agg* (*di età*) elderly; (*di carica*) senior ♦ *sm, f* (*vecchio*) senior citizen.

anziché *cong* rather than.

anzitutto *avv* first of all.

apatia *sf* apathy.

apatico, -a, -ci, -che *agg* apathetic.

ape *sf* bee.

aperitivo *sm* aperitif.

APERITIVO

The tradition of taking an alcoholic or a non-alcoholic drink before lunch or dinner is common throughout Italy. Italians are especially fond of having an aperitif at some point during their Sunday stroll or 'passeggiata'. Although an aperitif is sometimes served at home, it is more usual to go out to a bar where, in addition to the usual range of drinks, there may be local or house specialities on offer. Drinks are generally accompanied by olives, crisps or other savoury snacks.

---

aperto, -a ♦ *pp* → **aprire** ♦ *agg* open ♦ *sm*: **all'~** in the open air.

apertura *sf* opening.

apice *sm* peak; **essere all'~ di qc** to be at the height of sthg.

apicoltura *sf* beekeeping.

apnea *sf*: **in ~** (*subacqueo*) without breathing apparatus.

apolide ♦ *agg* stateless ♦ *smf* stateless person.

apostolo *sm* apostle.

apostrofo *sm* apostrophe.

appagare *vt* to satisfy.

appannare *vt* (*vetro*) to mist; (*fig: mente*) to dim.

▶ **appannarsi** *vr* (*vetro*) to mist up; (*fig: vista, mente*) to grow dim.

apparato *sm* (ANAT) system; (*impianto*) apparatus.

apparecchiare *vt*: **~ la tavola** to lay the table.

apparecchio *sm* (*congegno*) device; (*aereo*) aircraft; (*per i denti*) brace; **~ acustico** hearing aid.

apparente *agg* apparent.

apparentemente *avv* apparently.

apparenza *sf*: **in** o **all'~** apparently.

apparire *vi* (*mostrarsi*) to appear; (*sembrare*) to seem.

appariscente *agg* striking.

apparso, -a *pp* → **apparire**.

appartamento *sm* flat (Br), apartment (Am).

appartenere : appartenere a *v* + *prep* to belong to.

appassionato, -a ◆ *agg* passionate ◆ *sm, f* fan; **essere ~ di qc** to be keen on sthg.

appello *sm* (*chiamata*) rollcall; (DIR) appeal; **fare ~ a** to appeal to; **fare l'~** to call the roll.

appena ◆ *avv* (*a fatica*) hardly; (*da poco*) just; (*solo*) only, just ◆ *cong* as soon as; **non ~** as soon as.

appendere *vt* to hang up.

appendice *sf* appendix.

appendicite *sf* appendicitis.

Appennini *smpl*: **gli ~** the Apennines.

appeso, -a *pp* → **appendere**.

appetito *sm* appetite; **buon ~!** enjoy your meal!

appetitoso, -a *agg* appetizing.

appezzamento *sm* plot.

appiattire *vt* to flatten.

▶ **appiattirsi** *vr* (*al suolo, contro il muro*) to flatten o.s.; (*diventare piatto*) to become flatter.

appiccare *vt*: **~ il fuoco a qc** to set fire to sthg.

appiccicare *vt* to stick.

▶ **appiccicarsi** *vr*: **appiccicarsi (a)** to stick (to); (*fig: persona*) to cling (to).

appieno *avv* fully.

appigliarsi : appigliarsi a *vr* + *prep* (*afferrarsi*) to hold on to; (*fig: pretesto*) to cling to.

appiglio *sm* (*appoggio*) hold; (*fig: pretesto*) pretext.

appisolarsi *vr* to doze off.

applaudire *vt* to applaud.

applauso *sm* applause; **fare un ~** to give a round of applause.

applicare *vt* to apply.

▶ **applicarsi** *vr* to apply o.s.

applicazione *sf* (*di cerotto, pomata*) application; (*attuazione*) enforcement.

appoggiare *vt* (*per terra, sul tavolo*) to put (down); (*sostenere*) to support; (*al muro*): **~ qc a o contro qc** to lean sthg against sthg.

▶ **appoggiarsi a** *vr* + *prep* to lean against.

appoggiatesta *sm inv* headrest.

apporre *vt* (*form*) to add.

appositamente *avv* on purpose; **~ per te** specially for you.

apposito, -a *agg* appropriate.

apposta *avv* deliberately; **fare qc ~** to do sthg on purpose.

apposto, -a *pp* → **apporre**.

apprendere *vt* to learn.

apprendista, -i, -e *smf* apprentice.

apprensivo, -a *agg* apprehensive.

appreso, -a *pp* → **apprendere**.

appretto *sm* starch.

apprezzamento *sm* appreciation.

apprezzare *vt* to appreciate.

approccio *sm* approach.

approdare *vi* to land; **non ~ a niente** to come to nothing.

approdo *sm* (*atto*) landing; (*luogo*) landing-place.

approfittare : approfittare di *v* + *prep* to take advantage of.

approfondire *vt* (*accentuare*) to deepen; (*studiare*) to study in depth.

appropriarsi : appropriarsi di *vr* + *prep* to appropriate.

approssimativo, -a *agg* (*calcolo*) approximate; (*conoscenza*) superficial.

approvare *vt* (*legge, proposta*) to pass; (*comportamento*) to approve of.

approvazione *sf* approval.

appuntamento *sm* appointment; (*amoroso*) date; **dare (un) ~ a qn** to arrange to meet sb; **prendere un ~ con o da qn** to make an appointment with sb.

appuntare *vt* (*matita*) to sharpen; (*fissare*) to pin; (*annotare*) to note.

appunto ◆ *sm* (*annotazione*) note; (*rimprovero*) reprimand ◆ *avv* exactly.

apribottiglie *sm inv* bottle opener.

aprile *sm* April, → **settembre**.

aprire ♦ *vt* to open; (*gas, acqua*) to turn on ♦ *vi* to open; **vai tu ad ~?** can you answer the door?; **'non ~ prima che il treno sia fermo'** 'do not open before the train has stopped'.

▶ **aprirsi** *vr* (*porta*) to open; (*inchiesta*) to start up; (*confidarsi*): **aprirsi con qc** to open one's heart to sb.

apriscatole *sm inv* can opener.

aquila *sf* eagle.

aquilone *sm* kite.

Arabia Saudita *sf*: **l'~** Saudi Arabia.

arabo, -a ♦ *agg & sm, f* Arab ♦ *sm* (*lingua*) Arabic.

arachide *sf* peanut.

aragosta *sf* lobster.

arancia, -ce *sf* orange.

aranciata *sf* orange juice.

arancini *smpl* rice balls with a filling of tomatoes and mozzarella cheese (a Sicilian speciality).

arancio *sm* orange tree.

arancione *agg & sm* orange.

arare *vt* to plough.

aratro *sm* plough.

arazzo *sm* tapestry.

arbitrario, -a *agg* arbitrary.

arbitro *sm* referee.

arbusto *sm* shrub.

archeologia *sf* archaeology.

archeologico, -a, -ci, -che *agg* archaeological.

archeologo, -a, -gi, -ghe *sm, f* archaeologist.

architetto *sm* architect.

architettura *sf* architecture.

archivio *sm* (*luogo*) archives (*pl*); (*raccolta*) files (*pl*); (INFORM) file.

arcipelago, -ghi *sm* archipelago.

arcivescovo *sm* archbishop.

arco, -chi *sm* (*volta*) arch; (*arma*) bow; (*durata*): **nell'~ di due mesi** in the space of two months.

arcobaleno *sm* rainbow.

ardere *vt & vi* to burn.

ardesia *sf* (*pietra*) slate.

ardire ♦ *vi* to dare ♦ *sm* daring.

ardore *sm* ardour.

area *sf* area; **'~ pedonale'** 'pedestrian precinct'; **~ di servizio** services (*pl*).

arena *sf* arena.

arenarsi *vr* to run aground.

argenteria *sf* silverware.

Argentina *sf*: **l'~** Argentina.

argentino, -a *agg & sm, f* Argentinian.

argento *sm* silver; **d'~** silver.

argilla *sf* clay.

argine *sm* bank.

argomento *sm* (*tema*) subject; (*ragionamento*) argument.

arguto, -a *agg* (*persona*) quick-witted; (*discorso, battuta*) witty.

aria *sf* air; (*aspetto*) appearance; **ha l'~ familiare** he looks familiar; **mandare all'~ qc** to ruin sthg; **all'~ aperta** in the open air; **~ condizionata** air-conditioning; **darsi delle arie** to fancy o.s.

arido, -a *agg* (*secco*) arid; (*fig: persona, cuore*) cold.

ariete *sm* (*animale*) ram.

▶ **Ariete** *sm* Aries.

aringa, -ghe *sf* herring.

arista *sf* saddle of pork.

aristocratico, -a, -ci, -che ♦ *agg* aristocratic ♦ *sm, f* aristocrat.

aritmetica *sf* arithmetic.

Arlecchino *sm* Harlequin.

arma, -i *sf* (*strumento*) weapon; (*di esercito*) division; **~ da fuoco** firearm.

armadio *sm* cupboard; (*per vestiti*) wardrobe; **~ a muro** built-in cupboard.

armato, -a *agg* armed.

armatura *sf* armour.

armonia *sf* harmony.

arnese *sm* (*attrezzo*) tool; (*fam: oggetto*) thing.

arnia *sf* beehive.

Arno *sm*: **l'~** the Arno.

aroma, -i sm (odore) aroma; (essenza) flavouring.
▶ **aromi** smpl herbs.
arpa sf harp.
arpione sm harpoon.
arrabbiarsi vr to get angry.
arrabbiato, -a agg angry; all'arrabbiata → **penne**.
arrampicarsi vr to climb.
arrangiarsi vr to get by.
arredamento sm (arte, studio) interior design; (mobili) furnishings (pl).
arredare vt to furnish.
arrendersi vr to surrender.
arrestare vt (catturare) to arrest; (emorragia, flusso) to stop.
arresto sm (cattura) arrest; (fermata) stop; ~ **cardiaco** cardiac arrest.
arretrato, -a agg (pagamento, giornale) back (dav s); (sottosviluppato) backward; (sorpassato) old-fashioned.
▶ **arretrati** smpl arrears.
arricchire vt to enrich.
▶ **arricchirsi** vr to get rich.
arricciacapelli sm inv curling tongs (pl).
arricciare vt (capelli, nastro) to curl; ~ **il naso** to wrinkle one's nose.
arrivare vi to arrive; **arriverò a Firenze alle due** I'll get to Florence at two.
▶ **arrivare a** v + prep (grado, livello) to reach; ~ **a fare qc** (riuscire) to manage to do sthg; (giungere al punto di, osare) to go so far as to do sthg.
arrivederci esclam goodbye!
arrivederla esclam goodbye!
arrivista, -i, -e smf social climber.
arrivo sm arrival; (nello sport) finishing line; **essere in** ~ to be arriving; **'arrivi (nazionali/internazionali)'** '(domestic/international) arrivals'.
arrogante agg arrogant.

arrossire vi to blush.
arrostire vt to roast.
arrosto sm roast.
arrotolare vt to roll up.
arrotondare vt (render tondo) to round; (numero) to round off; (stipendio) to add to.
arrugginito, -a agg rusty.
arruolarsi vr to enlist.
arsenale sm (di armi) arsenal; (cantiere) dockyard.
arte sf art; (abilità) skill.
arteria sf artery.
artico, -a, -ci, -che agg Arctic.
articolare vt (parola) to articulate.
▶ **articolarsi: articolarsi in** vr + prep (testo, discorso) to be made up of.
articolazione sf joint.
articolo sm article; (merce) article, item; **articoli da regalo** gifts.
Artide sf: l'~ the Arctic.
artificiale agg artificial.
artigianato sm craftsmanship; **di** ~ handcrafted.
artigiano, -a ♦ agg craft (dav s) ♦ sm, f craftsman (f craftswoman).
artiglio sm claw.
artista, -i, -e smf artist.
artistico, -a, -ci, -che agg artistic.
arto sm limb.
artrite sf arthritis.
artrosi sf osteoarthritis.
ascella sf armpit.
ascendente sm (influsso) ascendancy; (astrologico) ascendant.
Ascensione sf: l'~ the Ascension.
ascensore sm lift (Br), elevator (Am).
ascesso sm abscess.
ascia (pl asce) sf axe.
asciugacapelli sm inv hairdryer.
asciugamano sm towel.
asciugare vt to dry.
▶ **asciugarsi** vr (persona) to dry o.s.; (tinta, vestiti) to dry.
asciutto, -a agg (secco) dry; (magro) thin.
ascoltare vt to listen to.

ascoltatore, -trice sm, f listener.

ascolto sm: **dare** o **prestare ~ a** to pay attention to; **essere in ~** to be listening.

asfaltato, -a agg asphalt (dav s).

asfalto sm asphalt.

asfissia sf asphyxia.

asfissiare vt & vi to suffocate.

Asia sf: **l'~** Asia.

asiatico, -a, -ci, -che agg & sm, f Asian.

asilo sm (scuola) nursery; **~ nido** crèche; **~ politico** political asylum.

asino sm donkey.

asma sf asthma.

asola sf buttonhole.

asparago sm asparagus.

aspettare vt to wait for; **aspetta!** wait!; **mi aspetto una risposta** I expect an answer; **~ un bambino** to be expecting a child.

aspettativa sf (previsione) expectation; (congedo) leave.

aspetto sm (apparenza) appearance; (punto di vista) point of view; (elemento) aspect.

aspirapolvere sm inv vacuum cleaner.

aspirare vt (inalare) to breathe in; (risucchiare) to suck up.

▶ **aspirare a** v + prep to aspire to.

aspiratore sm extractor.

aspirina® sf aspirin.

aspro, -a agg (sapore) sour.

assaggiare vt to taste.

assai avv (molto) very; (abbastanza) enough.

assalire vt to attack.

assassinare vt to murder.

assassinio sm murder.

assassino, -a sm, f murderer.

asse ♦ sf board ♦ sm (di auto) axle; (retta) axis.

assediare vt to besiege.

assedio sm siege.

assegnare vt: **~ qc (a qn)** (casa, rendita) to allocate sthg (to sb); (incarico, compiti) to assign sthg (to sb); (premio) to award sthg (to sb).

assegno sm (bancario) cheque; (sussidio) benefit; **~ a vuoto** bounced cheque; **~ circolare** bank draft; **~ di studio** study grant; **~ di viaggio** o **turistico** traveller's cheque; **contro ~** cash on delivery.

assemblea sf meeting.

assente ♦ agg (da luogo) absent; (distratto) vacant ♦ smf absentee.

assenza sf (lontananza) absence; (mancanza) lack.

assetato, -a agg thirsty.

assicurare vt (auto, casa) to insure; (garantire) to ensure; (fissare) to secure.

▶ **assicurarsi** vr to insure o.s.; **assicurarsi di fare qc** to be sure to do sthg; **assicurarsi che** to make sure that.

assicurata sf registered letter.

assicurato, -a agg insured.

assicurazione sf (contratto) insurance; (garanzia) assurance; **~ sulla vita** life assurance.

assieme avv together.

assillare vt (infastidire) to pester; (sog: pensiero) to torment.

Assisi sf Assisi.

assistente smf assistant; **~ sociale** social worker; **~ di volo** steward (f stewardess).

assistenza sf aid.

assistere ♦ vt to assist; (malato) to care for ♦ vi: **~ (a qc)** (a lezioni) to attend (sthg); (a scena) to be present (at sthg).

assistito, -a pp → **assistere**.

asso sm ace.

associare vt to associate.

▶ **associarsi** vr: **associarsi (a o con)** (ditta) to enter into a partnership (with); **associarsi a qc** (club) to join sthg.

associazione sf association.

assolto, -a pp → **assolvere**.

assolutamente avv absolutely.

assoluto, -a agg absolute.

assoluzione sf (accusato) acquittal; (RELIG) absolution.

assolvere vt (accusato) to acquit; (RELIG) to absolve; (compito) to carry out.

assomigliare : assomigliare a v + prep to resemble, to look like.

assonnato, -a agg sleepy.

assorbente ◆ agg (tampone) absorbent ◆ sm: ~ **(igienico)** (sanitary) towel; ~ **interno** tampon.

assorbire vt to absorb.

assordante agg deafening.

assortimento sm assortment.

assortito, -a agg (vario) assorted; (accordato) matching.

assumere vt (personale) to take on; (impegno) to accept; (atteggiamento) to assume.

assunto, -a pp → assumere.

assurdità sf inv absurdity.

assurdo, -a agg absurd.

asta sf (bastone) pole; (vendita) auction.

astemio, -a agg teetotal.

astenersi : astenersi da vr + prep to abstain from.

asterisco, -schi sm asterisk.

astigmatico, -a, -ci, -che agg astigmatic.

astratto, -a agg abstract.

astrologia sf astrology.

astronauta, -i, -e smf astronaut.

astronomia sf astronomy.

astuccio sm case.

astuto, -a agg (persona) cunning; (idea, azione) shrewd.

astuzia sf (furbizia) shrewdness; (stratagemma) trick.

A.T. abbr = **alta tensione**.

Atene sf Athens.

ateo, -a sm, f atheist.

ATI (abbr di Aerotrasporti Italiani) Italian domestic airline.

atlante sm (geografico) atlas.

atlantico, -a, -ci, -che agg Atlantic.

Atlantico sm: l'(Oceano) ~ the Atlantic (Ocean).

atleta, -i, -e smf athlete.

atletica sf athletics (sg).

atletico, -a, -ci, -che agg athletic.

atmosfera sf atmosphere.

atmosferico, -a, -ci, -che agg atmospheric.

atomico, -a, -ci, -che agg atomic.

atomo sm atom.

atroce agg atrocious.

attaccante sm forward.

attaccapanni sm inv clothes stand.

attaccare vt (unire) to attach; (apparecchio) to plug in; (appendere) to hang up; (assalire) to attack; (trasmettere) to give.

▶ **attaccarsi** vr to stick.

attacco, -chi sm attack; (presa) socket.

atteggiamento sm attitude.

attendere vt to wait for.

attentato sm attack.

attento, -a agg (che presta attenzione) attentive; (prudente) careful; **stai ~!** (non distrarti) pay attention!; (stai in guardia) be careful!; '**attenti al cane**' 'beware of the dog'; '**attenti al gradino**' 'mind the step'.

attenzione sf attention; ~! be careful!; **fare ~** (concentrarsi) to pay attention; (essere prudente) to be careful.

atterraggio sm landing.

atterrare vi to land.

attesa sf wait; **essere in ~ di** to be waiting for.

atteso, -a pp → attendere.

attestato sm certificate.

attico sm penthouse.

attillato, -a agg close-fitting.

attimo sm moment; **un ~** hold on (a moment).

attirare vt to attract.

attitudine sf aptitude.

attività sf inv activity; (occupazione) occupation; (COMM) assets (pl).

attivo, -a ◆ agg active ◆ sm assets (pl).

atto sm (azione, gesto) act, deed;

(*documento*) document; (*di dramma*) act; **mettere in ~** to put into action.

attonito, -a *agg* astonished.

attorcigliare *vt* to twist.

attore, -trice *sm, f* actor (*f* actress).

attorniare *vt* to surround.

attorno *avv* around.

attracco, -chi *sm* (*manovra*) docking; (*luogo*) mooring.

attraente *agg* attractive.

attrarre *vt* (*affascinare*) to attract; (*richiamare*) to draw.

attrattiva *sf* (*richiamo*) attraction; (*qualità*) attractiveness.

attratto, -a *pp* → **attrarre**.

attraversamento *sm* crossing; **~ pedonale** pedestrian crossing.

attraversare *vt* (*strada, città*) to cross; (*periodo*) to go through.

attraverso *prep* (*da parte a parte*) across; (*per mezzo di*) through.

attrazione *sf* attraction.

attrezzato, -a *agg* well-equipped.

attrezzatura *sf* equipment.

attrezzo *sm* tool.

attribuire : attribuire a *v + prep* (*opera*) to attribute to; **~ il merito a qn** to give sb the credit.

attrice → **attore**.

attrito *sm* friction.

attuale *agg* (*presente*) present; (*moderno*) topical.

attualità *sf inv* current events (*pl*); **d'~** topical.

attualmente *avv* at present.

attuare *vt* to carry out.

attutire *vt* (*colpo, rumore*) to reduce.

audace *agg* bold.

audacia *sf* audacity.

audiovisivo, -a *agg* audio-visual.

auditorio *sm* auditorium.

audizione *sf* audition.

augurare *vt*: **~ qc a qn** to wish sb sthg; **augurarsi di fare qc** to hope to do sthg; **mi auguro che tutto vada**

bene I hope that all goes well.

augurio *sm* wish; **auguri** greetings; **(tanti) auguri!** all the best!; (*per compleanno*) happy birthday!; **fare gli auguri a qn** to give sb one's best wishes.

aula *sf* classroom.

aumentare *vt & vi* to increase.

aumento *sm* increase; **~ (di stipendio)** pay rise.

aureola *sf* halo.

auricolare *sm* earphone.

aurora *sf* dawn.

ausiliare *agg & sm* auxiliary.

austero, -a *agg* austere.

Australia *sf*: **l'~** Australia.

australiano, -a *agg & sm, f* Australian.

Austria *sf*: **l'~** Austria.

austriaco, -a, -ci, -che *agg & sm, f* Austrian.

autenticare *vt* to authenticate.

autentico, -a, -ci, -che *agg* (*firma, quadro*) authentic; (*fatto*) true; **è un ~ cretino** he's a real cretin.

autista, -i, -e *smf* driver.

auto *sf inv* car.

autoabbronzante ♦ *agg* self-tanning ♦ *sm* fake tanning cream.

autoadesivo, -a ♦ *agg* self-adhesive ♦ *sm* sticker.

autoambulanza *sf* ambulance.

autobiografia *sf* autobiography.

autobus *sm inv* bus.

autocarro *sm* truck.

autocisterna *sf* tanker.

autocontrollo *sm* self-control.

autodidatta, -i, -e *smf* self-taught person.

autodromo *sm* racing track.

autofilotranviario, -a *agg* bus, trolley and tram (*dav s*).

autogol *sm inv* own goal.

autografo *sm* autograph.

autogrill® *sm inv* motorway restaurant.

autolinea *sf* bus service.

automa, -i *sm* automaton.

automatico, -a, -ci, -che *agg* automatic.

automazione *sf* automation.

automezzo *sm* motor vehicle.

automobile *sf* car (Br), automobile (Am).

automobilismo *sm* (*sport*) motor racing; (*industria*) car industry (Br), auto industry (Am).

automobilista, -i, -e *smf* motorist.

autonoleggio *sm* car hire.

autonomia *sf* (*indipendenza*) autonomy; (*di veicolo*) range.

autonomo, -a *agg* independent, autonomous.

autopsia *sf* autopsy.

autoradio *sf inv* car radio.

autore, -trice *sm, f* (*di libro*) author; (*di quadro*) painter; **l'~ del delitto** the person who committed the crime.

autorevole *agg* authoritative.

autorimessa *sf* garage.

autorità *sf inv* authority.

autoritario, -a *agg* authoritarian.

autorizzare *vt* to authorize.

autorizzazione *sf* authorization.

autoscatto *sm* timer.

autoscontro *sm* Dodgem® car.

autoscuola *sf* driving school.

autoservizi *smpl* bus services.

autostop *sm* hitchhiking; **fare l'~** to hitchhike.

autostoppista, -i, -e *smf* hitchhiker.

autostrada *sf* motorway (Br), freeway (Am).

autostradale *agg* motorway (Br) (*dav s*), freeway (Am) (*dav s*).

autoveicolo *sm* motor vehicle.

autovettura *sf* motorcar.

autunno *sm* autumn (Br), fall (Am).

avambraccio *sm* forearm.

avanguardia *sf:* **d'~** avant-garde; **essere all'~** to be in the vanguard.

avanti ♦ *avv* (*stato in luogo*) in front; (*moto*) forward ♦ *prep:* **~ a** (*stato in luogo*) ahead of; (*moto*) ahead of, in front of; **~!** (*invito a entrare*) come in!; (*esortazione*) come on!; **'avanti!'** (*al semaforo*) 'cross now', 'walk' (Am); (*in banca*) 'enter'; **~ e indietro** backwards and forwards; **andare ~** to go on; (*orologio*) to be fast; **il mio orologio va ~ di 5 minuti** my watch is 5 minutes fast; **essere ~** (*nel lavoro, studio*) to be well ahead; **essere ~ negli anni** to be getting on (in years); **farsi ~** to come forward; **passare ~ a qn** to go in front of sb.

avanzare ♦ *vt* (*spostare avanti*) to move forward; (*proposta*) to put forward ♦ *vi* (*procedere*) to advance; (*restare*) to be left (over).

avanzo *sm* (*di cibo*) leftovers (*pl*); (*di stoffa*) remnant.

avaria *sf* (*meccanico*) breakdown.

avariato, -a *agg* (*cibo*) off.

avaro, -a ♦ *agg* mean ♦ *sm, f* miser.

avena *sf* oats (*pl*).

avere *vt* **1.** (*possedere*) to have; **ha due fratelli** he's got two brothers; **non ho più soldi** I haven't got any money left.

2. (*come caratteristica*) to have; **~ occhi e capelli scuri** to have dark eyes and hair; **~ molta immaginazione** to have a lot of imagination.

3. (*età*): **quanti anni hai?** how old are you?; **ho 18 anni** I'm 18 (years old).

4. (*portare addosso*) to have on, to wear; **ha un cappotto grigio** she's wearing a grey coat, she's got a grey coat on.

5. (*sentire*): **~ caldo/freddo** to be hot/cold; **~ sonno** to be sleepy; **~ fame** to be hungry; **ho mal di testa** I've got a headache.

6. (*ottenere, ricevere*) to get.

7. (*in espressioni*): **non ha niente a che fare** o **vedere con lui** that's got nothing to do with him; **non ne ho per**

molto it won't take me long; **~ da fare** to have things to do; **avercela con qn** to be angry with sb; **quanti ne abbiamo oggi?** what's the date today?

♦ *v aus* to have; **non ho finito** I haven't finished; **gli ho parlato ieri** I spoke to him yesterday.

▶ **averi** *smpl* (*beni*) wealth (*sg*).

avi *smpl* ancestors.

aviazione *sf* aviation.

avido, -a *agg* greedy.

AVIS *sf* (*abbr di Associazione Volontari Italiani del Sangue*) blood donors' association.

avocado *sm inv* avocado.

avorio *sm* ivory.

avvallamento *sm* depression.

avvantaggiare *vt* to favour.

▶ **avvantaggiarsi** *vr*: **avvantaggiarsi negli studi** to get ahead with one's studies; **avvantaggiarsi sui concorrenti** to get ahead of one's competitors.

▶ **avvantaggiarsi di** *vr + prep* to take advantage of.

avvelenamento *sm* poisoning.

avvelenare *vt* to poison; (*aria*) to pollute.

avvenente *agg* attractive.

avvenimento *sm* event.

avvenire ♦ *sm* future ♦ *vi* to happen.

avventarsi *vr*: **~ su o contro** to rush at.

avventato, -a *agg* rash.

avventura *sf* adventure; (*amorosa*) affair.

avventurarsi *vr* to venture.

avventuroso, -a *agg* adventurous.

avvenuto, -a *pp* → **avvenire**.

avverarsi *vr* to come true.

avverbio *sm* adverb.

avversario, -a ♦ *agg* opposing ♦ *sm, f* opponent.

avvertenza *sf* (*avviso*) notice.

▶ **avvertenze** *sfpl* instructions.

avvertimento *sm* warning.

avvertire *vt* (*avvisare*) to warn; (*infor-*

mare) to notify; (*dolore, fastidio*) to feel.

avviamento *sm* (*di motore*) starting; (COMM) goodwill.

avviare *vt* (*cominciare*) to start; (*indirizzare*) to introduce.

▶ **avviarsi** *vr* to set off.

avvicinare *vt* to move closer.

▶ **avvicinarsi** *vr*: **avvicinarsi (a)** to move close (to).

avvilirsi *vr* to lose heart.

avvincente *agg* enthralling.

avvisare *vt* (*informare*) to inform; (*ammonire*) to warn.

avviso *sm* (*scritto*) notice; (*annuncio*) announcement; (*avvertimento*) warning; **a mio ~** in my opinion.

avvistare *vt* to sight.

avvitare *vt* (*lampadina*) to screw in; (*con viti*) to screw.

avvizzire *vi* to wither.

avvocato *sm* lawyer.

avvolgere *vt* (*fascia*) to wrap round; (*tappeto*) to roll up; (*avviluppare*) to wrap up.

▶ **avvolgersi** *vr* (*aggrovigliarsi*) to become tangled; (*avvilupparsi*) to wrap o.s. up.

avvolgibile *sm* roller blind.

avvolto, -a *pp* → **avvolgere**.

avvoltoio *sm* vulture.

azalea *sf* azalea.

azienda *sf* business, firm; **~ agricola** farm.

azionare *vt* to operate.

azione *sf* action; (COMM) share.

azionista, -i, -e *smf* shareholder.

azoto *sm* nitrogen.

azzannare *vt* to sink one's teeth into.

azzardare *vt* to venture.

▶ **azzardarsi** *vr*: **azzardarsi a fare qc** to dare to do sthg.

azzardo *sm* risk; **giocare d'~** to gamble.

azzeccare *vt* to get right.

azzuffarsi *vr* to scuffle.

azzurro, -a *agg* & *sm* blue.

▶ **Azzurri** *smpl*: **gli Azzurri** the Italian national team.

B

babà sm inv rum baba.

babbo sm (fam) dad, daddy; **Babbo Natale** Father Christmas.

baby-sitter [bɛbi'sitter] smf inv babysitter.

bacca, -che sf (frutto) berry.

baccalà sm inv dried salt cod; ~ **alla fiorentina** dried salt cod cooked with garlic and tomato sauce; ~ **alla vicentina** dried salt cod poached in milk with onions, anchovies and parsley.

bacheca, -che sf (pannello) notice board; (cassetta) display case.

baciare vt to kiss.

▶ **baciarsi** vr to kiss (each other).

bacinella sf bowl.

bacino sm (in geografia, catino) basin; (ANAT) pelvis.

bacio sm kiss; **baci di dama** sweet pastries sandwiched together with chocolate cream.

badare vi: ~ **a** (prendersi cura di) to look after; (fare attenzione a) to pay attention to; ~ **a o di fare qc** to take care to do sthg; **mio fratello non bada a spese** money's no object where my brother's concerned.

badia sf abbey.

baffi smpl moustache (sg).

bagagliaio sm (di macchina) boot (Br), trunk (Am); (di treno) luggage van (Br), baggage car (Am).

bagaglio sm luggage, baggage; ~ **a mano** hand luggage; **ho un solo** ~ I have only one piece of luggage.

▶ **bagagli** smpl luggage (sg); **fare i bagagli** to pack.

bagliore sm (di lampi) flash; (di fari) glare.

bagna cauda sf oil, garlic and anchovy dip from Piedmont kept warm at the table and served with vegetables.

bagnare vt to wet; (tovaglia, vestiti) to get wet; (annaffiare) to water; (sog: fiume) to flow through; (sog: mare) to wash.

▶ **bagnarsi** vr (in mare) to bathe; (di pioggia, spruzzi) to get wet.

bagnato, -a agg wet; ~ **fradicio** soaked through.

bagnino, -a sm, f lifeguard.

bagno sm (nella vasca) bath; (in piscina, mare) swim; (stanza) bathroom; **fare il** ~ (nella vasca) to have a bath; (in mare) to have a swim; ~ **pubblico** public baths (pl).

▶ **bagni** smpl (stabilimento) bathing establishment.

bagnomaria sm: **cuocere a** ~ to cook in a double saucepan.

bagnoschiuma sm inv bath foam.

baia sf bay.

baita sf chalet.

balaustra sf balustrade.

balbettare vi to stammer.

balcone sm balcony.

balena sf whale.

balla sf (frottola) fib; (di merci) bale.

ballare vi & vt to dance.

ballerina sf (scarpa) pump, → **ballerino**.

ballerino, -a sm, f dancer; (classico) ballet-dancer (f ballerina).

balletto sm ballet.

ballo sm dance; (festa) dance, ball; **essere in** ~ to be at stake; **tirare in** ~ (coinvolgere) to involve; (menzionare) to mention.

balneare agg bathing (dav s).

balneazione sf bathing; **'divieto di balneazione'** 'no bathing'.

balsamo sm (per capelli) conditioner; (pomata) ointment.

Baltico sm: **il (Mar)** ~ the Baltic (Sea).

balzare vi to leap.

bambinaia sf nanny.

bambino, -a *sm, f* child; (*neonato*) baby.

bambola *sf* doll.

banale *agg* banal.

banana *sf* banana.

banca, -che *sf* bank; **~ dati** data bank.

bancarella *sf* stall.

bancario, -a ♦ *agg* bank (*dav s*) ♦ *sm, f* bank employee.

bancarotta *sf* bankruptcy.

banchina *sf* (*di porto*) quay; (*di stazione*) platform; **'~ non transitabile'** 'soft verges'.

banco, -chi *sm* (*di scuola*) desk; (*di negozio, bar*) counter; (*di mercato*) stall; (*banca*) bank; **~ di corallo** coral reef; **~ di nebbia** fog bank.

bancomat® *sm inv* (*sportello*) cash dispenser; (*tessera*) cash card; (*sistema*) automated banking.

bancone *sm* counter.

banconota *sf* bank note.

banda *sf* (*musicale*) band; (*striscia*) band, strip; (*di malviventi*) gang; (*di amici*) group.

bandiera *sf* flag.

bandito *sm* bandit.

bando *sm* announcement; **~ alle chiacchiere!** that's enough talking!

bar *sm inv* bar; **~-tabacchi** *bar that also sells cigarettes and stamps.*

BAR

Italian bars are open throughout the day. You can have a coffee and a pastry for breakfast, a mid-morning snack, an aperitif or a toasted sandwich. You can eat standing at the counter, which is cheaper, but many bars also offer table service. Look out for the sign 'munirsi dello scontrino', as this means you have to pay at the cash desk before being served at the counter.

---

bara *sf* coffin.

baracca, -che *sf* hut; (*spreg: casa*) dump; **mandare avanti la ~** (*fam*) to keep things going.

baraccone *sm* booth.

baratro *sm* barter.

barattolo *sm* jar; (*di latta*) can.

barba *sf* beard; **farsi la ~** to shave; **che ~!** what a bore!

barbaro, -a ♦ *agg* barbaric ♦ *sm, f* barbarian.

barbecue ['ba:bikju:] *sm inv* barbecue.

barbiere *sm* barber.

barbone, -a *sm, f* tramp.

barca, -che *sf* boat; **~ a remi** rowing boat (Br), rowboat (Am); **~ a vela** sailing boat (Br), sailboat (Am).

barcollare *vi* to stagger.

barella *sf* stretcher.

barista, -i, -e *smf* barman (*f* barmaid).

barman *sm inv* barman.

barocco, -a, -chi, -che *agg & sm* baroque.

Barolo *sm* Barolo (*full-bodied red wine from Piedmont*).

barra *sf* rod, bar; (*lineetta*) stroke; (*di barca*) tiller.

barricare *vt* to barricade.

▶ **barricarsi** *vr*: **barricarsi in/dietro** to barricade o.s. in/behind.

barriera *sf* barrier.

basare *vt* to base.

▶ **basarsi su** *vr + prep* (*persona*) to base o.s. on.

base *sf* base; (*fondamento*) basis; **a ~ di whisky** whisky-based; **in ~ a qc** on the basis of sthg; **di ~** basic.

baseball ['beizbol] *sm* baseball.

basette *sfpl* sideboards.

basilica, -che *sf* basilica.

Basilicata *sf* Basilicata (*region of southern Italy*).

basilico *sm* basil.

basso, -a ♦ *agg* low; (*persona*) short; (*acqua*) shallow ♦ *sm* (*fondo*) bottom; (*strumento, cantante*) bass; **in ~** at the bottom.

basta *esclam* that's enough!

bastare *vi & v impers* to be enough; **~ a qn** to be enough for sb; **basta che** so long as; **basta così!** that's enough!

bastone *sm* stick; ~ **da passeggio** walking stick.

▶ **bastoni** *smpl* (*nelle carte*) suit in a Neapolitan pack of cards.

battaglia *sf* battle.

battello *sm* boat.

battere ♦ *vt* to beat; (*testa*) to hit; (*ore*) to strike; (*zona*) to scour ♦ *vi* (*cuore*) to beat; (*sole, pioggia*) to beat down; (*urtare*): ~ **contro** o **in qc** to hit sthg; **si batteva i denti dal freddo** our teeth were chattering with the cold; ~ **a macchina** to type; ~ **le mani** to clap; **in un batter d'occhio** in the twinkling of an eye.

▶ **battersi** *vr* to fight.

batteria *sf* (*elettrica*) battery; (*strumento*) drums (*pl*).

battesimo *sm* baptism, christening.

battezzare *vt* to baptize.

battigia *sf* water's edge.

battistrada *sm inv* tread.

battito *sm* beat, beating; (*di orologio*) ticking; ~ **cardiaco** heartbeat.

battuta *sf* (*spiritosaggine*) witty remark; (*teatrale*) cue; (*di tennis*) service.

baule *sm* (*da viaggio*) trunk; (*di auto*) boot (Br), trunk (Am).

bavaglino *sm* bib.

bavaglio *sm* gag.

bavarese *sf* (*dolce*) cold dessert made with eggs, milk and cream.

bavero *sm* collar.

bazzecola *sf* (*cosa poco importante*) trifle; (*cosa facile*): **è una** ~ it's no problem.

beato, -a *agg* (*felice*) happy; (RELIG) blessed; ~ **te!** lucky you!

beauty-case [ˈbjuːti ˈkeis] *sm inv* beauty case.

beccare *vt* to peck; (*fam: sorprendere*) to catch; **beccarsi qc** (*fam*) (*raffreddore*) to catch sthg; (*ceffone*) to get sthg.

becco, -chi *sm* beak.

Befana *sf* (*festa*) Epiphany; (*per-* *sonaggio*) *legendary old woman who brings children their presents at the Epiphany.*

BEFANA

According to legend, the 'Befana' is a kindly old hag who delivers presents to children on the night before the Epiphany. Children leave out a stocking before going to bed, and the 'Befana' comes down the chimney in the night, bringing sweets and other gifts to good boys and girls and lumps of coal to those who have been naughty.

beffa *sf* joke.

beffarsi : beffarsi di *vr + prep* to make fun of.

begli → **bello**.

bei → **bello**.

beige [bɛʒ] *agg inv & sm inv* beige.

bel → **bello**.

belga, -gi, -ghe *agg & smf* Belgian.

Belgio *sm*: **il** ~ Belgium.

bella *sf* (SPORT) decider.

bellezza *sf* beauty; **che** ~! fantastic!

bello, -a (*dav sm* **bel** (*pl* **bei**) + *consonante*; **bello** (*pl* **begli**) + *s+consonante, gn, ps, z*; **bell'** (*pl* **begli**) + *vocale*) *agg* **1.** (*donna, cosa*) beautiful; (*uomo*) handsome; **farsi** ~ to make o.s. beautiful; **le belle arti** fine arts.

2. (*piacevole*) pleasant, lovely.

3. (*tempo*) fine, beautiful; **la bella stagione** the summer months (*pl*); **fa** ~ it's lovely weather.

4. (*buono*) good.

5. (*lodevole*) good, kind.

6. (*grande*): **un bel piatto di spaghetti** a nice big plate of spaghetti; **una bella dormita** a good sleep; **è una bella cifra** it's a considerable sum of money.

7. (*rafforzativo*): **è bell'e (che) andato** he's already gone; **è una bugia bell'e buona** it's an absolute lie; **alla bell'e meglio** somehow or other; **un**

bel niente absolutely nothing.
♦ *sm* **1.** (*bellezza*) beauty.
2. (*punto culminante*): **sul più ~** at that very moment; **il ~ è che ...** the best bit is that ...

belva *sf* wild beast.

belvedere *sm inv* scenic viewpoint.

benché *cong* although, though.

benda *sf* (*fasciatura*) bandage; (*per occhi*) blindfold.

bendare *vt* (*ferita*) to bandage; (*occhi*) to blindfold.

bene *avv* (*compar & superl* **meglio**) **1.** (*in modo soddisfacente*) well; **avete mangiato ~?** did you enjoy your meal?
2. (*nel modo giusto*) well; **hai fatto ~** you did the right thing.
3. (*in buona salute*): **stare/sentirsi ~** to be/feel well, to be/feel fine.
4. (*a proprio agio*): **stare ~** to be o feel comfortable.
5. (*esteticamente*): **stare ~** to look good.
6. (*rafforzativo*): **è ben difficile** it's very difficult; **è ben più difficile del previsto** it's much more difficult than we thought; **lo credo ~** I can well believe it; **spero ~ che** I very much hope that.
7. (*in espressioni*): **è ~ che lo sappiate** it's as well that you know; **sarebbe ~ aspettare** it would be better to wait; **dire ~ di qn** to speak well of sb; **ti sta ~!** it serves you right!; **va ~** all right, OK.
♦ *esclam* fine!, OK!
♦ *sm* good; **è per il tuo ~** it's for your own good; **è un ~ per tutti** it is a good thing for everyone.
▶ **beni** *smpl* (*proprietà*) property (*sg*).

benedire *vt* to bless.

benedizione *sf* blessing.

beneducato, -a *agg* well-mannered.

beneficenza *sf* charity.

beneficio, -ci *sm* benefit.

benessere *sm* wellbeing.

benestante *agg* well-to-do.

benevolo, -a *agg* benevolent.

beninteso *avv* certainly, of course.

benvenuto, -a *agg & sm* welcome; **benvenuti a Roma!** welcome to Rome!; **dare il ~ a qn** to welcome sb.

benzina *sf* petrol (Br), gas (Am); **fare ~** to get petrol (Br), to get gas (Am); **finire la ~** to run out of petrol (Br), to run out of gas (Am).

benzinaio, -a *sm, f* forecourt attendant.

bere *vt* to drink; **bevi qualcosa?** would you like something to drink?; **offrire da ~ a qn** to offer sb a drink.

bergamotto *sm* bergamot.

Berlino *sf* Berlin.

bermuda *smpl* bermuda shorts.

bernoccolo *sm* bump.

bersaglio *sm* target.

besciamella *sf* béchamel sauce.

bestemmiare *vi* to curse, to swear.

bestia *sf* animal; **andare in ~** to fly into a rage.

bestiame *sm* livestock.

bevanda *sf* drink.

bevuto, -a *pp* → **bere**.

biancheria *sf* linen; **~ intima** underwear.

bianchetto *sm* correcting fluid.

bianco, -a, -chi, -che ♦ *agg & sm* white ♦ *sm, f* (*persona*) white man (*f* white woman); **riso in ~** plain rice; **pesce in ~** boiled fish; **in ~ e nero** black and white.

biasimare *vt* to blame.

bibbia *sf* bible.

biberon *sm inv* baby's bottle.

bibita *sf* drink.

biblioteca, -che *sf* library.

bicarbonato *sm*: **~ (di sodio)** bicarbonate (of soda).

bicchiere *sm* glass.

bici *sf inv* (*fam*) bike.

bicicletta *sf* bicycle; **andare in ~** to cycle.

bistecca

bidè *sm inv* bidet.

bidone *sm* bin; (*fam*) (*imbroglio*) swindle; **fare un ~ a qn** (*fam*) (*imbrogliare*) to cheat sb; (*mancare a un appuntamento*) to stand sb up.

biennale *agg* (*ogni due anni*) two-yearly; (*per due anni*) two-year (*dav s*).

▶ **Biennale** *sf*: **la Biennale** the Venice Arts Festival.

BIENNALE

Established in 1895, this international art festival takes place every two years in the gardens of the International Gallery of Modern Art in Venice. The selection of paintings and sculptures on view reflects the avant-garde emphasis of the festival, a trend which has become more pronounced in recent years and is not without its critics. Alongside the art festival there are festivals of music, theatre and architecture, as well as an annual film festival.

biforcarsi *vr* to fork.

BiGE *sm reduced-price train ticket for people under 26.*

bigiotteria *sf* costume jewellery; (*negozio*) costume jeweller's.

biglia = **bilia**.

bigliardo = **biliardo**.

bigliettaio, -a *sm, f* ticket inspector.

biglietteria *sf* ticket office; (*al teatro*) box office; **~ automatica** ticket machine.

biglietto *sm* (*scontrino*) ticket; (*messaggio*) note; (*banconota*) (bank) note; **fare il ~** to buy one's ticket; **~ d'andata e ritorno** return (ticket); **~ di (sola) andata** single (ticket); **~ collettivo** party ticket; **~ cumulativo** group ticket; **~ gratuito** complimentary ticket; **~ intero** full-price ticket; **~ ridotto** reduced-price ticket; **~ d'auguri** greetings card; **~ da visita** visiting card.

bignè *sm inv choux bun filled with custard or chocolate.*

bigodino *sm* curler.

bigoli *smpl*: **~ coi rovinazzi** *large spaghetti from Veneto in a sauce made with chicken giblets.*

bikini® *sm inv* bikini.

bilancia, -ce *sf* scales (*pl*).

▶ **Bilancia** *sf* Libra.

bilancio *sm* (COMM) balance sheet; **~ preventivo** budget.

bilia *sf* (*di vetro*) marble; (*da biliardo*) billiard ball.

biliardo *sm* (*gioco*) billiards (*sg*); (*tavolo*) billiard table.

bilico : in bilico *avv* balanced.

bilingue *agg* bilingual.

bimbo, -a *sm, f* little boy (*f* little girl).

binario *sm* (*rotaie*) railway track; (*marciapiede*) platform; '**ai binari**' 'to the trains'.

binocolo *sm* binoculars (*pl*).

biologia *sf* biology.

biologo, -a, gi, -ghe *sm, f* biologist.

biondo, -a *agg* blond (*f* blonde).

birichino, -a ♦ *agg* cheeky ♦ *sm, f* little rascal.

birillo *sm* skittle.

biro® *sf inv* Biro®.

birra *sf* beer; **~ chiara** lager; **~ scura** stout; **~ alla spina** draught beer.

birreria *sf* pub.

bis *esclam* encore!

bisbigliare *vi & vt* to whisper.

biscotto *sm* biscuit.

bisessuale *agg* bisexual.

bisestile *agg* → **anno**.

bisnonno, -a *sm, f* great-grandfather (*f* great-grandmother).

bisognare *v impers*: **bisogna stare attenti** we/I must be careful; **bisogna che tu venga subito** you have to come at once.

bisogno *sm* need, necessity; **aver ~ di** to need.

bistecca, -che *sf* steak; **~ al sangue** rare steak; **~ alla fiorentina**

T-bone steak grilled or cooked over char-coal.

bisticciare *vi* to bicker.

bitter *sm inv* bitters *(pl)*.

bivio *sm* fork, junction.

bizza *sf* tantrum.

bizzarro, -a *agg* odd, eccentric.

bloccare *vt* to block; *(città)* to cut off; *(meccanismo)* to jam; *(prezzi)* to freeze.

▶ **bloccarsi** *vr (ascensore)* to get stuck; *(porta)* to jam.

blocchetto *sm (quaderno)* note-book.

blocco, -chi *sm* block; *(quaderno)* notebook; *(di meccanismo)* blockage; *(di attività)* stoppage; **~ stradale** roadblock; **in ~** en bloc.

blu *agg inv & sm inv* blue.

blue-jeans [blu'dʒins] *smpl* jeans.

blusa *sf* blouse.

boa ◆ *sm inv (serpente)* boa ◆ *sf (galleggiante)* buoy.

bobina *sf (di auto)* coil; *(di pellicola)* reel.

bocca, -che *sf* mouth; **in ~ al lupo!** good luck!

boccaccia, -ce *sf:* **fare le boccacce** to pull faces.

boccale *sm* jug.

boccia, -ce *sf* bowl.

bocciare *vt (studente)* to fail; *(proposta, progetto)* to reject.

boccone *sm* mouthful; **mangiare un ~** to have a bite to eat.

bocconi *avv* face downwards.

boicottare *vt* to boycott.

bolla *sf* bubble; *(vescica)* blister; (COMM) bill.

bollente *agg* boiling.

bolletta *sf* bill; *(ricevuta)* receipt.

bollettino *sm* bulletin; **~ meteorologico** weather forecast.

bollire *vt & vi* to boil.

bollito, -a ◆ *agg* boiled ◆ *sm beef, veal or chicken, served with a parsley sauce.*

bollitore *sm* kettle.

bollo *sm (marchio)* stamp.

Bologna *sf* Bologna.

bolognese *agg* of/from Bologna; **alla ~** with meat and tomato sauce.

bomba *sf* bomb.

bombardare *vt* to bomb.

bombola *sf* cylinder.

bombolone *sm* doughnut.

bonaccia *sf* (dead) calm.

bonario, -a *agg* good-natured.

bonet *sm inv chocolate-flavoured egg custard.*

bontà *sf* goodness.

borbottare ◆ *vi* to grumble ◆ *vt* to mutter.

bordeaux [bor'do] *agg inv* maroon.

bordo *sm (orlo)* edge; *(guarnizione)* trim, border; *(di nave)* (ship's) side; **a ~ di** *(nave, aereo)* on board; *(auto)* in; *(moto)* on.

borghese *agg* middle-class; **in ~** in plain clothes.

borghesia *sf* middle classes *(pl)*.

borgo, -ghi *sm (paesino)* hamlet; *(quartiere)* district.

borotalco® *sm* talcum powder.

borraccia, -ce *sf* flask.

borsa *sf* bag; **~ dell'acqua calda** hot-water bottle; **~ del ghiaccio** ice bag; **~ della spesa** shopping bag; **~ di studio** grant.

▶ **Borsa** *sf* Stock Exchange.

borsaiolo *sm* pickpocket.

borsellino *sm* purse.

borsetta *sf* handbag.

boscaiola *sf* → **risotto**.

bosco, -schi *sm* wood.

botanico, -a, -ci, -che ◆ *agg* botanic ◆ *sm, f* botanist.

botta *sf* blow; *(rumore)* bang; **fare a botte** to come to blows.

botte *sf* barrel.

bottega, -ghe *sf* shop; *(laboratorio)* workshop.

bottegaio, -a *sm, f* shopkeeper.

bottiglia *sf* bottle.

bottiglione *sm* large bottle.

bottone *sm* button; **attaccare un ~ a qn** to buttonhole sb.

boutique [bu'tik] sf inv boutique.

box sm inv (garage) lock-up (garage); (per bambini) playpen; (per animali) pen.

boxe [bɔks] sf boxing.

boy-scout [bɔi'skaut] sm inv boy scout.

braccetto: a braccetto avv arm in arm.

bracciale sm bracelet.

braccialetto sm bracelet.

braccio sm (arto: pl f **braccia**) arm; (di edificio: pl m **bracci**) wing; (di gru, fiume: pl m **bracci**) arm; ~ **di ferro** arm wrestling; **in** ~ in one's arms; **sotto** ~ arm in arm.

bracciolo sm arm.

brace sf embers (pl); **alla** ~ charcoal-grilled.

braciola sf steak; (con osso) chop.

braille ['braj] sm braille.

branco, -chi sm (di animali) herd; (spreg: di persone) gang, bunch.

branda sf camp bed.

brasato sm braised beef.

Brasile sm: **il** ~ Brazil.

bravo, -a agg good; ~! well done!; ~ **a fare qc** good at doing sthg; ~ **in qc** good at sthg.

bresaola sf dried salt beef served thinly sliced.

bretelle sfpl (per pantaloni) braces; (spalline) straps.

breve agg short, brief; **in** ~ briefly; **tra** ~ shortly.

brevetto sm (di invenzione) patent; (patente) licence.

brezza sf breeze.

bricco, -chi sm jug.

briciola sf crumb.

briciolo sm: **un** ~ **di qc** a bit of sthg.

bridge [bridʒ] sm bridge.

brillante ♦ agg brilliant; (lucente) bright ♦ sm diamond.

brillare vi to shine.

brillo, -a agg tipsy.

brindisi sm inv toast; **fare un** ~ **a** to toast.

brioche [bri'ɔʃ] sf inv round, sweet bread roll made with butter and eaten for breakfast.

briscola sf Italian card game.

britannico, -a, -ci, -che agg British.

brivido sm shiver, shudder.

brocca, -che sf jug.

brodo sm broth; **pasta in** ~ noodle soup; **riso in** ~ rice soup.

bronchite sf bronchitis.

brontolare vi to grumble; (stomaco, tuono) to rumble.

bronzo sm bronze.

bruciapelo : a bruciapelo avv point-blank.

bruciare ♦ vt to burn; (distruggere) to burn down ♦ vi to burn; (produrre bruciore) to sting.

▶ **bruciarsi** vr (persona) to burn o.s.; (oggetto) to burn.

bruciato, -a agg burnt.

bruciatura sf burn.

bruno, -a agg dark.

bruschetta sf bread toasted with garlic and olive oil.

brusio sm buzz.

brutale agg brutal.

brutto, -a agg (di aspetto) ugly; (tempo, giornata, strada) bad; (situazione, sorpresa, malattia) nasty; (rafforzativo): ~ **imbroglione!** you rotten cheat!; **non è una brutta idea** it's not a bad idea; **brutti ma buoni** almond and hazelnut meringues.

Bruxelles [bru'ksɛl] sf Brussels.

buca, -che sf hole; ~ **delle lettere** letterbox.

bucare vt to make a hole o holes in; ~ **una gomma** to puncture a tyre.

▶ **bucarsi** vr (forarsi) to have a puncture; (pungersi) to prick o.s.; (fam: drogarsi) to mainline.

bucatini smpl: ~ **all'amatriciana** dish from Lazio consisting of long, thin pasta tubes in a sauce of tomatoes, bacon, chillies and pecorino cheese.

bucato sm washing.

buccellato *sm light, ring-shaped sponge cake from Sarzana and Lucca.*

buccia, -ce *sf* skin.

buco, -chi *sm* hole.

budino *sm type of egg custard baked in a mould;* ~ **di riso** *egg custard made with rice, sultanas and sometimes rum.*

bue *sm* ox.

bufera *sf* storm.

buffet [by'fɛ] *sm inv* buffet.

buffo, -a *agg* funny.

bugia *sf* lie; *(candeliere)* candle-holder.

bugiardo, -a ◆ *agg* lying ◆ *sm, f* liar.

buio, -a ◆ *agg* dark ◆ *sm* dark, darkness; **far** ~ to get dark.

Bulgaria *sf:* **la** ~ Bulgaria.

bulgaro, -a *agg* Bulgarian.

bullone *sm* bolt.

buonanotte *esclam* good night!

buonasera *esclam* good evening!; *(nel pomeriggio)* good afternoon!

buongiorno *esclam (in mattinata)* good morning!; *(nel pomeriggio)* good afternoon!

buongustaio, -a *sm, f* gourmet.

buono, -a *agg (dav* sm **buon** + consonante o vocale; **buono** + s + consonante, gn, ps, z) **1.** *(di qualità)* good.
2. *(gradevole)* good.
3. *(generoso):* ~ **(con)** good (to), kind (to).
4. *(bravo, efficiente)* good; **non essere** ~ **a nulla** to be no good at anything; **è** ~ **solo a criticare** all he can do is criticize.
5. *(valido: biglietto, passaporto)* valid.
6. *(temperamento)* good; **avere un buon carattere** to be good-natured; **essere di buon umore** to be in a good mood.
7. *(occasione, momento)* right.
8. *(negli auguri):* **buon appetito!** enjoy your meal!; **buon compleanno!** Happy Birthday!; **buona fortuna!** good luck!; **fate buon viaggio!** have a good journey!
9. *(rafforzativo):* **ci vuole un'ora buona** it takes a good hour.
10. *(in espressioni):* ~ **a sapersi** that's nice to know; **a buon mercato** cheap; **di buon'ora** early; **alla buona** *(cena)* simple; *(vestirsi)* simp-ly; **farai i compiti, con le buone o con le cattive** like it or not, you'll do your homework.
◆ *sm* **1.** *(aspetto positivo)* good; **il** ~ **è che ...** the good thing is that ...
2. *(tagliando)* voucher; *(invece di rimborso)* credit note; ~ **sconto** voucher; ~ **del tesoro** treasury bill.

buonsenso *sm* common sense.

buonumore *sm* good humour.

burattino *sm* puppet.

burla *sf* prank, trick.

burocrazia *sf* bureaucracy.

burrasca, -sche *sf* storm.

burrida *sf Sardinian dish made from dogfish cooked with garlic, vinegar, pine kernels and walnuts and served cold.*

burro *sm* butter; ~ **di cacao** cocoa butter.

burrone *sm* ravine.

bus [bʌs] *sm inv (abbr di* autobus*)* bus.

bussare *vi* to knock.

bussola *sf* compass.

busta *sf (per lettera)* envelope; *(di plastica, carta)* bag; ~ **paga** pay packet.

busto *sm* bust; *(indumento)* corset.

butano *sm* butane.

buttafuori *sm inv* bouncer.

buttare *vt (gettare)* to throw; ~ **all'aria** qc to turn sthg upside down; ~ **fuori** qn to throw sb out; ~ **giù** *(abbattere)* to knock down; *(inghiottire)* to gulp down; ~ **(via)** *(gettare)* to throw away; *(sprecare)* to waste.

▶ **buttarsi** *vr (gettarsi)* to jump; *(fig: tentare)* to have a go.

by-pass [bai'pas] *sm inv* bypass.

C

cabina *sf* (*di nave*) cabin; (*in spiaggia*) beach hut; (*in piscina*) cubicle; (*di camion*) cab; ~ **telefonica** telephone box.

cacao *sm* cocoa.

cacca *sf* (*fam*) poo.

caccia, -ce *sf* (*di animali*) hunting; (*inseguimento*) chase; ~ **al tesoro** treasure hunt.

cacciare *vt* (*animale*) to hunt; (*mandar via*) to get rid of; ~ **fuori qc** to throw sb out.

▶ **cacciarsi** *vr*: **dove si sarà cacciato?** where has he got to?; **cacciarsi nei guai** to get into trouble.

cacciatora *sf* → **pollo**.

cacciavite *sm inv* screwdriver.

cacciucco, -chi *sm fish soup from Livorno, served with toast rubbed with garlic.*

cachemire ['kaʃmir] *sm* cashmere.

caciocavallo *sm hard pear-shaped cheese from southern Italy.*

cadavere *sm* corpse, dead body.

cadere *vi* to fall; (*capelli*) to fall out; (*abito*) to hang; **far** ~ to knock over; **lasciar** ~ to drop.

caduta *sf* fall; **la** ~ **dei capelli** hair loss; **'~ massi'** 'beware falling rocks'.

caffè *sm inv* coffee; (*locale*) cafe; **prendere un** ~ to have a coffee; ~ **corretto** coffee with a dash of spirits; ~ **macchiato** coffee with a dash of milk.

CAFFÈ

Drunk at any time of day, 'caffè' (coffee) or 'espresso', served in the traditional 'tazzina' (little cup), is the typical Italian drink. In bars and restaurants, you can choose from a number of different versions: 'normale' (normal), 'ristretto' (concentrated), 'lungo' (more diluted), 'macchiato caldo' or 'macchiato freddo' (with a drop of hot or cold milk), or 'corretto' (with a drop of your chosen spirit). If you prefer coffee without caffeine, you can order a 'hag®', a 'decaffeinato' or, a recent addition, 'caffè d'orzo' (made with barley).

caffeina *sf* caffeine.

caffellatte *sm inv* hot milk with coffee.

caffettiera *sf* coffeepot.

cagna *sf* bitch.

CAI (*abbr di Club Alpino Italiano*) *Italian mountaineering association.*

cala *sf* bay.

Calabria *sf* Calabria (*region of southern Italy*).

calabrone *sm* hornet.

calamaretti *smpl* squid (*sg*).

calamaro *sm* squid; **calamari ripieni** *squid stuffed with anchovies, capers, breadcrumbs and parsley, and cooked in white wine.*

calamita *sf* magnet.

calare ♦ *vt* to lower ♦ *vi* (*prezzo, peso*) to go down; (*vento*) to drop; (*sole*) to set.

calca, -che *sf* throng.

calcagno *sm* heel.

calce *sf* lime.

calciatore, -trice *sm, f* footballer.

calcio *sm* (*pedata*) kick; (*sport*) football (Br), soccer; (*elemento chimico*) calcium; (*di arma*) butt; **dare un** ~ **a** to kick; **prendere a calci** to kick.

calcolare *vt* to calculate; (*prevedere*) to reckon on, to take into account.

calcolatrice *sf* calculator.

calcolo *sm* (*conteggio*) calculation; (MED) stone; **fare i calcoli** to do one's calculations; **è andato tutto secondo i calcoli** everything went according to plan.

caldaia *sf* boiler.

caldo, -a ♦ *agg* warm; (*a temperatura elevata*) hot ♦ *sm* (*calore*) heat;

avere ~ to be hot; **è o fa ~** it's hot.

calendario *sm* calendar.

calma ♦ *sf* calm ♦ *esclam* calm down!

calmante *sm* tranquillizer.

calmare *vt* to calm; (*dolore*) to soothe.

▶ **calmarsi** *vr* (*persona*) to calm down; (*mare*) to become calm; (*vento*) to drop.

calmo, -a *agg* (*tranquillo*) peaceful, calm; (*mare*) calm.

calore *sm* warmth.

caloria *sf* (*di cibo*) calorie.

calorifero *sm* radiator.

caloroso, -a *agg* warm.

calpestare *vt* to tread on.

calunnia *sf* slander.

calvizie *sf* baldness.

calvo, -a *agg* bald.

calza *sf* (*da donna*) stocking; (*da uomo*) sock; **fare la ~** to knit.

calzagatto *sm* dish from Emilia Romagna consisting of polenta with beans, onions and bacon.

calzamaglia (*pl* calzamaglie) *sf* tights (*pl*) (Br), panty hose (*pl*) (Am).

calzante *sm* shoehorn.

calzare ♦ *vt* to put on ♦ *vi* to fit.

calzature *sfpl* footwear (*sg*).

calzettone *sm* knee(-length) sock.

calzino *sm* (short) sock.

calzolaio *sm* (*riparatore*) cobbler; (*fabbricante*) shoemaker.

calzoleria *sf* shoe shop.

calzoncini *smpl* shorts.

calzone *sm* (*cibo*) pasty made from pizza dough stuffed with cheese, tomato, ham and egg.

▶ **calzoni** *smpl* trousers.

camaleonte *sm* chameleon.

cambiale *sf* bill.

cambiamento *sm* change.

cambiare *vt & vi* to change; **~ le lire in sterline** to change lire into sterling; **~ un biglietto da centomila** to change a hundred thousand lire note.

▶ **cambiarsi** *vr* to change (one's clothes).

cambio *sm* (*sostituzione*) change; (*di denaro*) exchange; (*di automobile*) gears (*pl*); **dare il ~ a qn** to take over from sb; **fare a ~ (con qn)** to swap (with sb); **in ~ di qc** in exchange for sthg; **~ automatico** automatic gearbox.

camera *sf* room; **~ (da letto)** bedroom; **~ d'aria** inner tube; **~ con bagno** room with a bath; **~ blindata** vault; **Camera di Commercio** Chamber of Commerce; **Camera dei Deputati** ≃ House of Commons (Br), ≃ House of Representatives (Am); **~ con doccia** room with a shower; **~ doppia** double room; **~ a due letti** twin-bedded room; **~ matrimoniale** room with a double bed; **~ degli ospiti** guestroom, spare room; **~ singola** single room.

cameriere, -a *sm, f* waiter (*f* waitress).

camice *sm* white coat.

camicetta *sf* blouse.

camicia *sf* (*da uomo*) shirt; (*da donna*) blouse, shirt; **~ da notte** (*da donna*) nightdress; (*da uomo*) nightshirt.

caminetto *sm* fireplace, hearth.

camino *sm* (*focolare*) fireplace, hearth; (*comignolo*) chimney.

camion *sm inv* truck.

camioncino *sm* van.

cammello *sm* camel; (*tessuto*) camelhair.

cammeo *sm* cameo.

camminare *vi* to walk.

camminata *sf* walk.

cammino *sm* way; **mettersi in ~** to set off.

camomilla *sf* camomile.

camorra *sf* Camorra.

camoscio *sm* chamois; **giacca di ~** suede jacket.

campagna *sf* country; (*propaganda, guerra*) campaign; **in ~** in the country; **andare in ~** to go to the country.

campana *sf* bell; (*per vetro, carta*) recycling bank; **a ~** bell-shaped.

campanello *sm* bell; **suonare il ~** to ring the bell.

Campania *sf* Campania (*region of southern Italy*).

campanile *sm* bell-tower.

campare *vi* to get by.

campato, -a *agg*: **~ in aria** unfounded.

campeggiare *vi* to camp.

campeggiatore, -trice *sm, f* camper.

campeggio *sm* (*luogo*) campsite; (*attività*) camping.

camper *sm inv* camper van.

campestre *agg* rural, country (*dav s*).

Campidoglio *sm*: **il ~** the Capitol.

camping *sm inv* campsite.

campionario *sm* (collection of) samples (*pl*).

campionato *sm* championship.

campione, -essa ♦ *sm, f* champion ♦ *sm* (*esemplare*) sample.

campo *sm* field; (*accampamento*) camp; **~ di concentramento** concentration camp; **~ di golf** golf course; **~ profughi** refugee camp; **~ da tennis** tennis court.

camposanto (*pl* **campisanti**) *sm* cemetery.

Canada *sm*: **il ~** Canada.

canadese ♦ *agg & smf* Canadian ♦ *sf* (*tenda*) ridge tent.

canaglia *sf* rogue.

canale *sm* channel; (*artificiale*) canal; **~ navigabile** ship canal.

canapa *sf* hemp.

canarino *sm* canary.

canasta *sf* canasta.

cancellare *vt* (*con gomma*) to rub out; (*con penna*) to cross out; (*annullare*) to cancel.

cancelleria *sf* (*materiale*) stationery.

cancello *sm* gate.

cancerogeno, -a *agg* carcinogenic.

cancrena *sf* (MED) gangrene.

cancro *sm* cancer.
▶ **Cancro** *sm* Cancer.

candeggina *sf* bleach.

candela *sf* candle; **~ (di accensione)** spark plug.

candelabro *sm* candelabra.

candeliere *sm* candlestick.

candidato, -a *sm, f* candidate.

candido, -a *agg* (*bianco*) (pure) white; (*puro*) pure, innocent.

candito, -a ♦ *agg* candied ♦ *sm* candied fruit.

cane *sm* dog; **~ da guardia** guard dog; **~ guida** guide dog; **~ lupo** Alsatian; **~ poliziotto** police dog; **non c'era un ~** there wasn't a soul there; **solo come un ~** all alone; **tempo da cani** lousy weather; **una vita da cani** a dog's life; **'cani al guinzaglio'** 'dogs must be kept on a lead'.

canestro *sm* basket.

cangiante *agg* iridescent.

canguro *sm* kangaroo.

canicola *sf* heat.

canile *sm* (*cuccia*) kennel; (*allevamento*) kennels (*pl*); **~ municipale** dog pound.

canino *sm* canine.

canna *sf* (*pianta*) reed; (*di bicicletta*) crossbar; (*di fucile*) barrel; **~ fumaria** chimney flue; **~ da pesca** fishing rod; **~ da zucchero** sugar cane.

cannariculi *smpl* thin curved pastry covered in honey.

cannella *sf* (*spezia*) cinnamon; (*rubinetto*) tap.

cannello *sm* blowlamp.

cannelloni *smpl* cannelloni (*sg*).

cannibale *smf* cannibal.

cannocchiale *sm* telescope.

cannolo *sm*: **~ alla crema** pastry tube filled with custard; **~ siciliano** 'cannolo' filled with sweetened ricotta cheese, candied fruit and chocolate.

cannone *sm* gun.

cannuccia, -ce *sf* straw.

canoa sf (barca) canoe; (sport) canoeing.

canone sm (quota) rent; (regola) rule.

canottaggio sm rowing.

canottiera sf (biancheria) vest (Br), undershirt (Am); (per esterno) sleeveless T-shirt.

canotto sm rubber dinghy; ~ di salvataggio lifeboat.

cantante smf singer.

cantare vt & vi to sing.

cantautore, -trice sm, f singer-songwriter.

cantiere sm (edile) building site; (navale) shipyard.

cantina sf (seminterrato) cellar; (per il vino) wine cellar; (negozio) wine shop.

canto sm (ARTE) singing; (canzone) song; (di uccello) chirping; d'altro ~ on the other hand.

cantonata sf: prendere una ~ to make a blunder.

cantone sm (in Svizzera) canton.

Canton Ticino sm: il ~ the canton of Ticino.

cantucci smpl wedge-shaped almond biscuits.

canzonare vt to tease.

canzone sf song.

canzonetta sf popular song, ditty.

caos sm chaos.

CAP abbr = codice di avviamento postale.

capace agg (esperto) able, capable; (ampio) capacious; essere ~ di fare qc to be able to do sthg; essere ~ di tutto to be capable of anything.

capacità sf inv (abilità) ability; (capienza) capacity.

capanna sf hut.

capannone sm (industriale) shed; (agricolo) barn.

caparbio, -a agg stubborn.

caparra sf deposit.

capello sm hair.

▶ **capelli** smpl hair (sg); averne fin sopra i capelli to be fed up to the back teeth.

capezzolo sm nipple.

capillare sm capillary.

capire vt & vi to understand; ho capito I see; non capisco I don't understand; scusi, non ho capito I'm sorry, I don't understand; si capisce! certainly!

▶ **capirsi** vr to understand each other.

capitale ♦ sf & sm capital ♦ agg (pena, peccato) capital; (fondamentale) fundamental.

capitaneria sf: ~ di porto port authorities (pl).

capitano sm captain.

capitare ♦ vi (accadere) to happen; (giungere) to turn up ♦ v impers to happen; ~ a qn to happen to sb; ~ a proposito to come at the right time.

capitello sm capital.

capitolino, -a agg Capitoline.

capitolo sm chapter.

capitombolo sm tumble.

capo sm (principale) boss; (testa, estremità) head; (di gruppo) leader; (di tribù) chief; ~ di vestiario item of clothing; andare a ~ to start a new paragraph; venire a ~ di qc to get through sthg; da ~ over again; da un ~ all'altro (di qc) from end to end (of sthg); in ~ a un mese within a month.

Capodanno sm New Year.

capofitto : a capofitto avv headfirst.

capolavoro sm masterpiece.

capolinea (pl capilinea) sm terminus.

capolino sm: fare ~ to peep in/out.

capoluogo, -ghi (pl -ghi) sm: ~ di provincia provincial capital, = county town (Br); ~ di regione regional capital.

capostazione (pl capistazione) smf station master.

capotavola (mpl capitavola, fpl

inv) *smf* head of the table; **a ~** at the head of the table.

capoufficio (*mpl* **capiufficio**, *fpl inv*) *smf* office manager (*f* manageress).

capoverso *sm* paragraph.

capovolgere *vt* (*barca, oggetto*) to overturn; (*fig: situazione*) to reverse.

▶ **capovolgersi** *vr* (*barca*) to capsize; (*macchina*) to overturn; (*fig: situazione*) to be reversed.

capovolto, -a *pp* → **capovolgere**.

cappa *sf* (*di camino*) hood; (*mantello*) cape.

cappella *sf* chapel.

cappello *sm* hat; **~ di paglia** straw hat.

cappero *sm* caper.

cappone *sm* capon; **~ ripieno al forno** *capon stuffed with beef, Parmesan cheese and breadcrumbs.*

cappotto *sm* coat.

cappuccino *sm* cappuccino.

cappuccio *sm* hood; (*di penna*) cap.

capra *sf* goat.

Capri *sf* Capri.

capriccio *sm* tantrum; (*voglia*) whim; **fare i capricci** to be naughty.

capriccioso, -a *agg* naughty, → **pizza**.

Capricorno *sm* Capricorn.

capriola *sf* somersault.

capriolo *sm* roe deer.

capro *sm*: **~ espiatorio** scapegoat.

capsula *sf* (*di farmaco*) capsule; (*di bottiglia*) cap.

carabiniere *sm* *member of the Italian police force responsible for civil and military matters.*

caraffa *sf* carafe, jug.

Caraibi *smpl*: **i ~** the Caribbean.

caramella *sf* sweet.

carato *sm* carat.

carattere *sm* character.

caratteristica, -che *sf* characteristic.

caratteristico, -a, -ci, -che *agg* characteristic.

caratterizzare *vt* to characterize.

carboidrato *sm* carbohydrate.

carbonara *sf* → **spaghetti**.

carbone *sm* coal.

carburante *sm* fuel.

carburatore *sm* carburettor.

carcerato, -a *sm, f* prisoner.

carcere (*pl f* **carceri**) *sm* prison.

carciofo *sm* artichoke; **carciofi alla romana** *sautéed or baked artichokes with parsley, mint and garlic.*

cardiaco, -a, -ci, -che *agg* cardiac, heart (*dav s*).

cardigan *sm inv* cardigan.

cardinale ♦ *agg* → **numero, punto** ♦ *sm* cardinal.

cardine *sm* hinge.

cardo *sm* thistle.

carenza *sf* lack, deficiency.

carestia *sf* famine.

carezza *sf* caress; (*a animale*) stroke.

carezzare *vt* to caress; (*animale*) to stroke.

carica, -che *sf* (*incarico*) position, office; (*elettrica, di arma*) charge; **in ~** in office.

caricare *vt* (*mettere su*) to load; (*sveglia*) to wind up; **~ qc di qc** to load sthg with sthg; **~ qn di qc** to weigh sb down with sthg.

carico, -a, -chi, -che ♦ *agg* (*arma, macchina fotografica*) loaded; (*batteria*) charged; (*orologio*) wound up ♦ *sm* load; **~ (di qc)** weighed down (with sthg); **a ~ di** (*spesa*) charged to.

carie *sf inv* (*dei denti*) decay.

carino, -a *agg* (*grazioso*) pretty, lovely; (*gentile*) nice.

carnagione *sf* complexion.

carne *sf* meat; (ANAT) flesh; **~ di maiale/vitello** pork/veal; **~ macinata o tritata** mince.

carneficina *sf* massacre.

carnevale *sm* carnival.

CARNEVALE

The period before Lent, from the Epiphany to Ash Wednesday, is carnival time in Italy. Most festivities take place during the last week of this period, Shrovetide. Both children and adults don masks, go to parties, play tricks on each other, and throw confetti ('coriandoli') and streamers. In some cities special organized events are held: Viareggio is particularly famous for its carnival procession, whilst in Venice the city gives itself over to open-air parties, theatre and concerts.

---

caro, -a *agg* expensive, dear; (*amato*) dear; **costare ~** to be expensive; **Caro Luca** Dear Luca.
carota *sf* carrot.
carovita *sm* high cost of living.
carpaccio *sm* *thin slices of raw beef served with oil, lemon and shavings of Parmesan cheese.*
carpire *vt:* **~ qc a qn** (*segreto*) to get sthg out of sb.
carponi *avv* on all fours.
carrabile *agg* → **passo.**
carraio *agg m* → **passo.**
carreggiata *sf* carriageway.
carrello *sm* trolley.
carriera *sf* career; **far ~** to get on.
carro *sm* cart, wagon; **~ armato** tank; **~ attrezzi** breakdown truck (Br), tow truck (Am).
carrozza *sf* (*cocchio*) coach, carriage; (*vagone*) carriage (Br), car (Am); '**~ letto**' sleeping car; '**~ ristorante**' restaurant car.
carrozzeria *sf* bodywork.
carrozziere *sm* coachbuilder.
carrozzina *sf* pram (Br), baby carriage (Am).
carta *sf* paper; (*tessera*) card; **alla ~** à la carte; **~ d'argento** *senior citizens' railcard*; **~ assegni** cheque card; **~ automobilistica o stradale** road map; **~ da bollo** *paper carrying a government duty stamp*; **~ di credito** credit card; **~ geografica** map; **~ d'identità** identity card; **~ igienica** toilet paper; **~ d'imbarco** boarding pass; **~ da let-**

tere notepaper; **~ da pacchi** brown paper, wrapping paper; **~ da parati** wallpaper; **~ stagnola** silver foil; **~ verde** green card; **~ dei vini** wine list; **carte da gioco** playing cards.

CARTA D'IDENTITÀ

Every Italian citizen is issued with an identity card, an official document listing details such as place and date of birth, home address, profession, colour of eyes and hair, and marital status. It also contains a photograph of the bearer. By law Italians must show their identity card when asked to do so by the police, and when booking in at hotels. The card can be used instead of a passport for travel inside the European Union.

---

cartacarbone *sf* carbon paper.
cartaccia, -ce *sf* waste paper.
cartapesta *sf* papier-mâché.
cartella *sf* (*di scolaro*) schoolbag; (*di professionista*) briefcase; (*per fogli*) folder; (*scheda*) file; **~ clinica** case history.
cartello *sm* (*avviso*) notice; (*in dimostrazioni*) placard; **~ stradale** road sign.
cartellone *sm* (*teatrale*) playbill; **~ (pubblicitario)** poster.
cartina *sf:* **~ (geografica)** map.
cartoccio *sm* paper bag; **al ~** in tin foil.
cartoleria *sf* stationer's.
cartolibreria *sf* stationer's and bookseller's.
cartolina *sf* (*illustrata*) (picture) postcard; **~ postale** postcard.
cartone *sm* cardboard.
▶ **cartoni animati** *smpl* cartoons.
casa *sf* (*costruzione*) house; (*dimora*) house, home; (*ditta*) firm; **andare a ~** to go home; **essere a o in ~** to be at home; **fatto in ~** homemade; **~ di cura** nursing home.
casale *sm* (*casa di campagna*) farmhouse.

casalinga, -ghe *sf* housewife.
casalingo, -a, -ghi, -ghe *agg* homemade; (*amante della casa*) home-loving.
▶ **casalinghi** *smpl* household articles.

cascare *vi* to fall down.

cascata *sf* waterfall.

cascina *sf* farmstead.

casco, -schi *sm* (*protettivo*) helmet; (*per capelli*) dryer; (*di banane*) bunch.

casella *sf* (*riquadro*) square; (*scomparto*) compartment; **~ postale** post office box; **~ vocale** electronic mailbox.

casello *sm* tollbooth.

caserma *sf* barracks (*pl*).

casino *sm* (*fam: confusione*) mess.

casinò *sm inv* casino.

caso *sm* chance; (*eventualità*) event; (*poliziesco, medico*) case; **fare ~ a** to pay attention to; **non è il ~ di offendersi** you shouldn't take offence; **a ~** at random; **in ~ contrario** otherwise; **in ogni ~** in any case; **nel ~ venisse** should he come; **per ~** by chance; **in tutti i casi** at any rate; **'in ~ d'emergenza rompere il vetro'** 'in case of emergency break glass'.

casomai *cong* if by any chance.

cassa *sf* (*contenitore*) case, box; (*di negozio*) cash register; (*di supermercato*) checkout; (*di banca*) counter; (*amplificatore*) speaker; (*di orologio*) case; **~ automatica prelievi** cash dispenser; **~ continua** night safe; **~ toracica** chest.

cassaforte (*pl* **casseforti**) *sf* safe.

cassata *sf* ice cream dessert containing candied fruit, served in slices like a cake; **~ siciliana** Sicilian dessert made with sponge, ricotta cheese, candied fruit and liqueur.

casseruola *sf* saucepan.

cassetta *sf* (*contenitore*) box; (*di musica, film*) tape; **~ delle lettere** letterbox (Br), mailbox (Am); **~ di sicurezza** strongbox.

cassetto *sm* drawer.

cassettone *sm* chest of drawers.

cassiere, -a *sm, f* (*di negozio*) cashier; (*di banca*) teller.

cassoela *sf* pork ribs with salami and savoy cabbage (a speciality of Lombardy).

cassonetto *sm* large dustbin on wheels.

castagna *sf* chestnut.

castagnaccio *sm* Tuscan cake made from chestnut flour, pine kernels and sometimes sultanas and rosemary.

castagno *sm* chestnut (tree).

castano, -a *agg* chestnut (brown).

castello *sm* castle.

castigo, -ghi *sm* punishment; **mettere qn in ~** to punish sb.

castoro *sm* beaver.

castrare *vt* to castrate.

casual ['kaʃwal] *agg inv* casual.

casuale *agg* chance (*dav s*).

catacomba *sf* catacomb.

catalogare *vt* to catalogue.

catalogo, -ghi *sm* catalogue.

catamarano *sm* catamaran.

catarifrangente *sm* reflector.

catarro *sm* catarrh.

catasta *sf* stack.

catastrofe *sf* catastrophe.

categoria *sf* (*gruppo*) category; (*di albergo*) class.

catena *sf* chain; **~ di montaggio** assembly line; **a ~** chain (*dav s*); **catene (da neve)** (snow) chains.

catinella *sf* basin; **piovere a catinelle** to pour down.

catino *sm* basin.

catrame *sm* tar.

cattedra *sf* teacher's desk.

cattedrale *sf* cathedral.

cattiveria *sf* (*qualità*) wickedness; (*commento*) spiteful remark; (*atto*) spiteful act.

cattività *sf* captivity.

cattivo, -a *agg* bad; (*bambino*) naughty; (*sapore, odore*) bad, nasty; (*incapace*) poor.

cattolico, -a, -ci, -che *agg & sm, f* Catholic.

cattura *sf* capture.

catturare *vt* to capture.

caucciù *sm* rubber.

causa *sf* cause; (DIR) case; **a o per ~ di** because of.

causare *vt* to cause.

cautela *sf* caution, prudence.

cautelare *vt* to protect.

▶ **cautelarsi da** *vr + prep* to take precautions against.

cauto, -a *agg* cautious, prudent.

cauzione *sf* security; (DIR) bail.

cava *sf* quarry.

cavalcare *vt* to ride.

cavalcavia *sm inv* flyover.

cavalcioni *avv*: **a ~ di** astride.

cavaliere *sm* (*chi cavalca*) rider; (*medioevale, titolo*) knight; (*in balli*) partner.

cavalleria *sf* (MIL) cavalry; (*cortesia*) chivalry.

cavallerizzo, -a *sm, f* (*istruttore*) riding instructor; (*di circo*) bareback rider.

cavalletta *sf* grasshopper.

cavalletto *sm* easel.

cavallo *sm* horse; (*di pantaloni*) crotch; (*negli scacchi*) knight; **a ~ on** horseback; **andare a ~** to ride; **~ da tiro** carthorse; **~ (vapore)** horsepower.

cavallone *sm* (*ondata*) breaker.

cavare *vt* to extract; **cavarsela** to manage, to cope.

cavatappi *sm inv* corkscrew.

cavatelli *smpl*: **~ alla foggiana** flat *'gnocchi' in a vegetable, cheese or meat sauce.*

caverna *sf* cave.

cavia *sf* guinea pig; **fare da ~** to be a guinea pig.

caviale *sm* caviar.

caviglia *sf* ankle.

cavità *sf inv* (*buca*) hollow; (ANAT) chamber.

cavo, -a ◆ *agg* hollow ◆ *sm* cable; (*corda*) rope.

cavolfiore *sm* cauliflower.

cavolo *sm* cabbage; **che ~ vuole?** (*fam*) what the hell does he want?

cazzotto *sm* (*fam*) punch.

cc (*abbr di centimetro cubico*) cc.

c/c (*abbr di conto corrente*) a/c.

C.C. *abbr* = **Carabinieri**.

C.D. *sm inv* CD.

ce → **ci**.

cece *sm* chickpea.

Cecoslovacchia *sf*: **la ~** Czechoslovakia.

cedere ◆ *vt*: **~ qc (a qn)** to give sthg up (to sb) ◆ *vi* (*soffitto, pavimento*) to give way; **~ (a qc)** (*fig: persona*) to give in (to sthg), to yield (to sthg).

cedola *sf* coupon.

cedro *sm* (*sempreverde*) cedar; (*albero da frutto, frutto*) citron.

CEE *sf* (*abbr di Comunità Economica Europea*) EEC.

ceffone *sm* slap.

celebrare *vt* to celebrate.

celebre *agg* famous.

celebrità *sf inv* fame.

celeste *agg & sm* sky-blue.

celibe ◆ *agg* single ◆ *sm* bachelor.

cella *sf* cell.

cellophane® ['tʃelofan] *sm* Cellophane®.

cellula *sf* cell; **~ fotoelettrica** photoelectric cell.

cellulare *sm* (*telefono*) mobile phone; (*furgone*) Black Maria.

cemento *sm* cement; **~ armato** reinforced concrete.

cena *sf* dinner.

cenare *vi* to have dinner.

cencio *sm* (*straccio*) rag.

▶ **cenci** *smpl* (CULIN) Tuscan speciality of deep-fried sticks of dough sprinkled with sugar.

cenere *sf* ash.

cenno *sm* (*con la mano*) gesture; (*col capo*) nod; (*allusione*) hint; (*sintomo*) sign; **fare ~ a qn** to beckon to sb; **fare ~ di sì/no** to nod/shake one's head.

cenone *sm* New Year's Eve dinner.

censimento *sm* census.

censura *sf* (*controllo*) censorship.

centenario, -a ♦ *agg* (*di età*) hundred-year-old; (*ogni cento anni*) centenary (*dav s*) ♦ *sm* centenary.

centerbe *sm inv* type of liqueur made from herbs.

centesimo, -a *num* hundredth, → **sesto**.

centigrado *agg m* → **grado**.

centimetro *sm* centimetre.

centinaio (*pl f* **centinaia**) *sm*: **un ~ (di)** about a hundred.

cento *num* a o one hundred; **~ per ~** 100 per cent, → **sei**.

centomila *num* a o one hundred thousand, → **sei**.

centotredici *sm* (*numero telefonico*) ≃ 999 (*Br*), ≃ 911 (*Am*); (*polizia*) police (*pl*).

centrale ♦ *agg* (*nel centro*) central; (*principale*) main ♦ *sf* head office; **~ elettrica** electric power station.

centralinista, -i, -e *smf* operator.

centralino *sm* telephone exchange; (*di albergo, ditta*) switchboard.

centrare *vt* to hit the centre of.

centrifuga, -ghe *sf* spin-dryer.

centro *sm* centre; **fare ~** (*colpire*) to hit the bull's eye; (*fig: risolvere*) to hit the nail on the head; **~ abitato** built-up area; **~ commerciale** shopping centre; **~ storico** old town.

ceppo *sm* (*di albero*) stump; (*ciocco*) log.

cera *sf* wax.

ceramica *sf* pottery.

cerbiatto *sm* fawn.

cerca *sf*: **essere in ~ di qc** to be in search of sthg.

cercare *vt* to look for.

▶ **cercare di** *v + prep*: **~ di fare qc** to try to do sthg.

cerchio *sm* circle; **mettersi in ~ (intorno a)** to form a circle (around).

cereale *sm* cereal.

cerimonia *sf* ceremony.

cerino *sm* match.

cernia *sf* grouper.

cerniera *sf* (*di porte, finestre*) hinge; **~ (lampo)** zip.

cerotto *sm* plaster.

certamente *avv* certainly.

certezza *sf* certainty; **sapere qc con ~** to know sthg for sure.

certificato *sm* certificate; **~ medico** medical certificate; **~ di nascita** birth certificate.

certo, -a *agg* **1.** (*convinto*) certain; **essere ~ di qc** to be certain of sthg; **sono ~ di aver prenotato** I'm positive I booked; **siete certi che sia lui?** are you sure it's him?

2. (*assicurato, evidente*) certain; **la vittoria è data per certa** victory is certain.

3. (*non specificato*) certain; **un ~ signor Rossi** a (certain) Mr Rossi; **c'è un ~ Paolo al telefono** there's someone called Paolo on the phone; **ho certe cose da fare** I have some things I need to do; **in certi casi** in some o certain cases.

4. (*qualche*): **certi(-e)** some.

5. (*limitativo*) some; **avere un ~ intuito** to have some insight.

6. (*rafforzativo*) some; **ha certe idee!** he has some strange ideas!; **ha certi occhi azzurri!** he's got really blue eyes!; **avere una certa età** to be getting on.

♦ *avv*: **vieni anche tu? - ~!** are you coming too? – of course!; **di ~** certainly.

▶ **certi, -e** *pron* (*persone*) some (people); **certi dicono che ...** some people say that ...

certosa *sf* charterhouse.

cervello *sm* brain.

Cervino *sm*: **il ~** the Cervino.

cervo *sm* deer; (*maschio*) stag; **~ volante** stag beetle.

cesoie *sfpl* shears.

cespuglio *sm* bush.

cessare *vt* to stop.

cesso *sm* loo.

cesta *sf* basket.

cestino *sm* (*cesto*) basket; (*per car-*

tacce) wastepaper basket; **~ da viaggio** packed lunch.

cesto *sm* basket.

ceto *sm* class.

cetriolo *sm* cucumber.

champagne [ʃamˈpaɲ] *sm inv* champagne.

charter [ˈtʃarter] *sm inv* charter.

che *pron relativo* **1.** (*soggetto: persona*) who, that; **il dottore ~ mi ha visitato** the doctor who examined me.

2. (*complemento oggetto: persona*) whom, that; **la ragazza ~ hai conosciuto** the girl (whom o that) you met.

3. (*cosa, animale*) that, which; **la macchina ~ è in garage** the car which o that is in the garage; **il treno ~ abbiamo perso** the train (which o that) we missed.

4. (*fam: in cui*): **la sera ~ siamo usciti** the evening we went out.

◆ *pron interr & esclam* what; **~ (cosa) ne pensi?** what do you think?; **~ (cosa) ti succede?** what's the matter?; **non so ~ (cosa) fare** I don't know what to do; **grazie! – non c'è di ~!** thank you! – don't mention it!; **ma ~ (cosa) dici!** what are you saying!

◆ *agg interr* **1.** (*tra molti*) what; (*tra pochi*) which; **~ libro vuoi, questo o quello?** which book do you want, this one or that one?; **~ tipo è il tuo amico?** what's your friend like?

2. (*in esclamazioni*): **~ strana idea!** what a strange idea!; **~ bello!** how lovely!

◆ *cong* **1.** (*introduce una subordinata*) that; **è difficile ~ venga** he's unlikely to come; **sai ~ non è vero** you know (that) it's not true; **sono così stanca ~ non mi reggo in piedi** I'm so tired (that) I can hardly stand up; **sono contenta ~ sia partito** I'm pleased (that) he left.

2. (*temporale*): **è già un anno ~ è partito** it's already a year since he left; **è un po' ~ non lo vedo** I haven't seen him for a while.

3. (*comparativa*) than; **è più furbo ~ intelligente** he's cunning rather than intelligent; **è più bello ~ mai** he's more handsome than ever.

4. (*introduce alternativa*) whether; **~ tu venga o no, io ci vado** I'm going, whether you come or not.

check-in [tʃɛˈkin] *sm inv* check-in.

chewing-gum [ˈtʃwingam] *sm* chewing-gum.

chi *pron relativo* **1.** (*colui che*) the person who.

2. (*qualcuno che*): **c'è ancora ~ crede alle sue storie** there are still people who believe his tales.

3. (*chiunque*) whoever, anyone who; **entra ~ vuole** anyone can come in.

◆ *pron interr* **1.** (*soggetto*) who; **~ è?** who is it?; **~ è stato?** who was it?

2. (*complemento diretto*) who; **non so ~** I don't know who; **~ si vede!** look who's here!

3. (*complemento indiretto*) who, whom; **a ~ devo chiedere?** who should I ask?; **con ~ parti?** who are you leaving with?; **di ~ è questo ombrello?** whose umbrella is this?; **a ~ lo dici!** you're telling me!

chiacchierare *vi* (*conversare*) to chat; (*spettegolare*) to gossip.

chiacchiere *sfpl* (*pettegolezzi*) rumours, gossip (*sg*); **fare due** o **quattro ~** to have a chat.

chiacchierone, -a *agg* (*loquace*) talkative; (*pettegolo*) gossipy.

chiamare *vt* to call.

▶ **chiamarsi** *vr* to be called; **come ti chiami?** what's your name?; **mi chiamo ...** my name is ...

chiamata *sf* call.

Chianti *sm* Chianti.

chiarezza *sf* clarity.

chiarire *vt* (*mettere in chiaro*) to make clear; (*spiegare*) to clarify; (*problema*) to clear up.

▶ **chiarirsi** *vr* to be cleared up.

chiaro, -a *agg* clear; (*colore*) light.

chiasso *sm* noise.

chiassoso, -a *agg* noisy.

chiave *sf* key; **chiudere a ~** to lock;

~ **d'accensione** ignition key; ~ **inglese** monkey wrench.

chiavetta *sf* (*dell'acqua, del gas*) tap; (*d'accensione*) key.

chic [sik] *agg inv* chic.

chicco, -chi *sm* (*di grano*) grain; (*di caffè*) bean; ~ **d'uva** grape.

chiedere *vt* (*per sapere*) to ask; (*per avere*) to ask for; ~ **qc a qn** to ask sb sthg.

▶ **chiedere di** *v + prep* (*per notizie*) to ask after; (*al telefono*) to ask for.

chiesa *sf* church.

chiesto, -a *pp* → **chiedere**.

chiglia *sf* keel.

chilo *sm* (*chilogrammo*) kilo; **mezzo** ~ **di** half a kilo of.

chilogrammo *sm* kilogram.

chilometro *sm* kilometre.

chimica *sf* (*disciplina*) chemistry, → **chimico**.

chimico, -a, -ci, -che ◆ *agg* chemical ◆ *sm, f* chemist.

chinarsi *vr* to bend.

chinotto *sm* (*bibita*) a type of soft drink.

chiocciola *sf* snail.

chiodo *sm* nail; ~ **fisso** fixed idea; **chiodi di garofano** cloves.

chioma *sf* (*di albero*) foliage; (*capigliatura*) (head of) hair.

chiosco, -schi *sm* kiosk.

chiostro *sm* cloister.

chiromante *smf* fortune-teller.

chirurgia *sf* surgery; ~ **estetica** plastic surgery.

chissà *avv* who knows?

chitarra *sf* guitar.

chiudere ◆ *vt* to close, to shut; (*acqua, gas*) to turn off; (*strada*) to close; (*definitivamente*) to close down, to shut down; (*concludere*) to end ◆ *vi* to close, to shut; (*definitivamente*) to close down, to shut down; ~ **a chiave** to lock.

▶ **chiudersi** *vr* to close, to shut; **chiudersi in casa** to lock o.s. in; **'si chiude da sé'** 'automatic door'.

chiunque *pron* (*indefinito*) anyone;

(*relativo*) whoever; ~ **sia** whoever it may be.

chiuso, -a ◆ *pp* → **chiudere** ◆ *agg* closed; (*persona*) reserved; **'~ per ferie'** 'closed for holidays'; **'~ per riposo settimanale'** 'weekly closing day'.

chiusura *sf* (*di negozio, ufficio, scuole*) closing; (*definitiva*) closure; (*termine*) end; (*dispositivo*) fastener; ~ **lampo** zip (Br), zipper (Am).

ci (*diventa* **ce** *se precede* **lo, la, li, le, ne**) *pron personale* **1.** (*complemento oggetto*) us; ~ **vedono** they can see us; **ascoltaci** listen to us.

2. (*complemento di termine*) (to) us; ~ **può fare un favore?** can you do us a favour?; **non ce lo ha detto** he didn't tell us.

3. (*riflessivo*) ourselves; ~ **laviamo** we wash ourselves.

4. (*reciproco*) each other; ~ **vediamo stasera** see you tonight.

◆ *pron dimostrativo* (*a ciò, in ciò, su ciò*): ~ **penso io** I'll take care of it; **mettici un po' d'impegno!** put a bit of effort into it!; **quella sedia è vuota: posso appoggiarci la borsa?** that seat is empty: can I put my bag on it?; ~ **puoi scommettere** you can bet on it.

◆ *avv* **1.** (*stato in luogo*: **qui**) here; (*stato in luogo*: **lì**) there; **non c'è** (*persona*) he's/she's not here, he's/she's not there; (*oggetto*) it's not here/there; ~ **fermiamo una sola notte** we are staying (here/there) for just one night.

2. (*moto a luogo*: **qui**) here; (*moto a luogo*: **lì**) there; ~ **si può andare a piedi** you can walk there; ~ **vengono spesso** they come here often.

3. (*moto per luogo*): ~ **passa l'autostrada** the motorway runs through it; **non ~ passa mai nessuno** nobody ever goes this/that way.

4. (*in espressioni*): **c'è** there is; ~ **sono** there are; ~ **vuole un po'** (*di tempo*) it takes a bit of time; **io ~ sto** I agree; **non ~ sento/vedo** I can't hear/see; **ce l'hai?** have you got it?

ciabatta *sf* (*pantofola*) slipper;

(pane) type of long, flat bread.

cialda *sf* wafer.

ciambella *sf (dolce)* ring-shaped cake; *(salvagente)* rubber ring; **~ di salvataggio** life buoy, life belt.

ciao *esclam (all'incontro)* hello!; *(di commiato)* bye!

ciascuno, -a *agg & pron* each; **~ di noi** each of us.

cibo *sm* food.

cicala *sf* cicada.

cicatrice *sf* scar.

cicca, -che *sf* cigarette end.

ciccione, -a *sm, f (fam)* fatty.

cicerone *sm* guide.

ciclabile *agg* → **pista**.

ciclamino *sm* cyclamen.

ciclismo *sm* cycling.

ciclista, -i, -e *smf* cyclist.

ciclo *sm* cycle.

ciclomotore *sm* moped.

ciclone *sm* cyclone.

cicogna *sf* stork.

cieco, -a, -chi, -che ♦ *agg* blind ♦ *sm, f* blind man (f woman).

cielo *sm* sky; *(paradiso)* heaven.

cifra *sf (numero)* figure; *(di denaro)* sum, figure.

ciglio *sm (di palpebra: pl f ciglia)* eyelash; *(di strada: pl m cigli)* edge.

cigno *sm* swan.

cigolare *vi* to squeak, to creak.

Cile *sm: il ~* Chile.

cilecca *sf: fare ~* to fail.

ciliegia, -gie o **-ge** *sf* cherry.

cilindro *sm (di motore)* cylinder; *(cappello)* top hat.

cima *sf* top; *(estremità)* end; **in ~ (a qc)** at the top (of sthg); **da ~ a fondo** from top to bottom, from beginning to end; **~ alla genovese** veal stuffed with bacon, sweetbreads, brains, mushrooms, peas and grated cheese, served cold in slices.

cimice *sf (insetto)* bug; *(puntina)* drawing pin (Br), thumbtack (Am).

ciminiera *sf* chimney; *(di nave)* funnel.

cimitero *sm* cemetery.

Cina *sf: la ~* China.

cin cin *esclam* cheers!

Cinecittà *sf* film studios in Rome.

CINECITTÀ

Meaning 'city of cinema', the name 'Cinecittà' has been given to the film complex built in the suburbs of Rome in 1937. 'Cinecittà' was most productive in the 1950s, when films like Fellini's La dolce vita were shot there, and it continues to be widely used by the Italian film industry.

cinema *sm inv* cinema.

cinepresa *sf* cine-camera.

cinese ♦ *agg & sm* Chinese ♦ *smf* Chinese person.

cingere *vt* to surround.

cinghia *sf* belt.

cinghiale *sm* wild boar.

cinguettare *vi* to chirp.

cinico, -a, -ci, -che *agg* cynical.

ciniglia *sf* chenille.

cinquanta *num* fifty, → **sei**.

cinquantesimo, -a *agg* fiftieth, → **sesto**.

cinquantina *sf (di età)*: **essere sulla ~** to be about 50; **una ~ (di)** about 50.

cinque *num* five, → **sei**.

cinquecento *num* five hundred, → **sei**.

▶ **Cinquecento** *sm*: **il Cinquecento** the sixteenth century.

cinto, -a *pp* → **cingere**.

cintura *sf* belt; *(punto vita)* waist; **~ di sicurezza** safety o seat belt; **'allacciare le cinture di sicurezza'** 'fasten your seat belts'.

ciò *pron* this, that; **~ che** what; **~ nonostante** nevertheless.

cioccolata *sf* chocolate; *(bevanda)* hot chocolate.

cioccolatino *sm* chocolate.

cioccolato *sm* chocolate.

cioè ♦ *avv* that is ♦ *cong (vale a dire)* that is; *(anzi)* or rather.

ciondolo *sm* pendant.

ciotola sf bowl.

ciottolo sm pebble.

cipolla sf onion.

cipresso sm cypress.

cipria sf face powder.

circa avv & prep about.

circo, -chi sm circus.

circolare ♦ agg & sf circular ♦ vi to circulate; (veicoli) to drive; (persone) to move along; (notizia) to go round.

circolazione sf (di merce, moneta, giornali) circulation; **mettere in ~** (notizia) to spread; (merce, moneta) to put into circulation; **~ sanguigna** circulation; **~ stradale** traffic.

circolo sm circle; (club) club.

circondare vt to surround.

circonferenza sf circumference.

circonvallazione sf ring road.

circoscrizione sf district.

circostante agg surrounding.

circostanza sf circumstance; **date le circostanze** in o under the circumstances.

circuito sm circuit.

ciste = **cisti**.

cisterna sf tank.

cisti sf inv cyst.

citare vt (DIR) to summon; (menzionare) to cite; (opera, autore) to quote.

citofono sm entry phone.

città sf inv town; (importante) city; **~ universitaria** (university) campus.

▶ **Città del Vaticano** sf Vatican City.

cittadinanza sf citizenship; (abitanti) citizens (pl).

cittadino, -a ♦ sm, f citizen ♦ agg town, city (dav s).

ciuco, -chi sm ass, donkey.

ciuffo sm tuft.

civetta sf owl; (fig: donna) flirt.

civico, -a, -ci, -che agg civic.

civile ♦ agg civil; (civilizzato) civilized ♦ sm civilian.

civiltà sf inv civilization.

clacson sm inv horn.

clamoroso, -a agg sensational.

clandestino, -a ♦ agg (illegale) illegal; (segreto) clandestine ♦ sm, f stowaway.

clarinetto sm clarinet.

classe sf class; (aula) classroom; **~ turistica** tourist class; **prima/seconda ~** first/second class; **che ~ fai?** what year are you in?

classico, -a, -ci, -che agg (letteratura, arte, musica) classical; (moda, esempio) classic.

classifica, -che sf (sportiva) league table; (d'esame) results (pl); (musicale) charts (pl).

classificare vt (ordinare) to classify; (valutare) to mark.

▶ **classificarsi** vr: **classificarsi primo** to come first.

claudicante agg (zoppicante) limping.

clausola sf (DIR) clause.

clavicembalo sm harpsichord.

clavicola sf clavicle.

claxon = **clacson**.

clero sm clergy.

cliente smf (di negozio, bar) customer; (di professionista) client.

clientela sf (di negozio, bar) clientele; (di professionista) clients (pl).

clima, -i sm climate.

clinica, -che sf clinic.

cloro sm chlorine.

club [klab] sm inv club.

cm (abbr di centimetro) cm.

coagulare vt (sangue) to coagulate; (latte) to curdle.

▶ **coagularsi** vr (sangue) to clot; (latte) to curdle.

coca sf (fam: bibita) Coke®.

Coca-Cola® sf Coca-Cola®.

cocaina sf cocaine.

coccinella sf ladybird.

coccio sm (terracotta) earthenware; (frammento) shard.

cocciuto, -a agg stubborn.

cocco, -chi sm (albero) coconut palm; (frutto) coconut.

coccodrillo sm crocodile.

coccolare vt to cuddle.

cocomero sm watermelon.

coda sf (fila) queue (Br), line (Am); (di animale) tail; **fare la ~** to queue (Br), to stand in line (Am); **mettersi in ~** to join the queue (Br) o line (Am); **~ (di cavallo)** ponytail.

codardo, -a agg cowardly.

codesto, -a agg & pron this.

codice sm code; **~ (di avviamento) postale** postcode; **~ fiscale** tax code; **~ della strada** highway code.

coerente agg consistent.

coetaneo, -a agg: **siamo coetanei** we are the same age.

cofano sm bonnet (Br), hood (Am).

cogliere vt to pick, to gather; (fig: occasione, momento) to seize; **~ qn sul fatto** to catch sb redhanded.

cognac sm inv cognac.

cognato, -a sm, f brother-in-law (f sister-in-law).

cognome sm surname.

coi = con + i, → con.

coincidenza sf (caso) coincidence; (aereo, treno) connection.

coincidere vi: **~ (con qc)** (oggetti) to coincide (with sthg); (versione dei fatti) to agree (with sthg); (date, eventi) to clash (with sthg).

coinciso, -a pp → coincidere.

coinvolgere vt: **~ qn (in qc)** to involve sb (in sthg).

coinvolto, -a pp → coinvolgere.

col = con + il, → con.

colapasta = scolapasta.

colare ♦ vt (filtrare) to filter; (pasta) to drain ♦ vi (liquido) to drip; (contenitore) to leak; (cera, burro) to melt; **~ a picco** to sink.

colazione sf (pranzo) lunch; **(prima) ~** breakfast; **fare ~** (al mattino) to have breakfast.

colera sm cholera.

colica, -che sf colic.

colino sm colander.

colla sf glue.

collaborare vi: **~ a** to collaborate on.

collaboratore, -trice sm, f collaborator.

collaborazione sf collaboration.

collana sf necklace; (serie) series.

collant [kol'lan] smpl tights.

collare sm collar.

collasso sm collapse.

collaudo sm test.

colle sm hill.

collega, -ghi, -ghe smf colleague.

collegare vt to connect.

▶ **collegarsi** vr to link up.

▶ **collegarsi con** vr + prep (per telefono, radio, TV) to link up with.

collegio sm boarding school.

collera sf anger; **essere in ~ (con qn)** to be angry (with sb).

colletta sf collection.

collettivo, -a agg (comune) common, general; (responsabilità) collective; (di gruppo) group (dav s).

colletto sm collar.

collezionare vt to collect.

collezione sf collection; **fare la ~ di qc** to collect sthg.

collina sf hill.

collirio sm eyewash.

collisione sf impact.

collo sm neck; (di abito) collar, neck; (pacco) package.

collocamento sm employment.

collocare vt (disporre) to place.

colloquio sm (conversazione) talk; (esame) oral exam; **~ di lavoro** interview.

colmo, -a ♦ agg full ♦ sm: **è il ~!** it's the last straw!

colomba sf dove; (dolce) Easter cake.

Colombia sf: **la ~** Colombia.

colonia sf colony; (per bambini) summer camp; **(acqua di) ~** (eau de) cologne.

colonna sf column; **~ vertebrale** spine, spinal column.

colorante sm (per alimenti) food colouring; (per tessuti) dye.

colorare vt to colour.

colore sm colour; **di che ~?** what colour?; **di ~** coloured; **a colori** colour (dav s).

coloro pron mpl: **~ che ...** those who ...

colosseo sm: **il Colosseo** the Colosseum.

IL COLOSSEO

One of Rome's most visited monuments, the Colosseum was built between 75 and 80 AD. In its arena spectators watched gladiatorial contests, fights between men and animals, chariot races and simulated naval battles. Pillaged over the centuries, and attacked more recently by pollution, the amphitheatre nevertheless still retains some of its outer walls.

---

colpa sf (responsabilità) fault; (reato) offence; **dare la ~** (di qc to blame sb/sthg (for sthg); **per ~ di** through, owing to.

colpire vt to hit; (impressionare, sog: malattia) to strike.

colpo sm (sparo) blow; (sparo) shot; (alla porta) knock; (fam: infarto) stroke; (fam: rapina) raid; **di ~** suddenly; **fare ~** to make a strong impression; **un ~ di fulmine** love at first sight; **~ di sole** sunstroke; **~ di stato** coup (d'état); **~ di telefono** phone call; **~ di testa** impulse; **~ di vento** gust of wind.

coltello sm knife.

coltivare vt to cultivate.

colto, -a ♦ pp → **cogliere** ♦ agg cultured.

coma sm inv coma.

comandante sm (di nave) captain; (di esercito) commanding officer.

comandare ♦ vi to be in command ♦ vt to order, to command.

comando sm command; (congegno) control.

combaciare vi to fit together.

combattere vt & vi to fight.

combinare vt (accordare) to combine; (organizzare) to arrange; (fam: fare) to do.

combinazione sf combination; (caso) coincidence; **per ~** by chance.

combustibile ♦ agg combustible ♦ sm fuel.

come avv **1.** (comparativo) like; **ho dormito ~ un ghiro** I slept like a log; **~ me** like me; **~ sempre** as always; **~ se niente fosse** as if nothing had happened.

2. (interrogativo) how; **non so ~ fare** I don't know what to do; **com'è?** what's it like?; **~ sarebbe?** what do you mean?; **~ stai?** how are you?; **~ mai?** how come?

3. (in qualità di) as; **viaggiare ~ turista** to travel as a tourist.

4. (in esclamazioni) how; **~ mi dispiace!** I'm so sorry!

5. (per esempio) like; **mi piacciono i colori accesi ~ il rosso** I like bright colours like red.

♦ cong **1.** (nel modo in cui) how; **mi ha spiegato ~ lo ha conosciuto** she told me how she met him; **fai ~ ti dico** do as I tell you; **~ vuole** as you like.

2. (comparativa) as; **non è caldo ~ pensavo** it's not as hot as I thought.

3. (quanto) how; **sai ~ mi piace il cioccolato** you know how much I like chocolate.

cometa sf comet.

comfort sm inv comfort; **l'hotel dispone di tutti i ~** the hotel offers a wide range of amenities.

comico, -a, -ci, -che ♦ agg funny; (genere) comic ♦ sm (attore) comedian.

cominciare vt & vi to begin, to start; **~ a fare qc** to begin to do sthg, to begin doing sthg; **~ col fare qc** to begin by doing sthg.

comitiva sf group.

comizio sm meeting.

commedia sf play; (opera comica) comedy.

commemorare vt to commemorate.

commentare vt to comment on.

commento sm comment; (a un testo, programma) commentary.

commerciale agg commercial.

commerciante smf (mercante) trader; (negoziante) shopkeeper.

commerciare : commerciare in v + prep to deal in.

commercio sm (vendita) trade; **essere fuori ~** not to be for sale; **essere in ~** to be on the market.

commesso, -a pp → **commettere** ♦ sm, f shop assistant.

commestibile agg edible.

▶ **commestibili** smpl foodstuffs.

commettere vt (crimine) to commit; (errore) to make.

commissario sm (di polizia) superintendent; (d'esami) member of an examining board; **~ tecnico** national coach.

commissione sf commission.

▶ **commissioni** sfpl errands.

commosso, -a ♦ pp → **commuovere** ♦ agg moved.

commovente agg touching.

commozione sf (emozione) emotion; **~ cerebrale** concussion.

commuovere vt to move, to touch.

▶ **commuoversi** vr to be moved, to be touched.

comò sm inv chest of drawers.

comodino sm bedside table.

comodità sf inv comfort.

comodo, -a ♦ agg comfortable; (conveniente) convenient; (utile) handy ♦ sm: **fare ~ a qn** to be handy for sb; **fare il proprio ~** to do as one pleases; **con ~** at one's convenience.

compact disc ['kɔmpat 'disk] sm inv compact disc.

compagnia sf company; (di amici) group; **fare ~ a qn** to keep sb company; **~ aerea** airline; **~ d'assicurazione** insurance company.

compagno, -a sm, f companion; (convivente) partner; **~ di scuola** school friend; **~ di squadra** team mate.

comparire vi to appear.

compartimento sm (di locale, spazio) section; (di treno) compartment.

compasso sm pair of compasses.

compatibile agg compatible; **un comportamento non ~** inexcusable behaviour.

compatire vt (aver compassione di) to feel sorry for; (scusare) to make allowances for.

compatto, -a agg (ben unito) compact; (folla) dense; (fig: solidale) united.

compensare vt to compensate; **~ qn di qc** to compensate sb for sthg.

compenso sm (paga) payment; (risarcimento) compensation; (ricompensa) recompense; **in ~** on the other hand.

comperare = **comprare**.

compere sfpl: **far ~** to do the shopping.

competente agg competent.

competere vi to compete.

▶ **competere a** v + prep to be due to.

competizione sf competition.

compiacere vt to please.

▶ **compiacersi** vr: **compiacersi di** o **per qc** to be delighted at sthg; **compiacersi con qn** to congratulate sb.

compiaciuto, -a pp → **compiacere**.

compiere vt (eseguire) to fulfil; (concludere) to complete; **quando compi gli anni?** when is your birthday?; **compie 15 anni a maggio** he'll be 15 in May.

compilare vt to fill in.

compito sm (incarico) task; (dovere) duty; (in classe) test.

▶ **compiti** smpl homework (sg); **fare i compiti** to do one's homework.

compleanno sm birthday; **buon ~!** Happy Birthday!

complessivo, -a agg overall.

complesso, -a ♦ *agg* complex ♦ *sm* complex; (*musicale*) band, group; **in** o **nel ~** on the whole.

completamente *avv* completely.

completare *vt* to complete.

completo, -a ♦ *agg* complete; (*pieno*) full ♦ *sm* (*vestiario*) suit; (*di oggetti*) set; **al ~** (*hotel, aereo*) fully booked; **c'era la famiglia al ~** the whole family was there.

complicare *vt* to complicate.

▶ **complicarsi** *vr* to become complicated.

complicato, -a *agg* complicated.

complicazione *sf* (*difficoltà*) snag; (*di malattia*) complication.

complice *smf* accomplice.

complimentarsi *vr*: **~ con qn** to congratulate sb.

complimento *sm* compliment; **complimenti!** congratulations!; **non fare complimenti** don't stand on ceremony.

componente ♦ *smf* (*membro*) member ♦ *sf* (*aspetto*) element.

componibile *agg* fitted.

comporre *vt* (*musica, poesia*) to compose; (*parola*) to make up; (*numero di telefono*) to dial.

comportamento *sm* behaviour.

comportare *vt* to involve.

▶ **comportarsi** *vr* to behave.

compositore, -trice *sm, f* composer.

composizione *sf* composition; '*~ principali treni*' *board showing the position of compartments, restaurant car etc making up main line trains.*

composto, -a ♦ *pp* → **comporre** ♦ *agg* (*persona, contegno*) composed; (*sostanza, parola*) compound ♦ *sm* compound; **~ da** composed of.

comprare *vt* to buy.

comprendere *vt* (*includere*) to include; (*capire*) to understand.

comprensione *sf* understanding.

comprensivo, -a *agg* (*tollerante*) understanding; (*inclusivo*) inclusive.

compreso, -a ♦ *pp* → **comprendere** ♦ *agg* inclusive; **~ nel prezzo** included in the price.

compressa *sf* tablet.

compromesso *sm* compromise.

compromettere *vt* to compromise.

computer [kom'pjuter] *sm inv* computer.

comunale *agg* municipal.

comune ♦ *agg* common; (*a più persone*) shared; (*ordinario*) ordinary ♦ *sm* (*edificio*) town hall; (*ente*) town council; (*area*) = borough; **avere qc in ~ (con qn)** to have sthg in common (with sb); **mettere qc in ~** to share sthg; **fuori del ~** out of the ordinary.

comunicare ♦ *vt* to communicate ♦ *vi* (*parlare, corrispondere*) to communicate; (*porta*): **~ con** to lead to.

comunicazione *sf* (*atto*) communication; (*annuncio*) announcement; (*telefonica*) call; **dare la ~ a qn** to put a call through to sb.

comunione *sf* (*eucaristia*) Communion; **~ dei beni** (DIR) joint ownership of property.

comunismo *sm* communism.

comunista, -i, -e *agg & smf* communist.

comunità *sf inv* community; **la Comunità (Economica) Europea** the European (Economic) Community.

comunque ♦ *avv* anyway ♦ *cong* (*tuttavia*) however; (*in qualsiasi modo*) no matter how.

con *prep* with; **~ piacere!** with pleasure!; **viaggiare ~ il treno/la macchina** to travel by train/car.

concavo, -a *agg* concave.

concedere *vt* (*dare, accordare*) to grant; (*ammettere*) to concede; **~ a qn di fare qc** to allow sb to do sthg; **concedersi qc** to treat o.s. to sthg.

concentrare *vt* to concentrate; (*riassumere*) to condense.

▶ **concentrarsi** *vr* to concentrate.

concentrato, -a ♦ *agg* concentrated, concentrating ♦ *sm* concentrate.

concentrazione *sf* concentration.

concepimento *sm* conception.

concepire *vt* (*figlio*) to conceive; (*idea*) to devise.

concerto *sm* concert.

concessionario *sm* agent.

concesso, -a *pp* → **concedere**.

concetto *sm* concept; (*opinione*) opinion.

conchiglia *sf* shell.

conciliare *vt* (*impegni, attività*) to reconcile; (*sonno*) to be conducive to; (*contravvenzione*) to settle on the spot.

concime *sm* fertilizer.

concludere *vt* to conclude.

▶ **concludersi** *vr* to conclude.

conclusione *sf* conclusion; **in ~** in conclusion.

concluso, -a *pp* → **concludere**.

concordare ♦ *vt* (*stabilire*) to agree on; (GRAMM) to make agree ♦ *vi* to agree.

concorde *agg* in agreement.

concorrente *smf* (*in gara, affari*) competitor; (*ad un concorso*) contestant.

concorrenza *sf* competition.

concorso *sm* competition; (*esame*) competitive examination; **~ di bellezza** beauty contest.

concreto, -a *agg* concrete.

condanna *sf* (*sentenza*) sentence; (*pena*) conviction; (*disapprovazione*) condemnation.

condannare *vt* (DIR) to sentence; (*disapprovare*) to condemn.

condensare *vt* to condense.

condimento *sm* (*per insalata*) dressing; (*per carne*) seasoning.

condire *vt* (*insalata*) to dress; (*carne*) to season.

condividere *vt* to share.

condizionale ♦ *agg & sm* conditional ♦ *sf* (DIR) suspended sentence.

condizionatore *sm* air-conditioner.

condizione *sf* condition; **a ~ che** on condition that.

condoglianze *sfpl* condolences.

condominio *sm* (*edificio*) block of flats (*jointly owned*); (*persone*) joint owners (*pl*).

condomino *sm* joint owner.

condotta *sf* conduct.

condotto, -a ♦ *pp* → **condurre** ♦ *sm* conduit; (ANAT) duct.

conducente *sm* driver; '**non parlare al ~**' 'please do not speak to the driver whilst the vehicle is in motion'.

condurre *vt* (*affare, azienda*) to run; (*bambino, prigioniero*) to take; (*vita*) to lead; (*gas, acqua*) to carry.

conduttore, -trice ♦ *sm, f* driver; (TV) presenter ♦ *sm* (*di calore, elettricità*) conductor.

confarsi : confarsi a *vr + prep* to suit.

confederazione *sf* confederation.

conferenza *sf* (*riunione*) conference; (*discorso*) lecture; **~ stampa** press conference.

conferire *vt* (*form*): **~ qc a qn** to confer sthg on sb.

conferma *sf* confirmation.

confermare *vt* to confirm.

confessare *vt* to confess.

▶ **confessarsi** *vr* (RELIG) to confess; (*dichiararsi*): **confessarsi colpevole** to plead guilty.

confessione *sf* confession.

confetto *sm* (*dolciume*) sugared almond; (*pastiglia*) pill.

confezionare *vt* (*merce*) to package; (*pacco*) to make up; (*vestiario*) to make.

confezione *sf* (*involucro*) packaging; (*di vestiario*) tailoring; **casa di ~** clothing manufacturer; **~ regalo** gift pack.

confidare *vt*: **~ qc a qn** to confide sthg to sb.

▶ **confidare in** *v + prep* to have confidence in.

▶ **confidarsi** *vr*: **confidarsi con qn**

to open one's heart to sb.

confidenziale *agg* confidential.

confinare : confinare con *v +
prep* to border on.

▶ **confinarsi in** *vr + prep* to shut
o.s. away in.

confine *sm* (*frontiera*) border; (*limite*) boundary.

confiscare *vt* to confiscate.

conflitto *sm* (*guerra*) conflict; (*contrasto*) clash.

confondere *vt* to confuse, to mix
up; ~ **le idee a qn** to confuse sb.

▶ **confondersi** *vr* (*mescolarsi*) to
merge; (*sbagliarsi*) to get mixed up;
(*turbarsi*) to become confused.

conformità *sf* conformity; **in ~ con**
in accordance with.

confortare *vt* to comfort.

confortevole *agg* comfortable.

confrontare *vt* to compare.

confronto *sm* comparison; **in ~ (a)**
in comparison (with); **nei miei confronti** towards me.

confusionario, -a *agg* muddle-
headed.

confusione *sf* (*caos*) confusion;
(*disordine*) mess; (*chiasso*) racket,
noise; **far ~** (*confondersi*) to get
mixed up; (*far rumore*) to make a
racket.

confuso, -a ♦ *pp* → **confondere**
♦ *agg* confused.

congedare *vt* (*lasciar andare*) to
dismiss; (MIL) to demobilize.

▶ **congedarsi** *vr* (*andar via*) to take
one's leave; (MIL) to be demobi-
lized.

congedo *sm* leave; (MIL) discharge.

congegno *sm* device.

congelare *vt* to freeze.

▶ **congelarsi** *vr* to freeze; (*fig: persona, mani*) to be frozen.

congelato, -a *agg* frozen.

congelatore *sm* freezer.

congeniale *agg* congenial.

congenito, -a *agg* congenital.

congestione *sf* congestion.

congettura *sf* conjecture.

congiungere *vt* to join (together).

▶ **congiungersi** *vr* (*strade*) to
meet.

congiuntivo *sm* subjunctive.

congiunto, -a ♦ *pp* → **congiungere** ♦ *sm, f* relative.

congiunzione *sf* conjunction.

congiura *sf* conspiracy.

congratularsi *vr*: ~ **con qn per qc**
to congratulate sb on sthg.

congratulazioni *sfpl* congratulations.

congresso *sm* congress.

coniglio *sm* rabbit.

coniugato, -a *agg* married.

coniuge *smf* spouse.

connazionale *smf* fellow country-
man (*f* fellow countrywoman).

connettere *vt* to connect.

connotati *smpl* description (*sg*).

cono *sm* cone; ~ **gelato** ice-cream
cone.

conoscente *smf* acquaintance.

conoscenza *sf* knowledge; (*persona*) acquaintance; **perdere ~** to
lose consciousness.

conoscere *vt* to know; (*incontrare*)
to meet.

conosciuto, -a ♦ *pp* → **conoscere** ♦ *agg* well-known.

conquista *sf* (*azione*) conquest;
(*risultato, cosa ottenuta*) achievement.

conquistare *vt* (*impadronirsi di*) to
conquer; (*ottenere*) to gain; (*persona*)
to win over.

consanguineo, -a *sm, f* blood
relation.

consapevole *agg*: ~ **di qc** aware
of sthg.

conscio, -a, -sci, -sce *agg*: ~ **di
qc** conscious of sthg.

consegna *sf* (*recapito*) delivery;
(*custodia*): **dare qc in ~ a qn** to
entrust sb with sthg.

consegnare *vt* (*recapitare*) to
deliver; (*affidare*) to entrust.

conseguenza *sf* consequence; **di**

~ consequently.

conseguire ♦ *vt* to obtain ♦ *vi*: **ne consegue che ...** it follows that ...

consenso *sm* consent.

consentire *vt* to allow.

▶ **consentire a** *v + prep* to consent to.

conserva *sf* preserve; ~ **di frutta** jam; ~ **di pomodoro** tomato sauce.

conservante *sm* preservative.

conservare *vt* (*tenere*) to keep; (*monumento, resti*) to preserve; '~ **in frigo**' 'keep refrigerated'.

▶ **conservarsi** *vr* (*cibo*) to keep; (*monumento, resti*) to be preserved.

conservatore, -trice *sm, f* conservative.

conservazione *sf* conservation; (*di cibo*) preservation.

considerare *vt* to consider.

▶ **considerarsi** *vr* to consider o.s.

considerazione *sf*: **prendere in** ~ to take into consideration.

considerevole *agg* considerable.

consigliare *vt* (*persona*) to advise; (*locale, metodo*) to recommend; ~ **a qn di fare qc** to advise sb to do sthg.

▶ **consigliarsi con** *vr + prep*: **consigliarsi con qn** to ask sb's advice.

consigliere *sm* (*funzionario*) adviser; (*politico*) councillor.

consiglio *sm* (*suggerimento*) piece of advice; (*riunione*) meeting; (*organo*) council; **dare un** ~ **a qn** to give sb some advice; ~ **d'amministrazione** board; **il Consiglio dei Ministri** = the Cabinet.

consistere : **consistere di** *v + prep* to consist of; **consistere in** *v + prep* to consist in.

consistito, -a *pp* → **consistere**.

consolare *vt* (*confortare*) to console; (*sollevare*) to cheer up.

▶ **consolarsi** *vr* to console o.s.

consolato *sm* consulate.

console *sm* consul.

consonante *sf* consonant.

constatare *vt* to notice.

consueto, -a *agg* usual.

consulente *smf* consultant.

consultare *vt* to consult.

▶ **consultarsi** *vr* to confer.

▶ **consultarsi con** *vr + prep* to consult with.

consultorio *sm* advice bureau.

consumare *vt* to consume; (*logorare*) to wear out.

▶ **consumarsi** *vr* to wear out.

consumatore *sm* consumer.

consumazione *sf* (*bibita*) drink; (*spuntino*) snack; **la** ~ **al tavolo è più cara** it's more expensive to eat/drink sitting at a table; '~ **obbligatoria**' 'minimum charge'.

consumismo *sm* consumerism.

consumo *sm* consumption.

contabile *smf* accountant.

contabilità *sf inv* (*operazioni*) accountancy; (*libri*) accounts (*pl*); (*ufficio*) accounts department.

contachilometri *sm inv* ≃ mileometer.

contadino, -a *sm, f* farmer; (STORIA, *spreg*) peasant.

contagiare *vt* to infect.

contagocce *sm inv* dropper.

contante ♦ *agg* → **denaro** ♦ *sm* cash; **pagare in contanti** to pay in cash.

contare *vt & vi* to count; **avere i soldi contati** not to have a penny to spare.

▶ **contare di** *v + prep*: ~ **di fare qc** to intend to do sthg.

▶ **contare su** *vr + prep* to count on.

contatore *sm* meter.

contattare *vt* to contact.

contatto *sm* contact; **mettersi in** ~ (**con qn**) to get in touch (with sb).

conte, -essa *sm, f* count (*f* countess).

contegno *sm* attitude.

contemporaneamente *avv* simultaneously.

contemporaneo, -a *agg* (*dello stesso tempo*) contemporaneous; (*attuale*) contemporary.

contendere *vt*: ~ qc a qn to compete with sb for sthg.

contenere *vt* to contain.

▶ **contenersi** *vr* to contain o.s.

contenitore *sm* container.

contento, -a *agg* (*lieto*) happy, glad; (*soddisfatto*): ~ **(di)** pleased (with).

contenuto *sm* (*cosa racchiusa*) contents (*pl*); (*argomento*) content.

contestare *vt* to object to.

contestazione *sf* (*obiezione*) objection; (*protesta*) protest.

contesto *sm* context.

contiguo, -a *agg*: ~ **(a qc)** adjacent (to sthg).

continentale *agg* continental.

continente *sm* (*geografico*) continent; (*terraferma*) mainland.

contingente *sm* contingent.

continuamente *avv* (*senza interruzioni*) continuously; (*di frequente*) continually.

continuare ♦ *vt & vi* to continue ♦ *v impers*: **continua a piovere** it's still raining; ~ **a fare qc** to continue doing sthg.

continuazione *sf* continuation.

continuo, -a *agg* (*incessante*) continuous; (*serie, fila*) continual; **di** ~ continually.

conto *sm* (*calcolo*) calculation; (*di ristorante, albergo*) bill; (*bancario*) account; **mi porta il ~, per favore?** could you bring me the bill, please?; **fare ~ su** to rely on; **rendersi ~ di qc** to realize sthg; **tenere ~ di qc** to take account of sthg; ~ **corrente** current account; ~ **alla rovescia** countdown; **per ~ di qn** on behalf of sb; **fare i conti con qn** (*fam*) to sort sb out; **in fin dei conti** all things considered.

contorno *sm* (*di pietanza*) vegetables (*pl*); (*linea*) outline.

contrabbando *sm* smuggling.

contrabbasso *sm* double bass.

contraccambiare *vt* to return.

contraccolpo *sm* rebound.

contraddire *vt* to contradict.

▶ **contraddirsi** *vr* to contradict o.s.

contraddizione *sf* contradiction.

contraffare *vt* to falsify; (*firma*) to forge.

contrapporre *vt* to set against.

contrariamente *avv*: ~ **a** contrary to.

contrario, -a ♦ *agg* (*opposto*) opposite; (*sfavorevole*) unfavourable; ♦ *sm* opposite; **essere** ~ **a qc** to be against sthg; **avere qualcosa in** ~ to have an objection; **al** ~ on the contrary.

contrarre *vt* to contract.

▶ **contrarsi** *vr* (*muscolo*) to contract.

contrassegno *sm* (*marchio*) mark; **spedire qc (in)** ~ to send sthg cash on delivery.

contrastare ♦ *vt* to hinder ♦ *vi*: ~ **(con)** to clash (with).

contrasto *sm* contrast; **essere in** ~ **con qc** (*opinione, esigenza*) to be in contrast with sthg.

contrattare *vt* to negotiate.

contrattempo *sm* hitch.

contratto, -a ♦ *pp* → **contrarre** ♦ *sm* contract.

contravvenzione *sf* fine.

contribuire : **contribuire a** *v + prep* to contribute to.

contributo *sm* (*partecipazione*) contribution; (*tassa*) levy.

contro *prep* against; ~ **di me** against me; **prendere qc** ~ **il mal di gola** to take sthg for one's sore throat.

controfigura *sf* stuntman (*f* stuntwoman).

controllare *vt* to control; (*verificare*) to check; '~ **il resto'** 'please check your change'.

▶ **controllarsi** *vr* to control o.s.

controllo *sm* (*verifica*) check; (*sorveglianza*) supervision; (*dominio*) control; **perdere il** ~ to lose control; ~ **doganale** customs inspection; '~ **elettronico della velocità'** 'speed checks'; '~ **passaporti** 'passport control'.

controllore sm (di autobus, treni) (ticket) inspector; ~ **di volo** air-traffic controller.

contromano avv in the wrong direction.

controproducente agg counter-productive.

controsenso sm contradiction in terms.

controvoglia avv reluctantly.

contusione sf bruise.

convalescenza sf convalescence.

convalidare vt (biglietto) to validate; (dubbio, sospetto) to confirm; '~ all'inizio del viaggio' 'stamp your ticket at the start of your journey'.

convegno sm conference.

convenevoli smpl civilities.

conveniente agg favourable; (prezzo) cheap; (affare) advantageous.

convenire ♦ vi (riunirsi) to gather; (concordare) to agree; (tornare utile) to be worthwhile ♦ v impers (essere consigliabile): **conviene avvertirli** it is advisable to inform them; **ti conviene aspettare** you'd better wait.

convento sm convent.

convenuto pp → **convenire**.

convenzioni sfpl conventions.

conversazione sf (chiacchierata) conversation.

convertire vt to convert.

► **convertirsi** vr: **convertirsi (a qc)** to convert (to sthg).

convincere vt: ~ **qn di qc** to convince sb of sthg; ~ **qn a fare qc** to persuade sb to do sthg.

convinto, -a ♦ pp → **convincere** ♦ agg convinced.

convivere vi to live together.

convocare vt to convene.

convoglio sm convoy.

convulsioni sfpl convulsions.

cooperativa sf cooperative.

coordinare vt to coordinate.

coperchio sm lid.

coperta sf (da letto) blanket; (di nave) deck.

copertina sf cover.

coperto, -a ♦ pp → **coprire** ♦ agg (piscina, campo) indoor (dav s); (persona) wrapped up; (cielo) overcast ♦ sm (a tavola) place; (al ristorante) cover charge; ~ **di qc** covered with sthg; **al** ~ under cover.

copertone sm (pneumatico) tyre.

copia sf copy; **bella** ~ final draft; **brutta** ~ rough draft.

copiare vt to copy.

copione sm script.

coppa sf (bicchiere) goblet; (di gelato) tub; (ciotola) bowl; (di reggiseno, trofeo) cup; ~ **dell'olio** oil sump.

coppia sf (paio) pair; (di sposi, amanti) couple; **a coppie** in pairs.

copricostume sm inv beach robe.

coprifuoco, -chi sm curfew.

copriletto sm inv bedspread.

coprire vt to cover; ~ **qn di qc** to cover sb with sthg; (insulti) to shower sb with sthg.

► **coprirsi** vr (con indumenti) to cover o.s.; **coprirsi di qc** (muffa, fango) to be covered in sthg.

coraggio ♦ sm (forza d'animo) courage; (faccia tosta) cheek ♦ esclam cheer up!; (forza) come on!; **avere il** ~ **di fare qc** (avere l'animo) to have the nerve to do sthg; (avere faccia tosta) to have the cheek to do sthg.

coraggioso, -a agg courageous, brave.

corallo sm coral.

Corano sm: **il** ~ the Koran.

corazzieri smpl the President's guard.

corda sf (fune) rope; (spago, di strumento) string; **tagliare la** ~ (fig) to sneak off; **corde vocali** vocal cords.

cordiale agg warm, cordial.

cordone sm cord; (di persone) cordon; ~ **ombelicale** umbilical cord.

coreografia sf choreography.

coriandolo sm (spezia, pianta) coriander.

▶ **coriandoli** *smpl* confetti (*sg*).

coricarsi *vr* to go to bed.

cornamusa *sf* bagpipes (*pl*).

cornetta *sf* receiver.

cornetto *sm* (*pasta*) croissant; (*gelato*) cone.

cornice *sf* frame.

cornicione *sm* cornice.

corno (*pl f* corna) *sm* horn; **facciamo le corna!** (*fam*) = touch wood!; **fare o mettere le corna a qn** (*fam*) to cheat on sb.

Cornovaglia *sf*: **la ~** Cornwall.

coro *sm* chorus; (*di chiesa*) choir.

corona *sf* (*reale*) crown; (*di fiori*) wreath.

corpo *sm* body; (*militare*) corps (*sg*); **~ insegnante** teaching staff; **(a) ~ a ~** hand to hand.

corporatura *sf* build.

corporeo, -a *agg* bodily.

corredare *vt*: **~ qc di qc** to equip sthg with sthg.

corredo *sm* (*da sposa*) trousseau; (*attrezzatura*) kit.

correggere *vt* to correct.

corrente ◆ *agg* (*moneta*) valid; (*mese, anno*) current; (*comune*) everyday ◆ *sf* current; (*tendenza*) trend ◆ *sm*: **essere al ~ (di qc)** to be informed (about sthg); **mettere qn al ~ (di qc)** to inform sb (about sthg); **~ alternata** alternating current; **~ continua** direct current.

correntemente *avv* (*speditamente*) fluently; (*comunemente*) commonly.

correre ◆ *vi* to run; (*affrettarsi*) to rush ◆ *vt* to run; **~ dietro a qn** to run after sb.

corretto, -a ◆ *pp* → correggere ◆ *agg* (*esatto*) correct; (*onesto*) proper.

correzione *sf* correction; (*di compiti*) marking.

corridoio *sm* corridor.

corridore *sm* (*atleta*) runner; (*pilota*) racer.

corriera *sf* coach, bus.

corriere *sm* courier.

corrimano *sm* handrail.

corrispondente ◆ *agg* corresponding ◆ *smf* correspondent.

corrispondenza *sf* correspondence.

corrispondere *vt* to return.

▶ **corrispondere a** *v + prep* to correspond to.

corrisposto, -a *pp* → corrispondere.

corrodere *vt* to corrode.

corrompere *vt* (*comprare*) to bribe; (*traviare*) to corrupt.

corroso, -a *pp* → corrodere.

corrotto, -a ◆ *pp* → corrompere ◆ *agg* (*disonesto*) corrupt.

corruzione *sf* (*disonestà*) corruption; (*con denaro*) bribery.

corsa *sf* (*a piedi*) running; (*gara*) race; (*di mezzo pubblico*) journey; **fare una ~** (*correre*) to run; (*sbrigarsi*) to dash; **di ~** in a rush; **~ campestre** (*gara*) cross-country race; (*attività*) cross-country running; **corse dei cavalli** horse races.

corsia *sf* (*di strada*) lane; (*di ospedale*) ward; **~ preferenziale** bus and taxi lane; **~ di sorpasso** overtaking lane; **'~ chiusa'** 'lane closed'.

Corsica *sf*: **la ~** Corsica.

corso, -a ◆ *pp* → correre ◆ *sm* course; (*strada*) main street; **fare un ~ (di qc)** to take a course (in sthg); **~ accelerato** crash course; **~ d'acqua** watercourse; **corsi estivi** summer courses; **corsi serali** evening classes; **in ~** (*denaro*) in circulation; (*riunione, lavori*) in progress; **fuori ~** out of circulation.

corte *sf* (*reale*) court; **fare la ~ a qn** to court sb.

corteccia, -ce *sf* bark.

corteggiare *vt* to court.

corteo *sm* (*manifestazione*) demonstration; (*processione*) procession.

cortese *agg* polite.

cortesia *sf* (*qualità*) politeness; (*atto*) favour; **per ~** please.

cortile *sm* courtyard.

corto, -a *agg* short; **essere a ~ di qc** to be short of sthg.

cortocircuito *sm* short circuit.

corvo *sm* raven.

cosa *sf* thing; (*faccenda*) matter; **è una ~ da niente** it's nothing; **~?** what?; **~ c'è?** what's the matter?; **per prima ~** firstly.

coscia, -sce *sf* (*di uomo*) thigh; (*di pollo, agnello*) leg.

cosciente *agg* (*sveglio*) conscious; (*consapevole*): **~ di qc** aware o conscious of sthg.

coscienza *sf* conscience; **avere qc sulla ~** to have sthg on one's conscience.

coscienzioso, -a *agg* conscientious.

coscio *sm* leg.

cosciotto *sm* leg.

così *avv* **1.** (*in questo modo*) like this/by that; **fai ~ do** it this way; **~ so-so** per **~ dire** so to speak; **meglio ~** it's better like this; **proprio ~!** just like that!; **e ~ via** and so on. **2.** (*per descrivere misure*) so; **una scatola larga ~ e lunga ~** a box so wide and so long. **3.** (*talmente*) so; **è ancora ~ presto!** it's still so early!; **~ poco/tanto** so little/much; **una ragazza ~ bella** such a beautiful girl. **4.** (*conclusivo*) so; **~, non hai ancora deciso** so you haven't decided yet. ♦ *cong* **1.** (*perciò*) so, therefore. **2.** (*a tal punto*): **~ ... che** so ... (that); **sono ~ stanco che non sto in piedi** I'm so tired I can hardly stand up; **~ ... da** enough ... to; **è ~ sciocco da dire di no** he's silly enough to say no. ♦ *agg inv*: **non ho mai visto una macchina ~** I've never seen a car like that.

▶ **così che** *cong*: (*affinché*) so (that).

cosicché *cong* so that.

cosiddetto, -a *agg* so-called.

cosmetici *smpl* cosmetics.

cosmopolita, -i, -e *agg* cosmopolitan.

coso *sm* (*fam*) thing.

cospargere *vt*: **~ qc di qc** to sprinkle sthg with sthg.

cosparso, -a *pp* → **cospargere**.

cospicuo, -a *agg* sizeable.

cospirare *vi* to conspire.

costa *sf* coast.

costante *agg* (*stabile, durevole*) constant; (*persona*) steadfast.

costare *vi* to cost; **quanto costa?** how much does it cost?; **~ caro** to be expensive.

costata *sf* chop.

costatare = **constatare**.

costeggiare *vt* (*fiancheggiare*) to go alongside; (*navigare*) to hug the coast of.

costellazione *sf* constellation.

costernato, -a *agg* dismayed.

costì *avv* there.

costiero, -a *agg* coastal.

costituire *vt* (*formare*) to constitute; (*fondare*) to set up.

▶ **costituirsi** *vr* to give o.s. up.

costituzione *sf* constitution; (*formazione*) setting-up.

costo *sm* cost; **a tutti i costi** at all costs.

costola *sf* rib.

costoletta *sf* cutlet.

costoso, -a *agg* expensive.

costretto, -a *pp* → **costringere**.

costringere *vt*: **~ qn (a fare qc)** to force sb (to do sthg).

costruire *vt* (*fabbricare*) to build.

costruzione *sf* construction.

costume *sm* (*uso*) custom; (*abito*) costume; **~ da bagno** swimsuit.

cotechino *sm* pork sausage.

cotoletta *sf* chop; (*di vitello*) cutlet; **~ alla milanese** escalope of veal, coated in egg and breadcrumbs then fried.

cotone *sm* cotton; **~ idrofilo** cotton wool.

cotta *sf*: **prendersi una ~ per qn** (*fam*) to have a crush on sb.

cotto, -a ♦ *pp* → **cuocere** ♦ *agg* cooked; (*fam: innamorato*) head over heels in love; **ben ~** welldone.

cottura sf cooking.

coupon [ku'pon] sm inv coupon.

cozza sf mussel.

C.P. (abbr di casella postale) P.O. Box.

cracker ['krɛker] sm inv cracker.

crampo sm cramp.

cranio sm skull.

cratere sm crater.

crauti smpl sauerkraut flavoured with cumin and juniper, a speciality of Trento.

cravatta sf tie.

creare vt to create.

creativo, -a agg creative.

creatore, -trice sm, f creator; **il Creatore** the Creator.

creatura sf creature.

credente smf believer.

credenza sf (convinzione) belief; (mobile) sideboard.

credere vt to believe; **credo di sì/no** I think/don't think so; **credo (che) sia vero** I think that's true; **credo di fare la cosa giusta** I think I'm doing the right thing.
▶ **credere a** v + prep to believe; **non ci credo!** I don't believe it!
▶ **credere in** v + prep to believe in.
▶ **credersi** vr to consider o.s.

credito sm (COMM) credit; (fiducia) trust.

crema sf cream; (dolce) egg custard; **~ di asparagi** cream of asparagus soup; **~ depilatoria** hair-removing cream; **~ pasticcera** confectioner's custard; **~ solare** suntan cream; **gelato alla ~** vanilla ice-cream.

crematorio sm crematorium.

cremazione sf cremation.

crème caramel ['krɛm'karamɛl] sm inv o sf inv crème caramel.

cremisi agg inv crimson.

cremoso, -a agg creamy.

crepaccio sm crevice.

crepapelle : a crepapelle avv: **ridere a ~** to split one's sides laughing.

crepare vi (fam: morire) to snuff it; **~ dal ridere** to die laughing.

crêpe [krɛp] sf inv pancake.

crepuscolo sm (tramonto) twilight.

crescere ♦ vi to grow; (diventare adulto) to grow up ♦ vt to bring up.

crescita sf growth.

cresima sf confirmation.

crespo, -a agg frizzy.

cresta sf crest.

creta sf clay.

cretino, -a agg idiot.

cric sm inv (attrezzo) jack.

criminale agg & smf (criminoso) criminal.

crimine sm crime.

criniera sf mane.

cripta sf crypt.

crisi sf inv (fase difficile) crisis; (attacco) fit; **in ~** in a state of crisis.

cristallo sm crystal.

cristianesimo sm Christianity.

cristiano, -a agg & sm, f Christian.

Cristo sm Christ; **avanti ~** BC; **dopo ~** AD.

criterio sm (regola) criterion; (buon senso) common sense.

critica, -che sf (biasimo) criticism; (i critici) critics (pl), → **critico**.

criticare vt to criticize.

critico, -a, -ci, -che ♦ agg critical ♦ sm, f (persona) critic.

croccante ♦ agg crisp ♦ sm almond crunch.

crocchetta sf croquette.

croce sf cross; **la Croce Rossa** the Red Cross.

crocevia sm inv crossroads (sg).

crociera sf cruise.

crocifisso sm crucifix.

crollare vi (edificio, ponte) to collapse; (fig: per stanchezza, dolore) to break down.

crollo sm (di edificio, ponte) collapse; (di prezzi) slump.

cronaca, -che sf (attualità) news (sg); (di partita) commentary; **~ nera** crime news (sg).

cronico, -a, -ci, -che agg chronic.

cronista, -i, -e smf reporter.

cronologico, -a, -ci, -che agg

chronological.

crosta sf (di pane) crust; (di formaggio) rind; (di ferita) scab.

crostacei smpl shellfish.

crostata sf fruit or jam tart with a pastry lattice topping.

crostino sm (per minestra) crouton; (tartina) canapé; **crostini di fegato** small pieces of toast spread with chicken liver pâté.

croupier [kru'pje] sm inv croupier.

cruciale agg crucial.

cruciverba sm inv crossword.

crudele agg cruel.

crudo, -a agg raw.

crusca sf bran.

cruscotto sm dashboard.

cubo sm cube.

cuccetta sf (di treno) couchette; (di nave) berth.

cucchiaiata sf spoonful.

cucchiaino sm teaspoon.

cucchiaio sm spoon.

cuccia, -ce sf dog's bed; **a ~!** down!

cucciolo sm cub; (di cane) puppy.

cucina sf (stanza) kitchen; (attività, cibi) cooking; (elettrodomestico) cooker; **la ~ italiana** Italian cooking, Italian cuisine; **~ casalinga** home cooking; **~ a gas** gas cooker.

cucinare vt to cook.

cucire vt to sew.

cucitura sf stitching.

cuculo sm cuckoo.

cuffia sf cap; (per l'ascolto) headphones (pl); '**è obbligatorio l'uso della ~**' 'swimming caps must be worn'.

cugino, -a sm, f cousin.

cui pron relativo **1**. (in complemento indiretto: persona) who, whom; **l'amico a ~ ho prestato il libro** the friend I lent the book to, the friend to whom I lent the book; **l'amico di ~ ti ho parlato** the friend I told you about; **la ragazza con ~ esco** the girl I'm going out with.
2. (in complemento indiretto: cosa) which; **il film a ~ mi riferisco** the film (which) I'm referring to; **l'appartamento in ~ vivo** the flat (which) I live in; **il motivo per ~ ti chiamo** the reason (that) I'm calling you.
3. (tra articolo e sostantivo): **la città il ~ nome mi sfugge** the town whose name escapes me; **la persona alla ~ domanda rispondo** the person whose question I'm answering.
▶ **per cui** cong (perciò) so; **sono stanco, per ~ vado a letto** I'm tired, so I'm going to bed.

culla sf cradle.

culmine sm peak.

culo sm (volg) arse (Br), ass (Am).

culto sm cult; (adorazione) worship.

cultura sf culture.

culturale agg cultural.

culturismo sm body-building.

cumulativo agg m → **biglietto**.

cumulo sm (mucchio) heap, pile.

cunetta sf (avvallamento) bump.

cuocere vt & vi to cook.

cuoco, -a, -chi, -che sm, f cook.

cuoio sm leather; **~ capelluto** scalp.

cuore sm heart; **avere a ~ qc** to care about sthg; **nel ~ della notte** in the middle of the night.

cupo, -a agg (scuro) dark; (voce) deep.

cupola sf dome.

cura sf care; (trattamento, terapia) treatment; **avere ~ di** to take care of; **prendersi ~ di** to look after; **~ dimagrante** diet.

curare vt (trattare) to treat; (guarire) to cure.

curiosare vi to look around.

curiosità sf inv curiosity.

curioso, -a agg (insolito) curious; (indiscreto) inquisitive.

curva sf bend; **in ~** on a bend; '**~ pericolosa**' 'dangerous bend'.

curvare ♦ vi (veicolo, autista) to turn; (strada) to bend ♦ vt to bend.

curvo, -a agg (linea) curved; (persona, spalle) bent.

cuscino sm (da divano) cushion; (guanciale) pillow.

custode smf attendant; (di scuola) janitor.

custodia sf (cura, controllo) custody; (astuccio) case.

custodire vt (assistere) to look after; (conservare) to keep.

cute sf skin.

D

da prep 1. (con verbo passivo) by; **il viaggio è pagato dalla ditta** the trip is paid for by the company.

2. (stato in luogo) at; **abito ~ una zia** I'm living at an aunt's.

3. (moto a luogo) to; **andare dal medico/dal parrucchiere** to go to the doctor's/the hairdresser's.

4. (moto per luogo) through; **è entrato dall'ingresso principale** he came in through the main entrance; **il treno passa ~ Roma** the train goes via Rome.

5. (indica l'origine, la provenienza) from; **venire ~ Roma** to come from Rome; **ricevere una lettera ~ un amico** to get a letter from a friend.

6. (indica tempo) for; **aspetto ~ ore** I've been waiting for hours; **lavoro dalle 9 alle 5** I work from 9 to 5; **non lo vedo ~ ieri** I haven't seen him since yesterday; **comincerò ~ domani** I'll start from tomorrow.

7. (indica condizione, funzione) as; **~ grande voglio fare il pompiere** when I grow up I want to be a fireman; **fare ~ guida** to act as a guide.

8. (indica la causa) with; **tremare dal freddo** to shiver; **piangere dalla felicità** to cry for joy.

9. (indica una caratteristica) with; **una ragazza dagli occhi verdi** a girl with green eyes, a green-eyed girl; **una stanza ~ 200 000 lire a notte** a 200,000 lira a night room; **una bottiglia ~ un litro** a litre bottle.

10. (indica il fine): **occhiali ~ sole** sunglasses; **qualcosa ~ mangiare** something to eat.

11. (indica separazione) from; **vedere ~ lontano/vicino** to see from a distance/close up; **essere lontano ~ casa** to be far from home; **la piscina è a 3 chilometri ~ qui** the swimming pool is 3 kilometres from here; **isolarsi ~ tutti** to cut o.s. off from everyone; **mettere qc ~ parte** to save sthg.

12. (indica modo) like; **trattare qn ~ amico** to treat sb like o as a friend; **puoi farlo ~ te** you can do it (for) yourself; **non è cosa ~ te!** it's not like you!

13. (indica la conseguenza): **essere stanco ~ morire** to be dead tired.

daccapo avv from the beginning.

dado sm (per gioco) dice; (estratto) stock cube; (per vite) nut.

dagli = da + gli, → da.

dai¹ = da + i, → da.

dai² esclam go on!

daino sm (animale) deer.

dal = da + il, → da.

dall' = da + l', → da.

dalla = da + la, → da.

dalle = da + le, → da.

dallo = da + lo, → da.

daltonico, -a, -ci, -che agg colour-blind.

dama sf (gioco) draughts (sg); (nel ballo) partner.

damigiana sf demijohn.

danaro = denaro.

dancing ['dɛnsɪŋ] sm inv dance hall.

danese ♦ agg & sm Danish ♦ smf Dane.

Danimarca sf: **la ~** Denmark.

danneggiare vt (rovinare) to damage; (nuocere a) to harm.

danno sm (materiale) damage; (morale) harm; **i danni** (DIR) damages.

dannoso, -a agg harmful.

danza sf: **la ~** dancing, dance; **una ~** a dance.

dappertutto avv everywhere.

dappoco agg inv (persona) inept; (questione) insignificant.

dapprima avv at first.

dare vt to give; (risultati) to produce; (film): **cosa danno all'Odeon?** what's on at the Odeon?; **~ qc a qn** to give sthg to sb, to give sb sthg; **~ la mano a qn** to shake hands with sb; **~ la nausea a qn** to make sb feel sick; **~ la buonanotte a qn** to say goodnight to sb; **~ da bere a qn** to give sb something to drink; **~ una festa** to throw a party; **~ del lei a qn** to address sb as 'lei'; **~ del tu a qn** to address sb as 'tu'; **~ qn per morto** to give sb up for dead; **~ qc per scontato** to take sthg for granted; **darsi il cambio** to take it in turns; **~ alla testa a qn** (sog: alcool, successo) to go to sb's head.

▶ **dare su** v + prep (finestra) to look out onto; (porta) to lead to.

▶ **darsi a** vr + prep (dedicarsi a) to devote o.s. to; **darsi al bere** to take to drink.

data sf date; **~ di nascita** date of birth.

dato, -a ♦ pp → **dare** ♦ agg particular ♦ sm datum; **~ che** given that; **un ~ di fatto** a fact; **i dati** the data.

datore, -trice sm, f: **~ di lavoro** employer.

dattero sm date.

dattilografo, -a sm, f typist.

davanti ♦ avv in front; (avanti) ahead; (nella parte anteriore) at the front ♦ agg inv front (dav s) ♦ sm front ♦ prep: **~ a** in front of; (dirimpetto) opposite.

davanzale sm windowsill.

davvero avv really.

d.C. (abbr di dopo Cristo) A.D.

dea sf goddess.

debito sm debt.

debole ♦ agg weak ♦ sm: **avere un**

~ per to have a weakness for.

debolezza sf weakness.

debuttare vi to make one's debut.

decaffeinato, -a agg decaffeinated.

decapitare vt to decapitate.

decappottabile agg & sf convertible.

deceduto, -a agg deceased.

decennio sm decade.

decente agg decent.

decesso sm (form) death.

decidere ♦ vt to decide on ♦ vi to decide; **~ di fare qc** to decide to do sthg.

▶ **decidersi** vr: **decidersi (a fare qc)** to make up one's mind (to do sthg).

decimale agg decimal.

decimo, -a num tenth, → **sesto**.

decina sf ten; (circa dieci) about ten; **decine di** dozens of.

decisione sf decision; **prendere una ~** to make a decision.

deciso, -a ♦ pp → **decidere** ♦ agg decisive; **~ a fare qc** determined to do sthg.

decollare vi to take off.

decollo sm takeoff.

decorare vt to decorate.

decotto sm decoction.

decreto sm decree.

dedica, -che sf dedication.

dedicare vt: **~ qc a qn** (poesia, canzone) to dedicate sthg to sb; (fig: consacrare) to devote sthg to sb.

▶ **dedicarsi a** vr + prep to devote o.s. to.

dedito, -a agg: **~ a qc** (studio) devoted to sthg; (droga, alcool) addicted to sthg.

dedotto, -a pp → **dedurre**.

dedurre vt (concludere) to deduce; (detrarre) to deduct.

deduzione sf deduction.

deficiente agg (spreg) idiotic.

deficit sm inv deficit.

definire vt to define.

definitivo, -a *agg* definitive.

definizione *sf* definition.

deformare *vt* to deform; (*fig:* *travisare*) to distort.

▶ **deformarsi** *vr* to become deformed.

defunto, -a *sm, f* deceased.

degenerare *vi* to degenerate.

degli = di + gli, → **di**.

degnarsi *vr*: ~ di fare qc to condescend to do sthg.

degno, -a *agg*: ~ di worthy of.

degradare *vt* (*peggiorare*) to degrade; (MIL) to demote.

degustazione *sf* (*assaggio*) tasting; (*negozio*) specialist shop where beverages, especially wine or coffee, are tasted.

dei = di + i, → **di**.

delegare *vt*: ~ qn (a fare qc) to delegate sb (to do sthg); ~ qc a qn to delegate sthg to sb.

delegazione *sf* delegation.

delfino *sm* dolphin.

delicatezza *sf* (*l'essere delicato*) delicacy; (*gentilezza*) consideration; (*atto gentile*) considerate act.

delicato, -a *agg* delicate; (*gentile*) considerate.

delineare *vt* to outline.

▶ **delinearsi** *vr* (*essere visibile*) to be outlined; (*fig: presentarsi*) to take shape.

delinquente *smf* delinquent, criminal.

delirio *sm* (MED) delirium; (*esaltazione*) frenzy.

delitto *sm* crime.

delizioso, -a *agg* (*cibo*) delicious; (*gradevole*) delightful.

dell' = di + l', → **di**.

della = di + la, → **di**.

delle = di + le, → **di**.

dello = di + lo, → **di**.

delta *sm inv* delta.

deltaplano *sm* hang glider.

deludere *vt* to disappoint.

delusione *sf* disappointment.

deluso, -a ♦ *pp* → **deludere** ♦ *agg* disappointed.

democratico, -a, -ci, -che *agg* democratic.

democrazia *sf* democracy.

demolire *vt* to demolish.

demonio *sm* devil.

demoralizzare *vt* to demoralize.

▶ **demoralizzarsi** *vr* to become demoralized.

denaro *sm* money; ~ **contante** cash.

denigrare *vt* to denigrate.

denominare *vt* to name.

denominazione *sf* name, denomination; ~ **d'origine controllata** a mark guaranteeing that the product, especially wine, is of a good quality.

densità *sf* density.

denso, -a *agg* thick.

dente *sm* tooth; ~ **da latte** milk tooth; ~ **del giudizio** wisdom tooth; **al** ~ al dente (*cooked enough to be still firm when bitten*); **mettere qc sotto i denti** to have a bite to eat; **armato fino ai denti** armed to the teeth.

dentiera *sf* (*denti finti*) dentures (*pl*).

dentifricio *sm* toothpaste.

dentista, -i, -e *smf* dentist.

dentro *avv & prep* inside; **darci** ~ (*fam*) to put one's back into it; ~ **di sé** inwardly, inside; **qui/là** ~ in here/there; **dal di** ~ from the inside; **in** ~ inwards.

denuncia, -ce o **-cie** *sf*: **fare la** ~ to make a statement to the police; ~ **dei redditi** income tax return.

denunciare *vt* (*sporgere denuncia contro*) to report; (*rendere noto*) to declare.

deodorante *sm* (*per il corpo*) deodorant; (*per ambiente*) air freshener.

deperibile *agg* perishable.

depilazione *sf* hair removal.

dépliant [depli'an] *sm inv* brochure, leaflet.

deplorevole *agg* deplorable.

deportare *vt* to deport.

depositare vt to deposit; (persona) to leave.
▶ **depositarsi** vr to settle.
deposito sm deposit; (per autobus) depot; (per merci) warehouse; (di liquido) sediment; ~ **bagagli** left luggage office; ~ **valori** safe deposit, safety deposit.
depravato, -a sm, f degenerate.
depressione sf depression.
depresso, -a ♦ pp → **deprimere**
♦ agg depressed.
deprimente agg depressing.
deprimere vt to depress.
▶ **deprimersi** vr to become depressed.
deputato, -a sm, f ≈ Member of Parliament (Br), ≈ Representative (Am).
derattizzazione sf rodent control.
deriva sf: andare alla ~ to drift.
derivare : derivare da v + prep to derive from.
dermatologo, -a, -gi o **-ghi, -ghe** sm, f dermatologist.
derubare vt to rob.
descritto, -a pp → **descrivere**.
descrivere vt to describe.
descrizione sf description.
deserto, -a ♦ agg (disabitato) deserted; (senza vegetazione) barren ♦ sm desert.
desiderare vt to want, to desire; (sessualmente) to desire; **desidera?** can I help you?; ~ **fare qc** to wish to do sthg; **lasciare a ~** to leave much to be desired.
desiderio sm wish.
desideroso, -a agg: ~ **di fare qc** eager to do sthg.
designare vt to designate.
desistere : desistere da v + prep (form) to give up.
desistito pp → **desistere**.
destinare vt (assegnare, riservare) to assign; (indirizzare) to address.
destinatario, -a sm, f addressee.

destinazione sf destination; **arrivare a** ~ to reach one's destination.
destino sm destiny, fate.
destra sf (mano) right hand; (lato) right; **la** ~ (POL) the right wing; **tenere la** ~ to keep to the right; **a** ~ (stato in luogo) on the right; (moto a luogo) right; **di** ~ (dal lato destro) right-hand.
destreggiarsi vr (nel traffico) to manoeuvre; (fig: tra difficoltà) to manage.
destro, -a agg (opposto a sinistra) right.
detenuto, -a sm, f prisoner.
detenzione sf detention.
detergente ♦ agg cleansing ♦ sm (cosmetico) cleansing cream; (detersivo) detergent.
deteriorare vt to impair.
▶ **deteriorarsi** vr to deteriorate.
determinante agg decisive.
determinare vt (stabilire) to determine.
determinazione sf determination.
detersivo sm detergent.
detestare vt to detest.
detrarre vt to deduct.
detratto, -a pp → **detrarre**.
dettagliato, -a agg detailed.
dettaglio sm detail; **al** ~ (COMM) retail.
dettare vt to dictate; ~ **legge** to lay down the law.
dettato sm dictation.
detto, -a ♦ pp → **dire** ♦ agg (soprannominato) known as ♦ sm saying.
devastare vt to devastate.
deviare ♦ vt to divert ♦ vi (di direzione): ~ **da qc** to turn off sthg.
deviazione sf (del traffico) detour; (di fiume) deviation.
devoto, -a agg devoted.
di prep 1. (indica appartenenza) of; **il libro** ~ **Marco** Marco's book; **la porta della camera** the bedroom door.

2. (*indica l'autore*) by; **un quadro ~ Giotto** a painting by Giotto.

3. (*partitivo*) of; **alcuni ~ noi** some of us.

4. (*nei paragoni*): **sono più alto ~ te** I'm taller than you; **il migliore ~ tutti** the best of all.

5. (*indica argomento*) about, of; **un libro ~ storia** a history book; **parlare ~** to talk about.

6. (*temporale*) in; **d'estate** in (the) summer; **~ mattina** in the morning; **~ notte** at/by night; **~ sabato** on Saturdays.

7. (*indica provenienza*) from; **~ dove sei?** where are you from?; **sono ~ Messina** I'm from Messina.

8. (*indica una caratteristica*): **un bambino ~ due anni** a two-year-old child, a child of two; **una statua ~ marmo** a marble statue; **una torre ~ 40 metri** a 40-metre tower; **un film ~ due ore** a two-hour film.

9. (*indica la causa*): **urlare ~ dolore** to scream with pain; **sto morendo ~ fame!** I'm starving!; **soffrire ~ mal di testa** to suffer from headaches; **morire ~ vecchiaia** to die of old age.

10. (*indica contenuto*) of; **una bottiglia ~ vino** a bottle of wine.

11. (*seguito da infinito*): **mi ha detto ~ non aspettare** he told me not to wait; **pensavo ~ uscire** I was thinking of going out; **capita ~ sbagliare** anyone can make a mistake; **mi sembra ~ conoscerlo** I think I know him.

12. (*in espressioni*): **a causa ~** because of; **~ modo che** so as to; **dare del bugiardo a qn** to call sb a liar.

♦ *art* some; (*in negative*) any; **vorrei del pane** I'd like some bread; **ha degli spiccioli?** have you got any change?

diabete *sm* diabetes.

diabetico, -a, -ci, -che *agg* diabetic.

diaframma, -i *sm* diaphragm.

diagnosi *sf inv* diagnosis.

diagonale *agg & sf* diagonal.

diagramma, -i *sm* diagram.

dialetto *sm* dialect.

dialisi *sf* (MED) dialysis.

dialogo, -ghi *sm* dialogue.

diamante *sm* diamond.

diametro *sm* diameter.

diamine *esclam* (*certo*) absolutely!; **che ~ stai facendo?** what on earth are you doing?

diapositiva *sf* slide.

diario *sm* diary; (*a scuola*) homework book; (*calendario*) timetable.

diarrea *sf* diarrhoea.

diavola *sf → pollo.

diavolo *sm* devil; **che ~ vuole?** (*fam*) what the hell does he want?; **va al ~!** (*fam*) go to hell!

dibattito *sm* debate.

**dica → dire.

dicembre *sm* December, **→ settembre.

diceria *sf* piece of gossip, rumour.

dichiarare *vt* to declare.

dichiarazione *sf* declaration.

diciannove *num* nineteen, **→ sei.

diciannovesimo, -a *num* nineteenth, **→ sesto.

diciassette *num* seventeen, **→ sei.

diciassettesimo, -a *num* seventeenth, **→ sesto.

diciottesimo, -a *num* eighteenth, **→ sesto.

diciotto *num* eighteen, **→ sei.

didattico, -a, -ci, -che *agg* educational.

dieci *num* ten, **→ sei.

**diecina = decina.

diesel ['dizel] *agg inv & sm inv* diesel.

dieta *sf* diet; **essere a ~** to be on a diet.

dietetico, -a, -ci, -che *agg* diet (*dav s*).

dietro ♦ *avv* (*nella parte posteriore*) at/in the back; (*indietro*) behind ♦ *sm* back ♦ *prep*: **~ (a)** (*dopo*) after; (*di là da*) behind; **~ di me** behind me; **di ~** back (dav s); **qui/lì ~** behind here/there; **~ pagamento** on payment.

difatti cong in fact.

difendere vt to defend.

▶ **difendersi** vr to defend o.s.

difensore sm defender.

difesa sf defence.

difeso, -a pp → **difendere**.

difetto sm defect; (morale) fault; **~ di fabbricazione** manufacturing defect.

difettoso, -a agg (meccanismo) faulty; (vista, abito) defective.

diffamare vt (a parole) to slander; (per iscritto) to libel.

differente agg different.

differenza sf difference; **non fa ~** it doesn't make any difference; **a ~ di** unlike.

difficile agg difficult; **è ~ che esca** (poco probabile) it's unlikely that he'll go out.

difficoltà sf inv difficulty.

diffidare : diffidare di v + prep to mistrust.

diffidente agg mistrustful.

diffondere vt to spread.

▶ **diffondersi** vr to spread.

diffusione sf diffusion.

diffuso, -a ◆ pp → **diffondere** ◆ agg widespread.

diga, -ghe sf dam.

digeribile agg digestible.

digerire vt to digest.

digestione sf digestion.

digestivo, -a ◆ agg digestive ◆ sm liqueur drunk to aid digestion, after meals.

digitale agg digital.

digitare vt (INFORM) to key in.

digiunare vi to fast.

digiuno, -a ◆ sm fasting ◆ agg: **essere ~** not to have eaten; **a ~** on an empty stomach.

dignità sf dignity.

dilagante agg (fenomeno) rampant.

dilagare vi to be rampant.

dilaniare vt to tear to pieces.

dilapidare vt to squander.

dilatare vt (pupille) to dilate; (gas, metallo, corpo) to expand.

▶ **dilatarsi** vr (pupille) to dilate; (gas, metallo, corpo) to expand.

dilazionare vt to defer.

dilemma, -i sm dilemma.

dilettante smf amateur.

diligente agg diligent.

diluire vt (allungare) to dilute; (sciogliere) to dissolve.

dilungarsi vr: **~ su** (argomento) to dwell upon; **~ in spiegazioni** to give a longwinded explanation.

diluvio sm downpour.

dimagrire vi to lose weight.

dimenare vt (fianchi) to swing; (corpo) to shake; (coda) to wag.

▶ **dimenarsi** vr to fling o.s. about.

dimensione sf dimension.

dimenticanza sf oversight.

dimenticare vt to forget; (lasciare) to leave; **dimenticarsi qc** to leave sthg.

▶ **dimenticarsi di** vr + prep to forget about; **dimenticarsi di fare qc** to forget to do sthg.

dimesso, -a ◆ pp → **dimettere** ◆ agg humble.

dimestichezza sf familiarity.

dimettere vt to discharge.

▶ **dimettersi** vr to resign.

dimezzare vt to halve.

diminuire ◆ vt to reduce ◆ vi to decrease; (prezzi) to drop.

diminuzione sf fall; (di prezzi) drop.

dimissioni sfpl resignation (sg); **dare le ~** to hand in one's resignation.

dimostrare vt (manifestare) to show; (provare) to prove; **dimostra meno di vent'anni** he doesn't look twenty.

▶ **dimostrarsi** vr to prove to be.

dimostrazione sf (d'affetto, simpatia) show; (di teoria) proof; (protesta, per prodotto) demonstration.

dinamico, -a, -ci, -che agg dynamic.

dinamite sf dynamite.

dinamo sf inv dynamo.

dinanzi prep: ~ **a** (davanti a) in front of; (alla presenza di) before.

dinosauro sm dinosaur.

dintorni smpl outskirts; **nei ~ di** in the vicinity of.

dio (pl **dei**) sm god.

▶ **Dio** sm God; **mio Dio!** my God!

diocesi sf inv diocese.

dipartimento sm department.

dipendente ♦ agg subordinate ♦ smf employee.

dipendenza sf (subordinazione) dependence; (assuefazione) addiction; **essere alle dipendenze di qn** to be employed by sb.

dipendere vi: ~ **da** to depend on; (derivare) to be due to; **dipende** it depends.

dipeso, -a pp → **dipendere**.

dipingere vt to paint.

dipinto, -a ♦ pp → **dipingere** ♦ sm painting.

diploma, -i sm diploma.

diplomarsi vr to obtain a diploma.

diplomatico, -a, -ci, -che ♦ agg diplomatic ♦ sm (funzionario) diplomat; (pasta) pastry made of layers of liqueur-soaked sponge, puff pastry and confectioner's custard, topped with icing sugar.

diplomazia sf diplomacy.

diradare vt to cut down on.

▶ **diradarsi** vr (nebbia, nubi) to clear; (vegetazione) to thin out.

dire vt **1.** (pronunciare) to say; ~ **di sì/no** to say yes/no.

2. (esprimere, raccontare) to say; ~ **qc a qn** to tell sb sthg; ~ **a qn che/perché** to tell sb that/why; ~ **la verità** to tell the truth; **dimmi tutto** tell me everything; **dica pure** (in un negozio) can I help you?

3. (ordinare): ~ **a qn di fare qc** to tell sb to do sthg.

4. (sostenere) to say; **dice che non è**

vero he says it isn't true.

5. (tradurre): **come si dice 'scusi' in inglese?** what's the English for 'scusi'?

6. (pensare) to think; **che ne dite di ...?** how about ...?; **e ~ che ...!** to think that ...!

7. (in espressioni): **diciamo che ...** let's say that ...; **a ~ il vero ...** to tell the truth ...; **vuol ~ che ...** it means (that) ...; **non c'è che ~** there's no doubt about it; **il nome non mi dice niente** the name doesn't mean much to me; **dico davvero** o **sul serio!** I'm serious!; **a dir poco** at least; **a dir tanto** at most; **volevo ben ~!** I thought so!

♦ v impers: **si dice che ...** they say (that) ...; **si direbbe che ...** it seems (that) ...

diretta sf: **in ~** (trasmissione) live.

direttamente avv (per via diretta) straight; (senza intermediari) directly.

direttissimo sm express train.

diretto, -a ♦ pp → **dirigere** ♦ agg direct ♦ sm (treno) through train; **essere ~ a** (aereo, passeggero) to be bound for; (indirizzato) to be intended for.

direttore, -trice sm, f manager (f manageress); (di scuola elementare) head (teacher) (Br), principal (Am); ~ **d'orchestra** conductor.

direzione sf direction; (di azienda) management.

dirigente smf executive.

dirigere vt (attenzione, sguardo) to direct; (scuola, azienda) to run; (orchestra) to conduct.

▶ **dirigersi** vr to head.

dirimpetto avv opposite.

diritto, -a ♦ agg & avv straight ♦ sm right; (leggi) law; (di abito, stoffa) right side; (nel tennis) forehand; (nella maglia) plain stitch; **andare ~** (in linea retta) to go straight on; **vai ~ a casa** go straight home; **sempre (a) ~** straight on; **avere ~ a qc** to be entitled to sthg.

dirittura sf: ~ **d'arrivo** home straight.

diroccato, -a agg in ruins.

dirottare vt to hijack; (traffico) to divert.

dirotto, -a agg: **piovere a ~** to pour.

dirupo sm precipice.

disabitato, -a agg uninhabited.

disaccordo sm disagreement.

disadattato, -a agg maladjusted.

disagio sm (scomodità) discomfort; (imbarazzo) uneasiness; **essere a ~** to be ill at ease.

disapprovare vt to disapprove.

disarmare vt to disarm.

disarmo sm disarmament.

disastro sm disaster; (danno) damage.

disastroso, -a agg disastrous.

disattento, -a agg inattentive.

disavanzo sm deficit.

disavventura sf mishap.

discapito sm: **a ~ di** to the detriment of.

discarica, -che sf dump.

discendente smf descendant.

discepolo, -a sm, f disciple.

discesa sf slope; (movimento) descent; **in ~** downhill; **~ libera** downhill race; **'~ a mare'** 'this way down to the sea'.

dischetto sm diskette.

disciplina sf (ubbidienza) discipline; (materia) subject.

disciplinato, -a agg disciplined.

disc-jockey [disk 'dʒɔkei] smf inv disc jockey.

disco, -schi sm (musicale) record; (per computer) disk; **~ orario** parking disc; **~ volante** flying saucer.

discolpare vt to clear.

discorde agg conflicting.

discorrere : discorrere di v + prep to talk about.

discorso ♦ pp → **discorrere ♦** sm speech; (conversazione) conversation, talk.

discoteca, -che sf disco.

discretamente avv (abbastanza

bene) fairly well; (con tatto) discreetly.

discreto, -a agg (persona) discreet; (abbastanza buono) reasonably good.

discrezione sf (tatto) discretion; (moderazione) moderation.

discriminare vt to discriminate.

discussione sf (dibattito) discussion; (litigio) argument.

discusso, -a pp → **discutere**.

discutere ♦ vt (parlare di) to discuss; (contestare) to question **♦** vi to argue; **~ di** o **su** (dibattere) to discuss.

disdetto, -a pp → **disdire**.

disdire vt to cancel.

disegnare ♦ vt to draw; (progettare) to design **♦** vi to draw.

disegno sm drawing; (materia) art; (motivo) pattern; (progetto) project; **~ di legge** bill.

diseredare vt to disinherit.

disertare vt & vi to desert.

disertore sm deserter.

disfare vt to undo; (valigia) to unpack; (maglia) to unravel; (sciogliere) to melt.

disfatto, -a pp → **disfare**.

disgelo sm thaw.

disgrazia sf (incidente) accident.

disgraziato, -a ♦ agg (persona) wretched; (viaggio) ill-fated; (anno) unlucky **♦** sm, f (sfortunato) poor wretch; (canaglia) rogue.

disguido sm error, mix-up.

disgustare vt to disgust.

disgusto sm disgust.

disgustoso, -a agg disgusting.

disidratare vt to dehydrate.

disinfestare vt to disinfest.

disinfettante agg & sm disinfectant.

disinfettare vt to disinfect.

disinibito, -a agg uninhibited.

disintegrare vt to cause to disintegrate.

disinteressarsi : disinteressarsi di vr + prep to take no interest in.

disinteresse *sm* (*indifferenza*) indifference; (*generosità*) unselfishness.

disintossicare *vt* to detoxify; ~ l'organismo to clear out one's system.

▶ **disintossicarsi** *vr* (*da droga*) to be treated for drug addiction.

disintossicazione *sf* (*da droga*) treatment for drug addiction.

disinvolto, -a *agg* free and easy.

disinvoltura *sf* ease.

dislivello *sm* (*di quota*) difference in height; (*fig: differenza*) gap.

disoccupato, -a ◆ *agg* unemployed ◆ *sm, f* unemployed person.

disoccupazione *sf* unemployment.

disonesto, -a *agg* dishonest.

disopra ◆ *avv* above; (*al piano superiore*) upstairs ◆ *agg inv* above.

disordinato, -a *agg* untidy; (*vita*) disorderly.

disordine *sm* (*materiale*) untidiness; (*mentale*) confusion; in ~ in a mess.

disorganizzazione *sf* disorganization.

disorientato, -a *agg* disorientated.

disossare *vt* to bone.

disotto ◆ *avv* below; (*al piano inferiore*) downstairs ◆ *agg inv* below.

dispari *agg inv* odd.

disparte *avv*: tenersi o starsene in ~ to keep to o.s.

dispendioso, -a *agg* expensive.

dispensa *sf* (*stanza*) larder; (*mobile*) sideboard; (*fascicolo*) instalment.

disperarsi *vr* to despair.

disperatamente *avv* desperately.

disperato, -a *agg* desperate.

disperazione *sf* desperation.

disperdere *vt* to disperse.

disperso, -a ◆ *pp* → disperdere ◆ *sm, f* missing person.

dispetto *sm* (*atto*) spiteful trick; (*stizza*) vexation; fare un ~ a qn to play a spiteful trick on sb; fare qc per ~ to do sthg out of spite; a ~ di despite.

dispiacere ◆ *sm* (*dolore*) grief; (*rammarico*) regret ◆ *v impers*: le dispiace se aspetto qui? do you mind if I wait here?; mi dispiace che sia andata così I'm sorry it worked out that way; mi dispiace di non potermi trattenere I'm afraid I can't stop.

dispiaciuto, -a ◆ *pp* → dispiacere ◆ *agg* sorry.

disponibile *agg* available; (*persona*) willing to help.

disponibilità *sf* (*di posto, camere*) availability; (*di persona*) willingness to help; (*di denaro*) liquid assets (*pl*).

disporre *vt* to arrange.

▶ **disporre di** *v + prep* (*poter usare*) to have at one's disposal; (*avere*) to have.

dispositivo *sm* device.

disposizione *sf* (*di mobili, oggetti*) arrangement; (*comando*) order; (*attitudine*) disposition; (DIR) provision; essere a ~ di qn to be at sb's disposal; mettere qc a ~ di qn to make sthg available to sb.

disposto, -a ◆ *pp* → disporre ◆ *agg*: ~ a fare qc prepared to do sthg.

disprezzare *vt* to despise.

disprezzo *sm* contempt.

disputa *sf* argument.

dissanguare *vt* (*fig: persona*) to bleed white.

disseminare *vt* to spread.

dissenso *sm* (*disapprovazione*) dissent; (*contrasto*) disagreement.

dissenteria *sf* dysentery.

disservizio *sm* inefficiency.

dissestato, -a *agg* uneven.

dissidente *smf* dissident.

dissidio *sm* disagreement.

dissimulare *vt* to conceal.

dissoluto, -a ◆ *pp* → dissolvere ◆ *agg* dissolute.

dissolvere vt (sciogliere) to dissolve; (nebbia, fumo) to disperse.

dissuadere vt: ~ qn dal fare qc to dissuade sb from doing sthg.

dissuaso, -a pp → **dissuadere**.

distaccare vt (oggetti) to remove; (dipendente) to transfer; (SPORT) to outdistance.

▶ **distaccarsi da** vr + prep (fig: allontanarsi) to withdraw from.

distacco, -chi sm separation; (indifferenza) detachment.

distante agg & avv far away; ~ da far from.

distanza sf distance; (temporale): **a ~ di due mesi** after two months; **tenere le distanze** to keep one's distance.

distanziare vt (separare) to space out; (SPORT) to outdistance.

distare vi: **quanto dista da qui?** how far is it from here?

distendere vt (gamba, mano) to stretch out; (telo, coperta) to spread; (rilassare) to relax.

▶ **distendersi** vr (sdraiarsi) to lie down; (rilassarsi) to relax.

distesa sf expanse.

disteso, -a pp → **distendere**.

distillare vt to distil.

distilleria sf distillery.

distinguere vt to distinguish.

distintivo, -a ◆ agg distinctive ◆ sm badge.

distinto, -a ◆ pp → **distinguere** ◆ agg (diverso) different; (immagine) distinct; (persona) distinguished; **Distinti saluti** (in lettera) Yours faithfully.

distinzione sf distinction.

distogliere vt: ~ qc da to take sthg away from sb; ~ qn da qc to deter sb from sthg.

distolto, -a pp → **distogliere**.

distorsione sf (MED) sprain; (di suono, immagine) distortion.

distrarre vt to distract; (divertire) to amuse, to entertain.

▶ **distrarsi** vr to be distracted; (divertirsi) to amuse o.s.

distratto, -a ◆ pp → **distrarre** ◆ agg (sbadato) absent-minded; (disattento) inattentive.

distrazione sf distraction; (svago) amusement.

distretto sm district.

distribuire vt (assegnare compiti) to allocate; (posta, giornali) to distribute.

distributore sm: ~ **automatico** vending machine; ~ **(di benzina)** petrol pump (Br), gasoline pump (Am).

distribuzione sf distribution; (ripartizione) allocation.

distruggere vt to destroy.

distrutto, -a ◆ pp → **distruggere** ◆ agg shattered.

distruzione sf destruction.

disturbare vt to disturb, to trouble; (interrompere) to interrupt; **la linea è disturbata** it's a bad line; **'non ~ il conducente'** 'do not distract the driver'.

▶ **disturbarsi** vr to bother.

disturbo sm (fastidio) bother; (malessere) disorder; (di comunicazione) interference.

disubbidiente agg disobedient.

disubbidire vi: ~ **(a qn)** to disobey (sb).

disumano, -a agg inhuman.

disuso sm: **in ~** obsolete.

ditale sm thimble.

dito (pl f **di**) sm finger; (misura) drop; ~ **(del piede)** toe.

ditta sf company, firm.

dittatura sf dictatorship.

dittongo, -ghi sm diphthong.

diurno, -a agg daytime (dav s).

diva → **divo**.

divampare vi to flare up.

divano sm sofa; ~ **letto** sofa-bed.

divaricare vt to open wide.

divenire vi to become.

diventare vi to become; ~ **rosso** (persona) to go red.

diversificare vt to diversify.

diversità sf inv diversity; (l'esser diverso) difference.

diversivo sm diversion.

diverso, -a agg different; ~ **da** different from.

▶ **diversi, -e ♦** agg pl various, several ♦ pron pl several; (varie persone) several (people).

divertente agg amusing.

divertimento sm amusement, entertainment; **per** ~ for fun.

divertire vt to amuse.

▶ **divertirsi** vr to enjoy o.s.

dividere vt to divide; (spartire) to share out; (separare) to separate; (condividere) to share.

▶ **dividersi** vr (ripartirsi) to split up; (coppia) to separate.

divieto sm prohibition; '~ **di sosta**' 'no waiting'; '~ **di transito**' 'no thoroughfare'.

divinità sf inv divinity.

divino, -a agg divine.

divisa sf uniform.

divisione sf division.

diviso, -a pp → **dividere**.

divisorio, -a agg dividing.

divo, -a sm, f star.

divorare vt to devour.

divorziare vi to divorce.

divorziato, -a ♦ agg divorced ♦ sm, f divorced person.

divorzio sm divorce.

divulgare vt (notizia) to divulge; (scienza, dottrina) to popularize.

▶ **divulgarsi** vr to spread.

dizionario sm dictionary.

D.J. [diːˈdʒeɪ] smf (abbr di disc-jockey) DJ.

D.N.A. sm DNA.

DOC (abbr di Denominazione di Origine Controllata) label guaranteeing the quality of an Italian wine.

doccia, -ce sf shower; **fare la** ~ to take o to have a shower.

docente ♦ agg teaching ♦ smf teacher; (di università) lecturer.

docile agg (animale) docile.

documentare vt to document.

▶ **documentarsi** vr to gather information.

documentario sm documentary.

documento sm document.

▶ **documenti** smpl documents.

dodicesimo, -a num twelfth, → **sesto**.

dodici num twelve, → **sei**.

dogana sf customs (pl); **passare la** ~ to go through customs.

doganale agg customs (dav s).

doganiere sm customs officer.

dolce ♦ agg sweet; (persona, carattere) gentle; (suono, musica, voce) soft ♦ sm (torta) cake; (portata) dessert.

dolcelatte sm dolcelatte (soft blue cheese).

dolcezza sf sweetness.

dolcificante sm sweetener.

dolciumi smpl confectionery (sg).

dolere vi to hurt.

▶ **dolersi di** vr + prep (essere spiacente di) to regret; (lamentarsi di) to complain of.

dollaro sm dollar.

dolo sm (DIR) malice.

Dolomiti sfpl: **le** ~ the Dolomites.

dolore sm (fisico) pain; (morale) sorrow, grief.

doloroso, -a agg (intervento) painful; (situazione) distressing.

domanda sf (per sapere) question; (per ottenere) request; (COMM) demand; **fare una** ~ **a qn** to ask sb a question; **fare** ~ to apply.

domandare vt (per sapere) to ask; (per ottenere) to ask for; ~ **qc a qn** to ask sb sthg.

▶ **domandarsi** vr to wonder.

domani ♦ avv tomorrow ♦ sm (giorno seguente) tomorrow; **a** ~! see you tomorrow!; ~ **l'altro** the day after tomorrow; **il** ~ the future; ~ **mattina** tomorrow morning; ~ **sera** tomorrow evening.

domare vt (animale) to tame; (rivolta) to put down; (incendio) to control.

domattina avv tomorrow morning.

domenica, -che sf Sunday, → **sabato**.

domestico, -a, -ci, -che agg & sm, f domestic.

domicilio sm domicile; **a ~** home (dav s).

dominante agg dominant.

dominare vt to dominate; (paese) to rule; (situazione, impulso) to control. ► **dominarsi** vr to control o.s.

dominio sm (potere) power; (controllo) control; (territorio) dominion; **essere di ~ pubblico** to be common knowledge.

domino sm dominoes (pl).

donare ♦ vt to give ♦ vi: **questo colore ti dona** this colour suits you; **~ il sangue** to give blood.

donatore, -trice sm, f giver; (di sangue, organi) donor.

dondolare ♦ vt to rock ♦ vi to sway. ► **dondolarsi** vr to sway.

dondolo sm swing hammock; **cavallo/sedia a ~** rocking horse/chair.

donna sf woman; (nelle carte) queen; **~ di servizio** maid.

dono sm gift.

doping ['dopiŋ] sm drug use (in sport).

dopo ♦ avv afterwards; (più tardi) later; (nello spazio) after ♦ prep (di tempo) after; (di luogo) past, after ♦ agg inv after ♦ cong: **~ aver fatto qc** after doing sthg; **il giorno ~** the following day; **un giorno ~** a day later; **a ~!** see you later!; **~ di me** after me.

dopobarba sm inv aftershave.

dopodiché avv after which.

dopodomani avv the day after tomorrow.

dopoguerra sm post-war period.

dopolavoro sm workers' club.

dopopranzo avv in the early afternoon.

doposcì sm inv après-ski.

doposcuola sm inv supervised after-school activities.

dopotutto avv after all.

doppiaggio sm dubbing.

doppiare vt (film) to dub; (SPORT) to lap; (NAUT) to round.

doppiato, -a agg dubbed.

doppio, -a ♦ agg & avv double ♦ sm (SPORT) doubles; **ne ha il ~ di me** (quantità) he has twice as much as me; (numero) he has twice as many as me.

doppione sm duplicate.

doppiopetto sm double-breasted jacket.

dorato, -a agg (di colore) golden; (ricoperto d'oro) gilt.

dormiglione, -a sm, f sleepyhead.

dormire vi to sleep.

dormitorio sm dormitory.

dorso sm back; (di libro) spine.

dosaggio sm dosage.

dosare vt to measure out; (MED) to dose.

dose sf amount; (MED) dose.

dosso sm bump; **togliersi o levarsi qc di ~** to take sthg off.

dotare vt: **~ qc di** to equip sthg with.

dotato, -a agg gifted.

dote sf (qualità) gift; (di sposa) dowry.

Dott. (abbr di dottore) Dr.

dottorato sm doctorate.

dottore, -essa sm, f (medico) doctor; (laureato) graduate.

dottrina sf doctrine.

Dott.ssa (abbr di dottoressa) Dr.

dove avv where; **da ~ vieni?** where do you come from?; **di ~ sei?** where are you from?; **dov'è?** where is it?; **~ vai?** where are you going?; **siediti ~ vuoi** sit wherever you like.

dovere vt **1.** (essere debitore di): **~ qc a qn** to owe sb sthg; **gli devo dei soldi/un favore** I owe him some money/a favour; **quanto le devo?** (in negozio) how much does it come to? **2.** (aver l'obbligo di): **~ fare qc** to have to do sthg; **comportarsi come si deve** to behave o.s. properly; **ora devo andare** I have to o must go now. **3.** (aver bisogno di): **~ fare qc** to have to do sthg; **devo dormire almeno otto ore** I need at least eight hours' sleep; **devi sapere che ...** you should know that ...

4. (*esprime un rimprovero*): **avreste dovuto pensarci prima** you should have thought of it earlier; **avrei dovuto saperlo** I should have known.

5. (*per suggerire*): **dovrebbe prendersi delle vacanze** he should o ought to take a holiday.

6. (*esprime probabilità*): **devono essere già le sette** it must be seven o'clock already; **il tempo dovrebbe rimettersi** the weather should improve.

7. (*esprime intenzione*): **dovevamo partire ieri, ma ...** we were due to leave yesterday, but ...

♦ *sm* duty; **avere dei doveri verso qn** to have a duty to sb.

dovunque *avv* (*in qualunque luogo*) wherever; (*dappertutto*) everywhere.

dovuto, -a *agg*: ~ **a** due to.

dozzina *sf* dozen; **una ~ di rose** a dozen roses.

drago, -ghi *sm* dragon.

dramma, -i *sm* drama.

drammatico, -a, -ci, -che *agg* dramatic.

drastico, -a, -ci, -che *agg* drastic.

drenare *vt* to drain.

dritto, -a *agg & avv* = **diritto**.

drizzare *vt* (*raddrizzare*) to straighten; ~ **le orecchie** to prick up one's ears.

▶ **drizzarsi** *vr*: **drizzarsi (in piedi)** to stand up.

droga, -ghe *sf* drug.

drogare *vt* to drug.

▶ **drogarsi** *vr* to take drugs.

drogato, -a *sm, f* drug addict.

drogheria *sf* grocer's.

droghiere *sm* grocer.

dromedario *sm* dromedary.

dubbio, -a ♦ *agg* (*incerto*) doubtful; (*equivoco*) questionable ♦ *sm* doubt; **ho il ~ che menta** I suspect that he's lying; **essere in ~** to be in doubt; **mettere in ~ qc** to question sthg; **senza ~** without a doubt.

dubbioso, -a *agg* uncertain.

dubitare : dubitare di *v + prep* to doubt; (*mettere in discussione*) to question; **dubito che venga** I doubt whether he'll come.

duca, -chi *sm* duke.

duchessa *sf* duchess.

due *num* two, → **sei**.

duecento *num* two hundred, → **sei**.

▶ **Duecento** *sm*: **il Duecento** the thirteenth century.

duemila *num* two thousand.

▶ **il Duemila** *sm* the year two thousand, → **sei**.

duepezzi *sm inv* (*bikini*) bikini; (*abito*) two-piece suit.

duna *sf* dune.

dunque ♦ *cong* (*perciò*) so; (*allora*) well, now (then) ♦ *sm*: **venire al ~** to get to the point.

duomo *sm* cathedral.

duplex *sm inv* party line.

duplicato *sm* duplicate.

duplice *agg* double; **in ~ copia** in duplicate.

durante *prep* during.

durare ♦ *vi* to last ♦ *vt*: ~ **fatica (a fare qc)** to tire o.s. out (doing sthg).

durata *sf* (*periodo*) duration.

durezza *sf* (*di materiale*) hardness; (*insensibilità*) severity.

duro, -a ♦ *agg* hard; (*carne*) tough; (*ostinato*) stubborn; (*severo*) harsh ♦ *sm, f* tough person; **tieni ~!** don't give in!

durone *sm* callus.

E

e (*spesso* **ed** + *vocale*) *cong* and; ~ **io?** what about me?; ~ **vacci!** well then, go!

E (*abbr di est*) E.

è → **essere**.

ebano *sm* ebony.

ebbene *cong* (*allora*) well.

ebbrezza *sf* (*ubriachezza*): **in stato di ~** drunk.

ebete *agg* idiotic.

ebollizione *sf* boiling.

ebraico, -a, -ci, -che *agg & sm* Hebrew.

ebreo, -a ♦ *agg* Jewish ♦ *sm, f* Jew.

Ebridi *sfpl*: **le (isole) ~** the Hebrides.

ecc. (*abbr di eccetera*) etc.

eccedenza *sf* excess.

eccedere *vt* to exceed.

▶ **eccedere in** *v + prep*: **~ nel bere/mangiare** to drink/eat too much.

eccellente *agg* excellent.

eccellenza *sf* excellence; (*titolo*) Excellency.

eccellere *vi*: **~ (in qc)** to excel (at sthg).

eccelso *pp* → **eccellere**.

eccentrico, -a, -ci, -che *agg* eccentric.

eccessivo, -a *agg* excessive.

eccesso *sm* excess; **~ di velocità** speeding; **all'~** excessively; **bagaglio in ~** excess baggage.

eccetera *avv* etcetera.

eccetto ♦ *prep* except ♦ *cong*: **~ che** unless.

eccettuare *vt* to except.

eccezionale *agg* exceptional.

eccezione *sf* exception; **a ~ di** with the exception of; **d'~** exceptional; **senza ~** without exception.

eccidio *sm* massacre.

eccitante *agg* (*stimolante*) stimulating; (*provocante*) exciting.

eccitare *vt* (*curiosità*) to arouse.

▶ **eccitarsi** *vr* to get excited; (*sessualmente*) to become aroused.

eccitazione *sf* excitement.

ecclesiastico, -a, -ci, -che ♦ *agg* ecclesiastical ♦ *sm* ecclesiastic.

ecco *avv* here is/are; **~ a lei** here you are; **~ fatto!** there, that's that!; **eccolo!** there he is!; **eccone uno!** there's one!

eccome *avv* you bet!

eclissi *sf inv* eclipse.

eco (*pl m* echi) *sf* echo.

ecologia *sf* ecology.

ecologico, -a, -ci, -che *agg* ecological.

economia *sf* economy; (*scienza*) economics (*sg*); **fare ~** to economize.

economico, -a, -ci, -che *agg* (*dell'economia*) economic; (*poco costoso*) economical.

ecosistema, -i *sm* ecosystem.

ECU *sm inv* ECU.

eczema *sm* eczema.

ed → **e**.

edera *sf* ivy.

edicola *sf* newsstand.

edificare *vt* to build.

edificio *sm* building.

edile *agg* building (*dav s*).

Edimburgo *sf* Edinburgh.

editore, -trice ♦ *agg* publishing (*dav s*) ♦ *sm* publisher.

editoria *sf* publishing (industry).

edizione *sf* edition; **~ speciale** special edition.

educare *vt* (*formare*) to educate; (*bambino*) to bring up.

educato, -a *agg* polite.

educazione *sf* (*maniere*) (good) manners (*pl*); (*formazione*) training; **~ fisica** physical education.

effervescente *agg* effervescent.

effettivamente *avv* in fact.

effettivo, -a *agg* actual, real.

effetto *sm* effect; **in effetti** in fact, actually.

effettuare *vt* to carry out.

efficace *agg* effective.

efficacia *sf* effectiveness.

efficiente *agg* efficient.

efficienza *sf* efficiency.

effimero, -a *agg* (*gioia, successo*) short-lived.

egemonia *sf* (*supremazia*) hegemony.

Egitto *sm*: l'~ Egypt.

egli *pron* he; ~ **stesso** he himself.

egocentrico, -a, -ci, -che *agg* egocentric.

egoismo *sm* selfishness.

egoista, -i, -e *agg* selfish.

egregio, -a, -gi, -gie *agg* (*nelle lettere*): Egregio Signore Dear Sir.

eguagliare = **uguagliare**.

ehi *esclam* hey!

E.I. *abbr* = **Esercito Italiano**.

elaborare *vt* (*progetto, piano*) to work out; (*con computer*) to process.

elaborato, -a *agg* elaborate.

elaboratore *sm*: ~ (**elettronico**) computer.

elaborazione *sf*: ~ **dei dati** data processing.

elasticità *sf* elasticity; (*di mente*) flexibility.

elasticizzato, -a *agg* stretch (*dav* s).

elastico, -a, -ci, -che ♦ *agg* elastic; (*mente*) flexible ♦ *sm* (*gommino*) rubber band; (*da cucito*) elastic.

Elba *sf*: l'(isola d')~ Elba.

elefante *sm* elephant.

elegante *agg* elegant, smart.

eleganza *sf* elegance.

eleggere *vt* to elect.

elementare *agg* elementary.

▶ **elementari** *sfpl*: le (scuole) elementari primary school (*sg*) (Br), grade school (*sg*) (Am).

elemento *sm* (*fattore*) element; (*di cucina*) unit; (*persona*) individual.

elemosina *sf* alms (*pl*); chiedere l'~ to beg.

elencare *vt* to list.

elenco, -chi *sm* list; ~ **telefonico** telephone directory.

eletto, -a *pp* → **eleggere**.

elettorale *agg* electoral.

elettore, -trice *sm, f* voter.

elettrauto *sm inv* (*officina*) workshop for electrical repairs on cars; (*persona*) car electrician.

elettricista, -i *sm* electrician.

elettricità *sf* electricity.

elettrico, -a, -ci, -che *agg* electric.

elettrodomestico, -ci *sm* electrical household appliance.

elettronico, -a, -ci, -che *agg* electronic.

elezione *sf* election.

elica, -che *sf* propeller.

elicottero *sm* helicopter.

eliminare *vt* to eliminate.

eliminatoria *sf* qualifying round.

ella *pron* she.

elmetto *sm* helmet.

elogio *sm* praise.

eloquente *agg* eloquent.

eludere *vt* to evade.

elusivo, -a *agg* elusive.

elvetico, -a, -ci, -che *agg* Swiss.

emaciato, -a *agg* emaciated.

emanare *vt* (*luce*) to send out; (*calore*) to give off; (*legge*) to issue.

emancipato, -a *agg* emancipated.

emarginato, -a *sm, f* social outcast.

ematoma, -i *sm* haematoma.

embrione *sm* embryo.

emergenza *sf* emergency.

emergere *vi* to emerge.

emerso, -a *pp* → **emergere**.

emicrania *sf* migraine.

emigrante *smf* emigrant.

emigrare *vi* (*persona*) to emigrate; (*animale*) to migrate.

emigrazione *sf* emigration.

Emilia Romagna *sf*: l'~ Emilia Romagna (*region in eastern central Italy*).

emisfero *sm* hemisphere.

emittente *sf* broadcasting station.

emorragia *sf* hemorrhage.

emozionante *agg* thrilling.

emozione *sf* emotion.

emulsione *sf* emulsion.

enciclopedia *sf* encyclopedia.

ENEL *abbr* Italian national electricity company.

energia *sf* energy; **~ elettrica** electrical energy.

energico, -a, -ci, -che *agg* energetic.

enfasi *sf inv* emphasis.

enigma, -i *sm* enigma.

ennesimo, -a *agg* umpteenth.

enorme *agg* enormous.

enoteca, -che *sf* (*negozio*) vintage wine store; (*bar*) wine bar.

ente *sm* body, organization.

entrambi, -e ♦ *pron pl* both (of them) ♦ *agg pl*: **entrambe le città** both towns.

entrare *vi* to enter, to go in; **~ in qc** (*trovar posto*) to fit into sthg; (*essere ammesso*) to join sthg; **entra!** come in!; **questo non c'entra niente** that has nothing to do with it; **~ in una stanza** to enter a room; **~ in guerra** to go to war; **far ~ qn** to let sb in.

entrata *sf* entrance; **'~ libera'** (*in museo*) 'admission free'; (*in negozio*) 'browsers welcome'.

▶ **entrate** *sfpl* (*incasso*) takings; (*guadagno*) income (*sg*).

entro *prep* (*periodo*) in, within; (*scadenza*) by.

entusiasmare *vt* to enthral.

▶ **entusiasmarsi** *vr*: **entusiasmarsi (per)** to get excited (about).

entusiasmo *sm* enthusiasm.

entusiasta, -i, -e *agg* enthusiastic.

enunciare *vt* to enunciate.

Eolie *sfpl*: **le (isole) ~** the Aeolian Islands.

epatite *sf* hepatitis.

epidemia *sf* epidemic.

epidermide *sf* epidermis.

Epifania *sf*: **l'~** the Epiphany, Twelfth Night.

epilessia *sf* epilepsy.

episodio *sm* episode.

epoca, -che *sf* (*era, età*) age; (*tempo*) time; **d'~** (*mobile, costume*) period (*dav s*).

eppure *cong* and yet, nevertheless.

equatore *sm* equator.

equazione *sf* equation.

equestre *agg* equestrian.

equilibrare *vt* to balance.

equilibrato, -a *agg* (*proporzionato*) balanced; (*persona*) well-balanced.

equilibrio *sm* (*stabilità*) balance; (*posizione, stato*) equilibrium; **perdere l'~** to lose one's balance.

equino, -a *agg* equine, horse (*dav s*).

equipaggiamento *sm* (*di nave, aereo*) fitting out; (*sportivo*) equipment.

equipaggio *sm* crew.

equitazione *sf* horse riding.

equivalente *agg & sm* equivalent.

equivalere : **equivalere a** *v + prep* to be equivalent to.

equivalso, -a *pp* → **equivalere**.

equivoco, -a, -ci, -che ♦ *agg* (*ambiguo*) equivocal; (*poco onesto*) dubious ♦ *sm* misunderstanding.

era *sf* age.

erba *sf* (*prato*) grass; (*pianta*) herb; **erbe aromatiche** herbs.

erbazzone *sm* spinach and Parmesan cheese tart topped with bacon and parsley (*a speciality of Emilia Romagna*).

erboristeria *sf* health food and beauty store.

erede *smf* heir (*f* heiress).

eredità *sf inv* inheritance; (*biologica*) heredity; **lasciare qc in ~ (a qn)** to bequeath sthg (to sb).

ereditare *vt* to inherit.

ereditario, -a *agg* hereditary.

eresia *sf* heresy.

eretico, -a, -ci, -che *sm, f* heretic.

eretto, -a ♦ *pp* → **erigere** ♦ *agg* erect.

ergastolo *sm* life imprisonment.

erigere *vt* to erect.

ernia *sf* hernia.

ero → **essere**.

eroe, eroina *sm, f* hero (*f* heroine).

erogare *vt* to supply.

eroico, -a, -ci, -che *agg* heroic.

eroina *sf* (*droga*) heroin, → **eroe**.

erosione *sf* erosion.

erotico, -a, -ci, -che *agg* erotic.

errare *vi* (*vagare*) to wander; (*sbagliare*) to be mistaken.

errore *sm* (*di ortografia, calcolo*) mistake; (*colpa*) error; **per ~** by mistake.

erta *sf*: **stare all'~** to be on the alert.

eruzione *sf* (*di vulcano*) eruption; (MED) rash.

esagerare *vt* & *vi* to exaggerate.

esagerato, -a *agg* excessive.

esalazione *sf* exhalation.

esaltare *vt* (*lodare*) to extol; (*entusiasmare*) to excite.

esame *sm* examination; **fare** o **dare un ~** to take an exam; **~ del sangue** blood test.

esaminare *vt* (*analizzare*) to examine; (*candidato*) to interview.

esattamente *avv* & *esclam* exactly.

esattezza *sf* accuracy.

esatto, -a ♦ *agg* (*giusto*) correct; (*preciso*) exact ♦ *esclam* exactly!

esattore *sm* collector.

esauriente *agg* exhaustive.

esaurimento *sm* exhaustion; **~ (nervoso)** nervous breakdown.

esaurire *vt* to exhaust.

▶ **esaurirsi** *vr* (*merce*) to run out; (*persona*) to wear o.s. out.

esaurito, -a *agg* (*provviste, pozzo*) exhausted; (*merce*) sold out; (*libro*) out of print; (*persona*) worn out; '**tutto ~**' 'sold out'.

esausto, -a *agg* worn out.

esca (*pl* **esche**) *sf* bait.

escandescenza *sf*: **dare in escan**descenze to lose one's temper.

eschimese *smf* Eskimo.

esclamare *vi* to exclaim.

esclamazione *sf* exclamation.

escludere *vt* to exclude.

esclusiva *sf* (*di notizia*) scoop; (DIR) exclusive rights (*pl*).

esclusivo, -a *agg* exclusive.

escluso, -a *pp* → **escludere**.

esco → **uscire**.

escogitare *vt* to come up with.

escursione *sf* excursion; **~ termica** temperature range.

escursionista, -i, -e *smf* walker; tripper.

esecutivo, -a *agg* & *sm* executive.

esecuzione *sf* execution; (*di concerto*) performance.

eseguire *vt* to carry out; (*in musica*) to perform.

esempio *sm* example; **ad** o **per ~** for example; **fare un ~** to give an example.

esemplare *sm* specimen; (*di libro*) copy.

esentare *vt*: **~ qn/qc da qc** to exempt sb/sthg from sthg.

esente *agg*: **~ da** (*esonerato da*) exempt from; (*libero da*) free from.

esequie *sfpl* funeral rites.

esercitare *vt* to exercise; (*professione*) to practise.

▶ **esercitarsi** *vr* to practise.

esercito *sm* army.

esercizio *sm* exercise; (*di professione*) practice; (*azienda, negozio*) business; **essere fuori ~** to be out of practice.

esibire *vt* to show.

▶ **esibirsi** *vr* to perform.

esigente *agg* demanding.

esigenza *sf* (*bisogno*) requirement; (*pretesa*) demand.

esigere *vt* (*pretendere*) to demand; (*richiedere*) to require; (*riscuotere*) to collect.

esile *agg* (*sottile*) thin; (*persona*) slim.

esilio *sm* exile.

esistente *agg* existing.

esistenza *sf* existence.

esistere *vi* to exist.

esitare *vi* to hesitate.

esitazione *sf* hesitation.

esito *sm* outcome.

esorbitante *agg* exorbitant.

esordio *sm* debut.

esortare *vt*: ~ qn a fare qc to urge sb to do sthg.

esotico, -a, -ci, -che *agg* exotic.

espandere *vt* to expand.

▶ **espandersi** *vr* (*ingrandirsi*) to expand; (*odori, liquidi*) to spread.

espansione *sf* (*allargamento*) expansion; (*di attività*) growth.

espansivo, -a *agg* expansive.

espanso, -a *pp* → **espandere**.

espediente *sm* expedient.

espellere *vt* (*da scuola*) to expel; (MED) to excrete.

esperienza *sf* experience.

esperimento *sm* (*prova*) test; (*scientifico*) experiment.

esperto, -a ♦ *agg* (*con esperienza*) experienced; (*bravo*) skilful ♦ *sm* expert.

espiare *vt* to expiate.

esplicito, -a *agg* explicit.

esplodere ♦ *vi* to explode ♦ *vt* to fire.

esplorare *vt* to explore.

esploratore, -trice *sm, f* explorer.

esplosione *sf* explosion; (*di gioia, ira*) outburst.

esplosivo, -a *agg & sm* explosive.

esploso, -a *pp* → **esplodere**.

esporre *vt* (*merce*) to display; (*opera d'arte*) to show; (*pellicola*) to expose; (*idea, fatto*) to explain.

esportare *vt* to export.

esportazione *sf* (*spedizione*) exportation; (*merce*) exports (*pl*).

esposizione *sf* (*di merce*) display; (*mostra*) exhibition; (*di pellicola*) exposure; (*resoconto*) account.

esposto, -a ♦ *pp* → **esporre** ♦ *sm* petition ♦ *agg*: ~ a sud facing south.

espressione *sf* expression.

espressivo, -a *agg* expressive.

espresso, -a ♦ *pp* → **esprimere** ♦ *sm* (*treno*) express; (*caffè*) espresso; (*lettera*) express letter.

esprimere *vt* (*pensiero, sentimento*) to express.

▶ **esprimersi** *vr* (*spiegarsi*) to express o.s.; (*parlare*) to speak.

espulso, -a *pp* → **espellere**.

essenziale *agg* essential.

essere *vi* **1.** (*per descrivere*) to be; **sono italiano** I'm Italian; **sei solo?** are you alone?; **siamo di Torino** we're from Turin; **Franco è (un) medico** Franco is a doctor.

2. (*trovarsi*) to be; **dove siete?** where are you?; **il museo è in centro** the museum is in the town centre; **sono a casa** I'm at home; **sono stato in Scozia tre volte** I've been to Scotland three times.

3. (*esistere*): **c'è** there is; **c'è un'altra possibilità** there's another possibility; **ci sono** there are; **ci sono vari alberghi** there are various hotels.

4. (*con data, ora*) to be; **oggi è martedì** today is Tuesday; **è l'una** it's one o'clock; **sono le due** it's two o'clock.

5. (*con prezzo, peso*): **quant'è? – (sono) 10 000 lire** how much is it? – (that's) 10,000 lira; **sono due chili e mezzo** that's two and a half kilos.

6. (*indica appartenenza*): ~ **di qn** to belong to sb; **questa macchina è di Paolo** this car is Paolo's.

7. (*indica bisogno, obbligo*): **è da fare** it's still to be done; **la camera è da prenotare** the room is to be booked.

♦ *v impers* to be; **è tardi** it's late; **è vero che ...** it's true that ...; **oggi è freddo** it's cold today; **è meglio telefonare** it's better to phone.

♦ *v aus* **1.** (*in tempi passati*) to have, to be; **sono tornato ieri** I came back yesterday; **erano già usciti** they'd already gone out; **sono nata a Roma** I was born in Rome; **ti sei lavato?** did you wash yourself?

2. (*in passivi*) to be; **questo oggetto è fatto a mano** this object is hand-made; **sono stato pagato ieri** I was paid yesterday.

♦ *sm* (*creatura*) being; **~ umano** human being; **gli esseri viventi** the living.

essi, -e → esso.

esso, -a *pron* it.

▶ **essi, -e** *pron pl* (*soggetto*) they; (*con preposizione*) them.

est *sm* east; **a ~ di Milano** east of Milan.

estate *sf* summer.

estendere *vt* to extend.

esteriore *agg* (*esterno*) external, outward; (*apparente*) superficial.

esterno, -a ♦ *agg* exterior; (*muro*) outer; (*pericolo*) external ♦ *sm* outside; **all'~** on the outside.

estero, -a ♦ *agg* foreign ♦ *sm*: **l'~** foreign countries (*pl*); **all'~** abroad.

esteso, -a ♦ *pp* → **estendere** ♦ *agg* extensive.

estetista, -i, -e *smf* beautician.

estinguere *vt* (*fuoco*) to extinguish; (*debito*) to settle.

▶ **estinguersi** *vr* (*fuoco*) to go out; (*specie*) to become extinct.

estinto, -a *pp* → **estinguere.**

estintore *sm* (fire) extinguisher.

estivo, -a *agg* summer (*dav s*).

estorcere *vt* to extort.

estraneo, -a ♦ *agg* unconnected ♦ *sm, f* stranger.

estrarre *vt* to extract; (*sorteggiare*) to draw.

estratto, -a ♦ *pp* → **estrarre** ♦ *sm* (*di sostanza*) essence; (*di libro*) extract; **~ conto** bank statement.

estrazione *sf* extraction; **~ a sorte** draw; **~ sociale** social class.

estremità ♦ *sf inv* end ♦ *sfpl* extremities.

estremo, -a ♦ *agg* (*grande*) extreme; (*drastico*) drastic; (*ultimo*) final, last ♦ *sm* (*punto*) extreme; (*fig*: *limite*) limit.

▶ **estremi** *smpl* details.

estroverso, -a *agg* extrovert.

estuario *sm* estuary.

esuberante *agg* exuberant.

età *sf inv* age; **abbiamo la stessa ~** we are the same age; **la maggiore ~** the legal age; **di mezza ~** middle-aged; **la terza ~** old age.

etere *sm* ether.

eternità *sf* eternity.

eterno, -a *agg* eternal.

eterogeneo, -a *agg* heterogeneous.

eterosessuale *agg & smf* heterosexual.

etica *sf* ethics.

etichetta *sf* (*di prodotto*) label; (*cerimoniale*) etiquette.

Etna *sm*: **l'~** Mount Etna.

etrusco, -a, -schi, -sche *agg* Etruscan.

▶ **Etruschi** *smpl*: **gli Etruschi** the Etruscans.

ettaro *sm* hectare.

etto *sm* = 100 grams.

ettogrammo *sm* hectogram.

eucaristia *sf*: **l'~** the Eucharist.

eufemismo *sm* euphemism.

euforia *sf* euphoria.

EUR *sm residential area of Rome built on the site of the Rome Exhibition.*

Europa *sf*: **l'~** Europe.

europeo, -a *agg & sm, f* European.

eurovisione *sf*: **in ~** Eurovision (*dav s*).

eutanasia *sf* euthanasia.

evacuare *vt* to evacuate.

evacuazione *sf* evacuation.

evadere ♦ *vt* (*tasse, fisco*) to evade; (*corrispondenza*) to deal with ♦ *vi*: **~ (da qc)** to escape (from sthg).

evaporare *vi* to evaporate.

evasione *sf* escape; **~ fiscale** tax evasion; **d'~** escapist.

evasivo, -a *agg* evasive.

evaso, -a ♦ *pp* → **evadere** ♦ *sm, f* escapee.

evenienza *sf*: **in ogni ~** should

the need arise.

evento sm event.

eventuale agg possible.

eventualità sf inv possibility.

eventualmente avv if necessary.

evidente agg (chiaro) clear; (ovvio) obvious.

evidenza sf evidence; **mettere in ~** to highlight.

evitare vt to avoid; **~ di fare qc** to avoid doing sthg; **~ qc a qn** to spare sb sthg.

evocare vt (ricordare) to recall; (spiriti) to evoke.

evoluto, -a agg (tecnica, paese) advanced; (persona) broadminded.

evoluzione sf (biologica) evolution; (progresso) progress.

evviva esclam hurrah!

ex prep: **l'~ presidente** the former president; **la sua ~ moglie** his ex-wife.

extra agg inv & sm inv extra.

extracomunitario, -a ♦ agg from outside the EU ♦ sm, f immigrant from a non-EU country.

extraconiugale agg extramarital.

extraterrestre smf alien.

F

fa¹ → **fare**.

fa² avv: **un anno ~** a year ago; **tempo ~** some time ago.

fabbisogno sm needs (pl).

fabbrica, -che sf factory.

fabbricare vt (costruire) to build; (produrre) to make.

faccenda sf (questione) affair, matter.

▶ **faccende** sfpl: **faccende (domestiche)** housework (sg).

facchino sm porter.

faccia, -ce sf face; **di ~ a** oppo-

site; **~ a ~** face to face; **che ~ tosta!** what a nerve!

facciata sf (di edificio) facade; (di pagina) side.

faccio → **fare**.

facile agg easy; **è ~ che il treno sia in ritardo** the train's quite likely to be late.

facilità sf (caratteristica) easiness; (attitudine) ease.

facilitare vt to make easier.

facoltà sf inv faculty; (potere) power.

facoltativo, -a agg optional.

facsimile sm inv facsimile.

faggio, -gi sm beech.

fagiano sm pheasant.

fagiolino sm French bean (Br), string bean (Am).

fagiolo sm bean; **fagioli all'uccelletto** white beans cooked with tomatoes and pepper (a Tuscan speciality).

fagotto sm bundle; (strumento) bassoon; **far ~** to pack one's bags and leave.

fai da te sm inv do-it-yourself.

falange sf finger bone.

falciare vt to mow.

falda sf (di cappello) brim; (d'acqua) water table; (di monte) slope.

falegname sm carpenter.

falla sf leak.

fallimento sm failure; (DIR) bankruptcy.

fallire ♦ vi (DIR) to go bankrupt; (non riuscire) **~ (in qc)** to fail (in sthg) ♦ vt to miss.

fallo sm foul.

falò sm inv bonfire.

falsificare vt to forge.

falso, -a ♦ agg false; (gioiello) fake; (banconota, quadro) forged ♦ sm forgery.

fama sf fame; (reputazione) reputation.

fame sf hunger; **aver ~** to be hungry.

famigerato, -a agg notorious.

famiglia sf family.

familiare agg (della famiglia) family (dav s); (noto) familiar; (atmosfera) friendly; (informale) informal.

▶ **familiari** smpl relations.

famoso, -a agg famous.

fanale sm light.

fanatico, -a, -ci, -che agg fanatical.

fango, -ghi sm mud.

fanno → fare.

fannullone, -a sm, f loafer.

fantacalcio sm fantasy football.

fantascienza sf science fiction.

fantasia ♦ sf (immaginazione) imagination ♦ agg inv patterned.

fantasma, -i sm ghost.

fantastico, -a, -ci, -che agg fantastic; (immaginario) fantasy (dav s).

fantino sm jockey.

fantoccio sm puppet.

farabutto sm crook.

faraglione sm stack.

faraona sf guinea fowl.

farcito, -a agg (pollo) stuffed; (torta) filled.

fard sm inv blusher.

fare vt 1. (fabbricare, preparare) to make; ~ progetti to make plans; ~ da mangiare to cook.

2. (attuare) to make; ~ un viaggio to go on a trip; ~ un sogno to dream.

3. (essere occupato in) to do; **cosa fai stasera?** what are you doing tonight?; **fa il meccanico** he's a mechanic; ~ l'università to go to university; **faccio tennis** I play tennis.

4. (percorrere) to do; **che percorso facciamo per rientrare?** which route shall we take to go back?

5. (suscitare) to make; **mi fa pena** I feel sorry for him; **farsi male** to hurt o.s.; ~ **paura** to be frightening; ~ **chiasso** to be noisy.

6. (atteggiarsi a) to play, to act; ~ lo **scemo** to behave like an idiot.

7. (indica il risultato): **2 più 2 fa 4** 2 and 2 makes 4; **quanto fa?** what's the total?

8. (credere): **ti facevo più furbo** I

thought you were smarter than that.

9. (acquisire): **farsi degli amici** to make friends; **farsi la macchina nuova** (fam) to get a new car.

10. (con infinito) to make; **far credere qc a qn** to make sb believe sthg; **far vedere qc a qn** to show sb sthg; **far costruire qc** to have sthg built; **far cuocere qc** to cook sthg.

11. (in espressioni): **non ~ caso a** not to pay attention to; **non fa niente** (non importa) it doesn't matter; **farcela** to manage; **non ce la faccio più** I can't go on; **far bene/male (a qn)** to be good/bad (for sb).

♦ vi 1. (agire) to do; **come si fa a uscire?** how do you get out?; **fai come ti pare** do as you like; **non fa che ripetere le stesse cose** all he does is repeat the same things; **darsi da ~** to get busy.

2. (fam: dire) to say.

♦ v impers to be; **fa bello/brutto** the weather's fine/bad; **fa caldo/freddo** it's hot/cold.

▶ **farsi** vr (diventare): **farsi grande** to grow up; **farsi furbo** to get smart; **farsi vivo** to get in touch; **farsi avanti/indietro** (spostarsi) to move forward/back.

farfalla sf butterfly; **cravatta a ~** bow tie.

farina sf flour; ~ **gialla** maize flour.

farinata sf type of bread similar to a very thin 'focaccia' but made from chickpea flour (a speciality of Liguria).

faringite sf pharyngitis.

farmacia sf (negozio) chemist's (Br), drugstore (Am); (scienza) pharmacy; **'farmacie di turno'** 'duty chemists'.

farmacista, -i, -e smf pharmacist.

farmaco, -ci sm medicine.

faro sm (per navi) lighthouse; (di veicoli) headlight; (per aerei) beacon.

farsa sf farce.

farsumagru sm inv beef roll stuffed with mince, pecorino cheese, sausage and boiled eggs, cooked in Marsala and tomato puree (a Sicilian speciality).

fascia, -sce sf (striscia) strip, band; (medica) bandage; (di territorio) strip; (di popolazione) band; **~ elastica** elastic bandage; **~ oraria** time band.

fasciare vt to bandage.

fasciatura sf bandage.

fascicolo sm (di rivista) issue; (di documenti) file.

fascino sm charm.

fascio sm (d'erba, di fibri) bunch; (di legna) bundle; (di luce) beam.

fascismo sm Fascism.

fascista, -i, -e agg & smf Fascist.

fase sf phase; (di motore) stroke.

fast food [fast'fud] sm inv fast-food restaurant.

fastidio sm bother, trouble; **dare ~ a qn** to annoy sb; **le dà ~ se fumo?** do you mind if I smoke?

fastidioso, -a agg inconvenient.

fastoso, -a agg sumptuous.

fasullo, -a agg (falso) fake.

fata sf fairy.

fatale agg (mortale) fatal; (inevitabile) inevitable; (sguardo) irresistible.

fatalità sf inv (inevitabilità) inevitability; (destino) fate; (disgrazia) misfortune.

fatica sf hard work; (stanchezza) fatigue; **fare ~ a fare qc** to have difficulty doing sthg; **a ~** hardly.

faticoso, -a agg (stancante) exhausting; (difficile) hard.

fatidico, -a, -ci, -che agg fateful.

fato sm fate.

fatto, -a ♦ pp → **fare** ♦ sm (cosa concreta) fact; (avvenimento) event ♦ agg: **~ a mano** hand-made; **~ in casa** home-made; **il ~ è che ...** the fact is that ...; **cogliere qn sul ~** to catch sb in the act; **in ~ di vini ...** when it comes to wine ...; **sono fatti miei** that's my business.

fattore sm (elemento, MAT) factor.

fattoria sf farm.

fattorino sm (per consegne) delivery man; (d'albergo) messenger.

fattura sf invoice; (magia) spell.

fauna sf fauna.

favola sf fairy tale; (cosa bella) dream.

favoloso, -a agg fabulous.

favore sm favour; **per ~** please.

favorevole agg favourable; (voto) in favour.

favorire vt (promuovere) to promote; (aiutare) to favour; **vuoi ~?** would you like some?

favorito, -a agg favourite.

fax sm inv fax.

fazzoletto sm (da naso) handkerchief; (per la testa) headscarf.

febbraio sm February, → **settembre**.

febbre sf fever; **avere la ~** to have a temperature.

feci sfpl excrement (sg).

fecondazione sf fertilization.

fede sf faith; (anello) wedding ring; **aver ~ in** to have faith in; **essere in buona/cattiva ~** to act in good/bad faith.

fedele ♦ agg faithful; (cliente) loyal; (preciso) accurate ♦ smf believer.

fedeltà sf (lealtà) faithfulness, loyalty; (precisione) accuracy.

federa sf pillowcase.

federazione sf federation.

fegato sm liver; (fig: coraggio) guts (pl); **~ alla veneziana** thinly sliced calves' liver and onions.

felice agg happy.

felicità sf happiness.

felicitarsi vr: **~ con qn per qc** to congratulate sb on sthg.

felino, -a agg & sm feline.

felpa sf (maglia) sweatshirt; (tessuto) plush.

feltro sm felt.

femmina sf (animale) female; (figlia, ragazza) girl.

femminile ♦ agg female; (rivista, modi) women's; (GRAMM) feminine ♦ sm feminine.

femminismo sm feminism.

fenomenale agg phenomenal.

fenomeno *sm* phenomenon.

feriale *agg* working (*dav s*).

ferie *sfpl* holidays (Br), vacation (*sg*) (Am); **andare in ~** to go on holiday (Br), to go on vacation (Am); **essere in ~** to be on holiday (Br), to be on vacation (Am).

ferire *vt* (*colpire*) to injure; (*addolorare*) to hurt.

▶ **ferirsi** *vr* to injure o.s.

ferita *sf* wound.

ferito, -a ♦ *agg* injured ♦ *sm, f* injured person.

fermaglio *sm* clip.

fermare ♦ *vt* to stop; (*bottone*) to fasten; (*sospetto*) to detain ♦ *vi* to stop.

▶ **fermarsi** *vr* to stop; (*sostare*) to stay; **fermarsi a fare qc** to stop to do sthg.

fermata *sf* stop; **~ dell'autobus** bus stop; '**~ prenotata**' 'bus stopping'; '**~ a richiesta**' 'request stop'.

fermento *sm* ferment.

fermo, -a *agg* (*persona*) still; (*veicolo*) stationary; (*mano, voce*) steady; (*orologio*) stopped; (*saldo*) firm; **stare ~** to keep still.

fermo posta *avv & sm inv* poste restante (Br), general delivery (Am).

feroce *agg* (*animale*) ferocious; (*dolore*) terrible.

ferragosto *sm* (*giorno*) *Italian public holiday which falls on 15 August*; (*periodo*) *August holidays* (*pl*).

FERRAGOSTO

August 15, the feast of the Assumption, is a national holiday in Italy and marks the peak of the holiday season. The Italian name, 'Ferragosto', comes from the Latin 'feriae augustae', meaning 'August holidays'. Cities become ghost towns, as families and groups of friends flock to the coast, the mountains and the lakes, and most factories and businesses close down.

ferramenta *sf* ironmonger's (Br), hardware store (Am).

ferro *sm* iron; **toccare ~** to touch wood; **~ battuto** wrought iron; **~ da calza** knitting needle; **~ da stiro** iron; **carne ai ferri** grilled meat.

ferrovia *sf* railway (Br), railroad (Am); **Ferrovie dello Stato** *Italian railway system*, ≃ British Rail (Br), ≃ Amtrak (Am).

ferroviario, -a *agg* railway (Br) (*dav s*), railroad (Am) (*dav s*).

fertile *agg* fertile.

fervido, -a *agg* fervent, ardent.

fesso, -a *agg* (*fam*) stupid.

fessura *sf* crack; (*per gettone, moneta*) slot.

festa *sf* (*religiosa*) feast; (*giorno festivo*) holiday; (*ricevimento*) party; (*ricorrenza*): **la ~ della mamma** Mother's Day; **far ~ a qn** to have a holiday; **far ~ a qn** to give sb a warm welcome; **buone feste!** (*a Natale*) Merry Christmas!

FESTA DELLE DONNE

Since the 1970s, March 8 has been celebrated as National Women's Day in Italy. Meetings, debates and conferences on women's issues are held, and there is now a tradition of presenting women with the gift of a bunch of mimosa.

festeggiare *vt* (*ricorrenza*) to celebrate; (*persona*) to throw a party for.

festival *sm inv* festival.

FESTIVAL DI SPOLETO

Also known as the 'Festival dei Due Mondi' (Festival of the Two Worlds), the Festival of Spoleto has been held every June and July since 1958. It hosts top-class performances of opera, theatre, music and ballet, attracting internationally renowned artists and a cosmopolitan audience.

festivo, -a *agg* festive; **giorno ~** holiday; **orario ~** *timetable for*

Sundays and public holidays.

festone sm festoon.

festoso, -a agg merry.

feto sm foetus.

fetta sf slice.

fettuccine sfpl ribbons of egg pasta.

fettunta sf toast flavoured with garlic and olive oil (a Tuscan speciality).

FF.SS. abbr = BR (Br), ≈ Amtrak (Am).

fiaba sf fairy tale.

fiaccola sf torch.

fiamma sf flame; **dare alle fiamme** to set on fire.

fiammifero sm match.

fiancheggiare vt to border.

fianco, -chi sm (di persona) hip; (di edificio, collina) side; **di ~ a** next to.

fiasco, -schi sm flask; **fare ~** to flop.

fiato sm (respiro) breath; (resistenza) stamina; **avere il ~ grosso** to be out of breath.

fibbia sf buckle.

fibra sf fibre.

ficcanaso (pl m **ficcanasi**, pl f inv) smf busybody.

ficcare vt to put.

▶ **ficcarsi** vr: **dove ti eri ficcato?** where did you get to?

fico, -chi sm fig; **~ d'India** prickly pear.

fidanzamento sm engagement.

fidanzarsi vr to get engaged.

fidanzato, -a ♦ agg engaged ♦ sm, f fiancé (f fiancée).

fidarsi vr: **~ di** to trust.

fidato, -a agg trustworthy.

fiducia sf confidence.

fiducioso, -a agg confident.

fieno sm hay.

fiera sf fair.

fiero, -a agg proud.

fifa sf (fam) fright.

figlio, -a sm, f son (f daughter), child; **~ di papà** (fig) spoilt brat; **~ unico** only child.

figura sf figure; (illustrazione) illustration, picture; **fare bella/brutta ~**

to create a good/bad impression.

figurare ♦ vi to appear ♦ vt: **figurarsi qc** to imagine sthg.

▶ **figurarsi** vr: **figurati!** of course not!

figurina sf picture card.

fila sf (coda) queue (Br), line (Am); (di macchine) line; (di posti) row; (serie) series; **fare la ~** to queue (Br), to stand in line (Am); **di ~** in succession.

filare ♦ vt (lana) to spin ♦ vi (ragno, baco) to spin; (formaggio) to go stringy; (discorso) to be coherent; (fam: andarsene) to split; **fila!** off you go!; **~ diritto** to toe the line.

filastrocca, -che sf nursery rhyme.

filatelia sf philately, stamp-collecting.

filatelli smpl thin strips of egg pasta served with a sauce made from pork, tomatoes, chillis and pecorino cheese (a speciality of Calabria).

filatieddi = filatelli.

filetto sm fillet; **~ al pepe verde** fillet steak with green peppercorns.

film sm inv film (Br), movie (Am).

filo sm thread; (cavo) wire; (di lama, rasoio) edge; (di pane) stick; **~ d'erba** blade of grass; **~ spinato** barbed wire; **fil di ferro** wire; **per ~ e per segno** word for word.

filobus sm inv trolleybus.

filosofia sf philosophy.

filtrare vt & vi to filter.

filtro sm (apparecchio) filter; (di sigarette) filter tip.

fin → fino.

finale ♦ agg & sf final ♦ sm end, ending.

finalmente avv at (long) last.

finanza sf finance; (di frontiera) ≈ Customs and Excise.

▶ **finanze** sfpl finances.

finanziere sm (banchiere) financier; (di frontiera) customs officer; (per tasse) ≈ Inland Revenue officer (Br), ≈ Internal Revenue officer (Am).

finché *cong* (*per tutto il tempo*) as long as; (*fino a quando*) until.

fine ◆ *agg* (*sottile*) thin; (*polvere*) fine; (*elegante*) refined; (*vista, udito*) keen, sharp ◆ *sf* (*conclusione*) end ◆ *sm* (*scopo*) aim; **lieto ~** happy ending; **~ settimana** weekend; **alla ~** in the end.

finestra *sf* window.

finestrino *sm* window.

fingere *vt* (*simulare*) to feign; **~ di fare qc** to pretend to do sthg.

▶ **fingersi** *vr*: **fingersi malato** to pretend to be ill.

finimondo *sm* pandemonium.

finire ◆ *vt* to finish ◆ *vi* to finish; (*avere esito*) to end; (*cacciarsi*) to get to; **~ col fare qc** to end up doing sthg; **~ di fare qc** to finish doing sthg.

finlandese ◆ *agg & sm* Finnish ◆ *smf* Finn.

Finlandia *sf*: **la ~** Finland.

fino, -a ◆ *agg* (*sottile*) thin; (*oro, argento*) pure; (*udito, vista*) keen, sharp ◆ *avv* even ◆ *prep*: **~ a** (*di tempo*) until; (*di luogo*) as far as; **~ da** (*luogo*) as far as; **fin da domani** from tomorrow; **fin da ieri** since yesterday; **~ qui/lì** as far as here/there.

finocchio *sm* fennel.

finora *avv* so far.

finta *sf* (*finzione*) pretence; (*nel pugilato*) feint; (*nel calcio*) dummy; **fare ~ di fare qc** to pretend to do sthg.

finto, -a ◆ *pp* → **fingere** ◆ *agg* false.

fiocco, -chi *sm* (*di nastro*) bow; (*di neve*) flake; **coi fiocchi** (*ottimo*) excellent, first-rate.

fiocina *sf* harpoon.

fioco, -a, -chi, -che *agg* (*voce*) faint; (*luce*) dim.

fioraio, -a *sm, f* florist.

fiore *sm* flower; **a fior d'acqua** on the surface of the water; **a fiori** (*stoffa*) with a floral pattern; **fiori di zucca ripieni** fried courgette flowers stuffed with breadcrumbs, parsley and anchovies.

▶ **fiori** *smpl* (*nelle carte*) clubs.

fiorentino, -a *agg & sm, f* Florentine.

fiorire *vi* (*albero*) to blossom; (*fiore*) to bloom.

fiorito, -a *agg* (*giardino*) in bloom; (*stile*) flowery.

Firenze *sf* Florence.

firma *sf* (*sottoscrizione*) signature; (*marca*) designer brand.

firmare *vt* to sign.

fiscale *agg* tax (*dav s*).

fischiare ◆ *vi* to whistle ◆ *vt* to whistle; (*disapprovare*) to boo.

fischio *sm* whistle.

fisco *sm* ≃ Inland Revenue (Br), ≃ Internal Revenue (Am).

fisica *sf* (*materia*) physics (*sg*), → **fisico**.

fisico, -a, -ci, -che ◆ *agg* physical ◆ *sm* (*corpo*) physique ◆ *sm, f* physicist.

fisionomia *sf* face.

fissare *vt* (*guardare*) to stare at; (*rendere fisso*) to fix; (*appuntamento*) to arrange; (*camera, volo*) to book.

▶ **fissarsi** *vr*: **fissarsi di fare qc** to set one's heart on doing sthg.

fisso, -a ◆ *agg* (*fissato*) fixed; (*impiego*) permanent; (*reddito*) regular ◆ *avv*: **guardare ~** to stare.

fitta *sf* sharp pain.

fitto, -a ◆ *agg* thick ◆ *sm* (*affitto*) rent.

fiume *sm* river.

fiutare *vt* (*sog: cane*) to smell; (*fig: accorgersi di*) to get wind of.

flacone *sm* bottle.

flagrante *agg*: **cogliere qc in ~** to catch sb in the act.

flash [flɛʃ] *sm inv* flash.

flauto *sm*: **~ (traverso)** flute.

flessibile *agg* flexible.

flessione *sf* (*sulle gambe*) kneebend; (*a terra*) sit-up; (*calo*) dip.

flesso, -a *pp* → **flettere**.

flettere *vt* to bend.

flipper *sm inv* pinball machine.

F.lli *abbr* Bros.

flora *sf* flora.

flotta *sf* fleet.

fluido, -a *agg & sm* fluid.

fluire *vi* to flow.

flusso *sm* flow; (*in fisica*) flux.

fluttuare *vi* (*ondeggiare*) to rise and fall; (FIN) to fluctuate.

F.M. (*abbr di Modulazione di frequenza*) FM.

focaccia, -ce *sf* (*dolce*) bun; (*pane*) *type of flat salted bread made with olive oil*; **~ alla valdostana** '*focaccia*' *filled with fontina cheese.*

foce *sf* mouth.

focolare *sm* hearth.

fodera *sf* (*interna*) lining; (*esterna*) cover.

foglia *sf* leaf.

foglio *sm* (*di carta, di metallo*) sheet; (*documento*) document; (*banconota*) note; **~ rosa** provisional driving licence; **~ di via** expulsion order.

fogna *sf* sewer.

fognature *sfpl* sewers.

föhn [fɔn] = **fon.**

folclore *sm* folklore.

folcloristico, -a, -ci, -che *agg* folk (*dav s*).

folgorare *vt* (*sog: fulmine*) to strike; (*sog: alta tensione*) to electrocute.

folla *sf* crowd.

folle *agg* (*pazzo*) mad; (TECNOL) idle; **in ~** (*di auto*) in neutral.

follia *sf* (*pazzia*) madness; (*atto*) act of madness.

folto, -a *agg* thick.

fon *sm inv* hairdryer.

fondale *sm* bottom (of the sea).

fondamentale *agg* fundamental, basic.

fondamento *sm* foundation.

▶ **fondamenta** *sfpl* foundations.

fondare *vt* to found; (*basare*) **~ qc su qc** to base sthg on sthg.

▶ **fondarsi su** *vr + prep* to be based on.

fondazione *sf* foundation.

fondere ♦ *vt* to melt; (*aziende*) to merge ♦ *vi* to melt.

▶ **fondersi** *vr* to melt.

fondo, -a ♦ *agg* (*profondo*) deep ♦ *sm* bottom; (*di strada*) surface; (*di liquido*) dregs (*pl*); (*sfondo*) background; (SPORT) long distance race; (*proprietà*) property; **andare a ~** (*affondare*) to sink; **conoscere a ~** to know very well; **in ~** (*fig: tutto sommato*) after all; **andare fino in ~ a qc** (*approfondire*) to get to the bottom of sthg; **in ~ (a qc)** at the bottom (of sthg); (*stanza*) at the back (of sthg); (*libro, mese*) at the end (of sthg).

▶ **fondi** *smpl* (*denaro*) funds.

fonduta *sf* fondue.

fonetica *sf* phonetics (*sg*).

fontana *sf* fountain.

fonte ♦ *sf* (*sorgente*) spring; (*origine*) source ♦ *sm*: **~ battesimale** font.

fontina *sf a hard cheese made from cow's milk (a speciality of the Valle d'Aosta).*

foraggio *sm* fodder.

forare *vt* (*praticare un foro in*) to pierce; (*gomma*) to puncture; (*biglietto*) to punch; (*pallone*) to burst.

forbici *sfpl* scissors.

forca, -che *sf* (*attrezzo*) pitchfork; (*patibolo*) gallows (*pl*).

forchetta *sf* fork.

forcina *sf* hairpin.

foresta *sf* forest.

forestiero, -a ♦ *agg* foreign ♦ *sm, f* foreigner.

forfora *sf* dandruff.

forma *sf* shape; (*tipo*) form; (*stampo*) mould; **essere/tenersi in ~** to be/keep fit; **a ~ di** in the shape of.

▶ **forme** *sfpl* (*del corpo*) figure (*sg*).

formaggino *sm* processed cheese.

formaggio *sm* cheese.

FORMAGGIO

Cheese is a mainstay of the Italian diet, whether used as a filling for a roll, eaten as part of a main course, or served as a course in its own right. The cheese course in Italy comes after the main course and before fruit or dessert. Between 250 and 300 varieties of cheese may be found: soft ones, like 'mozzarella', 'ricotta', 'robiola', 'gorgonzola' and 'bel paese'; and hard ones, like 'caciocavallo', 'provolone', 'grana', 'parmigiano' and 'pecorino'. These last three are grated onto pasta dishes and sprinkled on top of soups.

---

formale agg formal.

formalità sf inv formality.

formare vt to form; (comporre) to make up; (persona) to train.

▶ **formarsi** vr to form.

formato sm size.

formazione sf formation; (istruzione) education; ~ **professionale** professional training.

formica®1 sf Formica®.

formica², **-che** sf ant.

formicolio sm (intorpidimento) pins and needles (pl).

formidabile agg fantastic, amazing.

formula sf formula; (frase rituale) set phrase; ~ **uno** formula one.

fornaio, **-a** sm, f baker.

fornello sm (di elettrodomestico) ring; ~ **elettrico** hotplate.

fornire vt: ~ **qc a qn** to provide o supply sb with sthg; ~ **qn/qc di qc** to provide sb/sthg with sthg, to supply sb/sthg with sthg.

fornitore, **-trice** sm, f supplier; ~ **d'accesso** (INFORM) service provider.

forno sm oven; ~ **a legna** wood-burning stove; ~ **a microonde** microwave (oven).

foro sm (buco) hole; (romano) forum.

forse avv perhaps, maybe; (circa) about.

forte ◆ agg strong; (suono) loud; (luce, colore) bright ◆ avv (vigorosamente) hard; (ad alta voce) loudly;

(velocemente) fast ◆ sm (fortezza) fort; (specialità) strong point.

fortezza sf fortress.

fortuito, **-a** agg chance (dav s), fortuitous.

fortuna sf luck; (patrimonio) fortune; **buona ~!** good luck!; **portare ~** to bring luck; **per ~** luckily, fortunately.

fortunatamente avv luckily, fortunately.

fortunato, **-a** agg (persona) lucky; (evento) successful.

forviare = **fuorviare**.

forza sf strength; (in fisica, violenza) force; **~!** come on!; **a ~ di** by dint of; **per ~** (naturalmente) of course; (contro la volontà) against one's will; **le forze armate** the armed forces.

forzare vt (porta, finestra) to force open; (obbligare): ~ **qn a fare qc** to force sb to do sthg.

foschia sf haze.

fossa sf (buca) pit, hole; (tomba) grave.

fossato sm ditch; (di castello) moat.

fossile sm fossil.

fosso sm ditch.

foto sf inv photo.

fotocopia sf photocopy.

fotocopiare vt to photocopy.

fotogenico, **-a**, **-ci**, **-che** agg photogenic.

fotografare vt to photograph.

fotografia sf (ARTE) photography; (immagine) photograph; ~ **a colori** colour photograph; ~ **in bianco e nero** black and white photograph.

fotografo, **-a** sm, f photographer.

fotoromanzo sm photoromance.

fototessera sf passport-size photograph.

foulard [fu'lar] sm inv scarf.

fra = **tra**.

fracassare vt to smash.

fracasso sm crash.

fradicio, **-a**, **-ci**, **-ce** agg soaked.

fragile agg fragile; (persona) delicate.

fragola sf strawberry.

fragore *sm* loud noise.

fragranza *sf* fragrance.

fraintendere *vt* to misunderstand.

frammento *sm* fragment.

frana *sf* landslide; (*fig: persona*): **essere una ~** to be useless.

francese ♦ *agg & sm* French ♦ *smf* (*abitante*) Frenchman (*f* Frenchwoman); **i francesi** the French.

Francia *sf*: **la ~** France.

franco, -a, -chi, -che ♦ *agg* (*sincero*) frank; (COMM) free ♦ *sm* franc; **farla franca** to get away with it.

francobollo *sm* stamp.

frangia, -ge *sf* fringe.

frantumare *vt* to smash. ▶ **frantumarsi** *vr* to smash.

frantumi *smpl*: **andare in ~** to smash; (*sogno*) to be shattered.

frappé *sm inv* (milk) shake.

Frascati *sm* Frascati (*white wine from the Frascati area near Rome*).

frase *sf* (GRAMM) sentence; (*espressione*) expression, phrase.

frastuono *sm* din.

frate *sm* (*monaco*) friar; (*pasta*) ring doughnut.

fratellastro *sm* stepbrother.

fratello *sm* brother.

frattempo *sm*: **nel ~** in the meantime, meanwhile.

frattura *sf* fracture.

frazione *sf* (*parte*) fraction; (*di comune*) village.

freccia, -ce *sf* arrow; **~ di direzione** indicator; **mettere la ~** to put the indicator on.

freddo, -a *agg & sm* cold; **aver ~** to be cold; **è o fa ~** it's cold.

freddoloso, -a *agg*: **essere ~** to feel the cold.

freezer ['fridzer] *sm inv* freezer.

fregare *vt* (*strofinare*) to rub; (*fam: imbrogliare*) to trick; **~ qc a qn** (*fam: rubare*) to nick sthg from sb; **fregarsene (di qc)** (*volg*) not to give a damn (about sthg).

frenare ♦ *vi* to brake ♦ *vt* (*rabbia,* *entusiasmo*) to curb; (*lacrime*) to hold back; (*avanzata, progresso*) to hold up.

frenata *sf* braking; **fare una ~** to brake.

frenetico, -a, -ci, -che *agg* hectic.

freno *sm* (*di veicolo*) brake; (*per cavallo*) bit; **~ a mano** handbrake.

frequentare *vt* (*corso*) to attend; (*locale*) to go to; (*persona*) to mix with.

frequente *agg* frequent.

fresco, -a, -schi, -sche ♦ *agg* fresh; (*temperatura*) cool; (*notizie*) recent ♦ *sm* (*temperatura*) cool; **è o fa ~** it's cool; **mettere al ~** to put in a cool place; **stare ~** to be way out.

fretta *sf* (*urgenza*) hurry; (*rapidità*) haste; **avere ~** to be in a hurry; **in ~ e furia** in a hurry.

fricassea *sf* stewed meat and vegetables in an egg and lemon sauce.

friggere ♦ *vt* to fry ♦ *vi* to sizzle.

frigo *sm inv* fridge.

frigobar *sm inv* minibar.

frigorifero *sm* refrigerator.

frittata *sf* omelette.

frittella *sf* fritter; **frittelle di mele** apple fritters.

fritto, -a ♦ *pp* → **friggere** ♦ *agg* fried ♦ *sm*: **~ misto** mixed deep-fried fish and seafood.

frittura *sf*: **~ di pesce** deep-fried fish and seafood.

frivolo, -a *agg* frivolous.

frizione *sf* (*di auto*) clutch; (*massaggio*) massage.

frizzante *agg* fizzy; (*vino*) sparkling.

frode *sf* fraud.

frontale *agg* frontal; (*scontro*) head-on.

fronte ♦ *sf* forehead ♦ *sm* front; **di ~** opposite; **di ~ a** (*faccia a faccia*) opposite; (*in una fila*) in front of; (*in confronto a*) compared with.

frontiera *sf* frontier.

frottola *sf* (*bugia*) lie.

frugare *vi & vt* to search.

frullare *vt* to whisk.

frullato *sm* milk shake.

frullatore *sm* blender, liquidizer.

frullino *sm* whisker.

frusta *sf* (*per animali*) whip.

frustino *sm* (riding) crop.

frutta *sf* fruit; **~ secca** dried fruit and nuts.

fruttivendolo *sm* (*negozio*) greengrocer's.

frutto *sm* fruit; (*profitto*) profit; **frutti di bosco** forest fruits; **frutti di mare** seafood (*sg*).

F.S. = **FF.SS.**

fucile *sm* rifle.

fuga, -ghe *sf* escape; **~ di gas** gas leak.

fuggire *vi* (*allontanarsi*) to escape; (*rifugiarsi*) to run away.

fulmine *sm* bolt of lightning.

fumare ♦ *vt* to smoke ♦ *vi* to smoke; (*emettere vapore*) to steam; 'vietato ~' 'no smoking'.

fumatore, -trice *sm, f* smoker; **fumatori o non fumatori?** smoking or non-smoking?

fumetti *smpl* (*vignette*) cartoon strip (*sg*); (*giornalino*) comics.

fumo *sm* smoke; (*vapore*) steam.

fune *sf* rope.

funebre *agg* funeral (*dav s*); (*lugubre*) funereal.

funerale *sm* funeral.

fungo, -ghi *sm* mushroom; (MED) fungus; **~ mangereccio** edible mushroom.

funicolare *sf* funicular railway.

funivia *sf* cable way.

funzionamento *sm* functioning.

funzionare *vi* to work.
▶ **funzionare da** *v + prep* to act as.

funzione *sf* function; (*compito*) duty; (*religiosa*) service; **essere in ~** to be working; **in ~ di** (*secondo*) according to.

fuoco, -chi *sm* fire; (*fornello*) ring; (*in ottica*) focus; **al ~!** fire!; **dar ~ a qc** to set fire to sthg; **fare ~** to fire; **prender ~** to catch fire; **fuochi d'artificio** fireworks.

fuorché *cong* except.

fuori ♦ *avv* out, outside; (*fuori di casa*) out; (*all'aperto*) outdoors, outside ♦ *prep*: **~ (di)** out of, outside; **far ~ qn** (*fam*) to kill sb; **essere ~ di sé** to be beside oneself; **lasciare ~** to leave out; **tirare ~** to get out; **~ luogo** uncalled for; **~ mano** out of the way; **andare ~ strada** to leave the road; '**~ servizio**' 'out of order'.

fuoribordo *sm inv* outboard.

fuorilegge *smf inv* outlaw.

fuoristrada ♦ *sm inv* Jeep® ♦ *agg inv*: **moto ~** trail bike.

fuorviare *vt* to mislead.

furbo, -a *agg* clever, smart; (*spreg*) cunning.

furgone *sm* van.

furia *sf* (*ira*) fury; (*impeto*) violence; **a ~ di fare qc** by (means of) doing sthg; **andare su tutte le furie** to get into a towering rage.

furioso, -a *agg* furious.

furore *sm* fury; **far ~** to be all the rage.

furto *sm* theft; **~ con scasso** burglary.

fusa *sfpl*: **fare le ~** to purr.

fusilli *smpl* pasta spirals.

fusione *sf* (*di cera, metallo*) melting; (*unione*) fusion.

fuso, -a ♦ *pp* → **fondere** ♦ *sm*: **~ orario** time zone.

fustino *sm* tub.

fusto *sm* (*di pianta*) stem; (*contenitore*) drum; (*fam: ragazzo*) hunk.

futile *agg* futile.

futuro, -a *agg & sm* future.

G

gabbia *sf* cage.

gabbiano *sm* seagull.

gabinetto *sm* (*bagno*) toilet; (*ministero*) cabinet; (*di dentista*) surgery.

gaffe [gaf] *sf inv* blunder.

gala sf (sfarzo) pomp; (festa) gala.

galassia sf galaxy.

galateo sm etiquette.

galera sf prison.

galla sf: stare a ~ to float; venire a ~ (fig) to come out.

galleggiante ♦ agg floating ♦ sm (boa) buoy; (per la pesca) float.

galleria sf (traforo) tunnel; (museo) gallery; (di teatro) circle; (di cinema) balcony; (strada coperta) arcade.

galletta sf cracker.

gallina sf hen.

gallo sm cock.

gamba sf leg; essere in ~ to be very able.

gamberetto sm shrimp.

gambero sm prawn.

gamberoni smpl: ~ alla griglia grilled crayfish.

gambo sm stem.

gancio sm hook.

gangheri smpl: essere fuori dai ~ to fly off the handle.

gara sf (nello sport) race; (concorso) competitive bidding; fare a ~ to compete.

garage [ga'raʒ] sm inv garage.

garantire vt to guarantee.

garanzia sf (di merce) guarantee; (di debito) guarantee, security.

gareggiare vi to compete.

gargarismo sm: fare i gargarismi to gargle.

garza sf gauze.

garzone sm boy.

gas sm inv gas; dare ~ to step on the gas; ~ lacrimogeno tear gas.

gasato, -a = gassato.

gasolio sm diesel (oil).

gassato, -a agg (bevanda) fizzy.

gassosa sf fizzy drink.

gastronomia sf gastronomy; (negozio) delicatessen.

gastronomico, -a, -ci, -che agg gastronomic.

gattino, -a sm, f kitten.

gatto, -a sm, f cat; ~ delle nevi snow cat; eravamo in quattro gatti there were only a few of us.

gazzetta sf gazette.

G.d.F. abbr = Guardia di Finanza.

gel sm inv gel.

gelare vi, vt & v impers to freeze.

gelateria sf ice-cream shop (Br), ice-cream parlour (Am).

gelatina sf gelatine; ~ di frutta fruit jelly.

gelato, -a ♦ agg frozen ♦ sm ice cream.

GELATO

Although ice cream is associated with the summer months, it is eaten in Italy all year round and at any time of day. 'Gelaterie', or ice-cream shops, specialize in the production and sale of a seemingly endless variety of flavours, ranging from traditional fruit, chocolate and coffee to the more exotic. 'Gelato artigianale' means that the ice cream has been made on the premises.

gelido, -a agg freezing, icy.

gelo sm (freddo) intense cold; (ghiaccio) ice.

gelosia sf jealousy.

geloso, -a agg jealous.

gemello, -a agg & sm, f twin.
▶ **gemelli** smpl (di camicia) cuff links.
▶ **Gemelli** smpl Gemini (sg).

gemere vi to moan.

gemma sf (pietra) gem; (di pianta) bud.

generale agg & sm general; in ~ in general.

generalità sfpl particulars.

generalmente avv generally.

generare vt (produrre) to generate, to produce.

generatore sm generator.

generazione sf generation.

genere *sm* (*tipo*) kind, type; (*di arte*) genre; (GRAMM) gender; (*di animali, vegetali*) genus; **il ~ umano** mankind; **in ~** generally.
▶ **generi** *smpl*: **generi alimentari** foodstuffs.

generico, -a, -ci, -che *agg* (*generale*) generic; (*vago*) vague; **medico ~** general practitioner.

genero *sm* son-in-law.

generoso, -a *agg* generous.

gengiva *sf* gum.

geniale *agg* brilliant.

genio *sm* genius; **andare a ~ a qn** to be liked by sb.

genitali *smpl* genitals.

genitore *sm* parent; **i nostri genitori** our parents.

gennaio *sm* January, → **settembre**.

Genova *sf* Genoa.

gente *sf* people (*pl*).

gentile *agg* kind, nice; **Gentile Signore** Dear Sir; **Gentile Signor G. Paoli** Mr G. Paoli.

gentilezza *sf* kindness; **per ~** please.

gentiluomo (*pl* **gentiluomini**) *sm* gentleman.

genuino, -a *agg* genuine.

geografia *sf* geography.

geologia *sf* geology.

geometria *sf* geometry.

geranio *sm* geranium.

gerarchia *sf* hierarchy.

gergo, -ghi *sm* (*di giovani*) slang; (*specialistico*) jargon.

Germania *sf*: **la ~** Germany.

germe *sm* germ.

gerundio *sm* gerund.

gesso *sm* chalk; (*per frattura*) plaster.

gestione *sf* management.

gestire *vt* to run.

gesto *sm* gesture.

gestore *sm* manager.

Gesù *sm* Jesus.

gettare *vt* (*lanciare*) to throw; (*buttar via*) to throw away; (*grido*) to utter; (*acqua*) to spout; (*scultura*) to cast; **'non ~ alcun oggetto dal finestrino'** 'do not throw objects out of the window'.
▶ **gettarsi** *vr*: **gettarsi da/in** to throw o.s. from/into; **gettarsi in** (*fiume*) to flow into.

getto *sm* (*d'acqua, gas*) jet; (*vapore*) puff; **di ~** (*scrivere*) in one go.

gettone *sm* token; **~ telefonico** telephone token.

ghiacciaio *sm* glacier.

ghiacciato, -a *agg* frozen; (*freddo*) ice-cold.

ghiaccio *sm* ice.

ghiacciolo *sm* (*gelato*) ice lolly (Br), Popsicle® (Am); (*di fontana*) icicle.

ghiaia *sf* gravel.

ghiandola *sf* gland.

ghiotto, -a *agg* (*persona*) greedy; (*cibo*) appetizing.

già ◆ *avv* already; (*precedentemente*) already, before ◆ *esclam* of course!, yes!; **di ~?** already?

giacca, -che *sf* jacket; **~ a vento** windcheater.

giacché *cong* as, since.

giaccone *sm* heavy jacket.

giacere *vi* to lie.

giallo, -a ◆ *agg* (*colore*) yellow; (*carnagione*) sallow ◆ *sm* (*colore*) yellow; (*romanzo*) detective story; **film ~** thriller; **~ dell'uovo** yolk.

gianduiotto *sm* hazelnut chocolate.

Giappone *sm*: **il ~** Japan.

giapponese ◆ *agg & sm* Japanese ◆ *smf* Japanese person.

giardinaggio *sm* gardening.

giardiniera *sf* (*verdure*) starter of mixed pickled vegetables, → **giardiniere**.

giardiniere, -a *sm, f* gardener.

giardino *sm* garden; **~ botanico** botanical gardens (*pl*); **~ d'infanzia** nursery, kindergarten; **~ pubblico** park; **~ zoologico** zoo.

gigante ◆ *agg* (*enorme*) gigantic ◆ *sm* giant.

gigantesco, -a, -schi, -sche *agg* gigantic.

gilè *sm inv* waistcoat.

gin [dʒin] *sm inv* gin.

ginecologo, -a, -gi, -ghe *sm, f* gynaecologist.

ginestra *sf* broom.

Ginevra *sf* Geneva.

ginnastica *sf* gymnastics (*sg*); **fare ~** to do exercises.

ginocchio (*pl m* **ginocchi** o *pl f* **ginocchia**) *sm* knee; **stare in ~** to be on one's knees, to kneel.

giocare ♦ *vi* to play; (*scommettere*) to gamble ♦ *vt* to play; (*scommettere*) to gamble; (*ingannare*) to take in; **sai ~ a tennis?** can you play tennis?; **giocarsi il posto** to lose one's job.

giocatore, -trice *sm, f* player; **~ d'azzardo** gambler.

giocattolo *sm* toy.

gioco, -chi *sm* game; (*divertimento*) play; **mettere in ~ qc** to risk sthg; **~ d'azzardo** game of chance; **~ di parole** pun; **per ~** as a joke, for fun.

giocoliere *sm* juggler.

gioia *sf* joy; (*gioiello*) jewel; **darsi alla pazza ~** to live it up.

gioielleria *sf* jeweller's shop.

gioiello *sm* jewel, piece of jewellery.

giornalaio, -a *sm, f* newsagent (Br), newsdealer (Am).

giornale *sm* (*quotidiano*) newspaper; (*rivista*) magazine; **~ radio** news bulletin.

giornaliero, -a *agg* daily.

giornalista, -i, -e *smf* journalist.

giornata *sf* day; **oggi è una bella ~** it's lovely today; **~ lavorativa** working day; **vivere alla ~** to live for the day.

giorno *sm* (*ventiquattro ore*) day; (*opposto alla notte*) day, daytime; (*periodo di luce*) daylight; **a giorni alterni** on alternate days; **l'altro ~** the other day; **~ feriale** working day; **~ festivo** holiday; **~ libero** day off; **al ~** by the day, per day; **di ~** by day, during the day.

giostra *sf* merry-go-round.

giovane *agg* young; **da ~** as a young man/woman; **i giovani** young people.

giovanile *agg* youthful.

giovanotto *sm* young man.

giovare : giovare a *v + prep* to be good for.

▶ **giovarsi di** *vr + prep* to make use of.

giovedì *sm inv* Thursday; **~ grasso** *last Thursday of Carnival, before Lent,* → **sabato.**

gioventù *sf* (*età*) youth; (*giovani*) young people (*pl*).

giovinezza *sf* youth.

giradischi *sm inv* record player.

giraffa *sf* giraffe.

giramento *sm:* **~ di testa** dizziness.

girare ♦ *vt* to turn; (*visitare*) to go round; (*filmare*) to shoot; (*assegno, cambiale*) to endorse ♦ *vi* to turn; (*velocemente*) to spin; (*terra*) to revolve; (*andare in giro*) to go around.

▶ **girarsi** *vr* to turn around.

girarrosto *sm* spit.

girasole *sm* sunflower.

girata *sf* (*passeggiata*) stroll; (*in macchina*) drive; (FIN) endorsement.

girello *sm* (*di carne*) topside; (*per bambini*) baby-walker.

girevole *agg* turning, revolving.

giro *sm* (*viaggio*) tour; (*rotazione*) turn; (*di amici, colleghi*) circle; (*di pista*) lap; **fare un ~** (*a piedi*) to go for a walk; (*in macchina*) to go for a drive; (*in bicicletta*) to go for a ride; **fare un ~ per la Toscana** to go on a tour of Tuscany; **fare il ~ di** (*città, negozi*) to go round; **~ d'affari** turnover; **~ di parole** circumlocution; **~ di prova** test drive; **in ~** around; **nel ~ di un anno** in the space of a year; **prendere in ~ qn** to tease sb, to pull sb's leg; **essere su di giri** to be excited.

girotondo *sm* ring-a-ring-o'-roses.

gita sf trip; **andare in ~ a Roma** to go on a trip to Rome.

giù avv down; (al piano di sotto) downstairs; **in ~** down, downwards; **~ di lì** thereabouts; **~ per le scale** down the stairs; **essere ~** (fig: essere depresso) to be low.

giubbotto sm jacket.

giudicare ♦ vt (valutare) to judge; (reputare) to consider; (DIR) to find ♦ vi to judge.

giudice sm judge; (nello sport) umpire.

giudizio sm judgment; (opinione) opinion; (a scuola) report; **a mio ~** in my opinion.

giugno sm June, → **settembre**.

giungere vi: **~ a/in** to reach, to arrive at.

giungla sf jungle.

giunta sf committee; **per ~** in addition.

giunto, -a pp → **giungere**.

giuramento sm oath.

giurare ♦ vt to swear ♦ vi to take an oath.

giuria sf (di gare, concorsi) judges (pl); (di tribunale) jury.

giustificare vt to justify.

giustificazione sf (scusa) excuse; (SCOL) note (of absence).

giustizia sf justice.

giusto, -a ♦ agg (equo) fair, just; (vero, adeguato) right; (esatto) correct ♦ avv (esattamente) correctly; (proprio) just; **cercavo ~ te!** you're just the person I was looking for!

gli ♦ art mpl (dav s + consonante, gn, ps, z, vocale e h) the, → **il** ♦ pron (a lui) (to) him; (a esso) (to) it; (a loro) (to) them; **glielo hai detto?** have you told him/her?; **gliene devo due** I owe him/her two (of them).

gliela → **gli**.

gliele → **gli**.

glieli → **gli**.

glielo → **gli**.

gliene → **gli**.

globale agg global.

globo sm globe.

globulo sm: **~ rosso/bianco** red/white corpuscle.

gloria sf glory.

gnocchi smpl gnocchi (small dumplings made from potatoes and flour or from semolina).

goal [gɔl] sm inv goal.

gobba sf (su schiena) hump; (rigonfiamento) bump.

gobbo, -a ♦ agg hunchbacked; (curvo) round-shouldered ♦ sm hunchback.

goccia, -ce sf drop.

gocciolare vi & vt to drip.

godere vt: **godersi qc** to enjoy sthg.

▶ **godere di** v + prep (avere) to enjoy; **~ di una riduzione** to benefit from a reduction.

goffo, -a agg clumsy.

gola sf throat; (golosità) greed; (di monte) gorge.

golf sm inv (maglia) sweater, jumper; (sport) golf.

golfista, -i, -e smf golfer.

golfo sm gulf.

goloso, -a agg greedy.

gomito sm elbow.

gomma sf rubber; (per cancellare) rubber (Br), eraser (Am); (pneumatico) tyre; **bucare** o **forare una ~** to have a puncture; **~ a terra** flat tyre; **~ (da masticare)** chewing gum.

gommapiuma® sf foam rubber.

gommone sm rubber dinghy.

gondola sf gondola.

gondoliere sm gondolier.

gonfiare vt (pallone, gomme) to inflate; (dilatare, ingrossare) to swell; (notizia, impresa) to exaggerate.

▶ **gonfiarsi** vr to swell; (fiume) to rise.

gonfio, -a agg (piede, occhi) swollen; (stomaco) bloated.

gonna sf skirt; **~ a pieghe** pleated skirt; **~ pantalone** culottes (pl).

gorgogliare vi to gurgle.

gorgonzola sm Gorgonzola (a strong green-veined cheese made from cow's milk).

gorilla sm inv (animale) gorilla; (guardia del corpo) bodyguard.

goulash ['gulaʃ] sm goulash.

governante sf (per bambini) governess; (di casa) housekeeper.

governare vt to govern; (animale) to look after.

governatore sm governor.

governo sm government.

gracile agg delicate.

gradazione sf (di colori) scale; (sfumatura) shade; **~ alcolica** alcoholic strength.

gradevole agg pleasant.

gradinata sf (scalinata) (flight of) steps; (in stadi, teatri) tiers (pl).

gradino sm step.

gradire vt (regalo) to like, to appreciate; (desiderare) to like; **gradisce un caffè?** would you like a coffee?

grado sm degree; (sociale) level; (MIL) rank; **quanti gradi ha questo vino?** how strong is this wine?; **essere in ~ di fare qc** to be able to do sthg; **~ centigrado** centigrade.

graduale agg gradual.

graduatoria sf (ranked) list.

graffetta sf (fermaglio) clip; (di pinzatrice) staple.

graffiare vt to scratch.

graffio sm scratch.

grafica sf graphics (pl).

grafico, -a, -ci, -che ◆ agg (rappresentazione, arti) graphic ◆ sm, f (pubblicitario) designer ◆ sm graph.

grammatica, -che sf (disciplina) grammar; (libro) grammar book.

grammo sm gram.

grana ◆ sf (fam) (seccatura) trouble; (soldi) cash ◆ sm inv a hard cheese similar to Parmesan.

granaio sm granary, barn.

Gran Bretagna sf: **la ~** Great Britain.

granché pron: **non ne so (un) ~** I don't know much about it; **non è**

(un) ~ it's nothing special.

granchio sm crab; **prendere un ~** (fig) to blunder.

grande ◆ (a volte **gran**) agg (gen) big; (albero) tall; (rumore) loud; (scrittore, affetto, capacità) great ◆ sm (adulto) grown-up, adult; **grandi magazzini** department store; **cosa farai da ~?** what will you do when you grow up?; **fare le cose in ~** to do things on a grand scale; **è un gran bugiardo** he's such a liar; **fa un gran caldo** it's very hot.

grandezza sf (dimensioni) size; (eccellenza) greatness.

grandinare v impers to hail.

grandine sf hail.

granello sm (di sale, sabbia) grain.

granita sf granita (crushed ice with syrup, fruit juice or coffee poured over).

grano sm wheat.

granturco sm maize.

grappa sf (acquavite) grappa (spirit distilled from grape marc).

grappolo sm bunch.

grasso, -a ◆ agg (persona) fat; (cibo) fatty; (pelle, capelli) greasy ◆ sm fat; (unto) grease.

grassoccio, -a, -ci, -ce agg plump.

grata sf grating.

gratis avv free.

gratitudine sf gratitude.

grato, -a agg grateful.

grattacielo sm skyscraper.

gratta e vinci sm inv scratch card.

grattare vt to scratch; (formaggio) to grate; (fam: rubare) to pinch; **grattarsi il naso/la gamba** to scratch one's nose/leg.

▶ **grattarsi** vr to scratch o.s.

grattugia sf grater.

grattugiare vt to grate.

gratuito, -a agg free.

grave agg (malattia, ferita) serious; (danno, perdite) serious, great; (responsabilità) heavy; (sacrificio) great; (voce, suono) deep; (contegno) solemn.

gravemente avv seriously.

gravidanza sf pregnancy.

gravità sf (in fisica) gravity; (serietà) seriousness.

grazia sf grace; (DIR) pardon.

grazie esclam thank you!; **~ tante** o **mille!** thank you so much!; **~ dei fiori** o **per i fiori** thank you for the flowers; **~ a** thanks to.

grazioso, -a agg pretty, charming.

Grecia sf: **la ~** Greece.

greco, -a, -ci, -che agg & sm, f Greek.

gregge (pl f greggi) sm flock.

greggio, -a, -gi, -ge ♦ agg raw, unrefined; (tessuto) unbleached; (diamante) rough, uncut ♦ sm crude oil.

grembiule sm (da cucina) apron; (per bambini) smock.

grezzo = **greggio**.

gridare ♦ vi to shout; (di dolore) to yell, to cry out ♦ vt to shout.

grido (pl f grida) sm (di persona) shout, cry; **di ~** famous.

grigio, -a, -gi, -gie agg & sm grey.

griglia sf grill; **alla ~** grilled.

grigliata sf mixed grill (of meat or fish).

grill sm = **griglia**.

grilletto sm trigger.

grillo sm cricket.

grinta sf determination.

grinzoso, -a agg (tessuto) creased; (pelle) wrinkled.

grissini smpl bread-sticks.

grolla sf wooden goblet or bowl, typical of the Valle d'Aosta.

grondare vi to stream.

▶ **grondare di** v + prep to drip with.

groppa sf rump.

groppo sm tangle; **avere un ~ alla gola** to have a lump in one's throat.

grossista, -i, -e smf wholesaler.

grosso, -a ♦ agg big, large; (spesso) thick; (importante) important; (grave) great ♦ sm majority; **dirla grossa** to tell a whopping lie; **questa volta l'hai fatta grossa!** you've really done it this time!; **sbagliarsi di ~** to make a big mistake; **mare ~** rough sea; **pezzo ~** big shot; **sale ~** coarse salt.

grossolano, -a agg (persona) coarse; (lavoro) crude; (errore) gross.

grossomodo avv roughly, approximately.

grotta sf cave.

grottesco, -a, -schi, -sche agg grotesque.

groviera sm o sf Gruyère cheese.

groviglio sm tangle.

gru sf inv (macchina) crane.

gruccia, -ce sf (stampella) crutch; (per abiti) coat hanger.

grugnire vi to grunt.

grumo sm (di sangue) clot; (di farina) lump.

gruppo sm group; **~ sanguigno** blood group.

gruviera = **groviera**.

guadagnare vt (soldi) to earn; (ottenere) to gain; **guadagnarsi da vivere** to earn one's living.

guadagno sm (denaro) earnings (pl); (tornaconto) profit.

guado sm ford.

guai esclam **~ a te!** you'll be for it!

guaio sm (pasticcio) trouble; (inconveniente) problem; **essere nei guai** to be in trouble; **mettere qn nei guai** to get sb into trouble.

guancia, -ce sf cheek.

guanciale sm pillow.

guanto sm glove.

guardaboschi sm inv forest ranger.

guardacoste sm inv (persona) coastguard; (nave) (coastguard's) patrol boat.

guardalinee sm inv linesman.

guardamacchine sm inv car park attendant.

guardare ♦ vt (osservare) to look at, to watch; (televisione, film) to watch; (bambini, borsa) to look after ♦ vi (edificio) to look, to face; (badare): **non ~ a spese** to spare no expense; **guarda!** look!

▶ **guardarsi** vr to look at o.s.

▶ **guardarsi da** vr + prep qc to be wary of; **guardarsi dal fare qc** to be careful not to do sthg.

guardaroba sm inv wardrobe; (di locale) cloakroom.

guardia sf guard; (attività) watch, guard duty; **fare la ~ a** to guard; **mettere qn in ~ contro qc** to warn sb about sthg; **~ del corpo** bodyguard; **Guardia di Finanza** military body responsible for customs and fiscal matters; **~ forestale** forest ranger; **~ medica** first-aid station; **di ~** on duty.

guardiano sm caretaker; **~ notturno** night watchman.

guardrail [gar'dreil] sm inv crash barrier.

guarire ♦ vi to recover; (ferita) to heal ♦ vt to cure; (ferita) to heal.

guarnizione sf (ornamento) trim; (contorno) accompaniment, garnish; (per recipienti) seal; (di auto) gasket.

guastafeste smf inv spoilsport.

guastare vt to spoil.

▶ **guastarsi** vr (meccanismo) to break down; (cibo) to go bad; (tempo) to change for the worse.

guasto, -a ♦ agg (radio) broken; (ascensore, telefono) out of order; (cibo) bad ♦ sm breakdown; **un ~ al motore** engine trouble.

guerra sf war; **essere in ~** to be at war; **~ mondiale** World War.

guerriglia sf guerrilla warfare.

gufo sm owl.

guglia sf spire.

guida sf guide; (di veicolo) driving; **~ a destra** right-hand drive; **~ a sinistra** left-hand drive.

guidare vt (veicolo) to drive; (accompagnare) to guide; **sai ~?** can you drive?

guidatore, -trice sm, f driver.

guinzaglio sm lead.

guscio sm shell.

gustare vt (cibo) to taste; (godersi) to enjoy.

gusto sm taste; **al ~ di banana** banana-flavoured; **mangiare di ~** to enjoy one's food; **ridere di ~** to laugh heartily; **ci ha preso ~** he's come to like it.

gustoso, -a agg tasty.

H

ha → avere.

habitat sm inv habitat.

hai → avere.

hall [ol] sf inv hall, foyer.

hamburger [am'burger] sm inv hamburger.

handicap ['ɛndikap] sm inv handicap.

handicappato, -a ♦ agg handicapped ♦ sm, f handicapped person, disabled person.

hanno → avere.

henné sm inv henna.

hg (abbr di ettogrammo) hg.

hi-fi [ai'fai] sm inv hi-fi.

hippy agg inv & smf inv hippy.

ho → avere.

hobby sm inv hobby.

hockey sm hockey (Br), field hockey (Am); **~ su ghiaccio** ice hockey.

hostess sf inv (di volo) airhostess.

hotel sm inv hotel.

I

i *art mpl* the, → **il**.

IC *abbr* = **intercity**.

iceberg ['aizberg] *sm inv* iceberg.

Iddio *sm* God.

idea *sf* idea; (*opinione, impressione*) impression; (*progetto*): **avere ~ di fare qc** to think of doing sthg; **neanche per ~!** don't even think about it!; **non avere la più pallida ~ di qc** not to have the slightest idea about sthg; **non ne ho ~** I've no idea; **cambiare ~** to change one's mind.

ideale *agg & sm* ideal.

ideare *vt* (*metodo, sistema*) to devise; (*viaggio*) to plan.

idem *avv* (*fam: lo stesso*) the same.

identico, -a, -ci, -che *agg* identical.

identità *sf inv* identity.

ideologia, -gie *sf* ideology.

idiota, -i, -e ♦ *agg* idiotic, stupid ♦ *smf* idiot.

idolo *sm* idol.

idoneo, -a *agg* (*adatto*): **~ a** suitable for; (MIL) fit for.

idrante *sm* hydrant.

idratante *agg* moisturizing.

idratare *vt* to moisturize.

idraulico, -a, -ci, -che ♦ *agg* hydraulic ♦ *sm* plumber; **impianto ~** plumbing.

idrofilo *agg m* → **cotone**.

idrogeno *sm* hydrogen.

idromassaggio, -gi *sm* hydromassage.

idroscalo *sm* seaplane base.

idrosolubile *agg* soluble (in water).

iella *sf* (*fam*) bad luck.

ieri *avv* yesterday; **~ mattina** yesterday morning; **~ notte** last night; **l'altro ~, ~ l'altro** the day before yesterday; **la posta di ~** yesterday's mail.

igiene *sf* hygiene.

igienico, -a, -ci, -che *agg* hygienic.

ignorante *agg* ignorant.

ignorare *vt* (*non sapere*) not to know; (*trascurare*) to ignore.

ignoto, -a *agg* unknown.

il (*mpl* **i**; *dav sm* **lo** (*pl* **gli**) + *s+consonante, gn, ps, z*; *f* **la**, *fpl* **le**; *dav sm o sf* **l'** + *vocale o h*) *art* **1.** (*gen*) the.

2. (*con nome comune*) the; **~ lago** the lake; **la finestra** the window; **lo studente** the student; **l'isola** the island.

3. (*con nome astratto*): **~ tempo** time; **la vita** life.

4. (*con titolo*): **~ Signor Pollini** Mr Pollini; **la regina Elisabetta** Queen Elizabeth.

5. (*con nomi geografici*): **~ Po** the Po; **le Dolomiti** the Dolomites.

6. (*indica possesso*): **si è rotto ~ naso** he broke his nose; **ha i capelli biondi** she has fair hair.

7. (*indica il tempo*): **~ sabato** (*tutti i sabati*) on Saturdays; (*quel sabato*) on Saturday; **la sera** in the evening; **è ~ 29 dicembre** it's the 29th of December; **dopo le tre** after three o'clock.

8. (*ciascuno*): **5 000 lire l'uno** 5,000 lira each.

illazione *sf* inference.

illecito, -a *agg* illicit.

illegale *agg* illegal.

illegittimo, -a *agg* illegitimate.

illeso, -a *agg* unhurt.

illimitato, -a *agg* (*spazio, tempo*) unlimited; (*fiducia*) absolute.

illudere *vt* to deceive.

▶ **illudersi** *vr* to deceive o.s.

illuminare *vt* to light up, to illuminate.

illuminazione *sf* lighting; (*fig: intuizione*) enlightenment.

illusione *sf* (*falsa apparenza*) illusion; (*falsa speranza*) delusion.

illusionista, -i, -e *smf* conjurer.

illuso, -a ◆ *pp →* **illudere ◆** *sm, f*: **essere un ~** to be fooling o.s.

illustrare *vt* to illustrate.

illustrativo, -a *agg* illustrative.

illustrazione *sf* illustration, picture.

imballaggio *sm* packaging.

imballare *vt* to pack (up).

imbalsamare *vt* to embalm.

imbarazzante *agg* embarrassing.

imbarazzare *vt* to embarrass.

imbarazzato, -a *agg* embarrassed.

imbarcadero *sm* landing stage.

imbarcare *vt* (*passeggero*) to board; (*merce*) to load.

▶ **imbarcarsi** *vr* to board.

imbarcazione *sf* boat; **imbarcazioni da diporto** pleasure boats.

imbarco, -chi *sm* (*salita a bordo*) boarding; (*carico*) loading; (*luogo*) point of departure.

imbattersi : imbattersi in *vr + prep* to run into.

imbecille ◆ *agg* stupid, idiotic ◆ *smf* imbecile, idiot.

imbellire ◆ *vt* to embellish ◆ *vi* to become more beautiful.

imbiancare ◆ *vt* to whitewash ◆ *vi* (*diventare bianco*) to turn white.

imbianchino *sm* decorator.

imboccare *vt* (*bambino*) to feed; (*strada*) to turn into.

imboccatura *sf* (*di condotto*) mouth; (*di strada*) entrance; (*di strumento musicale*) mouthpiece.

imbocco, -chi *sm* entrance.

imbottigliare *vt* (*liquido*) to bottle; (*nave*) to blockade; **è rimasto imbottigliato** he got stuck in a traffic jam.

imbottire *vt* (*cuscino*) to stuff; (*giacca*) to pad.

imbottito, -a *agg* stuffed; (*indumento*) padded, quilted; **panino ~** filled roll.

imbranato, -a *agg* (*fam*) clumsy.

imbrattare *vt* to dirty.

imbrogliare *vt* (*ingannare*) to deceive; (*ingarbugliare*) to entangle.

imbroglio *sm* swindle.

imbroglione, -a *sm, f* swindler.

imbronciato, -a *agg* sulky.

imbucare *vt* to post (Br), to mail (Am).

imburrare *vt* to butter.

imbuto *sm* funnel.

imitare *vt* to imitate.

imitazione *sf* imitation.

immacolato, -a *agg* (*bianco*) pure white; (*puro*) immaculate, pure.

immaginare *vt* (*rappresentarsi*) to imagine; (*supporre*) to suppose; **si immagini!** don't mention it!; **~ di fare qc** to imagine doing sthg.

immaginazione *sf* imagination.

immagine *sf* image.

immatricolare *vt* (*auto*) to register; (*studente*) to enrol.

immaturo, -a *agg* immature.

immedesimarsi : immedesimarsi in *vr + prep* to identify with.

immediatamente *avv* immediately.

immediato, -a *agg* immediate.

immenso, -a *agg* immense, enormous.

immergere *vt* to immerse.

▶ **immergersi** *vr* to dive.

▶ **immergersi in** *vr + prep* (*dedicarsi a*) to immerse o.s. in.

immersione *sf* dive.

immerso, -a *pp →* **immergere**.

immesso, -a *pp →* **immettere**.

immettere *vt* to introduce.

immigrante *smf* immigrant.

immigrato, -a *sm, f* immigrant.

immigrazione *sf* immigration.

imminente *agg* imminent.

immobile ◆ *agg* immobile ◆ *sm* property (Br), real estate (Am).

immobiliare *agg* property (*dav s*) (Br), real estate (*dav s*) (Am).

immodesto, -a *agg* immodest.

immondizia *sf* rubbish.

immorale *agg* immoral.

immortale *agg* immortal.

immunità *sf* immunity.

immunizzare *vt* to immunize.

impacchettare *vt* to wrap.

impacciato, -a *agg* (*goffo*) awkward; (*imbarazzato*) embarrassed.

impacco, -chi *sm* compress.

impadronirsi : impadronirsi di *vr + prep* (*città, beni*) to take possession of; (*lingua*) to master.

impalcatura *sf* scaffolding.

impallidire *vi* to go pale.

impalpabile *agg* impalpable.

impappinarsi *vr* to stumble.

imparare *vt* to learn; ~ **a fare qc** to learn to do sthg.

imparziale *agg* impartial, unbiased.

impassibile *agg* impassive.

impastare *vt* (*pane*) to knead; (*mescolare*) to mix.

impasto *sm* (*di farina*) dough; (*amalgama*) mixture.

impatto *sm* impact.

impaurire *vt* to frighten.

▶ **impaurirsi** *vr* to get frightened.

impaziente *agg* impatient; **essere ~ di fare qc** to be impatient to do sthg.

impazzire *vi* to go mad o crazy; **mi piace da ~** I'm mad o crazy about it.

impedimento *sm* obstacle.

impedire *vt* (*ostacolare*) to obstruct; (*vietare*): ~ **a qn di fare qc** to prevent sb from doing sthg.

impegnare *vt* (*occupare*) to keep busy; (*dare in pegno*) to pawn.

▶ **impegnarsi** *vr* to commit o.s.; **impegnarsi a fare qc** to undertake to do sthg; **impegnarsi in qc** to commit o.s. to sthg.

impegnativo, -a *agg* (*lavoro*) demanding, exacting; (*promessa*) binding.

impegnato, -a *agg* (*occupato*) busy; (*militante*) committed.

impegno *sm* commitment; (*incombenza*) engagement, appointment.

impellente *agg* pressing, urgent.

impenetrabile *agg* impenetrable.

impennarsi *vr* (*cavallo*) to rear (up); (*moto*) to do a wheelie; (*aereo*) to climb.

impennata *sf* (*di cavallo*) rearing; (*di moto*) wheelie; (*di aereo*) climb.

impensabile *agg* unthinkable, inconceivable.

impepata *sf*: ~ **di cozze** mussels cooked with lots of pepper or chilli (*a speciality of Naples*).

imperativo *sm* imperative.

imperatore, -trice *sm, f* emperor (*f* empress).

imperfezione *sf* imperfection.

impermeabile ◆ *agg* waterproof ◆ *sm* raincoat.

impero *sm* empire.

impersonale *agg* impersonal.

impersonare *vt* to play.

impertinente *agg* impertinent.

imperturbabile *agg* imperturbable.

imperversare *vi* (*calamità*) to rage; (*fam: moda*) to be all the rage.

impervio, -a *agg* passable with difficulty.

impeto *sm* (*forza*) force; (*slancio*) surge.

impianto *sm* (*installazione*) installation; (*elettrico, del gas, antifurto*) system; (*macchinario*) plant; ~ **di riscaldamento** heating system; ~ **sportivo** sports complex; **impianti di risalita** ski lifts.

impiccare *vt* to hang.

▶ **impiccarsi** *vr* to hang o.s.

impiccione, -a *sm, f* busybody.

impiegare *vt* (*tempo*) to take; (*utilizzare*) to use; (*assumere*) to employ.

▶ **impiegarsi** *vr* to get a job.

impiegato, -a *sm, f* employee; ~ **di banca** bank clerk.

impiego, -ghi *sm* (*lavoro*) work, employment; (*uso*) use.

impigliare *vt* to entangle.

▶ **impigliarsi** *vr*: impigliarsi in qc to get entangled in sthg.

impigrire ◆ *vt* to make lazy ◆ *vi* to become lazy.

▶ **impigrirsi** *vr* to become lazy.

implacabile *agg* implacable, relentless.

implicare *vt* (*comportare*) to imply, to entail; (*coinvolgere*) to involve.

implicato, -a *agg*: essere ~ in qc to be implicated in sthg.

implicazione *sf* implication.

implicito, -a *agg* implicit.

implorare *vt* to implore.

impolverare *vt* to cover with dust.

▶ **impolverarsi** *vr* to get dusty.

imponente *agg* imposing.

impopolare *agg* unpopular.

imporre *vt* (*volontà, silenzio*) to impose; (*costringere*): ~ a qn di fare qc to make sb do sthg.

▶ **imporsi** *vr* (*farsi ubbidire*) to impose o.s., to assert o.s.; (*avere successo*) to be successful; imporsi di fare qc to make o.s. do sthg.

importante *agg* important.

importanza *sf* importance; avere ~ to be important, to matter; dare ~ a qc to give weight to sthg.

importare ◆ *vt* to import ◆ *vi* to matter, to be important ◆ *v impers* to matter; non importa! it doesn't matter!; non mi importa I don't care.

importato, -a *agg* imported.

importazione *sf* importation; (*prodotto*) import.

importo *sm* amount.

importunare *vt* to bother.

impossessarsi : impossessarsi di *vr + prep* to take possession of.

impossibile ◆ *agg* impossible ◆ *sm*: fare l'~ to do all one can.

imposto, -a ◆ *pp* → **imporre** ◆ *sf* (*tassa*) tax, duty; (*di finestra*) shutter.

impostare *vt* (*lettera*) to post (Br), to mail (Am); (*lavoro*) to plan; (*domanda*) to formulate.

imposto, -a *pp* → **imporre**.

impostore, -a *sm, f* impostor.

impotente *agg* powerless; (MED) impotent.

impraticabile *agg* impassable.

imprecare *vi* to curse.

imprecazione *sf* curse.

impregnare *vt*: ~ qc (di qc) (*inzuppare*) to soak sthg (with sthg); (*di fumo, odore*) to impregnate sthg (with sthg).

imprenditore, -trice *sm, f* (*industriale*) entrepreneur; (*appaltatore*) contractor.

impreparato, -a *agg* unprepared.

impresa *sf* (*azione*) undertaking; (*ditta*) business.

impresario, -a *sm, f* (*teatrale*) impresario; ~ edile building constructor.

impressionante *agg* impressive.

impressionare *vt* (*turbare*) to disturb; (*colpire*) to impress.

▶ **impressionarsi** *vr* to get upset.

impressione *sf* impression; (*sensazione*) impression, feeling; ho l'~ di conoscerlo I have the impression o feeling I know him; fare ~ (*colpire*) to impress; (*turbare*) to upset; fare buona/cattiva ~ to make a good/bad impression.

impresso, -a *pp* → **imprimere**.

imprestare *vt*: ~ qc a qn to lend sthg to sb.

imprevisto, -a ◆ *agg* unexpected ◆ *sm* unexpected event; salvo imprevisti circumstances permitting.

imprigionare *vt* (*incarcerare*) to imprison; (*tenere chiuso*) to confine.

imprimere *vt* to print; (*movimento*) to transmit.

improbabile *agg* improbable, unlikely.

impronta *sf* (*di piede, mano, zampa*) print; ~ digitale fingerprint.

improvvisamente *avv* suddenly, unexpectedly.

improvvisare *vt* to improvise.

▶ **improvvisarsi** *vr*: **si è improvvisato cuoco** he acted as cook.

improvvisata *sf* surprise.

improvviso, -a *agg* (*inatteso*) sudden, unexpected; (*istantaneo*) sudden; **all'~** suddenly.

imprudente *agg* (*persona*) unwise, imprudent; (*azione*) rash.

imprudenza *sf* rash action.

impudente *agg* impudent.

impugnare *vt* (*stringere*) to grasp; (DIR) to contest.

impugnatura *sf* handle.

impulsivo, -a *agg* impulsive.

impulso *sm* impulse; **d'~** on impulse.

impuntarsi *vr* (*bambino*) to stop dead; (*cavallo*) to jib; (*ostinarsi*) to dig one's heels in.

imputare *vt*: **~ qc a qn** to attribute sthg to sb; **~ qn di qc** to accuse sb of sthg.

imputato, -a *sm, f* defendant.

in *prep* **1.** (*stato in luogo*) in; **abitare ~ campagna** to live in the country; **essere ~ casa** to be at home; **l'ho lasciato ~ macchina/nella borsa** I left it in the car/in the bag; **vivo ~ Italia** I live in Italy; **avere qc ~ mente** to have sthg in mind. **2.** (*moto a luogo*) to; **andare ~ Italia** to go to Italy; **andare ~ montagna** to go to the mountains; **mettersi qc ~ testa** to get sthg into one's head; **entrare ~ macchina** to get into the car; **entrare nella stanza** to go into the room. **3.** (*indica un momento*) in; **~ primavera** in spring; **nel 1995** in 1995. **4.** (*indica durata*) in; **l'ho fatto ~ cinque minuti** I did it in five minutes; **~ giornata** within the day. **5.** (*indica modo*): **parlare ~ italiano** to speak in Italian; **~ silenzio** in silence; **sono ancora in pigiama** I'm still in my pyjamas; **quant'è ~ lire?** how much is that in lira?; **~ vacanza** on holiday (Br), on vacation (Am). **6.** (*indica mezzo*) by; **pagare ~ contanti** to pay cash; **viaggiare ~ macchina** to travel by car. **7.** (*indica materia*) made of; **statua ~ bronzo** bronze statue. **8.** (*indica fine*): **ha speso un capitale in libri** he spent a fortune on books; **dare ~ omaggio** to give as a free gift; **~ onore di** in honour of. **9.** (*con valore distributivo*): **siamo partiti ~ tre** three of us left; **~ tutto sono 10 000 lire** it's 10,000 lira in total.

inabile *agg*: **~ (a qc)** unfit (for sthg).

inaccessibile *agg* (*luogo*) inaccessible; (*persona*) unapproachable.

inaccettabile *agg* unacceptable.

inadatto, -a *agg* unsuitable.

inadeguato, -a *agg* (*insufficiente*) inadequate; (*non idoneo*) unsuitable.

inagibile *agg* unfit for use.

inalare *vt* to inhale.

inalberarsi *vr* to get angry.

inalterato, -a *agg* unchanged.

inamidare *vt* to starch.

inammissibile *agg* inadmissible.

inappetenza *sf* lack of appetite.

inappuntabile *agg* (*persona*) faultless, irreproachable; (*lavoro, vestito*) impeccable.

inarcare *vt* (*schiena*) to arch; **~ le sopracciglia** to raise one's eyebrows.

▶ **inarcarsi** *vr* to arch.

inaridire *vt* to dry (up).

▶ **inaridirsi** *vr* to dry up.

inaspettato, -a *agg* unexpected.

inasprire *vt* to make worse.

▶ **inasprirsi** *vr* to become bitter.

inattendibile *agg* unbelievable, unreliable.

inatteso, -a *agg* unexpected.

inattività *sf* inactivity.

inattuabile *agg* impractical, unfeasible.

inaudito, -a *agg* unheard-of, unprecedented.

inaugurare *vt* (*luogo, mostra*) to open; (*monumento*) to unveil.

inavvertenza *sf* carelessness.

inavvertitamente *avv* inadvertently.

incagliarsi *vr* (*nave*) to run aground; (*fig: trattative*) to break down.

incalcolabile *agg* incalculable.

incallito, -a *agg* (*mani, piedi*) calloused; (*fig: fumatore, giocatore*) inveterate.

incalzare ◆ *vt* (*inseguire*) to pursue; (*fig: premere*) to press ◆ *vi* to be imminent.

incamminarsi *vr* to set out.

incantevole *agg* enchanting.

incanto *sm* (*incantesimo*) enchantment; (*asta*) auction; **come per ~** as if by magic.

incapace *agg* incapable.

incapacità *sf* (*inettitudine*) incapacity; (DIR) incompetence.

incappare : incappare in *v + prep* to run into.

incaricare *vt* to entrust; **~ qn di qc** to entrust sb with sthg; **~ qn di fare qc** to ask sb to do sthg.

▶ **incaricarsi di** *vr + prep* to undertake to.

incaricato, -a ◆ *agg*: **~ di qc** entrusted with sthg ◆ *sm, f* representative.

incarico, -chi *sm* task.

incarnare *vt* to embody.

incarnirsi *vr* to become ingrown.

incartare *vt* to wrap up; **me lo può ~?** can you wrap it up for me?

incassare *vt* (*denaro*) to receive; (*assegno*) to cash; (*colpo, offesa*) to take; (*mobile*) to build in.

incasso *sm* takings (*pl*).

incastrare *vt* (*connettere*) to join; (*fam: intrappolare*) to catch.

▶ **incastrarsi** *vr* (*rimanere bloccato*) to get stuck; (*combaciare*) to fit together.

incastro *sm* joint; **a ~** interlocking.

incatenare *vt* (*legare*) to chain.

incauto, -a *agg* imprudent, rash.

incavato, -a *agg* hollow; (*occhi*) sunken.

incavo *sm* hollow.

incavolarsi *vr* (*fam*) to lose one's temper.

incendiare *vt* (*dare fuoco a*) to set fire to.

▶ **incendiarsi** *vr* to catch fire.

incendio *sm* fire.

incenerire *vt* to incinerate.

incenso *sm* incense.

incensurato, -a *agg*: **essere ~** to have no previous convictions.

incentivo *sm* incentive.

inceppare *vt* to block, to obstruct.

▶ **incepparsi** *vr* to jam.

incerata *sf* (*tela*) oilcloth; (*giaccone*) oilskin.

incertezza *sf* uncertainty.

incerto, -a *agg* uncertain; (*tempo*) variable.

incetta *sf*: **fare ~ di qc** to buy sthg up.

inchiesta *sf* enquiry.

inchinarsi *vr* (*uomo*) to bow; (*donna*) to curtsy.

inchino *sm* (*di uomo*) bow; (*di donna*) curtsy.

inchiodare *vt* to nail.

inchiostro *sm* ink.

inciampare *vi* to trip; **~ in qc** to trip over sthg.

incidente *sm* accident; **~ stradale** road accident.

incidere *vt* (*intagliare*) to engrave; (*canzone*) to record; (*ascesso*) to lance.

▶ **incidere su** *v + prep* to affect.

incinta *agg f* pregnant.

incirca *avv*: **all'~** approximately, about.

incisione *sf* (*taglio*) cut; (*in arte*) engraving; (*di disco, canzone*) recording; (MED) incision.

incisivo, -a ◆ *agg* incisive ◆ *sm* incisor.

inciso, -a ◆ *pp* → **incidere** ◆ *sm*: **per ~** incidentally.

incitare vt to incite.

incivile agg (non civilizzato) uncivilized; (maleducato) rude.

inclinazione sf inclination.

includere vt (accludere) to enclose; (comprendere) to include.

incluso, -a ♦ pp → **includere** ♦ agg (accluso) enclosed; (compreso) included; ~ **nel prezzo** included in the price.

incognito sm: **in** ~ incognito.

incollare vt (sovrapporre) to stick; (unire) to stick, to glue.

▶ **incollarsi** vr (stare vicino): **incollarsi a qn** to stick close to sb.

incolpare vt: ~ **qn (di qc)** to blame sb (for sthg).

incolume agg unhurt.

incominciare vt & vi to begin, to start; ~ **a fare qc** to begin to do sthg o doing sthg, to start to do sthg o doing sthg.

incompatibile agg incompatible.

incompetente agg incompetent.

incompiuto, -a agg unfinished, incomplete.

incompleto, -a agg incomplete.

incomprensibile agg incomprehensible.

incomprensione sf incomprehension.

inconcepibile agg inconceivable.

inconcludente agg (persona) ineffectual; (discorsi) inconclusive.

incondizionato, -a agg unconditional.

inconfondibile agg unmistakable.

inconsapevole agg unaware.

inconscio, -a, -sci, -sce agg unconscious.

incontaminato, -a agg uncontaminated.

incontentabile agg impossible to please.

incontinenza sf incontinence.

incontrare vt to meet; (difficoltà, favore) to meet with.

▶ **incontrarsi** vr to meet.

incontrario : all'incontrario avv (fam) (alla rovescia) back to front; (all'indietro) backwards.

incontro ♦ sm meeting; (casuale) encounter; (sportivo) match ♦ avv towards; **andare/venire** ~ **a qn** (avanzare verso) to go/to come towards sb; (incontrare) to go/to come to meet sb; (fig: con compromesso) to meet sb halfway; **andare** ~ **a qc** (spese) to incur; (difficoltà) to encounter.

inconveniente sm setback, problem.

incoraggiare vt to encourage.

incosciente agg (privo di coscienza) unconscious; (irresponsabile) irresponsible.

incredibile agg incredible.

incrementare vt to increase.

incremento sm increase.

incrociare vt to cross; (persona, veicolo) to pass; ~ **le gambe/braccia** to cross one's legs/arms; ~ **le dita** to cross one's fingers.

▶ **incrociarsi** vr (strade, linee) to cross; (persone, veicoli) to pass each other.

incrocio sm (crocevia) crossroads (sg); (combinazione) cross-breed.

incubatrice sf incubator.

incubo sm nightmare.

incurabile agg incurable.

incurante agg: ~ **di** careless of, indifferent to.

incuriosire vt to make curious.

▶ **incuriosirsi** vr to become curious.

incustodito, -a agg unattended.

indaco sm indigo.

indaffarato, -a agg busy.

indagine sf (di polizia) investigation; (studio) survey.

indebolire vt to weaken.

▶ **indebolirsi** vr to weaken, to become weak.

indecente agg indecent.

indecifrabile agg indecipherable.

indeciso, -a agg undecided; (titubante) indecisive.
indefinito, -a agg indefinite.
indegno, -a agg disgraceful.
indelebile agg indelible.
indenne agg unhurt.
indennità sf inv (rimborso) payment; (risarcimento) compensation, indemnity.
indescrivibile agg indescribable.
indeterminativo, -a agg indefinite.
indeterminato, -a agg indeterminate, vague.
india sf: l'~ India.
indiano, -a agg & sm, f Indian.
indicare vt (mostrare) to show; (col dito) to point to; (suggerire) to recommend.
indicatore sm (TECNOL) gauge; ~ della benzina petrol gauge; ~ di direzione indicator; ~ di velocità speedometer.
indicazione sf (segnalazione) indication; (informazione) piece of information; (prescrizione) direction.
indice sm (dito) index finger; (di libro) index; (lancetta) needle; (indizio) rating.
indietro avv back; (moto a luogo) backwards; (moto a luogo) backwards; **essere ~** (col lavoro) to be behind; (orologio) to be slow; **rimandare ~** to send back; **tornare ~** to go back; **all'~** backwards.
indifeso, -a agg defenceless.
indifferente agg (insensibile) indifferent; (irrilevante) insignificant; **mi è ~** it's all the same to me.
indigeno, -a sm, f native.
indigente agg destitute.
indigestione sf indigestion.
indigesto, -a agg indigestible.
indimenticabile agg unforgettable.
indipendente agg independent.
indipendenza sf independence.
indire vt (concorso) to announce; (elezioni) to call.
indiretto, -a agg indirect.

indirizzare vt (lettera, discorso) to address; (mandare) to refer; **un film indirizzato ai giovani** a film aimed at o intended for young people.
indirizzo sm address; **scuola a ~ tecnico** ≈ technical college.
indisciplinato, -a agg undisciplined.
indiscreto, -a agg indiscreet.
indiscrezione sf (invadenza) indiscretion; (notizia) unconfirmed report.
indiscusso, -a agg undisputed.
indiscutibile agg unquestionable.
indispensabile agg indispensable.
indispettire vt to annoy.
▶ **indispettirsi** vr to become annoyed.
indisponente agg annoying.
indistruttibile agg indestructible.
individuale agg individual.
individuare vt to identify.
individuo sm individual.
indiziato, -a ♦ agg suspected ♦ sm, f suspect.
indizio sm (segno) sign; (per polizia) clue; (DIR) piece of evidence.
indole sf nature.
indolenzito, -a agg aching, stiff.
indolore agg painless.
indomani sm: l'~ the next day.
indossare vt (mettere addosso) to put on; (avere addosso) to wear.
indossatore, -trice sm, f model.
indotto, -a pp → **indurre**.
indovinare vt to guess; (prevedere) to predict; (azzeccare) to get right.
indovinello sm riddle.
indovino, -a sm, f fortune-teller.
indubbiamente avv undoubtedly.
indugiare vi (temporeggiare) to take one's time.
indugio sm delay; **senza ~** without delay.
indulgente agg indulgent.

indumento sm garment; **indumenti** (abiti) clothes.

indurire vt to harden.

▶ **indurirsi** vr to harden.

indurre vt: ~ qn a fare qc to induce sb to do sthg.

industria sf industry; (stabilimento) industrial plant.

industriale ◆ agg industrial ◆ sm industrialist.

inebetito, -a agg stunned.

inebriante agg intoxicating.

ineccepibile agg unexceptionable.

inedito, -a agg unpublished.

inefficiente agg inefficient.

ineluttabile agg inescapable.

inerente agg: ~ a concerning.

inerme agg unarmed, defenceless.

inerzia sf inactivity.

inesatto, -a agg inaccurate.

inesauribile agg inexhaustible.

inesistente agg nonexistent.

inesperienza sf inexperience.

inesperto, -a agg inexperienced.

inestimabile agg inestimable.

inevaso, -a agg outstanding.

inevitabile agg inevitable.

inevitabilmente avv inevitably.

in extremis avv in extremis.

infallibile agg infallible.

infantile agg (di, per bambini) child (dav s); (immaturo) infantile.

infanzia sf (periodo) childhood; (bambini) children (pl); **prima ~** infancy.

infarinare vt (di farina) to cover with flour; (cospargere) to sprinkle.

infarto sm heart attack.

infastidire vt to annoy.

▶ **infastidirsi** vr to get annoyed.

infatti cong in fact.

infatuarsi : infatuarsi di vr + prep to become infatuated with.

infatuazione sf infatuation.

infedele agg unfaithful.

infedeltà sf inv infidelity.

infelice agg unhappy; (sfavorevole) unsuccessful; (mal riuscito) poor; (inopportuno) unfortunate.

infelicità sf unhappiness.

inferiore ◆ agg (sottostante) lower; (per qualità) inferior ◆ smf inferior; ~ a (minore) below; (peggiore) inferior to.

infermeria sf infirmary; (di scuola) sickbay.

infermiere, -a sm, f nurse.

infermo, -a agg infirm.

infernale agg (fam: terribile) terribile; (diabolico) diabolical.

inferno sm hell.

inferriata sf grating.

infestare vt to infest.

infettare vt to infect.

▶ **infettarsi** vr to become infected.

infettivo, -a agg infectious; **malattie infettive** infectious diseases.

infezione sf infection.

infiammabile agg flammable.

infiammare vt (incendiare) to set alight; (MED) to inflame.

▶ **infiammarsi** vr (incendiarsi) to catch fire; (MED) to become inflamed.

infiammazione sf inflammation.

infilare vt (introdurre) to insert; (ago) to thread; (anello, vestito) to slip on.

▶ **infilarsi in** vr + prep to slip into.

infine avv (alla fine) finally; (insomma) in short.

infinità sf infinity; **un'~ di** countless.

infinito, -a ◆ agg (illimitato) infinite; (enorme, innumerevole) countless ◆ sm (spazio, tempo) infinite; (GRAMM) infinitive.

infischiarsi : infischiarsene di vr + prep not to care about.

inflazione sf inflation.

inflessibile agg inflexible.

infliggere vt to inflict.

inflitto, -a pp → **infliggere**.

influente *agg* influential.

influenza *sf* influence; (*malattia*) flu; **avere ~ su** to have an influence on; **avere l'~** to have flu.

influenzare *vt* to influence.

influire : influire su *v + prep* to have an effect on.

influsso *sm* influence.

infondato, -a *agg* unfounded.

infondere *vt* to instil.

inforcare *vt* (*fieno*) to fork up; (*bicicletta, moto*) to get onto; (*occhiali*) to put on.

informale *agg* informal.

informare *vt*: **~ qn (di qc)** to inform sb (of sthg).

▶ **informarsi** *vr*: **informarsi di** o **su** to find out about.

informatica *sf* information technology.

informativo, -a *agg* informative.

informatore *sm* informer.

informazione *sf* piece of information; **chiedere informazioni (a qn)** to ask (sb) for information; '**informazioni**' 'information'.

informicolirsi *vr*: **mi si è informicolita una gamba** I've got pins and needles in my leg.

infortunio *sm* accident.

infossarsi *vr* (*terreno*) to sink; (*guance*) to become hollow.

infradito *sm inv* o *sf inv* flip-flop.

infrangere *vt* to break.

▶ **infrangersi** *vr* to break.

infrangibile *agg* unbreakable.

infranto, -a ◆ *pp* → **infrangere** ◆ *agg* broken.

infrazione *sf* infringement; **~ al codice stradale** traffic offence.

infreddolito, -a *agg* chilled.

infuori *avv*: **all'~** outwards; **all'~ di** apart from.

infusione *sf* infusion.

infuso, -a ◆ *pp* → **infondere** ◆ *sm* herb tea.

ingannare *vt* (*imbrogliare*) to deceive; (*tempo*) to while away.

▶ **ingannarsi** *vr* to be mistaken.

inganno *sm* deception.

ingarbugliare *vt* to tangle; (*situazione, conti*) to muddle.

▶ **ingarbugliarsi** *vr* to become tangled; (*situazione*) to become muddled; (*impapinarsi*) to falter.

ingegnere *sm* engineer.

ingegneria *sf* engineering.

ingegno *sm* (*intelligenza*) intelligence; (*creatività*) ingenuity.

ingegnoso, -a *agg* ingenious.

ingelosire *vt* to make jealous.

▶ **ingelosirsi** *vr* to become jealous.

ingente *agg* huge.

ingenuo, -a *agg* naive.

ingerire *vt* to ingest.

ingessare *vt* to put in plaster.

Inghilterra *sf*: **l'~** England.

inghiottire *vt* to swallow; (*sopportare*) to put up with.

ingiallire *vi* to yellow.

ingigantire *vt* (*foto*) to enlarge; (*fig: problema*) to exaggerate.

inginocchiarsi *vr* to kneel down.

ingiù *avv*: **(all')~** downwards.

ingiustizia *sf* (*qualità*) injustice; (*atto*) unjust act.

ingiusto, -a *agg* unfair.

inglese ◆ *agg* English ◆ *smf* Englishman (*f* Englishwoman) ◆ *sm* (*lingua*) English.

ingoiare *vt* (*inghiottire*) to swallow; (*fig: sopportare*) to put up with.

ingolfare *vt* to flood.

▶ **ingolfarsi** *vr* to flood.

ingombrante *agg* cumbersome.

ingombrare *vt* (*passaggio, strada*) to obstruct; (*tavolo, stanza*) to clutter up.

ingombro, -a ◆ *agg* obstructed ◆ *sm*: **essere d'~** to be in the way.

ingordo, -a *agg* greedy.

ingorgo, -ghi *sm* traffic jam.

ingranaggio *sm* (*meccanismo*) gear; (*fig: operazioni, attività*) machinery.

ingranare ◆ *vt* to engage ◆ *vi* (*ingranaggio*) to engage; (*fam: pren-*

dere avvio) to get going.

ingrandimento *sm* enlargement; (*ottico*) magnification.

ingrandire *vt* to enlarge; (*con microscopio, lente*) to magnify.

▶ **ingrandirsi** *vr* (*di misura*) to get bigger; (*d'importanza*) to become more important.

ingrassare ♦ *vi* to put on weight ♦ *vt* (*animali*) to fatten up; (*motore*) to grease.

ingrediente *sm* ingredient.

ingresso *sm* (*porta*) entrance; (*stanza*) hall; (*permesso di entrare*) admission; '~ **gratuito**' 'admission free'; '~ **libero**' 'admission free'.

ingrossare *vt* (*gambe, fegato*) to cause to swell.

▶ **ingrossarsi** *vr* (*gambe, fegato*) to swell.

ingrosso *avv*: **all'~** (*vendita*) wholesale; (*grossomodo*) about, roughly.

inguine *sm* groin.

inibire *vt* to inhibit.

iniettare *vt* to inject.

iniezione *sf* injection.

inimicare *vt*: **inimicarsi qn** to make an enemy of sb.

inimitabile *agg* inimitable.

ininterrottamente *avv* nonstop.

ininterrotto, -a *agg* continuous, unbroken.

iniziale *agg & sf* initial.

inizialmente *avv* initially.

iniziare *vt & vi* to begin, to start; ~ **qn a qc** to introduce sb to sthg; ~ **a fare qc** to begin o start to do sthg.

iniziativa *sf* initiative; **prendere l'~** to take the initiative.

inizio *sm* start, beginning; **all'~** at the start, at the beginning; **dare ~ a qc** to start o begin sthg; **avere ~** to start, to begin.

innaffiare = **annaffiare**.

innalzare *vt* to erect.

innamorarsi *vr*: ~ (**di qn**) to fall in love (with sb).

innamorato, -a *agg*: ~ (**di qn**) in love (with sb).

innanzi ♦ *avv* in front ♦ *prep* (*davanti a*) in front of; (*prima di*) before.

innanzitutto *avv* first of all.

innato, -a *agg* innate.

innervosire *vt* to make nervous.

▶ **innervosirsi** *vr* to get nervous.

innescare *vt* (*bomba*) to prime; (*fig: fenomeno, meccanismo*) to trigger.

innestare *vt* (*pianta*) to graft; (*meccanismo, marcia*) to engage.

inno *sm* hymn; ~ **nazionale** national anthem.

innocente *agg* innocent.

innocuo, -a *agg* harmless.

innovazione *sf* innovation.

innumerevole *agg* countless.

inodore *agg* odourless.

inoffensivo, -a *agg* inoffensive.

inoltrare *vt* to forward.

▶ **inoltrarsi** *vr* to advance.

inoltrato, -a *agg* late.

inoltre *avv* besides.

inondazione *sf* flood.

inopportuno, -a *agg* inappropriate.

inorridire ♦ *vt* to horrify ♦ *vi* to be horrified.

inosservato, -a *agg*: **passare ~** to go unnoticed.

inquadrare *vt* (*personaggio, avvenimento*) to place; (*con telecamera*): ~ **qn/qc** to get sb/sthg in the shot.

inquadratura *sf* shot.

inqualificabile *agg* contemptible.

inquietante *agg* disturbing.

inquilino, -a *sm, f* tenant.

inquinamento *sm* pollution.

inquinare *vt* (*contaminare*) to pollute; (*fig: prove*) to corrupt.

inquinato, -a *agg* polluted.

insabbiare *vt* to shelve.

▶ **insabbiarsi** *vr* (*nave*) to run aground; (*pratica, progetto*) to be shelved.

insaccato *sm* sausage.

insalata *sf* (*di verdure*) salad; (*lattuga*) lettuce; ~ **mista** mixed salad;

~ di mare seafood salad; **~ di riso** rice salad; **~ russa** Russian salad (*cold diced cooked vegetables mixed with mayonnaise*).

insalatiera *sf* salad bowl.

insaponare *vt* to soap.

▶ **insaponarsi** *vr* to soap o.s.

insapore *agg* tasteless.

insaporire *vt* to flavour.

insaputa *sf*: **all'~ di qn** without sb's knowledge.

inscenare *vt* to stage.

insegna *sf* sign.

insegnamento *sm* teaching.

insegnante *smf* teacher.

insegnare *vt & vi* to teach; **~ qc a qn** to teach sb sthg; **~ a qn a fare qc** to teach sb to do sthg.

inseguire *vt* to pursue.

insenatura *sf* inlet, creek.

insensato, -a *agg* (*persona*) foolish; (*discorso, idea*) senseless.

insensibile *agg* insensitive.

inseparabile *agg* inseparable.

inserire *vt* (*introdurre*) to insert; (*includere*) to put in.

▶ **inserirsi** *vr*: **inserirsi in qc** (*entrare a far parte di*) to become part of sthg.

inserto *sm* insert.

inserviente *smf* attendant.

inserzione *sf* advertisement.

insetticida, -i *sm* insecticide.

insetto *sm* insect.

insicurezza *sf* insecurity.

insicuro, -a *agg* insecure.

insidia *sf* hidden danger.

insieme ◆ *avv* together ◆ *sm* (*totalità*) whole; (MAT) set ◆ *prep*: **~ a o con** with; **mettere ~** (*raccogliere*) to put together; **tutto ~** all together; **tutti ~** all together; **nell'~** taken as a whole.

insignificante *agg* insignificant.

insinuare *vt* to insinuate.

insinuazione *sf* insinuation.

insipido, -a *agg* insipid.

insistente *agg* (*persona, richieste*) insistent; (*pioggia, dolore*) persistent.

insistere *vi* to insist; **~ a o col fare qc** to persist in doing sthg.

insoddisfacente *agg* unsatisfactory.

insoddisfatto, -a *agg*: **~ di** dissatisfied with.

insolazione *sf* sunstroke.

insolente *agg* insolent.

insolito, -a *agg* unusual.

insoluto, -a *agg* (*non risolto*) unsolved; (*non pagato*) outstanding.

insomma ◆ *avv* (*dunque*) well; (*in breve*) in short ◆ *esclam* for Heaven's sake!

insonne *agg* (*persona*) unable to sleep; (*notte*) sleepless.

insonnia *sf* insomnia.

insonnolito, -a *agg* sleepy.

insopportabile *agg* unbearable.

insorgere *vi* (*popolo*) to rise up; (*difficoltà*) to arise.

insospettire *vt* to arouse suspicions in.

▶ **insospettirsi** *vr* to become suspicious.

insozzare *vt* to dirty.

insperato, -a *agg* unhoped-for.

inspiegabile *agg* inexplicable.

inspirare *vt* to breathe in.

installare *vt* to install.

instaurare *vt* to establish.

insù *avv*: **(all')~** upwards.

insuccesso *sm* failure.

insudiciare *vt* to dirty.

▶ **insudiciarsi** *vr* to get dirty.

insufficiente *agg* insufficient.

insulina *sf* insulin.

insultare *vt* to insult.

insulto *sm* insult.

intaccare *vt* to attack; (*fare tacche in*) to cut into; (*risparmi*) to break into.

intanto *avv* (*nel frattempo*) meanwhile.

intarsio *sm* inlay.

intasare *vt* to block.

▶ **intasarsi** *vr* to become blocked.

intatto, -a *agg* (*intero*) intact; (*mai toccato*) untouched.

integrale agg (totale) complete; (pane, farina) wholemeal.

integrare vt to integrate.

▶ **integrarsi** vr to integrate.

integrità sf integrity.

integro, -a agg (intero) intact; (onesto) honest.

intelaiatura sf framework.

intelletto sm intellect.

intellettuale agg & smf intellectual.

intelligente agg intelligent.

intelligenza sf intelligence.

intemperie sfpl bad weather (sg).

intendere vt (capire) to understand; (udire) to hear; (avere intenzione di): ~ fare qc to intend to do sthg; non intende ragioni he won't listen to reason; intendersela con qn to have an affair with sb.

▶ **intendersi di** vr + prep to know about.

intenditore, -trice sm, f expert.

intensificare vt to intensify.

▶ **intensificarsi** vr to intensify.

intensità sf intensity.

intensivo, -a agg intensive.

intenso, -a agg intense.

intento, -a ♦ sm intention ♦ agg: ~ (a fare qc) intent (on doing sthg).

intenzione sf intention; aver ~ di fare qc to intend to do sthg.

interamente avv completely.

intercalare ♦ sm catchphrase ♦ vt to insert.

intercettare vt to intercept.

intercity [inter'siti] sm inv fast train connecting major Italian cities.

interdetto, -a agg taken aback.

interessamento sm (interesse) interest; (intervento) intervention.

interessante agg interesting; in stato ~ (incinta) expecting.

interessare ♦ vt (destare l'interesse di) to interest; (riguardare) to concern ♦ vi: ~ a qn to interest sb; ciò non mi interessa I'm not interested in it.

▶ **interessarsi a** vr + prep to be interested in.

▶ **interessarsi di** vr + prep (per informazioni) to find out about; (per lavoro, hobby) to be interested in.

interessato, -a agg (partecipe) interested; (calcolatore) self-interested.

interesse sm interest; (tornaconto) self-interest.

▶ **interessi** smpl interests.

interferire vi to interfere.

interiezione sf interjection.

interiora sfpl entrails.

interiore agg (lato, parte) interior.

interlocutore, -trice sm, f interlocutor.

intermezzo sm interval.

interminabile agg endless.

intermittente agg intermittent.

internazionale agg international.

Internet sm the Internet; navigare in ~ to surf the Internet.

interno, -a ♦ agg (di dentro) interior, internal; (nazionale) domestic ♦ sm interior; (telefono) extension; (in indirizzo): ~ 20 flat 20; all'~ inside.

▶ **interni** smpl: ministero degli Interni = Home Office (Br), Department of the Interior (Am).

intero, -a agg whole; (prezzo) full; (latte) full-cream; per ~ in full.

interpretare vt to interpret; (recitare) to perform.

interprete smf (traduttore) interpreter; (attore, musicista) performer.

interrogare vt (studente) to examine; (sospetto) to question.

interrogativo, -a ♦ agg (sguardo) enquiring; (GRAMM) interrogative ♦ sm question.

interrogazione sf oral examination.

interrompere vt to interrupt; (linea telefonica, strada) to cut off.

▶ **interrompersi** vr to stop.

interrotto, -a ♦ pp → interrompere ♦ agg cut off.

interruttore *sm* switch.

intersecare *vt* to intersect.

interurbana *sf* long-distance call.

interurbano, -a *agg* (*trasporti*) intercity; (*chiamata*) long-distance.

intervallo *sm* interval.

intervenire *vi* to intervene; (*partecipare*) to take part; (MED) to operate.

intervento *sm* (*intromissione*) intervention; (*partecipazione*) participation; (*discorso*) speech; (MED) operation.

intervenuto, -a *pp* → **intervenire**.

intervista *sf* interview.

intesa *sf* (*tra persone*) understanding; (*tra stati*) agreement.

inteso, -a ♦ *pp* → **intendere** ♦ *agg*: **resta ~ che** it is understood that; **siamo intesi?** are we agreed?

intestare *vt* (*lettera*) to address; **~ qc a qn** (*casa, auto*) to register sthg in sb's name; (*assegno*) to make sthg out to sb.

intestino *sm* intestine.

intimare *vt* to order.

intimidire *vt* to intimidate.

intimità *sf* (*spazio privato*) privacy; (*familiarità*) intimacy.

intimo, -a ♦ *agg* intimate; (*cerimonia, parti*) private; (*interiore*) innermost; (*igiene*) personal ♦ *sm* (*persona*) close friend.

intimorire *vt* to frighten.

intingolo *sm* sauce.

intitolare *vt* (*libro, film*) to entitle; (*via, piazza*): **~ a** to name after.

▶ **intitolarsi** *vr* to be entitled.

intollerabile *agg* unbearable.

intollerante *agg* intolerant.

intolleranza *sf* intolerance.

intonaco, -ci o **-chi** *sm* plaster.

intonare *vt* (*canto*) to intone; (*vestiti*): **~ qc a qc** to match sthg with sthg.

▶ **intonarsi** *vr* to go together.

intontire *vt* to stun.

intorno ♦ *avv* around, round ♦ *prep*: **~ a** around.

intossicare *vt* to poison.

intossicato, -a *agg* poisoned.

intossicazione *sf* poisoning.

intraducibile *agg* untranslatable.

intralciare *vt* to hamper.

intramontabile *agg* timeless.

intramuscolare *agg* → **iniezione**.

intransigente *agg* intransigent.

intransitivo, -a *agg* intransitive.

intraprendente *agg* enterprising.

intraprendere *vt* to undertake.

intrapreso, -a *pp* → **intraprendere**.

intrattabile *agg* (*persona*) intractable; (*prezzo*) non-negotiable.

intrattenere *vt* (*persona*) to entertain; (*relazioni, rapporti*) to maintain.

▶ **intrattenersi** *vr*: **intrattenersi su qc** to dwell on sthg.

intrecciare *vt* (*capelli*) to plait, to braid; (*nastri*) to intertwine.

▶ **intrecciarsi** *vr* (*fili*) to intertwine.

intrigante *agg* scheming.

intrigo, -ghi *sm* (*macchinazione*) intrigue.

introdurre *vt* to introduce; (*moneta*) to insert; '**vietato ~ cani**' 'dogs not allowed'.

▶ **introdursi** *vr* (*uso, tecnica*) to be introduced; (*entrare*) to enter.

introduzione *sf* introduction.

introito *sm* (*incasso*) income.

intromettersi *vr* (*immischiarsi*) to interfere; (*interporsi*) to intervene.

introvabile *agg* not to be found.

introverso, -a *agg* introverted.

intruso, -a *sm, f* intruder.

intuire *vt* (*cogliere*) to grasp; (*accorgersi*) to realize.

intuito *sm* intuition.

intuizione *sf* intuition.

inumidire *vt* to dampen.

▶ **inumidirsi** *vr* to become damp.

inutile *agg* useless; (*superfluo*) pointless.

inutilmente *avv* in vain.

invadente *agg* intrusive.

invadere *vt* to invade.

invaghirsi: invaghirsi di *vr + prep* to take a fancy to.

invalido, -a ♦ *agg* disabled ♦ *sm, f* disabled person.

invano *avv* in vain.

invasione *sf* invasion.

invasore *sm* invader.

invecchiare ♦ *vi* (*persona*) to grow old; (*vino*) to age ♦ *vt* (*vino, formaggio*) to age; (*persona*) to make look older.

invece ♦ *avv* but ♦ *prep*: ~ **di** instead of.

inveire *vi*: ~ **(contro)** to rail (against).

inventare *vt* to invent; **si è inventato tutto** he made it all up.

inventario *sm* (*registrazione*) stocktaking; (*lista*) inventory.

inventore, -trice *sm, f* inventor.

invenzione *sf* invention.

invernale *agg* winter (*dav s*).

inverno *sm* winter; **in** o **d'~** in (the) winter.

inverosimile *agg* unbelievable.

inversione *sf* (*di ordine, tendenza*) inversion; (*di marcia*) U-turn.

inverso, -a *agg & sm* opposite; **fare qc all'~** to do sthg the wrong way round.

invertire *vt* (*ordine*) to invert; ~ **la marcia** to do a U-turn.

investimento *sm* investment.

investire *vt* (*denaro*) to invest; (*persona, animale*) to knock down.

inviare *vt* to send.

inviato, -a *sm, f* (*incaricato*) envoy; (*giornalista*) correspondent.

invidia *sf* envy.

invidiare *vt* to envy; ~ **qc a qn** to envy sb sthg.

invidioso, -a *agg* envious.

invincibile *agg* (*imbattibile*) invincible.

invio *sm* (*spedizione*) dispatching;

(*merci*) consignment.

inviperito, -a *agg* furious.

invischiarsi : invischiarsi in *vr + prep* to get involved in.

invisibile *agg* invisible.

invitare *vt* to invite; ~ **qn a fare qc** (*proporre di*) to invite sb to do sthg; (*sollecitare*) to request sb to do sthg.

invitato, -a *sm, f* guest.

invito *sm* invitation.

invocare *vt* (*Dio*) to invoke; (*chiedere*) to beg for; (*legge, diritto*) to cite.

invogliare *vt* to tempt.

involontario, -a *agg* involuntary.

involtino *sm* thin slice of meat, rolled up and sometimes stuffed; ~ **primavera** spring roll.

involucro *sm* covering.

inzaccherare *vt* to splash with mud.

inzuppare *vt* to soak; (*biscotto*) to dip.

io *pron* I; **sono** ~ it's me; ~ **stesso** I myself.

iodio *sm* iodine.

iogurt = **yogurt**.

Ionio *sm*: **lo** ~, **il mar** ~ the Ionian (Sea).

ipertensione *sf* hypertension.

ipnosi *sf* hypnosis.

ipnotizzare *vt* to hypnotize.

ipocrisia *sf* hypocrisy.

ipocrita, -i, -e ♦ *agg* hypocritical ♦ *smf* hypocrite.

ipoteca, -che *sf* mortgage.

ipotesi *sf inv* hypothesis.

ippica *sf* horse racing.

ippico, -a, -ci, -che *agg* horse (*dav s*).

ippodromo *sm* racecourse.

ippopotamo *sm* hippopotamus.

Iran *sm*: **l'~** Iran.

Iraq *sm*: **l'~** Iraq.

iride *sf* (*di occhio*) iris; (*arcobaleno*) rainbow.

iris *sf inv* iris.

Irlanda *sf*: **l'~** Ireland; **l'~ del Nord** Northern Ireland.

irlandese ◆ *agg* Irish ◆ *smf* Irishman (*f* Irishwoman).

ironia *sf* irony.

ironico, -a, -ci, -che *agg* ironic.

irradiare ◆ *vt* to light up ◆ *vi* to radiate.

irraggiungibile *agg* unreachable.

irragionevole *agg* unreasonable.

irrazionale *agg* irrational.

irreale *agg* unreal.

irrecuperabile *agg* (*oggetto*) irretrievable; (*fig: persona*) irredeemable.

irregolare *agg* irregular; (*discontinuo*) uneven.

irregolarità *sf inv* irregularity; (*discontinuità*) unevenness.

irremovibile *agg* inflexible.

irreparabile *agg* irreparable.

irrequieto, -a *agg* restless.

irresponsabile *agg* irresponsible.

irreversibile *agg* irreversible.

irriducibile *agg* unyielding.

irrigare *vt* to irrigate.

irrigidirsi *vr* to stiffen.

irrilevante *agg* insignificant.

irrisorio, -a *agg* ridiculous.

irritabile *agg* irritable.

irritante *agg* irritating.

irritare *vt* to irritate.

▶ **irritarsi** *vr* to become irritated.

irrompere : irrompere in *v + prep* to burst into.

irrotto, -a *pp* → **irrompere**.

irruente *agg* impetuous.

irruzione *sf* raid.

iscritto, -a ◆ *pp* → **iscrivere** ◆ *agg*: **essere ~ a qc** (*ad un circolo, partito*) to be a member of sthg; (*all'università*) to be enrolled in sthg; (*ad un esame*) to be entered for sthg; **per ~** in writing.

iscrivere *vt*: **~ qn (a qc)** (*scuola*) to register sb (at sthg), to enrol sb (at sthg); (*corso*) to register sb (for sthg), to enrol sb (for sthg).

▶ **iscriversi** *vr*: **iscriversi (a)** (*circolo, partito*) to become a member (of); (*università*) to enrol (in); (*esame*) to enter.

iscrizione *sf* (*a università*) enrolment; (*a esame*) entry; (*a partito*) membership; (*funeraria*) inscription.

Islanda *sf*: **l'~** Iceland.

islandese ◆ *agg* Icelandic ◆ *smf* Icelander.

isola *sf* island; **~ pedonale** pedestrian precinct.

isolamento *sm* (*solitudine*) isolation; (*elettrico, termico*) insulation; (*acustico*) soundproofing.

isolante ◆ *agg* insulating ◆ *sm* insulator.

isolare *vt* (*tenere lontano*) to isolate; (*da freddo, corrente elettrica*) to insulate; (*da rumore*) to soundproof.

▶ **isolarsi** *vr* to cut o.s. off.

isolato, -a ◆ *agg* isolated ◆ *sm* block.

ispettore *sm* inspector.

ispezionare *vt* to inspect.

ispezione *sf* inspection.

ispirare *vt* to inspire.

▶ **ispirarsi a** *vr + prep* to draw one's inspiration from.

Israele *sm* Israel.

issare *vt* to hoist.

istantanea *sf* snapshot.

istantaneo, -a *agg* instantaneous, instant.

istante *sm* instant; **all'~** instantly, at once.

isterico, -a, -ci, -che *agg* hysterical.

istigare *vt*: **~ qn a fare qc** to incite sb to do sthg.

istinto *sm* instinct.

istituire *vt* to institute.

istituto *sm* (*organismo*) institute; (*universitario*) department; **~ di bellezza** beauty salon.

istituzione *sf* institution; **le istituzioni** (*le autorità*) the Establishment.

istmo *sm* (GEOG) isthmus.

istrice *sm* (*animale*) porcupine.

istruire vt (insegnare a) to teach; (informare) to instruct.
istruito, -a agg educated.
istruttore, -trice sm, f instructor.
istruzione sf (insegnamento) education; (cultura) learning.
▶ **istruzioni** sfpl: **istruzioni (per l'uso)** instructions (for use).
Italia sf: l'~ Italy.
italiano, -a agg & sm, f Italian.
itinerario sm (percorso) route; (descrizione) itinerary; ~ **turistico** (percorso) tourist route.
Iugoslavia sf: la ~ Yugoslavia.
IVA sf (abbr di imposta sul valore aggiunto) VAT.

J

jazz [dʒɛts] sm jazz.
jeans [dʒins] ◆ smpl jeans ◆ sm (tessuto) denim.
jeep® [dʒip] sf inv Jeep®.
jolly ['dʒɔlli] sm inv joker.
Jonio = **Ionio**.
jota sf bean soup with onions and turnips marinated in wine (speciality of Friuli).
Jugoslavia = **Iugoslavia**.
juke-box [dʒuːk'bɔks] sm inv juke-box.

K

karaoke sm inv (gioco) karaoke; (locale) karaoke bar.
karatè sm karate.
Kenia sm: il ~ Kenya.
kg (abbr di chilogrammo) kg.

killer smf inv killer.
kitsch [kitʃ] agg inv kitsch.
kiwi ['kiwi] sm inv kiwi fruit.
km (abbr di chilometro) km.
k.o. avv: **mettere qn ~** to knock sb out.
koala sm inv koala.
K-way® [ki'wei] sm inv cagoule.

L

l' → **la, lo**.
la ◆ (l' dav vocale e h) art f the, → **il** ◆ pron (persona) her; (animale, cosa) it; (forma di cortesia) you.
là avv there; **di ~** (nella stanza accanto) in there; (moto da luogo) from there; (nei paraggi) over there; **al di ~ di** beyond.
labbro (pl f **labbra**) sm (ANAT) lip.
labirinto sm (di strade, corridoi) labyrinth; (giardino) maze.
laboratorio sm (scientifico) laboratory; (artigianale) workshop; ~ **linguistico** language laboratory.
laburista, -i, -e agg: **il partito ~** the Labour Party.
lacca, -che sf (per capelli) lacquer, hair spray; (vernice) lacquer.
laccio sm lace.
lacerare vt to tear, to rip.
▶ **lacerarsi** vr to tear.
lacero, -a agg torn.
lacrima sf tear; **in lacrime** in tears.
lacrimogeno agg m → **gas**.
lacuna sf gap.
ladro, -a sm, f thief.
laggiù avv (in basso) down there; (lontano) over there.

lagnarsi vr (piagnucolare) to moan, to groan; (protestare): ~ **(di)** to complain (about).
lago, -ghi sm lake.

I LAGHI
The most fámous of the many Italian lakes are undoubtedly those in northern Italy: Lake Garda (the largest), Lake Maggiore and Lake Como. Millions of Italian and foreign tourists alike visit them every year, attracted by their scenic splendour and pleasant climate, the grand villas and lush gardens lining their shores, and the many varieties of wild flower to be found in the area. In summer the lakes attract swimmers, sunbathers and water-sports enthusiasts looking for an alternative to the coastal resorts.

laguna sf lagoon.
laico, -a, -ci, -che agg lay (dav s).
lama sf blade.
lamentarsi vr (emettere lamenti) to groan, to moan; ~ **(di)** (dimostrarsi insoddisfatto) to complain (about).
lamentela sf complaint, complaining (sg).
lametta sf razor blade.
lamiera sf sheet metal.
lampada sf lamp; **fare la** ~ to use a sunlamp; ~ **da tavolo** table lamp.
lampadario sm chandelier.
lampadina sf light bulb; ~ **tascabile** torch (Br), flashlight (Am).
lampeggiare vi to flash.
lampeggiatore sm (freccia) indicator; (di ambulanza) flashing light.
lampione sm streetlight.
lampo ◆ sm (fulmine) flash of lightning; (bagliore) flash ◆ sf inv (cerniera) zip (Br), zipper (Am).
lampone sm raspberry.
lana sf wool; **pura** ~ **vergine** pure new wool.
lancetta sf hand.
lancia, -ce sf (arma) lance; (imbar-

cazione) launch.
lanciare vt (pietra, palla) to throw; (missile) to launch; (grido) to give; (insulto) to hurl; (fig: appello, moda, prodotto) to launch.
▶ **lanciarsi** vr to throw o.s.; **lanciarsi in qc** (mare) to throw o.s. into sthg; (impresa) to embark on sthg.
lancinante agg piercing, shooting.
lancio sm (tiro) throw; (di prodotti, missile) launch.
languido, -a agg languid.
languore sm (di stomaco) hunger pangs (pl).
lapide sf (funeraria) tombstone; (commemorativa) plaque.
lapis sm inv pencil.
lapsus sm inv slip.
lardo sm lard, bacon fat.
larghezza sf (dimensione) width, breadth; (abbondanza) generosity.
largo, -a, -ghi, -ghe ◆ agg wide, broad; (indumento) loose; (percentuale, parte) large ◆ sm width; (piazza) square; (alto mare): **andare al** ~ to take to the open sea; **è ~ 10 metri** it's 10 metres wide; **stare** o **tenersi alla larga (da)** to keep one's distance (from); **farsi** ~ to push one's way.
larva sf (insetto) larva.
lasagne sfpl lasagne (sg).
lasciare ◆ vt to leave; (cessare di tenere) to let go of; **posso** ~ **i bagagli in camera?** can I leave the luggage in the room?; ~ **la porta aperta** to leave the door open; ~ **qn in pace** to leave sb in peace; **lasciar detto a qn che ...** to leave sb word that ...; ~ **a desiderare** to leave a lot to be desired; **prendere** o ~ take it or leave it; ~ **la presa** to let go ◆ v aus: **lasciami vedere** let me see; **lascia che faccia come vuole** let him do as he wants; **lascia perdere!** forget it!; **lasciar credere qc a qn** to let sb believe sthg; **lascialo stare!** leave him alone!
▶ **lasciarsi** vr (separarsi) to leave

each other; **lasciarsi andare** to let o.s. go; **lasciarsi convincere** to allow o.s. to be persuaded.

laser *sm inv & agg inv* laser.

lassativo *sm* laxative.

lassù *avv* up there.

lastra *sf* (*di ghiaccio, vetro*) sheet; (*di pietra*) slab; (*radiografia*) plate.

laterale *agg* lateral, side (*dav s*).

latino, -a *agg & sm* Latin.

latino-americano, -a *agg* Latin-American.

latitudine *sf* latitude.

lato *sm* side; **a ~** (*di qc*) beside (sthg); **da un ~ ... dall'altro ...** on the one hand ... on the other hand ...

latta *sf* tin.

lattaio, -a *sm, f* milkman (*f* milk-woman).

lattante *smf* baby.

latte *sm* milk; **~ detergente** cleansing milk; **~ intero** full cream milk; **~ magro** *o* **scremato** skimmed milk; **~ in polvere** powdered milk; **~ di soia** soya milk.

latteria *sf* dairy.

latticini *smpl* dairy products.

lattina *sf* can.

lattuga, -ghe *sf* lettuce.

laurea *sf* degree.

laurearsi *vr* to graduate; **~ in qc** to graduate in sthg.

laureato, -a *agg & sm, f* graduate; **è ~ in legge** he has a law degree.

lava *sf* lava.

lavabo *sm* washbasin (Br), wash-bowl (Am).

lavaggio *sm* washing; **~ automatico** (*per auto*) car wash.

lavagna *sf* blackboard.

lavanda *sf* lavender; **fare una ~ gastrica a qn** to pump sb's stomach.

lavanderia *sf* laundry; **~ automatica** launderette; **~ a secco** dry cleaner's.

lavandino *sm* sink.

lavapiatti *sf inv* dishwasher.

lavare *vt* to wash; **~ a secco qc** to dry-clean sthg; **lavarsi le mani** to wash one's hands; **lavarsi i denti** to clean one's teeth.

▶ **lavarsi** *vr* to wash o.s.

lavasecco *sm inv* o *sf inv* dry cleaner's.

lavastoviglie *sf inv* dishwasher.

lavatrice *sf* washing machine.

lavorare *vi & vt* to work; **~ a maglia** to knit.

lavorativo, -a *agg* working (*dav s*).

lavorato, -a *agg* (*mobile, tessuto*) elaborate; (*terreno*) cultivated.

lavoratore, -trice *sm, f* worker.

lavorazione *sf* (*di legno*) carving; (*di cotone*) manufacture.

lavoro *sm* work; (*occupazione*) work, job; **~ nero** moonlighting; '**lavori in corso**' 'men at work'; **lavori stradali** road works.

Lazio *sm* Lazio (*region of central Italy*).

le ◆ *art fpl* the, → **il** ◆ *pron* (*complemento oggetto*) them; (*a lei*) (to) her; (*forma di cortesia*) (to) you.

leader ['lider] *smf inv* leader.

leale *agg* loyal.

lecca lecca *sm inv* lollipop.

leccare *vt* to lick.

lecito, -a *agg* permitted.

lega, -ghe *sf* (*associazione*) league; (*alleanza politica*) alliance; (*di metalli*) alloy.

legale ◆ *agg* legal ◆ *smf* (*avvocato*) lawyer.

legalizzare *vt* to legalize.

legame *sm* (*sentimentale*) tie; (*nesso*) link.

legare *vt* (*con catena, laccio*) to tie (up); (*sog: sentimento, interesse*) to bind; (*fatti*) to link.

legge *sf* law.

leggenda *sf* (*favola*) legend; (*didascalia*) key.

leggendario, -a *agg* legendary.

leggere *vt & vi* to read.

leggerezza *sf* (*di materiale, corpo*)

lightness; (*fig: sconsideratezza*) thoughtlessness.

leggero, -a *agg* light; (*caffè, tè*) weak; (*di poca importanza*) slight.

legittimo, -a *agg* legitimate; legittima difesa self-defence.

legna *sf* firewood.

legname *sm* wood.

legno *sm* (*materia*) wood; (*pezzo*) piece of wood, stick.

legumi *smpl* pulses.

lei *pron* (*soggetto*) she; (*complemento oggetto, con preposizione*) her; (*forma di cortesia*) you; è ~ it's her; io sto bene, e ~? I'm fine, and you?; ~ stessa she herself/you yourself.

lentamente *avv* slowly.

lente *sf* lens; ~ di ingrandimento magnifying glass; lenti a contatto contact lenses.

lentezza *sf* slowness.

lenticchie *sfpl* lentils.

lento, -a *agg* slow; (*allentato*) loose *sm* slow dance.

lenza *sf* fishing line.

lenzuolo (*pl f* lenzuola) *sm* sheet.

leone *sm* lion.

► **Leone** *sm* Leo.

leopardo *sm* leopard.

lepre *sf* hare; ~ in salmì *marinated hare in a sauce made from its offal.*

lesbica, -che *sf* lesbian.

lesione *sf* lesion.

lesso, -a *agg* boiled *sm* boiled beef.

letale *agg* lethal.

letame *sm* manure.

lettera *sf* letter; alla ~ literally.

► **lettere** *sfpl* (*facoltà*) = arts.

letterario, -a *agg* literary.

letteratura *sf* literature.

lettino *sm* (*del medico*) couch; (*per bambini*) cot; ~ (solare) sunbed.

letto, -a *pp* → **leggere** *sm* bed; andare a ~ to go to bed; ~ matrimoniale o a due piazze double bed; ~ a una piazza single bed; letti a castello bunk beds; letti gemelli twin beds.

lettore, -trice *sm, f* (*di libro, giornale*) reader; (*di università*) foreign language assistant *sm*: ~ di compact CD player.

lettura *sf* reading.

leva *sf* lever; (*militare*) conscription; fare ~ su qc (*fig*) to play on sthg; ~ del cambio gear lever (Br), gear shift (Am).

levante *sm* east.

levare *vt* (*togliere*) to remove; (*alzare*) to raise.

► **levarsi** *vr* (*vento*) to get up, to rise.

levata *sf* collection.

levatoio *agg m* → **ponte**.

levigare *vt* to smooth.

lezione *sf* lesson; (*all'università*) lecture.

lezioso, -a *agg* affected.

lezzo *sm* stink.

li *pron mpl* them.

lì *avv* there; essere ~ (~) per fare qc to be on the point of doing sthg; da ~ in poi (*tempo*) from then on; (*spazio*) from that point onwards.

Libano *sm*: il ~ Lebanon.

libeccio *sm* southwest wind.

libellula *sf* dragonfly.

liberale *agg* liberal.

liberamente *avv* freely.

liberare *vt* (*prigioniero*) to free, to release; (*camera, posto*) to vacate.

► **liberarsi** *vr* (*annullare un impegno*) to free o.s.; liberarsi di to get rid of.

libero, -a *agg* free; essere ~ di fare qc to be free to do sthg; ~ professionista self-employed professional; 'libero' (*su taxi*) 'for hire'; (*in toilette*) 'vacant'.

libertà *sf inv* freedom; (*permesso*) liberty; mettere in ~ qn to free sb.

Libia *sf*: la ~ Libya.

libreria *sf* (*negozio*) bookshop; (*mobile*) bookcase.

libretto *sm* (MUS) libretto; ~ degli assegni cheque book; ~ di circolazione log book; ~ di risparmio savings book; ~ universitario university report card.

libro *sm* book; ~ **giallo** thriller.

licenza *sf* (*autorizzazione*) licence; (*militare*) leave; ~ **media** school-leaving certificate.

licenziamento *sm* dismissal.

licenziare *vt* to dismiss.

▶ **licenziarsi** *vr* to resign.

liceo *sm* secondary school (Br), high school (Am).

lido *sm* beach; **il Lido di Venezia** the Venice Lido.

lieto, -a *agg* (*contento*): ~ **di conoscerla!** pleased to meet you!; **molto ~!** pleased to meet you!

lievitare *vi* to rise.

lievito *sm* yeast; ~ **di birra** brewer's yeast.

Liguria *sf*: **la** ~ Liguria.

lillà *agg inv* & *sm inv* lilac.

lima *sf* file.

limetta *sf*: ~ **per unghie** nail file.

limitare *vt* to limit, to restrict.

▶ **limitarsi** *vr*: **limitarsi a fare qc** to limit o.s. to do sthg; **limitarsi nel bere** to restrict one's drinking.

limitato, -a *agg* limited.

limite *sm* (*confine*) border; (*punto estremo*) limit; ~ **di velocità** speed limit; **entro certi limiti** within certain limits; **al** ~ if the worst comes to the worst.

limitrofo, -a *agg* neighbouring.

limonata *sf* lemonade.

limone *sm* lemon.

limpido, -a *agg* clear.

linea *sf* line; (*itinerario*) route; **è caduta la** ~ (*al telefono*) we have been cut off; **rimanere** o **restare in** ~ (*al telefono*) to hold the line; **mantenere la** ~ to look after one's figure; **avere qualche** ~ **di febbre** to have a slight temperature; **linee urbane** local buses; **in** ~ **d'aria** as the crow flies; **in** ~ **di massima** as a general rule; **a grandi linee** in broad outline.

lineare *agg* linear.

lineetta *sf* dash.

lingua *sf* (ANAT & CULIN) tongue; (*linguaggio*) language; ~ **madre** mother tongue; ~ **straniera** foreign language.

linguaggio *sm* language; ~ **dei segni** sign language.

linguetta *sf* tongue.

linguistico, -a, -ci, -che *agg* linguistic.

lino *sm* linen.

linoleum *sm* linoleum.

liofilizzato, -a *agg* freeze-dried.

liquefare *vt* to melt.

▶ **liquefarsi** *vr* to melt.

liquefatto, -a *pp* → **liquefare**.

liquidare *vt* (*società, beni*) to liquidate; (*merce*) to sell off; (*sbarazzarsi di*) to get rid of; (*fig: questione, problema*) to solve.

liquidazione *sf* (*di merci*) selling off, clearance; (*indennità*) severance pay.

liquido, -a ◆ *agg* liquid ◆ *sm* liquid; (*denaro*) cash.

liquirizia *sf* liquorice.

liquore *sm* liqueur.

lira *sf* lira; **non avere una** ~ not to have a penny (Br), not to have a dime (Am).

lirica *sf* opera.

lirico, -a, -ci, -che *agg* (*musica*) opera (*dav s*), operatic.

lisca, -sche *sf* fishbone.

liscio, -a, -sci, -sce ◆ *agg* (*pietra, pelle*) smooth; (*capelli*) straight; (*whisky*) neat ◆ *sm* (*ballo*) ballroom dance; **andar** ~ to go smoothly.

lista *sf* list; **essere in** ~ **d'attesa** to be on a waiting list; ~ **dei vini** wine list.

listino *sm*: ~ **(dei) prezzi** price list; ~ **dei cambi** exchange rate.

Lit *abbr* = **lira**.

lite *sf* quarrel.

litigare *vi* to quarrel.

litigio *sm* quarrel.

litorale *sm* coast.

litoraneo, -a *agg* coastal.

litro *sm* litre.

livello *sm* (*altezza, piano*) level; ~ **del mare** sea level.

livido, -a ♦ *agg* (*per percosse*) black and blue ♦ *sm* bruise; **~ per il freddo** blue with cold.

lo ♦ *art* the, → **il** ♦ *pron* (*persona*) him; (*animale, cosa*) it; **~ so** I know.

locale ♦ *agg* local ♦ *sm* (*stanza*) room; (*luogo pubblico*) premises (*pl*); **~ notturno** night club.

località *sf inv* locality.

locanda *sf* inn.

locandina *sf* theatre poster.

locomotiva *sf* locomotive.

lodare *vt* to praise.

lode *sf* (*elogio*) praise; **laurearsi con 110 e ~** to graduate with first-class honours (Br), to graduate summa cum laude (Am).

loggia, -ge *sf* loggia.

loggione *sm*: **il ~** the gods (*pl*).

logica *sf* logic.

logico, -a, -ci, -che *agg* logical.

logorare *vt* to wear out.

▶ **logorarsi** *vr* to wear out.

logorio *sm* wear and tear.

Lombardia *sf*: **la ~** Lombardy.

lombardo, -a *agg* Lombard.

lombata *sf* loin.

lombrico, -chi *sm* earthworm.

Londra *sf* London.

longitudine *sf* longitude.

lontananza *sf* (*distanza*) distance; (*di persona*) absence; **in ~** in the distance.

lontano, -a ♦ *agg* (*luogo*) distant, faraway; (*nel tempo*) far off; (*assente*) absent; (*parente*) distant ♦ *avv* far; **è ~?** is it far?; **è ~ 3 chilometri** it's 3 kilometres from here; **~ da** far (away) from; **da ~** from far away; **più ~** farther.

loquace *agg* talkative.

lordo, -a *agg* gross.

loro *pron* (*soggetto*) they; (*complemento oggetto, con preposizione*) them; (*form: complemento di termine*) (to) them; **~ stessi** they themselves.

▶ **il loro** ♦ (*f* la loro, *mpl* i loro, *fpl* le loro) *agg* their ♦ *pron* theirs.

losco, -a, -schi, -sche *agg* suspicious, shady.

lotta *sf* struggle, fight.

lottare *vi* to fight, to struggle.

lotteria *sf* lottery.

lotto *sm* (*gioco*) lottery; (*di terreno*) lot.

lozione *sf* lotion.

L.P. *sm inv* LP.

lubrificante *sm* lubricant.

lucchetto *sm* padlock.

luccicare *vi* to sparkle.

lucciola *sf* glow-worm, firefly.

luce *sf* light; (*elettricità*) electricity; **dare alla ~** to give birth to; **mettere in ~ qc** to highlight sthg; **~ del sole** sunlight; **luci d'arresto** brake lights; **luci di direzione** indicators; **luci di posizione** parking lights; **film a luci rosse** porno film.

lucernario *sm* skylight.

lucertola *sf* lizard.

lucidare *vt* to polish.

lucidatrice *sf* floor polisher.

lucido, -a ♦ *agg* (*pavimento, tessuto*) shiny; (*fig: mente, persona*) lucid ♦ *sm* (*da proiettore*) acetate; **~ da scarpe** shoe polish.

lucro *sm* profit.

luganega, -ghe *sf* type of sausage (*a speciality of Veneto and Lombardy*).

luglio *sm* July, → **settembre**.

lugubre *agg* gloomy.

lui *pron* (*soggetto*) he; (*complemento oggetto, con preposizione*) him; **è ~** it's him; **~ stesso** he himself.

lumaca, -che *sf* snail.

lumacone *sm* (large) slug.

lume *sm* lamp; **a ~ di candela** by candlelight.

luminaria *sf* illuminations (*pl*).

luminoso, -a *agg* luminous, bright.

luna *sf* moon; **~ di miele** honeymoon; **~ park** funfair; **~ piena** full moon.

lunario *sm*: **sbarcare il ~** to make ends meet.

lunedì *sm inv* Monday, → **sabato**.

lunghezza *sf* length; **~ d'onda** wavelength.

lungo, -a, -ghi, -ghe agg long; (caffè) weak; **è ~ 3 metri** it's 3 metres long; **saperla lunga** to know what's what; **a ~** for a long time; **di gran lunga** by far; **in ~ e in largo** far and wide; **andare per le lunghe** to drag on.

lungofiume sm embankment.

lungolago, -ghi sm road around a lake.

lungomare sm promenade, seafront.

lunotto sm rear window.

luogo, -ghi sm place; (di delitto, incidente) scene; **aver ~** to take place; **dare ~ a qc** to give rise to sthg; **~ comune** commonplace; **~ di culto** place of worship; **~ di nascita** place of birth; **del ~** local; **in primo ~** in the first place.

lupini smpl lupins.

lupo sm wolf.

lurido, -a agg filthy.

lusinga, -ghe sf flattery.

lusingare vt to flatter.

lussare vt to dislocate.

Lussemburgo sm: **il ~** Luxembourg.

lusso sm luxury; **di ~** de luxe, luxury.

lussuoso, -a agg luxurious.

lussureggiante agg luxuriant.

lussuria sf lust.

lustrare vt to polish.

lustrino sm sequin.

lustro, -a agg shiny.

lutto sm mourning; **essere in ~** to be in mourning.

M

ma cong but.

macabro, -a agg macabre.

macché esclam of course not!

maccheroni smpl macaroni (sg); **~ alla chitarra** flat ribbons of egg pasta in a sauce of either tomatoes and chillis, or lamb (a speciality of Abruzzo).

macchia sf (chiazza) spot, stain; (di colore) spot; (bosco) scrub.

macchiare vt to stain, to mark.

▶ **macchiarsi** vr (persona) to get stains o marks on one's clothes; (abiti, tappeto) to become stained o marked.

macchiato, -a agg stained.

macchina sf (automobile) car; (apparecchio) machine; **andare in ~** to go by car, to drive; **~ fotografica** camera; **~ da scrivere** typewriter.

macchinario sm machinery.

macchinetta sf (caffettiera) percolator; **~ mangiasoldi** slot machine.

macchinista, -i sm (di treno) driver; (di nave) engineer.

macedonia sf fruit salad.

macellaio, -a sm, f butcher.

macelleria sf butcher's.

macerie sfpl rubble (sg).

macigno sm rock, boulder.

macinacaffè sm inv coffee grinder.

macinapepe sm inv pepper grinder.

macinare vt (grano) to mill, to grind; (caffè, pepe) to grind; (carne) to mince (Br), to grind (Am).

macinato, -a ◆ agg minced (Br), ground (Am) ◆ sm mince (Br), ground beef (Am).

macrobiotica sf health foods (pl).

Madonna sf Madonna.

madre sf mother.

madrelingua ◆ agg inv mother tongue (dav s) ◆ sf mother tongue.

madreperla sf mother-of-pearl.

madrina sf godmother.

maestrale sm northwest wind.

maestro, -a ◆ sm, f teacher ◆ sm (MUS) maestro; (artigiano, artista) master; **~ di tennis** tennis coach.

mafia sf Mafia.

mafioso, -a ◆ agg of the Mafia, Mafia (dav s) ◆ sm, f member of the Mafia.

magari ◆ *esclam* if only! ◆ *avv* maybe.

magazzino *sm* warehouse.

maggio *sm* May; **il primo ~** May Day, → **settembre**.

IL PRIMO MAGGIO

Since the end of the Second World War, May 1 has been celebrated all over Italy as a workers' festival. It is a national holiday and is the occasion of trade union meetings and marches in the cities.

---

maggiorana *sf* marjoram.

maggioranza *sf* majority; **nella ~ dei casi** in the majority of cases.

maggiore ◆ *agg* (*comparativo: più grande, più numeroso*) larger, bigger; (*di quantità*) greater; (*più importante*) major, more important; (*più vecchio*) elder, older; (*superlativo: più grande, più numeroso*) largest, biggest; (*di quantità*) greatest; (*più importante*) most important; (*più vecchio*) eldest, oldest ◆ *sm* (MIL) major; **andare per la ~** to be very popular; **la ~ età** the age of majority; **la maggior parte (di)** the majority (of).

maggiorenne ◆ *agg* of age ◆ *smf* person who has come of age.

maggiormente *avv* much more.

magia *sf* magic.

magico, -a, -ci, -che *agg* magic.

magistratura *sf* magistracy.

maglia *sf* (*indumento*) sweater, jersey; (*di sportivo, tessuto*) jersey; (*di catena*) link; **lavorare a ~** to knit.

maglieria *sf* knitwear.

maglietta *sf* T-shirt; (*canottiera*) vest (Br), undershirt (Am).

maglione *sm* sweater, jumper.

magnate *sm* magnate.

magnetico, -a, -ci, -che *agg* magnetic.

magnifico, -a, -ci, -che *agg* magnificent.

mago, -a, -ghi, -ghe *sm, f* (*stregone*) sorcerer (*f* sorceress); (*illusionista*) magician.

magro, -a *agg* (*persona*) thin; (*formaggio, yogurt*) low-fat; (*carne*) lean; (*fig: scarso*) meagre.

mai *avv* never; (*qualche volta*): **l'hai ~ visto?** have you ever seen him?; **non ... ~** never; **~ più** never again.

maiale *sm* (*animale*) pig; (*carne*) pork; **~ alle mele** pork with brandy-flavoured apple sauce.

maiolica *sf* majolica.

maionese *sf* mayonnaise.

mais *sm* maize.

maiuscola *sf* capital letter.

maiuscolo, -a *agg* capital.

mal = **male**.

malafede *sf* bad faith.

malaga *sm*: **gelato al ~** rum and raisin ice cream.

malandato, -a *agg* (*persona*) in poor shape; (*oggetto*) shabby.

malanno *sm* ailment.

malapena : a malapena *avv* hardly, scarcely.

malato, -a ◆ *agg* ill, sick ◆ *sm, f* sick person, patient; **essere ~ di cuore** to have a bad heart.

malattia *sf* illness, disease; **essere in ~** to be on sick leave.

malavita *sf* underworld.

malconcio, -a, -ci, -ce *agg* in a sorry state.

maldestro, -a *agg* (*poco abile*) inept; (*impacciato, goffo*) clumsy.

maldicenza *sf* malicious gossip.

male ◆ *sm* (*ingiustizia*) evil; (*dolore*) pain; (*malattia*) complaint ◆ *avv* badly; **ti fa ~?** does it hurt?; **mi fanno ~ i piedi** my feet hurt; **fare del ~ a qn** to hurt sb; **non c'è ~!** not bad!; **mal d'aereo** airsickness; **mal d'auto** carsickness; **mal di gola** sore throat; **mal di mare** seasickness; **mal di stomaco** stomachache; **mal di testa** headache; **andare a ~** to go off; **restarci o rimanerci ~** to be disappointed; **sentirsi ~** to feel ill; **di ~ in peggio** from bad to worse.

maledetto, -a ♦ pp → **maledire**
♦ agg damned.

maledire vt to curse.

maledizione sf curse.

maleducato, -a agg rude.

maleducazione sf rudeness.

maleodorante agg smelly.

malessere sm (fisico) ailment; (mentale) uneasiness.

malfamato, -a agg notorious.

malfattore, -trice sm, f wrongdoer.

malfermo, -a agg unsteady.

malformazione sf malformation, deformity.

malgrado ♦ prep in spite of ♦ cong although; **mio ~** against my will.

malignità sf inv (d'animo) malice; (insinuazione) spiteful remark.

maligno, -a agg (persona, commento) malicious; (MED) malignant.

malinconia sf melancholy.

malinconico, -a, -ci, -che agg gloomy.

malincuore : a malincuore avv reluctantly.

malintenzionato, -a agg ill-intentioned.

malinteso sm misunderstanding.

malizia sf cunning, malice.

malizioso, -a agg malicious.

malleabile agg malleable.

malmenare vt to beat up.

malnutrizione sf malnutrition.

malore sm: **ho avuto un ~** I suddenly felt ill.

malridotto, -a agg in a bad state.

malsano, -a agg unhealthy.

Malta sf Malta.

maltagliati smpl soup pasta, cut into irregular shapes.

maltempo sm bad weather.

malto sm malt.

maltrattare vt to ill-treat.

malumore sm bad temper; **essere di ~** to be in a bad mood.

malvagio, -a, -gi, -gie agg wicked.

malvolentieri avv unwillingly.

mamma sf mum (Br), mom (Am); **~ mia!** my goodness!

mammella sf (di donna) breast; (di animale) udder.

mammifero sm mammal.

mammismo sm close attachment between mother and son.

manager ['mɛnadʒɛr] smf inv manager (f manageress).

manata sf slap.

mancanza sf (scarsità, assenza) lack; (colpa) fault; **sentire la ~ di qn** to miss sb; **in ~ di** for lack of.

mancare ♦ vi (non esserci) to be missing; (essere lontano) to be away; (form: morire) to pass away ♦ vt (colpo, bersaglio) to miss; **è mancata la luce per due ore** the electricity was off for two hours; **mi manchi molto** I miss you a lot; **manca il latte** there's no milk; **mi manca il tempo** I haven't got the time; **mi mancano mille lire** I still need a thousand lire; **ci è mancato poco che cadesse** it nearly fell; **manca un quarto alle quattro** it's quarter to four.

▶ **mancare a** v + prep (promessa) to fail to keep.

▶ **mancare di** v + prep to lack.

mancia, -ce sf tip; **dare la ~ (a qn)** to tip (sb).

manciata sf handful.

mancino, -a agg left-handed.

manco avv (fam) not even; **~ per sogno** o **per idea** I wouldn't dream of it.

mandarancio sm clementine.

mandare vt to send; (grido) to give; **~ a chiamare qn** to send for sb; **~ via qn** to send sb away; **~ avanti qn** to send sb on ahead; **~ avanti qc** to provide for sthg; **~ giù** to swallow.

mandarino sm mandarin (orange), tangerine.

mandata sf (di chiave) turn; **chiudere a doppia ~** to double-lock.

mandato sm (DIR) warrant; **~ d'arresto** arrest warrant.

mandibola sf jaw.

mandolino sm mandolin.

mandorla sf almond.

maneggiare vt (strumenti, attrezzi) to handle; (denaro) to manage, to deal with.

maneggio sm riding school.

manetta sf handle.

▶ **manette** sfpl handcuffs.

mangereccio agg m → **fungo**.

mangiare ♦ vt (cibo) to eat; (fig: patrimonio) to squander; (negli scacchi) to take ♦ vi to eat; **far da ~** to do the cooking; **mangiarsi le parole** to mumble.

mangiasoldi agg inv → **macchinetta**.

mangime sm fodder.

mangione, -a sm, f glutton.

mania sf (fissazione) obsession; **avere la ~ di fare qc** to have a habit of doing sthg.

maniaco, -a, -ci, -che ♦ agg manic ♦ sm, f maniac.

manica, -che sf sleeve; **a maniche corte o a mezze maniche** short-sleeved.

▶ **Manica** sf: **la Manica, il Canale della Manica** the (English) Channel.

manicaretto sm delicacy.

manichino sm (di negozio) dummy; (per artisti) model.

manico, -ci sm handle.

manicomio sm (ospedale) mental hospital; (fig: confusione) madhouse.

manicure sf inv (persona) manicurist; (trattamento) manicure.

maniera sf way; (stile) style; **in ~ che** so that; **in ~ da fare qc** so as to do sthg; **in tutte le maniere** at all costs.

manifestare ♦ vt to show ♦ vi to demonstrate.

▶ **manifestarsi** vr to appear.

manifestazione sf (corteo) demonstration; (di sentimento) show; (di malattia) symptom; (spettacolo) event.

manifesto sm (cartellone) poster.

maniglia sf (di porta) handle; (di autobus) strap.

manipolare vt (con le mani) to handle; (fig: alterare) to manipulate.

mano, -i sf hand; (di vernice) coat; **dare una ~ a qn** to give sb a hand; **darsi la ~** to shake hands; **fatto a ~** handmade; **di seconda ~** second-hand; **man ~** gradually; **andare contro ~** to drive on the wrong side of the road; **essere alla ~** to be easygoing; **fare man bassa** to take everything; **fuori ~** out of the way; **stare con le mani in ~** to twiddle one's thumbs.

manodopera sf (lavoratori) workforce; (costo) labour.

manomesso, -a pp → **manomettere**.

manomettere vt (serratura) to force.

manopola sf knob, control.

manovale sm labourer.

manovella sf handle.

manovra sf manoeuvre.

manovrare ♦ vt (congegno) to operate; (fig: persona) to manipulate ♦ vi (MIL) to manoeuvre; (fig: tramare) to plot.

manrovescio sm slap.

mansarda sf attic.

mansione sf task, job.

mantella sf cape.

mantello sm (di animale) coat; (indumento) cloak.

mantenere vt to keep; (sostentare) to support.

▶ **mantenersi** vr (pagarsi da vivere) to support o.s.; (conservarsi) to stay, to keep.

mantenimento sm maintenance.

manuale agg & sm manual.

manubrio sm (di bicicletta, moto) handlebars (pl); (di congegno) handle.

manutenzione sf maintenance.

manzo sm (carne) beef.

mappa sf map.

mappamondo *sm (globo)* globe; *(su carta)* map of the world.

maraschino *sm* maraschino *(cherry liqueur)*.

maratona *sf* marathon.

marca, -che *sf (di prodotto)* brand; *(scontrino)* ticket; **~ da bollo** revenue stamp; **prodotto di ~** quality product.

marcare *vt* to mark; *(goal)* to score.

Marche *sfpl*: **le ~** the Marches *(region of central Italy)*.

marchio *sm* mark; *(di bestiame)* brand; **~ di fabbrica** trademark; **~ registrato** registered trademark.

marcia, -ce *sf* march; *(di auto)* gear; *(SPORT)* walking; **fare ~ indietro** to reverse; **mettersi in ~** to start off.

marciapiede *sm* pavement (Br), sidewalk (Am); *(di stazione)* platform.

marciare *vi* to march.

marcio, -a, -ci, -ce *agg* rotten.

marcire *vi (cibo)* to rot; *(ferita)* to fester.

marco, -chi *sm* mark.

mare *sm* sea; **andare al ~** to go to the seaside; **il Mare del Nord** the North Sea.

marea *sf* tide; **alta ~** high tide; **bassa ~** low tide.

mareggiata *sf* stormy sea.

maresciallo *sm* ≈ warrant officer.

margarina *sf* margarine.

margherita *sf* daisy, → **pizza**.

margine *sm (di pagina)* margin; *(di strada, bosco)* edge.

marina *sf* navy.

marinaio *sm* sailor.

marinare *vt* to marinate; **~ la scuola** to play truant.

marinaro, -a *agg (popoli, tradizioni)* seafaring; **alla marinara** cooked with seafood.

marinata *sf* marinade.

marino, -a *agg* sea *(dav s)*.

marionetta *sf* marionette.

marito *sm* husband.

maritozzo *sm* type of sweet bread containing sultanas, pine kernels and candied peel *(a speciality of Lazio)*.

marittimo, -a *agg (clima)* maritime; *(scalo)* coastal; **località marittima** seaside resort.

marmellata *sf* jam; *(di arance)* marmalade.

marmitta *sf (di auto, moto)* silencer; *(pentola)* large cooking pot.

marmo *sm* marble.

marocchino, -a *agg & sm, f* Moroccan.

Marocco *sm*: **il ~** Morocco.

marrone ♦ *agg inv* brown ♦ *sm (colore)* brown; *(frutto)* chestnut.

marron glacé [mar'ron gla'se] *sm inv* marron glacé *(crystallized chestnut)*.

marsala *sm inv* Marsala *(sweet fortified wine)*.

marsupio *sm (borsello)* bum bag (Br), fanny pack (Am); *(di animale)* pouch.

martedì *sm inv* Tuesday, → **sabato**.

martellare ♦ *vt* to hammer ♦ *vi* to throb.

martello *sm* hammer.

martini® *sm inv (vermut)* Martini; *(cocktail)* Martini cocktail.

martire *smf* martyr.

martirio *sm* martyrdom.

marzapane *sm* marzipan.

marziale *agg* martial.

marziano, -a *sm, f* Martian.

marzo *sm* March, → **settembre**.

mascalzone *sm* scoundrel.

mascara *sm inv* mascara.

mascarpone *sm* mascarpone *(type of cream cheese)*.

mascella *sf* jaw.

maschera *sf* mask; *(costume)* fancy dress; *(di bellezza)* face pack; *(di cinema, teatro)* usher (f usherette).

mascherare *vt (volto)* to mask; *(emozioni)* to conceal.

▶ **mascherarsi** *vr*: **mascherarsi (da)**

to dress up (as).

maschile agg (GRAMM) masculine; (sesso, anatomia) male; (abiti) men's (dav s); (per ragazzi) boy's (dav s).

maschio, -a ♦ agg male ♦ sm (animale, individuo) male; (ragazzo, figlio, neonato) boy; **figlio ~** son.

mascolino, -a agg masculine.

mascotte [maˈskɔt] sf inv mascot.

masochista, -i, -e smf masochist.

massa sf mass; **una ~ di** (errori, gente) loads of; (mattoni, legna) a pile of; **la ~** the masses (pl); **di ~** mass (dav s); **in ~** en masse.

massacro sm massacre.

massaggiare vt to massage.

massaggiatore, -trice sm, f masseur (f masseuse).

massaggio sm massage.

massaia sf housewife.

massiccio, -a, -ci, -ce ♦ agg (corporatura) stout, big; (edificio) solid; **oro ~** solid gold ♦ sm massif.

massima sf (detto) maxim; (temperatura) maximum temperature; **in linea di ~** generally speaking.

massimo, -a agg & sm maximum; **al ~** at most.

mass media smpl mass media.

masso sm rock.

masticare vt to chew.

mastice sm putty.

mastino sm mastiff.

matassa sf skein.

matematica sf mathematics (sg).

matematico, -a, -ci, -che agg mathematical; (sicuro) certain.

materassino sm air bed; (da ginnastica) mat.

materasso sm mattress.

materia sf (in fisica) matter; (materiale) material; (disciplina, argomento) subject; **materie prime** raw materials.

materiale ♦ agg material ♦ sm material; (attrezzatura) equipment; **beni ~** worldly goods; **~ sintetico** man-made material.

maternità sf inv (condizione) motherhood; (di ospedale) maternity ward; **essere in ~** to be on maternity leave.

materno, -a agg maternal; (paese, lingua) mother (dav s).

matita sf pencil.

matrigna sf stepmother.

matrimoniale agg matrimonial.

matrimonio sm marriage; (cerimonia) wedding.

mattatoio sm slaughterhouse.

mattina sf morning; **di ~** in the morning.

mattinata sf morning.

mattiniero, -a agg: **essere ~** to be an early riser.

mattino sm morning.

matto, -a ♦ agg mad ♦ sm, f madman (f madwoman); **andare ~ per** to be crazy about.

mattone sm brick.

mattonella sf tile.

maturare vi & vt (frutta, grano) to ripen; (persona) to mature.

maturità sf (diploma, esame) ≃ A levels (pl) (Br); ≃ SATs (pl) (Am).

MATURITÀ

The 'maturità' examination is sat by students aged 18 to 19 in the final year of 'scuola superiore'. Depending on the type of school, the 'maturità' is classed as either classical, scientific, technical or artistic, and a pass allows the student to go on to university. The exam consists of two written and two oral parts: the same written paper in Italian is sat at all schools. The final mark out of 60 covers all subjects, and is based on both the exam results and on continuous assessment over the previous three years.

---

maturo, -a agg (frutto) ripe; (persona) mature.

mazza sf (bastone) club; (da baseball, cricket) bat; **~ da golf** golf club.

mazzo *sm* (*di fiori, chiavi*) bunch; (*di carte*) pack.

me *pron* me, → **mi**.

MEC *abbr* = **Mercato Comune Europeo**.

meccanica *sf* (*scienza*) mechanics (*sg*), → **meccanico**.

meccanico, -a, -ci, -che ◆ *agg* mechanical ◆ *sm* mechanic.

meccanismo *sm* mechanism.

mèche [mɛʃ] *sfpl* streaks.

medaglia *sf* medal.

medaglione *sm* (*gioiello*) locket; ~ di vitello veal medallion.

medesimo, -a *agg* same.

media *sf* (*valore intermedio*) average; (*di voti*) average mark (*Br*), average grade (*Am*); **in ~** on average; **le (scuole) medie** = secondary school (*sg*) (*Br*), junior high school (*sg*) (*Am*).

mediante *prep* by means of.

mediatore, -trice *sm, f* mediator; (COMM) middleman.

medicare *vt* to dress.

medicina *sf* medicine.

medicinale ◆ *agg* medicinal ◆ *sm* medicine, drug.

medico, -a, -ci, -che ◆ *agg* medical ◆ *sm* doctor; ~ di guardia doctor on call.

medievale *agg* medieval.

medio, -a ◆ *agg* average; (*di mezzo*) middle ◆ *sm*: (**dito**) ~ middle finger.

mediocre *agg* mediocre.

medioevale = **medievale**.

medioevo *sm* Middle Ages (*pl*).

meditare ◆ *vt* to plan ◆ *vi* to meditate.

mediterraneo, -a *agg* Mediterranean.

▶ **Mediterraneo** *sm*: **il (mar) Mediterraneo** the Mediterranean (Sea).

medusa *sf* jellyfish.

megafono *sm* megaphone.

meglio *avv* 1. (*comparativo*) better; mi sento ~ di ieri I feel better than I did yesterday; andare ~ to get better; così va ~ that's better; per ~ dire or rather.

2. (*superlativo*) best; è la cosa che mi riesce ~ it's the thing I do best; le persone ~ vestite the best-dressed people.

◆ *agg inv* 1. (*migliore*) better; la tua macchina è ~ della mia your car is better than mine.

2. (*in costruzioni impersonali*) better; è ~ rimanere qui it would be better to stay here; è ~ che te lo dica I'd better tell you.

◆ *sm*: fare del proprio ~ to do one's best; agire per il ~ to do the right thing.

◆ *sf*: avere la ~ su qn to get the better of sb.

mela *sf* apple.

melagrana *sf* pomegranate.

melanzana *sf* aubergine (*Br*), eggplant (*Am*); melanzane alla parmigiana *fried aubergine slices covered in tomato and Parmesan cheese*.

melenso, -a *agg* dull.

melma *sf* mud.

melo *sm* apple tree.

melodia *sf* melody.

melodramma, -i *sm* melodrama.

melone *sm* melon.

membro, -i *sm* (*di club, associazione*) member.

memorabile *agg* memorable.

memoria *sf* memory; sapere qc a ~ to know sthg by heart.

mendicante *smf* beggar.

meno *avv* 1. (*in comparativi*) less; ~ di less than; ~ vecchio (di) younger (than); camminare ~ in fretta don't walk so fast; ne voglio (di) ~ I want less; ~ lo vedo meglio sto the less I see him, the better I feel.

2. (*in superlativi*) least; la camera ~ cara the cheapest room; il ~ interessante the least interesting; fare il ~ possibile to do as little as possible; la macchina che costa ~ (di tutte) the least expensive car (of

all); è **Luca** che mi preoccupa ~ Luca worries me the least.

3. (*no*): **non so se accettare o ~** I don't know whether to accept or not.

4. (*nelle ore*): **le nove ~ un quarto** a quarter to nine (*Br*), a quarter of nine (*Am*).

5. (*nelle sottrazioni, nelle temperature*) minus.

6. (*in espressioni*): **non essere da ~ (di qn)** to be just as good (as sb); **fare a ~ di** to do without; **~ male (che) c'eri tu!** thank goodness you were there!; **venir ~ a** (*promessa*) to break; (*impegno*) not to fulfil; **non poteva fare a ~ di urlare** he couldn't help screaming.

♦ *prep* except (for); **c'erano tutti ~ (che) lei** they were all there except (for) her; **pensa a tutto ~ che a divertirsi** enjoying himself is the last thing on his mind.

♦ *agg inv* less; **oggi c'è ~ gente** there are fewer people today.

▶ **a meno che** *cong* unless; **vengo a ~ che non piova** I'm coming unless it rains.

menopausa *sf* menopause.

mensa *sf* canteen.

mensile *agg* & *sm* monthly.

mensola *sf* shelf.

menta *sf* mint; (*bibita*) peppermint cordial.

mentale *agg* mental.

mentalmente *avv* mentally.

mente *sf* mind; **avere in ~ di fare qc** to be thinking of doing sthg; **imparare/sapere qc a ~ to** learn/know sthg by heart; **sfuggire o passare di ~ a qn** to slip sb's mind; **tenere a ~ qc** to bear sthg in mind.

mentire *vi* to lie.

mento *sm* chin.

mentre *cong* (*temporale*) while; (*avversativa*) while, whereas.

menu *sm inv* menu.

menzionare *vt* to mention.

menzogna *sf* lie.

meraviglia *sf* (*stupore*) amazement; (*cosa, persona*) marvel; **a ~** perfectly.

meravigliare *vt* to amaze.

▶ **meravigliarsi di** *vr + prep* to be amazed at.

meraviglioso, -a *agg* wonderful.

mercante *sm* trader.

mercantile ♦ *agg* merchant (*davs*) ♦ *sm* (*nave*) merchant ship.

mercanzia *sf* goods (*pl*), merchandise.

mercatino *sm* local market.

mercato *sm* market; **~ dei cambi** foreign exchange market; **~ nero** black market; **a buon ~** cheap; **Mercato Comune Europeo** Common Market.

MERCATO

Almost every Italian town has an indoor or outdoor market selling food, flowers and plants. Once or twice a week there will also be a general market with stalls selling clothes, shoes and household items among other things. Prices are generally lower than in shops, and shoppers and stallholders often haggle.

---

merce *sf* goods (*pl*), merchandise.

merceria *sf* haberdasher's (*Br*), notions store (*Am*).

mercoledì *sm inv* Wednesday, → **sabato**.

mercurio *sm* mercury.

merda *sf* & *esclam* (*volg*) shit.

merenda *sf* afternoon snack.

meridionale ♦ *agg* southern ♦ *smf* southerner.

Meridione *sm*: **il ~** the South of Italy.

meringa, -ghe *sf* meringue.

meritare ♦ *vt* to deserve ♦ *vi* to be good; **meritarsi qc** to deserve sthg.

merito *sm* (*qualità*) merit; (*riconoscimento*) credit; **per ~ di qn** thanks to sb; **finire a pari ~** to tie.

merlo sm (uccello) blackbird; (di mura) battlement.

merluzzo sm cod.

meschino, -a agg (spregevole) mean.

mescolare vt (mischiare) to mix; (insalata) to toss; (caffé) to stir; (mettere in disordine) to mix up.

▶ **mescolarsi** vr (confondersi) to mingle.

mese sm month.

messa sf mass.

messaggio sm message.

Messico sm: il ~ Mexico.

messinscena sf (teatrale) production; (finzione) act.

messo, -a pp → **mettere**.

mestiere sm (professione) job; (artigianale) craft; (manuale) trade.

mestolo sm ladle.

mestruazioni sfpl period (sg).

meta sf (destinazione) destination; (scopo) aim, goal.

metà sf inv (parte) half; (punto di mezzo) middle; **dividere qc a** ~ to divide sthg in half; **essere a** ~ **strada** to be halfway; **fare a** ~ **(con qn)** to go halves (with sb).

metabolismo sm metabolism.

metafora sf metaphor.

metallico, -a, -ci, -che agg (di metallo) metal (dav s); (rumore, voce) metallic.

metallo sm metal.

metano sm methane.

meteorologico, -a, -ci, -che agg meteorological, weather (dav s).

meticoloso, -a agg meticulous.

metodico, -a, -ci, -che agg methodical.

metodo sm method.

metrico, -a, -ci, -che agg metric.

metro sm (unità di misura) metre; (nastro) tape measure; (a stecche) rule; ~ **cubo** cubic metre; ~ **quadrato** square metre.

metronotte sm inv night security guard.

metropoli sf inv metropolis.

metropolitana sf underground (Br), subway (Am).

mettere vt **1.** (collocare) to put; ~ **un annuncio** to place an advert; ~ **i piatti in tavola** to set the table; ~ **qn alla prova** to put sb to the test; ~ **i libri in ordine** to tidy (up) the books; ~ **l'antenna dritta** to put the aerial straight.

2. (indossare): **mettersi qc** to put sthg on; **mettersi una sciarpa** to put a scarf on, to wear a scarf; **cosa mi metto oggi?** what shall I wear today?

3. (tempo): **metterci: ci si mette un'ora per andare** it takes an hour to get there.

4. (dedicare): ~ **attenzione in qc** to do sthg with care; **mettercela tutta** to do one's best.

5. (far funzionare) to put on; ~ **gli abbaglianti** to put one's headlights on full beam.

6. (suscitare): ~ **appetito a qn** to make sb hungry; ~ **paura a qn** to scare sb.

7. (supporre): **mettiamo che non venga** let's suppose he doesn't come.

8. (in espressioni): ~ **avanti/indietro l'orologio** to put the clock forward/back; ~ **in chiaro qc** to clear sthg up; ~ **in dubbio qc** to cast doubt on sthg; **mettersi in testa di fare qc** to get it into one's head to do sthg; ~ **insieme** to put together.

▶ **mettersi** vr **1.** (porsi): **mettiti a sedere qui** sit here; **mettersi a tavola** to sit down to eat; **mettersi nei guai** to get into trouble.

2. (vestirsi): **mettersi in pigiama** to put one's pyjamas on.

3. (cominciare): **mettersi a fare qc** to start doing sthg; **s'è messo a gridare** he started screaming; **mettersi in viaggio** to set off.

4. (in espressioni): **mettersi d'accordo** to agree; **mettersi bene/male** to turn out well/badly; **mettersi con qn** (in società) to go into partnership with sb; (*in coppia*) to go out with sb.

mezza *sf*: **la ~** (*mezzogiorno e mezzo*) half-past twelve.

mezzaluna (*pl* **mezzelune**) *sf* (*parte di luna*) half moon; (*coltello*) chopping blade; (*islamica*) crescent.

mezzanino *sm* mezzanine floor.

mezzanotte *sf* midnight.

mezzo, -a ◆ *agg* half ◆ *sm* (*metà*) half; (*parte centrale*) middle; (*strumento, procedimento*) means; (*veicolo*) vehicle ◆ *avv*: **~ pieno** half-full; **~ chilo** half a kilo; **~ litro** half a litre; **mezza pensione** half board; **abiti di mezza stagione** spring/autumn clothes; **a mezze maniche** short-sleeved; **di mezza età** middle-aged; **quello di ~** the one in the middle, the middle one; **per ~ di** by means of; **le cinque e mezza** o **~** half-past five; **non vuole andarci di ~** he doesn't want to get involved; **fare a ~ (con qn)** to share (with sb); **levarsi** o **togliersi di ~** to get out of the way; **mezzi di comunicazione (di massa)** (mass) media; **mezzi pubblici** public transport (*sg*); **mezzi di trasporto** means of transport.

▶ **mezzi** *smpl* (*economici*) means.

mezzogiorno *sm* (*ora*) midday, noon.

▶ **Mezzogiorno** *sm*: **il Mezzogiorno** Southern Italy.

MEZZOGIORNO

The south of Italy, including Sicily and Sardinia, is called 'il Mezzogiorno'. This area is less industrial than the rest of the country, but is rich in art and culture and is blessed with spectacular scenery.

---

mezzora *sf* half an hour.

mi (*diventa* **me** *se precede* lo, la, li, le, ne) *pron* (*complemento oggetto*) me; (*complemento di termine*) (to) me; (*riflessivo*) myself; **me li dai?** will you give them to me?

miagolare *vi* to miaow.

mica *avv* (*fam*): **non ci avrai ~ creduto?** you didn't believe it, did you?; **non sono ~ scemo!** I'm not stupid, am I!; **~ male** not bad (at all).

miccia, -ce *sf* fuse.

micidiale *agg* (*mortale*) deadly; (*dannoso*) murderous; (*insopportabile*) unbearable.

micosi *sf inv* (MED) fungus.

microfono *sm* microphone.

microscopio *sm* microscope.

midolla *sf* (*mollica*) crumb.

midollo (*pl f* **midolla**) *sm* marrow.

mie → **mio**.

miei → **mio**.

miele *sm* honey.

migliaio (*pl f* **migliaia**) *sm* thousand; **un ~ (di persone)** about a thousand (people); **a migliaia** by the thousand.

miglio *sm* (*unità di misura: pl f* **miglia**) mile; (*pianta*) millet.

miglioramento *sm* improvement.

migliorare ◆ *vt* to improve ◆ *vi* (*tempo, situazione*) to improve; (*malato*) to get better.

migliore *agg* (*comparativo*) better; **il/la ~** (*superlativo*) the best.

mignolo *sm* little finger (Br), pinkie (Am); (*del piede*) little toe.

mila *pl* → **mille**.

milanese ◆ *agg* Milanese ◆ *smf* person from Milan.

Milano *sf* Milan.

miliardo *sm* thousand million (Br), billion (Am).

milione *sm* million.

militare ◆ *agg* military ◆ *sm* serviceman; **fare il ~** to do one's military service.

mille (*pl* **mila**) *num* a o one thousand, → **sei**.

millefoglie *sm inv* millefeuille (Br), napoleon (Am).

millennio *sm* millennium.

millepiedi *sm inv* millipede.

misto

millesimo, -a num thousandth, → **sesto**.

millimetro sm millimetre.

milza sf spleen.

mimare vt to mime.

mimetizzare vt to camouflage.

▶ **mimetizzarsi** vr (animali, piante) to camouflage o.s.

mimo sm mime.

mimosa sf mimosa.

min. (abbr di minimo, di minuto) min.

mina sf (esplosiva) mine; (di matita) lead.

minaccia, -ce sf threat.

minacciare vt to threaten; ~ **di fare qc** to threaten to do sthg.

minaccioso, -a agg threatening, menacing.

minatore sm miner.

minerale agg & sm mineral.

minestra sf soup; ~ **in brodo** noodle soup; ~ **di verdure** vegetable soup.

minestrone sm minestrone.

miniatura sf miniature.

miniera sf mine.

minigolf sm minigolf.

minigonna sf miniskirt.

minima sf minimum temperature.

minimizzare vt to minimize.

minimo, -a ♦ agg (il più piccolo) slightest, least; (il più basso) lowest; (molto piccolo) very small, slight ♦ sm (parte più piccola) minimum; (di motore) idling speed; **come** ~ at the very least.

ministero sm (settore amministrativo) ministry.

ministro sm minister; ~ **degli Esteri** Foreign Secretary (Br), Secretary of State (Am).

minoranza sf minority; **essere in** ~ to be in a minority.

minore ♦ agg (comparativo: di età) younger; (di grandezza) smaller; (di importanza) minor; (numero) lower; (grado) lesser; (superlativo: di età) youngest; (di grandezza) smallest; (di importanza) least important; (di numero) lowest ♦ smf (minorenne) minor.

minorenne smf minor.

minuscola sf small letter.

minuscolo, -a agg (scrittura) small; (molto piccolo) tiny.

minuto, -a ♦ agg (persona, corpo) small; (piccolo) tiny, minute; (fine) fine ♦ sm (unità) minute.

mio (f **mia**, mpl **miei**, fpl **mie**) ♦ agg: **il** ~ **(la mia)** my ♦ pron: **il** ~ **(la mia)** mine; ~ **padre** my father; **un** ~ **amico** a friend of mine; **questa bici è mia** this bike is mine.

miope agg short-sighted.

mira sf aim; **prendere la** ~ to take aim; **prendere di** ~ **qc** (fig) to pick on sb.

miracolo sm miracle.

miraggio sm mirage.

mirare vi: ~ **a** to aim at.

miriade sf multitude; **una** ~ **di** a multitude of.

mirtillo sm blueberry.

miscela sf (miscuglio) mixture; (di caffè) blend; (benzina) petrol and oil mixture.

mischia sf brawl; (nel rugby) scrum.

mischiare vt to mix; ~ **le carte** to shuffle the cards.

▶ **mischiarsi** vr to mix.

miseria sf (extreme) poverty; (quantità insufficiente): **è costato una** ~ it cost next to nothing; **porca** ~! (volg: accidenti) damn!, bloody hell!

misericordia sf mercy.

misero, -a agg (povero) poor, poverty-stricken; (infelice) wretched, miserable; (insufficiente) miserable.

missile sm missile.

missionario, -a sm, f missionary.

missione sf mission.

misterioso, -a agg mysterious.

mistero sm mystery.

misto, -a ♦ agg mixed ♦ sm mixture; **insalata mista** mixed salad; ~

lana woollen blend; **~ cotone** cotton blend.

misura *sf* (*unità, provvedimento*) measure; (*dimensione*) measurement; (*taglia*) size; (*moderazione*) moderation; **prendere le misure di qc** to measure sthg; **su ~** made-to-measure.

misurare ◆ *vt* to measure; (*abito*) to try on; (*vista*) to test ◆ *vi* to measure.

▶ **misurarsi con** *vr + prep* to compete with.

misurino *sm* measure.

mite *agg* mild.

mito *sm* myth.

mitra *sm inv* submachine gun.

mitragliatrice *sf* machine gun.

mittente *smf* sender.

mobile ◆ *agg* movable ◆ *sm* piece of furniture; **mobili** (*mobilia*) furniture (*sg*).

mobilia *sf* furniture.

mobilitare *vt* to mobilize.

moca *sf inv* coffee machine.

mocassino *sm* mocassin.

moda *sf* fashion; **essere o andare di ~** to be in fashion; **passare di ~** to go out of fashion; **alla ~** fashionable; **di ~** fashionable.

modellare *vt* to model.

modellino *sm* model.

modello, -a ◆ *sm, f* model ◆ *sm* model; (*di vestito*) model, style; (*per sarta*) pattern; (*modulo*) form.

moderare *vt* to moderate.

moderato, -a *agg* moderate.

moderno, -a *agg* modern.

modestia *sf* modesty.

modesto, -a *agg* modest.

modico, -a, -ci, -che *agg* low.

modifica, -che *sf* alteration.

modo *sm* way; (*opportunità*) chance; (GRAMM: *verbale*) mood; **a ~ mio** in my way; **in ~ da fare qc** so as to do sthg; **~ di dire** expression; **di ~ che** so that; **in nessun ~** in no way; **in ogni ~** anyway; **in qualche ~** in some way; **in tutti i modi** in every way.

modulazione *sf*: **~ di frequenza** frequency modulation.

modulo *sm* form.

moglie, -gli *sf* wife.

mole *sf* (*dimensione*) massive shape; (*quantità*): **una ~ di lavoro** masses of work.

molestare *vt* to annoy.

molesto, -a *agg* annoying.

molla *sf* (*meccanica*) spring.

▶ **molle** *sfpl* (*per camino, ghiaccio*) tongs.

mollare ◆ *vt* (*allentare*) to slacken; (*lasciar andare*) to let go; (*fam: fidanzato*) to ditch ◆ *vi* (*desistere*) to give in; **~ un ceffone a qn** (*fam: dare uno schiaffo*) to slap sb.

molle *agg* (*morbido*) soft; (*fig: persona*) weak.

molletta *sf* (*per capelli*) hair grip; (*per panni*) clothes peg.

mollica, -che *sf* crumb.

molo *sm* (*di porto*) jetty.

molteplice *agg* (*complesso*) complex.

▶ **molteplici** *agg pl* (*numerosi*) numerous, various.

moltiplicare *vt* to multiply.

moltiplicazione *sf* (MAT) multiplication; (*accrescimento*) increase.

moltitudine *sf* multitude.

molto, -a ◆ *agg* **1.** (*in grande quantità*) a lot of, much; **non ho ~ tempo** I don't have (very) much time; **hai molta fame?** are you very hungry?
2. (*di numero elevato*) **molti(-e)** a lot of, many; **ci sono molti turisti** there are a lot of tourists.
◆ *pron* a lot, much; **molti** (*molta gente*) many (people); **molti di noi** many of us.
◆ *avv* **1.** (*con verbi*) a lot, (very) much; **mi piace ~** I like it a lot o very much.
2. (*con aggettivi, avverbi*) very; (*con participio passato*) much; **è ~ simpatica** she's very nice; **è ~ meglio così** it's much better like this; **è ~ presto/tardi** it's very early/late; **è ~ volentieri!** certainly!

momentaneamente *avv* at the moment.

momentaneo, -a *agg* momentary.

momento *sm* moment; (*circostanza*) time; **all'ultimo ~** at the last moment; **da un ~ all'altro** (*tra poco*) (at) any moment; **dal ~ che** since; **per il ~** for the time being; **a momenti** (*tra poco*) soon; (*quasi*) nearly.

monaca, -che *sf* nun.

monaco, -ci *sm* monk.

monarchia *sf* monarchy.

monastero *sm* (*di monaci*) monastery; (*di monache*) convent.

mondano, -a *agg* (*di società*) society (*dav s*); (*terreno*) earthly.

mondiale *agg* world (*dav s*).

mondo *sm* world.

moneta *sf* (*di metallo*) coin; (*valuta*) currency; **~ spicciola** change.

monetario, -a *agg* monetary.

monolocale *sm* studio flat (Br), studio apartment (Am).

monopattino *sm* scooter.

monopolio *sm* monopoly.

monosci *sm inv* monoski.

monotono, -a *agg* (*ripetitivo*) monotonous; (*noioso*) dull.

montacarichi *sm inv* goods lift.

montagna *sf* mountain; (*zona*) the mountains (*pl*); **andare in ~** to go to the mountains; **montagne russe** roller coaster (*sg*).

montanaro, -a *sm, f* mountain dweller.

montano, -a *agg* mountain (*dav s*).

montare ♦ *vi* (*salire*) to go up; (*cavalcare*) to ride ♦ *vt* (*congegno*) to assemble; (*cavallo, pietra preziosa*) to mount; (*panna*) to whip; (*albumi*) to whisk; (*fecondare*) to cover; **~ in macchina** to get into a car; **~ in treno** to get on a train; **montarsi la testa** to become bigheaded.

montatura *sf* (*di occhiali*) frames (*pl*); (*di gioiello*) setting.

monte *sm* mountain; **andare a ~** to come to nothing; **mandare a ~ qc** to upset sthg; **~ premi** prize money; **il Monte Bianco** Mont Blanc.

montone *sm* (*animale*) ram; (*carne*) mutton; (*giaccone*) sheepskin jacket.

montuoso, -a *agg* mountainous.

monumento *sm* monument.

moquette [mɔ'kɛt] *sf inv* fitted carpet.

mora *sf* (*commestibile*) blackberry; (*del gelso*) mulberry; (DIR) default.

morale ♦ *agg* moral ♦ *sf* morals (*pl*); (*insegnamento*) moral ♦ *sm* morale; **essere giù di ~** to be feeling down.

morbido, -a *agg* soft.

morbillo *sm* measles (*sg*).

morbo *sm* disease.

morboso, -a *agg* morbid.

mordere *vt* to bite.

morfina *sf* morphine.

moribondo, -a *agg* dying.

morire *vi* to die; (*estinguersi*) to die out; **~ di fame** to die of hunger; **~ di noia** to die of boredom; **~ dal ridere** to kill o.s. laughing; **bello da ~** stunning; **mi piace da ~** I adore it.

mormorare ♦ *vi* (*bisbigliare*) to whisper; (*sparlare*) to gossip ♦ *vt* to murmur.

moro, -a *agg* dark.

morso, -a ♦ *pp* → **mordere** ♦ *sm* bite; (*di briglia*) bit.

mortadella *sf* Mortadella (*large pork sausage served cold in thin slices*).

mortale ♦ *agg* mortal; (*letale*) deadly ♦ *sm* mortal.

mortalità *sf* mortality.

morte *sf* death; **avercela a ~ con qn** to have it in for sb.

mortificare *vt* to mortify.

morto, -a ♦ *pp* → **morire** ♦ *agg* dead ♦ *sm, f* dead man (*f* dead woman); **fare il ~** (*nell'acqua*) to float on one's back.

mosaico, -ci *sm* mosaic.

mosca, -sche *sf* fly; **~ cieca** blind man's buff.

Mosca sf Moscow.

moscato sm muscatel (*sweet wine*).

moscerino sm gnat.

moschettone sm spring clip.

moscone sm (*insetto*) bluebottle; (*imbarcazione*) pedalo.

mossa sf movement; (*negli scacchi*) move.

mosso, -a ♦ pp → **muovere** ♦ agg (*mare*) rough; (*capelli*) wavy; (*fotografia*) blurred.

mostarda sf mustard.

mostra sf exhibition; **mettersi in ~** to draw attention to o.s.; **in ~** on show; **la Mostra del cinema di Venezia** Venice Film Festival.

LA MOSTRA DEL CINEMA DI VENEZIA

The Venice Film Festival, or the 'Mostra internazionale d'arte cinematografica di Venezia', has been held every year since 1938 during the last week in August and the first week in September. Film fans flock to the Palazzo del Cinema in Lido di Venezia to see the celebrities, to watch important new films and retrospectives, and to attend premières. The festival concludes with the awarding of prizes, including the prestigious 'Leone d'oro' (golden lion).

---

mostrare vt to show.
▶ **mostrarsi** vr to look; **mostrarsi in pubblico** to appear in public.

mostro sm monster.

mostruoso, -a agg (*orrendo*) monstrous; (*feroce*) ferocious; (*smisurato*) incredible.

motel sm inv motel.

motivo sm (*causa*) reason; (*di stoffa*) pattern; (*musicale*) tune; **per quale ~?** for what reason?; **senza ~** without a reason.

moto ♦ sm (*in fisica*) motion; (*movimento*) movement; (*esercizio fisico*) exercise ♦ sf inv motorbike; **mettere in ~** (AUTO) to start.

motocicletta sf motorcycle.

motocross sm motocross.

motore sm motor, engine; **a ~** motor (*dav s*).

motorino sm moped; **~ d'avviamento** starter.

motoscafo sm motorboat.

motto sm maxim.

mousse [mus] sf inv mousse.

movimentare vt to liven up.

movimento sm (*attività*) activity.

mozzafiato agg inv breathtaking.

mozzare vt to cut off; **~ il fiato a qn** to take sb's breath away.

mozzarella sf mozzarella (*a round fresh cheese from Naples made from cow's or buffalo's milk*); **~ in carrozza** mozzarella sandwiched between two slices of bread, then dipped in egg and fried.

mozzicone sm stub.

mozzo, -a ♦ agg cut off ♦ sm ship's boy.

mucca, -che sf cow.

mucchio sm (*cumulo*) heap; **un ~ di** (*fig: grande quantità*) loads of.

muffa sf mould.

muffole sfpl mittens.

mugolare vi to whine.

mulattiera sf mule track.

mulatto, -a agg & sm, f mulatto.

mulinello sm (*vortice*) whirl; (*da pesca*) reel.

mulino sm mill; **~ a vento** windmill.

mulo sm mule.

multa sf fine; **fare la ~ a qn** to fine sb.

multare vt to fine.

multiplo, -a agg & sm multiple.

multiproprietà sf inv timeshare.

mungere vt to milk.

municipale agg municipal.

municipio sm town hall.

munire vt: **~ qn/qc di qc** to equip sb/sthg with sthg.
▶ **munirsi di** vr + prep to equip o.s. with.

muovere vt to move; (*critica, accusa*) to make.

▶ **muoversi** *vr* to move; (*fam: sbrigarsi*) to hurry up, to get a move on.

mura *sfpl* walls.

murare *vt* to wall up.

muratore *sm* bricklayer.

murena *sf* moray eel.

muro *sm* wall.

muscolare *agg* muscular, muscle (*dav s*).

muscolo *sm* muscle; **muscoli** (*forza*) brawn (*sg*).

muscoloso, -a *agg* muscular.

museo *sm* museum.

museruola *sf* muzzle.

musica *sf* music; ~ **da camera** chamber music; ~ **classica** classical music; ~ **leggera** light music; ~ **pop** pop music.

musicale *agg* musical.

musicista, -i, -e *smf* musician.

muso *sm* (*di animale*) muzzle; (*fam & spreg: di persona*) mug; (*di auto*) front end; (*aereo*) nose; **tenere il** ~ to sulk.

muta *sf* (*da sub*) wet suit; (*di cani*) pack.

mutamento *sm* change.

mutande *sfpl* pants.

mutandine *sfpl* knickers.

mutare *vt & vi* to change.

mutazione *sf* change; (*genetica*) mutation.

mutilato, -a *sm, f person who has lost a limb*; ~ **di guerra** disabled ex-serviceman (Br), disabled war veteran (Am).

muto, -a *agg* dumb; (*silenzioso*) silent; (*cinema, consonante*) silent.

mutua *sf* = National Health Service.

mutuo, -a ♦ *agg* mutual ♦ *sm* loan; (*per casa*) mortgage.

N

N (*abbr di nord*) N.

nafta *sf* (*olio combustibile*) fuel oil; (*gasolio*) diesel oil.

naftalina *sf* mothballs (*pl*).

nailon® *sm* nylon.

nanna *sf* (*fam*): **andare a** ~ to go to beddy-byes.

nano, -a *agg & sm, f* dwarf.

napoletana *sf a type of coffee percolator*.

napoletano, -a *agg & sm, f* Neapolitan, → **pizza**.

Napoli *sf* Naples.

narice *sf* nostril.

narrare *vt* to tell.

narrativa *sf* fiction.

nasale *agg* nasal.

nascere *vi* to be born; (*pianta*) to come up; (*sole*) to rise; (*fiume*) to have its source; (*dente*) to come through; (*attività, impresa*) to start up; **sono nata il 31 luglio del 1965** I was born on the 31st of July 1965.

▶ **nascere da** *v + prep* to arise from.

nascita *sf* (*di bambino, animale*) birth; (*di attività, movimento*) start; **data di** ~ date of birth; **luogo di** ~ place of birth.

nascondere *vt* to hide; (*dissimulare*) to hide, to conceal.

▶ **nascondersi** *vr* to hide.

nascondino *sm* hide and seek.

nascosto, -a ♦ *pp* → **nascondere** ♦ *agg* hidden; **di** ~ secretly.

naso *sm* nose; **ficcare il** ~ **in qc** to poke one's nose into sthg.

nastro *sm* ribbon; ~ **adesivo** adhesive tape; ~ **trasportatore** conveyor belt.

Natale *sm* Christmas.

NATALE

Italian Christmas celebrations begin on Christmas Eve with a dinner at which special regional dishes are served. The rest of the evening is normally spent playing 'tombola' (line bingo) or cards, and in some families the gifts which were placed under the Christmas tree or by the 'presepe' (crib) are exchanged now rather than on the 25th. Churchgoers then attend midnight mass. Christmas Day itself is usually spent with the family. Lunch is traditionally rounded off with a 'panettone', a domed cake containing raisins and candied fruit.

natalità *sf* birth rate.

natante *sm* craft.

nato, -a ♦ *pp* → **nascere** ♦ *agg* (*fig: per natura*) born; **nata Mattei** (*da nubile*) née Mattei.

NATO *sf* NATO.

natura *sf* nature; **~ morta** still life.

naturale *agg* natural.

naturalmente *avv* naturally; (*certamente sì*) naturally, of course.

naufragare *vi* (*nave*) to be wrecked; (*persona*) to be shipwrecked.

naufragio *sm* shipwreck.

naufrago, -a, -ghi, -ghe *sm, f* shipwrecked person.

nausea *sf* nausea.

nauseante *agg* nauseating.

nauseare *vt* to make sick.

nautico, -a, -ci, -che *agg* nautical.

navale *agg* naval.

navata *sf* nave.

nave *sf* ship; **~ passeggeri** passenger ship; **~ traghetto** ferry.

navetta *sf* shuttle; **~ (spaziale)** space shuttle.

navigabile *agg* navigable.

navigare *vi* (*nave*) to sail; (*persona*) to navigate.

navigazione *sf* navigation.

naviglio *sm* (*nave*) vessel; (*canale*) canal.

nazionale ♦ *agg* national ♦ *sf* (*squadra*) national team.

nazionalità *sf inv* nationality.

nazione *sf* nation.

ne *pron* 1. (*di lui*) of/about him; (*di lei*) of/about her; (*di loro*) of/about them; **~ apprezzo l'onestà** I value his honesty.

2. (*di un insieme*) of it, of them; **ha dei panini? – ~ vorrei due** have you got any rolls? – I'd like two (of them).

3. (*di ciò*) about it; **non parliamone più** let's not talk about it any more; **non ~ ho idea** I've no idea.

4. (*da ciò*): **~ deriva che …** it follows that …

♦ *avv* (*di là*) from there; **~ veniamo proprio ora** we've just come from there.

né *cong*: **né … né** neither … nor; **~ l'uno ~ l'altro sono italiani** neither of them are Italian; **non si è fatto ~ sentire ~ vedere** I haven't heard from him or seen him; **non voglio ~ il primo ~ il secondo** I don't want either the first one or the second.

neanche *cong & avv* not even; **non … ~** not even …; **~ io lo conosco** I don't know him either; **non ho mangiato – ~ io** I haven't eaten – neither have I; **~ per sogno** o **per idea!** not on your life!

nebbia *sf* fog.

nebulizzatore *sm* spray.

necessariamente *avv* necessarily.

necessario, -a ♦ *agg* necessary ♦ *sm* necessities (*pl*); **è ~ farlo** it must be done; **~ per toeletta** toiletries (*pl*).

necessità *sf inv* (*bisogno*) necessity.

necessitare : necessitare di *v + prep* to need, to require.

necrologio *sm* (*annuncio*) obituary.

negare *vt* to deny; (*rifiutare*): ~ qc (a qn) to refuse (sb) sthg; ~ di aver fatto qc to deny having done sthg.

negativo, -a *agg & sm* negative.

negato, -a *agg*: essere ~ per qc to be hopeless at sthg.

negli = in + gli, → in.

negligente *agg* negligent.

negoziante *smf* shopkeeper.

negozio *sm* shop; ~ di giocattoli toy shop.

negro, -a *agg & sm, f* black.

nei = in + i, → in.

nel = in + il, → in.

nell' = in + l', → in.

nella = in + la, → in.

nelle = in + le, → in.

nello = in + lo, → in.

nemico, -a, -ci, -che ◆ *agg* (*esercito, stato*) enemy (*dav s*); (*ostile*) hostile ◆ *sm, f* enemy.

nemmeno = neanche.

neo *sm* mole.

neofascismo *sm* neofascism.

neon *sm* neon.

neonato, -a *sm, f* newborn baby.

neozelandese ◆ *agg* New Zealand (*dav s*) ◆ *smf* New Zealander.

neppure = neanche.

nero, -a ◆ *agg* (*colore*) black; (*scuro*) dark; (*pane*) wholemeal ◆ *sm* black.

nervo *sm* nerve; dare ai o sui nervi a qc to get on sb's nerves.

nervosismo *sm* nervousness.

nervoso, -a ◆ *agg* nervous ◆ *sm*: avere il ~ to be on edge.

nespola *sf* medlar.

nessuno, -a ◆ *agg* no ◆ *pron* (*non una persona*) nobody, no one; (*non una cosa*) none; (*qualcuno*): c'è ~? is anybody in?; nessuna città è bella quanto Roma there's no city more beautiful than Rome; non c'è nessun posto libero there aren't any free seats; da nessuna parte nowhere; ~ lo sa nobody knows; non ho visto ~ I didn't see anybody; ~ di noi none of us; ~ dei due

neither of them; non me ne piace ~ I don't like any of them.

nettezza *sf*: ~ urbana refuse department.

netto, -a *agg* (*preciso*) clear; (*deciso*) definite; (*peso, stipendio*) net.

netturbino *sm* dustman.

neutrale *agg* neutral.

neutralizzare *vt* to neutralize.

neutro, -a ◆ *agg* neutral; essere ~ (*imparziale*) to be neutral ◆ *sm* (*in linguistica*) neuter.

neve *sf* snow.

nevicare *v impers* to snow; nevica it's snowing.

nevicata *sf* snowfall.

nevischio *sm* sleet.

nevralgia *sf* neuralgia.

nevrotico, -a, -ci, -che *agg* neurotic.

nicchia *sf* niche.

nicotina *sf* nicotine.

nido *sm* nest.

niente *pron* 1. (*nessuna cosa*) nothing; non ... ~ nothing; non faccio ~ la domenica I do nothing on Sundays, I don't do anything on Sundays; ~ di ~ nothing at all; grazie! – di ~! thank you – not at all. 2. (*qualcosa*) anything; le serve ~? do you need anything?; non per ~, ma ... not that it matters, but ... 3. (*poco*): da ~ (*cosa*) not important; (*persona*) worthless.

◆ *agg inv* (*fam*: nessuno): non ha ~ buon senso he has no common sense; ~ paura! never fear!

◆ *avv*: non ... ~ not ... at all; non me ne importa ~ I couldn't care less; questo non c'entra ~ this doesn't come into it at all; non fa ~ it doesn't matter; ti piace? – per ~! do you like it? – not at all!

◆ *sm*: basta un ~ per farlo contento the slightest thing makes him happy; un bel ~ nothing at all.

nientemeno ◆ *avv* no less, actually ◆ *esclam* you don't say!

night(-club) ['nait(-'klab)] *sm inv* nightclub.

Nilo *sm*: il ~ the Nile.

ninnananna *sf* lullaby.

ninnolo *sm* knick-knack.

nipote *smf* (*di zii*) nephew (*f* niece); (*di nonni*) grandson (*f* granddaughter).

nitido, -a *agg* well-defined.

nitrire *vi* to neigh.

no *avv* no; c'eri anche tu, ~? you were there too, weren't you?; lo sai, ~, com'è fatto you know, don't you, what he's like?; lo vuoi o ~? do you want it or not?; ~ di certo certainly not; perché ~? why not?

nobile *agg & smf* noble.

nobiltà *sf* (*aristocrazia*) nobility; (*di animo, azione*) nobleness.

nocciola ◆ *sf* hazelnut ◆ *agg inv* hazel.

nocciolina *sf*: ~ (americana) peanut.

nocciolo¹ *sm* (*di frutto*) stone; (*fig*) heart.

nocciolo² *sm* (*albero*) hazel.

noce *sf & sm* walnut; ~ di cocco coconut; ~ moscata nutmeg.

nocivo, -a *agg* harmful.

nodo *sm* knot; avere un ~ alla gola to have a lump in one's throat.

noi *pron* (*soggetto*) we; (*complemento oggetto, con preposizione*) us; da ~ (*nel nostro paese*) in our country; ~ stessi we ourselves.

noia *sf* (*tedio*) boredom; (*fastidio*) nuisance; gli è venuto a ~ he's tired of it; dar ~ a qn to annoy sb; avere delle noie con to have trouble with.

noioso, -a *agg* (*monotono*) boring; (*fastidioso*) annoying.

noleggiare *vt* (*prendere a nolo*) to hire; (*dare a nolo*) to hire out.

noleggio *sm* hire (Br), rental; prendere qc a ~ to hire sthg.

nolo = noleggio.

nome *sm* name; (GRAMM) noun; conoscere qn di ~ to know sb by name; a ~ di qn on behalf of sb; ~ di battesimo Christian name; ~ da ragazza maiden name.

nominare *vt* (*menzionare*) to men-

tion; (*eleggere*) to appoint; l'ho sentito ~ I've heard him mentioned.

nominativo *sm* (form: *nome*) name.

non *avv* not, → affatto, ancora ecc.

nonché *cong* (*e anche*) as well as; (*tanto meno*) let alone.

noncurante *agg*: ~ (di) indifferent (to).

nondimeno *cong* nevertheless, however.

nonno, -a *sm, f* grandfather (*f* grandmother).

nonnulla *sm inv*: un ~ a trifle.

nono, -a *num* ninth, → sesto.

nonostante ◆ *prep* in spite of ◆ *cong* although.

non vedente *smf* blind person.

nord ◆ *sm* north ◆ *agg inv* north, northern; a ~ (di) north (of); nel ~ in the north.

nordest *sm* northeast.

nordico, -a, -ci, -che *agg* Nordic.

nordovest *sm* northwest.

norma *sf* rule; di ~ as a rule; a ~ di legge according to the law.

normale *agg* normal.

normalità *sf* normality.

normanno, -a *agg* Norman.

norvegese *agg, smf & sm* Norwegian.

Norvegia *sf*: la ~ Norway.

nostalgia *sf* nostalgia; avere ~ di casa o di paese to be homesick.

nostro, -a ◆ *agg*: il ~ (la nostra) our ◆ *pron*: il ~ (la nostra) ours; ~ padre our father; un ~ amico a friend of ours; questa casa è nostra it's our house.

nota *sf* note; (*conto*) bill; (*elenco*) list; prendere ~ (di qc) to make a note (of sthg).

notaio *sm* notary public.

notare *vt* (*osservare, accorgersi di*) to notice; (*annotare*) to note down; farsi ~ to get o.s. noticed.

notevole *agg* (*differenza, prezzo*) considerable; (*persona*) remarkable.

notificare *vt* (*form*) to notify.

notizia *sf* (*informazione*) news (*sg*), piece of news; **le ultime notizie** the latest news; **avere notizie di qn** to hear from sb.

notiziario *sm* news (*sg*).

noto, -a *agg* well-known; **rendere ~ qc a qn** to make sthg known to sb.

nottambulo, -a *sm, f* night bird.

nottata *sf* night.

notte *sf* night; **di ~** at night; **una ~ in bianco** a sleepless night.

notturno, -a *agg* night (*dav s*); **animale ~** nocturnal animal.

novanta *num* ninety, → **sei**.

novantesimo, -a *num* ninetieth, → **sesto**.

nove *num* nine, → **sei**.

novecento *num* nine hundred, → **sei**.

▶ **Novecento** *sm*: **il Novecento** the twentieth century.

novella *sf* short story.

novembre *sm* November, → **settembre**.

novità *sf inv* (*cosa nuova*) something new; (*fatto, notizia recente*) (piece of) news (*sg*); **le ~ musicali** the latest releases.

nozione *sf* notion, idea; **nozioni** (*di matematica, francese*) rudiments.

nozze *sfpl* wedding (*sg*); **~ d'oro** golden wedding.

nube *sf* cloud.

nubifragio *sm* rainstorm.

nubile *agg* single.

nuca, -che *sf* nape of the neck.

nucleare *agg* nuclear.

nucleo *sm* (*di cellula, atomo*) nucleus; (*di persone*) group; (*di soldati, polizia*) squad; **~ familiare** family unit.

nudismo *sm* nudism.

nudista, -i, -e *smf* nudist.

nudo, -a ◆ *agg* (*persona*) naked; (*parete*) bare; **mettere a ~ qc** to lay sthg bare ◆ *sm* (ARTE) nude.

nugolo *sm*: **un ~ di** a host of.

nulla = **niente**.

nullità *sf inv* (*di ragionamento, documento*) nullity; (*persona*) nobody.

nullo, -a *agg* (*non valido*) (null and) void; (SPORT) drawn.

numerale *agg & sm* numeral.

numerare *vt* to number.

numero *sm* (MAT: *quantità*) number; (*segno, cifra*) numeral; (*di scarpe*) size; (*di rivista*) issue; **che ~ porta?** what size do you take?; **fare il ~** (*di telefono*) to dial (the number); **~ civico** house number; **~ chiuso** selective entry system; **~ di conto** account number; **~ di targa** numberplate; **~ di telefono** telephone number; **~ verde** ≃ freefone number (Br), ≃ toll-free number (Am); **dare i numeri** (*fig*) to be off one's head.

numeroso, -a *agg* (*molteplice*) numerous; (*grande*) large.

numismatica *sf* numismatics (*sg*).

nuocere : nuocere a *v + prep* to harm.

nuora *sf* daughter-in-law.

nuotare *vi* to swim.

nuoto *sm* swimming.

nuovamente *avv* again.

Nuova Zelanda *sf*: **la ~** New Zealand.

nuovo, -a *agg* new; **di ~** again; **~ di zecca** brand-new.

nuraghe, -ghi *sm prehistoric stone monument in Sardinia*.

nutriente *agg* nutritious.

nutrimento *sm* nourishment.

nutrire *vt* (*con cibo*) to feed; (*fig: sentimento*) to feel.

▶ **nutrirsi di** *vr + prep* to feed on.

nuvola *sf* cloud; **cascare dalle nuvole** to be flabbergasted.

nuvoloso, -a *agg* cloudy.

O

o *cong* or; **~ ... ~** either ... or.

O *(abbr di ovest)* W.

oasi *sf inv* oasis.

obbediente = **ubbidiente**.

obbedire = **ubbidire**.

obbligare *vt*: **~ qn a fare qc** to force sb to do sthg.

obbligato, -a *agg (percorso, passaggio)* fixed; *(costretto)*: **~ a fare qc** obliged to do sthg.

obbligatorio, -a *agg* compulsory.

obbligo, -ghi *sm* obligation; **avere l'~ di fare qc** to be obliged to do sthg.

obelisco, -schi *sm* obelisk.

obeso, -a *agg* obese.

obiettare *vt* to object.

obiettivo, -a ◆ *agg* objective ◆ *sm (fotografico)* lens; *(bersaglio, scopo)* objective.

obiettore *sm* objector; **~ di coscienza** conscientious objector.

obiezione *sf* objection.

obitorio *sm* mortuary.

obliquo, -a *agg* slanting.

obliterare *vt* to stamp.

oblò *sm inv* porthole.

oboe *sm* oboe.

obsoleto, -a *agg* obsolete.

oca *(pl* **oche)** *sf* goose.

occasione *sf (momento favorevole)* opportunity; *(affare)* bargain; *(causa, circostanza)* occasion; **avere ~ di fare qc** to have the chance to do sthg; **cogliere l'~ per fare qc** to take the opportunity to do sthg; **d'~** second-hand.

occhiaie *sfpl* bags, rings.

occhiali *smpl*: **~ (da vista)** glasses; **~ da sole** sunglasses.

occhiata *sf*: **dare un'~ a** to have a look at.

occhiello *sm* buttonhole.

occhio *sm* eye; **a ~ nudo** with the naked eye; **tenere o non perdere d'~ qn/qc** to keep an eye on sb/sthg; **a ~ e croce** roughly; **costare un ~ della testa** to cost a fortune; **saltare o balzare all'~** to be obvious; **a quattr'occhi** in private; **sognare a occhi aperti** to daydream.

occhiolino *sm*: **fare l'~ (a qn)** to wink (at sb).

occidentale *agg (zona)* west, western; *(cultura, società)* Western.

occidente *sm* west.

▶ **Occidente** *sm*: **l'Occidente** the West.

occorrente *sm* everything necessary.

occorrenza *sf*: **all'~** if need be.

occorrere *vi* to be necessary; **occorre aspettare** you/we have to wait; **mi occorre tempo** I need time.

occorso, -a *pp* → **occorrere**.

occulto, -a *agg* occult.

occupare *vt (ingombrare)* to take up; *(paese, università)* to occupy; *(impegnare)* to keep busy.

▶ **occuparsi di** *vr + prep (prendersi cura di)* to take care of, to look after; *(impicciarsi in)* to interfere in; *(interessarsi di)*: **si occupa di politica** he's in politics; **occupati dei fatti tuoi!** mind your own business!

occupato, -a *agg (sedia, posto)* taken; *(telefono, bagno)* engaged; *(impegnato)* busy.

occupazione *sf (impiego)* occupation; *(in economia)* employment.

Oceania *sf*: **l'~** Oceania.

oceano *sm* ocean.

oculista, -i, -e *smf* eye specialist.

odiare *vt* to hate.

odio *sm* hatred.

odioso, -a *agg* hateful, odious.

odorare *vt* to smell.

▶ **odorare di** *v + prep* to smell of.

odorato *sm (sense of)* smell.

odore *sm* smell.

▶ **odori** *(da cucina) smpl* herbs.

offendere *vt* to offend.
▶ **offendersi** *vr* to take offence.
offensivo, -a *agg* offensive.
offerto, -a ♦ *pp* → **offrire** ♦ *sf* (*proposta*) offer; (*donazione*) donation; (FIN) supply; ~ **speciale** special offer.
offesa *sf* offence.
offeso, -a ♦ *pp* → **offendere** ♦ *agg* offended.
officina *sf* (*di fabbrica*) workshop; (*per auto*) garage.
offrire *vt* to offer; (*cena, caffè*) to pay for; ~ **da bere a qn** to buy sb a drink.
▶ **offrirsi di** *vr + prep*: **offrirsi di fare qc** to offer to do sthg.
offuscare *vt* (*luce*) to darken; (*vista, mente, memoria*) to dim.
▶ **offuscarsi** *vr* (*vista*) to dim.
oggettivo, -a *agg* objective.
oggetto *sm* object; (*ufficio*) **oggetti smarriti** lost property (office) (Br), lost-and-found office (Am).
oggi *avv* today; (*attualmente*) nowadays; ~ **pomeriggio** this afternoon; **il giornale di** ~ today's newspaper; **dall'** ~ **al domani** from one day to the next.
oggigiorno *avv* nowadays.
ogni *agg inv* (*tutti*) every, each; (*distributivo*) every; **gente di** ~ **tipo** all sorts of people; ~ **giorno/mese/anno** every day/month/year; ~ **tre giorni** every three days; **in** ~ **caso** in any case; **ad** ~ **modo** anyway; ~ **quanto?** how often?; ~ **tanto** every so often; ~ **volta che** whenever.
Ognissanti *sm* All Saints' Day.
ognuno, -a *pron* everyone, everybody; ~ **di voi** each of you.
Olanda *sf*: **l'**~ Holland.
olandese ♦ *agg & sm* Dutch ♦ *smf* Dutchman (*f* Dutchwoman); **gli olandesi** the Dutch.
oleoso, -a *agg* oily.
olfatto *sm* sense of smell.
oliare *vt* to oil.
oliera *sf* oil and vinegar cruet.

olimpiadi *sfpl*: **le** ~ the Olympic Games.
olio *sm* oil; ~ **(extra-vergine) d'oliva** (extra-virgin) olive oil; ~ **di semi** vegetable oil; **sott'**~ in oil.
oliva *sf* olive; **olive farcite all'anconetana** olives stuffed with meat and vegetables, then covered in breadcrumbs and fried.
olivastro, -a *agg* (*carnagione*) sallow.
olivo *sm* olive tree.
olmo *sm* elm.
oltraggio *sm* (DIR) offence.
oltralpe : **d'oltralpe** *agg* on the other side of the Alps.
oltranza : **a oltranza** *avv* to the (bitter) end.
oltre ♦ *prep* (*di là da*) beyond; (*più di*) over, more than; (*in aggiunta a*) as well as, besides ♦ *avv* (*più in là*) further; ~ **a** (*all'infuori di*) apart from; (*in aggiunta a*) as well as; **non** ~ **le cinque** no later than five o'clock.
oltrepassare *vt* to go beyond.
omaggio *sm* (*tributo*) homage; (*regalo*) gift; **in** ~ (*con prodotto*) free.
ombelico, -chi *sm* navel.
ombra *sf* (*zona*) shade; (*figura*) shadow; **all'**~ in the shade.
ombrello *sm* umbrella.
ombrellone *sm* beach umbrella.
ombretto *sm* eye shadow.
omeopatia *sf* homeopathy.
omesso, -a *pp* → **omettere**.
omettere *vt* to omit; ~ **di fare qc** to omit to do sthg.
omicidio *sm* murder.
omissione *sf* omission.
omogeneizzato *sm* baby food.
omogeneo, -a *agg* (*uniforme*) homogeneous; (*armonico*) harmonious.
omonimo, -a *sm, f* (*persona*) namesake.
omosessuale *smf* homosexual.
On. (*abbr di onorevole*) Hon.
onda *sf* wave; **andare in** ~ to go on the air; **mandare in** ~ **qc** to broad-

cast sthg; **onde lunghe/medie/corte** long/medium/short wave (sg); **'onde pericolose'** sign warning swimmers to take care.

ondata sf wave; **a ondate** in waves.

ondulato, -a agg (terreno) undulating; (capelli) wavy; (lamiera, carta) corrugated.

onere sm (form) burden; **oneri fiscali** (DIR) taxes.

onestà sf honesty.

onesto, -a agg honest.

onnipotente agg omnipotent.

onomastico sm name day.

ONOMASTICO

Along with their birthdays, Italians also celebrate their 'onomastico', or name day, albeit in a minor way. This is the day when the saint after whom they are named is honoured. Relatives and friends send cards, small gifts or simply their best wishes.

---

onorare vt (celebrare) to honour; (fare onore a) to do credit to.

onorario, -a ♦ agg (cittadinanza, console) honorary ♦ sm fee.

onore sm honour; **fare ~ a qc** (pranzo) to do justice to sthg; (scuola, famiglia) to be a credit to sthg; **in ~ di** in honour of; **fare gli onori di casa** to be the host (f hostess); **farsi ~** to distinguish o.s.

onorevole ♦ agg (parlamentare) Honourable ♦ smf ≃ Member of Parliament (Br), ≃ Congressman (f Congresswoman) (Am).

ONU (abbr di Organizzazione delle Nazioni Unite) UN.

opaco, -a, -chi, -che agg (vetro) opaque; (colore, metallo) dull.

opera sf work; (in musica) opera; **è tutta ~ sua!** it's all his doing!; **mettersi all'~** to get down to work; **~ d'arte** work of art; **opere pubbliche** public works.

operaio, -a ♦ agg working-class ♦ sm, f worker.

operare ♦ vt (realizzare) to carry out; (MED) to operate on ♦ vi (agire) to act.

▶ **operarsi** vr (compiersi) to take place; (subire un'operazione) to have an operation.

operatore, -trice sm, f (di televisione, cinema) cameraman (f camerawoman); **~ turistico** tour operator.

operazione sf operation; (FIN) transaction.

opinione sf opinion; **l'~ pubblica** public opinion.

opporre vt (argomenti, ragioni) to put forward; **~ resistenza** to put up some resistance; **~ un rifiuto** to refuse.

▶ **opporsi** vr: **opporsi (a)** to oppose.

opportunità sf inv opportunity.

opportuno, -a agg opportune.

opposizione sf opposition.

opposto, -a ♦ pp → **opporre** ♦ agg (lato, senso) opposite; (idee) opposing ♦ sm opposite.

oppressione sf oppression.

oppresso, -a pp → **opprimere**.

opprimente agg oppressive.

opprimere vt (popolo) to oppress; (angosciare) to weigh down.

oppure cong (o invece) or; (se no) or else, otherwise.

optare : optare per v + prep to opt for.

opuscolo sm brochure.

ora ♦ sf hour; (momento) time ♦ avv now; **a che ~ parte il treno?** what time does the train leave?; **è ~ di partire** it's time to leave; **che ~ è?, che ore sono?** what's the time?; **e ~?** now what?; **~ come ~** right now; **~ legale** summertime; **~ locale** local time; **~ di punta** rush hour; **50 km all'~** 50 km an hour; **di buon'~** early; **d'~ in poi** o **in avanti** from now on; **fare le ore piccole** to stay up till the small hours.

orale agg & sm oral.

oramai → **ormai**.

orario, -a ♦ agg (segnale) time (dav

s); (*velocità*) per hour; (*tariffa*) hourly ◆ *sm* (*di lavoro, visite*) hours (*pl*); (*tabella*) timetable; **fuori ~** after hours; **in ~** on time; **~ di arrivo** arrival time; **~ di partenza** departure time; **~ di apertura** opening hours (*pl*); **~ di chiusura** closing time; **~ d'ufficio** office hours (*pl*).

orata *sf* sea bream.

orbita *sf* (*di satellite*) orbit; (*di occhio*) eye socket.

orchestra *sf* orchestra.

orchidea *sf* orchid.

ordigno *sm* device.

ordinare *vt* (*al ristorante, bar*) to order; (*disporre in ordine*) to put in order; (*comandare*): **~ a qn di fare qc** to order sb to do sth.

ordinario, -a *agg* (*normale*) ordinary; (*mediocre, scadente*) poor.

ordinato, -a *agg* tidy.

ordinazione *sf* order.

ordine *sm* order; **essere in ~** (*stanza*) to be tidy; (*documenti*) to be in order; **mettere in ~ qc** (*stanza*) to tidy sth; (*documenti*) to put sth in order; **~ pubblico** public order.

orecchiabile *agg* catchy.

orecchiette *sfpl tiny ear-shaped pasta from Puglia.*

orecchino *sm* earring.

orecchio (*pl f* **orecchie**) *sm* ear; **avere ~** to have a good ear (for music).

orecchioni *smpl* mumps (*sg*).

oreficeria *sf* (*negozio*) jeweller's.

orfano, -a *agg & sm, f* orphan.

organico, -a, -ci, -che ◆ *agg* organic ◆ *sm* staff.

organismo *sm* (*essere vivente*) organism; (*ente*) body.

organizzare *vt* to organize.

▶ **organizzarsi** *vr* to organize o.s.

organizzato, -a *agg* organized.

organizzatore, -trice *sm, f* organizer.

organizzazione *sf* organization.

organo *sm* organ.

orgasmo *sm* orgasm.

orgoglio *sm* pride.

orgoglioso, -a *agg* proud.

orientale ◆ *agg* (*paese, prodotto*) eastern; (*persona*) oriental ◆ *smf* Oriental.

orientamento *sm* (*posizione*) orientation; (*fig: indirizzo*) leanings (*pl*); **perdere l'~** to lose one's bearings; **~ professionale** careers guidance.

orientare *vt* (*carta*) to orientate.

▶ **orientarsi** *vr* to find one's bearings.

oriente *sm* east.

▶ **Oriente** *sm*: **l'Oriente** the East.

origano *sm* oregano.

originale ◆ *agg* original; (*stravagante*) eccentric ◆ *sm* original.

originario, -a *agg* (*iniziale*) original; (*paese, lingua*) native.

origine *sf* origin; (*causa*) origin, cause; **avere ~ da qc** to originate from sth; **dare ~ a qc** to cause sth; **di ~ italiana** of Italian origin.

origliare *vi* to eavesdrop.

orina = **urina**.

oriundo, -a *sm, f*: **essere ~ italiano** to be of Italian extraction.

orizzontale *agg* horizontal.

orizzonte *sm* horizon.

orlo *sm* (*di fosso*) edge; (*di bicchiere*) rim; (*di gonna, pantaloni*) hem.

orma *sf* footprint.

ormai *avv* (*a questo punto*) by now; (*a quel punto*) by then; (*quasi*) almost; **~ è tardi** it's too late now.

ormeggiare *vt & vi* to moor.

ormeggio *sm* mooring.

ormone *sm* hormone.

ornamento *sm* ornament.

ornare *vt* to decorate.

oro *sm* gold; **d'~** gold.

orologio *sm* clock; (*da polso*) watch.

oroscopo *sm* horoscope.

orrendo, -a *agg* (*spaventoso, atroce*) horrendous; (*brutto*) horrible, awful.

orribile *agg* horrible.

orrore *sm* horror.

orsacchiotto *sm* teddy bear.

orso *sm* bear.

ortaggio *sm* vegetable.

ortica, -che *sf* nettle.

orticaria *sf* hives (*pl*).

orto *sm* vegetable garden.

ortodosso, -a *agg* orthodox.

ortografia *sf* spelling.

orzaiolo *sm* stye.

orzo *sm* barley.

osare *vt*: ~ **(fare qc)** to dare (to do sthg).

osceno, -a *agg* obscene.

oscillare *vi* (*dondolare*) to swing; (*fig: variare*) to vary.

oscillazione *sf* (*di pendolo*) swing; (*di prezzi*) fluctuation; (*di temperatura*) variation.

oscurità *sf* darkness.

oscuro, -a ◆ *agg* dark ◆ *sm*: **essere all'~ di qc** to be in the dark about sthg.

ospedale *sm* hospital.

ospitale *agg* (*persona*) hospitable; (*paese*) friendly.

ospitalità *sf* hospitality; **mi ha dato ~ per una notte** he put me up for a night.

ospitare *vt* to put up.

ospite *smf* (*chi ospita*) host (*f* hostess); (*ospitato*) guest.

ospizio *sm* old people's home.

ossa *pl* → **osso**.

osseo, -a *agg* bone (*dav s*).

osservare *vt* (*guardare*) to observe, to watch; (*rilevare*) to notice; (*rispettare, mantenere*) to observe; **far ~ qc a qn** to point sthg out to sb.

osservatorio *sm* observatory.

osservazione *sf* (*esame*) observation; (*commento*) observation, remark; (*rimprovero*) criticism.

ossessionare *vt* to obsess.

ossessione *sf* obsession.

ossia *cong* that is.

ossidare *vt* to oxidize.

▶ **ossidarsi** *vr* to oxidize.

ossido *sm* oxide; ~ **di carbonio** carbon monoxide.

ossigenare *vt* to oxygenate; (*capelli*) to bleach.

ossigeno *sm* oxygen.

osso *sm* (*umano: pl f* **ossa**) bone; (*di carne: pl m* **ossi**) bone.

ossobuco (*pl* **ossibuchi**) *sm* veal knuckle cooked on the bone in tomatoes and white wine (*a speciality of Milan*).

ostacolare *vt* to obstruct.

ostacolo *sm* obstacle; (*in atletica*) hurdle; (*in equitazione*) fence.

ostaggio *sm* hostage.

ostello *sm*: ~ **(della gioventù)** (youth) hostel.

ostentare *vt* to flaunt.

osteria *sf* inn.

ostetrica, -che *sf* midwife.

ostia *sf* (RELIG) host.

ostile *agg* hostile.

ostilità ◆ *sf* hostility ◆ *sfpl* (MIL) hostilities.

ostinarsi *vr*: ~ **a fare qc** to persist in doing sthg.

ostinato, -a *agg* obstinate.

ostinazione *sf* persistence.

ostrica, -che *sf* oyster.

ostruire *vt* to obstruct, to block.

ottanta *num* eighty, → **sei**.

ottantesimo, -a *num* eightieth, → **sesto**.

ottantina *sf*: **una ~ (di)** about eighty; **essere sull'~** to be in one's eighties.

ottavo, -a *num* eighth, → **sesto**.

ottenere *vt* to get.

ottico, -a, -ci, -che ◆ *agg* (*nervo*) optic; (*strumento*) optical ◆ *sm* optician.

ottimale *agg* optimum.

ottimismo *sm* optimism.

ottimista, -i, -e *smf* optimist.

ottimo, -a *agg* excellent, very good.

otto ◆ *num* eight, → **sei** ◆ *sm*: ~ **volante** roller coaster.

ottobre *sm* October, → **settembre**.

ottocento *num* eight hundred, → **sei**.

▶ **Ottocento** *sm*: l'**Ottocento** the nineteenth century.
ottone *sm* brass.
otturare *vt* to fill.
otturazione *sf* filling.
ottuso, -a *agg* obtuse.
ovale *agg* oval.
ovatta *sf* cotton wool.
overdose *sf inv* overdose.
ovest *sm & agg inv* west; **a ~ (di qc)** west (of sthg).
ovile *sm* sheepfold.
ovino, -a *agg* sheep (*dav s*).
ovovia *sf* ski lift (*with oval cabins*).
ovunque = **dovunque**.
ovvero *cong* or, in other words.
ovviare *vi*: ~ **a qc** to avoid sthg.
ovvio, -a *agg* obvious.
ozio *sm* idleness.
ozono *sm* ozone.

P

pacato, -a *agg* calm.
pacca, -che *sf* pat.
pacchetto *sm* (*di sigarette, caramelle*) packet; (*pacco*) parcel.
pacchiano, -a *agg* garish.
pacco, -chi *sm* parcel.
pace *sf* peace; **in ~** in peace; **fare (la) ~** to make it up.
pacemaker [pei'smɛkər] *sm inv* pacemaker.
pacifico, -a, -ci, -che *agg* peaceful.
▶ **Pacifico** *sm*: il **Pacifico** the Pacific.
pacifista, -i, -e *agg & smf* pacifist.
padella *sf* (*da cucina*) frying pan; (*per malati*) bedpan.
padiglione *sm* (*di ospedale, fiera*) pavilion; (*di giardino*) marquee.

Padova *sf* Padua.
padre *sm* father.
padrino *sm* godfather.
padrone, -a *sm, f* owner; **essere ~ di fare qc** to be free to do sthg; **~ di casa** landlord (*f* landlady).
paesaggio *sm* landscape; (*panorama*) scenery.
paese *sm* (*nazione*) country; (*villaggio*) village; **~ di provenienza** country of origin; **mandare qn a quel ~** (*volg*) to tell sb to get lost.
▶ **Paesi Bassi** *smpl*: i **Paesi Bassi** the Netherlands.
paffuto, -a *agg* plump, chubby.
paga, -ghe *sf* pay.
pagamento *sm* payment; **'~ pedaggio'** 'toll to be paid here'.
pagano, -a *agg & sm, f* pagan.
pagare *vt* to pay; (*offrire*) to buy; **quanto l'hai pagato?** how much did you pay for it?; **~ con assegno** to pay by cheque; **~ con carta di credito** to pay by credit card; **~ in contanti** to pay cash.
pagella *sf* (school) report.
pagina *sf* page.
paglia *sf* straw.
pagliaccio *sm* clown.
pagnotta *sf* round loaf.
paio (*pl f* **paia**) *sm* pair; **un ~ di** (*alcuni*) a couple of; **un ~ di scarpe** a pair of shoes.
Pakistan *sm*: il **~** Pakistan.
pala *sf* (*vanga*) shovel; (*di mulino, elica*) blade.
palato *sm* palate.
palazzo *sm* (*signorile*) palace; (*edificio*) building; (*condominio*) block of flats (Br), apartment building (Am); **~ di giustizia** law courts (*pl*); **~ dello sport** indoor stadium.
palco, -chi *sm* (*palcoscenico*) stage; (*pedana*) stand; (*a teatro*) box.
palcoscenico, -ci *sm* stage.
Palermo *sf* Palermo.
Palestina *sf*: la **~** Palestine.
palestra *sf* gymnasium.
paletta *sf* (*giocattolo, per giardiniere*)

spade; (*per lo sporco*) dustpan; (*di polizia, capostazione*) signalling disc.

paletto *sm* stake.

palio *sm*: **mettere qc in ~** to offer sthg as a prize.

▶ **Palio** *sm*: **il Palio (di Siena)** the Palio (*traditional horse race held in the centre of Siena*).

IL PALIO DI SIENA

Siena's famous horse race attracts thousands of visitors to Tuscany on July 2 and August 16 every year. Representatives of Siena's 17 'contrade' (districts) parade in Renaissance costumes, and 10 districts enter a horse and rider in the race which follows. The race is very rough, and the walls of the Piazza del Campo are padded to protect the contestants. The winner is awarded a 'palio' (painted banner), and is paraded through the town.

---

palla *sf* ball; **che palle!** (*volg*) what a drag!

pallacanestro *sf* basketball.

pallanuoto *sf* water polo.

pallavolo *sf* volleyball.

pallido, -a *agg* pale.

palloncino *sm* balloon.

pallone *sm* (*palla*) ball; (*da calcio*) football; **~ aerostatico** hot air balloon.

pallottola *sf* bullet.

palma *sf* palm tree.

palmo *sm* palm.

palo *sm* (*di legno*) post; (*di telefono*) pole; **~ della luce** lamppost.

palombaro *sm* (deep sea) diver.

palpebra *sf* eyelid.

palude *sf* marsh, swamp.

panca, -che *sf* bench.

pancarrè *sm* sliced bread.

pancetta *sf* bacon.

panchina *sf* (*di parco*) bench; (*di giardino*) garden seat.

pancia, -ce *sf* (*fam*) belly.

panciotto *sm* waistcoat.

panda *sm inv* panda.

pandoro *sm conical sponge cake eaten at Christmas.*

pane *sm* bread; (*pagnotta*) loaf; (*di burro*) block; **~ a** o **in cassetta** sliced bread; **~ integrale** wholemeal bread; **~ tostato** toast; **pan dolce** *Christmas cake with candied fruit (a speciality of Genoa)*; **pan di Spagna** *sponge cake.*

PANE

A staple of the Mediterranean diet, bread is eaten with all Italian meals and waiters bring it automatically to the restaurant table. The main varieties are 'pane bianco' (white bread), which is either 'comune' (plain) or 'speciale' (made with oil), and 'pane integrale' (wholemeal bread). It is sold in loaves or sticks or as rolls, and its shapes and names differ from region to region and city to city.

---

panetteria *sf* bakery.

panettone *sm traditional dome-shaped Christmas cake containing raisins and candied fruit.*

panforte *sm very rich round, flat cake made with almonds, hazelnuts, candied fruits and spices (a speciality of Siena).*

pangrattato *sm* breadcrumbs (*pl*).

panico *sm* panic.

panificio *sm* baker's.

panino *sm* roll; **~ imbottito** o **ripieno** filled roll; **~ al prosciutto** ham roll.

paninoteca, -che *sf* sandwich bar.

panna *sf*: **~ (montata)** whipped cream; **~ cotta** *cold dessert made from cream and sugar, eaten with chocolate or fruit sauce*; **~ da cucina** cream.

panne : **in panne** *agg inv*: **ho l'auto in ~** my car has broken down.

pannello *sm* panel.

panno *sm* cloth; **mettersi nei panni di qn** to put o.s. in sb's shoes.

pannocchia *sf* cob.

pannolino *sm* nappy (Br), diaper (Am).

panorama, -i sm panorama.
panoramico, -a, -ci, -che agg panoramic.
panpepato sm ≃ gingerbread.
pantaloncini smpl shorts.
pantaloni smpl trousers (Br), pants (Am).
pantera sf panther.
pantofole sfpl slippers.
panzanella sf Tuscan salad of tomatoes, anchovies, tuna, onion and herbs, whose special ingredient is moistened bread.
panzerotti smpl large ravioli stuffed with cheese and tomato, and fried in oil.
paonazzo, -a agg purple.
papa, -i sm: **il ~** the Pope.
papà sm inv (fam) daddy, dad.
papavero sm poppy.
papera sf (errore): **fare una ~** to make a slip of the tongue, → **papero.**
papero, -a sm, f gosling.
papillon [papi'jɔn] sm inv bow tie.
pappa sf (fam) baby food.
pappagallo sm (animale) parrot; (per malati) bedpan.
pappardelle sfpl large noodles; **~ alla lepre** 'pappardelle' served with hare sauce.
paprica sf paprika.
para sf crepe rubber.
parabola sf (MAT) parabola; (RELIG) parable.
parabrezza sm inv windscreen.
paracadute sm inv parachute.
paracarro sm post.
paradiso sm (RELIG) paradise, heaven.
paradossale agg paradoxical.
paradosso sm paradox.
parafango, -ghi sm mudguard.
parafulmine sm lightning conductor.
paraggi smpl: **nei ~** in the neighbourhood.
paragonare vt: **~ con** to compare with.

paragone sm comparison.
paragrafo sm paragraph.
paralisi sf inv paralysis.
paralizzare vt to paralyse.
parallela sf parallel.
▶ **parallele** sfpl (attrezzo) parallel bars.
parallelo, -a agg & sm parallel.
paralume sm lampshade.
parapendio sm paragliding.
parapetto sm parapet.
parare vt (colpi) to parry; (occhi) to shield; (nel calcio) to save.
parassita, -i sm parasite.
parata sf (militare) parade; (nel calcio) save.
paraurti sm inv bumper.
paravento sm screen.
parcella sf fee.
parcheggiare vt to park.
parcheggio sm (area) car park (Br), parking lot (Am); (manovra) parking; **~ a pagamento** car park where drivers must pay to park; **~ riservato** private car park.
parchimetro sm parking meter.
parco, -chi sm park; **~ giochi** o **dei divertimenti** swing park.

PARCHI NAZIONALI

Five Italian national parks have been created by the government to protect the environment and preserve the balance of nature in these designated areas. They are areas of great natural beauty, and are well equipped to welcome visitors. In the Alps the Parco del Gran Paradiso shelters the ibex, and the Parco dello Stelvio the chamois. In the central Apennines are the Parco Nazionale d'Abruzzo and the Parco del Circeo, and in the south is the Parco Nazionale della Calabria.

---

parecchio, -a ♦ agg quite a lot of ♦ pron quite a lot ♦ avv (con agg) quite; (con verbo) quite a lot; **è ~ (tempo) che aspetto** I've been waiting for quite a while.

pareggiare ◆ vt (capelli, orlo) to make even; (terreno) to level; (bilancio, conti) to balance ◆ vi to draw.

pareggio sm (in partite) draw; (del bilancio) balance.

parente smf relative.

parentela sf (vincolo) relationship; (famiglia) relatives (pl).

parentesi sf inv (segno) bracket; (commento) digression; **tra ~** in brackets.

pareo sm pareo.

parere ◆ sm (opinione) opinion ◆ vi (sembrare) to seem; (apparire) to look ◆ v impers: **pare che** it seems that; **che te ne pare?** what do you think?; **fate come vi pare** do as you like; **mi pare di no** I don't think so; **mi pare di sì** I think so; **mi pare (che) vada bene** it seems (to be) all right; **pare (che) sia vero** it seems (to be) true.

parete sf (di stanza) wall; (di montagna) face.

pari ◆ agg inv (in partite, giochi, superficie) level; (numero) even ◆ sm inv equal; **alla ~** (ragazza) au pair; **ora siamo ~** now we're even; **essere ~ a** (uguale) to be the same as, to be equal to; **essere alla ~** to be even; **mettersi in ~ con qc** to catch up with sthg; **~ ~** word for word.

Parigi sf Paris.

parlamentare ◆ agg parliamentary ◆ smf = Member of Parliament (Br), = Congressman (f Congresswoman) (Am).

parlamento sm parliament.

parlantina sf (fam): **avere una buona ~** to have the gift of the gab.

parlare ◆ vi to talk, to speak ◆ vt (lingua) to speak; **~ (a qn) di** to talk o to speak (to sb) about; **parla italiano?** do you speak Italian?

Parma sf Parma.

parmigiano sm Parmesan (cheese).

parola sf word; **prendere la ~** to (begin to) speak; **rivolgere la ~ a qn**

to talk to sb; **rimangiarsi la ~** to go back on one's word; **~ d'onore** word of honour; **~ d'ordine** password; **parole crociate** crossword (puzzle) (sg); **è una ~!** it's not easy!

parolaccia, -ce sf swearword.

parrocchia sf (chiesa) parish church; (zona) parish.

parroco, -ci sm parish priest.

parrucca, -che sf wig.

parrucchiere, -a sm, f (per signora) hairdresser.

parso, -a pp → parere.

parte sf part; (lato) side; (direzione) way; (quota) share; (DIR) party; **fare ~ di qc** to be part of sthg; **mettere da ~ qc** (risparmiare) to put sthg aside; **prendere ~ a qc** to take part in sthg; **stare dalla ~ di** to be on the side of; **la maggior ~** di most of; **la maggior ~ degli italiani** most Italians; **a ~ questo** apart from that; **a ~** (spese, pacco) separate; (pagare, incartare) separately; **da ~ di qn** from; (ringraziare) on sb's behalf; **d'altra ~** on the other hand; **dall'altra ~** (essere) on the other side; (andare, guardare) the other way; **da che ~?** which way?; **da nessuna ~** nowhere; **da ogni ~** everywhere; **da qualche ~** somewhere; **da questa ~** this way; **in ~** partly.

partecipare : partecipare a v + prep (intervenire) to take part in; (spese) to contribute to; (gioia, dolore) to share in.

partenza sf departure; (nello sport) start; **essere in ~ (per Roma)** to be about to leave (for Rome); '**partenze nazionali/internaziona-li**' 'domestic/international departures'.

participio sm participle.

particolare ◆ agg particular; (caratteristico) distinctive ◆ sm detail; **niente di ~** nothing special; **in ~** in particular.

particolareggiato, -a agg detailed.

partigiano, -a sm, f partisan.

partire vi (persona) to leave; (treno, aereo) to depart; (nello sport) to start;

(*colpo*) to go off; **a ~ da** from; **parto da Milano alle cinque** I leave Milan at five.

partita *sf* (*competizione*) match; (*a carte, a tennis*) game; (*di merce*) consignment; **~ IVA** VAT registration number.

partito *sm* party.

parto *sm* birth.

partorire *vt* to give birth to.

parziale *agg* (*limitato*) partial; (*ingiusto*) biased.

pascolo *sm* pasture.

Pasqua *sf* Easter.

pasquale *agg* Easter (*dav s*).

Pasquetta *sf* Easter Monday.

PASQUETTA

In Italy, Easter still retains its religious significance. Holy Week culminates in a Mass celebrated by the Pope from the balcony of St Peter's, and on Easter Sunday families have a special lunch and exchange Easter eggs. In many regions Easter Monday, a national holiday, is called 'Pasquetta'. It is traditionally celebrated with a picnic in the country or by the sea.

---

passabile *agg* passable.

passaggio *sm* (*transito*) passage; (*varco*) thoroughfare; (*in macchina*) lift; (*cambiamento*) change; **essere di ~** to be passing through; **~ a livello** level crossing (Br), grade crossing (Am); **~ pedonale** pedestrian crossing.

passamontagna *sm inv* balaclava.

passante ◆ *smf* (*persona*) passerby ◆ *sm* (*per cintura*) loop.

passaporto *sm* passport.

passare ◆ *vi* to go by; (*da un'apertura*) to go through; (*fare una visita*) to call in; (*cessare*) to go away; (*proposta*) to be passed ◆ *vt* (*attraversare*) to cross; (*trascorrere*) to spend; (*cera, vernice*) to apply; (*esame*) to pass; (*oltrepassare*) to go beyond; (*verdure*) to puree; (*porgere*) to pass;

mi è passato di mente! it slipped my mind!; **ti passo Matteo** (*al telefono*) here's Matteo; **il treno passa da Firenze** the train goes via Florence; **~ l'aspirapolvere** to vacuum; **~ qc a qn** to pass o to give sb sthg; **~ avanti a qn** to push in front of sb; **~ da o per scemo** to be taken for a fool; **~ sopra qc** (*fig: tollerare*) to overlook; **passarsela bene** to get on well; **come te la passi?** how are you getting on?

passatempo *sm* pastime.

passato, -a ◆ *agg* (*trascorso*) over ◆ *sm* past; **~ di verdure** thin vegetable soup.

passaverdura *sm inv* vegetable mill.

passeggero, -a ◆ *agg* passing ◆ *sm, f* passenger.

passeggiare *vi* to walk; (*andare a spasso*) to stroll.

passeggiata *sf* (*camminata*) walk; (*strada*) promenade; **fare una ~** to take a walk.

PASSEGGIATA

The Italian custom of taking a stroll with friends or family has survived many changes in fashion and still brings different generations together. Courting couples, families and teenagers alike meet up on Sunday morning or in the late afternoon and stroll slowly round the main square or the park, or along the main street or the promenade. They may stop to say hello to friends and acquaintances, to have an aperitif or to buy cakes and pastries for dessert.

---

passeggino *sm* pushchair.

passeggio *sm*: **andare a ~** to go for a walk.

passerella *sf* (*passaggio*) footbridge; (*di aereo, nave*) gangway; (*di sfilata*) catwalk.

passerotto *sm* sparrow.

passione *sf* passion.

passivo, -a ◆ *agg* passive ◆ *sm*

(GRAMM) passive; (COMM) liabilities (pl).

passo sm (movimento) step; (andatura) pace; (rumore) footstep; (valico) pass; **allungare il ~** to quicken one's pace; **fare il primo ~** (fig) to make the first move; **a ~ d'uomo** dead slow; **'~ carraio** o **carrabile'** 'keep clear'; **fare due** o **quattro passi** to go for a short walk; **a due passi** a stone's throw away; **di questo ~** at this rate.

pasta sf pasta; (impasto) dough; (pasticcino) pastry, cake; (di colla) paste; **~ in brodo** soup with pasta in it; **~ frolla** shortcrust pastry; **~ sfoglia** puff pastry.

PASTA

Most Italians eat pasta at least once a day, and an infinite variety of types can be found: 'spaghetti', 'bucatini' and 'tagliatelle' are just a few examples of 'pasta lunga' (long pasta); 'penne', 'rigatoni' and 'fusilli' are common types of 'pasta corta' (short pasta). The basic dough is just flour and water, but it can be varied by using a different type of flour and by adding different ingredients and flavourings. 'Pasta integrale' is wholemeal pasta, 'pasta all'uovo' is enriched with egg, and 'pasta verde' is flavoured with spinach. The tradition of making one's own pasta ('pasta fatta in casa') still survives in many families.

---

pastasciutta sf pasta.
pastella sf batter.
pasticca, -che = **pastiglia**.
pasticceria sf ≈ cake shop.
pasticcino sm pastry.
pasticcio sm (vivanda) pie; (disordine) mess; (guaio) trouble; **essere nei pasticci** to be in trouble.
pasticcione, -a sm, f bungler.
pastiera sf Neapolitan Easter tart with a filling of ricotta cheese and candied fruit.

pastiglia sf pastille.
pastizzada sf horse meat or beef and vegetables marinated in wine, generally served with polenta (a speciality of Veneto).
pasto sm meal.
pastore sm (di greggi) shepherd; (sacerdote) minister; **~ tedesco** German shepherd, Alsatian (Br).
pastorizzato, -a agg pasteurized.
patata sf potato; **patate fritte** chips (Br), French fries (Am).
patatine sfpl crisps (Br), chips (Am).
pâté sm inv pâté.
patente sf licence; **~ (di guida)** driving licence (Br), driver's license (Am).
paternità sf paternity.
paterno, -a agg paternal.
patetico, -a, -ci, -che agg pathetic.
patire vt & vi to suffer.
patria sf homeland.
patrigno sm stepfather.
patrimonio sm (beni) property; (culturale, spirituale) heritage.
patrono sm patron saint.
pattinaggio sm skating; **~ su ghiaccio** ice skating.
pattinare vi to skate; **~ su ghiaccio** to ice-skate.
pattini smpl: **~ a rotelle** roller skates; **~ da ghiaccio** ice skates.
pattino sm pedalo with oars.
patto sm (accordo) pact; **a ~ che** on condition that.
pattuglia sf patrol.
pattumiera sf dustbin.
paura sf fear; **avere ~ (di)** to be afraid (of); **avere ~ di fare qc** to be afraid of doing sth; **fare ~ a qn** to frighten sb; **per ~ di fare qc** for fear of doing sth; **per ~ che** for fear that.
pauroso, -a agg (spaventoso) frightening; (timoroso) fearful.
pausa sf (intervallo) break; (MUS) pause; **fare una ~** to take a break.

pavimento *sm* floor.
pavone *sm* peacock.
paziente *agg & smf* patient.
pazienza *sf* patience; **perdere la ~** to lose one's patience; **~!** never mind!
pazzamente *avv* madly.
pazzesco, -a, -schi, -sche *agg* crazy.
pazzia *sf* madness; (*azione*) crazy thing.
pazzo, -a ◆ *agg* (*malato*) mad ◆ *sm, f* madman (*f* madwoman); **andare ~ per qc** to be crazy about sthg; **essere ~ di qn** to be crazy about sb; **darsi alla pazza gioia** to live it up.
peccare *vi* to sin; **~ di qc** to be guilty of sthg.
peccato *sm* sin; **è un ~ che ...** it's a pity that ...; (**che**) **~!** what a pity!
peccatore, -trice *sm, f* sinner.
pecora *sf* sheep.
pecorino *sm* a cheese made from ewe's milk.
pedaggio *sm* toll.
pedalare *vi* to pedal.
pedale *sm* pedal; **a pedali** pedal (*dav s*).
pedana *sf* (*poggiapiedi*) footboard; (*in atletica*) springboard; (*nella scherma*) piste.
pedata *sf* (*impronta*) footmark; (*calcio*) kick.
pediatra, -i, -e *smf* pediatrician.
pedicure *sm* pedicure.
pedina *sf* piece.
pedonale *agg* pedestrian (*dav s*).
pedone *sm* pedestrian; (*negli scacchi*) pawn.
peggio ◆ *avv & agg inv* worse ◆ *smf*: **il/la ~** the worst; **~ per te!** so much the worse for you!; **temere il ~** to fear the worst; **alla ~** if the worst comes to the worst; **~ che mai** worse than ever.
peggioramento *sm* deterioration.
peggiorare *vt & vi* to worsen.

peggiore ◆ *agg* (*comparativo*) worse; (*superlativo*) worst ◆ *smf*: **il/la ~** the worst.
pelare *vt* to peel.
pelato, -a *agg* bald.
▶ **pelati** *smpl* peeled tomatoes.
pelle *sf* skin; (*conciata*) leather; **avere la ~ d'oca** to have goose pimples.
pellegrinaggio *sm* pilgrimage.
pellegrino, -a *sm, f* pilgrim.
pelletteria *sf* (*prodotti*) leather goods (*pl*); (*negozio*) leather goods shop.
pellicceria *sf* fur shop.
pelliccia, -ce *sf* (*di animale*) fur; (*indumento*) fur coat.
pellicola *sf* film; **~ a colori** colour film.
pelo *sm* (*del corpo, di tessuto*) hair; (*di animale*) fur; **ce l'ho fatta per un ~** I made it by the skin of my teeth; **c'è mancato un ~ che lo investissero** they narrowly missed hitting him.
peloso, -a *agg* hairy.
peltro *sm* pewter.
peluche [pe'luʃ] *sm inv* (*tessuto*) plush; (*pupazzo*) cuddly toy.
pena *sf* (*condanna*) sentence; (*cruccio*) anxiety; (*pietà*) pity; (RELIG) torment; **mi fanno ~** I feel sorry for them; **(non) vale la ~ di andarci** it's (not) worth going; **~ di morte** death penalty; **a mala ~** hardly.
penalità *sf inv* penalty.
pendente ◆ *agg* (*appeso*) hanging; (*inclinato*) leaning; (*conto*) pending ◆ *sm* (*ciondolo*) pendant; (*orecchino*) drop earring.
pendenza *sf* (*inclinazione*) slope; (*di conto*) outstanding account.
pendere *vi* (*essere appeso*) to hang; (*essere inclinato*) to slope.
pendici *sfpl* slopes.
pendio *sm* slope.
pendola *sf* pendulum clock.
pendolare *smf* commuter.
pene *sm* penis.
penetrare *vi*: **~ in qc** (*entrare in*) to enter sthg; (*sog: chiodo, liquido*) to

penetrate sthg.
penicillina *sf* penicillin.
penisola *sf* peninsula.
penitenza *sf* (*religiosa*) penitence;
(*nei giochi*) forfeit.
penitenziario *sm* prison.
penna *sf* pen; (*di uccello*) feather; ~
a sfera ballpoint pen; ~ **stilografica**
fountain pen;.
▶ **penne** *sfpl* pasta quills; **penne**
all'arrabbiata '*penne*' *in a spicy sauce of*
tomatoes and chillies.
pennarello *sm* felt-tip pen.
pennello *sm* (*da pittore*) brush; (*per*
vernici, tinte) paintbrush; ~ **da barba**
shaving brush; **a** ~ like a glove.
penombra *sf* half-light.
penoso, -a *agg* painful.
pensare ♦ *vi* to think ♦ *vt* (*imma-*
ginare) to think; (*escogitare*) to think
up; **cosa ne pensi?** what do you
think (of it)?; ~ **a** (*riflettere su, ricor-*
dare) to think about; (*occuparsi di*) to
see to; **pensa a un numero** think of
a number; ~ **di fare qc** to be thinking of doing sthg; **penso di no** I
don't think so; **penso di sì** I think
so; **pensarci su** to think it over.
pensiero *sm* thought; (*preoccu-*
pazione) worry; **stare in** ~ **per qn** to
be worried about sb.
pensile ♦ *agg* hanging ♦ *sm* wall
cupboard.
pensilina *sf* (*di stazione*) platform
roof; (*per autobus*) bus shelter.
pensionante *smf* lodger.
pensionato, -a ♦ *sm, f* (*persona*)
pensioner ♦ *sm* (*per studenti*) hostel.
pensione *sf* (*somma*) pension;
(*albergo*) boardinghouse; (*vitto e*
alloggio) board and lodging; **andare**
in ~ to retire; **essere in** ~ to be
retired; ~ **completa** full board;
mezza ~ half board.
Pentecoste *sf* Whitsun.
pentirsi *vr*: ~ **di qc** to regret sthg;
~ **di aver fatto qc** to regret doing
sthg.
pentola *sf* pot; ~ **a pressione** pressure cooker.

penultimo, -a *agg* penultimate.
pepare *vt* to pepper.
pepato, -a *agg* peppery.
pepe *sm* pepper.
peperonata *sf* stewed sliced peppers,
tomatoes and onions.
peperoncino *sm* chilli pepper; ~
rosso red chilli pepper.
peperone *sm* (*capsicum*) pepper.
per *prep* **1.** (*indica lo scopo, la desti-*
nazione) for; **è** ~ **te** it's for you; **fare qc**
~ **i soldi** to do sthg for money;
equipaggiarsi ~ **la montagna** to kit
o.s. out for the mountains; ~ **fare**
qc (*in order*) to do sthg; **sono venu-**
to ~ **vederti** I've come to see you; **è**
abbastanza grande ~ **capire certe**
cose he's old enough to understand these things.
2. (*attraverso*) through; **ti ho cercato** ~
tutta la città I've been looking for
you all over town.
3. (*moto a luogo*) for, to; **il treno** ~
Genova the Genoa train; **partire** ~
Napoli to leave for Naples.
4. (*indica una durata, una scadenza*) for;
~ **tutta la vita** for one's whole life;
sarò di ritorno ~ **le cinque** I'll be back
by five; **l'ho vista** ~ **Pasqua** I saw her
at Easter; **fare qc** ~ **tempo** to do sthg
in time; ~ **sempre** forever.
5. (*indica il mezzo, il modo*) by; **gli ho**
parlato ~ **telefono** I talked to him
over the phone; **viaggiare** ~ **mare**
to travel by sea; **fare qc** ~ **scherzo**
to do sthg for a joke; ~ **caso** by
chance.
6. (*indica la causa*) for; **piangere** ~ **la**
rabbia to cry with rage; **viaggiare** ~
lavoro to travel on business; ~ **aver**
fatto qc for doing sthg.
7. (*con valore distributivo*) per; **entrare**
uno ~ **volta** to go in one at a time;
uno ~ **uno** one by one.
8. (*come*) as; **tenere qc** ~ **certo** to
take sthg for granted.
9. (*indica il prezzo*): **lo ha venduto** ~ **un**
milione he sold it for a million lira.
10. (MAT): **2** ~ **3 fa 6** 2 times 3
makes 6.

11. (*indica la conseguenza*): **è troppo bello ~ essere vero** it's too good to be true.

12. (*indica limitazione*) for; **~ me, vi sbagliate** as far as I'm concerned, you are wrong; **~ questa volta** this time.

pera *sf* pear.

peraltro *avv* what is more.

perbene ♦ *agg inv* decent ♦ *avv* properly.

percentuale *sf* percentage.

percepire *vt* (*sentire*) to perceive; (*ricevere*) to receive.

perché *avv* why; **~ corri?** why are you running?; **~ non ci andiamo?** why don't we go?; **spiegami ~ lo hai fatto** tell me why you did it; **~ no?** why not?; **chissà ~** who knows why; **ecco ~** that's why.

♦ *cong* **1.** (*per il fatto che*) because; **vado ~ ho fretta** I'm going because I'm in a hurry; **~ sì/no!** (just) because!

2. (*affinché*) so that; **telefona ~ non stiano in pensiero** phone so that (they) don't worry.

3. (*cosicché*): **è troppo complicato ~ si possa capire** it's too complicated for anyone to understand.

♦ *sm inv* (*ragione*) reason; **senza un ~** for no reason.

perciò *cong* therefore.

percorrere *vt* (*regione*) to travel over; (*distanza*) to cover.

percorso, -a ♦ *pp* → **percorrere** ♦ *sm* journey.

percosse *sfpl* blows.

percosso, -a *pp* → **percuotere**.

percuotere *vt* (*form*) to beat.

perdere *vt* to lose; (*treno, lezione, film*) to miss; (*tempo, denaro*) to waste; (*liquido, gas*) to leak; **~ sangue** to lose blood; **lasciare ~** not to bother; **non avere nulla da ~** to have nothing to lose; **~ la testa** to lose one's head.

► **perdersi** *vr* to get lost.

perdita *sf* loss; (*di acqua, gas*) leak; **una ~ di tempo** a waste of time; **a ~**

d'occhio as far as the eye can see.

perdonare *vt* to forgive.

perdono *sm* (*di colpa, peccato*) pardon; (*scusa*) forgiveness.

perdutamente *avv* desperately.

perfettamente *avv* perfectly.

perfetto, -a *agg* perfect.

perfezionare *vt* to perfect.

perfezione *sf* perfection; **alla ~** perfectly.

perfido, -a *agg* treacherous.

perfino *avv* even.

perforare *vt* to pierce.

pergola *sf* pergola.

pericolante *agg* unsafe.

pericolo *sm* danger; **essere fuori ~** to be out of danger; **essere in ~** to be in danger; **'~ (di morte)'** 'danger of death'.

pericoloso, -a *agg* dangerous.

periferia *sf* outskirts (*pl*), suburbs (*pl*); **in ~** in the suburbs.

perimetro *sm* perimeter.

periodico, -a, -ci, -che ♦ *agg* periodic ♦ *sm* periodical.

periodo *sm* period.

perito *sm* (*esperto*) expert; **~ chimico** qualified chemist.

perla *sf* pearl.

perlustrare *vt* to patrol.

permaloso, -a *agg* touchy.

permanente ♦ *agg* permanent ♦ *sf* perm; **'permanente'** 'at all times'.

permanenza *sf* continued stay.

permesso, -a ♦ *pp* → **permettere** ♦ *sm* (*autorizzazione*) permission; (*congedo*) leave; (*documento*) permit; **(è) ~?** (*per entrare*) may I come in?; **~!** (*per passare*) excuse me!; **~ di soggiorno** residence permit.

permettere *vt* to allow; **~ a qn di fare qc** to allow sb to do sthg; **potersi ~ qc** (*spesa, acquisto*) to be able to afford sthg; **permettersi di fare qc** (*prendersi la libertà*) to take the liberty of doing sthg; **potersi ~ di fare qc**

(*finanziariamente*) to be able to afford to do sth.

perno sm hinge.

pernottamento sm overnight stay.

però cong (*ma*) but; (*tuttavia*) however.

perpendicolare agg perpendicular.

perplesso, -a agg puzzled.

perquisire vt to search.

perquisizione sf search.

perseguitare vt to persecute.

perseverare vi to persevere.

persiana sf shutter.

persiano, -a ♦ agg Persian ♦ sm (*pelliccia*) Persian lamb.

persino = **perfino**.

persistente agg persistent, long-lasting.

perso, -a pp → **perdere**.

persona sf person; **c'è una ~ che ti aspetta** there's somebody waiting for you; **conoscere qn di ~** to know sb personally; **in ~** in person.

personaggio sm (*di libro, film*) character; (*pubblico, politico*) figure.

personale ♦ agg personal ♦ sm (*dipendenti*) personnel, staff; (*fisico*) build.

personalità sf inv personality.

personalmente avv personally.

persuadere vt to persuade; **~ qn a fare qc** to persuade sb to do sthg; **~ qn di qc** to convince sb of sthg.

persuaso, -a pp → **persuadere**.

pertanto cong (*perciò*) therefore.

perturbare vt to upset.

perturbazione sf disturbance.

Perugia sf Perugia.

pervenire vi: **~ a** to reach, to arrive at.

pervenuto, -a pp → **pervenire**.

pesante agg heavy; (*fig: persona, film*) boring; (*scherzo*) in bad taste.

pesare ♦ vt to weigh ♦ vi to weigh; (*essere pesante*) to be heavy; (*essere spiacevole*) to be hard.

▶ **pesarsi** vr to weigh o.s.

pesca, -sche sf (*frutto*) peach; (*attività*) fishing; **pesche ripiene** *peaches stuffed with macaroons and baked in white wine*; **andare a ~** to go fishing; **~ di beneficenza** lucky dip; **~ subacquea** underwater fishing.

pescare vt (*pesce*) to catch; (*carta*) to draw; (*trovare*) to find out; **mi piace ~** I like fishing.

pescatore sm fisherman.

pesce sm fish; **~ d'aprile!** April Fool!

▶ **Pesci** smpl Pisces (*sg*).

PESCE D'APRILE

April 1 is the occasion for tricks and practical jokes in Italy, as it is in Britain, but in Italy it is named after the paper fish which children secretly attach to the backs of their friends and of passers-by. Recently, newspapers have joined in the fun by publishing fake news stories to catch out the unwary.

pescheria sf fishmonger's.

pescivendolo, -a sm, f fishmonger.

peso sm weight; **lancio del ~** shot-put; **~ lordo** gross weight; **~ netto** net weight; **essere di ~ a qn** to be a burden on sb.

pessimismo sm pessimism.

pessimista, -i, -e smf pessimist.

pessimistico, -a, -ci, -che agg pessimistic.

pessimo, -a agg dreadful.

pestare vt (*calpestare*) to tread on; (*uva, aglio*) to crush; (*picchiare*) to beat up.

pesto, -a ♦ agg: **buio ~** pitch-black; **occhio ~** black eye ♦ sm: **~ (alla genovese)** pesto (*sauce made from basil, pine kernels, garlic, olive oil and cheese; a speciality of Genoa*).

petalo sm petal.

petardo sm firecracker.

petroliera sf oil tanker.

petrolio sm oil.

pettegolezzi smpl gossip (*sg*).

pettinare vt to comb.
▶ **pettinarsi** vr to comb one's hair, to do one's hair.
pettine sm comb.
petto sm (torace) chest; (seno) breast; ~ **di pollo** chicken breast; **a doppio** ~ double-breasted.
pezzo sm piece; (di spazio, tempo) bit; **è un bel** ~ **che ti cerco** I've been looking for you for quite a while; **andare in (mille) pezzi** to be smashed (to smithereens); **cadere a pezzi** to fall to pieces; ~ **di ricambio** spare part; ~ **grosso** (fig) big shot.
piacere ♦ sm pleasure; (favore) favour ♦ vi: **mi piace** I like it; **mi piacciono i tulipani** I like tulips; **mi ha fatto molto** ~ **vederla** I was delighted to see her; **per** ~ please; ~ **(di conoscerla)!** pleased to meet you!; ~ **mio!** the pleasure is mine!
piacevole agg pleasant.
piaga, -ghe sf (lesione) sore; (fig: flagello) plague.
pianerottolo sm landing.
pianeta, -i sm planet.
piangere vi to cry, to weep.
pianista, -i, -e smf pianist.
piano, -a ♦ agg (piatto) flat; (MAT) plane ♦ avv (lentamente) slowly; (a bassa voce) softly ♦ sm (di edificio) floor, storey; (GEOG & MAT) plane; (livello) level; (programma, disegno) plan; (pianoforte) piano; **andarci** ~ to act with caution; **piano piano** (poco a poco) little by little; (lentamente) very slowly; **abitano al primo** ~ they live on the first floor (Br), they live on the second floor (Am); **il** ~ **di sopra/di sotto** the floor above/below; ~ **di cottura** hob; **in primo** ~ in the foreground.
piano-bar sm inv bar with music provided by pianist.
pianoforte sm piano.
pianoterra = **pianterreno**.
pianta sf plant; (di piede) sole; (di città) map; (di casa) plan; ~ **grassa** succulent.

piantare vt (semi) to plant; (conficcare) to knock in; (fam: abbandonare) to leave; **piantala!** stop it!
pianterreno sm ground floor (Br), first floor (Am); **al** ~ on the ground floor (Br), on the first floor (Am).
pianto ♦ pp → **piangere** ♦ sm crying, weeping.
pianura sf plain; **la** ~ **padana** the Paduan Plain.
piastrella sf tile.
piattaforma sf (superficie piana) platform; (galleggiante) rig.
piattino sm saucer.
piatto, -a ♦ agg (piano) flat; (monotono) dreary ♦ sm (recipiente) plate, dish; (vivanda) dish; (portata) course; ~ **freddo** cold dish; ~ **del giorno** today's special; ~ **tipico** typical dish; **primo** ~ first course; **secondo** ~ second course; **lavare i piatti** to wash the dishes; **piatti pronti** ready meals.
piazza sf square; **fare** ~ **pulita di** to make a clean sweep of.
piazzale sm large square.
piazzare vt (collocare) to place; (vendere) to sell.
▶ **piazzarsi** vr (in gara) to be placed.
piccante agg spicy.
picchetto sm (di tenda) peg; (di scioperanti, soldati) picket.
picchiare ♦ vt (dar botte) to beat (up); (testa, pugni) to bang ♦ vi (alla porta, sul tavolo) to thump; (sole) to beat down; ~ **contro il muro** (urtare) to hit the wall.
▶ **picchiarsi** vr to fight.
piccino, -a agg small.
piccione sm pigeon.
picco, -chi sm (vetta) peak; **a** ~ vertically; **colare a** ~ to sink.
piccolo, -a agg small; (breve) short; (di poco conto) slight.
piccozza sf ice-axe.
picnic [pik'nik] sm inv picnic.
pidocchio sm louse.
piede sm foot; (di mobile) leg;

andare a piedi to go on foot; **essere a piedi** to be on foot; **in piedi** standing; **prendere ~** to gain ground.

piedistallo *sm* pedestal.

piega, -ghe *sf* fold; (*di gonna*) pleat; (*di pantaloni, grinza*) crease; **prendere una brutta ~** to take a turn for the worse.

piegare *vt* to bend; (*foglio, tovaglia*) to fold; (*letto, sedia*) to fold up.

▶ **piegarsi** *vr* (*curvarsi*) to bend; (*letto, sedia*) to fold up.

▶ **piegarsi a** *vr + prep* to give in to.

pieghevole *agg* (*flessibile*) pliable; (*sedia, tavolo*) folding.

Piemonte *sm*: **il ~** Piedmont.

piena *sf* flood.

pieno, -a ♦ *agg* full ♦ *sm* (*di carburante*) full tank; (*culmine*) peak; **~ di** full of; **~ di sé** full of oneself; **a stomaco ~** on a full stomach; **in ~ inverno** in the middle of winter; **il ~, per favore** fill her up, please.

pietà *sf* (*compassione*) pity; **avere ~ di qn** to take pity on sb; **come attore fa ~** as an actor he's useless.

pietanza *sf* dish, course.

pietoso, -a *agg* (*che sente pietà*) compassionate; (*che ispira pietà*) pitiful.

pietra *sf* stone; **~ dura** semi-precious stone; **~ preziosa** precious stone.

pigiama, -i *sm* pyjamas (*pl*).

pigiare *vt* to press.

pigliare *vt* (*prendere*) to take; (*afferrare*) to grab.

pigna *sf* pine cone.

pignolo, -a *agg* fussy, meticulous.

pignorare *vt* (DIR) to distrain.

pigrizia *sf* laziness.

pigro, -a *agg* lazy.

pila *sf* (*cumulo*) pile; (*batteria*) battery.

pilastro *sm* pillar.

pillola *sf* pill.

pilone *sm* pylon; (*di ponte*) pier.

pilota, -i, -e *smf* (*di aereo, nave*) pilot; (*di auto*) driver.

pinacoteca, -che *sf* art gallery.

pineta *sf* pinewood.

ping-pong *sm* table tennis.

pinguino *sm* (*animale*) penguin; (*gelato*) *chocolate-coated ice cream on a stick*.

pinna *sf* (*di pesce*) fin; (*per nuotare*) flipper.

pino *sm* (*albero*) pine tree; (*legno*) pine.

pinoccate *sfpl*: **~ alla perugina** *almond and pine kernel sweets*.

pinolo *sm* pine kernel.

pinzare *vt* (*con graffette*) to staple; (*sog: granchio*) to nip.

pinze *sfpl* (*utensile*) pliers.

pinzette *sfpl* tweezers.

pinzimonio *sm* dip of seasoned oil.

pioggia, -ge *sf* rain; **sotto la ~** in the rain.

piolo *sm* rung.

piombare *vi* (*giungere*) to arrive unexpectedly; (*fig: nella disperazione*) to plunge; (*gettarsi*): **~ su** to fall upon.

piombino *sm* (*per pacchi*) lead seal; (*da pesca*) sinker.

piombo *sm* lead; **senza ~** unleaded.

pioppo *sm* poplar.

piovere ♦ *v impers* to rain ♦ *vi* (*pietre, proiettili, insulti*) to rain down; (*proteste*) to pour in; **piove** it's raining.

piovigginare *v impers* to drizzle.

piovoso, -a *agg* rainy.

pipa *sf* pipe.

pipì *sf* (*fam*) **fare (la) ~** to have a wee.

pipistrello *sm* bat.

pirata, -i *agg & sm* pirate; **~ della strada** road hog.

Pirenei *smpl*: **i ~** the Pyrenees.

pirofila *sf* Pyrex® dish.

piromane *smf* pyromaniac.

piroscafo *sm* steamer.

Pisa *sf* Pisa.

pisarei *smpl*: **~ e fasò piacentini** *'gnocchi' in a sauce of beans, tomatoes and other vegetables.*

pisciare *vi (volg)* to piss.

piscina *sf* swimming pool.

pisello *sm* pea.

pisolino *sm*: **fare un ~** to take a nap.

pista *sf (traccia)* trail; *(per corse)* track; *(da sci)* run; *(di aeroporto)* runway; **~ da ballo** dance floor; **~ ciclabile** cycle lane.

pistacchio *sm* pistachio.

pistola *sf* pistol, gun.

pitta *sf* tart made with a yeasted dough and filled with tomatoes, anchovies, tuna and capers or ricotta cheese and boiled eggs.

pittore, -trice *sm, f* painter.

pittoresco, -a, -schi, -sche *agg* picturesque.

pittorico, -a, -ci, -che *agg* pictorial, of painting.

pittura *sf* painting; **'~ fresca'** 'wet paint'.

pitturare *vt* to paint.

più *avv* **1.** *(in comparativi)*: **~ (di)** more (than); **ho fatto ~ tardi del solito** I was later than usual; **~ triste che mai** sadder than ever; **poco ~ di** just over; **di ~** *(in maggior quantità)* more; **l'ho pagato di ~** I paid more for it.

2. *(in superlativi)*: **la ~ bella città** the most beautiful city; **la collina ~ alta** the highest hill; **il ~ grande** the biggest; **il ~ velocemente possibile** as quickly as possible.

3. *(oltre)* any more; **non parlo ~** I'm not saying any more; **mai ~** never again.

4. *(in espressioni)*: **~ o meno** more or less; **per di ~** what's more; **tre di o in ~** three more; **in ~** in addition; **~ ci pensi, peggio è** the more you think about it, the worse it seems.

♦ *prep* **1.** *(con l'aggiunta di)* plus; **siamo in sei ~ gli ospiti** there are six of us plus guests.

2. *(MAT)*: **3 ~ 3 fa 6** 3 plus 3 makes 6.

♦ *agg inv* **1.** *(in quantità, numero maggiore)* more; **ho ~ lavoro del solito** I've got more work than usual; **ho fatto ~ punti di te** I got more points than you; **~ siamo, meglio è** the more of us there are, the better.

2. *(diversi)* several; **l'ho ripetuto ~ volte** I repeated it several times.

♦ *sm inv* **1.** *(la maggior parte)* most; **il ~ delle volte** more often than not; **parlare del ~ e del meno** to talk about this and that.

2. *(la maggioranza)*: **i ~** the majority.

piuma *sf* feather.

piumino *sm (trapunta)* duvet; *(giaccone)* quilted jacket.

piumone® *sm (trapunta)* duvet.

piuttosto *avv* rather; **~ che** rather than.

pizza *sf* pizza; **~ capricciosa** *pizza with cheese, tomato, artichokes and capers*; **~ margherita** *pizza with cheese and tomato*; **~ napoletana** *pizza with cheese, tomato, anchovies and capers*; **~ quattro stagioni** *pizza with a different topping on each quarter.*

PIZZA

Originally from Naples, pizza is now internationally popular. In Italy it can be bought at the bar or the baker's, either 'al taglio' (cut into rectangles) or as 'pizzette' (small pizzas), as well as at pizzerias, which Italians generally go to in the evening. Besides the traditional 'margherita' (just cheese and tomato) and 'napoletana' (cheese, tomato, anchovies and capers), many other varieties can be found. Pizzas with a mixture of vegetables, with mushrooms, with cold meats, and with different cheeses are particularly popular.

pizzaiola *sf*: **alla ~** *in a tomato, garlic and oregano sauce.*

pizzeria *sf* pizzeria, pizza restaurant.

pizzetta *sf* small pizza eaten as a snack.

pizzicagnolo, -a *sm, f* delicatessen owner.

pizzicare ♦ *vt* (*con le dita*) to pinch; (*pungere*) to sting ♦ *vi* (*prudere*) to itch; (*cibo*) to be spicy.

pizzicheria *sf* delicatessen.

pizzico, -chi *sm* dash; **un ~ di sale** a pinch of salt.

pizzicotto *sm* pinch.

pizzo *sm* (*merletto*) lace; (*barba*) goatee.

placare *vt* (*ira*) to pacify; (*fame, sete*) to satisfy.

▶ **placarsi** *vr* (*vento*) to die down; (*mare*) to become calmer.

placca, -che *sf* (*targa*) plate; (*dentaria*) plaque.

placcare *vt* (*rivestire*) to plate; **placcato d'oro** gold-plated.

plagiare *vt* (*libro, canzone*) to plagiarize; (*persona*) to coerce.

plagio *sm* (*imitazione*) plagiarism; (*di persona*) coercion.

plancia, -ce *sf* bridge.

planetario, -a ♦ *agg* planetary ♦ *sm* planetarium.

plasmare *vt* to mould.

plastica, -che *sf* (*sostanza*) plastic; (MED) plastic surgery.

plastico, -a, -ci, -che ♦ *agg* plastic ♦ *sm* (*modello*) model; (*esplosivo*) plastic explosive.

plastificato, -a *agg* plastic-coated.

plastilina® *sf* Plasticine®.

platano *sm* plane tree.

platea *sf* (*settore*) stalls (*pl*); (*pubblico*) audience.

plausibile *agg* plausible.

plenilunio *sm* full moon.

plico, -chi *sm* parcel.

plurale *agg & sm* plural.

pneumatico, -ci *sm* tyre.

po' = poco.

Po *sm*: **il ~** the Po.

poco, -a, -chi, -che *agg* 1. (*in piccola quantità*) little, not much; **ha poca fantasia** he doesn't have much imagination; **a ~ prezzo** cheap.

2. (*in piccolo numero*): **pochi** few, not many; **in poche parole** in few words. ♦ *sm* little.

♦ *pron* 1. (*una piccola quantità*) (a) little; (*un piccolo numero*) few, not many; **pochi** (*non molta gente*) few (people); **pochi di noi** few of us.

2. (*in espressioni*): **aver ~ da fare** to have little to do; **ci vuole ~ a capire che ...** it doesn't take much to understand that ...; **siamo tornati da ~** we've just got back; **è una cosa da ~** it's nothing; **per ~** nearly; **tra ~** soon, shortly; **(a) ~ a ~** little by little.

♦ *avv* 1. (*con verbo*) little, not much; **mangia ~** he doesn't eat much.

2. (*con aggettivo, avverbio*) not very; **~ lontano da qui** not very far from here; **è ~ simpatica** she's not very nice; **sta ~ bene** he's not very well.

3. (*indica tempo*): **durare ~** not to last long; **~ dopo/prima** shortly afterwards/before.

▶ **un po'** *avv* a bit, a little; **un altro po'** a bit more; **restiamo ancora un po'** we'll stay a bit longer; **un po' di** a bit of, a little; **compra un po' di pane** buy some bread.

podere *sm* farm.

poderoso, -a *agg* powerful.

podio *sm* podium.

poesia *sf* (ARTE) poetry; (*componimento*) poem.

poeta, -essa, -i, -esse *sm, f* poet.

poetico, -a, -ci, -che *agg* poetic.

poggiare ♦ *vt* to rest ♦ *vi*: **~ su qc** to rest on sthg.

poggiatesta *sm inv* headrest.

poi *avv* then; (*dopo*) later.

poiché *cong* as, since.

polare *agg* polar.

polaroid® *sf inv* Polaroid®.

polemica, -che *sf* controversy.

polemico, -a, -ci, -che *agg* (*persona, tono*) argumentative; (*discorso*) controversial.

polenta *sf* polenta (*type of savoury porridge made with maize flour*); **~ concia valdostana** *'polenta' cooked with soft*

cheeses and served with Parmesan cheese;
~ e osei *'polenta' served with small birds*
wrapped in pork loin and flavoured with
sage (a speciality of Lombardy); **~ pa-**
sticciata alla veneta *'polenta' baked in*
a meat, tomato and sausage sauce.
poliambulatorio *sm* ≈ health
centre.
poliestere *sm* polyester.
polistirolo *sm* polystyrene.
politica, -che *sf* (*scienza*) politics
(*sg*); (*linea di condotta*) policy, →
politico.
politico, -a, -ci, -che ♦ *agg*
political ♦ *sm, f* politician.
polizia *sf* police; **~ stradale** traffic
police.
poliziesco, -a, -schi, -sche *agg*
police (*dav s*); (*romanzo, film*) detective (*dav s*).
poliziotto, -a *sm, f* policeman (*f*
policewoman).
polizza *sf* policy; **~ di assicu-**
razione insurance policy.
pollaio *sm* hen house.
pollame *sm* poultry.
pollice *sm* thumb; (*unità di misura*)
inch.
polline *sm* pollen.
pollo *sm* chicken; **~ arrosto** roast
chicken; **~ alla cacciatora** *chicken in a*
sauce of mushrooms, tomatoes, olives,
herbs and wine; **~ alla diavola** *chicken*
cut open and flattened out, marinated in
lemon juice.
polmone *sm* lung.
polmonite *sf* pneumonia.
polo ♦ *sm* pole ♦ *sf inv* polo shirt;
il ~ Nord/Sud the North/South
Pole.
Polonia *sf*: **la ~** Poland.
polpaccio *sm* calf.
polpastrello *sm* fingertip.
polpetta *sf* meatball.
polpettone *sm* meat loaf.
polpo *sm* octopus.
polsino *sm* cuff.
polso *sm* wrist; (MED) pulse.
poltiglia *sf* paste.

poltrona *sf* armchair; (*di teatro*)
seat in the stalls.
poltrone, -a *sm, f* lazy person.
polvere *sf* dust; **latte in ~** powdered milk; **sapone in ~** soap powder.
polveroso, -a *agg* dusty.
pomata *sf* ointment.
pomeridiano, -a *agg* afternoon
(*dav s*).
pomeriggio *sm* afternoon; **di ~** in
the afternoon.
pomice *sf* pumice.
pomo *sm* knob; **~ d'Adamo**
Adam's apple.
pomodoro *sm* tomato; **pomodori**
ripieni *tomatoes stuffed with bread-*
crumbs, parsley, garlic and egg.
pompa *sf* pump; (*sfarzo*) pomp;
pompe funebri undertaker's
(*sg*).
pompare *vt* to pump.
Pompei *n* Pompei.

POMPEI

One of the world's most famous
archaeological sites, the ancient
town of Pompei, not far from
Naples, was totally buried in 79 AD
when Mount Vesuvius erupted.
Today it is open to the public, and
offers a unique insight into the
ancient Roman way of life.

pompelmo *sm* grapefruit.
pompiere *sm* fireman.
pomposo, -a *agg* (*sfarzoso*) full of
pomp; (*ostentato*) pompous.
ponderare *vt & vi* to ponder.
ponente *sm* west.
ponte *sm* bridge; (*di nave*) deck;
(*impalcatura*) scaffolding; **~ levatoio**
drawbridge; **fare il ~** *to have the day*
off between a national holiday and a week-
end; **il Ponte Vecchio** the Ponte
Vecchio.

IL PONTE VECCHIO

One of Italy's most picturesque
bridges, the Ponte Vecchio has
come to be the symbol of Florence.

Built in 1345 and so the oldest bridge in the city (hence its name), it stands at the narrowest point of the Arno and is connected to the Uffizi Gallery and the Pitti Palace by an arcade. The Ponte Vecchio is famous for the goldsmiths and silversmiths which line it on both sides.

---

pontefice sm pontiff.

pony sm inv pony; ~ **express** express courier service.

popcorn sm popcorn.

popolare ♦ agg popular; (popolano) working-class (dav s) ♦ vt to populate.

popolarità sf popularity.

popolazione sf population.

popolo sm people (pl).

popone sm melon.

poppa sf (NAUT) stern.

poppare vt to suck (from the breast).

porcellana sf porcelain.

porcellino sm (maialino) piglet; ~ d'India guinea pig.

porcino sm cep (edible brown mushroom with nutty flavour).

porco, -ci sm (animale) pig; (carne) pork.

porcospino sm porcupine.

porgere vt (tendere) to hold out; (dare) to give; **porgo distinti saluti** (in lettera) yours sincerely.

pornografico, -a, -ci, -che agg pornographic.

poro sm pore.

porpora agg inv crimson.

porre vt to put; (condizioni, limiti) to set; (riporre) to place; (supporre): **poniamo che** ... let us suppose that ...; ~ **una domanda** to ask a question; ~ **fine a qc** to put an end to sthg.

porro sm (verdura) leek; (MED) wart.

porta sf door; (di città) gate; (nel calcio) goal.

portabagagli sm inv (bagagliaio)

boot (Br), trunk (Am); (sul tetto) roof rack.

portacenere sm inv ashtray.

portachiavi sm inv key ring.

portacipria sm inv compact.

portaerei sf inv aircraft carrier.

portafinestra (pl portefinestre) sf French window.

portafoglio sm (per denaro) wallet; (FIN & POL) portfolio.

portafortuna sm inv lucky charm.

portagioie sm inv jewel box.

portalettere = **postino**.

portamento sm bearing.

portamonete sm inv purse.

portapacchi sm inv luggage rack.

portare vt (trasportare) to carry; (condurre, prendere) to take; (abiti, occhiali) to wear; (barba, capelli lunghi) to have; (fig: spingere) to drive; ~ **qc a qn** (consegnare) to take sthg to sb; **portar via** to take; ~ **avanti** to carry on; ~ **fortuna** to bring luck.

portasapone sm inv soap dish.

portasigarette sm inv cigarette case.

portata sf (piatto) course; (di veicolo) capacity; (di fiume) flow; (importanza) importance; **essere a ~ di mano** to be within reach; **alla ~ di tutti** within everybody's grasp.

portatile agg portable; ~ **di handicap** disabled.

portatore, -trice sm, f (di assegno) bearer.

portatovagliolo sm napkin ring.

portauovo sm inv eggcup.

portico sm portico.

▶ **portici** smpl arcades.

portiera sf door.

portiere, -a sm, f (portinaio) concierge, caretaker; (di albergo) porter; (nel calcio) goalkeeper.

portineria sf (di palazzo) caretaker's lodge; (di albergo) reception.

porto, -a ♦ pp → porgere ♦ sm port; ~ **d'armi** licence to carry firearms.

Portogallo *sm*: il ~ Portugal.
portoghese *agg*, *sm* & *sf* Portuguese.
portone *sm* main entrance.
porzione *sf* portion; (*di cibo*) helping.
posa *sf* pose; **mettersi in** ~ to pose.
posacenere *sm inv* ashtray.
posare ♦ *vt* to put down ♦ *vi* to pose.
▶ **posarsi** *vr* (*uccello*) to perch.
posate *sfpl* cutlery (*sg*).
positivo, -a *agg* positive.
posizione *sf* position.
posologia *sf* dosage.
possedere *vt* (*cose*) to own, to possess; (*qualità*) to have, to possess.
possessivo, -a *agg* possessive.
possesso *sm* possession, ownership; **essere in** ~ **di qc** to be in possession of sthg.
possibile ♦ *agg* possible ♦ *sm*: **fare (tutto) il** ~ **(per fare qc)** to do everything possible (to do sthg); **ma non è** ~! it can't be true!; **il più presto** ~ as soon as possible; **se** ~ if possible; **il più** ~ (*quantità*) as much as possible; (*numero*) as many as possible.
possibilità *sf inv* (*eventualità*) possibility; (*occasione*) chance; (*capacità*): **avere la** ~ **di fare qc** to be able to do sthg.
posta *sf* (*negozio*) post office; (*lettere, servizio*) post, mail; **per** ~ by post o mail; ~ **aerea** air mail.
postale *agg* postal, post (*dav s*).
posteggiare *vt* to park.
posteggiatore, -trice *sm*, *f* car park attendant (Br), parking lot attendant (Am).
posteggio *sm* car park (Br), parking lot (Am); ~ **a pagamento** *car park where drivers must pay to park*.
poster *sm inv* poster.
posteriore *agg* (*nello spazio*) rear, back; (*nel tempo*) later.
posticipare *vt* to postpone.
postino, -a *sm*, *f* postman (*f* postwoman).

posto, -a ♦ *pp* → **porre** ♦ *sm* place; (*spazio*) room; (*per persona*) place, seat; (*impiego*) job; **mettere a** ~ to tidy (up); ~ **di blocco** roadblock; ~ **letto** bed; ~ **di polizia** police station; **al** ~ **di** in (the) place of.
potabile *agg* → **acqua**.
potare *vt* to prune.
potente *agg* powerful.
potere *vi* 1. (*essere in grado di*) can, to be able; **non ci posso andare** I can't go, I'm not able to go; **puoi farmi un favore?** can you do me a favour?; **non posso farci niente** I can't do anything about it.
2. (*avere il permesso di*) can, to be able; **non potete parcheggiare qui** you can't park here; **posso entrare?** can o may I come in?
3. (*esprime eventualità*): **può far freddo** it can get cold; **possono aver perso il treno** they might o could have missed the train; **potrei sbagliarmi** I could be wrong; **può darsi** perhaps; **può darsi che sia partito** he may o might have left.
4. (*esprime suggerimento*): **puoi provare** you can try.
5. (*in espressioni*): **non ne posso più!** (*sono stufo*) I can't take any more!; (*sono stanco*) I'm exhausted!; **a più non posso** (*correre*) really fast; (*lavorare*) really hard; **si può fare** it can be done.
♦ *sm* 1. (*comando*) power; **essere al** ~ to be in power.
2. (*facoltà*) power, ability.
povero, -a ♦ *agg* poor ♦ *sm*, *f* poor man (*f* woman); **i poveri** the poor; ~ **di qc** lacking in sthg.
pozza *sf* pool.
pozzanghera *sf* puddle.
pozzo *sm* well; ~ **petrolifero** oil well.
pranzare *vi* to have lunch.
pranzo *sm* (*di mezzogiorno*) lunch; (*banchetto*) dinner; **a** ~ at lunch; (*ora*) at lunchtime.
prassi *sf* usual procedure.

pratica, -che sf practice; (esperienza) practical experience; (documenti) paperwork; **mettere in ~ qc** to put sthg into practice; **in ~** in practice.

praticamente avv (quasi) practically; (concretamente) in a practical way.

praticare vt to practise (Br), to practice (Am); **~ uno sport** to do some sport; **~ il tennis** to play tennis.

pratico, -a, -ci, -che agg practical.

prato sm (distesa d'erba) meadow; (di giardino) lawn.

preavviso sm notice.

precario, -a agg precarious.

precauzione sf precaution.

precedente ♦ agg preceding, previous ♦ sm precedent; **senza precedenti** unprecedented; **precedenti penali** criminal record (sg).

precedenza sf (in auto) right of way; (priorità) priority; **dare la ~ (a)** (in auto) to give way (to).

precedere vt (nello spazio) to be ahead of; (nel tempo) to precede.

precipitare vi (cadere) to fall; (fig: situazione) to come to a head.

▶ **precipitarsi** vr to rush.

precipitazione sf (atmosferica) precipitation; (fretta) haste.

precipizio sm precipice.

precisare vt to specify.

precisione sf (esattezza) precision; (accuratezza) accuracy.

preciso, -a agg precise; **sono le due precise** it's exactly two o'clock.

precoce agg (bambino) precocious; (vecchiaia) premature.

preda sf prey; **essere in ~ a qc** to be prey to sthg.

predetto, -a pp → predire.

predica, -che sf (RELIG) sermon; (fam: ramanzina) telling-off.

predire vt to foretell.

predisporre vt to prepare; **~ qn/qc a qc** to predispose sb/sthg to sthg.

predisposizione sf tendency.

predominare vi to predominate.

prefabbricato, -a agg prefabricated.

preferenza sf preference.

preferire vt to prefer; **~ qn/qc a** to prefer sb/sthg to.

preferito, -a agg favourite.

prefiggersi vr: **~ uno scopo** to set o.s. a goal.

prefisso, -a ♦ pp → prefiggersi ♦ sm code.

pregare ♦ vi to pray ♦ vt (Dio) to pray to; **~ qn di fare qc** (supplicare) to beg sb to do sthg; (chiedere a) to ask sb to do sthg; **i passeggeri sono gentilmente pregati di non fumare** passengers are kindly requested not to smoke.

preghiera sf prayer.

pregiato, -a agg precious.

pregio sm (qualità) good quality; (valore) value.

pregiudicare vt to prejudice.

pregiudicato, -a sm, f previous offender.

pregiudizio sm prejudice.

prego esclam (risposta a ringraziamento) don't mention it!; (invito a sedersi) take a seat!; (invito ad entrare prima) after you!; **vorrei fare una domanda – ~!** I'd like to ask a question – go ahead!

preistorico, -a, -ci, -che agg prehistoric.

prelavaggio sm prewash.

prelevare vt (soldi) to withdraw; (campione, sangue) to take.

prelievo sm (in banca) withdrawal; (MED) sample.

preliminare agg & sm preliminary.

preludio sm prelude.

pre-maman agg inv maternity (dav s).

prematuro, -a agg premature.

premere ♦ vt to press ♦ vi: **~ su** to press on.

▶ **premere a** v + prep: **~ a qn** to matter to sb.

premiare vt (dare un premio) to give a prize to; (merito, onestà) to reward.

premiazione sf prize-giving.

premio sm (vincita) prize; (ricompensa) reward; ~ (di assicurazione) (insurance) premium.

premunirsi vr: ~ contro qc to protect o.s. against sthg.

premuroso, -a agg thoughtful.

prendere vt 1. (afferrare) to take.
2. (portare con sé) to take; **prendi l'ombrello** take the umbrella.
3. (mezzi di trasporto, strada) to take; ~ **il treno** to take the train; **prenda la prima a destra** take the first on the right.
4. (mangiare, bere) to have; **andiamo a ~ un caffè** let's go for a coffee; ~ **qualcosa da bere** to have something to drink; **che cosa prendete?** (da bere) what would you like to drink?
5. (lezioni, voto, stipendio) to get; ~ **qc in affitto** to rent sthg.
6. (interpretare) to take; **prenderla bene/male** to take it well/badly.
7. (catturare, sorprendere) to catch; **quanti pesci hai preso?** how many fish have you caught?; ~ **qn con le mani nel sacco** to catch sb redhanded.
8. (malattia, stato fisico): ~ **freddo** to catch cold; ~ **il sole** to sunbathe; **prendersi un raffreddore** to catch a cold.
9. (sottrarre): ~ **qc a qn** to take sthg (away) from sb.
10. (scambiare): ~ **qn per** to take sb for.
11. (in espressioni): **andare a ~** (persona) to meet; (cosa) to go to get; **prendersi cura di** to look after; ~ **fuoco** to catch fire; ~ **un impegno** to take on a commitment; ~ **le misure di** (oggetto, persona) to measure; **che ti prende?** what's the matter with you?; **prendersela** (offendersi) to get annoyed; (preoccupare) to worry; **prendersela con qn** (arrabbiarsi) to

get angry with sb.
◆ vi 1. (colla, cemento) to set; (fuoco) to catch.
2. (cominciare): ~ **a fare qc** to start doing sthg.

prendisole sm inv sundress.

prenotare vt to book; **ho prenotato una camera** I've booked a room.

prenotazione sf booking.

preoccupare vt to worry.
▶ **preoccuparsi** vr: **preoccuparsi (per)** to worry (about).
▶ **preoccuparsi di** vr + prep (occuparsi di) to think about.

preoccupato, -a agg worried.

preoccupazione sf worry.

preparare vt to prepare; (documenti, cose) to get ready; (esame, concorso) to prepare for; ~ **da mangiare** to cook.
▶ **prepararsi** vr (vestirsi) to get ready; ~ **a fare qc** to get ready to do sthg.

preparativi smpl preparations.

preposizione sf preposition.

prepotente ◆ agg domineering ◆ smf bully.

presa sf (il prendere) grip; (nello sport, appiglio) hold; (di acqua, gas) supply point; (di sale, pepe) pinch; (di colla, cemento) setting; (di città) capture; (per spina): ~ **(di corrente)** socket; **far ~** to set; **far ~ su qn** to captivate sb; ~ **d'aria** air intake; **essere alle prese con** to be up against.

presbite agg longsighted.

prescindere : **prescindere da** v + prep to leave aside; **a ~ da** apart from.

prescritto, -a pp → **prescrivere**.

prescrivere vt to prescribe.

presentare vt to present; (domanda, dimissioni) to submit; (persona): ~ **qn a qn** to introduce sb to sb; **le presento mia moglie** this is my wife.
▶ **presentarsi** vr (farsi conoscere) to introduce o.s.; (recarsi) to present o.s.; (capitare) to arise; (mostrarsi) to look.

presentatore, -trice sm, f presenter.

presentazione sf presentation; **fare le presentazioni** to make the introductions.

presente ♦ agg present ♦ smf: **i presenti** those present; **tener ~ che** to bear in mind that; **aver ~** to remember.

presentimento sm presentiment.

presenza sf presence; **in ~ di tutti** in front of everybody.

presepe = **presepio**.

presepio sm Nativity scene, crib.

preservativo sm condom.

preside smf headteacher (Br), principal (Am).

presidente smf president; **~ del Consiglio** Prime Minister; **il ~ della Repubblica** the Italian President.

preso, -a pp → **prendere**.

pressappoco avv more or less.

pressare vt to press.

pressione sf pressure; **far ~ su qn** to put pressure on sb; **essere sotto ~** to be under pressure.

presso prep (sulle lettere) c/o; (vicino a) near; (alle dipendenze di) for, with; **~ qn** (a casa di) at sb's home.

▶ **pressi** smpl: **nei pressi di Siena** in the vicinity of Siena.

prestare vt to lend; **~ qc (a qn)** (denaro, oggetti) to lend (sb) sthg, to lend sthg (to sb); **~ aiuto a qn** to lend sb a hand; **~ attenzione a** to pay attention to.

▶ **prestarsi a** vr + prep: **prestarsi a fare qc** to offer to do sthg.

prestazione sf performance.

▶ **prestazioni** sfpl services.

prestigiatore, -trice sm, f conjurer.

prestito sm loan; **dare in ~ qc (a qn)** to lend sthg (to sb); **prendere qc in ~ (da qn)** to borrow sthg (from sb).

presto avv (fra poco) soon; (in fretta) quickly; (nella giornata, nel tempo) early; **fai ~!** hurry up!; **a ~!** see you

soon!; **al più ~** as soon as possible.

presumere vt to presume.

presunto, -a pp → **presumere**.

presuntuoso, -a agg conceited.

prêt-à-porter ['pret a por'te] sm ready-to-wear (fashion).

prete sm priest.

pretendere vt to claim; (a torto) to pretend; **pretende che tutti lo ascoltino** he expects everyone to listen to him; **pretende di essere il migliore** he thinks he's the best.

preteso, -a pp → **pretendere**.

pretesto sm (scusa) excuse, pretext; (occasione) opportunity.

prevalente agg prevalent.

prevalere vi to prevail.

prevedere vt to foresee.

▶ **prevedere di** v + prep to expect.

prevenire vt (anticipare) to forestall; (evitare) to prevent.

preventivo, -a ♦ agg preventive ♦ sm estimate.

prevenzione sf prevention.

previdenza sf foresight; **~ sociale** social security (Br), welfare (Am).

previo, -a agg: **~ pagamento** upon payment.

previsione sf (valutazione) prediction; (aspettativa) expectation; **in ~ di** in anticipation of; **previsioni del tempo** o **meteorologiche** weather forecast.

previsto, -a ♦ pp → **prevedere** ♦ agg expected ♦ sm: **più/meno del ~** more/less than expected.

prezioso, -a agg precious, valuable.

prezzemolo sm parsley.

prezzo sm price; **~ comprensivo del servizio** price including service charge; **a buon ~** cheap.

prigione sf prison.

prigionia sf imprisonment.

prigioniero, -a ♦ agg (rinchiuso) imprisoned; (catturato) captive ♦ sm, f prisoner.

prima ♦ avv (in precedenza) before; (più presto) earlier; (per prima cosa, nello spazio) first; (un tempo) once ♦ sf (*di teatro*) first night; (*marcia*) first gear; (*in treno, aereo*) first class ♦ *cong* before ♦ *prep*: ~ **di** before; **fai ~ di qua** it's quicker this way; ~ **che arrivi** before he arrives; ~ **di fare qc** before doing sthg; ~ **o poi** sooner or later; ~ **d'ora** before now; ~ **di tutto** first of all; **l'anno ~** the year before.

primario, -a ♦ *agg* primary ♦ *sm* (MED) chief physician.

primato *sm* (*supremazia*) primacy; (SPORT) record.

primavera *sf* spring.

primeggiare *vi*: ~ (**in**) to excel (**in**).

primitivo, -a *agg* (*uomo, civiltà*) primitive; (*originario*) original.

primo, -a ♦ *agg* first; (*nel tempo*) early ♦ *sm* (*portata*) first course; (*giorno*) first; **il ~ (di) marzo** the first of March; **di prima qualità** first-class; **ai primi d'ottobre** in early October; **sulle prime** at first, in the beginning.

primogenito, -a *agg & sm, f* firstborn.

principale ♦ *agg* main, principal ♦ *smf* manager, boss.

principe *sm* prince.

principessa *sf* princess.

principiante *smf* beginner.

principio *sm* (*inizio, origine*) beginning; (*concetto, norma*) principle; **in** o **al ~** at first; **per ~** on principle.

priorità *sf inv* (*precedenza*) priority.

privare *vt*: ~ **qn di qc** to deprive sb of sthg.

▶ **privarsi** *vr* + *prep*: **privarsi di qc** to go without sthg.

privato, -a ♦ *agg* private ♦ *sm, f* (*cittadino*) private citizen ♦ *sm*: **in ~** in private.

privilegiare *vt* to favour.

privo, -a *agg*: ~ **di qc** without sthg, lacking in sthg.

pro *sm inv*: **a che ~?** for what purpose?; **i ~ e i contro** the pros and cons.

probabile *agg* probable; **è ~ che**

piova it will probably rain.

probabilità *sf inv* probability.

probabilmente *avv* probably.

problema, -i *sm* problem.

proboscide *sf* trunk.

procedere *vi* (*avanzare, progredire*) to proceed; (*agire*) to behave.

procedimento *sm* procedure.

processare *vt* to try.

processione *sf* procession.

processo *sm* (DIR) trial; (*operazione, metodo*) process.

procinto *sm*: **essere in ~ di fare qc** to be about to do sthg.

proclamare *vt* to proclaim.

procurare *vt*: ~ **qc a qn** to obtain sthg for sb, to get sthg for sb; **procurarsi qc** to get sthg.

prodotto, -a ♦ *pp* → **produrre** ♦ *sm* product.

produrre *vt* to produce; (*provocare*) to cause.

produttore, -trice *sm, f* producer.

produzione *sf* production.

Prof. (*abbr di professore*) Prof.

profano, -a ♦ *agg* profane ♦ *sm* layman.

professionale *agg* professional; (*scuola, istituto*) vocational.

professione *sf* profession.

professionista, -i, -e *smf* (*avvocato, medico*) professional person; (*non dilettante*) professional.

professore, -essa *sm, f* teacher; (*all'università*) professor.

profilo *sm* profile; **di ~** in profile.

profiterole [profite'rɔl] *sm inv* profiteroles (*pl*).

profitto *sm* profit; **trarre ~ da qc** to take advantage of sthg.

profondità *sf inv* depth.

profondo, -a *agg* deep.

Prof.ssa (*abbr di professoressa*) Prof.

profugo, -a, -ghi, -ghe *sm, f* refugee.

profumare ♦ *vt* to perfume ♦ *vi* to smell good; ~ **di** to smell of.

profumato, -a *agg* scented.

profumeria *sf* perfumery.

profumo *sm* (*odore*) scent, fragrance; (*cosmetico*) perfume.

progettare *vt* to plan.

progetto *sm* project; (*programma, di architetto*) plan.

programma, -i *sm* programme; (*per vacanze, serata*) plan; (SCOL) syllabus; (INFORM) program.

programmare *vt* (*pianificare*) to plan; (INFORM) to program.

progredire *vi* (*avanzare*) to advance; (*migliorare*) to progress.

progressivo, -a *agg* progressive.

progresso *sm* progress; **fare progressi** to make progress.

proibire *vt* to forbid; **~ a qn di fare qc** to forbid sb to do sthg; **è proibito fumare** smoking is prohibited.

proiettare *vt* (*film*) to show; (*luce, ombra*) to cast.

proiettile *sm* bullet.

proiezione *sf* (*di film*) projection, showing.

proletariato *sm* proletariat.

prolunga, -ghe *sf* extension.

prolungare *vt* to prolong.

▶ **prolungarsi** *vr* to go on.

promemoria *sm inv* memo.

promessa *sf* promise; **mantenere una ~** to keep a promise.

promesso, -a *pp* → **promettere**.

promettere *vt*: **~ qc (a qn)** to promise (sb) sthg; **~ (a qn) di fare qc** to promise (sb) to do sthg; **promette bene!** that's a good start!

promontorio *sm* promontory.

promosso, -a *pp* → **promuovere**.

promotore, -trice *sm, f* promoter.

promozione *sf* promotion; (SCOL): **avere la ~** to go up a class.

promulgare *vt* to promulgate.

promuovere *vt* (SCOL) to pass; (*impiegato, iniziativa*) to promote.

pronome *sm* pronoun.

pronto, -a ♦ *agg* ready ♦ *esclam*

hello! (*on the phone*); **essere ~ a fare qc** to be ready to do sthg; **~ soccorso** first aid; **~, chi parla?** hello, who's speaking?

pronuncia, -ce *sf* pronunciation.

pronunciare *vt* (*parola, lettera*) to pronounce; (*dire*) to say.

▶ **pronunciarsi** *vr* (*parola, lettera*) to be pronounced; (*dichiararsi*) to declare o.s.

pronunzia = **pronuncia**.

proporre *vt*: **~ qc (a qn)** to propose sthg (to sb); **~ di fare qc** to suggest doing sthg.

▶ **proporsi di** *vr + prep*: **proporsi di fare qc** to decide to do sthg.

proporzionato, -a *agg* well proportioned.

proporzione *sf* (MAT) ratio; **in ~ a** in proportion to.

proposito *sm* (*progetto*) intention; **fare qc di ~** to do sthg on purpose; **a ~, ...** by the way, ...; **a ~ di** on the subject of, with regard to; **capitare a ~** (*avvenimento*) to happen at the right time.

proposta *sf* proposal.

proposto, -a *pp* → **proporre**.

proprietà *sf inv* property; (*fatto di possedere*) ownership; **'~ privata'** 'private property'.

proprietario, -a *sm, f* owner.

proprio, -a ♦ *agg* (*possessivo*) own; (*senso*) literal, exact; (*tipico*) characteristic ♦ *avv* (*veramente*) really; (*precisamente*) just; (*affatto*) at all; **non ne ho ~ idea** I really have no idea; **~ così** that's just it; **non ~** not exactly; **mettersi in ~** to set up on one's own.

prora *sf* (*di nave*) prow; (*di aereo*) nose.

prosa *sf* prose.

prosciugare *vt* to dry up; (*terreno*) to drain, to reclaim.

prosciutto *sm* ham; **~ cotto** (cooked) ham; **~ crudo** cured ham.

proseguire ♦ *vt* to carry on with, to continue ♦ *vi* to carry on, to continue.

prospettiva *sf* (*di disegno, punto di*

vista) perspective; (*possibilità*) prospect.

prossimità *sf* proximity, nearness; **in ~ di** near.

prossimo, -a ♦ *agg* next ♦ *sm* neighbour.

prostituta *sf* prostitute.

protagonista, -i, -e *smf* protagonist.

proteggere *vt*: **~ qn/qc (da)** to protect sb/sthg (from).

protesta *sf* protest.

protestante *agg & smf* Protestant.

protestare *vi & vt* to protest.

protetto, -a *pp* → **proteggere**.

protezione *sf* protection.

prototipo *sm* prototype.

Prov. *abbr* = **provincia**.

prova *sf* (*dimostrazione, conferma*) proof; (*esperimento*) test, trial; (DIR) proof, evidence; (*di spettacolo*) rehearsal; (*esame*) exam; **dar ~ di abilità** to prove to be skilful; **mettere qn alla ~** to put sb to the test; **fino a ~ contraria** until (it's) proved otherwise; **in ~** on trial; **fare la prove** to rehearse.

provare *vt* (*cibo*) to try; (*vestito*) to try on; (*sentire*) to feel, to experience; (*dimostrare*) to show; (*tentare*): **~ a fare qc** to try to do sthg; **provarsi qc** to try sthg on.

▶ **provarsi** *vr + prep*: **provarsi a fare qc** to try to do sthg.

provenienza *sf* origin; **in ~ da** (*treno, aereo*) from.

provenire : provenire da *v + prep* to come from; **proveniente da** (*treno, aereo*) from.

provenuto, -a *pp* → **provenire**.

proverbio *sm* proverb.

provetta *sf* test tube.

provincia, -ce o **-cie** *sf* (*ente*) province; (*opposta a grandi città*) provinces (*pl*).

provinciale ♦ *agg* provincial ♦ *sf* main road.

provino *sm* (*audizione*) audition; (*fotografico*) screen test.

provocante *agg* provocative.

provocare *vt* (*causare*) to cause; (*sfidare*) to provoke.

provocazione *sf* provocation.

provolone *sm a hard cheese made from cow's milk.*

provvedere *vi* (*prendere provvedimenti*) to take measures; (*occuparsi di*): **~ (a qc)** to provide (for sthg).

provvedimento *sm* measure.

provvisorio, -a *agg* temporary, provisional.

provviste *sfpl* supplies.

prua *sf* prow.

prudente *agg* cautious, prudent.

prudenza *sf* caution, prudence; **'prudenza'** 'caution'.

prudere *vi* to itch; **mi prude una gamba** my leg is itchy.

prugna *sf* plum; **~ secca** prune.

pruno *sm* prickle, thorn.

prurito *sm* itch.

P.S. ♦ (*abbr di postscriptum*) PS ♦ *abbr* = **Pubblica Sicurezza**.

pseudonimo *sm* pseudonym.

psicanalisi *sf* psychoanalysis.

psiche *sf* psyche.

psichiatra, -i, -e *smf* psychiatrist.

psicologia *sf* psychology.

psicologo, -a, -gi, -ghe *sm, f* psychologist.

P.T. (*abbr di poste e telecomunicazioni*) PO.

P.T.P. (*abbr di posto telefonico pubblico*) payphone.

pubblicare *vt* to publish.

pubblicazione *sf* publication.

▶ **pubblicazioni** *sfpl*: **~ (matrimoniali)** (marriage) banns.

pubblicità *sf inv* (*annuncio*) advertisement; (*divulgazione*) publicity; (*attività*) advertising.

pubblico, -a, -ci, -che ♦ *agg* public; (*statale*) state (*dav s*) ♦ *sm* (*utenti*) public; (*spettatori*) audience; **in ~** in public; **la Pubblica Sicurezza** the police; **pubbliche relazioni** public relations.

pube *sm* pubis.

pudore *sm* modesty.
pugilato *sm* boxing.
pugile *sm* boxer.
Puglia *sf*: **la ~** Apulia.
pugnalare *vt* to stab.
pugno *sm* (*mano*) fist; (*colpo*) punch; (*quantità*) handful.
pulce *sf* flea.
Pulcinella *sm* Punch.
pulcino *sm* chick.
puledro, -a *sm, f* colt (*f* filly).
pulire *vt* to clean; **pulirsi il viso/le scarpe** to clean one's face/shoes.
pulita *sf*: **dare una ~** to clean up.
pulito, -a *agg* clean; (*coscienza*) clear.
pulizia *sf* (*stato*) cleanliness; (*atto*) cleaning; **fare le pulizie** to do the cleaning.
pullman *sm inv* coach.
pullover *sm inv* pullover.
pulmino *sm* minibus.
pulsante *sm* button.
pulsare *vi* to beat.
puma *sm inv* puma.
pungere *vt* to sting.
pungiglione *sm* sting.
punire *vt* to punish.
punizione *sf* (*castigo*) punishment; (*nel calcio*) free kick.
punta *sf* (*di matita, spillo, coltello*) point; (*di continente, dita*) tip; **in ~ dei piedi** (*camminare*) on tiptoe.
puntare *vt* (*arma*) to aim; (*scommettere*) to bet; **~ i piedi** to dig one's heels in.
puntata *sf* (*episodio*) episode; (*scommessa*) bet; **teleromanzo a puntate** serial.
punteggiatura *sf* punctuation.
punteggio *sm* score.
puntina *sf*: **~ (da disegno)** drawing pin.
puntino *sm* dot; **fare qc a ~** to do sthg properly; **puntini di sospensione** suspension points.
punto, -a ♦ *pp →* **pungere ♦** *sm* point; (*segno grafico*) full stop (Br), period (Am); (MED: *di cucito*) stitch; **~**

esclamativo exclamation mark; **~ interrogativo** question mark; **~ di riferimento** point of reference, landmark; **~ di ritrovo** meeting point; **~ vendita** point of sale; **~ e virgola** semi-colon; **~ di vista** point of view; **due punti** colon; **punti cardinali** points of the compass; **essere sul ~ di fare qc** to be about to do sthg; **essere a buon ~** to be at a good point; **fare il ~ della situazione** to take stock; **mettere a ~ qc** to adjust sthg; **di ~ in bianco** all of a sudden; **a tal ~ che** to such an extent that; **le tre in ~** three o'clock sharp.
puntuale *agg* punctual.
puntualità *sf* punctuality.
puntura *sf* (*di insetto*) sting; (*di spillo*) prick; (*fam: iniezione*) injection.
punzecchiare *vt* (*pungere*) to prick; (*fig: infastidire*) to tease.
pupazzo *sm* puppet.
pupilla *sf* pupil.
purché *cong* provided that.
pure ♦ *avv* (*anche*) also, too **♦** *cong* even if; **pur di fare qc** just to do sthg; **faccia ~!** please do!, go ahead!
purè *sm* (*di patate*) mashed potatoes with milk, butter and Parmesan cheese.
purezza *sf* purity.
purga, -ghe *sf* laxative.
purgatorio *sm* Purgatory.
puro, -a *agg* pure; (*verità*) simple.
purosangue *agg inv* thoroughbred.
purtroppo *avv* unfortunately.
pustola *sf* pimple.
putiferio *sm* row.
putrefare *vi* to putrefy, to rot.
putrefatto, -a ♦ *pp →* **putrefare ♦** *agg* rotten.
putrido, -a *agg* putrid.
puttana *sf* (*volg*) whore.
puttanesca *sf →* **spaghetti**.
puzza *sf* = **puzzo**.
puzzare *vi* to stink.

puzzo *sm* stink.
puzzola *sf* polecat.
puzzolente *agg* stinking.

Q

qua *avv* here; **al di ~ di** on this side of; **di ~ e di là** here and there; **per di ~** this way.

quaderno *sm* exercise book.

quadrante *sm* (*di orologio*) face; (*di bussola*) quarter.

quadrare *vi* (*bilancia*) to balance; (*coincidere*) to correspond; **non mi quadra** (*fam*) there's something not quite right about it.

quadrato, -a *agg & sm* square; **2 al ~** 2 squared.

quadretto *sm*: **a quadretti** (*tessuto*) checked; (*foglio*) squared.

quadrifoglio *sm* four-leaf clover.

quadrimestre *sm* (SCOL) term; (*periodo*) period of four months.

quadro *sm* (*pittura*) painting; (*fig: situazione*) picture; (TECNOL) board, panel; (*in azienda*) executive.

▶ **quadri** *smpl* (*nelle carte*) diamonds.

quadruplo, -a *agg & sm* quadruple.

quaggiù *avv* down here.

quaglia *sf* quail.

qualche *agg* 1. (*alcuni*) a few, some; **restiamo solo ~ giorno** we are only staying a few days; **~ volta** a few times; **c'è ~ novità?** is there any news?

2. (*indeterminato*) some; **l'ho letto in ~ articolo** I read it in some article; **hai ~ libro da prestarmi?** have you any books to lend me?; **in ~ modo** somehow; **da ~ parte** somewhere.

3. (*un certo*) some; **ci siamo frequentati per ~ tempo** we've been seeing

each other for some time; **~ cosa = qualcosa**.

qualcheduno, -a = qualcuno.

qualcosa *pron* something; (*nelle interrogative*) anything; **~ di nuovo** something new; **~ da bere** something to drink; **qualcos'altro** something else.

qualcuno, -a *pron* (*uno*) someone, somebody; (*nelle interrogative*) anyone, anybody; (*alcuni*) some; (*alcuni: nelle interrogative*) any; **qualcun altro** (*persona*) someone else; **~ di voi** some of you; (*nelle interrogative*) any of you.

quale *agg interr* 1. (*persona*) which; **qual è il tuo scrittore preferito?** who is your favourite writer?; **da ~ dentista sei stato?** which dentist have you been to?

2. (*cosa*) which, what; **non so ~ libro scegliere** I don't know which book to choose; **in ~ albergo hai prenotato?** which hotel have you booked?

♦ *agg relativo* such as, like; **alcuni animali quali il cane** some animals such as the dog.

♦ *pron interr* which (one); **~ vuole di questi cappelli?** which of these hats do you want?; **non so ~ scegliere** I don't know which (one) to choose.

♦ *pron relativo* 1. (*soggetto*): **il/la ~** (*persona*) who; (*cosa*) which, that; **suo fratello, il ~ è un mio amico** his brother, who is a friend of mine.

2. (*con preposizioni: persona*) who(m); (*cosa*) which, that; **l'albergo nel ~ alloggio** the hotel (that) I'm staying in; **la persona con la ~ parlavo** the person (whom) I was talking to; **l'uomo del ~ conosco il figlio** the man whose son I know.

3. (*in qualità di*) as; **vengo ~ accompagnatore** I'm coming as a tour guide.

qualifica, -che *sf* qualification.

qualificare *vt* to describe, to define.

▶ **qualificarsi** *vr* to qualify.

qualificativo, -a *agg* qualifying.

qualità *sf inv* quality; (*varietà*) type; **in ~ di** in one's capacity as.

qualsiasi = **qualunque**.

qualunque *agg* any; (*quale che*) whatever; **~ cosa** anything; **~ cosa succeda** whatever happens; **~ persona** anyone; **prendine uno ~** take whichever you want.

quando *avv & cong* when; **da ~ sono qui** from when I got here; **da ~ sei qui?** how long have you been here?; **da ~ in qua** since when; **di ~ sono queste foto?** when were these photos taken?

quantità *sf inv* quantity, amount; **una ~ di** a lot o lots of.

quanto, -a *agg interr* 1. (*quantità*) how much; (*numero*) how many; **~ tempo ci vuole?** how long does it take?; **quanti anni hai?** how old are you?

2. (*in frasi esclamative*) what; **quanta fatica sprecata!** what a waste of energy!

◆ *agg relativo* (*quantità*) as much as; (*numero*) as many as; **puoi restare quanti giorni vuoi** you can stay for as many days as you like.

◆ *pron interr* (*quantità*) how much; (*numero*) how many; **prima di comprare il pane guarda ~ ce n'è** before buying the bread see how much there is; **quanti ne vuoi?** how many do you want?; **quanti ne abbiamo oggi?** what's the date today?

◆ *pron relativo* (*quello che: quantità*) as much as; (*numero*) as many as; **dammene ~ ti pare** give me as much as you want; **per ~ ne so** as far as I know.

◆ *avv* 1. (*interrogativo: quantità*) how much; (*numero*) how many; **quant'è?** how much is it?; **~ ti fermi?** how long are you staying?; **~ è alta questa montagna?** how high is this mountain?; **~ mi dispiace!** I'm so sorry!; **~ costa/costano?** how much is it/are they?

2. (*relativo*) as much as; **mi sforzo ~ posso** I try as hard as I can; **~ prima** as soon as possible.

3. (*in espressioni*): **in ~** (*perché*) as; **per ~** however.

quaranta *num* forty, → **sei**.

quarantena *sf* quarantine.

quarantesimo, -a *num* fortieth, → **sesto**.

quarantina *sf*: **una ~ (di)** about forty; **essere sulla ~** to be in one's forties.

quaresima *sf* (RELIG): **la ~** Lent.

quarta *sf* (*marcia*) fourth gear.

quartetto *sm* quartet.

quartiere *sm* area, district; **quartier generale** headquarters (*pl*).

quarto, -a ◆ *num* fourth ◆ *sm* (*parte*) quarter; **un ~ d'ora** a quarter of an hour; **le tre e un ~** quarter past three (Br), quarter after three (Am); **le tre meno un ~** quarter to three (Br), quarter of three (Am); **un ~ di vino** a quarter litre of wine, → **sesto**.

quarzo *sm* quartz.

quasi ◆ *avv* nearly ◆ *cong* as if; **~ mai** hardly ever; **~ sempre** almost always; **~ ~ vengo anch'io** I might just come too.

quassù *avv* up here.

quattordicesimo, -a *num* fourteenth, → **sesto**.

quattordici *num* fourteen, → **sei**.

quattrini *smpl* (*fam*) money (*sg*).

quattro *num* four; **farsi in ~ (per fare qc)** to go out of one's way (to do sthg); **eravamo ~ gatti** (*fam*) there were only a few of us there; **in ~ e quattr'otto** in less than no time, → **sei**.

quattrocento *num* four hundred, → **sei**.

▶ **Quattrocento** *sm*: **il Quattrocento** the fifteenth century.

quei → **quello**.

quegli → **quello**.

quello, -a (*dav sm* **quel** (*pl* **quei**) + *consonante;* **quello** (*pl* **quegli**) + *s+consonante, gn, ps, x, z;* **quell'** (*pl* **quegli**) + *vocale*) *agg* 1. (*indica lontananza*) that, those (*pl*); **quella casa** that house; **quegli alberi** those trees;

quei bambini those children.

2. (*per sottolineare*): **spegni quella tv!** switch that TV off!

3. (*per cosa, persona già nota*) that, those (*pl*); **non mi piace quella gente** I don't like those people.

♦ *pron* **1.** (*indica lontananza*) that (one), those (ones) (*pl*); **quella è la mia macchina** that one's my car; **prendo ~ in offerta** I'll take the one on special offer; **~ lì** that one (there).

2. (*con pronome relativo*): **faccio ~ che posso** I'll do what I can; **quelli che potevano si sono fermati** those who could, stopped.

quercia, -ce *sf* oak.

querelare *vt* to bring a legal action against.

quesito *sm* query.

questionario *sm* questionnaire.

questione *sf* question; **è ~ di giorni** it's a matter of days; **in ~ in** question.

questo, -a *agg* **1.** (*indica prossimità*) this, these (*pl*); **questa finestra è aperta** this window is open; **partiamo ~ giovedì** we're leaving this Thursday.

2. (*simile*) such; **non uscire con questa pioggia** don't go out in this rain.

3. (*il seguente/precedente*) this, these (*pl*); **~ è il mio consiglio** this is my advice.

♦ *pron* **1.** (*indica prossimità*) this (one), these (ones) (*pl*); **~ è Franco** this is Franco; **~ qui** o **qua** this one (here).

2. (*per riassumere*) that; **~ è tutto** that's all; **questa è bella!** that's rich!

questura *sf* (*organo*) police headquarters (*pl*).

qui *avv* here; **da ~ in avanti** from now on; **di** o **da ~** from here; **di ~ a un anno** in a year's time; **di ~ a poco** in a little while.

quiete *sf* quiet.

quindi *cong* so, therefore.

quindicesimo, -a *num* fifteenth, → **sesto**.

quindici *num* fifteen; **~ giorni** a fortnight, → **sei**.

quindicina *sf* about fifteen; **una ~ di giorni** about a fortnight.

quinta *sf* (*marcia*) fifth gear.

▶ **quinte** *sfpl* (*di teatro*) wings.

quintale *sm* = 100 kilograms.

quinto, -a *num* fifth, → **sesto**.

quintuplo *sm*: **il ~ del prezzo normale** five times the normal price.

Quirinale *nm*: **il ~** *official residence of the President of Italy*.

IL QUIRINALE

The 'Palazzo del Quirinale' has been the official residence of the president of the Italian republic since 1947. It overlooks the square of the same name in Rome and is guarded by armed policemen in full dress uniform. It is here that the president receives foreign heads of state on official business.

---

quota *sf* (*altitudine*) altitude; (*di denaro, bene*) share; **perdere ~** to lose height; **prendere ~** to climb; **~ d'iscrizione** (*a circolo*) membership fee.

quotato, -a *agg* valued.

quotidianamente *avv* daily.

quotidiano, -a ♦ *agg* daily ♦ *sm* daily (newspaper).

quoziente *sm* quotient; **~ d'intelligenza** IQ.

R

rabarbaro *sm* rhubarb.

rabbia *sf* (*collera*) anger, rage; (*malattia*) rabies; **far ~ a qn** to drive sb mad.

rabbino *sm* rabbi.

rabbioso, -a *agg* angry; (MED) rabid.

rabbonire *vt* to calm down.

▶ **rabbonirsi** *vr* to calm down.

rabbrividire *vi* (*di freddo*) to shiver; (*di paura*) to shudder.

raccapezzarsi *vr*: **non mi ci raccapezzo** I can't make it out.

raccapricciante *agg* horrifying.

raccattapalle *smf inv* ball-boy (*f* ball-girl).

raccattare *vt* to pick up.

racchetta *sf* (*da tennis*) racket; (*da ping-pong*) bat (*Br*), paddle (*Am*); (*da sci*) ski pole.

raccogliere *vt* (*da terra*) to pick up; (*frutti, fiori*) to pick; (*mettere insieme*) to collect; (*voti*) to win.

▶ **raccogliersi** *vr* (*radunarsi*) to meet, to gather; (*in meditazione, preghiera*) to gather one's thoughts.

raccolta *sf* collection; (*agricola*) harvesting, gathering; **fare la ~ di qc** to collect sthg.

raccolto, -a ♦ *pp* → **raccogliere** ♦ *sm* harvest, crop.

raccomandare *vt* to recommend; (*affidare*) to entrust; **~ a qn di fare qc** to urge sb to do sthg.

▶ **raccomandarsi** *vr*: **raccomandarsi a** to appeal to; **mi raccomando, non fare tardi!** don't be late now, will you!

raccomandata *sf* registered letter.

raccomandato, -a *agg* (*lettera*) registered; (*candidato*) recommended.

raccomandazione *sf* (*consiglio*) recommendation.

raccontare *vt* to tell.

racconto *sm* (*esposizione*) account; (*romanzo*) short story.

raccordo *sm* connection, link; (*di autostrada*) slip road (*Br*), entrance/exit ramp (*Am*); **~ anulare** ring road (*Br*), beltway (*Am*).

racimolare *vt* to scrape together.

rada *sf* harbour.

radar *sm inv* radar.

raddoppiare ♦ *vt* (*rendere doppio*) to double; (*aumentare*) to redouble

♦ *vi* to double.

radente *agg* (*tiro, volo*) very low.

radere *vt* to shave; **~ qc al suolo** to raze sthg to the ground.

▶ **radersi** *vr* to shave.

radiare *vt* to strike off.

radiatore *sm* radiator.

radiazione *sf* radiation.

radicale *agg* radical.

radicalmente *avv* radically, completely.

radicchio *sm* radicchio (*an Italian variety of chicory*).

radice *sf* root; **~ quadrata** square root.

radio *sf inv* radio; (*stazione*) radio station; **alla ~** on the radio.

radioamatore, -trice *sm, f* radio ham.

radioascoltatore, -trice *sm, f* listener.

radioattivo, -a *agg* radioactive.

radiocomandato, -a *agg* remote-controlled.

radiografia *sf* X-ray.

radioso, -a *agg* bright.

radiotaxi *sm inv* minicab.

rado, -a *agg* sparse; **di ~** rarely.

radunare *vt* (*persone*) to gather; (*cose*) to assemble.

▶ **radunarsi** *vr* to gather.

raduno *sm* meeting.

rafano *sm* radish.

raffermo, -a *agg* stale.

raffica, -che *sf* (*di vento*) gust; (*di mitra*) burst.

raffigurare *vt* to portray.

raffinato, -a *agg* refined; (*stile*) sophisticated.

raffineria *sf* refinery.

rafforzare *vt* to strengthen.

raffreddare *vt* to cool; (*fig: rapporti, interesse*) to cool, to dampen.

▶ **raffreddarsi** *vr* (*bevanda, cibo*) to get cold; (*fig: persona, amicizia*) to cool down; (*ammalarsi*) to catch a cold.

raffreddato, -a *agg*: **essere ~** to have a cold.

raffreddore sm cold.

rafia sf raffia.

ragazza sf (giovane donna) girl; (fidanzata) girlfriend; ~ **madre** single mother.

ragazzata sf childish trick.

ragazzo sm (giovane) boy; (fidanzato) boyfriend.

raggiante agg radiant, beaming.

raggio sm (di sole, infrarosso) ray; (area) range; (MAT) radius; (di ruota) spoke.

raggirare vt to trick, to cheat.

raggiungere vt (persona) to catch up; (luogo) to reach; (fig: fine) to achieve.

raggiunto, -a pp → **raggiungere**.

raggomitolarsi vr to curl up.

raggranellare vt to scrape together.

raggrinzire vt & vi to shrivel up.

▶ **raggrinzirsi** vr to shrivel.

raggruppare vt (mettere insieme) to assemble; (a gruppi) to group together.

▶ **raggrupparsi** vr to assemble.

ragguagli smpl: **dare** ~ to give details.

ragionamento sm (riflessione) reasoning; (discorso) argument.

ragionare vi to reason.

▶ **ragionare di** v + prep (parlare di) to argue about.

ragione sf reason; **avere** ~ to be right; **dare** ~ **a qn** to side with sb; **a maggior** ~ even more so.

ragioneria sf (materia) accountancy; (scuola) commercial school; (reparto) accounts (pl).

ragionevole agg reasonable.

ragioniere, -a sm, f accountant.

ragliare vi to bray.

ragnatela sf cobweb, spider's web.

ragno sm spider.

ragù sm inv sauce of minced beef, tomatoes and onions.

RAI sf Italian broadcasting corporation.

rallegramenti smpl congratulations.

rallentare vt to slow down.

rally ['relli] sm inv rally.

ramaiolo sm ladle.

ramanzina sf telling-off.

rame sm copper.

ramino sm rummy.

rammaricarsi : rammaricarsi di vr + prep to regret.

rammendare vt (stoffa) to mend; (lana) to darn.

rammentare vt to remember; ~ **qc a qn** to remind sb of sthg.

▶ **rammentarsi di** vr + prep to remember.

rammollito, -a agg soft.

ramo sm branch.

ramoscello sm twig.

rampa sf flight (of stairs); ~ **di lancio** launch pad.

rampicante agg climbing.

rampone sm (fiocina) harpoon; (in alpinismo) crampon.

rana sf frog.

rancido, -a agg rancid.

rancore sm rancour.

randagio, -a, -gi, -gie o **-ge** agg stray.

randello sm club.

rango, -ghi sm rank.

rannicchiarsi vr to huddle up.

rannuvolarsi vr to cloud over.

ranocchio sm frog.

rantolo sm death rattle.

rapa sf turnip.

rapace ♦ agg predatory ♦ sm bird of prey.

rapare vt to crop.

rapida sf rapids (pl).

rapidamente avv rapidly, fast.

rapidità sf rapidity.

rapido, -a ♦ agg (svelto) fast; (breve) quick, rapid ♦ sm express (train).

rapimento sm kidnapping.

rapina sf robbery; ~ **a mano armata** armed robbery.

rapinare vt to rob.

rapinatore, -trice *sm, f* robber.
rapire *vt* to kidnap.
rapitore, -trice *sm, f* kidnapper.
rapporto *sm* (*resoconto*) report; (*tra persone*) relationship; (*connessione*) connection, relation; (MAT) ratio; **rapporti sessuali** sexual intercourse (*sg*).
rapprendersi *vr* to curdle.
rappresentante *smf* representative.
rappresentare *vt* to represent; (*raffigurare*) to depict; (*mettere in scena*) to stage, to perform.
rappresentazione *sf* (*spettacolo*) performance; (*raffigurazione*) representation.
rappreso, -a *pp* → **rapprendersi**.
raramente *avv* rarely.
rarità *sf inv* (*scarsità*) rarity; (*oggetto*) rare thing.
raro, -a *agg* rare.
rasare *vt* to shave.
▶ **rasarsi** *vr* to shave.
rasato, -a *agg* shaven.
raschiare *vt* to scrape.
rasentare *vt* (*sfiorare*) to graze; (*muro*) to hug, to keep close to; (*fig: avvicinarsi a*) to border on.
rasente *prep* close to.
raso, -a ♦ *pp* → **radere** ♦ *agg* (*cucchiaio*) level ♦ *sm* (*tessuto*) satin; **~ terra** close to the ground.
rasoio *sm* razor; **~ elettrico** electric razor.
rassegna *sf* review; (*cinematografica, teatrale*) season; **passare in ~** (MIL) to review.
rassegnare *vt*: **~ le dimissioni** to hand in one's resignation.
▶ **rassegnarsi** *vr* to resign o.s.
rasserenarsi *vr* to clear up.
rassettare *vt* (*stanza, capelli*) to tidy (up); (*vestito*) to mend.
rassicurare *vt* to reassure.
rassodare *vt* (*terreno*) to harden; (*muscoli*) to tone.
rassomigliare : rassomigliare

a *v + prep* to resemble.
rastrellare *vt* (*foglie*) to rake; (*fig: zona*) to comb.
rastrello *sm* rake.
rata *sf* instalment; **pagare qc a rate** to pay for sthg in instalments.
rateale *agg* by o in instalments.
ratificare *vt* (DIR) to ratify.
ratto *sm* rat.
rattoppare *vt* to patch.
rattrappire *vt* to numb.
▶ **rattrappirsi** *vr* to go numb.
rattristare *vt* to make sad.
▶ **rattristarsi** *vr* to become sad.
rauco, -a, -chi, -che *agg* raucous.
ravanello *sm* radish.
ravioli *smpl* ravioli.
ravvicinare *vt* (*avvicinare*) to bring closer; (*rappacificare*) to reconcile.
▶ **ravvicinarsi** *vr* to be reconciled.
ravvivare *vt* to brighten up.
razionale *agg* rational.
razionalità *sf* rationality.
razionare *vt* to ration.
razione *sf* ration.
razza *sf* (*di persone*) race; (*di animali*) breed; (*pesce*) ray; **che ~ di domanda è questa?** (*fam*) what sort of question is that?
razzia *sf* raid.
razziale *agg* racial.
razzismo *sm* racism.
razzista, -i, -e *agg & smf* racist.
razzo *sm* rocket.
razzolare *vi* to scratch about.
re *sm inv* king.
reagire *vi*: **~ (a qc)** to react (to sthg).
reale *agg* (*vero*) real; (*di re*) royal.
realista, -i, -e *smf* realist.
realizzare *vt* (*progetto*) to carry out; (*sogno*) to fulfil; (*film*) to make; (*rendersi conto di*, COMM) to realize.
▶ **realizzarsi** *vr* (*persona*) to be fulfilled; (*progetto*) to be carried out; (*sogno*) to come true.
realizzazione *sf* (*attuazione*) carrying-out.

realmente *avv* really.

realtà *sf inv* reality; **in ~** in reality.

reato *sm* offence, crime.

reattore *sm* (*aereo*) jet; (*motore*) jet engine; (*in fisica*) reactor.

reazionario, -a *agg* reactionary.

reazione *sf* reaction.

rebus *sm inv* game in which pictures represent the syllables of words.

recapitare *vt* to deliver.

recapito *sm* (*luogo*) address; (*consegna*) delivery; **~ telefonico** (tele)phone number.

recare *vt*: **~ disturbo a qn** to disturb sb.

▶ **recarsi** *vr* to go.

recensione *sf* review.

recente *agg* recent; **di ~** recently.

recentemente *avv* recently.

recessione *sf* recession.

recidere *vt* to cut off.

recintare *vt* to fence in.

recinto *sm* (*spazio*) enclosure; (*recinzione*) fence.

recipiente *sm* container.

reciproco, -a, -ci, -che *agg* reciprocal.

reciso, -a *pp* → **recidere**.

recita *sf* play.

recitare ◆ *vt* (*poesia*) to recite; (*ruolo*) to play ◆ *vi* to act.

reclamare ◆ *vi* to complain ◆ *vt* to claim.

réclame [re'klam] *sf inv* advertising.

reclamo *sm* (*protesta*) complaint.

reclinabile *agg* reclining.

reclusione *sf* (DIR) imprisonment.

reclutare *vt* to recruit.

record *sm inv* record.

recuperare *vt* (*riprendere*) to recover, to get back; (*svantaggio, tempo*) to make up; (*rottami*) to salvage.

redatto, -a *pp* → **redigere**.

redattore, -trice *sm, f* editor.

redazione *sf* (*stesura*) writing; (*ufficio*) editorial department; (*personale*) editorial staff.

redditizio, -a *agg* profitable.

reddito *sm* income.

redigere *vt* (*articolo, lettera*) to write; (*documento, contratto*) to draw up.

redimere *vt* to redeem.

redini *sfpl* reins.

referendum *sm inv* referendum.

referenze *sfpl* references.

referto *sm* medical report.

refettorio *sm* refectory, dining hall.

refrigerare *vt* to refrigerate.

refurtiva *sf* stolen goods (*pl*).

regalare *vt* (*dono*) to give (as a present); (*dare gratis*) to give away.

regalo *sm* (*dono*) present, gift.

regata *sf* regatta.

reggere ◆ *vt* (*tenere*) to hold; (*sostenere*) to bear, to support; (*sopportare*) to bear; (*governare*) to govern; (GRAMM) to take, to be followed by ◆ *vi* (*durare*) to last; (*essere logico*) to stand up, to hold good; (*resistere*): **~ a qc** to withstand sthg.

▶ **reggersi** *vr*: **non mi reggo in piedi** I can't stand up.

reggia, -ge *sf* palace.

reggicalze *sm inv* suspender belt.

reggimento *sm* regiment.

reggipetto = **reggiseno**.

reggiseno *sm* bra.

regista, -i, -e *smf* (CINEMA, TV) director; (TEATRO) producer.

regia *sf* (*di film*) direction; (*di dramma*) production.

regime *sm* (*politico*) regime; (*alimentare*) diet.

regina *sf* queen.

regionale *agg* regional.

regione *sf* region.

REGIONE

For administrative purposes Italy is divided up into 20 regions. Each region is made up of different provinces ('province'), and each province is made up of municipalities known as 'comuni'. Five of the regions have a special statute granting them a greater degree of autonomy than the others: they are Valle d'Aosta, Friuli-Venezia Giulia, Trentino-Alto Adige, Sicily and Sardinia.

---

regista, -i, -e *smf* director.

registrare *vt* to register; (*su cassetta*) to record; (COMM) to enter.

registratore *sm* tape recorder; ~ **di cassa** cash register.

registrazione *sf* (*di nascita, morte*) registration; (*di musica, programma*) recording; (COMM) entry.

registro *sm* register; ~ **di classe** attendance register.

regnare *vi* to reign.

regno *sm* kingdom; (*fig: ambito*) realm.

▶ **Regno Unito** *sm*: **il Regno Unito** the United Kingdom.

regola *sf* rule; **essere in ~** to be (all) in order; **fare qc a ~ d'arte** to do sthg perfectly.

regolabile *agg* adjustable.

regolamento *sm* regulations (*pl*).

regolare ◆ *agg* regular ◆ *vt* to regulate; (*apparecchio, macchina*) to adjust; (*questione, conto*) to settle

▶ **regolarsi** *vr* (*comportarsi*) to behave; (*moderarsi*) to control o.s.; **regolarsi nel bere/mangiare** to watch what one drinks/eats.

regolarmente *avv* regularly.

regolo *sm* ruler; ~ **calcolatore** slide rule.

regredire *vi* to regress.

reintegrare *vt* to reinstate.

relativamente *avv* relatively, comparatively; ~ **a** in relation to, as regards.

relativo, -a *agg* relative; ~ **a** relating to.

relax *sm* relaxation.

relazione *sf* relationship; (*amorosa*) affair; (*resoconto*) report.

relegare *vt* to relegate.

religione *sf* religion.

religioso, -a ◆ *agg* religious ◆ *sm, f* monk (*f* nun).

reliquia *sf* relic.

relitto *sm* wreck, piece of wreckage.

remare *vi* to row.

remo *sm* oar.

rendere ◆ *vt* (*restituire*) to give back, to return; (*far diventare*) to make; (*produrre*) to yield ◆ *vi* (*persona, azienda*) to do well; (*lavoro*) to pay well; ~ **possibile qc** to make sthg possible; ~ **l'idea** (*persona*) to make o.s. clear.

▶ **rendersi** *vr* (*diventare*) to become; **rendersi utile** to make o.s. useful.

rendiconto *sm* (*relazione*) report; (COMM) statement of accounts.

rendimento *sm* (*efficienza*) efficiency; (*di scolaro, macchina*) performance.

rendita *sf* unearned income; **vivere di ~** (*fig: studente*) to get by on one's past performance.

rene *sm* kidney.

renitente *agg* reluctant; **è ~ ai consigli** he won't listen to advice; **essere ~ alla leva** to fail to report for military service.

renna *sf* reindeer.

Reno *sm*: **il ~** the Rhine.

reparto *sm* (*di negozio*) department; (*d'ospedale*) ward; (MIL) unit.

repentaglio *sm*: **mettere a ~ qc** to put sthg at risk.

reperibile *agg* (*merce, persona*) available; (*al lavoro*) on call.

reperto *sm* (*resto*) find; (*resoconto*) report.

repertorio *sm* (*teatrale*) repertoire; (*elenco*) index.

replica, -che *sf* (*in televisione*) repeat; (*a teatro*) repeat performance.

replicare *vt* to reply.

repressione *sf* repression.

represso, -a *pp* → **reprimere**.

reprimere *vt* to repress.

▶ **reprimersi** *vr* to restrain o.s.

repubblica, -che sf republic.

repubblicano, -a agg republican.

repulsione sf repulsion.

reputare vt to consider.

reputazione sf reputation.

requisire vt to requisition.

requisito sm requisite.

resa sf (l'arrendersi) surrender; (restituzione) return; (rendimento) yield; **~ dei conti** (fig) day of reckoning.

residence ['rɛzidəns] sm inv residential hotel.

residente agg resident.

residenza sf residence.

residenziale agg residential.

residuo, -a ♦ agg residual, remaining ♦ sm (avanzo) remainder; (scoria) waste.

resina sf resin.

resistente agg (robusto) strong; (durevole) durable; **~ al calore** heatproof, heat-resistant.

resistenza sf resistance; (di materiale) strength; (a fatica, dolore) endurance; **~ (elettrica)** (electrical) resistance.

resistere vi (tener duro) to hold out.

▶ **resistere a** v + prep (opporsi) to resist; (sopportare) to withstand.

resistito, -a pp → **resistere**.

reso, -a pp → **rendere**.

resoconto sm account.

respingere vt to reject; (attacco, aggressore) to repel; (SCOL) to fail.

respinto, -a pp → **respingere**.

respirare vi & vt to breathe.

respiratore sm (per immersione) aqualung; (MED) respirator.

respirazione sf breathing; **~ artificiale** artificial respiration.

respiro sm (respirazione) breathing; (movimento) breath; **tirare un ~ di sollievo** to heave a sigh of relief.

responsabile ♦ agg responsible ♦ smf (in azienda, negozio) person in charge; (colpevole) culprit; **essere ~ di qc** (incaricato di) to be in charge of sthg; (colpevole di) to be responsible for sthg.

responsabilità sf inv responsibility; (colpa) responsibility, liability.

ressa sf crowd.

restare vi to stay, to remain; (avanzare) to be left, to remain; (trovarsi) to be; **~ a piedi** to remain standing; **mi restano pochi giorni** I only have a few days left.

restaurare vt to restore.

restauro sm restoration.

restituire vt to give back, to return.

resto sm rest, remainder; (di denaro) change; (MAT) remainder; **del ~** moreover, besides.

▶ **resti** smpl (ruderi) ruins; (di cibo) leftovers; (di persona, animale) remains.

restringere vt (dimensioni) to reduce; (abito) to take in; (limitare) to limit, to restrict.

▶ **restringersi** vr (strada) to (become) narrow; (stoffa) to shrink; (per numero, estensione) to reduce.

resurrezione sf resurrection.

resuscitare = **risuscitare**.

rete sf net; (recinzione) wire fence; (radiotelevisiva, stradale) network; (del letto) bedsprings (pl); (nel calcio: punto) goal.

▶ **Rete** sf (INFORM): **la Rete** the Net.

reticente agg reticent.

reticolato sm (intreccio di linee) network; (recinzione) fencing, wire netting.

retina sf (ANAT) retina.

retino sm net.

retorica sf rhetoric.

retorico, -a, -ci, -che agg (spreg) pompous.

retribuire vt to remunerate, to pay.

retribuzione sf remuneration, pay.

retro sm inv back; **sul ~** at the back; **vedi ~** see over.

retrocedere vi to recede; (SPORT) to be relegated.

retrocesso, -a pp → **retrocedere**.

retrogrado, -a agg retrograde.

retromarcia sf reverse.

retroscena sm inv (antefatti) background.

retrospettivo, -a agg retrospective.

retrovisore sm rear-view mirror.

retta sf (linea) straight line; (di pensionato) charge; **dar ~ a** to pay attention to.

rettangolare agg rectangular.

rettangolo sm rectangle.

rettificare vt (form) to rectify.

rettile sm reptile.

rettilineo, -a agg & sm straight.

retto, -a ♦ pp → **reggere** ♦ agg (diritto) straight; (persona, comportamento) honest; **angolo ~** right angle.

rettore sm rector.

reumatismi smpl rheumatism (sg).

reversibile agg reversible.

revisionare vt (apparecchio, macchina) to service, to overhaul; (testo) to revise.

revisione sf (di apparecchio) service; (di conti) audit(ing); (di scritto) revision.

revocare vt to revoke.

revolver sm inv revolver.

riabilitare vt to rehabilitate.

riacquistare vt to regain.

riaggiustare vt to readjust.

rialzare vt to raise.

▶ **rialzarsi** vr to get up.

rialzo sm rise.

rianimazione sf (reparto) intensive care.

riaperto, -a pp → **riaprire**.

riapertura sf reopening; **~ delle scuole** beginning of the school term.

riaprire vt & vi to reopen.

▶ **riaprirsi** vr to reopen.

riarmo sm rearming.

riassetto sm reorganization.

riassumere vt (ricapitolare) to summarize; (impiegato) to re-employ; (riprendere) to resume.

riassunto, -a ♦ pp → **riassumere** ♦ sm summary.

riattaccare vt (attaccare di nuovo) to re-attach; (bottone) to sew back on; (ricominciare) to start again; (al telefono) to hang up.

riavere vt (avere di nuovo) to have again; (avere indietro) to get back; (riacquistare) to regain, to recover.

▶ **riaversi da** vr + prep to recover from.

ribadire vt to confirm.

ribaltabile agg folding.

ribaltare vt to overturn.

ribassare ♦ vt to lower ♦ vi to fall.

ribasso sm fall, reduction.

ribattere ♦ vt (palla) to return ♦ vi (replicare) to answer back.

ribellarsi vr to rebel; **~ a qn** to rebel against sb.

ribelle agg rebellious.

ribellione sf rebellion.

ribes sm inv: **~ nero** blackcurrant; **~ rosso** redcurrant.

ribollire vi (fig) to seethe.

ribrezzo sm horror; **far ~ a qn** to revolt sb.

ricadere vi (cadere di nuovo) to fall again; (in errore, vizio) to relapse; (capelli, vestiti) to hang down.

▶ **ricadere su** v + prep to fall on.

ricalcare vt to trace.

ricamare vt to embroider.

ricambiare vt (sentimento, favore) to return; (cambiare di nuovo) to change again.

ricambio sm (sostituzione) exchange, replacement; **in ~** in return.

▶ **ricambi** smpl spare parts.

ricamo sm embroidery.

ricapitolare vt to summarize.

ricaricare vt (macchina fotografica, arma) to reload; (batteria) to recharge; (*orologio*) to wind up.

ricattare *vt* to blackmail.

ricatto *sm* blackmail.

ricavare *vt* (*estrarre*) to extract; (*ottenere*) to obtain.

ricavato *sm* (*guadagno*) proceeds (*pl*).

ricchezza *sf* wealth.

▶ **ricchezze** *sfpl* wealth (*sg*); ~ **naturali** natural resources.

ricciarelli *smpl* diamond-shaped sweets made from marzipan (*a speciality of Siena*).

riccio, -a, -ci, -ce ♦ *agg* curly ♦ *sm* (*di capelli*) curl; (*animale*) hedgehog; ~ **di mare** sea urchin.

ricciolo *sm* curl.

ricciuto, -a *agg* curly.

ricco, -a, -chi, -che *agg* rich, wealthy; ~ **di qc** rich in sthg.

ricerca, -che *sf* research; (*di persona, di cosa*) search; **essere alla ~ di** to be in search of.

ricercare *vt* (*cercare di nuovo*) to look for (again); (*ladro*) to look for, to search for.

ricercatezza *sf* refinement.

ricercato, -a *agg* (*elegante*) refined; (*apprezzato*) in demand, sought-after; **essere ~ dalla polizia** to be wanted by the police.

ricercatore, -trice *sm, f* researcher.

ricetta *sf* recipe; ~ **medica** prescription.

ricettazione *sf* receiving (stolen goods).

ricevere *vt* (*lettera, regalo*) to receive, to get; (*schiaffo, palla*) to get; (*accogliere*) to welcome; (*ospite*) to entertain; (*cliente, paziente*) to receive.

ricevimento *sm* reception.

ricevitore *sm* receiver.

ricevuta *sf* receipt; **mi può fare una ~?** may I have a receipt?

ricezione *sf* reception.

richiamare *vt* (*ritelefonare, per far tornare*) to call back; (*attirare*) to attract; (*rimproverare*) to reprimand; ~ **alla mente qc a qn** to remind sb of sthg.

richiamo *sm* (*per far tornare*) call; (*attrazione*) appeal, attraction; (*di vaccinazione*) booster.

richiedere *vt* (*ridomandare*) to ask again; (*aiuto, spiegazioni*) to ask for; (*necessitare di*) to require; **gli ho richiesto le chiavi** (*indietro*) I asked him for my keys back.

richiesta *sf* (*domanda*) request; (*esigenza*) demand; **a ~** on request.

richiesto, -a ♦ *pp* → **richiedere** ♦ *agg* in demand, sought-after.

richiudere *vt* to close again.

riciclare *vt* to recycle.

ricollegare *vt* (*centri isolati*) to reconnect; (*fatti, discorsi*) to connect, to relate.

▶ **ricollegarsi** *vr*: **ricollegarsi a** (*riferirsi a*) to refer to; (*fatto*) to be connected with.

ricominciare *vt & vi* to begin again, to start again; ~ **a fare qc** to begin again, to resume doing sthg.

ricompensa *sf* reward.

ricompensare *vt* to reward.

ricomporre *vt* to reconstruct.

▶ **ricomporsi** *vr* to regain one's composure.

ricomposto, -a *pp* → **ricomporre**.

riconciliare *vt* to reconcile.

▶ **riconciliarsi** *vr* to be reconciled.

ricondotto, -a *pp* → **ricondurre**.

ricondurre *vt* (*in luogo*) to take back, to bring back.

riconferma *sf* (*conferma ulteriore*) reconfirmation; (*dimostrazione*) proof.

riconfermare *vt* to reconfirm.

riconoscente *agg* grateful.

riconoscere *vt* to recognize; (*ammettere*) to admit.

riconquistare *vt* (*territorio*) to reconquer; (*stima, rispetto*) to regain.

riconsegnare *vt* to give back.

ricoperto, -a *pp* → **ricoprire**.

ricopiare *vt* to copy.

ricoprire vt (poltrona, dolce) to cover; (carica) to hold; ~ qn/qc di qc to cover sb/sth with sth.

ricordare vt to remember, to recall; ~ qc a qn to remind sb of sth; **non mi ricordo l'indirizzo** I don't remember the address.

▶ **ricordarsi di** vr + prep to remember; **ricordarsi di aver fatto qc** to remember doing o having done sth; **ricordarsi di fare qc** to remember to do sth.

ricordo sm (memoria) memory; (oggetto) souvenir.

ricorrente agg recurrent.

ricorrenza sf anniversary.

ricorrere vi (ripetersi) to recur.

▶ **ricorrere a** v + prep (rivolgersi a) to turn to; (utilizzare) to resort to.

ricorso, -a ♦ pp → **ricorrere** ♦ sm (DIR) appeal; **far ~ a qc** (utilizzare) to resort to sth.

ricostruire vt (edificio) to rebuild; (fatto) to reconstruct.

ricotta sf ricotta (soft cheese made from milk whey).

ricoverare vt: ~ qn in ospedale to admit sb to hospital.

ricreare vt (creare di nuovo) to recreate.

ricreazione sf (a scuola) break.

ricredersi vr to change one's mind.

ricucire vt to mend.

ricuperare = **recuperare**.

ridacchiare vi to snigger.

ridare vt (dare di nuovo) to give again; (restituire) to give back.

ridere vi to laugh; **morire dal ~** to die laughing.

▶ **ridere di** v + prep to laugh at.

ridetto, -a pp → **ridire**.

ridicolo, -a agg ridiculous.

ridimensionare vt: ~ un problema to get a problem into perspective.

ridire vt (ripetere) to repeat; **avere qualcosa da ~** to find fault.

ridondante agg redundant.

ridosso sm: **a ~ (di qc)** behind (sth).

ridotto, -a ♦ pp → **ridurre** ♦ agg (prezzo) reduced; (formato) smaller; ~ **male** in a bad state.

ridurre vt to reduce.

▶ **ridursi** vr (diminuire) to shrink.

▶ **ridursi a** vr + prep to be reduced to.

riduzione sf reduction.

rielaborare vt to redesign.

riempire vt to fill; (modulo) to fill in; ~ **di** to fill with.

▶ **riempirsi di** vr + prep (stadio, cinema) to fill with; (fam: mangiare) to stuff o.s. with.

rientrare vi (entrare di nuovo) to go/come back in; (a casa, in patria) to return; (essere compreso) to be included; (avere una rientranza) to curve inwards.

riepilogo, -ghi sm summary.

rievocare vt (ricordare) to recall; (far ricordare) to commemorate.

rifare vt (fare di nuovo) to do again; (ricostruire) to rebuild; ~ **il letto** to make the bed.

▶ **rifarsi di** vr + prep (perdita) to recover; **rifarsi di qc su qn** to get one's own back on sb for sth.

rifatto, -a pp → **rifare**.

riferimento sm reference; **fare ~ a** to refer to.

riferire vt: ~ qc (a qn) to report sth (to sb).

▶ **riferirsi a** vr + prep to refer to.

rifilare vt: ~ qc a qn (fam: merce) to palm sth off on sb; (fam: compito) to saddle sb with sth.

rifiniture sfpl finishing touches.

rifiorire vi to flower again.

rifiutare vt to refuse; ~ **di fare qc** to refuse to do sth.

rifiuto sm refusal.

▶ **rifiuti** smpl (spazzatura) rubbish (sg) (Br), trash (sg) (Am).

riflessione sf reflection.

riflessivo, -a agg reflexive.

riflesso, -a ♦ pp → **riflettere** ♦ sm (luce) reflection; (conseguenza) repercussion; (MED) reflex.

riflettere vt & vi to reflect; ~ **su** to reflect on, to think about.

▶ **riflettersi** vr to be reflected.

▶ **riflettersi su** vr + prep (influire) to influence, to have repercussions on.

riflettore sm (di teatro) spotlight; (di stadio) floodlight.

riflusso sm (flusso contrario) flow; (di marea) ebb.

riforma sf reform.

riformare vt to reform; (MIL) to invalid out.

rifornimento sm: **fare ~ di qc** to stock up with sthg.

▶ **rifornimenti** smpl supplies.

rifornire vt: ~ **qn/qc di** to supply sb/sthg with.

▶ **rifornirsi di** vr + prep to stock up with.

rifrangere vt to refract.

rifratto, -a pp → **rifrangere**.

rifugiarsi vr to take refuge.

rifugiato, -a sm, f refugee.

rifugio sm (riparo) shelter, refuge; ~ **alpino** mountain hut.

riga, -ghe sf line; (di capelli) parting; (righello) ruler; **mettersi in ~** to get into line; **a righe** (tessuto) striped; (foglio) lined.

rigare ♦ vt to scratch ♦ vi: ~ **diritto** to toe the line.

rigattiere sm junk dealer.

rigettare vt (gettare indietro) to throw back; (respingere) to reject; (fam: vomitare) to throw up.

rigetto sm (MED) rejection.

rigidità sf (di oggetto) rigidity; (del corpo) stiffness; (di clima) harshness; (di regolamento, persona) strictness.

rigido, -a agg (non elastico) rigid; (membra) stiff; (clima) harsh; (severo) strict.

rigirare vt (voltare) to turn (round); ~ **il discorso** to change the subject.

▶ **rigirarsi** vr (voltarsi) to turn round; (nel letto) to turn over.

rigo, -ghi sm line.

rigoglioso, -a agg luxuriant.

rigore sm rigour; (SPORT) penalty; **essere di ~** to be compulsory.

rigoroso, -a agg rigorous.

rigovernare vt to wash up.

riguardare vt (guardare di nuovo) to look at again; (controllare) to check; (concernere) to concern.

▶ **riguardarsi** vr to look after o.s.; **riguardati!** look after yourself!, take care!; **questo non ti riguarda** this has nothing to do with you.

riguardo sm (attenzione) care; (stima) regard, respect; ~ **a** with regard to.

rilanciare vt to relaunch.

rilancio sm relaunch; (economico) recovery.

rilasciare vt (intervista) to give; (ostaggio) to release; (documento, diploma) to issue.

rilassante agg relaxing.

rilassare vt to relax.

▶ **rilassarsi** vr to relax.

rilegare vt to bind.

rilegatura sf binding.

rilento avv: **a ~** slowly.

rilevante agg relevant.

rilevare vt (notare) to notice; (mettere in evidenza) to point out; (dati) to collect; (COMM) to take over.

rilievo sm relief; **mettere in ~ qc** to emphasize sthg.

riluttante agg reluctant.

rima sf rhyme.

rimandare vt (mandare di nuovo) to send again; (mandare indietro) to send back; (riunione, esame) to postpone; ~ **qn a qc** (in testo) to refer sb to sthg; ~ **qn in italiano** (SCOL) to make sb resit their Italian exam.

rimando sm cross-reference.

rimanente ♦ agg remaining ♦ sm remainder.

rimanenza sf remainder.

rimanere vi (in luogo) to stay, to remain; (nel tempo) to last, to remain; (avanzare) to be left; (essere) to be; **mi sono rimaste diecimila lire** I have ten thousand lire left; **siamo**

rimasti in due there are (only) two of us left; **sono rimasto solo** I was left on my own; **~ indietro** (*di luogo*) to be left behind; (*nel lavoro*) to fall behind.

rimarginare vt to heal.

▶ **rimarginarsi** vr to heal.

rimasto, -a pp → **rimanere**.

rimasuglio sm scrap.

rimbalzare vi (*palla*) bounce; (*proiettile*) to ricochet.

rimbalzo sm (*di palla*) bounce; (*di proiettile*) ricochet.

rimbambito, -a agg daft.

rimboccare vt (*lenzuola, coperta*) to tuck in; (*maniche, pantaloni*) to turn up; **rimboccarsi le maniche** to roll up one's sleeves.

rimbombare vi to rumble.

rimborsare vt to reimburse, to refund.

rimborso sm refund; **~ spese** refund of expenses.

rimediare ◆ vt (*fam: procurarsi*) to find ◆ vi: **~ a qc** (*sbaglio, danno*) to make amends for sthg.

rimedio sm remedy; **porre ~ a qc** to remedy sthg.

rimescolare vt (*liquido*) to mix well; (*carte*) to shuffle.

rimessa sf (*per veicoli*) garage; (*per aerei*) hangar; (*nel calcio*) throw-in.

rimesso, -a pp → **rimettere**.

rimettere vt (*mettere di nuovo*) to put back; (*indossare di nuovo*) to put back on; (*perdonare*) to forgive, to pardon; (*vomitare*) to vomit; **~ a posto** to tidy up; **rimetterci (qc)** to lose (sthg).

▶ **rimettersi** vr (*guarire*) to get better, to recover; (*tempo*) to clear up; **rimettersi a fare qc** to start doing sthg again.

rimmel® sm inv mascara.

rimodernare vt to modernize.

rimontare ◆ vt to reassemble ◆ vi to catch up.

rimorchiare vt (*veicolo*) to tow; (*fam: ragazza*) to pick up.

rimorchiatore sm tug.

rimorchio sm (*operazione*) towing; (*di veicolo*) trailer.

rimorso sm remorse.

rimosso, -a pp → **rimuovere**.

rimozione sf (*spostamento*) removal; (*da carica, impiego*) dismissal; **'~ forzata** o **coatta'** 'tow-away zone'.

rimpatriare ◆ vt to repatriate ◆ vi to go home.

rimpiangere vt: **~ di aver fatto qc** to regret doing sthg.

rimpianto, -a ◆ pp → **rimpiangere** ◆ sm regret.

rimpiattino sm hide-and-seek.

rimpiazzare vt to replace.

rimpicciolire ◆ vt to make smaller ◆ vi to become smaller.

rimpinzarsi : rimpinzarsi di vr + prep to stuff o.s. with.

rimproverare vt to scold.

rimprovero sm scolding.

rimuginare ◆ vt to brood over ◆ vi: **~ (su qc)** to ponder (sthg).

rimuovere vt (*spostare*) to remove; (*da carica*) to dismiss.

rinascimentale agg Renaissance (*dav s*), of the Renaissance.

Rinascimento sm: **il ~** the Renaissance.

rinascita sf (*di foglie, capelli*) regrowth; (*economica, sociale*) revival.

rincalzare vt (*lenzuola*) to tuck in; (*muro, scala*) to prop up.

rincarare vi to increase in price.

rincasare vi to return home.

rinchiudere vt to confine.

▶ **rinchiudersi in** vr + prep to shut o.s. up in.

rinchiuso, -a pp → **rinchiudere**.

rincorrere vt to chase.

rincorsa sf run-up.

rincorso, -a pp → **rincorrere**.

rincrescere vi: **mi rincresce che tu parta** I'm sorry you're leaving; **mi rincresce di non poterti aiutare** I'm sorry I can't help you.

rinculo sm recoil.

rinfacciare vt: **~ qc a qn** (*colpa,*

difetto) to reproach sb with o for sthg; (*favore*) to throw sthg in sb's face.

rinforzare *vt* (*muscoli, capelli*) to strengthen; (*rendere più solido*) to reinforce.

rinforzo *sm* reinforcement.

rinfrescante *agg* refreshing.

rinfrescare ♦ *vt* (*atmosfera*) to cool ♦ *v impers*: **è rinfrescato** it's got cooler; **~ la memoria a qn** to refresh sb's memory.

▸ **rinfrescarsi** *vr* (*ristorarsi*) to refresh o.s.; (*lavarsi*) to freshen up.

rinfresco, -schi *sm* reception.

rinfusa : alla rinfusa *avv* higgledy-piggledy.

ringhiare *vi* to snarl.

ringhiera *sf* (*di balcone*) railings (*pl*); (*di scala*) banisters (*pl*).

ringiovanire ♦ *vt*: **~ qn** to make sb look younger ♦ *vi* to look young again, to be rejuvenated.

ringraziamento *sm* thanks (*pl*).

ringraziare *vt* to thank; **~ qn di qc** to thank sb for sthg.

rinnegare *vt* (*persona*) to disown; (*fede*) to renounce.

rinnovamento *sm* (*cambiamento*) updating; (*di impianti, locale*) renovation.

rinnovare *vt* to renew; (*locale*) to renovate.

rinnovo *sm* (*di contratto, guardaroba*) renewal; (*di casa*) renovation.

rinoceronte *sm* rhinoceros.

rinomato, -a *agg* famous.

rinsaldare *vt* to strengthen.

rintocco, -chi *sm* (*di campana*) toll; (*di orologio*) chime.

rintracciare *vt* to track down.

rintronare ♦ *vt* to deafen ♦ *vi* to boom.

rinuncia, -ce *sf* renunciation.

rinunciare : rinunciare a *v + prep* (*rifiutare*) to renounce; (*privarsi di*) to give up; **~ a fare qc** to give up doing sthg.

rinunzia = **rinuncia**.

rinunziare = **rinunciare**.

rinvenire ♦ *vt* (*trovare*) to find; (*scoprire*) to find out ♦ *vi* to come round/to, to revive.

rinvenuto, -a *pp* → **rinvenire**.

rinviare *vt* to return; **~ qc (a)** (*posporre*) to postpone sthg (until).

rinvio *sm* (*di lettera, palla*) return; (*di appuntamento, riunione*) postponement; (*a pagina, capitolo*) cross-reference.

rione *sm* quarter.

riordinare *vt* (*mettere in ordine*) to tidy up; (*cambiare ordine*) to reorganize.

riorganizzare *vt* to reorganize.

riparare *vt* (*aggiustare*) to repair; (*proteggere*) to protect; (*rimediare*) to make up for.

▸ **ripararsi** *vr* to shelter; **ripararsi da qc** to shelter/protect o.s. from sthg.

riparazione *sf* repair.

riparo *sm* (*protezione*) protection; (*rifugio*) shelter.

ripartire ♦ *vt* (*eredità, guadagno*) to share out; (*compiti, responsabilità*) to allocate ♦ *vi* to leave again.

ripassare ♦ *vt* to go over ♦ *vi* to go/come back.

ripensare : ripensare a *v + prep* (*riflettere su*) to think over; (*cambiare idea*) to change one's mind about; (*ricordare*) to recall.

ripercosso, -a *pp* → **ripercuotersi**.

ripercuotersi : ripercuotersi su *vr + prep* to influence.

ripercussione *sf* repercussion.

ripescare *vt* (*dall'acqua*) to fish out; (*ritrovare*) to find.

ripetere *vt* to repeat.

▸ **ripetersi** *vr* (*persona*) to repeat o.s.; (*avvenimento*) to happen again.

ripetitivo, -a *agg* repetitive.

ripetizione *sf* (*replica*) repetition.

▸ **ripetizioni** *sfpl* private lessons.

ripiano *sm* shelf.

ripicca, -che *sf*: **per ~** out of spite.

ripido, -a agg steep.

ripiegare ♦ vt (lenzuola) to fold (up); (piegare di nuovo) to refold ♦ vi (indietreggiare) to retreat.

▶ **ripiegare su** v + prep (rassegnarsi a) to make do with.

ripiego, -ghi sm expedient; **per ~** as a makeshift.

ripieno, -a ♦ agg: ~ **(di qc)** (casa, cassetto) full (of sthg); (panino) filled (with sthg); (tacchino) stuffed (with sthg) ♦ sm (di panino) filling.

riporre vt (mettere al suo posto) to put back; (mettere via) to put away; ~ **la propria fiducia in qn** to place one's trust in sb.

riportare vt (restituire, ricondurre) to take/bring back; (riferire) to report, to tell; (ottenere) to obtain.

riposare ♦ vi (rilassarsi) to rest; (dormire) to sleep ♦ vt to rest.

▶ **riposarsi** vr (rilassarsi) to rest; (dormire) to sleep.

riposo sm rest; (sonno) sleep; **a ~** retired.

ripostiglio sm store room.

riposto, -a pp → riporre.

riprendere ♦ vt (prendere di nuovo) to take again; (ritirare) to take back; (ricominciare) to resume; (rimproverare) to reproach; (filmare) to shoot, to film ♦ vi: **~ a fare qc** to start doing sthg again.

▶ **riprendersi da** vr + prep to recover from.

ripresa sf (di attività) resumption; (da malattia) recovery; (di motore) acceleration; (cinematografica) shot; **a più riprese** several times.

ripreso, -a pp → riprendere.

riprodotto, -a pp → riprodurre.

riprodurre vt to reproduce.

▶ **riprodursi** vr to reproduce.

riproduzione sf reproduction.

riprova sf confirmation.

riprovevole agg reprehensible.

ripugnante agg disgusting.

ripugnare vi: **~ a qn** (disgustare qn) to repel o disgust sb.

ripulire vt (pulire) to clean up; (rubare) to clean out.

riquadro sm square; (di parete, soffitto) panel.

risalire vt to go back up.

▶ **risalire a** v + prep to go back to.

risaltare vi to stand out.

risalto sm prominence; **mettere in ~ qc** to make sthg stand out.

risaputo, -a agg: **è ~ che ...** it is common knowledge that ...

risarcimento sm compensation.

risarcire vt: **~ qn (di qc)** to compensate sb (for sthg).

risata sf laugh.

riscaldamento sm heating; **~ centrale** central heating.

riscaldare vt (stanza) to heat; (mani) to warm; (cibo) to heat up.

▶ **riscaldarsi** vr (persona) to warm up; (diventare caldo) to get warmer.

riscatto sm ransom.

rischiarare vt to light up.

▶ **rischiararsi** vr to clear.

rischiare ♦ vt to risk ♦ vi: **rischio di arrivare in ritardo** I'm likely to be late; **ha rischiato di essere investito** he nearly got run over.

rischio sm risk; **correre il ~ di fare qc** to run the risk of doing sthg.

rischioso, -a agg risky.

risciacquare vt to rinse.

riscontrare vt to find.

riscontro sm (conferma) confirmation.

riscoprire vt to rediscover.

riscosso, -a pp → riscuotere.

riscuotere vt (somma) to collect; (stipendio, pensione) to receive; (assegno) to cash; (successo, consenso) to win, to earn.

risentire : risentire di v + prep to be affected by.

▶ **risentirsi** vr: risentirsi di o per qc to take offence at sthg.

riserva sf (provvista, giocatore) reserve; (di caccia, pesca) preserve; (restrizione) reservation; **essere in ~** (AUTO) to be low on petrol (Br) o gas (Am); **di ~** in reserve; **~ naturale** nature reserve.

riservare vt to save; (prenotare) to book, to reserve.

riservato, -a agg (posto, carattere) reserved; (informazione, lettera) confidential.

risi e bisi smpl rice and pea soup (a speciality of Veneto).

risiedere vi to reside.

riso ◆ pp → **ridere** ◆ sm (cereale) rice; (il ridere: pl f **risa**) laughter.

risolto, -a pp → **risolvere**.

risoluto, -a agg (deciso) determined.

risoluzione sf (decisione) resolution.

risolvere vt (problema, caso) to solve; (questione) to resolve.

▶ **risolversi** vr (problema) to resolve itself.

▶ **risolversi a** vr + prep: **risolversi a fare qc** to make up one's mind to do sthg.

▶ **risolversi in** vr + prep (andare a finire) to turn out.

risonanza sf resonance; **avere grande ~** (fatto, notizia) to arouse a great deal of interest.

risorgere vi (risuscitare) to revive; (problema) to recur.

risorsa sf resort.

▶ **risorse** sfpl resources.

risorto, -a pp → **risorgere**.

risotto sm risotto; **~ alla boscaiola** risotto with tomatoes, mushrooms and parsley; **~ di mare** seafood risotto; **~ alla milanese** risotto with saffron and lots of Parmesan cheese; **~ ai tartufi** risotto with truffles.

risparmiare ◆ vi to save ◆ vt (non consumare) to save; (non uccidere) to spare; (evitare): **~ qc a qn** to spare sb sthg.

risparmio sm (somma) savings (pl); (di tempo, soldi, fatica) saving.

rispecchiare vt to reflect.

rispettabile agg respectable.

rispettare vt to respect; **farsi ~** to command respect.

rispettivamente avv respectively.

rispettivo, -a agg respective.

rispetto sm respect; **mancare di ~ (a qn)** to be disrespectful (to sb); **~ a** (a paragone di) compared to; (in relazione a) as for.

rispettoso, -a agg respectful.

risplendere vi to shine.

rispondere vi to answer, to reply; (freni) to respond.

▶ **rispondere a** v + prep (corrispondere) to meet; **~ a qn** to answer sb.

▶ **rispondere di** v + prep to be responsible for.

risposta sf answer; (azione) response; **in ~ a qc** in reply to sthg.

risposto pp → **rispondere**.

rissa sf brawl.

ristabilire vt to restore.

▶ **ristabilirsi** vr to recover.

ristagnare vi (acqua) to become stagnant; (fig: industria) to stagnate.

ristampa sf (opera) reprint.

ristorante sm restaurant.

ristoro sm refreshment.

ristretto, -a ◆ pp → **restringere** ◆ agg (numero) limited; (brodo) thick; (uso) restricted.

ristrutturare vt (azienda) to reorganize; (casa) to alter.

risucchiare vt to suck in.

risultare vi to turn out to be; **mi risulta che ...** I understand that ...; **non mi risulta** not as far as I know.

▶ **risultare da** v + prep to result from.

risultato sm result.

risuolare vt to resole.

risuscitare vt to resuscitate.

risvegliare vt (dal sonno) to wake up; (memoria, appetito) to awaken.

risvolto sm (di pantaloni) turn-up (Br), cuff (Am); (di giacca) lapel; (fig: conseguenza) implication.

ritagliare vt to cut out.

ritaglio sm (di giornale) cutting; (di stoffa) scrap; **nei ritagli di tempo** in one's spare time.

ritardare ◆ vi to be late ◆ vt

(*rimandare*) to delay; (*rallentare*) to slow down.

ritardatario, -a *sm, f* latecomer.

ritardo *sm* (*di treno, pagamento*) delay; **in ~** late.

ritenere *vt* (*giudicare*) to believe; (*somma*) to deduct.

ritentare *vt* to try again.

ritirare *vt* to withdraw; (*pacco, da lavanderia*) to collect; (*insulto, promessa*) to take back.

▶ **ritirarsi** *vr* (*da attività*) to retire; (*restringersi*) to shrink.

ritirata *sf* retreat.

ritiro *sm* (*di pacco*) collection; (*di patente, passaporto*) confiscation; (*sportivo, spirituale*) retreat; (*da attività*) retirement.

ritmo *sm* (MUS) rhythm; (*di pulsazioni*) beat; (*di vita, lavoro*) pace.

rito *sm* rite.

ritornare *vi* (*andare, venire di nuovo*) to return, to go/come back; (*ricomparire*) to recur; (*ridiventare*): **~ pulito** to be clean again.

ritornello *sm* chorus.

ritorno *sm* return; **essere di ~** to be back.

ritrarre *vt* (*ritirare*) to withdraw; (*rappresentare*) to portray.

ritratto, -a ♦ *pp* → **ritrarre** ♦ *sm* portrait.

ritrovare *vt* (*cosa persa*) to find; (*riacquistare*) to regain.

▶ **ritrovarsi** *vr* (*incontrarsi*) to meet; (*in situazione*) to find o.s.

ritrovo *sm* meeting place.

ritto, -a *agg* upright.

riunione *sf* (*incontro*) meeting; (*di famiglia, amici*) reunion.

riunire *vt* to bring together.

▶ **riunirsi** *vr* to meet.

riuscire *vi* (*avere esito*) to turn out; (*aver successo*) to succeed; **~ a fare qc** to manage to do sthg; **~ in qc** to succeed in sthg.

riva *sf* (*di fiume*) bank; (*di lago, mare*) shore.

rivale *agg & smf* rival.

rivalutare *vt* to revalue.

rivedere *vt* (*vedere di nuovo*) to see again; (*riesaminare*) to review; (*ripassare*) to revise.

▶ **rivedersi** *vr* to meet again.

rivelare *vt* to reveal.

rivendicare *vt* (*diritto, bene*) to claim; (*attentato*) to claim responsibility for.

rivendita *sf* (*negozio*) dealer.

rivenditore, -trice *sm, f* retailer; **~ autorizzato** authorized dealer.

riversare *vt* (*fig: affetto*) to lavish; (*colpa*) to heap.

▶ **riversarsi** *vr* to pour.

rivestimento *sm* covering.

rivestire *vt* (*poltrona*) to cover; (*carica*) to hold; (*ruolo*) to play.

▶ **rivestirsi** *vr* to get dressed again.

riviera *sf* coast.

LA RIVIERA ADRIATICA

The bathing resorts which line the winding Adriatic coast are collectively known as 'la Riviera Adriatica'. Tourists from the rest of Italy and from abroad flock to famous resorts like Jesolo near Venice and Rimini on the Romagna coast. Renowned for its beautiful beaches and its first-rate amenities, Rimini is the quintessential Italian seaside town, teeming with life 24 hours a day.

rivincita *sf* (*di partita*) return match; (*rivalsa*) revenge.

rivisto, -a ♦ *pp* → **rivedere** ♦ *sf* (*giornale*) magazine.

rivolgere *vt* (*parola*) to address; (*attenzione, occhiata*) to direct.

▶ **rivolgersi a** *vr + prep* to contact, to apply to.

rivoltante *agg* revolting.

rivoltare *vt* (*rigirare*) to turn over; (*disgustare*) to disgust.

▶ **rivoltarsi** *vr* to rebel.

rivoltella *sf* revolver.

rivolto, -a ♦ *pp* → **rivolgere** ♦ *sf* revolt.

rivoluzionario, -a *agg & sm, f* revolutionary.

rivoluzione *sf* revolution.

rizzare *vt* to stand on end.

▶ **rizzarsi** *vr* to stand up.

roastbeef ['rɔzbif] *sm inv joint of beef braised or grilled, then served sliced.*

roba *sf* (*cose*) stuff, things (*pl*); ~ **da mangiare** things to eat; ~ **da matti!** (well I) never!

robiola *sf a type of soft rindless cheese.*

robot *sm inv* (*automa*) robot; (*da cucina*) food processor.

robusto, -a *agg* robust, sturdy.

rocca, -che *sf* fortress.

roccaforte *sf* stronghold.

rocchetto *sm* reel, spool.

roccia, -ce *sf* rock.

roccioso, -a *agg* rocky.

rock [rɔk] *sm* rock (music).

roco, -a, -chi, -che *agg* hoarse.

rodaggio *sm* running-in.

rodere *vt* to gnaw.

▶ **rodersi di** *vr + prep* to be consumed with.

rogna *sf* (*malattia*) scabies; (*fam: guaio*) nuisance.

rognone *sm* kidney; **rognoni alla romana** kidneys fried with garlic, parsley and white wine.

Roma *sf* Rome.

Romania *sf*: **la** ~ Romania.

romanico, -a, -ci, -che *agg* Romanesque.

romano, -a *agg & sm, f* Roman.

romanticismo *sm* romanticism.

romantico, -a, -ci, -che *agg* romantic.

romanzo *sm* (*libro*) novel; ~ **rosa** romantic novel.

rombo *sm* (*rumore*) roar; (*pesce*) turbot; **a rombi** (*disegno*) diamond-patterned.

rompere ◆ *vt* to break; (*fidanzamento*) to break off; (*strappare*) to tear ◆ *vi* (*coppia*) to break up; **rompersi una gamba** to break one's leg; **smetti di ~!** (*fam*) lay off!

▶ **rompersi** *vr* to break.

rompicapo *sm* puzzle.

rompiscatole *smf inv* (*fam*) pest, pain in the neck.

rondine *sf* swallow.

ronzare *vi* to buzz.

ronzio *sm* (*di insetti*) buzzing; (*rumore*) drone.

rosa ◆ *agg inv* (*di colore*) pink; (*sentimentale*) sentimental ◆ *sf* rose ◆ *sm* (*colore*) pink.

rosé *sm inv* rosé.

rosicchiare *vt* to gnaw, to nibble.

rosmarino *sm* rosemary.

roso, -a *pp* → **rodere**.

rosolare *vt* to brown.

rosolia *sf* German measles (*sg*).

rosone *sm* (*di soffitti*) ceiling rose; (*vetrata*) rose window.

rospo *sm* toad.

rossetto *sm* lipstick.

rosso, -a *agg & sm* red; ~ **d'uovo** egg yolk.

rosticceria *sf shop selling cooked food such as roast chicken, lasagna etc.*

rosticciana *sf* grilled or fried pork.

rotaie *sfpl* rails.

rotazione *sf* rotation.

rotella *sf* cog.

rotolare *vi* (*palla, valanga*) to roll.

▶ **rotolarsi** *vr* to roll.

rotolo *sm* roll; **andare a rotoli** to go to rack and ruin.

rotonda *sf* circular terrace.

rotondo, -a *agg* round.

rotta *sf* route.

rottame *sm* scrap.

rotto, -a ◆ *pp* → **rompere** ◆ *agg* (*spezzato, guasto*) broken; (*strappato*) torn.

rottura *sf* (*azione*) breaking; (*interruzione*) breaking-off; (*fam: seccatura*) nuisance.

roulette [ru'lɛt] *sf* roulette.

roulotte [ru'lɔt] *sf inv* caravan.

routine [ru'tin] *sf inv* routine.

rovente *agg* red-hot.

rovescia *sf*: **alla** ~ upside down; (*sottosopra*) inside out.

rovesciare vt (*liquido*) to spill; (*tavolo, sedia*) to overturn; (*situazione*) to turn upside down.

▶ **rovesciarsi** vr (*versarsi*) to spill; (*capovolgersi*) to overturn; (*barca*) to capsize.

rovescio sm (*di vestito, stoffa*) wrong side; (*pioggia*) downpour; (*nel tennis*) backhand; **al ~** (*con l'interno all'esterno*) inside out; (*con il davanti didietro*) back to front.

rovina sf ruin; **andare in ~** to collapse.

▶ **rovine** sfpl ruins.

rovinare vt to ruin.

▶ **rovinarsi** vr (*cosa*) to be ruined; (*persona*) to be ruined.

rovo sm bramble bush.

rozzo, -a agg rough.

ruba sf: **andare a ~** to sell like hot cakes.

rubare ♦ vt to steal ♦ vi: **hanno rubato in casa mia** my house has been burgled; **~ qc a qn** to steal sthg from sb.

rubinetto sm tap.

rubino sm ruby.

rubrica, -che sf (*di indirizzi*) address book; (*di giornale*) column.

ruderi smpl ruins.

rudimentale agg rudimentary, basic.

ruffiano, -a sm, f creep.

ruga, -ghe sf wrinkle.

rugby ['rεgbi] sm rugby.

ruggine sf rust.

ruggire vi to roar.

rugiada sf dew.

rullino sm roll of film; **un ~ da 24** a 24-exposure film.

rullo sm (*rotolo, arnese*) roller; (*di tamburo*) roll.

rum sm inv rum.

rumore sm noise.

rumoroso, -a agg noisy.

ruolo sm role.

ruota sf wheel; **~ di scorta** spare wheel.

ruotare vi & vt to rotate.

rupe sf cliff.

ruscello sm stream.

ruspa sf excavator.

Russia sf: **la ~** Russia.

russo, -a agg, sm & sf Russian.

rustico, -a, -ci, -che agg rustic.

ruttare vi to belch.

ruvido, -a agg rough.

ruzzolare vi to tumble down.

ruzzolone sm tumble.

S

sabato sm Saturday; **torniamo ~** we'll be back on Saturday; **oggi è ~** it's Saturday today; **~ 6 maggio** Saturday 6 May; **~ pomeriggio** Saturday afternoon; **~ prossimo** next Saturday; **~ scorso** last Saturday; **di ~** on Saturdays; **a ~!** see you Saturday!

sabbia sf sand.

sabotare vt to sabotage.

sacca, -che sf (*borsa*) bag.

saccarina sf saccharin.

saccente agg conceited.

saccheggiare vt (*case, villaggi*) to loot; (*fig: con acquisti*) to buy up.

sacchetto sm bag.

sacco, -chi sm (*di carta, nylon®*) bag; (*di iuta*) sack; **un ~ di** a lot of; **~ a pelo** sleeping bag.

sacerdote sm priest.

sacrificare vt to sacrifice.

▶ **sacrificarsi** vr to make sacrifices.

sacrificio sm sacrifice.

sacro, -a agg sacred.

sadico, -a, -ci, -che ♦ agg sadistic ♦ sm, f sadist.

safari sm inv safari.

saggezza sf wisdom.

saggio, -a, -gi, -ge ♦ agg wise

♦ *sm* (*persona*) wise man, sage; (*campione*) sample; (*libro, ricerca*) essay.

Sagittario *sm* Sagittarius.

sagoma *sf* (*profilo, forma*) outline; (*fam: persona*) character.

sagra *sf* festival, feast.

SAGRA

A 'sagra' is a local festival held in celebration of the agricultural produce typical of a particular town or village (wine, truffles, cherries and so on). As well as sampling and buying the local produce, you can eat and drink in the open air and sometimes dance to the music of the local brass band.

sai → **sapere**.

saint-honoré [sɛ̃tɔnɔ're] *sm inv* *dessert consisting of a puff pastry base topped with cream and surrounded by choux buns.*

sala *sf* (*salotto*) living room; (*di palazzo*) hall; ~ **d'aspetto** o **d'attesa** waiting room; ~ **da gioco** gaming room; ~ **operatoria** operating theatre; ~ **da pranzo** dining room.

salame *sm* salami.

salare *vt* to salt.

salario *sm* wage.

salatini *smpl* salted crackers.

salato, -a *agg* (*con sale*) salted; (*con troppo sale*) salty; (*fam: caro*) expensive.

saldare *vt* (*metalli*) to weld; (*debito, conto*) to settle.

saldo, -a ♦ *agg* (*resistente, stabile*) firm ♦ *sm* balance.

▶ **saldi** *mpl* sales.

sale *sm* salt; ~ **grosso** cooking salt.

salice *sm* willow; ~ **piangente** weeping willow.

saliente *agg* salient.

saliera *sf* saltcellar (Br), salt shaker (Am).

salire ♦ *vt* (*scale*) to go up ♦ *vi* to go up; (*aereo*) to climb; ~ **in** o **su** (*treno, moto*) to get onto; (*auto*) to

get into; ~ **su** (*tetto, podio*) to climb onto; ~ **a bordo** to board.

salita *sf* climb; **in** ~ uphill.

saliva *sf* saliva.

salmì *sm* → **lepre**.

salmone *sm* salmon.

salone *sm* (*sala*) sitting room; (*mostra*) show.

salotto *sm* lounge.

salpare ♦ *vi* (*partire*) to set sail ♦ *vt*: ~ **l'ancora** to weigh anchor.

salsa *sf* sauce; ~ **di pomodoro** tomato sauce.

salsiccia, -ce *sf* sausage.

saltare ♦ *vt* (*scavalcare*) to jump (over); (*omettere*) to skip ♦ *vi* to jump; **fare** ~ **qc** to blow sth up; ~ **fuori (da qc)** to jump out (from sth); ~ **giù da qc** to jump down from sth; ~ **su (qc)** to jump on (sth).

saltimbocca *sm inv* *thin slices of veal rolled up with ham and sage.*

salto *sm* (*balzo*) jump; (*visita*): **fare un** ~ **in città** to pop into town; ~ **in alto/lungo** high/long jump; ~ **con l'asta** pole vault.

salumeria *sf* delicatessen.

salumi *smpl* cold meats and salami.

salutare *vt* (*incontrandosi*) to greet, to say hello to; (*andando via*) to say goodbye to.

▶ **salutarsi** *vr* (*incontrandosi*) to say hello; (*andando via*) to say goodbye; **salutamelo!** say hello to him from me!

salute *sf* health; ~! (*cin cin*) cheers!; (*per starnuto*) bless you!; **bere alla** ~ **di qn** to drink to sb's health.

saluto *sm* (*incontrandosi*) greeting; (*andando via*) goodbye; (*col capo*) nod; (*con la mano*) wave.

salvadanaio *sm* moneybox.

salvagente *sm* (*giubbotto*) life jacket; (*ciambella*) life buoy; (*spartitraffico*) traffic island.

salvaguardare *vt* to safeguard.

salvare *vt* (*vita, persona*) to sur-

vive; (*onore*) to protect.
▶ **salvarsi** *vr* to save o.s.
salvataggio *sm* rescue.
salvavita® *sm inv* fuse box.
salve *esclam* (*fam*) hello!
salvezza *sf* safety.
salvia *sf* sage.
salvietta *sf* wet wipe.
salvo, -a ♦ *agg* safe ♦ *prep* except
for; **essere in ~** to be safe; **~ imprevisti** barring accidents.
san → **santo**.
sandali *smpl* sandals.
sangue *sm* blood; **a ~ freddo** in
cold blood.
sanguinaccio, -ci *sm* black
pudding (Br).
sanguinare *vi* to bleed.
sanità *sf* health service.
sanitario, -a *agg* (*sistema, servizio*)
health (*dav s*); (*condizioni*) sanitary.
▶ **sanitari** *smpl* bathroom fittings.
San Marino *sf* San Marino.

SAN MARINO

In central northern Italy, not far
from the Adriatic coast, sits San
Marino, one of the world's smallest
countries. Although it is only 60
kilometres square, it is a fully independent sovereign state, and has
its own currency and stamps.

sano, -a *agg* healthy; **~ e salvo**
safe and sound; **~ come un pesce** as
fit as a fiddle.
San Silvestro *sf*: **la notte di ~** New
Year's Eve.

SAN SILVESTRO

New Year's Eve is known as 'San
Silvestro' in Italy. People either
spend the evening at home, with
family and friends, or go out to a
'veglione' (dance) which lasts until
the small hours of New Year's Day.
A 'cenone' (big dinner) is eaten,
and on the stroke of midnight bottles of 'spumante' (sparkling wine)
are uncorked and everyone wishes
each other 'buon anno' (Happy

New Year). Firecrackers are let off
and in some areas the tradition of
throwing old objects out of the
window still survives.

santo, -a ♦ *agg* holy ♦ *sm, f* saint;
Santo Stefano ≃ Boxing Day; **tutto il
~ giorno** all day long.

SANTO

Every village, town and city in Italy
has its own patron saint, honoured
once a year with a festival combin-
ing religious processions and cer-
emonies with other more secular
events. The streets are decorated
with illuminations and there is
often a funfair and sweet stalls.
Schools and businesses are closed
for the day.

santuario *sm* sanctuary.
sanzione *sf* sanction.
sapere *vt* to know; **mi sa che non
viene** I don't think he's coming; **~
fare qc** to know how to do sthg; **sai
sciare?** can you ski?; **far ~ qc a qn** to
let sb know sthg.
▶ **sapere di** *v + prep* to taste of.
sapiente *agg* (*colto*) learned; (*abile*)
masterly.
sapienza *sf* wisdom.
sapone *sm* soap; **~ da bucato** ≃
household soap.
saponetta *sf* bar of soap.
sapore *sm* taste, flavour.
saporito, -a *agg* tasty.
saracinesca, -sche *sf* shutter.
sarcastico, -a, -ci, -che *agg* sarcastic.
sarde *sfpl*: **~ e beccaficu** *fried sar-
dines stuffed with breadcrumbs, pecorino
cheese and tomatoes*.
Sardegna *sf*: **la ~** Sardinia.
sardina *sf* sardine.
sardo, -a *agg & sm, f* Sardinian.
sarto, -a *sm, f* dressmaker; (*per
azienda*) tailor.
sartoria *sf* dressmaker's shop;
tailor's shop.

sartù *sm inv*: ~ **di riso** rice mould filled with liver, mushrooms, peas, meatballs, mozzarella cheese and boiled eggs (*a speciality of Naples*).

sasso *sm* stone; (*roccia*) rock.

sassofono *sm* saxophone.

satellite *sm* (*naturale, artificiale*) satellite; (TV) satellite TV.

satira *sf* satire.

sauna *sf* sauna.

savoiardi *smpl* sponge fingers.

saziare *vt* to satisfy.

sazietà *sf*: **mangiare a ~** to eat one's fill.

sazio, -a *agg* full.

sbadato, -a *agg* careless.

sbadigliare *vi* to yawn.

sbadiglio *sm* yawn.

sbafo *sm*: **a ~** at somebody else's expense.

sbagliare ♦ *vt* to get wrong ♦ *vi* (*fare un errore*) to make a mistake; (*avere torto*) to be wrong; ~ **mira** to miss one's aim; ~ **numero** to dial the wrong number; ~ **strada** to take the wrong road; **ho sbagliato a contare** I counted wrong.

▶ **sbagliarsi** *vr* (*fare un errore*) to make a mistake; (*avere torto*) to be wrong; **sbagliarsi di grosso** to be completely wrong.

sbagliato, -a *agg* wrong.

sbaglio *sm* mistake; **fare uno ~** to make a mistake; **fare qc per ~** to do sthg by mistake.

sballottare *vt* to toss about.

sbalzare *vt* to throw.

sbalzo *sm* (*di temperatura*) sudden change.

sbandare *vi* to skid.

sbandata *sf* skid; **prendersi una ~ per qn** to fall for sb.

sbandierare *vt* (*sventolare*) to wave; (*ostentare*) to show off.

sbando *sm*: **allo ~** adrift.

sbaraglio *sm*: **andare allo ~** to risk everything.

sbarazzare *vt* to clear up.

▶ **sbarazzarsi di** *vr + prep* to get rid of.

sbarazzino, -a *agg* cheeky.

sbarcare ♦ *vt* (*merce*) to unload; (*passeggeri*) to disembark ♦ *vi* (*da nave*) to disembark.

sbarco *sm* (*di merci*) unloading; (*di passeggeri*) disembarkation.

sbarra *sf* (*spranga*) bar; (*segno grafico*) stroke; (*di passaggio a livello*) barrier.

sbarrare *vt* (*porta, finestra*) to bar; (*passaggio*) to block; ~ **gli occhi** to open one's eyes wide.

sbarrato, -a *agg* (*strada*) blocked; (*porta*) barred; (*casella*) crossed; (*parola*) crossed out; (*occhi*) wide open.

sbatacchiare *vt* to bang, to slam.

sbattere ♦ *vt* to beat; (*porta*) to bang, to slam ♦ *vi* to bang; ~ **contro** (*muro*) to bang against, to knock against; ~ **fuori qn** to throw sb out.

▶ **sbattersene** *vr* (*fam*) not to give a damn.

sbattuto, -a *agg* downcast.

sbavare *vi* to dribble.

sbellicarsi *vr*: ~ **dal ridere** to split one's sides laughing.

sbiadire *vt* to fade.

▶ **sbiadirsi** *vr* to fade.

sbiadito, -a *agg* faded.

sbiancare ♦ *vi* to grow pale ♦ *vt* to bleach.

sbieco, -a, -chi, -che *agg*: **di ~** (*obliquamente*) at an angle.

sbigottire *vt* to dismay.

▶ **sbigottirsi** *vr* to be dismayed.

sbigottito, -a *agg* dismayed, aghast.

sbilanciare *vt* to unbalance.

▶ **sbilanciarsi** *vr* (*perdere l'equilibrio*) to lose one's balance; (*fig: compromettersi*) to compromise o.s.

sbirciare *vt* (*con curiosità*) to eye; (*di sfuggita*) to peep at.

sbizzarrirsi *vr* to satisfy one's whims.

sbloccare *vt* to unblock; ~ **la situazione** to get things moving.

▶ **sbloccarsi** *vr* (*meccanismo*) to

become unblocked; (*situazione*) to return to normal.

sboccare : sboccare in *v + prep* (*fiume*) to flow into; (*strada*) to lead into; (*concludersi con*) to end in.

sboccato, -a *agg* foul-mouthed.

sbocciare *vi* to bloom.

sbocco, -chi *sm* (*di strada*) end; (*di fiume*) mouth; (*fig: esito*) way out.

sbornia *sf* (*fam*): **prendersi una ~** to get plastered.

sborsare *vt* (*pagare*) to pay out.

sbottare *vi* (*in risata*) to burst out; (*di rabbia*) to explode.

sbottonare *vt* to unbutton; **sbottonarsi la giacca** to undo one's jacket.

▶ **sbottonarsi** *vr* (*fam: confidarsi*) to open up.

sbracciarsi *vr* to wave one's arms about.

sbracciato, -a *agg* (*vestito*) sleeveless; (*persona*) with bare arms.

sbraitare *vi* to shout.

sbranare *vt* to tear to pieces.

sbriciolare *vt* to crumble.

▶ **sbriciolarsi** *vr* (*pane, muro*) to crumble.

sbrigare *vt* (*faccenda*) to deal with.

▶ **sbrigarsi** *vr* to hurry; **sbrigarsi a fare qc** to hurry up and do sthg.

sbrodolare *vt* to stain.

sbronza *sf* (*fam*): **prendersi una ~** to get plastered.

sbronzo, -a *agg* (*fam*) plastered.

sbucare *vi* (*uscire*) to come out; (*saltar fuori*) to spring out.

sbucciare *vt* to peel; **sbucciarsi un ginocchio** to graze one's knee.

sbuffare *vi* (*per fastidio, noia*) to snort; (*per caldo*) to pant.

scabroso, -a *agg* indecent.

scacchi *smpl* chess (*sg*); **a ~** (*tessuto*) checked.

scacciare *vt* (*persona, animale*) to drive away; (*preoccupazioni*) to dispel.

scadente *agg* (*prodotto*) poor-

quality; (*qualità*) poor.

scadenza *sf* (*di cibo*) sell-by date; (*di documento, contratto*) expiry date; (*di medicinali*) 'use-by' date; (*per iscrizione, consegna*) deadline.

scadere *vi* to expire; (*cibo*) to pass its sell-by date.

scaffale *sm* shelf.

scafo *sm* hull.

scaglia *sf* (*frammento*) flake, chip; (*di pesce*) scale.

scagliare *vt* to throw.

▶ **scagliarsi contro** *vr + prep* (*assalire*) to hurl o.s. against; (*fig: insultare*) to hurl abuse at.

scaglione *sm* echelon; **a scaglioni** in groups.

scala *sf* (*gradini*) stairs (*pl*), staircase; (*a pioli*) ladder; (*di valori*) scale; **su larga ~** on a large scale; **~ mobile** escalator; **le scale** the stairs.

scalare *vt* (*mura, montagna*) to climb; (*somma*) to knock off; (*capelli*) to layer.

scalata *sf* climb.

scalatore, -trice *sm, f* climber.

scalcinato, -a *agg* (*fig: casa*) shabby.

scaldabagno *sm* water heater.

scaldare *vt* to heat.

▶ **scaldarsi** *vr* (*al fuoco, al sole*) to warm o.s.; (*fig: accalorarsi*) to get excited.

scaleo *sm* stepladder.

scalfire *vt* to scratch.

scalinata *sf* flight of steps.

scalino *sm* step.

scalmanarsi *vr* to get worked up.

scalo *sm* call; **fare ~ a** (*in aereo*) to make a stopover at; (*in nave*) to call at; **~ merci** goods yard (Br), freight yard (Am).

scaloppina *sf* escalope.

scalpore *sm* (*risonanza*) stir; **fare o destare ~** to cause a stir.

scaltro, -a *agg* shrewd.

scalzo, -a *agg* barefooted.

scambiare *vt* to exchange, to

swap; **~ qn/qc per** (confondere) to mistake sb/sthg for; **scambiarsi qc** to exchange sthg.

scambio sm (di regali, opinioni) exchange; (confusione) mistake; (COMM) trade; **fare a ~ con qn** to swap with sb.

scampagnata sf trip to the country.

scampare vt to escape; **scamparla (bella)** to have a narrow escape.

▶ **scampare a** v + prep to escape.

scampo sm: **non c'è (via di) ~** there is no way out; **trovare ~ in qc** to find safety in sthg.

▶ **scampi** smpl scampi (sg).

scampolo sm remnant.

scandalizzare vt to make a spectacle of o.s.

▶ **scandalizzarsi** vr to be scandalized.

scandalo sm scandal; **dare ~ to** make a spectacle of o.s.; **fare ~ to** cause a scandal.

scandaloso, -a agg scandalous.

Scandinavia sf: **la ~** Scandinavia.

scandire vt to articulate.

scannare vt (animale) to butcher; (persona) to cut the throat of.

scansafatiche smf inv idler, waster.

scansare vt (spostare) to shift; (colpo) to ward off; (difficoltà, fatica) to avoid; (persona) to shun.

▶ **scansarsi** vr to step aside.

scanso sm: **a ~ di equivoci** (in order) to avoid any misunderstandings.

scantinato sm basement.

scanzonato, -a agg easygoing.

scapaccione sm slap.

scapestrato, -a agg dissolute.

scapito sm: **a ~ di** to the detriment of.

scapolo sm bachelor.

scappamento sm → **tubo.**

scappare vi (fuggire) to escape; (da casa) to run away; (andare) to rush; **mi è scappato detto** I let it slip; **mi è scappato di mano** it slipped

out of my hands; **mi è scappato di mente** it slipped my mind; **mi è scappato da ridere** I couldn't help laughing; **lasciarsi ~ l'occasione** to miss an opportunity.

scappatella sf casual affair.

scappatoia sf way out.

scarabocchiare ◆ vt to scrawl ◆ vi to scribble.

scarafaggio sm cockroach.

scaramanzia sf: **per ~** for luck.

scaraventare vt to hurl.

▶ **scaraventarsi** vr to fling o.s.

scarcerare vt to release.

scarica, -che sf (di pugni) hail; (di pistola) volley; **~ elettrica** electrical discharge.

scaricare vt (merci, camion, arma) to unload; (passeggeri) to let off; (batteria) to run down; (fig: colpa) to shift.

▶ **scaricarsi** vr (batteria) to go flat; (fig: rilassarsi) to unwind.

scarico, -a, -chi, -che ◆ agg (camion, arma) unloaded; (batteria) flat ◆ sm (di merci) unloading; (discarica) dump; **'divieto di ~'** 'no dumping'.

scarlatto, -a agg scarlet.

scarpa sf shoe; **che numero di scarpe porta?** what size shoe do you take?; **scarpe da ginnastica** plimsolls (Br), sneakers (Am).

scarpata sf slope.

scarponi smpl boots; **~ da sci** ski boots.

scarseggiare vi to be scarce.

▶ **scarseggiare di** v + prep to be short of.

scarsità sf inv scarcity, shortage.

scarso, -a agg scarce; **un chilo ~** just under a kilo.

scartare vt (regalo) to unwrap; (eliminare) to reject; (nelle carte) to discard.

scarto sm (scelta) discarding; (cosa scartata) reject; (differenza) gap, difference.

scassinare vt to break open.

scasso sm → **furto.**

scatenare vt to provoke, to stir up.

▶ **scatenarsi** vr (temporale) to break; (persona) to go wild.

scatenato, -a agg (persona, ballo) wild.

scatola sf box; (di latta) tin, can; **in ~** (cibo) tinned, canned; **rompere le scatole a qn** (fam) to get up sb's nose.

scattante agg agile.

scattare ♦ vt (foto) to take ♦ vi (balzare) to jump; (molla, congegno) to be released; (allarme) to go off; (manifestare ira) to fly into a rage; **far ~** (molla, congegno) to release; (allarme) to set off.

scatto sm (di congegno) release; (rumore) click; (di foto) shot; (di telefono) unit; (balzo) fit; **di ~** suddenly.

scaturire : scaturire da v + prep (sgorgare) to gush from; (fig: derivare) to come from.

scavalcare vt (muro, ostacolo) to climb over; (fig: concorrenti) to overtake.

scavare vt (fossa, terreno) to dig; (render cavo) to hollow out.

scavo sm excavation.

scegliere vt to choose.

scelta sf choice; (raccolta) selection; **non avere ~** to have no choice; **'frutta o formaggio a ~'** 'choice of fruit or cheese'.

scelto, -a ♦ pp → **scegliere** ♦ agg (gruppo) select; (frutta) choice.

scemo, -a agg (fam) stupid, silly.

scena sf scene.

scenata sf row, scene.

scendere ♦ vi (venir giù) to go/come down; (da treno) to get off; (diminuire) to go down ♦ vt to go/come down; **~ dal treno** to get off the train; **~ dalla macchina** to get out of the car.

sceneggiato sm serial.

sceneggiatura sf screenplay.

scervellarsi vr to rack one's brains.

sceso, -a pp → **scendere**.

scettico, -a, -ci, -che agg sceptical.

scheda sf (cartoncino) card; (modulo) form; **~ magnetica** magnetic card; **~ telefonica** phonecard.

schedare vt (libro) to catalogue; **è stato schedato dalla polizia** he has a police record.

schedario sm (raccolta) file; (mobile) filing cabinet.

schedina sf ≈ pools coupon.

SCHEDINA

The coupon you fill in to play 'toto-calcio' (the football pools) is called a 'schedina'; it can be bought at tobacconists and bars. Players must predict the results of 13 games, marking the coupon with 1 for a home win, 2 for an away win, and X for a draw. Winners receive prizes ranging from a few thousand to several billion lire.

scheggia, -ge sf splinter.

scheletro sm skeleton.

schema, -i sm plan.

scherma sf fencing.

schermo sm screen.

scherno sm derision.

scherzare vi to joke.

scherzo sm (battuta, gesto) joke; (brutto tiro) trick; **è uno ~** (cosa facile) it's child's play; **fare qc per ~** to do sthg for a laugh.

scherzoso, -a agg playful.

schiaccianoci sm inv nutcrackers (pl).

schiacciare vt (comprimere) to crush; (noce) to crack; (pulsante) to press; (fig: avversario) to overwhelm; (SPORT) to smash.

▶ **schiacciarsi** vr to get squashed.

schiacciata sf (focaccia) type of flat salted bread made with olive oil; (SPORT) smash.

schiacciato, -a agg (appiattito) flat; (deformato) squashed.

schiaffo sm slap.

schiamazzi smpl screams.

schiantare vt to break.
▶ **schiantarsi** vr to break up.
schianto sm (rumore) crash; **è uno ~!** (fam) she's/it's a knockout!
schiarire vt to lighten.
▶ **schiarirsi** vr (cielo) to clear up; (colore) to become lighter; **schiarirsi la voce** to clear one's throat.
schiavitù sf slavery.
schiavo, -a ♦ sm, f slave ♦ agg: **~ di** a slave to.
schiena sf back.
schienale sm back.
schiera sf group; **a ~** (casa) terraced.
schierare vt (esercito, squadra) to draw up; (libri, oggetti) to line up.
▶ **schierarsi** vr (mettersi in fila) to line up; **schierarsi con/contro qn** to side with/oppose sb.
schietto, -a agg (persona) frank; (vino) not watered-down.
schifezza sf: **essere una ~** (cibo) to be disgusting; (film) to be awful.
schifo sm disgust; **mi fa ~** it makes me sick; **fare ~** (cibo, insetto) to be disgusting; (film) to be awful.
schifoso, -a agg (disgustoso) disgusting; (pessimo, brutto) awful.
schioccare vt (dita) to snap; (lingua) to click.
schiuma sf (marina) foam; (di sapone) lather; **~ da barba** shaving foam.
schivare vt to dodge, to avoid.
schivo, -a agg reserved, shy.
schizzare ♦ vt to splash ♦ vi (acqua, getto) to spurt; (fig: saltar via) to dart away.
schizzo sm (spruzzo) stain, splash; (disegno) sketch.
sci sm inv (attrezzo) ski; (attività) skiing; **~ d'acqua** water skiing; **~ da fondo** cross-country skiing.
scia sf (di nave) wake; (di profumo, fumo) trail.
sciacquare vt to rinse; **sciacquarsi la bocca** to rinse out one's mouth.
sciacquone sm flush; **tirare lo ~** to flush the toilet.

sciagura sf disaster.
sciagurato, -a agg (sfortunato) unlucky; (cattivo) wicked.
scialacquare vt to squander.
scialbo, -a agg (colore) pale; (sapore) bland; (persona) dull.
scialle sm shawl.
scialuppa sf sloop; **~ di salvataggio** lifeboat.
sciame sm swarm.
sciangai sm (gioco) pick-up-sticks.
sciare vi to ski.
sciarpa sf scarf.
sciatore, -trice sm, f skier.
sciatto, -a agg untidy.
scientifico, -a, -ci, -che agg scientific.
scienza sf (studio della realtà) science; (sapere) knowledge.
▶ **scienze** sfpl science (sg).
scienziato, -a sm, f scientist.
scimmia sf monkey.
scimmiottare vt to ape.
scindere vt (dividere) to divide.
scintilla sf spark.
scintillare vi to sparkle.
scioccare vt to shock.
sciocchezza sf (cosa stupida) silly thing; (cosa poco importante) trifle.
sciocco, -a, -chi, -che agg silly.
sciogliere vt (nodo) to untie; (capelli) to loosen; (animale) to let loose; (ghiaccio, burro) to melt; (pastiglia, società) to dissolve; (mistero) to solve; (assemblea) to close.
▶ **sciogliersi** vr (nodo) to come untied; (neve, burro) to melt.
scioglilingua sm inv tongue twister.
sciolto, -a ♦ pp → **sciogliere** ♦ agg (disinvolto) easy; (agile) agile.
sciopero sm strike; **essere in ~, fare ~** to be on strike.
sciovia sf ski lift.
scippare vt: **~ qn** to snatch sb's bag.
scippo sm bagsnatching.
sciroppo sm (medicina) cough mixture; (di frutta) syrup.

scissione sf (separazione) split.

scisso, -a pp → **scindere**.

sciupare vt (vestito, libro) to spoil, to ruin.

▶ **sciuparsi** vr (rovinarsi) to get spoiled; (deperire) to become run down.

scivolare vi (scorrere) to glide; (perdere l'equilibrio) to slip, to slide.

scivolo sm (gioco) slide.

scivoloso, -a agg slippery.

scoccare ◆ vt (freccia) to shoot ◆ vi (ore) to strike.

scocciare vt (fam) to annoy.

▶ **scocciarsi** vr (fam) to be annoyed.

scodella sf bowl.

scodinzolare vi to wag its tail.

scogliera sf rocks (pl).

scoglio sm (roccia) rock; (fig) stumbling block.

scoiattolo sm squirrel.

scolapasta sm inv colander.

scolapiatti sm inv draining rack.

scolare vt to drain.

scolaro, -a sm, f schoolboy (f schoolgirl).

scolastico, -a, -ci, -che agg school (dav s).

scollare vt (staccare) to unstick.

▶ **scollarsi** vr to come unstuck.

scollato, -a agg (abito) low-cut.

scollatura sf neckline.

scolorire vt to fade.

▶ **scolorirsi** vr to fade.

scolpire vt to sculpt; (legno) to carve; (iscrizione) to engrave.

scombussolare vt to upset.

scommessa sf bet.

scommesso, -a pp → **scommettere**.

scommettere vt to bet.

scomodare vt to bother.

▶ **scomodarsi** vr to put o.s. out; scomodarsi a fare qc to go to the bother of doing sthg.

scomodo, -a agg (poltrona) uncomfortable; (orario) inconvenient.

scompagnato, -a agg (calzini) odd.

scomparire vi (sparire) to disappear.

scomparso, -a pp → **scomparire**.

scompartimento sm (di treno) compartment.

scomparto sm compartment.

scompigliare vt (capelli) to ruffle, to mess up.

scompiglio sm confusion.

scomporre vt (mobile, armadio) to take to pieces.

▶ **scomporsi** vr (perdere il controllo) to lose one's composure.

scomposto, -a pp → **scomporre**.

sconcertare vt to disconcert.

sconcio, -a, -ci, -ce agg (osceno) obscene.

sconfiggere vt to defeat.

sconfinare vi (uscire dai confini) to cross the border; (fig): ~ **da** to stray from.

sconfinato, -a agg boundless.

sconfitta sf defeat.

sconfitto, -a pp → **sconfiggere**.

sconforto sm dejection.

scongelare vt to defrost.

scongiurare vt (supplicare) to implore; (pericolo, minaccia) to ward off.

sconnesso, -a agg (ragionamento) incoherent.

sconosciuto, -a ◆ agg unknown ◆ sm, f stranger.

sconsiderato, -a agg thoughtless.

sconsigliare vt to advise against; ~ **qc a qn** to advise sb against sthg; ~ **a qn di fare qc** to advise sb against doing sthg.

scontare vt (detrarre) to deduct; (pena) to serve; (colpa, errore) to pay for.

scontato, -a agg (prezzo) discounted; (previsto) taken for granted; **dare qc per ~** to take sthg for granted.

scontento, -a *agg*: ~ **(di)** dissatisfied (with).

sconto *sm* discount; **fare uno** ~ to give a discount.

scontrarsi *vr* (*urtarsi*) to collide; (*combattere, discordare*) to clash.

scontrino *sm* (*di cassa*) receipt; (*biglietto*) ticket; **'munirsi dello scontrino alla cassa'** 'pay at the till and obtain a receipt' (*before being served at the counter*).

scontro *sm* (*urto*) collision; (*combattimento, fig*) clash.

scontroso, -a *agg* surly.

sconveniente *agg* (*indecente*) improper.

sconvolgente *agg* disturbing.

sconvolgere *vt* (*persona*) to disturb, to shake; (*ordine, piani*) to upset.

sconvolto, -a *pp* → **sconvolgere**.

scopa *sf* (*arnese*) broom.

scoperta *sf* discovery.

scoperto, -a ♦ *pp* → **scoprire** ♦ *agg* uncovered; (*capo, braccia*) bare.

scopo *sm* purpose, aim; **allo** ~ **di fare qc** in order to do sthg; **a che** ~? for what purpose?

scoppiare *vi* (*spaccarsi*) to burst; (*esplodere*) to explode; ~ **dal caldo** (*fam*) to be boiling (hot); ~ **a piangere** to burst into tears; ~ **a ridere** to burst out laughing.

scoppio *sm* (*rumore, di pneumatico*) bang; (*esplosione*) explosion; (*di risa*) burst; (*di guerra*) outbreak; **a** ~ **ritardato** delayed-action.

scoprire *vt* to discover; (*liberare da copertura*) to uncover.

▶ **scoprirsi** *vr* (*svestirsi*) to dress less warmly; (*rivelarsi*) to give o.s. away.

scoraggiare *vt* to discourage.

▶ **scoraggiarsi** *vr* to become discouraged.

scorbutico, -a, -ci, -che *agg* (*scontroso*) cantankerous.

scorciatoia *sf* short cut; **prendere una** ~ to take a short cut.

scordare *vt* to forget.

▶ **scordarsi di** *vr + prep* to forget; **scordarsi di fare qc** to forget to do sthg.

scorgere *vt* to see, to make out.

scorpacciata *sf*: **fare una** ~ **(di qc)** to stuff o.s. (with sthg).

scorpione *sm* scorpion.

▶ **Scorpione** *sm* Scorpio.

scorrazzare *vi* to run around.

scorrere ♦ *vi* (*liquido, fiume, traffico*) to flow; (*fune*) to run; (*tempo*) to pass ♦ *vt* (*giornale, libro*) to glance through.

scorretto, -a *agg* (*errato*) incorrect; (*sleale*) unfair.

scorrevole *agg* (*porta*) sliding; (*traffico, stile*) flowing.

scorrimento *sm* (*di traffico*) flow.

scorsa *sf*: **dare una** ~ **a qc** to glance through sthg.

scorso, -a ♦ *pp* → **scorrere** ♦ *agg* last.

scorta *sf*: **fare** ~ **di qc** to stock up with sthg; **di** ~ spare.

scortare *vt* to escort.

scortese *agg* impolite.

scorticare *vt* (*pelle*) to graze; (*animale*) to skin.

scorto, -a *pp* → **scorgere**.

scorza *sf* (*di albero*) bark; (*di frutto*) peel.

scorzanera *sf* type of bitter-tasting root vegetable.

scosceso, -a *agg* steep.

scossa *sf* (*movimento*) jolt; (*elettrica*) shock.

scosso, -a ♦ *pp* → **scuotere** ♦ *agg* shaken.

scossone *sm* jolt.

scostare *vt* to move aside.

▶ **scostarsi** *vr* to move aside.

scotch®¹ [skɔtʃ] *sm inv* (*nastro adesivo*) = Sellotape® (Br), Scotch® tape (Am).

scotch² [skɔtʃ] *sm inv* (*whisky*) Scotch.

scottadito : **a scottadito** *avv* piping hot.

scottare ♦ vt (ustionare) to burn; (cuocere) to scald ♦ vi (bevanda, pietanza) to be too hot.

▶ **scottarsi** vr to burn o.s.

scottatura sf burn.

scotto, -a agg overcooked.

scout ['skaut] smf inv scout.

scovare vt (negozio, ristorante) to discover.

Scozia sf: la ~ Scotland.

scozzese ♦ agg Scottish; (tessuto) tartan ♦ smf Scotsman (f Scotswoman); **gli scozzesi** the Scots.

screditare vt to discredit.

screpolare vt to crack.

▶ **screpolarsi** vr to crack.

screziato, -a agg streaked.

screzio sm disagreement.

scricchiolare vi to creak.

scricchiolio sm creaking.

scriminatura sf parting.

scritta sf inscription.

scritto, -a ♦ pp → **scrivere** ♦ agg written ♦ sm (opera) work, writing.

scrittore, -trice sm, f writer.

scrittura sf writing.

scrivania sf writing desk.

scrivere vt & vi to write; ~ **a qn** to write to sb; ~ **a macchina** to type.

▶ **scriversi** vr (parola): **come si scrive 'cuore'?** how do you write o spell 'cuore'?

scroccare vt (fam) to scrounge.

scrollare vt (agitare) to shake; (spalle) to shrug; **scrollarsi qc di dosso** to shake sthg off.

scrosciare vi (pioggia) to pelt down; (applausi) to thunder.

scroscio sm (d'acqua) pelting; (d'applausi) thunder.

scrostare vt (intonaco) to strip off.

▶ **scrostarsi** vr (pareti, tegame) to peel.

scrupolo sm (timore) scruple; (diligenza) conscientiousness; **senza scrupoli** unscrupulous.

scrupoloso, -a agg (persona) scrupulous; (resoconto, lavoro) meticulous.

scrutare vt to scrutinize; (orizzonte) to search.

scucire vt (cucitura) to unpick.

▶ **scucirsi** vr to come unstitched.

scuderia sf stable.

scudetto sm (SPORT) championship shield.

scudo sm shield.

sculacciare vt to spank.

scultore, -trice sm, f sculptor.

scultura sf sculpture.

scuola sf school; **andare a** ~ to go to school; ~ **elementare** = primary school (Br), grade school (Am)(for children aged from 6 to 11); ~ **guida** driving school; ~ **materna** nursery school (for children aged from 3 to 5); ~ **media** first three years of secondary school for children aged from 11 to 14; ~ **dell'obbligo** compulsory education; **scuole tecniche** schools which prepare their students for practical professions; **scuole serali** evening classes.

scuotere vt to shake; (spalle) to shrug.

▶ **scuotersi** vr to shake o.s.

scurire ♦ vt to darken ♦ vi to grow dark.

▶ **scurirsi** vr to grow dark.

scuro, -a ♦ agg dark ♦ sm (buio) darkness.

scusa sf excuse; **chiedere** ~ **(a qn)** to apologize (to sb).

scusare vt (perdonare) to forgive; (giustificare) to excuse.

▶ **scusarsi** vr to apologize; **(mi) scusi, dov'è la stazione?** excuse me, where is the station?; **scusi!** sorry!

sdebitarsi vr: ~ **con qn di qc** to repay sb for sthg.

sdentato, -a agg toothless.

sdolcinato, -a agg oversentimental.

sdraia sf deckchair.

sdraiarsi vr to lie down.

sdraio sm: (sedia a) ~ deckchair.

sdrammatizzare vt to play down.

sdrucciolare vi to slip.

se cong 1. (nel caso in cui) if; **rimani** ~

vuoi stay if you want; ~ **è possibile** if it's possible; ~ **fossi in te** if I were you; ~ **non sbaglio** ... if I'm not wrong ...

2. (*dato che*) if; ~ **lo dici, sarà vero** if you say so, it must be true.

3. (*con frasi dubitative & interrogative indirette*) whether, if; **vedi** ~ **puoi venire** see whether o if you can come; **chiedile** ~ **le piace** ask her if she likes it.

4. (*esprime un suggerimento*): **e** ~ **andassimo al cinema?** how about going to the cinema?

5. (*esprime un augurio*) if; ~ **solo potessi!** if only I could!

6. (*in espressioni*): **anche** ~ even if; ~ **mai** if; **neanche** ~ even if; ~ **non altro** if nothing else; ~ **no** otherwise.

♦ *pron* → **si**.

sé *pron* (*per cosa*) itself; (*per persona*) himself/herself/themselves; **tenere qc per** ~ to keep sthg for oneself; **pensa solo a se stesso** he only thinks of himself.

sebbene *cong* although.

sec. (*abbr di secolo*) c.

secca, -che *sf* (*di mare, fiume*) shallows (*pl*).

seccare *vt* to dry; (*prosciugare*) to dry up; (*infastidire*) to annoy.

▶ **seccarsi** *vr* to dry; (*prosciugarsi*) to dry up; (*infastidirsi*) to get annoyed.

seccato, -a *agg* (*infastidito*) annoyed.

seccatore, -trice *sm, f* nuisance.

seccatura *sf* (*fastidio*) nuisance.

secchiello *sm* (*contenitore*) bucket.

secchio *sm* bucket.

secchione, -a *sm, f* (*fam*) swot.

secco, -a, -chi, -che ♦ *agg* dry; (*funghi, prugne*) dried; (*brusco*) curt ♦ *sm*: **essere a** ~ **di qc** (*fig: non avere*) to be without sthg; **tirare in** ~ **una barca** to beach a boat; **lavare a** ~ to dry-clean.

secolare *agg* (*vecchio di secoli*) age-old.

secolo *sm* century; (*periodo lungo*):

non lo vedo da secoli I haven't seen him for ages.

seconda *sf* (*marcia*) second gear; **viaggiare in** ~ to travel second-class; **a** ~ **di** according to.

secondario, -a *agg* secondary; **scuola secondaria** secondary school.

secondo, -a ♦ *num* second ♦ *agg* (*altro*) second ♦ *sm* (*tempo*) second; (*portata*) main course ♦ *prep* according to; ~ **me** in my opinion; **di seconda mano** second-hand, → **sesto**.

sedano *sm* celery.

sedativo *sm* sedative.

sede *sf* (*di organizzazione*) headquarters (*pl*); (*di azienda*) head office.

sedentario, -a *agg* sedentary.

sedere ♦ *sm* (*parte del corpo*) bottom ♦ *vi*: **mettersi a** ~ to sit down.

▶ **sedersi** *vr* to sit down.

sedia *sf* chair.

sedicesimo, -a *num* sixteenth, → **sesto**.

sedici *num* sixteen, → **sei**.

sedile *sm* (*di veicolo*) seat.

sedotto, -a *pp* → **sedurre**.

seducente *agg* seductive.

sedurre *vt* (*uomo, donna*) to seduce; (*sog: idea, proposta*) to appeal to.

seduta *sf* session.

sega, -ghe *sf* saw.

segale *sf* rye.

segare *vt* to saw.

seggio *sm* seat; ~ **elettorale** polling station.

seggiola *sf* chair.

seggiolino *sm* (*sedia pieghevole*) folding chair.

seggiolone *sm* (*per bambini*) high chair.

seggiovia *sf* chair lift.

segnalare *vt* (*comunicare*) to point out; (*indicare*) to indicate.

segnalazione *sf* (*indicazione*) indication; (*raccomandazione*) recommendation.

segnale *sm* (*indicazione*) signal; (*stradale*) sign; ~ **acustico** sound signal; ~ **d'allarme** alarm; ~ **orario** time signal.

segnaletica *sf* (*stradale*) road signs (*pl*).

segnalibro *sm* bookmark.

segnaposto *sm* place card.

segnare *vt* (*mettere un segno*) to mark; (*indicare*) to indicate; (SPORT) to score; **segnarsi qc** to make a note of sthg.

segno *sm* sign; (*lettera, numero*) symbol; (*contrassegno, traccia*) mark; **fare ~ a qn di fare qc** to signal sb to do sthg; **fare ~ di no** to shake one's head; **fare ~ di sì** to nod one's head; **perdere il ~** to lose one's place; **cogliere o colpire nel ~** (*fig*) to hit the mark.

segretario, -a *sm, f* secretary.

segreteria *sf* (*di azienda, scuola*) secretary's office; (*di partito*) position of Secretary.

▶ **segreteria telefonica** *sf* answering machine.

segreto, -a *agg & sm* secret.

seguente *agg* following, next.

seguire ◆ *vt* to follow ◆ *vi* to follow; (*continuare*): **segue a pag. 70** continued on page 70.

seguito *sm* (*proseguimento*) continuation; (*risultato*) result; (*scorta*) retinue; (*favore*) following; **in ~ a** following; **di ~** at a stretch, on end; **in ~** subsequently.

sei[1] → **essere**.

sei[2] *agg num* six; **ha ~ anni** he/she is six (years old); **sono le ~** it's six o'clock; **il ~ gennaio** the sixth of January; **pagina ~** page six; **il ~ di picche** the six of spades; **erano in ~** there were six of them.

seicento *num* six hundred, → **sei**.

▶ **Seicento** *sm*: **il Seicento** the seventeenth century.

selciato *sm* cobbles (*pl*), cobbled surface.

selettivo, -a *agg* selective.

selezionare *vt* to select.

selezione *sf* selection.

self-service ['sɛl 'sɛrvis] *agg inv & sm inv* self-service.

sella *sf* saddle.

selvaggina *sf* game.

selvaggio, -a, -gi, -ge ◆ *agg* wild; (*tribù*) savage; (*delitto*) brutal ◆ *sm, f* savage.

selvatico, -a, -ci, -che *agg* wild.

semaforo *sm* (*apparecchio*) traffic lights (*pl*).

sembrare ◆ *vi* to seem ◆ *v impers*: **sembra che** it seems that; **mi sembra di conoscerlo** I think I know him; **sembra che stia per piovere** it looks like it's going to rain.

seme *sm* seed; (*nocciolo*) stone; (*di carte da gioco*) suit.

semestre *sm* six-month period; (SCOL) semester.

semifinale *sf* semifinal.

semifreddo *sm* dessert similar to ice cream.

seminare *vt* to sow.

seminario *sm* seminar; (RELIG) seminary.

seminterrato *sm* basement.

semmai ◆ *cong* if (ever) ◆ *avv* if anything.

semolino *sm* semolina.

semplice *agg* simple; (*corsa, filo, consonante*) single; **è una ~ proposta** it's just a suggestion.

semplicemente *avv* simply.

semplicità *sf* simplicity.

semplificare *vt* to simplify.

sempre *avv* always; (*ancora*) still; **va ~ meglio/peggio** things are getting better and better/worse and worse; **~ che ci riesca** provided he manages it; **da ~** always; **di ~** usual; **per ~** forever.

senape *sf* mustard.

senato *sm* senate.

senatore, -trice *sm, f* senator.

sennò *avv* (*altrimenti*) otherwise.

seno *sm* (*petto*) breast.

sensazionale *agg* sensational.

sensazione *sf* sensation, feeling; **fare ~** to cause a sensation.

sensibile *agg* sensitive; (*notevole*) noticeable; **~ a** (*caldo, freddo*) sensitive to; (*complimenti*) susceptible to.

sensibilità *sf* sensitivity.

senso *sm* (*facoltà, coscienza*) sense; (*sentimento, impressione*) feeling; (*significato*) meaning, sense; (*direzione*) direction; **non avere ~** to make no sense; **a ~ unico** one-way; **in ~ orario** clockwise; **perdere i sensi** to lose consciousness.

sentenza *sf* (*di processo*) sentence; (*massima*) maxim.

sentiero *sm* path.

sentimentale *agg* sentimental.

sentimento *sm* feeling.

sentire *vt* (*udire*) to hear; (*percepire, con il tatto*) to feel; (*odore*) to smell; (*sapore*) to taste; **senti!** listen!

▶ **sentirsi** *vr* (*bene, stanco, allegro*) to feel; **sentirsi di fare qc** to feel like doing sthg; **sentirsi bene/male** to feel well/ill; (*telefonarsi*): **ci sentiamo domani** speak to you tomorrow.

senza *prep & cong* without; **~ di me** without me; **senz'altro** certainly, of course; **~ dubbio** undoubtedly; **~ che tu te ne accorga** without you noticing it.

senzatetto *smf inv* homeless person.

separare *vt* to separate.

▶ **separarsi** *vr* (*coniugi*) to separate; (*gruppo*) to split up; **separarsi da** *vr + prep* (*coniuge*) to separate from.

separato, -a *agg* (*disgiunto*) separate; (*coniuge*) separated.

separazione *sf* separation.

sepolto, -a *pp* → **seppellire**.

seppellire *vt* to bury.

seppia *sf* cuttlefish.

sequenza *sf* sequence.

sequestrare *vt* (DIR) to sequestrate; (*persona*) to kidnap.

sequestro *sm* (DIR) sequestration; (*rapimento*) kidnapping.

sera *sf* evening; **di ~** in the evening.

serale *agg* evening (*dav s*).

serata *sf* evening; (*ricevimento*) party.

serbare *vt* to put aside, to keep; **~ rancore a qn** to bear sb a grudge.

serbatoio *sm* (*di veicolo*) tank.

serbo *sm*: **avere qc in ~** to have sthg in store; **tenere qc in ~** to put sthg aside.

serenata *sf* serenade.

sereno, -a ♦ *agg* (*tempo, cielo*) clear; (*persona*) calm ♦ *sm* (*bel tempo*) fine weather.

serie *sf inv* (*successione*) series (*inv*); (*insieme*) set; (SPORT) division; **produzione in ~** mass production.

serietà *sf* seriousness; (*coscienziosità*) reliability.

serio, -a ♦ *agg* serious; (*coscienzioso*) reliable ♦ *sm*: **sul ~** (*davvero*) seriously; **prendere qn/qc sul ~** to take sb/sthg seriously.

serpente *sm* snake; (*pelle*) snakeskin.

serra *sf* (*per piante*) greenhouse.

serranda *sf* rolling shutter.

serrare *vt* (*chiudere*) to close; (*stringere*) to shut tightly.

serratura *sf* lock.

servire ♦ *vt* to serve ♦ *vi* (*in tennis, pallavolo*) to serve; (*essere utile*) to be of use; **~ a fare qc** to be used for doing sthg; **~ a qn** to be of use to sb; **mi serve un martello** I need a hammer; **serve altro?** do you need anything else?; **~ da** to be used as.

▶ **servirsi** *vr* (*prendere da mangiare/bere*) to help o.s.

▶ **servirsi da** to shop at.

▶ **servirsi di** *vr + prep* (*utilizzare*) to use.

servitù *sf* (*condizione*) slavery; (*personale*) domestic staff.

servizio *sm* service; (*di piatti, bicchieri*) set; (*giornalistico*) report; **essere di ~** to be on duty; **'~ compreso'** 'service included'; **~ militare** military service.

▶ **servizi** smpl (di abitazione) kitchen and bathroom.

sessanta num sixty, → **sei**.

sessantesimo, -a num sixtieth, → **sesto**.

sessantina sf: una ~ (di) about sixty; **essere sulla ~** to be in one's sixties.

sesso sm sex.

sessuale agg sexual.

sesto, -a ♦ agg num & pron num sixth ♦ sm (frazione) sixth; **al ~ piano** on the sixth floor; **rimettersi in ~** to recover.

seta sf silk.

setacciare vt (separare) to sieve.

sete sf thirst; **avere ~** to be thirsty.

settanta num seventy, → **sei**.

settantesimo, -a num seventieth, → **sesto**.

settantina sf: una ~ (di) about seventy; **essere sulla ~** to be in one's seventies.

sette num seven, → **sei**.

settecento num seven hundred, → **sei**.

▶ **Settecento** sm: **il Settecento** the eighteenth century.

settembre sm September; **a** o **in ~** in September; **lo scorso ~** last September; **il prossimo ~** next September; **all'inizio di ~** at the beginning of September; **alla fine di ~** at the end of September; **il due ~** the second of September.

settentrionale agg northern.

settentrione sm north.

setter sm inv setter.

settimana sf week.

settimanale ♦ agg weekly ♦ sm weekly publication.

settimo, -a num seventh, → **sesto**.

settore sm sector.

severamente avv: **'è ~ vietato attraversare i binari'** 'crossing the track is strictly forbidden'.

severo, -a agg strict, severe.

sevizie sfpl torture (sg).

sexy agg inv sexy.

sezione sf section; (MED) dissection.

sfaccendato, -a agg lazy.

sfacchinata sf hard work.

sfacciato, -a agg (persona) cheeky.

sfacelo sm (rovina) ruin.

sfamare vt to feed.

▶ **sfamarsi** vr to satisfy one's hunger.

sfare vt to undo.

sfarzo sm pomp, magnificence.

sfasciare vt (sbendare) to unbandage; (rompere) to smash.

▶ **sfasciarsi** vr (rompersi) to fall to pieces.

sfaticato, -a agg lazy.

sfatto, -a pp → **sfare**.

sfavorevole agg unfavourable.

sfera sf sphere.

sferico, -a, -ci, -che agg spherical.

sferrare vt (attacco) to launch; **~ un colpo contro qn** to lash out at sb.

sfibrare vt to exhaust.

sfida sf challenge.

sfidare vt to challenge; (pericolo, morte) to defy; **~ qn a fare qc** to challenge sb to do sthg.

sfiducia sf distrust.

sfigurare ♦ vt to disfigure ♦ vi to make a bad impression.

sfilare ♦ vt (togliere) to take off ♦ vi (marciare) to parade; **sfilarsi le scarpe** to slip off one's shoes.

▶ **sfilarsi** vr (calze) to ladder.

sfilata sf (corteo) march; (di moda) fashion show.

sfinire vt to exhaust.

sfiorare vt to skim (over).

sfiorire vi to wither.

sfitto, -a agg vacant.

sfizioso, -a agg enticing.

sfocato, -a = sfuocato.

sfociare : **sfociare in** v + prep (fiume) to flow into.

sfoderare vt (giacca) to remove the lining from; (spada) to draw; (fig) to show off.

sfoderato, -a *agg* unlined.

sfogare *vt* to give vent to.

▶ **sfogarsi** *vr* (*aprirsi*) to pour out one's feelings; **sfogarsi su qn** (*scaricare la collera*) to vent one's anger on sb.

sfoggiare *vt* to show off.

sfogliare *vt* (*giornale*) to leaf through.

sfogliatelle *sfpl* puff pastries filled with spiced ricotta cheese and candied fruit.

sfogo, -ghi *sm* (*passaggio*) outlet; (*di sentimenti*) outburst; (*eruzione cutanea*) rash; **dare ~ a qc** to give vent to sthg.

sfoltire *vt* to thin.

sfondare *vt* (*contenitore*) to break the bottom of; (*porta*) to break down.

▶ **sfondarsi** *vr* (*contenitore*) to burst at the bottom.

sfondo *sm* background.

sformato *sm* savoury pudding made with vegetables and cheese or sometimes with meat, baked in a mould and then turned out.

sfornare *vt* (*pane, dolci*) to take out of the oven.

sfortuna *sf* misfortune; **portare ~** to bring bad luck.

sfortunatamente *avv* unfortunately.

sfortunato, -a *agg* unlucky.

sforzare *vt* to force; (*occhi, voce, motore*) to strain.

▶ **sforzarsi** *vr* to make an effort.

sforzo *sm* effort; **fare uno ~** to make an effort.

sfottere *vt* (*fam*) to tease.

sfratto *sm* eviction.

sfrecciare *vi* to shoot past.

sfregare *vt* (*strofinare*) to rub.

sfregio *sm* (*taglio*) gash.

sfrenato, -a *agg* unrestrained.

sfrontato, -a *agg* impudent.

sfruttamento *sm* exploitation.

sfruttare *vt* to exploit.

sfuggire *vi* (*scappare*) to escape.

▶ **sfuggire a** *v + prep* (*sottrarsi a*) to escape from; **~ di mano a qn** to slip out of sb's hands; **~ di mente a qn** to slip sb's mind; **non gli sfugge nulla** he misses nothing.

sfuggita : di sfuggita *avv* in passing.

sfumare ◆ *vt* (*colore*) to shade off; (*capelli*) to taper ◆ *vi* (*colore*) to shade off; (*svanire*) to vanish.

sfumato, -a *agg* (*colore*) soft.

sfumatura *sf* (*tonalità*) shade; (*fig: piccola differenza*) touch, hint; (*di capelli*) tapering.

sfuocato, -a *agg* blurred, out of focus.

sfuriata *sf* (*sfogo violento*) outburst of anger; (*rimprovero*) telling off.

sgabello *sm* stool.

sgabuzzino *sm* storage room.

sgambetto *sm*: **fare lo ~ a qn** to trip sb up.

sganciare *vt* (*vestito, allacciatura*) to unfasten; (*rimorchio, vagone*) to uncouple; (*bombe*) to drop; (*fam: soldi*) to fork out.

▶ **sganciarsi** *vr* (*staccarsi*) to come undone.

sgarbato, -a *agg* impolite.

sghignazzare *vi* to laugh scornfully.

sgobbare *vi* (*fam*) to slog.

sgocciolare ◆ *vt* (*bottiglia*) to drain ◆ *vi* to drip.

sgolarsi *vr* to make o.s. hoarse.

sgomb(e)rare *vt* (*strada, soffitta*) to clear.

sgombero, -a = **sgombro**.

sgombro, -a ◆ *agg* clear ◆ *sm* (*evacuazione*) evacuation; (*pesce*) mackerel.

sgomentare *vt* to dismay.

▶ **sgomentarsi** *vr* to be dismayed.

sgominare *vt* to rout.

sgonfiare *vt* to deflate.

▶ **sgonfiarsi** *vr* (*canotto*) to deflate; (*caviglia*) to go down.

sgorbio *sm* (*scarabocchio*) scribble; (*fig: persona*) fright.

sgradevole *agg* unpleasant.

sgradito, -a *agg* unwelcome.

sgranare *vt* (*fagioli*) to shell.

sgranchirsi *vr*: ~ **le gambe** to stretch one's legs.

sgranocchiare *vt* to munch.

sgraziato, -a *agg* graceless.

sgretolare *vt* (*frantumare*) to cause to crumble.

▶ **sgretolarsi** *vr* to crumble.

sgridare *vt* to scold.

sguaiato, -a *agg* coarse.

sgualcire *vt* to crumple.

▶ **sgualcirsi** *vr* to become crumpled.

sguardo *sm* (*occhiata*) look; (*espressione*) expression.

sguinzagliare *vt* (*cane*) to take off the lead.

sgusciare ♦ *vt* (*fagioli*) to shell ♦ *vi* (*sfuggire*) to slip away.

shampoo ['ʃampo] *sm inv* shampoo.

shock [ʃɔk] *sm inv* shock.

si (*diventa* **se** *quando precede* lo, la, li, le, ne) *pron* **1.** (*riflessivo: persona*) himself (*f* herself), themselves (*pl*); (*impersonale*) oneself; (*cosa, animale*) itself, themselves (*pl*); **lavarsi** to wash (oneself); ~ **stanno preparando** they are getting ready.

2. (*con verbo transitivo*): **lavarsi i denti** to brush one's teeth; ~ **è comprato un vestito** he bought himself a suit.

3. (*reciproco*) each other, one another; ~ **sono conosciuti a Roma** they met in Rome.

4. (*impersonale*): ~ **può sempre provare** one o you can always try; ~ **dice che ...** they say that ..., it is said that ...; ~ **vede che è stanco** one o you can see he's tired; '~ **prega di non fumare**' 'please do not smoke'; **non** ~ **sa mai** you never know.

5. (*passivo*): **questi prodotti** ~ **trovano dappertutto** these products are found everywhere.

sì *avv & sm inv* yes; **dire di** ~ to say yes; **uno** ~ **e uno no** every other one.

sia¹ → **essere**.

sia² *cong*: ~ ... **che**, ~ ... ~ both ... and; ~ **che** ... ~ **che** whether ... or; ~ **che tu venga**, ~ **che tu non venga** whether you come or not.

siamo → **essere**.

sicché *cong* (*e quindi*) and so.

siccità *sf inv* drought.

siccome *cong* as, since.

Sicilia *sf*: **la** ~ Sicily.

siciliano, -a *agg & sm, f* Sicilian.

sicura *sf* (*di auto*) safety lock; (*di arma*) safety catch.

sicurezza *sf* (*mancanza di pericolo*) safety, security; (*certezza*) certainty; **di** ~ safety (*dav s*), security (*dav s*).

sicuro, -a ♦ *agg* safe; (*amico, informazione*) reliable; (*fiducioso*) confident; (*certo*) certain ♦ *avv* certainly; **di** ~ certainly; **andare sul** ~ to play safe; **essere** ~ **di sé** to be sure of o.s.; **al** ~ in a safe place.

Siena *sf* Siena.

siepe *sf* hedge.

sieropositivo, -a *agg* HIV-positive.

siete → **essere**.

Sig. (*abbr di signor*) Mr.

Sig.a (*abbr di signora*) Ms.

sigaretta *sf* cigarette.

sigaro *sm* cigar.

Sigg. *abbr* Messrs.

sigla *sf* (*abbreviazione*) acronym; (*musicale*) signature tune; ~ **automobilistica** two-letter abbreviation of province on a vehicle's number plate.

Sig.na (*abbr di signorina*) Miss.

significare *vt* to mean; **che cosa significa?** what does it mean?

significativo, -a *agg* (*discorso*) significant; (*sguardo*) meaningful.

significato *sm* meaning.

signor *sm* → **signore**.

signora *sf* (*donna*) lady; (*moglie*) wife; **buon giorno** ~ good morning (Madam); **Gentile Signora** (*in una lettera*) Dear Madam; **la** ~ **Poli** Mrs

Poli; **signore e signori** ladies and gentlemen.

signore *sm* (*uomo*) gentleman; **buon giorno ~** good morning (Sir); **il ~ desidera?** what can I do for you, sir?; **Gentile Signore** (*in una lettera*) Dear Sir; **i Signori Rossi** (*marito e moglie*) Mr and Mrs Rossi; **il Signor Martini** Mr Martini.

signorile *agg* (*raffinato*) refined; (*elegante*) elegant; (*quartiere, alloggio*) exclusive.

signorina *sf* (*ragazza*) young lady; **buon giorno ~** good morning (Madam); **la ~ Logi** Miss Logi.

Sig.ra *abbr* Mrs.

silenzio *sm* silence; **fare ~** to be quiet.

silenzioso, -a *agg* quiet, silent.

sillaba *sf* syllable.

simbolico, -a, -ci, -che *agg* symbolic.

simbolo *sm* symbol.

simile *agg* (*analogo*) similar; (*tale*): **una persona ~** such a person; **~ a** similar to.

simmetrico, -a, -ci, -che *agg* symmetric(al).

simpatia *sf* (*inclinazione*) liking; (*qualità*) pleasantness.

simpatico, -a, -ci, -che *agg* nice.

simulare *vt* (*fingere*) to feign; (*imitare*) to simulate.

simultaneo, -a *agg* simultaneous.

sin = sino.

sinagoga, -ghe *sf* synagogue.

sincero, -a *agg* (*persona*) sincere; (*dolore, gioia*) genuine, heart-felt.

sindacalista, -i, -e *smf* trade unionist.

sindacato *sm* (*di lavoratori*) trade union.

sindaco, -ci *sm* mayor.

sinfonia *sf* symphony.

singhiozzo *sm* hiccups (*pl*).

▶ **singhiozzi** *smpl* sobs; **a singhiozzi** (*fig*) by fits and starts.

singolare ♦ *agg* (*originale*) unusual; (GRAMM) singular ♦ *sm* (GRAMM) singular.

singolo, -a *agg* single.

sinistra *sf*: **la ~** the left; (POL) the left (wing); **scrivere con la ~** to write with one's left hand; **a ~** left; **a ~ di** to the left of.

sinistro, -a ♦ *agg* left; (*minaccioso*) sinister ♦ *sm* accident.

sino = fino.

sinonimo *sm* synonym.

sintesi *sf inv* (*riassunto*) summary.

sintetico, -a, -ci, -che *agg* (*artificiale*) synthetic; (*succinto*) brief.

sintetizzare *vt* (*riassumere*) to summarize.

sintomo *sm* symptom.

sintonizzare *vt* to tune in.

▶ **sintonizzarsi su** *vr + prep* to tune in to.

sipario *sm* curtain.

sirena *sf* (*apparecchio*) siren; (*nella mitologia*) mermaid.

siringa, -ghe *sf* (*per iniezioni*) syringe; (*da cucina*) = piping bag.

sistema, -i *sm* system.

sistemare *vt* (*ordinare*) to tidy up; (*disporre*) to arrange; (*risolvere*) to sort out, to settle; (*alloggiare*) to find accommodation (Br) o accommodations (Am) for; (*procurare un lavoro a*) to find a job for; (*maritare*) to marry off.

▶ **sistemarsi** *vr* (*risolversi*) to be settled; (*trovare alloggio*) to find accommodation (Br) o accommodations (Am); (*trovare lavoro*) to find work; (*sposarsi*) to marry.

sistematico, -a, -ci, -che *agg* systematic.

sistemazione *sf* (*disposizione*) arrangement; (*alloggio*) accommodation (Br), accommodations (Am); (*lavoro*) employment.

sito *sm* (INFORM): **~ Web** Web site.

situare *vt* to situate, to locate.

situazione *sf* situation.

skate-board ['skeit 'bord] *sm inv* skateboard.

ski-lift [ski'lift] *sm inv* ski lift.

ski-pass [ski'pas] *sm inv* ski pass.

slacciare *vt* to undo.

slanciato, -a *agg* slender.

slancio *sm* (*balzo*) dash; (*fig*) burst.

slavina *sf* snowslide.

slavo, -a *agg* Slavonic, Slav.

sleale *agg* (*persona*) disloyal; (*azione*) treacherous.

slegare *vt* to untie.

slip *sm inv* briefs (*pl*).

slitta *sf* sledge.

slittare *vi* to slide; (*automobile*) to skid.

slogan *sm inv* slogan.

slogare *vt* to dislocate.

slogatura *sf* dislocation.

smacchiatore *sm* stain remover.

smagliante *agg* dazzling.

smagliare *vt* (*collant, calze*) to ladder.

smagliatura *sf* (*di calze*) ladder; (*della pelle*) stretch mark.

smaltire *vt* (*merce*) to sell off; (*rifiuti*) to discharge; (*cibo*) to digest; ~ **la sbornia** to get over one's hangover.

smalto *sm* (*per metalli, di denti*) enamel; (*per ceramica*) glaze; (*per unghie*) nail varnish.

smania *sf* (*agitazione*) restlessness; (*desiderio*) craving; **aver la ~ di qc** to have a craving for sthg.

smarrire *vt* to lose.

▶ **smarrirsi** *vr* to get lost.

smarrito, -a *agg* lost; (*sbigottito*) bewildered.

smascherare *vt* to unmask.

smemorato, -a *agg* absent-minded.

smentire *vt* (*notizia*) to deny; (*testimonianza*) to refute.

smentita *sf* (*di notizia*) denial.

smeraldo *sm* emerald.

smesso, -a *pp* → **smettere**.

smettere *vt* to stop; (*abito*) to stop wearing; ~ **di fare qc** to stop doing sthg; ~ **di fumare** to give up o stop smoking; **smettila!** stop it!

smidollato, -a *agg* spineless.

sminuire *vt* to belittle.

sminuzzare *vt* to crumble.

smistamento *sm* (*di posta, pacchi*) sorting; (*di treni*) shunting.

smistare *vt* (*posta*) to sort; (*treni*) to shunt.

smisurato, -a *agg* enormous, huge.

smodato, -a *agg* excessive.

smog *sm inv* smog.

smoking *sm inv* dinner jacket (Br), tuxedo (Am).

smontabile *agg* that can be dismantled.

smontare ◆ *vt* (*macchina, libreria*) to take to pieces; (*fig: far perdere l'entusiasmo a*) to discourage ◆ *vi* (*da cavallo*) to dismount; (*da turno di lavoro*) to finish (work).

smorfia *sf* grimace.

smorfioso, -a *agg* simpering.

smorzare *vt* (*suoni*) to muffle; (*colore*) to tone down; (*entusiasmo*) to dampen.

smosso, -a *pp* → **smuovere**.

smottamento *sm* landslide.

smunto, -a *agg* pinched.

smuovere *vt* (*spostare*) to shift; (*da proposito, intenzione*) to deter.

smussare *vt* (*spigolo*) to round off.

snack-bar *sm inv* snack bar.

snackeria *sf* snack bar.

snaturato, -a *agg* inhuman.

snello, -a *agg* slim, slender.

snervante *agg* exhausting.

snidare *vt* to flush out.

snobismo *sm* snobbery.

snodare *vt* (*slegare*) to untie; (*arti*) to loosen up.

▶ **snodarsi** *vr* (*slegarsi*) to come loose.

sobbalzare *vi* (*balzare*) to jolt; (*trasalire*) to jump.

sobborgo, -ghi *sm* suburb.

sobrio, -a *agg* sober.

socchiudere *vt* (*porta*) to leave ajar; (*occhi*) to half-close.

socchiuso, -a *pp* → **socchiudere**.

soccorrere *vt* to help.

soccorso, -a ♦ *pp* → **soccorrere** ♦ *sm* help, aid; ~ **stradale** breakdown service.

sociale *agg* social.

socialista, -i, -e *agg* socialist.

socializzare *vi* to socialize.

società *sf inv* (*gruppo umano*) society; (*associazione*) association, club; (COMM) company; ~ **per azioni** limited company (Br), incorporated company (Am).

socievole *agg* sociable.

socio, -a, -ci, cie *sm, f* (*di circolo*) member; (COMM) partner.

soda®1 *sf* soda.

soda2 *sf* (*bevanda*) soda water.

soddisfacente *agg* satisfactory.

soddisfare *vt* to satisfy.

soddisfatto, -a *agg* satisfied; **essere ~ di** (*contento*) to be satisfied with.

soddisfazione *sf* satisfaction.

sodo, -a *agg* hard, firm.

sofà *sm inv* sofa.

sofferente *agg* suffering.

sofferenza *sf* suffering.

sofferto, -a *pp* → **soffrire**.

soffiare ♦ *vi* to blow ♦ *vt* to blow; ~ **qn/qc a qn** to pinch sb/sthg from sb; **soffiarsi il naso** to blow one's nose.

soffiata *sf* (*fam*) tip-off.

soffice *agg* soft.

soffio *sm* (*di fiato, vento*) breath; ~ **al cuore** heart murmur.

soffitta *sf* attic.

soffitto *sm* ceiling.

soffocante *agg* suffocating, stifling.

soffocare ♦ *vt* to suffocate ♦ *vi* to suffocate.

soffriggere *vt & vi* to fry lightly.

soffrire ♦ *vt* (*patire*) to suffer; (*sopportare*) to bear ♦ *vi* to suffer ▶ **soffrire di** *v + prep* to suffer from.

soffritto *sm* lightly fried onions and herbs.

sofisticato, -a *agg* sophisticated.

software ['software] *sm* software.

soggetto, -a ♦ *agg*: **essere ~ a** to be subject to ♦ *sm* subject.

soggezione *sf* (*sottomissione*) subjection; (*imbarazzo*) uneasiness; **dare ~ a qn** to make sb ill at ease.

soggiorno *sm* (*permanenza*) stay; (*stanza*) living room.

soglia *sf* threshold.

sogliola *sf* sole.

sognare ♦ *vt* to dream of o about ♦ *vi* to dream; ~ **ad occhi aperti** to daydream.

sogno *sm* dream; **fare un brutto ~** to have a bad dream.

soia *sf* soya.

solaio *sm* attic.

solamente *avv* only, just.

solare *agg* solar, sun (*dav s*).

solarium *sm inv* solarium.

solco, -chi *sm* (*in terreno*) furrow; (*incisione*) groove; (*scia*) wake.

soldato *sm* soldier; ~ **semplice** private.

soldo *sm*: **non avere un ~** to be penniless.

▶ **soldi** *smpl* (*denaro*) money (*sg*).

sole *sm* sun; **prendere il ~** to sunbathe.

soleggiato, -a *agg* sunny.

solenne *agg* solemn.

solere *v impers*: **come si suol dire** as they say.

soletta *sf* (*suola*) insole.

solfo = **zolfo**.

solidale *agg*: **essere ~ con qn** to be in agreement with sb.

solidarietà *sf* solidarity.

solido, -a *agg & sm* solid.

solista, -i, -e *smf* soloist.

solitario, -a ♦ *agg* (*persona*) lonely, solitary; (*luogo*) lonely ♦ *sm* (*di carte*) patience (Br), solitaire (Am); (*brillante*) solitaire.

solito, -a *agg* usual; **essere ~ fare qc** to be in the habit of doing sthg; (**come**) **al ~** as usual; **di ~** usually.

solitudine *sf* solitude.

sollecitare *vt* (*risposta, pagamento*) to press for.

solleone *sm* (*caldo*) summer heat; (*periodo*) dog days (*pl*).

solletico *sm* tickling; **soffrire il ~ to** be ticklish.

sollevamento *sm* lifting; **~ pesi** (SPORT) weight lifting.

sollevare *vt* (*tirare su*) to lift, to raise; (*problema, questione*) to raise; (*fare insorgere*) to stir up.

▶ **sollevarsi** *vr* (*da terra*) to get up; (*insorgere*) to rise up.

sollevato, -a *agg* (*confortato*) relieved.

sollievo *sm* relief.

solo, -a ♦ *agg* (*senza compagnia*) alone; (*isolato*) lonely; (*unico*) only ♦ *avv* (*soltanto*) only, just; **c'è un ~ posto a sedere** there's only one seat; **da ~** by oneself; **ho ~ 5 000 lire** I only have 5,000 lire; **non ~ ... ma anche** not only ... but also; **a ~** (MUS) solo.

soltanto *avv* only.

solubile *agg* soluble; **caffè ~** instant coffee.

soluzione *sf* solution.

Somalia *sf*: **la ~** Somalia.

somaro, -a *sm, f* (*asino*) donkey, ass; (*fig: a scuola*) dunce.

somiglianza *sf* resemblance.

somigliare : somigliare a *v + prep* (*nell'aspetto*) to look like; (*nel modo di essere*) to be like.

▶ **somigliarsi** *vr* to be alike.

somma *sf* sum.

sommare *vt* (MAT) to add up.

sommario, -a ♦ *agg* brief ♦ *sm* (*di libro*) index.

sommergere *vt* to submerge; **~ di** (*fig*) to overwhelm with.

sommergibile *sm* submarine.

sommerso, -a ♦ *pp* → **sommergere** ♦ *agg* (*isola, città*) underwater.

somministrare *vt* to administer.

sommità *sf inv* (*cima*) summit.

sommo, -a *agg* highest; (*eccellente*) outstanding, excellent; **per sommi capi** in short, in brief.

sommossa *sf* uprising.

sommozzatore, -trice *sm, f* (deep-sea) diver.

sonda *sf* (*spaziale*, MED) probe.

sondaggio *sm* (*indagine*) survey.

sondare *vt* (*fondo marino*) to sound; (*intenzioni, opinioni*) to sound out.

sonetto *sm* sonnet.

sonnambulo, -a *agg*: **essere ~ to** sleepwalk.

sonnellino *sm* nap.

sonnifero *sm* sleeping pill.

sonno *sm* sleep; **avere ~ to** be sleepy; **prendere ~ to** fall asleep.

sono → **essere**.

sonoro, -a ♦ *agg* (*onde, film*) sound (*dav s*); (*voce, risata, schiaffo*) ringing ♦ *sm* (*di film*) soundtrack.

sontuoso, -a *agg* sumptuous.

soppiatto : di soppiatto *avv* secretly.

sopportare *vt* (*peso*) to support, to bear; (*umiliazione, dolore*) to bear; (*tollerare*) to put up with.

soppresso, -a *pp* → **sopprimere**.

sopprimere *vt* (*legge*) to abolish; (*servizio, treno*) to withdraw, to do away with; (*parola*) to delete.

sopra ♦ *prep* (*su*) on; (*al di sopra di*) above; (*al di là di*) over; (*riguardo a*) about, on ♦ *avv* (*in alto*) above; (*in lettera, scritto*): **come precisato ~** as detailed above; **al di ~ di** above; **di ~** upstairs.

soprabito *sm* overcoat.

sopracciglio (*pl f* **sopracciglia**) *sm* eyebrow.

sopraffare *vt* to overcome.

sopraffatto, -a *pp* → **sopraffare**.

sopraggiungere *vi* (*giungere all'improvviso*) to arrive (unexpectedly); (*accadere*) to occur (unexpectedly).

sopraggiunto, -a *pp* → **sopraggiungere**.

sopralluogo, -ghi *sm* (*di polizia*)

on-the-spot investigation; (*visita*) inspection.

soprammobile *sm* ornament.

soprannaturale *agg* supernatural.

soprannome *sm* nickname.

soprano *sm* soprano.

soprassalto : di soprassalto *avv* with a start.

soprattutto *avv* above all, especially.

sopravvalutare *vt* to overestimate.

sopravvento *sm*: avere il ~ su to have the upper hand over.

sopravvissuto, -a ♦ *pp* → **sopravvivere** ♦ *sm, f* survivor.

sopravvivere *vi* to survive.

▶ **sopravvivere a** *v + prep* to survive.

soprelevata *sf* elevated section.

soprintendente *smf* (*a attività, lavoro*) superintendent, supervisor.

soprintendenza *sf* (*attività*) supervision; (*ufficio*) superintendency.

sopruso *sm* abuse of power.

soqquadro *sm*: mettere qc a ~ to turn sthg upside down.

sorbetto *sm* sorbet.

sorbire *vt* to sip; sorbirsi qn/qc (*fig*) to put up with sb/sthg.

sorcio *sm* mouse.

sordido, -a *agg* sordid, squalid.

sordina *sf*: in ~ softly.

sordo, -a ♦ *agg* (*non udente*) deaf; (*rumore, tonfo*) muffled, dull ♦ *sm, f* deaf person.

sordomuto, -a ♦ *agg* deaf and dumb ♦ *sm, f* deaf and dumb person.

sorella *sf* sister.

sorellastra *sf* stepsister.

sorgente *sf* (*d'acqua*) spring; (*di fiume, elettricità, calore*) source.

sorgere *vi* to rise; (*sospetto, dubbio*) to arise.

sorpassare *vt* (AUTO) to overtake; (*superare*) to exceed.

sorpassato, -a *agg* old-fashioned.

sorpasso *sm* (*di veicolo*) overtaking; fare un ~ to overtake.

sorprendente *agg* surprising.

sorprendere *vt* (*cogliere*) to catch; (*stupire*) to surprise.

▶ **sorprendersi di** *vr + prep* to be surprised at.

sorpresa *sf* surprise; fare una ~ a qn to give sb a surprise; di ~ by surprise.

sorpreso, -a *pp* → **sorprendere**.

sorreggere *vt* to support.

sorretto, -a *pp* → **sorreggere**.

sorridente *agg* smiling.

sorridere *vi* to smile.

sorriso, -a ♦ *pp* → **sorridere** ♦ *sm* smile.

sorsata *sf* gulp.

sorso *sm* (*sorsata*) gulp; (*piccola quantità*) sip.

sorta *sf* kind, sort.

sorte *sf* fate; tirare a ~ to draw lots.

sorteggio *sm* draw.

sortilegio *sm* spell.

sorveglianza *sf* supervision; (POLIZIA) surveillance.

sorvegliare *vt* to watch.

sorvolare ♦ *vt* (*territorio*) to fly over ♦ *vi*: ~ su (*territorio*) to fly over; (*fig*) to pass over.

S.O.S. *sm* SOS; lanciare un ~ to send out an SOS.

sosia *smf inv* double.

sospendere *vt* (*attaccare*) to hang; (*attività, pagamenti, funzionario*) to suspend.

sospensione *sf* suspension.

sospeso, -a ♦ *pp* → **sospendere** ♦ *agg* (*interrotto*) suspended; lasciare qc in ~ to leave sthg unfinished; tenere qn in ~ to keep sb in suspense.

sospettare ♦ *vt* to suspect ♦ *vi*: ~ di qn (*avere sospetti su*) to suspect sb; (*diffidare di*) to be suspicious of sb.

sospetto, -a ♦ *agg* suspicious

♦ *sm, f* suspect ♦ *sm* suspicion.

sospirare *vi* to sigh; **farsi ~** to keep sb waiting.

sospiro *sm* sigh; **tirare un ~ di sollievo** to heave a sigh of relief.

sosta *sf* (*in luogo*) stop; (*pausa*) break; **fare ~ a/in** to make a stop at/in; **'divieto di ~'** 'no waiting'; **senza ~** nonstop; **'~ consentita solo per carico e scarico'** 'no waiting except for loading and unloading'.

sostantivo *sm* noun.

sostanza *sf* substance.

sostanzioso, -a *agg* (*cibo*) nourishing; (*notevole*) substantial.

sostare *vi* (*fermarsi*) to stop.

sostegno *sm* support.

sostenere *vt* to support; **~ che** to maintain (that); **~ gli esami** to sit exams.

▶ **sostenersi** *vr* (*tenersi dritto*) to hold o.s. up.

sostenitore, -trice *sm, f* supporter.

sostentamento *sm* maintenance.

sostenuto, -a *agg* (*tono, stile*) elevated; (*ritmo, passo*) sustained.

sostituire *vt* (*rimpiazzare*) to replace; (*prendere il posto di*) to take over from; **~ qn/qc con** to substitute sb/sthg with; **~ qn/qc a** to substitute sb/sthg for.

sostituto, -a *sm, f* substitute.

sostituzione *sf* substitution.

sottaceti *smpl* pickles.

sottana *sf* (*gonna*) skirt; (*di prete*) cassock.

sotterfugio *sm* subterfuge.

sotterraneo, -a ♦ *agg* underground; (*fig*) clandestine, secret ♦ *sm* cellar.

sottigliezza *sf* (*di spessore*) thinness; (*fig*) subtlety; (*dettaglio*) quibble.

sottile *agg* (*non spesso*) thin; (*capelli*) fine; (*slanciato*) slim; (*vista, odorato, ingegno*) sharp, keen; **non andare per il ~** not to mince matters.

sottintendere *vt* to imply.

sottinteso, -a ♦ *pp* → **sottintendere** ♦ *sm* allusion.

sotto ♦ *prep* under; (*più in basso di*) below ♦ *avv* (*in posizione inferiore*) underneath; (*più in basso, in scritto*) below; **al di ~ di** under, below; **sott'olio** in oil; **di ~** (*al piano inferiore*) downstairs.

sottobanco *avv* (*comprare*) under the counter.

sottobicchiere *sm* coaster.

sottobosco *sm* undergrowth.

sottobraccio *avv* (*prendere*) by the arm; (*camminare*) arm in arm.

sottofondo *sm* (MUS) background music.

sottolineare *vt* to underline; (*dare risalto a*) to emphasize.

sottolio → **sotto**.

sottomarino, -a ♦ *agg* underwater (*dav s*) ♦ *sm* submarine.

sottomesso, -a ♦ *pp* → **sottomettere** ♦ *agg* submissive.

sottomettere *vt* (*al proprio dominio*) to subdue.

▶ **sottomettersi a** *vr + prep* to submit to.

sottopassaggio *sm* (*per auto*) underpass; (*per pedoni, in stazione*) subway, underpass; **'servirsi del ~'** 'please use the subway'.

sottoporre *vt*: **~ qn a qc** to subject sb to sthg; **~ qc a qn** to submit sthg to sb.

▶ **sottoporsi a** *vr + prep* (*subire*) to undergo.

sottoposto, -a *pp* → **sottoporre**.

sottoscala *sm inv* cupboard under the stairs.

sottoscritto, -a ♦ *pp* → **sottoscrivere** ♦ *sm, f* undersigned.

sottoscrivere *vt* to sign.

▶ **sottoscrivere a** *v + prep* to subscribe to.

sottosopra *avv* upside down.

sottostante *agg* lower.

sottosuolo *sm* (*di terreno*) subsoil; (*locale*) basement.

sottosviluppato, -a *agg* underdeveloped.

sottoterra *avv* underground.
sottotitoli *smpl* subtitles.
sottovalutare *vt* to underestimate.
sottoveste *sf* underskirt, petticoat.
sottovoce *avv* in a low voice.
sottovuoto *avv* vacuum-packed.
sottrarre *vt* (MAT) to subtract; (*fondi*) to take away, to remove; ~ qc a qn (*rubare*) to steal sthg from sb.
▶ **sottrarsi a** *vr + prep* to escape, to avoid.
sottratto, -a *pp* → **sottrarre**.
sottrazione *sf* (MAT) subtraction; (*furto*) removal.
souvenir [suve'nir] *sm inv* souvenir.
sovietico, -a, -ci, -che *agg* soviet.
sovraccaricare *vt* to overload.
sovrano, -a *agg & sm, f* sovereign.
sovrapporre *vt* to put on top of.
sovrapposto, -a *pp* → **sovrapporre**.
sovrastare *vt* (*valle, paese*) to overhang.
sovrumano, -a *agg* superhuman.
sovvenzionare *vt* to subsidize.
sovversivo, -a *agg* subversive.
sozzo, -a *agg* filthy.
S.p.A. (*abbr di società per azioni*) ≃ Ltd (Br), ≃ Inc. (Am).
spaccare *vt* to break, to split.
▶ **spaccarsi** *vr* to break, to split.
spaccatura *sf* split.
spacciare *vt* (*droga*) to push.
▶ **spacciarsi per** *vr + prep* to pass o.s. off as.
spacciatore, -trice *sm, f* (*di droga*) pusher.
spacco, -chi *sm* split; (*di gonna*) slit.
spaccone, -a *sm, f* boaster.
spada *sf* sword.
▶ **spade** *sfpl* (*nelle carte*) suit in a

Neapolitan pack of cards.
spaesato, -a *agg* disorientated.
spaghetteria *sf* restaurant specializing in pasta dishes.
spaghetti *smpl* spaghetti (*sg*); ~ aglio, olio e peperoncino *spaghetti with garlic, chilli and olive oil*; ~ alla carbonara *spaghetti in an egg, bacon and cheese sauce*; ~ pomodoro e basilico *spaghetti in a fresh tomato and basil sauce*; ~ alla puttanesca *spaghetti in a sauce of tomatoes, anchovies, olives and capers*; ~ alle vongole *spaghetti in a clam sauce*.
Spagna *sf*: **la ~** Spain.
spagnolo, -a ♦ *agg* Spanish ♦ *sm, f* Spaniard ♦ *sm* (*lingua*) Spanish.
spago, -ghi *sm* string.
spaiato, -a *agg* odd.
spalancare *vt* to open wide.
spalla *sf* shoulder; **voltare le spalle a qn** to turn one's back on sb; **di spalle** from behind.
spalliera *sf* (*di letto*) head; (SPORT) wall bars (*pl*).
spallina *sf* (*di reggiseno, sottoveste*) strap; (*imbottitura*) shoulder pad.
spalmare *vt* to spread.
spalti *smpl* (*di stadio*) terraces.
spandere *vt* (*versare*) to pour; (*spargere*) to spread.
▶ **spandersi** *vr* to spread.
spappolare *vt* to pulp.
▶ **spappolarsi** *vr* to get mushy.
sparare ♦ *vi* to fire, to shoot ♦ *vt* (*colpo, fucilata*) to fire.
sparecchiare ♦ *vi* to clear the table ♦ *vt*: ~ **la tavola** to clear the table.
spareggio *sm* (SPORT) play-off.
spargere *vt* (*sparpagliare*) to scatter; (*versare*) to spill; (*divulgare*) to spread.
▶ **spargersi** *vr* (*sparpagliarsi*) to scatter; (*divulgarsi*) to spread.
sparire *vi* to disappear.
sparlare : **sparlare di** *v + prep* to run down.

sparo sm shot.

sparpagliare vt to scatter.

▶ **sparpagliarsi** vr to scatter.

sparso, -a ♦ pp → **spargere** ♦ agg scattered.

spartire vt (dividere) to share out.

spartitraffico sm inv central reservation (Br), median strip (Am).

spasmo sm spasm.

spassarsela vr to have a good time.

spasso sm (film, scena) amusement, fun; (persona) laugh, scream; (passeggiata): **andare a ~** to go for a walk; **essere a ~** (fig) to be out of work.

spauracchio sm scarecrow.

spaventapasseri sm inv scarecrow.

spaventare vt to frighten.

▶ **spaventarsi** vr to become frightened.

spavento sm (paura) fear, fright; **far ~ a qn** to give sb a fright.

spaventoso, -a agg frightening.

spazientirsi vr to lose one's patience.

spazio sm space.

spazioso, -a agg spacious.

spazzaneve sm inv snowplough.

spazzare vt (pavimento) to sweep; (sporco, foglie) to sweep up.

spazzatura sf (rifiuti) rubbish.

spazzino, -a sm, f road sweeper.

spazzola sf (per capelli) hairbrush; (per abiti) clothes brush; **~ da scarpe** shoe brush.

spazzolare vt to brush.

spazzolino sm: **~ (da denti)** toothbrush.

spazzolone sm scrubbing brush.

specchiarsi vr to look at o.s. (in a mirror).

specchietto sm (da borsetta) pocket mirror; (prospetto) scheme, table; **~ (retrovisore)** rear-view mirror.

specchio sm mirror.

speciale agg special.

specialista, -i, -e sm, f specialist.

specialità sf inv speciality; **~ della casa** speciality of the house.

specialmente avv especially.

specie ♦ sf inv (di piante, animali) species (inv); (sorta) kind ♦ avv especially; **una ~ di** a kind of.

specificare vt to specify.

specifico, -a, -ci, -che agg specific.

speculare vi to speculate.

speculazione sf speculation.

spedire vt to send; **~ (per posta)** to post.

spedizione sf (di lettera, merci) sending; (viaggio) expedition.

spegnere vt (fuoco, sigaretta) to put out; (luce, TV, gas) to turn off.

spellare vt (coniglio) to skin.

▶ **spellarsi** vr to peel.

spendaccione, -a sm, f spendthrift.

spendere vt & vi to spend.

spensierato, -a agg carefree.

spento, -a ♦ pp → **spegnere** ♦ agg (colore) dull; (sguardo) lifeless.

speranza sf hope.

sperare vt to hope for; **spero che venga** I hope he'll come; **spero di sì** I hope so; **~ di fare qc** to hope to do sthg.

▶ **sperare in** v + prep to trust in.

sperduto, -a agg (luogo) out-of-the-way; (persona) lost.

spericolato, -a agg fearless.

sperimentale agg experimental.

sperimentare vt (sottoporre a esperimento, fig) to test; (fare esperienza di) to experience.

sperma, -i sm sperm.

sperperare vt to squander.

spesa sf (somma) expense; (acquisti) shopping; **fare la ~** to do the shopping; **fare spese** (acquisti) to go shopping.

▶ **spese** sfpl (uscite) expenses; **spese postali** postage (sg); **spese di viaggio** travel expenses; **a spese di** at the expense of.

spesso, -a ♦ *agg* thick ♦ *avv* often.

spessore *sm* thickness.

Spett. *abbr* = **spettabile**.

spettabile *agg* (*nelle lettere*): ~ **ditta** Messrs … & Co.

spettacolo *sm* (*rappresentazione*) show, performance; (*vista*) sight.

spettare : spettare a *v* + *prep* to be up to; **spetta a te dirglielo** it's up to you to tell him.

spettatore, -trice *sm, f* (*di spettacolo*) member of the audience; (*di avvenimento*) onlooker.

spettinare *vt*: ~ **qn** to ruffle sb's hair.

▶ **spettinarsi** *vr* to get one's hair messed up.

spettro *sm* (*fantasma*) spectre.

spezia *sf* spice.

spezzare *vt* (*rompere*) to break; (*viaggio, giornata*) to break (up).

▶ **spezzarsi** *vr* to break.

spezzatino *sm* stew.

spezzato, -a ♦ *agg* (*diviso*) broken ♦ *sm* (*vestito*) jacket and trousers.

spezzettare *vt* to break into small pieces.

spia *sf* (*di polizia*) informer; (*agente*) spy; (*luminosa*) warning light; (*indizio*) indication, sign; **fare la** ~ to be a sneak.

spiacente *agg*: **essere** ~ (**di fare qc**) to be sorry (for doing sthg).

spiacevole *agg* unpleasant.

spiaggia, -ge *sf* beach; **andare/essere in** ~ to go to/be on the beach; ~ **privata** private beach.

spianare *vt* (*terreno*) to level; (*pasta*) to roll out; ~ **il terreno** (*fig*) to prepare the ground.

spiare *vt* to spy on.

spiazzo *sm* open space.

spiccare ♦ *vi* (*risaltare*) to stand out ♦ *vt*: ~ **un balzo** to jump; ~ **il volo** to fly off.

spiccato, -a *agg* marked, strong.

spicchio *sm* (*d'arancia*) segment; (*di mela, pera*) slice; ~ **d'aglio** clove of garlic.

spicciarsi *vr* to hurry up.

spicciolo, -a *agg*: **moneta spicciola** small change.

▶ **spiccioli** *smpl* small change.

spider ['spaidə] *sm inv* two-seater convertible sports car.

spiedino *sm* (*pietanza*) kebab.

spiedo *sm* spit; **allo** ~ spit-roasted.

spiegare *vt* (*far capire*) to explain; (*vele*) to unfurl; (*lenzuola*) to unfold; ~ **qc a qn** to explain sthg to sb.

▶ **spiegarsi** *vr* (*farsi capire*) to make o.s. clear; (*diventare chiaro*) to become clear; **spieghiamoci!** let's get things straight!

spiegazione *sf* explanation.

spietato, -a *agg* ruthless.

spiga, -ghe *sf* (*di grano*) ear.

spigolo *sm* (*di mobile, muro*) corner.

spilla *sf* brooch; ~ **da balia** safety pin.

spillare *vt* (*soldi*): ~ **qc a qn** to tap sb for sthg.

spillo *sm* (*da sarto*) pin.

spilorcio, -a, -ci, -ce *agg* mean, stingy.

spina *sf* (*di pianta*) thorn; (*di riccio*) spine; (*lisca*) bone; (*elettrica*) plug; **birra alla** ~ draught beer; ~ **dorsale** backbone.

spinaci *smpl* spinach (*sg*).

spinello *sm* (*fam: sigaretta*) joint.

spingere *vt* & *vi* to push; ~ **qn a fare qc** to press sb to do sthg.

▶ **spingersi** *vr* to push on.

spinoso, -a *agg* prickly, thorny.

spinta *sf* (*pressione, urto*) push; (*incoraggiamento*) incentive, spur; (*raccomandazione*): **dare una** ~ **a qn** to pull strings for sb.

spinto, -a ♦ *pp* → **spingere** ♦ *agg* (*scabroso*) risqué.

spintone *sm* push, shove.

spionaggio *sm* espionage.

spioncino sm peephole, spy hole.

spiraglio sm (fessura) chink; (di luce) gleam, glimmer.

spirale sf spiral; (anticoncezionale) coil.

spirito sm (intelletto) mind; (fantasma, disposizione d'animo, RELIG) spirit; (vivacità d'ingegno) wit; (senso dell'umorismo) humour; (alcol): ciliegie sotto ~ cherries preserved in alcohol.

spiritoso, -a agg witty.

spirituale agg spiritual.

splendente agg shining.

splendere vi to shine.

splendido, -a agg (bellissimo) magnificent.

splendore sm splendour; (luce) brilliance.

spogliare vt (svestire) to undress; ~ qn di qc (derubare, privare) to strip sb of sthg.
▶ **spogliarsi** vr to undress.

spogliarello sm striptease.

spogliatoio sm (di palestra, piscina) changing room; (di abitazione) dressing room.

spoglio sm (di schede elettorali) counting.

spola sf (bobina) spool; fare la ~ (tra) to go to and fro (between).

spolpare vt to strip the flesh off.

spolverare vt & vi to dust.

sponda sf (di fiume) bank; (di lago) shore; (di letto) edge; (di biliardo) cushion.

sponsorizzare vt sponsor.

spontaneo, -a agg spontaneous; (non artificioso) natural.

spopolare ◆ vt to depopulate ◆ vi to draw the crowds.
▶ **spopolarsi** vr to become depopulated.

sporadico, -a, -ci, -che agg sporadic.

sporcare vt to dirty; sporcarsi le mani to get one's hands dirty.
▶ **sporcarsi** vr to get dirty.

sporcizia sf (l'esser sporco) dirtiness; (cosa sporca) dirt.

sporco, -a, -chi, -che ◆ agg dirty ◆ sm dirt.

sporgente agg protruding; (occhi) bulging.

sporgere ◆ vt to put out ◆ vi to stick out.
▶ **sporgersi** vr to lean out.

sport sm inv sport.

sporta sf shopping bag.

sportello sm (di mobile, treno) door; (di banca, posta) window, counter; ~ automatico cash dispenser.

sportivo, -a ◆ agg (programma, campo) sports (dav s); (persona) sporty; (abbigliamento) casual; (comportamento, spirito) sporting ◆ sm, f sportsman (f sportswoman).

sporto, -a pp → sporgere.

sposare vt to marry.
▶ **sposarsi** vr to get married.
▶ **sposarsi con** vr + prep to marry.

sposato, -a agg married.

sposo, -a sm, f bridegroom (f bride); gli sposi the newlyweds.

spossante agg exhausting.

spostare vt to move; (cambiare) to change.
▶ **spostarsi** vr to move.

spot sm inv (faretto) spotlight; (pubblicità) advert.

spranga, -ghe sf bar.

spray sm inv spray.

sprecare vt to waste.

spreco, -chi sm waste.

spregiudicato, -a agg (senza scrupoli) unscrupulous.

spremere vt (arancia, limone) to squeeze.

spremiagrumi sm inv lemon squeezer.

spremuta sf fresh fruit juice; ~ di arancia freshly-squeezed orange juice.

sprezzante agg scornful.

sprigionare vt to emit.
▶ **sprigionarsi** vr to emanate.

sprint sm sprint.

stabilimento

sprizzare vi to spurt.

sprofondare vi (crollare) to collapse; (affondare) to sink.

sproporzionato, -a agg out of all proportion.

sproposito sm blunder; (somma esagerata): **costa uno ~** it costs a fortune; **parlare a ~** to talk out of turn.

sprovveduto, -a agg inexperienced.

sprovvisto, -a agg: **~ di** lacking in; **cogliere qn alla sprovvista** to catch sb unawares.

spruzzare vt (profumo) to spray; (acqua) to sprinkle; (persona) to splash.

spruzzatore sm spray.

spruzzo sm spray.

spugna sf (da bagno) sponge; (tessuto) towelling.

spuma sf (schiuma) foam, froth.

spumante sm sparkling wine.

SPUMANTE

The sparkling wine called 'spumante' can be drunk as an aperitif or as a dessert wine, and comes in sweet, dry or muscat versions, the latter being named after the grape variety. This Italian answer to champagne gets its name from the fact that it releases lots of bubbles, or foam ('spuma'), when uncorked. No birthday or wedding is complete without 'spumante', and it is also traditional to open a bottle at midnight on New Year's Eve.

---

spumone sm (dolce) a foamy dessert made from whisked egg white, milk and sugar.

spuntare ♦ vi (apparire) to appear ♦ vt (tagliare la punta di) to break the point of; **spuntarsi i capelli** to trim one's hair; **spuntarla** (fig) to make it.

spuntino sm snack.

spunto sm (punto di partenza) starting point.

sputare ♦ vt to spit out ♦ vi to spit.

sputo sm spit.

squadra sf (di operai, SPORT) squad, team; (strumento) set square.

squadrare vt (scrutare) to look at closely; (foglio, blocco) to square.

squagliare vt to melt; **squagliarsela** (fam) to clear off.

▸ **squagliarsi** vr to melt.

squalificare vt to disqualify.

squallido, -a agg wretched, miserable.

squallore sm wretchedness, misery.

squalo sm shark.

squama sf scale.

squamarsi vr to flake off.

squarciagola : a squarciagola avv at the top of one's voice.

squarciare vt to rip.

squartare vt to quarter.

squash [skwɔʃ] sm squash.

squattrinato, -a agg penniless.

squilibrato, -a agg unbalanced.

squilibrio sm (fisico) disequilibrium; (psichico) derangement; (disparità) imbalance.

squillare vi (telefono, campanello) to ring; (tromba) to blare.

squillo sm (di telefono, campanello) ring; (di tromba) blare.

squisito, -a agg (cibo) delicious; (raffinato) exquisite; (persona) delightful.

sradicare vt (albero) to uproot.

srotolare vt to unroll.

stabile ♦ agg stable; (lavoro, occupazione) steady ♦ sm (edificio) building.

stabilimento sm (complesso) factory, plant; **~ balneare** bathing establishment.

STABILIMENTI BALNEARI

Many Italian seaside resorts have their 'stabilimenti balneari', bathing clubs on the beach which provide a bar, showers and changing huts, and hire out beach umbrellas, deckchairs and pedalos. Some even organize volleyball tournaments, treasure hunts and dances.

stabilire *vt* to establish; (*fissare*) to fix; ~ **che** (*decidere*) to decide (that).

▶ **stabilirsi** *vr* to settle.

stabilità *sf* stability.

staccare ♦ *vt* (*separare*) to detach, to separate; (*elettrodomestico*) to unplug; (SPORT) to leave behind ♦ *vi* (*risaltare*) to stand out; (*fam: finire il lavoro*) to knock off.

▶ **staccarsi** *vr* (*bottone, cerotto*) to come off; **staccarsi da** (*venir via da*) to come off; (*fig: allontanarsi*) to move away from.

staccionata *sf* (*recinzione*) fence; (SPORT) hurdle.

stadio *sm* (SPORT) stadium; (*fase*) stage.

staffa *sf* (*di sella, pantaloni*) stirrup; **perdere le staffe** (*fig*) to fly off the handle.

staffetta *sf* (SPORT) relay race.

stagionale ♦ *agg* seasonal ♦ *smf* seasonal worker.

stagionato, -a *agg* seasoned.

stagione *sf* season; **alta/bassa ~** high/low season; **vestiti di mezza ~** clothes for spring and autumn.

stagno, -a ♦ *agg* (*a tenuta d'acqua*) watertight; (*a tenuta d'aria*) airtight ♦ *sm* (*laghetto*) pond; (*metallo*) tin.

stagnola *sf* tinfoil.

stalla *sf* (*per cavalli*) stable; (*per bovini*) cowshed.

stamattina *avv* this morning.

stambecco, -chi *sm* ibex.

stampa *sf* (*tecnica*) printing; (*con stampante, opera*) print; (*giornalisti*): **la ~** the press; **'stampe'** 'printed matter'.

stampante *sf* (INFORM) printer.

stampare *vt* to print; (*pubblicare*) to publish; (*nella memoria*) to impress.

stampatello *sm* block letters (*pl*).

stampella *sf* crutch.

stampo *sm* mould; (*fig: sorta*) type.

stancare *vt* (*affaticare*) to tire; (*stufare*) to bore.

▶ **stancarsi** *vr* to get tired; **stancarsi di** (*stufarsi di*) to grow tired of.

stanchezza *sf* tiredness.

stanco, -a, -chi, -che *agg* tired; (*stufo*): ~ **di** fed up with; ~ **morto** dead tired.

stanghetta *sf* (*di occhiali*) leg.

stanotte *avv* tonight; (*nella notte appena passata*) last night.

stante *agg*: **a sé ~** separate, independent.

stantio, -a *agg* (*cibo*) stale.

stanza *sf* (*camera*) room; ~ **da bagno** bathroom; ~ **da letto** bedroom.

stanziare *vt* to allocate.

stare *vi* (*rimanere*) to stay; (*abitare*) to live; (*con gerundio*): **sto leggendo** I'm reading; **come sta?** how are you?; **ti sta bene!** it suits you; **ci stai?** is that OK with you?; **sta a voi decidere** it's up to you to decide; **queste scarpe mi stanno strette** these shoes are tight; ~ **per fare qc** to be about to do sthg; ~ **bene/male** to be well/not very well; ~ **a guardare** to watch; ~ **in piedi** to stand (up); ~ **seduto** to sit, to be sitting; ~ **simpatico a qn** to like sb; ~ **zitto** to shut up; **starci** to fit.

starnutire *vi* to sneeze.

starnuto *sm* sneeze.

stasera *avv* this evening, tonight.

statale ♦ *agg* state (*dav s*), government (*dav s*) ♦ *smf* civil servant ♦ *sf* main road.

statistica, -che *sf* (*disciplina*) statistics (*pl*); (*dati*) statistic.

stato ♦ *pp* → **essere, stare** ♦ *sm* (*condizione*) state, condition; (*nazione*) state; **essere in ~ interessante** to be pregnant; ~ **d'animo** state of mind; ~ **civile** marital status; **gli Stati Uniti (d'America)** the United

States (of America).

statua sf statue.

statunitense agg United States (dav s), of the United States.

statura sf (fisica) height.

statuto sm statute.

stazionario, -a agg (immutato) unchanged.

stazione sf station; ~ degli autobus bus station; ~ balneare seaside resort; ~ centrale central station; ~ ferroviaria railway station (Br), railroad station (Am); ~ di polizia police station; ~ sciistica ski resort; ~ di servizio petrol station (Br), gas station (Am); ~ termale spa.

stecca, -che sf (asticella) stick; (di sigarette) carton; (da biliardo) cue.

steccato sm fence.

stella sf star; stelle filanti shooting stars; albergo a tre stelle three-star hotel.

stellato, -a agg starry.

stelo sm (di fiore) stem.

stemma, -i sm coat of arms.

stendere vt (allungare) to stretch (out); (panni, vele) to spread (out); (bucato) to hang out.

► **stendersi** vr (sdraiarsi) to lie down.

stenografare vt to take down in shorthand.

stentare vi: ~ a fare qc to find it hard to do sthg.

stento sm: a ~ with difficulty.

► **stenti** smpl (privazioni) hardship (sg).

sterco, -chi sm dung.

stereo sm inv stereo.

stereotipo sm stereotype.

sterile agg (uomo, donna) sterile.

sterilizzare vt to sterilize.

sterlina sf pound (sterling).

sterminare vt to exterminate.

sterminato, -a agg immense.

sterminio sm extermination.

sterzare vi to steer.

sterzo sm steering.

steso, -a pp → stendere.

stesso, -a ♦ agg same; (in persona, proprio): il presidente ~ the president himself o in person ♦ pron: lo ~/la stessa the same (one); io ~ I myself; lei stessa she herself; lo faccio per me ~ I'm doing it for myself; fare qc lo ~ to do sthg just the same; fa o è lo ~ it doesn't matter; per me è lo ~ it's all the same to me.

stesura sf (atto) drafting; (documento) draft.

stile sm style; ~ libero freestyle.

stilista, -i, -e smf designer.

stilografica, -che sf fountain pen.

stima sf (valutazione) valuation; (apprezzamento) esteem; fare la ~ di qc to estimate the value of sthg; avere ~ di qn to have a high opinion of sb.

stimare vt (valutare) to value; (ritenere) to consider; (apprezzare) to respect.

stimolare vt to stimulate; ~ qn a fare qc to spur sb on to do sthg.

stimolo sm stimulus.

stingere vi to fade.

► **stingersi** vr to fade.

stinto, -a pp → stingere.

stipendio sm salary.

stipite sm (di porta, finestra) jamb.

stipulare vt to draw up.

stirare vt (con il ferro) to iron.

stiro sm → asse, ferro.

stirpe sf stock, birth.

stitichezza sf constipation.

stivale sm boot.

stivaletto sm ankle boot.

stizza sf anger.

stizzirsi vr to get irritated.

stoccafisso sm wind-dried cod, stockfish.

stoffa sf material, fabric; avere la ~ di to have the makings of.

stola sf stole.

stolto, -a agg stupid.

stomaco, -chi o **-ci** sm stomach.

stonato, -a agg (MUS) off key.

stop ♦ *sm inv* (AUTO: *segnale*) stop sign; (AUTO: *luce*) brake light (Br), stoplight ♦ *esclam* stop!; **'stop con segnale rosso'** 'stop when light is on red'.

storcere *vt* to twist; **~ il naso** to turn up one's nose; **storcersi una caviglia** to twist one's ankle.

▶ **storcersi** *vr* to twist.

stordire *vt* to stun.

stordito, -a *agg* stunned.

storia *sf* (*avvenimenti umani, materia, opera*) history; (*vicenda, invenzione*) story; (*faccenda*) business (*no pl*); (*scusa*) excuse.

storico, -a, -ci, -che ♦ *agg* historic(al) ♦ *sm, f* historian.

stormo *sm* (*di uccelli*) flock.

storpiare *vt* (*rendere storpio*) to cripple; (*parola*) to mangle; (*concetto*) to twist.

storta *sf*: **prendere una ~ al piede** to sprain one's foot.

storto, -a ♦ *pp* → **storcere** ♦ *agg* (*chiodo*) twisted, bent; (*gambe, quadro*) crooked; **andare ~** to go wrong.

stoviglie *sfpl* dishes.

strabico, -a, -ci, -che *agg* (*persona*) squint-eyed; (*occhi*) squint.

straccadenti *smpl* type of very hard biscuit.

stracchino *sm* a creamy cow's milk cheese from Lombardy.

stracciare *vt* (*vestito, foglio*) to tear.

stracciatella *sf* (*gelato*) chocolate-chip ice cream; (*minestra*) broth enriched with eggs, semolina and Parmesan cheese.

straccio *sm* rag; (*per pulizie*) duster, cloth.

straccione, -a *sm, f* ragamuffin.

strada *sf* road; (*urbana*) street; (*percorso*) way; **~ facendo** on the way; **tagliare la ~ a qn** to cut across sb; **~ panoramica** scenic route; **~ senza uscita** dead end; **'~ deformata'** 'uneven road surface'; **'~ privata'** 'private road'; **'~ transitabile con catene'** 'road negotiable with chains'.

stradale ♦ *agg* road (*dav s*) ♦ *sf* traffic police.

strafalcione *sm* (*sproposito*) howler.

straforo : di straforo *avv* on the sly.

strafottente *agg* arrogant.

strage *sf* massacre.

stralunato, -a *agg* (*occhi*) rolling; (*persona*) dazed.

stramazzare *vi* to fall heavily.

strangolare *vt* to strangle.

straniero, -a ♦ *agg* foreign ♦ *sm, f* foreigner.

strano, -a *agg* strange.

straordinario, -a ♦ *agg* extraordinary; (*treno*) special ♦ *sm* (*lavoro*) overtime.

strapazzare *vt* to ill-treat.

▶ **strapazzarsi** *vr* to tire o.s. out.

strappo *sm* (*in tessuto*, MED) tear; (*fam: passaggio*) lift (Br), ride (Am); **fare uno ~ alla regola** to make an exception to the rule.

straripare *vi* to overflow.

strascico, -chi *sm* (*di abito*) train; (*fig: consequenza*) aftereffect.

strascinati *smpl* squares of pasta in a tomato and minced meat sauce (a speciality of Calabria).

stratagemma, -i *sm* stratagem.

strategia *sf* strategy.

strato *sm* (*di polvere, di crema*) layer; (*di vernice, smalto*) coat.

stravagante *agg* eccentric.

stravedere : stravedere per *v* + *prep* to be crazy about.

stravisto *pp* → **stravedere**.

stravolgere *vt* to distort.

stravolto, -a *pp* → **stravolgere**.

straziante *agg* (*dolore*) excruciating; (*scena*) harrowing.

strazio *sm*: **essere uno ~** (*libro, film*) to be awful; (*persona*) to be a pain.

strega, -ghe *sf* witch.

stregone *sm* (*mago*) sorcerer; (*di tribù*) witchdoctor.

stremare *vt* to exhaust.

stremo *sm*: **essere allo ~ delle forze**

to be at the end of one's tether.

strepitoso, -a agg resounding.

stress sm stress.

stressante agg stressful.

stretta sf grip; ~ **di mano** handshake; **mettere alle strette qn** to put sb in a tight corner.

strettamente avv (serratamente) tightly; (rigorosamente) strictly.

stretto, -a ♦ pp → **stringere** ♦ agg (strada, stanza) narrow; (vestito, scarpe) tight; (rigoroso, preciso) strict ♦ sm strait; **parenti stretti** close family (sg).

strettoia sf bottleneck.

striato, -a agg streaked.

stridere vi (freni) to creak; (cicale, grilli) to chirr; (colori) to clash.

strillare vi & vt to scream.

strillo sm scream.

striminzito, -a agg (vestito) shabby; (persona) skinny.

stringa, -ghe sf lace.

stringato, -a agg concise.

stringere ♦ vt (vite, nodo) to tighten; (denti, pugno) to clench; (labbra) to press; (tenere stretto) to grip; (abito) to take in; (patto, accordo) to conclude ♦ vi to be tight; ~ **qn tra le braccia** to hug sb; ~ **la mano a qn** to shake hands with sb; ~ **i tempi** to get a move on; **il tempo stringe** time is short.

▶ **stringersi** vr to squeeze up.

striscia, -sce sf (nastro) strip; (riga) stripe; **strisce (pedonali)** zebra crossing (sg).

strisciare ♦ vi (serpente) to slither; (passare rasente) to scrape ♦ vt (macchina) to scrape; (piedi) to drag.

striscione sm banner.

stritolare vt to crush.

strizzare vt to wring out; ~ **l'occhio** to wink.

strofinaccio sm cloth.

strofinare vt to rub.

stroncare vt to break off; (rivolta) to put down; (libro, film) to pan.

stropicciare vt (braccio, occhi) to rub; (vestito) to crease.

strozzapreti smpl 'gnocchi' either in a meat sauce, or made with eggs and spinach and served with butter and cheese.

strozzare vt (strangolare) to strangle; (sog: cibo) to choke.

▶ **strozzarsi** vr to choke.

strudel sm inv apple strudel.

strumento sm (musicale, di precisione) instrument; (di fabbro, meccanico) tool.

strusciare vt to rub.

▶ **strusciarsi** vr to rub o.s.

strutto sm lard.

struttura sf structure.

struzzo sm ostrich.

stuccare vt (buco) to plaster; (vetro) to putty.

stucco, -chi sm (malta) plaster; (decorazione) stucco; **rimanere di ~** to be dumbfounded.

studente, -essa sm, f student; (di liceo) pupil.

studentesco, -a, -schi, -sche agg student (dav s).

studentessa → **studente**.

studiare vt & vi to study.

studio sm (attività) studying; (ricerca, stanza) study; (di professionista) office; (di televisione, radio) studio; ~ **medico** surgery (Br), office (Am); **gli studi** (scuola, università) studies.

studioso, -a ♦ agg studious ♦ sm, f scholar.

stufa sf stove; ~ **elettrica** heater.

stufare vt (seccare): **mi hai stufato con le tue chiacchiere!** I'm sick and tired of you talking!

▶ **stufarsi** vr: **stufarsi (di)** (fam) to get fed up (with).

stufato sm stew.

stufo, -a agg (fam): **essere ~ (di)** to be fed up (with).

stuoia sf straw mat.

stupefacente ♦ agg amazing ♦ sm drug.

stupendo, -a agg marvellous.

stupidaggine sf stupid thing.

stupido, -a agg stupid.

stupire vt to amaze.

▶ **stupirsi di** *vr* + *prep* to be amazed by.

stupore *sm* astonishment.

stupro *sm* rape.

sturare *vt* to unblock.

stuzzicadenti *sm inv* toothpick.

stuzzicare *vt* (*irritare*) to tease; ~ l'appetito to whet one's appetite.

su *prep* 1. (*stato in luogo*) on; **le chiavi sono sul tavolo** the keys are on the desk; **a 2 000 metri sul livello del mare** at 2,000 metres above sea level; **una casa sul mare** a house by the sea.

2. (*moto a luogo*) on, onto; **venite sulla terrazza** come onto the terrace.

3. (*argomento*) about, on; **un libro sulla vita di Napoleone** a book about Napoleon's life.

4. (*tempo*) around; **vengo sul tardo pomeriggio** I'll come in the late afternoon; **sul momento** at that moment; **sul presto** fairly early.

5. (*prezzo e misura*) about; **costerà sulle 200 000 lire** it will cost about 200,000 lira; **peserà sui tre chili** he weighs about three kilos; **un uomo sulla quarantina** a man about forty years old.

6. (*modo*): **facciamo dolci solo ~ ordinazione** we only make cakes to order; **~ appuntamento** by appointment; **vestito ~ misura** made-to-measure suit; **parlare sul serio** to be serious; **nove volte ~ dieci** nine times out of ten.

◆ *avv* 1. (*in alto*) up; (*al piano di sopra*) upstairs; **in ~** (*verso l'alto*) up(wards); (*in poi*) onwards; **dai 18 anni in ~** from the age of 18 onwards.

2. (*per esortare*) come on; **~, sbrigatevi!** come on, hurry up!; **~ con la vita!** cheer up!

sub *smf inv* diver.

subacqueo, -a ◆ *agg* underwater ◆ *sm, f* diver.

subbuglio *sm* turmoil; **essere in ~** to be in a turmoil.

subdolo, -a *agg* sly.

subentrare *vi*: **~ a qn** to take sb's place.

subire *vt* (*ingiustizia, consequenze*) to suffer; (*operazione*) to undergo; **~ un torto** to be wronged.

subissare *vt*: **~ qn di qc** to shower sb with sthg.

subito *avv* (*immediatamente*) straightaway, immediately, at once; **torno ~** I'll be right back.

sublime *agg* sublime.

subordinato, -a *agg*: **~ a** (*dipendente da*) dependent on.

suburbano, -a *agg* suburban.

succedere *vi* (*accadere*) to happen; **~ a qn** (*subentrare*) to succeed sb; **che cos'è successo?** what happened?

▶ **succedersi** *vr* to follow one another.

successivamente *avv* afterwards.

successivo, -a *agg* following.

successo, -a ◆ *pp* → **succedere** ◆ *sm* success; **di ~** successful.

successore *sm* successor.

succhiare *vt* to suck.

succhiotto *sm* dummy.

succinto, -a *agg* (*conciso*) succinct; (*abito*) scanty.

succo, -chi *sm* juice; **~ di frutta** fruit juice; **~ di pomodoro** tomato juice.

sud ◆ *sm* south ◆ *agg inv* south; **a ~ (di qc)** south (of sthg); **nel ~** in the south.

Sudafrica *sm*: **il ~** South Africa.

Sudamerica *sm*: **il ~** South America.

sudare *vi* to sweat.

suddetto, -a *agg* abovementioned.

suddividere *vt* to subdivide.

sudest *sm* southeast.

sudicio, -a, -ci, -ce o **-cie** *agg* dirty.

sudore *sm* sweat.

sudovest *sm* southwest.

sue → **suo.**

sufficiente ♦ agg (che basta) enough, sufficient; (tono, atteggiamento) arrogant ♦ sm (SCOL) pass.

sufficienza sf: a ~ enough.

suffragio sm (voto) vote; ~ universale universal suffrage.

suggerimento sm suggestion.

suggerire vt (consigliare) to suggest; (risposta) to tell.

suggestionare vt to influence.

suggestivo, -a agg evocative.

sughero sm cork.

sugli = su + gli, → su.

sugo, -ghi sm (condimento) sauce; (di arrosto) juices (pl); (succo) juice; ~ di pomodoro tomato sauce.

sui = su + i, → su.

suicidarsi vr to commit suicide.

suicidio sm suicide.

suino, -a ♦ agg pork (dav s) ♦ sm pig.

sul = su + il, → su.

sull' = su + l', → su.

sulla = su + la, → su.

sulle = su + le, → su.

sullo = su + lo, → su.

suo (f sua, mpl suoi, fpl sue) ♦ agg (di lui) his; (di lei) her; (di esso, essa) its; (forma di cortesia) your; (proprio) one's ♦ pron (di lui) his; (di lei) hers; (di esso, essa) its; (forma di cortesia) yours; (proprio) one's; **i suoi** (di lui) his family; (di lei) her family.

suocero, -a sm, f father-in-law (f mother-in-law).

► **suoceri** smpl in-laws.

suoi → suo.

suola sf sole.

suolo sm (terra) ground; (terreno) soil.

suonare ♦ vt (strumento) to play; (campanello) to ring; (clacson) to sound; (allarme) to set off; (ore) to strike ♦ vi (musicista) to play; (telefono, campana) to ring; (allarme, sveglia) to go off; (fig: parole) to sound.

suono sm sound.

suora sf nun.

super sf inv four-star (petrol) (Br), premium (Am).

superare vt (confine, traguardo, fiume) to cross; (limite) to exceed; (veicolo) to overtake; (esame, concorso, prova) to pass; (ostacolo) to overcome; (essere migliore di) to beat; **ha superato la trentina** he is over 30.

superbo, -a agg (arrogante) haughty; (grandioso) superb.

superficiale agg superficial.

superficie, -ci sf surface; (MAT) area.

superfluo, -a agg superfluous.

superiore ♦ sm, f superior ♦ agg (di sopra) upper; (quantità, numero) larger, greater; (prezzo) higher; (qualità) superior; **di età ~ ai 26 anni** above 26.

superlativo sm superlative.

supermercato sm supermarket.

superstrada sf ≃ (toll-free) motorway (Br), ≃ (toll-free) expressway (Am).

suppergiù avv more or less.

supplementare agg extra.

supplemento sm supplement; (di prezzo) extra charge; ~ **rapido** additional charge for fast train.

supplente smf (SCOL) supply teacher.

supporre vt to suppose.

supposta sf suppository.

supposto, -a pp → supporre.

surriscaldare vt to overheat.

suscitare vt to arouse.

susina sf plum.

susseguire vt to follow.

► **susseguirsi** vr to follow one another.

sussidio sm subsidy.

sussulto sm (sobbalzo) start.

sussurrare vt to whisper.

svagarsi vr (divertirsi) to enjoy o.s.; (distrarsi) to take one's mind off things.

svago, -ghi sm (divertimento) fun; (passatempo) pastime.

svaligiare vt to burgle.

svalutare *vt* to devalue.

svanire *vi* to disappear, to vanish.

svantaggio *sm* (*aspetto negativo*) disadvantage; **essere in ~** (SPORT) to be behind.

svariato, -a *agg* (*vario*) varied; (*numeroso*) various.

svedese ♦ *agg* & *sm* Swedish ♦ *smf* Swede.

sveglia *sf* (*orologio*) alarm clock; **la ~ è alle sei** we have to get up at six.

svegliare *vt* to wake (up).

▶ **svegliarsi** *vr* to wake up.

sveglio, -a *agg* (*desto*) awake; (*intelligente*) smart.

svelare *vt* to reveal.

svelto, -a *agg* quick; **alla svelta** quickly.

svendita *sf* sale.

svenire *vi* to faint.

sventare *vt* to foil.

sventolare ♦ *vt* to wave ♦ *vi* to flutter.

sventura *sf* (*sfortuna*) bad luck, misfortune; (*disgrazia*) disaster.

svenuto, -a *pp* → svenire.

svestire *vt* to undress.

▶ **svestirsi** *vr* to get undressed.

Svezia *sf*: **la ~** Sweden.

sviare *vt* to distract; **~ il discorso** to change the subject.

svignarsela *vr* (*fam*) to sneak off.

sviluppare *vt* to develop.

▶ **svilupparsi** *vr* (*ragazzo*) to grow; (*industria, attività*) to expand, to grow; (*incendio, infezione*) to spread.

sviluppo *sm* development; **età dello ~** puberty.

svincolo *sm* (*stradale*) motorway junction.

svitare *vt* to unscrew.

Svizzera *sf*: **la ~** Switzerland.

svizzero, -a *agg* & *sm, f* Swiss.

svogliato, -a *agg* listless.

svolgere *vt* (*attività, lavoro*) to carry out; (*srotolare*) to unroll, to unwind; (*tema*) to write.

▶ **svolgersi** *vr* (*fatto, film*) to take

place; (*srotolarsi*) to unwind.

svolta *sf* turn; (*mutamento*) turning point.

svoltare *vi* to turn; **~ a sinistra** to turn left.

svolto, -a *pp* → svolgere.

svuotare *vt* to empty.

T

tabaccaio, -a *sm, f* tobacconist.

tabaccheria *sf* tobacconist's.

tabacco, -chi *sm* tobacco.

tabella *sf* (*cartellone*) board; (*prospetto*) table; **~ oraria** timetable.

tabellone *sm* (*con orari*) timetable (board); (*per affissioni*) billboard.

tabù *sm inv* taboo.

tacca, -che *sf* notch.

taccagno, -a *agg* mean.

tacchino *sm* turkey.

tacciare *vt*: **~ qn di qc** to accuse sb of sthg.

tacco, -chi *sm* heel; **tacchi a spillo** stilettos.

taccuino *sm* notebook.

tacere ♦ *vi* to be quiet ♦ *vt* to keep quiet about.

taciturno, -a *agg* taciturn.

tafano *sm* horsefly.

tafferuglio *sm* brawl.

taglia *sf* (*misura*) size; (*corporatura*) build; **~ unica** one size.

tagliacarte *sm inv* paper knife.

taglialegna *sm inv* woodcutter.

tagliando *sm* coupon.

tagliare *vt* to cut; (*affettare*) to slice; (*carne*) to carve; (*legna*) to chop; (*recidere*) to cut off; (*ritagliare*) to cut out; (*intersecare*) to cut across; (*vino*) to mix; **~ corto** to cut short; **~ la strada a qn** to cut in front of sb;

tagliarsi i capelli to have one's hair cut.

▶ **tagliarsi** *vr* to cut o.s.

tagliatelle *sfpl* tagliatelle (*sg*).

tagliaunghie *sm inv* nail clippers (*pl*).

tagliente *agg* sharp.

tagliere *sm* chopping board.

taglio *sm* cut; (*di stoffa*) length; (*parte tagliente*) edge; **~ cesareo** (MED) caesarean section; **banconote di piccolo/grosso ~** small/large denomination bank notes.

tagliuzzare *vt* to cut into small pieces.

tailleur [ta'jœr] *sm inv* suit (*for women*).

Taiwan *sm*: **il ~** Taiwan.

talco *sm* talcum powder.

tale *agg dimostrativo* **1.** (*di questo tipo*) such; **non ammetto tali atteggiamenti** I won't allow such behaviour.

2. (*così grande*): **mi hai fatto una ~ paura!** you gave me such a fright!; **è un ~ disordinato!** he's so untidy!; **fa un ~ freddo!** it's so cold!; **è di una gentilezza ~ che non si può dirgli di no** he's so nice (that) you can't say no to him; **fa un rumore ~ da farti venire il mal di testa** it makes so much noise (that) it gives you a headache.

3. (*in paragoni*): **~ ... ~** like ... like; **~ madre ~ figlia** like mother like daughter; **~ quale** just like; **è ~ quale lo ricordavo** he's just like I remembered.

◆ *agg indefinito* (*non precisato*): **ti cerca un tal signor Marchi** someone called Mr Marchi is looking for you; **il giorno ~ all'ora ~** on such and such a day at such and such a time.

◆ *pron indefinito* (*persona non precisata*): **un ~ mi ha chiesto di te** some man asked me about you; **quel ~** that person.

taleggio *sm a type of soft cheese from Lombardy*.

talento *sm* talent.

talloncino *sm* counterfoil.

tallone *sm* heel.

talmente *avv* so.

talora *avv* sometimes.

talpa *sf* mole.

talvolta *avv* sometimes.

tamburellare *vi* to drum.

tamburello *sm* (*strumento*) tambourine; (*gioco*) *ball game played with a round bat*.

tamburo *sm* drum.

Tamigi *sm*: **il ~** the Thames.

tamponamento *sm* collision; **~ a catena** pileup.

tamponare *vt* (AUTO) to bump into; (*ferita*) to plug.

tampone *sm* (MED) wad; (*assorbente interno*) tampon.

tana *sf* den.

tandem *sm inv* tandem.

tanfo *sm* stench.

tanga *sm inv* tanga.

tangente *sf* (MAT) tangent; (*quota*) share.

tangenziale *sf* bypass.

tango, -ghi *sm* tango.

tanica, -che *sf* (*recipiente*) (jerry) can.

tantino : **un tantino** *avv* a little, a bit.

tanto, -a *agg* **1.** (*in grande quantità*) a lot of, much; (*così tanto*) such a lot of, so much; **abbiamo ancora ~ tempo** we've still got a lot of time; **lo conosco da ~ tempo** I've known him for a long time.

2. (*in numero elevato*): **tanti(-e)** a lot of, many; (*così tanti*) such a lot of, so many; **ho tanti amici** I've got a lot of o many friends; **tanti auguri!** all the best!; (*di compleanno*) happy birthday!

3. (*in paragoni*): **~ ... quanto** (*quantità*) as much ... as; (*numero*) as many ... as; **non ho tanta immaginazione quanta ne hai tu** I haven't got as much imagination as you; **ha tanti fratelli quante sorelle** he's got as many brothers as sisters.

◆ *pron* **1.** (*una grande quantità*) a lot,

much; (*così tanto*) such a lot, so much; **mi piace il cioccolato e ne mangio ~** I like chocolate and eat a lot of it; **c'è ~ da fare** there's a lot o plenty to do.

2. (*un grande numero*): **tanti(-e)** many, a lot; (*così tanti*) so many, such a lot; **è una ragazza come tante** she's just an ordinary girl; **l'hanno visto in tanti** many people saw it.

3. (*una quantità indeterminata*): **di questi soldi tanti sono per la casa, tanti per le tue spese** so much of this money is for the house and so much for your expenses; **pago un ~ al mese** I pay so much per month.

4. (*in paragoni*): **~ quanto** as much as; **tanti quanti** as many as.

5. (*in espressioni*): **~ vale che tu stia a casa** you may as well stay at home; **di ~ in ~** from time to time.

♦ *avv* **1.** (*molto*) very; **ti ringrazio ~** thank you very much; **non ~** (*poco*) not much; **~ meglio!** so much the better!

2. (*così*) so; **è ~ sciocco da crederci** he's silly enough to believe it; **è ~ grasso che non ci passa** he's so fat that he can't get through; **non pensavo piovesse ~** I didn't think it rained so much.

3. (*in paragoni*): **~ ... quanto** as ... as; **non studia ~ quanto potrebbe** he doesn't study as much as he could.

4. (*soltanto*): **~ per divertirsi/parlare** just for enjoyment/for the sake of talking; **~ per cambiare** just for a change; **una volta ~** for once.

♦ *cong* after all.

tappa *sf* (*fermata*) stop; (*parte di tragitto, nel ciclismo*) stage.

tappare *vt* (*buco, falla*) to plug; (*bottiglia*) to cork; **tapparsi le orecchie** to turn a deaf ear.

tapparella *sf* store.

tappeto *sm* (*da pavimento*) carpet; (*più piccolo*) rug; **mandare qn al ~** (SPORT) to floor sb.

tappezzare *vt* (*pareti*) to paper; (*poltrona*) to cover.

tappezzeria *sf* (*tessuto*) soft furnishings (*pl*); (*carta da parati*) wallpaper.

tappo *sm* (*di plastica, metallo*) top; (*di sughero*) cork; (*fam: spreg: persona bassa*) shorty.

taralli *smpl* ring-shaped biscuits flavoured with aniseed and pepper (*a speciality of southern Italy*).

tarantella *sf* tarantella (*a folk dance from the South of Italy*).

tarantola *sf* tarantula.

tarchiato, -a *agg* stocky.

tardare ♦ *vi* (*arrivare tardi*) to be late ♦ *vt* (*ritardare*) to delay; **~ a fare qc** to be late in doing sthg.

tardi *avv* late; **fare ~** to be late; **più ~** later; **a più ~!** see you later!; **al più ~** at the latest; **sul ~** late in the day.

targa, -ghe *sf* (*di auto*) number-plate; (*con indicazione*) plate.

targhetta *sf* (*su campanello*) name-plate; (*piccola targa*) tag.

tariffa *sf* rate; (*di trasporti*) fare; **~ ridotta** reduced fare; **~ unica** flat rate.

tarlo *sm* woodworm.

tarma *sf* moth.

tarocchi *smpl* tarot cards.

tartagliare *vi* to stammer, to stutter.

tartaro *sm* tartar.

tartaruga, -ghe *sf* (*di terra*) tortoise; (*di mare*) turtle; (*materiale*) tortoiseshell.

tartina *sf* canapé.

tartufo *sm* (*fungo*) truffle; (*gelato*) type of chocolate ice cream.

tasca, -sche *sf* pocket.

tascabile ♦ *agg* pocket (*dav s*) ♦ *sm* paperback.

taschino *sm* breast pocket.

tassa *sf* (*imposta*) tax; (*per servizio*) fee; **~ di iscrizione** membership fee.

tassametro *sm* taximeter.

tassare *vt* to tax.

tassativo, -a *agg* peremptory.

tassello *sm* plug.

tassì = **taxi**.

tassista, -i, -e *smf* taxi driver.

tasso *sm* (*indice*) rate; (*percentuale*) percentage; (*animale*) badger; **~ di cambio** exchange rate.

tastare *vt* (*polso*) to take; **~ il terreno** (*fig*) to see how the land lies.

tastiera *sf* keyboard.

tasto *sm* (*di pianoforte, computer*) key; (*di TV, radio*) button.

tastoni *avv:* **procedere (a) ~** to feel one's way.

tattico, -a, -ci, -che *agg* tactical.

tatto *sm* (*senso*) touch; (*fig: accortezza*) tact.

tatuaggio *sm* tattoo.

tatuare *vt* to tattoo.

tavola *sf* (MATH, *mobile*) table; (*asse*) plank; **mettersi o andare a ~** to sit down to eat; **~ calda** snack bar.

tavoletta *sf* bar.

tavolino *sm* (*da salotto*) small table; (*di bar*) table; (*scrivania*) writing desk.

tavolo *sm* table.

taxi *sm inv* taxi.

tazza *sf* cup; (*del water*) toilet bowl; **una ~ di caffè** a cup of coffee.

tazzina *sf* coffee cup.

T.C.I. (*abbr di Touring Club Italiano*) = AA, ≃ RAC.

te *pron* you, → **ti**.

tè *sm inv* tea.

teatrale *agg* theatrical.

teatrino *sm* puppet theatre.

teatro *sm* theatre; **~ dell'opera** opera house; **~ tenda** *marquee used for public performances*.

tecnica, -che *sf* technique; (*tecnologia*) technology, → **tecnico**.

tecnico, -a, -ci, -che ◆ *agg* technical ◆ *sm, f* technician.

tecnologia *sf* technology.

tecnologico, -a, -ci, -che *agg* technological.

tedesco, -a, -schi, -sche *agg, sm & sf* German.

tegame *sm* pan.

teglia *sf* baking tin.

tegola *sf* tile.

teiera *sf* teapot.

tel. (*abbr di telefono*) tel.

tela *sf* (*tessuto*) cloth; (*quadro*) canvas; **~ cerata** oilcloth.

telaio *sm* (*per tessere*) loom; (*di macchina*) chassis; (*di finestra, letto*) frame.

telecamera *sf* television camera.

telecomando *sm* remote control.

telecronaca, -che *sf* television report.

teleferica, -che *sf* cableway.

telefilm *sm inv* TV film (Br), TV movie (Am).

telefonare *vi & vt* to (tele)phone; **~ a qn** to (tele)phone sb.

telefonata *sf* (tele)phone call; **~ a carico (del destinatario)** reverse charge call.

telefonico, -a, -ci, -che *agg* (tele)phone (*dav s*).

telefonino *sm* mobile phone.

telefonista, -i, -e *smf* switchboard operator.

telefono *sm* telephone; **~ cellulare** mobile phone; **~ a gettoni** payphone; **~ pubblico** public phone; (*cabina*) call box; **~ a scatti** metered phone; **~ a scheda (magnetica)** cardphone; **al ~** on the phone; **per ~** by phone.

telegiornale *sm* television news (*sg*).

telegrafare *vt & vi* to cable, to telegraph.

telegramma, -i *sm* telegram.

telenovela *sf* soap opera.

teleobiettivo *sm* telephoto lens.

Telepass® *sm inv* motorway toll card.

teleromanzo *sm* serial.

teleschermo *sm* television screen.

telescopio *sm* telescope.

teleselezione *sf* direct dialling.

televisione *sf* television; **alla ~** on television.

televisivo, -a agg television (dav s).

televisore sm television (set); ~ in bianco e nero black-and-white television; ~ a colori colour television.

telex sm inv telex.

telo sm cloth.

tema, -i sm (argomento, soggetto) topic, subject; (SCOL) essay; (MUS) theme.

temere ◆ vt to fear, to be afraid of ◆ vi to be afraid; **temo che non venga** I'm afraid he won't come; **temo di no** I'm afraid not; **temo di sì** I'm afraid so; **temo di non farcela** I'm afraid I can't make it ▶ **temere per** v + prep to fear for.

tempera sf tempera.

temperamatite sm inv pencil sharpener.

temperamento sm (carattere) temperament; (carattere forte) strong character.

temperato, -a agg (clima, stagione) temperate.

temperatura sf temperature.

temperino sm (coltello) penknife; (temperamatite) pencil sharpener.

tempesta sf storm; ~ di neve blizzard.

tempestare vt: ~ qn di domande to bombard sb with questions.

tempestivo, -a agg timely.

tempestoso, -a agg stormy.

tempia sf temple (ANAT).

tempio sm temple (building).

tempo sm (cronologico, ritmo) time; (meteorologico) weather; (GRAMM) tense; (di partita) half; (di film) part; **quanto ~ ci vuole?** how long does it take?; **avere il ~ di** o **per fare qc** to have the time to do sth; **fare qc per ~** to do sth in time; **perdere ~** to waste time; ~ **di cottura** cooking time; ~ **libero** free time; ~ **fa** some time ago; **in ~** in time; **allo stesso ~** at the same time.

temporale ◆ agg (GRAMM) of time ◆ sm (thunder)storm.

temporaneo, -a agg temporary.

temporeggiare vi to play for time.

tenace agg (persona, carattere) tenacious.

tenacia sf tenacity.

tenaglie sfpl pliers.

tenda sf (di finestra) curtain; (da campeggio) tent; ~ **canadese** ridge tent.

tendenza sf tendency.

tendere vt (elastico, muscoli) to stretch; (corda) to tighten; (mano) to hold out.

▶ **tendere a** v + prep: ~ **a qc** (propendere per) to be inclined to sth; (essere simile a) to verge on sth; ~ **a fare qc** to tend to do sth.

tendine sm tendon.

tenebre sfpl darkness (sg).

tenente sm lieutenant.

tenere vt 1. (reggere) to hold; ~ **qc in mano** to hold sth (in one's hand); ~ **qn per mano** to hold sb by the hand.

2. (mantenere) to keep; ~ **la finestra aperta** to keep the window open; ~ **le mani in tasca** to keep one's hands in one's pockets; ~ **qc a mente** to remember sth; ~ **il posto a qn** to keep a seat for sb; ~ **qn occupato** to keep sb busy; **tenga pure il resto** keep the change.

3. (promessa, segreto) to keep.

4. (conferenza, riunione) to hold; ~ **un discorso** to make a speech.

5. (non allontanarsi da): ~ **la destra/sinistra** to keep right/left; ~ **la strada** to hold the road.

6. (in espressioni): **tieni!** (dando qc) here!; **la lana tiene caldo** wool is warm; ~ **compagnia a qn** to keep sb company; ~ **conto di qc** to take sth into account; ~ **d'occhio qn** to keep an eye on sb.

◆ vi (corda, diga) to hold; **questa colla non tiene** this glue isn't sticking; ~ **duro** to hold out.

▶ **tenere a** v + prep (dare importanza a) to care about; ~ **a fare qc** to be keen to do sthg.

▶ **tenere per** *v + prep* (*fare il tifo per*) to support; **per che squadra tieni?** which team do you support?

▶ **tenersi** *vr* 1. (*reggersi*): **tenersi (a)** to hold on (to); **tieni forte!** hold on! 2. (*restare*): **tieni pronto** be ready; **tenersi in disparte** to stand apart; **tenersi a disposizione di qn** to be at sb's disposal; **tenersi a distanza** to keep one's distance. 3. (*aver luogo*) to be held.

tenerezza *sf* tenderness.

tenero, -a *agg* (*cibo*) tender; (*materia*) soft.

tenia *sf* tapeworm.

tennis *sm* tennis; **~ da tavolo** table tennis.

tennista, -i, -e *smf* tennis player.

tenore *sm* (*tono*) tone; (MUS) tenor; **~ di vita** standard of living.

tensione *sf* tension; **alta ~** high voltage.

tentacolo *sm* tentacle.

tentare *vt* (*sperimentare*) to try; (*allettare*) to tempt; **~ di fare qc** to try o to attempt to do sthg.

tentativo *sm* attempt.

tentazione *sf* temptation.

tentennare *vi* (*oscillare*) to wobble; (*esitare*) to hesitate.

tentoni *avv*: **andare (a) ~** to feel one's way.

tenuta *sf* (*abbigliamento*) clothes (*pl*); (*di liquidi, gas*) capacity; (*podere*) estate; **a ~ d'aria** airtight; **~ di strada** roadholding.

teoria *sf* theory; **in ~** in theory.

teoricamente *avv* theoretically.

teorico, -a, -ci, -che *agg* theoretical.

tepore *sm* warmth.

teppista, -i, -e *smf* hooligan.

tequila [te'kila] *sf inv* tequila.

terapeutico, -a, -ci, -che *agg* therapeutic.

terapia *sf* therapy.

tergicristallo *sm* windscreen wiper.

tergiversare *vi* to avoid the issue.

tergo *sm*: **a ~** overleaf.

terital® *sm* Terylene®.

termale *agg* thermal.

terme *sfpl* (*stabilimento*) spa (*sg*); (*nell'antica Roma*) baths.

termico, -a, -ci, -che *agg* (*di temperatura*) thermal.

terminal *sm inv* (air) terminal.

terminale ♦ *agg* final ♦ *sm* terminal.

terminare ♦ *vt* to finish ♦ *vi* to end.

termine *sm* (*fine*) end; (*scadenza*) deadline; (*parola*) term; **portare o condurre a ~ qc** to bring sthg to a conclusion; **a breve/lungo ~** short-/long-term; **senza mezzi termini** without beating about the bush.

▶ **termini** *smpl* terms.

termite *sf* termite.

termometro *sm* thermometer.

termos = **thermos**.

termosifone *sm* radiator.

termostato *sm* thermostat.

terra *sf* (*pianeta*) Earth; (*terraferma, territorio*) land; (*suolo*) ground; (*sostanza*) soil; (SPORT) clay; **a o per ~** (*sedere*) on the ground; (*cadere*) to the ground; **essere a ~** to feel low; **essere ~ ~** to be down to earth.

terracotta *sf* terracotta.

terraferma *sf* dry land.

terrapieno *sm* embankment.

terrazza *sf* terrace.

terrazzo *sm* (*balcone*) balcony; (*di terreno*) terrace.

terremoto *sm* earthquake.

terreno, -a ♦ *agg* (*vita*) earthly; (*beni*) worldly ♦ *sm* (*suolo*) land; (*appezzamento*) plot of land.

terreo, -a *agg* wan.

terrestre *agg* (*del pianeta*) of the Earth; (*di terraferma*) land (*dav s*).

terribile *agg* terrible; (*irrequieto*) wild.

terrificante agg terrifying.

terrina sf tureen.

territoriale agg territorial.

territorio sm (nazionale, straniero) territory; (montuoso, desertico) region.

terrore sm terror.

terrorismo sm terrorism.

terrorista, -i, -e smf terrorist.

terrorizzare vt to terrorize.

terso, -a agg clear.

terza sf (marcia) third gear.

terzetto sm trio.

terzino sm fullback.

terzo, -a num third; **la terza età** old age.

▶ **terzi** smpl (altri) others, → **sesto**.

terzultimo, -a sm, f third from last.

tesa sf brim.

teschio sm skull.

tesi sf inv theory; ~ **(di laurea)** thesis.

teso, -a ♦ pp → **tendere** ♦ agg (corda) taut; (faccia, situazione) tense; (rapporti) strained.

tesoreria sf treasury.

tesoro sm (oggetti preziosi, denaro) treasure; (naturale) resources (pl); (fam: appellativo) darling; **ministro del Tesoro** Chancellor of the Exchequer (Br), Secretary of the Treasury (Am).

tessera sf membership card; ~ **magnetica** magnetic card.

tessere vt to weave.

tessile agg textile (dav s).

tessitura sf weaving.

tessuto sm (stoffa) material; (muscolare, osseo) tissue.

test sm inv test; ~ **di gravidanza** pregnancy test.

testa sf head; **di** ~ (vagone) front; **mettersi in** ~ **di fare qc** to set one's mind on doing sthg; **dalla** ~ **ai piedi** from head to foot; **essere in** ~ **(a qc)** to be in the lead (in sthg); **fare qc di** ~ **propria** to do sthg off one's own bat; **montarsi la** ~ to become bigheaded; **perdere la** ~ to lose

one's head; **dare alla** ~ **a qn** to go to sb's head; **essere fuori di** ~ to be out of one's mind; **fare a** ~ **o croce** to toss up; **a** ~ each.

testamento sm will.

testardo, -a agg stubborn.

testaroli smpl broad pasta in a 'pesto' sauce (a speciality of La Spezia).

teste smf witness.

testicolo sm testicle.

testimone smf witness.

testimoniare ♦ vt (il vero, falso) to testify; (provare) to prove ♦ vi to testify.

testina sf head.

testo sm text.

testone, -a sm, f stubborn person.

testuggine sf tortoise.

tetano sm tetanus.

tetro, -a agg gloomy.

tettarella sf teat.

tette sfpl (fam) boobs.

tetto sm roof; **i senza** ~ the homeless.

tettoia sf canopy.

Tevere sm: **il** ~ the Tiber.

TG sm inv TV news (sg).

thermos sm inv Thermos flask®.

thriller sm inv thriller.

ti (diventa **te** se precede lo, la, li, le, ne) pron (complemento oggetto) you; (complemento di termine) (to) you; (riflessivo) yourself; **te lo do** I'll give them to you.

tibia sf tibia.

tic sm inv (nervoso) tic; (rumore) tick.

ticchettio sm ticking.

ticket sm inv (MED) prescription charge.

tiepido, -a agg lukewarm.

tifare : tifare per v + prep to support.

tifo sm (SPORT): **fare il** ~ **per** to be a fan of.

tifone sm typhoon.

tifoso, -a sm, f supporter, fan.

tiglio sm lime.

tigrato, -a agg striped.

tigre *sm o f* tiger.

tilt *sm*: **andare in ~** to stop functioning.

timballo *sm* pie.

timbrare *vt* to stamp.

timbro *sm* (*arnese, marchio*) stamp; (*di voce*) timbre.

timer ['taimer] *sm inv* timer.

timidezza *sf* shyness.

timido, -a *agg* (*persona, sguardo*) shy, timid; (*tentativo, accenno*) bashful.

timo *sm* thyme.

timone *sm* rudder.

timore *sm* fear.

timpano *sm* eardrum.

tinello *sm* small dining room.

tingere *vt* to dye; **tingersi i capelli** to dye one's hair.

tinozza *sf* tub.

tinta *sf* (*materiale*) paint; (*colore*) colour; **farsi la ~** (*dal parrucchiere*) to have one's hair dyed; **in ~ unita** in one colour.

tintarella *sf* (*fam*) suntan.

tintinnare *vi* to tinkle.

tinto, -a ♦ *pp* → **tingere** ♦ *agg* dyed.

tintoria *sf* dry cleaner's.

tintura *sf*: **~ di iodio** iodine.

tipa *sf* (*fam*) (*donna*) woman; (*ragazza*) girl.

tipico, -a, -ci, -che *agg* typical.

tipo *sm* (*specie*) type, kind; (*modello*) type; (*fam: individuo*) bloke (Br), guy (Am).

tipografia *sf* (*stabilimento*) printing works (*sg*).

tipografo, -a *sm, f* printer.

TIR *sm inv* (*abbr di Transports Internationaux Routiers*) HGV.

tiramisù *sm inv* dessert made from sponge soaked in coffee and covered with sweetened cream cheese and cocoa.

tiranno, -a *sm, f* tyrant.

tirare ♦ *vt* to pull; (*lanciare*) to throw; (*riga, tende*) to draw; (*sparare*) to fire ♦ *vi* to be tight; **tira vento** it's windy; **~ calci contro qc** to kick sthg;

~ diritto to go straight on; **~ fuori** to pull out; **~ a indovinare** to guess; **~ a sorte** to draw lots; **~ su** to lift; **tirarsi indietro** (*rinunciare*) to draw back; **'tirare'** (*su porta*) 'pull'.

tiratore *sm* shot.

tiratura *sf* (*di giornale*) circulation.

tirchio, -a *agg* (*fam*) mean.

tiro *sm* (*d'arma*) shooting; (SPORT) shot; (*traino*) draught; **~ con l'arco** archery; **giocare un brutto ~ a qn** to play a nasty trick on sb.

tirocinio *sm* apprenticeship.

tiroide *sf* thyroid.

tirrenico, -a, -ci, -che *agg* Tyrrhenian.

Tirreno *sm*: **il (mar) ~** the Tyrrhenian Sea.

tisana *sf* herb tea.

titolare *smf* owner.

titolo *sm* title; **~ di studio** academic qualification; **titoli di credito** instruments of credit.

titubante *agg* hesitant.

tivù *sf inv* (*fam*) TV, telly (Br).

tizio, -a *sm, f* person.

tizzone *sm* ember.

toast [tɔst] *sm inv* toasted sandwich.

toccare ♦ *vt* to touch; (*tastare*) to feel; (*argomento*) to touch on; (*riguardare*) to concern ♦ *vi* to touch the bottom; **'vietato ~'** 'do not touch'.

▶ **toccare a** *v + prep* (*spettare*) to be up to; (*capitare*) to happen to; **a chi tocca?** whose turn is it?; **mi tocca ricomprarlo** I have to buy it back.

tocco, -chi *sm* touch.

toga, -ghe *sf* (*di magistrato*) robe.

togliere *vt* (*rimuovere*) to take off; (*privare di*) to take away; (*liberare*) to get out; **~ qc a qn** to take sthg (away) from sb; **ciò non toglie che ...** this doesn't mean that ...; **togliersi gli occhiali** to take one's glasses off; **~ l'appetito a qn** to put sb off his food.

toilette [twa'lɛt] *sf inv* toilet.

tollerabile *agg* tolerable.

tollerante *agg* tolerant.

tollerare *vt* to tolerate.

tolto, -a *pp* → **togliere**.

tomba *sf* grave.

tombino *sm* manhole.

tombola *sf* = bingo.

tonaca, -che *sf* habit.

tonalità *sf inv* (*di colore*) shade; (MUS) key.

tondo, -a *agg* (*circolare*) round.

tonfo *sm* (*rumore*) thud; (*caduta*) fall.

tonico, -a, -ci, -che *agg & sm* tonic.

tonificante *agg* toning, invigorating.

tonificare *vt* to tone up.

tonnellata *sf* ton.

tonno *sm* tuna fish; ~ **in scatola** tinned tuna fish.

tono *sm* tone; **essere giù di ~** to be under the weather.

tonsille *sfpl* tonsils.

tonto, -a *agg* stupid; **fare il finto ~** to pretend not to understand.

top *sm inv* top.

topaia *sf* dump.

topazio *sm* topaz.

topless *sm inv*: **essere in ~** to be topless.

topo *sm* mouse.

toppa *sf* (*di stoffa*) patch; (*di serratura*) keyhole.

torace, -ci *sm* thorax, chest.

torbido, -a *agg* cloudy.

torcere *vt* (*panni*) to wring; (*piegare*) to twist.

▶ **torcersi** *vr* to double up.

torchio *sm* press.

torcia, -ce *sf* torch.

torcicollo *sm* stiff neck.

torero *sm* bullfighter.

Torino *sf* Turin.

tormenta *sf* blizzard.

tormentare *vt* (*procurare fastidio*) to annoy.

▶ **tormentarsi** *vr* to fret.

tormento *sm* (*angoscia*) torment; (*fastidio*) nuisance.

tornaconto *sm* advantage.

tornante *sm* hairpin bend.

tornare *vi* to go/come back; (*ridiventare*) to become again; (*riuscire giusto*) to be correct; ~ **utile** to come in handy; ~ **a casa** to go/come home.

torneo *sm* tournament.

toro *sm* bull.

▶ **Toro** *sm* Taurus.

torre *sf* (*edificio*) tower; (*negli scacchi*) rook; ~ **di controllo** control tower; **la ~ di Pisa** the Leaning Tower of Pisa.

TORRE DI PISA

The famous bell tower of Pisa cathedral, known as the 'Torre Pendente' (Leaning Tower), stands in the magnificent Campo dei Miracoli. The building dates back to the late xIIth century but is now closed to the public. A total of 294 steps lead up the spiral staircase to the bell chamber above. It was from here that Galileo conducted his famous experiments regarding the laws of gravity.

torrefazione *sf* (*negozio*) *shop where coffee is roasted and sold.*

torrente *sm* torrent.

torrido, -a *agg* torrid.

torrione *sm* keep.

torrone *sm* nougat.

torsione *sf* twisting.

torso *sm* torso; **a ~ nudo** barechested.

torsolo *sm* core.

torta *sf* (*dolce*) cake; ~ **gelato** icecream gâteau; ~ **di mele** apple tart; ~ **pasqualina** *puff-pastry tart filled with spinach, ricotta cheese, Parmesan cheese and eggs (a speciality of Genoa);* ~ **salata** flan.

tortellini *smpl* tortellini; ~ **all'emiliana** *'tortellini' filled with pork, ham, Parmesan cheese and spices, generally served in broth.*

tortiera *sf* cake tin.

tortino *sm* pie.

torto, -a ♦ *pp* → **torcere** ♦ *sm* (*ingiustizia*) wrong; (*colpa*): **avere ~** to be wrong; **a ~** wrongly.

tortora *sf* turtledove.

tortuoso, -a *agg* winding.

tortura *sf* torture.

torturare *vt* to torture.

tosaerba *sm inv o sf inv* lawn-mower.

tosare *vt* (*pecora*) to shear; (*siepe*) to clip.

Toscana *sf*: **la ~** Tuscany.

toscano, -a *agg* Tuscan.

tosse *sf* cough.

tossico, -a, -ci, -che *agg* toxic.

tossicomane *smf* drug addict.

tossire *vi* to cough.

tosta *agg f* → **faccia**.

tostapane *sm inv* toaster.

tostare *vt* to toast.

tot *agg inv & pron inv* (*quantità*) so much; (*numero*) so many (*pl*).

totale *agg & sm* total; **in ~** in total.

totalità *sf*: **la ~ di** all of.

totalizzare *vt* to score.

totano *sm* squid.

totip *sm betting game based on horse racing similar to the pools.*

totocalcio *sm* pools (*pl*).

toupet [tu'pe] *sm inv* toupee.

tournée [tur'ne] *sf inv* tour.

tovaglia *sf* tablecloth.

tovagliolo *sm* napkin.

tozzo, -a ♦ *agg* squat ♦ *sm*: **un ~ di pane** a crust of bread.

tra *prep* (*in mezzo a due*) between; (*in mezzo a molti*) among(st); (*di tempo, distanza*) in; **tenere qn ~ le braccia** to hold sb in one's arms; **quale preferisci ~ questi?** which one of these do you like best?; **detto ~ (di) noi** between me and you; **~ sé e sé** to oneself.

traballare *vi* to stagger.

trabiccolo *sm* (*fam*) car.

traboccare *vi* to overflow.

trabocchetto *sm* trap.

tracannare *vt* to gulp down.

traccia, -ce *sf* (*segno*) mark; (*indizio*) trace.

tracciare *vt* (*solco*) to trace; (*disegnare*) to draw.

tracciato *sm* (*percorso*) route; (*grafico*) graph.

trachea *sf* windpipe.

tracolla *sf* shoulder bag; **a ~** over one's shoulder.

tradimento *sm* (*slealtà*) treachery; (*adulterio*) infidelity; **a ~** by surprise.

tradire *vt* to betray; (*coniuge*) to be unfaithful to.

▶ **tradirsi** *vr* to give o.s. away.

traditore, -trice *sm, f* traitor.

tradizionale *agg* traditional.

tradizione *sf* tradition.

tradotto, -a *pp* → **tradurre**.

tradurre *vt* to translate.

traduttore, -trice *sm, f* translator.

traduzione *sf* translation.

trafelato, -a *agg* breathless.

trafficare ♦ *vt* to deal in ♦ *vi* to busy o.s.

traffico, -ci *sm* (*di veicoli*) traffic; (*di droga, armi*) dealing.

trafiggere *vt* to pierce.

trafiletto *sm* short article.

trafitto, -a *pp* → **trafiggere**.

traforo *sm* tunnel.

tragedia *sf* tragedy.

traghetto *sm* ferry.

tragico, -a, -ci, -che *agg* tragic.

tragitto *sm* journey.

traguardo *sm* finishing line.

traiettoria *sf* trajectory.

trainare *vt* (*tirare*) to tow.

traino *sm* (*operazione*) pulling; (*di auto*) towing.

tralasciare *vt* to leave out.

traliccio *sm* (*per elettricità*) pylon.

tram *sm inv* tram.

trama *sf* plot.

tramandare *vt* to pass on.

trambusto *sm* turmoil.

tramezzino *sm* sandwich.

tramite *prep* through.

tramontana *sf* north wind.

tramonto *sm* sunset.

tramortire *vt* to stun.

trampolino *sm* (*per tuffi*) springboard, divingboard; (*sci*) ski jump.

tramutare *vt*: ~ qn/qc in to change sb/sth into.

▶ **tramutarsi in** *vr + prep* to turn into.

trancio *sm* slice.

tranello *sm* trap.

trangugiare *vt* to gulp down.

tranne *prep* except (for); ~ che unless.

tranquillante *sm* tranquillizer.

tranquillità *sf* (*stato d'animo*) calm; (*di luogo*) peacefulness; (*sicurezza*) peace of mind.

tranquillizzare *vt* to reassure.

▶ **tranquillizzarsi** *vr* to calm down.

tranquillo, -a *agg* quiet; (*non preoccupato*) calm; **stai ~** don't worry.

transalpino, -a *agg* transalpine.

transatlantico, -a, -ci, -che ♦ *agg* transatlantic ♦ *sm* ocean liner.

transatto *pp* → **transigere**.

transazione *sf* transaction.

transenna *sf* barrier.

transigere *vi*: **in fatto di puntualità non transige** she won't stand for people being late.

transistor *sm inv* transistor.

transitabile *agg* passable.

transitare *vi* to pass.

transitivo, -a *agg* (GRAMM) transitive.

transito *sm* transit; **'divieto di ~'** 'no entry'.

transizione *sf* transition.

trapano *sm* drill.

trapassare *vt* to pierce.

trapelare *vi* to leak out.

trapezio *sm* (*di circo*) trapeze.

trapezista, -i, -e *smf* trapeze artist.

trapiantare *vt* to transplant.

trapianto *sm* transplant.

trappola *sf* trap.

trapunta *sf* quilt.

trarre *vt*: ~ **in inganno qn** to deceive sb; ~ **origine da qc** to come from sth; ~ **in salvo qn** to rescue sb; ~ **vantaggio da qc** to benefit from sth.

trasalire *vi* to jump.

trasandato, -a *agg* shabby.

trasbordare ♦ *vt* to transfer ♦ *vi* to change ship/plane/train.

trascinare *vt* to drag.

▶ **trascinarsi** *vr* (*strisciare*) to drag o.s. along; (*nel tempo*) to drag on.

trascorrere ♦ *vt* to spend ♦ *vi* to pass.

trascorso, -a *pp* → **trascorrere**.

trascritto, -a *pp* → **trascrivere**.

trascrivere *vt* to transcribe.

trascurabile *agg* negligible.

trascurare *vt* (*lavoro, persona*) to neglect; (*dettagli*) to disregard.

trascurato, -a *agg* neglected.

trasferibile ♦ *agg* (*biglietto*) transferable ♦ *sm* transfer.

trasferimento *sm* transfer.

trasferire *vt* (*impiegato*) to transfer; (*negozio, sede*) to move.

▶ **trasferirsi** *vr* to move.

trasferta *sf* (*viaggio*) transfer; (*indennità*) travelling expenses (*pl*); (SPORT) away game.

trasformare *vt* to transform; ~ **qc in qc** to turn sth into sth; (*edificio, stanza*) to convert sth into sth.

▶ **trasformarsi** *vr* to change completely; **trasformarsi in** to turn into.

trasformatore *sm* transformer.

trasformazione *sf* transformation.

trasfusione *sf* transfusion.

trasgredire *vt* to disobey.

traslocare *vi* to move.

trasloco, -chi *sm* (*di mobili*) removal; (*trasferimento*) move.

trasmesso, -a *pp* → **trasmettere**.

trasmettere *vt* (RADIO, TV) to broadcast; (*malattia*) to pass on;

(*far pervenire*) to send.

trasmissione *sf* (*programma*) programme; (TECNOL) transmission.

trasparente *agg* (*acqua*) transparent; (*vestito*) see-through.

trasparenza *sf* transparency.

traspirazione *sf* perspiration.

trasportare *vt* to transport.

trasporto *sm* transport.

trastullarsi *vr* (*divertirsi*) to amuse o.s.; (*perdere tempo*) to waste time.

trasversale *agg* (*obliquo*) cross (*dav s*); (*via*) side (*dav s*).

trattamento *sm* treatment.

trattare *vt* (*persona*) to treat; (*argomento*) to discuss; (*negoziare*) to negotiate; (*commerciare*) to deal in.
► **trattare di** *v + prep* to deal with.
► **trattarsi** *vr*: **di cosa si tratta?** what is it about?

trattative *sfpl* negotiations.

trattato *sm* (*patto*) treaty; (*testo*) treatise.

trattenere *vt* (*far rimanere*) to detain; (*lacrime, risa*) to hold back; (*somma*) to deduct; ~ **qn dal fare qc** to stop sb doing sth.
► **trattenersi** *vr* to stay; **quanto si trattiene?** how long are you staying?; **trattenersi dal fare qc** to stop o.s. doing sthg.

trattenuta *sf* deduction.

trattino *sm* (*tra parole*) hyphen; (*per discorso diretto*) dash.

tratto, -a ♦ *pp* → **trarre** ♦ *sm* (*di penna*) stroke; (*di strada, mare*) stretch; **ad un ~, d'un ~** suddenly.
► **tratti** *smpl* features.

trattore *sm* tractor.

trattoria *sf* restaurant specializing in local cuisine.

TRATTORIA

In the past the term 'trattoria' was used to describe an inexpensive family-run restaurant, but today 'trattorie' can be very expensive. They serve traditional Italian food typical of the region in rustic-looking but often upmarket surroundings.

trauma, -i *sm* (*shock*) shock; (MED) trauma.

travagliato, -a *agg* troubled.

travaglio *sm* labour.

travasare *vt* to decant.

trave *sf* beam.

traveggole *sfpl*: **avere le ~** to be seeing things.

traveller's cheque ['traveler 'tʃɛk] *sm inv* traveller's cheque.

traversa *sf* (*via*) side street; (SPORT) crossbar.

traversare *vt* to cross.

traversata *sf* (*marittima*) crossing; (*aerea*) flight.

traverso, -a ♦ *agg* side (*dav s*) ♦ *avv*: **di ~** crosswise.

travestimento *sm* disguise.

travestire *vt* to dress up.
► **travestirsi da** *vr + prep* to dress up as.

travisare *vt* to misinterpret.

travolgere *vt* to sweep away.

travolto, -a *pp* → **travolgere**.

tre *num* three, → **sei**.

treccia, -ce *sf* plait.

trecento *num* three hundred, → **sei**.
► **Trecento** *sm*: **il ~** the fourteenth century.

tredicesima *sf* Christmas bonus.

tredicesimo, -a *num* thirteenth, → **sesto**.

tredici *num* thirteen, → **sei**.

tregua *sf* (*armistizio*) truce; (*sosta*) rest.

trekking *sm* trekking.

tremare *vi*: ~ **(di)** (*paura*) to shake o tremble (with); (*freddo*) to shiver o tremble (with).

tremarella *sf* (*fam*) shivers (*pl*).

tremendo, -a *agg* terrible, awful.

trementina *sf* turpentine.

tremila *num* three thousand, → **sei**.

Tremiti *sfpl*: **le (isole)** ~ the Tremiti Islands.

tremito *sm* shudder.

trenino *sm* toy train.

treno *sm* train; ~ **diretto** fast train; ~ **espresso** express train; ~ **intercity** Intercity train®; ~ **interregionale** long-distance train; ~ **merci** goods train (Br), freight train (Am); ~ **regionale** local train; **'treni in arrivo'** 'arrivals'; **'treni in partenza'** 'departures'.

trenta *num* thirty, → **sei**.

trentesimo, -a *num* thirtieth, → **sesto**.

trentina *sf*: **una** ~ **(di)** about thirty; **essere sulla** ~ to be in one's thirties.

Trentino *sm*: **il** ~**-Alto Adige** Trentino-Alto Adige.

tresca, -sche *sf* intrigue.

triangolare *agg* triangular.

triangolo *sm* triangle.

tribolare *vi* to suffer.

tribù *sf inv* tribe.

tribuna *sf* stand.

tribunale *sm* court.

tributo *sm* tax.

tricheco, -chi *sm* walrus.

triciclo *sm* tricycle.

tricolore *agg* three-coloured.

tridimensionale *agg* three-dimensional.

triennio *sm* three-year period.

Trieste *sf* Trieste.

trifoglio *sm* clover.

trifolato, -a *agg* (*verdura, carne*) cooked in oil, garlic and parsley.

triglia *sf* red mullet.

trimestre *sm* (*tre mesi*) quarter; (SCOL) term.

trincea *sf* trench.

trinciapollo *sm inv* poultry shears (*pl*).

trio *sm* trio.

trionfale *agg* triumphal.

trionfare *vi* (*vincere*) to triumph.

trionfo *sm* triumph.

triplicare *vt* to triple.

triplice *agg* triple.

triplo, -a ◆ *agg* triple ◆ *sm*: **il** ~ three times as much.

trippa *sf* tripe.

triste *agg* sad; (*luogo*) gloomy.

tristezza *sf* (*afflizione*) sadness; (*squallore*) dreariness.

tritacarne *sm inv* mincer (Br), grinder (Am).

tritaghiaccio *sm inv* ice crusher.

tritare *vt* to chop; (*carne*) to mince (Br), to grind (Am).

trito, -a ◆ *agg* chopped ◆ *sm* chopped ingredients (*pl*); ~ **e ritrito** (*fig*) trite.

triturare *vt* to mince (Br), to grind (Am).

trivellare *vt* to drill.

triviale *agg* crude.

trofeo *sm* trophy.

tromba *sf* trumpet; ~ **d'aria** whirlwind; ~ **delle scale** stairwell.

trombone *sm* trombone.

troncare *vt* to cut off.

tronco, -chi *sm* trunk.

trono *sm* throne.

tropicale *agg* tropical.

tropico *sm* tropic; **i tropici** the tropics.

troppo, -a *agg* **1.** (*in quantità eccessiva*) too much; **c'è troppa acqua** there's too much water.

2. (*in numero eccessivo*): **troppi(-e)** too many; **ho mangiato troppi biscotti** I've eaten too many biscuits.

◆ *pron* **1.** (*una quantità eccessiva*) too much; **ho poco tempo libero, tu** ~ I have little free time, you have too much.

2. (*un numero eccessivo*): **troppi(-e)** too many; **non voglio altri problemi, ne ho fin troppi** I don't want any more problems, I've got too many already; **lo sanno in troppi** too many people know.

◆ *avv* **1.** (*in misura eccessiva*) too; **sei** ~ **stanco** you are too tired; **parla** ~ **velocemente** he speaks too quickly; **spendo** ~ I spend too much; **ho bevuto un bicchiere di** ~ I've had one drink too many; **essere di** ~ to

be in the way.
2. (*molto*): **non mi sento ~ bene** I'm not feeling too good.

trota *sf* trout.

trottare *vi* to trot.

trotterellare *vi* to trot along.

trotto *sm* trot.

trottola *sf* spinning top.

troupe [trup] *sf inv* troupe.

trovare *vt* to find; (*per caso*) to come across; **andare a ~ qn** to go and see sb.

▶ **trovarsi** *vr* (*essere, stare*) to be; (*incontrarsi*) to meet.

trovata *sf* good idea.

truccare *vt* (*attore*) to make up; (*motore*) to soup up; (*risultato, partita*) to fix.

▶ **truccarsi** *vr* to make o.s. up.

trucco, -chi *sm* (*artificio, inganno*) trick; (*cosmetico*) make-up; (*operazione*) making-up.

truce *agg* fierce.

trucidare *vt* to slaughter.

truciolo *sm* shaving.

truffa *sf* fraud.

truffare *vt* to swindle.

truffatore, -trice *sm, f* swindler.

trullo *sm* ancient round house with conical roof typical of Apulia.

truppa *sf* troop.

tu ♦ *pron* you ♦ *sm*: **a ~ per ~** face to face; **~ stesso** you yourself; **se lo dici ~!** if you say so!

tubare *vi* to coo.

tubatura *sf* piping, pipes (*pl*).

tubercolosi *sf* tuberculosis.

tubero *sm* tuber.

tubetto *sm* tube.

tubo *sm* pipe; **~ di scappamento** exhaust (pipe).

tue → **tuo**.

tuffarsi *vr* (*in acqua*) to dive.

tuffo *sm* dive.

tulipano *sm* tulip.

tumbada *sf* baked egg custard with crushed macaroons.

tumore *sm* tumour.

tunica, -che *sf* tunic.

Tunisia *sf*: **la ~** Tunisia.

tunnel *sm inv* tunnel.

tuo (*f* **tua**, *mpl* **tuoi**, *fpl* **tue**) ♦ *agg*: **il ~ (la tua)** your ♦ *pron*: **il ~ (la tua)** yours; **~ padre** your father; **un ~ amico** a friend of yours; **questi soldi sono tuoi** this is your money.

tuoi → **tuo**.

tuonare *v impers*: **tuona** it's thundering.

tuono *sm* (*di lampo*) thunder.

tuorlo *sm*: **~ (d'uovo)** yolk.

turacciolo *sm* (*di sughero*) cork; (*di plastica*) top.

turare *vt* (*buco*) to plug; (*orecchie, naso*) to block.

▶ **turarsi** *vr*: **~ il naso** to hold one's nose.

turbamento *sm* (*sconcerto*) anxiety.

turbante *sm* (*copricapo*) turban.

turbare *vt* (*sconcertare*) to trouble.

turbolento, -a *agg* (*persona*) boisterous.

turchese *agg & sm* turquoise.

Turchia *sf*: **la ~** Turkey.

turchino, -a *agg* deep blue.

turismo *sm* tourism.

turista, -i, -e *smf* tourist.

turistico, -a, -ci, -che *agg* tourist (*dav s*).

turno *sm* (*di lavoro*) shift; (*di gioco*) turn; **è il tuo ~** it's your turn; **fare ~ (a fare qc)** to take turns (to do sthg); **essere di ~** to be on duty.

tuta *sf* (*da lavoro*) overalls (*pl*); (*sportiva*) tracksuit.

tutela *sf* protection.

tutelare *vt* to protect.

▶ **tutelarsi** *vr* to protect o.s.

tutina *sf* romper suit.

tuttavia *cong* yet, nevertheless.

tutto, -a *agg* **1.** (*la totalità di*) all (of), the whole (of); **~ il vino** all the wine; **~ il giorno** all day, the whole day; **in tutta Europa** all over Europe; **tutti i presenti** everyone present; **tutte le piante** all the plants; **tutti e cinque** all five of

us/you/them; **tutti e due** both of us/you/them; **tutta una pizza** a whole pizza.
2. (*ogni*): **tutti(-e)** every; **telefona tutti i giorni** he phones every day; **in tutti i casi** in every case; **tutte le volte che** every time (that).
3. (*esclusivamente*) all; **è tutta colpa tua** it's all your fault; **è ~ casa e chiesa** he's a family man and a regular churchgoer.
4. (*molto*) very; **è tutta contenta** she's very happy; **sei ~ sporco** you're all dirty.
♦ *pron* **1.** (*la totalità*) all; **bevilo ~** drink all of it; **li ho visti tutti** I've seen all of them; **in ~** (*nel complesso*) in all; **in ~ fanno 300 000 lire** that's 300,000 lira in all.
2. (*la totalità della gente*): **tutti** everyone, all; **verremo tutti (quanti)** we will all come, everybody will come; **tutti voi** all of you.
3. (*ogni cosa*) everything; **mi ha raccontato ~** he told me everything; **non è ~** that's not everything; **vende di ~** it sells all sorts of things; **mangio un po' di ~** I eat a bit of everything; **in ~ e per ~** completely; **~ compreso** all in; **~ esaurito** sold out; **~ sommato** all things considered.
4. (*qualunque cosa*) anything; **è capace di ~** he's capable of anything.
♦ *avv* (*interamente*) completely; **tutt'altro** anything but; **~ il contrario** quite the opposite; **del ~** completely; **tutt'al più** at the most.
♦ *sm*: **il ~** the lot; **il ~ per ~** everything.
tuttora *avv* still.
tutù *sm inv* tutu.
T.V. *sf inv* TV.
tweed [twid] *sm* tweed.

U

ubbidiente *agg* obedient.
ubbidire *vi* to obey.
ubicazione *sf* location.
ubriacare *vt*: **~ qn** to get sb drunk.
▶ **ubriacarsi** *vr* to get drunk.
ubriaco, -a, -chi, -che *agg & sm, f* drunk.
uccello *sm* bird.
uccidere *vt* to kill.
▶ **uccidersi** *vr* to kill o.s.
udienza *sf* (*colloquio*) audience; (DIR) hearing.
udire *vt* to hear.
udito *sm* hearing.
uffa *esclam* tut!
ufficiale ♦ *agg* official ♦ *sm* (MIL) officer; (*funzionario*): **~ giudiziario** clerk of the court.
ufficialmente *avv* officially.
ufficio *sm* office; **~ cambi** bureau de change; **~ di collocamento** employment office; **~ informazioni** information bureau; **~ oggetti smarriti** lost property office (Br), lost-and-found office (Am); **~ postale** post office; **~ turistico** tourist office.
Uffizi *mpl*: **gli ~** the Uffizi (*art gallery in Florence*).

GLI UFFIZI

Situated by the Arno river in Florence, the Galleria degli Uffizi is one of the world's most important museums. It is called the 'Uffizi' because it was originally built in the xvith century to house government offices. Although it specializes in masterpieces from the Italian Renaissance, the U-shaped gallery also contains countless works of art from other periods and by non-Italian artists.

Ufo *sm inv* UFO.

uggioso, -a *agg* dull.

uguaglianza *sf* equality.

uguagliare *vt* to equal.

uguale ◆ *agg* (*identico*) the same; (*pari*) equal ◆ *avv:* **costano ~** they cost the same; **essere ~ a** (*identico*) to be the same as; (*pari*) to be equal to; (MAT) to equal.

ugualmente *avv* (*in modo uguale*) equally; (*lo stesso*) all the same.

ulcera *sf* ulcer.

uliva = **oliva**.

ulivo = **olivo**.

ulteriore *agg* further.

ultimare *vt* to finish.

ultimatum *sm inv* ultimatum.

ultimo, -a ◆ *agg* last; (*più recente*) latest ◆ *sm, f* last (one); **da ~** in the end; **fino all'~** till the end; **per ~** last; **l'~ piano** the top floor.

ultravioletto, -a *agg* ultraviolet.

umanità *sf* humanity.

umano, -a *agg* human; (*benevolo*) humane.

umidità *sf* (*di clima*) humidity; (*di stanza, muro*) dampness.

umido, -a ◆ *agg* (*bagnato*) damp; (*clima*) humid ◆ *sm:* **in ~** stewed.

umile *agg* humble.

umiliante *agg* humiliating.

umiliare *vt* to humiliate.

▶ **umiliarsi** *vr* to humble o.s.

umiliazione *sf* humiliation.

umore *sm* mood; **essere di buon/cattivo ~** to be in a good/bad mood.

umorismo *sm* humour.

umoristico, -a, -ci, -che *agg* humorous.

un → **uno**.

un' → **uno**.

unanime *agg* unanimous.

unanimità *sf* unanimity; **all'~** unanimously.

uncinetto *sm* crochet hook.

undice...

sesto.

undici *num*...

ungere *vt* (*pa...*) (*macchiare*) to get...

▶ **ungersi** *vr* (*macc...*) ered in grease; **ung... solare** to put suntan lot...

Ungheria *sf:* **l'~** Hungary.

unghia *sf* nail.

unicamente *avv* only.

unico, -a, -ci, -che *agg* (*singolo*) only; (*incomparabile*) unique.

unifamiliare *agg* one-family (*dav* s).

uniformare *vt* (*adeguare*) to adapt; (*superficie*) to level.

▶ **uniformarsi a** *vr + prep* to comply with.

uniforme *agg & sf* uniform.

unione *sf* union; **l'Unione Sovietica** the Soviet Union.

unire *vt* (*mettere insieme*) to join; (*persone*) to unite; (*collegare*) to link; (*mescolare*) to combine.

▶ **unirsi** *vr* (*associarsi*) to join together; (*strade*) to meet.

unità *sf inv* unit; (*unione*) unity; **~ di misura** unit of measurement.

unito, -a *agg* (*amici, parenti*) close; (*da uno scopo*) united; (*oggetti*) joined.

universale *agg* universal.

università *sf inv* university.

universitario, -a *agg* university (*dav* s).

universo *sm* universe.

uno, -a (*dav sm* **un** + *consonante o vocale,* **uno** + *s+consonante, gn, ps, x, z; dav sf* **un'** + *vocale,* **una** + *consonante*) *art indeterminativo* a, an; **~ studente** a student; **una donna** a woman; **un albero** a tree; **un'arancia** an orange; **un giorno ci andrò** one day I'll go; **ho avuto una fortuna!** it was such a stroke of luck!

◆ *pron* 1. (*uno qualunque*) one; **me ne dai ~?** can you give me one (of them)?; **~ dei miei libri/dei migliori** one of my books/of the best; **l'un** ach other, one another; mo tutto l'~ dell'altro they know everything about each other; l'~ o l'altro either (of you/them/us); né l'~ né l'altro neither (of you/them/us); l'~ e l'altro both (of you/them/us).

2. (un tale) someone, somebody; **sta parlando con una** he's talking to some woman.

3. (uso impersonale) one, you; **se ~ può** if one o you can.

♦ num one, → **sei**.

unto, -a ♦ pp → **ungere** ♦ sm grease.

untuoso, -a agg greasy.

uomo (pl **uomini**) sm man; ~ **d'affari** businessman; **da ~** men's.

uovo (pl f **uova**) sm egg; ~ **in camicia** poached egg; ~ **alla coque** boiled egg; ~ **di Pasqua** Easter egg; ~ **sodo** hard-boiled egg; ~ **al tegamino** fried egg; **uova strapazzate** scrambled eggs.

uragano sm hurricane.

urbano, -a agg urban; (telefonata) local.

urgente agg urgent.

urgenza sf (necessità) urgency; (MED) emergency; **essere operato d'~** to have emergency surgery.

urgere vi to be needed urgently.

urina sf urine.

urlare ♦ vi (persona) to scream; (animale) to howl ♦ vt to yell.

urlo sm (di persona: pl f **urla**) scream; (di animale: pl m **urli**) howl.

urna sf: **andare alle urne** to go to the polls.

urrà esclam hurrah!

URSS sf: **l'(ex) ~** the former USSR.

urtare ♦ vt (scontrare) to bump into; (irritare) to annoy ♦ vi: ~ **contro** o **in qc** to bump into sthg.

▶ **urtarsi** vr (scontrarsi) to collide; (irritarsi) to get annoyed.

urto sm crash.

USA smpl: **gli ~** the USA (sg).

usanza sf custom.

usare vt to use; ~ **fare qc** to be in

the habit of doing sthg; **qui usa così** it's the custom here.

usato, -a ♦ agg (consumato) worn; (di seconda mano) used ♦ sm second-hand goods (pl).

usciere, -a sm, f usher.

uscio sm door.

uscire vi to go out; (libro, numero) to come out; ~ **di strada** to go off the road.

uscita sf (porta) exit, way out; (al cinema, ristorante) evening out; (di autostrada) junction; (di libro) publication; (di film) release; (COMM) expenditure; **ci vediamo all'~ da scuola** I'll meet you after school; ~ **di sicurezza** o **emergenza** emergency exit.

usignolo sm nightingale.

uso sm (impiego) use; (abitudine) custom; **fuori ~** out of use; **'per ~ esterno'** 'for external use'.

USSL (abbr di Unità Socio-Sanitaria Locale) local health and social centre.

ustionare vt to burn; **ustionarsi un braccio** to burn one's arm.

ustione sf burn.

usuale agg common.

usufruire : usufruire di v + prep to make use of.

usuraio, -a sm, f moneylender.

utensile sm tool; **utensili da cucina** kitchen utensils.

utente smf user.

utero sm uterus.

utile ♦ agg useful ♦ sm (COMM) profit; **rendersi ~** to be helpful; **posso esserle ~?** can I help you?

utilità sf usefulness; **essere di grande ~** to be of great use.

utilitaria sf economy car.

utilizzare vt to use, to make use of.

utopia sf utopia.

uva sf grapes (pl).

uvetta sf raisins (pl).

V

va → **andare**.

vacanza *sf* holiday (Br), vacation (Am); **andare/essere in ~** to go/be on holiday (Br), to go/be on vacation (Am).

vacca, -che *sf* cow.

vaccinare *vt* to vaccinate.

vaccinazione *sf* vaccination.

vacillare *vi* (*barcollare*) to sway; (*fig: memoria, coraggio*) to be failing.

vado → **andare**.

vagabondo, -a *sm, f* (*senza dimora fissa*) tramp; (*fannullone*) loafer.

vagare *vi* to wander.

vagina *sf* vagina.

vagito *sm* wailing.

vaglia *sm inv* money order; **~ postale** postal order.

vagliare *vt* (*valutare*) to weigh up.

vago, -a, -ghi, -ghe *agg* vague.

vagone *sm* carriage (Br), car (Am); **~ letto** sleeper; **~ ristorante** restaurant car.

vai → **andare**.

valanga, -ghe *sf* avalanche.

Val d'Aosta = **Valle d'Aosta**.

valere ◆ *vi* (*biglietto*) to be valid; (*regola*) to apply; (*avere valore*) to be worth ◆ *vt* (*avere un valore di*) to be worth; (*equivalere a*) to be equal to; **~ la pena di fare qc** to be worth doing sthg; **far ~ qc** to assert sthg; **vale a dire** that is to say.

▶ **valersi di** *vr + prep* to take advantage of.

valevole *agg* valid.

valico, -chi *sm* pass.

validità *sf* validity.

valido, -a *agg* (*valevole*) valid; (*efficace*) effective; (*abile*) capable.

valigia, -gie o **-ge** *sf* suitcase; **fare le valigie** to pack.

vallata *sf* valley.

valle *sf* valley.

▶ **Valle d'Aosta** *sf*: **la Valle d'Aosta** Valle d'Aosta.

valore *sm* value; (*validità*) validity; (*talento*) merit.

▶ **valori** *smpl* (*gioielli*) valuables; (*ideali*) values.

valorizzare *vt* to bring out.

valoroso, -a *agg* courageous.

valso, -a *pp* → **valere**.

valuta *sf* currency.

valutare *vt* (*quadro, persona*) to value; (*valore, peso*) to estimate.

valutazione *sf* (*di un bene*) valuation; (*calcolo sommario*) estimate; (SCOL) assessment.

valvola *sf* (*in meccanica*) valve; (*in elettrotecnica*) fuse.

valzer *sm inv* waltz.

vampata *sf* blaze.

vampiro *sm* vampire.

vandalismo *sm* vandalism.

vandalo, -a *sm, f* vandal.

vanga, -ghe *sf* spade.

vangelo *sm* gospel.

vanificare *vt* to nullify.

vaniglia *sf* vanilla.

vanità *sf* vanity.

vanitoso, -a *agg* vain.

vanno → **andare**.

vano, -a ◆ *agg* vain ◆ *sm* (*stanza*) room; (*apertura*) opening.

vantaggio *sm* advantage; (*in competizioni*) lead; **trarre ~ da qc** to benefit from sthg; **essere in ~** to be in the lead.

vantaggioso, -a *agg* favourable.

vantarsi *vr* to boast; **~ di fare qc** to boast about doing sthg.

vanvera *sf*: **parlare a ~** to talk nonsense.

vapore *sm*: **~ (acqueo)** steam; **cuocere a ~** to steam.

vaporetto *sm* waterbus.

vaporizzatore *sm* spray.

vaporoso, -a *agg* (*abito*) floaty.

varare *vt* (*legge*) to pass; (*nave*) to launch.

varcare vt to cross.

varco, -chi sm passage.

variabile agg variable.

variante sf variation.

variare ♦ vt to vary ♦ vi (modificarsi) to vary; (essere diverso) to fluctuate.

variazione sf variation.

varice sf varicose vein.

varicella sf chickenpox.

variegato, -a agg variegated.

varietà ♦ sf inv variety ♦ sm inv variety show.

vario, -a agg (svariato) varied; (numeroso, diverso) various.

variopinto, -a agg multi-coloured.

vasca, -sche sf (contenitore) tank; (di fontana) basin; (nel nuoto) length; ~ (da bagno) bath.

vaschetta sf basin.

vasellame sm crockery.

vasetto sm (di yogurt) pot; (di marmellata) jar.

vaso sm vase; (per piante) pot.

vassoio sm tray.

vasto, -a agg (superficie) vast.

Vaticano sm: il ~ the Vatican.

IL VATICANO

The Vatican City, situated on the right bank of the Tiber in Rome, is the Pope's official residence. The Basilica of Saint Peter, one of the most magnificent Catholic churches in the world, stands here. The Vatican is an independent country, with its own currency and stamps, and the Pope is the head of state. The vast number of works of art concentrated here make it one of Italy's most important cultural centres.

---

ve → vi.

vecchiaia sf old age.

vecchio, -a ♦ agg old; (sorpassato) old-fashioned ♦ sm, f old man (f old woman).

vece sf: **fare le veci di qn** to take sb's place.

vedere vt & vi to see; **vedrò di fare qualcosa** I'll see what I can do; **questo non ha niente a che ~ con me** this has nothing to do with me; **non la posso ~** (fig) I can't stand her; **non ~ l'ora di fare qc** to look forward to doing sth; **non vedo l'ora di arrivare** I can't wait to get there; **farsi ~ da uno specialista** to see a specialist; **da qui si vede il mare** you can see the sea from there.

▶ **vedersi** vr (guardarsi) to see o.s.; (incontrarsi) to meet; **ci vediamo!** see you!

vedovo, -a sm, f widower (f widow).

veduta sf view.

vegetale ♦ agg vegetable (dav s) ♦ sm plant.

vegetariano, -a agg vegetarian.

vegetazione sf vegetation.

veglia sf wakefulness; ~ **funebre** wake.

veglione sm ball.

veicolo sm vehicle; '**veicoli lenti**' 'slow lane'.

vela sf (tela) sail; (sport) sailing.

velare vt to veil.

veleno sm poison.

velenoso, -a agg (sostanza) poisonous.

velina sf tissue paper.

vellutato, -a agg velvety.

velluto sm velvet; ~ **a coste** cord, corduroy.

velo sm (indumento) veil.

veloce agg fast.

velocemente avv quickly.

velocità sf speed; '~ **max 15 kmh**' = 'maximum speed 10 mph'.

vena sf vein; **non essere in ~ di qc** not to be in the mood for sth.

vendemmia sf grape harvest.

vendemmiare vi to harvest the grapes.

vendere vt to sell; '**vendesi**' 'for sale'.

vendetta sf revenge.

vendicare vt to avenge.

▶ **vendicarsi** *vr* to avenge o.s.; **vendicarsi di** to take one's revenge for; **vendicarsi su qn** to take one's revenge on sb.

vendita *sf* sale; **essere in ~** to be on sale; **'in ~ qui'** 'on sale here'.

venditore, -trice *sm, f* seller; **~ ambulante** pedlar.

venerdì *sm inv* Friday, → **sabato**.

Venezia *sf* Venice.

veneziana *sf* venetian blind, → **veneziano**.

veneziano, -a *agg & sm, f* Venetian.

venire *vi* to come; **mi viene da piangere** I feel like crying; **quanto vengono le mele?** how much are the apples?; **~ bene/male** to turn out well/badly; **~ giù** to come down; **~ via** (*persona*) to leave; (*macchia*) to come out; (*etichetta*) to come off; **~ a sapere qc** to learn sthg.

ventata *sf* gust.

ventesimo, -a *num* twentieth, → **sesto**.

venti *num* twenty, → **sei**.

ventilare *vt* to ventilate.

ventilatore *sm* (*apparecchio*) fan; (*nel muro*) ventilator.

ventina *sf*: **una ~ (di)** about twenty; **essere sulla ~** to be in one's twenties.

vento *sm* wind; **'forte ~ laterale'** 'strong side wind'.

ventosa *sf* (*di gomma*) suction pad.

ventoso, -a *agg* windy.

ventre *sm* stomach.

venturo, -a *agg* next.

venuto, -a → **venire**.

veramente *avv* really.

veranda *sf* veranda.

verbale *sm* (*di riunione*) minutes (*pl*); (*di polizia*) statement.

verbo *sm* verb.

verde ◆ *agg* green ◆ *sm* (*colore*) green; (*vegetazione*) greenery.

verdetto *sm* verdict.

verdura *sf* vegetables (*pl*).

verduraio, -a *sm, f* greengrocer.

vergine *agg* virgin; (*cassetta*) blank.

▶ **Vergine** *sf* Virgo.

vergogna *sf* (*pentimento, scandalo*) shame; (*timidezza*) shyness; (*imbarazzo*) embarrassment; **avere ~ (di)** to be ashamed (of).

vergognarsi *vr*: **~ (di)** (*per disonore*) to be ashamed (of); (*per timidezza*) to be embarrassed (about).

vergognoso, -a *agg* (*scandaloso*) shameful; (*timido*) shy.

verifica, -che *sf* check.

verificare *vt* to check.

▶ **verificarsi** *vr* to happen.

verità *sf* truth; **dire la ~** to tell the truth.

verme *sm* worm.

vermicelli *smpl* vermicelli (*sg*).

vermut *sm inv* vermouth.

vernice *sf* (*sostanza*) paint; (*pelle*) patent leather; **'~ fresca'** 'wet paint'.

verniciare *vt* to paint.

vero, -a ◆ *agg* (*reale*) true; (*autentico*) real, genuine ◆ *sm* truth; **~?** (isn't that) right?

verosimile *agg* likely, probable.

verruca, -che *sf* wart.

versamento *sm* deposit.

versante *sm* slopes (*pl*).

versare *vt* (*in recipiente*) to pour; (*rovesciare*) to spill; (*pagare*) to pay; (*depositare*) to deposit.

▶ **versarsi** *vr* to spill.

versatile *agg* versatile.

versione *sf* version; (*traduzione*) translation.

verso ◆ *sm* (*di poesia*) line; (*di animale*) cry; (*direzione*) direction ◆ *prep* (*in direzione di, nei confronti di*) towards; (*in prossimità di*) near; (*di tempo, età*) around, about; **non c'è ~ di convincerlo** there's no way of convincing him; **fare il ~ a qn** to mimic sb.

vertebra *sf* vertebra.

verticale *agg & sf* vertical.

vertice *sm* peak; (MAT) vertex.

vertigine *sf* dizziness; **soffrire di vertigini** to be afraid of heights.

vescovo *sm* bishop.

vespa *sf* wasp.

vestaglia *sf* dressing gown.

veste *sf*: **in ~ di** as.

vestiario *sm* wardrobe, clothes (*pl*).

vestire *vt & vi* to dress.

▶ **vestirsi** *vr* to get dressed.

vestito *sm* (*da uomo*) suit; (*da donna*) dress.

▶ **vestiti** *smpl* (*indumenti*) clothes.

Vesuvio *sm*: **il ~** Vesuvius.

veterinario, -a *sm, f* vet(erinary surgeon) (Br), veterinarian (Am).

vetrata *sf* (*di casa*) glass door/window; (*di chiesa*) stained glass window.

vetrina *sf* (*di negozio*) shop window.

vetro *sm* (*materiale*) glass; (*frammento*) piece of glass; (*di finestra*) windowpane; (*di auto*) window.

vetta *sf* top.

vettovaglie *sfpl* supplies.

vettura *sf* (*automobile*) car; (*di treno*) carriage (Br), car (Am).

vezzeggiativo *sm* term of endearment.

vezzo *sm* habit.

vi ◆ (*diventa* **ve** *se precede lo, la, li, le, ne*) *pron* (*complemento oggetto*) you; (*complemento di termine*) (to) you; (*riflessivo*) yourselves; (*reciproco*) each other ◆ *avv* = **ci**; **ve li do** I'll give them to you.

via ◆ *sf* way; (*strada*) street, road ◆ *avv* away ◆ *prep* via ◆ *esclam* (*per scacciare*) go away!; (*in gara, gioco*) go! ◆ *sm inv*: **dare il ~** (SPORT) to give the starting signal; **dare il ~ a qc** (*progetto*) to give the green light to sthg; **~ aerea** (*posta*) by airmail; **~ mare** by sea; **~ terra** overland; **in ~ eccezionale** as an exception; **per ~ di** (*a causa di*) because of; **in ~ di guarigione** on the road to recovery;

una ~ di mezzo a middle course; **e così ~** and so on.

viabilità *sf* practicability.

Viacard® *sf inv* credit card for motorway tolls.

viaggiare *vi* to travel.

viaggiatore, -trice *sm, f* passenger.

viaggio *sm* travel; (*tragitto*) journey; (*gita*) trip; **buon ~!** have a good trip!; **essere in ~** to be away; **fare un ~** to go on a trip; **~ d'affari** business trip; **~ di nozze** honeymoon; **~ organizzato** package tour.

viale *sm* (*corso*) avenue; (*in un parco*) path.

viavai *sm* coming and going.

vibrare *vi* to vibrate.

vibrazione *sf* vibration.

vice *smf inv* deputy.

vicenda *sf* event.

▶ **a vicenda** *avv* in turn.

viceversa *avv* vice versa.

vicinanza *sf* proximity; **nelle vicinanze (di qc)** in the vicinity (of sthg).

vicinato *sm* (*zona*) neighbourhood; (*vicini*) neighbours (*pl*).

vicino, -a ◆ *agg* (*nello spazio*) near, nearby; (*nel tempo*) close at hand ◆ *sm, f* neighbour ◆ *avv* nearby ◆ *prep*: **~ a** (*accanto a*) next to; (*nei pressi di*) near; **~ di casa** neighbour; **da ~** close up.

vicolo *sm* alley; **~ cieco** blind alley.

video *sm inv* (*musicale*) video; (*schermo*) screen.

videocassetta *sf* video(cassette).

videocitofono *sm* entryphone with closed circuit TV.

videogame ['videogeim] = **videogioco**.

videogioco, -chi *sm* video game.

videoregistratore *sm* video(recorder) (Br), VCR (Am).

Videotel® *sm* = Viewdata®.

vietare *vt* to forbid; **~ a qn di fare qc** to forbid sb to do sthg; **~ qc a qn**

to forbid sthg to sb.

vietato, -a *agg* forbidden; **'~ l'accesso'** 'no entry'; **'~ l'accesso ai mezzi non autorizzati'** 'no entry for unauthorized vehicles'; **'è ~ fare il bagno nelle ore notturne'** 'no swimming at night'; **'~ fumare'** 'no smoking'; **'~ ai minori'** 'adults only'.

Vietnam *sm*: **il ~** Vietnam.

vigilare *vt* to watch over.

vigile ◆ *agg* watchful ◆ *smf*: **~ (urbano)** *local police officer who deals mainly with traffic offences*; **i vigili del fuoco** the fire brigade.

vigilia *sf* eve; **~ di Natale** Christmas Eve.

vigliacco, -a, -chi, -che ◆ *agg* cowardly ◆ *sm, f* coward.

vigna *sf* vines (*pl*).

vigore *sm* vigour; **in ~** (DIR) in force.

vile *agg* cowardly.

villa *sf* (*al mare*) villa; (*in campagna*) country house; (*in città*) detached house.

villaggio *sm* village; **~ turistico** holiday village.

villano, -a ◆ *agg* rude ◆ *sm, f* boor.

villeggiatura *sf* holiday (Br), vacation (Am).

villetta *sf* = **villino**.

villino *sm* small detached house (*with garden*).

vimini *smpl* wicker (*sg*).

vinavil® *sm* glue.

vincere ◆ *vt* (*gioco, partita, battaglia*) to win; (*avversario*) to beat ◆ *vi* to win.

vincita *sf* (*vittoria*) win; (*premio*) winnings (*pl*).

vincitore, -trice *sm, f* winner.

vinicolo, -a *agg* wine-producing, wine-making.

vino *sm* wine; **~ bianco** white wine; **~ rosso** red wine.

VINO

Wines are produced in every Italian region, and their names reflect either the area where they are produced (like 'Chianti') or the grape varieties they are made from ('moscato'). 'Vino da tavola' on a label indicates an inexpensive table wine, while DOC ('denominazione d'origine controllata'), DOCG ('denominazione d'origine controllata e garantita'), and VQPRD ('vino di qualità prodotto in regioni delimitate') all indicate that the wine is of superior quality.

---

vinto, -a ◆ *pp → vincere* ◆ *agg* (*partita*) won; (*concorrente*) beaten; **darla vinta a qn** to let sb have their way; **non darsi per ~** not to give up.

viola ◆ *agg inv & sm inv* purple ◆ *sf* (*fiore*) violet; (MUS) viola.

violare *vt* to violate.

violentare *vt* to rape.

violento, -a *agg* violent.

violenza *sf* violence.

violinista, -i, -e *smf* violinist.

violino *sm* violin.

violoncello *sm* cello.

viottolo *sm* track.

vipera *sf* viper.

virare *vi* (NAUT) to come about; (*aereo*) to turn.

virgola *sf* (GRAMM) comma; (MAT) point.

virgolette *sfpl* quotation marks.

virile *agg* manly.

virtù *sf inv* virtue.

virus *sm inv* virus.

viscere *sfpl* entrails.

viscido, -a *agg* slimy.

viscosa *sf* viscose.

visibile *agg* (*che si vede*) visible; (*chiaro*) evident.

visibilità *sf* visibility.

visiera *sf* peak.

visionare *vt* to examine.

visione *sf* (*vista*) sight; (*modo di vedere*) view; (*apparizione*) vision; **prendere ~ di qc** to look over sthg; **prima ~** TV premiere.

visita *sf* (*di amico*) visit; (*di medico*) examination; **fare ~ a qn** to pay sb a visit; **~ medica** medical examination.

visitare vt to visit; (sog: medico) to examine.

viso sm face.

vispo, -a agg lively.

vissuto, -a pp → **vivere**.

vista sf (facoltà) (eye)sight; (possibilità di vedere) sight; (panorama) view; **conoscere qn di ~** to know sb by sight; **a prima ~** at first sight.

visto, -a ◆ pp → **vedere** ◆ sm visa.

vistoso, -a agg gaudy.

vita sf life; (ANAT) waist.

vitale agg vital.

vitamina sf vitamin.

vite sf (pianta) vine; (utensile) screw.

vitello sm (animale) calf; (carne) veal; (pelle) calfskin; **~ tonnato** boiled veal served cold with tuna mayonnaise.

vittima sf victim.

vitto sm food; **~ e alloggio** board and lodging.

vittoria sf victory.

viva esclam: **~ le vacanze!** hurray for the holidays!

vivace agg (persona) lively; (colore) bright.

vivacità sf vivacity.

vivaio sm (di piante) nursery; (di pesci) hatchery.

vivanda sf food.

vivente agg → **essere**.

vivere ◆ vi to live ◆ vt (vita) to live; (passare) to live through.

viveri smpl food (sg).

vivo, -a agg (vivente) alive, living; (persona) lively; (colore) bright; **dal ~** from life; **farsi ~ (con qn)** to get in touch (with sb).

viziare vt to spoil.

viziato, -a agg (bambino) spoilt; (aria) stale.

vizio sm (cattiva abitudine) bad habit; (morale) vice; (difetto) defect.

V.le (abbr di viale) Ave.

vocabolario sm (dizionario) dictionary; (lessico) vocabulary.

vocabolo sm word.

vocale ◆ agg vocal ◆ sf vowel.

vocazione sf (inclinazione) natural bent.

voce sf (suono) voice; (diceria) rumour; (di elenco) entry; **a bassa/alta ~** in a low/loud voice; **sotto ~** in a whisper.

voga sf: **essere in ~** to be in fashion.

vogatore, -trice ◆ sm, f oarsman (f oarswoman) ◆ sm rowing machine.

voglia sf (desiderio) desire; (sulla pelle) birthmark; **avere ~ di fare qc** to feel like doing sthg; **avere ~ di qc** to feel like sthg; **levarsi la ~ di qc** to satisfy one's desire for sthg; **contro ~** unwillingly.

voi pron you; **~ stessi** you yourselves.

volano sm shuttlecock.

volante ◆ agg flying ◆ sm (di veicolo) steering wheel ◆ sf (polizia) flying squad.

volantino sm leaflet.

volare vi to fly.

volatile sm bird.

vol-au-vent [volo'van] sm inv vol-au-vent.

volenteroso, -a agg willing.

volentieri avv (con piacere) willingly; (come risposta) with pleasure.

volere vt 1. (desiderare, esigere) to want; **cosa vuoi?** what do you want?; **voglio delle spiegazioni** I want some explanations; **~ fare qc** to want to do sthg; **voglio che tu venga** I want you to come; **cosa volete fare stasera?** what do you want to do tonight?; **ti vogliono al telefono** you're wanted on the phone; **come vuoi** as you like; **vorrei un cappuccino** I'd like a cappuccino; **vorrei andare** I'd like to go; **senza volerlo** unintentionally; **se si vuole accomodare?** if you would care to take a seat?

2. (consentire a): **se tua madre vuole, ti porto al cinema** if your mother

agrees, I'll take you to the cinema; **vogliamo andare?** shall we go?

3. (*soldi*): **quanto vuole per questo orologio?** how much do you want for this watch?

4. (*credere*) to think; **la leggenda vuole che ...** legend has it that ...

5. (*decidersi a*): **la macchina non vuole partire** the car won't start.

6. (*necessitare di*) to need; **volerci** (*coraggio, materiale*) to need; (*tempo*) to take; **ci vuole pazienza** you must be patient; **ci vogliono ancora dieci minuti per finire** it'll take another ten minutes to finish.

7. (*in espressioni*): **voler bene a qn** (*affetto*) to be fond of sb; (*amare*) to love sb; **voler dire** to mean; **volerne a qn** to have a grudge against sb.
♦ *sm* will, wish; **contro il ~ di qn** against sb's wishes.

volgare *agg* vulgar.

volgere *vt* to turn; **il tempo volge al bello** the weather's getting better; **~ al termine** to draw to an end.

volo *sm* flight; **~ charter** charter flight; **~ di linea** scheduled flight; **capire qc al ~** to understand sthg straightaway.

volontà *sf inv* will; **buona ~** goodwill; **a ~** as much as one likes.

volontario, -a ♦ *agg* voluntary ♦ *sm, f* volunteer.

volpe *sf* fox.

volt *sm inv* volt.

volta *sf* (*circostanza*) time; (*di edificio*) vault; **a sua ~** in his/her turn; **di ~ in** from time to time; **una ~** once; **due volte** twice; **tre volte** three times; **una ~ che** once; **una ~ tanto** just for once; **uno per o alla ~** one at a time; **a volte** sometimes.

voltafaccia *sm inv* about-turn.

voltare *vt & vi* to turn; **~ l'angolo** to turn the corner; **~ pagina** to turn over a new leaf.
▶ **voltarsi** *vr* to turn.

voltastomaco *sm* nausea; **dare il ~ a qn** to make sb feel sick.

volto, -a ♦ *pp* → **volgere** ♦ *sm* face.

volubile *agg* fickle.

volume *sm* volume.

voluminoso, -a *agg* voluminous, bulky.

vomitare *vt & vi* to vomit, to throw up.

vomito *sm* vomit.

vongola *sf* clam.

vorace *agg* (*animale*) voracious; (*persona*) greedy.

voragine *sf* abyss.

vortice *sm* whirl.

vostro, -a ♦ *agg*: **il ~ (la vostra)** your ♦ *pron*: **il ~ (la vostra)** yours; **~ padre** your father; **un ~ amico** a friend of yours; **sono vostri questi bagagli?** is this your luggage?

votare ♦ *vt* to vote on ♦ *vi* to vote.

votazione *sf* (*procedimento*) vote; (SCOL) marks (*pl*).

voto *sm* (DIR) vote; (SCOL) marks (*pl*).

vulcanico, -a, -ci, -che *agg* volcanic.

vulcano *sm* volcano.

vulnerabile *agg* vulnerable.

vuotare *vt* to empty.
▶ **vuotarsi** *vr* to empty.

vuoto, -a ♦ *agg* empty; (*pagina*) blank ♦ *sm* (*spazio vuoto*) empty space; (*bottiglia*) empty (bottle); (*in fisica*) vacuum; **andare a ~** to fail; **parlare a ~** to waste one's breath.

WXY

wafer ['vafer] *sm inv* wafer.

Walkman® *sm inv* Walkman®, personal stereo.

water (closet) ['vater ('kloz)] *sm inv* toilet.

watt [vat] *sm inv* watt.

wc (*abbr di water closet*) WC.
week-end [wi'kɛnd] *sm inv* week-end.
western ['wɛstern] *agg inv*: **film ~** western.
whisky ['wiski] *sm inv* whisky.
windsurf ['windsərf] *sm inv* (*tavola*) windsurf board; (*sport*) windsurfing.
würstel ['vurstel] *sm inv* frank-furter.

xenofobia *sf* xenophobia.
xilofono *sm* xylophone.

yacht [jɔt] *sm inv* yacht.
yoga *sm* yoga.
yogurt *sm inv* yoghurt.

Z

zabaglione *sm* = **zabaione**.
zabaione *sm cream dessert made from egg yolks whipped with sugar and Marsala.*
zafferano *sm* saffron.
zaino *sm* rucksack.
zampa *sf* paw; **a quattro zampe** on all fours.
zampillo *sm* spurt.
zampirone *sm* mosquito repellent.
zampone *sm boiled pig's trotter stuffed with minced meat and spices.*
zanna *sf* (*di elefante*) tusk; (*di carnivori*) fang.
zanzara *sf* mosquito.
zanzariera *sf* mosquito net.
zappa *sf* hoe.
zappare *vt* to hoe.
zattera *sf* raft.
zavorra *sf* ballast.
zazzera *sf* fringe.
zebra *sf* zebra.

▶ **zebre** *sfpl* (*fam*) zebra crossing (*sg*) (Br), crosswalk (*sg*) (Am).
zecca, -che *sf* (*insetto*) tick; (*officina di monete*) mint.
zelante *agg* zealous.
zelo *sm* zeal.
zenzero *sm* ginger.
zeppo, -a *agg* crammed.
zeppole *sfpl type of ring doughnut eaten at carnival time in the south of Italy.*
zerbino *sm* doormat.
zero *sm* zero; (SPORT) nil; **sotto ~** subzero.
zigomo *sm* cheekbone.
zigzag *sm inv* zigzag.
zimbello *sm* laughingstock.
zingaro, -a *sm, f* gipsy.
zio, -a *sm, f* uncle (*f* aunt).
zip *sm inv* zip.
zitella *sf* (*spreg*) spinster.
zitto, -a *agg* silent; **state zitti!** be quiet!
zoccolo *sm* (*calzatura*) clog; (*di cavallo*) hoof.
zodiaco *sm* zodiac.
zolfo *sm* sulphur.
zolla *sf* clod.
zolletta *sf* lump.
zona *sf* area; **~ blu** o **verde** *zone where traffic is restricted*; **~ disco** parking meter zone; **~ industriale** industrial estate; **'~ militare'** 'army property'; **~ pedonale** pedestrian precinct (Br), pedestrian zone (Am).
zonzo : a zonzo *avv*: **andare a ~** to wander about.
zoo *sm inv* zoo.
zoom [dzum] *sm inv* zoom.
zoppicare *vi* to limp.
zoppo, -a *agg* lame.
zucca, -che *sf* pumpkin.
zuccherato, -a *agg* sweetened.
zuccheriera *sf* sugar bowl.
zucchero *sm* sugar; **~ filato** candy-floss; **~ vanigliato** vanilla sugar; **~ a velo** icing sugar (Br), confectioner's sugar (Am).

zuccheroso, -a *agg* sugary.

zucchina *sf* courgette; **zucchine ripiene** *courgettes stuffed with minced meat, breadcrumbs, eggs and spices.*

zucchino = **zucchina**.

zuccone, -a *sm, f (sciocco)* blockhead; *(testardo)* stubborn person.

zuccotto *sm* ice-cream sponge.

zuffa *sf* brawl.

zuppa *sf* soup; **~ inglese** ≃ trifle (Br), *dessert made from sponge soaked in liqueur, with custard and chocolate.*

zuppiera *sf* tureen.

zuppo, -a *agg*: **~ (di)** soaked (with).

Zurigo *sf* Zurich.

a [stressed eɪ, unstressed ə] (**an** *before vowel or silent 'h'*) *indefinite article* **1.** un/uno (una/un'); **a restaurant** un ristorante; **a brush** uno spazzolino; **a chair** una sedia; **an island** un'isola; **a friend** un amico (un'amica); **to be a doctor** essere medico, fare il medico. **2.** (*instead of the number one*) un/uno (una/un'); **a month ago** un mese fa; **a hundred and twenty pounds** centoventi sterline; **a thousand** mille; **four and a half** quattro e mezzo. **3.** (*in prices, ratios*) a; **£2 a kilo** 2 sterline al chilo; **three times a week** tre volte alla settimana.

AA *n* (Br: *abbr of Automobile Association*) ≃ ACI *m*.

aback [ə'bæk] *adv*: **to be taken ~** restare sbalordito(-a).

abandon [ə'bændən] *vt* abbandonare.

abattoir ['æbətwɑːʳ] *n* mattatoio *m*.

abbey ['æbɪ] *n* abbazia *f*.

abbreviation [ə,briːvɪ'eɪʃn] *n* abbreviazione *f*.

abdomen ['æbdəmən] *n* addome *m*.

abide [ə'baɪd] *vt*: **I can't ~ him** non lo sopporto.

▶ **abide by** *vt fus* rispettare.

ability [ə'bɪlətɪ] *n* capacità *f inv*.

able ['eɪbl] *adj* capace; **to be ~ to do sthg** essere capace di fare qc, poter fare qc.

abnormal [æb'nɔːml] *adj* anormale.

aboard [ə'bɔːd] ◆ *adv* a bordo ◆ *prep* a bordo di, su.

abolish [ə'bɒlɪʃ] *vt* abolire.

aborigine [,æbə'rɪdʒənɪ] *n* aborigeno *m* (-a *f*).

abort [ə'bɔːt] *vt* (*call off*) sospendere.

abortion [ə'bɔːʃn] *n* aborto *m*; **to have an ~** abortire.

about [ə'baʊt] ◆ *adv* **1.** (*approximately*) circa, più o meno; **~ 50 people** una cinquantina di persone; **~ a thousand** un migliaio; **at ~ six o'clock** verso le sei. **2.** (*referring to place*) qua e là; **to walk ~** camminare. **3.** (*on the point of*): **to be ~ to do sthg** stare per fare qc. ◆ *prep* **1.** (*concerning*) su, a proposito di; **a book ~ Scotland** un libro sulla Scozia; **what's it ~?** di che cosa si tratta?; **I'll talk to you ~ it** te ne parlerò; **what ~ a coffee?** cosa ne diresti di un caffè? **2.** (*referring to place*) per, in giro per; **there are lots of hotels ~ the town** ci sono molti alberghi nella città.

above [ə'bʌv] ◆ *prep* sopra ◆ *adv*

(*higher*) (di) sopra; (*more*) oltre; ~ **all** soprattutto.

abroad [ə'brɔːd] *adv* all'estero.

abrupt [ə'brʌpt] *adj* (*sudden*) improvviso(-a).

abscess ['æbses] *n* ascesso *m*.

absence ['æbsəns] *n* assenza *f*.

absent ['æbsənt] *adj* assente.

absent-minded [-'maɪndɪd] *adj* distratto(-a).

absolute ['æbsəluːt] *adj* assoluto(-a).

absolutely [*adv* 'æbsəluːtlɪ, *excl* ˌæbsə'luːtlɪ] *adv* (*completely*) assolutamente ♦ *excl* assolutamente!

absorb [əb'sɔːb] *vt* assorbire.

absorbed [əb'sɔːbd] *adj*: **to be ~ in** sthg essere assorto(-a) in qc.

absorbent [əb'sɔːbənt] *adj* assorbente.

abstain [əb'steɪn] *vi*: **to ~ (from)** astenersi (da).

absurd [əb'sɜːd] *adj* assurdo(-a).

ABTA ['æbtə] *n* associazione delle agenzie di viaggio britanniche.

abuse [*n* ə'bjuːs, *vb* ə'bjuːz] ♦ *n* (*insults*) insulti *mpl*; (*wrong use*) abuso *m*; (*maltreatment*) maltrattamento *m* ♦ *vt* (*insult*) insultare; (*use wrongly*) abusare di; (*maltreat*) maltrattare.

abusive [ə'bjuːsɪv] *adj* offensivo(-a).

AC (*abbr of alternating current*) c.a.

academic [ˌækə'demɪk] ♦ *adj* (*educational*) accademico(-a) ♦ *n* professore *m* universitario (professoressa *f* universitaria).

academy [ə'kædəmɪ] *n* accademia *f*.

accelerate [ək'seləreɪt] *vi* accelerare.

accelerator [ək'seləreɪtər] *n* acceleratore *m*.

accent ['æksent] *n* accento *m*.

accept [ək'sept] *vt* accettare.

acceptable [ək'septəbl] *adj* accettabile.

access ['ækses] *n* accesso *m*.

accessible [ək'sesəbl] *adj* (*place*) accessibile.

accessories [ək'sesərɪz] *npl* accessori *mpl*.

access road *n* strada *f* d'accesso.

accident ['æksɪdənt] *n* incidente *m*; **by ~** per caso.

accidental [ˌæksɪ'dentl] *adj* accidentale.

accident insurance *n* assicurazione *f* contro gli infortuni.

accident-prone *adj* soggetto(-a) a frequenti infortuni.

acclimatize [ə'klaɪmətaɪz] *vi* acclimatarsi.

accommodate [ə'kɒmədeɪt] *vt* alloggiare.

accommodation [əˌkɒmə'deɪʃn] *n* alloggio *m*.

accommodations [əˌkɒmə'deɪʃnz] *npl* (*Am*) = **accommodation**.

accompany [ə'kʌmpənɪ] *vt* accompagnare.

accomplish [ə'kʌmplɪʃ] *vt* realizzare.

accord [ə'kɔːd] *n*: **of one's own ~** di propria iniziativa.

accordance [ə'kɔːdəns] *n*: **in ~ with** in conformità a.

according [ə'kɔːdɪŋ]: **according to** *prep* secondo.

accordion [ə'kɔːdɪən] *n* fisarmonica *f*.

account [ə'kaunt] *n* (*at bank, shop*) conto *m*; (*report*) resoconto *m*; **to take into ~** tener conto di; **on no ~** in nessun caso; **on ~ of** a causa di. ► **account for** *vt fus* (*explain*) spiegare; (*constitute*) rappresentare.

accountant [ə'kauntənt] *n* ragioniere *m* (-a *f*).

account number *n* numero *m* di conto.

accumulate [ə'kjuːmjʊleɪt] *vt* accumulare.

accurate ['ækjurət] *adj* preciso(-a).

accuse [ə'kjuːz] *vt*: **to ~ sb of sthg** accusare qn di qc.

accused [ə'kjuːzd] *n*: **the ~** l'imputato *m* (-a *f*).

ace [eɪs] n (card) asso m.

ache [eɪk] ♦ n dolore m ♦ vi: **my head ~s** mi fa male la testa.

achieve [ə'tʃiːv] vt ottenere.

acid ['æsɪd] ♦ adj acido(-a) ♦ n acido m.

acid rain n pioggia f acida.

acknowledge [ək'nɒlɪdʒ] vt (accept) riconoscere; (letter) accusare ricevuta di.

acne ['æknɪ] n acne f.

acorn ['eɪkɔːn] n ghianda f.

acoustic [ə'kuːstɪk] adj acustico(-a).

acquaintance [ə'kweɪntəns] n (person) conoscente mf.

acquire [ə'kwaɪər] vt acquisire.

acre ['eɪkər] n = 4 046,9 m², acro m.

acrobat ['ækrəbæt] n acrobata mf.

across [ə'krɒs] ♦ prep (to, on other side of) dall'altra parte di; (from one side to the other of) attraverso, da una parte all'altra di ♦ adv (to other side) dall'altra parte; **to walk ~ sthg** attraversare qc (a piedi); **to drive ~ sthg** attraversare qc (in macchina); **10 miles ~** largo 10 miglia; **~ from** di fronte a.

acrylic [ə'krɪlɪk] n acrilico m.

act [ækt] ♦ vi agire; (behave) comportarsi; (in play, film) recitare ♦ n atto m; (POL) legge f; (performance) numero m; **to ~ as** (serve as) fare da.

action ['ækʃn] n azione f; **to take ~** agire; **to put sthg into ~** mettere in pratica qc; **out of ~** (machine) fuori uso; (person) fuori combattimento.

active ['æktɪv] adj (busy) attivo(-a).

activity [æk'tɪvətɪ] n attività f inv.

activity holiday n vacanza organizzata per ragazzi con attività ricreative di vario genere.

act of God n causa f di forza maggiore.

actor ['æktər] n attore m.

actress ['æktrɪs] n attrice f.

actual ['æktʃuəl] adj (real) effettivo(-a), reale; (itself) in sé.

actually ['æktʃuəlɪ] adv (really) veramente; (in fact) in effetti.

acupuncture ['ækjupʌŋktʃər] n agopuntura f.

acute [ə'kjuːt] adj acuto(-a).

ad [æd] n (inf) (for product) pubblicità f inv; (for job) annuncio m.

AD (abbr of Anno Domini) d.C.

adapt [ə'dæpt] ♦ vt adattare ♦ vi adattarsi.

adapter [ə'dæptər] n (for foreign plug) adattatore m; (for several plugs) presa f multipla.

add [æd] vt (put, say in addition) aggiungere; (numbers, prices) sommare.

▶ **add up** vt sep sommare.

▶ **add up to** vt fus (total) ammontare a.

adder ['ædər] n vipera f.

addict ['ædɪkt] n tossicodipendente mf.

addicted [ə'dɪktɪd] adj: **to be ~ to sthg** essere assuefatto(-a) a qc.

addiction [ə'dɪkʃn] n dipendenza f.

addition [ə'dɪʃn] n (added thing) aggiunta f; (in maths) addizione f; **in ~** inoltre; **in ~ to** oltre a.

additional [ə'dɪʃənl] adj supplementare.

additive ['ædɪtɪv] n additivo m.

address [ə'dres] ♦ n (on letter) indirizzo m ♦ vt (speak to) rivolgersi a; (letter) indirizzare.

address book n rubrica f.

addressee [,ædre'siː] n destinatario m (-a f).

adequate ['ædɪkwət] adj adeguato(-a).

adhere [əd'hɪər] vi: **to ~ to** (stick to) aderire a; (obey) rispettare.

adhesive [əd'hiːsɪv] ♦ adj adesivo(-a) ♦ n adesivo m.

adjacent [ə'dʒeɪsənt] adj adiacente.

adjective ['ædʒɪktɪv] n aggettivo m.

adjoining [ə'dʒɔɪnɪŋ] adj contiguo(-a).

adjust [ə'dʒʌst] ♦ vt aggiustare ♦ vi: **to ~ to** adattarsi a.

adjustable [ə'dʒʌstəbl] adj regolabile.

adjustment [ə'dʒʌstmənt] n (of machine) regolazione f; (of plan) modifica f.

administration [ədˌmɪnɪ'streɪʃn] n amministrazione f.

administrator [əd'mɪnɪstreɪtər] n amministratore m (-trice f).

admiral ['ædmərəl] n ammiraglio m.

admire [əd'maɪər] vt ammirare.

admission [əd'mɪʃn] n (permission to enter, entrance cost) ingresso m.

admission charge n ingresso m.

admit [əd'mɪt] vt (confess) ammettere; (allow to enter) far entrare; **to ~ to sthg** ammettere qc; **'~s one'** (on ticket) 'valido per una sola persona'.

adolescent [ˌædə'lesnt] n adolescente mf.

adopt [ə'dɒpt] vt adottare.

adopted [ə'dɒptɪd] adj adottivo(-a).

adorable [ə'dɔːrəbl] adj adorabile.

adore [ə'dɔːr] vt adorare.

Adriatic [eɪdrɪ'ætɪk] n: **the ~ (Sea)** l'Adriatico m, il mar Adriatico.

adult ['ædʌlt] ♦ n adulto m (-a f) ♦ adj (entertainment, films) per adulti; (animal) adulto(-a).

adult education n ≃ educazione f permanente.

adultery [ə'dʌltəri] n adulterio m.

advance [əd'vɑːns] ♦ n (money) anticipo m; (movement) avanzamento m ♦ adj (payment) anticipato(-a) ♦ vt anticipare ♦ vi (move forward) avanzare; (improve) fare progressi; **~ warning** preavviso m.

advance booking n prenotazione f anticipata.

advanced [əd'vɑːnst] adj (student) di livello avanzato; (level) avanzato(-a).

advantage [əd'vɑːntɪdʒ] n vantaggio m; **to take ~ of** approfittare di.

adventure [əd'ventʃər] n avventura f.

adventurous [əd'ventʃərəs] adj avventuroso(-a).

adverb ['ædvɜːb] n avverbio m.

adverse ['ædvɜːs] adj avverso(-a).

advert ['ædvɜːt] = **advertisement**.

advertise ['ædvətaɪz] vt (product, event) fare pubblicità a.

advertisement [əd'vɜːtɪsmənt] n (for product) pubblicità f inv; (for job) annuncio m.

advice [əd'vaɪs] n consigli mpl; **a piece of ~** un consiglio; **to ask for sb's ~** chiedere consiglio a qn.

advisable [əd'vaɪzəbl] adj consigliabile.

advise [əd'vaɪz] vt consigliare; **to ~ sb to do sthg** consigliare a qn di fare qc; **to ~ sb against doing sthg** sconsigliare a qn di fare qc.

advocate [n 'ædvəkət, vb 'ædvəkeɪt] ♦ n (JUR) avvocato m (difensore) ♦ vt sostenere.

aerial ['eərɪəl] n antenna f.

aerobic [eə'rəubɪk] adj aerobico (-a).

aerobics [eə'rəubɪks] n aerobica f.

aerodynamic [ˌeərəudaɪ'næmɪk] adj aerodinamico(-a).

aeroplane ['eərəpleɪn] n aeroplano m.

aerosol ['eərəsɒl] n aerosol m.

affair [ə'feər] n (event) affare m; (love affair) relazione f.

affect [ə'fekt] vt (influence) incidere su.

affection [ə'fekʃn] n affetto m.

affectionate [ə'fekʃnət] adj affettuoso(-a).

affluent ['æfluənt] adj ricco(-a).

afford [ə'fɔːd] vt: **to be able to ~ sthg** potersi permettere qc; **I can't ~ it** non me lo posso permettere; **I can't ~ the time** non ho tempo.

affordable [ə'fɔːdəbl] adj accessibile.

afloat [ə'fləʊt] *adj* a galla.

afraid [ə'freɪd] *adj* spaventato(-a); **to be ~ of** aver paura di; **I'm ~ so/not** temo di sì/di no.

Africa ['æfrɪkə] *n* l'Africa *f*.

African ['æfrɪkən] ♦ *adj* africano(-a) ♦ *n* africano *m* (-a *f*).

after ['ɑːftər] ♦ *prep & adv* dopo ♦ *conj* dopo che; **he arrived ~ me** arrivò dopo di me; **a quarter ~ ten** (*Am*) le dieci e un quarto; **to be ~ sb/sthg** (*in search of*) cercare qn/qc; **~ all** dopo tutto.

► **afters** *npl* dessert *m*.

aftercare ['ɑːftəkeər] *n* assistenza *f* postospedaliera.

aftereffects ['ɑːftərɪˌfekts] *npl* conseguenze *fpl*, (*of illness*) postumi *mpl*.

afternoon [ˌɑːftə'nuːn] *n* pomeriggio *m*; **good ~!** buon giorno! (*il pomeriggio*).

afternoon tea *n* spuntino pomeridiano a base di tramezzini, dolci, tè o caffè.

aftershave ['ɑːftəʃeɪv] *n* dopobarba *m*.

aftersun ['ɑːftəsʌn] *n* doposole *m*.

afterwards ['ɑːftəwədz] *adv* dopo.

again [ə'gen] *adv* ancora, di nuovo; **~ and ~** più volte; **never ... ~** non ... mai più.

against [ə'genst] *prep* contro; **to lean ~ sthg** appoggiarsi a qc; **~ the law** contro la legge.

age [eɪdʒ] *n* età *f*; **under ~** minorenne; **I haven't seen him for ~s** (*inf*) non lo vedo da secoli.

aged [eɪdʒd] *adj*: **~ eight** di otto anni.

age group *n* fascia *f* d'età.

age limit *n* limite *m* d'età.

agency ['eɪdʒənsɪ] *n* agenzia *f*.

agenda [ə'dʒendə] *n* ordine *m* del giorno.

agent ['eɪdʒənt] *n* agente *mf*.

aggression [ə'greʃn] *n* aggressività *f*; **act of ~** aggressione *f*.

aggressive [ə'gresɪv] *adj* aggressivo(-a).

agile [*Br* 'ædʒaɪl, *Am* 'ædʒəl] *adj* agile.

agility [ə'dʒɪlətɪ] *n* agilità *f*.

agitated ['ædʒɪteɪtɪd] *adj* agitato(-a).

ago [ə'gəʊ] *adv*: **a month ~** un mese fa; **how long ~?** quanto tempo fa?

agonizing ['ægənaɪzɪŋ] *adj* (*pain*) atroce; (*decision*) straziante.

agony ['ægənɪ] *n* (*physical*) dolore *m* atroce; (*mental*) agonia *f*.

agree [ə'griː] *vi* (*be in agreement*) essere d'accordo; (*consent*) acconsentire; (*correspond*) concordare; **it doesn't ~ with me** (*food*) mi fa male; **to ~ to sthg** accettare qc; **to ~ to do sthg** accettare di fare qc.

► **agree on** *vt fus* (*time, price*) concordare, mettersi d'accordo su.

agreed [ə'griːd] *adj* stabilito(-a); **to be ~** (*person*) essere d'accordo.

agreement [ə'griːmənt] *n* accordo *m*; **in ~ with** d'accordo con.

agriculture ['ægrɪkʌltʃər] *n* agricoltura *f*.

ahead [ə'hed] *adv* (*in front*) davanti; (*forwards*) avanti; **the months ~** i prossimi mesi; **to be ~** (*winning*) condurre; **~ of** (*in front of*) davanti a; (*in better position than*) in vantaggio su; (*in time*) in anticipo su.

aid [eɪd] ♦ *n* aiuto *m* ♦ *vt* aiutare; **in ~ of** a favore di; **with the ~ of** con l'aiuto di.

AIDS [eɪdz] *n* AIDS *m*.

ailment ['eɪlmənt] *n* (*fml*) acciacco *m*.

aim [eɪm] ♦ *n* (*purpose*) scopo *m* ♦ *vt* (*gun, camera, hose*) puntare ♦ *vi*: **to ~ (at)** mirare (a); **to ~ to do sthg** avere l'intenzione di fare qc.

air [eər] ♦ *n* aria *f* ♦ *vt* (*room*) arieggiare ♦ *adj* aereo(-a); (*travel*) in aereo; **by ~** (*travel*) in aereo; (*send*) via aerea.

airbed ['eəbed] *n* materassino *m*.

airborne ['eəbɔ:n] *adj* in volo.

air-conditioned [-kən'dɪʃnd] *adj* con aria condizionata.

air-conditioning [-kən'dɪʃnɪŋ] *n* aria *f* condizionata.

aircraft ['eəkrɑ:ft] (*pl inv*) *n* aeromobile *m*.

aircraft carrier [-,kærɪər] *n* portaerei *f inv*.

airfield ['eəfi:ld] *n* campo *m* d'aviazione.

airforce ['eəfɔ:s] *n* aeronautica *f* militare.

air freshener [-,freʃnər] *n* deodorante *m* per ambienti.

airhostess ['eə,həustɪs] *n* hostess *f inv*.

airing cupboard ['eərɪŋ-] *n* sgabuzzino della caldaia dove viene riposta la biancheria ad asciugare.

airletter ['eə,letər] *n* aerogramma *m*.

airline ['eəlaɪn] *n* compagnia *f* aerea.

airliner ['eə,laɪnər] *n* aereo *m* di linea.

airmail ['eəmeɪl] *n* posta *f* aerea; **by ~** per via aerea.

airplane ['eərpleɪn] *n* (*Am*) aeroplano *m*.

airport ['eəpɔ:t] *n* aeroporto *m*.

air raid *n* incursione *f* aerea.

airsick ['eəsɪk] *adj*: **to be ~** soffrire di mal d'aria.

air steward *n* assistente *m* di volo.

air stewardess *n* assistente *f* di volo.

air traffic control *n* (*people*) controllori *mpl* di volo.

airy ['eərɪ] *adj* arioso(-a).

aisle [aɪl] *n* (*in church*) navata *f*; (*in plane, cinema*) corridoio *m*; (*in supermarket*) corsia *f*.

aisle seat *n* posto *m* corridoio.

ajar [ə'dʒɑ:r] *adj* socchiuso(-a).

alarm [ə'lɑ:m] ♦ *n* allarme *m* ♦ *vt* allarmare.

alarm clock *n* sveglia *f*.

alarmed [ə'lɑ:md] *adj* (*door, car*) dotato(-a) di allarme.

alarming [ə'lɑ:mɪŋ] *adj* allarmante.

Albania [æl'beɪnjə] *n* l'Albania *f*.

Albert Hall ['ælbət-] *n*: **the ~** l'Albert Hall *f* (*sala concerti di Londra*).

album ['ælbəm] *n* album *m inv*.

alcohol ['ælkəhɒl] *n* alcool *m*.

alcohol-free *adj* analcolico(-a).

alcoholic [,ælkə'hɒlɪk] ♦ *adj* alcolico(-a) ♦ *n* alcolizzato *m* (-a *f*).

alcoholism ['ælkəhɒlɪzm] *n* alcolismo *m*.

alcopop ['ælkəupɒp] *n* bibita leggermente alcolica.

alcove ['ælkəuv] *n* rientranza *f*.

ale [eɪl] *n* birra *f*.

alert [ə'lɜ:t] ♦ *adj* vigile ♦ *vt* allertare.

A levels *npl* ≈ esami *mpl* di maturità.

algebra ['ældʒɪbrə] *n* algebra *f*.

alias ['eɪlɪəs] *adv* alias.

alibi ['ælɪbaɪ] *n* alibi *m inv*.

alien ['eɪlɪən] *n* (*foreigner*) straniero *m* (-a *f*); (*from outer space*) alieno *m* (-a *f*).

alight [ə'laɪt] ♦ *adj* in fiamme ♦ *vi* (*fml: from train, bus*): **to ~ (from)** scendere (da).

align [ə'laɪn] *vt* allineare.

alike [ə'laɪk] ♦ *adj* simile ♦ *adv* allo stesso modo; **to look ~** assomigliarsi.

alive [ə'laɪv] *adj* (*living*) vivo(-a).

all [ɔ:l] *adj* tutto(-a); **~ the food** tutto il cibo; **~ the money** tutti i soldi; **~ the houses** tutte le case; **~ trains stop at Tonbridge** tutti i treni fermano a Tonbridge; **~ the time** sempre; **~ day** tutto il giorno.

♦ *adv* 1. (*completely*) completamente, interamente; **~ alone** tutto solo (tutta sola).

2. (*in scores*): **it's two ~** sono due pari.

3. (*in phrases*): **~ but empty** quasi vuoto; **~ over** (*finished*) finito.

♦ *pron* **1.** (*the whole amount*) tutto(-a); ~ **of the work** tutto il lavoro; **is that ~?** (*in shop*) basta così?
2. (*everybody, everything*) tutti(-e); ~ **of the girls/rooms** tutte le ragazze/camere; ~ **of us went** ci siamo andati tutti.
3. (*with superlative*): **the best of ~** il migliore di tutti.
4. (*in phrases*): **in ~** (*in total*) in tutto; (*in summary*) nel complesso; **can I help you at ~?** posso esserle di aiuto?

Allah [ˈælə] *n* Allah *m*.

allege [əˈledʒ] *vt* asserire.

allergic [əˈlɜːdʒɪk] *adj*: **to be ~ to** essere allergico(-a) a.

allergy [ˈælədʒɪ] *n* allergia *f*.

alleviate [əˈliːvɪeɪt] *vt* alleviare.

alley [ˈælɪ] *n* (*narrow street*) vicolo *m*.

alligator [ˈælɪgeɪtəʳ] *n* alligatore *m*.

all-in *adj* (Br: *inclusive*) tutto compreso (*inv*).

all-night *adj* (*bar, petrol station*) aperto(-a) tutta la notte.

allocate [ˈæləkeɪt] *vt* (*money, task*) assegnare.

allotment [əˈlɒtmənt] *n* (Br: *for vegetables*) piccolo lotto di terra preso in affitto per coltivarvi ortaggi.

allow [əˈlaʊ] *vt* (*permit*) permettere; (*time, money*) calcolare; **to ~ sb to do sthg** permettere a qn di fare qc; **to be ~ed to do sthg** avere il permesso di fare qc, poter fare qc.
▶ **allow for** *vt fus* tener conto di.

allowance [əˈlaʊəns] *n* (*state benefit*) assegno *m*; (*for expenses*) indennità *f inv*; (Am: *pocket money*) paghetta *f*.

all right ♦ *adv* (*satisfactorily*) bene; (*yes, okay*) va bene ♦ *adj*: **is everything ~?** va tutto bene?; **is it ~ if I smoke?** Le dispiace se fumo?; **are you ~?** ti senti bene?; **how was the film? – it was ~** com'era il film? – niente di speciale; **how are you? – I'm ~** come stai? – non c'è male.

ally [ˈælaɪ] *n* alleato *m* (-a *f*).

almond [ˈɑːmənd] *n* mandorla *f*.

almost [ˈɔːlməʊst] *adv* quasi.

alone [əˈləʊn] ♦ *adj* solo(-a) ♦ *adv* da solo(-a); **to leave sb ~** lasciare qn in pace; **to leave sthg ~** lasciar stare qc.

along [əˈlɒŋ] ♦ *prep* lungo ♦ *adv*: **to walk ~** camminare; **to bring sthg ~** portare qc; **all ~** sempre; **~ with** insieme a.

alongside [əˌlɒŋˈsaɪd] ♦ *prep* accanto a ♦ *adv*: **to come ~** accostare.

aloof [əˈluːf] *adj* distaccato(-a).

aloud [əˈlaʊd] *adv* a voce alta.

alphabet [ˈælfəbet] *n* alfabeto *m*.

Alps [ælps] *npl*: **the ~** le Alpi.

already [ɔːlˈredɪ] *adv* già.

also [ˈɔːlsəʊ] *adv* anche.

altar [ˈɔːltəʳ] *n* altare *m*.

alter [ˈɔːltəʳ] *vt* cambiare.

alteration [ˌɔːltəˈreɪʃn] *n* modifica *f*.

alternate [Br ɔːlˈtɜːnət, Am ˈɔːltərnət] *adj* alterni(-e).

alternating current [ˈɔːltəneɪtɪŋ-] *n* corrente *f* alternata.

alternative [ɔːlˈtɜːnətɪv] ♦ *adj* alternativo(-a) ♦ *n* alternativa *f*.

alternatively [ɔːlˈtɜːnətɪvlɪ] *adv* in alternativa.

alternator [ˈɔːltəneɪtəʳ] *n* alternatore *m*.

although [ɔːlˈðəʊ] *conj* sebbene, benché.

altitude [ˈæltɪtjuːd] *n* altitudine *f*.

altogether [ˌɔːltəˈgeðəʳ] *adv* (*completely*) del tutto; (*in total*) in tutto.

aluminium [ˌæljʊˈmɪnɪəm] *n* (Br) alluminio *m*.

aluminum [əˈluːmɪnəm] (Am) = **aluminium**.

always [ˈɔːlweɪz] *adv* sempre.

am [æm] → **be**.

a.m. (*abbr of ante meridiem*): **at two ~** alle due di notte; **at ten ~** alle dieci di mattina.

amateur [ˈæmətəʳ] *n* dilettante *mf*.

amazed [əˈmeɪzd] *adj* stupito(-a).

amazing [ə'meɪzɪŋ] *adj* incredibile.

Amazon ['æməzn] *n* (*river*): **the ~** il Rio delle Amazzoni.

ambassador [æm'bæsədəʳ] *n* ambasciatore *m* (-trice *f*).

amber ['æmbəʳ] *adj* (*traffic lights*) giallo(-a); (*jewellery*) d'ambra.

ambiguous [æm'bɪgjuəs] *adj* ambiguo(-a).

ambition [æm'bɪʃn] *n* ambizione *f*.

ambitious [æm'bɪʃəs] *adj* ambizioso(-a).

ambulance ['æmbjʊləns] *n* ambulanza *f*.

ambush ['æmbuʃ] *n* imboscata *f*.

amenities [ə'miːnətɪz] *npl* (*in hotel*) comfort *m inv*; (*in town*) strutture *fpl* (*sportive, ricreative ecc.*).

America [ə'merɪkə] *n* l'America *f*.

American [ə'merɪkən] ♦ *adj* americano(-a) ♦ *n* (*person*) americano *m* (-a *f*).

amiable ['eɪmɪəbl] *adj* amabile.

ammunition [ˌæmjʊ'nɪʃn] *n* munizioni *fpl*.

amnesia [æm'niːzɪə] *n* amnesia *f*.

among(st) [ə'mʌŋ(st)] *prep* tra, fra.

amount [ə'maʊnt] *n* (*quantity*) quantità *f inv*; (*sum*) somma *f*.

▶ **amount to** *vt fus* (*total*) ammontare a.

amp [æmp] *n* ampere *m inv*; **a 13-~ plug** una spina con fusibile da 13 ampere.

ample ['æmpl] *adj* più che sufficiente.

amplifier ['æmplɪfaɪəʳ] *n* amplificatore *m*.

amputate ['æmpjʊteɪt] *vt* amputare.

Amtrak ['æmtræk] *n* compagnia ferroviaria statunitense.

amuse [ə'mjuːz] *vt* divertire.

amusement arcade [ə'mjuːz-mənt-] *n* sala *f* giochi.

amusement park *n* luna park *m inv*.

amusements [ə'mjuːzmənts] *npl*

giostre e giochi al luna park.

amusing [ə'mjuːzɪŋ] *adj* divertente.

an [*stressed* æn, *unstressed* ən] → **a**.

anaemic [ə'niːmɪk] *adj* (Br: *person*) anemico(-a).

anaesthetic [ˌænɪs'θetɪk] *n* (Br) anestetico *m*.

analgesic [ˌænæl'dʒiːzɪk] *n* analgesico *m*.

analyse ['ænəlaɪz] *vt* analizzare.

analyst ['ænəlɪst] *n* analista *mf*.

analyze ['ænəlaɪz] (Am) = **analyse**.

anarchy ['ænəkɪ] *n* anarchia *f*.

anatomy [ə'nætəmɪ] *n* (*science*) anatomia *f*; (*of animal*) struttura *f*; (*of person*) corpo *m*.

ancestor ['ænsestəʳ] *n* antenato *m* (-a *f*).

anchor ['æŋkəʳ] *n* àncora *f*.

anchovy ['æntʃəvɪ] *n* acciuga *f*.

ancient ['eɪnʃənt] *adj* (*customs, monument*) antico(-a).

and [*strong form* ænd, *weak form* ənd, ən] *conj* e, ed (*before vowel*); **more ~ more** sempre più; **~ you?** e tu?; **a hundred ~ one** centouno; **to try ~ do sthg** cercare di fare qc; **to go ~ see** andare a vedere.

Andes ['ændiːz] *npl*: **the ~** le Ande.

anecdote ['ænɪkdəʊt] *n* aneddoto *m*.

anemic [ə'niːmɪk] (Am) = **anaemic**.

anesthetic [ˌænɪs'θetɪk] (Am) = **anaesthetic**.

angel ['eɪndʒl] *n* angelo *m*.

anger ['æŋgəʳ] *n* rabbia *f*.

angina [æn'dʒaɪnə] *n* angina *f* pectoris.

angle ['æŋgl] *n* angolo *m*; **at an ~** storto(-a).

angler ['æŋgləʳ] *n* pescatore *m* (-trice *f*).

angling ['æŋglɪŋ] *n* pesca *f*.

angry ['æŋgrɪ] *adj* (*person*) arrabbiato(-a); (*words*) pieno(-a) di rabbia; **to get ~ (with sb)** arrabbiarsi (con qn).

animal ['ænɪml] n animale m.

aniseed ['ænɪsiːd] n semi mpl d'anice.

ankle ['æŋkl] n caviglia f.

annex ['æneks] n (building) edificio m annesso.

annihilate [ə'naɪəleɪt] vt annientare.

anniversary [ænɪ'vɜːsərɪ] n anniversario m.

announce [ə'naʊns] vt annunciare.

announcement [ə'naʊnsmənt] n annuncio m.

announcer [ə'naʊnsə'] n annunciatore m (-trice f).

annoy [ə'nɔɪ] vt dare fastidio a.

annoyed [ə'nɔɪd] adj seccato(-a); **to get ~ (with sb)** arrabbiarsi (con qn).

annoying [ə'nɔɪɪŋ] adj seccante, irritante.

annual ['ænjʊəl] adj annuale.

anonymous [ə'nɒnɪməs] adj anonimo(-a).

anorak ['ænəræk] n giacca f a vento.

another [ə'nʌðə'] ♦ adj un altro (un'altra) ♦ pron un'altro (un'altra f); **can I have ~ (one)?** posso prenderne un altro?; **in ~ two weeks** fra altre due settimane; **one ~** l'un l'altro (l'un l'altra); **to help one ~** aiutarsi (l'un l'altro); **to talk to one ~** parlarsi; **one after ~** uno dopo l'altro (una dopo l'altra).

answer ['ɑːnsə'] ♦ n risposta f ♦ vt rispondere a ♦ vi rispondere; **to ~ the door** andare ad aprire (la porta); **to ~ the phone** rispondere al telefono.

▶ **answer back** vi rispondere male.

answering machine ['ɑːnsərɪŋ-] = **answerphone**.

answerphone ['ɑːnsəfəʊn] n segreteria f telefonica.

ant [ænt] n formica f.

Antarctic [æn'tɑːktɪk] n: **the ~** l'Antartide f.

antenna [æn'tenə] n (Am: aerial) antenna f.

anthem ['ænθəm] n inno m.

antibiotics [æntɪbaɪ'ɒtɪks] npl antibiotici mpl.

anticipate [æn'tɪsɪpeɪt] vt (expect) aspettarsi; (guess correctly) prevedere.

anticlimax [æntɪ'klaɪmæks] n delusione f.

anticlockwise [æntɪ'klɒkwaɪz] adv (Br) in senso antiorario.

antidote ['æntɪdəʊt] n antidoto m.

antifreeze ['æntɪfriːz] n antigelo m.

antihistamine [æntɪ'hɪstəmɪn] n antistaminico m.

antiperspirant [æntɪ'pɜːspərənt] n deodorante m (ad azione antitraspirante).

antiquarian bookshop [æntɪ'kweərɪən-] n libreria f antiquaria.

antique [æn'tiːk] n pezzo m d'antiquariato.

antique shop n negozio m d'antiquariato.

antiseptic [æntɪ'septɪk] n antisettico m.

antisocial [æntɪ'səʊʃl] adj (person) asociale; (behaviour) incivile.

antlers ['æntləz] npl palchi mpl.

anxiety [æŋ'zaɪətɪ] n ansia f.

anxious ['æŋkʃəs] adj (worried) preoccupato(-a); (eager) ansioso(-a).

any ['enɪ] adj 1. (in questions): **have you got ~ money?** hai (dei) soldi?; **have you got ~ postcards?** ha delle cartoline?; **is there ~ coffee left?** c'è ancora del caffè?

2. (in negatives): **I haven't got ~ money** non ho soldi; **I haven't got ~ Italian stamps** non ho nessun francobollo italiano; **we don't have ~ rooms** non abbiamo camere libere.

3. (no matter which) qualunque, qualsiasi; **take ~ one you like** pren-

di quello che preferisci.

♦ *pron* **1.** (*in questions*) ne; **I'm look-ing for a hotel – are there ~ nearby?** sto cercando un albergo – ce ne sono da queste parti?

2. (*in negatives*) ne; **I don't want ~ (of them)** non ne voglio.

3. (*no matter which one*): **you can sit at ~ of the tables** potete sedere a qualsiasi tavolo.

♦ *adv* **1.** (*in questions*): **is that ~ better?** così va un po' meglio?; **is there ~ more ice cream?** c'è ancora un po' di gelato?; **~ other questions?** altre domande?

2. (*in negatives*): **he's not ~ better** non c'è nessun miglioramento; **we can't wait ~ longer** non possiamo più aspettare.

anybody ['enɪˌbɒdɪ] = **anyone**.

anyhow ['enɪhaʊ] *adv* comunque; (*carelessly*) alla rinfusa.

anyone ['enɪwʌn] *pron* (*someone*) qualcuno; (*any person*) chiunque; **is ~ there?** c'è nessuno?; **there wasn't ~ in** non c'era nessuno.

anything ['enɪθɪŋ] *pron* (*something*) qualcosa; (*no matter what*) qualunque cosa, qualsiasi cosa; **have you ~ bigger?** ha niente di più grande?; **I don't want ~ to eat** non voglio mangiare niente.

anyway ['enɪweɪ] *adv* comunque.

anywhere ['enɪweər] *adv* (*in ques-tions*) da qualche parte; (*with nega-tive*) da nessuna parte; (*any place*) dovunque, da qualunque OR qual-siasi parte; **did you go ~ else?** siete andati da qualche altra parte?; **~ you like** dove vuoi.

apart [ə'pɑːt] *adv* (*separated*): **the towns are 5 miles ~** le due città di-stano 8 km l'una dall'altra; **we live ~** non viviamo insieme; **to come ~** andare in pezzi; **~ from** (*except for*) a parte; (*as well as*) oltre a.

apartheid [ə'pɑːtheɪt] *n* apartheid *f*.

apartment [ə'pɑːtmənt] *n* (Am) appartamento *m*.

apathetic [ˌæpə'θetɪk] *adj* apati-co(-a).

ape [eɪp] *n* scimmia *f*.

aperitif [ə,perɪ'tiːf] *n* aperitivo *m*.

aperture ['æpətʃər] *n* (*of camera*) apertura *f*.

APEX ['eɪpeks] *n* (*plane ticket*) biglietto *m* APEX; (Br: *train ticket*) *biglietto ferroviario con data prefissata e dal prezzo ridotto comprato due settimane prima della partenza.*

apiece [ə'piːs] *adv* (*for each item*) l'uno (l'una); (*to, for each person*) cia-scuno(-a).

apologetic [ə,pɒlə'dʒetɪk] *adj*: **to be ~** scusarsi.

apologize [ə'pɒlədʒaɪz] *vi*: **to ~ (to sb for sthg)** scusarsi (con qn per qc).

apology [ə'pɒlədʒɪ] *n* scuse *fpl*.

apostrophe [ə'pɒstrəfɪ] *n* apo-strofo *m*.

appal [ə'pɔːl] *vt* (Br) sconvolgere.

appall [ə'pɔːl] (Am) = **appal**.

appalling [ə'pɔːlɪŋ] *adj* spavento-so(-a).

apparatus [ˌæpə'reɪtəs] *n* (*device*) apparecchio *m*; (*in gym*) attrezzatu-ra *f*.

apparently [ə'pærəntlɪ] *adv* (*it seems*) a quanto pare; (*evidently*) evi-dentemente.

appeal [ə'piːl] ♦ *n* (JUR) appello *m*; (*fundraising campaign*) raccolta *f* di fondi ♦ *vi* (JUR) fare appello; **to ~ to sb for help** chiedere aiuto a qn; **it doesn't ~ to me** non mi attira.

appear [ə'pɪər] *vi* apparire; (*seem*) sembrare; (*before court*) comparire; **it ~s that** sembra che.

appearance [ə'pɪərəns] *n* (*arrival*) comparsa *f*; (*look*) aspetto *m*.

appendices [ə'pendɪsiːz] *pl* → **appendix**.

appendicitis [ə,pendɪ'saɪtɪs] *n* appendicite *f*.

appendix [ə'pendɪks] (*pl* -dices) *n* appendice *f*.

appetite ['æpɪtaɪt] *n* appetito *m*.

appetizer ['æpɪtaɪzəʳ] *n* stuzzichino *m*.

appetizing ['æpɪtaɪzɪŋ] *adj* appetitoso(-a).

applaud [ə'plɔːd] *vt* & *vi* applaudire.

applause [ə'plɔːz] *n* applauso *m*.

apple ['æpl] *n* mela *f*.

apple charlotte [-'ʃɑːlət] *n* dolce di pane o pan di Spagna, ripieno di mele e pane sbriciolato e cotto in forno.

apple crumble *n* mele cotte ricoperte da uno strato di pasta frolla sbriciolata.

apple juice *n* succo *m* di mela.

apple pie *n* torta *f* di mele ricoperta di pasta.

apple sauce *n* mele *fpl* grattugiate.

apple tart *n* crostata *f* di mele.

apple turnover [-'tɜːn,əʊvəʳ] *n* sfogliatella *f* di mele.

appliance [ə'plaɪəns] *n* apparecchio *m*; **electrical/domestic ~** elettrodomestico *m*.

applicable [ə'plɪkəbl] *adj*: **to be ~ (to)** essere applicabile (a); **if ~ se** pertinente.

applicant ['æplɪkənt] *n* candidato *m* (-a *f*).

application [æplɪ'keɪʃn] *n* (*for job, membership*) domanda *f*.

application form *n* modulo *m* di domanda.

apply [ə'plaɪ] ◆ *vt* (*lotion, paint*) dare; (*brakes*) azionare ◆ *vi*: **to ~ (to sb for sthg)** (*make request*) fare domanda (per qc presso qn); **to ~ (to sb)** (*be applicable*) essere valido (per qn); **to ~ for a job** fare domanda di lavoro.

appointment [ə'pɔɪntmənt] *n* (*with doctor, hairdresser, businessman*) appuntamento *m*; **to have/make an ~ (with)** avere/prendere un appuntamento (con); **by ~** per OR su appuntamento.

appreciable [ə'priːʃəbl] *adj* apprezzabile.

appreciate [ə'priːʃɪeɪt] *vt* apprez-

zare; (*understand*) rendersi conto di.

apprehensive [æprɪ'hensɪv] *adj* preoccupato(-a).

apprentice [ə'prentɪs] *n* apprendista *mf*.

apprenticeship [ə'prentɪsʃɪp] *n* apprendistato *m*.

approach [ə'prəʊtʃ] ◆ *n* (*road*) accesso *m*; (*to problem, situation*) approccio *m* ◆ *vt* (*come nearer to*) avvicinare; (*problem, situation*) affrontare ◆ *vi* avvicinarsi.

appropriate [ə'prəʊprɪət] *adj* adatto(-a).

approval [ə'pruːvl] *n* approvazione *f*.

approve [ə'pruːv] *vi*: **to ~ (of sb/sthg)** approvare (qn/qc).

approximate [ə'prɒksɪmət] *adj* approssimativo(-a).

approximately [ə'prɒksɪmətlɪ] *adv* circa.

Apr. (*abbr of* April) apr.

apricot ['eɪprɪkɒt] *n* albicocca *f*.

April ['eɪprəl] *n* aprile *m*, → **September**.

April Fools' Day *n* il primo aprile, giorno in cui si fanno i 'pesci d'aprile'.

apron ['eɪprən] *n* grembiule *m* (da cucina).

apt [æpt] *adj* (*appropriate*) appropriato(-a); **to be ~ to do sthg** avere tendenza a fare qc.

aquarium [ə'kweərɪəm] (*pl* **-ria** [-rɪə]) *n* acquario *m*.

Aquarius [ə'kweərɪəs] *n* Acquario *m*.

aqueduct ['ækwɪdʌkt] *n* acquedotto *m*.

Arab ['ærəb] ◆ *adj* arabo(-a) ◆ *n* (*person*) arabo *m* (-a *f*).

Arabic ['ærəbɪk] ◆ *adj* arabo(-a) ◆ *n* (*language*) arabo *m*.

arbitrary ['ɑːbɪtrərɪ] *adj* arbitrario(-a).

arc [ɑːk] *n* arco *m*.

arcade [ɑː'keɪd] *n* (*for shopping*) galleria *f*; (*of video games*) sala *f* giochi.

arch [ɑːtʃ] n arco m.

archaeologist [ˌɑːkɪˈɒlədʒɪst] n archeologo m (-a f).

archaeology [ˌɑːkɪˈɒlədʒɪ] n archeologia f.

archbishop [ˌɑːtʃˈbɪʃəp] n arcivescovo m.

archery [ˈɑːtʃərɪ] n tiro m con l'arco.

archipelago [ˌɑːkɪˈpeləgəʊ] n arcipelago m.

architect [ˈɑːkɪtekt] n architetto mf.

architecture [ˈɑːkɪtektʃər] n architettura f.

archives [ˈɑːkaɪvz] npl archivi mpl.

Arctic [ˈɑːktɪk] n: **the ~** l'Artide f.

are [weak form ər, strong form ɑːr] → **be**.

area [ˈeərɪə] n (region) zona f; (space, zone) area f; (surface size) superficie f; **dining ~** zona pranzo.

area code n (Am) prefisso m.

arena [əˈriːnə] n (at circus) pista f; (sports ground) campo m.

aren't = are not.

Argentina [ˌɑːdʒənˈtiːnə] n l'Argentina f.

argue [ˈɑːgjuː] ◆ vi (quarrel): **to ~ (with sb about sthg)** litigare (con qn per qc) ◆ vt: **to ~ (that) ...** sostenere (che) ...

argument [ˈɑːgjʊmənt] n (quarrel) discussione f; (reason) argomento m.

arid [ˈærɪd] adj arido(-a).

Aries [ˈeəriːz] n Ariete m.

arise [əˈraɪz] (pt **arose**, pp **arisen** [əˈrɪzn]) vi (problem, opportunity) presentarsi; **to ~ from** derivare da.

aristocracy [ˌærɪˈstɒkrəsɪ] n aristocrazia f.

arithmetic [əˈrɪθmətɪk] n aritmetica f.

arm [ɑːm] n (of person) braccio m; (of chair) bracciolo m; (of garment) manica f; **to hold in one's ~s** (baby) tenere in braccio.

armbands [ˈɑːmbændz] npl (for swimming) braccioli mpl.

armchair [ˈɑːmtʃeər] n poltrona f.

armed [ɑːmd] adj armato(-a).

armed forces npl: **the ~** le forze armate.

armor (Am) = **armour**.

armour [ˈɑːmər] n (Br) armatura f.

armpit [ˈɑːmpɪt] n ascella f.

arms [ɑːmz] npl (weapons) armi fpl.

army [ˈɑːmɪ] n esercito m.

A road n (Br) strada f statale.

aroma [əˈrəʊmə] n aroma m.

aromatic [ˌærəˈmætɪk] adj aromatico(-a).

arose [əˈrəʊz] pt → **arise**.

around [əˈraʊnd] ◆ adv in giro ◆ prep (surrounding) intorno a; (to the other side of) dall'altra parte di; (near) vicino a; (all over) per; (approximately) circa; **~ here** (in the area) da queste parti; **~ the corner** dietro l'angolo; **to turn ~** girarsi; **to look ~** (turn head) guardarsi intorno; (in shop, city) dare un'occhiata in giro; **at ~ two o'clock** verso le due; **is Paul ~?** c'è Paul?

arouse [əˈraʊz] vt destare.

arrange [əˈreɪndʒ] vt (flowers, books) sistemare; (meeting, event) organizzare; **to ~ to do sthg (with sb)** mettersi d'accordo (con qn) per fare qc.

arrangement [əˈreɪndʒmənt] n (agreement) accordo m; (layout) disposizione f; **by ~** su richiesta; **to make ~s (to do sthg)** fare il necessario (per fare qc).

arrest [əˈrest] ◆ n arresto m ◆ vt arrestare; **under ~** in arresto.

arrival [əˈraɪvl] n arrivo m; **on ~** all'arrivo; **new ~** (person) nuovo arrivato m (nuova arrivata f).

arrive [əˈraɪv] vi arrivare; **to ~ at** (place) arrivare in/a.

arrogant [ˈærəgənt] adj arrogante.

arrow [ˈærəʊ] n freccia f.

arson [ˈɑːsn] n incendio m doloso.

art [ɑːt] n arte f; (SCOL: subject) disegno m.

▶ **arts** *npl* (*humanities*) discipline *fpl* umanistiche; **the ~s** (*fine arts*) l'arte *f*.

artefact ['ɑːtɪfækt] *n* manufatto *m*.

artery ['ɑːtəri] *n* arteria *f*.

art gallery *n* galleria *f* d'arte.

arthritis [ɑːˈθraɪtɪs] *n* artrite *f*.

artichoke ['ɑːtɪtʃəʊk] *n* carciofo *m*.

article ['ɑːtɪkl] *n* articolo *m*.

articulate [ɑːˈtɪkjʊlət] *adj* chiaro(-a).

artificial [ˌɑːtɪˈfɪʃl] *adj* artificiale.

artist ['ɑːtɪst] *n* artista *mf*.

artistic [ɑːˈtɪstɪk] *adj* (*design*) artistico(-a); (*person*) dotato(-a) di senso artistico.

arts centre *n* centro *m* artistico.

as [*unstressed* əz, *stressed* æz] *adv* (*in comparisons*): **~ ... ~** (così) ... come; **~ white ~ snow** bianco come la neve; **he's ~ tall ~ I am** è alto quanto to me; **~ many ~** tanti ... quanti (tante ... quante); **~ much ~** tanto ... quanto (tanta ... quanta); **twice ~ big** due volte più grande.

♦ *conj* **1.** (*referring to time*) mentre, nel momento in cui; **~ the plane was coming in to land** nel momento in cui l'aereo si preparava ad atterrare.

2. (*referring to manner*) come; **~ expected ...** come previsto ...; **do ~ you like** fa' come vuoi.

3. (*introducing a statement*) come; **~ you know ...** come sai ...

4. (*because*) poiché, dato che.

5. (*in phrases*): **~ for** quanto a; **~ from** (a partire) da; **~ if** come se; **it looks ~ if it will rain** sembra che stia per piovere.

♦ *prep* (*referring to function, job*) come; **to work ~ a teacher** fare l'insegnante.

asap (*abbr of as soon as possible*) il più presto possibile.

ascent [əˈsent] *n* (*climb*) scalata *f*.

ascribe [əˈskraɪb] *vt*: **~ sthg to** attribuire qc a.

ash [æʃ] *n* (*from cigarette, fire*) cenere *f*; (*tree*) frassino *m*.

ashamed [əˈʃeɪmd] *adj* vergognoso(-a); **to be ~ (of)** vergognarsi (di), avere vergogna (di).

ashore [əˈʃɔːr] *adv* a riva.

ashtray ['æʃtreɪ] *n* portacenere *m inv*.

Asia [Br 'eɪʃə, Am 'eɪʒə] *n* l'Asia *f*.

Asian [Br 'eɪʃn, Am 'eɪʒn] ♦ *adj* asiatico(-a) ♦ *n* asiatico *m* (-a *f*).

aside [əˈsaɪd] *adv* (*to one side*) di lato; **to move ~** spostarsi.

ask [ɑːsk] ♦ *vt* (*person*) chiedere a; (*request*) chiedere; (*invite*) invitare ♦ *vi*: **to ~ about sthg** chiedere informazioni su qc; **to ~ sb sthg** chiedere qc a qn; **to ~ sb about sthg** chiedere a qn di qc; **to ~ sb to do sthg** chiedere a qn di fare qc; **to ~ sb for sthg** chiedere qc a qn; **to ~ a question** fare una domanda; **can I ~ you about this translation?** posso farti qualche domanda su questa traduzione?

▶ **ask for** *vt fus* (*ask to talk to*) chiedere di; (*request*) chiedere.

asleep [əˈsliːp] *adj* addormentato(-a); **to be ~** dormire; **to fall ~** addormentarsi.

asparagus [əˈspærəgəs] *n* asparagi *mpl*.

asparagus tips *npl* punte *fpl* d'asparagi.

aspect ['æspekt] *n* aspetto *m*.

aspirin ['æsprɪn] *n* aspirina® *f*.

ass [æs] *n* (*animal*) asino *m*.

assassinate [əˈsæsɪneɪt] *vt* assassinare.

assault [əˈsɔːlt] ♦ *n* aggressione *f* ♦ *vt* aggredire.

assemble [əˈsembl] ♦ *vt* (*bookcase, model*) montare ♦ *vi* riunirsi.

assembly [əˈsemblɪ] *n* (*at school*) riunione quotidiana di alunni e professori.

assembly hall *n* (*at school*) locale di una scuola dove alunni e professori si riuniscono ogni giorno prima delle lezioni.

assembly point *n* punto di raduno in caso di emergenza.

assert [əˈsɜːt] vt (*fact, innocence*) sostenere; (*authority*) far valere; to ~ o.s. farsi valere.

assess [əˈses] vt (*person, situation, effect*) valutare; (*value, damage, cost*) stimare.

assessment [əˈsesmənt] n (*of person, situation, effect*) valutazione f; (*of value, damage, cost*) stima f.

asset [ˈæset] n (*valuable person, thing*) punto m di forza.

assign [əˈsaɪn] vt: to ~ sthg to sb (*give*) assegnare qc a qn; to ~ sb to do sthg (*designate*) incaricare qn di fare qc.

assignment [əˈsaɪnmənt] n (*task*) incarico m; (SCH) ricerca f.

assist [əˈsɪst] vt aiutare.

assistance [əˈsɪstəns] n aiuto m; to be of ~ (to sb) essere d'aiuto (a qn).

assistant [əˈsɪstənt] n assistente mf.

associate [n əˈsəʊsɪət, vb əˈsəʊsɪeɪt] ◆ n (*partner*) socio m (-a f); (*colleague*) collega mf ◆ vt: to ~ sb/sthg with associare qn/qc a; to be ~d with venire associato a.

association [ə,səʊsɪˈeɪʃn] n associazione f.

assorted [əˈsɔːtɪd] adj assortito(-a).

assortment [əˈsɔːtmənt] n assortimento m.

assume [əˈsjuːm] vt (*suppose*) supporre; (*control*) assumere; (*responsibility*) assumersi.

assurance [əˈʃʊərəns] n (*promise*) promessa f; (*insurance*) assicurazione f.

assure [əˈʃʊəʳ] vt assicurare; to ~ sb (that) ... assicurare a qn che ...

asterisk [ˈæstərɪsk] n asterisco m.

asthma [ˈæsmə] n asma f.

asthmatic [æsˈmætɪk] adj asmatico(-a).

astonished [əˈstɒnɪʃt] adj stupito(-a).

astonishing [əˈstɒnɪʃɪŋ] adj incredibile.

astound [əˈstaʊnd] vt sbalordire.

astray [əˈstreɪ] adv: to go ~ smarrirsi.

astrology [əˈstrɒlədʒɪ] n astrologia f.

astronomy [əˈstrɒnəmɪ] n astronomia f.

asylum [əˈsaɪləm] n (*mental hospital*) manicomio m.

at [unstressed ət, stressed æt] prep **1.** (*indicating place, position*) a; ~ school a scuola; ~ the hotel in OR all'albergo; ~ home a casa; ~ my mother's da mia madre.

2. (*indicating direction*): to throw sthg ~ tirare qc contro; to look ~ sb/sthg guardare qn/qc; to smile ~ sb sorridere a qn.

3. (*indicating time*) a; ~ nine o'clock alle nove; ~ night di notte.

4. (*indicating rate, level, speed*) a; it works out ~ £5 each viene 5 sterline a testa; ~ 60 km/h a 60km/h.

5. (*indicating activity*): she's ~ lunch sta pranzando; to be good/bad ~ sthg essere/non essere bravo in qc.

6. (*indicating cause*): shocked ~ sthg scioccato da qc; angry ~ sb arrabbiato con qn; delighted ~ sthg contentissimo di qc.

ate [Br et, Am eɪt] pt → eat.

atheist [ˈeɪθɪɪst] n ateo m (-a f).

Athens [ˈæθɪnz] n Atene f.

athlete [ˈæθliːt] n atleta mf.

athletics [æθˈletɪks] n atletica f.

Atlantic [ətˈlæntɪk] n: the ~ (Ocean) l'Atlantico m, l'Oceano m Atlantico.

atlas [ˈætləs] n atlante m.

atmosphere [ˈætməsfɪəʳ] n atmosfera f; (*air in room*) aria f.

atom [ˈætəm] n atomo m.

A to Z n (*map*) stradario m.

atrocious [əˈtrəʊʃəs] adj (*very bad*) orrendo(-a).

attach [əˈtætʃ] vt attaccare; to ~ sthg to sthg attaccare qc a qc.

attachment [əˈtætʃmənt] n (*device*) accessorio m.

attack [ə'tæk] ♦ n attacco m ♦ vt aggredire.

attacker [ə'tækər] n aggressore m.

attain [ə'teɪn] vt (fml) conseguire.

attempt [ə'tempt] ♦ n tentativo m ♦ vt tentare; **to ~ to do sthg** tentare di fare qc.

attend [ə'tend] vt (meeting) partecipare a; (school) frequentare; (mass) ascoltare.

▶ **attend to** vt fus (deal with) occuparsi di.

attendance [ə'tendəns] n (people at concert, match) affluenza f; (at school) frequenza f.

attendant [ə'tendənt] n (at public toilets, cloakroom) addetto m (-a f); (at museum) custode mf.

attention [ə'tenʃn] n attenzione f; **to pay ~ (to)** fare attenzione (a).

attic ['ætɪk] n soffitta f.

attitude ['ætɪtjuːd] n atteggiamento m.

attorney [ə'tɜːnɪ] n (Am) avvocato m.

attract [ə'trækt] vt attirare.

attraction [ə'trækʃn] n (liking) attrazione f; (attractive feature) attrattiva f.

attractive [ə'træktɪv] adj attraente.

attribute [ə'trɪbjuːt] vt: **to ~ sthg to** attribuire qc a.

aubergine ['əʊbəʒiːn] n (Br) melanzana f.

auburn ['ɔːbən] adj castano ramato (inv).

auction ['ɔːkʃn] n asta f.

audience ['ɔːdɪəns] n (of play, concert, film) pubblico m; (of TV) telespettatori mpl; (of radio) ascoltatori mpl.

audio ['ɔːdɪəʊ] adj audio (inv).

audio-visual [-'vɪʒʊəl] adj audio-visivo(-a).

auditorium [ˌɔːdɪ'tɔːrɪəm] n sala f.

Aug. (abbr of August) ago.

August ['ɔːgəst] n agosto m, → **September**.

aunt [ɑːnt] n zia f.

au pair [ˌəʊ'peər] n ragazza f alla pari.

aural ['ɔːrəl] adj uditivo(-a).

Australia [ɒ'streɪlɪə] n l'Australia f.

Australian [ɒ'streɪlɪən] ♦ adj australiano(-a) ♦ n australiano m (-a f).

Austria ['ɒstrɪə] n l'Austria f.

Austrian ['ɒstrɪən] ♦ adj austriaco(-a) ♦ n austriaco m (-a f).

authentic [ɔː'θentɪk] adj autentico(-a).

author ['ɔːθər] n (of book, article) autore m (-trice f); (by profession) scrittore m (-trice f).

authority [ɔː'θɒrətɪ] n autorità f inv; **the authorities** le autorità.

authorization [ˌɔːθəraɪ'zeɪʃn] n autorizzazione f.

authorize ['ɔːθəraɪz] vt autorizzare; **to ~ sb to do sthg** autorizzare qn a fare qc.

autobiography [ˌɔːtəbaɪ'ɒgrəfɪ] n autobiografia f.

autograph ['ɔːtəgrɑːf] n autografo m.

automatic [ˌɔːtə'mætɪk] ♦ adj automatico(-a) ♦ n (car) automobile f con cambio automatico.

automatically [ˌɔːtə'mætɪklɪ] adv automaticamente.

automobile ['ɔːtəməbiːl] n (Am) automobile f.

autumn ['ɔːtəm] n autunno m; **in (the) ~** in autunno.

auxiliary (verb) [ɔːg'zɪljərɪ-] n ausiliare m.

available [ə'veɪləbl] adj disponibile.

avalanche ['ævəlɑːnʃ] n valanga f.

Ave. (abbr of avenue) V.le.

avenue ['ævənjuː] n viale m.

average ['ævərɪdʒ] ♦ adj medio(-a); (not very good) mediocre ♦ n media f; **on ~** in media.

aversion [ə'vɜːʃn] n avversione f.

aviation [ˌeɪvɪ'eɪʃn] n aviazione f.

avid [ˈævɪd] *adj* avido(-a).

avocado [ˌævəˈkɑːdəʊ] (*pl* **-s** OR **-es**) *n*: ~ **(pear)** avocado *m inv*.

avoid [əˈvɔɪd] *vt* evitare; **to ~ doing sthg** evitare di fare qc.

await [əˈweɪt] *vt* attendere.

awake [əˈweɪk] (*pt* **awoke,** *pp* **awoken)** ◆ *adj* sveglio(-a) ◆ *vi* svegliarsi.

award [əˈwɔːd] ◆ *n* premio *m* ◆ *vt*: **to ~ sb sthg** (*prize*) assegnare qc a qn; (*damages, compensation*) accordare qc a qn.

aware [əˈweər] *adj* consapevole; **to be ~ of** rendersi conto di.

away [əˈweɪ] *adv* via; (*look, turn*) da un'altra parte; **to drive ~** allontanarsi; **to walk ~** allontanarsi; **to go ~ on holiday** partire per le vacanze; **to put sthg ~** mettere via qc, mettere a posto qc; **to take sthg ~** (**from sb)** portare via qc (a qn), prendere qc (a qn); **far ~** molto lontano; **it's 10 miles ~ (from here)** è a 10 miglia (da qui); **the festival is two weeks ~** mancano due settimane al festival.

awesome [ˈɔːsəm] *adj* (*impressive*) imponente; (*inf: excellent*) fantastico(-a).

awful [ˈɔːfəl] *adj* orribile; **I feel ~** sto malissimo; **an ~ lot of** un mucchio di.

awfully [ˈɔːflɪ] *adv* (*very*) molto, terribilmente.

awkward [ˈɔːkwəd] *adj* (*movement*) sgraziato(-a); (*position*) goffo(-a); (*shape, size*) poco funzionale; (*situation, question*) imbarazzante; (*task, time*) difficile.

awning [ˈɔːnɪŋ] *n* tenda *f*.

awoke [əˈwəʊk] *pt* → **awake.**

awoken [əˈwəʊkən] *pp* → **awake.**

axe [æks] *n* scure *f*.

axle [ˈæksl] *n* asse *m*.

B

BA (*abbr of Bachelor of Arts*) (*degree*) laurea *f* in materie umanistiche; (*person*) laureato *m* (-a *f*) in materie umanistiche.

babble [ˈbæbl] *vi* balbettare.

baby [ˈbeɪbɪ] *n* bambino *m* (-a *f*); **to have a ~** avere un bambino; **~ sweetcorn** piccole spighe di mais.

baby carriage *n* (Am) carrozzina *f*.

baby food *n* alimenti *mpl* per l'infanzia.

baby-sit *vi* fare da baby-sitter.

baby wipe *n* salvietta *f* umidificata (per bambini).

back [bæk] ◆ *adv* indietro ◆ *n* (*of person*) schiena *f*; (*of chair*) schienale *m*; (*of car, book, bank note*) retro *m*; (*of room*) fondo *m*; (*of hand*) dorso *m* ◆ *adj* (*seat, wheels*) posteriore ◆ *vi* (*car, driver*) fare retromarcia ◆ *vt* (*support*) appoggiare; **to put sthg ~** rimettere qc (a posto); **to arrive ~** ritornare; **to give sthg ~** restituire OR dare indietro qc; **to write ~ to sb** rispondere a qn; **at the ~ of** sul retro di, dietro; **in ~ of** (Am) sul retro di, dietro; **~ to front** davanti di dietro.

▶ **back up** ◆ *vt sep* (*support*) appoggiare ◆ *vi* (*car, driver*) fare retromarcia.

backache [ˈbækeɪk] *n* mal *m* di schiena.

backbone [ˈbækbəʊn] *n* spina *f* dorsale.

back door *n* porta *f* posteriore.

backfire [ˌbækˈfaɪər] *vi* (*car*) fare un'autoaccensione.

background [ˈbækgraʊnd] *n* sfondo *m*; (*of person*) background *m inv*.

backlog [ˈbæklɒg] *n* cumulo *m*; **a ~ of work** del lavoro arretrato.

backpack [ˈbækpæk] *n* zaino *m*.

backpacker [ˈbækpækəʳ] n *persona che viaggia con zaino e sacco a pelo.*

back seat n *sedile m posteriore.*

backside [ˌbækˈsaɪd] n (*inf*) *sedere m.*

back street n *viuzza f.*

backstroke [ˈbækstrəʊk] n *dorso m (nel nuoto).*

backwards [ˈbækwədz] adv (*look*) indietro; (*fall, move*) all'indietro; (*wrong way round*) al contrario.

bacon [ˈbeɪkən] n *pancetta f, bacon m;* ~ **and eggs** *uova fpl e pancetta.*

bacteria [bækˈtɪərɪə] npl *batteri mpl.*

bad [bæd] (*compar* **worse**, *superl* **worst**) *adj* cattivo(-a); (*harmful*) dannoso(-a); (*accident, wound*) brutto(-a); (*eyesight, heart*) debole; (*arm, leg*) malandato(-a); **drinking is ~ for you** *bere ti fa male;* **to go ~** (*milk, yoghurt*) *andare a male;* **not ~** (*film, food, journey*) *niente male;* **how are you? – not ~** *come stai? – non c'è male.*

badge [bædʒ] n *distintivo m.*

badger [ˈbædʒəʳ] n *tasso m.*

badly [ˈbædlɪ] (*compar* **worse**, *superl* **worst**) *adv* male; (*injured*) gravemente; (*affected*) profondamente; (*very much*) tanto.

badly paid [-peɪd] *adj* mal pagato(-a).

badminton [ˈbædmɪntən] n *badminton m.*

bad-tempered [-ˈtempəd] *adj* irascibile.

bag [bæg] n *sacchetto m;* (*handbag*) *borsa f;* (*piece of luggage*) *borsone m;* **a ~ of crisps** *un sacchetto di patatine.*

bagel [ˈbeɪgəl] n *panino a forma di ciambella.*

baggage [ˈbægɪdʒ] n *bagagli mpl.*

baggage allowance n *franchigia f bagaglio.*

baggage reclaim n *ritiro m bagagli.*

baggy [ˈbægɪ] *adj* largo(-a).

bagpipes [ˈbægpaɪps] npl *cornamusa f.*

bail [beɪl] n *cauzione f.*

bait [beɪt] n *esca f.*

bake [beɪk] ♦ vt *cuocere (al forno)* ♦ n: **vegetable** ~ *verdure fpl al forno.*

baked [beɪkt] *adj* cotto(-a) al forno.

baked Alaska [-əˈlæskə] n *meringata f.*

baked beans npl *fagioli mpl al sugo di pomodoro.*

baked potato n *patata f cotta al forno con la buccia.*

baker [ˈbeɪkəʳ] n *fornaio m (-a f);* ~**'s** (*shop*) *panificio m, panetteria f.*

Bakewell tart [ˈbeɪkwel-] n *torta con una base di pasta frolla, uno strato di marmellata e uno di pan di Spagna alle mandorle, ricoperta da una glassa dal caratteristico aspetto a onde.*

balance [ˈbæləns] ♦ n (*of person*) *equilibrio m;* (*of bank account, remainder*) *saldo m* ♦ vt (*object*) *tenere in equilibrio.*

balcony [ˈbælkənɪ] n *balcone m.*

bald [bɔːld] *adj* calvo(-a).

bale [beɪl] n *balla f.*

ball [bɔːl] n (SPORT) *palla f;* (*in football, rugby*) *pallone m;* (*in golf, table tennis*) *pallina f;* (*of wool, string*) *gomitolo m;* (*dance*) *ballo m;* **on the ~** (*fig*) *in gamba.*

ballad [ˈbæləd] n *ballata f.*

ballerina [ˌbæləˈriːnə] n *ballerina f.*

ballet [ˈbæleɪ] n *balletto m.*

ballet dancer n *ballerino m classico (ballerina classica f).*

balloon [bəˈluːn] n (*at party etc*) *palloncino m.*

ballot [ˈbælət] n (*vote*) *votazione f a scrutinio segreto.*

ballpoint pen [ˈbɔːlpɔɪnt-] n *penna f a sfera.*

ballroom [ˈbɔːlrum] n *sala f da ballo.*

ballroom dancing n *ballo m liscio.*

balti ['bɔːltɪ] *n* (*pan*) pentola utilizzata nella cucina indiana; (*food*) piatto indiano cucinato e servito in un 'balti'.

bamboo [bæm'buː] *n* bambù *m*.

bamboo shoots *npl* germogli *mpl* di bambù.

ban [bæn] ◆ *n* divieto *m* ◆ *vt* vietare; **to ~ sb from doing sthg** vietare a qn di fare qc.

banana [bə'nɑːnə] *n* banana *f*.

banana split *n* banana split *f inv*.

band [bænd] *n* (*musical group*) banda *f*; (*for rock, jazz*) complesso *m*, gruppo *m*; (*strip of paper, rubber*) striscia *f*.

bandage ['bændɪdʒ] ◆ *n* benda *f* ◆ *vt* fasciare.

B and B *abbr* = **bed and breakfast**.

bandstand ['bændstænd] *n* palco *m* dell'orchestra.

bang [bæŋ] ◆ *n* (*of gun, explosion*) scoppio *m* ◆ *vt* sbattere.

banger ['bæŋər] *n* (*Br: inf: sausage*) salsiccia *f*; **~s and mash** salsicce e purè di patate.

bangle ['bæŋgl] *n* braccialetto *m*.

bangs [bæŋz] *npl* (*Am*) frangia *f*.

banister ['bænɪstər] *n* ringhiera *f*.

banjo ['bændʒəʊ] (*pl* **-s** OR **-es**) *n* banjo *m inv*.

bank [bæŋk] *n* (*for money*) banca *f*; (*of river, lake*) riva *f*; (*slope*) scarpata *f*.

bank account *n* conto *m* bancario.

bank book *n* libretto *m* di banca.

bank charges *npl* commissioni *fpl* bancarie.

bank clerk *n* impiegato *m* (-a *f*) di banca.

bank draft *n* assegno *m* circolare.

banker ['bæŋkər] *n* banchiere *m*.

banker's card *n* carta *f* assegni.

bank holiday *n* (*Br*) giorno *m* festivo.

bank manager *n* direttore *m* (-trice *f*) di banca.

bank note *n* banconota *f*.

bankrupt ['bæŋkrʌpt] *adj* fallito(-a).

bank statement *n* estratto *m* conto.

banner ['bænər] *n* striscione *m*.

bannister ['bænɪstər] = **banister**.

banquet ['bæŋkwɪt] *n* (*formal dinner*) banchetto *m*; (*at Indian restaurant etc*) menu per più persone.

bap [bæp] *n* (*Br*) panino *m*.

baptize [*Br* bæp'taɪz, *Am* 'bæptaɪz] *vt* battezzare.

bar [bɑːr] ◆ *n* (*pub, in hotel*) bar *m inv*; (*counter in pub*) banco *m*; (*of metal, wood*) sbarra *f*; (*of chocolate*) tavoletta *f* ◆ *vt* (*obstruct*) sbarrare; **a ~ of soap** una saponetta.

barbecue ['bɑːbɪkjuː] ◆ *n* barbecue *m inv* ◆ *vt* arrostire alla griglia.

barbecue sauce *n* salsa piccante usata per condire carne o pesce alla griglia.

barbed wire [bɑːbd-] *n* filo *m* spinato.

barber ['bɑːbər] *n* barbiere *m*; **~'s** (*shop*) barbiere *m*.

bar code *n* codice *m* a barre.

bare [beər] *adj* (*feet, arms*) nudo(-a); (*head*) scoperto(-a); (*room, cupboard*) vuoto(-a); **the ~ minimum** il minimo indispensabile.

barefoot [,beə'fʊt] *adv* a piedi nudi.

barely ['beəlɪ] *adv* (*hardly*) appena; (*with difficulty*) a malapena.

bargain ['bɑːgɪn] ◆ *n* (*agreement*) accordo *m*; (*cheap buy*) occasione *f* ◆ *vi* (*haggle*) contrattare sul prezzo.
▶ **bargain for** *vt fus* aspettarsi.

bargain basement *n* reparto *m* occasioni.

barge [bɑːdʒ] *n* chiatta *f*.
▶ **barge in** *vi* fare irruzione; **to ~ in on sb** interrompere qn.

bark [bɑːk] ◆ *n* (*of tree*) corteccia *f* ◆ *vi* abbaiare.

barley ['bɑːlɪ] *n* orzo *m*.

barmaid ['bɑːmeɪd] n barista f.

barman ['bɑːmən] (pl -men [-mən]) n barista m.

bar meal n pasto leggero servito in un bar o un pub.

barn [bɑːn] n granaio m.

barometer [bə'rɒmɪtəʳ] n barometro m.

baron ['bærən] n barone m.

baroque [bə'rɒk] adj barocco(-a).

barracks ['bærəks] npl caserma f.

barrage ['bærɑːʒ] n (of questions) raffica f; (of criticism) ondata f.

barrel ['bærəl] n (of beer, wine, oil) barile m; (of gun) canna f.

barren ['bærən] adj (land, soil) sterile.

barricade [ˌbærɪ'keɪd] n barricata f.

barrier ['bærɪəʳ] n barriera f.

barrister ['bærɪstəʳ] n (Br) avvocato m.

bartender ['bɑːtendəʳ] n (Am) barista m.

barter ['bɑːtəʳ] vi barattare.

base [beɪs] ◆ n base f ◆ vt: **to ~ sthg on** basare qc su; **I'm ~d in London** ho base a Londra.

baseball ['beɪsbɔːl] n baseball m.

baseball cap n cappellino m da baseball.

basement ['beɪsmənt] n seminterrato m.

bases ['beɪsiːz] pl → **basis**.

bash [bæʃ] vt (inf) sbattere.

basic ['beɪsɪk] adj (fundamental) fondamentale; (accommodation, meal) semplice.

▶ **basics** npl: **the ~s** i rudimenti.

basically ['beɪsɪklɪ] adv (in conversation) in sostanza; (fundamentally) fondamentalmente.

basil ['bæzl] n basilico m.

basin ['beɪsn] n (washbasin) lavabo m; (bowl) terrina f.

basis ['beɪsɪs] (pl -ses) n base f; **on a weekly ~** settimanalmente; **on the ~ of** sulla base di.

basket ['bɑːskɪt] n cesto m.

basketball ['bɑːskɪtbɔːl] n (game) pallacanestro f.

basmati rice [bəz'mæti-] n tipo di riso aromatico utilizzato nella cucina indiana.

bass[1] [beɪs] ◆ n (singer) basso m ◆ adj: **~ guitar** basso m.

bass[2] [bæs] n (freshwater fish) pesce m persico; (sea fish) spigola f, branzino m.

bassoon [bə'suːn] n fagotto m.

bastard ['bɑːstəd] n (vulg) stronzo m (-a f).

bat [bæt] n (in cricket, baseball) mazza f; (in table tennis) racchetta f; (animal) pipistrello m.

batch [bætʃ] n (of goods) lotto m; (of people) scaglione m.

bath [bɑːθ] ◆ n bagno m; (tub) vasca f (da bagno) ◆ vt fare il bagno a; **to have a ~** fare il OR un bagno.

▶ **baths** npl (Br: public swimming pool) piscina f.

bathe [beɪð] vi fare il bagno.

bathing ['beɪðɪŋ] n (Br) balneazione f.

bathrobe ['bɑːθrəʊb] n (for bathroom, swimming pool) accappatoio m; (dressing gown) vestaglia f.

bathroom ['bɑːθrʊm] n bagno m.

bathroom cabinet n armadietto m del bagno.

bathtub ['bɑːθtʌb] n vasca f da bagno.

baton ['bætən] n (of conductor) bacchetta f; (truncheon) manganello m.

batter ['bætəʳ] ◆ n (CULIN) pastella f ◆ vt (wife, child) picchiare.

battered ['bætəd] adj (CULIN) ricoperto di pastella e fritto.

battery ['bætərɪ] n batteria f.

battery charger [-ˌtʃɑːdʒəʳ] n caricabatteria m inv.

battle ['bætl] n battaglia f.

battlefield ['bætlfiːld] n campo m di battaglia.

battlements ['bætlmənts] npl parapetto m.

battleship ['bætlʃɪp] n corazzata f.

bay [beɪ] n (on coast) baia f; (for parking) posto m macchina.

bay leaf n foglia f d'alloro.

bay window n bow-window m inv.

B & B abbr = **bed and breakfast.**

BC (abbr of before Christ) a.C.

be [biː] (pt **was, were,** pp **been**) vi **1.** (exist) essere; **there is** c'è; **there are** ci sono; **are there any shops near here?** ci sono dei negozi qui vicino?

2. (referring to location) essere; **the hotel is near the airport** l'albergo è OR si trova vicino all'aeroporto.

3. (referring to movement): **has the postman been?** è venuto il postino?; **have you ever been to Ireland?** sei mai stato in Irlanda?; **I'll ~ there in ten minutes** sarò lì tra dieci minuti.

4. (occur) essere; **my birthday is in November** il mio compleanno è in novembre.

5. (identifying, describing) essere; **he's a doctor** è medico; **I'm Italian** sono italiano; **I'm hot/cold** ho caldo/freddo.

6. (referring to health) stare; **how are you?** come sta?; **I'm fine** sto bene; **she's ill** è malata.

7. (referring to age): **how old are you?** quanti anni hai?; **I'm 14 (years old)** ho 14 anni.

8. (referring to cost) costare; **how much is it?** (item) quanto costa?; (meal, shopping) quant'è?; **it's £10** (item) costa 10 sterline; (meal, shopping) sono 10 sterline.

9. (referring to time, dates) essere; **what time is it?** che ore sono?; **it's ten o'clock** sono le dieci; **it's the 9th of April** è il 9 aprile.

10. (referring to measurement) essere; **it's 2 m wide/long** è largo/lungo 2 m; **I'm 6 feet tall** sono alto 1 metro e 80; **I'm 8 stone** peso 50 chili.

11. (referring to weather) fare; **it's hot/cold** fa caldo/freddo; **it's sunny** c'è il sole; **it's windy** c'è vento; **it's going to be nice today** oggi farà bello.

♦ aux vb **1.** (forming continuous tense): **I'm learning Italian** sto imparando l'italiano; **what are you reading?** cosa stai leggendo?, cosa leggi?; **he's arriving tomorrow** arriva domani, arriverà domani; **we've been visiting the museum** abbiamo visitato il museo.

2. (forming passive) essere; **the flight was delayed** il volo è stato ritardato.

3. (with infinitive to express order): **all rooms are to ~ vacated by 10 a.m.** tutte le camere devono essere lasciate libere per le 10.

4. (with infinitive to express future tense): **the race is to start at noon** la corsa è prevista per mezzogiorno.

5. (in tag questions): **it's cold, isn't it?** fa freddo, (non è) vero?

beach [biːtʃ] n spiaggia f; **on the ~** in spiaggia.

bead [biːd] n (of glass, wood etc) grano m.

beak [biːk] n becco m.

beaker ['biːkəʳ] n bicchiere m.

beam [biːm] ♦ n (of light) raggio m; (of wood, concrete) trave f ♦ vi (smile) sorridere.

bean [biːn] n fagiolo m; (of coffee) chicco m.

bean curd [-kɜːd] n tofu m.

beansprouts ['biːnspraʊts] npl germogli mpl di soia.

bear [beəʳ] (pt **bore,** pp **borne**) ♦ n (animal) orso m ♦ vt (support) reggere; (endure) sopportare; **to ~ left/right** tenersi sulla sinistra/destra.

bearable ['beərəbl] adj sopportabile.

beard [bɪəd] n barba f.

bearer ['beərəʳ] n (of cheque) portatore m; (of passport) titolare mf.

bearing ['beərɪŋ] n (relevance) attinenza f; **to get one's ~s** orizzontarsi.

beast [biːst] n bestia f.

beat [biːt] (pt **beat**, pp **beaten** [biːtn]) ◆ n (of heart, pulse) battito m; (MUS) tempo m ◆ vt battere; (eggs, cream) sbattere.

▶ **beat down** ◆ vi (sun, rain) battere ◆ vt sep: **I ~ him down to £20** gli ho fatto abbassare il prezzo a 20 sterline.

▶ **beat up** vt sep pestare.

beautiful [ˈbjuːtɪful] adj bello(-a).

beauty [ˈbjuːtɪ] n bellezza f.

beauty parlour n istituto m di bellezza.

beauty spot n (place) bellezza f naturale.

beaver [ˈbiːvəʳ] n castoro m.

became [bɪˈkeɪm] pt → **become**.

because [bɪˈkɒz] conj perché; **~ of** a causa di.

beckon [ˈbekən] vi: **to ~ (to)** fare cenno (a).

become [bɪˈkʌm] (pt **became**, pp **become**) vi diventare; **what became of him?** cosa ne è stato di lui?

bed [bed] n letto m; (of sea) fondo m; (CULIN) strato m; **in ~** a letto; **to get out of ~** alzarsi; **to go to ~** andare a letto; **to go to ~ with sb** andare a letto con qn; **to make the ~** fare il letto.

bed and breakfast n (Br) ≃ pensione f.

bedclothes [ˈbedkləʊðz] npl lenzuola fpl e coperte fpl.

bedding [ˈbedɪŋ] n biancheria f da letto.

bed linen n lenzuola fpl (e federe fpl).

bedroom [ˈbedrʊm] n camera f da letto.

bedside table [ˈbedsaɪd-] n comodino m.

bedsit [ˈbedˌsɪt] n (Br) camera f ammobiliata.

bedspread [ˈbedspred] n copriletto m inv.

bedtime [ˈbedtaɪm] n ora f di andare a letto.

bee [biː] n ape f.

beech [biːtʃ] n faggio m.

beef [biːf] n manzo m; **~ Wellington** pasticcio m di manzo.

beefburger [ˈbiːfˌbɜːgəʳ] n hamburger m inv.

beehive [ˈbiːhaɪv] n alveare m.

been [biːn] pp → **be**.

beer [bɪəʳ] n birra f.

beer garden n giardino per i clienti di un pub.

beer mat n sottobicchiere m.

beetle [ˈbiːtl] n scarabeo m.

beetroot [ˈbiːtruːt] n barbabietola f.

before [bɪˈfɔːʳ] ◆ adv prima ◆ prep prima di; (fml: in front of) davanti a ◆ conj: **~ it gets too late** prima che sia troppo tardi; **I've been there ~** ci sono già stato; **~ doing sthg** prima di fare qc; **~ you leave** prima di partire; **the day ~** il giorno prima; **the week ~ last** due settimane fa.

beforehand [bɪˈfɔːhænd] adv in anticipo.

befriend [bɪˈfrend] vt trattare da amico.

beg [beg] ◆ vi elemosinare ◆ vt: **to ~ sb to do sthg** supplicare qn di fare qc; **to ~ for sthg** elemosinare qc.

began [bɪˈgæn] pt → **begin**.

beggar [ˈbegəʳ] n mendicante mf.

begin [bɪˈgɪn] (pt **began**, pp **begun**) vt & vi cominciare, iniziare; **to ~ doing** OR **to do sthg** cominciare a fare qc; **to ~ by doing sthg** cominciare col fare qc; **to ~ with** (at the start) all'inizio; (firstly) per prima cosa.

beginner [bɪˈgɪnəʳ] n principiante mf.

beginning [bɪˈgɪnɪŋ] n inizio m.

begun [bɪˈgʌn] pp → **begin**.

behalf [bɪˈhɑːf] n: **on ~ of** a nome di.

behave [bɪˈheɪv] vi comportarsi; **to ~ (o.s.)** (be good) comportarsi bene.

behavior [bɪˈheɪvjəʳ] (Am) = **behaviour**.

behaviour [bɪˈheɪvjər] n comportamento m.

behind [bɪˈhaɪnd] ◆ adv (at the back) dietro; (late) indietro ◆ prep (at the back of) dietro ◆ n (inf) didietro m; **to leave sthg** ~ dimenticare qc; **to stay** ~ restare indietro; **we're all** ~ **you** (supporting) siamo tutti con te.

beige [beɪʒ] adj beige (inv).

being [ˈbiːɪŋ] n essere m; **to come into** ~ nascere.

belated [bɪˈleɪtɪd] adj tardivo(-a).

belch [beltʃ] vi ruttare.

Belgian [ˈbeldʒən] ◆ adj belga ◆ n belga mf.

Belgian waffle n (Am) cialda dalla caratteristica superficie a quadretti che si mangia con sciroppo d'acero, panna o frutta.

Belgium [ˈbeldʒəm] n il Belgio.

belief [bɪˈliːf] n (faith) fede f; (opinion) convinzione f.

believe [bɪˈliːv] ◆ vt credere ◆ vi: **to** ~ **in** (God) credere in; **to** ~ **in doing sthg** credere che sia giusto fare qc.

believer [bɪˈliːvər] n credente mf.

bell [bel] n (of church) campana f; (of phone) suoneria f; (of door) campanello m.

bellboy [ˈbelbɔɪ] n fattorino m d'albergo.

bellow [ˈbeləʊ] vi muggire.

belly [ˈbelɪ] n (inf) pancia f.

belly button n (inf) ombelico m.

belong [bɪˈlɒŋ] vi (be in right place) essere al suo posto; **to** ~ **to** (property) appartenere a; (to club, party) far parte di; **where does this** ~? dove sta questo?

belongings [bɪˈlɒŋɪŋz] npl effetti mpl personali.

below [bɪˈləʊ] ◆ adv sotto; (downstairs) di sotto; (in text) qui sotto ◆ prep sotto.

belt [belt] n (for clothes) cintura f; (TECH) cinghia f.

beltway [ˈbeltweɪ] n (Am) raccordo m anulare.

bench [bentʃ] n panchina f.

bend [bend] (pt & pp **bent**) ◆ n (in road) curva f; (in river) ansa f; (in pipe) gomito m ◆ vt piegare ◆ vi (road, river, pipe) fare una curva.

▶ **bend down** vi abbassarsi.

▶ **bend over** vi chinarsi.

beneath [bɪˈniːθ] adv & prep sotto.

beneficial [ˌbenɪˈfɪʃl] adj benefico(-a).

benefit [ˈbenɪfɪt] ◆ n (advantage) beneficio m; (money) indennità f inv ◆ vt giovare a ◆ vi: **to** ~ **(from)** beneficiare (di); **for the** ~ **of** per.

benign [bɪˈnaɪn] adj (MED) benigno(-a).

bent [bent] pt & pp → **bend**.

bereaved [bɪˈriːvd] adj (family) del defunto.

beret [ˈbereɪ] n basco m.

bergamot [ˈbɜːɡəmɒt] n bergamotto m.

Berlin [bɜːˈlɪn] n Berlino f.

Bermuda shorts [bəˈmjuːdə-] npl bermuda mpl.

berry [ˈberɪ] n bacca f.

berserk [bəˈzɜːk] adj: **to go** ~ andare su tutte le furie.

berth [bɜːθ] n (for ship) ormeggio m; (in ship, train) cuccetta f.

beside [bɪˈsaɪd] prep (next to) accanto a; **that's** ~ **the point** questo non c'entra.

besides [bɪˈsaɪdz] ◆ adv inoltre ◆ prep oltre a.

besiege [bɪˈsiːdʒ] vt assediare.

best [best] ◆ adj migliore ◆ adv meglio ◆ n: **the** ~ il migliore (la migliore); **a pint of** ~ (beer) ≃ un boccale di birra scura; **I like this one** ~ questo mi piace più di tutti; **she played** ~ ha giocato meglio di tutti; **the** ~ **thing to do is ...** la miglior cosa da fare è ...; **to make the** ~ **of sthg** accontentarsi di qc; **to do one's** ~ fare del proprio meglio; '~ **before** ...' 'da consumarsi preferibilmente entro ...'; **at** ~ per bene che vada; **all the** ~! auguri!

best man n testimone m (di nozze).

best-seller [-'selə^r] n (book) best seller m inv.

bet [bet] (pt & pp bet) ♦ n scommessa f ♦ vt scommettere ♦ vi: **to ~ (on)** scommettere (su); **I ~ (that) you can't do it** scommetto che non sei capace di farlo.

betray [bɪ'treɪ] vt tradire.

better ['betə^r] ♦ adj migliore ♦ adv meglio; **she's ~ at tennis than me** è più brava di me a tennis; **are you ~ now?** stai meglio adesso?; **you had ~ ...** faresti meglio a ...; **to get ~** migliorare.

betting ['betɪŋ] n scommesse fpl.

betting shop n (Br) = sala f scommesse.

between [bɪ'twiːn] ♦ prep tra, fra ♦ adv (in time) nel frattempo; **in ~** (in space) in mezzo; (in time) nel frattempo.

beverage ['bevərɪdʒ] n (fml) bevanda f.

beware [bɪ'weə^r] vi: **to ~ of** stare attento a; **'~ of the dog'** 'attenti al cane'.

bewildered [bɪ'wɪldəd] adj sconcertato(-a).

beyond [bɪ'jɒnd] ♦ prep oltre ♦ adv più avanti; **~ doubt** senza dubbio; **~ reach** irraggiungibile.

biased ['baɪəst] adj di parte.

bib [bɪb] n (for baby) bavaglino m.

bible ['baɪbl] n bibbia f.

biceps ['baɪseps] n bicipite m.

bicycle ['baɪsɪkl] n bicicletta f.

bicycle path n pista f ciclabile.

bicycle pump n pompa f per la bicicletta.

bid [bɪd] (pt & pp bid) n (at auction) offerta f; (attempt) tentativo m ♦ vt (money) fare un'offerta di ♦ vi: **to ~ (for)** fare un'offerta (per).

bidet [ˈbiːdeɪ] n bidè m inv.

big [bɪg] adj grande; (problem, mistake, risk) grosso(-a); **my ~ brother**
mio fratello maggiore; **how ~ is it?** quanto è grande?

bike [baɪk] n (inf) (bicycle) bici f inv; (motorcycle) moto f inv.

biking ['baɪkɪŋ] n: **to go ~** (on bicycle) andare in bicicletta; (on motorcycle) andare in moto.

bikini [bɪ'kiːnɪ] n bikini® m inv.

bikini bottom n pezzo m di sotto del bikini®.

bikini top n pezzo m di sopra del bikini®.

bilingual [baɪ'lɪŋgwəl] adj bilingue.

bill [bɪl] n (for meal, hotel room) conto m; (for electricity etc) bolletta f; (Am: bank note) banconota f; (at cinema, theatre) programma m; (POL) proposta f di legge; **can I have the ~, please?** il conto, per favore.

billboard ['bɪlbɔːd] n tabellone m.

billfold ['bɪlfəʊld] n (Am) portafoglio m.

billiards ['bɪljədz] n biliardo m.

billion ['bɪljən] n (thousand million) miliardo m; (Br: million million) mille miliardi.

bin [bɪn] n (rubbish bin) pattumiera f; (wastepaper bin) cestino m; (for flour) barattolo m; (on plane) armadietto m in alto; **bread ~** portapane m inv.

bind [baɪnd] (pt & pp bound) vt (tie up) legare.

binding ['baɪndɪŋ] n (of book) rilegatura f; (for ski) attacco m.

bingo ['bɪŋgəʊ] n = tombola f.

binoculars [bɪ'nɒkjʊləz] npl binocolo m.

biodegradable [ˌbaɪəʊdɪ'greɪdəbl] adj biodegradabile.

biography [baɪ'ɒgrəfɪ] n biografia f.

biological [ˌbaɪə'lɒdʒɪkl] adj biologico(-a).

biologist [baɪ'ɒlədʒɪst] n biologo m (-a f).

biology [baɪ'ɒlədʒɪ] n biologia f.

birch [bɜːtʃ] n betulla f.

bird [bɜːd] n uccello m; (Br: inf: woman) pollastrella f.

bird-watching [-ˌwɒtʃɪŋ] n osservazione f degli uccelli.

Biro® [ˈbaɪərəʊ] (pl -s) n biro® f inv.

birth [bɜːθ] n nascita f; **by ~** di nascita; **to give ~ to** dare alla luce, partorire.

birth certificate n certificato m di nascita.

birth control n controllo m delle nascite.

birthday [ˈbɜːθdeɪ] n compleanno m; **happy ~!** buon compleanno!

birthday card n biglietto m d'auguri di compleanno.

birthday party n festa f di compleanno.

birthplace [ˈbɜːθpleɪs] n luogo m di nascita.

biscuit [ˈbɪskɪt] n (Br) biscotto m; (Am: scone) focaccina di pasta non lievitata da mangiare con burro e marmellata o insieme a piatti salati.

bishop [ˈbɪʃəp] n (RELIG) vescovo m; (in chess) alfiere m.

bistro [ˈbiːstrəʊ] (pl -s) n ristorantino m.

bit [bɪt] ♦ pt → **bite** ♦ n (piece) pezzetto m; (of drill) punta f; (of bridle) morso m; (amount): **a ~** un po'; **a ~ of money** un po' di soldi; **to do a ~ of reading** leggere un po'; **not a ~** per niente; **~ by ~** a poco a poco.

bitch [bɪtʃ] n (vulg: woman) stronza f; (dog) cagna f.

bite [baɪt] (pt **bit**, pp **bitten**) ♦ n morso m; (from insect) puntura f ♦ vt mordere; (subj: insect) pungere; **to have a ~ to eat** mangiare un boccone.

bitter [ˈbɪtər] ♦ adj (taste, food) amaro(-a); (weather, wind) pungente; (person) amareggiato(-a); (argument, conflict) aspro(-a) ♦ n (Br: beer) tipo di birra amarognola.

bitter lemon n limonata f amara.

bizarre [bɪˈzɑːr] adj bizzarro(-a).

black [blæk] ♦ adj nero(-a) ♦ n (colour) nero m; (person) negro m (-a f).

▶ **black out** vi perdere conoscenza.

black and white adj in bianco e nero.

blackberry [ˈblækbrɪ] n mora f.

blackbird [ˈblækbɜːd] n merlo m.

blackboard [ˈblækbɔːd] n lavagna f.

black cherry n ciliegia f nera.

blackcurrant [ˌblækˈkʌrənt] n ribes m inv nero.

black eye n occhio m nero.

Black Forest gâteau n torta f di cioccolato e panna.

black ice n strato m di ghiaccio invisibile.

blackmail [ˈblækmeɪl] ♦ n ricatto m ♦ vt ricattare.

blackout [ˈblækaʊt] n (power cut) black-out m inv.

black pepper n pepe m nero.

black pudding n (Br) sanguinaccio m.

blacksmith [ˈblæksmɪθ] n fabbro m.

bladder [ˈblædər] n vescica f.

blade [bleɪd] n (of knife, saw) lama f; (of propeller, oar) pala f; (of grass) filo m.

blame [bleɪm] ♦ n colpa f ♦ vt incolpare; **to ~ sb for sthg** incolpare qn di qc; **to ~ sthg on sb** dare a qn la colpa di qc.

bland [blænd] adj (food) insipido(-a).

blank [blæŋk] ♦ adj (space, cassette) vuoto(-a); (page) bianco(-a); (expression) assente ♦ n (empty space) spazio m (in) bianco.

blank cheque n assegno m in bianco.

blanket [ˈblæŋkɪt] n coperta f.

blast [blɑːst] ♦ n (explosion) esplosione f; (of wind) raffica f; (of air) folata f ♦ excl (inf) maledizione!; **at full ~** a tutto volume.

blaze [bleɪz] ♦ n (fire) incendio m

♦ vi (fire) ardere; (sun, light) risplen-dere.

blazer [ˈbleɪzəʳ] n blazer m inv.

bleach [bliːtʃ] ♦ n candeggina f ♦ vt (clothes) candeggiare; (hair) decolorare.

bleak [bliːk] adj triste.

bleed [bliːd] (pt & pp bled [bled]) vi sanguinare.

blend [blend] ♦ n (of coffee, whisky) miscela f ♦ vt mescolare.

blender [ˈblendəʳ] n frullatore m.

bless [bles] vt benedire; ~ you! (said after sneeze) salute!

blessing [ˈblesɪŋ] n benedizione f.

blew [bluː] pt → blow.

blind [blaɪnd] ♦ adj cieco(-a) ♦ n (for window) tendina f avvolgibile ♦ npl: the ~ i non vedenti.

blind corner n svolta f senza visibilità.

blindfold [ˈblaɪndfəʊld] ♦ n benda f ♦ vt bendare.

blind spot n (AUT) punto m senza visibilità.

blink [blɪŋk] vi battere le palpebre.

blinkers [ˈblɪŋkəz] npl (Br) paraocchi mpl.

bliss [blɪs] n estasi f.

blister [ˈblɪstəʳ] n vescica f.

blizzard [ˈblɪzəd] n bufera f di neve.

bloated [ˈbləʊtɪd] adj (after eating) strapieno(-a).

blob [blɒb] n (of paint) chiazza f.

block [blɒk] ♦ n (of stone, wood, ice) blocco m; (building) palazzo m; (Am: in town, city) isolato m ♦ vt (obstruct) bloccare; to have a ~ed (up) nose avere il naso chiuso.

► **block up** vt sep ostruire.

blockage [ˈblɒkɪdʒ] n ostruzione f.

block capitals npl stampatello m maiuscolo.

block of flats n condominio m.

bloke [bləʊk] n (Br: inf) tipo m, tizio m.

blond [blɒnd] ♦ adj biondo(-a) ♦ n biondo m.

blonde [blɒnd] ♦ adj biondo(-a) ♦ n bionda f.

blood [blʌd] n sangue m.

blood donor n donatore m (-trice f) di sangue.

blood group n gruppo m sanguigno.

blood poisoning n setticemia f.

blood pressure n pressione f sanguigna; to have high ~ avere la pressione alta; to have low ~ avere la pressione bassa.

bloodshot [ˈblʌdʃɒt] adj arrossato(-a).

blood test n analisi f inv del sangue.

blood transfusion n trasfusione f di sangue.

bloody [ˈblʌdɪ] ♦ adj (hands, handkerchief) insanguinato(-a); (Br: vulg: damn) maledetto(-a) ♦ adv (Br: vulg) veramente.

bloody mary [-ˈmeərɪ] n Bloody Mary m inv.

bloom [bluːm] ♦ n fiore m ♦ vi fiorire; in ~ in fiore.

blossom [ˈblɒsəm] n fiori mpl.

blot [blɒt] n macchia f.

blotch [blɒtʃ] n chiazza f.

blotting paper [ˈblɒtɪŋ-] n carta f assorbente.

blouse [blauz] n camicetta f.

blow [bləʊ] (pt blew, pp blown) ♦ vt (subj: wind) soffiare; (whistle, trumpet) suonare; (bubbles) fare ♦ vi soffiare; (fuse) saltare ♦ n colpo m; to ~ one's nose soffiarsi il naso.

► **blow up** ♦ vt sep (cause to explode) far saltare in aria; (inflate) gonfiare ♦ vi (explode) saltare in aria.

blow-dry ♦ n piega f föhn ♦ vt fonare.

blown [bləʊn] pp → blow.

BLT n panino imbottito con pancetta, lattuga e pomodoro.

blue [bluː] ♦ adj azzurro(-a); (film) spinto(-a) ♦ n azzurro m.

► **blues** n (MUS) blues m.

bluebell ['blu:bel] n campanula f.

blueberry ['blu:bərɪ] n mirtillo m.

bluebottle ['blu:ˌbɒtl] n moscone m.

blue cheese n formaggio con muffa di stagionatura.

bluff [blʌf] ◆ n (cliff) promontorio m ◆ vi bleffare.

blunder ['blʌndəʳ] n cantonata f.

blunt [blʌnt] adj (pencil) spuntato(-a); (knife) non affilato(-a); (fig: person) brusco(-a).

blurred [blɜ:d] adj (photo) sfocato(-a); (vision) offuscato(-a).

blush [blʌʃ] vi arrossire.

blusher ['blʌʃəʳ] n fard m inv.

blustery ['blʌstərɪ] adj burrascoso(-a).

board [bɔ:d] ◆ n (plank) tavola f; (notice board, for games) tabellone m; (for chess) scacchiera f; (blackboard) lavagna f; (of company) consiglio m d'amministrazione ◆ vt (plane, ship) imbarcarsi su; (bus) salire su; ~ and lodging vitto e alloggio; full ~ pensione f completa; half ~ mezza pensione; on ~ adv a bordo ◆ prep su.

board game n gioco m di società.

boarding ['bɔ:dɪŋ] n imbarco m.

boarding card n carta f d'imbarco.

boardinghouse ['bɔ:dɪŋhaʊs, pl -haʊzɪz] n pensione f.

boarding school n collegio m.

board of directors n consiglio m d'amministrazione.

boast [bəʊst] vi: to ~ (about sthg) vantarsi (di qc).

boat [bəʊt] n (small) barca f; (large) nave f; by ~ in barca.

bob [bɒb] n (hairstyle) carré m inv.

bobby pin ['bɒbɪ-] n (Am) forcina f.

bodice ['bɒdɪs] n corpino m.

body ['bɒdɪ] n corpo m; (of car) carrozzeria f; (organization) organismo m.

bodyguard ['bɒdɪgɑ:d] n (person) guardia f del corpo.

bodywork ['bɒdɪwɜ:k] n carrozzeria f.

bog [bɒg] n pantano m.

bogus ['bəʊgəs] adj falso(-a).

boil [bɔɪl] ◆ vt (water) bollire, far bollire; (kettle) mettere a bollire; (food) lessare ◆ vi bollire ◆ n (on skin) foruncolo m.

boiled egg [bɔɪld-] n uovo m alla coque.

boiled potatoes [bɔɪld-] npl patate fpl lesse.

boiler ['bɔɪləʳ] n caldaia f.

boiling (hot) ['bɔɪlɪŋ-] adj (inf) (water) bollente; I'm ~ sto morendo di caldo; it's ~ si scoppia dal caldo.

bold [bəʊld] adj (brave) audace.

bollard ['bɒlɑ:d] n (Br: on road) colonnina f spartitraffico.

bolt [bəʊlt] ◆ n (on door, window) chiavistello m; (screw) bullone m ◆ vt (door, window) sprangare.

bomb [bɒm] ◆ n bomba f ◆ vt bombardare.

bombard [bɒm'bɑ:d] vt bombardare.

bomb scare n allarme causato dalla presunta presenza di una bomba.

bomb shelter n rifugio m antiaereo.

bond [bɒnd] n (tie, connection) legame m.

bone [bəʊn] n (of person, animal) osso m; (of fish) lisca f.

boned [bəʊnd] adj (chicken) disossato(-a); (fish) senza lische.

boneless ['bəʊnləs] adj (chicken, pork) disossato(-a).

bonfire ['bɒnˌfaɪəʳ] n falò m inv.

bonnet ['bɒnɪt] n (Br: of car) cofano m.

bonus ['bəʊnəs] (pl -es) n (extra money) gratifica f; (additional advantage) extra m inv.

bony ['bəʊnɪ] adj (fish) pieno(-a) di spine; (chicken) pieno di ossi.

boo [bu:] vi fischiare.

boogie ['buːgɪ] *vi* (*inf*) ballare.

book [bʊk] ◆ *n* libro *m*; (*for writing in*) quaderno *m*; (*of tickets, stamps*) blocchetto *m*; (*of matches*) pacchetto *m* ◆ *vt* (*reserve*) prenotare.

▶ **book in** *vi* (*at hotel*) registrarsi.

bookable ['bʊkəbl] *adj* (*seats, flight*) prenotabile.

bookcase ['bʊkkeɪs] *n* libreria *f*.

booking ['bʊkɪŋ] *n* (*reservation*) prenotazione *f*.

booking office *n* (*at theatre*) botteghino *m*; (*at station*) ufficio *m* prenotazioni.

bookkeeping ['bʊkˌkiːpɪŋ] *n* contabilità *f*.

booklet ['bʊklɪt] *n* opuscolo *m*.

bookmaker's ['bʊkˌmeɪkəz] *n* = sala *f* scommesse.

bookmark ['bʊkmɑːk] *n* segnalibro *m*.

bookshelf ['bʊkʃelf] (*pl* **-shelves** [-ʃelvz]) *n* scaffale *m*.

bookshop ['bʊkʃɒp] *n* libreria *f*.

bookstall ['bʊkstɔːl] *n* bancarella *f* di libri.

bookstore ['bʊkstɔːr] = **bookshop**.

book token *n* buono *m* libri.

boom [buːm] ◆ *n* (*sudden growth*) boom *m inv* ◆ *vi* (*voice, guns*) tuonare.

boost [buːst] *vt* (*profits, production*) incrementare; (*confidence*) aumentare; (*spirits*) sollevare.

booster ['buːstər] *n* (*injection*) richiamo *m*.

boot [buːt] *n* (*shoe*) stivale *m*; (*for walking*) scarpone *m*; (*for football*) scarpetta *f*; (*Br: of car*) bagagliaio *m*.

booth [buːð] *n* (*for telephone*) cabina *f*; (*at fairground*) baraccone *m*.

booze [buːz] ◆ *n* (*inf*) alcool *m* ◆ *vi* (*inf*) sbevazzare.

bop [bɒp] *n* (*inf: dance*): **to have a ~** ballare.

border ['bɔːdər] *n* (*of country*) frontiera *f*; (*edge*) orlo *m*; **the Borders** zona di confine fra Inghilterra e Scozia.

bore [bɔːr] ◆ *pt* → **bear** ◆ *n* (*inf*) noia *f* ◆ *vt* (*person*) annoiare; (*hole*) praticare.

bored [bɔːd] *adj* annoiato(-a).

boredom ['bɔːdəm] *n* noia *f*.

boring ['bɔːrɪŋ] *adj* noioso(-a).

born [bɔːn] *adj*: **to be ~** nascere.

borne [bɔːn] *pp* → **bear**.

borough ['bʌrə] *n* = comune *m*.

borrow ['bɒrəʊ] *vt*: **to ~ sthg (from sb)** prendere in prestito qc (da qn).

bosom ['bʊzəm] *n* seno *m*.

boss [bɒs] *n* capo *m*.

▶ **boss around** *vt sep* dare ordini a.

bossy ['bɒsɪ] *adj* autoritario(-a).

botanical garden [bə'tænɪkl-] *n* giardino *m* botanico.

both [bəʊθ] ◆ *adj & pron* tutti(-e) e due, entrambi(-e) ◆ *adv*: **~ ... and** sia ... sia, sia ... che; **it is ~ stupid and dangerous** è stupido e pericoloso insieme; **~ of them** entrambi, tutti e due; **~ of us** entrambi, tutti e due.

bother ['bɒðər] ◆ *vt* (*worry*) preoccupare; (*annoy, pester*) disturbare ◆ *vi* preoccuparsi ◆ *n* (*trouble*) fatica *f*; **I can't be ~ed** non ne ho voglia; **don't ~, I'll go!** non ti scomodare, vado io!; **it's no ~!** non c'è problema!

bottle ['bɒtl] *n* bottiglia *f*; (*for baby*) biberon *m inv*.

bottle bank *n* campana *f* per la raccolta del vetro.

bottled ['bɒtld] *adj* imbottigliato(-a); **~ beer** birra in bottiglia; **~ water** acqua minerale.

bottle opener [-ˌəʊpnər] *n* apribottiglie *m inv*.

bottom ['bɒtəm] ◆ *adj* (*lowest, last*) ultimo(-a); (*worst*) più basso(-a) ◆ *n* fondo *m*; (*of hill*) piedi *mpl*; (*buttocks*) sedere *m*; **the ~ shelf** l'ultimo scaffale in basso; **~ gear** prima *f*.

bought [bɔːt] *pt & pp* → **buy**.

boulder ['bəʊldər] *n* masso *m*.

bounce [bauns] vi (rebound) rimbalzare; (jump) saltare; (cheque) essere scoperto.

bouncer ['baunsə'] n (inf) buttafuori m inv.

bouncy ['baunsɪ] adj (person) pimpante.

bound [baund] ♦ pt & pp → **bind** ♦ vi saltellare ♦ adj: **it's ~ to rain** pioverà di sicuro; **to be ~ for** essere diretto(-a) a; **it's out of ~s** l'accesso è vietato.

boundary ['baundrɪ] n confine m.

bouquet [bu'keɪ] n bouquet m inv; (big bunch of flowers) mazzo m di fiori.

bourbon ['bɜ:bən] n bourbon m inv.

bout [baut] n (of illness) attacco m; (of activity) periodo m.

boutique [bu:'ti:k] n boutique f inv.

bow¹ [bau] ♦ n (of head) inchino m; (of ship) prua f ♦ vi inchinarsi.

bow² [bəu] n (knot) fiocco m; (weapon) arco m; (MUS) archetto m.

bowels ['bauəlz] npl (ANAT) intestino m.

bowl [bəul] n ciotola f; (for washing) bacinella f; (of toilet) tazza f; **fruit ~** fruttiera f; **salad ~** insalatiera f; **sugar ~** zuccheriera f.
▶ **bowls** npl bocce fpl.

bowling alley ['bəulɪŋ-] n (building) bowling m inv.

bowling green ['bəulɪŋ-] n campo m di bocce.

bow tie [bəu-] n farfalla f.

box [bɒks] ♦ n scatola f; (on form) casella f; (in theatre) palco m ♦ vi fare del pugilato; **a ~ of chocolates** una scatola di cioccolatini; **jewellery ~** portagioie m inv; **tool ~** cassetta f degli attrezzi.

boxer ['bɒksə'] n (fighter) pugile m.

boxer shorts npl boxer mpl.

boxing ['bɒksɪŋ] n pugilato m.

Boxing Day n Santo Stefano m.

boxing gloves npl guantoni mpl.

boxing ring n ring m inv.

box office n botteghino m.

boy [bɔɪ] ♦ n ragazzo m; (son) figlio m ♦ excl (inf): **(oh) ~!** accidenti!

boycott ['bɔɪkɒt] vt boicottare.

boyfriend ['bɔɪfrend] n ragazzo m.

boy scout n boy-scout m inv.

BR abbr = **British Rail**.

bra [brɑ:] n reggiseno m.

brace [breɪs] n (for teeth) apparecchio m (per i denti).
▶ **braces** npl (Br) bretelle fpl.

bracelet ['breɪslɪt] n braccialetto m.

bracken ['brækn] n felce f.

bracket ['brækɪt] n (written symbol) parentesi f inv; (support) reggimensola m inv.

brag [bræg] vi vantarsi.

braid [breɪd] n (hairstyle) treccia f; (on clothes) passamano m.

brain [breɪn] n cervello m.

brainy ['breɪnɪ] adj (inf) sveglio(-a).

braised [breɪzd] adj brasato(-a).

brake [breɪk] ♦ n freno m ♦ vi frenare.

brake block n freno m.

brake fluid n fluido m dei freni.

brake light n stop m inv.

brake pad n pastiglia f (del freno).

brake pedal n (pedale m del) freno m.

bran [bræn] n crusca f.

branch [brɑ:ntʃ] n ramo m; (of bank, company) filiale f.
▶ **branch off** vi diramarsi.

branch line n diramazione f.

brand [brænd] ♦ n marca f ♦ vt: **to ~ sb (as)** bollare qn (come).

brand-new adj nuovo(-a) di zecca.

brandy ['brændɪ] n brandy m inv.

brash [bræʃ] adj (pej) sfrontato(-a).

brass [brɑ:s] n ottone m.

brass band n fanfara f.

brasserie ['bræsərɪ] n ≃ trattoria f.

brassiere [Br 'bræsɪə', Am brə'zɪr] n

reggiseno *m*.

brat [bræt] *n* (*inf*) discolo *m* (-a *f*).

brave [breɪv] *adj* coraggioso(-a).

bravery ['breɪvərɪ] *n* coraggio *m*.

bravo [ˌbrɑː'vəʊ] *excl* bravo(-a)!

brawl [brɔːl] *n* rissa *f*.

Brazil [brə'zɪl] *n* il Brasile.

brazil nut *n* noce *f* del Brasile.

breach [briːtʃ] *vt* (*contract*) rompere; (*confidence*) tradire.

bread [bred] *n* pane *m*; ~ **and butter** pane *m* imburrato.

bread bin *n* (Br) portapane *m inv*.

breadboard ['bredbɔːd] *n* tagliere *m* (per il pane).

bread box (Am) = **bread bin**.

breadcrumbs ['bredkrʌmz] *npl* pangrattato *m*.

breaded ['bredɪd] *adj* impanato(-a).

bread knife *n* coltello *m* da pane.

bread roll *n* panino *m*.

breadth [bretθ] *n* larghezza *f*, ampiezza *f*.

break [breɪk] (*pt* **broke**, *pp* **broken**)
◆ *n* (*interruption*) interruzione *f*; (*rest, pause*) pausa *f*; (SCH) ricreazione *f*
◆ *vt* rompere; (*law, rule*) infrangere; (*promise, contract*) non rispettare; (*a record*) battere ◆ *vi* rompersi; (*dawn*) spuntare; (*voice*) cambiare; **without a ~** senza sosta; **a lucky ~** un colpo di fortuna; **to ~ one's leg** rompersi la gamba; **to ~ the news to sb** dare una notizia a qn; **to ~ one's journey** fare una sosta.

▶ **break down** ◆ *vi* (*car, machine*) guastarsi ◆ *vt sep* (*door, barrier*) abbattere.

▶ **break in** *vi* (*enter by force*) fare irruzione.

▶ **break off** ◆ *vt* (*detach*) staccare; (*holiday*) interrompere ◆ *vi* (*stop suddenly*) interrompersi.

▶ **break out** *vi* (*fire, war, panic*) scoppiare; **he broke out in a rash** gli è venuto uno sfogo.

▶ **break up** *vi* (*with spouse, partner*)

lasciarsi; (*meeting, marriage, school*) finire.

breakage ['breɪkɪdʒ] *n* danni *mpl*.

breakdown ['breɪkdaʊn] *n* (*of car*) guasto *m*; (*in communications, negotiation*) interruzione *f*; (*mental*) esaurimento *m* nervoso.

breakdown truck *n* carro *m* attrezzi.

breakfast ['brekfəst] *n* colazione *f*; **to have ~** fare colazione; **to have sthg for ~** mangiare qc a colazione.

breakfast cereal *n* cereali *mpl*.

break-in *n* scasso *m*.

breakwater ['breɪkˌwɔːtəʳ] *n* frangiflutti *m inv*.

breast [brest] *n* (*of woman*) seno *m*; (*of chicken, duck*) petto *m*.

breastbone ['brestbəʊn] *n* sterno *m*.

breast-feed *vt* allattare (al seno).

breaststroke ['breststrəʊk] *n* nuoto *m* a rana.

breath [breθ] *n* (*of person*) alito *m*; (*air inhaled*) respiro *m*; **out of ~** senza fiato; **to go for a ~ of fresh air** andare a prendere una boccata d'aria.

Breathalyser® ['breθəlaɪzəʳ] *n* (Br) etilometro *m*.

Breathalyzer® ['breθəlaɪzər] (Am) = **Breathalyser**®.

breathe [briːð] *vi* respirare.

▶ **breathe in** *vi* inspirare.

▶ **breathe out** *vi* espirare.

breathtaking ['breθˌteɪkɪŋ] *adj* mozzafiato (*inv*).

breed [briːd] (*pt & pp* **bred** [bred])
◆ *n* (*of animal*) razza *f*; (*of plant*) varietà *f inv* ◆ *vt* (*animals*) allevare ◆ *vi* riprodursi.

breeze [briːz] *n* brezza *f*.

breezy ['briːzɪ] *adj* (*weather, day*) ventilato(-a).

brew [bruː] ◆ *vt* (*tea*) fare ◆ *vi*: **the tea/coffee is ~ed** il tè/caffè è pronto.

brewery ['bruərɪ] *n* fabbrica *f* di birra.

bribe [braɪb] ◆ *n* bustarella *f*, tangente *f* ♦ *vt* corrompere.

bric-a-brac ['brɪkəbræk] *n* cianfrusaglie *fpl*.

brick [brɪk] *n* mattone *m*.

bricklayer ['brɪkˌleɪəʳ] *n* muratore *m*.

brickwork ['brɪkwɜːk] *n* muratura *f* di mattoni.

bride [braɪd] *n* sposa *f*.

bridegroom ['braɪdgrʊm] *n* sposo *m*.

bridesmaid ['braɪdzmeɪd] *n* damigella *f* d'onore.

bridge [brɪdʒ] *n* ponte *m*; (*card game*) bridge *m*.

bridle ['braɪdl] *n* briglia *f*.

bridle path *n* sentiero *m* (*per cavalli*).

brief [briːf] ♦ *adj* breve ♦ *vt* mettere al corrente; **in ~** in breve.

▶ **briefs** *npl* mutande *fpl*.

briefcase ['briːfkeɪs] *n* (*hard*) ventiquattr'ore *f inv*; (*soft*) cartella *f*.

briefly ['briːflɪ] *adv* brevemente.

brigade [brɪ'geɪd] *n* brigata *f*.

bright [braɪt] *adj* (*light, sun*) vivido(-a); (*weather, room, idea*) luminoso(-a); (*clever*) sveglio(-a); (*lively, cheerful, in colour*) vivace.

brilliant ['brɪljənt] *adj* brillante; (*inf: wonderful*) stupendo(-a).

brim [brɪm] *n* (*of hat*) tesa *f*; **it's full to the ~** è pieno fino all'orlo.

brine [braɪn] *n* salamoia *f*.

bring [brɪŋ] (*pt & pp* **brought**) *vt* portare.

▶ **bring along** *vt sep* portare.

▶ **bring back** *vt sep* riportare.

▶ **bring in** *vt sep* (*introduce*) introdurre; (*earn*) rendere.

▶ **bring out** *vt sep* (*new product*) far uscire.

▶ **bring up** *vt sep* (*child*) allevare; (*subject*) sollevare; (*food*) vomitare.

brink [brɪŋk] *n*: **on the ~ of sthg** sull'orlo di qc; **on the ~ of doing sthg** sul punto di fare qc.

brisk [brɪsk] *adj* (*quick*) rapido(-a);

(*efficient*) energico(-a); (*wind*) pungente.

bristle ['brɪsl] *n* (*of brush*) setola *f*; (*on chin*) pelo *m* ispido.

Britain ['brɪtn] *n* la Gran Bretagna.

British ['brɪtɪʃ] ♦ *adj* britannico(-a) ♦ *npl*: **the ~** i Britannici.

British Rail *n* ≃ le Ferrovie dello Stato.

British Telecom [-'telɪkɒm] *n* ≃ la Telecom Italia.

Briton ['brɪtn] *n* britannico *m* (-a *f*).

brittle ['brɪtl] *adj* friabile.

broad [brɔːd] *adj* ampio(-a); (*accent*) marcato(-a).

B road *n* (Br) ≃ strada *f* provinciale.

broad bean *n* fava *f*.

broadcast ['brɔːdkɑːst] (*pt & pp* **broadcast**) ♦ *n* trasmissione *f* ♦ *vt* trasmettere.

broadly ['brɔːdlɪ] *adv* (*in general*) grossomodo; **~ speaking** in linea di massima.

broccoli ['brɒkəlɪ] *n* broccoli *mpl*.

brochure ['brəʊʃəʳ] *n* opuscolo *m*.

broiled [brɔɪld] *adj* (Am) alla griglia.

broke [brəʊk] ♦ *pt* → **break** ♦ *adj* (*inf*) al verde.

broken ['brəʊkn] ♦ *pp* → **break** ♦ *adj* rotto(-a); (*English, Italian*) stentato(-a).

bronchitis [brɒŋ'kaɪtɪs] *n* bronchite *f*.

bronze [brɒnz] *n* bronzo *m*.

brooch [brəʊtʃ] *n* spilla *f*.

brook [brʊk] *n* ruscello *m*.

broom [bruːm] *n* scopa *f*.

broomstick ['bruːmstɪk] *n* manico *m* di scopa.

broth [brɒθ] *n* brodo *m*.

brother ['brʌðəʳ] *n* fratello *m*.

brother-in-law *n* cognato *m*.

brought [brɔːt] *pt & pp* → **bring**.

brow [braʊ] *n* (*forehead*) fronte *f*; (*eyebrow*) sopracciglio *m*.

brown [braʊn] ♦ *adj* (*tanned*) abbronzato(-a); (*eyes, hair*) castano(-a) ♦ *n* marrone *m*.

brown bread n pane m integrale.

brownie ['braʊnɪ] n (CULIN) biscotto con noci e cioccolato.

Brownie ['braʊnɪ] n giovane esploratrice f, coccinella f.

brown rice n riso m integrale.

brown sauce n (Br) salsa piccante, usata con la carne e i salumi.

brown sugar n zucchero m di canna.

browse [braʊz] vi (in shop) dare un'occhiata; **to ~ through** (book, paper) sfogliare.

browser ['braʊzə'] n: '**~s welcome**' 'entrata libera'.

bruise [bruːz] n livido m.

brunch [brʌntʃ] n brunch m inv.

brunette [bruːˈnet] n bruna f.

brush [brʌʃ] ♦ n (for hair) spazzola f; (for teeth) spazzolino m; (for painting) pennello m ♦ vt spazzolare; (clean, tidy) spazzare; (move with hand) scostare; **to ~ one's hair** spazzolarsi i capelli; **to ~ one's teeth** lavarsi i denti.

Brussels ['brʌslz] n Bruxelles f.

brussels sprouts npl cavoletti mpl di Bruxelles.

brutal ['bruːtl] adj brutale.

BSc n (abbr of Bachelor of Science) (titolare di una) laurea in discipline scientifiche.

BT abbr = British Telecom.

bubble ['bʌbl] n bolla f.

bubble bath n bagnoschiuma m inv.

bubble gum n gomma f da masticare (con cui si può fare le bolle).

bubbly ['bʌblɪ] n (inf) spumante m.

buck [bʌk] n (Am: inf: dollar) dollaro m; (male animal) maschio m.

bucket ['bʌkɪt] n secchio m.

Buckingham Palace ['bʌkɪŋəm-] n il Palazzo di Buckingham (residenza della famiglia reale britannica).

buckle ['bʌkl] ♦ n fibbia f ♦ vt (fasten) allacciare ♦ vi (warp) piegarsi.

buck's fizz [ˌbʌksˈfɪz] n bibita a base di champagne e succo d'arancia.

bud [bʌd] ♦ n germoglio m ♦ vi germogliare.

Buddhist ['bʊdɪst] n buddista mf.

buddy ['bʌdɪ] n (inf) amico m.

budge [bʌdʒ] vi spostarsi.

budgerigar ['bʌdʒərɪgɑː'] n pappagallino m.

budget ['bʌdʒɪt] ♦ adj (holiday, travel) a basso prezzo ♦ n bilancio m preventivo; **the Budget** (Br) la Legge finanziaria.

▶ **budget for** vt fus: **to ~ for sthg** preventivare la spesa di qc.

budgie ['bʌdʒɪ] n (inf) pappagallino m.

buff [bʌf] n (inf) patito m (-a f).

buffalo ['bʌfələʊ] (pl **-s** OR **-es**) n bufalo m.

buffalo wings npl (Am) ali fpl di pollo fritte.

buffer ['bʌfə'] n (on train) respingente m.

buffet [Br 'bʊfeɪ, Am bəˈfeɪ] n buffet m inv.

buffet car n vagone m ristorante.

bug [bʌg] ♦ n (insect) insetto m; (inf: mild illness) virus m inv ♦ vt (inf: annoy) dare fastidio a.

buggy ['bʌgɪ] n (pushchair) passeggino m; (Am: pram) carrozzina f.

bugle ['bjuːgl] n tromba f.

build [bɪld] (pt & pp **built**) ♦ n corporatura f ♦ vt costruire.

▶ **build up** ♦ vt sep aumentare ♦ vi accumularsi.

builder ['bɪldə'] n costruttore m (-trice f).

building ['bɪldɪŋ] n edificio m.

building site n cantiere m edile.

building society n (Br) = istituto m di credito edilizio.

built [bɪlt] pt & pp → **build**.

built-in adj incorporato(-a).

built-up area n agglomerato m urbano.

bulb [bʌlb] n (for lamp) lampadina f; (of plant) bulbo m.

Bulgaria [bʌlˈgeərɪə] n la Bulgaria.

bulge [bʌldʒ] vi essere rigonfio(-a).

bulk [bʌlk] n: **the ~ of** la maggior parte di; **in ~** all'ingrosso.

bulky [ˈbʌlkɪ] adj ingombrante.

bull [bʊl] n toro m.

bulldog [ˈbʊldɒg] n bulldog m inv.

bulldozer [ˈbʊldəʊzəʳ] n bulldozer m inv.

bullet [ˈbʊlɪt] n proiettile m, pallottola f.

bulletin [ˈbʊlətɪn] n (on radio, TV) notiziario m; (publication) bollettino m.

bullfight [ˈbʊlfaɪt] n corrida f.

bull's-eye n centro m (del bersaglio).

bully [ˈbʊlɪ] ◆ n prepotente mf ◆ vt fare il prepotente con.

bum [bʌm] n (inf: bottom) sedere m; (Am: inf: tramp) barbone m (-a f).

bum bag n (Br) marsupio m.

bumblebee [ˈbʌmblbiː] n bombo m.

bump [bʌmp] ◆ n (on knee, leg) rigonfiamento m; (on head) bernoccolo m; (on road) cunetta f; (sound) tonfo m; (minor accident) scontro m leggero ◆ vt (head, leg) sbattere.

▶ **bump into** vt fus (hit) sbattere contro; (meet) imbattersi in.

bumper [ˈbʌmpəʳ] n (on car) paraurti m inv; (Am: on train) respingente m.

bumpy [ˈbʌmpɪ] adj (road) dissestato(-a); **the flight was ~** c'è stata un po' di turbolenza durante il volo.

bun [bʌn] n (cake) focaccina f; (bread roll) panino m; (hairstyle) crocchia f.

bunch [bʌntʃ] n (of people) gruppo m; (of flowers, keys) mazzo m; (of grapes) grappolo m; (of bananas) casco m.

bundle [ˈbʌndl] n fascio m.

bung [bʌŋ] n tappo m.

bungalow [ˈbʌŋgələʊ] n casa a un solo piano.

bunion [ˈbʌnjən] n rigonfiamento m dell'alluce.

bunk [bʌŋk] n (bed) cuccetta f.

bunk bed n letto m a castello.

bunker [ˈbʌŋkəʳ] n bunker m inv; (for coal) carbonaia f.

bunny [ˈbʌnɪ] n coniglietto m.

buoy [Br bɔɪ, Am ˈbuːɪ] n boa f.

buoyant [ˈbɔɪənt] adj galleggiante.

BUPA [ˈbuːpə] n compagnia d'assicurazione britannica per assistenza medica privata.

burden [ˈbɜːdn] n (load) carico m; (responsibility) peso m.

bureaucracy [bjʊəˈrɒkrəsɪ] n burocrazia f.

bureau de change [ˌbjʊərəʊdə-ˈʃɒndʒ] n agenzia f di cambio.

burger [ˈbɜːgəʳ] n hamburger m inv; (made with nuts, vegetables etc) hamburger vegetariano.

burglar [ˈbɜːgləʳ] n scassinatore m (-trice f).

burglar alarm n allarme m antifurto.

burglarize [ˈbɜːgləraɪz] (Am) = **burgle**.

burglary [ˈbɜːglərɪ] n furto m con scasso.

burgle [ˈbɜːgl] vt scassinare.

burial [ˈberɪəl] n sepoltura f.

burn [bɜːn] (pt & pp burnt OR burned) ◆ n bruciatura f ◆ vt & vi bruciare.

▶ **burn down** ◆ vt sep incendiare ◆ vi: **the building was ~ed down** l'edificio è stato interamente distrutto dalle fiamme.

burning (hot) [ˈbɜːnɪŋ-] adj rovente.

Burns' Night [bɜːnz-] n festa celebrata in onore del poeta scozzese Robert Burns il 25 gennaio.

burnt [bɜːnt] pt & pp → **burn**.

burp [bɜːp] vi (inf) ruttare.

burrow [ˈbʌrəʊ] n tana f.

burst [bɜːst] (pt & pp burst) ◆ n scoppio m ◆ vt far scoppiare ◆ vi scoppiare; **he ~ into the room** irruppe nella stanza; **to ~ into tears** scoppiare in lacrime; **to ~ open** (*door*) spalancarsi.

bury ['bɛrɪ] *vt* seppellire.

bus [bʌs] *n* autobus *m inv*; **by ~** in autobus.

bus conductor [-,kən'dʌktər] *n* bigliettaio *m* (-a *f*).

bus driver *n* conducente *mf*.

bush [buʃ] *n* cespuglio *m*.

business ['bɪznɪs] *n* affari *mpl*; (*shop, firm*) impresa *f*; (*affair*) faccenda *f*; **mind your own ~!** fatti gli affari tuoi!; **'~ as usual'** 'aperto (regolarmente)'.

business card *n* biglietto *f* da visita.

business class *n* business class *f inv*.

business hours *npl* orario *m* di apertura.

businessman ['bɪznɪsmæn] (*pl* -**men** [-men]) *n* uomo *m* d'affari.

business studies *npl* ≃ amministrazione *f* aziendale.

businesswoman ['bɪznɪs,wumən] (*pl* -**women** [-wɪmɪn]) *n* donna *f* d'affari.

busker ['bʌskər] *n* (Br) musicista *mf* ambulante.

bus lane *n* corsia *f* preferenziale (per autobus).

bus pass *n* abbonamento *m* all'autobus.

bus shelter *n* pensilina *f*.

bus station *n* stazione *f* degli autobus.

bus stop *n* fermata *f* dell'autobus.

bust [bʌst] ◆ *n* (*of woman*) seno *m* ◆ *adj*: **to go ~** (*inf*) fallire.

bustle ['bʌsl] *n* (*activity*) trambusto *m*.

bus tour *n* gita *f* in autobus.

busy ['bɪzɪ] *adj* occupato(-a); (*day, schedule*) pieno(-a); (*street, office*) affollato(-a); **to be ~ doing sthg** essere occupato a fare qc.

busy signal *n* (Am) segnale *m* di occupato.

but [bʌt] ◆ *conj* ma, però ◆ *prep* tranne; **the last ~ one** il penultimo (la penultima); **~ for** a parte.

butcher ['butʃər] *n* macellaio *m* (-a *f*); **~'s** (*shop*) macelleria *f*.

butt [bʌt] *n* (*of rifle*) calcio *m*; (*of cigarette, cigar*) mozzicone *m*.

butter ['bʌtər] ◆ *n* burro *m* ◆ *vt* imburrare.

butter bean *n* fagiolo *m* bianco.

buttercup ['bʌtəkʌp] *n* ranuncolo *m*.

butterfly ['bʌtəflaɪ] *n* farfalla *f*.

butterscotch ['bʌtəskɒtʃ] *n* caramella dura di zucchero e burro.

buttocks ['bʌtəks] *npl* natiche *fpl*.

button ['bʌtn] *n* bottone *m*; (Am: *badge*) distintivo *m*.

buttonhole ['bʌtnhəul] *n* (*hole*) occhiello *m*.

button mushroom *n* champignon *m inv*.

buttress ['bʌtrɪs] *n* contrafforte *m*.

buy [baɪ] (*pt & pp* **bought**) ◆ *vt* comprare ◆ *n*: **a good ~** un buon acquisto; **to ~ sthg for sb, to ~ sb sthg** comprare qc per qn, comprare qc a qn.

buzz [bʌz] ◆ *vi* ronzare ◆ *n* (*inf*: *phone call*): **to give sb a ~** dare un colpo di telefono a qn.

buzzer ['bʌzər] *n* cicalino *m*.

by [baɪ] *prep* **1.** (*expressing cause, agent*) da; **he was hit ~ a car** è stato investito da un'automobile; **funded ~ the government** finanziato dal governo; **a book ~ Joyce** un libro di Joyce.

2. (*expressing method, means*): **~ car/train/plane** in macchina/treno/aereo; **~ post/phone** per posta/telefono; **to pay ~ credit card** pagare con la carta di credito; **to win ~ cheating** vincere con l'imbroglio.

3. (*near to, beside*) vicino a, accanto a; **~ the sea** (*holiday*) al mare; (*town*) sul mare.

4. (*past*) davanti a; **a car went ~ the**

house un'automobile è passata davanti alla casa.

5. (*via*) da; **go out ~ the door on the left** uscite dalla porta sulla sinistra.

6. (*with time*): **be there ~ nine** trovati lì per le nove; **~ day/night** di giorno/notte; **~ now** ormai.

7. (*expressing quantity*) a; **sold ~ the dozen/thousand** venduti a dozzine/migliaia; **prices fell ~ 20%** i prezzi sono diminuiti del 20%; **we charge ~ the hour** facciamo pagare a ore.

8. (*expressing meaning*): **what do you mean ~ that?** cosa intendi dire con questo?

9. (*in sums, measurements*) per; **two metres ~ five** due metri per cinque.

10. (*according to*) per, secondo; **~ law** per legge; **it's fine ~ me** per me va bene.

11. (*expressing gradual process*): **bit ~ bit** (a) poco a poco; **one ~ one** uno per uno; **year ~ year** di anno in anno.

12. (*in phrases*): **~ mistake** per errore; **~ oneself** (*alone*) (da) solo; (*unaided*) da solo; **he's a lawyer ~ profession** è avvocato di professione. ♦ *adv* (*past*): **to go ~** passare.

bye(-bye) [baɪ(baɪ)] *excl* (*inf*) ciao!

bypass ['baɪpɑːs] *n* (*road*) circonvallazione *f*.

C

C (*abbr of Celsius, centigrade*) C.

cab [kæb] *n* (*taxi*) taxi *m inv*; (*of lorry*) cabina *f*.

cabaret ['kæbəreɪ] *n* spettacolo *m* di cabaret.

cabbage ['kæbɪdʒ] *n* cavolo *m*.

cabin ['kæbɪn] *n* cabina *f*; (*wooden house*) capanna *f*.

cabin crew *n* personale *m* di bordo.

cabinet ['kæbɪnɪt] *n* (*cupboard*) armadietto *m*; (POL) consiglio *m* di gabinetto.

cable ['keɪbl] *n* cavo *m*.

cable car *n* funivia *f*.

cable television *n* televisione *f* via cavo.

cactus ['kæktəs] (*pl* -**tuses** OR -**ti** [-taɪ]) *n* cactus *m inv*.

Caesar salad [ˌsiːzə-] *n* insalata di lattuga, acciughe, olive, crostini e parmigiano.

cafe ['kæfeɪ] *n* caffè *m*.

cafeteria [ˌkæfɪ'tɪərɪə] *n* ristorante *m* self-service.

cafetière [kæf'tjeəʳ] *n* tipo di caffettiera con pressa che separa la polvere dal caffè ottenuto.

caffeine ['kæfiːn] *n* caffeina *f*.

cage [keɪdʒ] *n* gabbia *f*.

cagoule [kə'guːl] *n* (Br) K-way® *m inv*.

Cajun ['keɪdʒən] *adj* tipico della popolazione di origine francese della Louisiana.

cake [keɪk] *n* (*large*) torta *f*; (*small*) pasta *f*; (*of soap*) pezzo *m*.

calculate ['kælkjʊleɪt] *vt* calcolare.

calculator ['kælkjʊleɪtəʳ] *n* calcolatrice *f*.

calendar ['kælɪndəʳ] *n* calendario *m*.

calf [kɑːf] (*pl* **calves**) *n* (*of cow*) vitello *m*; (*part of leg*) polpaccio *m*.

call [kɔːl] ♦ *n* (*visit*) visita *f*; (*phone call*) telefonata *f*; (*of bird*) richiamo *m*; (*at airport*) chiamata *f*; (*at hotel*) sveglia *f* ♦ *vt* chiamare; (*meeting*) convocare; (*elections, strike*) indire ♦ *vi* (*visit*) passare; (*phone*) chiamare; **on ~** (*nurse, doctor*) reperibile; **to pay sb a ~** fare una visita a qn; **to be ~ed** chiamarsi; **what is he ~ed?** come si chiama?; **to ~ sb a liar** dare del bugiardo a qn; **to ~ sb's name** chiamare qn; **this train ~s at ...** questo treno ferma a ...; **who's ~ing?** chi parla?

▶ **call back** ♦ vt sep richiamare ♦ vi (*phone again*) richiamare; (*visit again*) ripassare.

▶ **call for** vt fus (*come to fetch*) passare a prendere; (*demand*) chiedere; (*require*) richiedere.

▶ **call on** vt fus (*visit*) fare visita a; **to ~ on sb to do sthg** chiedere a qn di fare qc.

▶ **call out** ♦ vt sep (*name, winner*) annunciare; (*doctor, fire brigade*) chiamare ♦ vi gridare.

▶ **call up** vt sep (MIL) chiamare alle armi; (*telephone*) chiamare.

call box n cabina f telefonica.

caller ['kɔ:lər] n (*visitor*) visitatore m (-trice f); (*on phone*) persona che chiama.

calm [kɑːm] ♦ adj calmo(-a) ♦ vt calmare.

▶ **calm down** ♦ vt sep calmare ♦ vi calmarsi.

Calor gas® ['kælə-] n butano m.

calorie ['kælərɪ] n caloria f.

calves [kɑːvz] pl → **calf**.

camcorder ['kæm,kɔːdər] n videocamera f.

came [keɪm] pt → **come**.

camel ['kæml] n cammello m.

camembert ['kæməmbeər] n camembert m inv.

camera ['kæmərə] n (*for photographs*) macchina f fotografica; (*for filming*) macchina da presa.

cameraman ['kæmərəmæn] (pl -men [-men]) n cameraman m inv.

camera shop n fotografo m.

camisole ['kæmɪsəʊl] n canottiera f.

camp [kæmp] ♦ n (*for holiday-makers*) campeggio m, camping m inv; (*for soldiers, prisoners*) campo m ♦ vi accamparsi.

campaign [kæm'peɪn] ♦ n campagna f ♦ vi: **to ~ (for/against)** fare una campagna (per/contro).

camp bed n branda f.

camper ['kæmpər] n (*person*) cam-

peggiatore m (-trice f); (*van*) camper m inv.

camping ['kæmpɪŋ] n: **to go ~** andare in campeggio.

camping stove n fornello m da campeggio.

campsite ['kæmpsaɪt] n campeggio m, camping m inv.

campus ['kæmpəs] (pl -es) n campus m inv.

can¹ [kæn] n (*of food*) scatola f; (*of drink*) lattina f; (*of paint*) barattolo m; (*of oil*) latta f.

can² [weak form kən, strong form kæn] (pt & conditional **could**) aux vb **1.** (*be able to*) potere; **~ you help me?** puoi aiutarmi?; **I ~ see you** ti vedo.

2. (*know how to*) sapere; **~ you drive?** sai guidare?; **I ~ speak Italian** parlo (l')italiano.

3. (*be allowed to*) potere; **you can't smoke here** è proibito fumare qui.

4. (*in polite requests*) potere; **~ you tell me the time?** mi può dire l'ora?, mi sa dire l'ora?; **~ I speak to the manager?** posso parlare al direttore?

5. (*expressing occasional occurrence*): **it ~ get cold at night** può fare freddo la notte.

6. (*expressing possibility*) potere; **they could be lost** si potrebbero essere persi.

Canada ['kænədə] n il Canada.

Canadian [kə'neɪdɪən] ♦ adj canadese ♦ n canadese mf.

canal [kə'næl] n canale m.

canapé ['kænəpeɪ] n tartina f.

cancel ['kænsl] vt annullare.

cancellation [,kænsə'leɪʃn] n annullamento m.

cancer ['kænsər] n cancro m.

Cancer ['kænsər] n Cancro m.

candidate ['kændɪdət] n candidato m (-a f).

candle ['kændl] n candela f.

candlelit dinner ['kændllɪt-] n cena f a lume di candela.

candy ['kændɪ] n (Am) (*confectionery*)

dolciumi *mpl;* (*sweet*) caramella *f.*

candyfloss ['kændɪflɒs] *n* (*Br*) zucchero *m* filato.

cane [keɪn] *n* (*for walking*) bastone *m;* (*for punishment*) bacchetta *f;* (*for furniture, baskets*) vimini *mpl.*

canister ['kænɪstər] *n* (*for tea*) barattolo *m;* (*for gas*) bombola *f.*

cannabis ['kænəbɪs] *n* cannabis *f.*

canned [kænd] *adj* (*food*) in scatola; (*drink*) in lattina.

cannon ['kænən] *n* cannone *m.*

cannot ['kænɒt] = **can not**.

canoe [kə'nu:] *n* canoa *f.*

canoeing [kə'nu:ɪŋ] *n* canottaggio *m.*

canopy ['kænəpɪ] *n* (*over bed etc*) baldacchino *m.*

can't [kɑ:nt] = **cannot**.

cantaloup(e) ['kæntəlu:p] *n* melone *m* (cantalupo).

canteen [kæn'ti:n] *n* mensa *f.*

canvas ['kænvəs] *n* (*for tent, bag*) tela *f.*

cap [kæp] *n* (*hat*) berretto *m;* (*of pen, bottle*) tappo *m;* (*contraceptive*) diaframma *m.*

capable ['keɪpəbl] *adj* (*competent*) capace; **to be ~ of doing sthg** essere capace di fare qc.

capacity [kə'pæsɪtɪ] *n* (*ability*) capacità *f inv;* (*of stadium, theatre*) capienza *f.*

cape [keɪp] *n* (*of land*) capo *m;* (*cloak*) cappa *f.*

capers ['keɪpəz] *npl* capperi *mpl.*

capital ['kæpɪtl] *n* (*of country*) capitale *f;* (*money*) capitale *m;* (*letter*) maiuscola *f.*

capital punishment *n* pena *f* capitale.

cappuccino [ˌkæpʊ'tʃi:nəʊ] (*pl* **-s**) *n* cappuccino *m.*

Capricorn *n* Capricorno *m.*

capsicum ['kæpsɪkəm] *n* peperone *m.*

capsize [kæp'saɪz] *vi* rovesciarsi.

capsule ['kæpsju:l] *n* (*for medicine*) capsula *f.*

captain ['kæptɪn] *n* capitano *m.*

caption ['kæpʃn] *n* didascalia *f.*

capture ['kæptʃər] *vt* (*person, animal*) catturare; (*town, castle*) conquistare.

car [kɑ:r] *n* (*motorcar*) automobile *f*, macchina *f;* (*railway wagon*) vagone *m.*

carafe [kə'ræf] *n* caraffa *f.*

caramel ['kærəmel] *n* (*sweet*) caramella *f* mou®; (*burnt sugar*) caramello *m.*

carat ['kærət] *n* carato *m;* **24-~ gold** oro a 24 carati.

caravan ['kærəvæn] *n* (*Br*) roulotte *f inv.*

caravanning ['kærəvænɪŋ] *n* (*Br*): **to go ~** andare in vacanza in roulotte.

caravan site *n* (*Br*) campeggio *m* per roulotte.

carbohydrate [ˌkɑ:bəʊ'haɪdreɪt] *n* (*in foods*) carboidrato *m.*

carbon ['kɑ:bən] *n* carbone *m.*

carbon copy *n* copia *f* fatta con carta carbone.

carbon dioxide [-daɪ'ɒksaɪd] *n* anidride *f* carbonica.

carbon monoxide [-mɒ'nɒksaɪd] *n* monossido *m* di carbonio.

car boot sale *n* (*Br*) mercatino di oggetti usati esposti nei bagagliai aperti delle automobili dei venditori.

carburetor [ˌkɑ:bə'retər] (*Am*) = **carburettor**.

carburettor [ˌkɑ:bə'retər] *n* (*Br*) carburatore *m.*

car crash *n* incidente *m* automobilistico.

card [kɑ:d] *n* (*for filing, notes*) scheda *f;* (*for greetings*) biglietto *m;* (*showing membership*) tessera *f;* (*of businessperson*) biglietto da visita; (*postcard*) cartolina *f;* (*playing card*) carta *f;* (*cardboard*) cartoncino *m;* **~s** (*game*) carte *fpl.*

cardboard ['kɑ:dbɔ:d] *n* cartone *m.*

car deck *n* ponte *m* auto.

cardiac arrest [ˌkɑːdɪæk-] n arresto m cardiaco.

cardigan ['kɑːdɪgən] n cardigan m inv.

care [keəʳ] ◆ n cura f ◆ vi: **I don't ~** non me ne importa; **to take ~ of** (look after) prendersi cura di; (deal with) occuparsi di; **would you ~ to ...?** (fml) se vuole ...; **to take ~ to do sthg** stare attento a fare qc; **take ~!** (goodbye) stammi bene!; **with ~** con cura; **to ~ about** (think important) avere a cuore; (person) voler bene a.

career [kəˈrɪəʳ] n carriera f.

carefree ['keəfriː] adj spensierato(-a).

careful ['keəfʊl] adj (cautious) attento(-a); (driver) prudente; (thorough) accurato(-a); **be ~!** attento(-a)!

carefully ['keəflɪ] adv (cautiously) con cautela; (thoroughly) attentamente.

careless ['keələs] adj (inattentive) sbadato(-a); (unconcerned) spensierato(-a).

caretaker ['keəˌteɪkəʳ] n (Br) custode mf.

car ferry n traghetto m.

cargo ['kɑːgəʊ] (pl -es OR -s) n carico m.

car hire n (Br) autonoleggio m.

Caribbean [Br ˌkærɪˈbiːən, Am kəˈrɪbɪən] n: **the ~** (area) i Caraibi.

caring ['keərɪŋ] adj premuroso(-a).

carnation [kɑːˈneɪʃn] n garofano m.

carnival ['kɑːnɪvl] n carnevale m.

carousel [ˌkærəˈsel] n (for luggage) nastro m trasportatore; (Am: merry-go-round) giostra f.

carp [kɑːp] n carpa f.

car park n (Br) parcheggio m.

carpenter ['kɑːpəntəʳ] n falegname m.

carpentry ['kɑːpəntrɪ] n falegnameria f.

carpet ['kɑːpɪt] n (rug) tappeto m;

(wall-to-wall) moquette f inv.

car rental n (Am) autonoleggio m.

carriage ['kærɪdʒ] n carrozza f.

carriageway ['kærɪdʒweɪ] n (Br) carreggiata f.

carrier (bag) ['kærɪəʳ-] n sacchetto m.

carrot ['kærət] n carota f.

carrot cake n torta f di carote.

carry ['kærɪ] ◆ vt portare; (disease) essere portatore di ◆ vi (voice, sound) arrivare.

▶ **carry on** ◆ vi continuare ◆ vt fus (continue) continuare; (conduct) compiere; **to ~ on doing sthg** continuare a fare qc.

▶ **carry out** vt sep (work, repairs, investigation) effettuare; (plan) portare a compimento; (order) eseguire; (promise) adempiere.

carrycot ['kærɪkɒt] n (Br) culla f portatile.

carryout ['kærɪaʊt] n (Am & Scot: meal) cibo m da asporto.

carsick ['kɑːˌsɪk] adj: **to be ~** soffrire il mal d'auto.

cart [kɑːt] n (for transport) carro m; (inf: video game cartridge) cartuccia f; (Am: in supermarket) carrello m.

carton ['kɑːtn] n (of milk, juice) cartone m; (box) scatola f.

cartoon [kɑːˈtuːn] n (drawing) vignetta f; (comic strip) fumetto m; (film) cartone m animato.

cartridge ['kɑːtrɪdʒ] n cartuccia f.

carve [kɑːv] vt (wood, stone) intagliare; (meat) tagliare.

carvery ['kɑːvərɪ] n ristorante dove si mangia carne arrosto, tagliata appositamente al banco per il cliente.

car wash n autolavaggio m.

case [keɪs] n (Br: suitcase) valigia f; (container) custodia f; (instance, patient) caso m; (JUR: trial) causa f; **in any ~** in ogni caso; **in ~ it rains** nel caso che piova; **in ~ of** in caso di; **(just) in ~** in caso di necessità; **in that ~** allora.

cash [kæʃ] ◆ n (coins, notes) contanti mpl; (money in general) soldi mpl ◆ vt: **to ~ a cheque** incassare un assegno; **to pay ~** pagare in contanti.

cash desk n cassa f.

cash dispenser [-ˌdɪˈspensər] n cassa f automatica.

cashew (nut) [ˈkæʃuː-] n noce f di acagiù.

cashier [kæˈʃɪər] n cassiere m (-a f).

cashmere [kæʃˈmɪər] n cachemire m.

cashpoint [ˈkæʃpɔɪnt] n (Br) cassa f automatica.

cash register n registratore m di cassa.

casino [kəˈsiːnəʊ] (pl -s) n casinò m inv.

cask [kɑːsk] n barile m.

cask-conditioned [-ˌkənˈdɪʃnd] adj fermentato(-a) in barili.

casserole [ˈkæsərəʊl] n (stew) stufato m; ~ (dish) casseruola f.

cassette [kæˈset] n cassetta f.

cassette recorder n registratore m (a cassette).

cast [kɑːst] (pt & pp **cast**) ◆ n (actors) cast m inv; (for broken bone) ingessatura f ◆ vt (shadow, light, look) gettare; **to ~ doubt on** mettere in dubbio; **to ~ one's vote** votare.

▶ **cast off** vi (boat, ship) salpare.

caster [ˈkɑːstər] n rotella f.

caster sugar n (Br) zucchero m semolato.

castle [ˈkɑːsl] n (building) castello m; (in chess) torre f.

casual [ˈkæʒʊəl] adj (relaxed) disinvolto(-a); (offhand) noncurante; (clothes) casual (inv); ~ **work** lavoro occasionale.

casualty [ˈkæʒjʊəltɪ] n (injured person) ferito m (-a f); (dead person) morto m (-a f); ~ (ward) pronto soccorso m.

cat [kæt] n gatto m.

catalog [ˈkætəlɒg] (Am) = **catalogue**.

catalogue [ˈkætəlɒg] n catalogo m.

catapult [ˈkætəpʌlt] n fionda f.

cataract [ˈkætərækt] n (in eye) cateratta f.

catarrh [kəˈtɑːr] n catarro m.

catastrophe [kəˈtæstrəfɪ] n catastrofe f.

catch [kætʃ] (pt & pp **caught**) ◆ vt prendere; (surprise, hear) cogliere; (attention) attirare ◆ vi (become hooked) impigliarsi ◆ n (of window, door) fermo m; (snag) intoppo m.

▶ **catch up** ◆ vt sep raggiungere ◆ vi: **to ~ up (with sthg)** (sleep, work) recuperare (qc); **to ~ up with sb** raggiungere qn.

catching [ˈkætʃɪŋ] adj (inf) contagioso(-a).

category [ˈkætəgərɪ] n categoria f.

cater [ˈkeɪtər]: **cater for** vt fus (Br) (needs) provvedere a; (anticipate) tenere conto di; (tastes) soddisfare.

caterpillar [ˈkætəpɪlər] n bruco m.

cathedral [kəˈθiːdrəl] n cattedrale f, duomo m.

Catholic [ˈkæθlɪk] ◆ adj cattolico(-a) ◆ n cattolico m (-a f).

Catseyes® [ˈkætsaɪz] npl (Br) catarifrangenti mpl.

cattle [ˈkætl] npl bestiame m.

cattle grid n griglia metallica posta sul suolo stradale per impedire il passaggio di pecore, mucche etc.

caught [kɔːt] pt & pp → **catch**.

cauliflower [ˈkɒlɪflaʊər] n cavolfiore m.

cauliflower cheese n cavolfiore gratinato con besciamella.

cause [kɔːz] ◆ n causa f; (justification) ragione f ◆ vt causare; **to ~ sb to make a mistake** far fare un errore a qn.

causeway [ˈkɔːzweɪ] n strada f rialzata.

caustic soda [ˌkɔːstɪk-] n soda f caustica.

caution [ˈkɔːʃn] n (care) cautela f; (warning) avvertimento m.

cautious ['kɔːʃəs] *adj* cauto(-a).

cave [keɪv] *n* grotta *f*.

▶ **cave in** *vi* crollare.

caviar(e) ['kævɪɑːʳ] *n* caviale *m*.

cavity ['kævətɪ] *n* (*in tooth*) carie *f inv*.

CD *n* (*abbr of compact disc*) CD *m inv*.

CDI *n* (*abbr of compact disc interactive*) CDI *m inv*.

CD player *n* lettore *m* di compact disc.

CDW *n* (*abbr of collision damage waiver*) franchigia *f*.

cease [siːs] *vt & vi* (*fml*) cessare.

ceasefire ['siːsˌfaɪəʳ] *n* cessate il fuoco *m inv*.

cedar ['siːdəʳ] *n* cedro *m*.

ceilidh ['keɪlɪ] *n* festa scozzese o irlandese con danze folcloristiche.

ceiling ['siːlɪŋ] *n* soffitto *m*.

celebrate ['selɪbreɪt] ◆ *vt* (*win, birthday*) festeggiare; (*Mass*) celebrare ◆ *vi* festeggiare.

celebration [ˌselɪ'breɪʃn] *n* (*event*) festa *f*.

▶ **celebrations** *npl* (*festivities*) festeggiamenti *mpl*.

celebrity [sɪ'lebrətɪ] *n* (*person*) celebrità *f inv*.

celeriac [sɪ'lerɪæk] *n* sedano *m* rapa.

celery ['selərɪ] *n* sedano *m*.

cell [sel] *n* (*of plant, body*) cellula *f*; (*in prison*) cella *f*.

cellar ['seləʳ] *n* cantina *f*.

cello ['tʃeləʊ] (*pl* **-s**) *n* violoncello *m*.

Cellophane® ['seləfeɪn] *n* cellophane® *m*.

Celsius ['selsɪəs] *adj* Celsius (*inv*).

cement [sɪ'ment] *n* cemento *m*.

cement mixer *n* betoniera *f*.

cemetery ['semɪtrɪ] *n* cimitero *m*.

cent [sent] *n* (*Am*) cent *m inv*.

center ['sentər] (*Am*) = **centre**.

centigrade ['sentɪgreɪd] *adj* centigrado(-a).

centimetre ['sentɪˌmiːtəʳ] *n* centimetro *m*.

centipede ['sentɪpiːd] *n* centopiedi *m inv*.

central ['sentrəl] *adj* centrale.

central heating *n* riscaldamento *m* autonomo.

central locking [-'lɒkɪŋ] *n* chiusura *f* delle porte centralizzata.

central reservation *n* (*Br*) zona *f* spartitraffico.

centre ['sentəʳ] ◆ *n* (*Br*) centro *m* ◆ *adj* (*Br*) centrale; **the ~ of attention** il centro dell'attenzione.

century ['sentʃʊrɪ] *n* secolo *m*.

ceramic [sɪ'ræmɪk] *adj* di ceramica.

▶ **ceramics** *npl* oggetti *mpl* di ceramica.

cereal ['sɪərɪəl] *n* (*breakfast food*) cereali *mpl*.

ceremony ['serɪmənɪ] *n* cerimonia *f*.

certain ['sɜːtn] *adj* certo(-a); **she's ~ to be late** farà tardi di sicuro; **to be ~ of sthg** essere certo di qc; **to make ~ (that)** assicurarsi che.

certainly ['sɜːtnlɪ] *adv* certamente, certo.

certificate [sə'tɪfɪkət] *n* certificato *m*.

certify ['sɜːtɪfaɪ] *vt* (*declare true*) attestare.

chain [tʃeɪn] ◆ *n* catena *f*; (*of islands*) arcipelago *m* ◆ *vt*: **to ~ sthg to sthg** incatenare qc a qc.

chain store *n* negozio che fa parte di una catena.

chair [tʃeəʳ] *n* sedia *f*.

chair lift *n* seggiovia *f*.

chairman ['tʃeəmən] (*pl* **-men** [-mən]) *n* presidente *m*.

chairperson ['tʃeəˌpɜːsn] (*pl* **-s**) *n* presidente *m* (-essa *f*).

chairwoman ['tʃeəˌwʊmən] (*pl* **-women** [-ˌwɪmɪn]) *n* presidentessa *f*.

chalet ['ʃæleɪ] *n* chalet *m inv*; (*at holiday camp*) bungalow *m inv*.

chalk [tʃɔːk] *n* gesso *m*; **a piece of ~** un gesso.

chalkboard [ˈtʃɔːkbɔːd] n (Am) lavagna f.

challenge [ˈtʃælɪndʒ] ◆ n sfida f ◆ vt (question) mettere in discussione; **to ~ sb (to sthg)** sfidare qn (a qc).

chamber [ˈtʃeɪmbəʳ] n (room) sala f.

chambermaid [ˈtʃeɪmbəmeɪd] n cameriera f (d'albergo).

chamber music n musica f da camera.

champagne [ˌʃæmˈpeɪn] n champagne m inv.

champion [ˈtʃæmpjən] n campione m (-essa f).

championship [ˈtʃæmpjənʃɪp] n campionato m.

chance [tʃɑːns] ◆ n (luck) caso m; (possibility) probabilità f inv; (opportunity) possibilità f inv, occasione f ◆ vt: **to ~ it** (inf) provarci; **to take a ~** rischiare; **by ~** per caso; **I came on the off ~ you'd be here** sono venuto per vedere se per caso ci fossi.

Chancellor of the Exchequer [ˌtʃɑːnsələrəvðəɪksˈtʃekəʳ] n (Br) ≈ ministro m del Tesoro.

chandelier [ˌʃændəˈlɪəʳ] n lampadario m.

change [tʃeɪndʒ] ◆ n (alteration) cambiamento m; (money received back) resto m; (coins) spiccioli mpl ◆ vt cambiare ◆ vi cambiare; (change clothes) cambiarsi; **a ~ of clothes** vestiti mpl di ricambio; **do you have ~ for a pound?** mi può cambiare una sterlina?; **for a ~** per cambiare; **to get ~d** cambiarsi; **to ~ money** cambiare i soldi; **to ~ a nappy** cambiare un pannolino; **to ~ a wheel** cambiare una ruota; **to ~ trains/planes** cambiare treno/aereo; **all ~!** (on train) per tutte le altre stazioni si cambia!

changeable [ˈtʃeɪndʒəbl] adj (weather) variabile.

change machine n distributore automatico di monete.

changing room [ˈtʃeɪndʒɪŋ-] n (for sport) spogliatoio m; (in shop)

camerino m.

channel [ˈtʃænl] n canale m; **the (English) Channel** la Manica.

Channel Islands npl: **the ~** le Isole della Manica.

Channel Tunnel n: **the ~** il tunnel sotto la Manica.

chant [tʃɑːnt] vt (RELIG) cantare; (words, slogan) scandire.

chaos [ˈkeɪɒs] n caos m.

chaotic [keɪˈɒtɪk] adj caotico(-a).

chap [tʃæp] n (Br: inf) tipo m.

chapatti [tʃəˈpætɪ] n pane m azzimo indiano.

chapel [ˈtʃæpl] n cappella f.

chapped [tʃæpt] adj screpolato(-a).

chapter [ˈtʃæptəʳ] n capitolo m.

character [ˈkærəktəʳ] n carattere m; (in film, book, play) personaggio m; (inf: person, individual) tipo m.

characteristic [ˌkærəktəˈrɪstɪk] ◆ adj caratteristico(-a) ◆ n caratteristica f.

charcoal [ˈtʃɑːkəʊl] n (for barbecue) carbone m di legna.

charge [tʃɑːdʒ] ◆ n (price) spesa f; (JUR) accusa f ◆ vt (customer) far pagare; (money) chiedere; (JUR) accusare; (battery) ricaricare ◆ vi (ask money) far pagare; (rush) precipitarsi; **to be in ~ (of)** essere responsabile (di); **to take ~ (of)** assumere la responsabilità (di); **free of ~** gratis; **extra ~** supplemento m; **there is no ~ for service** il servizio è gratuito.

char-grilled [tʃɑːɡrɪld] adj alla brace.

charity [ˈtʃærətɪ] n (organization) ente m di beneficenza; **to give to ~** dare soldi in beneficenza.

charity shop n negozio che vende articoli vari, il cui ricavato è destinato ad un ente di beneficenza.

charm [tʃɑːm] ◆ n (attractiveness) fascino m ◆ vt affascinare.

charming [ˈtʃɑːmɪŋ] adj affascinante.

chart [tʃɑːt] n (*diagram*) grafico m; (*map*) carta f; **the ~s** l'hit-parade f inv.

chartered accountant [tʃɑːtəd-] n esperto m (-a f) contabile.

charter flight [tʃɑːtə-] n volo m charter.

chase [tʃeɪs] ♦ n inseguimento m ♦ vt inseguire.

chat [tʃæt] ♦ n chiacchierata f ♦ vi chiacchierare; **to have a ~ (with)** fare quattro chiacchiere (con).

▶ **chat up** vt sep (Br: inf) agganciare.

château [ʃætəu] n castello m.

chat show n (Br) talk show m inv.

chatty [tʃætɪ] adj (*person*) chiacchierone(-a); (*letter*) pieno di pettegolezzi.

chauffeur [ʃəufər] n autista m.

cheap [tʃiːp] adj a buon mercato; (*pej: low-quality*) dozzinale.

cheap day return n biglietto di andata e ritorno a prezzo ridotto, valido per un solo giorno e soggetto a restrizioni di orario.

cheaply [tʃiːplɪ] adv a basso prezzo.

cheat [tʃiːt] ♦ n imbroglione m (-a f) ♦ vi imbrogliare ♦ vt: **to ~ sb out of sthg** sottrarre qc a qn con l'inganno.

check [tʃek] ♦ n (*inspection*) controllo m; (Am: *bill*) conto m; (Am: *tick*) segno m; (Am) = **cheque** ♦ vt controllare; (Am: *tick*) spuntare ♦ vi verificare; **to ~ for sthg** controllare qc; **to ~ on sthg** controllare qc.

▶ **check in** ♦ vt sep (*luggage*) far passare al check-in ♦ vi (*at hotel*) farsi registrare; (*at airport*) fare il check-in.

▶ **check off** vt sep spuntare.

▶ **check out** vi saldare il conto e andarsene.

▶ **check up** vi: **to ~ up (on)** fare delle indagini (su).

checked [tʃekt] adj a quadri.

checkers [tʃekəz] n (Am) dama f.

check-in desk n banco m dell'accettazione bagagli OR del check-in.

checkout [tʃekaut] n cassa f.

checkpoint [tʃekpɔɪnt] n posto m di blocco.

checkroom [tʃekrʊm] n (Am) deposito m bagagli.

checkup [tʃekʌp] n check-up m inv.

cheddar (cheese) [tʃedər-] n tipo di formaggio semi-stagionato.

cheek [tʃiːk] n guancia f; **what a ~!** che faccia tosta!

cheeky [tʃiːkɪ] adj sfacciato(-a).

cheer [tʃɪər] ♦ n acclamazione f ♦ vi acclamare.

cheerful [tʃɪəfʊl] adj allegro(-a); (*colour*) vivace.

cheerio [tʃɪərɪˈəu] excl (Br: inf) ciao!

cheers [tʃɪəz] excl (*when drinking*) cincin!, salute!; (Br: inf: *thank you*) grazie!

cheese [tʃiːz] n formaggio m.

cheeseboard [tʃiːzbɔːd] n (*cheese and biscuits*) piatto m di formaggi.

cheeseburger [tʃiːzˌbɜːgər] n cheeseburger m inv (*panino con hamburger e formaggio fuso*).

cheesecake [tʃiːzkeɪk] n cheesecake m inv (*dolce a base di biscotti, formaggio fresco e panna*).

chef [ʃef] n chef m inv.

chef's special n specialità f inv della casa.

chemical [kemɪkl] ♦ adj chimico(-a) ♦ n sostanza f chimica.

chemist [kemɪst] n (Br: *pharmacist*) farmacista mf; (*scientist*) chimico m (-a f); **~'s** (Br: *shop*) farmacia f.

chemistry [kemɪstrɪ] n chimica f.

cheque [tʃek] n (Br) assegno m; **to pay by ~** pagare con un assegno.

chequebook [tʃekbʊk] n libretto m degli assegni.

cheque card n carta f assegni.

cherry [tʃerɪ] n ciliegia f.

chess [tʃes] n scacchi mpl.

chest [tʃest] n (of body) torace m; (box) cassa f.

chestnut ['tʃesnʌt] ♦ n castagna f ♦ adj (colour) castano(-a); ~ (tree) castagno m.

chest of drawers n cassettone m.

chew [tʃuː] ♦ vt masticare ♦ n (sweet) caramella f (morbida).

chewing gum ['tʃuːɪŋ-] n gomma f da masticare.

chic [ʃiːk] adj alla moda, chic (inv).

chicken ['tʃɪkɪn] n (bird) gallina f; (meat) pollo m.

chicken breast n petto m di pollo.

chicken Kiev [-'kiːev] n filetto di pollo farcito con burro all'aglio, impanato e fritto.

chicken pox [-pɒks] n varicella f.

chickpea ['tʃɪkpiː] n cece m.

chicory ['tʃɪkərɪ] n cicoria f.

chief [tʃiːf] ♦ adj (highest-ranking) capo (inv); (main) principale ♦ n capo m.

chiefly ['tʃiːflɪ] adv (mainly) principalmente; (especially) soprattutto.

child [tʃaɪld] (pl children) n (young boy, girl) bambino m (-a f); (son, daughter) figlio m (-a f).

child abuse n maltrattamento m di minori.

child benefit n (Br) ≃ assegno m di famiglia.

childhood ['tʃaɪldhʊd] n infanzia f.

childish ['tʃaɪldɪʃ] adj (pej) infantile.

childminder ['tʃaɪld,maɪndər] n (Br) bambinaia f.

children ['tʃɪldrən] pl → child.

childrenswear ['tʃɪldrənzweər] n abbigliamento m per bambini.

child seat n (in car) seggiolino m per bambini.

Chile ['tʃɪlɪ] n il Cile.

chill [tʃɪl] ♦ n (illness) infreddatura f ♦ vt raffreddare; there's a ~ in the air l'aria è fredda.

chilled [tʃɪld] adj freddo(-a); 'serve ~' 'servire fresco'.

chilli ['tʃɪlɪ] (pl -ies) n (vegetable) peperoncino m piccante; (dish) = **chilli con carne**.

chilli con carne ['tʃɪlɪkɒn'kɑːnɪ] n piatto messicano a base di carne e fagioli rossi cotti in spezie e salsa piccante.

chilly ['tʃɪlɪ] adj freddo(-a).

chimney ['tʃɪmnɪ] n camino m.

chimneypot ['tʃɪmnɪpɒt] n comignolo m.

chimpanzee [,tʃɪmpən'ziː] n scimpanzé m inv.

chin [tʃɪn] n mento m.

china ['tʃaɪnə] n (material) porcellana f.

China ['tʃaɪnə] n la Cina.

Chinese [,tʃaɪ'niːz] ♦ adj cinese ♦ n (language) cinese m ♦ npl: the ~ i cinesi; a ~ restaurant un ristorante cinese.

chip [tʃɪp] ♦ n (small piece) scheggia f; (mark) scheggiatura f; (counter) fiche f inv; (COMPUT) chip m inv ♦ vt scheggiare.
▶ **chips** npl (Br: French fries) patate fpl fritte; (Am: crisps) patatine fpl.

chiropodist [kɪ'rɒpədɪst] n callista mf.

chisel ['tʃɪzl] n cesello m.

chives [tʃaɪvz] npl erba f cipollina.

chlorine ['klɔːriːn] n cloro m.

choc-ice ['tʃɒkaɪs] n (Br) blocco di gelato ricoperto di cioccolato.

chocolate ['tʃɒkələt] ♦ n (food) cioccolato m, cioccolata f; (sweet) cioccolatino m; (drink) cioccolata f ♦ adj al cioccolato.

chocolate biscuit n biscotto m al cioccolato.

choice [tʃɔɪs] ♦ n scelta f ♦ adj (meat, ingredients) di prima qualità; the dressing of your ~ il condimento di vostra scelta.

choir ['kwaɪər] n coro m.

choke [tʃəʊk] ♦ n (AUT) (valvola f dell')aria f inv ♦ vt soffocare ♦ vi (on fishbone etc) strozzarsi; (to death) soffocare.

cholera ['kɒlərə] n colera m.

choose [tʃuːz] (pt **chose**, pp **chosen**) vt & vi scegliere; **to ~ to do sthg** scegliere di fare qc.

chop [tʃɒp] ◆ n (of meat) braciola f ◆ vt tagliare.

▶ **chop down** vt sep abbattere.

▶ **chop up** vt sep tagliare a pezzetti.

chopper ['tʃɒpər] n (inf: helicopter) elicottero m.

chopping board ['tʃɒpɪŋ-] n tagliere m.

choppy ['tʃɒpɪ] adj increspato(-a).

chopsticks ['tʃɒpstɪks] npl bastoncini mpl cinesi.

chop suey [,tʃɒp'suːɪ] n piatto cinese a base di riso, striscioline di maiale o pollo, verdura e germogli di soia.

chord [kɔːd] n accordo m.

chore [tʃɔːr] n faccenda f.

chorus ['kɔːrəs] n (part of song) ritornello m; (group of singers, dancers) coro m.

chose [tʃəʊz] pt → **choose**.

chosen ['tʃəʊzn] pp → **choose**.

choux pastry [ʃuː-] n pasta f per bignè.

chowder ['tʃaʊdər] n zuppa di pesce o frutti di mare.

chow mein [,tʃaʊ'meɪn] n piatto cinese di tagliolini fritti con verdure, carne o frutti di mare.

Christ [kraɪst] n Cristo m.

christen ['krɪsn] vt (baby) battezzare.

christening ['krɪsnɪŋ] n battesimo m.

Christian ['krɪstʃən] ◆ adj cristiano(-a) ◆ n cristiano m (-a f).

Christian name n nome m di battesimo.

Christmas ['krɪsməs] n Natale m; **Happy ~!** Buon Natale!

Christmas card n biglietto m d'auguri di Natale.

Christmas carol [-'kærəl] n canto m di Natale.

Christmas Day n il giorno di Natale.

Christmas Eve n la vigilia di Natale.

Christmas pudding n dolce tradizionale natalizio a base di uva passa e frutta candita.

Christmas tree n albero m di Natale.

chrome [krəʊm] n cromo m.

chuck [tʃʌk] vt (inf) (throw) buttare; (boyfriend, girlfriend) mollare.

▶ **chuck away** vt sep buttare via.

chunk [tʃʌŋk] n pezzo m.

church [tʃɜːtʃ] n chiesa f; **to go to ~** andare in chiesa.

churchyard [tʃɜːtʃjɑːd] n cimitero m.

chute [ʃuːt] n scivolo m.

chutney ['tʃʌtnɪ] n salsa piccante agrodolce a base di frutta e spezie.

cider ['saɪdər] n sidro m.

cigar [sɪ'gɑːr] n sigaro m.

cigarette [,sɪgə'ret] n sigaretta f.

cigarette lighter n accendino m.

cinema ['sɪnəmə] n cinema m inv.

cinnamon ['sɪnəmən] n cannella f.

circle ['sɜːkl] ◆ n (shape, ring) cerchio m; (in theatre) galleria f ◆ vt (draw circle around) cerchiare; (move round) girare intorno a ◆ vi (plane) girare in circolo.

circuit ['sɜːkɪt] n (track) circuito m; (lap) giro m.

circular ['sɜːkjʊlər] ◆ adj circolare ◆ n circolare f.

circulation [,sɜːkjʊ'leɪʃn] n (of blood) circolazione f; (of newspaper, magazine) tiratura f.

circumstances ['sɜːkəmstənsɪz] npl circostanze fpl; **in OR under the ~** date le circostanze.

circus ['sɜːkəs] n circo m.

cistern ['sɪstən] n (of toilet) serbatoio m dell'acqua.

citizen ['sɪtɪzn] n cittadino m (-a f).

city ['sɪtɪ] n città f inv; **the City** la City (il centro finanziario di Londra).

city centre n centro m (della) città.

city hall n (Am) municipio m.

civilian [sɪˈvɪljən] n civile m.

civilized [ˈsɪvɪlaɪzd] adj (society) civilizzato(-a); (person, evening) cortese.

civil rights [ˌsɪvl-] npl diritti mpl civili.

civil servant [ˌsɪvl-] n impiegato m (-a f) statale.

civil service [ˌsɪvl-] n amministrazione f pubblica.

civil war [ˌsɪvl-] n guerra f civile.

cl (abbr of centilitre) cl.

claim [kleɪm] ◆ n (assertion) affermazione f; (demand) richiesta f, domanda f; (for insurance) domanda di indennizzo ◆ vt (allege) affermare, sostenere; (demand) richiedere; (credit, responsibility) rivendicare ◆ vi (on insurance) richiedere l'indennizzo.

claimant [ˈkleɪmənt] n (of benefit) richiedente mf.

claim form n modulo m per il rimborso.

clam [klæm] n vongola f.

clamp [klæmp] ◆ n (for car) ganascia f (bloccaruota) ◆ vt (car) bloccare con ganasce.

clap [klæp] vi applaudire.

claret [ˈklærət] n vino rosso di Bordeaux.

clarinet [ˌklærəˈnet] n clarinetto m.

clash [klæʃ] ◆ n (noise) rumore m metallico; (confrontation) scontro m ◆ vi (colours) stonare; (event, date) coincidere.

clasp [klɑːsp] ◆ n (fastener) fermaglio m ◆ vt stringere.

class [klɑːs] ◆ n classe f; (teaching period) lezione f ◆ vt: **to ~ sb/sthg (as)** classificare qn/qc (come).

classic [ˈklæsɪk] ◆ adj classico(-a) ◆ n classico m.

classical [ˈklæsɪkl] adj classico(-a).

classical music n musica f classica.

classification [ˌklæsɪfɪˈkeɪʃn] n classificazione f.

classified ads [ˌklæsɪfaɪd-] npl piccoli annunci mpl.

classroom [ˈklɑːsrʊm] n aula f.

claustrophobic [ˌklɔːstrəˈfəʊbɪk] adj (person) claustrofobo(-a); (place, situation) claustrofobico(-a).

claw [klɔː] n (of bird, cat, dog) artiglio m; (of crab, lobster) pinza f.

clay [kleɪ] n argilla f.

clean [kliːn] ◆ vt pulire ◆ adj pulito(-a); **to ~ one's teeth** lavarsi i denti; **I have a ~ driving licence** non sono mai stato multato per infrazioni gravi.

cleaner [ˈkliːnər] n (person) addetto m (-a f) alle pulizie; (substance) detergente m.

cleanse [klenz] vt pulire.

cleanser [ˈklenzər] n detergente m.

clear [klɪər] ◆ adj chiaro(-a); (transparent) trasparente; (unobstructed) libero(-a); (view) sgombro(-a); (day, sky) sereno(-a) ◆ vt (road, path) sgombrare; (pond) ripulire; (jump over) saltare; (declare not guilty) scagionare; (authorize) autorizzare; (cheque) autorizzare l'accreditamento di ◆ vi (weather) schiarirsi; (fog) levarsi; **to be ~ (about sthg)** avere capito esattamente (qc); **to be ~ of sthg** (not touching) essere staccato da qc; **to ~ one's throat** schiarirsi la voce; **to ~ the table** sparecchiare.

▶ **clear up** ◆ vt sep (room, toys) mettere a posto; (problem, confusion) chiarire ◆ vi (weather) schiarirsi; (tidy up) mettere a posto.

clearance [ˈklɪərəns] n (authorization) autorizzazione f; (free distance) distanza f; (for takeoff) autorizzazione (al decollo).

clearance sale n liquidazione f totale della merce.

clearing [ˈklɪərɪŋ] n radura f.

clearly [ˈklɪəlɪ] adv chiaramente.

clearway [ˈklɪəweɪ] n (Br) strada f con divieto di fermata.

clementine [ˈkleməntaɪn] n mandarancio m.

clerk [Br klɑːk, Am klɜːrk] n (in of-

fice) impiegato *m* (-a *f*); (Am: *in shop*) commesso *m* (-a *f*).

clever ['klevə^r] *adj* (*person*) intelligente; (*idea, device*) ingegnoso(-a).

click [klɪk] ♦ *n* scatto *m* ♦ *vi* (*make sound*) schioccare.

client ['klaɪənt] *n* cliente *mf*.

cliff [klɪf] *n* (*by the sea*) scoglio *m*; (*inland*) rupe *f*.

climate ['klaɪmɪt] *n* clima *m*.

climax ['klaɪmæks] *n* culmine *m*.

climb [klaɪm] ♦ *vt* salire su; (*tree*) arrampicarsi su; (*mountain*) scalare ♦ *vi* salire; (*plane*) prendere quota.

▶ **climb down** ♦ *vt fus* scendere da ♦ *vi* scendere.

▶ **climb up** *vt fus* salire su.

climber ['klaɪmə^r] *n* (*person*) scalatore *m* (-trice *f*).

climbing ['klaɪmɪŋ] *n* alpinismo *m*; **to go ~** fare alpinismo.

climbing frame *n* (Br) castello *m* (*gioco per bambini*).

clingfilm ['klɪŋfɪlm] *n* (Br) pellicola *f* (*per alimenti*).

clinic ['klɪnɪk] *n* clinica *f*.

clip [klɪp] ♦ *n* (*fastener*) fermaglio *m*; (*for paper*) graffetta *f*; (*of film, programme*) sequenza *f* ♦ *vt* (*fasten*) fermare insieme; (*cut*) tagliare; (*tickets*) forare.

cloak [kləʊk] *n* mantello *m*.

cloakroom ['kləʊkrʊm] *n* (*for coats*) guardaroba *m inv*; (Br: *toilet*) toilettes *fpl*.

clock [klɒk] *n* orologio *m*; (*mileometer*) contachilometri *m inv*; **round the ~** 24 ore su 24.

clockwise ['klɒkwaɪz] *adv* in senso orario.

clog [klɒg] ♦ *n* zoccolo *m* ♦ *vt* intasare.

close¹ [kləʊs] ♦ *adj* vicino(-a); (*relation, contact, resemblance*) stretto(-a); (*friend*) intimo(-a); (*examination*) attento(-a); (*race, contest*) combattuto(-a) ♦ *adv* vicino; **~ by** vicino; **~ to** (*near*) vicino a; (*on the verge of*) sull'orlo di.

close² [kləʊz] ♦ *vt* chiudere ♦ *vi* (*door, jar, eyes*) chiudersi; (*shop, office*) chiudere; (*deadline, offer, meeting*) finire.

▶ **close down** *vt sep & vi* chiudere (*definitivamente*).

closed [kləʊzd] *adj* chiuso(-a).

closely ['kləʊslɪ] *adv* (*related, involved*) strettamente; (*follow, examine*) da vicino, attentamente.

closet ['klɒzɪt] *n* (Am) armadio *m*.

close-up ['kləʊs-] *n* primo piano *m*.

closing time ['kləʊzɪŋ-] *n* orario *m* di chiusura.

clot [klɒt] *n* (*of blood*) grumo *m*.

cloth [klɒθ] *n* (*fabric*) stoffa *f*, tessuto *m*; (*piece of cloth*) strofinaccio *m*, panno *m*.

clothes [kləʊðz] *npl* vestiti *mpl*, abiti *mpl*.

clothesline ['kləʊðzlaɪn] *n* filo *m* della biancheria.

clothes peg *n* (Br) molletta *f*.

clothespin ['kləʊðzpɪn] (Am) = **clothes peg**.

clothes shop *n* negozio *m* di abbigliamento.

clothing ['kləʊðɪŋ] *n* abbigliamento *m*.

clotted cream [,klɒtɪd-] *n panna molto densa tipica della Cornovaglia.*

cloud [klaʊd] *n* nuvola *f*.

cloudy ['klaʊdɪ] *adj* (*sky, day*) nuvoloso(-a); (*liquid*) torbido(-a).

clove [kləʊv] *n* (*of garlic*) spicchio *m*.

▶ **cloves** *npl* (*spice*) chiodi *mpl* di garofano.

clown [klaʊn] *n* pagliaccio *m*.

club [klʌb] *n* (*organization*) club *m inv*, circolo *m*; (*nightclub*) locale *m* notturno; (*stick*) mazza *f*.

▶ **clubs** *npl* (*in cards*) fiori *mpl*.

clubbing ['klʌbɪŋ] *n*: **to go ~** (*inf*) andare in discoteca.

club class *n* club class *f inv*.

club sandwich *n* (Am) *sandwich a due o più strati.*

club soda n (Am) acqua f di seltz.

clue [kluː] n (information) indizio m; (in crossword) definizione f; **I haven't got a ~** non ho la minima idea.

clumsy ['klʌmzɪ] adj (person) goffo(-a).

clutch [klʌtʃ] ♦ n frizione f ♦ vt tenere stretto, afferrare.

cm (abbr of centimetre) cm.

c/o (abbr of care of) c/o.

Co. (abbr of company) C.ia.

coach [kəʊtʃ] n (bus) pullman m inv, autobus m inv; (of train) carrozza f; (SPORT) allenatore m (-trice f).

coach party n (Br) gruppo in viaggio organizzato in pullman.

coach station n stazione f dei pullman.

coach trip n (Br) escursione f in pullman.

coal [kəʊl] n carbone m.

coal mine n miniera f di carbone.

coarse [kɔːs] adj (rough) ruvido(-a); (vulgar) rozzo(-a).

coast [kəʊst] n costa f.

coaster ['kəʊstər] n (for glass) sottobicchiere m.

coastguard ['kəʊstgɑːd] n guardia f costiera.

coastline ['kəʊstlaɪn] n costa f.

coat [kəʊt] ♦ n cappotto m; (of animal) pelo m ♦ vt: **to ~ sthg (with)** ricoprire qc (con OR di).

coat hanger n gruccia f (per abiti).

coating ['kəʊtɪŋ] n rivestimento m.

cobbled street ['kɒbld-] n strada f in acciottolato.

cobbles ['kɒblz] npl ciottoli mpl.

cobweb ['kɒbweb] n ragnatela f.

Coca-Cola® [,kəʊkə'kəʊlə] n Coca-Cola® f.

cocaine [kəʊ'keɪn] n cocaina f.

cock [kɒk] n (male chicken) gallo m.

cock-a-leekie [,kɒkə'liːkɪ] n zuppa f di porri e pollo.

cockerel ['kɒkrəl] n galletto m.

cockles ['kɒklz] npl cardii mpl.

cockpit ['kɒkpɪt] n cabina f di pilotaggio.

cockroach ['kɒkrəʊtʃ] n scarafaggio m.

cocktail ['kɒkteɪl] n cocktail m inv.

cocktail party n cocktail m inv.

cock-up n (Br: vulg) casino m.

cocoa ['kəʊkəʊ] n (drink) cacao m.

coconut ['kəʊkənʌt] n noce f di cocco.

cod [kɒd] (pl inv) n merluzzo m.

code [kəʊd] n codice m; (dialling code) prefisso m.

cod-liver oil n olio m di fegato di merluzzo.

coeducational [,kəʊedjuː'keɪʃənl] adj misto(-a).

coffee ['kɒfɪ] n caffè m inv; **black/white ~** caffè nero/macchiato; **ground/instant ~** caffè macinato/istantaneo.

coffee bar n (Br) caffè m inv.

coffee break n pausa f per il caffè.

coffeepot ['kɒfɪpɒt] n caffettiera f.

coffee shop n (cafe) caffè m inv, bar m inv; (in store etc) caffetteria f.

coffee table n tavolino m (basso).

coffin ['kɒfɪn] n bara f.

cog(wheel) ['kɒg(wiːl)] n ingranaggio m.

coil [kɔɪl] ♦ n (of rope) rotolo m; (Br: contraceptive) spirale f ♦ vt avvolgere, arrotolare.

coin [kɔɪn] n moneta f.

coinbox ['kɔɪnbɒks] n (Br) telefono m a monete.

coincide [,kəʊɪn'saɪd] vi: **to ~ (with)** coincidere (con).

coincidence [kəʊ'ɪnsɪdəns] n coincidenza f.

Coke® [kəʊk] n coca® f.

colander ['kʌləndər] n colino m.

cold [kəʊld] ♦ adj freddo(-a) ♦ n (illness) raffreddore m; (low temperature) freddo m; **I'm ~** ho freddo; **it's ~** fa freddo; **to get ~** (food, drink) raffreddarsi; (person) avere freddo;

(*weather*) venire freddo; **to catch ~** prendere freddo; **to catch a ~** prendere il raffreddore.

cold cuts (Am) = **cold meats**.

cold meats *npl* affettati *mpl*.

coleslaw ['kəʊlslɔː] *n* insalata di cavolo, carote, cipolle e maionese.

colic ['kɒlɪk] *n* colica *f*.

collaborate [kə'læbəreɪt] *vi* collaborare.

collaboration [kə,læbə'reɪʃn] *n* collaborazione *f*.

collapse [kə'læps] *vi* (*building, tent*) crollare; (*person*) avere un collasso.

collar ['kɒlə'] *n* (*of shirt, coat*) colletto *m*; (*of dog, cat*) collare *m*.

collarbone ['kɒləbəʊn] *n* clavicola *f*.

colleague ['kɒliːg] *n* collega *mf*.

collect [kə'lekt] ♦ *vt* raccogliere; (*as a hobby*) collezionare; (*go and get*) andare a prendere ♦ *vi* (*dust, leaves, crowd*) raccogliersi ♦ *adv* (Am): **to call ~** fare una telefonata a carico del destinatario.

collection [kə'lekʃn] *n* (*of stamps, coins etc*) collezione *f*, raccolta *f*; (*of stories, poems*) raccolta *f*; (*of money*) colletta *f*; (*of mail*) levata *f*.

collective [kə'lektɪv] *adj* collettivo(-a).

collector [kə'lektə'] *n* (*as a hobby*) collezionista *mf*.

college ['kɒlɪdʒ] *n* (*school*) istituto *m* superiore; (Br: *of university*) tipo di organizzazione indipendente di studenti e professori in cui si dividono certe università; (Am: *university*) università *f inv*.

collide [kə'laɪd] *vi*: **to ~ (with)** scontrarsi (con).

collision [kə'lɪʒn] *n* collisione *f*.

cologne [kə'ləʊn] *n* (acqua *f* di) colonia *f*.

colon ['kəʊlən] *n* (GRAMM) due punti *mpl*.

colonel ['kɜːnl] *n* colonnello *m*.

colony ['kɒlənɪ] *n* colonia *f*.

color ['kʌlər] (Am) = **colour**.

colour ['kʌlə'] ♦ *n* colore *m* ♦ *adj*

(*photograph, film*) a colori ♦ *vt* (*hair*) tingere; (*food*) colorare.

► **colour in** *vt sep* colorare.

colour-blind *adj* daltonico(-a).

colourful ['kʌləfʊl] *adj* vivace.

colouring ['kʌlərɪŋ] *n* (*of food*) colorante *m*; (*complexion*) colorito *m*.

colouring book *n* album *m inv* da colorare.

colour supplement *n* supplemento *m* a colori.

colour television *n* televisione *f* a colori.

column ['kɒləm] *n* colonna *f*; (*newspaper article*) rubrica *f*.

coma ['kəʊmə] *n* coma *m*.

comb [kəʊm] ♦ *n* pettine *m* ♦ *vt*: **to ~ one's hair** pettinarsi.

combination [,kɒmbɪ'neɪʃn] *n* combinazione *f*.

combine [kəm'baɪn] *vt*: **to ~ sthg (with)** combinare qc (con).

combine harvester ['kɒmbaɪn-'haːvɪstə'] *n* mietitrebbia *f*.

come [kʌm] (*pt* came, *pp* come) *vi* **1.** (*move*) venire; **we came by taxi** siamo venuti in taxi; **~ and see!** vieni a vedere!; **~ here!** vieni qui!

2. (*arrive*) arrivare; **they still haven't ~** non sono ancora arrivati; **to ~ home** tornare a casa; **'coming soon'** 'prossimamente'.

3. (*in order*): **to ~ first** (*in sequence*) venire per primo; (*in competition*) arrivare primo; **to ~ last** (*in sequence*) venire per ultimo; (*in competition*) arrivare ultimo.

4. (*reach*): **to ~ up/down to** arrivare a.

5. (*become*): **to ~ undone** slacciarsi; **to ~ true** realizzarsi.

6. (*be sold*): **they ~ in packs of six** si vendono in confezioni da sei.

► **come across** *vt fus* (*person*) imbattersi in; (*thing*) trovare (per caso).

► **come along** *vi* (*progress*) procedere; (*arrive*) arrivare; **~ along!** (*as encouragement*) forza!; (*hurry up*) sbrigati!

▶ **come apart** vi cadere a pezzi.

▶ **come back** vi tornare.

▶ **come down** vi (price) calare.

▶ **come down with** vt fus (illness) buscarsi.

▶ **come from** vt fus venire da.

▶ **come in** vi (enter) entrare; (arrive) arrivare; (tide) salire; ~ **in!** avanti!

▶ **come off** vi (become detached) staccarsi, venir via; (succeed) riuscire.

▶ **come on** vi (project) procedere; (student) fare progressi; ~ **on!** (as encouragement) forza!; (hurry up) sbrigati!

▶ **come out** vi uscire; (photo) venire, riuscire; (stain) scomparire; (sun, moon) apparire.

▶ **come over** vi (visit) venire.

▶ **come round** vi (visit) venire; (regain consciousness) riprendere conoscenza.

▶ **come to** vt fus (subj: bill): **it ~s to £10** viene 10 sterline.

▶ **come up** vi (go upstairs) salire; (be mentioned) essere sollevato(-a); (happen, arise) presentarsi; (sun, moon) sorgere.

▶ **come up with** vt fus (idea) proporre.

comedian [kə'miːdjən] n comico m (-a f).

comedy ['kɒmədɪ] n commedia f; (humour) humour m.

comfort ['kʌmfət] ◆ n (ease) benessere m; (luxury) comfort m inv, comodità f inv; (consolation) conforto m ◆ vt confortare, consolare.

comfortable ['kʌmftəbl] adj comodo(-a); (after operation) in condizioni stazionarie; (financially) agiato(-a); **I don't feel ~ here** non mi sento a mio agio qui.

comic ['kɒmɪk] ◆ adj comico(-a) ◆ n (person) comico m (-a f); (magazine) giornalino m.

comical ['kɒmɪkl] adj comico(-a).

comic strip n fumetto m.

comma ['kɒmə] n virgola f.

command [kə'mɑːnd] ◆ n (order) comando m, ordine m; (mastery) padronanza f ◆ vt (order) ordinare a; (be in charge of) comandare.

commander [kə'mɑːndər] n comandante m.

commemorate [kə'meməreɪt] vt commemorare.

commence [kə'mens] vi (fml) cominciare.

comment ['kɒment] ◆ n commento m ◆ vi commentare.

commentary ['kɒməntrɪ] n (on TV) telecronaca f; (on radio) radiocronaca f.

commentator ['kɒmənteɪtər] n (on TV) telecronista mf; (on radio) radiocronista mf.

commerce ['kɒmɜːs] n commercio m.

commercial [kə'mɜːʃl] ◆ adj commerciale ◆ n pubblicità f inv.

commercial break n intervallo m pubblicitario.

commission [kə'mɪʃn] n commissione f.

commit [kə'mɪt] vt (crime, sin) commettere; **to ~ o.s. (to doing sthg)** impegnarsi (a fare qc); **to ~ suicide** suicidarsi.

committee [kə'mɪtɪ] n comitato m.

commodity [kə'mɒdətɪ] n merce f, articolo m.

common ['kɒmən] ◆ adj comune; (pej: vulgar) volgare ◆ n (Br: land) prato m pubblico; **in ~** (shared) in comune.

commonly ['kɒmənlɪ] adv (generally) comunemente.

Common Market n Mercato m comune.

common room n (for teachers) sala f professori; (for students) sala di ritrovo.

common sense n buon senso m.

Commonwealth ['kɒmənwelθ] n: **the ~** il Commonwealth.

communal ['kɒmjunl] adj (bathroom, kitchen) in comune.

communicate [kə'mjuːnɪkeɪt] vi: **to**

~ (with) comunicare (con).

communication [kə,mjuːnɪ'keɪʃn] *n* comunicazione *f*.

communication cord *n* (Br) freno *m* di emergenza.

communist ['kɒmjʊnɪst] *n* comunista *mf*.

community [kə'mjuːnətɪ] *n* comunità *f inv*.

community centre *n* centro *m* sociale.

commute [kə'mjuːt] *vi* fare il pendolare.

commuter [kə'mjuːtə^r] *n* pendolare *mf*.

compact [*adj* kəm'pækt, *n* 'kɒmpækt] ◆ *adj* compatto(-a) ◆ *n* (*for make-up*) portacipria *m inv*; (Am: *car*) utilitaria *f*.

compact disc [,kɒmpækt-] *n* compact disc *m inv*.

compact disc player *n* lettore *m* di compact disc.

company ['kʌmpənɪ] *n* (*business*) società *f inv*, compagnia *f*; (*companionship, guests*) compagnia; **to keep sb ~** fare OR tenere compagnia a qn.

company car *n* auto *f* della ditta.

comparatively [kəm'pærətɪvlɪ] *adv* relativamente.

compare [kəm'peə^r] *vt*: **to ~ sthg (with)** confrontare qc (con); **~d with** paragonato a.

comparison [kəm'pærɪsn] *n* confronto *m*, paragone *m*; **in ~ with** in confronto a.

compartment [kəm'pɑːtmənt] *n* (*of train*) scompartimento *m*; (*section*) compartimento *m*.

compass ['kʌmpəs] *n* (*magnetic*) bussola *f*; **(a pair of) ~es** un compasso.

compatible [kəm'pætəbl] *adj* compatibile.

compensate ['kɒmpenseɪt] ◆ *vt* risarcire ◆ *vi*: **to ~ (for sthg)** compensare (qc); **to ~ sb for sthg** com-

pensare qn di OR per qc.

compensation [,kɒmpen'seɪʃn] *n* (*money*) risarcimento *m*.

compete [kəm'piːt] *vi* (*take part*) gareggiare, concorrere; **to ~ with sb for sthg** competere con qn per qc.

competent ['kɒmpɪtənt] *adj* competente.

competition [,kɒmpɪ'tɪʃn] *n* (*race, contest*) gara *f*, competizione *f*; (*rivalry*) concorrenza *f*; **the ~** (*rivals*) la concorrenza.

competitive [kəm'petətɪv] *adj* (*price*) competitivo(-a); (*person*) che ha spirito di competizione.

competitor [kəm'petɪtə^r] *n* concorrente *mf*.

complain [kəm'pleɪn] *vi*: **to ~ (about)** lamentarsi (di).

complaint [kəm'pleɪnt] *n* (*statement*) lamentela *f*, reclamo *m*; (*illness*) malattia *f*.

complement ['kɒmplɪ,ment] *vt* completare.

complete [kəm'pliːt] ◆ *adj* completo(-a) ◆ *vt* completare; (*a form*) riempire; **~ with** completo di.

completely [kəm'pliːtlɪ] *adv* completamente.

complex ['kɒmpleks] ◆ *adj* complesso(-a) ◆ *n* complesso *m*.

complexion [kəm'plekʃn] *n* (*of skin*) carnagione *f*.

complicated ['kɒmplɪkeɪtɪd] *adj* complicato(-a).

compliment [*n* 'kɒmplɪmənt, *vb* 'kɒmplɪment] ◆*n* complimento *m* ◆ *vt* fare i complimenti a.

complimentary [,kɒmplɪ'mentərɪ] *adj* (*seat, ticket*) (in) omaggio (*inv*); (*words, person*) lusinghiero(-a).

compose [kəm'pəʊz] *vt* comporre; **to be ~d of** essere composto da OR di.

composed [kəm'pəʊzd] *adj* composto(-a), calmo(-a).

composer [kəm'pəʊzə^r] *n* compositore *m* (-trice *f*).

composition [,kɒmpə'zɪʃn] *n*

(*essay*) composizione *f*.

compound ['kɒmpaʊnd] *n* (*substance*) composto *m*; (*word*) parola *f* composta.

comprehensive [ˌkɒmprɪ'hensɪv] *adj* esauriente, completo(-a).

comprehensive (school) *n* (Br) *scuola secondaria ad ammissione non selettiva*.

compressed air [kəm'prest-] *n* aria *f* compressa.

comprise [kəm'praɪz] *vt* comprendere.

compromise ['kɒmprəmaɪz] *n* compromesso *m*.

compulsory [kəm'pʌlsərɪ] *adj* obbligatorio(-a).

computer [kəm'pjuːtər] *n* computer *m inv*.

computer game *n* gioco *m* su computer.

computerized [kəm'pjuːtəraɪzd] *adj* computerizzato(-a).

computer operator *n* operatore *m* (-trice *f*) di computer.

computer programmer [-'prəʊgræmər] *n* programmatore *m* (-trice *f*).

computing [kəm'pjuːtɪŋ] *n* informatica *f*.

con [kɒn] *n* (*inf: trick*) truffa *f*; **all mod ~s** tutti i comfort.

conceal [kən'siːl] *vt* nascondere.

conceited [kən'siːtɪd] *adj* (*pej*) presuntuoso(-a).

concentrate ['kɒnsəntreɪt] ◆ *vi* concentrarsi ◆ *vt*: **to be ~d** (*in one place*) essere concentrato; **to ~ on sthg** concentrarsi su qc.

concentrated ['kɒnsəntreɪtɪd] *adj* (*juice, soup, baby food*) concentrato(-a).

concentration [ˌkɒnsən'treɪʃn] *n* concentrazione *f*.

concentration camp *n* campo *m* di concentramento.

concern [kən'sɜːn] ◆ *n* (*worry*) preoccupazione *f*; (*matter of interest*) affare *m*; (COMM) azienda *f* ◆ *vt* (*be*

about) trattare di; (*worry*) preoccupare; (*involve*) riguardare; **to be ~ed about** essere preoccupato per; **to be ~ed with riguardare**; **to ~ o.s. with sthg** preoccuparsi di qc; **as far as I'm ~ed** per quanto mi riguarda.

concerned [kən'sɜːnd] *adj* (*worried*) preoccupato(-a).

concerning [kən'sɜːnɪŋ] *prep* riguardo a, circa.

concert ['kɒnsət] *n* concerto *m*.

concession [kən'seʃn] *n* (*reduced price*) riduzione *f*.

concise [kən'saɪs] *adj* conciso(-a).

conclude [kən'kluːd] ◆ *vt* concludere ◆ *vi* (*fml: end*) concludersi.

conclusion [kən'kluːʒn] *n* conclusione *f*.

concrete ['kɒnkriːt] ◆ *adj* (*building, path*) di cemento; (*idea, plan*) concreto(-a) ◆ *n* calcestruzzo *m*, cemento *m* armato.

concussion [kən'kʌʃn] *n* commozione *f* cerebrale.

condensation [ˌkɒnden'seɪʃn] *n* condensazione *f*.

condense [kən'dens] ◆ *vt* condensare ◆ *vi* condensarsi.

condensed milk [kən'denst-] *n* latte *m* condensato.

condition [kən'dɪʃn] *n* condizione *f*; (*illness*) malattia *f*; **to be out of ~** non essere in forma; **on ~ that** a condizione che (+ *subjunctive*).

conditioner [kən'dɪʃnər] *n* (*for hair*) balsamo *m*; (*for clothes*) ammorbidente *m*.

condo ['kɒndəʊ] (Am: *inf*) = **condominium**.

condom ['kɒndəm] *n* preservativo *m*.

condominium [ˌkɒndə'mɪnɪəm] *n* (Am) (*block of flats*) condominio *m*; (*flat*) appartamento *m* in un condominio.

conduct [*vb* kən'dʌkt, *n* 'kɒndʌkt] ◆ *vt* (*investigation, business*) dirigere, condurre; (MUS) dirigere ◆ *n* (*fml: behaviour*) condotta *f*; **to ~ o.s.** (*fml*) comportarsi.

conductor [kən'dʌktər] *n* (MUS) direttore *m* (-trice *f*) d'orchestra; (*on bus*) bigliettaio *m* (-a *f*); (Am: *on train*) capotreno *mf*.

cone [kəun] *n* cono *m*; (*on roads*) cono spartitraffico.

confectioner's [kən'fekʃnəz] *n* (*shop*) negozio *m* di dolciumi.

confectionery [kən'fekʃnəri] *n* dolciumi *mpl*.

conference ['kɒnfərəns] *n* conferenza *f*.

confess [kən'fes] *vi*: to ~ (to sthg) confessare (qc).

confession [kən'feʃn] *n* confessione *f*.

confidence ['kɒnfɪdəns] *n* (*self-assurance*) sicurezza *f* di sé; (*trust*) fiducia *f*; to have ~ in avere fiducia in.

confident ['kɒnfɪdənt] *adj* (*self-assured*) sicuro(-a) di sé; (*certain*) sicuro.

confined [kən'faɪnd] *adj* ristretto(-a).

confirm [kən'fɜːm] *vt* confermare.

confirmation [ˌkɒnfə'meɪʃn] *n* conferma *f*; (RELIG) cresima *f*.

conflict [*n* 'kɒnflɪkt, *vb* kən'flɪkt] ◆ *n* conflitto *m* ◆ *vi*: to ~ (with) essere in conflitto (con).

conform [kən'fɔːm] *vi*: to ~ (to) conformarsi (a).

confuse [kən'fjuːz] *vt* confondere; to ~ sthg with sthg confondere qc con qc.

confused [kən'fjuːzd] *adj* confuso(-a).

confusing [kən'fjuːzɪŋ] *adj* (*explanation, plot*) confuso(-a).

confusion [kən'fjuːʒn] *n* confusione *f*.

congested [kən'dʒestɪd] *adj* (*street*) congestionato(-a).

congestion [kən'dʒestʃn] *n* (*traffic*) congestione *f*.

congratulate [kən'grætʃuleɪt] *vt*: to ~ sb (on sthg) congratularsi con qn (per OR di qc).

congratulations [kənˌgrætʃu-'leɪʃənz] *excl* congratulazioni!

congregate ['kɒŋgrɪgeɪt] *vi* riunirsi.

Congress ['kɒŋgres] *n* (Am) il Congresso.

conifer ['kɒnɪfər] *n* conifera *f*.

conjunction [kən'dʒʌŋkʃn] *n* (GRAMM) congiunzione *f*.

conjurer ['kʌndʒərər] *n* prestigiatore *m* (-trice *f*).

connect [kə'nekt] ◆ *vt* collegare, connettere; (*telephone, machine*) collegare; (*caller on phone*) dare la linea a ◆ *vi*: to ~ with (*train, plane*) avere la coincidenza con; to ~ sthg with sthg (*associate*) collegare qc con OR a qc.

connecting flight [kə'nektɪŋ-] *n* volo *m* di coincidenza.

connection [kə'nekʃn] *n* (*link*) collegamento *m*; (*train, plane*) coincidenza *f*; it's a bad ~ (*on phone*) la linea è disturbata; a loose ~ (*in machine*) un contatto difettoso; in ~ with riguardo a, a proposito di.

conquer ['kɒŋkər] *vt* (*country*) conquistare.

conscience ['kɒnʃəns] *n* coscienza *f*.

conscientious [ˌkɒnʃɪ'enʃəs] *adj* coscienzioso(-a).

conscious ['kɒnʃəs] *adj* (*awake*) cosciente; (*deliberate*) consapevole; to be ~ of (*aware*) essere consapevole di.

consent [kən'sent] *n* consenso *m*.

consequence ['kɒnsɪkwəns] *n* (*result*) conseguenza *f*.

consequently ['kɒnsɪkwəntlɪ] *adv* di conseguenza.

conservation [ˌkɒnsə'veɪʃn] *n* tutela *f* dell'ambiente.

conservative [kən'sɜːvətɪv] *adj* conservatore(-trice).

▶ **Conservative** ◆ *adj* conservatore(-trice) ◆ *n* conservatore *m* (-trice *f*).

conservatory [kən'sɜːvətrɪ] *n* veranda *f* vetrata.

consider [kən'sɪdə^r] vt considerare; **to ~ doing sthg** pensare di fare qc.

considerable [kən'sɪdrəbl] adj considerevole.

consideration [kən,sɪdə'reɪʃn] n considerazione f; **to take sthg into ~** prendere qc in considerazione.

considering [kən'sɪdərɪŋ] prep considerando.

consist [kən'sɪst] : **consist in** vt fus consistere in; **to ~ in doing sthg** consistere nel fare qc.

▶ **consist of** vt fus essere composto di OR da.

consistent [kən'sɪstənt] adj (coherent) coerente; (worker, performance) costante.

consolation [,kɒnsə'leɪʃn] n consolazione f.

console ['kɒnsəʊl] n console f inv.

consonant ['kɒnsənənt] n consonante f.

conspicuous [kən'spɪkjʊəs] adj cospicuo(-a).

constable ['kʌnstəbl] n (Br) agente m di polizia.

constant ['kɒnstənt] adj (unchanging) costante; (continuous) continuo(-a).

constantly ['kɒnstəntlɪ] adv (all the time) continuamente.

constipated ['kɒnstɪpeɪtɪd] adj stitico(-a).

constitution [,kɒnstɪ'tjuːʃn] n costituzione f.

construct [kən'strʌkt] vt costruire.

construction [kən'strʌkʃn] n costruzione f; **under ~** in costruzione.

consul ['kɒnsəl] n console m.

consulate ['kɒnsjʊlət] n consolato m.

consult [kən'sʌlt] vt consultare.

consultant [kən'sʌltənt] n (Br: doctor) specialista mf.

consume [kən'sjuːm] vt consumare.

consumer [kən'sjuːmə^r] n consu-

matore m (-trice f).

contact ['kɒntækt] ◆ n (communication) contatto m; (person) conoscenza f ◆ vt mettersi in contatto con; **in ~ with** (in communication with) in contatto con; (touching) a contatto con.

contact lens n lente f a contatto.

contagious [kən'teɪdʒəs] adj contagioso(-a).

contain [kən'teɪn] vt contenere.

container [kən'teɪnə^r] n (box etc) contenitore m, recipiente m.

contaminate [kən'tæmɪneɪt] vt contaminare.

contemporary [kən'tempərərɪ] ◆ adj contemporaneo(-a) ◆ n contemporaneo m (-a f).

contend [kən'tend] : **contend with** vt fus affrontare.

content [adj kən'tent, n 'kɒntent] ◆ adj contento(-a) ◆ n (of vitamins, fibre etc) contenuto m.

▶ **contents** npl (things inside) contenuto m; (at beginning of book) indice m.

contest [n 'kɒntest, vb kən'test] ◆ n (competition) gara f, concorso m; (struggle) lotta f ◆ vt (election, seat) candidarsi per; (decision, will) contestare.

context ['kɒntekst] n contesto m.

continent ['kɒntɪnənt] n continente m; **the Continent** (Br) l'Europa f continentale.

continental [,kɒntɪ'nentl] adj (Br: European) (dell'Europa) continentale.

continental breakfast n colazione f continentale.

continental quilt n (Br) piumone® m.

continual [kən'tɪnjʊəl] adj continuo(-a).

continually [kən'tɪnjʊəlɪ] adv continuamente, di continuo.

continue [kən'tɪnjuː] vt & vi continuare; **to ~ doing sthg** continuare a fare qc; **to ~ with sthg** continuare con qc.

continuous [kən'tɪnjʊəs] adj continuo(-a).

continuously [kən'tɪnjʊəslɪ] adv continuamente, senza interruzione.

contraception [ˌkɒntrə'sepʃn] n contraccezione f.

contraceptive [ˌkɒntrə'septɪv] n contraccettivo m.

contract [n 'kɒntrækt, vb kən'trækt] ◆ n contratto m ◆ vt (fml: illness) contrarre.

contradict [ˌkɒntrə'dɪkt] vt contraddire.

contraflow ['kɒntrəfləʊ] n (Br) sistema che permette il traffico nei due sensi su una stessa carreggiata dell'autostrada per lavori in corso o per un incidente.

contrary ['kɒntrərɪ] n: **on the ~** al contrario.

contrast [n 'kɒntrɑːst, vb kən'trɑːst] ◆ n contrasto m ◆ vt mettere in contrasto; **in ~ to** contrariamente a.

contribute [kən'trɪbjuːt] ◆ vt (help, money) dare (come contributo) ◆ vi: **to ~ to** contribuire a.

contribution [ˌkɒntrɪ'bjuːʃn] n contributo m.

control [kən'trəʊl] ◆ n controllo m; (operating device) comando m ◆ vt controllare; (machine) regolare; **to be in ~** avere la situazione sotto controllo; **to get out of ~** (situation) sfuggire di mano; **to go out of ~** (car, plane) non rispondere ai comandi; **under ~** sotto controllo.

▶ **controls** npl comandi mpl.

control tower n torre f di controllo.

controversial [ˌkɒntrə'vɜːʃl] adj controverso(-a); (person) polemico(-a).

convenience [kən'viːnjəns] n comodità f inv; **at your ~** quando Le è più comodo.

convenient [kən'viːnjənt] adj comodo(-a); **would tomorrow be ~?** domani andrebbe bene?

convent ['kɒnvənt] n convento m.

conventional [kən'venʃənl] adj convenzionale.

conversation [ˌkɒnvə'seɪʃn] n conversazione f.

conversion [kən'vɜːʃn] n (change) trasformazione f; (of currency) conversione f; (to building) ristrutturazione f.

convert [kən'vɜːt] vt (change) trasformare; (currency, person) convertire; **to ~ sthg into** trasformare qc in.

converted [kən'vɜːtɪd] adj (barn, loft) ristrutturato(-a).

convertible [kən'vɜːtəbl] n cabriolet m inv.

convey [kən'veɪ] vt (fml: transport) trasportare; (idea, impression) dare.

convict [n 'kɒnvɪkt, vb kən'vɪkt] ◆ n carcerato m (-a f) ◆ vt: **to ~ sb (of)** giudicare qn colpevole (di).

convince [kən'vɪns] vt: **to ~ sb (of sthg)** convincere qn (di qc); **to ~ sb to do sthg** convincere qn a fare qc.

convoy ['kɒnvɔɪ] n convoglio m.

cook [kʊk] ◆ n cuoco m (-a f) ◆ vt (meal) cucinare; (food) cuocere ◆ vi (person) cucinare; (food) cuocere.

cookbook ['kʊkˌbʊk] = **cookery book**.

cooker ['kʊkər] n cucina f (elettrodomestico).

cookery ['kʊkərɪ] n cucina f.

cookery book n libro m di cucina.

cookie ['kʊkɪ] n (Am) biscotto m.

cooking ['kʊkɪŋ] n cucina f.

cooking apple n mela f da cuocere.

cooking oil n olio m per cucinare.

cool [kuːl] ◆ adj (temperature) fresco(-a); (calm) calmo(-a); (unfriendly) freddo(-a); (inf: great) fantastico(-a) ◆ vt raffreddare.

▶ **cool down** vi (become colder) raffreddarsi; (become calmer) calmarsi.

cooperate [kəʊ'ɒpəreɪt] vi collaborare, cooperare.

cooperation [kəʊˌɒpə'reɪʃn] n collaborazione f.

cooperative [kəʊ'ɒpərətɪv] adj

(*helpful*) disposto(-a) a collaborare.

coordinates [kəu'ɔːdɪnəts] *npl* (*clothes*) coordinati *mpl*.

cope [kəup] *vi*: **to ~ with** far fronte a; **I can't ~!** non ce la faccio!

copilot ['kəu,paɪlət] *n* secondo pilota *m*.

copper ['kɒpər] *n* (*metal*) rame *m*; (*Br: inf: coin*) moneta in rame da uno o due penny.

copy ['kɒpɪ] ◆ *n* copia *f* ◆ *vt* copiare.

cord(uroy) ['kɔːd(ərɔɪ)] *n* velluto *m* a coste.

core [kɔːr] *n* (*of fruit*) torsolo *m*.

coriander [,kɒrɪ'ændər] *n* coriandolo *m* (*spezia*).

cork [kɔːk] *n* (*in bottle*) tappo *m* (di sughero).

corkscrew ['kɔːkskruː] *n* cavatappi *m inv*.

corn [kɔːn] *n* (*Br: crop*) cereali *mpl*; (*Am: maize*) granturco *m*; (*on foot*) callo *m*.

corned beef [,kɔːnd-] *n* carne *f* di manzo in scatola.

corner ['kɔːnər] *n* angolo *m*; (*bend in road*) curva *f*; (*in football*) calcio *m* d'angolo; **it's just around the ~** è qui dietro l'angolo.

corner shop *n* (*Br*) negozietto *m* (*di alimentari e prodotti per la casa*).

cornet ['kɔːnɪt] *n* (*Br: ice-cream cone*) cornetto *m*.

cornflakes ['kɔːnfleɪks] *npl* cornflakes *mpl*.

corn-on-the-cob *n* pannocchia *f* bollita.

Cornwall ['kɔːnwɔːl] *n* la Cornovaglia.

corporal ['kɔːpərəl] *n* caporale *m*.

corpse [kɔːps] *n* cadavere *m*.

correct [kə'rekt] ◆ *adj* giusto(-a) ◆ *vt* correggere.

correction [kə'rekʃn] *n* correzione *f*.

correspond [,kɒrɪ'spɒnd] *vi*: **to ~ (to)** (*match*) corrispondere (a); **to ~ (with)** (*exchange letters*) essere in cor-

rispondenza (con).

corresponding [,kɒrɪ'spɒndɪŋ] *adj* corrispondente.

corridor ['kɒrɪdɔːr] *n* corridoio *m*.

corrugated iron ['kɒrəgeɪtɪd-] *n* lamiera *f* ondulata.

corrupt [kə'rʌpt] *adj* corrotto(-a).

cosmetics [kɒz'metɪks] *npl* cosmetici *mpl*.

cosmopolitan [,kɒzmə'pɒlɪtn] *adj* cosmopolita.

cost [kɒst] (*pt & pp* **cost**) ◆ *n* costo *m*; (*fig: loss*) prezzo *m* ◆ *vt* costare; **how much does it ~?** quanto costa?

costly ['kɒstlɪ] *adj* (*expensive*) costoso(-a).

costume ['kɒstjuːm] *n* costume *m*.

cosy ['kəuzɪ] *adj* (*Br: room, house*) accogliente.

cot [kɒt] *n* (*Br: for baby*) lettino *m* (per bambini); (*Am: camp bed*) brandina *f*.

cottage ['kɒtɪdʒ] *n* cottage *m inv*.

cottage cheese *n* formaggio *m* magro in fiocchi.

cottage pie *n* (*Br*) pasticcio a base di carne macinata e purè di patate.

cotton ['kɒtn] ◆ *adj* di cotone ◆ *n* cotone *m*.

cotton candy *n* (*Am*) zucchero *m* filato.

cotton wool *n* cotone *m* idrofilo.

couch [kautʃ] *n* divano *m*; (*at doctor's*) lettino *m*.

couchette [kuː'ʃet] *n* cuccetta *f*.

cough [kɒf] ◆ *n* tosse *f* ◆ *vi* tossire; **to have a ~** avere la tosse.

cough mixture *n* sciroppo *m* per la tosse.

could [kud] *pt* → **can**.

couldn't ['kudnt] = **could not**.

could've ['kudəv] = **could have**.

council ['kaunsl] *n* (*Br: of town*) comune *m*; (*Br: of county*) = regione *f*; (*organization*) consiglio *m*.

council house *n* (*Br*) casa *f* popolare.

councillor ['kaunsələr] *n* (*Br: of town, county*) consigliere *m* (-a *f*).

council tax n (Br) ≈ tassa f comunale.

count [kaʊnt] ♦ vt & vi contare ♦ n (nobleman) conte m.

▶ **count on** vt fus contare su.

counter ['kaʊntər] n (in shop) banco m; (in bank) sportello m; (in board game) fiche f inv.

counterclockwise [,kaʊntə-'klɒkwaɪz] adv (Am) in senso antiorario.

counterfoil ['kaʊntəfɔɪl] n matrice f.

countess ['kaʊntɪs] n contessa f.

country ['kʌntrɪ] ♦ n paese m; (countryside) campagna f ♦ adj di campagna.

country and western n (musica f) country m.

country house n villa f di campagna.

country road n strada f di campagna.

countryside ['kʌntrɪsaɪd] n campagna f.

county ['kaʊntɪ] n contea f.

couple ['kʌpl] n coppia f; **a ~ (of)** un paio (di).

coupon ['kuːpɒn] n (for discount etc) buono m; (for orders, enquiries) tagliando m.

courage ['kʌrɪdʒ] n coraggio m.

courgette [kɔːˈʒet] n (Br) zucchino m.

courier ['kʊrɪər] n (for holidaymakers) accompagnatore m (-trice f); (for delivering letters) corriere m.

course [kɔːs] n corso m; (of meal) portata f; (of treatment, injections) ciclo m; (of ship, plane) rotta f; (for golf) campo m; **of ~** (certainly) certo; (evidently) naturalmente; **of ~ not** certo che no; **in the ~ of** nel corso di, durante.

court [kɔːt] n (JUR: building, room) tribunale m; (SPORT) campo m; (of king, queen) corte f.

courtesy coach ['kɜːtɪsɪ-] n pullman m inv gratuito (di hotel, aeroporto ecc.).

court shoes npl scarpe fpl décolleté.

courtyard ['kɔːtjɑːd] n cortile m.

cousin ['kʌzn] n cugino m (-a f).

cover ['kʌvər] ♦ n (covering) fodera f; (lid) coperchio m; (of book, magazine) copertina f; (blanket) coperta f; (insurance) copertura f ♦ vt coprire; (apply to) comprendere; (discuss) trattare; (report) fare un servizio su; **to be ~ed in** essere ricoperto di OR da; **to ~ sthg with sthg** coprire qc con qc; **to take ~** mettersi al riparo.

▶ **cover up** vt sep (put cover on) coprire; (facts, truth) nascondere.

cover charge n coperto m.

cover note n (Br) polizza f di assicurazione provvisoria.

cow [kaʊ] n vacca f.

coward ['kaʊəd] n vigliacco m (-a f).

cowboy ['kaʊbɔɪ] n cow-boy m inv.

crab [kræb] n granchio m.

crack [kræk] ♦ n (in cup, glass) incrinatura f, crepa f; (gap) fessura f ♦ vt (cup, glass, wood) incrinare; (nut) schiacciare; (egg) rompere; (whip) schioccare ♦ vi (cup, glass, wood) incrinarsi; **to ~ a joke** (inf) fare una battuta.

cracker ['krækər] n (biscuit) cracker m inv; (for Christmas) tubo di cartone rivestito di carta da regalo che quando viene aperto produce uno scoppio e fa uscire una sorpresa. Tipico delle feste natalizie.

cradle ['kreɪdl] n culla f.

craft [krɑːft] n (skill) arte f; (trade) artigianato m; (boat: pl inv) imbarcazione f.

craftsman ['krɑːftsmən] (pl -men [-mən]) n artigiano m.

cram [kræm] vt: **to ~ sthg into** stipare qc in; **to be crammed with** essere stipato di.

cramp [kræmp] n crampo m; **stomach ~s** crampi allo stomaco.

cranberry ['krænbərɪ] n mirtillo m.

cranberry sauce n salsa f di mirtilli.

crane [kreɪn] n (machine) gru f inv.

crap [kræp] ◆ adj (vulg) di merda ◆ n (vulg) merda f.

crash [kræʃ] ◆ n (accident) incidente m; (noise) schianto m ◆ vt (car) sfasciare ◆ vi (car, train) schiantarsi; (plane) precipitare.

▶ **crash into** vt fus schiantarsi contro.

crash helmet n casco m.

crash landing n atterraggio m di fortuna.

crate [kreɪt] n cassa f.

crawl [krɔːl] ◆ vi (baby) andare carponi; (person) strisciare; (insect) muoversi lentamente; (traffic) andare a passo d'uomo ◆ n (swimming stroke) stile m libero.

crawler lane ['krɔːlə'-] n (Br) corsia f per veicoli lenti.

crayfish ['kreɪfɪʃ] (pl inv) n gambero m di fiume.

crayon ['kreɪɒn] n matita f colorata.

craze [kreɪz] n mania f.

crazy ['kreɪzɪ] adj matto(-a), pazzo(-a); **to be ~ about** andare matto per.

crazy golf n minigolf m.

cream [kriːm] ◆ n crema f; (fresh) panna f ◆ adj (in colour) color crema (inv).

cream cake n (Br) torta f alla panna.

cream cheese n formaggio m cremoso.

cream sherry n sherry m inv dolce.

cream tea n (Br) merenda a base di tè e 'scones', serviti con marmellata e panna.

creamy ['kriːmɪ] adj (food) alla panna; (texture) cremoso(-a).

crease [kriːs] n grinza f.

creased [kriːst] adj sgualcito(-a).

create [kriː'eɪt] vt creare.

creative [kriː'eɪtɪv] adj creativo(-a).

creature ['kriːtʃə'] n creatura f.

crèche [kreʃ] n (Br) nursery f inv.

credit ['kredɪt] n (praise) merito m; (money) credito m; (part of school, university course) sezione completata di un corso di studio; **to be in ~** essere in attivo.

▶ **credits** npl (of film) titoli mpl.

credit card n carta f di credito; **to pay by ~** pagare con la carta di credito; **'all major ~s accepted'** 'si accettano tutte le maggiori carte di credito'.

creek [kriːk] n (inlet) insenatura f; (Am: river) ruscello m.

creep [kriːp] (pt & pp **crept**) ◆ vi (crawl) strisciare; (walk) muoversi furtivamente ◆ n (inf: groveller) leccapiedi mf inv.

cremate [krɪ'meɪt] vt cremare.

crematorium [,kremə'tɔːrɪəm] n crematorio m.

crepe [kreɪp] n (thin pancake) crêpe f inv.

crept [krept] pt & pp → **creep**.

cress [kres] n crescione m.

crest [krest] n cresta f; (emblem) stemma m.

Creutzfeldt-Jakob disease [,krɔɪtsfelt'jækɒb-] n morbo m di Creutzfeldt-Jakob.

crew [kruː] n (of ship, plane) equipaggio m.

crew neck n girocollo m.

crib [krɪb] n (Am: cot) lettino m (per bambini).

cricket ['krɪkɪt] n (game) cricket m; (insect) grillo m.

crime [kraɪm] n crimine m.

criminal ['krɪmɪnl] ◆ adj criminale ◆ n criminale mf.

cripple ['krɪpl] ◆ n storpio m (-a f) ◆ vt (subj: disease, accident) storpiare.

crisis ['kraɪsɪs] (pl **crises** ['kraɪsiːz]) n crisi f inv.

crisp [krɪsp] adj (bacon, pastry) croccante; (fruit, vegetable) sodo(-a).

▶ **crisps** npl (Br) patatine fpl.

crispy ['krɪspɪ] *adj* croccante.

critic ['krɪtɪk] *n* critico *m* (-a *f*).

critical ['krɪtɪkl] *adj* critico(-a).

criticize ['krɪtɪsaɪz] *vt* criticare.

crockery ['krɒkərɪ] *n* stoviglie *fpl*.

crocodile ['krɒkədaɪl] *n* coccodrillo *m*.

crocus ['krəʊkəs] (*pl* -es) *n* croco *m*.

crooked ['krʊkɪd] *adj* (*bent, twisted*) storto(-a).

crop [krɒp] *n* (*kind of plant*) coltivazione *f*; (*harvest*) raccolto *m*.

▶ **crop up** *vi* saltare fuori.

cross [krɒs] ◆ *adj* arrabbiato(-a) ◆ *n* croce *f*; (*mixture*) incrocio *m* ◆ *vt* (*road, river, ocean*) attraversare; (*arms, legs*) incrociare; (Br: *cheque*) sbarrare ◆ *vi* (*intersect*) incrociarsi.

▶ **cross out** *vt sep* sbarrare.

▶ **cross over** *vt fus* (*road*) attraversare.

crossbar ['krɒsbɑːr] *n* (*of goal*) traversa *f*; (*of bicycle*) canna *f*.

cross-Channel ferry *n* traghetto *m* di servizio sulla Manica.

cross-country (running) *n* corsa *f* campestre.

crossing ['krɒsɪŋ] *n* (*on road*) attraversamento *m*; (*sea journey*) traversata *f*.

crossroads ['krɒsrəʊdz] (*pl inv*) *n* incrocio *m*.

crosswalk ['krɒswɔːk] *n* (Am) passaggio *m* pedonale.

crossword (puzzle) ['krɒswɜːd-] *n* cruciverba *m inv*.

crotch [krɒtʃ] *n* (*of person*) inforcatura *f*.

crouton ['kruːtɒn] *n* crostino *m*.

crow [krəʊ] *n* cornacchia *f*.

crowbar ['krəʊbɑːr] *n* piede *m* di porco.

crowd [kraʊd] *n* folla *f*; (*at match*) spettatori *mpl*.

crowded ['kraʊdɪd] *adj* affollato(-a).

crown [kraʊn] *n* (*of king, queen, on tooth*) corona *f*; (*of head*) sommità *f inv*.

Crown Jewels *npl*: **the ~** i gioielli della Corona.

crucial ['kruːʃl] *adj* cruciale.

crude [kruːd] *adj* (*drawing*) abbozzato(-a); (*estimate*) approssimativo(-a); (*rude*) rozzo(-a).

cruel [krʊəl] *adj* crudele.

cruelty ['krʊəltɪ] *n* crudeltà *f*.

cruet (set) ['kruːɪt-] *n* ampolliera *f*.

cruise [kruːz] ◆ *n* crociera *f* ◆ *vi* (*car, plane, ship*) andare a velocità di crociera.

cruiser ['kruːzər] *n* (*pleasure boat*) cabinato *m*.

crumb [krʌm] *n* briciola *f*.

crumble ['krʌmbl] ◆ *n* frutta cotta ricoperta da uno strato di pasta frolla sbriciolata ◆ *vi* (*building, cliff*) sgretolarsi; (*pastry, cake, cheese*) sbriciolarsi.

crumpet ['krʌmpɪt] *n* tipo di focaccina da mangiarsi calda con burro, marmellata ecc.

crunchy ['krʌntʃɪ] *adj* croccante.

crush [krʌʃ] ◆ *n* (*drink*) spremuta *f* ◆ *vt* schiacciare; (*ice*) frantumare.

crust [krʌst] *n* crosta *f*.

crusty ['krʌstɪ] *adj* croccante.

crutch [krʌtʃ] *n* (*stick*) stampella *f*; (*between legs*) = **crotch**.

cry [kraɪ] ◆ *n* urlo *m*, grido *m*; (*of bird*) verso *m* ◆ *vi* (*weep*) piangere; (*shout*) urlare, gridare.

▶ **cry out** *vi* urlare, gridare.

crystal ['krɪstl] *n* (*in jewellery etc*) cristallo *m*; (*glass*) cristallo *m*.

cub [kʌb] *n* (*animal*) cucciolo *m*.

Cub [kʌb] *n* lupetto *m*.

cube [kjuːb] *n* cubo *m*; (*of sugar, ice*) cubetto *m*.

cubicle ['kjuːbɪkl] *n* cabina *f*.

Cub Scout = **Cub**.

cuckoo ['kʊkuː] *n* cuculo *m*.

cucumber ['kjuːkʌmbər] *n* cetriolo *m*.

cuddle ['kʌdl] *n* coccola *f*.

cuddly toy ['kʌdlɪ-] *n* pupazzo *m* di peluche.

cue [kju:] n (in snooker, pool) stecca f.

cuff [kʌf] n (of sleeve) polsino m; (Am: of trousers) risvolto m.

cuff links npl gemelli mpl.

cuisine [kwɪ'zi:n] n cucina f.

cul-de-sac [ˈkʌldəsæk] n vicolo m cieco.

cult [kʌlt] ♦ n (RELIG) culto m ♦ adj di culto.

cultivate [ˈkʌltɪveɪt] vt (grow) coltivare.

cultivated [ˈkʌltɪveɪtɪd] adj (person) raffinato(-a).

cultural [ˈkʌltʃərəl] adj culturale.

culture [ˈkʌltʃəʳ] n cultura f.

cumbersome [ˈkʌmbəsəm] adj ingombrante.

cumin [ˈkjuːmɪn] n cumino m.

cunning [ˈkʌnɪŋ] adj furbo(-a).

cup [kʌp] n tazza f; (trophy, competition, of bra) coppa f.

cupboard [ˈkʌbəd] n (for food, dishes) credenza f; (for clothes) armadio m.

curator [ˌkjʊəˈreɪtəʳ] n conservatore m (di museo).

curb [kɜːb] (Am) = **kerb**.

curd cheese [ˌkɜːd-] n cagliata f.

cure [kjʊəʳ] ♦ n (for illness) cura f ♦ vt (illness, person) curare; (food) trattare.

curious [ˈkjʊərɪəs] adj curioso(-a).

curl [kɜːl] ♦ n (of hair) riccio m ♦ vt (hair) arricciare.

curler [ˈkɜːləʳ] n bigodino m.

curly [ˈkɜːlɪ] adj riccio(-a).

currant [ˈkʌrənt] n uvetta f.

currency [ˈkʌrənsɪ] n (money) moneta f.

current [ˈkʌrənt] ♦ adj attuale ♦ n corrente f.

current account n (Br) conto m corrente.

current affairs npl attualità f.

currently [ˈkʌrəntlɪ] adv attualmente.

curriculum [kəˈrɪkjələm] n curricolo m.

curriculum vitae [-ˈviːtaɪ] n (Br) curriculum vitae m inv.

curried [ˈkʌrɪd] adj al curry.

curry [ˈkʌrɪ] n piatto m al curry.

curse [kɜːs] vi bestemmiare.

cursor [ˈkɜːsəʳ] n cursore m.

curtain [ˈkɜːtn] n (in house) tenda f; (in theatre) sipario m.

curve [kɜːv] ♦ n curva f ♦ vi curvare.

curved [kɜːvd] adj curvo(-a).

cushion [ˈkʊʃn] n (for sitting on) cuscino m.

custard [ˈkʌstəd] n crema f gialla.

custom [ˈkʌstəm] n (tradition) usanza f; 'thank you for your ~' 'arrivederci e grazie'.

customary [ˈkʌstəmrɪ] adj abituale.

customer [ˈkʌstəməʳ] n (of shop) cliente mf.

customer services n (department) servizio m clienti.

customs [ˈkʌstəmz] n dogana f; **to go through ~** passare la dogana.

customs duty n dazio m doganale.

customs officer n doganiere m.

cut [kʌt] (pt & pp cut) ♦ n taglio m; (in taxes) riduzione f ♦ vt & vi tagliare; **~ and blow-dry** taglio e piega föhn; **to ~ o.s.** tagliarsi; **to ~ one's finger** tagliarsi un dito; **to have one's hair ~** tagliarsi i capelli; **to ~ the grass** tagliare l'erba; **to ~ sthg open** aprire qc.

▸ **cut back** vi: **to ~ back on sthg** ridurre qc.

▸ **cut down** vt sep (tree) tagliare.

▸ **cut down on** vt fus ridurre.

▸ **cut off** vt sep tagliare; (supply) sospendere; **I've been ~ off** (on phone) è caduta la linea; **to be ~ off** (isolated) rimanere isolato.

▸ **cut out** ♦ vt sep (newspaper article, photo) ritagliare ♦ vi (engine) spegnersi; **to ~ out smoking** smettere di fumare; **~ it out!** (inf) dacci un taglio!

▸ **cut up** vt sep tagliare a pezzetti.

cute [kjuːt] adj carino(-a).

cut-glass adj in vetro intagliato.

cutlery ['kʌtlərɪ] n posate fpl.

cutlet ['kʌtlɪt] n (of meat) costoletta f; (of nuts, vegetables) crocchetta f.

cut-price adj a prezzo scontato.

cutting ['kʌtɪŋ] n (from newspaper) ritaglio m.

CV n (Br: abbr of curriculum vitae) curriculum m inv.

cwt abbr = **hundredweight**.

cybercafe ['saɪbə,kæfeɪ] n locale fornito di computer in cui si può consumare navigando in Internet.

cyberspace ['saɪbəspeɪs] n cyberspace m.

cycle ['saɪkl] ♦ n (bicycle) bicicletta f; (series) ciclo m ♦ vi andare in bicicletta.

cycle hire n noleggio m bicilette.

cycle lane n pista f ciclabile.

cycle path n pista f ciclabile.

cycling ['saɪklɪŋ] n ciclismo m; **to go ~** andare in bicicletta.

cycling shorts npl pantaloncini mpl da ciclista.

cyclist ['saɪklɪst] n ciclista mf.

cylinder ['sɪlɪndər] n (of gas) bombola f; (in engine) cilindro m.

cynical ['sɪnɪkl] adj cinico(-a).

Czech [tʃek] ♦ adj ceco(-a) ♦ n (person) ceco m (-a f); (language) ceco m.

Czechoslovakia [,tʃekəslə'vækɪə] n la Cecoslovacchia.

Czech Republic n: **the ~** la Repubblica Ceca.

D

dab [dæb] vt (wound) tamponare.

dad [dæd] n (inf) papà m inv, babbo m.

daddy ['dædɪ] n (inf) papà m inv, babbo m.

daddy longlegs [-'lɒŋlegz] (pl inv) n tipula f.

daffodil ['dæfədɪl] n giunchiglia f.

daft [dɑːft] adj (Br: inf) stupido (-a).

daily ['deɪlɪ] ♦ adj quotidiano(-a) ♦ adv quotidianamente ♦ n: **a ~ (newspaper)** un quotidiano.

dairy ['deərɪ] n (on farm) caseificio m; (shop) latteria f.

dairy product n latticino m.

daisy ['deɪzɪ] n margherita f.

dam [dæm] n diga f.

damage ['dæmɪdʒ] ♦ n danno m ♦ vt danneggiare; (back, leg) lesionare.

damn [dæm] ♦ excl (inf) accidenti! ♦ adj (inf) maledetto(-a); **I don't give a ~** non me ne importa un accidente.

damp [dæmp] ♦ adj umido(-a) ♦ n umidità f.

damson ['dæmzn] n susina f damaschina.

dance [dɑːns] ♦ n danza f; (social event) ballo m ♦ vi ballare; **to have a ~** ballare.

dance floor n (in club) pista f da ballo.

dancer ['dɑːnsər] n ballerino m (-a f).

dancing ['dɑːnsɪŋ] n danza f; **to go ~** andare a ballare.

dandelion ['dændɪlaɪən] n dente m di leone.

dandruff ['dændrʌf] n forfora f.

Dane [deɪn] n danese mf.

danger ['deɪndʒər] n pericolo m; **in ~** in pericolo.

dangerous ['deɪndʒərəs] adj pericoloso(-a).

Danish ['deɪnɪʃ] ♦ adj danese ♦ n (language) danese m.

Danish pastry n sfoglia f alla frutta.

dare [deər] vt: **to ~ to do sthg** osare fare qc; **to ~ sb to do sthg** sfidare qn a fare qc; **how ~ you!** come ti permetti!

daring ['deərɪŋ] *adj* audace.

dark [dɑːk] ◆ *adj (room, night)* buio(-a); *(colour, skin)* scuro(-a); *(person)* bruno(-a) ◆ *n*: **after ~** col buio; **the ~** il buio.

dark chocolate *n* cioccolata *f* fondente.

dark glasses *npl* occhiali *mpl* scuri.

darkness ['dɑːknɪs] *n* oscurità *f*.

darling ['dɑːlɪŋ] *n (term of affection)* caro *m* (-a *f*).

dart [dɑːt] *n* freccia *f*.

▶ **darts** *n (game)* freccette *fpl*.

dartboard ['dɑːtbɔːd] *n* bersaglio *m* per freccette.

dash [dæʃ] ◆ *n (of liquid)* goccio *m*; *(in writing)* trattino *m* ◆ *vi* precipitarsi.

dashboard ['dæʃbɔːd] *n* cruscotto *m*.

data ['deɪtə] *n* dati *mpl*.

database ['deɪtəbeɪs] *n* data base *m inv*.

date [deɪt] ◆ *n (day)* data *f*; *(meeting)* appuntamento *m*; *(Am: person)* ragazzo *m* (-a *f*); *(fruit)* dattero *m* ◆ *vt (cheque, letter)* datare; *(person)* uscire con ◆ *vi (become unfashionable)* passare di moda; **what's the ~?** quanti ne abbiamo oggi?; **to have a ~ with sb** avere (un) appuntamento con qn.

date of birth *n* data *f* di nascita.

daughter ['dɔːtər] *n* figlia *f*.

daughter-in-law *n* nuora *f*.

dawn [dɔːn] *n* alba *f*.

day [deɪ] *n (of week)* giorno *m*; *(period, working day)* giornata *f*; **what ~ is it today?** che giorno è oggi?; **what a lovely ~!** che bella giornata!; **to have a ~ off** avere un giorno libero; **to have a ~ out** trascorrere una giornata fuori; **by ~** *(travel)* di giorno; **the ~ after tomorrow** dopodomani; **the ~ before** il giorno prima; **the ~ before yesterday** l'altro ieri, ieri l'al-

tro; **the following ~** il giorno dopo; **have a nice ~!** buona giornata!

daylight ['deɪlaɪt] *n (light)* luce *f* (del giorno); *(dawn)* alba *f*.

day return *n (Br: railway ticket)* biglietto di andata e ritorno valido per un giorno.

dayshift ['deɪʃɪft] *n* turno *m* di giorno.

daytime ['deɪtaɪm] *n* giorno *m*.

day-to-day *adj (everyday)* quotidiano(-a).

day trip *n* gita *f* (di un giorno).

dazzle ['dæzl] *vt* abbagliare.

DC *(abbr of direct current)* c.c.

dead [ded] ◆ *adj* morto(-a); *(battery)* scarico(-a) ◆ *adv* proprio; **the line has gone ~** è caduta la linea; **~ on time** in perfetto orario; **it's ~ ahead** è proprio a diritto; **'~ slow'** 'a passo d'uomo'.

dead end *n (street)* strada *f* senza uscita.

deadline ['dedlaɪn] *n* termine *m* ultimo, scadenza *f*.

deaf [def] ◆ *adj* sordo(-a) ◆ *npl*: **the ~** i non udenti.

deal [diːl] *(pt & pp* **dealt)** ◆ *n (agreement)* accordo *m* ◆ *vt (cards)* dare; **a good/bad ~** un buon/cattivo affare; **a great ~ of** una gran quantità di; **it's a ~!** affare fatto!

▶ **deal in** *vt fus* commerciare in.

▶ **deal with** *vt fus (handle)* affrontare; *(be about)* trattare di.

dealer ['diːlər] *n (COMM)* commerciante *mf*; *(in drugs)* spacciatore *m* (-trice *f*).

dealt [delt] *pt & pp* → **deal**.

dear [dɪər] ◆ *adj* caro(-a) ◆ *n*: **my ~** mio caro (mia cara); **Dear Sir** Gentile Signore; **Dear Madam** Gentile Signora; **Dear John** Caro John; **oh ~!** oh Dio!

death [deθ] *n* morte *f*.

debate [dɪ'beɪt] ◆ *n* dibattito *m* ◆ *vt (wonder)* riflettere su.

debit ['debɪt] ◆ *n* debito *m* ◆ *vt (account)* addebitare su.

debt [det] n (money owed) debito m; **to be in ~** essere indebitato.

Dec. (abbr of December) dic.

decaff ['di:kæf] n (inf) caffè m inv decaffeinato.

decaffeinated [dɪ'kæfɪneɪtd] adj decaffeinato(-a).

decanter [dɪ'kæntər] n bottiglia f da liquore.

decay [dɪ'keɪ] ♦ n (of wood) disfacimento m; (of building) rovina f; (of tooth) carie f ♦ vi (rot) putrefarsi.

deceive [dɪ'si:v] vt ingannare.

decelerate [,di:'seləreɪt] vi decelerare.

December [dɪ'sembər] n dicembre m, → **September**.

decent ['di:snt] adj (adequate, respectable) decente; (kind) carino(-a); (people) perbene inv.

decide [dɪ'saɪd] vt & vi decidere; **to ~ to do sthg** decidere di fare qc.
▶ **decide on** vt fus scegliere.

decimal ['desɪml] adj decimale.

decimal point n = virgola f.

decision [dɪ'sɪʒn] n decisione f; **to make a ~** prendere una decisione.

decisive [dɪ'saɪsɪv] adj (person) deciso(-a); (event, factor) decisivo(-a).

deck [dek] n (level of ship) ponte m; (exposed part of ship) coperta f; (of bus) piano m; (of cards) mazzo m.

deckchair ['dektʃeər] n sedia f a sdraio.

declare [dɪ'kleər] vt dichiarare; **to ~ (that)** dichiarare che; **'goods to ~'** 'articoli da dichiarare'; **'nothing to ~'** 'nulla da dichiarare'.

decline [dɪ'klaɪn] ♦ n calo m; (of country) declino m ♦ vi (get worse) peggiorare; (refuse) declinare.

decorate ['dekəreɪt] vt (with wallpaper) tappezzare; (with paint) pitturare; (make attractive) decorare.

decoration [,dekə'reɪʃn] n (decorative object) decorazione f.

decorator ['dekəreɪtər] n imbianchino m.

decrease [n 'di:kri:s, vb di:'kri:s] ♦ n diminuzione f ♦ vi diminuire.

dedicated ['dedɪkeɪtɪd] adj (committed) devoto(-a).

deduce [dɪ'dju:s] vt dedurre.

deduct [dɪ'dʌkt] vt dedurre.

deduction [dɪ'dʌkʃn] n deduzione f.

deep [di:p] ♦ adj profondo(-a); (colour) intenso(-a) ♦ adv in profondità; **the pool is 2 metres ~** la piscina è profonda 2 metri.

deep end n (of swimming pool) parte dove l'acqua è più alta.

deep freeze n congelatore m.

deep-fried [-'fraɪd] adj fritto(-a).

deep-pan adj: **~ pizza** pizza a pasta alta e soffice.

deer [dɪər] (pl inv) n cervo m.

defeat [dɪ'fi:t] ♦ n sconfitta f ♦ vt (team, army, government) sconfiggere.

defect ['di:fekt] n difetto m.

defective [dɪ'fektɪv] adj difettoso(-a).

defence [dɪ'fens] n difesa f.

defend [dɪ'fend] vt difendere.

defense [dɪ'fens] (Am) = **defence**.

deficiency [dɪ'fɪʃnsɪ] n (lack) carenza f.

deficit ['defɪsɪt] n deficit m inv.

define [dɪ'faɪn] vt definire.

definite ['defɪnɪt] adj (clear) preciso(-a); (certain) sicuro(-a); (improvement) deciso(-a).

definite article n articolo m determinativo.

definitely ['defɪnɪtlɪ] adv (certainly) senz'altro.

definition [,defɪ'nɪʃn] n (of word) definizione f.

deflate [dɪ'fleɪt] vt (tyre) sgonfiare.

deflect [dɪ'flekt] vt (ball) deviare.

defogger [,di:'fɒgər] n (Am) deumidificatore m.

deformed [dɪ'fɔ:md] adj deformato(-a).

defrost [,di:'frɒst] vt (food) scongelare; (fridge) sbrinare; (Am: demist) disappannare.

degree [dɪ'griː] n (unit of measurement, amount) grado m; (qualification) ≃ laurea f; **to have a ~ in sthg** avere una laurea in qc.

dehydrated [ˌdiːhaɪ'dreɪtɪd] adj (food) liofilizzato(-a); (person) disidratato(-a).

de-ice [diː'aɪs] vt togliere il ghiaccio da.

de-icer [diː'aɪsər] n antighiaccio m.

dejected [dɪ'dʒektɪd] adj sconsolato(-a).

delay [dɪ'leɪ] ◆ n ritardo m ◆ vt (flight, departure) ritardare; (person) trattenere ◆ vi indugiare; **without ~** senza indugio.

delayed [dɪ'leɪd] adj (train, flight) in ritardo.

delegate [n 'delɪgət, vb 'delɪgeɪt] ◆ n delegato m (-a f) ◆ vt (person) delegare.

delete [dɪ'liːt] vt cancellare.

deli ['delɪ] n (inf: abbr of delicatessen) negozio m di specialità gastronomiche.

deliberate [dɪ'lɪbərət] adj (intentional) intenzionale.

deliberately [dɪ'lɪbərətlɪ] adv (intentionally) deliberatamente.

delicacy ['delɪkəsɪ] n (food) leccornia f.

delicate ['delɪkət] adj delicato(-a).

delicatessen [ˌdelɪkə'tesn] n negozio m di specialità gastronomiche.

delicious [dɪ'lɪʃəs] adj squisito(-a).

delight [dɪ'laɪt] ◆ n (feeling) gioia f ◆ vt deliziare; **to take (a) ~ in doing sthg** provare piacere a fare qc.

delighted [dɪ'laɪtɪd] adj felicissimo(-a).

delightful [dɪ'laɪtfʊl] adj delizioso(-a).

delinquent [dɪ'lɪŋkwənt] n delinquente mf.

deliver [dɪ'lɪvər] vt (goods, letters, newspaper) consegnare; (speech, lecture) tenere; (baby) far nascere.

delivery [dɪ'lɪvərɪ] n (of goods, letters) consegna f; (birth) parto m.

delude [dɪ'luːd] vt illudere.

de luxe [də'lʌks] adj di lusso.

demand [dɪ'mɑːnd] ◆ n (request) richiesta f; (claim) rivendicazione f; (COMM) domanda f; (requirement) esigenza f ◆ vt (request forcefully) pretendere; (require) richiedere; **to ~ to do sthg** esigere di fare qc; **in ~** richiesto.

demanding [dɪ'mɑːndɪŋ] adj esigente.

demerara sugar [deməˈreərə-] n zucchero m di canna.

demist [ˌdiː'mɪst] vt (Br) disappannare.

demister [ˌdiː'mɪstər] n (Br) deumidificatore m.

democracy [dɪ'mɒkrəsɪ] n democrazia f.

Democrat ['deməkræt] n (Am) democratico m (-a f).

democratic [demə'krætɪk] adj democratico(-a).

demolish [dɪ'mɒlɪʃ] vt (building) demolire.

demonstrate ['demənstreɪt] ◆ vt (prove) dimostrare; (machine, appliance) mostrare il funzionamento di ◆ vi dimostrare.

demonstration [demən'streɪʃn] n dimostrazione f.

denial [dɪ'naɪəl] n (refusal) rifiuto m; (statement) smentita f.

denim ['denɪm] n denim m.
▶ **denims** npl jeans mpl.

denim jacket n giubbotto m di jeans.

Denmark ['denmɑːk] n la Danimarca.

dense [dens] adj (crowd, forest) fitto(-a); (smoke) denso(-a).

dent [dent] n ammaccatura f.

dental ['dentl] adj dentale.

dental floss [-flɒs] n filo m interdentale.

dental surgeon n dentista mf.

dental surgery n (place) studio m dentistico.

dentist ['dentɪst] n dentista mf; **to**

go to the ~'s andare dal dentista.
dentures ['dentʃəz] *npl* dentiera *f*.
deny [dɪ'naɪ] *vt* negare.
deodorant [di:'əudərənt] *n* deodorante *m*.
depart [dɪ'pɑːt] *vi* partire.
department [dɪ'pɑːtmənt] *n (of business, shop)* reparto *m*; *(of government)* ministero *m*; *(of school, university)* dipartimento *m*.
department store *n* grandi magazzini *mpl*.
departure [dɪ'pɑːtʃər] *n* partenza *f*; **'~s'** *(at airport)* 'partenze'.
departure lounge *n* sala *f* partenze.
depend [dɪ'pend] *vi*: **it ~s** dipende.
▶ **depend on** *vt fus* dipendere da; **~ing on** a seconda di.
dependable [dɪ'pendəbl] *adj* affidabile.
deplorable [dɪ'plɔːrəbl] *adj* deplorevole.
deport [dɪ'pɔːt] *vt* deportare.
deposit [dɪ'pɒzɪt] ◆ *n* deposito *m* ◆ *vt* depositare.
deposit account *n* (*Br*) conto *m* vincolato.
depot ['di:pəu] *n* (*Am: for buses, trains*) stazione *f*.
depressed [dɪ'prest] *adj* depresso(-a).
depressing [dɪ'presɪŋ] *adj* deprimente.
depression [dɪ'preʃn] *n* depressione *f*.
deprive [dɪ'praɪv] *vt*: **to ~ sb of sthg** privare qn di qc.
depth [depθ] *n* (*distance down*) profondità *f inv*; **out of one's ~** (*when swimming*) dove non si tocca; (*fig: unable to cope*) non all'altezza; **~ of field** (*in photography*) profondità di campo.
deputy ['depjutɪ] *adj* vice (*inv*).
derailleur [də'reɪljər] *n* deragliatore *m*.
derailment [dɪ'reɪlmənt] *n* deragliamento *m*.

derelict ['derəlɪkt] *adj* abbandonato(-a).
derv [dɜːv] *n* (*Br*) benzina *f* diesel.
descend [dɪ'send] *vt & vi* scendere.
descendant [dɪ'sendənt] *n* discendente *mf*.
descent [dɪ'sent] *n* discesa *f*.
describe [dɪ'skraɪb] *vt* descrivere.
description [dɪ'skrɪpʃn] *n* descrizione *f*.
desert [*n* 'dezət, *vb* dɪ'zɜːt] ◆ *n* deserto *m* ◆ *vt* abbandonare.
deserted [dɪ'zɜːtɪd] *adj* deserto(-a).
deserve [dɪ'zɜːv] *vt* meritare.
design [dɪ'zaɪn] ◆ *n* (*pattern*) disegno *m*; (*art*) design *m*; (*of machine, building*) progetto *m* ◆ *vt* (*dress*) disegnare; (*machine, building*) progettare; **to be ~ed for** essere concepito per.
designer [dɪ'zaɪnər] ◆ *n* (*of clothes*) stilista *mf*; (*of building*) architetto *m*; (*of product*) designer *mf inv* ◆ *adj* (*clothes, sunglasses*) firmato(-a).
desirable [dɪ'zaɪərəbl] *adj* desiderabile.
desire [dɪ'zaɪər] ◆ *n* desiderio *m* ◆ *vt* desiderare; **it leaves a lot to be ~d** lascia molto a desiderare.
desk [desk] *n* (*in home, office*) scrivania *f*; (*at airport, station, of pupil*) banco *m*; (*at hotel*) portineria *f*.
desktop publishing ['desk,tɒp-] *n* desktop publishing *m*.
despair [dɪ'speər] *n* disperazione *f*.
despatch [dɪ'spætʃ] = **dispatch**.
desperate ['desprət] *adj* disperato(-a); **to be ~ for sthg** avere un disperato bisogno di qc.
despicable [dɪ'spɪkəbl] *adj* spregevole.
despise [dɪ'spaɪz] *vt* disprezzare.
despite [dɪ'spaɪt] *prep* nonostante.
dessert [dɪ'zɜːt] *n* dessert *m inv*.
dessertspoon [dɪ'zɜːtspuːn] *n* cucchiaino *m*.
destination [,destɪ'neɪʃn] *n* destinazione *f*.

destroy [dɪ'strɔɪ] *vt* distruggere.

destruction [dɪ'strʌkʃn] *n* distruzione *f*.

detach [dɪ'tætʃ] *vt* staccare.

detached house [dɪ'tætʃt-] *n* villetta *f* unifamiliare.

detail ['di:teɪl] *n* dettaglio *m*; **in ~** dettagliatamente.

▸ **details** *npl* (*facts*) informazioni *fpl*.

detailed ['di:teɪld] *adj* dettagliato(-a).

detect [dɪ'tekt] *vt* (*sense*) avvertire; (*find*) scoprire.

detective [dɪ'tektɪv] *n* detective *mf inv*; **a ~ story** un racconto poliziesco.

detention [dɪ'tenʃn] *n* (SCH) *punizione che consiste nel trattenere un alunno a scuola oltre l'orario scolastico.*

detergent [dɪ't3:dʒənt] *n* detersivo *m*.

deteriorate [dɪ'tɪərɪəreɪt] *vi* deteriorarsi.

determination [dɪ,t3:mɪ'neɪʃn] *n* determinazione *f*.

determine [dɪ't3:mɪn] *vt* (*control*) determinare; (*find out*) accertare.

determined [dɪ't3:mɪnd] *adj* risoluto(-a); **to be ~ to do sthg** essere determinato a fare qc.

deterrent [dɪ'terənt] *n* deterrente *m*.

detest [dɪ'test] *vt* detestare.

detour ['di:,tuər] *n* deviazione *f*.

detrain [,di:'treɪn] *vi* (*fml*) scendere dal treno.

deuce [dju:s] *n* (*in tennis*) parità *f*.

devastate ['devəsteɪt] *vt* devastare.

develop [dɪ'veləp] ◆ *vt* sviluppare; (*machine, method*) perfezionare; (*illness, habit*) contrarre ◆ *vi* (*evolve*) svilupparsi.

developing country [dɪ'veləpɪŋ-] *n* paese *m* in via di sviluppo.

development [dɪ'veləpmənt] *n* sviluppo *m*; **a housing ~** un complesso residenziale.

device [dɪ'vaɪs] *n* congegno *m*.

devil ['devl] *n* diavolo *m*; **what the ~ ...?** (*inf*) che diavolo ...?

devise [dɪ'vaɪz] *vt* escogitare.

devoted [dɪ'vəʊtɪd] *adj* (*person*) affezionato(-a).

dew [dju:] *n* rugiada *f*.

diabetes [,daɪə'bi:ti:z] *n* diabete *m*.

diabetic [,daɪə'betɪk] ◆ *adj* (*person*) diabetico(-a); (*chocolate*) per diabetici ◆ *n* diabetico *m* (-a *f*).

diagnosis [,daɪəg'nəʊsɪs] (*pl* -oses [-əʊsi:z]) *n* diagnosi *f inv*.

diagonal [daɪ'ægənl] *adj* diagonale.

diagram ['daɪəgræm] *n* diagramma *m*.

dial ['daɪəl] ◆ *n* (*of telephone*) disco *m* combinatore; (*of clock*) quadrante *m*; (*of radio*) scala *f* ◆ *vt* (*number*) comporre.

dialling code ['daɪəlɪŋ-] *n* (Br) prefisso *m* telefonico.

dialling tone ['daɪəlɪŋ-] *n* (Br) segnale *m* di libero.

dial tone (Am) = **dialling tone**.

diameter [daɪ'æmɪtər] *n* diametro *m*.

diamond ['daɪəmənd] *n* (*gem*) diamante *m*.

▸ **diamonds** *npl* (*in cards*) quadri *mpl*.

diaper ['daɪpər] *n* (Am) pannolino *m*.

diarrhoea [,daɪə'rɪə] *n* diarrea *f*.

diary ['daɪərɪ] *n* (*for appointments*) agenda *f*; (*journal*) diario *m*.

dice [daɪs] (*pl inv*) *n* dado *m*.

diced [daɪst] *adj* a dadini.

dictate [dɪk'teɪt] *vt* dettare.

dictation [dɪk'teɪʃn] *n* dettato *m*.

dictator [dɪk'teɪtər] *n* dittatore *m* (-trice *f*).

dictionary ['dɪkʃənrɪ] *n* dizionario *m*.

did [dɪd] *pt* → **do**.

die [daɪ] (*pt & pp* died, *cont* dying

['daɪɪŋ]) *vi* morire; **to be dying for sthg** (*inf*) morire dalla voglia di qc; **to be dying to do sthg** (*inf*) morire dalla voglia di fare qc.

▶ **die away** *vi* spegnersi.

▶ **die out** *vi* scomparire.

diesel ['diːzl] *n* (*fuel*) gasolio *m*; (*car*) diesel *m inv*.

diet ['daɪət] ◆ *n* (*for slimming, health*) dieta *f*; (*food eaten*) alimentazione *f* ◆ *vi* essere a dieta ◆ *adj* dietetico(-a).

diet Coke® *n* coca *f* light®.

differ ['dɪfər] *vi*: **to ~ (from)** (*disagree*) non essere d'accordo (con); (*be dissimilar*) essere diverso (da).

difference ['dɪfrəns] *n* differenza *f*; **it makes no ~** è lo stesso; **a ~ of opinion** una divergenza di opinioni.

different ['dɪfrənt] *adj* diverso(-a); **to be ~ (from)** essere diverso (da); **a ~ route** un'altra strada.

differently ['dɪfrəntlɪ] *adv* in modo diverso.

difficult ['dɪfɪkəlt] *adj* difficile.

difficulty ['dɪfɪkəltɪ] *n* difficoltà *f inv*.

dig [dɪg] (*pt & pp* **dug**) *vt & vi* scavare.

▶ **dig out** *vt sep* (*rescue*) estrarre; (*find*) scovare.

▶ **dig up** *vt sep* (*from ground*) dissotterrare.

digest [dɪ'dʒest] *vt* digerire.

digestion [dɪ'dʒestʃn] *n* digestione *f*.

digestive (biscuit) [dɪ'dʒestɪv-] *n* (Br) biscotto di frumento con farina integrale.

digit ['dɪdʒɪt] *n* (*figure*) cifra *f*; (*finger, toe*) dito *m*.

digital ['dɪdʒɪtl] *adj* digitale.

dill [dɪl] *n* aneto *m*.

dilute [daɪ'luːt] *vt* (*liquid*) diluire.

dim [dɪm] ◆ *adj* (*light*) debole; (*room*) buio(-a); (*inf: stupid*) ottuso(-a) ◆ *vt* (*light*) abbassare.

dime [daɪm] *n* (Am) moneta *f* da dieci centesimi di dollaro.

dimensions [dɪ'menʃnz] *npl* dimensioni *fpl*.

din [dɪn] *n* baccano *m*.

dine [daɪn] *vi* cenare.

▶ **dine out** *vi* cenare fuori.

diner ['daɪnər] *n* (Am: *restaurant*) ≃ tavola *f* calda; (*person*) cliente *mf*.

dinghy ['dɪŋɪ] *n* (*with sail, oars*) barca *f*; (*for racing*) dinghy *m inv*; (*made of rubber*) canotto *m*.

dingy ['dɪndʒɪ] *adj* (*clothes*) sporco(-a); (*town, hotel*) squallido(-a).

dining car ['daɪnɪŋ-] *n* carrozza *f* ristorante.

dining hall ['daɪnɪŋ-] *n* refettorio *m*.

dining room ['daɪnɪŋ-] *n* sala *f* da pranzo.

dinner ['dɪnər] *n* (*at lunchtime*) pranzo *m*; (*in evening*) cena *f*; **to have ~** (*at lunchtime*) pranzare; (*in evening*) cenare.

dinner jacket *n* giacca *f* dello smoking.

dinner party *n* cena *f*.

dinner set *n* servizio *m* da tavola.

dinner suit *n* smoking *m inv*.

dinnertime ['dɪnətaɪm] *n* (*at lunchtime*) ora *f* di pranzo; (*in evening*) ora di cena.

dinosaur ['daɪnəsɔːr] *n* dinosauro *m*.

dip [dɪp] ◆ *n* (*in road, land*) avvallamento *m*; (*food*) salsetta cremosa in cui intingere patatine o verdure crude ◆ *vt* (*into liquid*) immergere ◆ *vi* (*road, land*) digradare; **to have a ~** (*swim*) fare una nuotatina; **to ~ one's headlights** (Br) spegnere gli abbaglianti.

diploma [dɪ'pləumə] *n* diploma *m*.

dipstick ['dɪpstɪk] *n* asta *f* di livello.

direct [dɪ'rekt] ◆ *adj* diretto(-a) ◆ *adv* (*go*) direttamente; (*travel*) senza fermarsi ◆ *vt*: **can you ~ me to the railway station?** mi può indicare la strada per la stazione?

direct current *n* corrente *f* continua.

direction [dɪ'rekʃn] n (of movement) direzione f; **to ask for ~s** chiedere indicazioni.

▶ **directions** npl (instructions) istruzioni fpl.

directly [dɪ'rektlɪ] adv (exactly) proprio; (soon) subito.

director [dɪ'rektər] n (of company) amministratore m (-trice f); (of film, play, TV programme) regista mf; (organizer) direttore m (-trice f).

directory [dɪ'rektərɪ] n elenco m.

directory enquiries n (Br) informazioni fpl elenco abbonati.

dirt [dɜːt] n sporcizia f; (earth) terra f.

dirty ['dɜːtɪ] adj sporco(-a).

disability [,dɪsə'bɪlətɪ] n handicap m inv; (through old age, illness) invalidità f inv.

disabled [dɪs'eɪbld] ♦ adj disabile ♦ npl: **the ~** i portatori di handicap; **'~ toilet'** 'toilette per portatori di handicap'.

disadvantage [,dɪsəd'vɑːntɪdʒ] n svantaggio m.

disagree [,dɪsə'griː] vi non essere d'accordo; **to ~ with sb (about)** non essere d'accordo con qn (su); **those mussels ~d with me** quelle cozze mi hanno fatto male.

disagreement [,dɪsə'griːmənt] n (argument) discussione f; (dissimilarity) disaccordo m.

disappear [,dɪsə'pɪər] vi sparire.

disappearance [,dɪsə'pɪərəns] n scomparsa f.

disappoint [,dɪsə'pɔɪnt] vt deludere.

disappointed [,dɪsə'pɔɪntɪd] adj deluso(-a).

disappointing [,dɪsə'pɔɪntɪŋ] adj deludente.

disappointment [,dɪsə'pɔɪntmənt] n delusione f.

disapprove [,dɪsə'pruːv] vi: **to ~ of** disapprovare.

disarmament [dɪs'ɑːməmənt] n disarmo m.

disaster [dɪ'zɑːstər] n disastro m.

disastrous [dɪ'zɑːstrəs] adj disastroso(-a).

disc [dɪsk] n (Br) disco m; (Br: CD) compact disc m inv; **I slipped a ~** mi è venuta l'ernia al disco.

discard [dɪ'skɑːd] vt scartare.

discharge [dɪs'tʃɑːdʒ] vt (prisoner) rilasciare; (patient) dimettere; (soldier) congedare; (smoke, gas) emettere; (liquid) scaricare.

discipline ['dɪsɪplɪn] n disciplina f.

disc jockey n disc-jockey mf inv.

disco ['dɪskəʊ] (pl -s) n (place) discoteca f; (event) festa f.

discoloured [dɪs'kʌləd] adj scolorito(-a).

discomfort [dɪs'kʌmfət] n fastidio m.

disconnect [,dɪskə'nekt] vt staccare; (gas supply) chiudere; (pipe) scollegare.

discontinued [,dɪskən'tɪnjuːd] adj (product) di fine serie.

discotheque ['dɪskəʊtek] n (place) discoteca f; (event) festa f.

discount ['dɪskaʊnt] n sconto m.

discover [dɪ'skʌvər] vt scoprire.

discovery [dɪ'skʌvərɪ] n scoperta f.

discreet [dɪ'skriːt] adj discreto(-a).

discrepancy [dɪ'skrepənsɪ] n discrepanza f.

discriminate [dɪ'skrɪmɪneɪt] vi: **to ~ against sb** discriminare contro qn.

discrimination [dɪ,skrɪmɪ'neɪʃn] n (unfair treatment) discriminazione f.

discuss [dɪ'skʌs] vt discutere.

discussion [dɪ'skʌʃn] n discussione f.

disease [dɪ'ziːz] n malattia f.

disembark [,dɪsɪm'bɑːk] vi sbarcare.

disgrace [dɪs'greɪs] n (shame) vergogna f; **it's a ~!** è una vergogna!

disgraceful [dɪs'greɪsfʊl] adj vergognoso(-a).

disguise [dɪs'gaɪz] ♦ n travestimento m ♦ vt travestire; **in ~** travestito.

disgust [dɪs'gʌst] ♦ *n* disgusto *m*
♦ *vt* disgustare.

disgusting [dɪs'gʌstɪŋ] *adj* disgustoso(-a).

dish [dɪʃ] *n* piatto *m*; **to do the ~es** fare i piatti; **'~ of the day**' 'piatto del giorno'.
▶ **dish up** *vt sep* servire.

dishcloth ['dɪʃklɒθ] *n* strofinaccio *m*.

disheveled [dɪ'ʃevəld] (Am) = **dishevelled**.

dishevelled [dɪ'ʃevəld] *adj* (Br: *hair*) arruffato(-a); (*appearance*) trasandato(-a).

dishonest [dɪs'ɒnɪst] *adj* disonesto(-a).

dish towel *n* (Am) strofinaccio *m*.

dishwasher ['dɪʃ,wɒʃə'] *n* (*machine*) lavastoviglie *f inv*.

disinfectant [,dɪsɪn'fektənt] *n* disinfettante *m*.

disintegrate [dɪs'ɪntɪgreɪt] *vi* disintegrarsi.

disk [dɪsk] *n* (Am) = **disc**; (COMPUT) dischetto *m*.

disk drive *n* drive *m inv*.

dislike [dɪs'laɪk] ♦ *n* (*poor opinion*) antipatia *f* ♦ *vt*: **I ~ them** non mi piacciono; **to take a ~ to** prendere in antipatia.

dislocate ['dɪsləkeɪt] *vt*: **to ~ one's shoulder** slogarsi la spalla.

dismal ['dɪzml] *adj* (*weather, place*) deprimente; (*terrible*) pessimo(-a).

dismantle [dɪs'mæntl] *vt* smontare.

dismay [dɪs'meɪ] *n* sgomento *m*.

dismiss [dɪs'mɪs] *vt* (*not consider*) ignorare; (*from job*) licenziare; (*from classroom*) congedare.

disobedient [,dɪsə'biːdjənt] *adj* disubbidiente.

disobey [,dɪsə'beɪ] *vt* disubbidire.

disorder [dɪs'ɔːdər] *n* (*confusion*) disordine *m*; (*illness*) disturbo *m*.

disorganized [dɪs'ɔːgənaɪzd] *adj* disorganizzato(-a).

dispatch [dɪ'spætʃ] *vt* inviare.

dispense [dɪ'spens]: **dispense with** *vt fus* fare a meno di.

dispenser [dɪ'spensər] *n* (*device*) distributore *m*.

dispensing chemist [dɪ'spensɪŋ-] *n* (Br: *shop*) farmacia *f*.

disperse [dɪ'spɜːs] ♦ *vt* disperdere ♦ *vi* dispersi.

display [dɪ'spleɪ] ♦ *n* (*of goods*) esposizione *f*; (*public event*) spettacolo *m*; (*readout*) schermo *m* ♦ *vt* (*goods, information*) esporre; (*feeling, quality*) manifestare; **on ~** in mostra.

displeased [dɪs'pliːzd] *adj* contrariato(-a).

disposable [dɪ'spəuzəbl] *adj* usa e getta (*inv*).

dispute [dɪ'spjuːt] ♦ *n* (*argument*) controversia *f*; (*industrial*) vertenza *f* ♦ *vt* mettere in discussione.

disqualify [,dɪs'kwɒlɪfaɪ] *vt* squalificare; **he is disqualified from driving** (Br) gli hanno ritirato la patente.

disregard [,dɪsrɪ'gɑːd] *vt* ignorare.

disrupt [dɪs'rʌpt] *vt* disturbare.

disruption [dɪs'rʌpʃn] *n* disordine *m*.

dissatisfied [,dɪs'sætɪsfaɪd] *adj* insoddisfatto(-a).

dissolve [dɪ'zɒlv] ♦ *vt* sciogliere ♦ *vi* sciogliersi.

dissuade [dɪ'sweɪd] *vt*: **to ~ sb from doing sthg** dissuadere qn dal fare qc.

distance ['dɪstəns] *n* distanza *f*; **from a ~** da lontano; **in the ~** in lontananza.

distant ['dɪstənt] *adj* distante; (*in time*) lontano(-a).

distilled water [dɪ'stɪld-] *n* acqua *f* distillata.

distillery [dɪ'stɪlərɪ] *n* distilleria *f*.

distinct [dɪ'stɪŋkt] *adj* (*separate*) distinto(-a); (*noticeable*) chiaro(-a).

distinction [dɪ'stɪŋkʃn] *n* (*difference*) distinzione *f*; (*mark in exam*) lode *f*.

distinctive [dɪ'stɪŋktɪv] *adj* inconfondibile.

distinguish [dɪ'stɪŋgwɪʃ] *vt* (*perceive*) distinguere; **to ~ sthg from sthg** distinguere qc da qc.

distorted [dɪ'stɔːtɪd] *adj* distorto(-a).

distract [dɪ'strækt] *vt* distrarre.

distraction [dɪ'strækʃn] *n* distrazione *f*.

distress [dɪ'stres] *n* (*pain*) sofferenza *f*; (*anxiety*) angoscia *f*.

distressing [dɪ'stresɪŋ] *adj* doloroso(-a).

distribute [dɪ'strɪbjuːt] *vt* distribuire.

distributor [dɪ'strɪbjutər] *n* (COMM) distributore *m*; (AUT) spinterogeno *m*.

district ['dɪstrɪkt] *n* regione *f*; (*of town*) quartiere *m*.

district attorney *n* (Am) = procuratore *m* della Repubblica.

disturb [dɪ'stɜːb] *vt* (*interrupt*) disturbare; (*worry*) turbare; (*move*) muovere; **'do not ~'** 'non disturbare'.

disturbance [dɪ'stɜːbəns] *n* (*violence*) disordini *mpl*.

ditch [dɪtʃ] *n* fossato *m*.

ditto ['dɪtəu] *adv* idem.

divan [dɪ'væn] *n* divano *m*.

dive [daɪv] (*pt Am* **-d** OR **dove**, *pt Br* **-d**) ♦ *n* (*of swimmer*) tuffo *m* ♦ *vi* tuffarsi; (*under sea*) immergersi.

diver ['daɪvər] *n* (*from divingboard, rock*) tuffatore *m* (-trice *f*); (*under sea*) sommozzatore *m* (-trice *f*).

diversion [daɪ'vɜːʃn] *n* (*of traffic*) deviazione *f*; (*amusement*) diversivo *m*.

divert [daɪ'vɜːt] *vt* (*traffic, river*) deviare; (*attention*) distrarre.

divide [dɪ'vaɪd] *vt* dividere.

▶ **divide up** *vt sep* dividere.

diving ['daɪvɪŋ] *n* (*from divingboard, rock*) tuffi *mpl*; (*under sea*) immersioni *fpl*; **to go ~** fare sub.

divingboard ['daɪvɪŋbɔːd] *n* trampolino *m*.

division [dɪ'vɪʒn] *n* divisione *f*; (*in football league*) serie *f*.

divorce [dɪ'vɔːs] ♦ *n* divorzio *m* ♦ *vt* divorziare da.

divorced [dɪ'vɔːst] *adj* divorziato(-a).

DIY *n* (*abbr of do-it-yourself*) il fai da te.

dizzy ['dɪzɪ] *adj*: **I feel ~** mi gira la testa.

DJ *n* (*abbr of disc jockey*) disc-jockey *mf inv*.

do [duː] (*pt* **did**, *pp* **done**, *pl* **dos**) *aux vb* **1.** (*in negatives*): **don't ~ that!** non farlo!; **she didn't listen** non ha ascoltato.

2. (*in questions*): **~ you like it?** ti piace?; **how ~ you do it?** come si fa?

3. (*referring to previous verb*): **I eat more than you** ~ io mangio più di te; **you made a mistake – no I didn't!** ti sei sbagliato – non è vero!; **so ~ I** anch'io.

4. (*in question tags*) vero?, non è vero?; **so, you like Scotland, ~ you?** e così ti piace la Scozia, non è vero?

5. (*for emphasis*): **I ~ like this bedroom** questa camera mi piace proprio; **~ come in!** si accomodi!

♦ *vt* **1.** (*perform*) fare; **to ~ one's homework** fare i compiti; **what is she doing?** cosa sta facendo?; **what can I ~ for you?** in cosa posso esserle utile?

2. (*attend to*): **to ~ one's hair** pettinarsi; **to ~ one's make-up** truccarsi; **to ~ one's teeth** lavarsi i denti.

3. (*cause*) fare; **to ~ damage** danneggiare; **to ~ sb good** fare bene a qn.

4. (*have as job*): **what do you ~?** che lavoro fai?

5. (*provide, offer*) fare; **we ~ pizzas for under £4** facciamo pizze a meno di 4 sterline.

6. (*study*) fare.

7. (*subj: vehicle*) fare; **the car was doing 50 mph** la macchina andava a 80 all'ora.

8. (*inf: visit*) fare; **we're doing Scotland next week** la settimana prossima facciamo la Scozia.

♦ *vi* **1.** (*behave, act*) fare; ~ **as I say** fai come ti dico.

2. (*progress, get on*) andare; **to ~ badly** andare male; **to ~ well** andare bene.

3. (*be sufficient*) bastare; **will £5 ~?** bastano 5 sterline?

4. (*in phrases*): **how do you ~?** piacere!; **what has that got to ~ with it?** e questo che c'entra?

♦ *n* (*party*) festa *f*; **the ~s and don'ts** le cose da fare e da non fare.

▶ **do out of** *vt sep* (*inf*): **to ~ sb out of sthg** fregare qc a qn.

▶ **do up** *vt sep* (*fasten*) allacciare; (*decorate*) rinnovare; (*wrap up*) impacchettare.

▶ **do with** *vt fus* (*need*): **I could ~ with a drink** mi ci vuole proprio un bicchierino.

▶ **do without** *vt fus* fare a meno di.

dock [dɒk] ♦ *n* (*for ships*) molo *m*; (JUR) banco *m* degli imputati ♦ *vi* attraccare.

doctor ['dɒktər] *n* dottore *m* (-essa *f*); **to go to the ~'s** andare dal dottore.

document ['dɒkjʊmənt] *n* documento *m*.

documentary [ˌdɒkjʊ'mentəri] *n* documentario *m*.

Dodgems® ['dɒdʒəmz] *npl* (Br) autoscontri *mpl*.

dodgy ['dɒdʒɪ] *adj* (Br: *inf: plan*) rischioso(-a); (*car*) poco sicuro(-a).

does [*weak form* dəz, *strong form* dʌz] → **do**.

doesn't ['dʌznt] = **does not**.

dog [dɒg] *n* cane *m*.

dog food *n* cibo *m* per cani.

doggy bag ['dɒgɪ-] *n* sacchetto per portar via gli avanzi di un pasto consumato al ristorante.

do-it-yourself *n* il fai da te.

dole [dəʊl] *n*: **to be on the ~** (Br) prendere il sussidio di disoccupazione.

doll [dɒl] *n* bambola *f*.

dollar ['dɒlər] *n* dollaro *m*.

Dolomites ['dɒləmaɪts] *npl*: **the ~** le Dolomiti.

dolphin ['dɒlfɪn] *n* delfino *m*.

dome [dəʊm] *n* cupola *f*.

domestic [də'mestɪk] *adj* (*of house, family*) domestico(-a); (*of country*) nazionale, interno(-a).

domestic appliance *n* elettrodomestico *m*.

domestic flight *n* volo *m* nazionale.

domestic science *n* economia *f* domestica.

dominate ['dɒmɪneɪt] *vt* dominare.

dominoes ['dɒmɪnəʊz] *n* domino *m*.

donate [də'neɪt] *vt* donare.

donation [də'neɪʃn] *n* donazione *f*.

done [dʌn] ♦ *pp* → **do** ♦ *adj* (*finished*) finito(-a); (*cooked*) cotto(-a).

donkey ['dɒŋkɪ] *n* asino *m*.

don't [dəʊnt] = **do not**.

door [dɔːr] *n* (*of building*) porta *f*; (*of vehicle, cupboard*) sportello *m*.

doorbell ['dɔːbel] *n* campanello *m*.

doorknob ['dɔːnɒb] *n* pomello *m*.

doorman ['dɔːmən] (*pl* -**men**) *n* portiere *m*.

doormat ['dɔːmæt] *n* zerbino *m*.

doormen ['dɔːmən] *pl* → **doorman**.

doorstep ['dɔːstep] *n* gradino *m* della porta; (Br: *inf: piece of bread*) grossa fetta *f* di pane.

doorway ['dɔːweɪ] *n* porta *f*.

dope [dəʊp] *n* (*inf: any illegal drug*) roba *f*; (*marijuana*) erba *f*.

dormitory ['dɔːmətrɪ] *n* dormitorio *m*.

Dormobile® ['dɔːmə,biːl] *n* camper *m inv*.

dosage ['dəʊsɪdʒ] *n* dosaggio *m*.

dose [dəʊs] *n* (*amount*) dose *f*; (*of ill-*

ness) attacco *m*.

dot [dɒt] *n* punto *m*; **on the ~** (*fig*) in punto.

dotted line ['dɒtɪd-] *n* linea *f* punteggiata.

double ['dʌbl] ◆ *adj* doppio(-a) ◆ *adv* (*twice*) due volte ◆ *n* (*twice the amount*) doppio *m*; (*alcohol*) dose *f* doppia ◆ *vt & vi* raddoppiare; **~ three, two, eight** trentatrè, ventotto; **a ~ whisky** un doppio whisky; **to bend sthg ~** piegare qc in due.
▶ **doubles** *n* (*in tennis*) doppio *m*.

double bed *n* letto *m* matrimoniale.

double-breasted [-'brestɪd] *adj* a doppio petto.

double cream *n* (*Br*) panna molto densa ad alto contenuto di grassi.

double-decker (bus) [-'dekər-] *n* autobus *m inv* a due piani.

double doors *npl* porte *fpl* a due battenti.

double-glazing [-'gleɪzɪŋ] *n* doppi vetri *mpl*.

double room *n* camera *f* per due.

doubt [daʊt] ◆ *n* dubbio *m* ◆ *vt* dubitare di; **I ~ it** ne dubito; **I ~ she'll be there** dubito che ci sarà; **in ~** in dubbio; **no ~** (*almost certainly*) senza dubbio.

doubtful ['daʊtfʊl] *adj* (*uncertain*) incerto(-a); **it's ~ that ...** è improbabile che ... (+ *subjunctive*).

dough [dəʊ] *n* pasta *f*, impasto *m* (*per pane, dolci*).

doughnut ['dəʊnʌt] *n* bombolone *m*.

dove[1] [dʌv] *n* (*bird*) colomba *f*.

dove[2] [dəʊv] *pt* (*Am*) → **dive**.

Dover ['dəʊvər] *n* Dover.

Dover sole *n* sogliola *f* di Dover.

down [daʊn] *adv* 1. (*towards the bottom*) giù; **~ here** quaggiù; **~ there** laggiù; **to fall ~** cadere.
2. (*along*): **I'm going ~ to the shops** vado ai negozi.

3. (*downstairs*): **I'll come ~ later** scenderò più tardi.
4. (*southwards*): **we're going ~ to London** andiamo a Londra.
5. (*in writing*): **to write sthg ~** scrivere qc.
◆ *prep* 1. (*towards the bottom of*): **they ran ~ the hill** corsero giù per la collina.
2. (*along*) lungo; **I was walking ~ the street** camminavo lungo la strada.
◆ *adj* (*inf: depressed*) giù (*inv*).
◆ *n* (*feathers*) piumino *m*.
▶ **downs** *npl* (*Br*) colline *fpl*.

downhill [,daʊn'hɪl] *adv* in discesa.

Downing Street ['daʊnɪŋ] *n* Downing Street *f* (*strada di Londra dove si trova la residenza del primo ministro*).

downpour ['daʊnpɔːr] *n* acquazzone *m*.

downstairs [,daʊn'steəz] ◆ *adj* di sotto ◆ *adv* al piano di sotto; **to go ~** scendere giù.

downtown [,daʊn'taʊn] ◆ *adj* (*hotel*) del centro; (*train*) per il centro ◆ *adv* in centro; **~ New York** il centro di New York.

down under *adv* (*Br: inf: in Australia*) in Australia.

downwards ['daʊnwədz] *adv* verso il basso.

doz. *abbr* = **dozen**.

doze [dəʊz] *vi* fare un pisolino.

dozen ['dʌzn] *n* dozzina *f*; **a ~ eggs** una dozzina di uova.

Dr (*abbr of doctor*) Dott. *m* (Dott.ssa *f*)

drab [dræb] *adj* grigio(-a).

draft [drɑːft] *n* (*early version*) bozza *f*; (*money order*) tratta *f*; (*Am*) = **draught**.

drag [dræg] ◆ *vt* (*pull along*) trascinare ◆ *vi* (*along ground*) strascicare; **what a ~!** (*inf*) che seccatura!
▶ **drag on** *vi* trascinarsi.

dragonfly ['drægnflaɪ] *n* libellula *f*.

drain [dreɪn] ◆ *n* (*sewer*) fogna *f*; (*grating in street*) tombino *m* ◆ *vt* (*tank, radiator*) svuotare ◆ *vi* (*vegetables, washing-up*) scolare.

draining board ['dreɪnɪŋ-] *n* scolatoio *m*.

drainpipe ['dreɪnpaɪp] *n* tubo *m* di scarico.

drama ['drɑːmə] *n* (*play, exciting event*) dramma *m*; (*art*) teatro *m*; (*excitement*) emozioni *fpl*.

dramatic [drə'mætɪk] *adj* (*impressive*) sensazionale.

drank [dræŋk] *pt* → **drink**.

drapes [dreɪps] *npl* (*Am*) tende *fpl*.

drastic ['dræstɪk] *adj* drastico(-a); (*improvement*) netto(-a).

drastically ['dræstɪklɪ] *adv* sensibilmente.

draught [drɑːft] *n* (*Br*: *of air*) corrente *f* d'aria.

draught beer *n* birra *f* alla spina.

draughts [drɑːfts] *n* (*Br*) dama *f*.

draughty ['drɑːftɪ] *adj* pieno(-a) di correnti d'aria.

draw [drɔː] (*pt* drew, *pp* drawn) ◆ *vt* (*with pen, pencil*) disegnare; (*line*) tracciare; (*pull*) tirare; (*attract*) attirare; (*conclusion*) trarre; (*comparison*) fare ◆ *vi* (*with pen, pencil*) disegnare; (*SPORT*) pareggiare ◆ *n* (*SPORT*: *result*) pareggio *m*; (*lottery*) estrazione *f*; **to ~ the curtains** tirare le tende.

▶ **draw out** *vt sep* (*money*) prelevare.

▶ **draw up** ◆ *vt sep* (*list, plan*) stendere ◆ *vi* (*car, bus*) accostarsi.

drawback ['drɔːbæk] *n* inconveniente *m*.

drawer [drɔːr] *n* cassetto *m*.

drawing ['drɔːɪŋ] *n* disegno *m*.

drawing pin *n* (*Br*) puntina *f* da disegno.

drawing room *n* salotto *m*.

drawn [drɔːn] *pp* → **draw**.

dreadful ['dredfʊl] *adj* terribile.

dream [driːm] ◆ *n* sogno *m* ◆ *vt* sognare ◆ *vi*: **to ~ (of)** sognare (di); **a ~ house** una casa di sogno.

dress [dres] ◆ *n* vestito *m*; (*clothes*) abbigliamento *m* ◆ *vt* vestire;

(*wound*) fasciare; (*salad*) condire ◆ *vi* (*get dressed*) vestirsi; (*in particular way*) vestire; **to be ~ed in** essere vestito di; **to get ~ed** vestirsi.

▶ **dress up** *vi* mettersi in ghingheri.

dress circle *n* prima galleria *f*.

dresser ['dresər] *n* (*Br*: *for crockery*) credenza *f*; (*Am*: *chest of drawers*) comò *m inv*.

dressing ['dresɪŋ] *n* (*for salad*) condimento *m*; (*for wound*) fasciatura *f*.

dressing gown *n* vestaglia *f*.

dressing room *n* camerino *m*.

dressing table *n* toilette *f inv*.

dressmaker ['dres,meɪkər] *n* sarta *f*.

dress rehearsal *n* prova *f* generale.

drew [druː] *pt* → **draw**.

dribble ['drɪbl] *vi* (*liquid*) gocciolare; (*baby*) sbavare.

drier ['draɪər] = **dryer**.

drift [drɪft] ◆ *n* (*of snow*) cumulo *m* ◆ *vi* (*in wind*) essere spinto dal vento; (*in water*) essere spinto dalla corrente.

drill [drɪl] ◆ *n* trapano *m* ◆ *vt* (*hole*) fare.

drink [drɪŋk] (*pt* drank, *pp* drunk) ◆ *n* bevanda *f*; (*alcoholic*) bicchierino *m* ◆ *vt* & *vi* bere; **would you like a ~?** vuoi qualcosa da bere?; **to have a ~** (*alcoholic*) bere un bicchierino.

drinkable ['drɪŋkəbl] *adj* (*safe to drink*) potabile; (*wine*) bevibile.

drinking water ['drɪŋkɪŋ-] *n* acqua *f* potabile.

drip [drɪp] ◆ *n* (*drop*) goccia *f*; (*MED*) flebo *f inv* ◆ *vi* gocciolare.

drip-dry *adj* che non si stira.

dripping (wet) ['drɪpɪŋ-] *adj* fradicio(-a).

drive [draɪv] (*pt* drove, *pp* driven) ◆ *n* (*journey*) viaggio *m* (in macchina); (*in front of house*) viale *m* d'accesso ◆ *vi* (*drive car*) guidare; (*travel in car*) andare in macchina

◆ vt (car, bus, train) guidare; (take in car) portare (in macchina); (operate, power): **it's driven by electricity** funziona a elettricità; **it's two hours' ~ from here** è a due ore di macchina da qui; **to go for a ~** andare a fare un giro in macchina; **to ~ sb to do sthg** spingere qn a fare qc; **to ~ sb mad** far diventare matto qn; **can you ~ me to the station?** mi accompagni alla stazione?

drivel ['drɪvl] n scemenze fpl.

driven ['drɪvn] pp → drive.

driver ['draɪvəʳ] n (of car, bus) conducente mf; (of train) macchinista mf; (of taxi) tassista mf.

driver's license (Am) = **driving licence**.

driveshaft ['draɪvʃɑ:ft] n albero m motore.

driveway ['draɪvweɪ] n vialetto m d'accesso.

driving lesson ['draɪvɪŋ-] n lezione f di guida.

driving licence ['draɪvɪŋ-] n (Br) patente f di guida.

driving test ['draɪvɪŋ-] n esame m di guida.

drizzle ['drɪzl] n pioggerellina f.

drop [drɒp] ◆ n (drip) goccia f; (small amount) goccio m; (distance down) salto m; (decrease) calo m; (in wages) riduzione f ◆ vt lasciar cadere; (reduce) ridurre; (from vehicle) far scendere; (omit) saltare ◆ vi (fall) cadere; (decrease) diminuire; **to ~ a hint that** far capire che; **to ~ sb a line** scrivere due righe a qn.

▶ **drop in** vi (inf) fare un salto.

▶ **drop off** ◆ vt sep (from vehicle) far scendere ◆ vi (fall asleep) addormentarsi; (fall off) staccarsi.

▶ **drop out** vi (of college, race) ritirarsi.

drought [draʊt] n siccità f inv.

drove [drəʊv] pt → drive.

drown [draʊn] vi annegare.

drug [drʌg] ◆ n (MED) farmaco m; (stimulant) droga f ◆ vt drogare.

drug addict n tossicodipendente mf.

druggist ['drʌgɪst] n (Am) farmacista mf.

drum [drʌm] n (MUS) tamburo m; (container) fusto m.

▶ **drums** npl batteria f.

drummer ['drʌməʳ] n batterista mf.

drumstick ['drʌmstɪk] n (of chicken) coscia f (di pollo).

drunk [drʌŋk] ◆ pp → drink ◆ adj ubriaco(-a) ◆ n ubriaco m (-a f); **to get ~** ubriacarsi.

dry [draɪ] ◆ adj secco(-a); (weather, day) asciutto(-a) ◆ vt asciugare ◆ vi asciugarsi; **to ~ o.s.** asciugarsi; **to ~ one's hair** asciugarsi i capelli.

▶ **dry up** vi (become dry) seccarsi; (dry the dishes) asciugare i piatti.

dry-clean vt pulire a secco.

dry cleaner's n lavanderia f (a secco).

dryer ['draɪəʳ] n (for clothes) asciugabiancheria m inv; (for hair) asciugacapelli m inv.

dry-roasted peanuts [-'rəʊstɪd-] npl arachidi fpl tostate.

DSS n (Br) ministero britannico per la previdenza sociale.

DTP n (abbr of desktop publishing) desktop publishing m.

dual carriageway ['dju:əl-] n (Br) strada f a doppia carreggiata.

dubbed [dʌbd] adj (film) doppiato(-a).

dubious ['dju:bjəs] adj (suspect) dubbio(-a).

duchess ['dʌtʃɪs] n duchessa f.

duck [dʌk] ◆ n anatra f ◆ vi abbassarsi.

due [dju:] adj (expected) atteso(-a); (owed) dovuto(-a); **to be ~** (bill, rent) scadere; **in ~ course** a tempo debito; **~ to** a causa di.

duet [dju:'et] n duetto m.

duffel bag ['dʌfl-] n sacca f da viaggio.

duffel coat ['dʌfl-] n montgomery m inv.

dug [dʌg] pt & pp → **dig**.

duke [djuːk] n duca m.

dull [dʌl] adj (boring) noioso(-a); (not bright) spento(-a); (weather) coperto(-a); (pain) sordo(-a).

dumb [dʌm] adj (inf: stupid) stupido(-a); (unable to speak) muto(-a).

dummy ['dʌmɪ] n (Br: for baby) ciuccio m; (for clothes) manichino m.

dump [dʌmp] ◆ n (for rubbish) discarica f; (inf: place) porcile m ◆ vt (drop carelessly) gettare; (get rid of) scaricare.

dumpling ['dʌmplɪŋ] n gnocco di pasta cotto al vapore e servito insieme agli stufati.

dune [djuːn] n duna f.

dungarees [ˌdʌŋgə'riːz] npl (for work) tuta f; (Br: fashion item) salopette f inv.

dungeon ['dʌndʒən] n segreta f.

duplicate ['djuːplɪkət] n duplicato m.

during ['djʊərɪŋ] prep durante.

dusk [dʌsk] n crepuscolo m.

dust [dʌst] ◆ n polvere f ◆ vt spolverare.

dustbin ['dʌstbɪn] n (Br) pattumiera f.

dustcart ['dʌstkɑːt] n (Br) camion m inv delle immondizie.

duster ['dʌstər] n straccio m (per spolverare).

dustman ['dʌstmən] (pl -men [-mən]) n (Br) netturbino m.

dustpan ['dʌstpæn] n paletta f (per la spazzatura).

dusty ['dʌstɪ] adj polveroso(-a).

Dutch [dʌtʃ] ◆ adj olandese ◆ n (language) olandese m ◆ npl: **the ~** gli olandesi.

Dutchman ['dʌtʃmən] (pl -men [-mən]) n olandese m.

Dutchwoman ['dʌtʃˌwʊmən] (pl -women [-ˌwɪmɪn]) n olandese f.

duty ['djuːtɪ] n (moral obligation) dovere m; (tax) dazio m, tassa f; **to be on ~** essere in OR di servizio; **to be off ~** essere fuori servizio, essere libero.

▶ **duties** npl (job) mansioni fpl.

duty chemist's n farmacia f di turno.

duty-free ◆ adj esente da dazio ◆ n: duty free m inv.

duty-free shop n duty free shop m inv.

duvet ['duːveɪ] n piumone® m.

dwarf [dwɔːf] (pl **dwarves** [dwɔːvz]) n nano m (-a f).

dwelling ['dwelɪŋ] n (fml) abitazione f.

dye [daɪ] ◆ n tinta f ◆ vt tingere.

dynamite ['daɪnəmaɪt] n dinamite f.

dynamo ['daɪnəməʊ] (pl -s) n (on bike) dinamo f inv.

dyslexic [dɪs'leksɪk] adj dislessico(-a).

E

E (abbr of east) E.

E111 n E111 m.

each [iːtʃ] ◆ adj ogni (inv), ciascuno(-a) ◆ pron ciascuno m (-a f), ognuno m (-a f); **~ one** ognuno; **~ of them** ognuno di loro; **one ~** uno ciascuno; **one of ~** uno di ognuno; **they know ~ other** si conoscono.

eager ['iːgər] adj (pupil, expression) entusiasta; **to be ~ to do sthg** essere impaziente di fare qc.

eagle ['iːgl] n (bird) aquila f.

ear [ɪər] n orecchio m; (of corn) spiga f.

earache ['ɪəreɪk] n: **to have ~** avere mal m d'orecchi.

earl [ɜːl] n conte m.

early ['ɜːlɪ] ◆ adj (childhood) primo(-a); (train) di buon'ora; (before *usual or arranged time)* anticipato(-a), precoce ♦ *adv* presto; **in the ~ morning** di primo mattino; **in the ~ 20th century** all'inizio del xx secolo; **at the earliest** al più presto; **~ on** presto; **to have an ~ night** andare a letto presto.

earn [ɜːn] *vt (money)* guadagnare; *(praise, success)* guadagnarsi; **to ~ a living** guadagnarsi da vivere.

earnings ['ɜːnɪŋz] *npl* guadagni *mpl.*

earphones ['ɪəfəʊnz] *npl* cuffie *fpl.*

earplugs ['ɪəplʌgz] *npl* tappi *mpl* per le orecchie.

earrings ['ɪərɪŋz] *npl* orecchini *mpl.*

earth [ɜːθ] ♦ *n* terra *f* ♦ *vt* (Br: *appliance)* mettere a terra; **how on ~ ...?** come diavolo ...?

earthenware ['ɜːθnweər] *adj* di terracotta.

earthquake ['ɜːθkweɪk] *n* terremoto *m.*

ease [iːz] ♦ *n (lack of difficulty)* facilità *f* ♦ *vt (pain, problem)* alleviare; **at ~** a proprio agio; **with ~** con facilità.
▶ **ease off** *vi (pain, rain)* attenuarsi.

easily ['iːzɪlɪ] *adv* facilmente; *(by far)* senza dubbio.

east [iːst] ♦ *n* est *m* ♦ *adj* dell'est ♦ *adv* a est; **in the ~ of England** nell'Inghilterra orientale; **the East** *(Asia)* l'Oriente *m.*

eastbound ['iːstbaʊnd] *adj* diretto(-a) a est.

Easter ['iːstər] *n* Pasqua *f.*

eastern ['iːstən] *adj* orientale, dell'est.
▶ **Eastern** *adj (Asian)* orientale.

Eastern Europe *n* l'Europa *f* dell'Est.

eastwards ['iːstwədz] *adv* verso est.

easy ['iːzɪ] *adj* facile; *(without problems)* tranquillo(-a); **to take it ~** prendersela con calma.

easygoing [ˌiːzɪ'gəʊɪŋ] *adj* rilassato(-a).

eat [iːt] *(pt* **ate**, *pp* **eaten** ['iːtn]) *vt & vi* mangiare.
▶ **eat out** *vi* mangiare fuori.

eating apple ['iːtɪŋ-] *n* mela *f* (da mangiare cruda).

ebony ['ebənɪ] *n* ebano *m.*

EC *n (abbr of European Community)* CE *f.*

eccentric [ɪk'sentrɪk] *adj* eccentrico(-a).

echo ['ekəʊ] *(pl* **-es**) ♦ *n* eco *f* ♦ *vi* fare eco.

ecology [ɪ'kɒlədʒɪ] *n* ecologia *f.*

economic [ˌiːkə'nɒmɪk] *adj* economico(-a).
▶ **economics** *n* economia *f.*

economical [ˌiːkə'nɒmɪkl] *adj (car, system)* economico(-a); *(person)* parsimonioso(-a).

economize [ɪ'kɒnəmaɪz] *vi* economizzare, risparmiare.

economy [ɪ'kɒnəmɪ] *n* economia *f.*

economy class *n* classe *f* economica.

economy size *adj* in confezione economica.

ecstasy ['ekstəsɪ] *n (joy)* estasi *f inv;* *(drug)* ecstasy *f.*

ECU ['ekjuː] *n* ECU *m inv.*

eczema ['eksɪmə] *n* eczema *m.*

edge [edʒ] *n* bordo *m;* *(of knife)* taglio *m.*

edible ['edɪbl] *adj* commestibile.

Edinburgh ['edɪnbrə] *n* Edimburgo *f.*

Edinburgh Festival *n:* **the ~** il festival di Edimburgo.

edition [ɪ'dɪʃn] *n* edizione *f;* *(of TV programme)* puntata *f.*

editor ['edɪtər] *n (of newspaper, magazine)* direttore *m* (-trice *f*); *(of book)* curatore *m* (-trice *f*); *(of film, TV programme)* tecnico *m* (-a *f*) del montaggio.

editorial [ˌedɪ'tɔːrɪəl] *n* editoriale *m.*

educate ['edʒʊkeɪt] *vt* istruire.

education [ˌedʒʊ'keɪʃn] *n* istruzione *f.*

EEC n C.E.E. f.

eel [iːl] n anguilla f.

effect [ɪ'fekt] n effetto m; **to put sthg into ~** mettere qc in atto; **to take ~** (drug) fare effetto; (law) entrare in vigore.

effective [ɪ'fektɪv] adj (successful) efficace; (law, system) effettivo(-a).

effectively [ɪ'fektɪvlɪ] adv (successfully) efficacemente; (in fact) effettivamente.

efficient [ɪ'fɪʃənt] adj efficiente.

effort ['efət] n sforzo m; **to make an ~ to do sthg** fare uno sforzo per fare qc; **it's not worth the ~** non ne vale la pena.

e.g. adv ad es.

egg [eg] n uovo m.

egg cup n portauovo m inv.

egg mayonnaise n uova fpl sode in maionese.

eggplant ['egplɑːnt] n (Am) melanzana f.

egg white n albume m.

egg yolk n tuorlo m.

Egypt ['iːdʒɪpt] n l'Egitto m.

eiderdown ['aɪdədaʊn] n piumone® m.

eight [eɪt] num otto, → **six**.

eighteen [ˌeɪ'tiːn] num diciotto, → **six**.

eighteenth [ˌeɪ'tiːnθ] num diciottesimo(-a), → **sixth**.

eighth [eɪtθ] num ottavo(-a), → **sixth**.

eightieth ['eɪtɪθ] num ottantesimo(-a), → **sixth**.

eighty ['eɪtɪ] num ottanta, → **six**.

Eire ['eərə] n la Repubblica d'Irlanda.

Eisteddfod [aɪ'stedfəd] n festival culturale gallese.

either ['aɪðəʳ, 'iːðəʳ] ♦ adj: **~ book will do** va bene sia l'uno che l'altro libro ♦ pron: **I'll take ~ (of them)** prendo o l'uno(-a) o l'altro(-a); **I don't like ~ (of them)** non mi piace né l'uno(-a) né l'altro(-a). ♦ adv: **I can't ~** non posso neanch'io; **~ ... or ...**

o; **on ~ side** su entrambi i lati.

eject [ɪ'dʒekt] vt (cassette) espellere.

elaborate [ɪ'læbrət] adj (needlework, design) elaborato(-a).

elastic [ɪ'læstɪk] n elastico m.

elastic band n (Br) elastico m.

elbow ['elbəʊ] n (of person) gomito m.

elder ['eldəʳ] adj più vecchio(-a), maggiore.

elderly ['eldəlɪ] ♦ adj anziano(-a) ♦ npl: **the ~** gli anziani.

eldest ['eldɪst] adj: **the ~ son/daughter** il figlio/la figlia maggiore.

elect [ɪ'lekt] vt eleggere; **to ~ to do sthg** (fml: choose) scegliere di fare qc.

election [ɪ'lekʃn] n elezione f.

electric [ɪ'lektrɪk] adj elettrico(-a).

electrical goods [ɪ'lektrɪkl-] npl apparecchi mpl elettrici.

electric blanket n coperta f elettrica.

electric drill n trapano m elettrico.

electric fence n recinto m elettrificato.

electrician [ˌɪlek'trɪʃn] n elettricista mf.

electricity [ˌɪlek'trɪsətɪ] n elettricità f.

electric shock n scossa f elettrica.

electrocute [ɪ'lektrəkjuːt] vt fulminare.

electronic [ˌɪlek'trɒnɪk] adj elettronico(-a).

elegant ['elɪgənt] adj elegante.

element ['elɪmənt] n elemento m; (of fire, kettle) resistenza f; **the ~s** (weather) gli elementi.

elementary [ˌelɪ'mentərɪ] adj elementare.

elephant ['elɪfənt] n elefante m.

elevator ['elɪveɪtəʳ] n (Am) ascensore m.

eleven [ɪ'levn] num undici, → **six**.

eleventh [ɪ'levnθ] num undicesimo(-a), → **sixth**.

eligible ['elɪdʒəbl] *adj* che ha i requisiti.

eliminate [ɪ'lɪmɪneɪt] *vt* eliminare.

Elizabethan [ɪˌlɪzə'biːθn] *adj* elisabettiano(-a) *(seconda metà del XVI secolo)*.

elm [elm] *n* olmo *m*.

else [els] *adv*: **I don't want anything ~** non voglio nient'altro; **anything ~?** altro?; **everyone ~** tutti gli altri; **nobody ~** nessun altro; **nothing ~** nient'altro; **somebody ~** qualcun altro; **something ~** qualcos'altro; **somewhere ~** da qualche altra parte; **what ~?** che altro?; **who ~?** chi altri?; **or ~** altrimenti.

elsewhere [els'weər] *adv* altrove.

embankment [ɪm'bæŋkmənt] *n* (*next to river*) argine *m*; (*next to road, railway*) terrapieno *m*.

embark [ɪm'bɑːk] *vi* (*board ship*) imbarcarsi.

embarkation card [ˌembɑː-'keɪʃn-] *n* carta *f* d'imbarco.

embarrass [ɪm'bærəs] *vt* imbarazzare.

embarrassed [ɪm'bærəst] *adj* imbarazzato(-a).

embarrassing [ɪm'bærəsɪŋ] *adj* imbarazzante.

embarrassment [ɪm'bærəsmənt] *n* imbarazzo *m*.

embassy ['embəsɪ] *n* ambasciata *f*.

emblem ['embləm] *n* emblema *m*.

embrace [ɪm'breɪs] *vt* abbracciare.

embroidered [ɪm'brɔɪdəd] *adj* ricamato(-a).

embroidery [ɪm'brɔɪdərɪ] *n* ricamo *m*.

emerald ['emərəld] *n* smeraldo *m*.

emerge [ɪ'mɜːdʒ] *vi* emergere.

emergency [ɪ'mɜːdʒənsɪ] ◆ *n* emergenza *f* ◆ *adj* di emergenza; **in an ~** in caso di emergenza.

emergency exit *n* uscita *f* di sicurezza.

emergency landing *n* atterraggio *m* di emergenza.

emergency services *npl* servizi *mpl* di pronto intervento.

emigrate ['emɪgreɪt] *vi* emigrare.

emigration [ˌemɪ'greɪʃn] *n* emigrazione *f*.

emit [ɪ'mɪt] *vt* emettere.

emotion [ɪ'məʊʃn] *n* emozione *f*.

emotional [ɪ'məʊʃənl] *adj* emotivo(-a).

emphasis ['emfəsɪs] (*pl* **-ases** [-əsiːz]) *n* enfasi *f*; **to put the ~ on** sthg dare importanza a qc.

emphasize ['emfəsaɪz] *vt* sottolineare.

empire ['empaɪər] *n* impero *m*.

employ [ɪm'plɔɪ] *vt* impiegare.

employed [ɪm'plɔɪd] *adj* impiegato(-a).

employee [ɪm'plɔɪiː] *n* dipendente *mf*.

employer [ɪm'plɔɪər] *n* datore *m* (-trice *f*) di lavoro.

employment [ɪm'plɔɪmənt] *n* impiego *m*.

employment agency *n* agenzia *f* di collocamento.

empty ['emptɪ] ◆ *adj* vuoto(-a); (*threat, promise*) vano(-a) ◆ *vt* vuotare.

EMU *n* (*abbr of Economic Monetary Union*) unione *f* economica e monetaria.

emulsion (paint) [ɪ'mʌlʃn-] *n* pittura *f* a emulsione.

enable [ɪ'neɪbl] *vt*: **to ~ sb to do sthg** permettere a qn di fare qc.

enamel [ɪ'næml] *n* smalto *m*.

enclose [ɪn'kləʊz] *vt* (*surround*) cingere, circondare; (*with letter*) allegare.

enclosed [ɪn'kləʊzd] *adj* (*space*) contenuto(-a), limitato(-a).

encounter [ɪn'kaʊntər] *vt* incontrare.

encourage [ɪn'kʌrɪdʒ] *vt* incoraggiare; **to ~ sb to do sthg** incoraggiare qn a fare qc.

encouragement [ɪn'kʌrɪdʒmənt] *n* incoraggiamento *m*.

encyclopedia [ɪnˌsaɪklə'piːdjə] n enciclopedia f.

end [end] ♦ n fine f; (purpose) fine m ♦ vt (story, evening, holiday) finire; (war, practice) finire, mettere fine a ♦ vi finire; **to come to an ~** finire, giungere alla fine; **to put an ~ to sthg** mettere fine a qc; **for days on ~** per giorni e giorni; **in the ~** alla fine; **to make ~s meet** sbarcare il lunario.

▶ **end up** vi finire; **to ~ up doing sthg** finire con il fare qc.

endangered species [ɪn'deɪn-dʒəd-] n specie f inv in via d'estinzione.

ending ['endɪŋ] n (of story, film, book) fine f; (GRAMM) desinenza f.

endive ['endaɪv] n (curly) indivia f (riccia); (chicory) cicoria f.

endless ['endlɪs] adj interminabile, senza fine.

endorsement [ɪn'dɔːsmənt] n (of driving licence) infrazione registrata sulla patente.

endurance [ɪn'djʊərəns] n resistenza f, sopportazione f.

endure [ɪn'djʊər] vt sopportare.

enemy ['enɪmɪ] n nemico m (-a f).

energy ['enədʒɪ] n energia f.

enforce [ɪn'fɔːs] vt (law) applicare, far rispettare.

engaged [ɪn'geɪdʒd] adj (to be married) fidanzato(-a); (Br: phone) occupato(-a); (toilet) occupato(-a); **to get ~** fidanzarsi.

engaged tone n (Br) segnale m di occupato.

engagement [ɪn'geɪdʒmənt] n (to marry) fidanzamento m; (appointment) appuntamento m.

engagement ring n anello m di fidanzamento.

engine ['endʒɪn] n (of vehicle) motore m; (of train) locomotiva f.

engineer [ˌendʒɪ'nɪər] n (of roads, machinery) ingegnere m; (to do repairs) tecnico m (-a f).

engineering [ˌendʒɪ'nɪərɪŋ] n ingegneria f.

engineering works npl (on railway line) lavori mpl in corso.

England ['ɪŋglənd] n l'Inghilterra f.

English ['ɪŋglɪʃ] ♦ adj inglese ♦ n (language) inglese m ♦ npl: **the ~** gli inglesi.

English breakfast n colazione f all'inglese.

English Channel n: **the ~** la Manica.

Englishman ['ɪŋglɪʃmən] (pl **-men** [-mən]) n inglese m.

Englishwoman ['ɪŋglɪʃˌwʊmən] (pl **-women** [-ˌwɪmɪn]) n inglese f.

engrave [ɪn'greɪv] vt incidere.

engraving [ɪn'greɪvɪŋ] n incisione f.

enjoy [ɪn'dʒɔɪ] vt godersi; **to ~ doing sthg** divertirsi a fare qc; **I ~ swimming** mi piace nuotare; **to ~ o.s.** divertirsi; **~ your meal!** buon appetito!

enjoyable [ɪn'dʒɔɪəbl] adj piacevole.

enjoyment [ɪn'dʒɔɪmənt] n piacere m.

enlargement [ɪn'lɑːdʒmənt] n (of photo) ingrandimento m.

enormous [ɪ'nɔːməs] adj enorme.

enough [ɪ'nʌf] ♦ adj abbastanza (inv), sufficiente ♦ pron & adv abbastanza; **~ time** abbastanza tempo; **is that ~?** è abbastanza?, basta?; **it's not big ~** non è abbastanza grande; **to have had ~ (of)** averne abbastanza (di).

enquire [ɪn'kwaɪər] vi informarsi.

enquiry [ɪn'kwaɪərɪ] n (question) domanda f; (investigation) indagine f, inchiesta f; **'Enquiries'** 'Informazioni'.

enquiry desk n banco m informazioni.

enrol [ɪn'rəʊl] vi (Br) iscriversi.

enroll [ɪn'rəʊl] (Am) = **enrol**.

en suite bathroom [ɒn'swiːt] n bagno m privato.

ensure [ɪn'ʃʊər] vt garantire, assicurare.

entail [ɪn'teɪl] vt comportare.

enter ['entər] ♦ vt entrare in; (college, competition) iscriversi a; (on form) scrivere ♦ vi entrare; (in competition) iscriversi.

enterprise ['entəpraɪz] n (company) impresa f; (plan) iniziativa f.

entertain [,entə'teɪn] vt (amuse) divertire.

entertainer [,entə'teɪnər] n intrattenitore m (-trice f).

entertaining [,entə'teɪnɪŋ] adj divertente.

entertainment [,entə'teɪnmənt] n (amusement) divertimento m; (show) spettacolo m.

enthusiasm [ɪn'θjuːzɪæzm] n entusiasmo m.

enthusiast [ɪn'θjuːzɪæst] n appassionato m (-a f).

enthusiastic [ɪn,θjuːzɪ'æstɪk] adj entusiasta.

entire [ɪn'taɪər] adj intero(-a).

entirely [ɪn'taɪəlɪ] adv completamente.

entitle [ɪn'taɪtl] vt: to ~ sb to sthg dare a qn diritto a qc; to ~ sb to do sthg dare diritto a qn di fare qc.

entrance ['entrəns] n entrata f, ingresso m.

entrance fee n biglietto m d'ingresso.

entry ['entrɪ] n (door, gate, admission) entrata f, ingresso m; (in dictionary) voce f; (piece in competition) cosa f presentata; 'no ~' (sign on door) 'ingresso vietato'; (road sign) 'divieto d'accesso'.

envelope ['envələʊp] n busta f.

envious ['envɪəs] adj invidioso(-a).

environment [ɪn'vaɪərənmənt] n ambiente m; the ~ l'ambiente (naturale).

environmental [ɪn,vaɪərən'mentl] adj ambientale.

environmentally friendly [ɪn,vaɪərən'mentəlɪ-] adj che rispetta l'ambiente, ecologico(-a).

envy ['envɪ] vt invidiare.

epic ['epɪk] n epopea f.

epidemic [,epɪ'demɪk] n epidemia f.

epileptic [,epɪ'leptɪk] adj epilettico(-a).

episode ['epɪsəʊd] n episodio m.

equal ['iːkwəl] ♦ adj (of same amount) uguale; (with equal rights) uguale, pari (inv) ♦ vt (number) fare; to be ~ to (number) essere uguale a.

equality [ɪ'kwɒlətɪ] n uguaglianza f.

equalize ['iːkwəlaɪz] vi pareggiare.

equally ['iːkwəlɪ] adv (bad, good, matched) ugualmente; (pay, treat, share) equamente; (at the same time) allo stesso modo.

equation [ɪ'kweɪʒn] n equazione f.

equator [ɪ'kweɪtər] n: the ~ l'equatore m.

equip [ɪ'kwɪp] vt: to ~ sb/sthg with fornire qn/qc di.

equipment [ɪ'kwɪpmənt] n attrezzatura f.

equipped [ɪ'kwɪpt] adj: to be ~ with essere fornito(-a) di.

equivalent [ɪ'kwɪvələnt] ♦ adj equivalente ♦ n equivalente m.

erase [ɪ'reɪz] vt (letter, word) cancellare.

eraser [ɪ'reɪzər] n gomma f.

erect [ɪ'rekt] ♦ adj (person, posture) eretto(-a) ♦ vt (tent) montare; (monument) erigere.

ERM n meccanismo m di cambio (dello SME).

erotic [ɪ'rɒtɪk] adj erotico(-a).

errand ['erənd] n commissione f.

erratic [ɪ'rætɪk] adj irregolare, incostante.

error ['erər] n errore m.

escalator ['eskəleɪtər] n scala f mobile.

escalope ['eskəlɒp] n cotoletta f alla milanese.

escape [ɪ'skeɪp] ♦ n fuga f ♦ vi: to ~ (from) (from prison) evadere (da); (from danger) fuggire (da); (leak) fuoriuscire (da).

escort [n 'eskɔːt, vb ɪ'skɔːt] ◆ n (guard) scorta f ◆ vt accompagnare.

espadrilles ['espəˌdrɪlz] npl espadrilles fpl.

especially [ɪ'speʃəlɪ] adv (in particular) specialmente, soprattutto; (on purpose) apposta; (very) particolarmente.

esplanade [ˌesplə'neɪd] n passeggiata f (a mare).

essay ['eseɪ] n (at school, university) composizione f, tema m.

essential [ɪ'senʃl] adj (indispensable) essenziale.

▶ **essentials** npl: **the ~s** l'essenziale m; **the bare ~s** il minimo indispensabile.

essentially [ɪ'senʃəlɪ] adv essenzialmente.

establish [ɪ'stæblɪʃ] vt (set up, create) fondare; (fact, truth) stabilire.

establishment [ɪ'stæblɪʃmənt] n (business) azienda f.

estate [ɪ'steɪt] n (land in country) proprietà f inv; (for housing) complesso m residenziale; (Br: car) = **estate car**.

estate agent n (Br) agente mf immobiliare.

estate car n (Br) station wagon f inv.

estimate [n 'estɪmət, vb 'estɪmeɪt] ◆ n (guess) stima f; (from builder, plumber) preventivo m ◆ vt stimare, valutare.

estuary ['estjuərɪ] n estuario m.

ethnic minority [ˌeθnɪk-] n minoranza f etnica.

EU n (abbr of European Union) U.E. f.

euphemism ['juːfəmɪzm] n eufemismo m.

Eurocheque ['juərəʊˌtʃek] n eurochèque m inv.

Europe ['juərəp] n l'Europa f.

European [ˌjuərə'pɪən] ◆ adj europeo(-a) ◆ n europeo m (-a f).

European Community n Comunità f Europea.

evacuate [ɪ'vækjueɪt] vt evacuare.

evade [ɪ'veɪd] vt (person, issue) evitare; (responsibility) sottrarsi a.

evaporated milk [ɪ'væpəreɪtɪd-] n latte m concentrato.

eve [iːv] n: **on the ~ of** alla vigilia di.

even ['iːvn] ◆ adj (uniform, equal) regolare, uniforme; (level, flat) liscio(-a), piano(-a); (contest) alla pari; (number) pari (inv) ◆ adv perfino, anche; **to break ~** fare pari; **not ~** nemmeno; **so ~** ciò nonostante; **~ though** anche se.

evening ['iːvnɪŋ] n sera f; (event, period) serata f; **good ~!** buona sera!; **in the ~** di or la sera.

evening classes npl corsi mpl serali.

evening dress n (formal clothes) abito m da sera; (woman's garment) vestito m da sera.

evening meal n cena f.

event [ɪ'vent] n (occurrence) evento m, avvenimento m; (SPORT) prova f; **in the ~ of** (fml) in caso di.

eventual [ɪ'ventʃuəl] adj finale.

eventually [ɪ'ventʃuəlɪ] adv alla fine.

ever ['evər] adv mai; **it's the worst ~** è il peggiore che sia mai esistito; **he was ~ so angry** era veramente arrabbiato; **for ~** (eternally) per sempre; **we've been waiting for ~** aspettiamo da tantissimo; **hardly ~** quasi mai.

▶ **ever since** ◆ adv fin da allora ◆ prep da … in poi ◆ conj fin da quando.

every ['evrɪ] adj ogni (inv); **~ day** ogni giorno, tutti i giorni; **~ other day** ogni due giorni; **one in ~ ten** uno su dieci; **we make ~ effort …** facciamo ogni sforzo …; **~ so often** ogni tanto.

everybody ['evrɪˌbɒdɪ] = **everyone**.

everyday ['evrɪdeɪ] adj di ogni giorno, quotidiano(-a).

everyone ['evrɪwʌn] pron ognuno m (-a f), tutti mpl (-e fpl).

everyplace ['evrɪˌpleɪs] (Am) = **everywhere**.

everything ['evrɪθɪŋ] *pron* tutto, ogni cosa.

everywhere ['evrɪweəʳ] *adv* dappertutto; (*wherever*) dovunque.

evidence ['evɪdəns] *n* (*proof*) prova *f*; (*legal statement*) testimonianza *f*.

evident ['evɪdənt] *adj* evidente.

evidently ['evɪdəntlɪ] *adv* evidentemente.

evil ['iːvl] ◆ *adj* cattivo(-a), malvagio(-a) ◆ *n* male *m*.

ex [eks] *n* (*inf: wife, husband, partner*) ex *mf*.

exact [ɪg'zækt] *adj* esatto(-a); '**~ fare ready please'** 'si prega di munirsi dell'esatta somma per il biglietto'.

exactly [ɪg'zæktlɪ] *adv & excl* esattamente.

exaggerate [ɪg'zædʒəreɪt] *vt & vi* esagerare.

exaggeration [ɪgˌzædʒə'reɪʃn] *n* esagerazione *f*.

exam [ɪg'zæm] *n* esame *m*; **to take an ~** fare un esame.

examination [ɪgˌzæmɪ'neɪʃn] *n* esame *m*; (MED) visita *f*.

examine [ɪg'zæmɪn] *vt* esaminare; (MED) visitare.

example [ɪg'zɑːmpl] *n* esempio *m*; **for ~** per esempio.

exceed [ɪk'siːd] *vt* (*be greater than*) superare; (*go beyond*) oltrepassare.

excellent ['eksələnt] *adj* eccellente.

except [ɪk'sept] *prep & conj* eccetto, tranne; **~ for** a parte, all'infuori di; '**~ for access**' 'escluso residenti'; '**~ for loading**' 'escluso (per le operazioni di) carico'.

exception [ɪk'sepʃn] *n* (*thing excepted*) eccezione *f*.

exceptional [ɪk'sepʃnəl] *adj* eccezionale.

excerpt ['eksɜːpt] *n* estratto *m*.

excess [ɪk'ses, ◆ *before nouns* 'ekses] *adj* in eccesso ◆ *n* eccesso *m*.

excess baggage *n* bagaglio *m* in eccedenza.

excess fare *n* (Br) supplemento *m*.

excessive [ɪk'sesɪv] *adj* eccessivo(-a).

exchange [ɪks'tʃeɪndʒ] ◆ *n* (*of telephones*) centralino *m*; (*of students*) scambio *m* ◆ *vt* scambiare; **to ~ sthg for sthg** scambiare qc con qc; **we're here on an ~** siamo qui con uno scambio.

exchange rate *n* tasso *m* di cambio.

excited [ɪk'saɪtɪd] *adj* eccitato(-a).

excitement [ɪk'saɪtmənt] *n* eccitazione *f*; (*exciting thing*) cosa *f* eccitante.

exciting [ɪk'saɪtɪŋ] *adj* eccitante, emozionante.

exclamation mark [ˌekskləˈmeɪʃn-] *n* (Br) punto *m* esclamativo.

exclamation point [ˌekskləˈmeɪʃn-] (Am) = **exclamation mark**.

exclude [ɪk'skluːd] *vt* escludere.

excluding [ɪk'skluːdɪŋ] *prep* escluso(-a).

exclusive [ɪk'skluːsɪv] ◆ *adj* esclusivo(-a) ◆ *n* esclusiva *f*; **~ of** escluso(-a).

excruciating [ɪk'skruːʃɪeɪtɪŋ] *adj* straziante.

excursion [ɪk'skɜːʃn] *n* escursione *f*.

excuse [*n* ɪk'skjuːs, *vb* ɪk'skjuːz] ◆ *n* scusa *f* ◆ *vt* (*forgive*) scusare; (*let off*) dispensare; **~ me!** mi scusi!

ex-directory *adj* (Br) fuori elenco.

execute ['eksɪkjuːt] *vt* (*kill*) giustiziare.

executive [ɪg'zekjʊtɪv] ◆ *adj* (*room*) per dirigenti ◆ *n* (*person*) dirigente *mf*.

exempt [ɪg'zempt] *adj:* **~ (from)** esente (da).

exemption [ɪg'zempʃn] *n* esenzione *f*.

exercise ['eksəsaɪz] ◆ n esercizio m ◆ vi fare esercizio OR del moto; **to do ~s** fare degli esercizi.

exercise book n quaderno m.

exert [ɪg'zɜːt] vt esercitare.

exhaust [ɪg'zɔːst] ◆ vt esaurire ◆ n: ~ **(pipe)** tubo m di scappamento.

exhausted [ɪg'zɔːstɪd] adj esausto(-a).

exhibit [ɪg'zɪbɪt] ◆ n (in museum, gallery) oggetto m esposto ◆ vt (in exhibition) esporre.

exhibition [ˌeksɪ'bɪʃn] n (of art) esposizione f, mostra f.

exist [ɪg'zɪst] vi esistere.

existence [ɪg'zɪstəns] n esistenza f; **to be in ~** esistere.

existing [ɪg'zɪstɪŋ] adj esistente.

exit ['eksɪt] ◆ n uscita f ◆ vi uscire.

exotic [ɪg'zɒtɪk] adj esotico(-a).

expand [ɪk'spænd] vi (in size) espandersi; (in number) aumentare.

expect [ɪk'spekt] vt (believe likely) aspettarsi, prevedere; (await) aspettare; **to ~ to do sthg** prevedere di fare qc; **to ~ sb to do sthg** (require) aspettarsi che qn faccia qc; **to be ~ing** (be pregnant) aspettare un bambino.

expedition [ˌekspɪ'dɪʃn] n spedizione f; (short outing) gita f.

expel [ɪk'spel] vt (from school) espellere.

expense [ɪk'spens] n spesa f, costo m; **at the ~ of** (fig) a spese di. ▶ **expenses** npl (of business trip) spese fpl.

expensive [ɪk'spensɪv] adj costoso(-a), caro(-a).

experience [ɪk'spɪərɪəns] ◆ n esperienza f ◆ vt provare.

experienced [ɪk'spɪərɪənst] adj esperto(-a).

experiment [ɪk'sperɪmənt] ◆ n esperimento m ◆ vi fare esperimenti.

expert ['ekspɜːt] ◆ adj (advice) esperto(-a); (treatment) apposi-

to(-a) ◆ n esperto m (-a f).

expire [ɪk'spaɪəʳ] vi scadere.

expiry date [ɪk'spaɪərɪ-] n data f di scadenza.

explain [ɪk'spleɪn] vt spiegare.

explanation [ˌeksplə'neɪʃn] n spiegazione f.

explode [ɪk'spləʊd] vi (bomb) esplodere.

exploit [ɪk'splɔɪt] vt (person) sfruttare.

explore [ɪk'splɔːʳ] vt (place) esplorare.

explosion [ɪk'spləʊʒn] n (of bomb etc) esplosione f.

explosive [ɪk'spləʊsɪv] n esplosivo m.

export [n 'ekspɔːt, vb ɪk'spɔːt] ◆ n (of goods) esportazione f; (goods themselves) merce f d'esportazione ◆ vt esportare.

exposed [ɪk'spəʊzd] adj (place) non riparato(-a).

exposure [ɪk'spəʊʒəʳ] n (photograph) foto f inv; (MED) assideramento m; (to heat, radiation) esposizione f.

express [ɪk'spres] ◆ adj (letter, delivery, train) espresso(-a) ◆ n (train) espresso m ◆ vt esprimere ◆ adv per espresso.

expression [ɪk'spreʃn] n espressione f.

expresso [ɪk'spresəʊ] (pl **-s**) n espresso m.

expressway [ɪk'spresweɪ] n (Am) autostrada f (urbana).

extend [ɪk'stend] ◆ vt prolungare; (hand) offrire ◆ vi estendersi.

extension [ɪk'stenʃn] n (of building) sala f annessa; (for phone at work) interno m; (for phone in private house) apparecchio m supplementare; (for permit, essay) proroga f.

extension lead n prolunga f.

extensive [ɪk'stensɪv] adj (area) esteso(-a), ampio(-a); (damage) grave; (selection) ampio.

extent [ɪk'stent] n (of damage,

knowledge) estensione *f;* **to a certain ~** fino ad un certo punto; **to what ~ ...?** fino a che punto ...?

exterior [ɪk'stɪərɪəʳ] ♦ *adj* esterno(-a) ♦ *n (of car, building)* esterno *m.*

external [ɪk'stɜːnl] *adj* esterno(-a).

extinct [ɪk'stɪŋkt] *adj* estinto(-a).

extinction [ɪk'stɪŋkʃn] *n* estinzione *f.*

extinguish [ɪk'stɪŋgwɪʃ] *vt (fire, cigarette)* spegnere.

extinguisher [ɪk'stɪŋgwɪʃəʳ] *n* estintore *m.*

extortionate [ɪk'stɔːʃnət] *adj* esorbitante.

extra ['ekstrə] ♦ *adj (additional)* extra *(inv),* supplementare; *(spare)* altro(-a), in più ♦ *n* extra *m inv* ♦ *adv (especially)* eccezionalmente; *(more)* di più; **~ charge** supplemento *m;* **~ large** extra-large *(inv).*

▶ **extras** *npl (in price)* spese *fpl* supplementari.

extract [*n* 'ekstrækt, *vb* ɪk'strækt] ♦ *n (of yeast, malt etc)* estratto *m;* *(from book, opera)* brano *m* ♦ *vt (tooth)* estrarre.

extractor fan [ɪk'stræktə-] *n (Br)* aspiratore *m.*

extraordinary [ɪk'strɔːdnrɪ] *adj* straordinario(-a).

extravagant [ɪk'strævəgənt] *adj* dispendioso(-a).

extreme [ɪk'striːm] ♦ *adj* estremo(-a) ♦ *n* estremo *m.*

extremely [ɪk'striːmlɪ] *adv* estremamente.

extrovert ['ekstrəvɜːt] *n* estroverso *m (-a f).*

eye [aɪ] ♦ *n* occhio *m;* *(of needle)* cruna *f* ♦ *vt* osservare attentamente; **to keep an ~ on** tenere d'occhio.

eyebrow ['aɪbraʊ] *n* sopracciglio *m.*

eye drops *npl* collirio *m,* gocce *fpl* per gli occhi.

eyeglasses ['aɪglɑːsɪz] *npl (Am)* occhiali *mpl.*

eyelash ['aɪlæʃ] *n* ciglio *m.*

eyelid ['aɪlɪd] *n* palpebra *f.*

eyeliner ['aɪˌlaɪnəʳ] *n* eye-liner *m inv.*

eye shadow *n* ombretto *m.*

eyesight ['aɪsaɪt] *n* vista *f.*

eye test *n* esame *m* oculistico.

eyewitness [ˌaɪ'wɪtnɪs] *n* testimone *mf* oculare.

F

F *(abbr of Fahrenheit)* F.

fabric ['fæbrɪk] *n (cloth)* stoffa *f,* tessuto *m.*

fabulous ['fæbjʊləs] *adj* favoloso(-a).

facade [fə'sɑːd] *n* facciata *f.*

face [feɪs] ♦ *n* faccia *f;* *(of cliff, mountain)* parete *f;* *(of clock, watch)* quadrante *m* ♦ *vt* essere di fronte a; *(accept, cope with)* affrontare; **to be ~d with** avere di fronte.

▶ **face up to** *vt fus* affrontare.

facecloth ['feɪsklɒθ] *n (Br)* panno *m* di spugna.

facial ['feɪʃl] *n* trattamento *m* del viso.

facilitate [fə'sɪlɪteɪt] *vt (fml)* facilitare.

facilities [fə'sɪlɪtiːz] *npl* attrezzature *fpl.*

facsimile [fæk'sɪmɪlɪ] *n* facsimile *m inv.*

fact [fækt] *n* fatto *m;* **in ~** in effetti.

factor ['fæktəʳ] *n* fattore *m;* **~ ten suntan lotion** crema *f* abbronzante a fattore di protezione dieci.

factory ['fæktərɪ] *n* fabbrica *f.*

faculty ['fækltɪ] *n* facoltà *f inv.*

FA Cup *n* ≃ coppa *f* Italia *(di calcio).*

fade [feɪd] *vi (light, sound)* affievolirsi; (*flower*) appassire; (*jeans, wallpaper*) sbiadire, sbiadirsi.

faded ['feɪdɪd] *adj* (*jeans*) sbiadito(-a).

fag [fæg] *n* (Br: *inf*: *cigarette*) sigaretta *f*.

Fahrenheit ['færənhaɪt] *adj* Fahrenheit (*inv*).

fail [feɪl] ◆ *vt* (*exam*) non superare ◆ *vi* fallire; (*in exam*) essere bocciato; (*engine*) guastarsi; **to ~ to do sthg** (*not do*) non fare qc.

failing ['feɪlɪŋ] ◆ *n* difetto *m* ◆ *prep*: **~ that** se no.

failure ['feɪljər] *n* fallimento *m*; (*unsuccessful person*) fallito *m* (-a *f*); (*act of neglecting*) mancanza *f*.

faint [feɪnt] ◆ *vi* svenire ◆ *adj* debole; (*outline*) indistinto(-a); **I haven't the ~est idea** non ho la più pallida idea.

fair [feər] ◆ *adj* (*just*) giusto(-a), equo(-a); (*quite large, quite good*) discreto(-a); (*hair, person*) biondo(-a); (*skin*) chiaro(-a); (*weather*) bello(-a) ◆ *n* (*funfair*) luna park *m inv*; (*trade fair*) fiera *f*; **~ enough!** mi sembra giusto!

fairground ['feəgraʊnd] *n* luna park *m inv*.

fair-haired [-'heəd] *adj* biondo(-a).

fairly ['feəlɪ] *adv* (*quite*) abbastanza.

fairy ['feərɪ] *n* fata *f*.

fairy tale *n* fiaba *f*.

faith [feɪθ] *n* fede *f*.

faithfully ['feɪθfʊlɪ] *adv*: **Yours ~** Distinti saluti.

fake [feɪk] ◆ *n* (*painting etc*) falso *m* ◆ *vt* (*signature, painting*) falsificare.

fall [fɔːl] (*pt* **fell**, *pp* **fallen** ['fɔːln]) ◆ *vi* cadere; (*number, pound, night*) scendere ◆ *n* caduta *f*; (*decrease*) abbassamento *m*; (Am: *autumn*) autunno *m*; **to ~ asleep** addormentarsi; **to ~ ill** ammalarsi; **to ~ in love** innamorarsi.

▶ **falls** *npl* (*waterfall*) cascate *fpl*.

▶ **fall behind** *vi* (*with work, rent*) rimanere indietro.

▶ **fall down** *vi* (*lose balance*) cadere.

▶ **fall off** *vi* cadere.

▶ **fall out** *vi* (*hair, teeth*) cadere; (*argue*) litigare.

▶ **fall over** *vi* cadere per terra.

▶ **fall through** *vi* fallire.

false [fɔːls] *adj* falso(-a).

false alarm *n* falso allarme *m*.

false teeth *npl* dentiera *f*.

fame [feɪm] *n* fama *f*.

familiar [fə'mɪljər] *adj* (*known*) familiare; (*informal*) (troppo) confidenziale; **to be ~ with** (*know*) conoscere.

family ['fæmlɪ] ◆ *n* famiglia *f* ◆ *adj* (*size*) familiare, da famiglia; (*film, holiday*) per famiglie.

family planning clinic [-'plænɪŋ-] *n* ≃ consultorio *m* familiare.

family room *n* (*at hotel*) camera *f* familiare; (*at pub, airport*) sala *f* per famiglie con bambini.

famine ['fæmɪn] *n* carestia *f*.

famished ['fæmɪʃt] *adj* (*inf*) molto affamato(-a).

famous ['feɪməs] *adj* famoso(-a).

fan [fæn] *n* (*held in hand*) ventaglio *m*; (*electric*) ventilatore *m*; (*enthusiast*) ammiratore *m* (-trice *f*); (*supporter*) tifoso *m* (-a *f*).

fan belt *n* cinghia *f* del ventilatore.

fancy ['fænsɪ] ◆ *vt* (*inf*: *feel like*) avere voglia di ◆ *adj* (*elaborate*) ricercato(-a); **I ~ her** (*inf*) mi piace; **~ (that)!** pensa un po'!

fancy dress *n* costume *m* (per maschera).

fan heater *n* stufa *f* elettrica con ventilatore.

fanlight ['fænlaɪt] *n* (Br) lunetta *f*.

fantastic [fæn'tæstɪk] *adj* fantastico(-a).

fantasy ['fæntəsɪ] *n* (*imagined thing*) fantasia *f*.

fantasy football *n* fantacalcio *m*.

far [fɑ:r] (*compar* **further** OR **farther,** *superl* **furthest** OR **farthest**) ♦ *adv* lontano; (*in degree*) molto, assai ♦ *adj* **at the ~ end (of)** in fondo (a); **how ~ is it (to London)?** quanto è lontano (da Londra)?; **as ~ as** (*place*) fino a; **as ~ as I'm concerned** per quanto mi riguarda; **as ~ as I know** per quel che ne so; **~ better** assai migliore; **by ~** di gran lunga; **so ~** (*until now*) finora; **to go too ~** (*behave unacceptably*) oltrepassare i limiti.

farce [fɑ:s] *n* (*ridiculous situation*) farsa *f*.

fare [feər] ♦ *n* (*on bus, train etc*) tariffa *f*; (*fml: food*) cibo *m* ♦ *vi* passarsela.

Far East *n*: **the ~** l'Estremo Oriente *m*.

fare stage *n* (Br) *fermata di autobus dove il prezzo del biglietto cambia*.

farm [fɑ:m] *n* fattoria *f*.

farmer [ˈfɑ:mər] *n* agricoltore *m*.

farmhouse [ˈfɑ:mhaʊs, *pl* -haʊzɪz] *n* casa *f* colonica.

farming [ˈfɑ:mɪŋ] *n* agricoltura *f*; (*of animals*) allevamento *m*.

farmland [ˈfɑ:mlænd] *n* terreno *m* coltivabile.

farmyard [ˈfɑ:mjɑ:d] *n* aia *f*.

farther [ˈfɑ:ðər] → **far**.

farthest [ˈfɑ:ðəst] → **far**.

fascinating [ˈfæsɪneɪtɪŋ] *adj* affascinante.

fascination [ˌfæsɪˈneɪʃn] *n* fascino *m*.

fashion [ˈfæʃn] *n* moda *f*; (*manner*) modo *m*, maniera *f*; **to be in ~** essere di moda; **to be out of ~** essere fuori moda.

fashionable [ˈfæʃnəbl] *adj* di moda, alla moda.

fashion show *n* sfilata *f* di moda.

fast [fɑ:st] ♦ *adv* (*quickly*) velocemente, rapidamente; (*securely*) saldamente ♦ *adj* veloce, rapido(-a); **to be ~** (*clock*) andare avanti; **~ asleep** profondamente addormentato; **a ~ train** un treno diretto.

fasten [ˈfɑ:sn] *vt* (*belt*) allacciare; (*coat*) abbottonare; (*two things*) fissare.

fastener [ˈfɑ:snər] *n* chiusura *f*, fermaglio *m*.

fast food *n*: **~ outlet** fast food *m inv*.

fat [fæt] ♦ *adj* grasso(-a) ♦ *n* grasso *m*.

fatal [ˈfeɪtl] *adj* (*accident, disease*) mortale.

father [ˈfɑ:ðər] *n* padre *m*.

Father Christmas *n* (Br) Babbo *m* Natale.

father-in-law *n* suocero *m*.

fattening [ˈfætnɪŋ] *adj* che fa ingrassare.

fatty [ˈfætɪ] *adj* grasso(-a).

faucet [ˈfɔ:sɪt] *n* (Am) rubinetto *m*.

fault [fɔ:lt] *n* (*responsibility*) colpa *f*; (*flaw*) difetto *m*; (*in machine*) guasto *m*; **it's your ~** è colpa tua.

faulty [ˈfɔ:ltɪ] *adj* difettoso(-a).

favor [ˈfeɪvər] (Am) = **favour**.

favour [ˈfeɪvər] ♦ *n* (Br: *kind act*) favore *m* ♦ *vt* (*prefer*) preferire; **to be in ~ of** essere in favore di; **to do sb a ~** fare un favore a qn.

favourable [ˈfeɪvrəbl] *adj* favorevole.

favourite [ˈfeɪvrɪt] ♦ *adj* favorito(-a) ♦ *n* favorito *m* (-a *f*).

fawn [fɔ:n] *adj* fulvo chiaro (*inv*).

fax [fæks] ♦ *n* fax *m inv* ♦ *vt* (*document*) inviare per fax, faxare; (*person*) inviare un fax a.

fax modem *n* modem-fax *m inv*.

fear [fɪər] ♦ *n* paura *f* ♦ *vt* (*be afraid of*) avere paura di, temere; **for ~ of** per paura di.

feast [fi:st] *n* (*meal*) banchetto *m*.

feather [ˈfeðər] *n* penna *f*, piuma *f*.

feature [ˈfi:tʃər] ♦ *n* (*characteristic*) caratteristica *f*; (*in newspaper, on radio, TV*) servizio *m* (speciale) ♦ *vt* (*subj: film*) avere come protagonista; **~s** (*of face*) lineamenti *mpl*.

feature film *n* lungometraggio *m*.

Feb. (*abbr of February*) feb.
February ['februǝri] *n* febbraio *m*,
→ **September**.
fed [fed] *pp* → **feed**.
fed up *adj* stufo(-a); **to be ~ with** essere stufo di.
fee [fiː] *n* pagamento *m*; (*of doctor, lawyer*) onorario *m*.
feeble ['fiːbǝl] *adj* debole.
feed [fiːd] (*pt & pp* **fed**) *vt* (*person, animal*) dare da mangiare a; (*baby*) allattare; (*insert*) immettere.
feel [fiːl] (*pt & pp* **felt**) ◆ *vt* (*touch*) tastare, toccare; (*experience*) sentire; (*think*) credere, pensare ◆ *vi* sentirsi; (*seem*) essere ◆ *n* (*of material*): **I like the ~ of it** è piacevole al tatto; **to ~ cold/hungry** avere freddo/fame; **to ~ like** (*fancy*) avere voglia di; **to ~ up to doing sthg** sentirsela di fare qc.
feeling ['fiːlɪŋ] *n* (*emotion*) sentimento *m*; (*sensation*) sensazione *f*; (*belief*) opinione *f*; **to hurt sb's ~s** ferire i sentimenti di qn.
feet [fiːt] → **foot**.
fell [fel] ◆ *pt* → **fall** ◆ *vt* (*tree*) abbattere.
fellow ['felǝu] ◆ *n* (*man*) tipo *m*, individuo *m* ◆ *adj*: **my ~ students** i miei compagni di classe.
felt [felt] ◆ *pt & pp* → **feel** ◆ *n* feltro *m*.
felt-tip pen *n* pennarello *m*.
female ['fiːmeɪl] ◆ *adj* femminile; (*child, animal*) femmina ◆ *n* (*animal*) femmina *f*.
feminine ['feminin] *adj* femminile.
feminist ['feminist] *n* femminista *mf*.
fence [fens] *n* recinto *m*.
fencing ['fensɪŋ] *n* (SPORT) scherma *f*.
fend [fend] *vi*: **to ~ for o.s.** provvedere a se stesso.
fender ['fendǝr] *n* (*for fireplace*) parafuoco *m*; (*Am: on car*) parafango *m*.
fennel ['fenl] *n* finocchio *m*.

fern [fɜːn] *n* felce *f*.
ferocious [fǝ'rǝuʃǝs] *adj* feroce.
ferry ['feri] *n* traghetto *m*.
fertile ['fɜːtaɪl] *adj* (*land*) fertile.
fertilizer ['fɜːtɪlaɪzǝr] *n* fertilizzante *m*.
festival ['festǝvl] *n* (*of music, arts etc*) festival *m inv*; (*holiday*) festa *f*.
feta cheese ['fetǝ-] *n* formaggio *bianco di latte di pecora di origine greca*.
fetch [fetʃ] *vt* andare a prendere; (*be sold for*) essere venduto per.
fete [feɪt] *n* festa *f* all'aperto (*a scopo di beneficenza*).
fever ['fiːvǝr] *n* (MED) febbre *f*; **to have a ~** avere la febbre.
feverish ['fiːvǝrɪʃ] *adj* (*having a fever*) febbricitante.
few [fjuː] ◆ *adj* pochi(-e); ◆ *pron* pochi *mpl* (-e *fpl*).
▶ **a few** ◆ *adj* qualche (*inv*) ◆ *pron* alcuni *mpl* (-e *fpl*); **quite a ~** parecchi.
fewer ['fjuːǝr] *adj & pron* meno (*inv*).
fiancé [fɪ'ɒnseɪ] *n* fidanzato *m*.
fiancée [fɪ'ɒnseɪ] *n* fidanzata *f*.
fib [fɪb] *n* (*inf*) (piccola) bugia *f*.
fiber ['faɪbǝr] (Am) = **fibre**.
fibre ['faɪbǝr] *n* fibra *f*.
fibreglass ['faɪbǝglɑːs] *n* fibra *f* di vetro.
fickle ['fɪkl] *adj* incostante, volubile.
fiction ['fɪkʃn] *n* narrativa *f*.
fiddle ['fɪdl] ◆ *n* (*violin*) violino *m* ◆ *vi*: **to ~ with sthg** giocherellare con qc.
fidget ['fɪdʒɪt] *vi* agitarsi.
field [fiːld] *n* campo *m*.
field glasses *npl* binocolo *m*.
fierce [fɪǝs] *adj* feroce; (*storm, heat*) violento(-a).
fifteen [fɪf'tiːn] *num* quindici, → **six**.
fifteenth [fɪf'tiːnθ] *num* quindicesimo(-a), → **sixth**.

fifth [fɪfθ] *num* quinto(-a), → **sixth**.

fiftieth ['fɪftɪəθ] *num* cinquantesimo(-a), → **sixth**.

fifty ['fɪftɪ] *num* cinquanta, → **six**.

fig [fɪg] *n* fico *m*.

fight [faɪt] (*pt & pp* **fought**) ♦ *n* rissa *f*; (*argument*) lite *f*; (*struggle*) lotta *f* ♦ *vt* combattere; (*person*) azzuffarsi con ♦ *vi* (*physically*) combattere; (*quarrel*) litigare; (*struggle*) lottare; **to have a ~ with sb** fare a pugni con qn.

▸ **fight back** *vi* difendersi.

▸ **fight off** *vt sep* (*attacker*) respingere; (*illness*) vincere.

fighting ['faɪtɪŋ] *n* combattimento *m*.

figure [Br 'fɪgər, Am 'fɪgjər] *n* figura *f*; (*number, statistic*) cifra *f*.

▸ **figure out** *vt sep* riuscire a capire.

file [faɪl] ♦ *n* (*folder*) cartella *f*; (*box*) schedario *m*; (*information on person*) scheda *f*; (COMPUT) file *m inv*; (*tool*) lima *f* ♦ *vt* (*complaint, petition*) presentare; (*nails*) limare; **in single ~** in fila indiana.

filing cabinet ['faɪlɪŋ-] *n* schedario *m*.

fill [fɪl] *vt* riempire; (*role*) ricoprire; (*tooth*) otturare.

▸ **fill in** *vt sep* (*form*) riempire.

▸ **fill out** = **fill in**.

▸ **fill up** *vt sep* riempire; **~ her up!** (*with petrol*) il pieno, per favore!

filled roll ['fɪld-] *n* panino *m* imbottito.

fillet ['fɪlɪt] *n* filetto *m*.

fillet steak *n* bistecca *f* di filetto.

filling ['fɪlɪŋ] ♦ *n* (*of cake, sandwich*) ripieno *m*; (*in tooth*) otturazione *f* ♦ *adj*: **it's very ~** sazia molto.

filling station *n* stazione *f* di servizio.

film [fɪlm] ♦ *n* (*at cinema*) film *m inv*; (*for camera*) pellicola *f* ♦ *vt* filmare.

film star *n* divo *m* (-a *f*) del cinema.

filter ['fɪltər] *n* filtro *m*.

filthy ['fɪlθɪ] *adj* sudicio(-a).

fin [fɪn] *n* pinna *f*.

final ['faɪnl] ♦ *adj* ultimo(-a); (*decision*) definitivo(-a) ♦ *n* finale *f*.

finalist ['faɪnəlɪst] *n* finalista *mf*.

finally ['faɪnəlɪ] *adv* (*at last*) finalmente; (*lastly*) infine.

finance [*n* 'faɪnæns, *vb* faɪ'næns] ♦ *n* (*money*) finanziamento *m*; (*profession*) finanza *f* ♦ *vt* finanziare.

▸ **finances** *npl* finanze *fpl*.

financial [fɪ'nænʃl] *adj* finanziario(-a).

find [faɪnd] (*pt & pp* **found**) ♦ *vt* trovare; (*find out*) scoprire ♦ *n* scoperta *f*; **to ~ the time to do sthg** trovare il tempo di fare qc.

▸ **find out** ♦ *vt sep* (*fact, truth*) scoprire ♦ *vi*: **to ~ out (about sthg)** (*learn*) scoprire (qc); (*get information*) informarsi (su qc).

fine [faɪn] ♦ *adv* (*thinly*) finemente; (*well*) bene ♦ *n* multa *f* ♦ *vt* multare ♦ *adj* (*good*) buono(-a); (*weather, day*) bello(-a); (*thin*) sottile; **it's ~** (*satisfactory*) va bene; **I'm ~** (*in health*) sto bene.

fine art *n* belle arti *fpl*.

finger ['fɪŋgər] *n* dito *m*.

fingernail ['fɪŋgəneɪl] *n* unghia *f*.

fingertip ['fɪŋgətɪp] *n* polpastrello *m*.

finish ['fɪnɪʃ] ♦ *n* fine *f*; (*on furniture*) finitura *f* ♦ *vt & vi* finire; **to ~ doing sthg** finire di fare qc.

▸ **finish off** *vt sep* finire; **finish up** *vi* finire; **to ~ up doing sthg** finire a fare qc.

Finland ['fɪnlənd] *n* la Finlandia.

Finn [fɪn] *n* finlandese *mf*.

Finnan haddock ['fɪnən-] *n* (*Scot*) eglefino *m* affumicato (*tipico della Scozia*).

Finnish ['fɪnɪʃ] ♦ *adj* finlandese ♦ *n* (*language*) finlandese *m*.

fir [fɜːr] *n* abete *m*.

fire ['faɪər] ♦ *n* fuoco *m*; (*uncontrolled*) incendio *m*; (*device*) stufa *f*

♦ vt (from job) licenziare; **to ~ a gun** sparare; **on ~** in fiamme; **to catch ~** prendere fuoco; **to make a ~** accendere un fuoco.

fire alarm n allarme m antincendio.

fire brigade n (Br) vigili mpl del fuoco.

fire department (Am) = **fire brigade**.

fire engine n autopompa f.

fire escape n scala f antincendio.

fire exit n uscita f di sicurezza.

fire extinguisher n estintore m.

fire hazard n: **it's a ~** rappresenta un pericolo di incendio.

fireman ['faɪəmən] (pl -**men** [-mən]) n vigile m del fuoco.

fireplace ['faɪəpleɪs] n caminetto m.

fire regulations npl norme fpl antincendio.

fire station n caserma f dei vigili del fuoco.

firewood ['faɪəwʊd] n legna f da ardere.

firework display ['faɪəwɜːk-] n fuochi mpl d'artificio.

fireworks ['faɪəwɜːks] npl (rockets) fuochi mpl d'artificio.

firm [fɜːm] ♦ adj (fruit) sodo(-a); (mattress) duro(-a); (structure) solido(-a); (grip) saldo(-a); (decision, belief) fermo(-a) ♦ n ditta f.

first [fɜːst] ♦ adj primo(-a) ♦ adv prima; (for the first time) per la prima volta ♦ n (event) novità f inv ♦ pron: **the ~** il primo (la prima); **~ (gear)** prima f; **~ thing (in the morning)** per prima cosa; **for the ~ time** per la prima volta; **the ~ of January** il primo gennaio; **at ~** dapprima; **~ of all** prima di tutto.

first aid n pronto soccorso m.

first-aid kit n cassetta f del pronto soccorso.

first class n (mail) posta celere, di solito consegnata entro uno o due giorni; (on train, plane, ship) prima classe f.

first-class adj (stamp) per consegna celere; (ticket) di prima (classe); (very good) di prima qualità.

first floor n (Br: floor above ground floor) primo piano m; (Am: ground floor) pianterreno m.

firstly ['fɜːstlɪ] adv in primo luogo.

First World War n: **the ~** la prima guerra mondiale.

fish [fɪʃ] ♦ (pl inv) n pesce m ♦ vi pescare.

fish and chips n pesce m e patate fritti.

fishcake ['fɪʃkeɪk] n crocchetta f di pesce.

fisherman ['fɪʃəmən] (pl -**men** [-mən]) n pescatore m.

fish farm n vivaio m.

fish fingers npl (Br) bastoncini mpl di pesce.

fishing ['fɪʃɪŋ] n pesca f; **to go ~** andare a pesca.

fishing boat n barca f da pesca.

fishing rod n canna f da pesca.

fishmonger's ['fɪʃˌmʌŋgəz] n (shop) pescheria f.

fish sticks (Am) = **fish fingers**.

fish supper n (Scot) pesce m e patate fritti.

fist [fɪst] n pugno m.

fit [fɪt] ♦ adj (healthy) in forma ♦ vt (be right size for) andare (bene) a; (kitchen, bath) installare; (a lock) mettere; (insert) inserire ♦ vi (be right size) andare bene ♦ n (of coughing, anger) attacco m; (epileptic) crisi f inv epilettica; **they're a good ~** (clothes, shoes) sono della misura giusta; **to be ~ for** sthg (suitable) essere adatto(-a) a qc; **~ to eat** buono(-a) da mangiare; **it doesn't ~** (object) non c'entra; **it doesn't ~ me** (jacket, skirt) non mi sta OR va; **to get ~** rimettersi in forma; **to keep ~** tenersi in forma.

▶ **fit in** ♦ vt sep (find time to do) trovare il tempo per ♦ vi (belong) inserirsi.

fitness ['fɪtnɪs] n (health) forma f.

fitted carpet [ˌfɪtəd-] n moquette f inv.

fitted sheet [ˌfɪtəd-] n lenzuolo m con gli angoli.

fitting room ['fɪtɪŋ-] n camerino m.

five [faɪv] num cinque, → **six**.

fiver ['faɪvər] n (Br: inf) cinque sterline fpl; (note) banconota f da cinque sterline.

fix [fɪks] vt (attach, decide on) fissare; (mend) riparare; (drink, food) preparare; (arrange) organizzare.

▶ **fix up** vt sep: **to ~ sb up with sthg** procurare qc a qn.

fixture ['fɪkstʃər] n (SPORT) incontro m; **~s and fittings** installazioni fpl.

fizzy ['fɪzɪ] adj frizzante.

flag [flæg] n bandiera f.

flake [fleɪk] ◆ n (of snow) fiocco m ◆ vi sfaldarsi.

flame [fleɪm] n fiamma f.

flammable ['flæməbl] adj infiammabile.

flan [flæn] n flan m inv.

flannel ['flænl] n (material) flanella f; (Br: for washing face) panno m di spugna.

▶ **flannels** npl pantaloni mpl di flanella.

flap [flæp] ◆ n (of envelope) linguetta f; (of pocket) risvolto m ◆ vt (wings) battere.

flapjack ['flæpdʒæk] n (Br) biscotto m di avena.

flare [fleər] n (signal) razzo m.

flared [fleəd] adj (trousers) a zampa d'elefante; (skirt) scampanato(-a).

flash [flæʃ] ◆ n (of light) lampo m; (for camera) flash m inv ◆ vi (light) lampeggiare; **a ~ of lightning** un lampo; **to ~ one's headlights** lampeggiare.

flashlight ['flæʃlaɪt] n torcia f elettrica.

flask [flɑːsk] n (Thermos) thermos® m inv; (hip flask) borraccia f.

flat [flæt] ◆ adj piatto(-a); (battery) scarico(-a); (drink) sgasato(-a); (rate, fee) unico(-a) ◆ adv (level) in piano ◆

n (Br: apartment) appartamento m; **a ~ (tyre)** una gomma a terra; **~ out** a più non posso.

flatter ['flætər] vt adulare.

flavor ['fleɪvər] (Am) = **flavour**.

flavour ['fleɪvər] n (Br: taste) sapore m; (of ice cream) gusto m.

flavoured ['fleɪvəd] adj: **lemon-~** al gusto di limone.

flavouring ['fleɪvərɪŋ] n aroma m.

flaw [flɔː] n difetto m.

flea [fliː] n pulce f.

flea market n mercato m delle pulci.

fleece [fliːs] n (downy material) vello m.

fleet [fliːt] n (of ships) flotta f.

Flemish ['flemɪʃ] ◆ adj fiammingo(-a) ◆ n (language) fiammingo m.

flesh [fleʃ] n (of person, animal) carne f; (of fruit, vegetable) polpa f.

flew [fluː] pt → **fly**.

flex [fleks] n cavetto m.

flexible ['fleksəbl] adj flessibile.

flick [flɪk] vt (a switch) premere; (with finger) colpire con il dito.

▶ **flick through** vt fus sfogliare.

flies [flaɪz] npl (of trousers) patta f.

flight [flaɪt] n volo m; **a ~ (of stairs)** una rampa (di scale).

flight attendant n assistente mf di volo.

flimsy ['flɪmzɪ] adj (object) poco consistente; (clothes) leggero(-a).

fling [flɪŋ] (pt & pp flung) vt lanciare.

flint [flɪnt] n (of lighter) pietrina f.

flip-flop [flɪp-] n (Br: shoe) infradito m inv or f inv.

flipper ['flɪpər] n (Br: of swimmer) pinna f.

flirt [flɜːt] vi: **to ~ (with sb)** flirtare (con qn).

float [fləut] ◆ n (for swimming) tavoletta f; (for fishing) galleggiante m; (in procession) carro m; (drink) bevanda con del gelato aggiunto ◆ vi galleggiare.

flock [flɒk] ◆ n (of birds) stormo m;

(of sheep) gregge m ◆ vi (people) accalcarsi.

flood [flʌd] ◆ n alluvione f ◆ vt inondare ◆ vi straripare.

floodlight ['flʌdlaɪt] n riflettore m.

floor [flɔːʳ] n (of room) pavimento m; (storey) piano m; (of nightclub) pista f.

floorboard ['flɔːbɔːd] n asse f del pavimento.

floor show n varietà m inv.

flop [flɒp] n (inf) fiasco m.

floppy disk ['flɒpɪ-] n floppy disk m inv.

floral ['flɔːrəl] adj (pattern) floreale.

Florence ['flɒrəns] n Firenze f.

Florida Keys ['flɒrɪdə-] npl: the ~ l'arcipelago m Keys.

florist's ['flɒrɪsts] n (shop) fioraio m.

flour ['flaʊəʳ] n farina f.

flow [fləʊ] ◆ n (of river, blood) flusso m ◆ vi (river, blood) scorrere.

flower ['flaʊəʳ] n fiore m.

flowerbed ['flaʊəbed] n aiuola f.

flowerpot ['flaʊəpɒt] n vaso m da fiori.

flown [fləʊn] pp → **fly**.

fl oz abbr = **fluid ounce**.

flu [fluː] n influenza f.

fluent ['fluːənt] adj: to be ~ in Italian, to speak ~ Italian parlare italiano correntemente.

fluff [flʌf] n (on clothes) pelucchi mpl.

fluid ounce [fluːɪd-] n = 0,03 l.

flume [fluːm] n canale m.

flung [flʌŋ] pp → **fling**.

flunk [flʌŋk] vt (Am: inf: exam) essere bocciato(-a) a.

fluorescent [flʊəˈresənt] adj fluorescente.

flush [flʌʃ] ◆ vi (toilet) funzionare ◆ vt: to ~ the toilet tirare lo sciacquone.

flute [fluːt] n flauto m traverso.

fly [flaɪ] (pt flew, pp flown) ◆ n (insect) mosca f; (of trousers) patta f ◆ vt (plane, helicopter) pilotare; (airline) volare con; (transport) traspor-

tare in aereo ◆ vi volare; (passenger) andare in aereo; (pilot a plane) pilotare un aereo; (flag) sventolare.

fly-drive n fly and drive m inv.

flying ['flaɪɪŋ] n: **I'm frightened of** ~ ho paura di volare.

flyover ['flaɪˌəʊvəʳ] n (Br) cavalcavia m inv.

flypaper ['flaɪˌpeɪpəʳ] n carta f moschicida.

flysheet ['flaɪʃiːt] n telo m protettivo.

FM n FM f.

foal [fəʊl] n puledro m.

foam [fəʊm] n (bubbles) schiuma f; (foam rubber) gommapiuma® f.

focus ['fəʊkəs] ◆ n (of camera) fuoco m ◆ vi (with camera, binoculars) mettere a fuoco; **in** ~ a fuoco; **out of** ~ sfocato.

fog [fɒg] n nebbia f.

fogbound ['fɒgbaʊnd] adj bloccato(-a) dalla nebbia.

foggy ['fɒgɪ] adj nebbioso(-a).

fog lamp n antinebbia m inv.

foil [fɔɪl] n (thin metal) carta f di alluminio.

fold [fəʊld] ◆ n (in paper, material) piega f ◆ vt piegare; (wrap) avvolgere; to ~ one's arms incrociare le braccia.

▶ **fold up** vi (chair, bed, bicycle) piegarsi.

folder ['fəʊldəʳ] n cartella f.

foliage ['fəʊlɪdʒ] n fogliame m.

folk [fəʊk] ◆ npl (people) gente f ◆ n: ~ (music) folk m.

▶ **folks** npl (inf: relatives): **my** ~**s** i miei.

follow ['fɒləʊ] ◆ vt seguire; (in order, time) seguire a ◆ vi seguire; ~**ed by** (in time) seguito da; **as** ~**s** come segue.

▶ **follow on** vi (come later) seguire.

following ['fɒləʊɪŋ] ◆ adj (next) successivo(-a); (mentioned below) seguente ◆ prep dopo.

follow on call n chiamata f successiva.

fond [fɒnd] *adj*: **to be ~ of** amare.
fondue ['fɒndu:] *n* fonduta *f*.
food [fu:d] *n* cibo *m*.
food poisoning [-,pɔɪznɪŋ] *n* avvelenamento *m* da cibo.
food processor [-,prəʊsesər] *n* tritatutto-frullatore *m inv* elettrico.
foodstuffs ['fu:dstʌfs] *npl* generi *mpl* alimentari.
fool [fu:l] ♦ *n* (*idiot*) stupido *m* (-a *f*); (*pudding*) mousse *f inv* di frutta ♦ *vt* ingannare.
foolish ['fu:lɪʃ] *adj* stupido(-a).
foot [fʊt] (*pl* **feet**) *n* (*of person*) piede *m*; (*of animal*) zampa *f*; (*measurement*) = 30,48 cm, piede; (*of hill, cliff, bed*) piedi *mpl*; (*of wardrobe, tripod, stairs*) base *f*; **by ~** a piedi; **on ~** a piedi.
football ['fʊtbɔ:l] *n* (Br: *soccer*) calcio *m*; (Am: *American football*) football *m* americano; (*ball*) pallone *m*.
footballer ['fʊtbɔ:lər] *n* (Br) calciatore *m* (-trice *f*).
football pitch *n* (Br) campo *m* di calcio.
footbridge ['fʊtbrɪdʒ] *n* sovrappassaggio *m*.
footpath ['fʊtpɑ:θ, *pl* -pɑ:ðz] *n* sentiero *m*.
footprint ['fʊtprɪnt] *n* orma *f*.
footstep ['fʊtstep] *n* passo *m*.
footwear ['fʊtweər] *n* calzature *fpl*.
for [fɔ:r] *prep* **1.** (*expressing intention, purpose, reason*) per; **this book is ~ you** questo libro è per te; **what did you do that ~?** perché l'hai fatto?; **what's it ~?** a cosa serve?; **a town famous ~ its wine** una città famosa per il suo vino; **~ this reason** per questo motivo; **to go ~ a walk** andare a fare una passeggiata; **'~ sale'** 'vendesi'.
2. (*during*): **I've lived here ~ ten years** abito qui da dieci anni, sono dieci anni che abito qui; **we talked ~ hours** abbiamo chiacchierato per ore.

3. (*by, before*) per; **be there ~ eight p.m.** trovati lì per le otto di sera; **I'll do it ~ tomorrow** lo farò per domani.
4. (*on the occasion of*) per); **I got socks ~ Christmas** ho avuto dei calzini per Natale; **what's ~ dinner?** cosa c'è per cena?
5. (*on behalf of*) per); **to do sthg ~ sb** fare qc per qn.
6. (*with time and space*) per; **there's no room ~ your suitcase** non c'è posto per la tua valigia; **have you got time ~ a coffee?** hai tempo per un caffè?; **it's time ~ dinner** è ora di cena.
7. (*expressing distance*) per; **'road works ~ 20 miles'** 'lavori in corso per 32 chilometri'.
8. (*expressing destination*) per; **a ticket ~ Edinburgh** un biglietto per Edimburgo; **this train is ~ London only** questo treno ferma solo a Londra.
9. (*expressing price*): **I bought it ~ £5** l'ho comprato per 5 sterline, l'ho pagato 5 sterline.
10. (*expressing meaning*) per; **what's the Italian ~ 'boy'?** come si dice 'boy' in italiano?
11. (*with regard to*) per; **it's warm ~ November** fa caldo per essere novembre; **it's easy ~ you** è facile per te; **it's too far ~ us to walk** è troppo lontano per andarci a piedi.
forbid [fə'bɪd] (*pt* **-bade** [-'beɪd], *pp* **-bidden**) *vt* proibire, vietare; **to ~ sb to do sthg** proibire OR vietare a qn di fare qc.
forbidden [fə'bɪdn] *adj* proibito(-a).
force [fɔ:s] ♦ *n* forza *f* ♦ *vt* forzare; **to ~ sb to do sthg** costringere qn a fare qc; **to ~ one's way through** farsi strada con la forza; **the ~s** le forze armate.
ford [fɔ:d] *n* guado *m*.
forecast ['fɔ:kɑ:st] *n* previsione *f*.
forecourt ['fɔ:kɔ:t] *n* spiazzo *m*.

forefinger [ˈfɔːˌfɪŋgəʳ] n indice m.

foreground [ˈfɔːgraʊnd] n primo piano m.

forehead [ˈfɔːhed] n fronte f.

foreign [ˈfɒrən] adj straniero(-a); (travel) all'estero.

foreign currency n valuta f estera.

foreigner [ˈfɒrənəʳ] n straniero m (-a f).

foreign exchange n cambio m.

Foreign Secretary n (Br) ministro m degli Esteri.

foreman [ˈfɔːmən] (pl -men [-mən]) n (of workers) capo operaio m.

forename [ˈfɔːneɪm] n (fml) nome m (di battesimo).

foresee [fɔːˈsiː] (pt -saw [-ˈsɔː], pp -seen [-ˈsiːn]) vt prevedere.

forest [ˈfɒrɪst] n foresta f.

forever [fəˈrevəʳ] adv (eternally) per sempre; (continually) in continuazione.

forgave [fəˈgeɪv] pt → forgive.

forge [fɔːdʒ] vt (copy) falsificare.

forgery [ˈfɔːdʒərɪ] n (copy) falso m.

forget [fəˈget] (pt -got, pp -gotten) ◆ vt dimenticare; (give up) lasciar perdere ◆ vi dimenticarsi; to ~ about sthg dimenticarsi di qc; to ~ how to do sthg dimenticare come si fa qc; to ~ to do sthg dimenticare di fare qc; ~ it! lascia perdere!

forgetful [fəˈgetfʊl] adj smemorato(-a).

forgive [fəˈgɪv] (pt -gave, pp -given [-ˈgɪvn]) vt perdonare.

forgot [fəˈgɒt] pt → forget.

forgotten [fəˈgɒtn] pp → forget.

fork [fɔːk] n (for eating with) forchetta f; (for gardening) forca f; (of road, path) bivio m.

▶ **forks** npl (of bike, motorbike) forcelle fpl.

form [fɔːm] ◆ n (type, shape) forma f; (piece of paper) modulo m; (SCH) classe f ◆ vt formare; (constitute) costituire; (produce) creare ◆ vi formarsi; **off** ~ giù di forma; **on** ~ in forma; **to** ~ **part of** fare parte di.

formal [ˈfɔːml] adj formale.

formality [fɔːˈmælətɪ] n formalità f inv; **it's just a** ~ è solo una formalità.

format [ˈfɔːmæt] n formato m.

former [ˈfɔːməʳ] ◆ adj (previous) precedente; (first) primo(-a) ◆ pron: **the** ~ il primo; **the** ~ **President** l'ex Presidente.

formerly [ˈfɔːməlɪ] adv precedentemente.

formula [ˈfɔːmjʊlə] (pl -as OR -ae [iː]) n formula f.

fort [fɔːt] n forte m.

forthcoming [fɔːθˈkʌmɪŋ] adj (future) prossimo(-a).

fortieth [ˈfɔːtɪɪθ] num quarantesimo(-a), → sixth.

fortnight [ˈfɔːtnaɪt] n (Br) quindici giorni mpl.

fortunate [ˈfɔːtʃnət] adj fortunato(-a).

fortunately [ˈfɔːtʃnətlɪ] adv fortunatamente.

fortune [ˈfɔːtʃuːn] n fortuna f; **it costs a** ~ (inf) costa una fortuna.

forty [ˈfɔːtɪ] num quaranta, → six.

forward [ˈfɔːwəd] ◆ adv (move, lean) in avanti ◆ n (SPORT) attaccante mf ◆ vt spedire; **to look** ~ **to doing sthg** non vedere l'ora di fare qc.

forwarding address [ˈfɔːwədɪŋ-] n recapito m nuovo.

fought [fɔːt] pp → fight.

foul [faʊl] ◆ adj (unpleasant) disgustoso(-a) ◆ n fallo m.

found [faʊnd] ◆ pp → find ◆ vt fondare.

foundation (cream) [faʊnˈdeɪʃn-] n fondotinta m inv.

foundations [faʊnˈdeɪʃnz] npl fondamenta fpl.

fountain [ˈfaʊntɪn] n fontana f.

fountain pen n penna f stilografica.

four [fɔːʳ] num quattro, → six.

four-star (petrol) n super f inv.

fourteen [ˌfɔːˈtiːn] num quattordici, → six.

fourteenth [ˌfɔːˈtiːnθ] *num* quattordicesimo(-a), → **sixth**.

fourth [fɔːθ] *num* quarto(-a), → **sixth**.

four-wheel drive *n* (*car*) veicolo *m* a quattro ruote motrici.

fowl [faʊl] (*pl inv*) *n* volatile *m*.

fox [fɒks] *n* volpe *f*.

foyer [ˈfɔɪeɪ] *n* (*of hotel*) hall *f inv*; (*of theatre*) foyer *m inv*.

fraction [ˈfrækʃn] *n* frazione *f*.

fracture [ˈfræktʃər] ♦ *n* frattura *f* ♦ *vt* fratturare.

fragile [ˈfrædʒaɪl] *adj* fragile.

fragment [ˈfrægmənt] *n* frammento *m*.

fragrance [ˈfreɪgrəns] *n* profumo *m*.

frail [freɪl] *adj* debole.

frame [freɪm] ♦ *n* (*of window, tent, bicycle*) telaio *m*; (*of picture, photo*) cornice *f*; (*of glasses*) montatura *f* ♦ *vt* (*photo, picture*) incorniciare.

France [frɑːns] *n* la Francia.

frank [fræŋk] *adj* franco(-a).

frankfurter [ˈfræŋkfɜːtər] *n* würstel *m inv*.

frankly [ˈfræŋklɪ] *adv* francamente.

frantic [ˈfræntɪk] *adj* frenetico(-a).

fraud [frɔːd] *n* (*crime*) frode *f*.

freak [friːk] ♦ *adj* strano(-a) ♦ *n* (*inf: fanatic*) fanatico *m* (*-a f*).

freckles [ˈfreklz] *npl* lentiggini *fpl*.

free [friː] ♦ *adj* libero(-a); (*costing nothing*) gratuito(-a) ♦ *vt* (*prisoner*) liberare ♦ *adv* gratis; **for ~** gratis; **~ of charge** gratis; **to be ~ to do sthg** essere libero di fare qc.

freedom [ˈfriːdəm] *n* libertà *f*.

freefone [ˈfriːfəʊn] *n* (*Br*) = numero *m* verde.

free gift *n* omaggio *m*.

free house *n* (*Br*) pub *m inv* (*che può vendere qualsiasi birra, non appartenendo a nessuna ditta*).

free kick *n* calcio *m* di punizione.

freelance [ˈfriːlɑːns] *adj* free-lance (*inv*).

freely [ˈfriːlɪ] *adv* liberamente; (*available*) facilmente.

free period *n* (SCH) ora *f* di buco.

freepost [ˈfriːpəʊst] *n* affrancatura *f* a carico del destinatario.

free-range *adj* (*chicken*) ruspante; (*eggs*) di galline ruspanti.

free time *n* tempo *m* libero.

freeway [ˈfriːweɪ] *n* (Am) superstrada *f*.

freeze [friːz] (*pt* **froze**, *pp* **frozen**) ♦ *vt* congelare ♦ *vi* gelare ♦ *v impers*: **it's freezing** fa un freddo polare.

freezer [ˈfriːzər] *n* (*deep freeze*) congelatore *m*; (*part of fridge*) freezer *m inv*.

freezing [ˈfriːzɪŋ] *adj* gelato(-a); (*temperatures*) sotto zero.

freezing point *n* temperatura *f* di congelamento.

freight [freɪt] *n* (*goods*) carico *m*.

French [frentʃ] ♦ *adj* francese ♦ *n* (*language*) francese *m* ♦ *npl*: **the ~** i francesi.

French bean *n* fagiolino *m*.

French bread *n* baguette *f inv*.

French dressing *n* (in UK) condimento per insalata a base di olio e aceto; (in US) condimento per insalata a base di maionese e ketchup.

French fries *npl* patatine *fpl* fritte.

Frenchman [ˈfrentʃmən] (*pl* **-men** [-mən]) *n* francese *m*.

French toast *n* (*fried bread*) fetta di pane passata nell'uovo e fritta.

French windows *npl* portafinestra *f*.

Frenchwoman [ˈfrentʃˌwʊmən] (*pl* **-women** [-ˌwɪmɪn]) *n* francese *f*.

frequency [ˈfriːkwənsɪ] *n* frequenza *f*.

frequent [ˈfriːkwənt] *adj* frequente.

frequently [ˈfriːkwəntlɪ] *adv* frequentemente.

fresh [freʃ] *adj* fresco(-a); (*water*) dolce; (*new*) nuovo(-a); **to get some ~ air** prendere un po' d'aria fresca.

fresh cream *n* panna *f* fresca.

freshen [ˈfreʃn]: **freshen up** *vi* rinfrescarsi.

freshly [ˈfreʃlɪ] *adv* appena.

fresh orange (juice) *n* spremuta *f* d'arancia.

Fri. (*abbr of Friday*) ven.

Friday [ˈfraɪdɪ] *n* venerdì *m inv*, → **Saturday**.

fridge [frɪdʒ] *n* frigorifero *m*.

fried egg [fraɪd-] *n* uovo *m* al tegame.

fried rice [fraɪd-] *n* piatto cinese a base di riso fritto.

friend [frend] *n* amico *m* (-a *f*); **to be ~s with sb** essere amico di qn; **to make ~s with sb** fare amicizia con qn.

friendly [ˈfrendlɪ] *adj* cordiale; **to be ~ with sb** essere amico di qn.

friendship [ˈfrendʃɪp] *n* amicizia *f*.

fries [fraɪz] = **French fries**.

fright [fraɪt] *n* spavento *m*, paura *f*; **to give sb a ~** fare paura a qn.

frighten [ˈfraɪtn] *vt* spaventare, far paura a.

frightened [ˈfraɪtnd] *adj* (*scared*) spaventato(-a); **to be ~ (that)** ... (*worried*) avere paura che ...; **to be ~ of** avere paura di.

frightening [ˈfraɪtnɪŋ] *adj* spaventoso(-a).

frightful [ˈfraɪtfʊl] *adj* (*very bad, unpleasant*) terribile.

frilly [ˈfrɪlɪ] *adj* arricciato(-a).

fringe [frɪndʒ] *n* frangia *f*.

frisk [frɪsk] *vt* perquisire.

fritter [ˈfrɪtəʳ] *n* frittella *f*.

fro [frəʊ] *adv* → **to**.

frog [frɒg] *n* rana *f*.

from [frɒm] *prep* **1**. (*expressing origin, source*) da; **I'm ~ England** sono inglese; **I bought it ~ a supermarket** l'ho comprato al supermercato; **the train ~ Manchester** il treno (proveniente) da Manchester.

2. (*expressing removal, deduction*) da; **away ~ home** lontano da casa; **to take sthg (away) ~ sb** prendere qc a

qn; **10% will be deducted ~ the total** dal totale verrà dedotto il 10%.

3. (*expressing distance*) da; **5 miles ~ London** a 5 miglia da Londra; **it's not far ~ here** non è lontano (da qui).

4. (*expressing position*) da; **~ here you can see the valley** da qui si vede la valle.

5. (*expressing starting time*) da; **open ~ nine to five** aperto dalle nove alle cinque; **~ next year** dall'anno prossimo.

6. (*expressing change*) da; **the price has gone up ~ £1 to £2** il prezzo è salito da 1 a 2 sterline.

7. (*expressing range*) da; **tickets are ~ £10** i biglietti vanno dalle 10 sterline in su.

8. (*as a result of*): **I'm tired ~ walking all day** sono stanco per aver camminato tutto il giorno.

9. (*expressing protection*) da; **sheltered ~ the wind** al riparo dal vento.

10. (*in comparisons*): **different ~** diverso da.

fromage frais [ˌfrɒmɑːʒˈfreɪ] *n* formaggio fresco cremoso.

front [frʌnt] ◆ *adj* anteriore ◆ *n* parte *f* anteriore; (*of weather*) fronte *m*; (*by the sea*) lungomare *m*; **in ~** (*further forward*) avanti; (*in the lead*) d'avanti; **in ~ of** davanti a.

front door *n* porta *f* principale.

frontier [frʌnˈtɪəʳ] *n* frontiera *f*.

front page *n* prima pagina *f*.

front seat *n* sedile *m* anteriore.

frost [frɒst] *n* gelo *m*.

frosty [ˈfrɒstɪ] *adj* (*morning, weather*) gelato(-a).

froth [frɒθ] *n* spuma *f*.

frown [fraʊn] ◆ *n* fronte *f* aggrottata ◆ *vi* aggrottare la fronte.

froze [frəʊz] *pt* → **freeze**.

frozen [ˈfrəʊzn] ◆ *pp* → **freeze** ◆ *adj* gelato(-a); (*food*) congelato(-a).

fruit [fruːt] *n* (*food*) frutta *f*; (*variety, single fruit*) frutto *m*; **a piece of ~** un frutto; **~s of the forest** frutti di bosco.

fruit cake n torta con frutta secca.

fruiterer ['fru:tərər] n (Br) frutti-vendolo m (-a f).

fruit juice n succo m di frutta.

fruit machine n (Br) slot-machine f inv.

fruit salad n macedonia f.

frustrating [frʌ'streɪtɪŋ] adj fru-strante.

frustration [frʌ'streɪʃn] n frustra-zione f.

fry [fraɪ] vt soffriggere; (deep-fry) friggere.

frying pan ['fraɪŋ-] n padella f.

ft abbr = **foot, feet**.

fudge [fʌdʒ] n dolciume gommoso fatto con burro, latte e zucchero.

fuel [fjʊəl] n (for engine) carburante m; (for heating) combustibile m.

fuel pump n pompa f del carbu-rante.

fulfil [fʊl'fɪl] vt (Br) (promise) mante-nere; (duty, role, need) adempiere; (conditions, request) soddisfare; (in-structions) eseguire.

fulfill [fʊl'fɪl] (Am) = **fulfil**.

full [fʊl] ♦ adj pieno(-a); (extent, fare) intero(-a); (name) completo(-a) ♦ adv (directly) in pieno; **I'm ~ (up)** sono pieno; **at ~ speed** a tutta velo-cità; **in ~** per esteso.

full board n pensione f comple-ta.

full-cream milk n latte m intero.

full-length adj (skirt, dress) lungo(-a).

full moon n luna f piena.

full stop n punto m.

full-time adj & adv a tempo pieno.

fully ['fʊlɪ] adv (completely) comple-tamente.

fully-licensed adj autorizzato a ven-dere alcolici.

fumble ['fʌmbl] vi (search clumsily) rovistare.

fun [fʌn] n divertimento m; **it's good ~** è divertente; **for ~** per divertimento; **to have ~** divertirsi; **to make ~ of** prendere in giro.

function ['fʌŋkʃn] ♦ n (role) funzio-ne f; (formal event) ricevimento m ♦ vi funzionare.

fund [fʌnd] ♦ n (of money) fondo m ♦ vt finanziare.

▶ **funds** npl fondi mpl.

fundamental [,fʌndə'mentl] adj fondamentale.

funeral ['fju:nərəl] n funerale m.

funfair ['fʌnfeər] n luna park m inv.

funky ['fʌŋkɪ] adj (inf: music) funky (inv).

funnel ['fʌnl] n (for pouring) imbuto m; (on ship) fumaiolo m.

funny ['fʌnɪ] adj (amusing) diver-tente; (strange) strano(-a); **to feel ~** (ill) sentirsi strano.

fur [fɜ:r] n pelliccia f.

fur coat n pelliccia f.

furious ['fjʊərɪəs] adj (angry) furio-so(-a).

furnished ['fɜ:nɪʃt] adj ammobi-liato(-a).

furnishings ['fɜ:nɪʃɪŋz] npl arreda-mento m.

furniture ['fɜ:nɪtʃər] n mobilia f; **a piece of ~** un mobile.

furry ['fɜ:rɪ] adj peloso(-a).

further ['fɜ:ðər] → **far** ♦ adv (in distance) più lontano; (more) di più ♦ adj (additional) ulteriore; **until ~ no-tice** fino a nuovo avviso.

furthermore [,fɜ:ðə'mɔ:r] adv inol-tre.

furthest ['fɜ:ðɪst] → **far** ♦ adj (most distant) il più lontano (la più lontana) ♦ adv (in distance) il più lon-tano (possibile).

fuse [fju:z] ♦ n (of plug) fusibile m; (on bomb) detonatore m ♦ vi (plug, device) saltare.

fuse box n scatola f dei fusibili.

fuss [fʌs] n (agitation) confusione f; (complaints) storie fpl.

fussy ['fʌsɪ] adj (person) difficile.

future ['fju:tʃər] ♦ n futuro m ♦ adj futuro(-a); **in ~** in futuro.

G

g (*abbr of gram*) g.

gable ['geɪbl] *n* timpano *m*.

gadget ['gædʒɪt] *n* aggeggio *m*.

Gaelic ['geɪlɪk] *n* gaelico *m*.

gag [gæg] *n* (*inf: joke*) gag *f inv*.

gain [geɪn] ◆ *n* (*improvement*) avanzamento *m*; (*profit*) guadagno *m* ◆ *vt* guadagnare; (*weight*) aumentare di; (*confidence, speed, popularity*) acquistare; (*achieve*) ottenere; (*subj: clock, watch*) andare avanti di ◆ *vi* (*get benefit*): **to ~ from sthg** trarre vantaggio da qc.

gale [geɪl] *n* burrasca *f*.

gallery ['gælərɪ] *n* galleria *f*.

gallon ['gælən] *n* (*Br*) = 4,546 l, gallone *m*; (*Am*) = 3,791 l, gallone.

gallop ['gæləp] *vi* galoppare.

gamble ['gæmbl] ◆ *n* azzardo *m* ◆ *vi* (*bet money*) giocare d'azzardo.

gambling ['gæmblɪŋ] *n* gioco *m* d'azzardo.

game [geɪm] *n* (*gen, in tennis*) gioco *m*; (*of football, squash, cards*) partita *f*; (*wild animals, meat*) cacciagione *f*.

▶ **games** ◆ *n* (SCH) = attività *fpl* sportive ◆ *npl* (*sporting event*) gare *fpl*.

gammon ['gæmən] *n* coscia di maiale da cuocere.

gang [gæŋ] *n* (*of criminals*) banda *f*; (*of friends*) gruppo *m*.

gangster ['gæŋstər] *n* gangster *m inv*.

gangway ['gæŋweɪ] *n* (*for ship*) passerella *f*; (*Br: in bus, aeroplane, theatre*) corridoio *m*.

gaol [dʒeɪl] (*Br*) = **jail**.

gap [gæp] *n* (*space*) buco *m*; (*of time*) intervallo *m*; (*difference*) divario *m*.

garage ['gærɑːʒ, 'gærɪdʒ] *n* (*for keeping car*) garage *m inv*; (*Br: for*

petrol) stazione *f* di servizio; (*for repairs*) autofficina *f*; (*Br: for selling cars*) concessionaria *f*.

garbage ['gɑːbɪdʒ] *n* (*Am: refuse*) spazzatura *f*.

garbage can *n* (*Am*) pattumiera *f*.

garbage truck *n* (*Am*) camion *m inv* della nettezza urbana.

garden ['gɑːdn] ◆ *n* giardino *m* ◆ *vi* fare giardinaggio.

▶ **gardens** *npl* (*public park*) giardini *mpl* pubblici.

garden centre *n* vivaio *m*.

gardener ['gɑːdnər] *n* giardiniere *m* (-a *f*).

gardening ['gɑːdnɪŋ] *n* giardinaggio *m*.

garden peas *npl* piselli *mpl*.

garlic ['gɑːlɪk] *n* aglio *m*.

garlic bread *n* = bruschetta *f*.

garlic butter *n* burro *m* all'aglio.

garment ['gɑːmənt] *n* indumento *m*.

garnish ['gɑːnɪʃ] ◆ *n* guarnizione *f* ◆ *vt* guarnire.

gas [gæs] *n* gas *m inv*; (*Am: petrol*) benzina *f*.

gas cooker *n* (*Br*) cucina *f* a gas.

gas cylinder *n* bombola *f* del gas.

gas fire *n* (*Br*) stufa *f* a gas.

gasket ['gæskɪt] *n* guarnizione *f*.

gas mask *n* maschera *f* antigas.

gasoline ['gæsəliːn] *n* (*Am*) benzina *f*.

gasp [gɑːsp] *vi* (*in shock*) rimanere senza fiato.

gas pedal *n* (*Am*) acceleratore *m*.

gas station *n* (*Am*) stazione *f* di servizio.

gas stove (*Br*) = **gas cooker**.

gas tank *n* (*Am*) serbatoio *m* della benzina.

gasworks ['gæswɜːks] (*pl inv*) *n* officina *f* del gas.

gate [geɪt] *n* (*to garden, field*) cancello *m*; (*at airport*) uscita *f*.

gâteau ['gætəʊ] (*pl* **-x** [-z]) *n* (*Br*) torta *f*.

gateway ['geɪtweɪ] n (entrance) entrata f.

gather ['gæðər] ◆ vt (collect) raccogliere; (speed) acquistare; (understand) dedurre ◆ vi (come together) riunirsi.

gaudy ['gɔːdɪ] adj vistoso(-a).

gauge [geɪdʒ] ◆ n (for measuring) indicatore m; (of railway track) scartamento m ◆ vt (calculate) misurare.

gauze [gɔːz] n garza f.

gave [geɪv] pt → **give**.

gay [geɪ] adj (homosexual) gay (inv).

gaze [geɪz] vi: **to ~ at** fissare.

GB (abbr of Great Britain) GB.

GCSE n esami sostenuti a conclusione della scuola dell'obbligo.

gear [gɪər] n (wheel) ingranaggio m; (speed) marcia f; (belongings) roba f; (equipment, clothes) attrezzatura f; **in ~** con la marcia inserita.

gearbox ['gɪəbɒks] n cambio m.

gear lever n leva f del cambio.

gear shift (Am) = **gear lever**.

gear stick (Br) = **gear lever**.

geese [giːs] pl → **goose**.

gel [dʒel] n gel m inv.

gelatine [ˌdʒeləˈtiːn] n gelatina f.

gem [dʒem] n gemma f.

Gemini ['dʒemɪnaɪ] n Gemelli mpl.

gender ['dʒendər] n genere m.

general ['dʒenərəl] ◆ adj generale; (idea, statement) generico(-a) ◆ n generale m; **in ~** in generale; (usually) in genere.

general anaesthetic n anestesia f totale.

general election n elezioni fpl politiche.

generally ['dʒenərəlɪ] adv generalmente.

general practitioner [-prækˈtɪʃənər] n medico m generico.

general store n drogheria f.

generate ['dʒenəreɪt] vt generare.

generation [ˌdʒenəˈreɪʃn] n generazione f.

generator ['dʒenəreɪtər] n generatore m.

generosity [ˌdʒenəˈrɒsətɪ] n generosità f.

generous ['dʒenərəs] adj generoso(-a).

genitals ['dʒenɪtlz] npl genitali mpl.

genius ['dʒiːnjəs] n genio m.

gentle ['dʒentl] adj (careful) delicato(-a); (kind) gentile; (movement, breeze) leggero(-a).

gentleman ['dʒentlmən] (pl **-men** [-mən]) n signore m; (with good manners) gentiluomo m; **'gentlemen'** (men's toilets) 'uomini'.

gently ['dʒentlɪ] adv (carefully) delicatamente.

gents [dʒents] n (Br) toilette f inv degli uomini.

genuine ['dʒenjʊɪn] adj (authentic) autentico(-a); (sincere) sincero(-a).

geographical [dʒɪəˈgræfɪkl] adj geografico(-a).

geography [dʒɪˈɒgrəfɪ] n geografia f.

geology [dʒɪˈɒlədʒɪ] n geologia f.

geometry [dʒɪˈɒmətrɪ] n geometria f.

Georgian ['dʒɔːdʒən] adj (architecture etc) georgiano(-a) (del periodo dei re Giorgio I–IV, 1714–1830).

geranium [dʒɪˈreɪnjəm] n geranio m.

German ['dʒɜːmən] ◆ adj tedesco(-a) ◆ n (person) tedesco m (-a f); (language) tedesco m.

German measles n rosolia f.

Germany ['dʒɜːmənɪ] n la Germania.

germs [dʒɜːmz] npl germi mpl.

gesture ['dʒestʃər] n (movement) gesto m.

get [get] (pt & pp **got**, Am pp **gotten**) vt 1. (obtain) ottenere; (job, house) trovare; **I got some crisps from the shop** ho comprato delle patatine al negozio; **she got a job** ha trovato lavoro.

2. (receive) ricevere; **I got a book for Christmas** mi hanno regalato un

libro per Natale; **you ~ a lot of rain here in winter** qui piove molto in inverno.

3. (*means of transport*) prendere; **let's ~ a taxi** prendiamo un taxi.

4. (*fetch*) andare a prendere; **could you ~ me the manager?** (*in shop*) mi può chiamare il direttore?; (*on phone*) mi può passare il direttore?

5. (*illness*) avere, prendere; **I've got a headache** ho mal di testa.

6. (*cause to become, do*): **to ~ sthg done** (*do*) fare qc; (*have done*) fare qc; **to ~ sb to do sthg** far fare qc a qn; **I can't ~ it open** non riesco ad aprirlo; **can I ~ my car repaired here?** posso far riparare qui la mia macchina?

7. (*move*): **to ~ sthg in/out** far entrare/uscire qc; **I can't ~ it through the door** non riesco a farlo passare dalla porta.

8. (*understand*) capire; **to ~ a joke** capire una barzelletta.

9. (*time, chance*) avere, trovare; **we didn't ~ the chance to see everything** non siamo riusciti a vedere tutto.

10. (*answer*): **I'll ~ it!** (*phone*) rispondo io!; (*door*) vado io!, → **have**.

♦ *vi* **1.** (*become*) diventare; **it's getting late** si sta facendo tardi; **to ~ bored** annoiarsi; **to ~ ready** prepararsi; **to ~ lost** perdersi; **~ lost!** (*inf*) vattene!

2. (*arrive*) arrivare; **when does the train ~ here?** a che ora arriva il treno?

3. (*go*): **to ~ to/from** andare a/da.

4. (*manage*): **to ~ to do sthg** riuscire a fare qc.

♦ *aux vb*: **to ~ delayed** essere trattenuto; **to ~ killed** essere ucciso.

▶ **get back** *vi* (*return*) ritornare.

▶ **get in** *vi* (*arrive*) arrivare; (*enter*) entrare.

▶ **get into** *vt fus* (*enter*) entrare in; **to ~ into the car** salire in macchina; **to ~ into bed** mettersi a letto; **to ~ into trouble** mettersi nei guai.

▶ **get off** *vi* (*leave train, bus*) scendere; (*depart*) partire.

▶ **get on** *vi* (*enter train, bus*) salire; (*in relationship*) andare d'accordo; **how are you getting on?** come va la vita?

▶ **get out** *vi* (*of car, bus, train*) scendere.

▶ **get through** *vi* (*on phone*) ottenere la comunicazione.

▶ **get up** *vi* alzarsi.

get-together *n* (*inf*) riunione *f*.

ghastly ['gɑːstlɪ] *adj* (*inf*) terribile.

gherkin ['gɜːkɪn] *n* cetriolino *m*.

ghetto blaster ['getəʊˌblɑːstər] *n* (*inf*) stereo *m* portatile.

ghost [gəʊst] *n* fantasma *m*.

giant ['dʒaɪənt] ♦ *adj* gigantesco(-a) ♦ *n* (*in stories*) gigante *m*.

giblets ['dʒɪblɪts] *npl* rigaglie *fpl*.

giddy ['gɪdɪ] *adj* (*dizzy*): **I feel ~** mi gira la testa.

gift [gɪft] *n* regalo *m*; (*talent*) talento *m*.

gifted ['gɪftɪd] *adj* dotato(-a).

gift shop *n* negozio *m* di articoli da regalo.

gift voucher *n* (*Br*) buono *m* acquisto.

gig [gɪg] *n* (*inf: concert*) concerto *m*.

gigantic [dʒaɪˈgæntɪk] *adj* gigantesco(-a).

giggle ['gɪgl] *vi* ridacchiare.

gill [dʒɪl] *n* (*measurement*) = 0,142 l.

gimmick ['gɪmɪk] *n* trovata *f*.

gin [dʒɪn] *n* gin *m inv*; **~ and tonic** gin tonic.

ginger ['dʒɪndʒər] ♦ *n* zenzero *m* ♦ *adj* (*colour*) rosso(-a).

ginger ale *n* bibita analcolica gassata allo zenzero.

ginger beer *n* bibita analcolica allo zenzero.

gingerbread ['dʒɪndʒəbred] *n* torta o biscotto allo zenzero.

gipsy ['dʒɪpsɪ] *n* zingaro *m* (-a *f*).

giraffe [dʒɪˈrɑːf] *n* giraffa *f*.

girdle ['gɜːdl] *n* panciera *f*.

girl [gɜːl] *n* (*child*) bambina *f*; (*young woman*) ragazza *f*; (*daughter*) femmina *f*.

girlfriend ['gɜːlfrend] n (of boy, man) ragazza f; (of girl, woman) amica f.

girl guide n (Br) giovane f esploratrice.

girl scout (Am) = **girl guide**.

giro ['dʒaɪrəʊ] n (system) giroconto m.

give [gɪv] (pt **gave**, pp **given** ['gɪvn]) vt dare; (a smile, speech) fare; (attention) prestare; (time) dedicare; **to ~ sb sthg** dare qc a qn; (as present) regalare qc a qn; **to ~ sthg a push** dare una spinta a qc; **to ~ sb a kiss** dare un bacio a qn; **it took an hour, ~ or take a few minutes** c'è voluta un'ora, minuto più minuto meno; **'~ way'** 'dare la precedenza'.

▶ **give away** vt sep (get rid of) dare via; (reveal) rivelare.

▶ **give back** vt sep restituire.

▶ **give in** vi arrendersi.

▶ **give off** vt fus emettere.

▶ **give out** vt sep (distribute) distribuire.

▶ **give up** ◆ vt sep (cigarettes, chocolate) rinunciare a; (seat) cedere ◆ vi (admit defeat) arrendersi; **to ~ up smoking** smettere di fumare.

glacier ['glæsjər] n ghiacciaio m.

glad [glæd] adj contento(-a); **to be ~ to do sthg** essere contento di fare qc.

gladly ['glædlɪ] adv (willingly) volentieri.

glamorous ['glæmərəs] adj affascinante.

glance [glɑːns] ◆ n sguardo m ◆ vi: **to ~ (at)** dare uno sguardo (a).

gland [glænd] n ghiandola f.

glandular fever ['glændjʊlə-] n mononucleosi f.

glare [gleər] vi (person) lanciare sguardi truci; (sun, light) abbagliare.

glass [glɑːs] ◆ n (material) vetro m; (container, glassful) bicchiere m ◆ adj di vetro.

▶ **glasses** npl occhiali mpl.

glassware ['glɑːsweər] n oggetti mpl in vetro.

glen [glen] n (Scot) valle f.

glider ['glaɪdər] n aliante m.

glimpse [glɪmps] vt intravedere.

glitter ['glɪtər] vi luccicare.

global warming [ˌgləʊbl'wɔːmɪŋ] n effetto m serra.

globe [gləʊb] n globo m; **the ~** (Earth) il globo.

gloomy ['gluːmɪ] adj cupo(-a).

glorious ['glɔːrɪəs] adj (weather, sight) magnifico(-a); (victory, history) glorioso(-a).

glory ['glɔːrɪ] n gloria f.

gloss [glɒs] n (shine) lucido m; **~ (paint)** vernice f lucida.

glossary ['glɒsərɪ] n glossario m.

glossy ['glɒsɪ] adj (magazine) patinato(-a); (photo) lucido(-a).

glove [glʌv] n guanto m.

glove compartment n vano m portaoggetti.

glow [gləʊ] ◆ n barlume m ◆ vi brillare.

glucose ['gluːkəʊs] n glucosio m.

glue [gluː] ◆ n colla f ◆ vt incollare.

gnat [næt] n pappataci m inv.

gnaw [nɔː] vt rosicchiare.

go [gəʊ] (pt **went**, pp **gone**, pl **goes**) vi **1.** (move, travel, attend) andare; **to ~ home** andare a casa; **to ~ to Italy** andare in Italia; **to ~ by bus** andare con l'autobus; **to ~ to school** andare a scuola; **to ~ for a walk** andare a fare una passeggiata; **to ~ and do sthg** andare a fare qc; **to ~ shopping** andare a fare spesa.

2. (leave) andarsene; (bus, train) partire; **it's time to ~** è ora d'andare; **~ away!** vattene!

3. (become) diventare; **she went pale** è impallidita; **the milk has gone sour** il latte è inacidito.

4. (expressing future tense): **to be going to do sthg** stare per fare qc; (intend to do) avere intenzione di fare qc; **I'm going to be sick** sto per vomita-

re; **I'm going to phone them tonight** ho intenzione di chiamarli stasera.
5. (*function*) funzionare; **the car won't ~** la macchina non parte.
6. (*stop working*) rompersi; **the fuse has gone** è saltato il fusibile.
7. (*time*) passare.
8. (*progress*) andare; **to ~ well** andar bene.
9. (*bell, alarm*) suonare.
10. (*match, be appropriate*): **to ~ (with)** andare (con).
11. (*be sold*) essere venduto(-a); **'everything must ~'** 'svendita totale'.
12. (*fit*) entrare.
13. (*lead*) andare, portare; **where does this path ~?** dove porta questo sentiero?
14. (*belong*) andare.
15. (*in phrases*): **to let ~ of sthg** (*drop*) lasciare (andare) qc; **to ~** (Am: *to take away*) da asportare; **there are only three weeks to ~** mancano solo tre settimane.
♦ *n* 1. (*turn*) turno *m*; **it's your ~** tocca a te.
2. (*attempt*) prova *f*, tentativo *m*; **to have a ~ at sthg** provare qc; **'50p a ~'** (*in game*) '50 pence a partita'.
▶ **go ahead** *vi* (*take place*) aver luogo; **~ ahead!** fai pure!
▶ **go back** *vi* (*return*) ritornare.
▶ **go down** *vi* (*decrease*) abbassarsi, scendere; (*sun*) tramontare; (*tyre*) sgonfiarsi.
▶ **go down with** *vt fus* (*inf: illness*) prendere.
▶ **go in** *vi* (*enter*) entrare.
▶ **go off** *vi* (*alarm, bell*) suonare; (*go bad*) andare a male; (*lights, heating*) spegnersi.
▶ **go on** *vi* (*happen*) succedere; (*lights, heating*) accendersi; (*continue*): **to ~ on doing sthg** continuare a fare qc.
▶ **go out** *vi* (*leave house*) uscire; (*light, fire, cigarette*) spegnersi; (*have relationship*): **to ~ out (with sb)** stare

insieme (a qn); **to ~ out for a meal** andare a mangiare fuori.
▶ **go over** *vt fus* (*check*) controllare.
▶ **go round** *vi* (*revolve*) girare; (*be enough*) bastare per tutti.
▶ **go through** *vt fus* (*experience*) passare; (*spend*) spendere; (*search*) esaminare.
▶ **go up** *vi* (*increase*) aumentare.
▶ **go without** *vt fus* fare a meno di.

goal [gəʊl] *n* (*posts*) porta *f*; (*point scored*) goal *m inv*; (*aim*) scopo *m*.
goalkeeper ['gəʊl,ki:pər] *n* portiere *m*.
goalpost ['gəʊlpəʊst] *n* palo *m*.
goat [gəʊt] *n* capra *f*.
gob [gɒb] *n* (Br: *inf: mouth*) bocca *f*.
god [gɒd] *n* dio *m*.
▶ **God** *n* Dio *m*.
goddaughter ['gɒd,dɔ:tər] *n* figlioccia *f*.
godfather ['gɒd,fɑ:ðər] *n* padrino *m*.
godmother ['gɒd,mʌðər] *n* madrina *f*.
gods [gɒdz] *npl*: **the ~** (Br: *inf: in theatre*) il loggione.
godson ['gɒdsʌn] *n* figlioccio *m*.
goes [gəʊz] → **go**.
goggles ['gɒglz] *npl* (*for swimming*) occhialini *mpl*; (*for skiing*) occhiali *mpl* da neve.
going ['gəʊɪŋ] *adj* (*available*) disponibile; **the ~ rate** la tariffa corrente.
go-kart [-kɑːt] *n* go-kart *m inv*.
gold [gəʊld] ♦ *n* oro *m* ♦ *adj* d'oro.
goldfish ['gəʊldfɪʃ] (*pl inv*) *n* pesce *m* rosso.
gold-plated [-'pleɪtɪd] *adj* placcato(-a) d'oro.
golf [gɒlf] *n* golf *m*.
golf ball *n* pallina *f* da golf.
golf club *n* (*place*) circolo *m* del golf; (*piece of equipment*) mazza *f* da golf.
golf course *n* campo *m* di golf.
golfer ['gɒlfər] *n* golfista *mf*.
gone [gɒn] ♦ *pp* → **go** ♦ *prep* (Br:

past): it's ~ ten sono le dieci passate.

good [gʊd] (*compar* **better**, *superl* **best**) ◆ *adj* buono(-a); (*enjoyable*) bello(-a); (*skilled, well-behaved*) bravo(-a); (*kind*) gentile ◆ *n* bene *m*; **the weather's** ~ fa bel tempo; **to have a** ~ **time** divertirsi; **to be** ~ **at sthg** saper fare qc bene; **a** ~ **ten minutes** dieci minuti buoni; **in** ~ **time** in anticipo; **to make** ~ **sthg** compensare qc; **for** ~ per sempre; **for the** ~ **of** per il bene di; **to do sb** ~ far bene a qn; **it's no** ~ (*there's no point*) è inutile; ~ **afternoon!** buon giorno!; ~ **evening!** buona sera!; ~ **morning!** buon giorno!; ~ **night!** buona notte!

▶ **goods** *npl* merce *f*.

goodbye [ˌgʊdˈbaɪ] *excl* arrivederci!

Good Friday *n* Venerdì *m* Santo.

good-looking [-ˈlʊkɪŋ] *adj* attraente.

goods train [gʊdz-] *n* treno *m* merci.

goose [guːs] (*pl* **geese**) *n* oca *f*.

gooseberry [ˈgʊzbərɪ] *n* uva *f* spina.

gorge [gɔːdʒ] *n* gola *f*.

gorgeous [ˈgɔːdʒəs] *adj* stupendo(-a).

gorilla [gəˈrɪlə] *n* gorilla *m inv*.

gossip [ˈgɒsɪp] ◆ *n* (*about someone*) pettegolezzi *mpl* ◆ *vi* (*about someone*) fare pettegolezzi; (*chat*) chiacchierare; **to have a** ~ chiacchierare.

gossip column *n* cronaca *f* rosa.

got [gɒt] *pt & pp* → **get**.

gotten [ˈgɒtn] *pp* (*Am*) → **get**.

goujons [ˈguːdʒɒnz] *npl* (*of fish*) frittelle *fpl*.

goulash [ˈguːlæʃ] *n* gulasch *m inv*.

gourmet [ˈgʊəmeɪ] ◆ *n* buongustaio *m* (-a *f*) ◆ *adj* per intenditori.

govern [ˈgʌvən] *vt* (*country, city*) governare.

government [ˈgʌvnmənt] *n* governo *m*.

gown [gaʊn] *n* (*dress*) abito *m* lungo.

GP *abbr* = **general practitioner**.

grab [græb] *vt* (*take hold of*) afferrare.

graceful [ˈgreɪsfʊl] *adj* (*elegant*) aggraziato(-a).

grade [greɪd] *n* (*quality*) categoria *f*; (*in exam*) voto *m*; (*Am: year at school*) classe *f*.

gradient [ˈgreɪdjənt] *n* pendenza *f*.

gradual [ˈgrædʒʊəl] *adj* graduale.

gradually [ˈgrædʒʊəlɪ] *adv* gradualmente.

graduate [*n* ˈgrædʒʊət, *vb* ˈgrædʒʊeɪt] ◆ *n* (*from university*) laureato *m* (-a *f*); (*Am: from high school*) diplomato *m* (-a *f*) ◆ *vi* (*from university*) laurearsi; (*Am: from high school*) diplomarsi.

graduation [ˌgrædʒʊˈeɪʃn] *n* (*ceremony at university*) consegna *f* delle lauree; (*Am: ceremony at school*) consegna dei diplomi.

graffiti [grəˈfiːtɪ] *n* graffiti *mpl*.

grain [greɪn] *n* (*seed*) chicco *m*; (*crop*) cereali *mpl*; (*of sand, salt*) granello *m*.

gram [græm] *n* grammo *m*.

grammar [ˈgræmər] *n* grammatica *f*.

grammar school *n* (*in UK*) scuola secondaria più selettiva e tradizionale delle altre.

gramme [græm] = **gram**.

gramophone [ˈgræməfəʊn] *n* grammofono *m*.

gran [græn] *n* (*Br: inf*) nonna *f*.

grand [grænd] ◆ *adj* (*impressive*) grandioso(-a) ◆ *n* (*inf*) (£1,000) mille sterline *fpl*; ($1,000) mille dollari *mpl*.

grandad [ˈgrændæd] *n* (*inf*) nonno *m*.

grandchild [ˈgræntʃaɪld] (*pl* **-children** [-ˌtʃɪldrən]) *n* nipote *mf*.

granddaughter [ˈgrænˌdɔːtər] *n* nipote *f*.

grandfather [ˈgrænd,fɑːðər] *n* nonno *m*.

grandma [ˈgrænmɑː] *n* (*inf*) nonna *f*.

grandmother [ˈgræn,mʌðər] *n* nonna *f*.

grandpa [ˈgrænpɑː] *n* (*inf*) nonno *m*.

grandparents [ˈgræn,peərənts] *npl* nonni *mpl*.

grandson [ˈgrænsʌn] *n* nipote *m*.

granite [ˈgrænɪt] *n* granito *m*.

granny [ˈgrænɪ] *n* (*inf*) nonna *f*.

grant [grɑːnt] ◆ *n* (POL) sovvenzione *f*; (*for university*) borsa *f* di studio ◆ *vt* (*fml: give*) concedere; **to take sthg for ~ed** dare qc per scontato; **to take sb for ~ed** pensare di poter sempre contare su qn.

grapefruit [ˈgreɪpfruːt] *n* pompelmo *m*.

grapefruit juice *n* succo *m* di pompelmo.

grapes [greɪps] *npl* uva *f*.

graph [grɑːf] *n* grafico *m*.

graph paper *n* carta *f* millimetrata.

grasp [grɑːsp] *vt* afferrare.

grass [grɑːs] *n* (*plant*) erba *f*; (*lawn*) prato *m*; **'keep off the ~'** 'non calpestare il prato'.

grasshopper [ˈgrɑːs,hɒpər] *n* cavalletta *f*.

grate [greɪt] *n* grata *f*.

grated [ˈgreɪtɪd] *adj* grattugiato(-a).

grateful [ˈgreɪtfʊl] *adj* (*person*) grato(-a).

grater [ˈgreɪtər] *n* grattugia *f*.

gratitude [ˈgrætɪtjuːd] *n* gratitudine *f*.

gratuity [grəˈtjuːɪtɪ] *n* (*fml*) mancia *f*.

grave¹ [greɪv] ◆ *adj* (*mistake, news, concern*) grave ◆ *n* tomba *f*.

grave² [grɑːv] *adj* (*accent*) grave.

gravel [ˈgrævl] *n* ghiaia *f*.

graveyard [ˈgreɪvjɑːd] *n* cimitero *m*.

gravity [ˈgrævətɪ] *n* gravità *f*.

gravy [ˈgreɪvɪ] *n* salsa ottenuta dal sugo di carne arrosto e resa più densa con della farina.

gray [greɪ] (*Am*) = **grey**.

graze [greɪz] *vt* (*injure*) scorticare, escoriare.

grease [griːs] *n* (*for machine*) olio *m*, lubrificante *m*; (*animal fat*) grasso *m*.

greaseproof paper [ˈgriːspruːf-] *n* (Br) carta *f* oleata.

greasy [ˈgriːsɪ] *adj* (*food, skin, hair*) grasso(-a); (*tools, clothes*) unto(-a).

great [greɪt] *adj* grande; (*very good*) eccellente, fantastico(-a); **(that's) ~!** fantastico!

Great Britain *n* la Gran Bretagna.

great-grandfather *n* bisnonno *m*.

great-grandmother *n* bisnonna *f*.

greatly [ˈgreɪtlɪ] *adv* molto.

Greece [griːs] *n* la Grecia.

greed [griːd] *n* avidità *f*.

greedy [ˈgriːdɪ] *adj* avido(-a).

Greek [griːk] ◆ *adj* greco(-a) ◆ *n* (*person*) greco *m* (-a *f*); (*language*) greco *m*.

Greek salad *n* insalata *f* greca (*a base di pomodori, cetriolo, formaggio greco e olive nere*).

green [griːn] ◆ *adj* verde; (*environmentalist*) ambientalista; (*inf: inexperienced*) inesperto(-a) ◆ *n* (*colour*) verde *m*; (*in village*) prato *m* pubblico; (*on golf course*) green *m inv*.

▶ **greens** *npl* (*vegetables*) verdura *f*.

green beans *npl* fagiolini *mpl*.

green card *n* (Br: *for car*) carta *f* verde; (Am: *work permit*) permesso *m* di soggiorno.

green channel *n* uscita di porto o aeroporto riservata ai passeggeri che non hanno niente da dichiarare.

greengage [ˈgriːngeɪdʒ] *n* susina *f* Regina Claudia.

greengrocer's [ˈgriːn,grəʊsəz] *n*

(*shop*) negozio *m* di frutta e verdura.

greenhouse ['gri:nhaʊs, *pl* -haʊzɪz] *n* serra *f*.

greenhouse effect *n* effetto *m* serra.

green light *n* (*go-ahead*): **to give sb the ~** dare il via libera a qn.

green pepper *n* peperone *m* verde.

Greens [gri:nz] *npl*: **the ~** i Verdi.

green salad *n* insalata *f* verde.

greet [gri:t] *vt* (*say hello to*) salutare.

greeting ['gri:tɪŋ] *n* saluto *m*.

grenade [grə'neɪd] *n* granata *f*.

grew [gru:] *pt* → **grow**.

grey [greɪ] ◆ *adj* grigio(-a) ◆ *n* grigio *m*; **to go ~** diventar grigio.

greyhound ['greɪhaʊnd] *n* levriero *m*.

grid [grɪd] *n* (*grating*) grata *f*; (*on map etc*) reticolato *m*.

grief [gri:f] *n* dolore *m*; **to come to ~** (*plan*) naufragare; (*person*) finire male.

grieve [gri:v] *vi* affliggersi.

grill [grɪl] ◆ *n* (*on cooker*) grill *m inv*; (*for open fire*) griglia *f*; (*part of restaurant*) area di un ristorante dove si cucina alla griglia ◆ *vt* cuocere ai ferri OR alla griglia.

grille [grɪl] *n* (AUT) griglia *f*.

grilled [grɪld] *adj* alla griglia, ai ferri.

grim [grɪm] *adj* (*expression*) severo(-a); (*place*) lugubre; (*news*) triste.

grimace ['grɪməs] *n* smorfia *f*.

grimy ['graɪmɪ] *adj* sudicio(-a).

grin [grɪn] ◆ *n* (*gran*) sorriso *m* ◆ *vi* fare un gran sorriso.

grind [graɪnd] (*pt & pp* ground) *vt* (*pepper, coffee*) macinare.

grip [grɪp] ◆ *n* (*hold*) presa *f*; (*of tyres*) tenuta *f* di strada; (*handle*) impugnatura *f*; (*bag*) borsa *f* da viaggio ◆ *vt* (*hold*) afferrare.

gristle ['grɪsl] *n* cartilagine *f*.

groan [grəʊn] ◆ *n* lamento *m*

◆ *vi* lamentarsi.

groceries ['grəʊsərɪz] *npl* generi *mpl* alimentari.

grocer's ['grəʊsəz] *n* (*shop*) drogheria *f*.

grocery ['grəʊsərɪ] *n* (*shop*) drogheria *f*.

groin [grɔɪn] *n* inguine *m*.

groove [gru:v] *n* solco *m*.

grope [grəʊp] *vi* andare a tastoni; **to ~ for sthg** cercare qc a tastoni.

gross [grəʊs] *adj* (*weight, income*) lordo(-a).

grossly ['grəʊslɪ] *adv* (*extremely*) estremamente.

grotty ['grɒtɪ] *adj* (Br: *inf*) squallido(-a).

ground [graʊnd] ◆ *pt & pp* → **grind** ◆ *n* (*surface of earth*) terra *f*; (*soil*) terreno *m*; (SPORT) campo *m* ◆ *adj* (*coffee*) macinato(-a) ◆ *vt* (Am: *electrical connection*) mettere a terra; **to be ~ed** (*plane*) essere trattenuto a terra; **on the ~** OR per terra.

▶ **grounds** *npl* (*of building*) terreni *mpl*; (*of coffee*) fondi *mpl*; (*reason*) motivo *m*, ragione *f*.

ground floor *n* pianterreno *m*.

groundsheet ['graʊndʃi:t] *n* telo *m* impermeabile.

group [gru:p] *n* gruppo *m*.

grouse [graʊs] (*pl inv*) *n* (*bird*) gallo *m* cedrone.

grovel ['grɒvl] *vi* (*be humble*) umiliarsi.

grow [grəʊ] (*pt* grew, *pp* grown) ◆ *vi* (*person, animal, plant*) crescere; (*fears, traffic*) aumentare; (*company, city*) espandersi; (*become*) diventare ◆ *vt* (*plant, crop*) coltivare; (*beard*) farsi crescere; **to ~ old** invecchiare.

▶ **grow up** *vi* crescere, diventare grande.

growl [graʊl] *vi* (*dog*) ringhiare.

grown [grəʊn] *pp* → **grow**.

grown-up ◆ *adj* adulto(-a) ◆ *n* adulto *m* (-a *f*).

growth [grəʊθ] *n* (*increase*) crescita *f*; (MED) tumore *m*.

grub [grʌb] n (inf: food) cibo m.

grubby ['grʌbɪ] adj (inf) sporco(-a).

grudge [grʌdʒ] ♦ n rancore m ♦ vt: **to ~ sb sthg** invidiare qc a qn.

grueling ['gruəlɪŋ] (Am) = **gruelling**.

gruelling ['gruəlɪŋ] adj (Br) estenuante.

gruesome ['gruːsəm] adj raccapricciante.

grumble ['grʌmbl] vi (complain) lagnarsi.

grumpy ['grʌmpɪ] adj (inf) scorbutico(-a).

grunt [grʌnt] vi grugnire.

guarantee [ˌgærən'tiː] ♦ n garanzia f ♦ vt garantire.

guard [gɑːd] ♦ n (of prisoner etc) guardia f; (Br: on train) capotreno mf; (protective cover) schermo m di protezione ♦ vt (watch over) sorvegliare; **to be on one's ~** stare in guardia.

guess [ges] ♦ n supposizione f ♦ vt & vi indovinare; **I ~ (so)** penso di sì; **have a ~!** indovina!

guest [gest] n (in home) ospite mf; (in hotel) cliente mf.

guesthouse ['gesthaus, pl -hauzɪz] n pensione f.

guestroom ['gestrum] n camera f degli ospiti.

guidance ['gaɪdəns] n guida f, direzione f.

guide [gaɪd] ♦ n guida f ♦ vt guidare.

▶ **Guide** n (Br) giovane esploratrice f.

guidebook ['gaɪdbuk] n guida f.

guide dog n cane m guida.

guided tour ['gaɪdɪd-] n visita f guidata.

guidelines ['gaɪdlaɪnz] npl direttive fpl.

guilt [gɪlt] n colpa f.

guilty ['gɪltɪ] adj colpevole; **to feel ~** sentirsi in colpa.

guinea pig ['gɪnɪ-] n cavia f.

guitar [gɪ'tɑːʳ] n chitarra f.

guitarist [gɪ'tɑːrɪst] n chitarrista mf.

gulf [gʌlf] n (of sea) golfo m.

Gulf War n: **the ~** la guerra del Golfo.

gull [gʌl] n gabbiano m.

gullible ['gʌləbl] adj credulone (-a).

gulp [gʌlp] n (of drink) sorso m.

gum [gʌm] n gomma f da masticare; (adhesive) colla f.

▶ **gums** npl gengive fpl.

gun [gʌn] n (pistol) pistola f; (rifle) fucile m; (cannon) cannone m.

gunfire ['gʌnfaɪəʳ] n sparatoria f.

gunshot ['gʌnʃɒt] n sparo m.

gust [gʌst] n (of wind) raffica f.

gut [gʌt] n (inf: stomach) stomaco m.

▶ **guts** npl (inf) (intestines) budella fpl; (courage): **to have ~s** avere fegato.

gutter ['gʌtəʳ] n (beside road) cunetta f; (of house) grondaia f.

guy [gaɪ] n (inf: man) tipo m.

▶ **guys** npl (Am: inf: people) gente f.

Guy Fawkes Night [-'fɔːks-] n festa che si celebra il 5 novembre per ricordare il fallimento della Congiura delle polveri.

guy rope n cavo m.

gym [dʒɪm] n palestra f; (school lesson) ginnastica f.

gymnast ['dʒɪmnæst] n ginnasta mf.

gymnastics [dʒɪm'næstɪks] n ginnastica f.

gym shoes npl scarpe fpl da ginnastica.

gynaecologist [ˌgaɪnə'kɒlədʒɪst] n ginecologo m (-a f).

gypsy ['dʒɪpsɪ] = **gipsy**.

H

H ◆ (*abbr of hospital*) H ◆ *abbr* = **hot**.
habit ['hæbɪt] *n* (*custom*) abitudine *f*.
hacksaw ['hæksɔː] *n* seghetto *m*.
had [hæd] *pt & pp* → **have**.
haddock ['hædək] (*pl inv*) *n* eglefino *m* (*pesce simile al merluzzo*).
hadn't ['hædnt] = **had not**.
haggis ['hægɪs] *n* piatto tipico scozzese a base di avena e frattaglie di pecora.
haggle ['hægl] *vi* mercanteggiare.
hail [heɪl] ◆ *n* grandine *f* ◆ *v impers* grandinare.
hailstone ['heɪlstəʊn] *n* chicco *m* di grandine.
hair [heəʳ] *n* (*on head*) capelli *mpl*; (*on animal*) pelo *m*; (*on human skin*) peli *mpl*; (*individual hair on head*) capello *m*; (*individual hair on skin*) pelo *m*; **to have one's ~ cut** tagliarsi i capelli.
hairband ['heəbænd] *n* cerchietto *m* per capelli.
hairbrush ['heəbrʌʃ] *n* spazzola *f* per capelli.
hairclip ['heəklɪp] *n* fermaglio *m* per capelli.
haircut ['heəkʌt] *n* (*style*) taglio *m* di capelli; **to have a ~** farsi tagliare i capelli.
hairdo ['heəduː] (*pl* -s) *n* acconciatura *f*, pettinatura *f*.
hairdresser ['heə,dresəʳ] *n* parrucchiere *m* (-a *f*); **~'s** (*salon*) negozio *m* di parrucchiere; **to go to the ~'s** andare dal parrucchiere.
hairdryer ['heə,draɪəʳ] *n* asciugacapelli *m inv*, föhn *m inv*.
hair gel *n* gel *m inv* per capelli, gommina *f*.
hairgrip ['heəgrɪp] *n* (*Br*) molletta *f* (per capelli).

hairnet ['heənet] *n* retina *f* (per capelli).
hairpin bend ['heəpɪn-] *n* tornante *m*.
hair remover [-rɪ,muːvəʳ] *n* crema *f* depilatoria.
hair rollers [-'rəʊləz] *npl* bigodini *mpl*.
hair slide *n* fermacapelli *m inv*.
hairspray ['heəspreɪ] *n* lacca *f* per capelli.
hairstyle ['heəstaɪl] *n* acconciatura *f*, pettinatura *f*.
hairy ['heərɪ] *adj* (*person, chest, legs*) peloso(-a).
half [Br haːf, Am hæf] (*pl* **halves**) *n* metà *f inv*; (*of match*) tempo *m*; (*half pint*) mezza pinta *f*; (*child's ticket*) biglietto *m* ridotto ◆ *adj* mezzo(-a) ◆ *adv*: **~ cooked** cotto a metà; **~ full** mezzo pieno; **I'm ~ Scottish** per metà sono scozzese; **a day and a ~** un giorno e mezzo; **four and a ~** quattro e mezzo; **~ past seven** sette e mezza; **~ as big as** la metà di; **an hour and a ~** un'ora e mezza; **~ an hour** mezz'ora; **~ a dozen** mezza dozzina; **~ price** a metà prezzo.
half board *n* mezza pensione *f*.
half-day *n* mezza giornata *f*.
half fare *n* mezza tariffa *f*.
half portion *n* mezza porzione *f*.
half-price *adj* a metà prezzo.
half term *n* (*Br*) vacanza a metà trimestre.
half time *n* intervallo *m*.
halfway [haːf'weɪ] *adv* (*in space*) a metà strada; (*in time*) a metà.
halibut ['hælɪbət] (*pl inv*) *n* halibut *m inv*.
hall [hɔːl] *n* (*of house*) ingresso *m*; (*large room, building*) sala *f*, salone *m*; (*country house*) maniero *m*.
hallmark ['hɔːlmaːk] *n* (*on silver, gold*) marchio *m*.
hallo [hə'ləʊ] = **hello**.
hall of residence *n* casa *f* dello studente.

Halloween [ˌhæləʊˈiːn] *n vigilia d'Ognissanti*.

halt [hɔːlt] ◆ *vi* fermarsi ◆ *n*: **to come to a ~** fermarsi.

halve [Br hɑːv, Am hæv] *vt* dimezzare.

halves [Br hɑːvz, Am hævz] *pl* → **half**.

ham [hæm] *n (meat)* prosciutto *m* (cotto).

hamburger [ˈhæmbɜːgəʳ] *n (beefburger)* hamburger *m inv*; (Am: *mince*) carne *f* macinata.

hamlet [ˈhæmlɪt] *n* paesino *m*.

hammer [ˈhæməʳ] ◆ *n* martello *m* ◆ *vt (nail)* piantare.

hammock [ˈhæmək] *n* amaca *f*.

hamper [ˈhæmpəʳ] *n* cesta *f*.

hamster [ˈhæmstəʳ] *n* criceto *m*.

hamstring [ˈhæmstrɪŋ] *n* tendine *m* del ginocchio.

hand [hænd] *n* mano *f*; (*of clock, watch, dial*) lancetta *f*; **to give sb a ~** dare una mano a qn; **to get out of ~** sfuggire di mano; **by ~** a mano; **in ~** (*time*) a disposizione; **on the one ~** da una parte; **on the other ~** d'altra parte.

► **hand in** *vt sep* consegnare.

► **hand out** *vt sep* distribuire.

► **hand over** *vt sep (give)* consegnare.

handbag [ˈhændbæg] *n* borsetta *f*.

handbasin [ˈhændbeɪsn] *n* lavabo *m*.

handbook [ˈhændbʊk] *n* manuale *m*.

handbrake [ˈhændbreɪk] *n* freno *m* a mano.

hand cream *n* crema *f* per le mani.

handcuffs [ˈhændkʌfs] *npl* manette *fpl*.

handful [ˈhændfʊl] *n (amount)* manciata *f*.

handicap [ˈhændɪkæp] *n* handicap *m inv*.

handicapped [ˈhændɪkæpt] ◆ *adj* handicappato(-a) ◆ *npl*: **the ~** i portatori di handicap.

handkerchief [ˈhæŋkətʃɪf] (*pl* -**chiefs** OR -**chieves** [-tʃiːvz]) *n* fazzoletto *m*.

handle [ˈhændl] ◆ *n (of door, window)* maniglia *f*; (*of knife, pan, suitcase*) manico *m* ◆ *vt (touch)* toccare; (*deal with*) occuparsi di; **'~ with care'** 'fragile'.

handlebars [ˈhændlbɑːz] *npl* manubrio *m*.

hand luggage *n* bagaglio *m* a mano.

handmade [ˌhændˈmeɪd] *adj* fatto(-a) a mano.

handout [ˈhændaʊt] *n (leaflet)* volantino *m*.

handrail [ˈhændreɪl] *n* corrimano *m*.

handset [ˈhændset] *n* ricevitore *m*; **'please replace the ~'** 'si prega di riporre il ricevitore'.

handshake [ˈhændʃeɪk] *n* stretta *f* di mano.

handsome [ˈhænsəm] *adj (man)* bello(-a).

handstand [ˈhændstænd] *n* verticale *f*.

handwriting [ˈhændˌraɪtɪŋ] *n* calligrafia *f*.

handy [ˈhændɪ] *adj (useful)* utile; (*convenient*) comodo(-a); (*good with one's hands*) abile; (*near*) vicino(-a), a portata di mano; **to come in ~** (*inf*) tornare utile.

hang [hæŋ] (*pt & pp* **hung**) ◆ *vt* appendere; (*execute: pt & pp* **hanged**) impiccare ◆ *vi (be suspended)* penzolare, pendere ◆ *n*: **to get the ~ of sthg** fare la mano a qc.

► **hang about** *vi* (Br: *inf*) ciondolare.

► **hang around** (*inf*) = **hang about**.

► **hang down** *vi* penzolare.

► **hang on** *vi* (*inf: wait*) aspettare.

► **hang out** ◆ *vt sep (washing)* stendere ◆ *vi* (*inf*) stare.

► **hang up** *vi* (*on phone*) riagganciare.

hangar ['hæŋəʳ] n hangar m inv.

hanger ['hæŋəʳ] n gruccia f, stampella f.

hang gliding n deltaplano m.

hangover ['hæŋ,əʊvəʳ] n postumi mpl di sbornia.

hankie ['hæŋkɪ] n (inf) fazzoletto m.

happen ['hæpən] vi succedere, accadere; **I ~ed to catch sight of him** mi è capitato di vederlo.

happily ['hæpɪlɪ] adv (luckily) fortunatamente.

happiness ['hæpɪnɪs] n felicità f.

happy ['hæpɪ] adj felice; **to be ~ about sthg** essere contento(-a) di qc; **to be ~ to do sthg** (willing) fare qc volentieri; **to be ~ with sthg** essere soddisfatto di qc; **Happy Birthday!** buon compleanno!; **Happy Christmas!** buon Natale!; **Happy New Year!** buon anno!

happy hour n (inf) momento della giornata, di solito nel tardo pomeriggio, in cui, nei bar, le bevande vengono vendute a prezzo ridotto.

harassment ['hærəsmənt] n molestie fpl.

harbor ['hɑːbər] (Am) = **harbour**.

harbour ['hɑːbəʳ] n (Br) porto m.

hard [hɑːd] ♦ adj duro(-a); (difficult) difficile; (strenuous) faticoso(-a); (forceful) forte; (winter, frost) rigido(-a); (drugs) pesante ♦ adv (work) duro; (listen) attentamente; (hit) con forza; (rain) a dirotto.

hardback ['hɑːdbæk] n edizione f rilegata.

hardboard ['hɑːdbɔːd] n pannello m di legno compresso.

hard-boiled egg [-bɔɪld-] n uovo m sodo.

hard disk n hard disk m inv, disco m rigido.

hardly ['hɑːdlɪ] adv a malapena, appena; **~ ever** quasi mai.

hardship ['hɑːdʃɪp] n (difficult conditions) privazioni fpl; (difficult circumstance) avversità fpl.

hard shoulder n (Br) corsia f d'emergenza.

hard up adj (inf) in bolletta.

hardware ['hɑːdweəʳ] n (tools, equipment) ferramenta fpl; (COMPUT) hardware m.

hardwearing [,hɑːd'weərɪŋ] adj (Br) resistente.

hardworking [,hɑːd'wɜːkɪŋ] adj instancabile.

hare [heəʳ] n lepre f.

harm [hɑːm] ♦ n (injury) male m; (damage) danno m ♦ vt (injure) far male a; (damage) danneggiare.

harmful ['hɑːmfʊl] adj nocivo(-a).

harmless ['hɑːmlɪs] adj innocuo(-a).

harmonica [hɑːˈmɒnɪkə] n armonica f.

harmony ['hɑːmənɪ] n armonia f.

harness ['hɑːnɪs] n (for horse) finimenti mpl; (for child) briglie fpl.

harp [hɑːp] n arpa f.

harpsichord ['hɑːpsɪkɔːd] n clavicembalo m.

harsh [hɑːʃ] adj (weather) rigido(-a); (conditions) duro(-a); (cruel) severo(-a); (sound) sgradevole.

harvest ['hɑːvɪst] n (of corn, fruit) raccolto m; (of grapes) vendemmia f.

has [weak form həz, strong form hæz] → **have**.

hash browns [hæʃ-] npl (Am) frittelle fpl di patate.

hasn't ['hæznt] = **has not**.

hassle ['hæsl] n (inf: problem) seccatura f.

hastily ['heɪstɪlɪ] adv (rashly) precipitosamente.

hasty ['heɪstɪ] adj (hurried) affrettato(-a); (rash) precipitoso(-a).

hat [hæt] n cappello m.

hatch [hætʃ] ♦ n (for food) passavivande m inv ♦ vi (egg) schiudersi.

hatchback ['hætʃ,bæk] n (car) tre OR cinque porte f inv.

hatchet ['hætʃɪt] n accetta f.

hate [heɪt] ♦ n odio m ♦ vt odiare, detestare; **to ~ doing sthg** detestare fare qc.

hatred ['heɪtrɪd] n odio m.

haul [hɔːl] ◆ vt trascinare ◆ n: a long ~ un percorso lungo e faticoso.

haunted ['hɔːntɪd] adj (house) abitato(-a) da fantasmi.

have [hæv] (pt & pp **had**) aux vb 1. (to form perfect tenses: gen) avere; (with many intransitive verbs) essere; **I** ~ **finished** ho finito; ~ **you been there? – no, I haven't** ci sei stato? – no; **the train had already gone** il treno era già partito.

2. (must): **to** ~ **(got) to do sthg** dover fare qc; **do you** ~ **to pay?** si deve pagare?

◆ vt 1. (possess): **to** ~ **(got)** avere; **do you** ~ OR ~ **you got a double room?** avete una camera doppia?; **she has (got) brown hair** ha i capelli castani.

2. (experience) avere; **to** ~ **a cold** avere il raffreddore; **we had a great time** ci siamo divertiti un mondo.

3. (replacing other verbs): **to** ~ **breakfast** fare colazione; **to** ~ **dinner** cenare; **to** ~ **lunch** pranzare; **to** ~ **a drink** bere qualcosa; **to** ~ **a shower** fare una doccia; **to** ~ **a swim** fare una nuotata; **to** ~ **a walk** fare una passeggiata.

4. (cause to be): **to** ~ **sthg done** far fare qc; **to** ~ **one's hair cut** farsi tagliare i capelli.

5. (be treated in a certain way): **I've had my wallet stolen** mi hanno rubato il portafoglio.

haversack ['hævəsæk] n zaino m.

havoc ['hævək] n caos m.

hawk [hɔːk] n falco m.

hawker ['hɔːkər] n venditore m (-trice f) ambulante.

hay [heɪ] n fieno m.

hay fever n raffreddore m da fieno.

haystack ['heɪˌstæk] n pagliaio m.

hazard ['hæzəd] n rischio m, pericolo m.

hazardous ['hæzədəs] adj rischioso(-a), pericoloso(-a).

hazard warning lights npl (Br) luci fpl di emergenza.

haze [heɪz] n foschia f.

hazel ['heɪzl] adj nocciola (inv).

hazelnut ['heɪzlˌnʌt] n nocciola f.

hazy ['heɪzɪ] adj (misty) offuscato(-a).

he [hiː] pron lui, egli; ~'**s tall** è alto.

head [hed] ◆ n (of body) testa f, capo m; (of queue, page, bed) cima f; (of company, department, table) capo; (head teacher of primary or lower secondary school) direttore m (-trice f) di scuola; (head teacher of upper secondary school) preside mf; (of beer) schiuma f ◆ vt (list) essere in testa a; (organization) dirigere, essere a capo di ◆ vi dirigersi; £10 a ~ 10 sterline a testa; ~s or tails? testa o croce?

▸ **head for** vt fus dirigersi verso OR a.

headache ['hedeɪk] n (pain) mal m di testa; **to have a** ~ avere mal di testa.

heading ['hedɪŋ] n intestazione f.

headlamp ['hedlæmp] (Br) = **headlight**.

headlight ['hedlaɪt] n fanale m anteriore.

headline ['hedlaɪn] n (in newspaper) titolo m; (on TV, radio) notizie fpl principali.

headmaster [ˌhedˈmɑːstər] n (of primary or lower secondary school) direttore m di scuola; (of upper secondary school) preside m.

headmistress [ˌhedˈmɪstrɪs] n (of primary or lower secondary school) direttrice f di scuola; (of upper secondary school) preside f.

head of state n capo m di Stato.

headphones ['hedfəʊnz] npl cuffie fpl.

headquarters [ˌhedˈkwɔːtəz] npl (of company, bank) sede f centrale; (of police, army) quartiere m generale.

headrest ['hedrest] n poggiatesta m inv.

headroom ['hedrʊm] n (under bridge) altezza f massima.

headscarf ['hedskɑːf] (pl **-scarves** [-skɑːvz]) n foulard m inv.

head start n vantaggio m.

head teacher n (of primary or lower secondary school) direttore m (-trice f) di scuola; (of upper secondary school) preside mf.

head waiter n capocameriere m.

heal [hiːl] ◆ vt curare ◆ vi guarire.

health [helθ] n salute f; **to be in good ~** essere in buona salute; **to be in poor ~** essere in cattive condizioni di salute; **your (very) good ~!** alla tua salute!

health centre n centro m sanitario.

health food n cibo m naturale.

health food shop n negozio m di prodotti naturali.

health insurance n assicurazione f contro le malattie.

healthy ['helθɪ] adj sano(-a).

heap [hiːp] n mucchio m; **~s of** (inf) un mucchio di.

hear [hɪəʳ] (pt & pp **heard** [hɜːd]) ◆ vt sentire; (case, evidence) esaminare ◆ vi sentire; **to ~ about sthg** sapere OR sentire di qc; **to ~ from sb** ricevere notizie da qn; **to have heard of** aver sentito parlare di.

hearing ['hɪərɪŋ] n (sense) udito m; (at court) udienza f; **to be hard of ~** esser duro d'orecchi.

hearing aid n apparecchio m acustico.

heart [hɑːt] n cuore m; **to know sthg (off) by ~** sapere qc a memoria; **to lose ~** scoraggiarsi.

▶ **hearts** npl (in cards) cuori mpl.

heart attack n infarto m.

heartbeat ['hɑːtbiːt] n (rhythm) battito m cardiaco.

heartburn ['hɑːtbɜːn] n bruciore m di stomaco.

heart condition n: **to have a ~** avere un disturbo cardiaco.

hearth [hɑːθ] n focolare m.

hearty ['hɑːtɪ] adj (meal) abbondante, sostanzioso(-a).

heat [hiːt] n (warmth) calore m; (warm weather) caldo m; (of oven) temperatura f.

▶ **heat up** vt sep riscaldare.

heater ['hiːtəʳ] n (for room) stufa f; (radiator) radiatore m; (in car) riscaldamento m; (for water) scaldabagno m.

heath [hiːθ] n brughiera f.

heather ['heðəʳ] n erica f.

heating ['hiːtɪŋ] n riscaldamento m.

heat wave n ondata f di caldo.

heave [hiːv] vt (push) spingere (con forza); (pull) tirare (con forza); (lift) sollevare (con forza).

Heaven ['hevn] n paradiso m.

heavily ['hevɪlɪ] adv (smoke, drink) molto; (rain) a dirotto.

heavy ['hevɪ] adj pesante; (rain, traffic) intenso(-a); (fighting) violento(-a); (losses, defeat) grave; **how ~ is it?** quanto pesa?; **to be a ~ smoker** essere un fumatore accanito.

heavy cream n (Am) panna molto densa ad alto contenuto di grassi.

heavy goods vehicle n (Br) veicolo m per trasporti pesanti.

heavy industry n industria f pesante.

heavy metal n heavy metal m.

heckle ['hekl] vt interrompere di continuo.

hectic ['hektɪk] adj frenetico(-a).

hedge [hedʒ] n siepe f.

hedgehog ['hedʒhɒg] n riccio m.

heel [hiːl] n (of person) calcagno m; (of shoe) tacco m.

hefty ['heftɪ] adj (person) robusto(-a); (fine) salato(-a).

height [haɪt] n altezza f; (peak period) apice m; **what ~ is it?** quanto è alto?

heir [eəʳ] n erede m.

heiress ['eərɪs] n erede f.

held [held] pt & pp → **hold**.

helicopter ['helɪkɒptər] n elicottero m.

he'll [hiːl] = **he will**, = **he shall**.

Hell [hel] n inferno m.

hello [hə'ləʊ] excl (as greeting) ciao!; (more formal) buongiorno!; (on phone) pronto!; (to attract attention) ehi!

helmet ['helmɪt] n casco m.

help [help] ♦ n aiuto m ♦ vt aiutare; (contribute to) contribuire a ♦ vi aiutare, essere d'aiuto ♦ excl aiuto!; **I can't ~ it** non ci posso fare niente; **to ~ sb (to) do sthg** aiutare qn a fare qc; **to ~ o.s. (to sthg)** servirsi (di qc); **can I ~ you?** (in shop) desidera?

► **help out** vi aiutare, dare una mano.

helper ['helpər] n (assistant) aiutante mf; (Am: cleaner) uomo m (donna f) delle pulizie.

helpful ['helpfʊl] adj (person) di grande aiuto; (useful) utile.

helping ['helpɪŋ] n porzione f.

helpless ['helplɪs] adj impotente; (child) indifeso(-a).

hem [hem] n orlo m.

hemophiliac [ˌhiːməˈfɪliæk] n emofiliaco m (-a f).

hemorrhage ['hemərɪdʒ] n emorragia f.

hen [hen] n gallina f.

hepatitis [ˌhepəˈtaɪtɪs] n epatite f.

her [hɜːr] ♦ adj il suo (la sua), i suoi (le sue) (pl) ♦ pron (direct) la; (indirect) le; (after prep, stressed) lei; ~ **brother** suo fratello; **I know ~** la conosco; **it's ~** è lei; **send it to ~** mandaglielo, mandalo a lei; **tell ~** diglielo; **tell ~ that ...** dille che ...; **he's worse than ~** lui è peggio di lei.

herb [hɜːb] n erba f.

herbal tea ['hɜːbl-] n tè m inv d'erbe.

herd [hɜːd] n (of cattle) mandria f.

here [hɪər] adv qui, qua; ~**'s your book** eccoti il libro; ~ **you are** eccoti (qui OR qua).

heritage ['herɪtɪdʒ] n eredità f,

patrimonio m.

heritage centre n centro informazioni in luoghi di interesse storico.

hernia ['hɜːnjə] n ernia f.

hero ['hɪərəʊ] (pl -es) n eroe m.

heroin ['herəʊɪn] n eroina f (droga).

heroine ['herəʊɪn] n eroina f.

heron ['herən] n airone m.

herring ['herɪŋ] n aringa f.

hers [hɜːz] pron il suo (la sua), i suoi (le sue) (pl); **a friend of ~** un suo amico.

herself [hɜːˈself] pron (reflexive) si; (after prep) se stessa, sé; **she did it ~** l'ha fatto da sola.

hesitant ['hezɪtənt] adj esitante.

hesitate ['hezɪteɪt] vi esitare.

hesitation [ˌhezɪˈteɪʃn] n esitazione f.

heterosexual [ˌhetərəʊˈsekʃʊəl] ♦ adj eterosessuale ♦ n eterosessuale mf.

hey [heɪ] excl (inf) ehi!

HGV abbr = **heavy goods vehicle**.

hi [haɪ] excl (inf) ciao!

hiccup ['hɪkʌp] n: **to have (the) ~s** avere il singhiozzo.

hide [haɪd] (pt hid [hɪd], pp hidden ['hɪdn]) ♦ vt nascondere ♦ vi nascondersi ♦ n (of animal) pelle f.

hideous ['hɪdɪəs] adj raccapricciante.

hi-fi ['haɪfaɪ] n hi-fi m inv.

high [haɪ] ♦ adj alto(-a); (price, speed, temperature) alto, elevato(-a); (wind) forte; (sound, voice) acuto(-a), alto; (inf: from drugs) fatto(-a) ♦ n (weather front) anticiclone m ♦ adv alto, in alto; **how ~ is it?** quanto è alto?; **it's 10 metres ~** è alto 10 metri.

high chair n seggiolone m.

high-class adj di lusso.

Higher ['haɪər] n (Scot) esame sostenuto alla fine di studi secondari.

higher education n istruzione f universitaria.

high heels npl tacchi mpl alti.

high jump n salto m in alto.

Highland Games ['haɪlənd-] npl: **the ~** gare sportive disputate all'aperto nelle Highlands scozzesi.

Highlands ['haɪləndz] npl: **the ~** le Highlands fpl (regione montuosa nel nord della Scozia).

highlight ['haɪlaɪt] ◆ n (best part) clou m inv ◆ vt (emphasize) evidenziare.

▶ **highlights** npl (of football match etc) sintesi f inv; (in hair) colpi mpl di sole.

highly ['haɪlɪ] adv (extremely) molto; (very well) molto bene; **to think ~ of sb** avere grande stima di qn.

high-pitched [-'pɪtʃt] adj acuto(-a).

high-rise adj con tanti piani.

high school n (in UK) ≃ scuola f secondaria inferiore e superiore; (in US) ≃ scuola secondaria superiore.

high season n alta stagione f.

high-speed train n treno m ad alta velocità.

high street n (Br) strada f principale.

high tide n alta marea f.

highway ['haɪweɪ] n (Am: between towns) superstrada f; (Br: any main road) strada f principale.

Highway Code n (Br) codice m stradale.

hijack ['haɪdʒæk] vt dirottare.

hijacker ['haɪdʒækər] n dirottatore m (-trice f).

hike [haɪk] ◆ n lunga camminata f ◆ vi fare una lunga camminata.

hiking ['haɪkɪŋ] n: **to go ~** andare a fare lunghe camminate.

hilarious [hɪ'leərɪəs] adj spassoso(-a).

hill [hɪl] n collina f, colle m.

hillwalking ['hɪlwɔːkɪŋ] n: **to go ~** fare lunghe camminate.

hilly ['hɪlɪ] adj collinoso(-a).

him [hɪm] pron (direct) lo; (indirect) gli; (after prep, stressed) lui; **I know ~** lo conosco; **it's ~** è lui; **send it to ~** mandaglielo, mandalo a lui; **tell ~** diglielo; **tell ~ that** … digli che …; **she's worse than ~** lei è peggio di lui.

himself [hɪm'self] pron (reflexive) si; (after prep) se stesso, sé; **he did it ~** l'ha fatto da solo.

hinder ['hɪndər] vt ostacolare.

Hindu ['hɪnduː] (pl -s) ◆ adj indù (inv) ◆ n (person) indù mf inv.

hinge [hɪndʒ] n cardine m.

hint [hɪnt] ◆ n (indirect suggestion) accenno m, allusione f; (piece of advice) consiglio m; (slight amount) accenno, punta f ◆ vi: **to ~ at sthg** alludere a qc.

hip [hɪp] n fianco m.

hippopotamus [ˌhɪpə'pɒtəməs] n ippopotamo m.

hippy ['hɪpɪ] n hippy mf inv.

hire ['haɪər] vt (car, bicycle, television) noleggiare; **'for ~'** (boats) 'a noleggio'; (taxi) 'libero'.

▶ **hire out** vt sep (car, bicycle, television) dare a noleggio.

hire car n (Br) vettura f a noleggio.

hire purchase n (Br) acquisto m rateale.

his [hɪz] ◆ adj il suo (la sua), i suoi (le sue) (pl) ◆ pron il suo (la sua), i suoi (le sue) (pl); **~ brother** suo fratello; **a friend of ~** un suo amico.

historical [hɪ'stɒrɪkəl] adj storico(-a).

history ['hɪstərɪ] n storia f; (record) passato m.

hit [hɪt] (pt & pp **hit**) ◆ vt colpire; (bang) sbattere, picchiare ◆ n (record, play, film) successo m.

hit-and-run adj: **~ accident** incidente in cui l'automobilista colpevole non si ferma a prestare soccorso.

hitch [hɪtʃ] ◆ n (problem) contrattempo m ◆ vt: **to ~ a lift** farsi dare un passaggio ◆ vi fare l'autostop.

hitchhike ['hɪtʃhaɪk] vi fare l'autostop.

hitchhiker ['hɪtʃhaɪkəʳ] n autostoppista mf.

hive [haɪv] n (of bees) alveare m.

HIV-positive adj sieropositivo(-a).

hoarding ['hɔːdɪŋ] n (Br: for adverts) tabellone m per pubblicità.

hoarse [hɔːs] adj rauco(-a).

hoax [həʊks] n burla f.

hob [hɒb] n piano m di cottura.

hobby ['hɒbɪ] n hobby m inv, passatempo m.

hock [hɒk] n (wine) vino m bianco del Reno.

hockey ['hɒkɪ] n (on grass) hockey m su prato; (Am: ice hockey) hockey su ghiaccio.

hoe [həʊ] n zappa f.

Hogmanay ['hɒgmənei] n (Scot) l'ultimo m dell'anno.

hold [həʊld] (pt & pp **held**) ◆ vt tenere; (contain) contenere; (possess) avere, possedere ◆ vi (weather) mantenersi; (luck, offer) permanere; (on telephone) restare in linea ◆ n (grip) presa f; (of ship) stiva f; (of aircraft) bagagliaio m; **to ~ sb prisoner** tenere prigioniero qn; **~ the line, please** resti in linea, per favore.

▶ **hold back** vt sep (restrain) trattenere; (keep secret) tenere segreto.

▶ **hold on** vi (wait) aspettare, attendere; (on telephone) restare in linea; **to ~ on to sthg** (grip) tenersi (stretto) a qc.

▶ **hold out** vt sep (hand) porgere, tendere.

▶ **hold up** vt sep (delay) bloccare.

holdall ['həʊldɔːl] n (Br) borsone m da viaggio.

holder ['həʊldəʳ] n (of passport, licence) titolare mf, proprietario m (-a f); (container) contenitore m.

holdup ['həʊldʌp] n (delay) ritardo m.

hole [həʊl] n (in sock, wall) buco m; (in ground, golf) buca f.

holiday ['hɒlɪdeɪ] ◆ n (Br: period of time) vacanze fpl; (time off work) ferie fpl; (public holiday) festa f ◆ vi (Br) trascorrere le vacanze; **to be on ~** essere in vacanza; **to go on ~** andare in vacanza.

holidaymaker ['hɒlɪdɪˌmeɪkəʳ] n (Br) villeggiante mf.

holiday pay n (Br) retribuzione f delle ferie.

Holland ['hɒlənd] n l'Olanda f.

hollow ['hɒləʊ] adj cavo(-a).

holly ['hɒlɪ] n agrifoglio m.

Hollywood ['hɒlɪwʊd] n Hollywood f.

holy ['həʊlɪ] adj sacro(-a).

home [həʊm] ◆ n casa f; (own country) patria f; (for old people) istituto m, ricovero m ◆ adv a casa ◆ adj (not foreign) interno(-a), nazionale; (cooking) casereccio(-a); **at ~** (in one's house) a casa; **to make o.s. at ~** fare come se si fosse a casa propria; **to go ~** andare a casa; **to leave ~** (for good) andarsene di casa; **~ address** indirizzo m di casa; **~ number** numero m (telefonico) di casa.

home economics n economia f domestica.

home help n (Br) collaboratore m domestico (collaboratrice domestica f).

homeless ['həʊmlɪs] npl: **the ~** i senzatetto.

homemade [ˌhəʊm'meɪd] adj (food) casereccio(-a).

homeopathic [ˌhəʊmɪəʊ'pæθɪk] adj omeopatico(-a).

home page n (COMPUT) home page f inv.

Home Secretary n (Br) ministro m degli Interni.

homesick ['həʊmsɪk] adj: **to be ~** avere nostalgia di casa.

homework ['həʊmwɜːk] n compiti mpl a casa.

homosexual [ˌhɒmə'sekʃʊəl] ◆ adj omosessuale ◆ n omosessuale mf.

honest ['ɒnɪst] adj (trustworthy) onesto(-a); (frank) sincero(-a), franco(-a).

honestly [ˈɒnɪstlɪ] adv (truthfully) onestamente; (frankly) sinceramente, francamente.

honey [ˈhʌnɪ] n miele m.

honeymoon [ˈhʌnɪmuːn] n luna f di miele, viaggio m di nozze.

honor [ˈɒnər] (Am) = **honour**.

honour [ˈɒnər] n (Br) onore m.

honourable [ˈɒnrəbl] adj onorevole.

hood [hʊd] n (of jacket, coat) cappuccio m; (on convertible car) cápote f inv; (Am: car bonnet) cofano m.

hoof [huːf] n zoccolo m.

hook [hʊk] n gancio m; (for fishing) amo m; **off the ~** (telephone) staccato.

hooligan [ˈhuːlɪɡən] n teppista mf, hooligan mf inv.

hoop [huːp] n cerchio m.

hoot [huːt] vi (driver) suonare il clacson.

Hoover® [ˈhuːvər] n (Br) aspirapolvere m inv.

hop [hɒp] vi (person) saltellare su una gamba.

hope [həʊp] ♦ n speranza f ♦ vt sperare; **to ~ for sthg** sperare in qc; **to ~ to do sthg** sperare di fare qc; **I ~ so** spero di sì.

hopeful [ˈhəʊpfʊl] adj (optimistic) fiducioso(-a).

hopefully [ˈhəʊpfəlɪ] adv (with luck) se tutto va bene.

hopeless [ˈhəʊplɪs] adj (without any hope) disperato(-a); **he's ~!** (inf) è un disastro!

hops [hɒps] npl luppolo m.

horizon [həˈraɪzn] n orizzonte m.

horizontal [ˌhɒrɪˈzɒntl] adj orizzontale.

horn [hɔːn] n (of car) clacson m inv; (on animal) corno m.

horoscope [ˈhɒrəskəʊp] n oroscopo m.

horrible [ˈhɒrəbl] adj orribile.

horrid [ˈhɒrɪd] adj (very bad) orrendo(-a); (unkind) odioso(-a); (food, drink) pessimo(-a).

horrific [hɒˈrɪfɪk] adj orripilante, terrificante.

hors d'oeuvre [ɔːˈdɜːvrə] n antipasto m.

horse [hɔːs] n cavallo m.

horseback [ˈhɔːsbæk] n: **on ~** a cavallo.

horse chestnut n ippocastano m.

horse-drawn carriage n carrozza f a cavalli.

horsepower [ˈhɔːsˌpaʊər] n cavallo m vapore.

horse racing n ippica f.

horseradish (sauce) [ˈhɔːsˌrædɪʃ-] n salsa f di rafano.

horse riding n equitazione f.

horseshoe [ˈhɔːsʃuː] n ferro m di cavallo.

hose [həʊz] n (hosepipe) tubo m per annaffiare.

hosepipe [ˈhəʊzpaɪp] n tubo m per annaffiare.

hosiery [ˈhəʊzɪərɪ] n calzetteria f.

hospitable [hɒˈspɪtəbl] adj ospitale.

hospital [ˈhɒspɪtl] n ospedale m; **in ~** all'ospedale.

hospitality [ˌhɒspɪˈtælətɪ] n ospitalità f.

host [həʊst] n (of party, event) ospite m; (of show, TV programme) conduttore m (-trice f).

hostage [ˈhɒstɪdʒ] n ostaggio m.

hostel [ˈhɒstl] n (youth hostel) ostello m.

hostess [ˈhəʊstes] n (on aeroplane) hostess f inv; (of party, event) ospite f.

hostile [Br ˈhɒstaɪl, Am ˈhɒstl] adj ostile.

hostility [hɒˈstɪlətɪ] n ostilità f.

hot [hɒt] adj caldo(-a); (spicy) piccante; **to be ~** (person) aver caldo; **it's ~** fa caldo.

hot chocolate n cioccolata f calda.

hot-cross bun n panino dolce con uvetta e spezie tipico del periodo pasquale.

hot dog n hot dog m inv (panino imbottito con würstel e senape).

hotel [həu'tel] *n* hotel *m inv*, albergo *m*.

hot line *n* telefono *m* rosso.

hotplate ['hɒtpleɪt] *n* piastra *f*.

hotpot ['hɒtpɒt] *n* spezzatino di carne con patate.

hot-water bottle *n* borsa *f* dell'acqua calda.

hour ['auər] *n* ora *f*; **I've been waiting for ~s** è un secolo che aspetto.

hourly ['auəlɪ] ♦ *adj* (*per hour*) orario(-a); (*every hour*) ogni ora ♦ *adv* (*per hour*) a ore; (*every hour*) ogni ora.

house (*n* haus, *pl* 'hauzɪz, *vb* hauz] *n* casa *f*; (SCH) uno dei gruppi in cui sono divisi gli alunni di una scuola media o superiore in occasione di competizioni sportive ecc. ♦ *vt* (*person*) alloggiare.

household ['haushəuld] *n* famiglia *f*.

housekeeping ['haus,ki:pɪŋ] *n* amministrazione *f* della casa.

House of Commons *n* (Br) Camera *f* dei Comuni.

House of Lords *n* (Br) Camera *f* dei Lord.

Houses of Parliament *npl* (Br: *building*) palazzo *m* del Parlamento.

housewife ['hauswaɪf] (*pl* **-wives** [-waɪvz]) *n* casalinga *f*.

house wine *n* vino *m* della casa.

housewives *pl* → **housewife**.

housework ['hausw3:k] *n* lavori *mpl* di casa.

housing ['hauzɪŋ] *n* alloggi *mpl*.

housing estate *n* (Br) complesso *m* residenziale.

housing project (Am) = **housing estate**.

hovercraft ['hɒvəkrɑːft] *n* hovercraft *m inv*.

hoverport ['hɒvəpɔːt] *n* porto *m* per hovercraft.

how [hau] *adv* **1.** (*asking about way or manner*) come; **~ do you get there?** come ci si arriva?; **~ does it work?** come funziona?; **tell me ~ to do it** dimmi come devo fare.

2. (*asking about health, quality*) come; **~ are you?** come stai?; **~ are you doing?** come va?; **~ are things?** come vanno le cose?; **~ do you do?** piacere!; **~ is your room?** com'è la tua camera?

3. (*asking about degree, amount*): **~ tall is he?** quanto è alto?; **~ far is it?** quanto dista?; **~ long will it take?** quanto tempo ci vorrà?; **~ many?** quanti(-e)?; **~ much?** quanto(-a)?; **~ much is it?** quant'è?; **~ old are you?** quanti anni hai?

4. (*in phrases*): **~ about some coffee?** cosa ne diresti di un caffè?; **~ lovely!** che bello!

however [hau'evər] *adv* (*nevertheless*) tuttavia; **~ difficult it is** per quanto sia difficile.

howl [haul] *vi* ululare.

HP *abbr* = **hire purchase**.

HQ *n* (*abbr of headquarters*) Q.G. *m*.

hub airport [hʌb-] *n* aeroporto *m* principale.

hubcap ['hʌbkæp] *n* coprimozzo *m*.

hug [hʌg] ♦ *vt* abbracciare ♦ *n*: **to give sb a ~** abbracciare qn.

huge [hju:dʒ] *adj* enorme.

hull [hʌl] *n* scafo *m*.

hum [hʌm] *vi* (*bee, machine*) ronzare; (*person*) canterellare.

human ['hju:mən] ♦ *adj* umano(-a) ♦ *n*: **~ (being)** essere *m* umano.

humanities [hju:'mænətɪz] *npl* materie *fpl* umanistiche.

human rights *npl* diritti *mpl* dell'uomo.

humble ['hʌmbl] *adj* umile.

humid ['hju:mɪd] *adj* umido(-a).

humidity [hju:'mɪdətɪ] *n* umidità *f*.

humiliating [hju:'mɪlɪeɪtɪŋ] *adj* umiliante.

humiliation [hju:,mɪlɪ'eɪʃn] *n* umiliazione *f*.

hummus ['huməs] *n* salsetta cremosa a base di ceci, aglio e pasta di sesamo.

humor ['hju:mər] (Am) = **humour**.

humorous ['hju:mərəs] *adj* (*story*) umoristico(-a); (*person*) spiritoso(-a).

humour ['hju:mə^r] *n* umorismo *m*; **sense of ~** senso *m* dell'umorismo.

hump [hʌmp] *n* (*bump*) dosso *m*; (*of camel*) gobba *f*.

humpbacked bridge ['hʌmpbækt-] *n* ponte *m* a schiena d'asino.

hunch [hʌntʃ] *n* impressione *f*.

hundred ['hʌndrəd] *num* cento; **a ~** cento; (**about**) **a ~ people** un centinaio di persone, → **six**.

hundredth ['hʌndrətθ] *num* centesimo(-a), → **sixth**.

hundredweight ['hʌndrədweɪt] *n* (*in UK*) = 50,8 kg; (*in US*) = 45,4 kg.

hung [hʌŋ] *pt & pp* → **hang**.

Hungarian [hʌŋ'geərɪən] ◆ *adj* ungherese ◆ *n* (*person*) ungherese *mf*; (*language*) ungherese *m*.

Hungary ['hʌŋɡərɪ] *n* l'Ungheria *f*.

hunger ['hʌŋɡə^r] *n* fame *f*.

hungry ['hʌŋɡrɪ] *adj* affamato(-a); **to be ~** avere fame.

hunt [hʌnt] ◆ *n* (*Br: for foxes*) caccia *f* ◆ *vt & vi* cacciare; **to ~ (for sb/sthg)** (*search*) cercare (qn/qc).

hunting ['hʌntɪŋ] *n* caccia *f*.

hurdle ['hɜ:dl] *n* (SPORT) ostacolo *m*.

hurl [hɜ:l] *vt* (*throw*) scaraventare, scagliare.

hurricane ['hʌrɪkən] *n* uragano *m*.

hurry ['hʌrɪ] ◆ *vt* (*person*) mettere fretta a ◆ *vi* affrettarsi, sbrigarsi ◆ *n*: **to be in a ~** avere fretta; **to do sthg in a ~** fare qc in fretta.

▶ **hurry up** *vi* sbrigarsi.

hurt [hɜ:t] (*pt & pp* **hurt**) ◆ *vt* (*injure*) fare male a; (*emotionally*) ferire ◆ *vi* far male; **my arm ~s** mi fa male il braccio; **I ~ my arm** mi sono fatto male al braccio; **to ~ o.s.** farsi male.

husband ['hʌzbənd] *n* marito *m*.

hustle ['hʌsl] *n*: **~ and bustle** attività *f* febbrile.

hut [hʌt] *n* capanna *f*.

hyacinth ['haɪəsɪnθ] *n* giacinto *m*.

hydrofoil ['haɪdrəfɔɪl] *n* aliscafo *m*.

hydromassage ['haɪdrəmæsɑ:ʒ] *n* idromassaggio *m*.

hygiene ['haɪdʒi:n] *n* igiene *f*.

hygienic [haɪ'dʒi:nɪk] *adj* igienico(-a).

hymn [hɪm] *n* inno *m*.

hypermarket ['haɪpə,mɑ:kɪt] *n* ipermercato *m*.

hyphen ['haɪfn] *n* trattino *m*.

hypocrite ['hɪpəkrɪt] *n* ipocrita *mf*.

hypodermic needle [,haɪpə'dɜ:mɪk-] *n* ago *m* ipodermico.

hysterical [hɪs'terɪkl] *adj* (*person*) isterico(-a); (*inf: very funny*) esilarante.

I

I [aɪ] *pron* io; **I'm tall** sono alto.

ice [aɪs] *n* ghiaccio *m*; (*ice cream*) gelato *m*.

iceberg ['aɪsbɜ:g] *n* iceberg *m inv*.

iceberg lettuce *n* lattuga *f* iceberg.

icebox ['aɪsbɒks] *n* (Am: *fridge*) frigorifero *m*.

ice-cold *adj* ghiacciato(-a).

ice cream *n* gelato *m*.

ice cube *n* cubetto *m* di ghiaccio.

ice hockey *n* hockey *m* su ghiaccio.

Iceland ['aɪslənd] *n* l'Islanda *f*.

ice lolly *n* (Br) ghiacciolo *m*.

ice rink *n* pista *f* di pattinaggio su ghiaccio.

ice skates *npl* pattini *mpl* da ghiaccio.

ice-skating *n* pattinaggio *m* su ghiaccio; **to go ~** andare a pattinare sul ghiaccio.

icicle ['aɪsɪkl] *n* ghiacciolo *m*.

icing ['aɪsɪŋ] *n* glassa *f*.

icing sugar *n* zucchero *m* a velo.

icy ['aɪsɪ] *adj* (*covered with ice*) ghiacciato(-a); (*very cold*) gelido(-a), gelato(-a).

I'd [aɪd] = **I would, I had**.

ID n (*abbr of identification*) documento m (d'identità).

ID card n carta f d'identità.

IDD code n prefisso m (teleselettivo) internazionale.

idea [aɪˈdɪə] n idea f; **I've no ~** non ne ho idea.

ideal [aɪˈdɪəl] ♦ adj ideale ♦ n ideale m.

ideally [aɪˈdɪəlɪ] adv idealmente; (*suited*) perfettamente.

identical [aɪˈdentɪkl] adj identico(-a).

identification [aɪˌdentɪfɪˈkeɪʃn] n (*document*) documento m d'identità.

identify [aɪˈdentɪfaɪ] vt identificare.

identity [aɪˈdentətɪ] n identità f inv.

idiom [ˈɪdɪəm] n (*phrase*) espressione f idiomatica.

idiot [ˈɪdɪət] n idiota mf.

idle [ˈaɪdl] ♦ adj (*lazy*) ozioso(-a); (*not working*) inattivo(-a); (*unemployed*) disoccupato(-a) ♦ vi (*engine*) girare al minimo.

idol [ˈaɪdl] n (*person*) idolo m.

idyllic [ɪˈdɪlɪk] adj idilliaco(-a).

i.e. (*abbr of id est*) cioè.

if [ɪf] conj se; **~ I were you** se fossi in te; **~ not** (*otherwise*) se no.

ignition [ɪgˈnɪʃn] n (AUT) accensione f.

ignorant [ˈɪgnərənt] adj ignorante.

ignore [ɪgˈnɔːr] vt ignorare.

ill [ɪl] adj (*in health*) malato(-a); (*bad*) cattivo(-a).

I'll [aɪl] = **I will, I shall**.

illegal [ɪˈliːgl] adj illegale.

illegible [ɪˈledʒəbl] adj illeggibile.

illegitimate [ˌɪlɪˈdʒɪtɪmət] adj illegittimo(-a).

illiterate [ɪˈlɪtərət] adj analfabeta.

illness [ˈɪlnɪs] n malattia f.

illuminate [ɪˈluːmɪneɪt] vt illuminare.

illusion [ɪˈluːʒn] n illusione f.

illustration [ˌɪləˈstreɪʃn] n illustrazione f.

illustrative [ˈɪləstrətɪv] adj illustrativo(-a).

I'm [aɪm] = **I am**.

image [ˈɪmɪdʒ] n immagine f.

imaginary [ɪˈmædʒɪnrɪ] adj immaginario(-a).

imagination [ɪˌmædʒɪˈneɪʃn] n immaginazione f.

imagine [ɪˈmædʒɪn] vt immaginare.

imitate [ˈɪmɪteɪt] vt imitare.

imitation [ˌɪmɪˈteɪʃn] ♦ n imitazione f ♦ adj finto(-a).

immaculate [ɪˈmækjʊlət] adj (*very clean*) immacolato(-a), lindo(-a); (*perfect*) impeccabile.

immature [ˌɪməˈtjʊər] adj immaturo(-a).

immediate [ɪˈmiːdjət] adj (*without delay*) immediato(-a).

immediately [ɪˈmiːdjətlɪ] ♦ adv (*at once*) immediatamente, subito ♦ conj (Br) non appena.

immense [ɪˈmens] adj immenso(-a).

immersion heater [ɪˈmɜːʃn-] n scaldabagno m inv elettrico.

immigrant [ˈɪmɪgrənt] n immigrato m (-a f).

immigration [ˌɪmɪˈgreɪʃn] n (*to country*) immigrazione f; (*section of airport, port*) dogana f.

imminent [ˈɪmɪnənt] adj imminente.

immune [ɪˈmjuːn] adj: **to be ~ to** (MED) essere immune da.

immunity [ɪˈmjuːnətɪ] n (MED) immunità f.

immunize [ˈɪmjuːnaɪz] vt immunizzare.

impact [ˈɪmpækt] n impatto m.

impair [ɪmˈpeər] vt danneggiare.

impatient [ɪmˈpeɪʃnt] adj impaziente; **to be ~ to do sthg** essere impaziente di fare qc.

imperative [ɪmˈperətɪv] n (GRAMM) imperativo m.

imperfect [ɪmˈpɜːfɪkt] n (GRAMM)
imperfetto m.

impersonate [ɪmˈpɜːsəneɪt] vt (for
amusement) imitare.

impertinent [ɪmˈpɜːtɪnənt] adj
impertinente.

implement [n ˈɪmplɪmənt, vb ˈɪmplɪ-
ment] n attrezzo m; (for cooking)
utensile m ♦ vt mettere in atto,
realizzare.

implication [ˌɪmplɪˈkeɪʃn] n (consequence) implicazione f.

imply [ɪmˈplaɪ] vt (suggest) lasciar
intendere, sottintendere.

impolite [ˌɪmpəˈlaɪt] adj scortese.

import [n ˈɪmpɔːt, vb ɪmˈpɔːt] n
merce f d'importazione ♦ vt
importare.

importance [ɪmˈpɔːtns] n importanza f.

important [ɪmˈpɔːtnt] adj importante.

impose [ɪmˈpəʊz] ♦ vt imporre ♦ vi
approfittare; **to ~ sthg on** imporre
qc a.

impossible [ɪmˈpɒsəbl] adj impossibile.

impractical [ɪmˈpræktɪkl] adj non
pratico(-a).

impress [ɪmˈpres] vt fare una
buona impressione a.

impression [ɪmˈpreʃn] n impressione f.

impressive [ɪmˈpresɪv] adj impressionante.

imprisonment [ɪmˈprɪznmənt] n
prigionia f.

improbable [ɪmˈprɒbəbl] adj
(event) improbabile; (story, excuse)
inverosimile.

improper [ɪmˈprɒpəʳ] adj (incorrect,
illegal) scorretto(-a); (rude) sconveniente.

improve [ɪmˈpruːv] vt & vi migliorare.

▶ **improve on** vt fus migliorare.

improvement [ɪmˈpruːvmənt] n (in
weather, health) miglioramento m; (to
home) miglioria f.

improvise [ˈɪmprəvaɪz] vi improvvisare.

impulse [ˈɪmpʌls] n impulso m; **on
~** d'impulso.

impulsive [ɪmˈpʌlsɪv] adj impulsi-
vo(-a).

in [ɪn] prep 1. (expressing place, position) in; **~ a box** in una scatola; **~ the
bedroom** in camera da letto; **~ the
street** per strada; **~ Scotland** in
Scozia; **~ Sheffield** a Sheffield; **~ the
United States** negli Stati Uniti; **~
here/there** qui/là dentro; **~ the sun**
al sole; **~ the rain** sotto la pioggia;
~ the middle al centro; **an article ~
the paper** un articolo sul giornale.
2. (participating in) in; **who's ~ the
play?** chi recita nella commedia?
3. (expressing arrangement); **~ a row**
in fila; **they come ~ packs of three**
vengono venduti in pacchetti da
tre.
4. (with time): **~ April** in aprile; **~ the
afternoon** di OR nel pomeriggio; **at
ten o'clock ~ the morning** alle dieci
del mattino; **~ 1994** nel 1994; **it'll
be ready ~ an hour** sarà pronto fra
un'ora; **they're arriving ~ two weeks**
arriveranno fra due settimane.
5. (expressing means): **to write ~ ink**
scrivere a penna; **~ writing** per
iscritto; **they were talking ~ English**
parlavano in inglese.
6. (wearing): **the man ~ the blue
jacket** l'uomo con la giacca blu;
dressed ~ white vestito di bianco.
7. (expressing state): **~ a bad mood** di
pessimo umore; **to be ~ a hurry**
essere di fretta; **to cry ~ pain** gridare di dolore; **to be ~ pain** soffrire; **~
ruins** in rovina.
8. (with regard to): **a rise ~ prices** un
aumento dei prezzi; **to be 50
metres ~ length** essere lungo 50
metri.
9. (with numbers, ratios): **one ~ ten**
uno su dieci; **~ dozens** a dozzine.
10. (expressing age): **she's ~ her thirties** è sulla trentina.
11. (with colours): **it comes ~ green or**

blue è disponibile in verde o in blu.

12. (*with superlatives*) di; **the best ~ the world** il migliore del mondo.

♦ *adv* **1.** (*inside*) dentro; **you can go ~ now** ora può entrare; **come ~!** avanti!

2. (*at home, work*): **she's not ~** non c'è; **to stay ~** stare a casa.

3. (*train, bus, plane*): **the train's not ~ yet** il treno non è ancora arrivato.

4. (*tide*): **the tide is ~** c'è alta marea.

♦ *adj* (*inf: fashionable*) alla moda.

inability [ˌɪnəˈbɪlətɪ] *n*: **~ (to do sthg)** incapacità *f* (di fare qc).

inaccessible [ˌɪnəkˈsesəbl] *adj* inaccessibile.

inaccurate [ɪnˈækjʊrət] *adj* inesatto(-a), impreciso(-a).

inadequate [ɪnˈædɪkwət] *adj* inadeguato(-a).

inappropriate [ˌɪnəˈprəʊprɪət] *adj* non adatto(-a).

inauguration [ɪˌnɔːgjʊˈreɪʃn] *n* inaugurazione *f*; (*of president etc*) insediamento *m* in carica.

incapable [ɪnˈkeɪpəbl] *adj*: **to be ~ of doing sthg** essere incapace di fare qc.

incense [ˈɪnsens] *n* incenso *m*.

incentive [ɪnˈsentɪv] *n* incentivo *m*.

inch [ɪntʃ] *n* = 2,5 cm, pollice *m*.

incident [ˈɪnsɪdənt] *n* episodio *m*, caso *m*.

incidentally [ˌɪnsɪˈdentəlɪ] *adv* a proposito.

incline [ˈɪnklaɪn] *n* pendio *m*.

inclined [ɪnˈklaɪnd] *adj* (*sloping*) inclinato(-a); **to be ~ to do sthg** essere propenso(-a) a fare qc.

include [ɪnˈkluːd] *vt* includere, comprendere.

included [ɪnˈkluːdɪd] *adj* (*in price*) compreso(-a); **to be ~ in sthg** essere compreso in qc.

including [ɪnˈkluːdɪŋ] *prep* compreso(-a).

inclusive [ɪnˈkluːsɪv] *adj*: **from the 8th to the 16th ~** dall'8 al 16 com-

preso; **~ of VAT** IVA compresa.

income [ˈɪŋkʌm] *n* reddito *m*.

income support *n* (*Br*) = sussidio *m* di indigenza.

income tax *n* imposta *f* sul reddito.

incoming [ˈɪnˌkʌmɪŋ] *adj* in arrivo.

incompetent [ɪnˈkɒmpɪtənt] *adj* incompetente.

incomplete [ˌɪnkəmˈpliːt] *adj* incompleto(-a).

inconsiderate [ˌɪnkənˈsɪdərət] *adj* sconsiderato(-a).

inconsistent [ˌɪnkənˈsɪstənt] *adj* incoerente.

incontinent [ɪnˈkɒntɪnənt] *adj* incontinente.

inconvenient [ˌɪnkənˈviːnjənt] *adj* scomodo(-a).

incorporate [ɪnˈkɔːpəreɪt] *vt* incorporare.

incorrect [ˌɪnkəˈrekt] *adj* (*answer, number*) sbagliato(-a); (*information*) inesatto(-a).

increase [*n* ˈɪnkriːs, *vb* ɪnˈkriːs] ♦ *n* aumento *m* ♦ *vt & vi* aumentare; **an ~ in sthg** un aumento di qc.

increasingly [ɪnˈkriːsɪŋlɪ] *adv* sempre più.

incredible [ɪnˈkredəbl] *adj* incredibile.

incredibly [ɪnˈkredəblɪ] *adv* (*very*) incredibilmente.

incur [ɪnˈkɜːr] *vt* incorrere in.

indecisive [ˌɪndɪˈsaɪsɪv] *adj* indeciso(-a).

indeed [ɪnˈdiːd] *adv* (*for emphasis*) davvero; (*certainly*) certamente.

indefinite [ɪnˈdefɪnɪt] *adj* (*time, number*) indefinito(-a), indeterminato(-a); (*answer, opinion*) vago(-a).

indefinitely [ɪnˈdefɪnətlɪ] *adv* (*closed, delayed*) indefinitamente.

indemnity [ɪnˈdemnətɪ] *n* indennità *f inv*.

independence [ˌɪndɪˈpendəns] *n* indipendenza *f*.

independent [ˌɪndɪˈpendənt] *adj* indipendente.

independently [ˌɪndɪ'pendəntlɪ] *adv* indipendentemente.

independent school *n* (Br) scuola *f* privata.

index ['ɪndeks] *n* (*of book*) indice *m*; (*in library*) catalogo *m*.

index finger *n* dito *m* indice.

India ['ɪndjə] *n* l'India *f*.

Indian ['ɪndjən] ◆ *adj* indiano(-a) ◆ *n* indiano *m* (-a *f*); **an ~ restaurant** un ristorante indiano.

Indian Ocean *n*: **the ~** l'oceano *m* Indiano.

indicate ['ɪndɪkeɪt] ◆ *vi* (AUT) mettere la freccia ◆ *vt* indicare.

indicator ['ɪndɪkeɪtər] *n* (AUT) indicatore *m* di direzione, freccia *f*.

indifferent [ɪn'dɪfrənt] *adj* (*uninterested*) indifferente; (*not very good*) mediocre.

indigestion [ˌɪndɪ'dʒestʃn] *n* indigestione *f*.

indigo ['ɪndɪɡəʊ] *adj* indaco (*inv*).

indirect [ˌɪndɪ'rekt] *adj* non diretto(-a).

individual [ˌɪndɪ'vɪdʒʊəl] ◆ *adj* individuale ◆ *n* individuo *m*.

individually [ˌɪndɪ'vɪdʒʊəlɪ] *adv* individualmente.

Indonesia [ˌɪndə'niːzjə] *n* l'Indonesia *f*.

indoor ['ɪndɔːr] *adj* (*swimming pool*) coperto(-a); (*sports*) praticato(-a) al coperto.

indoors [ˌɪn'dɔːz] *adv* dentro.

indulge [ɪn'dʌldʒ] *vi*: **to ~ in sthg** concedersi qc.

industrial [ɪn'dʌstrɪəl] *adj* industriale.

industrial estate *n* (Br) zona *f* industriale.

industry ['ɪndəstrɪ] *n* industria *f*.

inedible [ɪn'edɪbl] *adj* (*unpleasant*) immangiabile; (*unsafe*) non commestibile.

inefficient [ˌɪnɪ'fɪʃnt] *adj* inefficiente.

inequality [ˌɪnɪ'kwɒlətɪ] *n* disuguaglianza *f*.

inevitable [ɪn'evɪtəbl] *adj* inevitabile.

inevitably [ɪn'evɪtəblɪ] *adv* inevitabilmente.

inexpensive [ˌɪnɪk'spensɪv] *adj* poco costoso(-a).

infamous ['ɪnfəməs] *adj* infame.

infant ['ɪnfənt] *n* bambino *m* (-a *f*).

infant school *n* (Br) scuola *f* elementare (*per bambini da 5 a 7 anni*).

infatuated [ɪn'fætjʊeɪtd] *adj*: **to be ~ with** essere infatuato(-a) di.

infected [ɪn'fektɪd] *adj* infetto(-a).

infectious [ɪn'fekʃəs] *adj* contagioso(-a).

inferior [ɪn'fɪərɪər] *adj* (*person*) inferiore; (*goods, quality*) scadente.

infinite ['ɪnfɪnət] *adj* infinito(-a).

infinitely ['ɪnfɪnətlɪ] *adv* infinitamente.

infinitive [ɪn'fɪnɪtɪv] *n* infinito *m*.

infinity [ɪn'fɪnətɪ] *n* (*in space*, MATH) infinito *m*.

infirmary [ɪn'fɜːmərɪ] *n* ospedale *m*.

inflamed [ɪn'fleɪmd] *adj* (MED) infiammato(-a).

inflammation [ˌɪnflə'meɪʃn] *n* (MED) infiammazione *f*.

inflatable [ɪn'fleɪtəbl] *adj* gonfiabile.

inflate [ɪn'fleɪt] *vt* gonfiare.

inflation [ɪn'fleɪʃn] *n* (*of prices*) inflazione *f*.

inflict [ɪn'flɪkt] *vt* infliggere.

in-flight *adj* durante il volo.

influence ['ɪnflʊəns] ◆ *vt* influenzare ◆ *n*: **~ (on)** influenza *f* (su).

inform [ɪn'fɔːm] *vt* informare.

informal [ɪn'fɔːml] *adj* (*occasion*, *dress*) informale.

information [ˌɪnfə'meɪʃn] *n* informazioni *fpl*; **a piece of ~** un'informazione.

information desk *n* banco *m* informazioni.

information office *n* ufficio *m* informazioni.

informative [ɪnˈfɔːmətɪv] *adj* istruttivo(-a).

infuriating [ɪnˈfjʊərɪeɪtɪŋ] *adj* molto irritante.

ingenious [ɪnˈdʒiːnjəs] *adj* ingegnoso(-a).

ingredient [ɪnˈgriːdjənt] *n* ingrediente *m*.

inhabit [ɪnˈhæbɪt] *vt* abitare.

inhabitant [ɪnˈhæbɪtənt] *n* abitante *mf*.

inhale [ɪnˈheɪl] *vi* aspirare.

inhaler [ɪnˈheɪlər] *n* inalatore *m*.

inherit [ɪnˈherɪt] *vt* ereditare.

inhibition [ˌɪnhɪˈbɪʃn] *n* inibizione *f*.

initial [ɪˈnɪʃl] ♦ *adj* iniziale ♦ *vt* siglare.

▶ **initials** *npl* iniziali *fpl*.

initially [ɪˈnɪʃəlɪ] *adv* inizialmente.

initiative [ɪˈnɪʃətɪv] *n* iniziativa *f*.

injection [ɪnˈdʒekʃn] *n* iniezione *f*.

injure [ˈɪndʒər] *vt* (*physically*) ferire; **to ~ o.s.** ferirsi; **to ~ one's arm** ferirsi al braccio.

injured [ˈɪndʒəd] *adj* (*physically*) ferito(-a).

injury [ˈɪndʒərɪ] *n* (*physical*) ferita *f*.

ink [ɪŋk] *n* inchiostro *m*.

inland [*adj* ˈɪnlənd, *adv* ɪnˈlænd] ♦ *adj* interno(-a) ♦ *adv* nell'interno.

Inland Revenue *n* (*Br*) = Fisco *m*.

inn [ɪn] *n* locanda *f*.

inner [ˈɪnər] *adj* interno(-a), interiore.

inner city *n* quartieri vicino al centro di una città, generalmente sinonimo di problemi sociali.

inner tube *n* camera *f* d'aria.

innocence [ˈɪnəsəns] *n* innocenza *f*.

innocent [ˈɪnəsənt] *adj* innocente.

inoculate [ɪˈnɒkjʊleɪt] *vt*: **to ~ sb (against sthg)** vaccinare qn (contro qc).

inoculation [ɪˌnɒkjʊˈleɪʃn] *n* vaccinazione *f*.

input [ˈɪnpʊt] (*pt* & *pp* **input** OR **-ted**)

vt (COMPUT) immettere.

inquire [ɪnˈkwaɪər] = **enquire**.

inquiry [ɪnˈkwaɪərɪ] = **enquiry**.

insane [ɪnˈseɪn] *adj* pazzo(-a), matto(-a).

insect [ˈɪnsekt] *n* insetto *m*.

insect repellent [-rəˈpelənt] *n* insettifugo *m*.

insensitive [ɪnˈsensətɪv] *adj* insensibile.

insert [ɪnˈsɜːt] *vt* inserire, introdurre.

inside [ɪnˈsaɪd] ♦ *prep* dentro, all'interno di ♦ *adv* dentro ♦ *adj* (*internal*) interno(-a) ♦ *n*: **the ~** (*interior*) l'interno *m*; (AUT: *in UK*) la sinistra; (AUT: *in Europe, US*) la destra; **~ out** (*clothes*) a rovescio.

inside lane *n* (AUT) (*in UK*) corsia *f* di sinistra; (*in Europe, US*) corsia di destra.

inside leg *n* interno *m* gamba.

insight [ˈɪnsaɪt] *n* (*glimpse*) idea *f*.

insignificant [ˌɪnsɪgˈnɪfɪkənt] *adj* insignificante.

insinuate [ɪnˈsɪnjʊeɪt] *vt* insinuare.

insist [ɪnˈsɪst] *vi* insistere; **to ~ on doing sthg** insistere nel fare qc.

insole [ˈɪnsəʊl] *n* soletta *f*.

insolent [ˈɪnsələnt] *adj* insolente.

insomnia [ɪnˈsɒmnɪə] *n* insonnia *f*.

inspect [ɪnˈspekt] *vt* (*object*) ispezionare; (*ticket, passport*) controllare.

inspection [ɪnˈspekʃn] *n* (*of object*) ispezione *f*; (*of ticket, passport*) controllo *m*.

inspector [ɪnˈspektər] *n* (*on bus, train*) controllore *m*; (*in police force*) ispettore *m* (-trice *f*).

inspiration [ˌɪnspəˈreɪʃn] *n* ispirazione *f*.

instal [ɪnˈstɔːl] (*Am*) = **install**.

install [ɪnˈstɔːl] *vt* (*Br*) installare.

installment [ɪnˈstɔːlmənt] (*Am*) = **instalment**.

instalment [ɪnˈstɔːlmənt] *n* (*payment*) rata *f*; (*episode*) puntata *f*, parte *f*.

instance [ˈɪnstəns] *n* (*example, case*)

esempio *m*, caso *m*; **for ~** per OR ad esempio.

instant ['ɪnstənt] ◆ *adj* (*results, success*) immediato(-a); (*coffee*) solubile ◆ *n* (*moment*) istante *m*.

instant coffee *n* caffè *m* inv solubile.

instead [ɪn'sted] *adv* invece; **~ of** invece di.

instep ['ɪnstep] *n* collo *m* del piede.

instinct ['ɪnstɪŋkt] *n* istinto *m*.

institute ['ɪnstɪtjuːt] *n* istituto *m*.

institution [,ɪnstɪ'tjuːʃn] *n* istituzione *f*.

instructions [ɪn'strʌkʃnz] *npl* istruzioni *fpl*.

instructor [ɪn'strʌktər] *n* istruttore *m* (-trice *f*).

instrument ['ɪnstrʊmənt] *n* strumento *m*.

insufficient [,ɪnsə'fɪʃnt] *adj* insufficiente.

insulating tape ['ɪnsjʊleɪtɪŋ-] *n* nastro *m* isolante.

insulation [,ɪnsjʊ'leɪʃn] *n* (*material*) isolante *m*.

insulin ['ɪnsjʊlɪn] *n* insulina *f*.

insult [*n* 'ɪnsʌlt, *vb* ɪn'sʌlt] ◆ *n* insulto *m* ◆ *vt* insultare.

insurance [ɪn'ʃʊərəns] *n* assicurazione *f*.

insurance certificate *n* certificato *m* di assicurazione.

insurance company *n* compagnia *f* di assicurazione.

insurance policy *n* polizza *f* di assicurazione.

insure [ɪn'ʃʊər] *vt* assicurare.

insured [ɪn'ʃʊəd] *adj*: **to be ~** essere assicurato(-a).

intact [ɪn'tækt] *adj* intatto(-a).

intellectual [,ɪntə'lektjʊəl] ◆ *adj* intellettuale ◆ *n* intellettuale *mf*.

intelligence [ɪn'telɪdʒəns] *n* (*cleverness*) intelligenza *f*.

intelligent [ɪn'telɪdʒənt] *adj* intelligente.

intend [ɪn'tend] *vt* (*mean*): **to ~ to do**

sthg avere intenzione di fare qc; **you weren't ~ed to know** non dovevi saperlo.

intense [ɪn'tens] *adj* intenso(-a).

intensity [ɪn'tensətɪ] *n* intensità *f*.

intensive [ɪn'tensɪv] *adj* intensivo(-a).

intensive care *n* terapia *f* intensiva.

intent [ɪn'tent] *adj*: **to be ~ on doing sthg** essere deciso(-a) a fare qc.

intention [ɪn'tenʃn] *n* intenzione *f*.

intentional [ɪn'tenʃənl] *adj* intenzionale.

intentionally [ɪn'tenʃənəlɪ] *adv* intenzionalmente, apposta.

interchange ['ɪntətʃeɪndʒ] *n* (*on motorway*) svincolo *m*.

Intercity® [,ɪntə'sɪtɪ] *n* (Br) intercity *m* inv.

intercom ['ɪntəkɒm] *n* interfono *m*.

interest ['ɪntrəst] *n* interesse *m* ◆ *vt* interessare; **to take an ~ in sthg** interessarsi di OR a qc.

interested ['ɪntrəstɪd] *adj* interessato(-a); **to be ~ in sthg** interessarsi di qc.

interesting ['ɪntrəstɪŋ] *adj* interessante.

interest rate *n* tasso *m* d'interesse.

interfere [,ɪntə'fɪər] *vi* (*meddle*) immischiarsi; **to ~ with sthg** (*damage*) interferire con qc.

interference [,ɪntə'fɪərəns] *n* (*on TV, radio*) interferenza *f*.

interior [ɪn'tɪərɪər] ◆ *adj* interno(-a) ◆ *n* interno *m*.

interior design *n* arredamento *m*.

intermediate [,ɪntə'miːdjət] *adj* intermedio(-a).

intermission [,ɪntə'mɪʃn] *n* (*at cinema, theatre*) intervallo *m*.

internal [ɪn'tɜːnl] *adj* interno(-a).

internal flight *n* volo *m* interno.

international [,ɪntə'næʃənl] *adj* internazionale.

international flight *n* volo *m*

internazionale.

Internet ['ɪntənet] *n*: **the ~** Internet *m*.

interpret [ɪn'tɜːprɪt] *vi* fare da interprete.

interpreter [ɪn'tɜːprɪtər] *n* interprete *mf*.

interrogate [ɪn'terəgeɪt] *vt* interrogare.

interrupt [ˌɪntə'rʌpt] *vt* interrompere.

intersection [ˌɪntə'sekʃn] *n* (*of roads*) incrocio *m*.

interval ['ɪntəvl] *n* intervallo *m*.

intervene [ˌɪntə'viːn] *vi* (*person, event*) intervenire.

interview ['ɪntəvjuː] ♦ *n* (*on TV, in magazine*) intervista *f*; (*for job*) colloquio *m* ♦ *vt* (*on TV, in magazine*) intervistare; (*for job*) fare un colloquio a.

interviewer ['ɪntəvjuːər] *n* (*on TV, in magazine*) intervistatore *m* (-trice *f*).

intestine [ɪn'testɪn] *n* intestino *m*.

intimate ['ɪntɪmət] *adj* intimo(-a).

intimidate [ɪn'tɪmɪdeɪt] *vt* intimidire.

into ['ɪntʊ] *prep* (*inside*) in, dentro; (*against*) contro, in; (*concerning*) su; **4 ~ 20 goes 5** (*times*) il 4 nel 20 ci sta 5 volte; **to translate ~ Italian** tradurre in italiano; **to change ~ sthg** trasformarsi in qc; **to be ~ sthg** (*inf*: *like*) essere appassionato di qc.

intolerable [ɪn'tɒlrəbl] *adj* intollerabile.

intransitive [ɪn'trænzətɪv] *adj* intransitivo(-a).

intricate ['ɪntrɪkət] *adj* intricato(-a).

intriguing [ɪn'triːgɪŋ] *adj* affascinante.

introduce [ˌɪntrə'djuːs] *vt* presentare; **I'd like to ~ you to Fred** ti presento Fred.

introduction [ˌɪntrə'dʌkʃn] *n* (*to book, programme*) introduzione *f*; (*to person*) presentazione *f*.

introverted ['ɪntrə,vɜːtɪd] *adj* introverso(-a).

intruder [ɪn'truːdər] *n* intruso *m* (-a *f*).

intuition [ˌɪntjuː'ɪʃn] *n* (*feeling*) intuizione *f*; (*faculty*) intuito *m*.

invade [ɪn'veɪd] *vt* invadere.

invalid [*adj* ɪn'vælɪd, *n* 'ɪnvəlɪd] ♦ *adj* (*ticket, cheque*) non valido(-a) ♦ *n* invalido *m* (-a *f*).

invaluable [ɪn'væljʊəbl] *adj* inestimabile.

invariably [ɪn'veərɪəblɪ] *adv* sempre, invariabilmente.

invasion [ɪn'veɪʒn] *n* invasione *f*.

invent [ɪn'vent] *vt* inventare.

invention [ɪn'venʃn] *n* invenzione *f*.

inventory ['ɪnventrɪ] *n* inventario *m*.

inverted commas [ɪn'vɜːtɪd-] *npl* virgolette *fpl*.

invest [ɪn'vest] ♦ *vt* investire ♦ *vi*: **to ~ in sthg** investire in qc.

investigate [ɪn'vestɪgeɪt] *vt* indagare.

investigation [ɪnˌvestɪ'geɪʃn] *n* indagine *f*.

investment [ɪn'vestmənt] *n* investimento *m*.

invisible [ɪn'vɪzɪbl] *adj* invisibile.

invitation [ˌɪnvɪ'teɪʃn] *n* invito *m*.

invite [ɪn'vaɪt] *vt* invitare; **to ~ sb to do sthg** (*ask*) invitare qn a fare qc; **to ~ sb round** invitare qn.

invoice ['ɪnvɔɪs] *n* fattura *f*.

involve [ɪn'vɒlv] *vt* (*entail*) richiedere, comportare; **what does it ~?** che cosa comporta?; **to be ~d in sthg** essere coinvolto in qc.

involved [ɪn'vɒlvd] *adj* (*entailed*) richiesto(-a), necessario(-a).

inwards ['ɪnwədz] *adv* verso l'interno.

IOU *n* pagherò *m inv*.

IQ *n* Q.I. *m*.

Iran [ɪ'rɑːn] *n* l'Iran *m*.

Iraq [ɪ'rɑːk] *n* l'Iraq *m*.

Ireland ['aɪələnd] *n* l'Irlanda *f*.

iris ['aɪərɪs] (pl **-es**) n (flower) giaggiolo m, iris f inv.

Irish ['aɪrɪʃ] ◆ adj irlandese ◆ n (language) irlandese m ◆ npl: **the ~** gli irlandesi.

Irish coffee n Irish coffee m inv (caffè con whisky e panna).

Irishman ['aɪrɪʃmən] (pl **-men** [-mən]) n irlandese m.

Irish stew n spezzatino di agnello con patate e cipolle.

Irishwoman ['aɪrɪʃ,wʊmən] (pl **-women** [-,wɪmɪn]) n irlandese f.

iron ['aɪən] ◆ n (metal) ferro m; (for clothes) ferro da stiro; (golf club) mazza f da golf ◆ vt stirare.

ironic [aɪ'rɒnɪk] adj ironico(-a).

ironing board ['aɪənɪŋ-] n asse f da stiro.

ironmonger's ['aɪən,mʌŋgəz] n (Br) ferramenta f.

irrelevant [ɪ'reləvənt] adj non pertinente, irrilevante.

irresistible [,ɪrɪ'zɪstəbl] adj irresistibile.

irrespective [,ɪrɪ'spektɪv]: **irrespective of** prep a prescindere da.

irresponsible [,ɪrɪ'spɒnsəbl] adj irresponsabile.

irrigation [,ɪrɪ'geɪʃn] n irrigazione f.

irritable ['ɪrɪtəbl] adj irritabile.

irritate ['ɪrɪteɪt] vt irritare.

irritating ['ɪrɪteɪtɪŋ] adj irritante.

IRS n (Am) = Fisco m.

is [ɪz] → **be**.

Islam ['ɪzlɑːm] n (religion) islamismo m.

island ['aɪlənd] n isola f.

isle [aɪl] n isola f.

isolated ['aɪsəleɪtɪd] adj isolato(-a).

Israel ['ɪzreɪəl] n Israele m.

issue ['ɪʃuː] ◆ n (problem, subject) questione f, problema m; (of newspaper, magazine) numero m ◆ vt (statement, passport, document) rilasciare; (stamps, bank notes) emettere.

it [ɪt] pron 1. (referring to specific thing: subject, after prep) esso(-a); (direct object) lo (la); (indirect object) gli (le); **~'s big** è grande; **she hit ~** l'ha colpito; **give ~ to me** dammelo; **tell me about ~** parlamene; **we went to ~** ci siamo andati.
2. (nonspecific): **~'s nice here** si sta bene qui; **~'s me** sono io; **who is ~?** chi è?
3. (used impersonally): **~'s hot** fa caldo; **~'s six o'clock** sono le sei; **~'s Sunday** è domenica.

Italian [ɪ'tæljən] ◆ adj italiano(-a) ◆ n (person) italiano m (-a f); (language) italiano m; **an ~ restaurant** un ristorante italiano.

Italian Riviera n: **the ~** la Riviera Ligure.

Italy ['ɪtəlɪ] n l'Italia f.

itch [ɪtʃ] vi (arm, leg) prudere; (person) avere prurito.

item ['aɪtəm] n (object) articolo m; (on agenda) punto m; **news ~** notizia f.

itemized bill ['aɪtəmaɪzd-] n bolletta f con lettura dettagliata.

its [ɪts] adj il suo (la sua), i suoi (le sue) (pl).

it's [ɪts] = **it is**, **it has**.

itself [ɪt'self] pron (reflexive) si; (after prep), se stesso(-a) sé; **the house ~ is fine** la casa in sé va bene.

I've [aɪv] = **I have**.

ivory ['aɪvərɪ] n avorio m.

ivy ['aɪvɪ] n edera f.

J

jab [dʒæb] n (Br: inf: injection) puntura f.

jack [dʒæk] n (for car) cric m inv; (playing card) fante m.

jacket ['dʒækɪt] n (garment) giacca f; (of book) sopraccoperta f; (Am: of *record*) copertina f; (*of potato*) buccia f.

jacket potato n patata cotta al forno con la buccia.

jack-knife vi piegarsi su se stesso (*camion*).

Jacuzzi® [dʒə'ku:zı] n vasca f con idromassaggio.

jade [dʒeɪd] n giada f.

jail [dʒeɪl] n prigione f.

jam [dʒæm] ♦ n (*food*) marmellata f; (*of traffic*) ingorgo m; (*inf: difficult situation*) pasticcio m ♦ vt (*pack tightly*) stipare ♦ vi (*get stuck*) bloccarsi; **the roads are jammed** le strade sono intasate.

jam-packed [-'pækt] adj (*inf*) stipato(-a).

Jan. [dʒæn] (*abbr of* January) gen.

janitor ['dʒænɪtəʳ] n (*Am & Scot*) bidello m (-a f).

January ['dʒænjʊərɪ] n gennaio m, → **September**.

Japan [dʒə'pæn] n il Giappone.

Japanese [,dʒæpə'ni:z] ♦ adj giapponese ♦ n (*language*) giapponese m ♦ npl: **the ~ i** giapponesi.

jar [dʒɑ:ʳ] n barattolo m, vasetto m.

javelin ['dʒævlɪn] n giavellotto m.

jaw [dʒɔ:] n mascella f.

jazz [dʒæz] n jazz m.

jealous ['dʒeləs] adj geloso(-a).

jeans [dʒi:nz] npl jeans mpl.

Jeep® [dʒi:p] n jeep® f inv.

Jello® ['dʒeləʊ] n (*Am*) gelatina f.

jelly ['dʒelɪ] n (*dessert*) gelatina f; (*Am: jam*) marmellata f.

jellyfish ['dʒelɪfɪʃ] (*pl inv*) n medusa f.

jeopardize ['dʒepədaɪz] vt mettere a repentaglio.

jerk [dʒɜ:k] n (*movement*) strattone m, scossa f; (*inf: idiot*) imbecille mf.

jersey ['dʒɜ:zɪ] (*pl* -s) n (*garment*) maglia f.

jet [dʒet] n (*aircraft*) aviogetto m; (*of liquid, gas*) getto m; (*outlet*) ugello m.

jetfoil ['dʒetfɔɪl] n aliscafo m.

jet lag n jetleg m.

jet-ski n acqua-scooter m inv.

jetty ['dʒetɪ] n molo m.

Jew [dʒu:] n ebreo m (-a f).

jewel ['dʒu:əl] n gioiello m.

► **jewels** npl (*jewellery*) gioielli mpl.

jeweler's ['dʒu:ələz] (*Am*) = **jeweller's**.

jeweller's ['dʒu:ələz] n (*Br*) gioielleria f.

jewellery ['dʒu:əlrɪ] n (*Br*) gioielli mpl.

jewelry ['dʒu:əlrɪ] (*Am*) = **jewellery**.

Jewish ['dʒu:ɪʃ] adj ebreo(-a).

jigsaw (puzzle) ['dʒɪgsɔ:-] n puzzle m inv.

jingle ['dʒɪŋgl] n (*of advert*) motivo m musicale di pubblicità.

job [dʒɒb] n lavoro m; **to lose one's ~** perdere il lavoro.

job centre n (*Br*) ufficio m di collocamento.

jockey ['dʒɒkɪ] (*pl* -s) n fantino m (-a f).

jog [dʒɒg] ♦ vt (*bump*) urtare lievemente ♦ vi fare footing ♦ n: **to go for a ~** andare a fare del footing.

jogging ['dʒɒgɪŋ] n footing m; **to go ~** fare del footing.

join [dʒɔɪn] vt (*club, organization*) iscriversi a; (*fasten together*) unire; (*other people, celebrations*) unirsi a; (*road, river*) congiungersi con; (*connect*) collegare; **to ~ a queue** mettersi in fila.

► **join in** ♦ vt fus prendere parte a ♦ vi partecipare.

joint [dʒɔɪnt] ♦ adj comune ♦ n (*of body*) articolazione f; (*Br: of meat*) taglio m di carne per arrosto; (*in structure*) giuntura f.

joke [dʒəʊk] ♦ n scherzo m; (*story*) barzelletta f ♦ vi scherzare.

joker ['dʒəʊkəʳ] n (*playing card*) jolly m inv, matta f.

jolly ['dʒɒlɪ] ♦ adj (*cheerful*) allegro(-a) ♦ adv (*Br: inf: very*) molto.

jolt [dʒəʊlt] n scossa f, sobbalzo m.

jot [dʒɒt]: **jot down** *vt sep* annotare in fretta.

journal ['dʒɜːnl] *n* (*professional magazine*) rivista *f*; (*diary*) diario *m*.

journalist ['dʒɜːnəlɪst] *n* giornalista *mf*.

journey ['dʒɜːnɪ] (*pl* -s) *n* viaggio *m*.

joy [dʒɔɪ] *n* gioia *f*.

joypad ['dʒɔɪpæd] *n* (*of video game*) comandi *mpl*.

joyrider ['dʒɔɪraɪdər] *n* chi ruba un'auto per farci un giro e poi l'abbandona.

joystick ['dʒɔɪstɪk] *n* (*of video game*) joystick *m inv*.

judge [dʒʌdʒ] ♦ *n* giudice *mf* ♦ *vt* giudicare.

judg(e)ment ['dʒʌdʒmənt] *n* giudizio *m*.

judo ['dʒuːdəʊ] *n* judo *m*.

jug [dʒʌg] *n* brocca *f*, caraffa *f*.

juggernaut ['dʒʌgənɔːt] *n* (Br) grosso autotreno *m*, bestione *m*.

juggle ['dʒʌgl] *vi* fare giochi di destrezza (*con palle, birilli ecc.*).

juice [dʒuːs] *n* succo *m*; (*from meat*) sugo *m*.

juicy ['dʒuːsɪ] *adj* (*food*) succoso (-a).

jukebox ['dʒuːkbɒks] *n* juke-box *m inv*.

Jul. (*abbr of* July) lug.

July [dʒuːˈlaɪ] *n* luglio *m*, → **September**.

jumble sale ['dʒʌmbl-] *n* (Br) vendita *f* di cose usate (*a scopo di beneficenza*).

jumbo ['dʒʌmbəʊ] *adj* (*inf: big*) gigante.

jumbo jet *n* jumbo-jet *m inv*.

jump [dʒʌmp] ♦ *n* salto *m*, balzo *m* ♦ *vi* saltare, balzare; (*with fright*) sussultare; (*increase*) salire ♦ *vt* (Am): **to ~ the train/bus** viaggiare sul treno/sull'autobus senza pagare; **to ~ the queue** (Br) saltare la fila.

jumper ['dʒʌmpər] *n* (Br: *pullover*) maglione *m*, pullover *m inv*; (Am: *dress*) scamiciato *m*.

jump leads *npl* cavi *mpl* per batteria.

Jun. (*abbr of* June) giu.

junction ['dʒʌŋkʃn] *n* (*of roads*) incrocio *m*; (*of railway lines*) nodo *m* ferroviario; (*on motorways*) uscita *f*.

June [dʒuːn] *n* giugno *m*, → **September**.

jungle ['dʒʌŋgl] *n* giungla *f*.

junior ['dʒuːnjər] ♦ *adj* (*of lower rank*) di grado inferiore, subalterno(-a); (Am: *after name*) junior ♦ *n* (*younger person*): **to be sb's ~** essere più giovane di qn.

junior school *n* (Br) scuola *f* elementare (*per bambini da 7 a 11 anni*).

junk [dʒʌŋk] *n* (*inf: unwanted things*) cianfrusaglie *fpl*.

junk food *n* (*inf*) porcherie *fpl*.

junkie ['dʒʌŋkɪ] *n* (*inf*) drogato *m* (-a *f*).

junk shop *n* negozio *m* di rigattiere.

jury ['dʒʊərɪ] *n* giuria *f*.

just [dʒʌst] ♦ *adv* (*recently, slightly*) appena; (*in the next moment*) giusto; (*exactly*) proprio; (*only*) solo ♦ *adj* giusto(-a); **to be ~ about to do sthg** stare per fare qc; **to have ~ done sthg** avere appena fatto qc; **~ about** (*almost*) praticamente, quasi; (*only*) **~ per un pelo**; **I've (only) ~ arrived** sono arrivato (appena) adesso; **I'm ~ coming** vengo (subito); **~ a minute!** (solo) un minuto!

justice ['dʒʌstɪs] *n* giustizia *f*.

justify ['dʒʌstɪfaɪ] *vt* giustificare.

jut [dʒʌt]: **jut out** *vi* sporgersi.

juvenile ['dʒuːvənaɪl] *adj* (*young*) giovanile; (*childish*) puerile; (*crime*) minorile.

K

kangaroo [ˌkæŋgəˈruː] n canguro m.

karate [kəˈrɑːtɪ] n karate m.

kebab [kɪˈbæb] n: **(shish) ~** spiedino m di carne; **(doner) ~** pane azzimo imbottito con carne di agnello, insalata e salsa piccante.

keel [kiːl] n chiglia f.

keen [kiːn] adj (enthusiastic) entusiasta; (eyesight, hearing) acuto(-a); **to be ~ on sthg** essere appassionato(-a) di qc; **to be ~ to do sthg** avere voglia di fare qc.

keep [kiːp] (pt & pp **kept**) ◆ vt tenere; (promise) mantenere; (appointment) rispettare; (delay) trattenere ◆ vi (food) mantenersi; (remain) restare; **to ~ (on) doing sthg** (continuously) continuare a fare qc; (repeatedly) fare qc di continuo; **to ~ sb from doing sthg** impedire a qn di fare qc; **~ back!** state indietro!; **'~ in lane!'** 'restare in corsia'; **'~ left'** 'tenere la sinistra'; **'~ off the grass!'** 'vietato calpestare l'erba'; **'~ out!'** 'vietato l'accesso'; **'~ your distance!'** 'mantenere la distanza (di sicurezza)'; **to ~ clear (of)** stare lontano (da).

▶ **keep up** ◆ vt sep mantenere, continuare ◆ vi: **to ~ up (with)** tenersi al passo (con).

keep-fit n (Br) ginnastica f.

kennel [ˈkenl] n canile m.

kept [kept] pt & pp → **keep**.

kerb [kɜːb] n (Br) orlo m del marciapiede.

kerosene [ˈkerəsiːn] n (Am) cherosene m.

ketchup [ˈketʃəp] n ketchup m.

kettle [ˈketl] n bollitore m; **to put the ~ on** mettere l'acqua a bollire.

key [kiː] ◆ n chiave f; (of piano, type-

writer) tasto m; (of map) leggenda f ◆ adj chiave (inv).

keyboard [ˈkiːbɔːd] n tastiera f.

keyhole [ˈkiːhəʊl] n buco m della serratura.

keypad [ˈkiːpæd] n tastiera f.

key ring n portachiavi m inv.

kg (abbr of kilogram) kg.

kick [kɪk] ◆ n (of foot) calcio m ◆ vt dare calci a, prendere a calci.

kickoff [ˈkɪkɒf] n calcio m d'inizio.

kid [kɪd] ◆ n (inf) (child) bimbo m (-a f), bambino m (-a f); (young person) ragazzo m (-a f) ◆ vi (joke) scherzare.

kidnap [ˈkɪdnæp] vt rapire.

kidnaper [ˈkɪdnæpər] (Am) = **kidnapper**.

kidnapper [ˈkɪdnæpər] n (Br) rapitore m (-trice f).

kidney [ˈkɪdnɪ] (pl -s) n (organ) rene m; (food) rognone m.

kidney bean n fagiolo m comune.

kill [kɪl] vt (person) uccidere, ammazzare; (time) ammazzare; **my feet are ~ing me!** i piedi mi fanno un male!

killer [ˈkɪlər] n assassino m (-a f).

kilo [ˈkiːləʊ] (pl -s) n chilo m.

kilogram n [ˈkɪləˌgræm] n chilogrammo m.

kilometre [ˈkɪləˌmiːtər] n chilometro m.

kilt [kɪlt] n kilt m inv.

kind [kaɪnd] ◆ adj gentile, buono(-a) ◆ n (sort, type) genere m, tipo m; **~ of** (Am: inf) un po'.

kindergarten [ˈkɪndəˌgɑːtn] n asilo m infantile.

kindly [ˈkaɪndlɪ] adv: **would you ~ ...?** potrebbe ..., per favore?

kindness [ˈkaɪndnɪs] n gentilezza f, cortesia f.

king [kɪŋ] n re m inv.

kingfisher [ˈkɪŋˌfɪʃər] n martin m inv pescatore.

king prawn n gambero m.

king-size bed n letto largo 160 cm.

kiosk ['kiːɒsk] n (for newspapers etc) chiosco m, edicola f; (Br: phone box) cabina f (telefonica).

kipper ['kɪpər] n aringa f affumicata.

kiss [kɪs] ♦ n bacio m ♦ vt baciare.

kiss of life n respirazione f bocca a bocca.

kit [kɪt] n (set) attrezzatura f; (clothes) completo m; (for assembly) scatola f di montaggio.

kitchen ['kɪtʃɪn] n cucina f.

kitchen unit n mobile m componibile (da cucina).

kite [kaɪt] n (toy) aquilone m.

kitten ['kɪtn] n gattino m (-a f).

kitty ['kɪtɪ] n (of money) cassa f comune.

kiwi fruit ['kiːwiː-] n kiwi m inv.

Kleenex® ['kliːneks] n fazzoletto m di carta.

km (abbr of kilometre) km.

km/h (abbr of kilometres per hour) km/h.

knack [næk] n: **to have the ~ of doing sthg** avere l'abilità di fare qc.

knackered ['nækəd] adj (Br: inf) stanco morto (stanca morta).

knapsack ['næpsæk] n zaino m.

knee [niː] n ginocchio m.

kneecap ['niːkæp] n rotula f.

kneel [niːl] (pt & pp **knelt** [nelt]) vi inginocchiarsi.

knew [njuː] pt → **know**.

knickers ['nɪkəz] npl (Br: underwear) mutandine fpl.

knife [naɪf] (pl **knives**) n coltello m.

knight [naɪt] n (in history) cavaliere m; (in chess) cavallo m.

knit [nɪt] vt fare a maglia.

knitted ['nɪtɪd] adj fatto(-a) a maglia.

knitting ['nɪtɪŋ] n lavoro m a maglia.

knitting needle n ferro m (da calza).

knitwear ['nɪtweər] n maglieria f.

knives [naɪvz] pl → **knife**.

knob [nɒb] n (on door etc) pomello m; (on machine) manopola f.

knock [nɒk] ♦ n (at door) colpo m ♦ vt (head, elbow) battere; (chair, table) battere contro ♦ vi (at door etc) bussare.

▶ **knock down** vt sep (pedestrian) investire; (building) demolire; (price) ribassare.

▶ **knock out** vt sep (make unconscious) tramortire; (of competition) eliminare.

▶ **knock over** vt sep (glass, vase) rovesciare; (pedestrian) investire.

knocker ['nɒkər] n (on door) battente m.

knot [nɒt] n nodo m.

know [nəʊ] (pt **knew**, pp **known**) vt sapere; (person, place) conoscere; **to get to ~ sb** imparare a conoscere qc; **to ~ about sthg** (understand) saperne di qc; (have heard) sapere di qc; **to ~ how to do sthg** saper fare qc; **to ~ of** sapere di; **to be ~n as** essere noto come; **to let sb ~ sthg** far sapere qc a qn; **you ~** (for emphasis) sai.

knowledge ['nɒlɪdʒ] n conoscenza f; **to my ~** che io sappia.

known [nəʊn] pp → **know**.

knuckle ['nʌkl] n (of hand) nocca f; (of pork) garretto m.

Koran [kɒˈrɑːn] n: **the ~** il Corano.

l (abbr of litre) l.

L (abbr of learner) = P.

lab [læb] n (inf) laboratorio m.

label ['leɪbl] n cartellino m, etichetta f.

labor ['leɪbər] (Am) = **labour**.

laboratory [Br ləˈbɒrətrɪ, Am

ˈlæbrəˌtɔːrɪ] *n* laboratorio *m*.

labour [ˈleɪbər] *n* (*work*) lavoro *m*; **to be in ~** (MED) avere le doglie.

labourer [ˈleɪbərər] *n* manovale *m*.

Labour Party *n* (Br) partito *m* laburista.

labour-saving *adj* che fa risparmiare fatica.

lace [leɪs] *n* (*material*) merletto *m*; (*for shoe*) laccio *m*.

lace-ups *npl* scarpe *fpl* con i lacci.

lack [læk] ◆ *n* carenza *f* ◆ *vt* non avere ◆ *vi*: **to be ~ing** mancare.

lacquer [ˈlækər] *n* (*for hair*) lacca *f*; (*paint*) vernice *f*.

lad [læd] *n* (*inf*) ragazzo *m*.

ladder [ˈlædər] *n* (*for climbing*) scala *f*; (Br: *in tights*) smagliatura *f*.

ladies [ˈleɪdɪz] *n* (Br: *toilet*) toilette *f inv* per signore.

ladies room (Am) = **ladies**.

ladieswear [ˈleɪdɪzˌweər] *n* abbigliamento *m* da donna.

ladle [ˈleɪdl] *n* mestolo *m*.

lady [ˈleɪdɪ] *n* signora *f*.

ladybird [ˈleɪdɪbɜːd] *n* coccinella *f*.

ladybug [ˈleɪdɪbʌg] *n* (Am) = **ladybird**.

lag [læg] *vi* (*trade*) ristagnare; **to ~ behind** (*move more slowly*) restare indietro.

lager [ˈlɑːgər] *n* birra *f* (chiara).

lagoon [ləˈguːn] *n* laguna *f*.

laid [leɪd] *pt* & *pp* → **lay**.

lain [leɪn] *pp* → **lie**.

lake [leɪk] *n* lago *m*.

Lake District *n*: **the ~** la regione dei laghi (*nel nordovest dell'Inghilterra*).

lamb [læm] *n* agnello *m*.

lamb chop *n* braciola *f* OR costoletta *f* d'agnello.

lame [leɪm] *adj* zoppo(-a).

lamp [læmp] *n* lampada *f*; (*bicycle lamp*) fanale *m*; (*in street*) lampione *m*.

lamppost [ˈlæmppəʊst] *n* lampione *m*.

lampshade [ˈlæmpʃeɪd] *n* paralume *m*.

land [lænd] ◆ *n* terra *f* ◆ *vi* (*plane*) atterrare; (*passengers*) sbarcare; (*fall*) cadere.

landing [ˈlændɪŋ] *n* (*of plane*) atterraggio *m*; (*on stairs*) pianerottolo *m*.

landlady [ˈlændˌleɪdɪ] *n* (*of house*) padrona *f* di casa; (*of pub*) proprietaria *f*.

landlord [ˈlændlɔːd] *n* (*of house*) padrone *m* di casa; (*of pub*) proprietario *m*.

landmark [ˈlændmɑːk] *n* punto *m* di riferimento.

landscape [ˈlændskeɪp] *n* paesaggio *m*.

landslide [ˈlændslaɪd] *n* (*of earth, rocks*) frana *f*.

lane [leɪn] *n* (*narrow road*) stradina *f*; (*on road, motorway*) corsia *f*; **'get in ~'** 'disporsi su più file'.

language [ˈlæŋgwɪdʒ] *n* (*of a people, country*) lingua *f*; (*system, words*) linguaggio *m*.

lap [læp] *n* (*of person*) grembo *m*; (*of race*) giro *m*.

lapel [ləˈpel] *n* risvolto *m*.

lapse [læps] *vi* (*passport, membership*) scadere.

lard [lɑːd] *n* strutto *m*.

larder [ˈlɑːdər] *n* dispensa *f*.

large [lɑːdʒ] *adj* grande; (*person, dog, sum*) grosso(-a).

largely [ˈlɑːdʒlɪ] *adv* in gran parte.

large-scale *adj* su vasta scala.

lark [lɑːk] *n* allodola *f*.

laryngitis [ˌlærɪnˈdʒaɪtɪs] *n* laringite *f*.

lasagne [ləˈzænjə] *n* lasagne *fpl*.

laser [ˈleɪzər] *n* laser *m inv*.

lass [læs] *n* (*inf*) ragazza *f*.

last [lɑːst] ◆ *adj* ultimo(-a); (*week, year, month*) scorso(-a) ◆ *adv* (*most recently*) l'ultima volta; (*after everything else*) per ultimo ◆ *vi* (*continue*) durare ◆ *pron*: **the ~ to come** l'ultimo ad arrivare; **the ~ but one** il penultimo (la penultima); **the day before ~** l'altro ieri; **~ year** l'anno scorso; **the ~ year** l'ultimo anno; **at ~** finalmente; **to arrive ~** arrivare (per) ultimo; **it won't ~ till tomorrow** (*food*) non va fino a domani.

lastly ['lɑːstlɪ] *adv* infine.

last-minute *adj* dell'ultimo momento.

latch [lætʃ] *n* serratura *f* a scatto; **the door is on the ~** la porta non è chiusa a chiave.

late [leɪt] ♦ *adj* (*not on time*) in ritardo; (*after usual time*) tardi (*inv*); (*dead*) defunto(-a); (*morning, afternoon*) tardo(-a) ♦ *adv* (*not on time*) in ritardo; (*after usual time*) tardi; **in ~ June, ~ in June** verso la fine di giugno; **the train is running two hours ~** il treno viaggia con due ore di ritardo.

lately ['leɪtlɪ] *adv* ultimamente.

late-night *adj* aperto(-a) fino a tardi; **~ opening** apertura prolungata (*di negozi*).

later ['leɪtər] ♦ *adj* (*train*) successivo(-a) ♦ *adv*: **~ (on)** più tardi; **at a ~ date** in futuro.

latest ['leɪtɪst] *adj*: **the ~ fashion** l'ultima moda; **the ~** l'ultimo(-a); **at the ~** al più tardi.

lather ['lɑːðər] *n* schiuma *f*.

Latin ['lætɪn] *n* latino *m*.

Latin America *n* l'America *f* Latina.

Latin American ♦ *adj* latinoamericano(-a) ♦ *n* latino-americano *m* (-a *f*).

latitude ['lætɪtjuːd] *n* (*distance from Equator*) latitudine *f*.

latter ['lætər] *n*: **the ~** quest'ultimo(-a).

laugh [lɑːf] ♦ *n* risata *f* ♦ *vi* ridere; **to have a ~** (Br: *inf*) farsi due risate.
▶ **laugh at** *vt fus* (*mock*) ridere di.

laughter ['lɑːftər] *n* riso *m*.

launch [lɔːntʃ] *vt* (*boat*) varare; (*new product*) lanciare.

laund(e)rette [lɔːn'dret] *n* lavanderia *f* (automatica).

laundry ['lɔːndrɪ] *n* (*washing*) bucato *m*; (*place*) lavanderia *f*.

lavatory ['lævətrɪ] *n* gabinetto *m*.

lavender ['lævəndər] *n* lavanda *f*.

lavish ['lævɪʃ] *adj* (*meal, decoration*) sontuoso(-a).

law [lɔː] *n* legge *f*; **to be against the ~** essere contro la legge.

lawn [lɔːn] *n* prato *m*.

lawnmower ['lɔːn,məʊər] *n* tagliaerba *m inv*.

lawyer ['lɔːjər] *n* (*in court*) avvocato *m*; (*solicitor*) notaio *m*.

laxative ['læksətɪv] *n* lassativo *m*.

lay [leɪ] (*pt & pp* **laid**) ♦ *pt* → **lie** ♦ *vt* (*place*) poggiare; (*egg*) fare; **to ~ the table** apparecchiare la tavola.
▶ **lay off** *vt sep* (*worker*) licenziare.
▶ **lay on** *vt sep* (*food, transport*) fornire; (*entertainment*) organizzare.
▶ **lay out** *vt sep* (*display*) disporre.

lay-by (*pl* **lay-bys**) *n* piazzola *f* di sosta.

layer ['leɪər] *n* strato *m*.

layman ['leɪmən] (*pl* **-men** [-mən]) *n* profano *m* (-a *f*).

layout ['leɪaʊt] *n* (*of building*) struttura *f*; (*of streets*) tracciato *m*.

lazy ['leɪzɪ] *adj* pigro(-a).

lb *abbr* = **pound**.

lead¹ [liːd] (*pt & pp* **led**) ♦ *vt* (*take*) condurre; (*team, party, march*) guidare; (*procession*) aprire ♦ *vi* (*be winning*) condurre ♦ *n* (*for dog*) guinzaglio *m*; (*cable*) cavo *m*; **to ~ sb to do sthg** indurre qn a fare qc; **to ~ to** portare a; **to ~ the way** fare strada; **to be in the ~** essere in testa.

lead² [led] ♦ *n* piombo *m*; (*for pencil*) mina *f* ♦ *adj* di piombo.

leaded petrol ['ledɪd-] *n* benzina *f* con piombo.

leader ['liːdər] *n* (*of group*) capo *m*; (*of union, party*) leader *mf inv*; (*in race*) chi è in testa.

leadership ['liːdəʃɪp] *n* (*position*) direzione *f*.

lead-free [led-] *adj* senza piombo.

leading ['liːdɪŋ] *adj* (*most important*) principale.

leisure

lead singer [li:d-] n cantante mf (solista).

leaf [li:f] (pl **leaves**) n (of tree) foglia f.

leaflet ['li:flɪt] n dépliant m inv.

league [li:g] n (SPORT) campionato m; (association) lega f.

leak [li:k] ◆ n (hole) buco m; (of gas, water) perdita f ◆ vi (tank) perdere; (roof) gocciolare.

lean [li:n] (pt & pp **leant** [lent] OR **-ed**) ◆ adj (meat) magro(-a); (person, animal) asciutto(-a) ◆ vi (bend) piegarsi; (building) pendere ◆ vt: **to ~ sthg against sthg** appoggiare qc a qc; **to ~ on** appoggiarsi a.

▶ **lean forward** vi sporgersi (in avanti).

▶ **lean over** vi sporgersi.

leap [li:p] (pt & pp **leapt** [lept] OR **-ed**) vi (jump) balzare.

leap year n anno m bisestile.

learn [lɜ:n] (pt & pp **learnt** OR **-ed**) vt imparare; **to ~ (how) to do sthg** imparare a fare qc; **to ~ about sthg** (hear about) venire a sapere di qc; (study) studiare qc.

learner (driver) ['lɜ:nər-] n guidatore m (-trice f) principiante.

learnt [lɜ:nt] pt & pp → **learn**.

lease [li:s] ◆ n contratto m d'affitto ◆ vt affittare; **to ~ sthg from sb** affittare qc da qn; **to ~ sthg to sb** affittare qc a qn.

leash [li:ʃ] n guinzaglio m.

least [li:st] ◆ adv meno (di tutti) ◆ adj meno … di tutti ◆ pron: **(the) ~** meno di tutti; **at ~** almeno; **the ~ he could do** il minimo che potesse fare.

leather ['leðər] n cuoio m, pelle f.

▶ **leathers** npl (of motorcyclist) tuta f in pelle da motociclista.

leave [li:v] (pt & pp **left**) ◆ vt lasciare; (school) finire ◆ vi (go away) andarsene; (train, bus) partire ◆ n (time off work) permesso m; **to ~ a message** lasciare un messaggio, → **left**.

▶ **leave behind** vt sep (not take

away) lasciare.

▶ **leave out** vt sep tralasciare.

leaves [li:vz] pl → **leaf**.

Lebanon ['lebənən] n il Libano.

lecture ['lektʃər] n (at university) lezione f; (at conference) conferenza f.

lecturer ['lektʃərər] n docente mf (universitario).

lecture theatre n aula f (ad anfiteatro).

led [led] pt & pp → **lead**[1].

ledge [ledʒ] n (of window) davanzale m.

leek [li:k] n porro m.

left [left] ◆ pt & pp → **leave** ◆ adj (not right) sinistro(-a) ◆ adv a sinistra ◆ n sinistra f; **on the ~** a sinistra; **there are none ~** sono finiti.

left-hand adj (side) sinistro(-a); (lane) di sinistra.

left-hand drive n guida f a sinistra.

left-handed [-'hændɪd] adj (person) mancino(-a); (implement) per mancini.

left-luggage locker n (Br) armadietto m per deposito bagagli.

left-luggage office n (Br) deposito m bagagli.

left-wing adj di sinistra.

leg [leg] n gamba f; (of animal) zampa f; **~ of lamb** coscia f d'agnello.

legal ['li:gl] adj legale.

legal aid n assistenza f legale gratuita.

legalize ['li:gəlaɪz] vt legalizzare.

legal system n sistema f legale.

legend ['ledʒənd] n leggenda f.

leggings ['legɪnz] npl fuseaux mpl, pantacollant mpl.

legible ['ledʒɪbl] adj leggibile.

legislation [ˌledʒɪs'leɪʃn] n legislazione f.

legitimate [lɪ'dʒɪtɪmət] adj legittimo(-a).

leisure [Br 'leʒər, Am 'li:ʒər] n

tempo *m* libero.
leisure centre *n* centro *m* sportivo.
leisure pool *n* piscina *f*.
lemon ['lemən] *n* limone *m*.
lemonade [ˌleməˈneɪd] *n* limonata *f*.
lemon curd [-kɜːd] *n* (Br) sorta di marmellata a base di succo e scorza di limone, uova, burro e zucchero.
lemon juice *n* succo *m* di limone.
lemon meringue pie *n* dolce composto da una base di pasta frolla e uno strato di crema al limone rivestito di meringa.
lemon sole *n* limanda *f* (varietà di sogliola).
lemon tea *n* tè *m* al limone.
lend [lend] (*pt & pp* **lent**) *vt* prestare; **to ~ sb sthg** prestare qc a qn.
length [leŋθ] *n* (in distance) lunghezza *f*; (in time) durata *f*; (of swimming pool) vasca *f*.
lengthen ['leŋθən] *vt* allungare.
lens [lenz] *n* lente *f*.
lent [lent] *pt & pp* → **lend**.
Lent [lent] *n* la Quaresima.
lentils ['lentlz] *npl* lenticchie *fpl*.
Leo (*pl* **-s**) *n* Leone *m*.
leopard ['lepəd] *n* leopardo *m*.
leopard-skin *adj* a pelle di leopardo.
leotard ['liːətɑːd] *n* calzamaglia *f*.
leper ['lepəʳ] *n* lebbroso *m* (-a *f*).
lesbian ['lezbiən] ◆ *adj* lesbico(-a) ◆ *n* lesbica *f*.
less [les] *adj, adv & pron* meno; ~ **than 20** meno di 20.
lesson ['lesn] *n* (class) lezione *f*.
let [let] (*pt & pp* **let**) *vt* (allow) lasciare; (rent out) affittare; **to ~ sb do sthg** lasciar fare qc a qn; **to ~ go of sthg** mollare qc; **to ~ sb have sthg** (give) dare qc a qn; **to ~ sb know sthg** far sapere qc a qn; **~'s go!** andiamo!; **'to ~'** 'affittasi'.
▶ **let in** *vt sep* (allow to enter) far entrare.
▶ **let off** *vt sep* (excuse): **to ~ sb off**

doing sthg dispensare qn dal fare qc; **can you ~ me off at the station?** mi fa scendere alla stazione?
▶ **let out** *vt sep* (allow to go out) far uscire.
letdown ['letdaʊn] *n* (inf) delusione *f*.
lethargic [ləˈθɑːdʒɪk] *adj* apatico(-a).
letter ['letəʳ] *n* lettera *f*.
letterbox ['letəbɒks] *n* (Br) buca *f* delle lettere.
lettuce ['letɪs] *n* lattuga *f*.
leuk(a)emia [luːˈkiːmɪə] *n* leucemia *f*.
level ['levl] ◆ *adj* (flat) piano(-a); (horizontal) orizzontale ◆ *n* livello *m*; (storey) piano *m*; **to be ~ with** essere allo stesso livello di.
level crossing *n* (Br) passaggio *m* a livello.
lever [Br 'liːvəʳ, Am 'levəʳ] *n* leva *f*.
liability [ˌlaɪəˈbɪlɪtɪ] *n* (responsibility) responsabilità *f*.
liable ['laɪəbl] *adj*: **to be ~ to do sthg** avere la tendenza a fare qc; **to be ~ for sthg** rispondere di qc.
liaise [lɪˈeɪz] *vi*: **to ~ with** mantenere i contatti con.
liar ['laɪəʳ] *n* bugiardo *m* (-a *f*).
liberal ['lɪbərəl] *adj* (tolerant) liberale; (generous) generoso(-a).
Liberal Democrat Party *n* Partito *m* Liberaldemocratico.
liberate ['lɪbəreɪt] *vt* liberare.
liberty ['lɪbətɪ] *n* libertà *f inv*.
Libra *n* Bilancia *f*.
librarian [laɪˈbreərɪən] *n* bibliotecario *m* (-a *f*).
library ['laɪbrərɪ] *n* biblioteca *f*.
Libya ['lɪbɪə] *n* la Libia.
lice [laɪs] *npl* pidocchi *mpl*.
licence ['laɪsəns] ◆ *n* (Br: official document) licenza *f* ◆ *vt* (Am) = **license**; **driving ~** patente *f* (di guida); **TV ~** abbonamento *m* alla televisione.
license ['laɪsəns] ◆ *vt* (Br) autorizzare ◆ *n* (Am) = **licence**.

licensed ['laɪsənst] *adj (restaurant, bar)* munito di licenza per la vendita di alcolici.

licensing hours ['laɪsənsɪŋ-] *npl* (Br) orario in cui è consentita la vendita di alcolici.

lick [lɪk] *vt* leccare.

lid [lɪd] *n (cover)* coperchio *m*.

lie [laɪ] *(pt* lay, *pp* lain, *cont* lying) ♦ *n* bugia *f* ♦ *vi (tell lie: pt & pp* lied) mentire; *(be horizontal)* essere disteso; *(lie down)* sdraiarsi; *(be situated)* trovarsi; **to tell ~s** dire bugie; **to ~ about sthg** mentire su qc.

▶ **lie down** *vi* sdraiarsi.

lieutenant [Br lefˈtenənt, Am luːˈtenənt] *n* tenente *m*.

life [laɪf] *(pl* lives) *n* vita *f*.

life assurance *n* assicurazione *f* sulla vita.

life belt *n* salvagente *m*.

lifeboat ['laɪfbəʊt] *n* scialuppa *f* di salvataggio.

lifeguard ['laɪfgɑːd] *n* bagnino *m* (-a *f*).

life jacket *n* giubbotto *m* di salvataggio.

lifelike ['laɪflaɪk] *adj* fedele.

life preserver [-prɪˈzɜːvər] *n (Am)* (*life belt*) salvagente *m*; (*life jacket*) giubbotto *m* di salvataggio.

life-size *adj* a grandezza naturale.

lifespan ['laɪfspæn] *n* vita *f*.

lifestyle ['laɪfstaɪl] *n* stile *m* di vita.

lift [lɪft] ♦ *n* (Br: *elevator*) ascensore *m* ♦ *vt (raise)* sollevare, alzare ♦ *vi (fog)* alzarsi; **to give sb a ~** dare un passaggio a qn.

▶ **lift up** *vt sep* sollevare, alzare.

light [laɪt] *(pt & pp* lit OR -ed) ♦ *adj* leggero(-a); *(not dark)* chiaro(-a); *(traffic)* scorrevole ♦ *n* luce *f*; *(of car, bike)* faro *m* ♦ *vt (fire, cigarette)* accendere; *(room, stage)* illuminare; **have you got a ~?** hai da accendere?; **to set ~ to sthg** dar fuoco a qc.

▶ **lights** *npl (traffic lights)* semaforo *m*.

▶ **light up** ♦ *vt sep (house, road)* illu-

minare ♦ *vi (inf: light a cigarette)* accendersi una sigaretta.

light bulb *n* lampadina *f*.

lighter ['laɪtər] *n* accendino *m*.

light-hearted [-ˈhɑːtɪd] *adj* gioviale.

lighthouse ['laɪthaʊs, *pl* -haʊzɪz] *n* faro *m*.

lighting ['laɪtɪŋ] *n* illuminazione *f*.

light meter *n* contatore *m* della luce.

lightning ['laɪtnɪŋ] *n* lampi *mpl*, fulmini *mpl*.

lightweight ['laɪtweɪt] *adj (clothes, object)* leggero(-a).

like [laɪk] ♦ *prep* come; *(typical of)* tipico di ♦ *vt (want)* volere; **I ~ it** mi piace; **I ~ them** mi piacciono; **I ~ going out** mi piace uscire; **I'd ~ to sit down** vorrei sedermi; **I'd ~ a drink** vorrei bere qualcosa; **what's it ~?** com'è?; **to look ~ sb** assomigliare a qn; **do it ~ this** fallo così; **it's not ~ him** non è da lui.

likelihood ['laɪklɪhʊd] *n* probabilità *f*.

likely ['laɪklɪ] *adj* probabile.

likeness ['laɪknɪs] *n* somiglianza *f*.

likewise ['laɪkwaɪz] *adv* allo stesso modo; **to do ~** fare lo stesso.

lilac ['laɪlək] *adj* lilla *(inv)*.

Lilo® ['laɪləʊ] *(pl* -s) *n* (Br) materassino *m* (pneumatico).

lily ['lɪlɪ] *n* giglio *m*.

lily of the valley *n* mughetto *m*.

limb [lɪm] *n* arto *m*.

lime [laɪm] *n (fruit)* limetta *f*; **~ (juice)** succo *m* di limetta.

limestone ['laɪmstəʊn] *n* calcare *m*.

limit ['lɪmɪt] ♦ *n* limite *m* ♦ *vt* limitare; **the city ~s** i confini della città.

limited ['lɪmɪtɪd] *adj (restricted)* limitato(-a); *(in company name)* a responsabilità limitata.

limp [lɪmp] ♦ *adj* floscio(-a) ♦ *vi* zoppicare.

line [laɪn] ♦ *n* linea *f*; *(row)* fila *f*; (Am: *queue*) coda *f*, fila; *(of words on page)* riga *f*; *(of poem, song)* verso *m*;

(*for fishing*) lenza *f*; (*rope, washing line*) corda *f*; (*of business, work*) settore *m*, ramo *m* ♦ *vt* (*coat, drawers*) foderare; **in ~** (*aligned*) allineato; **it's a bad ~** la linea è disturbata; **the ~ is engaged** la linea è occupata; **to drop sb a ~** (*inf*) mandare due righe a qn; **to stand in ~** (*Am*) stare in fila.

▶ **line up** ♦ *vt sep* (*arrange*) organizzare ♦ *vi* allinearsi.

lined [laɪnd] *adj* (*paper*) rigato(-a), a righe.

linen ['lɪnɪn] *n* (*cloth*) lino *m*; (*tablecloths, sheets*) biancheria *f*.

liner ['laɪnər] *n* (*ship*) nave *f* di linea.

linesman ['laɪnzmən] (*pl* -**men** [-mən]) *n* guardalinee *m inv*.

linger ['lɪŋgər] *vi* (*in place*) attardarsi.

lingerie ['lænʒərɪ] *n* biancheria *f* intima (*femminile*).

lining ['laɪnɪŋ] *n* (*of coat, jacket*) fodera *f*; (*of brake*) guarnizione *f*.

link [lɪŋk] ♦ *n* (*connection*) collegamento *m*; (*between countries, companies*) relazione *f* ♦ *vt* (*connect*) collegare; **rail ~** collegamento ferroviario; **road ~** collegamento stradale.

lino ['laɪnəʊ] *n* (*Br*) linoleum *m*.

lion ['laɪən] *n* leone *m*.

lioness ['laɪənes] *n* leonessa *f*.

lip [lɪp] *n* (*of person*) labbro *m*.

lip salve [-sælv] *n* burro *m* di cacao.

lipstick ['lɪpstɪk] *n* rossetto *m*.

liqueur [lɪ'kjʊər] *n* liquore *m* (*dolce*).

liquid ['lɪkwɪd] *n* liquido *m*.

liquor ['lɪkər] *n* (*Am*) superalcolico *m*.

liquorice ['lɪkərɪs] *n* liquirizia *f*.

lisp [lɪsp] *n* difetto *f* di pronuncia (*relativo alla lettera s*).

list [lɪst] ♦ *n* lista *f*, elenco *m* ♦ *vt* elencare.

listen ['lɪsn] *vi*: **to ~ (to)** ascoltare.

listener ['lɪsnər] *n* (*on radio*) ascoltatore *m* (-trice *f*).

lit [lɪt] *pt & pp* → **light**.

liter ['liːtər] (*Am*) = **litre**.

literally ['lɪtərəlɪ] *adv* letteralmente.

literary ['lɪtərərɪ] *adj* letterario(-a).

literature ['lɪtrətʃər] *n* letteratura *f*; (*printed information*) materiale *m* illustrativo.

litre ['liːtər] *n* (*Br*) litro *m*.

litter ['lɪtər] *n* (*rubbish*) rifiuti *mpl*.

litterbin ['lɪtəbɪn] *n* (*Br*) cestino *m* dei rifiuti.

little ['lɪtl] ♦ *adj* piccolo(-a); (*not much*) poco(-a) ♦ *pron & adv* poco; **as ~ as possible** il meno possibile; **~ by ~** poco a poco.

▶ **a little** ♦ *pron & adv* un po' ♦ *adj* un po' di.

little finger *n* mignolo *m*.

live¹ [lɪv] *vi* vivere; (*have home*) vivere, abitare; **to ~ with sb** vivere con qn.

▶ **live together** *vi* vivere insieme.

live² [laɪv] ♦ *adj* (*alive*) vivo(-a); (*programme, performance*) dal vivo; (*wire*) sotto tensione ♦ *adv* in diretta.

liveliness ['laɪvlɪnɪs] *n* (*of person*) vivacità *f*; (*of place, atmosphere*) animazione *f*.

lively ['laɪvlɪ] *adj* (*person*) vivace; (*place, atmosphere*) animato(-a).

liver ['lɪvər] *n* fegato *m*.

lives [laɪvz] *pl* → **life**.

living ['lɪvɪŋ] ♦ *adj* vivente ♦ *n*: **to earn a ~** guadagnarsi da vivere; **what do you do for a ~?** che lavoro fa?

living room *n* soggiorno *m*.

lizard ['lɪzəd] *n* lucertola *f*.

load [ləʊd] ♦ *n* (*thing carried*) carico *m* ♦ *vt* caricare; **~s of** (*inf*) un sacco di.

loaf [ləʊf] (*pl* **loaves**) *n*: **a ~ (of bread)** una pagnotta.

loan [ləʊn] ♦ *n* prestito *m* ♦ *vt* prestare.

loathe [ləʊð] *vt* detestare.

loaves [ləʊvz] *pl* → **loaf**.

lobby ['lɒbɪ] *n* (*hall*) atrio *m*.

lobster ['lɒbstər] n aragosta f.

local ['ləʊkl] ♦ adj locale; (train) regionale ♦ n (inf: local person) abitante mf del posto; (Br: pub) bar m vicino; (Am: train) regionale m; (Am: bus) autobus m inv.

local anaesthetic n anestesia f locale.

local call n chiamata f urbana.

local government n amministrazione f locale.

locate [Br ləʊ'keɪt, Am 'ləʊkeɪt] vt (find) localizzare; **to be ~d** essere situato.

location [ləʊ'keɪʃn] n (place) posizione f.

loch [lɒk] n (Scot) lago m.

lock [lɒk] ♦ n (on door, drawer) serratura f; (for bike) lucchetto m; (on canal) chiusa f ♦ vt (door, drawer, car) chiudere a chiave; (keep safely) chiudere ♦ vi (become stuck) bloccarsi.
▶ **lock in** vt sep chiudere dentro.
▶ **lock out** vt sep chiudere fuori.
▶ **lock up** ♦ vt sep (imprison) mettere dentro ♦ vi chiudere porte e finestre.

locker ['lɒkər] n armadietto m.

locker room n (Am) spogliatoio m.

locket ['lɒkɪt] n medaglione m.

locomotive [,ləʊkə'məʊtɪv] n locomotiva f.

locum ['ləʊkəm] n (doctor) medico m sostituto.

locust ['ləʊkəst] n locusta f.

lodge [lɒdʒ] ♦ n (for skiers) rifugio m; (for hunters) casino m di caccia ♦ vi (stay) alloggiare; (get stuck) conficcarsi.

lodger ['lɒdʒər] n pensionante mf.

lodgings ['lɒdʒɪŋz] npl camera f ammobiliata.

loft [lɒft] n soffitta f.

log [lɒg] n (piece of wood) ceppo m.

logic ['lɒdʒɪk] n logica f.

logical ['lɒdʒɪkl] adj logico(-a).

logo ['ləʊgəʊ] (pl -s) n logo m inv.

loin [lɔɪn] n lombata f.

loiter ['lɔɪtər] vi (remain) attardarsi; (walk around) bighellonare.

lollipop ['lɒlɪpɒp] n lecca lecca m inv.

lolly ['lɒlɪ] n (inf: lollipop) lecca lecca m inv; (Br: ice lolly) ghiacciolo m.

Lombardy n la Lombardia.

London ['lʌndən] n Londra f.

Londoner ['lʌndənər] n londinese mf.

lonely ['ləʊnlɪ] adj (person) solo(-a); (place) isolato(-a).

long [lɒŋ] ♦ adj lungo(-a) ♦ adv molto; **it's 2 metres ~** è lungo 2 metri; **it's two hours ~** dura due ore; **how ~ is it?** (in length) quanto è lungo?; (in time) quanto dura?; **a ~ time** molto tempo; **all day ~** tutto il giorno; **as ~ as** (provided that) purché; **for ~** per molto tempo; **no ~er** non più; **so ~!** (inf) ciao!
▶ **long for** vt fus desiderare ardentemente.

long-distance adj (phone call) interurbano(-a).

long drink n long drink m inv.

long-haul adj su lunga distanza.

longitude ['lɒndʒɪtjuːd] n longitudine f.

long jump n salto m in lungo.

long-life adj (milk, fruit juice) a lunga conservazione; (battery) a lunga durata.

longsighted [,lɒŋ'saɪtɪd] adj presbite.

long-term adj a lungo termine.

long wave n onde fpl lunghe.

longwearing [,lɒŋ'weərɪŋ] adj (Am) resistente.

loo [luː] (pl -s) n (Br: inf) gabinetto m.

look [lʊk] ♦ n (glance) sguardo m, occhiata f; (appearance) aspetto m ♦ vi guardare; (seem) sembrare; **you don't ~ well** non hai una gran bella cera; **to ~ onto** (building, room) dare su; **to have a ~** dare un'occhiata; (good) **~s** bellezza f; **I'm just ~ing** (in *shop*) sto solo guardando; **~ out!** attento!

▶ **look after** *vt fus* occuparsi di.

▶ **look at** *vt fus* (*observe*) guardare; (*examine*) vedere.

▶ **look for** *vt fus* cercare.

▶ **look forward to** *vt fus* non veder l'ora di.

▶ **look out for** *vt fus* cercare.

▶ **look round** ♦ *vt fus* (*city, museum*) visitare; (*shop*) fare un giro da ♦ *vi* girarsi.

▶ **look up** *vt sep* (*in dictionary, phone book*) cercare.

loony ['lu:nɪ] *n* (*inf*) pazzo *m* (-a *f*).

loop [lu:p] *n* cappio *m*.

loose [lu:s] *adj* (*not fixed firmly*) allentato(-a); (*sweets, sheets of paper*) sciolto(-a); (*clothes*) largo(-a); **to let sb/sthg ~** lasciar libero qn/qc.

loosen ['lu:sn] *vt* allentare.

lop-sided [-'saɪdɪd] *adj* storto(-a).

lord [lɔ:d] *n* lord *m inv*.

lorry ['lɒrɪ] *n* (*Br*) camion *m inv*.

lorry driver *n* (*Br*) camionista *mf*.

lose [lu:z] (*pt & pp* **lost**) *vt & vi* perdere; **to ~ weight** dimagrire.

loser ['lu:zər] *n* (*in contest*) perdente *mf*.

loss [lɒs] *n* perdita *f*.

lost [lɒst] ♦ *pt & pp* → **lose** ♦ *adj* (*person*) perso(-a); **to get ~** (*lose way*) perdersi.

lost-and-found office *n* (*Am*) ufficio *m* oggetti smarriti.

lost property office *n* (*Br*) ufficio *m* oggetti smarriti.

lot [lɒt] *n* (*group of people*) gruppo *m*; (*at auction*) lotto *m*; (*Am: car park*) parcheggio *m*; **a ~** (*large amount*) molto(-a), molti(-e) (*pl*); (*to a great extent, often*) molto; **a ~ of time** molto tempo; **a ~ of problems** molti problemi; **~s (of)** molto(-a), molti(-e) (*pl*), un sacco (di); **the ~** (*everything*) tutto quanto (tutta quanta).

lotion ['ləʊʃn] *n* lozione *f*.

lottery ['lɒtərɪ] *n* lotteria *f*.

loud [laʊd] *adj* (*music, noise*) forte; (*voice*) alto(-a); (*colour, clothes*) sgargiante.

loudspeaker [,laʊd'spi:kər] *n* altoparlante *m*.

lounge [laʊndʒ] *n* (*in house*) salotto *m*, soggiorno *m*; (*at airport*) sala *f* partenze.

lounge bar *n* (*Br*) sala di un pub più confortevole e più cara del 'public bar'.

lousy ['laʊzɪ] *adj* (*inf: poor-quality*) schifoso(-a).

lout [laʊt] *n* teppista *mf*.

love [lʌv] ♦ *n* amore *m*; (*in tennis*) zero *m* ♦ *vt* amare; **I ~ reading** mi piace molto leggere; **I'd ~ a coffee** mi andrebbe un caffè; **I'd ~ to help** vorrei tanto aiutare; **to be in ~ (with)** essere innamorato (di); **(with) ~ from** (*in letter*) con affetto.

love affair *n* relazione *f*.

lovely ['lʌvlɪ] *adj* (*very beautiful*) bello(-a); (*very nice*) delizioso(-a).

lover ['lʌvər] *n* (*sexual partner*) amante *mf*; (*enthusiast*) appassionato *m* (-a *f*).

loving ['lʌvɪŋ] *adj* affettuoso(-a).

low [ləʊ] ♦ *adj* basso(-a); (*quantity*) piccolo(-a); (*supply*) scarso(-a); (*standard, quality, opinion*) scadente; (*depressed*) depresso(-a) ♦ *n* (*area of low pressure*) area *f* di bassa pressione; **we're ~ on petrol** abbiamo poca benzina.

low-alcohol *adj* a basso contenuto alcolico.

low-calorie *adj* ipocalorico(-a).

low-cut *adj* scollato(-a).

lower ['ləʊər] ♦ *adj* inferiore ♦ *vt* abbassare.

lower sixth *n* (*Br*) *primo anno di studi superiori per studenti di 17 anni che prepareranno gli 'A levels'*.

low-fat *adj* magro(-a).

low tide *n* bassa marea *f*.

loyal ['lɔɪəl] *adj* fedele.

loyalty ['lɔɪəltɪ] *n* fedeltà *f*.

lozenge ['lɒzɪndʒ] *n* (*sweet*) pasticca *f*, pastiglia *f*.

LP *n* LP *m inv*.

L-plate n (Br) targa indicante che chi guida la vettura non ha ancora preso la patente.

Ltd (abbr of limited) ≃ Srl.

lubricate ['lu:brɪkeɪt] vt lubrificare.

luck [lʌk] n fortuna f; **bad ~** sfortuna f; **good ~!** buona fortuna!; **with ~** con un po' di fortuna.

luckily ['lʌkɪlɪ] adv fortunatamente.

lucky ['lʌkɪ] adj fortunato(-a); **to be ~** essere fortunato.

ludicrous ['lu:dɪkrəs] adj ridicolo(-a).

lug [lʌg] vt (inf) trascinare.

luggage ['lʌgɪdʒ] n bagagli mpl.

luggage compartment n bagagliaio m.

luggage locker n armadietto m per deposito bagagli.

luggage rack n (on train) portabagagli m.

lukewarm ['lu:kwɔ:m] adj tiepido(-a).

lull [lʌl] n pausa f.

lullaby ['lʌləbaɪ] n ninnananna f.

lumbago [lʌm'beɪgəʊ] n lombaggine f.

lumber ['lʌmbər] n (Am: timber) legname m.

luminous ['lu:mɪnəs] adj fosforescente.

lump [lʌmp] n (of coal, mud, butter) pezzo m; (of sugar) zolletta f; (on body) nodulo m.

lump sum n compenso m forfettario.

lumpy ['lʌmpɪ] adj (sauce) grumoso(-a); (mattress) pieno(-a) di bozzi.

lunatic ['lu:nətɪk] n pazzo m (-a f).

lunch [lʌntʃ] n pranzo m; **to have ~** pranzare.

luncheon ['lʌntʃən] n (fml) pranzo m.

luncheon meat n ≃ carne di maiale f in scatola.

lunch hour n pausa f pranzo.

lunchtime ['lʌntʃtaɪm] n ora f di pranzo.

lung [lʌŋ] n polmone m.

lunge [lʌndʒ] vi: **to ~ at** gettarsi su.

lurch [lɜ:tʃ] vi barcollare.

lure [ljʊər] vt attirare.

lurk [lɜ:k] vi (person) stare in agguato.

lush [lʌʃ] adj (grass, field) rigoglioso(-a).

lust [lʌst] n (sexual desire) libidine f.

Luxembourg ['lʌksəmbɜ:g] n il Lussemburgo.

luxurious [lʌg'ʒʊərɪəs] adj di lusso.

luxury ['lʌkʃərɪ] ♦ adj di lusso ♦ n lusso m.

lying ['laɪɪŋ] cont → **lie**.

lyrics ['lɪrɪks] npl parole fpl.

M

m ♦ (abbr of metre) m ♦ abbr = **mile**.

M (Br: abbr of motorway) A; (abbr of medium) M.

MA n (abbr of Master of Arts) (titolare di) master in materie umanistiche.

mac [mæk] n (Br: inf: coat) impermeabile m.

macaroni [ˌmækə'rəʊnɪ] n maccheroni mpl.

macaroni cheese n maccheroni mpl gratinati.

machine [mə'ʃi:n] n macchina f.

machinegun [mə'ʃi:ngʌn] n mitragliatrice f.

machinery [mə'ʃi:nərɪ] n macchine fpl.

machine-washable adj lavabile in lavatrice.

mackerel ['mækrəl] (pl inv) n sgombro m.

mackintosh ['mækɪntɒʃ] n (Br) impermeabile m.

mad [mæd] adj pazzo(-a),

matto(-a); (*angry*) arrabbiato(-a); (*uncontrolled*) furioso(-a); **to be ~ about** (*inf: like a lot*) andare pazzo per; **like ~** come un matto.

Madam ['mædəm] *n* (*form of address*) signora *f*.

made [meɪd] *pt & pp* → **make.**

madeira [məˈdɪərə] *n* madera *m*.

made-to-measure *adj* fatto(-a) su misura.

madness [ˈmædnɪs] *n* pazzia *f*.

magazine [ˌmægəˈziːn] *n* (*journal*) rivista *f*.

maggot [ˈmægət] *n* verme *m*.

magic [ˈmædʒɪk] *n* magia *f*.

magician [məˈdʒɪʃn] *n* (*conjurer*) mago *m* (-a *f*).

magistrate [ˈmædʒɪstreɪt] *n* magistrato *m*.

magnet [ˈmægnɪt] *n* calamita *f*.

magnetic [mægˈnetɪk] *adj* magnetico(-a).

magnificent [mægˈnɪfɪsənt] *adj* magnifico(-a).

magnifying glass [ˈmægnɪfaɪɪŋ-] *n* lente *f* d'ingrandimento.

mahogany [məˈhɒgənɪ] *n* mogano *m*.

maid [meɪd] *n* cameriera *f*.

maiden name [ˈmeɪdn-] *n* nome *m* da nubile.

mail [meɪl] ◆ *n* posta *f* ◆ *vt* (*Am*) spedire.

mailbox [ˈmeɪlbɒks] *n* (*Am*) cassetta *f* delle lettere.

mailman [ˈmeɪlmən] (*pl* **-men** [-mən]) *n* (*Am*) postino *m*.

mail order *n* vendita *f* per corrispondenza.

main [meɪn] *adj* principale.

main course *n* portata *f* principale.

main deck *n* ponte *m* principale, coperta *f*.

mainland [ˈmeɪnlənd] *n*: **the ~** il continente.

main line *n* linea *f* principale.

mainly [ˈmeɪnlɪ] *adv* principalmente.

main road *n* strada *f* principale.

mains [meɪnz] *npl*: **the ~** le condutture.

main street *n* (*Am*) corso *m*.

maintain [meɪnˈteɪn] *vt* (*keep*) mantenere; (*in good condition*) provvedere alla manutenzione di.

maintenance [ˈmeɪntənəns] *n* (*of car, machine*) manutenzione *f*; (*money*) alimenti *mpl*.

maisonette [ˌmeɪzəˈnet] *n* (*Br*) appartamento *m* (su due piani).

maize [meɪz] *n* granturco *m*, mais *m*.

major [ˈmeɪdʒəʳ] ◆ *adj* (*important*) importante; (*most important*) principale ◆ *n* (MIL) maggiore *m* ◆ *vi* (*Am*): **to ~ in** laurearsi in.

majority [məˈdʒɒrətɪ] *n* maggioranza *f*.

major road *n* strada *f* principale.

make [meɪk] (*pt & pp* **made**) *vt* 1. (*produce, manufacture*) fare; **to be made of** essere (fatto) di; **to ~ lunch/supper** preparare il pranzo/la cena; **made in Japan** fabbricato in Giappone.

2. (*perform, do*) fare; (*decision*) prendere; **to ~ a mistake** fare un errore; **to ~ a phone call** fare una telefonata.

3. (*cause to be*) rendere; **to ~ sthg better** migliorare qc; **to ~ sb happy** rendere felice qn.

4. (*cause to do, force*) fare; **to ~ sb do sthg** far fare qc a qn, costringere qn a fare qc; **it made her laugh** l'ha fatta ridere.

5. (*amount to, total*) fare; **that ~s £5** fanno 5 sterline.

6. (*calculate*): **I ~ it £4** mi viene 4 sterline; **I ~ it seven o'clock** io faccio le sette.

7. (*earn*) fare; **to ~ a loss** registrare una perdita.

8. (*inf: arrive in time for*): **I don't think we'll ~ the 10 o'clock train** non credo che ce la faremo per il treno delle 10.

9. (*friend, enemy*) farsi.

10. (*have qualities for*): **this would ~ a lovely bedroom** sarebbe una camera (da letto) molto carina.

11. (*bed*) fare, rifare.

12. (*in phrases*): **to ~ do** (*with*) arrangiarsi (con); **to ~ good** (*damage*) risarcire; **to ~ it** (*arrive on time, be able to go*) farcela.

♦ *n* (*of product*) marca *f*.

▶ **make out** *vt sep* (*cheque, receipt*) fare; (*form*) compilare; (*see, hear*) distinguere, capire.

▶ **make up** *vt sep* (*invent*) inventare; (*comprise*) costituire, comporre; (*difference*) coprire.

▶ **make up for** *vt fus* compensare.

makeshift ['meɪkʃɪft] *adj* di fortuna.

make-up *n* (*cosmetics*) trucco *m*.

malaria [mə'leərɪə] *n* malaria *f*.

Malaysia [mə'leɪzɪə] *n* la Malesia.

male [meɪl] ♦ *adj* maschile; (*child, animal*) maschio ♦ *n* (*animal*) maschio *m*.

malfunction [mæl'fʌŋkʃn] *vi* (*fml*) funzionare male.

malignant [mə'lɪɡnənt] *adj* (*tumour*) maligno(-a).

mall [mɔːl] *n* (*shopping centre*) centro *m* commerciale.

mallet ['mælɪt] *n* maglio *m*.

malt [mɔːlt] *n* malto *m*.

maltreat [,mæl'triːt] *vt* maltrattare.

malt whisky *n* whisky *m inv* di malto.

mammal ['mæml] *n* mammifero *m*.

man [mæn] (*pl* **men**) ♦ *n* uomo *m* ♦ *vt* (*office*) dotare di personale; (*phones*) rispondere a.

manage ['mænɪdʒ] ♦ *vt* (*company, business*) dirigere; (*suitcase*) farcela a portare; (*job*) riuscire a fare; (*food*) farcela a mangiare ♦ *vi* (*cope*) farcela; **can you ~ Friday?** venerdì ti andrebbe bene?; **to ~ to do sthg** riuscire a fare qc.

management ['mænɪdʒmənt] *n* direzione *f*.

manager ['mænɪdʒəʳ] *n* (*of business, bank, shop*) direttore *m*; (*of sports team*) allenatore *m*.

manageress [,mænɪdʒə'res] *n* (*of business, bank, shop*) direttrice *f*.

managing director ['mænɪdʒɪŋ-] *n* amministratore *m* delegato.

mandarin ['mændərɪn] *n* mandarino *m*.

mane [meɪn] *n* criniera *f*.

maneuver [mə'nuːvəʳ] (*Am*) = **manoeuvre**.

mangetout [,mɒnʒ'tuː] *n* pisello *m* mangiatutto.

mangle ['mæŋgl] *vt* (*body*) straziare.

mango ['mæŋɡəʊ] (*pl* **-es** OR **-s**) *n* mango *m*.

Manhattan [mæn'hætən] *n* Manhattan *f*.

manhole ['mænhəʊl] *n* pozzo *m* d'ispezione.

maniac ['meɪnɪæk] *n* (*inf*) pazzo *m* (*-a f*).

manicure ['mænɪkjʊəʳ] *n* manicure *f inv*.

manifold ['mænɪfəʊld] *n* (AUT) collettore *m*.

manipulate [mə'nɪpjʊleɪt] *vt* (*person*) manipolare; (*machine, controls*) manovrare.

mankind [,mæn'kaɪnd] *n* l'umanità *f*.

manly ['mænlɪ] *adj* virile.

man-made *adj* artificiale.

manner ['mænəʳ] *n* (*way*) modo *m*.

▶ **manners** *npl* maniere *fpl*.

manoeuvre [mə'nuːvəʳ] ♦ *n* (Br) manovra *f* ♦ *vt* (Br) manovrare.

manor ['mænəʳ] *n* grande casa *f* di campagna.

mansion ['mænʃn] *n* casa *f* signorile.

manslaughter ['mæn,slɔːtəʳ] *n* omicidio *m* colposo.

mantelpiece ['mæntlpiːs] *n* mensola *f* del caminetto.

manual ['mænjʊəl] ♦ *adj* manuale ♦ *n* manuale *m*.

manufacture [,mænjʊ'fæktʃər] ♦ n
fabbricazione f ♦ vt (produce) fabbricare.

manufacturer [,mænjʊ'fæktʃərər]
n fabbricante m.

manure [mə'njʊər] n concime m.

many ['menɪ] (compar **more**, superl
most) ♦ adj molti(-e) ♦ pron molti
mpl (-e fpl); **how ~?** quanti(-e)?; **so ~**
così tanti(-e); **too ~** troppi(-e); **take
as ~ as you like** prendine quanti ne
vuoi; **twice as ~ as** il doppio di.

map [mæp] n (of country) carta f
geografica; (of town) pianta f.

Mar. (abbr of March) mar.

marathon ['mærəθn] n maratona f.

marble ['mɑːbl] n (stone) marmo m;
(glass ball) bilia f, pallina f (di vetro).

march [mɑːtʃ] ♦ n (demonstration)
marcia f ♦ vi (walk quickly) avanzare
con passo deciso.

March [mɑːtʃ] n marzo m, →
September.

mare [meər] n giumenta f.

margarine [,mɑːdʒə'riːn] n margarina f.

margin ['mɑːdʒɪn] n margine m.

marina [mə'riːnə] n porto m turistico.

marinated ['mærɪneɪtɪd] adj mari-
nato(-a).

marital status ['mærɪtl-] n stato
m civile.

marjoram ['mɑːdʒərəm] n maggiorana f.

mark [mɑːk] ♦ n (spot) macchia f;
(cut, symbol) segno m; (SCH) voto m;
(of gas oven) numero corrispondente a
una certa temperatura ♦ vt (blemish)
macchiare; (put symbol on) segnare;
(correct) correggere; (show position of)
indicare.

marker pen ['mɑːkə-] n (grosso)
pennarello m.

market ['mɑːkɪt] n mercato m.

marketing ['mɑːkɪtɪŋ] n marketing m.

marketplace ['mɑːkɪtpleɪs] n
(place) piazza f del mercato.

markings ['mɑːkɪŋz] npl (on road)
segnaletica f orizzontale.

marmalade ['mɑːməleɪd] n marmellata f di agrumi.

marquee [mɑː'kiː] n padiglione m.

marriage ['mærɪdʒ] n matrimonio
m.

married ['mærɪd] adj sposato(-a);
to get ~ sposarsi.

marrow ['mærəʊ] n (vegetable)
zucca f.

marry ['mærɪ] ♦ vt sposare ♦ vi
sposarsi.

marsh [mɑːʃ] n palude f.

martial arts [,mɑːʃl-] npl arti fpl
marziali.

martyr ['mɑːtər] n martire mf.

martyrdom ['mɑːtədəm] n martirio m.

marvellous ['mɑːvələs] adj (Br)
meraviglioso(-a).

marvelous ['mɑːvələs] (Am) =
marvellous.

marzipan ['mɑːzɪpæn] n marzapane m.

mascara [mæs'kɑːrə] n mascara m
inv.

masculine ['mæskjʊlɪn] adj maschile; (woman) mascolino(-a).

mashed potatoes [mæʃt-] npl
purè m inv di patate.

mask [mɑːsk] n maschera f.

masonry ['meɪsnrɪ] n muratura f.

mass [mæs] n (large amount) massa
f; (RELIG) messa f; **~es (of)** (inf: lots)
un sacco (di).

massacre ['mæsəkər] n massacro m.

massage [Br 'mæsɑːʒ, Am mə'sɑːʒ]
♦ n massaggio m ♦ vt massaggiare.

masseur [mæ'sɜːr] n massaggiatore m.

masseuse [mæ'sɜːz] n massaggia-
trice f.

massive ['mæsɪv] adj enorme.

mast [mɑːst] n (on boat) albero m.

master ['mɑːstər] ♦ n (at school)
insegnante m; (of servant, dog)
padrone m ♦ vt (learn) imparare a
fondo.

masterly [ˈmɑːstəlɪ] adj magistrale, sapiente

masterpiece [ˈmɑːstəpiːs] n capolavoro m.

mat [mæt] n (small rug) tappetino m; (on table) sottopiatto m.

match [mætʃ] ♦ n (for lighting) fiammifero m; (game) partita f, incontro m ♦ vt (in colour, design) intonarsi a OR con; (be the same as) corrispondere a; (be as good as) uguagliare ♦ vi (in colour, design) intonarsi.

matchbox [ˈmætʃbɒks] n scatola f di fiammiferi.

matching [ˈmætʃɪŋ] adj intonato(-a).

mate [meɪt] ♦ n (inf: friend) amico m (-a f) ♦ vi accoppiarsi.

material [məˈtɪərɪəl] n materiale m; (cloth) stoffa f.
▶ **materials** npl (equipment) occorrente m.

maternity leave [məˈtɜːnətɪ-] n congedo m di maternità.

maternity ward [məˈtɜːnətɪ-] n reparto m maternità.

math [mæθ] (Am) = **maths**.

mathematics [ˌmæθəˈmætɪks] n matematica f.

maths [mæθs] n (Br) matematica f.

matinée [ˈmætɪneɪ] n matinée f inv.

matt [mæt] adj opaco(-a).

matter [ˈmætər] ♦ n (issue, situation) questione f; (physical material) materia f ♦ vi importare; **it doesn't ~** non importa; **no ~ what happens** qualsiasi cosa accada; **there's something the ~ with my car** c'è qualcosa che non va con la mia macchina; **what's the ~?** che cosa c'è (che non va)?; **as a ~ of course** come è naturale; **as a ~ of fact** in realtà.

mattress [ˈmætrɪs] n materasso m.

mature [məˈtjʊər] adj (person, behaviour) maturo(-a); (cheese, wine) stagionato(-a).

mauve [məʊv] adj (color) malva (inv).

max. [mæks] (abbr of maximum) max.

maximum [ˈmæksɪməm] ♦ adj massimo(-a) ♦ n massimo m.

may [meɪ] aux vb 1. (expressing possibility): **it ~ be done as follows** si può procedere come segue; **it ~ rain** può darsi che piova; **they ~ have got lost** può darsi che si siano persi.
2. (expressing permission): **~ I smoke?** posso fumare?; **you ~ sit, if you wish** può sedersi, se vuole.
3. (when conceding a point): **it ~ be a long walk, but it's worth it** sarà anche lontano a piedi, ma ne vale la pena.

May [meɪ] n maggio m, → **September**.

maybe [ˈmeɪbiː] adv forse.

mayonnaise [ˌmeɪəˈneɪz] n maionese f.

mayor [meər] n sindaco m.

mayoress [ˈmeərɪs] n sindaco m (donna).

maze [meɪz] n labirinto m.

me [miː] pron mi; (after prep, stressed) me; **she knows ~** (lei) mi conosce; **it's ~** sono io; **send it to ~** mandalo a me; **tell ~** dimmi; **he's worse than ~** lui è peggio di me.

meadow [ˈmedəʊ] n prato m.

meal [miːl] n pasto m.

mealtime [ˈmiːltaɪm] n ora f di mangiare.

mean [miːn] (pt & pp meant) ♦ adj (miserly) avaro(-a), gretto(-a); (unkind) scortese, villano(-a) ♦ vt (signify, matter) significare, voler dire; (intend, be serious about) intendere; (be a sign of) significare; **I didn't ~ it** non dicevo sul serio; **to ~ to do sthg** avere l'intenzione di fare qc; **the bus was meant to leave at 8.30** l'autobus sarebbe dovuto partire alle 8.30; **it's meant to be good** dovrebbe essere buono.

meaning [ˈmiːnɪŋ] n significato m, senso m.

meaningless ['mi:nɪŋlɪs] *adj* (*irrelevant*) insignificante.

means [mi:nz] ♦ (*pl inv*) *n* (*method*) mezzo *m* ♦ *npl* (*money*) mezzi *mpl*; **by all ~!** ma certo!; **by ~ of** per mezzo di.

meant [ment] *pt & pp* → **mean**.

meantime ['mi:n,taɪm]: **in the meantime** *adv* nel frattempo.

meanwhile ['mi:n,waɪl] *adv* nel frattempo.

measles ['mi:zlz] *n* morbillo *m*.

measure ['meʒə'] ♦ *vt* misurare ♦ *n* (*step, action*) misura *f*, provvedimento *m*; (*of alcohol*) dose *f*; **the room ~s 10 m²** la stanza misura 10 m².

measurement ['meʒəmənt] *n* misura *f*.

meat [mi:t] *n* carne *f*; **red ~** carne rossa; **white ~** carne bianca.

meatball ['mi:tbɔ:l] *n* polpetta *f* (di carne).

mechanic [mɪ'kænɪk] *n* meccanico *m*.

mechanical [mɪ'kænɪkl] *adj* (*device*) meccanico(-a).

mechanism ['mekənɪzm] *n* meccanismo *m*.

medal ['medl] *n* medaglia *f*.

media ['mi:djə] *n or npl*: **the ~** i (mass) media.

medical ['medɪkl] ♦ *adj* medico(-a) ♦ *n* visita *f* medica.

medication [,medɪ'keɪʃn] *n* medicine *fpl*.

medicinal [me'dɪsɪnl] *adj* medicinale.

medicine ['medsɪn] *n* medicina *f*.

medicine cabinet *n* armadietto *m* dei medicinali.

medieval [,medɪ'i:vl] *adj* medievale.

mediocre [,mi:dɪ'əukə'] *adj* mediocre.

Mediterranean [,medɪtə'reɪnjən] *n*: **the ~** (*region*) la regione del Mediterraneo; **the ~ (Sea)** il (Mare) Mediterraneo.

medium ['mi:djəm] *adj* medio(-a); (*sherry*) semisecco(-a).

medium-dry *adj* semisecco(-a).

medium-sized [-saɪzd] *adj* di misura media.

medley ['medlɪ] *n*: **a ~ of cold meats** affettati *mpl* misti.

meet [mi:t] (*pt & pp* **met**) ♦ *vt* incontrare; (*get to know*) fare la conoscenza di, conoscere; (*go to collect*) andare a prendere; (*need, requirement*) soddisfare; (*cost, expenses*) far fronte a ♦ *vi* incontrarsi; (*get to know each other*) conoscersi.

▶ **meet up** *vi* incontrarsi.

▶ **meet with** *vt fus* incontrare.

meeting ['mi:tɪŋ] *n* (*for business*) incontro *m*.

meeting point *n* (*at airport, station*) punto *m* d'incontro.

melody ['melədɪ] *n* melodia *f*.

melon ['melən] *n* melone *m*.

melt [melt] *vi* sciogliersi; (*metal*) fondersi.

member ['membə'] *n* membro *m*.

Member of Congress [-'kɒŋgres] *n* membro *m* del Congresso (Americano).

Member of Parliament *n* ≈ deputato *m* (-a *f*).

membership ['membəʃɪp] *n* (*state of being a member*) appartenenza *f*; (*members*) (numero dei) membri *mpl*.

memo ['meməu] (*pl* **-s**) *n* promemoria *m inv*; (*in office*) comunicazione *f* di servizio.

memorial [mɪ'mɔ:rɪəl] *n* monumento *m*.

memorize ['meməraɪz] *vt* memorizzare.

memory ['memərɪ] *n* memoria *f*; (*thing remembered*) ricordo *m*.

men [men] *pl* → **man**.

menacing ['menəsɪŋ] *adj* minaccioso(-a).

mend [mend] *vt* accomodare, aggiustare; (*clothes*) rammendare.

menopause ['menəpɔ:z] n menopausa f.

men's room n (Am) gabinetto m degli uomini.

menstruate ['menstruert] vi avere le mestruazioni.

menswear ['menzweə'] n abbigliamento m da uomo.

mental ['mentl] adj mentale.

mental hospital n ospedale m psichiatrico.

mentally handicapped ['mentəlɪ-] ◆ adj mentalmente handicappato(-a) ◆ npl: **the ~** i portatori di handicap mentale.

mentally ill ['mentəlɪ-] adj malato(-a) di mente.

mention ['menʃn] vt accennare a; **don't ~ it!** non c'è di che!

menu ['menju:] n menu m inv; **children's ~** menu per bambini.

merchandise ['mɜ:tʃəndaɪz] n mercanzia f, merce f.

merchant marine [,mɜ:tʃənt-mə'ri:n] (Am) = **merchant navy**.

merchant navy [,mɜ:tʃənt-] n (Br) marina f mercantile.

mercury ['mɜ:kjʊrɪ] n mercurio m.

mercy ['mɜ:sɪ] n pietà f.

mere [mɪə'] adj semplice; **a ~ £5** solo 5 sterline.

merely ['mɪəlɪ] adv soltanto.

merge [mɜ:dʒ] vi (combine) fondersi, unirsi; **'merge'** (Am: AUT) segnale che indica agli automobilisti che si immettono su un'autostrada di disporsi sulla corsia di destra.

merger ['mɜ:dʒə'] n fusione f.

meringue [mə'ræŋ] n (egg white) meringa f; (cake) meringa alla panna.

merit ['merɪt] n merito m.

merry ['merɪ] adj allegro(-a); **Merry Christmas!** Buon Natale!

merry-go-round n giostra f.

mess [mes] n (untidiness) disordine m, confusione f; (difficult situation) pasticcio m; **in a ~** (untidy) in disordine.

▶ **mess about** vi (inf) (have fun) divertirsi; (behave foolishly) fare lo scemo; **to ~ about with sthg** (interfere) intromettersi in qc.

▶ **mess up** vt sep (inf: ruin, spoil) mandare a monte.

message ['mesɪdʒ] n messaggio m.

messenger ['mesɪndʒə'] n messaggero m (-a f).

messy ['mesɪ] adj disordinato(-a).

met [met] pt & pp → **meet**.

metal ['metl] ◆ adj metallico(-a), di metallo ◆ n metallo m.

metalwork ['metəlwɜ:k] n (craft) lavorazione f dei metalli.

meter ['mi:tə'] n (device) contatore m; (Am) = **metre**.

method ['meθəd] n metodo m.

methodical [mɪ'θɒdɪkl] adj metodico(-a).

meticulous [mɪ'tɪkjʊləs] adj meticoloso(-a).

metre ['mi:tə'] n (Br) metro m.

metric ['metrɪk] adj metrico(-a).

mews [mju:z] (pl inv) n (Br) stradina o cortile di antiche scuderie trasformate in appartamenti.

Mexican ['meksɪkn] ◆ adj messicano(-a) ◆ n messicano m (-a f).

Mexico ['meksɪkəʊ] n il Messico.

mg (abbr of milligram) mg.

miaow [mi:'aʊ] vi (Br) miagolare.

mice [maɪs] pl → **mouse**.

microchip ['maɪkrəʊtʃɪp] n microcircuito m integrato, microchip m inv.

microphone ['maɪkrəfəʊn] n microfono m.

microscope ['maɪkrəskəʊp] n microscopio m.

microwave (oven) ['maɪkrəweɪv-] n forno m a microonde.

midday [,mɪd'deɪ] n mezzogiorno m.

middle ['mɪdl] ◆ n mezzo m, parte f centrale ◆ adj (central) di mezzo; **in the ~ of the road** in mezzo alla strada; **in the ~ of April** a metà aprile; **to**

be in the ~ of doing sthg stare facendo qc.

middle-aged adj di mezza età.

middle-class adj borghese.

Middle East n: **the ~** il Medio Oriente.

middle name n secondo nome m.

middle school n (in UK) scuola f media (per ragazzi dagli 8 ai 13 anni).

midge [mɪdʒ] n pappataci m inv.

midget ['mɪdʒɪt] n nano m (-a f).

Midlands ['mɪdləndz] npl: **the ~** le contee dell'Inghilterra centrale.

midnight ['mɪdnaɪt] n mezzanotte f.

midsummer [ˌmɪd'sʌmər] n piena estate f.

midway [ˌmɪd'weɪ] adv (in space) a metà strada; (in time) a metà.

midweek [adj 'mɪdwiːk, adv mɪd'wiːk] ◆ adj di metà settimana ◆ adv a metà settimana.

midwife ['mɪdwaɪf] (pl **-wives** [-waɪvz]) n levatrice f.

midwinter ['mɪd'wɪntər] n pieno inverno m.

might [maɪt] aux vb **1.** (expressing possibility): **we ~ go to Wales this year** forse andremo in Galles quest'anno; **I suppose they ~ still come** può ancora darsi che arrivino; **they ~ have been killed** avrebbero potuto rimanere uccisi. **2.** (fml: expressing permission): **~ I have a few words?** posso parlarle un attimo? **3.** (when conceding a point): **it ~ be expensive, but it's good quality** sarà anche caro, ma è di buona qualità. **4.** (would): **I'd hoped you ~ come too** speravo che venissi anche tu. ◆ n (physical strength) forza f.

migraine ['miːgreɪn, 'maɪgreɪn] n emicrania f.

Milan [mɪ'læn] n Milano f.

mild [maɪld] ◆ adj (cheese, person) dolce; (detergent, taste) delicato(-a); (effect, flu) leggero(-a); (weather, climate) mite; (curiosity, surprise) lieve ◆ n (Br: beer) birra f leggera.

mile [maɪl] n miglio m; **it's ~s away** è lontanissimo.

mileage ['maɪlɪdʒ] n distanza f in miglia, ≃ chilometraggio m.

mileometer [maɪ'lɒmɪtər] n ≃ contachilometri m inv.

military ['mɪlɪtrɪ] adj militare.

milk [mɪlk] ◆ n latte m ◆ vt (cow) mungere.

milk chocolate n cioccolato m al latte.

milkman ['mɪlkmən] (pl **-men** [-mən]) n lattaio m.

milk shake n frappé m inv.

milky ['mɪlkɪ] adj (drink) con tanto latte.

mill [mɪl] n (flour-mill) mulino m; (for pepper, coffee) macinino m; (factory) fabbrica f.

milligram ['mɪlɪgræm] n milligrammo m.

millilitre ['mɪlɪˌliːtər] n millilitro m.

millimetre ['mɪlɪˌmiːtər] n millimetro m.

million ['mɪljən] n milione m; **~s of** (fig) milioni di.

millionaire [ˌmɪljə'neər] n ≃ miliardario m (-a f).

mime [maɪm] vi mimare.

min. [mɪn] (abbr of minute, minimum) min.

mince [mɪns] n (Br) carne f macinata.

mincemeat ['mɪnsmiːt] n (sweet filling) miscuglio a base di uvetta e spezie; (Am: mince) carne f macinata.

mince pie n pasticcino con ripieno a base di uvetta e spezie che si mangia durante il periodo natalizio.

mind [maɪnd] ◆ n mente f ◆ vt (be careful of) fare attenzione a; (look after) badare a ◆ vi: **I don't ~** non m'importa; **do you ~ if ...?** le dispiace se ...?; **never ~!** (don't worry) non preoccuparti!, non importa!; **it slipped my ~** mi è sfuggito di mente; **to my ~** secondo me, a mio parere; **to bear sthg in ~** tenere presente qc; **to change one's ~** cambiare idea; **to have sthg in ~** avere in mente qc; **to have sthg on one's ~** essere preoccupato per qc; **to make one's ~ up** decidersi; **do you ~ the noise?** le dà fastidio il rumore?; **I wouldn't ~ a drink** non mi dispiacerebbe bere qualcosa; **'~ the gap!'** (on underground) annuncio che avverte i viaggiatori sulla metropolitana di fare attenzione alla buca tra le carrozze e il marciapiede.

mine¹ [maɪn] pron il mio (la mia), i miei (le mie) (pl); **a friend of ~** un mio amico.

mine² [maɪn] n (for coal etc) miniera f; (bomb) mina f.

miner ['maɪnər] n minatore m.

mineral ['mɪnərəl] n minerale m.

mineral water n acqua f minerale.

minestrone [ˌmɪnɪ'strəʊnɪ] n minestrone m.

mingle ['mɪŋgl] vi mescolarsi.

miniature ['mɪnətʃər] ◆ adj in miniatura ◆ n (bottle) bottiglia f mignon.

minibar ['mɪnɪbɑːr] n minibar m inv.

minibus ['mɪnɪbʌs] (pl -es) n minibus m inv.

minicab ['mɪnɪkæb] n (Br) radiotaxi m inv.

minimal ['mɪnɪml] adj minimo(-a).

minimum ['mɪnɪməm] ◆ adj minimo(-a) ◆ n minimo m.

miniskirt ['mɪnɪskɜːt] n minigonna f.

minister ['mɪnɪstər] n (in government) ministro m; (in church) pastore m.

ministry ['mɪnɪstrɪ] n (of government) ministero m.

minor ['maɪnər] ◆ adj minore, di secondaria importanza ◆ n (fml) minorenne mf.

minority [maɪ'nɒrətɪ] n minoranza f.

minor road n strada f secondaria.

mint [mɪnt] n (sweet) caramella f alla menta; (plant) menta f.

minus ['maɪnəs] prep (in subtraction) meno; **it's ~ 10 (degrees C)** è meno 10 (gradi).

minuscule ['mɪnəskjuːl] adj minuscolo(-a).

minute¹ ['mɪnɪt] n minuto m; **any ~** da un momento all'altro; **just a ~!** (solo) un minuto!

minute² [maɪ'njuːt] adj minuscolo(-a).

minute steak [ˌmɪnɪt-] n fettina f (di carne).

miracle ['mɪrəkl] n miracolo m.

miraculous [mɪ'rækjʊləs] adj miracoloso(-a).

mirror ['mɪrər] n specchio m; (on car) specchietto m.

misbehave [ˌmɪsbɪ'heɪv] vi comportarsi male.

miscarriage [ˌmɪs'kærɪdʒ] n aborto m spontaneo.

miscellaneous [ˌmɪsə'leɪnjəs] adj (things) vario(-a); (collection) misto(-a).

mischievous ['mɪstʃɪvəs] adj birichino(-a).

misconduct [ˌmɪs'kɒndʌkt] n condotta f scorretta.

miser ['maɪzər] n avaro m (-a f).

miserable ['mɪzrəbl] adj (unhappy) infelice; (place, news, weather) deprimente; (amount) misero(-a).

misery ['mɪzərɪ] n (unhappiness) tristezza f; (poor conditions) miseria f.

misfire [ˌmɪs'faɪər] vi (car) perdere colpi.

misfortune [mɪs'fɔːtʃuːn] n (bad luck) sfortuna f.

mishap ['mɪshæp] n disavventura f.

misjudge [ˌmɪs'dʒʌdʒ] vt giudicare male.

mislay [ˌmɪs'leɪ] (pt & pp -laid) vt smarrire.

mislead [ˌmɪs'liːd] (pt & pp -led) vt

trarre in inganno.

miss [mɪs] ♦ *vt* perdere; (*not notice*) non vedere; (*fail to hit*) mancare ♦ *vi* sbagliare; **I ~ you** mi manchi.

► **miss out** ♦ *vt sep* saltare, omettere ♦ *vi:* **to ~ out on sthg** perdersi qc.

Miss [mɪs] *n* Signorina *f*.

missile [Br 'mɪsaɪl, Am 'mɪsl] *n* (*weapon*) missile *m*; (*thing thrown*) oggetto *m* (*scagliato*).

missing ['mɪsɪŋ] *adj* (*lost*) scomparso(-a); (*after accident*) disperso(-a); **to be ~** (*not there*) mancare.

missing person *n* persona *f* scomparsa.

mission ['mɪʃn] *n* missione *f*.

missionary ['mɪʃənrɪ] *n* missionario *m* (-a *f*).

mist [mɪst] *n* foschia *f*.

mistake [mɪ'steɪk] (*pt* **-took**, *pp* **-taken**) ♦ *n* sbaglio *m*, errore *m* ♦ *vt* (*misunderstand*) fraintendere; **by ~** per sbaglio; **to make a ~** fare uno sbaglio; **to ~ sb/sthg for** scambiare qn/qc per.

Mister ['mɪstər] *n* Signor *m*.

mistook [mɪ'stʊk] *pt* → **mistake**.

mistress ['mɪstrɪs] *n* (*lover*) amante *f*; (*Br: teacher*) insegnante *f*.

mistrust [mɪs'trʌst] *vt* diffidare di.

misty ['mɪstɪ] *adj* nebbioso(-a).

misunderstanding [ˌmɪsʌndə-'stændɪŋ] *n* malinteso *m*.

misuse [ˌmɪs'juːs] *n* cattivo uso *m*.

mitten ['mɪtn] *n* muffola *f*, manopola *f*.

mix [mɪks] ♦ *vt* mescolare ♦ *n* (*for cake, sauce*) (miscuglio) preparato *m* ♦ *vi* (*socially*): **to ~ with people** veder gente; **to ~ sthg with sthg** mescolare qc a OR con qc.

► **mix up** *vt sep* (*confuse*) confondere; (*put into disorder*) mescolare.

mixed [mɪkst] *adj* (*school*) misto(-a).

mixed grill *n* grigliata *f* mista.

mixed salad *n* insalata *f* mista.

mixed vegetables *npl* verdure *fpl* miste.

mixer ['mɪksər] *n* (*for food*) frullatore *m*; (*drink*) *bevanda analcolica usata nella preparazione di cocktail.*

mixture ['mɪkstʃər] *n* (*combination*) mescolanza *f*.

mix-up *n* (*inf*) confusione *f*.

ml (*abbr of millilitre*) ml.

mm (*abbr of millimetre*) mm.

moan [məʊn] *vi* (*in pain, grief*) gemere; (*inf: complain*) lamentarsi.

moat [məʊt] *n* fossato *m*.

mobile ['məʊbaɪl] *adj* mobile.

mobile phone *n* telefono *m* cellulare, telefonino *m*.

mock [mɒk] ♦ *adj* finto(-a) ♦ *vt* deridere, prendersi gioco di ♦ *n* (Br: *exam*) esercitazione *f* d'esame.

mode [məʊd] *n* modo *m*.

model ['mɒdl] *n* modello *m*; (*fashion model*) modello *m* (-a *f*).

modem ['məʊdem] *n* modem *m inv*.

moderate ['mɒdərət] *adj* moderato(-a).

modern ['mɒdən] *adj* moderno (-a).

modernized ['mɒdənaɪzd] *adj* rimodernato(-a).

modern languages *npl* lingue *fpl* moderne.

modest ['mɒdɪst] *adj* modesto(-a).

modify ['mɒdɪfaɪ] *vt* modificare.

mohair ['məʊheər] *n* mohair *m*.

moist [mɔɪst] *adj* umido(-a).

moisture ['mɔɪstʃər] *n* umidità *f*.

moisturizer ['mɔɪstʃəraɪzər] *n* idratante *m*.

molar ['məʊlər] *n* molare *m*.

mold [məʊld] (Am) = **mould**.

mole [məʊl] *n* (*animal*) talpa *f*; (*spot*) neo *m*.

molest [mə'lest] *vt* molestare.

mom [mɒm] *n* (Am: *inf*) mamma *f*.

moment ['məʊmənt] *n* momento *m*; **at the ~** al momento; **for the ~** per il momento.

Mon. (*abbr of Monday*) lun.

monarchy ['mɒnəkɪ] *n*: **the ~** la monarchia.

monastery ['mɒnəstrɪ] n monastero m.

Monday ['mʌndɪ] n lunedì m inv, → **Saturday**.

money ['mʌnɪ] n denaro m, soldi mpl.

money belt n marsupio m.

money order n vaglia m inv (postale).

mongrel ['mʌŋgrəl] n cane m bastardo.

monitor ['mɒnɪtə'] ♦ n (computer screen) monitor m inv ♦ vt (check, observe) controllare.

monk [mʌŋk] n monaco m.

monkey ['mʌŋkɪ] (pl **monkeys**) n scimmia f.

monkfish ['mʌŋkfɪʃ] n bottatrice f.

monopoly [mə'nɒpəlɪ] n monopolio m.

monorail ['mɒnəʊreɪl] n monorotaia f.

monotonous [mə'nɒtənəs] adj monotono(-a).

monsoon [mɒn'su:n] n monsone m.

monster ['mɒnstə'] n mostro m.

month [mʌnθ] n mese m; **every ~** ogni mese; **in a ~'s time** fra un mese.

monthly ['mʌnθlɪ] ♦ adj mensile ♦ adv mensilmente, ogni mese.

monument ['mɒnjʊmənt] n monumento m.

mood [mu:d] n umore m; **to be in a (bad) ~** essere di cattivo umore; **to be in a good ~** essere di buon umore.

moody ['mu:dɪ] adj (in a bad mood) di malumore; (changeable) lunatico(-a), volubile.

moon [mu:n] n luna f.

moonlight ['mu:nlaɪt] n chiaro m di luna.

moonlighting ['mu:nlaɪtɪŋ] n lavoro m nero.

moor [mɔ:'] ♦ n brughiera f ♦ vt ormeggiare.

moose [mu:s] (pl inv) n alce m.

mop [mɒp] ♦ n (for floor) lavapavimenti m inv ♦ vt (floor) lavare con lo straccio.

▸ **mop up** vt sep (clean up) asciugare con uno straccio.

moped ['məʊped] n ciclomotore m.

moral ['mɒrəl] ♦ adj morale ♦ n (lesson) morale f.

morality [mə'rælɪtɪ] n moralità f.

more [mɔ:'] adj 1. (a larger amount of) più; **there are ~ tourists than usual** ci sono più turisti del solito. 2. (additional) altro(-a); **are there any ~ cakes?** ci sono altri OR ancora pasticcini?; **I'd like two ~ bottles** vorrei altre due bottiglie; **there's no ~ wine** non c'è più vino. 3. (in phrases): **~ and more** sempre più.

♦ adv 1. (in comparatives) più; **it's ~ difficult than before** è più difficile di prima; **speak ~ clearly** parla più chiaramente. 2. (to a greater degree) di più; **we ought to go to the cinema ~** dovremmo andare più spesso al cinema. 3. (in phrases): **not ... any ~** non ... più; **I don't go there any ~** non ci vado più; **once ~** ancora una volta, un'altra volta; **~ or less** più o meno; **we'd be ~ than happy to help** saremmo più che lieti di dare una mano.

♦ pron 1. (a larger amount) più; **I've got ~ than you** ne ho più di te; **~ than 20 types of pizza** oltre 20 tipi di pizza. 2. (an additional amount) ancora; **is there any ~?** ce n'è ancora?; **there's no ~** non ce n'è più.

moreover [mɔ:'rəʊvə'] adv (fml) inoltre.

morning ['mɔ:nɪŋ] n mattina f, mattino m; **two o'clock in the ~** le due di notte; **good ~!** buon giorno!; **in the ~** (early in the day) di mattina; (tomorrow morning) domattina.

morning-after pill n pillola f del giorno dopo.

morning sickness n nausea f mattutina.

Morocco [məˈrɒkəʊ] n il Marocco.

moron [ˈmɔːrɒn] n (inf) deficiente mf.

Morse (code) [mɔːs-] n alfabeto m Morse.

mortgage [ˈmɔːgɪdʒ] n mutuo m (ipotecario).

mosaic [məˈzeɪɪk] n mosaico m.

Moslem [ˈmɒzləm] = **Muslim**.

mosque [mɒsk] n moschea f.

mosquito [məˈskiːtəʊ] (pl -es) n zanzara f.

mosquito net n zanzariera f.

moss [mɒs] n muschio m.

most [məʊst] adj 1. (the majority of) la maggior parte di; ~ **people agree** la maggior parte della gente è d'accordo.

2. (the largest amount of): **I drank (the)** ~ **beer** sono quello che ha bevuto più birra.

◆ adv 1. (in superlatives) più; **the ~ expensive hotel in town** l'albergo più caro della città.

2. (the largest amount): **she earns (the)** ~ è quella che guadagna di più.

3. (fml: very) molto, estremamente; **they were ~ welcoming** sono stati estremamente accoglienti.

◆ pron 1. (the majority) la maggior parte; ~ **of the villages** la maggior parte dei paesi; ~ **of the time** la maggior parte del tempo.

2. (to the greatest degree) di più, maggiormente; **I like this one** ~ questo è quello che mi piace di più.

3. (in phrases): **at** ~ al massimo; **to make the ~ of sthg** sfruttare al massimo qc.

mostly [ˈməʊstlɪ] adv per lo più.

MOT n (Br: test) revisione annuale obbligatoria degli autoveicoli di più di tre anni.

motel [məʊˈtel] n motel m inv.

moth [mɒθ] n farfalla f notturna.

mother [ˈmʌðər] n madre f.

mother-in-law n suocera f.

mother-of-pearl n madreperla f.

motif [məʊˈtiːf] n motivo m.

motion [ˈməʊʃn] ◆ n (movement) movimento m, moto m ◆ vi: **to ~ to sb** fare cenno a qn.

motionless [ˈməʊʃənlɪs] adj immobile.

motivate [ˈməʊtɪveɪt] vt (encourage) motivare, stimolare.

motive [ˈməʊtɪv] n motivo m.

motor [ˈməʊtər] n (engine) motore m.

Motorail® [ˈməʊtəreɪl] n treno m auto-cuccette.

motorbike [ˈməʊtəbaɪk] n moto f inv.

motorboat [ˈməʊtəbəʊt] n motoscafo m.

motorcar [ˈməʊtəkɑːr] n automobile f.

motorcycle [ˈməʊtəˌsaɪkl] n motocicletta f.

motorcyclist [ˈməʊtəˌsaɪklɪst] n motociclista mf.

motorist [ˈməʊtərɪst] n automobilista mf.

motor racing n corse fpl automobilistiche.

motorway [ˈməʊtəweɪ] n (Br) autostrada f.

motto [ˈmɒtəʊ] (pl -s) n motto m.

mould [məʊld] ◆ n (Br) (shape) forma f, stampo m; (substance) muffa f ◆ vt (Br) formare, modellare.

mouldy [ˈməʊldɪ] adj (Br) ammuffito(-a).

mound [maʊnd] n (hill) monticello m, collinetta f; (pile) mucchio m.

mount [maʊnt] ◆ n (for photo) supporto m; (mountain) monte m ◆ vt (horse) montare a OR su; (photo) sistemare ◆ vi (increase) aumentare.

mountain [ˈmaʊntɪn] n montagna f.

mountain bike n mountain bike f inv.

mountaineer [ˌmaʊntɪˈnɪər] n alpinista mf.

mountaineering [ˌmauntɪˈnɪərɪŋ] n: **to go ~** fare alpinismo.

mountainous [ˈmauntɪnəs] adj montagnoso(-a).

Mount Rushmore [-ˈrʌʃmɔːr] n il monte Rushmore.

mourning [ˈmɔːnɪŋ] n: **to be in ~** essere in lutto.

mouse [maus] (pl **mice**) n (animal) topo m; (COMPUT) mouse m inv.

moussaka [muːˈsɑːkə] n piatto tipico della cucina greca e turca, composto da strati di carne macinata, melanzane e besciamella.

mousse [muːs] n mousse f inv.

moustache [məˈstɑːʃ] n (Br) baffi mpl.

mouth [mauθ] n bocca f; (of cave, tunnel) entrata f, imboccatura f; (of river) foce f, bocca f.

mouthful [ˈmauθful] n (of food) boccone m; (of drink) sorsata f.

mouthorgan [ˈmauθˌɔːgən] n armonica f (a bocca).

mouthpiece [ˈmauθpiːs] n (of telephone) microfono m; (of musical instrument) bocchino m.

mouthwash [ˈmauθwɒʃ] n collutorio m.

move [muːv] ◆ n mossa f; (change of house) trasloco m ◆ vt (shift) muovere, spostare; (emotionally) commuovere ◆ vi (shift) muoversi, spostarsi; **to ~ (house)** cambiare casa, traslocare; **to make a ~** (leave) andarsene.

▶ **move along** vi circolare, andare avanti.

▶ **move in** vi (to house) andare/venire ad abitare.

▶ **move off** vi (train, car) partire.

▶ **move on** vi (after stopping) ripartire.

▶ **move out** vi (from house) sgombrare.

▶ **move over** vi spostarsi.

▶ **move up** vi (make room) spostarsi.

movement [ˈmuːvmənt] n movimento m.

movie [ˈmuːvɪ] n film m inv.

movie theater n (Am) cinema m inv.

moving [ˈmuːvɪŋ] adj (emotionally) commovente.

mow [məu] vt: **to ~ the lawn** tagliare l'erba (del prato).

mozzarella [ˌmɒtsəˈrelə] n mozzarella f.

MP n (abbr of Member of Parliament) = deputato m (-a f).

mph (abbr of miles per hour) miglia all'ora.

Mr [ˈmɪstər] abbr Sig.

Mrs [ˈmɪsɪz] abbr Sig.ra.

Ms [mɪz] abbr abbreviazione che comprende sia Mrs che Miss.

MSc n (abbr of Master of Science) (degree) master m inv in materie scientifiche.

much [mʌtʃ] (compar **more**, superl **most**) adj molto(-a); **I haven't got ~ money** non ho molti soldi; **as ~ food as you can eat** tanto cibo quanto ne riesci a mangiare; **how ~ time is left?** quanto tempo resta?; **they have so ~ money** hanno tanti di quei soldi; **we have too ~ work** abbiamo troppo lavoro.

◆ adv **1.** (to a great extent) molto; **it's ~ better** è molto meglio; **I like it very ~** mi piace moltissimo; **it's not ~ good** (inf) non è un granché; **thank you very ~** grazie tante.

2. (often) spesso, molto; **we don't go there ~** non ci andiamo spesso.

◆ pron molto; **I haven't got ~** non ne ho molto; **as ~ as you like** quanto ne vuoi; **how ~ is it?** quant'è?, quanto costa?

muck [mʌk] n (dirt) sudiciume m.

▶ **muck about** vi (Br) ((inf) (have fun) divertirsi; (waste time) gingillarsi.

▶ **muck up** vt sep (Br: inf) pasticciare.

mud [mʌd] n fango m.

muddle [ˈmʌdl] n: **to be in a ~** (confused) essere confuso; (in a mess) essere in disordine.

muddy ['mʌdɪ] *adj* fangoso(-a).

mudguard ['mʌdgɑːd] *n* parafango *m*.

muesli ['mjuːzlɪ] *n* muesli *m*.

muffin ['mʌfɪn] *n* (*roll*) panino *m* soffice (*mangiato caldo, con burro*); (*cake*) pasticcino *m* soffice.

muffler ['mʌflər] *n* (Am: *silencer*) marmitta *f*.

mug [mʌg] ◆ *n* (*cup*) tazza *f* (cilindrica) ◆ *vt* aggredire e derubare.

mugging ['mʌgɪn] *n* aggressione *f* (*a scopo di rapina*).

muggy ['mʌgɪ] *adj* afoso(-a).

mule [mjuːl] *n* mulo *m*.

multicoloured ['mʌltɪˌkʌləd] *adj* multicolore.

multigym ['mʌltɪdʒɪm] *n* attrezzo *m* ginnico.

multiple ['mʌltɪpl] *adj* multiplo(-a).

multiplex cinema ['mʌltɪpleks-] *n* cinema *m inv* multisala.

multiplication [ˌmʌltɪplɪ'keɪʃn] *n* moltiplicazione *f*.

multiply ['mʌltɪplaɪ] ◆ *vt* moltiplicare ◆ *vi* moltiplicarsi.

multistorey (car park) [ˌmʌltɪ'stɔːrɪ-] *n* parcheggio *m* multipiano.

mum [mʌm] *n* (Br: *inf*) mamma *f*.

mummy ['mʌmɪ] *n* (Br: *inf*: *mother*) mamma *f*.

mumps [mʌmps] *n* orecchioni *mpl*.

munch [mʌntʃ] *vt* sgranocchiare.

municipal [mjuː'nɪsɪpl] *adj* municipale.

mural ['mjuːərəl] *n* dipinto *m* murale.

murder ['mɜːdər] ◆ *n* assassinio *m*, omicidio *m* ◆ *vt* assassinare.

murderer ['mɜːdərər] *n* assassino *m* (-a *f*), omicida *mf*.

muscle ['mʌsl] *n* muscolo *m*.

museum [mjuː'ziːəm] *n* museo *m*.

mushroom ['mʌʃrom] *n* fungo *m*.

music ['mjuːzɪk] *n* musica *f*.

musical ['mjuːzɪkl] ◆ *adj* musicale; (*person*) portato(-a) per la musica ◆ *n* musical *m inv*.

musical instrument *n* strumento *m* musicale.

musician [mjuː'zɪʃn] *n* musicista *mf*.

Muslim ['mozlɪm] ◆ *adj* musulmano(-a) ◆ *n* musulmano *m* (-a *f*).

mussels ['mʌslz] *npl* cozze *fpl*.

must [mʌst] ◆ *aux vb* dovere ◆ *n* (*inf*): **it's a ~** è d'obbligo; **I ~ go** devo andare; **the room ~ be vacated by ten** la camera deve essere lasciata entro le dieci; **you ~ have seen it** devi averlo visto; **you ~ see that film** devi vedere quel film; **you ~ be joking!** stai scherzando!

mustache ['mʌstæʃ] (Am) = **moustache**.

mustard ['mʌstəd] *n* senape *f*, mostarda *f*.

mustn't ['mʌsənt] = **must not**.

mutter ['mʌtər] *vt* borbottare.

mutton ['mʌtn] *n* carne *f* di montone.

mutual ['mjuːtʃʊəl] *adj* (*feeling*) reciproco(-a), mutuo(-a); (*friend, interest*) comune.

muzzle ['mʌzl] *n* (*for dog*) museruola *f*.

my [maɪ] *adj* il mio (la mia), i miei (le mie) (*pl*); **~ brother** mio fratello.

myself [maɪ'self] *pron* (*reflexive*) mi; (*after prep*) me; **I did it ~** l'ho fatto da solo.

mysterious [mɪ'stɪərɪəs] *adj* misterioso(-a).

mystery ['mɪstərɪ] *n* mistero *m*.

myth [mɪθ] *n* mito *m*.

navy

N

N (*abbr of North*) N.

nag [næg] *vt* tormentare.

nail [neɪl] ♦ *n* (*of finger, toe*) unghia *f*; (*metal*) chiodo *m* ♦ *vt* (*fasten*) inchiodare.

nailbrush ['neɪlbrʌʃ] *n* spazzolino *m* da unghie.

nail file *n* limetta *f* per unghie.

nail scissors *npl* forbicine *fpl* da unghie.

nail varnish *n* smalto *m* per unghie.

nail varnish remover [-rə-'muːvəʳ] *n* acetone *m*, solvente *m* per unghie.

naive [naɪˈiːv] *adj* ingenuo(-a).

naked ['neɪkɪd] *adj* (*person*) nudo(-a).

name [neɪm] ♦ *n* nome *m* ♦ *vt* (*baby, animal*) chiamare; (*place*) denominare; (*identify*) dire il nome di, nominare; (*date, price*) fissare; **first ~** nome di battesimo; **last ~** cognome *m*; **what's your ~?** come si chiama?; **my ~ is ...** mi chiamo ...

namely ['neɪmlɪ] *adv* cioè, vale a dire.

nan bread [næn-] *n* pane indiano schiacciato e soffice.

nanny ['nænɪ] *n* (*childminder*) bambinaia *f*; (*inf: grandmother*) nonna *f*.

nap [næp] *n*: **to have a ~** fare un pisolino.

napkin ['næpkɪn] *n* tovagliolo *m*.

Naples ['neɪplz] *n* Napoli *f*.

nappy ['næpɪ] *n* pannolino *m*.

nappy liner *n* pannolino *m*.

narcotic [nɑːˈkɒtɪk] *n* narcotico *m*.

narrow ['nærəʊ] ♦ *adj* (*road, gap*) stretto(-a) ♦ *vi* (*road, gap*) restringersi.

narrow-minded [-ˈmaɪndɪd] *adj*

di idee ristrette.

nasty ['nɑːstɪ] *adj* (*person, comment, taste*) cattivo(-a); (*accident, moment, feeling*) brutto(-a).

nation ['neɪʃn] *n* nazione *f*.

national ['næʃənl] ♦ *adj* nazionale ♦ *n* cittadino *m* (-a *f*).

national anthem *n* inno *m* nazionale.

National Health Service *n* ≃ Servizio *m* Sanitario Nazionale.

National Insurance *n* (Br: *contributions*) ≃ Previdenza *f* Sociale.

nationality [ˌnæʃəˈnælətɪ] *n* nazionalità *f inv*.

national park *n* parco *m* nazionale.

nationwide ['neɪʃənwaɪd] *adj* su scala nazionale.

native ['neɪtɪv] ♦ *adj* (*customs, population*) indigeno(-a); (*country*) d'origine ♦ *n* nativo *m* (-a *f*); **a ~ speaker of English** una persona di madrelingua inglese.

Native American ♦ *adj* indiano(-a) (d'America) ♦ *n* indiano *m* (-a *f*) (d'America).

NATO ['neɪtəʊ] *n* NATO *f*.

natural ['nætʃrəl] *adj* (*charm*) naturale; (*ability*) innato(-a); (*swimmer, actor*) nato(-a).

natural gas *n* metano *m*, gas *m* naturale.

naturally ['nætʃrəlɪ] *adv* (*of course*) naturalmente.

natural yoghurt *n* yogurt *m inv* naturale.

nature ['neɪtʃəʳ] *n* natura *f*.

nature reserve *n* riserva *f* naturale.

naughty ['nɔːtɪ] *adj* (*child*) birichino(-a).

nausea ['nɔːzɪə] *n* nausea *f*.

navigate ['nævɪgeɪt] *vi* (*in boat, plane*) calcolare la rotta; (*in car*) fare da navigatore.

navy ['neɪvɪ] ♦ *n* (*ships*) marina *f* (militare) ♦ *adj*: **~ (blue)** blu scuro (*inv*).

NB (*abbr of nota bene*) N.B.

near [nɪə^r] ♦ *adv* vicino ♦ *adj* (*place, object*) vicino(-a); (*relation*) prossimo(-a) ♦ *prep*: **~ (to)** (*edge, object, place*) vicino a, presso; **in the ~ future** nel prossimo futuro.

nearby [nɪə'baɪ] ♦ *adv* vicino ♦ *adj* vicino(-a).

nearly ['nɪəlɪ] *adv* quasi.

near side *n* (*for right-hand drive*) destra *f*; (*for left-hand drive*) sinistra *f*.

neat [niːt] *adj* (*room*) ordinato(-a); (*writing*) chiaro(-a); (*work*) preciso(-a); (*whisky, vodka etc*) liscio(-a).

neatly ['niːtlɪ] *adv* (*placed, arranged*) in modo ordinato; (*written*) in modo chiaro.

necessarily [,nesə'serɪlɪ, Br 'nesəsrəlɪ] *adv*: **not ~** non necessariamente.

necessary ['nesəsrɪ] *adj* necessario(-a); **it is ~ to do it** è necessario farlo.

necessity [nɪ'sesətɪ] *n* necessità *f inv*.
▶ **necessities** *npl* necessità *fpl*.

neck [nek] *n* collo *m*.

necklace ['neklɪs] *n* collana *f*.

nectarine ['nektərɪn] *n* pescanoce *f*.

need [niːd] ♦ *n* bisogno *m* ♦ *vt* avere bisogno di; **to ~ to do sthg** dover fare qc; **you don't ~ to go** non c'è bisogno che tu ci vada.

needle ['niːdl] *n* ago *m*; (*for record player*) puntina *f*.

needlework ['niːdlwɜːk] *n* (SCH) cucito *m*.

needn't ['niːdənt] = **need not**.

needy ['niːdɪ] *adj* bisognoso(-a).

negative ['negətɪv] ♦ *adj* negativo(-a) ♦ *n* (*in photography*) negativo *m*; (GRAMM) negazione *f*.

neglect [nɪ'glekt] *vt* trascurare.

negligence ['neglɪdʒəns] *n* negligenza *f*.

negotiations [nɪ,gəʊʃɪ'eɪʃnz] *npl* negoziati *mpl*, trattative *fpl*.

negro ['niːgrəʊ] (*pl* **-es**) *n* negro *m* (-a *f*).

neighbour ['neɪbə^r] *n* vicino *m* (-a *f*).

neighbourhood ['neɪbəhʊd] *n* quartiere *m*, vicinato *m*.

neighbouring ['neɪbərɪŋ] *adj* vicino(-a), confinante.

neither ['naɪðə^r, niː'ðə^r] ♦ *adj*: **~ bag is big enough** nessuna delle due borse è abbastanza grande ♦ *pron*: **~ of us** nessuno(-a) di noi (due) ♦ *conj*: **~ do I** neanch'io, nemmeno io; **~ ... nor ...** né ... né ...

neon light ['niːɒn-] *n* luce *f* al neon.

nephew ['nefjuː] *n* nipote *m*.

nerve [nɜːv] *n* (*in body*) nervo *m*; (*courage*) coraggio *m*; **what a ~!** che faccia tosta!

nervous ['nɜːvəs] *adj* nervoso(-a).

nervous breakdown *n* esaurimento *m* nervoso.

nest [nest] *n* nido *m*.

net [net] ♦ *n* rete *f* ♦ *adj* netto(-a).

Net [net] *n* (COMPUT): **the ~** la Rete; **to surf the ~** navigare in Internet.

netball ['netbɔːl] *n* specie di pallacanestro femminile.

Netherlands ['neðələndz] *npl*: **the ~** i Paesi Bassi.

nettle ['netl] *n* ortica *f*.

network ['netwɜːk] *n* rete *f*.

neurotic [,njʊə'rɒtɪk] *adj* nevrotico(-a).

neutral ['njuːtrəl] ♦ *adj* (*country, person*) neutrale; (*in colour*) neutro(-a) ♦ *n* (AUT): **in ~** in folle.

never ['nevə^r] *adv* (non ...) mai; **she's ~ late** non è mai in ritardo; **I ~ knew he was married** non sapevo che fosse sposato; **~ mind!** non preoccuparti!

nevertheless [,nevəðə'les] *adv* tuttavia, ciononostante.

new [njuː] *adj* nuovo(-a).

newly ['njuːlɪ] *adv* di recente.

new potatoes *npl* patate *fpl* novelle.

news [njuːz] *n* (*information*) notizie *fpl*; (*on TV*) telegiornale *m*; (*on radio*)

giornale m radio; **a piece of ~** una notizia.

newsagent ['njuːzeɪdʒənt] n (shop) giornalaio m.

newspaper ['njuːzˌpeɪpəʳ] n giornale m.

New Year n anno m nuovo.

New Year's Day n Capodanno.

New Year's Eve n l'ultimo m dell'anno, San Silvestro m.

New York [-'jɔːk] n New York f.

New Zealand [-'ziːlənd] n la Nuova Zelanda.

next [nekst] ♦ adj prossimo(-a); (room, house) accanto ♦ adv (afterwards) dopo; (on next occasion) di nuovo; **when does the ~ bus leave?** quando parte il prossimo autobus?; **~ to** (by the side of) accanto a; **the week after ~** la settimana dopo la prossima.

next door adv accanto.

next of kin [-kɪn] n parente m prossimo (parente prossima f).

NHS n (abbr of National Health Service) = S.S.N. m.

nib [nɪb] n pennino m.

nibble ['nɪbl] vt (eat) mangiucchiare; (bite) mordicchiare.

nice [naɪs] adj (taste, meal) buono(-a); (day, clothes, house) bello(-a); (person, gesture) simpatico(-a), gentile; (feeling, job) piacevole; **to have a ~ time** divertirsi; **~ to see you!** piacere di rivederti!

nickel ['nɪkl] n (metal) nichel m; (Am: coin) moneta da cinque centesimi di dollaro.

nickname ['nɪkneɪm] n soprannome m.

niece [niːs] n nipote f.

night [naɪt] n notte f; (evening) sera f; **at ~** (not in daytime) di notte; (in evening) di sera; **by ~** di notte; **last ~** (yesterday evening) ieri sera; (very late) ieri notte.

nightclub ['naɪtklʌb] n locale m notturno.

nightdress ['naɪtdres] n camicia f da notte.

nightie ['naɪtɪ] n (inf) camicia f da notte.

nightlife ['naɪtlaɪf] n vita f notturna.

nightly ['naɪtlɪ] adv ogni notte; (every evening) ogni sera.

nightmare ['naɪtmeəʳ] n incubo m.

night safe n cassa f continua.

night school n scuola f serale.

nightshift ['naɪtʃɪft] n turno m di notte.

nil [nɪl] n (SPORT) zero m.

Nile [naɪl] n: **the ~** il Nilo.

nine [naɪn] num nove, → **six**.

nineteen [ˌnaɪn'tiːn] num diciannove; **~ ninety-five** millenovecentonovantacinque, → **six**.

nineteenth [ˌnaɪn'tiːnθ] num diciannovesimo(-a), → **sixth**.

ninetieth ['naɪntɪəθ] num novantesimo(-a), → **sixth**.

ninety ['naɪntɪ] num novanta, → **six**.

ninth [naɪnθ] num nono(-a), → **sixth**.

nip [nɪp] vt (pinch) pizzicare.

nipple ['nɪpl] n (of breast) capezzolo m; (of bottle) tettarella f.

nitrogen ['naɪtrədʒən] n azoto m.

no [nəʊ] ♦ adv no ♦ adj nessuno(-a) ♦ n no m inv; **I've got ~ time** non ho tempo; **I've got ~ money left** non ho più soldi.

noble ['nəʊbl] adj nobile.

nobody ['nəʊbədɪ] pron nessuno.

nod [nɒd] vi (in agreement) annuire.

noise [nɔɪz] n rumore m.

noisy ['nɔɪzɪ] adj rumoroso(-a).

nominate ['nɒmɪneɪt] vt (choose) nominare; (suggest) proporre come candidato.

non-alcoholic adj analcolico(-a).

none [nʌn] pron nessuno m (-a f); **there's ~ left** non ce n'è più.

nonetheless [ˌnʌnðə'les] adv tuttavia, nondimeno.

non-fiction n opere fpl non narrative (saggistica ecc.).

non-iron adj: 'non-iron' 'lava e

indossa', 'non stiro'.

nonsense ['nɒnsəns] n sciocchez-
ze fpl, fesserie fpl.

non-smoker n non fumatore m
(-trice f).

non-stick adj antiaderente.

non-stop ◆ adj (flight) diretto(-a);
(talking, arguing) continuo(-a) ◆ adv
(fly) senza scalo; (run, rain) ininterrottamente, senza sosta.

noodles ['nuːdlz] npl taglierini mpl.

noon [nuːn] n mezzogiorno m.

no-one = **nobody**.

nor [nɔːʳ] conj neanche, nemmeno;
~ **do I** neanch'io, nemmeno io, →
neither.

normal ['nɔːml] adj normale.

normally ['nɔːməlɪ] adv normal-
mente.

north [nɔːθ] ◆ n nord m, settentrione m ◆ adj del nord ◆ adv (fly,
walk) verso nord; (be situated) a
nord; **in the ~ of England** nel nord
dell'Inghilterra.

North America n l'America f del
Nord.

northbound ['nɔːθbaʊnd] adj
diretto(-a) a nord.

northeast [ˌnɔːθiːst] n nord-est m.

northern ['nɔːðən] adj settentrionale, del nord.

Northern Ireland n l'Irlanda f
del Nord.

North Pole n Polo m Nord.

North Sea n Mare m del Nord.

northwards ['nɔːθwədz] adv verso
nord.

northwest n nord-ovest m.

Norway ['nɔːweɪ] n la Norvegia.

Norwegian [nɔːwiːdʒən] ◆ adj
norvegese ◆ n (person) norvegese
mf; (language) norvegese m.

nose [nəʊz] n (of person) naso m; (of
animal, plane) muso m; (of rocket)
punta f.

nosebleed ['nəʊzbliːd] n emorragia f nasale.

no-smoking area n zona f non
fumatori.

nostril ['nɒstrəl] n narice f.

nosy ['nəʊzɪ] adj curioso(-a).

not [nɒt] adv non; **she's ~ there** non
c'è; ~ **yet** non ancora; ~ **at all**
(pleased, interested) per niente; (in
reply to thanks) di niente, prego.

notably ['nəʊtəblɪ] adv (in particular) in particolare.

note [nəʊt] ◆ n nota f; (message,
bank note) biglietto m ◆ vt (notice)
notare; (write down) annotare; **to
take ~s** prendere appunti.

notebook ['nəʊtbʊk] n taccuino m.

noted ['nəʊtɪd] adj celebre.

notepaper ['nəʊtpeɪpəʳ] n carta f
da lettere.

nothing ['nʌθɪŋ] pron niente, nulla;
he did ~ non ha fatto niente; ~
new/interesting niente di
nuovo/interessante; **for ~** per
niente.

notice ['nəʊtɪs] ◆ vt notare, accorgersi di ◆ n (written announcement)
avviso m; (warning) preavviso m; **to
take ~ of** fare caso a; **to hand in
one's ~** dare il preavviso, licenziarsi.

noticeable ['nəʊtɪsəbl] adj evidente.

notice board n tabellone m per
avvisi.

notion ['nəʊʃn] n idea f.

notorious [nəʊtɔːrɪəs] adj famige-
rato(-a).

nougat ['nuːgɑː] n torrone m.

nought [nɔːt] n zero m.

noun [naʊn] n nome m, sostantivo
m.

nourishment ['nʌrɪʃmənt] n nutrimento m.

Nov. (abbr of November) nov.

novel ['nɒvl] ◆ n romanzo m ◆ adj
nuovo(-a).

novelist ['nɒvəlɪst] n romanziere m
(-a f).

November [nəʊvembəʳ] n novembre m, → **September**.

now [naʊ] ◆ adv ora, adesso
◆ conj: ~ **(that)** adesso che, ora che;

153

observant

~ **(then)** dunque; **just** ~ proprio ora; **right** ~ (*at the moment*) in questo momento; (*immediately*) subito; **by** ~ ormai; **from** ~ **on** d'ora in poi.

nowadays ['nauədeiz] *adv* oggigiorno.

nowhere ['nəuweə^r] *adv* da nessuna parte, in nessun posto.

nozzle ['nɒzl] *n* boccaglio *m*.

nuclear ['nju:klıə^r] *adj* nucleare.

nude [nju:d] *adj* nudo(-a).

nudge [nʌdʒ] *vt* dare un colpetto di gomito a.

nuisance ['nju:sns] *n*: **it's a real ~!** è una vera seccatura!; **he's such a ~!** è un tale scocciatore!

numb [nʌm] *adj* intorpidito(-a).

number ['nʌmbə^r] ◆ *n* numero *m* ◆ *vt* (*give number to*) numerare.

numberplate ['nʌmbəpleit] *n* targa *f*.

numeral ['nju:mərəl] *n* numero *m*, cifra *f*.

numerous ['nju:mərəs] *adj* numeroso(-a).

nun [nʌn] *n* suora *f*.

nurse [nɜ:s] ◆ *n* infermiera *f* ◆ *vt* (*look after*) avere cura di, curare; **male** ~ infermiere *m*.

nursery ['nɜ:sərı] *n* (*in house*) stanza *f* dei bambini; (*for plants*) vivaio *m*.

nursery (school) *n* scuola *f* materna.

nursery slope *n* pista *f* per sciatori principianti.

nursing ['nɜ:sıŋ] *n* (*profession*) professione *f* d'infermiera.

nut [nʌt] *n* (*to eat*) frutta *f* secca (*noci, nocciole, ecc.*); (*of metal*) dado *m*.

nutcrackers ['nʌt,krækəz] *npl* schiaccianoci *m inv*.

nutmeg ['nʌtmeg] *n* noce *f* moscata.

nylon ['nailɒn] ◆ *n* nailon *m* ◆ *adj* di nailon.

o' [ə] *abbr* = **of**.

O *n* (*zero*) zero *m*.

oak [əuk] ◆ *n* quercia *f* ◆ *adj* di quercia.

OAP *abbr* = **old age pensioner**.

oar [ɔ:^r] *n* remo *m*.

oatcake ['əutkeik] *n* biscotto *m* di farina d'avena.

oath [əuθ] *n* (*promise*) giuramento *m*.

oatmeal ['əutmi:l] *n* farina *f* d'avena.

oats [əuts] *npl* avena *f*.

obedient [ə'bi:djənt] *adj* ubbidiente.

obey [ə'bei] *vt* (*person, command*) ubbidire a; (*regulations*) osservare.

object [*n* 'ɒbdʒıkt, *vb* ɒb'dʒekt] ◆ *n* (*thing*) oggetto *m*; (*purpose*) scopo *m*; (GRAMM) complemento *m* oggetto ◆ *vi*: **to ~ (to)** (*disapprove of*) disapprovare; (*oppose*) opporsi (a), protestare (contro).

objection [əb'dʒekʃn] *n* obiezione *f*.

objective [əb'dʒektıv] *n* obiettivo *m*.

obligation [ɒblı'geıʃn] *n* obbligo *m*, dovere *m*.

obligatory [ə'blıgətrı] *adj* obbligatorio(-a).

oblige [ə'blaidʒ] *vt*: **to ~ sb to do sthg** obbligare qn a fare qc.

oblique [ə'bli:k] *adj* obliquo(-a).

oblong ['ɒblɒŋ] ◆ *adj* oblungo(-a), rettangolare ◆ *n* rettangolo *m*.

obnoxious [əb'nɒkʃəs] *adj* odioso(-a).

oboe ['əubəu] *n* oboe *m*.

obscene [əb'si:n] *adj* osceno(-a).

obscure [əb'skjuə^r] *adj* oscuro(-a).

observant [əb'zɜ:vnt] *adj* dotato(-a) di spirito d'osservazione.

observation [ˌɒbzə'veɪʃn] n osservazione f.

observatory [əb'zɜːvətrɪ] n osservatorio m.

observe [əb'zɜːv] vt (watch, see) osservare.

obsessed [əb'sest] adj ossessionato(-a).

obsession [əb'seʃn] n ossessione f.

obsolete ['ɒbsəliːt] adj obsoleto(-a).

obstacle ['ɒbstəkl] n ostacolo m.

obstinate ['ɒbstənət] adj ostinato(-a).

obstruct [əb'strʌkt] vt (road, path) ostruire.

obstruction [əb'strʌkʃn] n (in road, path) ostruzione f.

obtain [əb'teɪn] vt ottenere.

obtainable [əb'teɪnəbl] adj ottenibile.

obvious ['ɒbvɪəs] adj ovvio(-a), evidente.

obviously ['ɒbvɪəslɪ] adv ovviamente.

occasion [ə'keɪʒn] n occasione f; (important event) avvenimento m.

occasional [ə'keɪʒənl] adj saltuario(-a), occasionale.

occasionally [ə'keɪʒnəlɪ] adv saltuariamente, di tanto in tanto.

occupant ['ɒkjupənt] n occupante mf.

occupation [ˌɒkju'peɪʃn] n lavoro m; (on form) occupazione f.

occupied ['ɒkjupaɪd] adj (toilet) occupato(-a).

occupy ['ɒkjupaɪ] vt occupare.

occur [ə'kɜːr] vi (happen) accadere, avvenire; (exist) trovarsi, essere presente.

occurrence [ə'kʌrəns] n (event) evento m, caso m.

ocean ['əʊʃn] n oceano m; **the ~** (Am: sea) il mare.

o'clock [ə'klɒk] adv: **it's one ~** è l'una; **it's seven ~** sono le sette; **at**

one ~ all'una; **at seven ~** alle sette.

Oct. (abbr of October) ott.

October [ɒk'təʊbər] n ottobre m, → **September**.

octopus ['ɒktəpəs] n polpo m, piovra f.

odd [ɒd] adj (strange) strano(-a); (number) dispari (inv); (not matching) spaiato(-a); (occasional) saltuario(-a), occasionale; **60 ~ miles** una sessantina di miglia; **some ~ bits of paper** vari pezzetti di carta; **~ jobs** lavori mpl occasionali.

odds [ɒdz] npl (in betting) quota f; (chances) probabilità fpl; **~ and ends** un po' di tutto.

odor ['əʊdər] (Am) = **odour**.

odour ['əʊdər] n (Br) odore m.

of [ɒv] prep 1. (gen) di; **the handle ~ the door** la maniglia della porta; **a group ~ schoolchildren** un gruppo di scolari; **a great love ~ art** un grande amore per l'arte.

2. (expressing amount) di; **a piece ~ cake** una fetta di torta; **a fall ~ 20%** un ribasso del 20%; **a town ~ 50,000 people** una città di 50 000 abitanti.

3. (made from) di, in; **a house ~ stone** una casa di pietra; **it's made ~ wood** è di OR in legno.

4. (referring to time) di; **the summer ~ 1969** l'estate del 1969; **the 26th ~ August** il 26 agosto.

5. (indicating cause) di; **he died ~ cancer** è morto di cancro.

6. (on the part of) da parte di; **that was very kind ~ you** è stato molto gentile da parte tua.

7. (Am: in telling the time): **it's ten ~ four** sono le quattro meno dieci.

off [ɒf] adv 1. (away): **to drive ~** partire; **to get ~** (from bus, train, plane, boat) scendere; **we're ~ to Austria next week** partiamo per l'Austria la settimana prossima.

2. (expressing removal): **to cut sthg ~** tagliare qc; **to take sthg ~** togliere qc.

3. (so as to stop working): **to turn sthg**

~ (*TV, radio, engine*) spegnere qc; (*tap*) chiudere qc.

4. (*expressing distance or time away*): **it's 10 miles ~** è a 10 miglia (da qui); **it's two months ~** mancano due mesi; **it's a long way ~** è lontano.

5. (*not at work*): **I'm ~ next Tuesday** martedì prossimo non lavoro; **I'm taking a week ~** prendo una settimana di ferie.

♦ *prep* **1.** (*away from*) da; **to get ~ sthg** scendere da qc; **~ the coast** al largo della costa; **just ~ the main road** poco lontano dalla strada principale.

2. (*indicating removal*) da; **take the lid ~ the jar** togli il tappo dal barattolo; **they've taken £20 ~ the price** mi hanno fatto uno sconto di 20 sterline.

3. (*absent from*): **to be ~ work** essere assente dal lavoro.

4. (*inf: from*) da; **I bought it ~ her** l'ho comprato da lei.

5. (*inf: no longer liking*): **I'm ~ my food** non ho appetito, non mi va di mangiare.

♦ *adj* **1.** (*food*) andato(-a) a male.

2. (*TV, radio, engine*) spento(-a); (*tap*) chiuso(-a).

3. (*cancelled*) annullato(-a).

4. (*not available*) esaurito(-a).

offence [ə'fens] *n* (*Br*) (*minor crime*) infrazione *f*; (*serious crime*) reato *m*; **to take ~ (at)** offendersi (per).

offend [ə'fend] *vt* (*upset*) offendere.

offender [ə'fendəʳ] *n* (*criminal*) delinquente *mf*.

offense [ə'fens] (*Am*) = **offence**.

offensive [ə'fensɪv] *adj* (*insulting*) offensivo(-a).

offer ['ɒfəʳ] ♦ *n* offerta *f* ♦ *vt* offrire; **on ~** (*at reduced price*) in offerta; **to ~ to do sthg** offrirsi di fare qc; **to ~ sb sthg** offrire qc a qn.

office ['ɒfɪs] *n* (*room*) ufficio *m*.

office block *n* palazzo *m* di uffici.

officer ['ɒfɪsəʳ] *n* (MIL) ufficiale *m*; (*policeman*) agente *m* (di polizia).

official [ə'fɪʃl] ♦ *adj* ufficiale ♦ *n* funzionario *m* (-a *f*).

officially [ə'fɪʃəlɪ] *adv* ufficialmente.

off-licence *n* (*Br*) negozio *m* di bevande alcoliche.

off-peak *adj* (*train*) delle ore non di punta; (*ticket*) a tariffa ridotta.

off sales *npl* (*Br*) vendita *f* di bevande alcoliche da asporto.

off-season *n* bassa stagione *f*.

offshore ['ɒfʃɔːʳ] *adj* (*breeze*) di terra.

off side *n* (*for right-hand drive*) lato *m* destro; (*for left-hand drive*) lato sinistro.

off-the-peg *adj* confezionato(-a).

often ['ɒfn, 'ɒftn] *adv* spesso; **how ~ do the buses run?** ogni quanto passano gli autobus?; **every so ~** ogni tanto.

oh [əʊ] *excl* oh!

oil [ɔɪl] *n* olio *m*; (*fuel*) petrolio *m*.

oilcan ['ɔɪlkæn] *n* oliatore *m*.

oil filter *n* filtro *m* dell'olio.

oil rig *n* piattaforma *f* petrolifera.

oily ['ɔɪlɪ] *adj* unto(-a).

ointment ['ɔɪntmənt] *n* unguento *m*, pomata *f*.

OK [əʊ'keɪ] ♦ *adv* (*inf*) (*expressing agreement*) va bene, d'accordo; (*satisfactorily, well*) bene ♦ *adj* (*of average quality*) non male; **is that ~?** va bene?; **are you ~?** tutto bene?

okay [əʊ'keɪ] = **OK**.

old [əʊld] *adj* vecchio(-a); (*person*) vecchio, anziano(-a); **how ~ are you?** quanti anni hai?; **I'm 36 years ~** ho 36 anni; **to get ~** invecchiare.

old age *n* vecchiaia *f*.

old age pensioner *n* pensionato *m* (-a *f*).

O-level *n esame oggi sostituito dal* 'GCSE'.

olive ['ɒlɪv] *n* oliva *f*.

olive oil *n* olio *m* d'oliva.

Olympic Games [ə'lɪmpɪk-] *npl* giochi *mpl* olimpici, Olimpiadi *fpl*.

omelette ['ɒmlɪt] *n* frittata *f*, omelette *f inv*; **mushroom ~** frittata ai funghi.

ominous ['ɒmɪnəs] *adj* sinistro(-a).

omit [ə'mɪt] *vt* omettere.

on [ɒn] *prep* 1. (*expressing position, location*) su; **it's ~ the table** è sul tavolo; **a picture ~ the wall** un quadro alla parete; **the exhaust ~ the car** il tubo di scappamento dell'automobile; **~ my right** alla mia destra; **~ the right** a OR sulla destra; **we stayed ~ a farm** ci siamo fermati in una fattoria; **a hotel ~ George Street** un albergo in George Street.

2. (*with forms of transport*): **~ the train/plane** in treno/aereo; **to get ~ a bus** salire su un autobus.

3. (*expressing means, method*): **~ foot** a piedi; **~ the radio** alla radio; **~ TV** in TV, alla televisione; **~ the piano** al piano.

4. (*using*): **it runs ~ unleaded petrol** va a benzina verde; **to be ~ medication** prendere medicine.

5. (*about*) su; **a book ~ Germany** un libro sulla Germania.

6. (*expressing time*): **~ arrival** all'arrivo; **~ Tuesday** martedì; **~ 25th August** il 25 agosto.

7. (*with regard to*) su; **a tax ~ imports** una tassa sulle importazioni; **the effect ~ Britain** l'effetto sulla Gran Bretagna.

8. (*describing activity, state*) in; **~ holiday** in vacanza; **~ offer** in offerta; **~ sale** in vendita.

9. (*in phrases*): **do you have any money ~ you?** (*inf*) hai un po' di soldi con te?; **the drinks are ~ me** offro io da bere.

♦ *adv* 1. (*in place, covering*): **to have sthg ~** (*clothes*) indossare qc; **put the lid ~** mettici il coperchio; **to put one's clothes ~** vestirsi.

2. (*film, play, programme*): **the news is ~** c'è il telegiornale; **what's ~ at the cinema?** cosa danno al cinema?

3. (*with transport*): **to get ~** salire.

4. (*functioning*): **to turn sthg ~** (TV, radio, engine) accendere qc; (*tap*) aprire qc.

5. (*taking place*): **how long is the festival ~?** quanto (tempo) dura il festival?

6. (*further forward*): **to drive ~** continuare a guidare.

7. (*in phrases*): **do you have anything ~ tonight?** fai qualcosa stasera?

♦ *adj* (TV, engine, light) acceso(-a); (*tap*) aperto(-a).

once [wʌns] ♦ *adv* una volta ♦ *conj* una volta che, non appena; **at ~** (*immediately*) subito; (*at the same time*) insieme, contemporaneamente; **for ~** per una volta; **~ more** ancora una volta.

oncoming ['ɒn,kʌmɪŋ] *adj* (*traffic*) che procede in senso opposto.

one [wʌn] ♦ *num* uno(-a) ♦ *adj* (*only*) unico(-a) ♦ *pron* uno(-a); **thirty-~** trentuno; **~ fifth** un quinto; **that ~** quello(-a); **which ~?** quale?; **this ~** questo(-a); **I want ~** ne voglio uno; **the ~ I told you about** quello di cui ti ho detto; **~ of my friends** uno dei miei amici; **~ day** un giorno.

one-piece (swimsuit) *n* costume *m* intero.

oneself [wʌn'self] *pron* (*reflexive*) si; (*after prep*) se stesso(-a), sé.

one-way *adj* (*street*) a senso unico; (*ticket*) di sola andata.

onion ['ʌnjən] *n* cipolla *f*.

onion bhaji [-'bɑːdʒɪ] *n polpetta a base di cipolla e spezie varie, fritta e servita come antipasto nella cucina indiana.*

onion rings *npl* rondelle *fpl* di cipolle fritte.

only ['əʊnlɪ] ♦ *adj* solo(-a), unico(-a) ♦ *adv* solo, soltanto; **he's an ~ child** è figlio unico; **I ~ want one** ne voglio solo uno; **we've ~ just arrived** siamo appena arrivati; **there's ~ just enough** ce n'è appena a sufficienza; **'members ~'** 'riservato ai soci'; **not ~** non solo.

onto ['ɒntuː] *prep* (*with verbs of movement*) su; **to get ~ sb** (*telephone*) chiamare qn.

onward ['ɒnwəd] ♦ adv =
onwards ♦ adj: **the ~ journey** il
proseguimento.

onwards ['ɒnwədz] adv (forwards)
in avanti; **from now ~** da ora in poi;
from October ~ da ottobre in poi.

opal ['əupl] n opale m o f.

opaque [əu'peɪk] adj (not transparent) opaco(-a).

open ['əupn] ♦ adj aperto(-a) ♦ vt
aprire ♦ vi (door, lock, meeting) aprirsi; (shop, office, bank) aprire; (play,
film) cominciare; **are you ~ at the
weekend?** siete aperti il fine settimana?; **wide ~** spalancato(-a); **in
the ~ (air)** all'aperto.
► **open onto** vt fus dare su.
► **open up** vi aprire.

open-air adj all'aperto.

opening ['əupnɪŋ] n apertura f;
(opportunity) opportunità f inv.

opening hours npl orario m di
apertura.

open-minded [-'maɪndɪd] adj
aperto(-a).

open-plan adj senza pareti divi-
sorie.

open sandwich n tartina f.

opera ['ɒpərə] n opera f.

opera house n teatro m del-
l'opera.

operate ['ɒpəreɪt] ♦ vt (machine)
azionare, far funzionare ♦ vi (work)
funzionare, agire; **to ~ on sb** operare qn.

operating room ['ɒpəreɪtɪŋ-] n
(Am) = **operating theatre**.

operating theatre ['ɒpəreɪtɪŋ-] n
(Br) sala f operatoria.

operation [,ɒpə'reɪʃn] n operazione f; **to be in ~** (law, system) essere in
vigore; **to have an ~** operarsi.

operator ['ɒpəreɪtər] n (on phone)
centralinista mf.

opinion [ə'pɪnjən] n opinione f,
parere m; **in my ~** a mio parere,
secondo me.

opponent [ə'pəunənt] n avversario
m (-a f).

opportunity [,ɒpə'tjuːnətɪ] n
opportunità f inv, occasione f.

oppose [ə'pəuz] vt opporsi a.

opposed [ə'pəuzd] adj: **to be ~ to**
essere contrario(-a) a.

opposite ['ɒpəzɪt] ♦ adj (facing) di
fronte; (totally different) opposto(-a),
contrario(-a) ♦ n: **the ~ (of)** il contrario (di).

opposition [,ɒpə'zɪʃn] n opposizione f; (SPORT) avversari mpl.

opt [ɒpt] vt: **to ~ to do sthg** scegliere di fare qc.

optician's [ɒp'tɪʃnz] n (shop) ottico
m.

optimist ['ɒptɪmɪst] n ottimista mf.

optimistic [,ɒptɪ'mɪstɪk] adj otti-
mistico(-a).

option ['ɒpʃn] n (alternative) scelta f,
alternativa f; (optional extra) optional
m inv.

optional ['ɒpʃənl] adj facoltati-
vo(-a).

or [ɔːr] conj o, oppure; (otherwise) se
no, altrimenti; (after negative): **I can't
read ~ write** non so (né) leggere né
scrivere.

oral ['ɔːrəl] ♦ adj orale ♦ n orale m.

orange ['ɒrɪndʒ] ♦ adj arancione
♦ n (fruit) arancia f; (colour) arancione
m.

orange juice n succo m d'arancia.

orange squash n (Br) aranciata
f non gassata.

orbit ['ɔːbɪt] n orbita f.

orbital (motorway) ['ɔːbɪtl-] n
(Br) raccordo m anulare.

orchard ['ɔːtʃəd] n frutteto m.

orchestra ['ɔːkɪstrə] n orchestra f.

orchid ['ɔːkɪd] n orchidea f.

ordeal [ɔː'diːl] n (durissima) esperienza f, travaglio m.

order ['ɔːdər] ♦ n ordine m; (in restaurant, for goods) ordinazione f ♦ vt
& vi ordinare; **in ~ to** allo scopo di,
per; **out of ~** (not working) guasto; **in
working ~** funzionante; **to ~ sb to do
sthg** ordinare a qn di fare qc.

order form n modulo m d'ordinazione.

ordinary [ˈɔːdənrɪ] adj ordinario(-a), comune.

ore [ɔːʳ] n minerale m (grezzo).

oregano [ˌɒrɪˈgɑːnəʊ] n origano m.

organ [ˈɔːgən] n organo m.

organic [ɔːˈgænɪk] adj (food) biologico(-a).

organization [ˌɔːgənaɪˈzeɪʃn] n organizzazione f.

organize [ˈɔːgənaɪz] vt organizzare.

organizer [ˈɔːgənaɪzəʳ] n (person) organizzatore m (-trice f); (diary) agenda f.

oriental [ˌɔːrɪˈentl] adj orientale.

orientate [ˈɔːrɪenteɪt] vt: to ~ o.s. orientarsi.

origin [ˈɒrɪdʒɪn] n origine f.

original [əˈrɪdʒənl] adj (first) originario(-a); (novel) originale.

originally [əˈrɪdʒənəlɪ] adv (formerly) originariamente.

originate [əˈrɪdʒəneɪt] vi: to ~ (from) avere origine (da).

ornament [ˈɔːnəmənt] n (object) soprammobile m.

ornamental [ˌɔːnəˈmentl] adj ornamentale.

ornate [ɔːˈneɪt] adj molto ornato(-a).

orphan [ˈɔːfn] n orfano m (-a f).

orthodox [ˈɔːθədɒks] adj ortodosso(-a).

ostentatious [ˌɒstənˈteɪʃəs] adj pretenzioso(-a); (action, behaviour) ostentato(-a).

ostrich [ˈɒstrɪtʃ] n struzzo m.

other [ˈʌðəʳ] ♦ adj altro(-a) ♦ pron altro(-a) ♦ adv: ~ than a parte; the ~ (one) l'altro; the ~ day l'altro giorno; one after the ~ uno dopo l'altro.

otherwise [ˈʌðəwaɪz] adv altrimenti.

otter [ˈɒtəʳ] n lontra f.

ought [ɔːt] aux vb dovere; you ~ to have gone avresti dovuto andarci; you ~ to see a doctor dovresti anda-

re dal dottore; **the car ~ to be ready by Friday** la macchina dovrebbe essere pronta per venerdì.

ounce [aʊns] n (unit of measurement) = 28,35 g, oncia f.

our [ˈaʊəʳ] adj il nostro (la nostra), i nostri (le nostre) (pl); ~ **mother** nostra madre.

ours [ˈaʊəz] pron il nostro (la nostra), i nostri (le nostre) (pl); **a friend of ~** un nostro amico.

ourselves [aʊəˈselvz] pron (reflexive) ci; (after prep) noi stessi (-e), noi; **we did it ~** l'abbiamo fatto da soli.

out [aʊt] adj 1. (light, cigarette) spento(-a).

2. (wrong) inesatto(-a); **the bill's £10 ~** c'è un errore di 10 sterline nel conto.

♦ adv 1. (outside) fuori; **to get ~ (of)** (car) scendere (da); **to go ~ (of)** uscire (da); **it's cold ~** fa freddo fuori.

2. (not at home, work) fuori; **to go ~** uscire, andare fuori.

3. (so as to be extinguished): **to turn sthg ~** spegnere qc; **put your cigarette ~** spegni la sigaretta.

4. (expressing removal): **to pour sthg ~** versare qc; **to take sthg ~ (of)** tirar fuori qc (da); (from bank) ritirare qc (da).

5. (outwards): **to stick ~** sporgere.

6. (expressing distribution): **to hand sthg ~** distribuire qc.

7. (in phrases): **to stay ~ of the sun** evitare il sole; **made ~ of wood** in OR di legno; **five ~ of ten women** cinque donne su dieci; **I'm ~ of cigarettes** ho finito le sigarette.

outback [ˈaʊtbæk] n: the ~ l'outback m, l'entroterra m australiano.

outboard (motor) [ˈaʊtbɔːd-] n motore m fuoribordo.

outbreak [ˈaʊtbreɪk] n (of fighting) scoppio m; (of disease) epidemia f.

outburst [ˈaʊtbɜːst] n scoppio m.

outcome [ˈaʊtkʌm] n esito m, risultato m.

outcrop ['aʊtkrɒp] n affioramento m.

outdated [,aʊt'deɪtɪd] adj antiquato(-a).

outdo [,aʊt'duː] (pt **-did**, pp **-done**) vt fare meglio di, superare.

outdoor ['aʊtdɔːr] adj all'aperto.

outdoors [aʊt'dɔːz] adv all'aperto, fuori.

outer ['aʊtər] adj esterno(-a).

outer space n spazio m cosmico.

outfit ['aʊtfɪt] n (clothes) completo m.

outing ['aʊtɪŋ] n gita f.

outlet ['aʊtlet] n (pipe) scarico m, sbocco m; **'no ~'** (Am) 'strada senza uscita'.

outline ['aʊtlaɪn] n profilo m.

outlook ['aʊtlʊk] n (for future) prospettiva f; (of weather) previsioni fpl; (attitude) modo m di vedere.

out-of-date adj (old-fashioned) superato(-a); (passport, licence) scaduto(-a).

outpatients' (department) ['aʊt,peɪʃnts-] n reparto m pazienti esterni.

output ['aʊtpʊt] n (of factory) produzione f; (COMPUT: printout) output m inv, tabulato m.

outrage ['aʊtreɪdʒ] n (cruel act) atrocità f inv.

outrageous [aʊt'reɪdʒəs] adj (shocking) scandaloso(-a).

outright [,aʊt'raɪt] adv (tell, deny) apertamente; (own) completamente.

outside [adv ,aʊt'saɪd, adj, prep & n 'aʊtsaɪd] ♦ adv fuori, all'esterno ♦ prep fuori di ♦ adj esterno(-a) ♦ n: **the ~** (of building, car, container) l'esterno m; (AUT: in UK) la destra; (AUT: in Europe, US) la sinistra; **an ~ line** una linea esterna; **~ of** (Am) (on the outside of) fuori di; (apart from) all'infuori di.

outside lane n corsia f di sorpasso.

outsize ['aʊtsaɪz] adj (clothes) di taglia forte.

outskirts ['aʊtskɜːts] npl periferia f.

outstanding [,aʊt'stændɪŋ] adj (remarkable) eccellente; (problem) rilevante; (debt) da pagare, in sospeso.

outward ['aʊtwəd] adj (journey) di andata; (external) esteriore.

outwards ['aʊtwədz] adv verso l'esterno, in fuori.

oval ['əʊvl] adj ovale.

ovation [əʊ'veɪʃn] n ovazione f.

oven ['ʌvn] n forno m.

oven glove n guanto m da forno.

ovenproof ['ʌvnpruːf] adj da forno.

oven-ready adj pronto(-a) per mettere in forno.

over ['əʊvər] prep 1. (above) sopra, su; **a bridge ~ the river** un ponte sul fiume.

2. (across) oltre, al di là di; **with a view ~ the park** con vista sul parco; **to walk ~ sthg** attraversare qc a piedi; **it's just ~ the road** è proprio qui di fronte.

3. (covering) su; **put a plaster ~ the wound** mettere un cerotto sulla ferita.

4. (more than) più di; **it cost ~ £1,000** è costato più di 1 000 sterline.

5. (during) durante; **~ the past two years** negli ultimi due anni.

6. (with regard to) su; **an argument ~ the price** una discussione sul prezzo.

7. (in phrases): **all ~ the world/country** in tutto il mondo/paese.

♦ adv 1. (downwards): **to fall ~** cadere; **to bend ~** piegarsi (in avanti).

2. (referring to position, movement): **to fly ~ to Canada** andare in Canada in aereo; **~ here** qui; **~ there** là.

3. (round to other side): **to turn sthg ~** rigirare qc.

4. (more): **children aged 12 and ~** ragazzi dai 12 anni in su.

5. (remaining): **to be (left) ~** restare.

6. (to one's house): **to invite sb ~ for dinner** invitare qn a cena; **we have**

some friends coming ~ verranno da noi OR a trovarci degli amici.

◆ *adj* (*finished*): **to be ~** essere finito(-a).

overall [*adv* ˌəuvər'ɔːl, *n* 'əuvərɔːl] ◆ *adv* (*in general*) complessivamente, nell'insieme ◆ *n* (Br: *coat*) grembiule *m*; (Am: *boiler suit*) tuta *f* (da lavoro); **how much does it cost ~?** quanto costa in tutto?

▶ **overalls** *npl* (Br: *boiler suit*) tuta *f* (da lavoro); (Am: *dungarees*) salopette *f inv*.

overboard ['əuvəbɔːd] *adv* (*from ship*) in mare.

overbooked [ˌəuvə'bukt] *adj*: **to be ~** avere più prenotazioni dei posti disponibili.

overcame [ˌəuvə'keɪm] *pt* → **overcome**.

overcast [ˌəuvə'kɑːst] *adj* coperto(-a).

overcharge [ˌəuvə'tʃɑːdʒ] *vt* far pagare un prezzo eccessivo.

overcoat ['əuvəkəut] *n* cappotto *m*.

overcome [ˌəuvə'kʌm] (*pt* **-came**, *pp* **-come**) *vt* (*defeat*) sopraffare; (*problem*) superare.

overcooked [ˌəuvə'kukt] *adj* troppo cotto(-a).

overcrowded [ˌəuvə'kraudɪd] *adj* sovraffollato(-a).

overdo [ˌəuvə'duː] (*pt* **-did**, *pp* **-done**) *vt* (*exaggerate*) esagerare con; **to ~ it** esagerare.

overdone [ˌəuvə'dʌn] ◆ *pp* → **overdo** ◆ *adj* (*food*) troppo cotto(-a).

overdose ['əuvədəus] *n* overdose *f inv*.

overdraft ['əuvədrɑːft] *n* scoperto *m* (di conto).

overdue [ˌəuvə'djuː] *adj* (*bus, flight*) in ritardo; (*rent, payment*) in arretrato.

over easy *adj* (Am: *egg*): **eggs ~** uova al tegamino fritte da entrambe le parti.

overexposed [ˌəuvərɪk'spəuzd] *adj*

(*photograph*) sovraesposto(-a).

overflow [*vb* ˌəuvə'fləu, *n* 'əuvəfləu] ◆ *vi* (*container, bath*) traboccare; (*river*) straripare ◆ *n* (*pipe*) troppopieno *m*.

overgrown [ˌəuvə'grəun] *adj* (*garden, path*) ricoperto(-a) di erbacce.

overhaul [ˌəuvə'hɔːl] *n* (*of machine, car*) revisione *f*.

overhead [*adj* 'əuvəhed, *adv* ˌəuvə'hed] ◆ *adj* aereo(-a) ◆ *adv* in alto, al di sopra.

overhead locker *n* (*on plane*) scomparto *m* in alto.

overhear [ˌəuvə'hɪər] (*pt & pp* **-heard**) *vt* sentire (per caso).

overheat [ˌəuvə'hiːt] *vi* surriscaldarsi.

overland ['əuvəlænd] *adv* via terra.

overlap [ˌəuvə'læp] *vi* sovrapporsi.

overleaf [ˌəuvə'liːf] *adv* a tergo.

overload [ˌəuvə'ləud] *vt* sovraccaricare.

overlook [*vb* ˌəuvə'luk, *n* 'əuvəluk] ◆ *vt* (*subj: building, room*) dare su; (*miss*) lasciarsi sfuggire, trascurare ◆ *n*: **(scenic) ~** (Am) punto *m* panoramico.

overnight [*adv* ˌəuvə'naɪt *adj* 'əuvənaɪt] ◆ *adv* (*during the night*) durante la notte; (*until next day*) per la notte ◆ *adj* (*train, journey*) di notte.

overnight bag *n* piccola borsa *f* da viaggio.

overpass ['əuvəpɑːs] *n* cavalcavia *m inv*.

overpowering [ˌəuvə'pauərɪŋ] *adj* (*heat, smell*) opprimente, soffocante.

oversaw [ˌəuvə'sɔː] *pt* → **oversee**.

overseas [*adv* ˌəuvə'siːz, *adj* 'əuvəsiːz] ◆ *adv* all'estero (*oltremare*) ◆ *adj* straniero(-a); (*trade*) estero(-a).

oversee [ˌəuvə'siː] (*pt* **-saw**, *pp* **-seen**) *vt* sovrintendere a.

overshoot [ˌəuvə'ʃuːt] (*pt & pp* **-shot**) *vt* (*turning, motorway exit*) oltrepassare.

oversight ['əʊvəsaɪt] n svista f.

oversleep [,əʊvə'sli:p] (pt & pp **-slept**) vi non svegliarsi (all'ora prevista).

overtake [,əʊvə'teɪk] (pt **-took**, pp **-taken**) vt & vi sorpassare; '**no overtaking**' 'divieto di sorpasso'.

overtime ['əʊvətaɪm] n straordinario m.

overtook [,əʊvə'tʊk] pt → **overtake**.

overture ['əʊvə,tjʊər] n (MUS) ouverture f inv.

overturn [,əʊvə'tɜ:n] vi rovesciarsi.

overweight [,əʊvə'weɪt] adj sovrappeso (inv).

overwhelm [,əʊvə'welm] vt sopraffare.

owe [əʊ] vt dovere; **to ~ sb sthg** dovere qc a qn; **owing to** a causa di.

owl [aʊl] n gufo m.

own [əʊn] ◆ adj proprio(-a) ◆ vt possedere ◆ pron: **my ~** il mio (la mia), i miei (le mie) (pl); **a room of my ~** una stanza (solo) per me; **on my ~** da solo; **to get one's ~ back** prendersi la rivincita.

▶ **own up** vi: **to ~ up to sthg** ammettere qc.

owner ['əʊnər] n proprietario m (-a f).

ownership ['əʊnəʃɪp] n proprietà f, possesso m.

ox [ɒks] (pl **oxen** ['ɒksən]) n bue m.

oxtail soup ['ɒksteɪl-] n minestra f di coda di bue.

oxygen ['ɒksɪdʒən] n ossigeno m.

oyster ['ɔɪstər] n ostrica f.

oz abbr = **ounce**.

ozone-friendly ['əʊzəʊn-] adj che non danneggia l'ozono.

P

p ◆ (abbr of page) p., pag. ◆ abbr = **penny, pence**.

pace [peɪs] n passo m.

pacemaker ['peɪs,meɪkər] n (for heart) pacemaker m inv.

Pacific [pə'sɪfɪk] n: **the ~ (Ocean)** il Pacifico, l'Oceano m Pacifico.

pacifier ['pæsɪfaɪər] n (Am: for baby) succhiotto m.

pacifist ['pæsɪfɪst] n pacifista mf.

pack [pæk] ◆ n (of washing powder) pacco m; (of cigarettes, crisps) pacchetto m; (Br: of cards) mazzo m; (rucksack) zaino m ◆ vt (suitcase, bag) preparare, fare; (clothes, camera etc) mettere in valigia; (to package) impacchettare, imballare ◆ vi (for journey) fare i bagagli or le valigie; **a ~ of lies** un mucchio di bugie; **to ~ sthg into sthg** stipare qc in qc; **to ~ one's bags** fare i bagagli or le valigie.

▶ **pack up** vi (pack suitcase) fare la valigia; (tidy up) riordinare; (Br: inf: machine, car) guastarsi.

package ['pækɪdʒ] ◆ n pacchetto m ◆ vt imballare.

package holiday n vacanza f organizzata.

package tour n viaggio m organizzato.

packaging ['pækɪdʒɪŋ] n (material) imballaggio m, confezione f.

packed [pækt] adj (crowded) stipato(-a).

packed lunch n pranzo m al sacco.

packet ['pækɪt] n pacchetto m; **it cost a ~** (Br: inf) è costato un mucchio di soldi.

packing ['pækɪŋ] n (material) imballaggio m; **to do one's ~** fare i bagagli or le valigie.

pad [pæd] n (of paper) blocco m; (of cloth, cotton wool) tampone m; (for protection) imbottitura f.

padded ['pædɪd] adj (jacket, seat) imbottito(-a).

padded envelope n busta f imbottita.

paddle ['pædl] ♦ n (pole) pagaia f ♦ vi (wade) sguazzare; (in canoe) remare (con la pagaia).

paddling pool ['pædlɪŋ-] n piscina f per bambini.

paddock ['pædək] n (at racecourse) paddock m inv.

padlock ['pædlɒk] n lucchetto m.

page [peɪdʒ] ♦ n (of book, newspaper) pagina f ♦ vt chiamare.

paid [peɪd] ♦ pt & pp → **pay** ♦ adj (holiday, work) pagato(-a).

pain [peɪn] n dolore m; **to be in ~** avere dolore, soffrire; **he's such a ~!** (inf) è un tale rompiscatole!

▶ **pains** npl (trouble) disturbo m.

painful ['peɪnfʊl] adj doloroso(-a).

painkiller ['peɪn,kɪlər] n analgesico m, antidolorifico m.

paint [peɪnt] ♦ n vernice f, colore m ♦ vt & vi dipingere; **to ~ one's nails** dipingersi le unghie.

▶ **paints** npl (tubes, pots etc) colori mpl.

paintbrush ['peɪntbrʌʃ] n pennello m.

painter ['peɪntər] n (artist) pittore m (-trice f); (decorator) imbianchino m.

painting ['peɪntɪŋ] n (picture) dipinto m, quadro m; (artistic activity) pittura f; (by decorator) tinteggiatura f.

pair [peər] n (of two things) paio m; **in ~s** a coppie, a due a due; **a ~ of pliers** un paio di pinze; **a ~ of scissors** un paio di forbici; **a ~ of shorts** un paio di calzoncini; **a ~ of tights** un paio di collant; **a ~ of trousers** un paio di pantaloni.

pajamas [pə'dʒɑːməz] (Am) = **pyjamas**.

Pakistan [Br ,pɑːkɪ'stɑːn, Am ,pækɪ'stæn] n il Pakistan.

Pakistani [Br ,pɑːkɪ'stɑːnɪ, Am ,pækɪ'stænɪ] ♦ adj pakistano(-a) ♦ n pakistano m (-a f).

pakora [pə'kɔːrə] npl frittelle piccanti a base di verdura e spezie varie servite come antipasto nella cucina indiana.

pal [pæl] n (inf) amico m (-a f).

palace ['pælɪs] n palazzo m.

palatable ['pælətəbl] adj (food, drink) gustoso(-a).

palate ['pælət] n palato m.

pale [peɪl] adj pallido(-a).

pale ale n birra f chiara.

palm [pɑːm] n (of hand) palmo m; **~ (tree)** palma f.

palpitations [,pælpɪ'teɪʃnz] npl palpitazioni fpl.

pamphlet ['pæmflɪt] n opuscolo m.

pan [pæn] n (saucepan) pentola f; (frying pan) padella f.

pancake ['pænkeɪk] n crêpe f inv.

pancake roll n involtino m primavera.

panda ['pændə] n panda m inv.

panda car n (Br) auto f inv della polizia.

pane [peɪn] n vetro m.

panel ['pænl] n (of wood) pannello m; (group of experts) gruppo m di esperti; (on TV, radio) giuria f.

paneling ['pænəlɪŋ] (Am) = **panelling**.

panelling ['pænəlɪŋ] n (Br) rivestimento m a pannelli.

panic ['pænɪk] (pt & pp -**ked**, cont -**king**) ♦ n panico m ♦ vi farsi prendere dal panico.

panniers ['pænɪəz] npl (for bicycle) borse fpl da bicicletta.

panorama [,pænə'rɑːmə] n panorama m.

panoramic [,pænə'ræmɪk] adj panoramico(-a).

pant [pænt] vi ansare.

panties ['pæntɪz] npl (inf) mutandine fpl.

pantomime ['pæntəmaɪm] n (Br)

spettacolo natalizio per bambini.

pantry ['pæntrɪ] *n* dispensa *f*.

pants [pænts] *npl* (Br: *underwear*) mutande *fpl*; (Am: *trousers*) pantaloni *mpl*.

panty hose ['pæntɪ-] *npl* (Am) collant *m inv*.

papadum ['pæpədəm] = **poppadom**.

paper ['peɪpər] ♦ *n* (*material*) carta *f*; (*newspaper*) giornale *m*; (*exam*) esame *m* (scritto) ♦ *adj* di carta ♦ *vt* tappezzare (con carta da parati); **a piece of ~** un pezzo di carta.

▶ **papers** *npl* (*documents*) documenti *mpl*.

paperback ['peɪpəbæk] *n* libro *m* in brossura.

paper bag *n* sacchetto *m* di carta.

paperboy ['peɪpəbɔɪ] *n* ragazzo che recapita i giornali a domicilio.

paper clip *n* graffetta *f*.

papergirl ['peɪpəgɜːl] *n* ragazza che recapita i giornali a domicilio.

paper handkerchief *n* fazzoletto *m* di carta.

paper shop *n* giornalaio *m*.

paperweight ['peɪpəweɪt] *n* fermacarte *m inv*.

paprika ['pæprɪkə] *n* paprica *f*.

par [pɑːr] *n* (*in golf*) norma *f*.

paracetamol [ˌpærə'siːtəmɒl] *n* paracetamolo *m*.

parachute ['pærəʃuːt] *n* paracadute *m inv*.

parade [pə'reɪd] *n* (*procession*) parata *f*; (*of shops*) fila *f* di negozi.

paradise ['pærədaɪs] *n* paradiso *m*.

paraffin ['pærəfɪn] *n* cherosene *m*.

paragliding ['pærəˌglaɪdɪŋ] *n* parapendio *m*.

paragraph ['pærəgrɑːf] *n* paragrafo *m*.

parallel ['pærəlel] *adj*: ~ **(to)** parallelo(-a) (a).

paralysed ['pærəlaɪzd] *adj* (Br) paralizzato(-a).

paralyzed ['pærəlaɪzd] (Am) = **paralysed**.

paramedic [ˌpærə'medɪk] *n* paramedico *m*.

paranoid ['pærənɔɪd] *adj* paranoico(-a).

parasite ['pærəsaɪt] *n* parassita *m*.

parasol ['pærəsɒl] *n* parasole *m inv*.

parcel ['pɑːsl] *n* pacco *m*, pacchetto *m*.

parcel post *n* servizio *m* pacchi postali.

pardon ['pɑːdn] *excl*: ~? prego?; ~ **(me)!** mi scusi!; **I beg your ~!** (*apologizing*) scusi!; **I beg your ~?** (*asking for repetition*) prego?

parent ['peərənt] *n* genitore *m*.

Paris ['pærɪs] *n* Parigi *f*.

parish ['pærɪʃ] *n* (*of church*) parrocchia *f*; (*village area*) ≃ comune *m*.

park [pɑːk] ♦ *n* parco *m* ♦ *vt & vi* parcheggiare.

park and ride *n* parcheggio decentrato presso una stazione di mezzi pubblici locali.

parking ['pɑːkɪŋ] *n* parcheggio *m*; **'no ~'** 'sosta vietata'.

parking brake *n* (Am) freno *m* a mano.

parking lot *n* (Am) parcheggio *m*, posteggio *m*.

parking meter *n* parchimetro *m*.

parking space *n* posto *m* per parcheggiare.

parking ticket *n* multa *f* per sosta vietata.

parkway ['pɑːkweɪ] *n* (Am) viale con alberi o piante nella banchina spartitraffico.

parliament ['pɑːləmənt] *n* parlamento *m*.

Parmesan (cheese) [ˌpɑːmɪ'zæn-] *n* parmigiano *m*, grana *f*.

parrot ['pærət] *n* pappagallo *m*.

parsley ['pɑːslɪ] *n* prezzemolo *m*.

parsnip ['pɑːsnɪp] *n* pastinaca *f*.

parson ['pɑːsn] *n* curato *m*, parroco *m*.

part [pɑːt] ♦ *n* parte *f*; (*of machine, car*) pezzo *m*; (*of serial*) puntata *f*;

(Am: *in hair*) scriminatura *f* ◆ *adv* in parte ◆ *vi* (*couple*) separarsi; **in this ~ of Italy** in questa zona dell'Italia; **to form ~ of** costituire parte di; **to play a ~ in** avere un ruolo in; **to take ~ in** prendere parte a; **for my ~** da parte mia; **for the most ~** per lo più, in generale; **in these ~s** da queste parti.

partial ['pɑːʃl] *adj* (*not whole*) parziale; **to be ~ to sthg** avere un debole per qc.

participant [pɑːˈtɪsɪpənt] *n* partecipante *mf*.

participate [pɑːˈtɪsɪpeɪt] *vi*: **to ~ (in)** partecipare (a).

particular [pəˈtɪkjʊləʳ] *adj* particolare; (*fussy*) esigente; **in ~** in particolare, specialmente; **nothing in ~** niente di particolare.

▶ **particulars** *npl* (*details*) particolari *mpl*.

particularly [pəˈtɪkjʊləlɪ] *adv* particolarmente, soprattutto.

parting ['pɑːtɪŋ] *n* (Br: *in hair*) scriminatura *f*.

partition [pɑːˈtɪʃn] *n* (*wall*) tramezzo *m*.

partly ['pɑːtlɪ] *adv* parzialmente, in parte.

partner ['pɑːtnəʳ] *n* (*husband*) marito *m*; (*wife*) moglie *f*; (*lover, in game, dance*) compagno *m* (-a *f*); (COMM) socio *m* (-a *f*).

partnership ['pɑːtnəʃɪp] *n* associazione *f*; (COMM) società *f* inv.

partridge ['pɑːtrɪdʒ] *n* pernice *f*.

part-time *adj & adv* part time.

party ['pɑːtɪ] *n* (*for fun*) festa *f*; (POL) partito *m*; (*group of people*) gruppo *m*; **to have a ~** fare una festa.

pass [pɑːs] ◆ *vt* passare; (*move past*) oltrepassare, passare davanti a; (*test, exam*) passare, superare; (*overtake*) sorpassare; (*law*) approvare ◆ *vi* passare ◆ *n* (*document*) lasciapassare *m* inv, permesso *m*; (*in mountain*) passo *m*; (*in exam*) sufficienza *f*; (SPORT) passaggio *m*; **to ~**

sb sthg passare qc a qn.

▶ **pass by** ◆ *vt fus* (*building, window etc*) passare davanti a ◆ *vi* passare.

▶ **pass on** *vt sep* (*message*) passare.

▶ **pass out** *vi* (*faint*) svenire.

▶ **pass up** *vt sep* (*opportunity*) lasciarsi sfuggire.

passable ['pɑːsəbl] *adj* (*road*) transitabile; (*satisfactory*) passabile.

passage ['pæsɪdʒ] *n* (*corridor*) passaggio *m*, corridoio *m*; (*in book*) brano *m*, passo *m*; (*sea journey*) traversata *f*.

passageway ['pæsɪdʒweɪ] *n* corridoio *m*.

passenger ['pæsɪndʒəʳ] *n* passeggero *m* (-a *f*).

passerby [ˌpɑːsəˈbaɪ] *n* passante *mf*.

passing place ['pɑːsɪŋ-] *n* (*for cars*) piazzola *f*.

passion ['pæʃn] *n* passione *f*.

passionate ['pæʃənət] *adj* (*showing strong feeling*) appassionato(-a); (*sexually*) passionale.

passive ['pæsɪv] *n* passivo *m*.

passport ['pɑːspɔːt] *n* passaporto *m*.

passport control *n* controllo *m* passaporti.

passport photo *n* fototessera *f*.

password ['pɑːswɜːd] *n* (*for computer*) password *f* inv, parola *f* d'accesso.

past [pɑːst] ◆ *adj* passato(-a); (*last*) ultimo(-a); (*former*) ex (*inv*) ◆ *prep* (*in times*) dopo; (*further than*) oltre, al di là di; (*in front of*) davanti a ◆ *adv* oltre ◆ *n* (*former time*) passato *m*; **~ (tense)** (GRAMM) passato; **the ~ month** il mese scorso; **twenty ~ four** le quattro e venti; **to run ~** passare di corsa; **in the ~** nel passato.

pasta ['pæstə] *n* pasta *f*.

paste [peɪst] *n* (*spread*) pasta *f*, crema *f* (da spalmare); (*glue*) colla *f*.

pastel ['pæstl] *n* (*for drawing*) pastello *m*; (*colour*) colore *m* pastello.

pasteurized ['pɑːstʃəraɪzd] *adj*

pastorizzato(-a).

pastille ['pæstɪl] n pastiglia f.

pastime ['pɑːstaɪm] n passatempo m.

pastry ['peɪstrɪ] n pasta f.

pasture ['pɑːstʃəʳ] n pascolo m.

pasty ['pæstɪ] n (Br) pasticcio m.

pat [pæt] vt dare un colpetto (affettuoso) a.

patch [pætʃ] n (for clothes) toppa f; (of colour, cloud, damp) macchia f; (for skin) cerotto m; (for eye) benda f; **a bad ~** (fig) un brutto periodo.

pâté ['pæteɪ] n pâté m inv.

patent [Br 'peɪtənt, Am 'pætənt] n brevetto m.

path [pɑːθ] n (in park, country) sentiero m, viottolo m; (in garden) vialetto m.

pathetic [pə'θetɪk] adj (pej: useless) penoso(-a).

patience ['peɪʃns] n (quality) pazienza f; (Br: card game) solitario m.

patient ['peɪʃnt] ♦ adj paziente ♦ n paziente mf, malato m (-a f).

patio ['pætɪəʊ] n terrazza f.

patriotic [Br ˌpætrɪ'ɒtɪk, Am ˌpeɪtrɪ'ɒtɪk] adj patriottico(-a).

patrol [pə'trəʊl] ♦ vt pattugliare ♦ n (group) pattuglia f.

patrol car n auto f inv di pattuglia.

patron ['peɪtrən] n (fml: customer) cliente mf; **'~s only'** 'riservato ai clienti'.

patronizing ['pætrənaɪzɪŋ] adj (person) che tratta con aria di superiorità.

pattern ['pætn] n (of shapes, colours) disegno m, motivo m; (for sewing) modello m.

patterned ['pætənd] adj fantasia (inv).

pause [pɔːz] ♦ n pausa f ♦ vi fare una pausa, soffermarsi.

pavement ['peɪvmənt] n (Br: beside road) marciapiede m; (Am: roadway) pavimentazione f.

pavilion [pə'vɪljən] n edificio annesso a campo sportivo, adibito a spogliatoio.

paving stone ['peɪvɪŋ-] n lastra f di pietra.

pavlova n dolce composto da due strati di meringa farciti di panna montata e frutta.

paw [pɔː] n zampa f.

pawn [pɔːn] ♦ vt impegnare, dare in pegno ♦ n (in chess) pedone m.

pay [peɪ] (pt & pp paid) ♦ vt pagare ♦ vi (give money) pagare; (be profitable) rendere ♦ n paga f, stipendio m; **to ~ sb for sthg** pagare qn per qc; **to ~ money into an account** versare dei soldi su un conto; **to ~ attention (to)** fare attenzione (a); **to ~ sb a visit** fare visita a qn; **to ~ by credit card** pagare con la carta di credito.

▶ **pay back** vt sep (money) restituire; (person) rimborsare.

▶ **pay for** vt fus (purchase) pagare.

▶ **pay in** vt sep (cheque, money) versare.

▶ **pay out** vt sep (money) sborsare.

▶ **pay up** vi saldare il debito.

payable ['peɪəbl] adj (bill) pagabile; **~ to** (cheque) pagabile a, intestato(-a) a.

payment ['peɪmənt] n (of money, bill) pagamento m; (amount) pagamento, versamento m.

payphone ['peɪfəʊn] n telefono m pubblico.

PC ♦ n (abbr of personal computer) PC m inv ♦ abbr (Br) = **police constable**.

PE abbr = **physical education**.

pea [piː] n pisello m.

peace [piːs] n pace f; **to leave sb in ~** lasciare qn in pace; **~ and quiet** pace e tranquillità.

peaceful ['piːsfʊl] adj (place, day, feeling) tranquillo(-a), calmo(-a); (demonstration) pacifico(-a).

peach [piːtʃ] n pesca f.

peach melba [-'melbə] n pesche fpl melba.

peacock ['piːkɒk] n pavone m.

peak [piːk] n (of mountain) cima f,

vetta f; (of hat) visiera f; (fig: highest point) apice m, culmine m.

peak hours npl ore fpl di punta.

peak rate n tariffa f ore di punta.

peanut ['pi:nʌt] n arachide f, nocciolina f americana.

peanut butter n burro m di arachidi.

pear [peər] n pera f.

pearl [pɜ:l] n perla f.

peasant ['peznt] n contadino m (-a f).

pebble ['pebl] n ciottolo m.

pecan pie ['pi:kæn-] n torta di noci pecan.

peck [pek] vi (bird) beccare.

peculiar [pɪ'kju:ljər] adj (strange) strano(-a), singolare; **to be ~ to** (exclusive) essere peculiare di.

peculiarity [pɪ,kju:lɪ'ærətɪ] n (special feature) particolarità f inv.

pedal ['pedl] ◆ n pedale m ◆ vi pedalare.

pedal bin n pattumiera f a pedale.

pedalo ['pedələʊ] (pl -s) n moscone m a pedali, pedalò® m inv.

pedestrian [pɪ'destrɪən] n pedone m (-a f).

pedestrian crossing n passaggio m pedonale.

pedestrianized [pɪ'destrɪənaɪzd] adj riservato(-a) ai pedoni.

pedestrian precinct n (Br) zona f pedonale.

pedestrian zone (Am) = **pedestrian precinct**.

pee [pi:] ◆ vi (inf) fare la pipì ◆ n: **to have a ~** (inf) fare la pipì.

peel [pi:l] ◆ n buccia f; (of orange, lemon) scorza f ◆ vt (fruit, vegetables) sbucciare ◆ vi (paint) staccarsi; (skin) spellarsi.

peep [pi:p] n: **to have a ~** dare una sbirciatina.

peer [pɪər] vi: **to ~ at** fissare, scrutare.

peg [peg] n (for tent) picchetto m; (hook) attaccapanni m inv; (for wash-

ing) molletta f.

pelican crossing ['pelɪkən-] n (Br) passaggio pedonale con semaforo a comando manuale.

pelvis ['pelvɪs] n bacino m.

pen [pen] n (for writing) penna f; (for animals) recinto m.

penalty ['penltɪ] n (fine) multa f, sanzione f; (in football) rigore m.

pence [pens] npl penny m inv; **it costs 20 ~** costa 20 penny.

pencil ['pensl] n matita f.

pencil case n portamatite m inv.

pencil sharpener n temperamatite m inv.

pendant ['pendənt] n pendente m, ciondolo m.

pending ['pendɪŋ] prep (fml) in attesa di.

penetrate ['penɪtreɪt] vt penetrare.

penfriend ['penfrend] n amico m (-a f) per corrispondenza.

penguin ['peŋgwɪn] n pinguino m.

penicillin [,penɪ'sɪlɪn] n penicillina f.

peninsula [pə'nɪnsjʊlə] n penisola f.

penis ['pi:nɪs] n pene m.

penknife ['pennaɪf] (pl -knives) n temperino m.

penny ['penɪ] (pl pennies) n (in UK) penny m inv; (in US) centesimo m.

pension ['penʃn] n pensione f.

pensioner ['penʃənər] n pensionato m (-a f).

penthouse ['penthaʊs, pl -haʊzɪz] n superattico m.

penultimate [pe'nʌltɪmət] adj penultimo(-a).

people ['pi:pl] ◆ npl (persons) persone fpl; (in general) gente f ◆ n (nation) popolo m; **the ~** (citizens) il popolo.

pepper ['pepər] n (spice) pepe m; (vegetable) peperone m.

peppercorn ['pepəkɔ:n] n grano m di pepe.

peppermint ['pepəmɪnt] ◆ adj alla

menta (piperita) ♦ n (*sweet*) caramella *f* di menta.

pepper pot n pepiera *f*.

pepper steak n bistecca *f* al pepe.

Pepsi® ['pepsɪ] n Pepsi® *f inv*.

per [pɜːʳ] *prep* per, a; ~ **person** a persona; ~ **week** alla settimana; **£20** ~ **night** 20 sterline a notte.

perceive [pəˈsiːv] *vt* percepire.

per cent *adv* per cento.

percentage [pəˈsentɪdʒ] n percentuale *f*.

perch [pɜːtʃ] n (*for bird*) posatoio *m*, asticella *f*.

percolator ['pɜːkəleɪtəʳ] n caffettiera *f* a filtro.

perfect [*adj* & n 'pɜːfɪkt, *vb* pəˈfekt] ♦ *adj* perfetto(-a) ♦ *vt* perfezionare ♦ *n*: **the** ~ **(tense)** il passato prossimo.

perfection [pəˈfekʃn] *n*: **to do sthg to** ~ fare qc alla perfezione.

perfectly ['pɜːfɪktlɪ] *adv* (*very well*) perfettamente, alla perfezione.

perform [pəˈfɔːm] ♦ *vt* (*task, operation*) eseguire, fare; (*play*) rappresentare; (*concert*) eseguire ♦ *vi* (*actor*) recitare; (*singer*) cantare.

performance [pəˈfɔːməns] n (*of play, concert, film*) spettacolo *m*; (*by actor*) interpretazione *f*; (*musician*) esecuzione *f*; (*of car*) prestazioni *fpl*.

performer [pəˈfɔːməʳ] n artista *mf*.

perfume ['pɜːfjuːm] n profumo *m*.

perhaps [pəˈhæps] *adv* forse.

perimeter [pəˈrɪmɪtəʳ] n perimetro *m*.

period ['pɪərɪəd] ♦ n periodo *m*; (SCH) lezione *f*; (*menstruation*) mestruazioni *fpl*; (*Am: full stop*) punto *m* ♦ *adj* (*costume, furniture*) d'epoca.

periodic [ˌpɪərɪˈɒdɪk] *adj* periodico(-a).

period pains *npl* dolori *mpl* mestruali.

periphery [pəˈrɪfərɪ] n periferia *f*.

perishable ['perɪʃəbl] *adj* deperibile.

perk [pɜːk] n vantaggio *m*.

perm [pɜːm] ♦ n permanente *f* ♦ *vt*: **to have one's hair** ~**ed** farsi la permanente.

permanent ['pɜːmənənt] *adj* permanente.

permanent address n residenza *f*.

permanently ['pɜːmənəntlɪ] *adv* permanentemente.

permissible [pəˈmɪsəbl] *adj* (*fml*) permissibile, ammissibile.

permission [pəˈmɪʃn] n permesso *m*.

permit [*vb* pəˈmɪt, n 'pɜːmɪt] ♦ *vt* permettere ♦ n permesso *m*; **to** ~ **sb to do sthg** permettere a qn di fare qc; '~ **holders only**' 'solo autorizzati'.

perpendicular [ˌpɜːpənˈdɪkjʊləʳ] *adj* perpendicolare.

persevere [ˌpɜːsɪˈvɪəʳ] *vi* perseverare.

persist [pəˈsɪst] *vi* persistere; **to** ~ **in doing sthg** ostinarsi a fare qc.

persistent [pəˈsɪstənt] *adj* persistente; (*person*) ostinato(-a).

person ['pɜːsn] (*pl* **people**) n persona *f*; **in** ~ di persona.

personal ['pɜːsənl] *adj* personale.

personal assistant n segretario *m* (-a *f*) personale.

personal belongings *npl* effetti *mpl* personali.

personal computer n personal computer *m inv*.

personality [ˌpɜːsəˈnælətɪ] n personalità *f inv*.

personally ['pɜːsnəlɪ] *adv* personalmente.

personal property n beni *mpl* mobili.

personal stereo n walkman® *m inv*.

personnel [ˌpɜːsəˈnel] *npl* personale *m*.

perspective [pəˈspektɪv] n prospettiva *f*.

Perspex® ['pɜːspeks] n (Br) ≃

plexiglas® m.

perspiration [ˌpɜːspəˈreɪʃn] n traspirazione f, sudore m.

persuade [pəˈsweɪd] vt: **to ~ sb (to do sthg)** persuadere qn (a fare qc); **to ~ sb that ...** persuadere qn che ...

persuasive [pəˈsweɪsɪv] adj persuasivo(-a), convincente.

pervert ['pɜːvɜːt] n pervertito m (-a f).

pessimist ['pesɪmɪst] n pessimista mf.

pessimistic [ˌpesɪˈmɪstɪk] adj pessimistico(-a).

pest [pest] n (insect) insetto m nocivo; (animal) animale m nocivo; (inf: person) peste f.

pester ['pestər] vt tormentare.

pesticide ['pestɪsaɪd] n pesticida m.

pet [pet] n animale m domestico; **the teacher's ~** il favorito dell'insegnante.

petal ['petl] n petalo m.

pet food n cibo m per animali (domestici).

petition [pɪˈtɪʃn] n (letter) petizione f.

petits pois npl pisellini mpl.

petrified ['petrɪfaɪd] adj (frightened) impietrito(-a) (dalla paura).

petrol ['petrəl] n (Br) benzina f.

petrol can n (Br) tanica f per la benzina.

petrol cap n (Br) tappo m del serbatoio.

petrol gauge n (Br) indicatore m di livello della benzina.

petrol pump n (Br) pompa f di benzina.

petrol station n (Br) stazione f di rifornimento.

petrol tank n (Br) serbatoio m della benzina.

pet shop n negozio m di animali.

petticoat ['petɪkəut] n sottoveste f.

petty ['petɪ] adj (pej: person, rule) meschino(-a).

petty cash n piccola cassa f.

pew [pjuː] n panca f (di chiesa).

pewter ['pjuːtər] adj di peltro.

PG (abbr of parental guidance) sigla che contraddistingue i film non vietati ai minori, per i quali è però consigliato l'accompagnamento dei genitori.

pharmacist ['fɑːməsɪst] n farmacista mf.

pharmacy ['fɑːməsɪ] n (shop) farmacia f.

phase [feɪz] n fase f.

PhD n (degree) ≃ dottorato m di ricerca.

pheasant ['feznt] n fagiano m.

phenomena [fɪˈnɒmɪnə] pl → **phenomenon**.

phenomenal [fɪˈnɒmɪnl] adj fenomenale.

phenomenon [fɪˈnɒmɪnən] (pl -mena) n fenomeno m.

Philippines ['fɪlɪpiːnz] npl: **the ~** le Filippine.

philosophy [fɪˈlɒsəfɪ] n filosofia f.

phlegm [flem] n (in throat) catarro m.

phone [fəun] ◆ n telefono m ◆ vt (Br) telefonare a ◆ vi (Br) telefonare; **to be on the ~** (talking) essere al telefono; (connected) avere il telefono.

▶ **phone up** ◆ vt sep telefonare a, chiamare ◆ vi telefonare.

phone book n elenco m telefonico.

phone booth n cabina f telefonica.

phone box n (Br) cabina f telefonica.

phone call n telefonata f.

phonecard ['fəunkɑːd] n scheda f telefonica.

phone number n numero m di telefono.

photo ['fəutəu] (pl -s) n foto f inv; **to take a ~ of** fare una foto a.

photo album n album m inv portafotografie.

photocopier [ˌfəutəuˈkɒpɪər] n fotocopiatrice f.

photocopy ['fəʊtəʊˌkɒpɪ] ♦ n fotocopia f ♦ vt fotocopiare.

photograph ['fəʊtəgrɑːf] ♦ n fotografia f ♦ vt fotografare.

photographer [fə'tɒgrəfər] n fotografo m (-a f).

photography [fə'tɒgrəfɪ] n fotografia f.

phrase [freɪz] n espressione f.

phrasebook ['freɪzbʊk] n vocabolarietto m con frasi tipiche.

physical ['fɪzɪkl] ♦ adj fisico(-a) ♦ n visita f medica.

physical education n educazione f fisica.

physically handicapped ['fɪzɪklɪ-] adj handicappato fisico (handicappata fisica).

physics ['fɪzɪks] n fisica f.

physiotherapy [ˌfɪzɪəʊ'θerəpɪ] n fisioterapia f.

pianist ['pɪənɪst] n pianista mf.

piano [pɪ'ænəʊ] (pl -s) n pianoforte m.

pick [pɪk] ♦ vt (select) scegliere; (fruit, flowers) cogliere ♦ n (pickaxe) piccone m; **to ~ a fight** attaccar briga; **to ~ one's nose** mettersi le dita nel naso; **to take the ~** scegliere.

▶ **pick on** vt fus prendersela con, prendere di mira.

▶ **pick out** vt sep (select) scegliere; (see) individuare, riconoscere.

▶ **pick up** ♦ vt sep (lift up) raccogliere; (collect) passare a prendere; (learn) imparare; (habit) prendere; (bargain) trovare; (hitchhiker) far salire; (inf: woman, man) rimorchiare ♦ vi (improve) riprendersi; **to ~ up the phone** (answer) rispondere al telefono.

pickaxe ['pɪkæks] n piccone m.

pickle ['pɪkl] n (Br: food) sottaceti mpl; (Am: pickled cucumber) cetriolo m sottaceto.

pickled onion ['pɪkld-] n cipollina f sottaceto.

pickpocket ['pɪkˌpɒkɪt] n borsaiolo m.

pick-up (truck) n camioncino m.

picnic ['pɪknɪk] n picnic m inv.

picnic area n area per picnic.

picture ['pɪktʃər] n (painting) quadro m; (drawing) disegno m; (photograph) fotografia f; (on TV) immagine f; (film) film m inv.

▶ **pictures** npl: **the ~s** (Br) il cinema.

picture frame n cornice f.

picturesque [ˌpɪktʃə'resk] adj pittoresco(-a).

pie [paɪ] n (savoury) pasticcio m; (sweet) torta f.

piece [piːs] n pezzo m; **a 20p ~** un pezzo da 20 penny; **a ~ of advice** un consiglio; **a ~ of clothing** un capo di vestiario; **a ~ of furniture** un mobile; **to fall to ~s** andare in pezzi; **in one ~** tutto intero.

pier [pɪər] n molo m.

pierce [pɪəs] vt forare, perforare; **to have one's ears ~d** farsi i buchi alle orecchie.

pig [pɪg] n maiale m, porco m.

pigeon ['pɪdʒɪn] n piccione m.

pigeonhole ['pɪdʒɪnhəʊl] n casella f.

pigskin ['pɪgskɪn] adj di cinghiale.

pigtails ['pɪgteɪlz] npl trecce fpl.

pike [paɪk] n (fish) luccio m.

pilau rice ['pɪlaʊ-] n riso m pilaf.

pilchard ['pɪltʃəd] n sardina f.

pile [paɪl] ♦ n (heap) mucchio m; (neat stack) pila f ♦ vt ammucchiare; **~s of** (inf: a lot) mucchi di.

▶ **pile up** ♦ vt sep ammucchiare ♦ vi (accumulate) ammucchiarsi.

piles [paɪlz] npl (MED) emorroidi fpl.

pileup ['paɪlʌp] n tamponamento m a catena.

pilgrim ['pɪlgrɪm] n pellegrino m (-a f).

pill [pɪl] n pillola f.

pillar ['pɪlər] n colonna f.

pillar box n (Br) cassetta f delle lettere.

pillion ['pɪljən] n: **to ride ~** viaggiare sul sellino posteriore.

pillow ['pɪləʊ] n cuscino m.

pillowcase ['pɪləʊkeɪs] n federa f.

pilot ['paɪlət] n pilota mf.

pilot light n fiamma f pilota.

pimple ['pɪmpl] n foruncolo m.

pin [pɪn] ◆ n (for sewing, safety pin) spillo m; (drawing pin) puntina f; (Am: brooch, badge) spilla f ◆ vt (fasten) attaccare con uno spillo; **a two-~ plug** una spina bipolare; **~s and needles** formicolio m.

pinafore ['pɪnəfɔːʳ] n (apron) grembiule m; (Br: dress) scamiciato m.

pinball ['pɪnbɔːl] n flipper m inv.

pincers ['pɪnsəz] npl (tool) tenaglie fpl.

pinch [pɪntʃ] ◆ vt (squeeze) pizzicare, dare un pizzicotto a; (Br: inf: steal) fregare ◆ n (of salt) pizzico m.

pine [paɪn] ◆ n (of pino m ◆ adj di pino.

pineapple ['paɪnæpl] n ananas m inv.

pink [pɪŋk] ◆ adj rosa (inv) ◆ n (colour) rosa m inv.

pinkie ['pɪŋkɪ] n (Am) mignolo m.

PIN number n numero m di codice segreto.

pint [paɪnt] n (in UK) = 0,568 l, pinta f; (in US) = 0,473 l, pinta; **a ~ (of beer)** (Br) ≃ una birra grande.

pip [pɪp] n (of fruit) seme m.

pipe [paɪp] n (for smoking) pipa f; (for gas, water) tubo m.

pipe cleaner n scovolino m.

pipeline ['paɪplaɪn] n conduttura f; (for oil) oleodotto m.

pipe tobacco n tabacco m da pipa.

pirate ['paɪrət] n pirata m.

Pisces ['paɪsiːz] n Pesci mpl.

piss [pɪs] ◆ vi (vulg) pisciare ◆ n: **to have a ~** (vulg) pisciare; **it's ~ing down** (vulg) piove a dirotto.

pissed [pɪst] adj (Br: vulg: drunk) sbronzo(-a); (Am: vulg: angry) incazzato(-a).

pissed off adj (vulg) incazzato(-a).

pistachio [pɪˈstɑːʃɪəʊ] (pl -s) ◆ n pistacchio m ◆ adj al pistacchio.

pistol ['pɪstl] n pistola f.

piston ['pɪstən] n pistone m.

pit [pɪt] n (hole) buca f, fossa f; (coalmine) miniera f (di carbone); (for orchestra) fossa dell'orchestra; (Am: in fruit) nocciolo m.

pitch [pɪtʃ] ◆ n (Br: SPORT) campo m ◆ vt (throw) lanciare; **to ~ a tent** piantare una tenda.

pitcher ['pɪtʃəʳ] n brocca f.

pitfall ['pɪtfɔːl] n insidia f, pericolo m.

pith [pɪθ] n (of orange) parte f interna della scorza.

pitta (bread) ['pɪtə-] n tipo di schiacciatina di origine mediorientale.

pitted ['pɪtɪd] adj (olives) snocciolato(-a).

pity ['pɪtɪ] n (compassion) pietà f; **to have ~ on sb** avere pietà di qn; **it's a ~ that ...** è un peccato che ...; **what a ~!** che peccato!

pivot ['pɪvət] n perno m.

pizza ['piːtsə] n pizza f.

pizzeria [ˌpiːtsəˈriːə] n pizzeria f.

Pl. (abbr of Place) abbreviazione di strada in alcuni indirizzi.

placard ['plækɑːd] n cartello m.

place [pleɪs] ◆ n (location) posto m, luogo m; (house, flat) casa f; (seat, proper position, in race, list) posto ◆ vt (put) collocare, mettere; (an order, bet) fare; **in the first ~** (firstly) in primo luogo; **to take ~** avere luogo, avvenire; **to take sb's ~** (replace) prendere il posto di qn; **all over the ~** dappertutto; **in ~ of** al posto di.

place mat n (heat-resistant) sottopiatto m; (linen) tovaglietta f.

placement ['pleɪsmənt] n (work experience) stage m inv.

place of birth n luogo m di nascita.

plague [pleɪg] n peste f.

plaice [pleɪs] (pl inv) n platessa f.

plain [pleɪn] ◆ adj (simple) semplice; (in one colour) in tinta unita;

(clear) chiaro(-a); *(paper)* non rigato(-a); *(pej: not attractive)* scialbo(-a) ◆ *n* pianura *f.*

plain chocolate *n* cioccolato *m* fondente.

plainly ['pleɪnlɪ] *adv* chiaramente.

plait [plæt] ◆ *n* treccia *f* ◆ *vt* intrecciare.

plan [plæn] ◆ *n* *(scheme, project)* piano *m*, progetto *m*; *(drawing)* pianta *f* ◆ *vt* *(organize)* programmare, progettare; **have you any ~s for tonight?** hai qualche programma per stasera?; **according to ~** secondo i piani; **to ~ to do sthg, to ~ on doing sthg** progettare di fare qc.

plane [pleɪn] *n* *(aeroplane)* aereo *m*; *(tool)* pialla *f.*

planet ['plænɪt] *n* pianeta *m.*

plank [plæŋk] *n* asse *f*, tavola *f.*

plant [plɑːnt] ◆ *n* pianta *f*; *(factory)* stabilimento *m*, fabbrica *f* ◆ *vt* piantare; **'heavy ~ crossing'** 'uscita mezzi pesanti'.

plantation [plæn'teɪʃn] *n* piantagione *f.*

plaque [plɑːk] *n* placca *f.*

plaster ['plɑːstər] *n* *(Br: for cut)* cerotto *m*; *(for walls)* intonaco *m*; **in ~** *(arm, leg)* ingessato.

plaster cast *n* *(for broken bones)* ingessatura *f.*

plastic ['plæstɪk] ◆ *n* plastica *f* ◆ *adj* di plastica.

plastic bag *n* sacchetto *m* di plastica.

Plasticine® ['plæstɪsiːn] *n* *(Br)* plastilina® *f.*

plate [pleɪt] *n* *(for food)* piatto *m*; *(of metal, glass)* piastra *f.*

plateau ['plætəʊ] *n* altopiano *m.*

plate-glass *adj* di vetro piano.

platform ['plætfɔːm] *n* *(at railway station)* marciapiede *m* *(di binario)*; *(raised structure)* piattaforma *f*; *(stage)* palco *m*; **~ 12** binario 12.

platinum ['plætɪnəm] *n* platino *m.*

platter ['plætər] *n* *(CULIN)* piatto *m* *(di affettati, frutti di mare assortiti ecc.).*

play [pleɪ] ◆ *vt* *(sport, game)* giocare a; *(musical instrument, music)* suonare; *(opponent)* giocare contro; *(CD, tape, record)* mettere *(su)*; *(role, character)* interpretare ◆ *vi* giocare; *(musician)* suonare ◆ *n* *(in theatre, on TV)* dramma *m*, commedia *f*; *(button on CD, tape recorder)* play *m inv.*

▶ **play back** *vt sep* *(tape)* riascoltare; *(video)* rivedere.

▶ **play up** *vi* *(machine, car)* fare i capricci.

player ['pleɪər] *n* *(of sport, game)* giocatore *m* *(-trice f)*; *(of musical instrument)* suonatore *m* *(-trice f)*.

playful ['pleɪfʊl] *adj* scherzoso(-a), giocoso(-a).

playground ['pleɪgraʊnd] *n* *(in school)* cortile *m* per la ricreazione; *(in park etc)* parco *m* giochi.

playgroup ['pleɪgruːp] *n* asilo *m* infantile.

playing card ['pleɪɪŋ-] *n* carta *f* da gioco.

playing field ['pleɪɪŋ-] *n* campo *m* sportivo.

playroom ['pleɪrʊm] *n* stanza *f* dei giochi.

playschool ['pleɪskuːl] *n* = **play-group**.

playtime ['pleɪtaɪm] *n* ricreazione *f.*

playwright ['pleɪraɪt] *n* drammaturgo *m* *(-a f)*.

plc *(Br: abbr of public limited company)* = S.r.l. *(quotata in borsa)*.

pleasant ['pleznt] *adj* piacevole, gradevole; *(person)* simpatico(-a).

please [pliːz] ◆ *adv* per favore, per piacere ◆ *vt* far piacere a; **~ take a seat** prego, si sieda; **yes ~!** si, grazie!; **whatever you ~** quello che ti pare.

pleased [pliːzd] *adj* contento(-a); **to be ~ with** essere contento di; **~ to meet you!** piacere!

pleasure ['pleʒər] *n* piacere *m*; **with ~** con piacere; **it's a ~!** non c'è di che!, prego!

pleat [pli:t] n piega f.

pleated ['pli:tɪd] adj pieghetta-to(-a).

plentiful ['plentɪful] adj abbondan-te.

plenty ['plentɪ] pron: **there's ~** ce n'è in abbondanza; **~ of** un sacco di.

pliers ['plaɪəz] npl pinze fpl.

plimsoll ['plɪmsəl] n (Br) scarpa f da tennis.

plonk [plɒŋk] n (Br: inf: wine) vino m da poco.

plot [plɒt] n (scheme) complotto m; (of story, film, play) trama f; (of land) appezzamento m.

plough [plaʊ] ◆ n (Br) aratro m ◆ vt (Br) arare.

ploughman's (lunch) ['plaʊ-mənz-] n (Br) piatto a base di formaggi, sottaceti e pane, spesso servito nei pub.

plow [plaʊ] (Am) = **plough**.

ploy [plɔɪ] n tattica f.

pluck [plʌk] vt (eyebrows) depilare; (chicken) spennare.

plug [plʌg] n (electrical) spina f; (for bath, sink) tappo m.

▶ **plug in** vt sep attaccare (a una presa).

plughole ['plʌghəʊl] n buco m (della vasca, ecc.).

plum [plʌm] n susina f, prugna f.

plumber ['plʌmər] n idraulico m.

plumbing ['plʌmɪŋ] n (pipes) tuba-ture fpl.

plump [plʌmp] adj grassoccio(-a).

plunge [plʌndʒ] vi (fall) precipita-re, cadere; (dive) tuffarsi; (decrease) precipitare.

plunge pool n piscina f piccola.

plunger ['plʌndʒər] n (for unblocking pipe) sturalavandini m inv.

pluperfect (tense) [plu:'pɜːfɪkt-] n: **the ~** il piuccheperfetto.

plural ['plʊərəl] n plurale m; **in the ~** al plurale.

plus [plʌs] ◆ prep più ◆ adj: **30 ~** più di 30.

plush [plʌʃ] adj lussuoso(-a).

plywood ['plaɪwʊd] n compensa-to m.

p.m. (abbr of post meridiem): **at 3 ~** alle 3 del pomeriggio; **at 10 ~** alle 10 di sera.

PMT n (abbr of premenstrual tension) sindrome f premestruale.

pneumatic drill [njuː'mætɪk-] n martello m pneumatico.

pneumonia [njuː'məʊnjə] n pol-monite f.

poached egg [pəʊtʃt-] n uovo m in camicia.

poached salmon [pəʊtʃt-] n sal-mone m bollito.

poacher ['pəʊtʃər] n bracconiere m.

PO Box n (abbr of Post Office Box) C.P.

pocket ['pɒkɪt] ◆ n tasca f ◆ adj tascabile.

pocketbook ['pɒkɪtbʊk] n (note-book) taccuino m; (Am: handbag) bor-setta f.

pocket money n (Br) paghetta f, settimana f.

podiatrist [pə'daɪətrɪst] n (Am) pedicure mf, callista mf.

poem ['pəʊɪm] n poesia f.

poet ['pəʊɪt] n poeta m (-essa f).

poetry ['pəʊɪtrɪ] n poesia f.

point [pɔɪnt] ◆ n punto m; (tip) punta f; (Br: electric socket) presa f ◆ vi: **to ~ to** indicare; **five ~ seven** cinque virgola sette; **what's the ~?** a che serve?; **there's no ~** è inutile; **to be on the ~ of doing sthg** essere sul punto di fare qc.

▶ **points** npl (Br: on railway) scam-bio m.

▶ **point out** vt sep (object, person) indicare; (fact, mistake) far notare.

pointed ['pɔɪntɪd] adj (in shape) appuntito(-a).

pointless ['pɔɪntlɪs] adj inutile.

point of view n punto m di vista.

poison ['pɔɪzn] ◆ n veleno m ◆ vt avvelenare.

poisoning ['pɔɪznɪŋ] n avvelenamento m, intossicazione f.

poisonous ['pɔɪznəs] adj veleno-so(-a).

poke [pəuk] vt (with finger, stick, elbow) dare un colpetto a.

poker ['pəukər] n (card game) poker m.

Poland ['pəulənd] n la Polonia.

polar bear ['pəulə-] n orso m bianco.

Polaroid® ['pəulərɔɪd] n (photograph) foto f inv polaroid®; (camera) polaroid® f inv.

pole [pəul] n (of wood) palo m.

Pole [pəul] n (person) polacco m (-a f).

police [pə'liːs] npl: the ~ la polizia.

police car n auto f inv della polizia.

police force n forze fpl di polizia OR dell'ordine.

policeman [pə'liːsmən] (pl -men [-mən]) n poliziotto m.

police officer n agente m di polizia.

police station n posto m di polizia.

policewoman [pə'liːsˌwumən] (pl -women [-ˌwɪmɪn]) n donna f poliziotto.

policy ['pɒləsɪ] n (approach, attitude) politica f; (for insurance) polizza f.

policy-holder n assicurato m (-a f).

polio ['pəulɪəu] n polio f.

polish ['pɒlɪʃ] ♦ n (for cleaning) lucido m, cera f ♦ vt lucidare.

Polish ['pəulɪʃ] ♦ adj polacco(-a) ♦ n (language) polacco m ♦ npl: the ~ i polacchi.

polite [pə'laɪt] adj cortese, gentile.

political [pə'lɪtɪkl] adj politico(-a).

politician [ˌpɒlɪ'tɪʃn] n politico m.

politics ['pɒlətɪks] n politica f.

poll [pəul] n (survey) sondaggio m (d'opinioni); the ~s (election) le elezioni.

pollen ['pɒlən] n polline m.

Poll Tax n (Br) tassa comunale pro capite.

pollute [pə'luːt] vt inquinare.

pollution [pə'luːʃn] n inquinamento m.

polo neck ['pəuləu-] n (Br: jumper) maglione m a collo alto.

polyester [ˌpɒlɪ'estər] n poliestere m.

polystyrene [ˌpɒlɪ'staɪriːn] n polistirolo m.

polytechnic [ˌpɒlɪ'teknɪk] n = politecnico m.

polythene bag ['pɒlɪθiːn-] n sacchetto m di plastica.

pomegranate ['pɒmɪˌgrænɪt] n melagrana f.

pompous ['pɒmpəs] adj pomposo(-a).

pond [pɒnd] n stagno m.

pontoon [pɒn'tuːn] n (Br: card game) ventuno m.

pony ['pəunɪ] n pony m inv.

ponytail ['pəunɪteɪl] n coda f di cavallo.

pony-trekking [-ˌtrekɪŋ] n (Br) escursione f a dorso di pony.

poodle ['puːdl] n barboncino m.

pool [puːl] n pozza f; (for swimming) piscina f; (game) biliardo m a buca.
▶ **pools** npl (Br): the ~s = il totocalcio.

poor [pɔːr] ♦ adj povero(-a); (bad) mediocre, scadente ♦ npl: the ~ i poveri.

poorly ['pɔːlɪ] ♦ adv malamente, male ♦ adj (Br: ill): to be ~ stare poco bene.

pop [pɒp] ♦ n (music) musica f pop ♦ vt (inf: put) mettere ♦ vi (balloon) scoppiare; my ears popped mi si sono stappate le orecchie.
▶ **pop in** vi (Br: visit) fare un salto.

popcorn ['pɒpkɔːn] n popcorn m.

Pope [pəup] n: the ~ il papa.

pop group n gruppo m pop.

poplar (tree) ['pɒplər-] n pioppo m.

pop music n musica f pop.

poppadom ['pɒpədəm] n *pane indiano molto sottile e croccante.*

popper ['pɒpə'] n (Br) bottone m a pressione.

poppy ['pɒpɪ] n papavero m.

Popsicle® ['pɒpsɪkl] n (Am) ghiacciolo m.

pop socks npl gambaletti mpl.

pop star n pop star f inv.

popular ['pɒpjʊlə'] adj popolare; (fashionable) in voga.

popularity [,pɒpjʊ'lærətɪ] n popolarità f.

populated ['pɒpjʊleɪtɪd] adj popolato(-a).

population [,pɒpjʊ'leɪʃn] n popolazione f.

porcelain ['pɔːsəlɪn] n porcellana f.

porch [pɔːtʃ] n (entrance) portico m; (Am: outside house) veranda f.

pork [pɔːk] n carne f di maiale.

pork chop n braciola f OR costoletta f di maiale.

pork pie n pasticcio m di maiale.

pornographic [,pɔːnə'græfɪk] adj pornografico(-a).

porridge ['pɒrɪdʒ] n porridge m, farinata f d'avena.

port [pɔːt] n porto m.

portable ['pɔːtəbl] adj portatile.

porter ['pɔːtə'] n (at hotel, museum) portiere m; (at station, airport) facchino m.

porthole ['pɔːthəʊl] n oblò m inv.

portion ['pɔːʃn] n porzione f.

portrait ['pɔːtreɪt] n ritratto m.

Portugal ['pɔːtʃʊgl] n il Portogallo.

Portuguese [,pɔːtʃʊ'giːz] ◆ adj portoghese ◆ n (language) portoghese m ◆ npl: **the ~** i portoghesi.

pose [pəʊz] ◆ vt (problem, threat) porre ◆ vi (for photo) posare.

posh [pɒʃ] adj (inf) (person, accent) snob inv, raffinato(-a); (hotel, restaurant) elegante, di lusso.

position [pə'zɪʃn] n posizione f; (fml: job) posto m; '**~ closed**' (in bank, post office etc) 'sportello chiuso'.

positive ['pɒzətɪv] adj positivo(-a); (certain, sure) sicuro(-a), certo(-a).

possess [pə'zes] vt possedere.

possession [pə'zeʃn] n (thing owned) bene m.

possessive [pə'zesɪv] adj possessivo(-a).

possibility [,pɒsə'bɪlətɪ] n possibilità f inv.

possible ['pɒsəbl] adj possibile; **it's ~ that we may be late** può darsi che facciamo tardi; **would it be ~ ...?** sarebbe possibile ...?; **as much as ~** il più possibile; **if ~** se possibile.

possibly ['pɒsəblɪ] adv (perhaps) forse.

post [pəʊst] ◆ n (system, letters, delivery) posta f; (pole) palo m; (fml: job) posto m ◆ vt (letter, parcel) spedire (per posta); **by ~** per posta.

postage ['pəʊstɪdʒ] n affrancatura f, spese fpl postali; **~ and packing** spese di spedizione (postale); **~ paid** franco di porto, affrancatura pagata.

postage stamp n (fml) francobollo m.

postal order ['pəʊstl-] n vaglia m inv postale.

postbox ['pəʊstbɒks] n (Br) cassetta f delle lettere.

postcard ['pəʊstkɑːd] n cartolina f.

postcode ['pəʊstkəʊd] n (Br) codice m (di avviamento) postale.

poster ['pəʊstə'] n manifesto m, poster m inv.

poste restante [,pəʊstres'tɑːnt] n (Br) fermo posta m.

post-free adv in franchigia postale, con affrancatura pagata.

postgraduate [,pəʊst'grædʒʊət] n laureato(-a) che frequenta un corso di specializzazione.

postman ['pəʊstmən] (pl **-men** [-mən]) n postino m.

postmark ['pəʊstmɑːk] n timbro m postale.

postmen pl → **postman**.

post office n (building) ufficio m

postale; **the Post Office** ≃ le Poste e Telecomunicazioni.

postpone [,pəʊst'pəʊn] *vt* rinviare, rimandare.

posture ['pɒstʃər] *n* postura *f*.

postwoman ['pəʊst,wʊmən] (*pl* **-women** [-,wɪmɪn]) *n* postina *f*.

pot [pɒt] *n* (*for cooking*) pentola *f*; (*for jam, paint*) vasetto *m*, barattolo *m*; (*for coffee*) caffettiera *f*; (*for tea*) teiera *f*; (*inf: cannabis*) erba *f*; **a ~ of tea** un tè (*servito in una teiera*).

potato [pə'teɪtəʊ] (*pl* **-es**) *n* patata *f*.

potato salad *n* patate *fpl* in insalata.

potential [pə'tenʃl] ◆ *adj* potenziale ◆ *n* potenziale *m*.

pothole ['pɒthəʊl] *n* (*in road*) buca *f*.

pot plant *n* pianta *f* da vaso.

pot scrubber [-'skrʌbər] *n* paglietta *f*.

potted ['pɒtɪd] *adj* (*meat, fish*) in vasetto, in scatola; (*plant*) in vaso.

pottery ['pɒtərɪ] *n* (*clay objects*) ceramiche *fpl*; (*craft*) ceramica *f*.

potty ['pɒtɪ] *n* (*inf*) vasino *m*.

pouch [paʊtʃ] *n* (*for money, tobacco*) borsellino *f*.

poultry ['pəʊltrɪ] *n & npl* pollame *m*.

pound [paʊnd] ◆ *n* (*unit of money*) sterlina *f*; (*unit of weight*) = 453,6 g, libbra *f* ◆ *vi* (*heart*) battere forte; (*head*) martellare.

pour [pɔːr] ◆ *vt* versare ◆ *vi* (*flow*) riversarsi; **it's ~ing (with rain)** sta piovendo a dirotto.

▶ **pour out** *vt sep* (*drink*) versare.

poverty ['pɒvətɪ] *n* povertà *f*, miseria *f*.

powder ['paʊdər] *n* polvere *f*; (*cosmetic*) cipria *f*.

power ['paʊər] ◆ *n* (*control, authority*) potere *m*; (*ability*) capacità *f inv*; (*strength, force*) potenza *f*; (*energy*) energia *f*; (*electricity*) corrente *f* ◆ *vt* azionare; **to be in ~** essere al potere.

power cut *n* interruzione *f* di corrente.

power failure *n* interruzione *f* di corrente.

powerful ['paʊəfʊl] *adj* potente.

power point *n* (*Br*) presa *f* di corrente.

power station *n* centrale *f* elettrica.

power steering *n* servosterzo *m*.

practical ['præktɪkl] *adj* pratico(-a).

practically ['præktɪklɪ] *adv* (*almost*) praticamente.

practice ['præktɪs] ◆ *n* (*training*) pratica *f*; (*training session*) allenamento *m*, esercizio *m*; (*of doctor, lawyer*) studio *m*; (*regular activity, custom*) consuetudine *f* ◆ *vt* (*Am*) = **practise**; **out of ~** fuori allenamento.

practise ['præktɪs] ◆ *vt* (*sport, music, technique*) allenarsi a, esercitarsi a OR in ◆ *vi* (*train*) allenarsi, esercitarsi; (*doctor, lawyer*) esercitare ◆ *n* (*Am*) = **practice**.

praise [preɪz] ◆ *n* elogio *m*, lode *f* ◆ *vt* elogiare, lodare.

pram [præm] *n* (*Br*) carrozzina *f*.

prank [præŋk] *n* burla *f*.

prawn [prɔːn] *n* gamberetto *m*.

prawn cocktail *n* cocktail *m inv* di gamberetti.

prawn crackers *npl* nuvolette *fpl* di drago.

pray [preɪ] *vi* pregare; **to ~ for sthg** (*fig*) pregare per qc, invocare qc.

prayer [preər] *n* preghiera *f*.

precarious [prɪ'keərɪəs] *adj* precario(-a).

precaution [prɪ'kɔːʃn] *n* precauzione *f*.

precede [prɪ'siːd] *vt* (*fml*) precedere.

preceding [prɪ'siːdɪŋ] *adj* precedente.

precinct ['priːsɪŋkt] *n* (*Br: for shop-*

ping) centro *m* commerciale (*chiuso al traffico*); (Am: *area of town*) circoscrizione *f*.

precious ['preʃəs] *adj* prezioso(-a).

precious stone *n* pietra *f* preziosa.

precipice ['presɪpɪs] *n* precipizio *m*.

precise [prɪ'saɪs] *adj* preciso(-a).

precisely [prɪ'saɪslɪ] *adv* precisamente.

predecessor ['priːdɪsesər] *n* predecessore *m*.

predicament [prɪ'dɪkəmənt] *n* situazione *f* difficile.

predict [prɪ'dɪkt] *vt* predire.

predictable [prɪ'dɪktəbl] *adj* prevedibile.

prediction [prɪ'dɪkʃn] *n* predizione *f*.

preface ['prefɪs] *n* prefazione *f*.

prefect ['priːfekt] *n* (Br: *at school*) studente *m* (-essa *f*) con funzioni disciplinari.

prefer [prɪ'fɜːr] *vt*: **to ~ sthg (to)** preferire qc (a); **to ~ to do sthg** preferire fare qc.

preferable ['prefrəbl] *adj* preferibile.

preferably ['prefrəblɪ] *adv* preferibilmente.

preference ['prefərəns] *n* preferenza *f*.

prefix ['priːfɪks] *n* prefisso *m*.

pregnancy ['pregnənsɪ] *n* gravidanza *f*.

pregnant ['pregnənt] *adj* incinta.

prejudice ['predʒudɪs] *n* pregiudizio *m*.

prejudiced ['predʒudɪst] *adj*: **~ (against)** prevenuto(-a) (contro); **~ (in favour of)** bendisposto(-a) (verso).

preliminary [prɪ'lɪmɪnərɪ] *adj* preliminare.

premature ['premə,tjuər] *adj* prematuro(-a).

premier ['premjər] ♦ *adj* primo(-a) ♦ *n* primo ministro *m*.

premiere ['premɪeər] *n* prima *f*.

premises ['premɪsɪz] *npl* locali *mpl*; **on the ~** sul posto.

premium ['priːmjəm] *n* (*for insurance*) premio *m*.

premium-quality *adj* (*meat*) di prima qualità.

preoccupied [priː'ɒkjupaɪd] *adj* preoccupato(-a).

prepacked [,priː'pækt] *adj* preconfezionato(-a).

prepaid ['priːpeɪd] *adj* (*envelope*) con affrancatura pagata.

preparation [,prepə'reɪʃn] *n* preparazione *f*.

▶ **preparations** *npl* (*arrangements*) preparativi *mpl*.

preparatory school [prɪ'pærətrɪ-] *n* (*in* UK) scuola *f* elementare privata; (*in* US) scuola *f* secondaria privata (*che prepara agli studi universitari*).

prepare [prɪ'peər] ♦ *vt* preparare ♦ *vi* prepararsi.

prepared [prɪ'peəd] *adj* (*ready*) preparato(-a), pronto(-a); **to be ~ to do sthg** essere disposto(-a) a fare qc.

preposition [,prepə'zɪʃn] *n* preposizione *f*.

prep school [prep-] = **preparatory school**.

prescribe [prɪ'skraɪb] *vt* prescrivere.

prescription [prɪ'skrɪpʃn] *n* (*paper*) ricetta *f*; (*medicine*) medicine *fpl*.

presence ['prezns] *n* presenza *f*; **in sb's ~** in presenza di qn.

present [*adj* & *n* 'preznt, *vb* prɪ'zent] ♦ *adj* (*in attendance*) presente; (*current*) attuale ♦ *n* (*gift*) regalo *m* ♦ *vt* presentare; (*offer*) offrire; **the ~ (tense)** il (tempo) presente; **at ~** al momento, attualmente; **the ~** il presente; **to ~ sb to sb** presentare qn a qn.

presentable [prɪ'zentəbl] *adj* presentabile.

presentation [,prezn'teɪʃn] *n* (*way*

of presenting) presentazione f; (ceremony) consegna f (ufficiale).

presenter [prɪˈzentər] n (of TV, radio programme) presentatore m (-trice f).

presently [ˈprezntlɪ] adv (soon) fra poco, a momenti; (now) attualmente.

preservation [ˌprezəˈveɪʃn] n tutela f, protezione f.

preservative [prɪˈzɜːvətɪv] n conservante m.

preserve [prɪˈzɜːv] ♦ n (jam) marmellata f ♦ vt (conserve) mantenere; (keep) preservare, proteggere; (food) conservare.

president [ˈprezɪdənt] n presidente mf.

press [pres] ♦ vt (push) premere, pigiare; (iron) stirare ♦ n: the ~ la stampa; to ~ sb to do sthg insistere perché qn faccia qc.

press conference n conferenza f stampa.

press-stud n bottone m a pressione, automatico m.

press-ups npl flessioni fpl (sulle braccia).

pressure [ˈpreʃər] n pressione f.

pressure cooker n pentola f a pressione.

prestigious [preˈstɪdʒəs] adj prestigioso(-a).

presumably [prɪˈzjuːməblɪ] adv presumibilmente.

presume [prɪˈzjuːm] vt (assume) presumere, supporre.

pretend [prɪˈtend] vt: to ~ to do sthg far finta di fare qc.

pretentious [prɪˈtenʃəs] adj pretenzioso(-a).

pretty [ˈprɪtɪ] ♦ adj grazioso(-a), carino(-a) ♦ adv (inf) (quite) piuttosto, abbastanza; (very) assai.

prevent [prɪˈvent] vt evitare; to ~ sb/sthg from doing sthg impedire a qn/qc di fare qc.

prevention [prɪˈvenʃn] n prevenzione f.

preview [ˈpriːvjuː] n anteprima f.

previous [ˈpriːvjəs] adj precedente.

previously [ˈpriːvjəslɪ] adv (formerly) precedentemente, in precedenza; (earlier, before) prima.

price [praɪs] ♦ n prezzo m ♦ vt fissare il prezzo di.

priceless [ˈpraɪslɪs] adj inestimabile, senza prezzo.

price list n listino m prezzi.

pricey [ˈpraɪsɪ] adj (inf) costoso(-a).

prick [prɪk] vt pungere.

prickly [ˈprɪklɪ] adj (plant, bush) spinoso(-a).

prickly heat n sudamina f.

pride [praɪd] ♦ n (satisfaction, self-respect) orgoglio m; (arrogance) superbia f ♦ vt: to ~ o.s. on sthg vantarsi di qc.

priest [priːst] n prete m, sacerdote m.

primarily [ˈpraɪmərɪlɪ] adv principalmente.

primary school [ˈpraɪmərɪ-] n scuola f elementare.

prime [praɪm] adj (chief) fondamentale; (beef, cut) di prima qualità.

prime minister n primo ministro m.

primitive [ˈprɪmɪtɪv] adj primitivo(-a).

primrose [ˈprɪmrəʊz] n primula f.

prince [prɪns] n principe m.

Prince of Wales n Principe m di Galles.

princess [prɪnˈses] n principessa f.

principal [ˈprɪnsəpl] ♦ adj principale ♦ n (of school) direttore m (-trice f); (of university) rettore m (-trice f).

principle [ˈprɪnsəpl] n principio m; in ~ in linea di principio.

print [prɪnt] ♦ n (words) caratteri mpl; (photo, of painting) stampa f; (mark) impronta f ♦ vt (book, newspaper, photo) stampare; (publish) pubblicare; (*write*) scrivere a stampatello; **out of ~** esaurito.

▶ **print out** *vt sep* stampare.

printed matter ['prɪntɪd-] *n* stampe *fpl*.

printer ['prɪntər] *n* (*machine*) stampante *f*; (*person*) tipografo *m* (-a *f*).

printout ['prɪntaʊt] *n* stampato *m*.

prior ['praɪər] *adj* (*previous*) precedente; **~ to** (*fml*) precedente.

priority [praɪˈɒrɪtɪ] *n* (*important thing*) elemento *m* prioritario; **to have ~ over** avere la priorità rispetto a.

prison ['prɪzn] *n* prigione *f*.

prisoner ['prɪznər] *n* prigioniero *m* (-a *f*).

prisoner of war *n* prigioniero *m* (-a *f*) di guerra.

prison officer *n* guardia *f* carceraria.

privacy ['prɪvəsɪ, Am 'praɪvəsɪ] *n* privacy *f*.

private ['praɪvɪt] ◆ *adj* privato(-a); (*confidential*) confidenziale; (*place*) appartato(-a); (*bathroom*) in camera ◆ *n* (MIL) soldato *m* semplice; **in ~** in privato.

private health care *n* assistenza *f* medica privata.

private property *n* proprietà *f* privata.

private school *n* scuola *f* privata.

privilege ['prɪvɪlɪdʒ] *n* privilegio *m*; **it's a ~!** è un onore!

prize [praɪz] *n* premio *m*.

prize-giving [-ˌgɪvɪŋ] *n* premiazione *f*.

pro [prəʊ] (*pl* **-s**) *n* (*inf: professional*) professionista *mf*.

▶ **pros** *npl*: **the ~s and cons** i pro e i contro.

probability [ˌprɒbəˈbɪlətɪ] *n* probabilità *f*.

probable ['prɒbəbl] *adj* probabile.

probably ['prɒbəblɪ] *adv* probabilmente.

probation officer [prəˈbeɪʃn-] *n*

persona incaricata di seguire i criminali in libertà vigilata.

problem ['prɒbləm] *n* problema *m*; **no ~!** (*inf*) non c'è problema!

procedure [prəˈsiːdʒər] *n* procedura *f*.

proceed [prəˈsiːd] *vi* (*fml*) procedere; **'~ with caution'** 'procedere con cautela'.

proceeds ['prəʊsiːdz] *npl* ricavato *m*.

process ['prəʊses] *n* processo *m*; **to be in the ~ of doing sthg** star facendo qc.

processed cheese ['prəʊsest-] *n* formaggio *m* fuso.

procession [prəˈseʃn] *n* processione *f*.

prod [prɒd] *vt* (*poke*) pungolare.

produce [prəˈdjuːs] ◆ *vt* produrre; (*cause*) creare ◆ *n* prodotti *mpl* agricoli.

producer [prəˈdjuːsər] *n* (*of film, manufacturer*) produttore *m* (-trice *f*); (TEATRO) regista *mf*.

product ['prɒdʌkt] *n* prodotto *m*.

production [prəˈdʌkʃn] *n* produzione *f*.

productivity [ˌprɒdʌkˈtɪvətɪ] *n* produttività *f*.

profession [prəˈfeʃn] *n* professione *f*.

professional [prəˈfeʃənl] ◆ *adj* (*relating to work*) professionale; (*not amateur*) professionista ◆ *n* professionista *mf*.

professor [prəˈfesər] *n* professore *m* (-essa *f*).

profile ['prəʊfaɪl] *n* profilo *m*.

profit ['prɒfɪt] ◆ *n* profitto *m* ◆ *vi*: **to ~ (from)** trarre profitto (da).

profitable ['prɒfɪtəbl] *adj* (*financially*) rimunerativo(-a); (*useful*) vantaggioso(-a).

profiteroles [prəˈfɪtərəʊlz] *npl* profiterole *m inv*.

profound [prəˈfaʊnd] *adj* profondo(-a).

program ['prəʊgræm] ◆ *n* (COMPUT) programma *m*; (Am) = **pro-**

gramme ♦ *vt* (COMPUT) programmare.

programme ['prəʊgræm] *n* (Br) programma *m*.

progress [*n* 'prəʊgres, *vb* prə'gres] ♦ *n* (*improvement*) progresso *m*; (*forward movement*) moto *m* ♦ *vi* (*work, talks, student*) progredire; (*day, meeting*) andare avanti; **to make ~** (*improve*) fare progressi; (*in journey*) avanzare; **in ~** in corso.

progressive [prə'gresɪv] *adj* (*forward-looking*) progressista.

prohibit [prə'hɪbɪt] *vt* proibire; '**smoking strictly ~ed**' 'è severamente vietato fumare'.

project ['prɒdʒekt] *n* progetto *m*; (*at school*) ricerca *f*.

projector [prə'dʒektər] *n* proiettore *m*.

prolong [prə'lɒŋ] *vt* prolungare.

prom [prɒm] *n* (Am: *dance*) ballo *m* (*per studenti*).

promenade [ˌprɒmə'nɑːd] *n* (Br: *by the sea*) lungomare *m inv*.

prominent ['prɒmɪnənt] *adj* (*person*) importante; (*noticeable*) evidente.

promise ['prɒmɪs] ♦ *n* promessa *f* ♦ *vt & vi* promettere; **to show ~** promettere (bene); **I ~!** te lo prometto; **I ~ (that) I'll come** prometto che verrò; **to ~ sb sthg** promettere qc a qn; **to ~ to do sthg** promettere di fare qc.

promising ['prɒmɪsɪŋ] *adj* promettente.

promote [prə'məʊt] *vt* (*in job*) promuovere.

promotion [prə'məʊʃn] *n* promozione *f*.

prompt [prɒmpt] ♦ *adj* (*quick*) pronto(-a) ♦ *adv*: **at six o'clock ~** alle sei in punto.

prone [prəʊn] *adj*: **to be ~ to sthg** essere incline a qc; **to be ~ to do sthg** essere incline a fare qc.

prong [prɒŋ] *n* (*of fork*) dente *m*.

pronoun ['prəʊnaʊn] *n* pronome *m*.

pronounce [prə'naʊns] *vt* (*word*) pronunciare.

pronunciation [prəˌnʌnsɪ'eɪʃn] *n* pronuncia *f*.

proof [pruːf] *n* (*evidence*) prova *f*; **to be 12% ~** (*alcohol*) avere 12 gradi.

prop [prɒp]: **prop up** *vt sep* (*support*) sostenere.

propeller [prə'pelər] *n* elica *f*.

proper ['prɒpər] *adj* (*suitable*) adatto(-a); (*correct*) giusto(-a); (*socially acceptable*) decoroso(-a).

properly ['prɒpəlɪ] *adv* (*suitably*) adeguatamente; (*correctly*) correttamente.

property ['prɒpətɪ] *n* proprietà *f inv*.

proportion [prə'pɔːʃn] *n* proporzione *f*; (*in art*) proporzioni *fpl*.

proposal [prə'pəʊzl] *n* (*suggestion*) proposta *f*.

propose [prə'pəʊz] ♦ *vt* (*suggest*) proporre ♦ *vi*: **to ~ (to sb)** fare una proposta di matrimonio (a qn).

proposition [ˌprɒpə'zɪʃn] *n* (*offer*) proposta *f*.

proprietor [prə'praɪətər] *n* (*fml*) proprietario *m* (-a *f*).

prose [prəʊz] *n* (*not poetry*) prosa *f*; (SCH) traduzione *f* (*dalla madrelingua*).

prosecution [ˌprɒsɪ'kjuːʃn] *n* (JUR: *charge*) azione *f* giudiziaria.

prospect ['prɒspekt] *n* (*possibility*) prospettiva *f*; **I don't relish the ~** non mi attira la prospettiva.

▶ **prospects** *npl* (*for the future*) prospettive *fpl*.

prospectus [prə'spektəs] (*pl* **-es**) *n* prospetto *m*.

prosperous ['prɒspərəs] *adj* prospero(-a).

prostitute ['prɒstɪtjuːt] *n* prostituta *f*.

protect [prə'tekt] *vt* proteggere; **to ~ sb/sthg from** proteggere qn/qc da; **to ~ sb/sthg against** proteggere qn/qc da.

protection [prə'tekʃn] *n* protezione *f*.

protection factor n fattore m di protezione.

protective [prə'tektɪv] adj (person) protettivo(-a); (clothes) di protezione.

protein ['prəuti:n] n proteina f.

protest [n 'prəutest, vb prə'test] ◆ n protesta f ◆ vt (Am: protest against) protestare contro ◆ vi: **to ~ (against)** protestare (contro).

Protestant ['prɒtɪstənt] n protestante mf.

protester [prə'testər] n dimostrante mf.

protractor [prə'træktər] n goniometro m.

protrude [prə'tru:d] vi sporgere.

proud [praud] adj (pleased) orgoglioso(-a); (pej: arrogant) superbo(-a); **to be ~ of** essere orgoglioso di.

prove [pru:v] (pp **-d** OR **proven** [pru:vn]) vt (show to be true) dimostrare; (turn out to be) dimostrarsi.

proverb ['prɒvɜːb] n proverbio m.

provide [prə'vaɪd] vt fornire; **to ~ sb with sthg** fornire qc a qn.

▶ **provide for** vt fus (person) provvedere a.

provided (that) [prə'vaɪdɪd-] conj purché.

providing (that) [prə'vaɪdɪŋ-] = **provided (that)**.

province ['prɒvɪns] n regione f.

provisional [prə'vɪʒənl] adj provvisorio(-a).

provisions [prə'vɪʒnz] npl provviste fpl.

provocative [prə'vɒkətɪv] adj provocatorio(-a).

provoke [prə'vəuk] vt provocare.

prowl [praul] vi muoversi furtivamente.

prune [pru:n] ◆ n prugna f secca ◆ vt (tree, bush) potare.

PS (abbr of postscript) P.S.

psychiatrist [saɪ'kaɪətrɪst] n psichiatra mf.

psychic ['saɪkɪk] adj dotato(-a) di poteri paranormali.

psychological [saɪkə'lɒdʒɪkl] adj psicologico(-a).

psychologist [saɪ'kɒlədʒɪst] n psicologo m (-a f).

psychology [saɪ'kɒlədʒɪ] n psicologia f.

psychotherapist [saɪkəʊ'θerəpɪst] n psicoterapeuta mf.

pt (abbr of pint) pt.

PTO (abbr of please turn over) v.r.

pub [pʌb] n pub m inv.

puberty ['pju:bətɪ] n pubertà f.

public ['pʌblɪk] ◆ adj pubblico(-a) ◆ n: **the ~** il pubblico; **in ~** in pubblico.

publican ['pʌblɪkən] n (Br) gestore m (-trice f) di un pub.

publication [pʌblɪ'keɪʃn] n pubblicazione f.

public bar n (Br) sala di un pub, in cui le bevande costano meno.

public convenience n (Br) gabinetti mpl pubblici.

public footpath n (Br) sentiero m.

public holiday n giorno m festivo.

public house n (Br: fml) pub m inv.

publicity [pʌb'lɪsɪtɪ] n pubblicità f.

public relations npl pubbliche relazioni fpl.

public school n (in UK) scuola f privata; (in US) scuola statale.

public telephone n telefono m pubblico.

public transport n trasporti mpl pubblici.

publish ['pʌblɪʃ] vt pubblicare.

publisher ['pʌblɪʃər] n (person) editore m (-trice f); (company) casa f editrice.

publishing ['pʌblɪʃɪŋ] n (industry) editoria f.

pub lunch n pranzo semplice e a basso costo servito in un pub.

pudding ['pudɪŋ] n (sweet dish)

budino m; (Br: course) dessert m inv.
puddle ['pʌdl] n pozzanghera f.
puff [pʌf] ♦ vi (breathe heavily) ansare ♦ n (of air, smoke) sbuffo m; **to ~ at** tirare una boccata di.
puff pastry n pasta f sfoglia.
pull [pʊl] ♦ vt tirare; (trigger) premere ♦ vi tirare ♦ n: **to give sthg a ~** dare una tirata a qc; **to ~ a face** fare una smorfia; **to ~ a muscle** farsi uno strappo muscolare; **'pull'** (on door) 'tirare'.
▶ **pull apart** vt sep (machine, book) fare a pezzi.
▶ **pull down** vt sep (lower) abbassare; (demolish) demolire.
▶ **pull in** vi (train) arrivare; (car) accostare.
▶ **pull out** ♦ vt sep (tooth, cork, plug) estrarre ♦ vi (train) partire; (car) entrare in corsia; (withdraw) ritirarsi.
▶ **pull over** vi (car) accostare.
▶ **pull up** ♦ vt sep (socks, trousers, sleeve) tirare su ♦ vi (stop) fermarsi.
pulley ['pʊlɪ] (pl **pulleys**) n carrucola f.
pull-out n (Am: beside road) piazzola f (di sosta).
pullover ['pʊl,əʊvəʳ] n pullover m inv.
pulpit ['pʊlpɪt] n pulpito m.
pulse [pʌls] n (MED) polso m.
pump [pʌmp] n pompa f.
▶ **pumps** npl (sports shoes) scarpe fpl da ginnastica.
▶ **pump up** vt sep gonfiare.
pumpkin ['pʌmpkɪn] n zucca f.
pun [pʌn] n gioco m di parole.
punch [pʌntʃ] ♦ n (blow) pugno m; (drink) punch m inv ♦ vt (hit) sferrare un pugno a; (ticket) forare.
Punch and Judy show [-'dʒuːdɪ-] n spettacolo di burattini.
punctual ['pʌŋktʃʊəl] adj puntuale.
punctuation [,pʌŋktʃʊ'eɪʃn] n punteggiatura f.
puncture ['pʌŋktʃəʳ] ♦ vt forare ♦ n: **to get a ~** forare (una gomma).

punish ['pʌnɪʃ] vt: **to ~ sb (for sthg)** punire qn (per qc).
punishment ['pʌnɪʃmənt] n punizione f.
punk [pʌŋk] n (person) punk mf inv; (music) musica f punk.
punnet ['pʌnɪt] n (Br) cestino m.
pupil ['pjuːpl] n (student) alunno m (-a f); (of eye) pupilla f.
puppet ['pʌpɪt] n burattino m.
puppy ['pʌpɪ] n cucciolo m.
purchase ['pɜːtʃəs] ♦ vt (fml) acquistare ♦ n (fml) acquisto m.
pure [pjʊəʳ] adj puro(-a).
puree ['pjʊəreɪ] n purè m inv.
purely ['pjʊəlɪ] adv (only) soltanto.
purity ['pjʊərətɪ] n purezza f.
purple ['pɜːpl] adj viola (inv).
purpose ['pɜːpəs] n scopo m; **on ~** apposta.
purr [pɜːʳ] vi (cat) fare le fusa.
purse [pɜːs] n (Br: for money) portamonete m inv; (Am: handbag) borsa f.
pursue [pə'sjuː] vt (follow) inseguire; (study) continuare; (matter, inquiry) approfondire.
pus [pʌs] n pus m.
push [pʊʃ] ♦ vt spingere; (button, doorbell) premere; (product) pubblicizzare ♦ vi spingere ♦ n: **to give sb/sthg a ~** dare una spinta a qn/qc; **to ~ sb into doing sthg** spingere qn a fare qc; **'push'** (on door) 'spingere'.
▶ **push in** vi (in queue) passare avanti.
▶ **push off** vi (inf: go away) andarsene.
push-button telephone n telefono m a tastiera.
pushchair ['pʊʃtʃeəʳ] n (Br) passeggino m.
pushed [pʊʃt] adj (inf): **to be ~ (for time)** essere a corto di tempo.
push-ups npl flessioni fpl (sulle braccia).
put [pʊt] (pt & pp **put**) vt mettere; (responsibility) dare; (pressure) eserci-

tare; (*express*) esprimere; (*a question*) porre; (*estimate*) stimare; **to ~ a child to bed** mettere a letto un bambino; **to ~ money into sthg** investire soldi in qc.

▶ **put aside** *vt sep* (*money*) mettere da parte.

▶ **put away** *vt sep* (*tidy up*) mettere via.

▶ **put back** *vt sep* (*replace*) mettere a posto; (*postpone*) posporre; (*clock, watch*) mettere indietro.

▶ **put down** *vt sep* (*on floor, table*) posare; (*passenger*) far scendere; (Br: *animal*) abbattere; (*deposit*) dare in acconto.

▶ **put forward** *vt sep* (*clock, watch*) mettere avanti; (*suggest*) suggerire.

▶ **put in** *vt sep* (*insert*) inserire; (*install*) installare.

▶ **put off** *vt sep* (*postpone*) rimandare; (*distract*) distrarre; (*repel*) disgustare; (*passenger*) far scendere.

▶ **put on** *vt sep* (*clothes, glasses, make-up*) mettersi; (*weight*) mettere su; (*television, light, radio*) accendere; (CD, *tape, record*) mettere; (*play, show*) mettere in scena.

▶ **put out** *vt sep* (*cigarette, fire, light*) spegnere; (*publish*) pubblicare; (*hand, arm, leg*) stendere; (*inconvenience*) disturbare; **to ~ one's back out** farsi male alla schiena.

▶ **put together** *vt sep* (*assemble*) montare; (*combine*) mettere insieme.

▶ **put up** ◆ *vt sep* (*tent, statue, building*) erigere; (*umbrella*) aprire; (*a notice, sign*) mettere; (*price, rate*) aumentare; (*provide with accommodation*) ospitare ◆ *vi* (Br: *in hotel*) alloggiare.

▶ **put up with** *vt fus* sopportare.

putter ['pʌtər] *n* (*club*) putter *m inv*.

putting green ['pʌtɪŋ-] *n* campo *m* da minigolf.

putty ['pʌtɪ] *n* stucco *m*.

puzzle ['pʌzl] ◆ *n* (*game*) rompicapo *m*; (*jigsaw*) puzzle *m inv*; (*mystery*) enigma *m* ◆ *vt* confondere.

puzzling ['pʌzlɪŋ] *adj* sconcertante.

pyjamas [pə'dʒɑːməz] *npl* (Br) pigiama *m*.

pylon ['paɪlən] *n* traliccio *m*.

pyramid ['pɪrəmɪd] *n* piramide *f*.

Pyrenees [ˌpɪrə'niːz] *npl*: **the ~** i Pirenei.

Pyrex® ['paɪreks] *n* pyrex® *m*.

Q

quail [kweɪl] *n* quaglia *f*.

quail's eggs *npl* uova *fpl* di quaglia.

quaint [kweɪnt] *adj* pittoresco(-a).

qualification [ˌkwɒlɪfɪ'keɪʃn] *n* (*diploma*) qualifica *f*; (*ability*) qualità *f inv*.

qualified ['kwɒlɪfaɪd] *adj* (*having qualifications*) qualificato(-a).

qualify ['kwɒlɪfaɪ] *vi* (*for competition*) qualificarsi; (*pass exam*) abilitarsi.

quality ['kwɒlətɪ] ◆ *n* qualità *f inv* ◆ *adj* di qualità.

quarantine ['kwɒrəntiːn] *n* quarantena *f*.

quarrel ['kwɒrəl] ◆ *n* lite *f* ◆ *vi* litigare.

quarry ['kwɒrɪ] *n* (*for stone, sand*) cava *f*.

quart [kwɔːt] *n* (*in UK*) = 1,136 l, ≃ litro *m*; (*in US*) = 0,946 l, ≃ litro.

quarter ['kwɔːtər] *n* (*fraction*) quarto *m*; (Am: *coin*) quarto di dollaro; (4 *ounces*) quarto di libbra; (*three months*) trimestre *m*; (*part of town*) quartiere *m*; **(a) ~ to five** (Br) le cinque meno un quarto; **(a) ~ of five** (Am) le cinque meno un quarto; **(a) ~ past five** (Br) le cinque e un quarto; **(a) ~ after five** (Am) le cinque e un quarto; **(a) ~ of an hour** un quarto d'ora.

quarterpounder [ˌkwɔːtəˈpaʊndər] n grosso hamburger m inv.

quartet [kwɔːˈtet] n quartetto m.

quartz [kwɔːts] adj (watch) al quarzo.

quay [kiː] n banchina f.

queasy [ˈkwiːzɪ] adj (inf): **to feel ~** avere la nausea.

queen [kwiːn] n regina f.

queer [kwɪər] adj (strange) strano(-a); (inf: homosexual) omosessuale; **to feel ~** (ill) sentirsi male.

quench [kwentʃ] vt: **to ~ one's thirst** dissetarsi.

query [ˈkwɪərɪ] n quesito m.

question [ˈkwestʃn] ◆ n (query, in exam, on questionnaire) domanda f; (issue) questione f ◆ vt (person) interrogare; **it's out of the ~** è fuori discussione.

question mark n punto m interrogativo.

questionnaire [ˌkwestʃəˈneər] n questionario m.

queue [kjuː] ◆ n (Br) coda f ◆ vi (Br) fare la coda.

▶ **queue up** vi (Br) fare la coda.

quiche [kiːʃ] n torta f salata.

quick [kwɪk] ◆ adj rapido(-a) ◆ adv rapidamente.

quickly [ˈkwɪklɪ] adv rapidamente.

quid [kwɪd] (pl inv) n (Br: inf) sterlina f.

quiet [ˈkwaɪət] ◆ adj silenzioso(-a); (calm, peaceful) tranquillo(-a) ◆ n quiete f; **in a ~ voice** a bassa voce; **keep ~!** silenzio!; **to keep ~** (not say anything) tacere; **to keep ~ about sthg** tenere segreto qc.

quieten [ˈkwaɪətn]: **quieten down** vi calmarsi.

quietly [ˈkwaɪətlɪ] adv silenziosamente; (calmly) tranquillamente.

quilt [kwɪlt] n (duvet) piumino m; (eiderdown) trapunta f.

quince [kwɪns] n mela f cotogna.

quirk [kwɜːk] n stranezza f.

quit [kwɪt] (pt & pp quit) ◆ vi (resign) dimettersi; (give up) smettere ◆ vt (Am: school, job) lasciare; **to ~ doing sthg** smettere di fare qc.

quite [kwaɪt] adv (fairly) abbastanza; (completely) proprio; **not ~** non proprio; **~ a lot (of)** un bel po' (di).

quiz [kwɪz] (pl -zes) n quiz m inv.

quota [ˈkwəʊtə] n quota f.

quotation [kwəʊˈteɪʃn] n (phrase) citazione f; (estimate) preventivo m.

quotation marks npl virgolette fpl.

quote [kwəʊt] ◆ vt (phrase, writer) citare ◆ n (phrase) citazione f; (estimate) preventivo m; **he ~d me a price of £50** mi ha dato un prezzo indicativo di 50 sterline.

R

rabbit [ˈræbɪt] n coniglio m.

rabies [ˈreɪbiːz] n rabbia f.

RAC n ≃ ACI m.

race [reɪs] ◆ n (competition) gara f; (ethnic group) razza f ◆ vi (compete) gareggiare; (go fast) correre; (engine) imballarsi ◆ vt (compete against) gareggiare con.

racecourse [ˈreɪskɔːs] n ippodromo m.

racehorse [ˈreɪshɔːs] n cavallo m da corsa.

racetrack [ˈreɪstræk] n (for horses) ippodromo m.

racial [ˈreɪʃl] adj razziale.

racing [ˈreɪsɪŋ] n: **(horse) ~** corse fpl (di cavalli).

racing car n automobile f da corsa.

racism [ˈreɪsɪzm] n razzismo m.

racist [ˈreɪsɪst] n razzista mf.

rack [ræk] n (for coats) attaccapanni m inv; (for plates) scolapiatti m inv;

(*for bottles*) portabottiglie *m inv*;
(**luggage**) ~ portabagagli *m inv*; ~ **of
lamb** carrè *m inv* di agnello.

racket ['rækɪt] *n* (*for tennis, badminton, squash*) racchetta *f*; (*noise*) baccano *m*.

racquet ['rækɪt] *n* racchetta *f*.

radar ['reɪdɑːr] *n* radar *m inv*.

radiation [ˌreɪdɪ'eɪʃn] *n* (*nuclear*) radiazione *f*.

radiator ['reɪdɪeɪtər] *n* radiatore *m*.

radical ['rædɪkl] *adj* radicale.

radii ['reɪdɪaɪ] *pl* → **radius**.

radio ['reɪdɪəʊ] (*pl* **-s**) ♦ *n* radio *f inv*
♦ *vt* (*person*) chiamare via radio; **on
the** ~ alla radio.

radioactive [ˌreɪdɪəʊ'æktɪv] *adj*
radioattivo(-a).

radio alarm *n* radiosveglia *f*.

radish ['rædɪʃ] *n* ravanello *m*.

radius ['reɪdɪəs] (*pl* **radii**) *n* raggio *m*.

raffle ['ræfl] *n* lotteria *f*.

raft [rɑːft] *n* (*of wood*) zattera *f*; (*inflatable*) materassino *m* (gonfiabile).

rafter ['rɑːftər] *n* travicello *m*.

rag [ræg] *n* (*old cloth*) straccio *m*.

rage [reɪdʒ] *n* rabbia *f*.

raid [reɪd] ♦ *n* raid *m inv*; (*robbery*)
scorreria *f* ♦ *vt* (*subj: police*) fare irruzione in; (*subj: thieves*) fare razzia in.

rail [reɪl] ♦ *n* (*bar*) sbarra *f*; (*for curtain*) asta *f*; (*on stairs*) corrimano *m
inv*; (*for train, tram*) rotaia *f* ♦ *adj* ferroviario(-a); **by** ~ in treno.

railcard ['reɪlkɑːd] *n* (*Br*) (*for young
people*) tessera per riduzione ferroviaria;
(*for pensioners*) = carta d'argento.

railings ['reɪlɪŋz] *npl* ringhiera *f*.

railroad ['reɪlrəʊd] (*Am*) = **railway**.

railway ['reɪlweɪ] *n* ferrovia *f*.

railway line *n* (*route*) linea *f* ferroviaria; (*track*) binario *m*.

railway station *n* stazione *f* ferroviaria.

rain [reɪn] ♦ *n* pioggia *f* ♦ *v impers*
piovere; **it's ~ing** sta piovendo.

rainbow ['reɪnbəʊ] *n* arcobaleno
m.

raincoat ['reɪnkəʊt] *n* impermeabile *m*.

raindrop ['reɪndrɒp] *n* goccia *f* di
pioggia.

rainfall ['reɪnfɔːl] *n* precipitazione
f.

rainy ['reɪnɪ] *adj* piovoso(-a).

raise [reɪz] ♦ *vt* sollevare; (*increase*)
aumentare; (*money*) raccogliere;
(*child, animals*) allevare ♦ *n* (*Am: pay
increase*) aumento *m*.

raisin ['reɪzn] *n* uva *f* passa.

rake [reɪk] *n* (*gardening tool*) rastrello *m*.

rally ['rælɪ] *n* (*public meeting*) comizio *m*; (*motor race*) rally *m inv*; (*in tennis, badminton, squash*) serie di scambi
della palla.

ram [ræm] ♦ *n* montone *m* ♦ *vt*
(*bang into*) speronare.

Ramadan [ˌræmə'dæn] *n* Ramadan
m inv.

ramble ['ræmbl] *n* camminata *f*.

ramp [ræmp] *n* (*slope*) rampa *f*; (*in
roadworks*) dislivello *m*; (*Am: to freeway*) rampa *f* d'accesso; **'ramp'** (*Br:
bump*) 'fondo dissestato'.

ramparts ['ræmpɑːts] *npl* bastioni
mpl.

ran [ræn] *pt* → **run**.

ranch [rɑːntʃ] *n* ranch *m inv*.

ranch dressing *n* (*Am*) maionese
piuttosto liquida e piccante.

rancid ['rænsɪd] *adj* rancido(-a).

random ['rændəm] ♦ *adj* a caso
♦ *n*: **at** ~ a caso.

rang [ræŋ] *pt* → **ring**.

range [reɪndʒ] ♦ *n* (*of radio, telescope*) portata *f*; (*of aircraft*) raggio *m*;
(*for shooting*) campo *m* di tiro; (*of
prices, temperatures, goods*) gamma *f*;
(*of hills, mountains*) catena *f*; (*cooker*)
cucina *f* economica ♦ *vi* (*vary*)
variare.

ranger ['reɪndʒər] *n* (*of park, forest*)
guardia *f* forestale.

rank [ræŋk] ♦ *n* (*in armed forces, police*) rango *m* ♦ *adj* (*smell, taste*) rancido(-a).

ransom ['rænsəm] n riscatto m.

rap [ræp] n (music) rap m inv.

rape [reɪp] ♦ n stupro m ♦ vt stuprare.

rapid ['ræpɪd] adj rapido(-a).
► **rapids** npl rapide fpl.

rapidly ['ræpɪdlɪ] adv rapidamente.

rapist ['reɪpɪst] n stupratore m.

rare [reər] adj (not common) raro(-a); (meat) al sangue.

rarely ['reəlɪ] adv raramente.

rash [ræʃ] ♦ n eruzione f cutanea ♦ adj impulsivo(-a).

rasher ['ræʃər] n fettina f di pancetta.

raspberry ['rɑːzbərɪ] n lampone m.

rat [ræt] n ratto m.

ratatouille [rætə'tuːɪ] n ratatouille f inv.

rate [reɪt] ♦ n (level) tasso m; (charge) tariffa f; (speed) ritmo m ♦ vt (consider) reputare; (deserve) meritare; ~ **of exchange** tasso di cambio; **at any** ~ in ogni caso; **at this** ~ di questo passo.

rather ['rɑːðər] adv (quite) piuttosto; **I'd** ~ **not** preferirei di no; **would you** ~ **...?** preferisci ...?; ~ **than** piuttosto che; ~ **a lot** molto.

ratio ['reɪʃɪəʊ] (pl -s) n rapporto m.

ration ['ræʃn] n (share) razione f.
► **rations** npl (food) razioni fpl.

rational ['ræʃnl] adj razionale.

rattle ['rætl] ♦ n (of baby) sonaglio m ♦ vi sbatacchiare.

rave [reɪv] n (party) rave m inv.

raven ['reɪvn] n corvo m.

ravioli [rævɪ'əʊlɪ] n ravioli mpl.

raw [rɔː] adj (uncooked) crudo(-a); (unprocessed) grezzo(-a).

raw material n materia f prima.

ray [reɪ] n raggio m.

razor ['reɪzər] n rasoio m.

razor blade n lametta f (da barba).

Rd abbr = **Road**.

re [riː] prep in merito a.

RE n (abbr of religious education) religione f (materia).

reach [riːtʃ] ♦ vt raggiungere ♦ n: **out of** ~ lontano; **within** ~ **of the beach** a poca distanza dalla spiaggia.
► **reach out** vi: **to** ~ **out (for)** allungarsi (per raggiungere).

react [rɪ'ækt] vi reagire.

reaction [rɪ'ækʃn] n reazione f.

read [riːd] (pt & pp **read** [red]) ♦ vt leggere; (subj: sign, note) dire; (subj: meter, gauge) segnare ♦ vi leggere; **to** ~ **about sthg** leggere di qc.
► **read out** vt sep leggere ad alta voce.

reader ['riːdər] n (of newspaper, book) lettore m (-trice f).

readily ['redɪlɪ] adv (willingly) prontamente; (easily) facilmente.

reading ['riːdɪŋ] n (of books, papers) lettura f; (of meter, gauge) valore m indicato.

reading matter n qualcosa da leggere.

ready ['redɪ] adj pronto(-a); **to be** ~ **for sthg** (prepared) essere preparato(-a) per qc; **to be** ~ **to do sthg** (willing) essere pronto a fare qc; (likely) essere sul punto di fare qc; **to get** ~ prepararsi; **to get sthg** ~ preparare qc.

ready cash n contante m.

ready-cooked [-kʊkt] adj precotto(-a).

ready-to-wear adj prêt-à-porter inv.

real ['rɪəl] ♦ adj vero(-a); (world) reale ♦ adv (Am) davvero.

real ale n (Br) birra rossa prodotta secondo metodi tradizionali.

real estate n proprietà fpl immobiliari.

realistic [rɪə'lɪstɪk] adj realistico(-a).

reality [rɪ'ælətɪ] n realtà f inv; **in** ~ in realtà.

realize ['rɪəlaɪz] vt rendersi conto

di; (*ambition, goal*) realizzare; **to ~ (that) ...** rendersi conto che OR di ...

really ['rɪəlɪ] *adv* veramente; (*in reality*) realmente; **do you like it? – no, not ~** ti piace? – veramente no; **~?** (*expressing surprise*) davvero?

realtor ['rɪəltər] *n* (Am) agente *mf* immobiliare.

rear [rɪər] ♦ *adj* posteriore ♦ *n* (*back*) retro *m inv*.

rearrange [ˌriːəˈreɪndʒ] *vt* spostare.

rearview mirror ['rɪəvjuː-] *n* specchietto *m* retrovisore.

rear-wheel drive *n* trazione *f* posteriore.

reason ['riːzn] *n* motivo *m*; **for some ~** per qualche motivo.

reasonable ['riːznəbl] *adj* ragionevole; (*quite big*) buono(-a).

reasonably ['riːznəblɪ] *adv* (*quite*) piuttosto.

reasoning ['riːznɪŋ] *n* ragionamento *m*.

reassure [ˌriːəˈʃɔːr] *vt* rassicurare.

reassuring [ˌriːəˈʃɔːrɪŋ] *adj* rassicurante.

rebate ['riːbeɪt] *n* rimborso *m*.

rebel [*n* 'rebl, *vb* rɪ'bel] ♦ *n* ribelle *mf* ♦ *vi* ribellarsi.

rebound [rɪ'baʊnd] *vi* (*ball*) rimbalzare.

rebuild [ˌriː'bɪld] (*pt & pp* **rebuilt** [ˌriː'bɪlt]) *vt* ricostruire.

rebuke [rɪ'bjuːk] *vt* rimproverare.

recall [rɪ'kɔːl] *vt* (*remember*) ricordare.

receipt [rɪ'siːt] *n* (*for goods, money*) ricevuta *f*; **on ~ of** al ricevimento di.

receive [rɪ'siːv] *vt* ricevere.

receiver [rɪ'siːvər] *n* (*of phone*) ricevitore *m*.

recent ['riːsnt] *adj* recente.

recently ['riːsntlɪ] *adv* recentemente.

receptacle [rɪ'septəkl] *n* (*fml*) ricettacolo *m*.

reception [rɪ'sepʃn] *n* (*in hotel*) reception *f inv*; (*at hospital*) accettazione *f*; (*party*) ricevimento *m*; (*welcome*) accoglienza *f*; (*of TV, radio*) ricezione *f*.

reception desk *n* banco *m* della reception.

receptionist [rɪ'sepʃənɪst] *n* receptionist *mf inv*.

recess ['riːses] *n* (*in wall*) nicchia *f*; (Am: SCH) intervallo *m*.

recession [rɪ'seʃn] *n* recessione *f*.

recipe ['resɪpɪ] *n* ricetta *f*.

recite [rɪ'saɪt] *vt* (*poem*) recitare; (*list*) elencare.

reckless ['reklɪs] *adj* avventato(-a).

reckon ['rekn] *vt* (*inf: think*) pensare.
▶ **reckon on** *vt fus* aspettarsi.
▶ **reckon with** *vt fus* (*expect*) aspettarsi.

reclaim [rɪ'kleɪm] *vt* (*baggage*) ritirare.

reclining seat [rɪ'klaɪnɪŋ-] *n* sedile *m* reclinabile.

recognition [ˌrekəg'nɪʃn] *n* riconoscimento *m*.

recognize ['rekəgnaɪz] *vt* riconoscere.

recollect [ˌrekə'lekt] *vt* ricordare.

recommend [ˌrekə'mend] *vt* raccomandare; **to ~ sb to do sthg** consigliare a qn di fare qc.

recommendation [ˌrekəmən'deɪʃn] *n* (*suggestion*) indicazione *f*.

reconsider [ˌriːkən'sɪdər] *vt* riconsiderare.

reconstruct [ˌriːkən'strʌkt] *vt* ricostruire.

record [*n* 'rekɔːd, *vb* rɪ'kɔːd] ♦ *n* (MUS) disco *m*; (*best performance, highest level*) record *m inv*; (*account*) nota *f* ♦ *vt* (*keep account of*) annotare; (*on tape*) registrare.

recorded delivery [rɪ'kɔːdɪd-] *n* (Br) ≃ raccomandata *f*.

recorder [rɪ'kɔːdər] *n* (*tape recorder*) registratore *m*; (*instrument*) flauto *m* diritto.

recording [rɪ'kɔːdɪŋ] *n* registrazione *f*.

record player n giradischi m inv.

record shop n negozio m di dischi.

recover [rɪ'kʌvəʳ] ♦ vt (stolen goods, lost property) recuperare ♦ vi riprendersi.

recovery [rɪ'kʌvərɪ] n (from illness) guarigione f.

recovery vehicle n (Br) carro m attrezzi.

recreation [,rekrɪ'eɪʃn] n divertimento m.

recreation ground n parco m (giochi).

recruit [rɪ'kruːt] ♦ n recluta mf ♦ vt (staff) assumere.

rectangle ['rek,tæŋgl] n rettangolo m.

rectangular [rek'tæŋgjʊləʳ] adj rettangolare.

recycle [,riː'saɪkl] vt riciclare.

red [red] ♦ adj rosso(-a) ♦ n (colour) rosso m; **in the ~** in rosso.

red cabbage n cavolo m rosso.

Red Cross n Croce f Rossa.

redcurrant ['redkʌrənt] n ribes m inv.

redecorate [,riː'dekəreɪt] vt rimbiancare.

redeem [rɪ'diːm] vt (RELIG) redimere; (from pawnbroker) disimpegnare; (debt) estinguere.

redhead ['redhed] n rosso m (-a f).

red-hot adj (metal) rovente.

redial [riː'daɪəl] vi rifare il numero.

redirect [,riːdɪ'rekt] vt (letter) spedire a un nuovo indirizzo; (traffic, plane) dirottare.

rediscover [,riːdɪ'skʌvəʳ] vt riscoprire.

red pepper n peperone m rosso.

reduce [rɪ'djuːs] ♦ vt ridurre ♦ vi (Am: slim) dimagrire.

reduced price [rɪ'djuːst-] n prezzo m ridotto.

reduction [rɪ'dʌkʃn] n riduzione f.

redundancy [rɪ'dʌndənsɪ] n (Br) licenziamento m (per esubero).

redundant [rɪ'dʌndənt] adj (Br): **to be made ~** essere licenziato(-a).

red wine n vino m rosso.

reed [riːd] n canna f.

reef [riːf] n scogliera f.

reek [riːk] vi puzzare.

reel [riːl] n (of thread) rocchetto m; (on fishing rod) mulinello m.

refectory [rɪ'fektərɪ] n refettorio m.

refer [rɪ'fɜːʳ]: **refer to** vt fus (speak about) fare riferimento a; (relate to) riferirsi a; (consult) consultare.

referee [,refə'riː] n (SPORT) arbitro m (-a f).

reference ['refrəns] ♦ n (mention) riferimento m; (letter for job) lettera f di referenze ♦ adj (book, library) di consultazione; **with ~ to** con riferimento a.

referendum [,refə'rendəm] n referendum m inv.

refill [n 'riːfɪl, vb ,riː'fɪl] ♦ n (for pen) ricambio m; (inf: drink) rifornimento m ♦ vt riempire.

refinery [rɪ'faɪnərɪ] n raffineria f.

reflect [rɪ'flekt] vt & vi riflettere.

reflection [rɪ'flekʃn] n (image) riflesso m.

reflector [rɪ'flektəʳ] n catarifrangente m.

reflex ['riːfleks] n riflesso m.

reflexive [rɪ'fleksɪv] adj riflessivo(-a).

reform [rɪ'fɔːm] ♦ n riforma f ♦ vt riformare.

refresh [rɪ'freʃ] vt rinfrescare.

refreshing [rɪ'freʃɪŋ] adj (drink, breeze, sleep) rinfrescante; (change) piacevole.

refreshments [rɪ'freʃmənts] npl rinfreschi mpl.

refrigerator [rɪ'frɪdʒəreɪtəʳ] n frigorifero m.

refugee [,refjʊ'dʒiː] n rifugiato m (-a f).

refund [n 'riːfʌnd, vb rɪ'fʌnd] ♦ n rimborso m ♦ vt rimborsare.

refundable [rɪ'fʌndəbl] adj rimborsabile.

refusal [rɪ'fjuːzl] n rifiuto m.

refuse¹ [rɪ'fjuːz] ♦ vt (not accept) rifiutare; (not allow) negare ♦ vi rifiutare; **to ~ to do sthg** rifiutare di fare qc.

refuse² ['refjuːs] n (fml) rifiuti mpl.

refuse collection ['refjuːs-] n (fml) raccolta f dei rifiuti.

regard [rɪ'gɑːd] ♦ vt (consider) considerare ♦ n: **with ~ to** riguardo a; **as ~s** per quanto riguarda.

▶ **regards** npl (in greetings) saluti mpl; **give them my ~s** li saluti da parte mia.

regarding [rɪ'gɑːdɪŋ] prep riguardo a.

regardless [rɪ'gɑːdlɪs] adv lo stesso; **~ of** senza tener conto di.

reggae ['regeɪ] n reggae m inv.

regiment ['redʒɪmənt] n reggimento m.

region ['riːdʒən] n regione f; **in the ~ of** circa.

regional ['riːdʒənl] adj regionale.

register ['redʒɪstər] ♦ n registro m ♦ vt registrare; (subj: machine, gauge) segnare ♦ vi (put one's name down) iscriversi; (at hotel) firmare il registro.

registered ['redʒɪstəd] adj (letter, parcel) assicurato(-a).

registration [,redʒɪ'streɪʃn] n (for course, at conference) iscrizione f.

registration (number) n (of car) numero m di targa.

registry office ['redʒɪstrɪ-] n anagrafe f.

regret [rɪ'gret] ♦ n (thing regretted) rimpianto m ♦ vt rimpiangere; **I ~ telling her** mi dispiace (di) averglielo detto; **we ~ any inconvenience caused** ci scusiamo per il disagio causato.

regrettable [rɪ'gretəbl] adj spiacevole.

regular ['regjʊlər] ♦ adj regolare; (normal, in size) normale; (customer, reader) abituale ♦ n (customer) cliente mf abituale.

regularly ['regjʊləlɪ] adv regolarmente.

regulate ['regjʊleɪt] vt regolare.

regulation [,regjʊ'leɪʃn] n (rule) norma f.

rehearsal [rɪ'hɜːsl] n prova f.

rehearse [rɪ'hɜːs] vt provare.

reign [reɪn] ♦ n regno m ♦ vi regnare.

reimburse [,riːɪm'bɜːs] vt (fml) rimborsare.

reindeer ['reɪn,dɪər] (pl inv) n renna f.

reinforce [,riːɪn'fɔːs] vt (wall, handle) rinforzare; (argument, opinion) rafforzare.

reinforcements [,riːɪn'fɔːsmənts] npl rinforzi mpl.

reins [reɪnz] npl redini fpl.

reject [rɪ'dʒekt] vt (proposal, request, coin) respingere; (applicant, plan) scartare.

rejection [rɪ'dʒekʃn] n rifiuto m.

rejoin [,riː'dʒɔɪn] vt (motorway) riprendere.

relapse [rɪ'læps] n ricaduta f.

relate [rɪ'leɪt] ♦ vt (connect) collegare ♦ vi: **to ~ to** (be connected with) essere collegato a; (concern) riguardare.

related [rɪ'leɪtɪd] adj (of same family) imparentato(-a); (connected) collegato(-a).

relation [rɪ'leɪʃn] n (member of family) parente mf; (connection) rapporto m; **in ~ to** in rapporto a.

▶ **relations** npl parenti mpl.

relationship [rɪ'leɪʃnʃɪp] n rapporto m, relazione f.

relative ['relətɪv] ♦ adj relativo(-a) ♦ n parente mf.

relatively ['relətɪvlɪ] adv relativamente.

relax [rɪ'læks] vi (person) rilassarsi.

relaxation [,riːlæk'seɪʃn] n (of person) relax m.

relaxed [rɪ'lækst] adj rilassato(-a).

relaxing [rɪ'læksɪŋ] adj rilassante.

relay ['riːleɪ] n (race) staffetta f.

release [rɪ'liːs] ♦ vt (set free) liberare; (let go of) mollare; (record, film) far uscire; (handbrake, catch) togliere ♦ n (record, film) uscita f.

relegate ['relɪgeɪt] vt: **to be ~d** (SPORT) essere retrocesso.

relevant ['reləvənt] adj (connected) pertinente; (important) importante; (appropriate) appropriato(-a).

reliable [rɪ'laɪəbl] adj (person, machine) affidabile.

relic ['relɪk] n (object) reperto m (archeologico).

relief [rɪ'liːf] n (gladness) sollievo m; (aid) aiuto m.

relief road n strada f di smaltimento.

relieve [rɪ'liːv] vt (pain, headache) alleviare.

relieved [rɪ'liːvd] adj sollevato(-a).

religion [rɪ'lɪdʒn] n religione f.

religious [rɪ'lɪdʒəs] adj religioso(-a).

relish ['relɪʃ] n (sauce) salsa f.

reluctant [rɪ'lʌktənt] adj riluttante.

rely [rɪ'laɪ] : **rely on** vt fus (trust) contare su; (depend on) dipendere da.

remain [rɪ'meɪn] vi rimanere.
▶ **remains** npl resti mpl.

remainder [rɪ'meɪndər] n resto m.

remaining [rɪ'meɪnɪŋ] adj restante.

remark [rɪ'mɑːk] ♦ n commento m ♦ vt commentare.

remarkable [rɪ'mɑːkəbl] adj notevole.

remedy ['remədɪ] n rimedio m.

remember [rɪ'membər] ♦ vt (recall) ricordare; (not forget) ricordarsi (di) ♦ vi (recall) ricordarsi; **to ~ doing sthg** ricordarsi di aver fatto qc; **to ~ to do sthg** ricordarsi di fare qc.

remind [rɪ'maɪnd] vt: **to ~ sb of sthg** ricordare qc a qn; **to ~ sb to do sthg** ricordare a qn di fare qc.

reminder [rɪ'maɪndər] n (for bill, library book) sollecito m.

remittance [rɪ'mɪtns] n rimessa f.

remnant ['remnənt] n resto m.

remote [rɪ'məʊt] adj remoto(-a).

remote control n telecomando m.

removal [rɪ'muːvl] n (taking away) rimozione f.

removal van n camion m inv dei traslochi.

remove [rɪ'muːv] vt togliere; (clothes) togliersi.

Renaissance [rə'neɪsəns] n: **the ~** il Rinascimento.

renew [rɪ'njuː] vt rinnovare.

renovate ['renəveɪt] vt rinnovare.

renowned [rɪ'naʊnd] adj rinomato(-a).

rent [rent] ♦ n affitto m ♦ vt (flat) affittare; (car, TV) noleggiare.

rental ['rentl] n (fee) affitto m.

repaid [riː'peɪd] pt & pp → **repay**.

repair [rɪ'peər] ♦ vt riparare ♦ n: **in good ~** in buone condizioni.
▶ **repairs** npl riparazioni fpl.

repair kit n (for bicycle) borsetta f degli attrezzi.

repay [riː'peɪ] (pt & pp **repaid**) vt restituire.

repayment [riː'peɪmənt] n (of loan) rimborso m.

repeat [rɪ'piːt] ♦ vt ripetere; (gossip, news) riferire ♦ n (on TV, radio) replica f.

repetition [ˌrepɪ'tɪʃn] n ripetizione f.

repetitive [rɪ'petɪtɪv] adj ripetitivo(-a).

replace [rɪ'pleɪs] vt rimpiazzare; (put back) mettere a posto.

replacement [rɪ'pleɪsmənt] n (substitute) sostituto m (-a f).

replay ['riːpleɪ] n (rematch) partita f ripetuta; (on TV) replay m inv.

reply [rɪ'plaɪ] ♦ n risposta f ♦ vt & vi rispondere.

report [rɪ'pɔːt] ♦ n (account) relazione f; (in newspaper, on TV, radio) servizio m; (Br: SCH) = scheda f ♦ vt (announce) riportare; (theft, disappearance, person) denunciare ♦ vi (*give account*) riferire; (*for newspaper, TV, radio*) fare un servizio; **to ~ to sb** (*go to*) presentarsi a qn.

report card n = scheda f (*scolastica*).

reporter [rɪ'pɔːtə^r] n reporter mf inv.

represent [ˌreprɪ'zent] vt rappresentare.

representative [ˌreprɪ'zentətɪv] n rappresentante mf.

repress [rɪ'pres] vt (*feelings*) reprimere; (*people*) opprimere.

reprieve [rɪ'priːv] n (*delay*) sospensione f.

reprimand ['reprɪmɑːnd] vt rimproverare.

reproach [rɪ'prəʊtʃ] vt rimproverare.

reproduction [ˌriːprə'dʌkʃn] n riproduzione f.

reptile ['reptaɪl] n rettile m.

republic [rɪ'pʌblɪk] n repubblica f.

Republican [rɪ'pʌblɪkən] ♦ n repubblicano m (-a f) ♦ adj repubblicano(-a).

repulsive [rɪ'pʌlsɪv] adj repellente.

reputable ['repjʊtəbl] adj di buona reputazione.

reputation [ˌrepjʊ'teɪʃn] n reputazione f.

reputedly [rɪ'pjuːtɪdlɪ] adv per quanto si dice.

request [rɪ'kwest] ♦ n richiesta f ♦ vt chiedere; **to ~ sb to do sthg** chiedere a qn di fare qc; **available on ~** (disponibile) su richiesta.

request stop n (Br) fermata f a richiesta.

require [rɪ'kwaɪə^r] vt (*subj: person*) avere bisogno di; (*subj: situation*) richiedere; **passengers are ~d to show their tickets** i passeggeri sono pregati di presentare i biglietti.

requirement [rɪ'kwaɪəmənt] n (*condition*) requisito m; (*need*) esigenza f.

resat [ˌriː'sæt] pt & pp → **resit**.

rescue ['reskjuː] vt salvare.

research [rɪ'sɜːtʃ] n ricerca f.

resemblance [rɪ'zembləns] n somiglianza f.

resemble [rɪ'zembl] vt somigliare a.

resent [rɪ'zent] vt risentirsi per.

reservation [ˌrezə'veɪʃn] n (*booking*) prenotazione f; (*doubt*) riserva f; **to make a ~** fare una prenotazione.

reserve [rɪ'zɜːv] ♦ n riserva f ♦ vt (*book*) prenotare; (*save*) riservare.

reserved [rɪ'zɜːvd] adj riservato(-a).

reservoir ['rezəvwɑː^r] n bacino m (idrico).

reset [ˌriː'set] (pt & pp **reset**) vt (*watch, device*) rimettere; (*meter*) azzerare.

reside [rɪ'zaɪd] vi (fml) risiedere.

residence ['rezɪdəns] n (fml) residenza f; **place of ~** (fml) luogo m di residenza.

residence permit n permesso m di soggiorno.

resident ['rezɪdənt] n (*of country*) residente mf; (*of hotel*) cliente mf; (*of area, house*) abitante mf; **'~s only'** (*for parking*) 'parcheggio riservato ai residenti'.

residential [ˌrezɪ'denʃl] adj (*area*) residenziale.

residue ['rezɪdjuː] n residuo m.

resign [rɪ'zaɪn] ♦ vi dare le dimissioni ♦ vt: **to ~ o.s. to sthg** rassegnarsi a qc.

resignation [ˌrezɪg'neɪʃn] n (*from job*) dimissioni fpl.

resilient [rɪ'zɪlɪənt] adj (*person*) che ha buone capacità di ripresa.

resist [rɪ'zɪst] vt (*fight against*) opporre resistenza a; (*temptation*) resistere a; **I can't ~ chocolate** non so resistere al cioccolato; **to ~ doing sthg** trattenersi dal fare qc.

resistance [rɪ'zɪstəns] n (*refusal to accept*) opposizione f; (*fighting*) resistenza f.

resit [ˌriː'sɪt] (*pt & pp* **resat**) *vt* ridare.

resolution [ˌrezə'luːʃn] *n* (*promise*) proposito *m*.

resolve [rɪ'zɒlv] *vt* (*solve*) risolvere.

resort [rɪ'zɔːt] *n* (*for holidays*) luogo *m* di villeggiatura; **as a last ~** come ultima risorsa.

▶ **resort to** *vt fus* ricorrere a; **to ~ to doing sthg** ricorrere a fare qc.

resource [rɪ'sɔːs] *n* risorsa *f*.

resourceful [rɪ'sɔːsful] *adj* pieno(-a) di risorse.

respect [rɪ'spekt] ♦ *n* rispetto *m* ♦ *vt* rispettare; **in some ~s** sotto certi aspetti; **with ~ to** per quanto riguarda.

respectable [rɪ'spektəbl] *adj* (*person, job etc*) rispettabile; (*acceptable*) decente.

respective [rɪ'spektɪv] *adj* rispettivo(-a).

respond [rɪ'spɒnd] *vi* rispondere.

response [rɪ'spɒns] *n* risposta *f*.

responsibility [rɪˌspɒnsə'bɪlətɪ] *n* responsabilità *f inv*.

responsible [rɪ'spɒnsəbl] *adj* responsabile; **to be ~ (for)** (*accountable*) essere responsabile (di).

rest [rest] ♦ *n* (*relaxation*) riposo *m*; (*support*) sostegno *m* ♦ *vi* (*relax*) riposarsi; **the ~** (*remainder*) il resto; **to have a ~** riposarsi; **to ~ against** appoggiarsi contro.

restaurant ['restərɒnt] *n* ristorante *m*.

restaurant car *n* (Br) carrozza *f* ristorante.

restful ['restful] *adj* riposante.

restless ['restlɪs] *adj* (*bored, impatient*) insofferente; (*fidgety*) agitato(-a).

restore [rɪ'stɔːr] *vt* (*building, painting*) restaurare; (*order*) ripristinare.

restrain [rɪ'streɪn] *vt* controllare.

restrict [rɪ'strɪkt] *vt* limitare.

restricted [rɪ'strɪktɪd] *adj* limitato(-a).

restriction [rɪ'strɪkʃn] *n* restrizione *f*.

rest room *n* (Am) toilette *f inv*.

result [rɪ'zʌlt] ♦ *n* risultato *m* ♦ *vi*: **to ~ in** avere come conseguenza; **as a ~ of** in seguito a.

resume [rɪ'zjuːm] *vi* riprendere.

résumé ['rezjuːmeɪ] *n* (*summary*) riassunto *m*; (Am: *curriculum vitae*) curriculum vitae *m inv*.

retail ['riːteɪl] ♦ *n* vendita *f* al dettaglio ♦ *vt* (*sell*) vendere al dettaglio ♦ *vi*: **to ~ at** essere venduto a.

retailer ['riːteɪlər] *n* dettagliante *mf*.

retail price *n* prezzo *m* al dettaglio.

retain [rɪ'teɪn] *vt* (*fml*) conservare.

retaliate [rɪ'tælɪeɪt] *vi* fare rappresaglie.

retire [rɪ'taɪər] *vi* (*stop working*) andare in pensione.

retired [rɪ'taɪəd] *adj* in pensione.

retirement [rɪ'taɪəmənt] *n* (*leaving job*) pensionamento *m*; (*period after retiring*) periodo *m* dopo il pensionamento.

retreat [rɪ'triːt] ♦ *vi* (*move away*) indietreggiare ♦ *n* (*place*) rifugio *m*.

retrieve [rɪ'triːv] *vt* (*get back*) recuperare.

return [rɪ'tɜːn] ♦ *n* ritorno *m*; (Br: *ticket*) biglietto *m* (di) andata e ritorno ♦ *vt* (*put back*) rimettere; (*give back*) restituire; (*ball, serve*) rimandare ♦ *vi* ritornare; (*happen again*) ricomparire ♦ *adj* (*journey*) di ritorno; **to ~ sthg (to sb)** (*give back*) restituire qc a qn; **by ~ of post** (Br) a giro di posta; **many happy ~s!** cento di questi giorni!; **in ~ (for)** in cambio (di).

return flight *n* (*journey back*) volo *m* di ritorno.

return ticket *n* (Br) biglietto *m* (di) andata e ritorno.

reunion [ˌriː'juːnjən] *n* riunione *f*.

reunite [ˌriːjuː'naɪt] *vt* riunire.

reveal [rɪ'viːl] *vt* rivelare.

revelation [ˌrevəˈleɪʃn] n rivelazione f.

revenge [rɪˈvendʒ] n vendetta f.

reverse [rɪˈvɜːs] ◆ adj inverso(-a) ◆ n (AUT) retromarcia f; (of coin) rovescio m; (of document) retro m ◆ vt (decision) ribaltare ◆ vi (car, driver) fare marcia indietro; **in ~ order** in ordine inverso; **the ~** (opposite) l'inverso; **to ~ the car** fare marcia indietro; **to ~ the charges** (Br) fare una telefonata a carico del destinatario.

reverse-charge call n (Br) telefonata f a carico del destinatario.

review [rɪˈvjuː] ◆ n (of book, record, film) recensione f; (examination) esame m ◆ vt (Am: for exam) ripassare.

revise [rɪˈvaɪz] ◆ vt rivedere ◆ vi (Br: for exam) ripassare.

revision [rɪˈvɪʒn] n (Br: for exam) ripasso m.

revive [rɪˈvaɪv] vt (person) rianimare; (economy) far riprendere; (custom) riportare in uso.

revolt [rɪˈvəʊlt] n rivolta f.

revolting [rɪˈvəʊltɪŋ] adj disgustoso(-a).

revolution [ˌrevəˈluːʃn] n rivoluzione f.

revolutionary [ˌrevəˈluːʃnərɪ] adj rivoluzionario(-a).

revolver [rɪˈvɒlvər] n revolver m inv.

revolving door [rɪˈvɒlvɪŋ-] n porta f girevole.

revue [rɪˈvjuː] n rivista f (spettacolo).

reward [rɪˈwɔːd] ◆ n ricompensa f ◆ vt ricompensare.

rewind [ˌriːˈwaɪnd] (pt & pp rewound [ˌriːˈwaʊnd]) vt riavvolgere.

rhetoric [ˈretərɪk] n retorica f.

rheumatism [ˈruːmətɪzm] n reumatismo m.

rhinoceros [raɪˈnɒsərəs] (pl inv OR -es) n rinoceronte m.

rhubarb [ˈruːbɑːb] n rabarbaro m.

rhyme [raɪm] ◆ n (poem) rima f ◆ vi fare rima.

rhythm [ˈrɪðm] n ritmo m.

rib [rɪb] n (of body) costola f.

ribbon [ˈrɪbən] n nastro m.

rice [raɪs] n riso m.

rice pudding n budino m di riso (dolce).

rich [rɪtʃ] ◆ adj ricco(-a) ◆ npl: **the ~** i ricchi; **to be ~ in sthg** essere ricco di qc.

ricotta cheese [rɪˈkɒtə-] n ricotta f.

rid [rɪd] vt: **to get ~ of** sbarazzarsi di.

ridden [ˈrɪdn] pp → **ride**.

riddle [ˈrɪdl] n indovinello m.

ride [raɪd] (pt **rode**, pp **ridden**) ◆ n (on horse) cavalcata f; (in vehicle, on bike) giro m ◆ vi (on horse) andare a cavallo; (on bike) andare in bicicletta; (in vehicle) viaggiare ◆ vt: **to ~ a horse** andare a cavallo; **to go for a ~** (in car) andare a fare un giro.

rider [ˈraɪdər] n (on horse) persona f a cavallo; (on bike) ciclista mf.

ridge [rɪdʒ] n (of mountain) cresta f; (raised surface) increspatura f.

ridiculous [rɪˈdɪkjʊləs] adj ridicolo(-a).

riding [ˈraɪdɪŋ] n equitazione f.

riding school n scuola f d'equitazione.

rifle [ˈraɪfl] n fucile m.

rig [rɪg] ◆ n (oilrig at sea) piattaforma f; (on land) pozzo m petrolifero ◆ vt (fix) manipolare.

right [raɪt] adj 1. (correct) giusto(-a), corretto(-a); **to be ~** (person) avere ragione; **to be ~ to do sthg** fare bene a fare qc; **have you got the ~ time?** ha l'ora esatta?; **that's ~!** esatto!; **is this the ~ way?** è la strada giusta?

2. (fair) giusto(-a); **that's not ~!** non è giusto!

3. (on the right) destro(-a); **the ~ side of the road** il lato destro della strada.

◆ n 1. (side): **the ~** la destra.

2. (entitlement) diritto m; **to have the**

~ **to do sthg** avere il diritto di fare qc.

♦ adv **1.** (towards the right) a destra; **turn ~ at the post office** all'ufficio postale giri a destra.

2. (correctly) bene, correttamente; **am I pronouncing it ~?** lo pronuncio bene?

3. (for emphasis) proprio; ~ **here** proprio qui; **I'll be ~ back** torno subito; ~ **away** subito.

right angle n angolo m retto.

right-hand adj di destra.

right-hand drive n guida f a destra.

right-handed [-'hændɪd] adj (person) destrimano(-a); (implement) per destrimani.

rightly ['raɪtlɪ] adv (correctly) correttamente; (justly) giustamente.

right of way n (AUT) diritto m di precedenza; (path) sentiero m.

right-wing adj di destra.

rigid ['rɪdʒɪd] adj rigido(-a).

rim [rɪm] n (of cup) bordo m; (of glasses) montatura f; (of wheel) cerchione m.

rind [raɪnd] n (of fruit) buccia f; (of bacon) cotenna f; (of cheese) crosta f.

ring [rɪŋ] (pt **rang**, pp **rung**) ♦ n anello m; (of people) cerchio m; (sound) trillo m; (on cooker) fornello m; (for boxing) ring m inv; (in circus) pista f ♦ vt (Br: on phone) telefonare a; (bell) suonare ♦ vi (bell, telephone) suonare; (Br: make phone call) telefonare; **to give sb a ~** fare una telefonata a qn; **to ~ the bell** suonare il campanello.

▶ **ring back** ♦ vt sep (Br) ritelefonare a ♦ vi (Br) ritelefonare.

▶ **ring off** vi (Br) mettere giù (il telefono).

▶ **ring up** ♦ vt sep (Br) telefonare a ♦ vi (Br) telefonare.

ringing tone ['rɪŋɪŋ-] n segnale m di libero.

ring road n circonvallazione f.

rink [rɪŋk] n pista f di pattinaggio.

rinse [rɪns] vt sciacquare.

▶ **rinse out** vt sep sciacquare.

riot ['raɪət] n sommossa f.

rip [rɪp] ♦ n strappo m ♦ vt strappare ♦ vi strapparsi.

▶ **rip up** vt sep strappare.

ripe [raɪp] adj (fruit, vegetable) maturo(-a); (cheese) stagionato(-a).

ripen ['raɪpn] vi maturare.

rip-off n (inf) fregatura f.

rise [raɪz] (pt **rose**, pp **risen** ['rɪzn]) ♦ vi alzarsi; (sun, moon) sorgere; (increase) aumentare ♦ n aumento m; (slope) salita f.

risk [rɪsk] ♦ n rischio m ♦ vt rischiare; **to take a ~** correre un rischio; **at your own ~** a suo rischio (e pericolo); **to ~ doing sthg** rischiare di fare qc; **to ~ it** arrischiarsi.

risky ['rɪskɪ] adj rischioso(-a).

risotto [rɪ'zɒtəʊ] (pl -s) n risotto m.

ritual ['rɪtʃʊəl] n rituale m.

rival ['raɪvl] ♦ adj rivale ♦ n rivale mf.

river ['rɪvər] n fiume m.

river bank n sponda f del fiume.

riverside ['rɪvəsaɪd] n riva f del fiume.

Riviera [,rɪvɪ'eərə] n: **the (Italian) ~** la riviera (ligure).

roach [rəʊtʃ] n (Am: cockroach) scarafaggio m.

road [rəʊd] n strada f; **by ~** in macchina.

road book n atlante m stradale.

road map n carta f stradale.

road rage n accesso di collera di un automobilista spesso accompagnato da atti di violenza.

road safety n sicurezza f sulle strade.

roadside ['rəʊdsaɪd] n: **the ~** il bordo della strada.

road sign n segnale m stradale.

road tax n tassa f di circolazione.

roadway ['rəʊdweɪ] n carreggiata f.

road works npl lavori mpl stradali.

roam [rəʊm] vi vagabondare.

roar [rɔːr] ♦ n (of crowd) strepito m; (of plane) rombo m ♦ vi (lion) ruggire; (crowd) strepitare; (traffic) rombare.

roast [rəʊst] ♦ n arrosto m ♦ vt arrostire ♦ adj arrosto (inv); ~ **beef** roast beef m; ~ **chicken** pollo m arrosto; ~ **lamb** arrosto di agnello; ~ **pork** arrosto di maiale; ~ **potatoes** patate fpl arrosto.

rob [rɒb] vt (house, bank) svaligiare; (person) derubare; **to ~ sb of sthg** derubare qn di qc.

robber [ˈrɒbər] n rapinatore m (-trice f).

robbery [ˈrɒbərɪ] n rapina f.

robe [rəʊb] n (Am: bathrobe) accappatoio m.

robin [ˈrɒbɪn] n pettirosso m.

robot [ˈrəʊbɒt] n robot m inv.

rock [rɒk] ♦ n roccia f; (Am: stone) pietra f; (music) rock m; (Br: sweet) bastoncini mpl di zucchero ♦ vt (baby) cullare; (boat) far rollare; **on the ~s** (drink) con ghiaccio.

rock climbing n roccia f (sport); **to go ~** fare scalate.

rocket [ˈrɒkɪt] n (missile) missile m; (space rocket, firework) razzo m.

rocking chair [ˈrɒkɪŋ-] n sedia f a dondolo.

rock 'n' roll [ˌrɒkənˈrəʊl] n rock and roll m.

rocky [ˈrɒkɪ] adj roccioso(-a).

rod [rɒd] n (pole) asta f; (for fishing) canna f (da pesca).

rode [rəʊd] pt → ride.

roe [rəʊ] n uova fpl di pesce.

role [rəʊl] n ruolo m.

roll [rəʊl] ♦ n (of bread) panino m; (of film) rullino m; (of paper) rotolo m ♦ vi (ball, rock) rotolare; (ship) rollare ♦ vt (ball, rock) far rotolare; (cigarette) arrotolare; (dice) tirare.
▶ **roll over** vi (person, animal) rivoltarsi; (car) ribaltarsi.
▶ **roll up** vt sep arrotolare.

roller coaster [ˈrəʊləˌkəʊstər] n otto m volante.

roller skate [ˈrəʊlə-] n pattino m a rotelle.

roller-skating [ˈrəʊlə-] n pattinaggio m a rotelle.

rolling pin [ˈrəʊlɪŋ-] n matterello m.

Roman [ˈrəʊmən] ♦ adj romano(-a) ♦ n romano m (-a f).

Roman Catholic n cattolico m romano (cattolica romana f).

romance [rəʊˈmæns] n (love) amore m; (love affair) avventura f; (novel) romanzo m sentimentale.

Romania [ruːˈmeɪnjə] n la Romania.

romantic [rəʊˈmæntɪk] adj romantico(-a); **a ~ novel** un romanzo rosa.

Rome [rəʊm] n Roma f.

romper suit [ˈrɒmpə-] n pagliaccetto m.

roof [ruːf] n tetto m; (of cave) volta f.

roof rack n portapacchi m inv.

room [ruːm, rʊm] n stanza f, camera f; (space) spazio m.

room number n numero m di stanza.

room service n servizio m in camera.

room temperature n temperatura f ambiente.

roomy [ˈruːmɪ] adj spazioso(-a).

root [ruːt] n radice f.

rope [rəʊp] ♦ n corda f ♦ vt legare.

rose [rəʊz] ♦ pt → rise ♦ n (flower) rosa f.

rosé [ˈrəʊzeɪ] n vino m rosé.

rosemary [ˈrəʊzmərɪ] n rosmarino m.

rot [rɒt] vi marcire.

rota [ˈrəʊtə] n turni mpl.

rotate [rəʊˈteɪt] vi ruotare.

rotten [ˈrɒtn] adj (food, wood) marcio(-a); (inf: not good) schifoso(-a); **I feel ~** (ill) mi sento uno schifo.

rouge [ruːʒ] n fard m inv.

rough [rʌf] ♦ adj (surface, skin, cloth) ruvido(-a); (sea) burrascoso(-a); (person) rude; (approximate) approssimativo(-a); (*conditions*) disagiato(-a); (*area, town*) brutto(-a); (*wine*) scadente ◆ *n* (*on golf course*) rough *m*; **to have a ~ time** passarsela male.

roughly ['rʌflɪ] *adv* (*approximately*) approssimativamente; (*push, handle*) sgarbatamente.

roulade [ruːˈlɑːd] *n* rotolo *m*.

roulette [ruːˈlet] *n* roulette *f*.

round [raʊnd] *adj* rotondo(-a); (*cheeks*) paffuto(-a).

◆ *n* **1.** (*of drinks*) giro *m*; **it's my ~** tocca a me offrire (questo giro).

2. (*of sandwiches*) tramezzini *mpl*.

3. (*of toast*) fetta *f*.

4. (*of competition*) turno *m*.

5. (*in golf*) partita *f*; (*in boxing*) round *m inv*, ripresa *f*.

6. (*of policeman, postman, milkman*) giro *m*.

◆ *adv* **1.** (*in a circle*): **to go ~** girare; **to spin ~** ruotare.

2. (*surrounding*): **all (the way) ~** tutt'intorno.

3. (*near*): **~ about** nei dintorni.

4. (*to one's house*): **to ask some friends ~** invitare (a casa propria) degli amici; **we went ~ to her place** siamo andati da lei OR a casa sua.

5. (*continuously*): **all year ~** tutto l'anno.

◆ *prep* **1.** (*surrounding, circling*) intorno a; **to go ~ the corner** girare l'angolo; **we walked ~ the lake** abbiamo fatto il giro del lago a piedi.

2. (*visiting*): **to go ~ a museum** visitare un museo; **to show sb ~ sthg** far fare il giro di qc a qn.

3. (*approximately*) circa, pressappoco; **~ (about) 100** circa 100; **~ ten o'clock** verso le dieci.

4. (*near*): **~ here** da queste parti.

5. (*in phrases*): **it's just ~ the corner** (*nearby*) è qui vicino; **~ the clock** 24 ore su 24.

▶ **round off** *vt sep* (*meal, day*) terminare.

roundabout ['raʊndəbaʊt] *n* (Br) (*in road*) isola *f* rotazionale; (*in playground, at fairground*) giostra *f*.

rounders ['raʊndəz] *n* (Br) gioco a squadre simile al baseball.

round trip *n* viaggio *m* di andata e ritorno.

route [ruːt] ◆ *n* (*way*) strada *f*; (*of bus, train*) percorso *m*; (*of plane*) rotta *f* ◆ *vt* (*change course of*) dirottare.

routine [ruːˈtiːn] ◆ *n* routine *f inv* ◆ *adj* di routine.

row¹ [rəʊ] ◆ *n* (*line*) fila *f* ◆ *vt & vi* remare; **in a ~** (*in succession*) di fila.

row² [raʊ] *n* (*argument*) lite *f*; (*inf: noise*) baccano *m*; **to have a ~** litigare.

rowboat ['rəʊbəʊt] (Am) = **rowing boat**.

rowdy ['raʊdɪ] *adj* turbolento(-a).

rowing ['rəʊɪŋ] *n* canottaggio *m*.

rowing boat *n* (Br) barca *f* a remi.

royal ['rɔɪəl] *adj* reale.

royal family *n* famiglia *f* reale.

royalty ['rɔɪəltɪ] *n* (*royal family*) reali *mpl*.

RRP (*abbr of recommended retail price*) prezzo *m* consigliato.

rub [rʌb] *vt & vi* strofinare; **to ~ sb's back** massaggiare la schiena a qn; **my shoes are rubbing** mi fanno male le scarpe.

▶ **rub in** *vt sep* (*lotion, oil*) far penetrare sfregando.

▶ **rub out** *vt sep* cancellare.

rubber ['rʌbə'] ◆ *adj* di gomma ◆ *n* gomma *f*; (*Am: inf: condom*) preservativo *m*.

rubber band *n* elastico *m*.

rubber gloves *npl* guanti *mpl* di gomma.

rubber ring *n* ciambella *f*.

rubbish ['rʌbɪʃ] *n* spazzatura *f*; (*inf: nonsense*) cretinate *fpl*.

rubbish bin *n* (Br) pattumiera *f*.

rubbish dump *n* (Br) discarica *f*.

rubble ['rʌbl] *n* macerie *fpl*.

ruby ['ruːbɪ] *n* rubino *m*.

rucksack [ˈrʌksæk] n zaino m.

rudder [ˈrʌdəʳ] n timone m.

rude [ruːd] adj (person) sgarbato(-a); (behaviour, joke, picture) volgare.

rug [rʌg] n (for floor) tappeto m; (Br: blanket) coperta f.

rugby [ˈrʌgbɪ] n rugby m.

ruin [ˈruːɪn] vt rovinare.

▶ **ruins** npl rovine fpl.

ruined [ˈruːɪnd] adj (building) in rovina; (clothes, meal, holiday) rovinato(-a).

rule [ruːl] ◆ n (law) regola f ◆ vt (country) governare; **to be the ~** (normal) essere la regola; **against the ~s** contro le regole; **as a ~** di regola.

▶ **rule out** vt sep escludere.

ruler [ˈruːləʳ] n (of country) capo m di Stato; (for measuring) righello m.

rum [rʌm] n rum m inv.

rumor [ˈruːmər] (Am) = **rumour**.

rumour [ˈruːməʳ] n (Br) voce f.

rump steak [ˌrʌmp-] n bistecca f di girello.

run [rʌn] (pt **ran**, pp **run**) vi 1. (on foot) correre; **we had to ~ for the bus** abbiamo dovuto fare una corsa per prendere l'autobus.

2. (train, bus) fare servizio; **the bus ~s every hour** c'è un autobus ogni ora; **the train is running an hour late** il treno ha un'ora di ritardo.

3. (operate) funzionare; **to ~ on sthg** andare a qc.

4. (tears, liquid, river) scorrere; **to ~ through** (river, road) passare per; **the path ~s along the coast** il sentiero corre lungo la costa; **she left the tap running** ha lasciato il rubinetto aperto.

5. (play, event) durare; **'now running at the Palladium'** 'in cartellone al Palladium'.

6. (nose) gocciolare, colare; (eyes) lacrimare.

7. (colour, dye, clothes) stingere.

◆ vt 1. (on foot) correre.

2. (compete in): **to ~ a race** partecipa-

re a una corsa.

3. (business, hotel) dirigere.

4. (bus, train): **we're running a special bus to the airport** mettiamo a disposizione una navetta per andare all'aeroporto.

5. (take in car): **I'll ~ you home** ti do un passaggio (fino) a casa.

6. (water) far correre.

◆ n 1. (on foot) corsa f; **to go for a ~** andare a fare una corsa.

2. (in car) giro m; **to go for a ~** andare a fare un giro (in macchina).

3. (for skiing) pista f.

4. (Am: in tights) smagliatura f.

5. (in phrases): **in the long ~** alla lunga.

▶ **run away** vi scappare.

▶ **run down** ◆ vt sep (run over) investire; (criticize) criticare ◆ vi (battery) scaricarsi.

▶ **run into** vt fus (meet) incontrare per caso; (hit) sbattere contro; (problem, difficulty) incontrare.

▶ **run out** vi (be used up) esaurirsi.

▶ **run out of** vt fus finire, esaurire.

▶ **run over** vt sep (hit) investire.

runaway [ˈrʌnəweɪ] n fuggiasco m (-a f).

rung [rʌŋ] ◆ pp → **ring** ◆ n (of ladder) piolo m.

runner [ˈrʌnəʳ] n (person) corridore m; (for door, drawer) guida f; (for sledge) pattino m.

runner bean n fagiolo m rampicante.

runner-up (pl **runners-up**) n secondo m classificato (seconda classificata f).

running [ˈrʌnɪŋ] ◆ n (SPORT) corsa f; (management) amministrazione f ◆ adj: **three days ~** tre giorni di fila; **to go ~** andare a correre.

running water n acqua f corrente.

runny [ˈrʌnɪ] adj (sauce, egg, omelette) troppo liquido(-a); (nose) che cola; (eye) che lacrima.

runway ['rʌnweɪ] n pista f (di volo).

rural ['rʊərəl] adj rurale.

rush [rʌʃ] ♦ n (hurry) fretta f; (of crowd) grosso afflusso m ♦ vi (move quickly) precipitarsi; (hurry) affrettarsi ♦ vt (work) fare in fretta; (food) mangiare in fretta; (transport quickly) portare d'urgenza; **to be in a ~** avere fretta; **there's no ~!** non c'è fretta!; **don't ~ me!** non mettermi fretta!

rush hour n ora f di punta.

Russia ['rʌʃə] n la Russia.

Russian ['rʌʃn] ♦ adj russo(-a) ♦ n (person) russo m (-a f); (language) russo m.

rust [rʌst] ♦ n ruggine f ♦ vi arrugginirsi.

rustic ['rʌstɪk] adj rustico(-a).

rustle ['rʌsl] vi frusciare.

rustproof ['rʌstpruːf] adj inossidabile.

rusty ['rʌstɪ] adj arrugginito(-a).

RV n (Am: abbr of recreational vehicle) camper m inv.

rye [raɪ] n segale f.

rye bread n pane m di segale.

S

S (abbr of south, small) S.

saccharin ['sækərɪn] n saccarina f.

sachet ['sæʃeɪ] n bustina f.

sack [sæk] ♦ n (bag) sacco m ♦ vt licenziare; **to get the ~** essere licenziato.

sacrifice ['sækrɪfaɪs] n (fig) sacrificio m.

sad [sæd] adj triste.

saddle ['sædl] n sella f.

saddlebag ['sædlbæg] n bisaccia f.

sadly ['sædlɪ] adv (unfortunately) sfortunatamente; (unhappily) tristemente.

sadness ['sædnɪs] n tristezza f.

s.a.e. n (Br: abbr of stamped addressed envelope) busta affrancata e completa d'indirizzo.

safari park [sə'fɑːrɪ-] n zoosafari m inv.

safe [seɪf] ♦ adj sicuro(-a); (out of harm) salvo(-a); (valuables) al sicuro ♦ n cassaforte f; **a ~ place** un posto sicuro; **(have a) ~ journey!** buon viaggio!; **~ and sound** sano(-a) e salvo(-a).

safe-deposit box n cassetta f di sicurezza.

safely ['seɪflɪ] adv (not dangerously) senza pericolo; (arrive) senza problemi; (out of harm) al sicuro.

safety ['seɪftɪ] n sicurezza f.

safety belt n cintura f di sicurezza.

safety pin n spilla f da balia.

sag [sæg] vi avvallarsi.

sage [seɪdʒ] n (herb) salvia f.

Sagittarius [,sædʒɪ'teərɪəs] n Sagittario m.

said [sed] pt & pp → **say**.

sail [seɪl] ♦ n vela f ♦ vi (boat, ship) navigare; (person) andare in barca; (depart) salpare ♦ vt: **to ~ a boat** condurre una barca; **to set ~** salpare.

sailboat ['seɪlbəʊt] (Am) = **sailing boat**.

sailing ['seɪlɪŋ] n (activity) vela f; (departure) partenza f; **to go ~** fare della vela.

sailing boat n barca f a vela.

sailor ['seɪlər] n marinaio m.

saint [seɪnt] n santo m (-a f).

sake [seɪk] n: **for my/their ~** per il mio/il loro bene; **for God's ~!** per l'amor di Dio!

salad ['sæləd] n insalata f.

salad bar n (Br: area in restaurant) tavolo m delle insalate; (restaurant) locale specializzato in insalate.

salad bowl n insalatiera f.

salad cream n (Br) salsa per l'insalata, simile alla maionese.

salad dressing n condimento m per l'insalata.

salami [sə'lɑːmɪ] n salame m.

salary ['sælərɪ] n stipendio m.

sale [seɪl] n (selling) vendita f; (at reduced prices) svendita f; **'for ~'** 'vendesi'; **on ~** in vendita.

▶ **sales** npl (COMM) vendite fpl; **the ~s** (at reduced prices) i saldi.

sales assistant ['seɪlz-] n commesso m (-a f).

salesclerk ['seɪlzklɜːrk] (Am) = **sales assistant**.

salesman ['seɪlzmən] (pl **-men** [-mən]) n (in shop) commesso m; (rep) rappresentante m.

sales rep(resentative) n rappresentante mf.

saleswoman ['seɪlz,wʊmən] (pl **-women** [-,wɪmɪn]) n (in shop) commessa f.

saliva [sə'laɪvə] n saliva f.

salmon ['sæmən] (pl inv) n salmone m.

salon ['sælɒn] n (hairdresser's) salone m.

saloon [sə'luːn] n (Br: car) berlina f; (Am: bar) saloon m inv; **~ (bar)** (Br) sala f interna.

salopettes [,sælə'pets] npl salopette f inv.

salt [sɔːlt, sɒlt] n sale m.

saltcellar ['sɔːlt,selər] n (Br) saliera f.

salted peanuts ['sɔːltɪd-] npl noccioline fpl salate.

salt shaker [-,ʃeɪkər] (Am) = **saltcellar**.

salty ['sɔːltɪ] adj salato(-a).

salute [sə'luːt] ◆ n saluto m ◆ vi fare il saluto.

same [seɪm] ◆ adj stesso(-a) ◆ pron: **the ~** lo stesso (la stessa); **they look the ~** sembrano uguali; **I'll have the ~ as her** prendo lo stesso che ha preso lei; **you've got the ~ book as me** hai lo stesso libro che

ho io; **it's all the ~ to me** per me è tutto uguale.

samosa [sə'məʊsə] n fagottino fritto triangolare, ripieno di carne o verdure, tipico della cucina indiana.

sample ['sɑːmpl] ◆ n campione m; (of blood, urine) prelievo m ◆ vt assaggiare.

sanctions ['sæŋkʃnz] npl sanzioni fpl.

sanctuary ['sæŋktʃʊərɪ] n (for birds, animals) riserva f.

sand [sænd] ◆ n sabbia f ◆ vt (wood) smerigliare.

▶ **sands** npl spiaggia f.

sandal ['sændl] n sandalo m.

sandcastle ['sænd,kɑːsl] n castello m di sabbia.

sandpaper ['sænd,peɪpər] n carta f vetrata.

sandwich ['sænwɪdʒ] n tramezzino m.

sandwich bar n paninoteca f.

sandy ['sændɪ] adj (beach) sabbioso(-a); (hair) color sabbia (inv).

sang [sæŋ] pt → **sing**.

sanitary ['sænɪtrɪ] adj (conditions, measures) sanitario(-a); (hygienic) igienico(-a).

sanitary napkin (Am) = **sanitary towel**.

sanitary towel n (Br) assorbente m igienico.

sank [sæŋk] pt → **sink**.

sapphire ['sæfaɪər] n zaffiro m.

sarcastic [sɑːˈkæstɪk] adj sarcastico(-a).

sardine [sɑːˈdiːn] n sardina f.

Sardinia [sɑːˈdɪnjə] n la Sardegna.

SASE n (Am: abbr of self-addressed stamped envelope) busta affrancata e completa del proprio indirizzo.

sat [sæt] pt & pp → **sit**.

Sat. (abbr of Saturday) sab.

satchel ['sætʃəl] n cartella f.

satellite ['sætəlaɪt] n (in space) satellite m; (at airport) zona f satellite.

satellite dish n antenna f parabolica.

satellite TV *n* televisione *f* via satellite.

satin ['sætɪn] *n* raso *m*.

satisfaction [,sætɪsˈfækʃn] *n* soddisfazione *f*.

satisfactory [,sætɪsˈfæktərɪ] *adj* soddisfacente.

satisfied ['sætɪsfaɪd] *adj* soddisfatto(-a).

satisfy ['sætɪsfaɪ] *vt* soddisfare.

satsuma [,sætˈsuːmə] *n* (Br) mandarino *m*.

saturate ['sætʃəreɪt] *vt* (with liquid) impregnare.

Saturday ['sætədɪ] *n* sabato *m*; **it's ~** è sabato; **~ morning** sabato mattina; **on ~** sabato; **on ~s** il OR di sabato; **last ~** sabato scorso; **this ~** questo sabato; **next ~** sabato prossimo; **~ week, a week on ~** sabato a otto.

sauce [sɔːs] *n* salsa *f*.

saucepan ['sɔːspən] *n* casseruola *f*.

saucer ['sɔːsər] *n* piattino *m*.

Saudi Arabia [,saʊdɪəˈreɪbjə] *n* l'Arabia *f* Saudita.

sauna ['sɔːnə] *n* sauna *f*.

sausage ['sɒsɪdʒ] *n* salsiccia *f*.

sausage roll *n* rustico *m* con salsiccia.

sauté [Br 'səʊteɪ, Am səʊˈteɪ] *adj* saltato(-a).

savage ['sævɪdʒ] *adj* selvaggio(-a).

save [seɪv] ◆ *vt* (rescue, COMPUT) salvare; (money, time) risparmiare; (reserve) tenere; (SPORT) parare ◆ *n* parata *f*.

▶ **save up** *vi* risparmiare; **to ~ up (for sthg)** mettere da parte i soldi (per qc).

saver ['seɪvər] *n* (Br: ticket) biglietto *m* ridotto.

savings ['seɪvɪŋz] *npl* risparmi *mpl*.

savings and loan association *n* (Am) ≈ istituto *m* di credito fondiario.

savings bank *n* cassa *f* di risparmio.

savory ['seɪvərɪ] (Am) = **savoury**.

savoury ['seɪvərɪ] *adj* (Br: not sweet) salato(-a).

saw [sɔː] (Br pt **-ed**, pp **sawn**, Am pt & pp **-ed**) ◆ *pt* → **see** ◆ *n* (tool) sega *f* ◆ *vt* segare.

sawdust ['sɔːdʌst] *n* segatura *f*.

sawn [sɔːn] *pp* → **saw**.

saxophone ['sæksəfəʊn] *n* sassofono *m*.

say [seɪ] (pt & pp **said**) ◆ *vt* dire; (subj: clock, meter) segnare ◆ *n*: **to have a ~ in sthg** avere voce in capitolo riguardo a qc; **could you ~ that again?** può ripetere, per favore?; **~ we met at nine?** diciamo che ci vediamo alle nove?; **what did you ~?** che cosa hai detto?

saying ['seɪɪŋ] *n* detto *m*.

scab [skæb] *n* (on skin) crosta *f*.

scaffolding ['skæfəldɪŋ] *n* impalcatura *f*.

scald [skɔːld] *vt* scottare.

scale [skeɪl] *n* scala *f*; (of fish, snake) squama *f*; (in kettle) incrostazione *f*.

▶ **scales** *npl* (for weighing) bilancia *f*.

scallion ['skæljən] *n* (Am) cipollina *f*.

scallop ['skɒləp] *n* pettine *m* (mollusco).

scalp [skælp] *n* cuoio *m* capelluto.

scampi ['skæmpɪ] *n* gamberoni *mpl* impanati e fritti.

scan [skæn] ◆ *vt* (consult quickly) scorrere ◆ *n* (MED) esame *m* eseguito con scanner.

scandal ['skændl] *n* scandalo *m*.

Scandinavia [,skændɪˈneɪvjə] *n* la Scandinavia.

scar [skɑːr] *n* cicatrice *f*.

scarce ['skeəs] *adj* scarso(-a).

scarcely ['skeəslɪ] *adv* (hardly) a malapena.

scare [skeər] *vt* spaventare.

scarecrow ['skeəkrəʊ] *n* spaventapasseri *m inv*.

scared ['skeəd] *adj* spaventato(-a).

scarf [skɑːf] (pl **scarves**) *n* (woollen) sciarpa *f*; (for women) foulard *m inv*.

scarlet ['skɑːlət] adj scarlatto(-a).

scarves [skɑːvz] pl → **scarf**.

scary ['skeərɪ] adj (inf) terrificante.

scatter ['skætər] ◆ vt spargere ◆ vi sparpagliarsi.

scene [siːn] n scena f; (view) vista f; **the music ~** il mondo della musica; **to make a ~** fare una scenata.

scenery ['siːnərɪ] n (countryside) paesaggio m; (in theatre) scenario m.

scenic ['siːnɪk] adj pittoresco(-a).

scent [sent] n odore m; (perfume) profumo m.

sceptical ['skeptɪkl] adj (Br) scettico(-a).

schedule [Br 'ʃedjuːl, Am 'skedʒʊl] ◆ n (of work, things to do) tabella f di marcia; (timetable) orario m; (list) tabella ◆ vt programmare; **according to ~** secondo la tabella di marcia; **behind ~** in ritardo sulla tabella di marcia; **on ~** puntualmente.

scheduled flight [Br 'ʃedjuːld-, Am 'skedʒʊld-] n volo m di linea.

scheme [skiːm] n (plan) piano m; (pej: dishonest plan) intrigo m.

scholarship ['skɒləʃɪp] n (award) borsa f di studio.

school [skuːl] ◆ n scuola f; (university department) facoltà f inv; (Am: university) università f inv ◆ adj scolastico(-a); **at ~** a scuola.

schoolbag ['skuːlbæg] n cartella f.

schoolbook ['skuːlbʊk] n libro m di testo.

schoolboy ['skuːlbɔɪ] n scolaro m.

school bus n scuolabus m inv.

schoolchild ['skuːltʃaɪld] (pl -children [-tʃɪldrən]) n scolaro m (-a f).

schoolgirl ['skuːlgɜːl] n scolara f.

schoolmaster ['skuːl,mɑːstər] n (Br) maestro m.

schoolmistress ['skuːl,mɪstrɪs] n (Br) maestra f.

schoolteacher ['skuːl,tiːtʃər] n insegnante mf.

school uniform n divisa f.

science ['saɪəns] n scienza f; (SCH) scienze fpl.

science fiction n fantascienza f.

scientific [,saɪən'tɪfɪk] adj scientifico(-a).

scientist ['saɪəntɪst] n scienziato m (-a f).

scissors ['sɪzəz] npl: **(a pair of) ~** (un paio di) forbici fpl.

scold [skəʊld] vt sgridare.

scone [skɒn] n pasta rotonda con uvette che si mangia con burro e marmellata durante il tè.

scoop [skuːp] n (for ice cream, flour) paletta f; (of ice cream) pallina f; (in media) scoop m inv.

scooter ['skuːtər] n (motor vehicle) scooter m inv.

scope [skəʊp] n (possibility) opportunità fpl; (range) portata f.

scorch [skɔːtʃ] vt bruciare.

score [skɔːr] ◆ n (total, final result) punteggio m; (current position) situazione f ◆ vt (SPORT) segnare; (in test) totalizzare ◆ vi (SPORT) segnare.

scorn [skɔːn] n disprezzo m.

Scorpio ['skɔːpɪəʊ] n Scorpione m.

scorpion ['skɔːpjən] n scorpione m.

Scot [skɒt] n scozzese mf.

scotch [skɒtʃ] n scotch m inv (whisky).

Scotch broth n minestra a base di brodo di carne, verdure e orzo perlato.

Scotch tape® n (Am) scotch® m.

Scotland ['skɒtlənd] n la Scozia.

Scotsman ['skɒtsmən] (pl -men [-mən]) n scozzese m.

Scotswoman ['skɒtswʊmən] (pl -women [-wɪmɪn]) n scozzese f.

Scottish ['skɒtɪʃ] adj scozzese.

scout [skaʊt] n (child) scout mf inv.

scowl [skaʊl] vi aggrottare le ciglia.

scrambled eggs [,skræmbld-] npl uova fpl strapazzate.

scrap [skræp] n (of paper, cloth) pezzo m; (old metal) rottami mpl (di metallo).

scrapbook ['skræpbʊk] n album m inv.

scrape [skreɪp] vt (rub) raschiare; (scratch) graffiare.

scrap paper n (Br) carta f da brutta copia.

scratch [skrætʃ] ◆ n graffio m ◆ vt (cut, mark) graffiare; (rub) grattare; **to be up to ~** essere all'altezza della situazione; **to start from ~** cominciare da zero.

scratch card n gratta e vinci m inv.

scratch paper (Am) = **scrap paper**.

scream [skriːm] ◆ n strillo m ◆ vi strillare.

screen [skriːn] ◆ n schermo m; (hall in cinema) sala f; (panel) paravento m ◆ vt (film) proiettare; (TV programme) trasmettere.

screening ['skriːnɪŋ] n (of film) proiezione f.

screen wash n detergente m per il parabrezza.

screw [skruː] ◆ n vite f ◆ vt (fasten) avvitare; (twist) torcere.

screwdriver ['skruːˌdraɪvəʳ] n cacciavite m inv.

scribble ['skrɪbl] vi scarabocchiare.

script [skrɪpt] n (of play, film) copione m.

scrub [skrʌb] vt strofinare.

scruffy ['skrʌfɪ] adj trasandato(-a).

scrumpy ['skrʌmpɪ] n sidro ad alta gradazione alcolica tipico del sudovest dell'Inghilterra.

scuba diving ['skuːbə-] n immersioni fpl (con autorespiratore).

sculptor ['skʌlptəʳ] n scultore m.

sculpture ['skʌlptʃəʳ] n scultura f.

sea [siː] n mare m; **by ~** via mare; **by the ~** sul mare.

seafood ['siːfuːd] n frutti mpl di mare.

seafront ['siːfrʌnt] n lungomare m.

seagull ['siːgʌl] n gabbiano m.

seal [siːl] ◆ n (animal) foca f; (on bottle, container, official mark) sigillo m ◆ vt (envelope, container) sigillare.

seam [siːm] n (in clothes) cucitura f.

search [sɜːtʃ] ◆ n ricerca f ◆ vt perquisire ◆ vi: **to ~ for** cercare.

seashell ['siːʃel] n conchiglia f.

seashore ['siːʃɔːʳ] n riva f del mare.

seasick ['siːsɪk] adj: **to be ~** avere il mal di mare.

seaside ['siːsaɪd] n: **the ~** il mare.

seaside resort n località f inv balneare.

season ['siːzn] ◆ n stagione f ◆ vt condire; **in ~** (fruit, vegetables) di stagione; (holiday) in alta stagione; **out of ~** (fruit, vegetables) fuori stagione; (holiday) in bassa stagione.

seasoning ['siːznɪŋ] n condimento m.

season ticket n abbonamento m.

seat [siːt] ◆ n (place, chair) posto m; (in parliament) seggio m ◆ vt: **the minibus ~s 12** il minibus ha 12 posti a sedere; **'please wait to be ~ed'** cartello che avvisa i clienti di un ristorante di attendere il cameriere per essere condotti al tavolo.

seat belt n cintura f di sicurezza.

seaweed ['siːwiːd] n alghe fpl.

secluded [sɪˈkluːdɪd] adj appartato(-a).

second ['sekənd] ◆ n secondo m ◆ num secondo(-a); **~ gear** seconda f, → **sixth**.

▶ **seconds** npl (goods) merce f di seconda scelta; (inf: of food) bis m inv.

secondary school ['sekəndrɪ-] n ≈ scuola f media inferiore e superiore.

second-class adj (ticket) di seconda classe; (stamp) per posta ordinaria sul territorio nazionale; (inferior) di seconda categoria.

second-hand adj di seconda mano.

Second World War n: **the ~** la seconda guerra mondiale.

secret ['siːkrɪt] ◆ adj segreto(-a) ◆ n segreto m.

secretary [Br 'sekrətrı, Am 'sekrə,terı] n segretario m (-a f).

Secretary of State n (Am: foreign minister) segretario m di Stato, ≃ ministro m degli Esteri; (Br: government minister) ministro.

section ['sekʃn] n sezione f.

sector ['sektər] n settore m.

secure [sı'kjuər] ♦ adj (safe, protected) sicuro(-a); (firmly fixed) saldamente assicurato(-a); (free from worry) tranquillo(-a) ♦ vt (fix) assicurare; (fml: obtain) assicurarsi.

security [sı'kjuərətı] n (protection) sicurezza f; (freedom from worry) tranquillità f.

security guard n guardia f giurata.

sedative ['sedətıv] n sedativo m.

seduce [sı'dju:s] vt sedurre.

see [si:] (pt **saw**, pp **seen**) ♦ vt vedere; (accompany) accompagnare ♦ vi vedere; **I ~** (understand) capisco; **to ~ if** one can do sthg vedere se si può fare qc; **to ~ to** sthg (deal with) occuparsi di qc; (repair) riparare qc; **~ you!** arrivederci!; **~ you later!** a più tardi!; **~ you soon!** a presto!; **~ p 14** vedi pag. 14.

▶ **see off** vt sep (say goodbye to) (andare a) salutare.

seed [si:d] n seme m.

seedy ['si:dı] adj squallido(-a).

seeing (as) ['si:ıŋ-] conj visto che.

seek [si:k] (pt & pp **sought**) vt (fml) (look for) cercare; (request) chiedere.

seem [si:m] ♦ vi sembrare ♦ v impers: **it ~s (that)** ... sembra (che) ...

seen [si:n] pp → **see**.

seesaw ['si:sɔ:] n altalena f.

segment ['segmənt] n (of fruit) spicchio m.

seize [si:z] vt (grab) afferrare; (drugs, arms) sequestrare.

▶ **seize up** vi bloccarsi.

seldom ['seldəm] adv raramente.

select [sı'lekt] ♦ vt scegliere ♦ adj selezionato(-a).

selection [sı'lekʃn] n selezione f.

self-assured [,selfə'ʃuəd] adj sicuro(-a) di sé.

self-catering [,self'keıtərıŋ] adj (flat) con uso di cucina.

self-confident [,self-] adj sicuro(-a) di sé.

self-conscious [,self-] adj timido(-a).

self-contained [,selfkən'teınd] adj (flat) autosufficiente.

self-defence [,self-] n autodifesa f.

self-employed [,self-] adj che lavora in proprio.

selfish ['selfıʃ] adj egoista.

self-raising flour [,self'reızıŋ-] n (Br) farina f con lievito.

self-rising flour [,self'raızıŋ-] (Am) = **self-raising flour**.

self-service [,self-] adj self-service (inv).

sell [sel] (pt & pp **sold**) vt & vi vendere; **to ~ for** essere venduto per; **to ~ sb** sthg vendere qc a qn.

sell-by date n data f di scadenza.

seller ['selər] n (person) venditore m (-trice f).

Sellotape® ['seləteıp] n (Br) nastro m adesivo.

semester [sı'mestər] n semestre m.

semicircle ['semı,sɜ:kl] n semicerchio m.

semicolon [,semı'kəulən] n punto m e virgola.

semidetached [,semıdı'tætʃt] adj bifamiliare.

semifinal [,semı'faınl] n semifinale f.

seminar ['semına:r] n seminario m.

semolina [,semə'li:nə] n semolino m.

send [send] (pt & pp **sent**) vt (letter, parcel, goods) spedire, mandare; (person) mandare; (TV or radio signal) trasmettere; **to ~ sthg to sb** mandare qc a qn.

▶ **send back** *vt sep* (*faulty goods*) rimandare.

▶ **send off** ◆ *vt sep* (*letter, parcel*) spedire; (SPORT) espellere ◆ *vi*: **to ~ off (for sthg)** ordinare (qc) per corrispondenza.

sender ['sendə^r] *n* mittente *mf*.

senile ['si:nail] *adj* senile.

senior ['si:njə^r] ◆ *adj* di grado superiore ◆ *n* (Br: SCH) studente *m* più grande; (Am: SCH) *studente dell'ultimo anno di scuola superiore o università*.

senior citizen *n* anziano *m* (-a *f*).

sensation [sen'seɪʃn] *n* sensazione *f*; **to cause a ~** fare colpo.

sensational [sen'seɪʃənl] *adj* (*very good*) fantastico(-a).

sense [sens] ◆ *n* senso *m*; (*common sense*) buonsenso *m*; (*of word, expression*) senso, significato *m* ◆ *vt* sentire, percepire; **to make ~** avere senso; **~ of direction** senso dell'orientamento; **~ of humour** senso dell'umorismo.

sensible ['sensəbl] *adj* (*person*) ragionevole, assennato(-a); (*clothes, shoes*) pratico(-a).

sensitive ['sensɪtɪv] *adj* sensibile; (*subject, issue*) delicato(-a).

sent [sent] *pt* & *pp* → **send**.

sentence ['sentəns] ◆ *n* (GRAMM) proposizione *f*; (*for crime*) sentenza *f*, condanna *f* ◆ *vt* condannare.

sentimental [,sentɪ'mentl] *adj* (*pej*) sentimentale.

Sep. (*abbr of September*) set.

separate [*adj* 'seprət, *vb* 'sepəreɪt] ◆ *adj* separato(-a); (*different*) diverso(-a) ◆ *vt* separare ◆ *vi* separarsi.

▶ **separates** *npl* (Br) coordinati *mpl*.

separately ['seprətlɪ] *adv* separatamente.

separation [sepə'reɪʃn] *n* separazione *f*.

September [sep'tembə^r] *n* settembre *m*; **at the beginning of ~** all'inizio di settembre; **at the end**

of ~ alla fine di settembre; **during ~** durante il mese di settembre; **every ~** ogni anno a settembre; **in ~** a settembre; **last ~** lo scorso settembre; **next ~** il prossimo settembre; **this ~** a settembre (di quest'anno); **2 ~ 1995** (*in letters etc*) 2 settembre 1995.

septic ['septɪk] *adj* infetto(-a).

septic tank *n* fossa *f* settica.

sequel ['si:kwəl] *n* (*to book, film*) seguito *m*.

sequence ['si:kwəns] *n* (*series*) serie *f inv*; (*order*) ordine *m*.

sequin ['si:kwɪn] *n* lustrino *m*, paillette *f inv*.

sergeant ['sɑ:dʒənt] *n* (*in police force*) ≃ brigadiere *m*; (*in army*) sergente *m*.

serial ['sɪərɪəl] *n* (*on TV, radio*) sceneggiato *m*, serial *m inv*; (*in magazine*) romanzo *m* a puntate.

series ['sɪəri:z] (*pl inv*) *n* serie *f inv*.

serious ['sɪərɪəs] *adj* serio(-a); (*illness, problem*) grave, serio; **are you ~?** dici sul serio?

seriously ['sɪərɪəslɪ] *adv* (*really*) seriamente; (*badly*) gravemente.

sermon ['sɜ:mən] *n* sermone *m*.

servant ['sɜ:vənt] *n* domestico *m* (-a *f*).

serve [sɜ:v] ◆ *vt* servire ◆ *vi* (SPORT) servire; (*work*) prestare servizio ◆ *n* (SPORT) servizio *m*; **to ~ as** (*be used for*) servire da; **the town is ~d by two airports** la città è servita da due aeroporti; '**~s two**' (*on packaging, menu*) 'per due persone'; **it ~s you right!** ben ti sta!

service ['sɜ:vɪs] ◆ *n* servizio *m*; (*at church*) rito *m*; (*of car*) revisione *f* ◆ *vt* (*car*) revisionare; '**out of ~**' 'fuori servizio'; '**~ included**' 'servizio incluso'; '**~ not included**' 'servizio escluso'; **to be of ~ to sb** (*fml*) essere d'aiuto a qn.

▶ **services** *npl* (*on motorway*) stazione *f* di servizio; (*of person*) servigi *mpl*.

service area *n* area *f* di servizio.

service charge n servizio m.

service department n servizio m clienti.

service station n stazione f di servizio.

serviette [,sɜ:vɪ'et] n tovagliolo m.

serving ['sɜ:vɪŋ] n (helping) porzione f.

serving spoon n cucchiaio m da portata.

sesame seeds ['sesəmɪ-] npl semi mpl di sesamo.

session ['seʃn] n seduta f; a drinking ~ una bevuta.

set [set] (pt & pp set) adj 1. (price, time) fisso(-a); a ~ lunch un menu fisso.

2. (text, book) assegnato(-a).

3. (situated) situato(-a).

♦ n 1. (of tools etc) serie f inv; (of cutlery, dishes) servizio m; chess ~ gioco m degli scacchi.

2. (TV): a (TV) ~ un apparecchio televisivo, un televisore.

3. (in tennis) set m inv.

4. (of play) scenario m.

5. (at hairdresser's): a shampoo and ~ uno shampoo e messa in piega.

♦ vt 1. (put) mettere, posare; to ~ the table apparecchiare.

2. (cause to be): to ~ a machine going avviare una macchina; to ~ fire to sthg dar fuoco a qc.

3. (clock, alarm, controls) regolare; ~ the alarm for 7 a.m. metti la sveglia alle 7.

4. (price, time) fissare.

5. (a record) stabilire.

6. (homework, essay) dare.

7. (play, film, story): to be ~ essere ambientato(-a).

♦ vi 1. (sun) tramontare.

2. (glue) fare presa; (jelly) rapprendersi.

▶ **set down** vt sep (Br: passengers) far scendere.

▶ **set off** ♦ vt sep (alarm) far scattare ♦ vi (on journey) mettersi in viaggio.

▶ **set out** ♦ vt sep (arrange) disporre ♦ vi (on journey) mettersi in viaggio.

▶ **set up** vt sep (barrier) erigere; (equipment) installare.

set meal n menu m inv fisso.

set menu n menu m inv fisso.

settee [se'ti:] n divano m.

setting ['setɪŋ] n (on machine) posizione f; (physical surroundings) scenario m; (atmosphere) ambiente m.

settle ['setl] ♦ vt (argument) sistemare, appianare; (bill) saldare, regolare; (stomach, nerves) calmare; (arrange, decide on) stabilire, decidere ♦ vi (start to live) stabilirsi; (come to rest) posarsi; (sediment, dust) depositarsi.

▶ **settle down** vi (calm down) calmarsi; (sit comfortably) accomodarsi.

▶ **settle up** vi (pay bill) saldare il conto.

settlement ['setlmənt] n (agreement) accordo m; (place) insediamento m.

seven ['sevn] num sette, → six.

seventeen [,sevn'ti:n] num diciassette, → six.

seventeenth [,sevn'ti:nθ] num diciassettesimo(-a), → sixth.

seventh ['sevnθ] num settimo(-a), → sixth.

seventieth ['sevntjəθ] num settantesimo(-a), → sixth.

seventy ['sevntɪ] num settanta, → six.

several ['sevrəl] adj & pron parecchi(-chie), diversi(-e).

severe [sɪ'vɪər] adj (conditions, damage, illness) grave; (criticism, person, punishment) severo(-a); (pain) violento(-a), forte.

sew [səʊ] (pp sewn) vt & vi cucire.

sewage ['su:ɪdʒ] n acque fpl di scarico.

sewing ['səʊɪŋ] n (activity) cucito m; (things sewn) lavoro m.

sewing machine n macchina f da cucire.

sewn [səʊn] *pp* → **sew**.

sex [seks] *n* (*gender*) sesso *m*; (*sexual intercourse*) rapporto *m* sessuale; **to have ~ (with)** avere rapporti sessuali (con).

sexist ['seksɪst] *n* sessista *mf*.

sexual ['sekʃʊəl] *adj* sessuale.

sexy ['seksɪ] *adj* sexy (*inv*).

shabby ['ʃæbɪ] *adj* trasandato(-a).

shade [ʃeɪd] ◆ *n* (*shadow*) ombra *f*; (*lampshade*) paralume *m*; (*of colour*) sfumatura *f*, tonalità *f inv* ◆ *vt* (*protect*) fare ombra a.

▶ **shades** *npl* (*inf: sunglasses*) occhiali *mpl* da sole.

shadow ['ʃædəʊ] *n* ombra *f*.

shady ['ʃeɪdɪ] *adj* (*place*) ombroso(-a); (*inf: person, deal*) losco(-a).

shaft [ʃɑːft] *n* (*of machine*) albero *m*; (*of lift*) pozzo *m*.

shake [ʃeɪk] (*pt* **shook**, *pp* **shaken** ['ʃeɪkn]) ◆ *vt* (*tree, rug, person*) scuotere; (*bottle, dice*) agitare; (*shock*) scuotere, turbare ◆ *vi* tremare; **to ~ hands (with sb)** dare OR stringere la mano (a qn); **to ~ one's head** (*saying no*) scuotere la testa.

shall [weak form ʃəl, strong form ʃæl] *aux vb* **1**. (*expressing future*): **I ~ be ready soon** sarò pronto tra poco. **2**. (*in questions*): **~ I buy some wine?** devo comprare del vino?; **~ we listen to the radio?** vogliamo ascoltare la radio?; **where ~ we go?** dove andiamo?, dove vogliamo andare? **3**. (*fml: expressing order*): **payment ~ be made within a week** il pagamento dovrà essere effettuato entro una settimana.

shallot [ʃəˈlɒt] *n* scalogno *m*.

shallow ['ʃæləʊ] *adj* poco profondo(-a).

shallow end *n* (*of swimming pool*) lato *m* meno profondo.

shambles ['ʃæmblz] *n* macello *m*, casino *m*.

shame [ʃeɪm] *n* vergogna *f*; **it's a ~** è un peccato; **what a ~!** che peccato!

shampoo [ʃæmˈpuː] (*pl* **-s**) *n* shampoo *m inv*.

shandy ['ʃændɪ] *n* bevanda a base di birra e limonata.

shape [ʃeɪp] *n* forma *f*; **to be in good/bad ~** essere in/fuori forma.

share [ʃeəʳ] ◆ *n* (*part*) parte *f*; (*in company*) azione *f* ◆ *vt* dividere.

▶ **share out** *vt sep* dividere.

shark [ʃɑːk] *n* squalo *m*, pescecane *m*.

sharp [ʃɑːp] ◆ *adj* (*knife, razor*) affilato(-a); (*pin, nails*) appuntito(-a); (*teeth*) aguzzo(-a); (*clear*) nitido(-a); (*quick, intelligent*) acuto(-a), scaltro (-a); (*rise, change, bend*) brusco(-a); (*painful*) acuto, lancinante; (*food, taste*) aspro(-a) ◆ *adv* (*exactly*) in punto.

sharpen ['ʃɑːpn] *vt* (*pencil*) temperare; (*knife*) affilare.

shatter ['ʃætəʳ] ◆ *vt* (*break*) frantumare ◆ *vi* frantumarsi.

shattered ['ʃætəd] *adj* (Br: inf: tired) distrutto(-a).

shave [ʃeɪv] ◆ *vt* radere, rasare ◆ *vi* radersi, rasarsi ◆ *n*: **to have a ~** farsi la barba.

shaver ['ʃeɪvəʳ] *n* rasoio *m* elettrico.

shaver point *n* presa *f* per rasoio elettrico.

shaving brush ['ʃeɪvɪŋ-] *n* pennello *m* da barba.

shaving cream ['ʃeɪvɪŋ-] *n* crema *f* da barba.

shaving foam ['ʃeɪvɪŋ-] *n* schiuma *f* da barba.

shawl [ʃɔːl] *n* scialle *m*.

she [ʃiː] *pron* lei; **~'s tall** è alta.

sheaf [ʃiːf] (*pl* **sheaves**) *n* (*of paper, notes*) fascio *m*.

shears [ʃɪəz] *npl* cesoie *fpl*.

sheaves [ʃiːvz] *pl* → **sheaf**.

shed [ʃed] (*pt* & *pp* **shed**) ◆ *n* capanno *m* ◆ *vt* (*tears, blood*) versare.

she'd [weak form ʃɪd, strong form ʃiːd] = **she had, she would**.

sheep [ʃiːp] (pl inv) n pecora f.

sheepdog [ʃiːpdɒg] n cane m pastore.

sheepskin [ʃiːpskɪn] adj di pelle di pecora.

sheer [ʃɪər] adj (pure, utter) puro(-a); (cliff) a picco, a strapiombo; (stockings) velato(-a).

sheet [ʃiːt] n (for bed) lenzuolo m; (of paper) foglio m; (of glass, metal) lastra f; (of wood) pannello m.

shelf [ʃelf] (pl shelves) n scaffale m.

shell [ʃel] n (of egg, nut, animal) guscio m; (on beach) conchiglia f; (bomb) granata f.

she'll [ʃiːl] = she will, she shall.

shellfish [ʃelfɪʃ] n (food) frutti mpl di mare.

shell suit n (Br) tuta f in acetato.

shelter [ʃeltər] ♦ n riparo m, rifugio m; (at bus stop) pensilina f ♦ vt (protect) proteggere, riparare ♦ vi proteggersi, ripararsi; **to take ~** mettersi al riparo.

sheltered [ʃeltəd] adj (place) riparato(-a).

shelves [ʃelvz] pl → shelf.

shepherd [ʃepəd] n pastore m.

shepherd's pie [ʃepədz-] n tortino a base di carne macinata coperta da uno spesso strato di purè di patate.

sheriff [ʃerɪf] n (in US) sceriffo m.

sherry [ʃerɪ] n sherry m inv.

she's [ʃiːz] = she is, she has.

shield [ʃiːld] ♦ n scudo m ♦ vt proteggere.

shift [ʃɪft] ♦ n (change) cambiamento m; (period of work) turno m ♦ vt spostare ♦ vi (move) spostarsi; (change) mutare, cambiare.

shin [ʃɪn] n stinco m.

shine [ʃaɪn] (pt & pp shone) ♦ vi brillare, splendere ♦ vt (shoes) lucidare, lustrare; (torch) puntare.

shiny [ʃaɪnɪ] adj scintillante, lucido(-a).

ship [ʃɪp] n nave f; **by ~** (travel) con la nave; (send, transport) via mare.

shipwreck [ʃɪprek] n (accident) naufragio m; (wrecked ship) relitto m.

shirt [ʃɜːt] n camicia f.

shit [ʃɪt] ♦ n (vulg) merda f ♦ excl (vulg) merda!

shiver [ʃɪvər] vi rabbrividire.

shock [ʃɒk] ♦ n (surprise) shock m inv; (force) urto m, scossa f ♦ vt (surprise) colpire, scioccare; (horrify) scioccare; **to be in ~** (MED) essere sotto shock.

shock absorber [-əb,zɔːbər] n ammortizzatore m.

shocking [ʃɒkɪŋ] adj (very bad) terribile.

shoe [ʃuː] n scarpa f.

shoelace [ʃuːleɪs] n stringa f.

shoe polish n lucido m da scarpe.

shoe repairer's [-rɪ,peərəz] n calzolaio m.

shoe shop n negozio m di calzature.

shone [ʃɒn] pt & pp → shine.

shook [ʃʊk] pt → shake.

shoot [ʃuːt] (pt & pp shot) ♦ vt (kill, injure) sparare a; (gun) sparare; (arrow) tirare, scoccare; (film) girare ♦ vi (with gun) sparare; (move quickly) sfrecciare; (SPORT) tirare ♦ n (of plant) germoglio m.

shop [ʃɒp] ♦ n negozio m ♦ vi fare acquisti.

shop assistant n (Br) commesso m (-a f).

shop floor n (place) area di una fabbrica dove lavorano gli operai.

shopkeeper [ʃɒp,kiːpər] n negoziante mf.

shoplifter [ʃɒp,lɪftər] n taccheggiatore m (-trice f).

shopper [ʃɒpər] n cliente mf, acquirente mf.

shopping [ʃɒpɪŋ] n spesa f; **to do the ~** fare la spesa; **to go ~** andare a fare spese.

shopping bag n borsa f per la spesa.

shopping basket n sporta f per la spesa.

shower

shopping centre n centro m commerciale.

shopping list n lista f della spesa.

shopping mall n centro m commerciale.

shop steward n rappresentante mf sindacale.

shop window n vetrina f.

shore [ʃɔːʳ] n riva f; **on ~** a terra.

short [ʃɔːt] ◆ adj (not tall) basso(-a); (letter, speech) corto(-a), breve; (hair, skirt) corto; (in time, distance) breve ◆ adv (cut hair) corti ◆ n (Br: drink) bicchierino m; (film) cortometraggio m; **to be ~ of sthg** (time, money) essere a corto di qc; **to be ~ for sthg** (be abbreviation of) essere l'abbreviazione di qc; **to be ~ of breath** essere senza fiato; **in ~** in breve.

▶ **shorts** npl (short trousers) calzoncini mpl, pantaloncini mpl; (Am: underpants) boxer mpl.

shortage [ʃɔːtɪdʒ] n carenza f.

shortbread [ʃɔːtbred] n biscotto m di pasta frolla.

short-circuit vi fare cortocircuito.

shortcrust pastry [ʃɔːtkrʌst-] n pasta f frolla.

short cut n scorciatoia f.

shorten [ʃɔːtn] vt accorciare.

shorthand [ʃɔːthænd] n stenografia f.

shortly [ʃɔːtlɪ] adv (soon) presto, fra poco; **~ before** poco prima di.

shortsighted [ˌʃɔːtˈsaɪtɪd] adj miope.

short-sleeved [-ˌsliːvd] adj a maniche corte.

short-stay car park n parcheggio m a tempo limitato.

short story n racconto m, novella f.

short wave n onde fpl corte.

shot [ʃɒt] ◆ pt & pp → **shoot** ◆ n (of gun) sparo m; (in football, tennis, golf etc) tiro m; (photo) foto f inv; (in film) ripresa f; (inf: attempt) prova f, tentativo m; (drink) bicchierino m.

shotgun [ʃɒtgʌn] n fucile m da caccia.

should [ʃʊd] aux vb **1.** (expressing desirability): **we ~ leave now** ora dovremmo OR sarebbe meglio andare.

2. (asking for advice): **~ I go too?** devo andarci anch'io?

3. (expressing probability): **she ~ be home soon** dovrebbe arrivare a momenti.

4. (ought to): **they ~ have won the match** avrebbero dovuto vincere la partita.

5. (fml: in conditionals): **~ you need anything, call reception** se dovesse aver bisogno di qualcosa, chiami la reception.

6. (fml: expressing wish): **I ~ like to come with you** mi piacerebbe venire con voi.

shoulder [ʃəʊldəʳ] n spalla f; (Am: of road) corsia f d'emergenza.

shoulder pad n spallina f.

shouldn't [ʃʊdnt] = **should not**.

should've [ʃʊdəv] = **should have**.

shout [ʃaʊt] ◆ n grido m, urlo m ◆ vt & vi gridare, urlare.

▶ **shout out** vt sep gridare.

shove [ʃʌv] vt (push) spingere; (put carelessly) ficcare, cacciare.

shovel [ʃʌvl] n pala f.

show [ʃəʊ] (pp -ed OR shown) ◆ n (at theatre, on TV) spettacolo m; (on radio) programma m; (exhibition) mostra f ◆ vt mostrare; (represent, depict) raffigurare; (accompany) accompagnare; (film, TV programme) dare ◆ vi (be visible) vedersi, essere visibile; (film) essere in programmazione; **to ~ sthg to sb** mostrare qc a qn; **to ~ sb how to do sthg** mostrare a qn come fare qc.

▶ **show off** vi mettersi in mostra.

▶ **show up** vi (come along) farsi vivo, arrivare; (be visible) risaltare.

shower [ʃaʊəʳ] ◆ n (for washing)

doccia *f*; (*of rain*) acquazzone *m* ◆ *vi* fare la doccia; **to have a ~** fare la doccia.

shower gel *n* gel *m inv* per la doccia.

shower unit *n* blocco *m* doccia.

showing ['ʃəuɪŋ] *n* (*of film*) proiezione *f*.

shown [ʃəun] *pp* → show.

showroom ['ʃəurum] *n* salone *m* d'esposizione.

shrank [ʃræŋk] *pt* → shrink.

shrimp [ʃrɪmp] *n* gamberetto *m*.

shrine [ʃraɪn] *n* santuario *m*.

shrink [ʃrɪŋk] (*pt* **shrank**, *pp* **shrunk**) ◆ *n* (*inf: psychoanalyst*) strizzacervelli *mf inv* ◆ *vi* (*clothes*) restringersi; (*number, amount*) ridursi, diminuire.

shrub [ʃrʌb] *n* arbusto *m*.

shrug [ʃrʌg] ◆ *n* scrollata *f* di spalle ◆ *vi* scrollare le spalle.

shrunk [ʃrʌŋk] *pp* → shrink.

shuffle ['ʃʌfl] ◆ *vt* (*cards*) mischiare ◆ *vi* (*walk*) camminare strascicando i piedi.

shut [ʃʌt] (*pt & pp* **shut**) ◆ *adj* chiuso(-a) ◆ *vt* chiudere ◆ *vi* (*door, mouth, eyes*) chiudersi; (*shop, restaurant*) chiudere.

▶ **shut down** *vt sep* chiudere i battenti.

▶ **shut up** *vi* (*inf: stop talking*) tacere, stare zitto; **~ up!** chiudi il becco!

shutter ['ʃʌtər] *n* (*on window*) imposta *f*; (*on camera*) otturatore *m*.

shuttle ['ʃʌtl] *n* (*plane, bus etc*) navetta *f*.

shuttlecock ['ʃʌtlkɒk] *n* volano *m*.

shy [ʃaɪ] *adj* timido(-a).

Sicily ['sɪsɪlɪ] *n* la Sicilia.

sick [sɪk] *adj* (*ill*) malato(-a); **to be ~** (*vomit*) vomitare; **to feel ~** (*nauseous*) avere la nausea; **to be ~ of** (*fed up with*) essere stufo(-a) di.

sick bag *n* sacchetto di emergenza per viaggiatori che soffrono di nausea e vomito.

sickness ['sɪknɪs] *n* (*illness*) malattia *f*.

sick pay *n* indennità *f* per malattia.

side [saɪd] ◆ *n* lato *m*; (*of road, pitch*) margine *m*; (*of river*) sponda *f*; (*team*) squadra *f*; (*in argument*) parte *f*; (Br: TV *channel*) canale *m* ◆ *adj* (*door, pocket*) laterale; **at the ~ of** a fianco di; (*road*) al margine di; (*river*) sulla riva di; **on the other ~** dall'altra parte; **on this ~** da questo lato; **~ by ~** fianco a fianco.

sideboard ['saɪdbɔːd] *n* credenza *f*.

sidecar ['saɪdkɑːr] *n* sidecar *m inv*.

side dish *n* contorno *m*.

side effect *n* effetto *m* collaterale.

sidelight ['saɪdlaɪt] *n* (Br: *of car*) luce *f* di posizione.

side order *n* contorno *m*.

side salad *n* insalata *f* di contorno.

side street *n* traversa *f*.

sidewalk ['saɪdwɔːk] *n* (Am) marciapiede *m*.

sideways ['saɪdweɪz] *adv* (*move*) di lato, di fianco; (*look*) di traverso.

sieve [sɪv] *n* setaccio *m*.

sigh [saɪ] ◆ *n* sospiro *m* ◆ *vi* sospirare.

sight [saɪt] *n* (*eyesight*) vista *f*; (*thing seen*) spettacolo *m*; **at first ~** a prima vista; **to catch ~ of** intravedere; **in ~** in vista; **to lose ~ of** perdere di vista; **to be out of ~** non essere visibile.

▶ **sights** *npl* (*of city, country*) luoghi *mpl* di maggiore interesse.

sightseeing ['saɪt,siːɪŋ] *n*: **to go ~** fare un giro turistico.

sign [saɪn] ◆ *n* (*in shop, station*) insegna *f*; (*next to road*) segnale *m*, cartello *m*; (*symbol, indication*) segno *m*; (*signal*) segnale ◆ *vt & vi* firmare; **there's no ~ of her** non c'è traccia di lei.

▶ **sign in** *vi* (*at hotel, club*) firmare il

registro (all'arrivo).

signal ['sɪgnl] ◆ n segnale m; (Am: traffic lights) semaforo m ◆ vi (in car, on bike) segnalare.

signature ['sɪgnətʃəʳ] n firma f.

significant [sɪg'nɪfɪkənt] adj (large) considerevole; (important) importante.

signpost ['saɪnpəʊst] n cartello m stradale.

sikh [siːk] n Sikh mf inv.

silence ['saɪləns] n silenzio m.

silencer ['saɪlənsəʳ] n (Br: AUT) marmitta f.

silent ['saɪlənt] adj silenzioso(-a).

silk [sɪlk] n seta f.

sill [sɪl] n davanzale m.

silly ['sɪlɪ] adj sciocco(-a), stupido(-a).

silver ['sɪlvəʳ] ◆ n (substance) argento m; (coins) monete fpl d'argento ◆ adj d'argento.

silver foil n stagnola f, carta f argentata.

silver-plated [-'pleɪtɪd] adj placcato(-a) d'argento.

similar ['sɪmɪləʳ] adj simile; to be ~ to essere simile a.

similarity [ˌsɪmɪ'lærətɪ] n (resemblance) somiglianza f; (similar point) affinità f inv.

simmer ['sɪməʳ] vi cuocere a fuoco lento.

simple ['sɪmpl] adj semplice.

simplify ['sɪmplɪfaɪ] vt semplificare.

simply ['sɪmplɪ] adv semplicemente.

simulate ['sɪmjʊleɪt] vt simulare.

simultaneous [Br ˌsɪməl'teɪnjəs, Am ˌsaɪməl'teɪnjəs] adj simultaneo(-a).

simultaneously [Br ˌsɪməl'teɪnjəslɪ, Am ˌsaɪməl'teɪnjəslɪ] adv simultaneamente.

sin [sɪn] ◆ n peccato m ◆ vi peccare.

since [sɪns] ◆ adv da allora ◆ prep da ◆ conj (in time) da quando, da

che; (as) dato che, poiché; **ever ~** prep fin da ◆ conj da che, fin da quando.

sincere [sɪn'sɪəʳ] adj sincero(-a).

sincerely [sɪn'sɪəlɪ] adv sinceramente; **Yours ~** Distinti saluti.

sing [sɪŋ] (pt sang, pp sung) vt & vi cantare.

singer ['sɪŋəʳ] n cantante mf.

single ['sɪŋgl] ◆ adj solo(-a); (man) celibe; (woman) nubile ◆ n (Br: ticket) biglietto m di sola andata; (record) 45 giri m inv; **every ~** ogni.

▶ **singles** ◆ n (SPORT) singolo m ◆ adj (bar, club) per single.

single bed n letto m a una piazza.

single cream n (Br) panna f liquida.

single parent n genitore m single.

single room n camera f singola.

single track road n strada f a una carreggiata.

singular ['sɪŋgjʊləʳ] n singolare m; **in the ~** al singolare.

sinister ['sɪnɪstəʳ] adj sinistro(-a).

sink [sɪŋk] (pt sank, pp sunk) ◆ n lavandino m ◆ vi (in water, mud) affondare; (decrease) calare, diminuire.

sink unit n blocco m lavello.

sinuses ['saɪnəsɪz] npl seni mpl paranasali.

sip [sɪp] ◆ n sorso m ◆ vt sorseggiare.

siphon ['saɪfn] ◆ n sifone m ◆ vt travasare.

sir [sɜːʳ] n signore m; **Dear Sir** Egregio Signore; **Sir Richard Blair** Sir Richard Blair.

siren ['saɪərən] n sirena f.

sirloin steak [ˌsɜːlɔɪn-] n bistecca f di lombo.

sister ['sɪstəʳ] n sorella f; (Br: nurse) caposala f.

sister-in-law n cognata f.

sit [sɪt] (pt & pp sat) ◆ vi sedere; (be situated) trovarsi ◆ vt (to place) far sedere; (Br: *exam*) sostenere, dare; **to be sitting** essere seduto.

▶ **sit down** *vi* sedersi; **to be sitting down** essere seduto.

▶ **sit up** *vi* (*after lying down*) tirarsi su a sedere; (*stay up late*) stare in piedi fino a tardi.

site [saɪt] *n* luogo *m*; (*building site*) cantiere *m*.

sitting room ['sɪtɪŋ-] *n* salotto *m*.

situated ['sɪtjʊeɪtɪd] *adj*: **to be ~** essere situato(-a).

situation [ˌsɪtjʊ'eɪʃn] *n* (*state of affairs*) situazione *f*; (*fml: location*) ubicazione *f*; **'~s vacant'** 'offerte di lavoro'.

six [sɪks] *num adj* & *n* sei; **to be ~ (years old)** avere sei anni; **it's ~ (o'clock)** sono le sei; **a hundred and ~** centosei; **~ Hill Street** Hill Street (numero) sei; **it's minus ~ (degrees)** è meno sei.

sixteen [sɪks'tiːn] *num* sedici, → **six**.

sixteenth [sɪks'tiːnθ] *num* sedicesimo(-a), → **sixth**.

sixth [sɪksθ] ◆ *num adj, adv* & *pron* sesto(-a) ◆ *num n* sesto *m*; **the ~ (of September)** il sei (di settembre).

sixth form *n* (Br) ultimi due anni facoltativi della scuola superiore.

sixth-form college *n* (Br) istituto che prepara agli esami dell'ultimo anno di scuola superiore.

sixtieth ['sɪkstɪəθ] *num* sessantesimo(-a), → **sixth**.

sixty ['sɪkstɪ] *num* sessanta, → **six**.

size [saɪz] *n* dimensioni *fpl*; (*of clothes, hats*) taglia *f*, misura *f*; (*of shoes*) numero *m*; **what ~ do you take?** che taglia porta?; **what ~ is this?** che taglia è?

sizeable ['saɪzəbl] *adj* notevole.

skate [skeɪt] ◆ *n* (*ice skate, roller skate*) pattino *m*; (*fish: pl inv*) razza *f* ◆ *vi* pattinare.

skateboard ['skeɪtbɔːd] *n* skateboard *m inv*.

skater ['skeɪtər] *n* pattinatore *m* (-trice *f*).

skating ['skeɪtɪŋ] *n*: **to go ~** andare a pattinare.

skeleton ['skelɪtn] *n* scheletro *m*.

skeptical ['skeptɪkl] (Am) = **sceptical**.

sketch [sketʃ] ◆ *n* (*drawing*) schizzo *m*; (*humorous*) sketch *m inv*, scenetta *f* ◆ *vt* schizzare.

skewer ['skjʊər] *n* spiedo *m*.

ski [skiː] (*pt* & *pp* **skied**, *cont* **skiing**) ◆ *n* sci *m inv* ◆ *vi* sciare.

ski boots *npl* scarponi *mpl* da sci.

skid [skɪd] ◆ *n* slittamento *m*, sbandamento *m* ◆ *vi* slittare, sbandare.

skier ['skiːər] *n* sciatore *m* (-trice *f*).

skiing ['skiːɪŋ] *n* sci *m*; **to go ~** andare a sciare; **a ~ holiday** una vacanza sulla neve.

skilful ['skɪlful] *adj* (Br) abile.

ski lift *n* sciovia *f*.

skill [skɪl] *n* (*ability*) abilità *f inv*; (*technique*) tecnica *f*.

skilled [skɪld] *adj* (*worker, job*) qualificato(-a); (*driver, chef*) provetto(-a).

skillful ['skɪlful] (Am) = **skilful**.

skimmed milk ['skɪmd-] *n* latte *m* scremato.

skin [skɪn] *n* pelle *f*; (*on fruit, vegetable*) buccia *f*; (*on milk*) pellicola *f*.

skin freshener [-ˌfreʃnər] *n* tonico *m*.

skinny ['skɪnɪ] *adj* magrissimo(-a).

skip [skɪp] ◆ *vi* (*with rope*) saltare la corda; (*jump*) saltellare ◆ *vt* (*omit*) saltare ◆ *n* (*container*) cassonetto *m*.

ski pants *npl* pantaloni *mpl* da sci.

ski pass *n* ski-pass *m inv*.

ski pole *n* racchetta *f* da sci.

skipping rope ['skɪpɪŋ-] *n* corda *f* per saltare.

skirt [skɜːt] *n* gonna *f*.

ski slope *n* pista *f* da sci.

ski tow *n* ski-lift *m inv*.

skittles ['skɪtlz] *n* birilli *mpl*.

skull [skʌl] *n* cranio *m*.

sky [skaɪ] *n* cielo *m*.

skylight ['skaɪlaɪt] n lucernario m.

skyscraper ['skaɪˌskreɪpəʳ] n grattacielo m.

slab [slæb] n (of stone, concrete) lastra f.

slack [slæk] adj (rope) non tirato(-a); (careless) negligente; (not busy) calmo(-a); (period) morto(-a).

slacks [slæks] npl pantaloni mpl.

slam [slæm] vt & vi sbattere.

slander ['slɑːndəʳ] n calunnia f; (in law) diffamazione f.

slang [slæŋ] n slang m, gergo m.

slant [slɑːnt] ◆ n (slope) pendenza f ◆ vi pendere.

slap [slæp] ◆ n (smack) schiaffo m ◆ vt schiaffeggiare.

slash [slæʃ] ◆ vt (cut) tagliare; (face) sfregiare; (fig: prices) ridurre ◆ n (written symbol) barra f.

slate [sleɪt] n (rock) ardesia f; (on roof) tegola f di ardesia.

slaughter ['slɔːtəʳ] vt (people, team) massacrare; (animal) macellare.

slave [sleɪv] n schiavo m (-a f).

sled [sled] = **sledge**.

sledge [sledʒ] n slitta f.

sleep [sliːp] (pt & pp slept) ◆ n sonno m ◆ vi dormire ◆ vt: the house ~s six la casa ha sei posti letto; did you ~ well? hai dormito bene?; I couldn't get to ~ non riuscivo a prender sonno; to go to ~ addormentarsi; to ~ with sb andare a letto con qn.

sleeper ['sliːpəʳ] n (train) treno m con vagoni letto; (sleeping car) vagone m letto; (Br: on railway track) traversina f; (Br: earring) campanella f.

sleeping bag ['sliːpɪŋ-] n sacco m a pelo.

sleeping car ['sliːpɪŋ-] n vagone m letto.

sleeping pill ['sliːpɪŋ-] n sonnifero m.

sleeping policeman ['sliːpɪŋ-] n (Br) piccolo dosso stradale che ha la funzione di rallentare il traffico.

sleepy ['sliːpɪ] adj insonnolito(-a);

I'm ~ ho sonno.

sleet [sliːt] ◆ n nevischio m ◆ v impers: it's ~ing sta nevischiando.

sleeve [sliːv] n (of garment) manica f; (of record) copertina f.

sleeveless ['sliːvlɪs] adj senza maniche.

slept [slept] pt & pp → **sleep**.

slice [slaɪs] ◆ n fetta f ◆ vt affettare, tagliare a fette.

sliced bread [ˌslaɪst-] n pane m a cassetta.

slide [slaɪd] (pt & pp slid [slɪd]) ◆ n (in playground) scivolo m; (of photograph) diapositiva f; (Br: hair slide) fermacapelli m inv ◆ vi (slip) scivolare.

sliding door [ˌslaɪdɪŋ-] n porta f scorrevole.

slight [slaɪt] adj (minor) lieve; the ~est il minimo (la minima); not in the ~est affatto.

slightly ['slaɪtlɪ] adv (a bit) leggermente; I know him ~ lo conosco appena.

slim [slɪm] ◆ adj (person, waist) snello(-a) ◆ vi dimagrire.

slimming ['slɪmɪŋ] n dimagrimento m.

sling [slɪŋ] (pt & pp slung) ◆ vt (inf: throw) buttare ◆ n: to have one's arm in a ~ portare il braccio al collo.

slip [slɪp] ◆ vi scivolare ◆ n (mistake) errore m; (of paper) foglietto m; (petticoat) sottoveste f.

▶ **slip up** vi (make a mistake) fare un errore.

slipper ['slɪpəʳ] n pantofola f.

slippery ['slɪpərɪ] adj scivoloso(-a).

slip road n (Br) raccordo m autostradale.

slit [slɪt] n fessura f.

slob [slɒb] n (inf) sciattone m (-a f).

slogan ['sləʊgən] n slogan m inv.

slope [sləʊp] ◆ n (incline) pendio m; (hill) fianco m; (for skiing) pista f da sci ◆ vi (hill, path) scendere;

(*floor, roof, shelf*) essere inclinato.

sloping ['sləʊpɪŋ] *adj* (*floor, roof, shelf*) inclinato(-a); (*hill*) degradante.

slot [slɒt] *n* (*for coin*) fessura *f*; (*groove*) scanalatura *f*.

slot machine *n* (*vending machine*) distributore *m* automatico; (*for gambling*) slot-machine *f inv*.

Slovakia [slə'vækɪə] *n* la Slovacchia.

slow [sləʊ] ◆ *adj* lento(-a); (*business*) fiacco(-a) ◆ *adv* lentamente; 'slow' (*sign on road*) 'rallentare'; **a ~ train** (*sign on road*) 'rallentare'; **a ~ train** un accelerato; **to be ~** (*clock*) essere indietro.

▶ **slow down** *vt sep & vi* rallentare.

slowly ['sləʊlɪ] *adv* lentamente.

slug [slʌg] *n* (*animal*) lumacone *m*.

slum [slʌm] *n* (*building*) baracca *f*.

▶ **slums** *npl* (*district*) bassifondi *mpl*.

slung [slʌŋ] *pt & pp* → **sling**.

slush [slʌʃ] *n* neve *f* in parte sciolta.

sly [slaɪ] *adj* (*cunning*) astuto(-a); (*deceitful*) scaltro(-a).

smack [smæk] ◆ *n* (*slap*) schiaffo *m* ◆ *vt* schiaffeggiare.

small [smɔːl] *adj* piccolo(-a); (*in height*) basso(-a).

small change *n* spiccioli *mpl*.

smallpox ['smɔːlpɒks] *n* vaiolo *m*.

smart [smɑːt] *adj* (*elegant, posh*) elegante; (*clever*) intelligente.

smart card *n* carta *f* intelligente.

smash [smæʃ] ◆ *n* (SPORT) smash *m inv*, schiacciata *f*; (*inf: car crash*) scontro *m* ◆ *vt* (*plate, window*) frantumare ◆ *vi* (*plate, vase etc*) frantumarsi.

smashing ['smæʃɪŋ] *adj* (Br: inf) fantastico(-a).

smear test ['smɪə-] *n* striscio *m*, pap-test *m inv*.

smell [smel] (*pt & pp* **-ed** OR **smelt**) ◆ *n* odore *m*; (*bad odour*) puzza *f* ◆ *vt* (*sniff at*) annusare; (*detect*) sentire odore di ◆ *vi* avere un odore; (*have*

bad odour) puzzare; **to ~ of sthg** (*pleasant*) profumare di qc; (*unpleasant*) puzzare di qc.

smelly ['smelɪ] *adj* puzzolente.

smelt [smelt] *pt & pp* → **smell**.

smile [smaɪl] ◆ *n* sorriso *m* ◆ *vi* sorridere.

smoke [sməʊk] ◆ *n* fumo *m* ◆ *vt & vi* fumare; **to have a ~** fumare una sigaretta.

smoked [sməʊkt] *adj* affumicato(-a).

smoked salmon *n* salmone *m* affumicato.

smoker ['sməʊkə^r] *n* (*person*) fumatore *m* (-trice *f*).

smoking ['sməʊkɪŋ] *n* fumo *m*; 'no ~' 'vietato fumare'.

smoking area *n* area *f* per fumatori.

smoking compartment *n* scompartimento *m* per fumatori.

smoky ['sməʊkɪ] *adj* (*room*) fumoso(-a).

smooth [smuːð] *adj* (*surface, skin, road*) liscio(-a); (*takeoff, landing*) dolce, morbido(-a); (*flight, journey, life*) tranquillo(-a); (*mixture, liquid*) vellutato(-a), omogeneo(-a); (*wine, beer*) amabile; (*pej: suave*) mellifluo(-a).

▶ **smooth down** *vt sep* lisciare.

smother ['smʌðə^r] *vt* (*cover*) coprire.

smudge [smʌdʒ] *n* sbavatura *f*.

smuggle ['smʌgl] *vt* contrabbandare.

snack [snæk] *n* spuntino *m*, snack *m inv*.

snack bar *n* snack-bar *m inv*, tavola *f* calda.

snail [sneɪl] *n* chiocciola *f*.

snake [sneɪk] *n* (*animal*) serpente *m*.

snap [snæp] ◆ *vt* (*break*) spezzare ◆ *vi* (*break*) spezzarsi ◆ *n* (*inf: photo*) foto *f inv*; (Br: *card game*) rubamazzo *m*.

snare [sneə^r] *n* (*trap*) trappola *f*.

snatch [snætʃ] *vt* strappare.

sneakers ['sni:kəz] *npl* (Am) scarpe *fpl* da ginnastica.

sneeze [sni:z] ◆ *n* starnuto *m* ◆ *vi* starnutire.

sniff [snɪf] ◆ *vi* tirar su col naso ◆ *vt* (*smell*) annusare.

snip [snɪp] *vt* tagliare.

snob [snɒb] *n* snob *mf inv.*

snog [snɒg] *vi* (Br: *inf*) pomiciare.

snooker ['snu:kər] *n* snooker *m* (*specie di biliardo giocato con 22 palle*).

snooze [snu:z] *n* pisolino *m.*

snore [snɔ:ʳ] *vi* russare.

snorkel ['snɔ:kl] *n* respiratore *m* (subacqueo).

snout [snaʊt] *n* muso *m*, grugno *m.*

snow [snəʊ] ◆ *n* neve *f* ◆ *v impers*: **it's ~ing** sta nevicando.

snowball ['snəʊbɔ:l] *n* palla *f* di neve.

snowdrift ['snəʊdrɪft] *n* cumulo *m* di neve.

snowflake ['snəʊfleɪk] *n* fiocco *m* di neve.

snowman ['snəʊmæn] (*pl* **-men** [-men]) *n* pupazzo *m* di neve.

snowplough ['snəʊplaʊ] *n* spazzaneve *m inv.*

snowstorm ['snəʊstɔ:m] *n* bufera *f* di neve.

snug [snʌg] *adj* (*person*) comodo(-a); (*place*) accogliente.

so [səʊ] *adv* 1. (*emphasizing degree*) così, talmente; **it's ~ difficult (that ...)** è così difficile (che ...).

2. (*referring back*): **I don't think ~** credo di no; **I'm afraid ~** temo proprio di sì; **if ~** se è così, in tal caso.

3. (*also*): **~ do I** anch'io.

4. (*in this way*) così, in questo modo.

5. (*expressing agreement*): **~ there is** proprio così, già.

6. (*in phrases*): **or ~** all'incirca; **~ as** per, così da; **~ that** affinché, perché.

◆ *conj* 1. (*therefore*) quindi, perciò; **nobody answered ~ we went away** non rispondeva nessuno perciò ce

ne siamo andati.

2. (*summarizing*) allora; **~ what have you been up to?** allora come vanno le cose?

3. (*in phrases*): **~ what?** (*inf*) e allora?; **~ there!** (*inf*) ecco!

soak [səʊk] ◆ *vt* (*leave in water*) mettere a bagno OR a mollo; (*make very wet*) impregnare, infradiciare ◆ *vi*: **to ~ through sthg** infiltrarsi in qc.

▶ **soak up** *vt sep* assorbire.

soaked [səʊkt] *adj* fradicio(-a).

soaking ['səʊkɪŋ] *adj* fradicio(-a).

soap [səʊp] *n* sapone *m.*

soap opera *n* soap opera *f inv*, telenovela *f.*

soap powder *n* detersivo *m* in polvere.

sob [sɒb] ◆ *n* singhiozzo *m* ◆ *vi* singhiozzare.

sober ['səʊbər] *adj* (*not drunk*) sobrio(-a).

soccer ['sɒkər] *n* calcio *m.*

sociable ['səʊʃəbl] *adj* socievole.

social ['səʊʃl] *adj* (*problem, conditions, class*) sociale.

social club *n* circolo *m* sociale.

socialist ['səʊʃəlɪst] ◆ *adj* socialista ◆ *n* socialista *mf.*

social life *n* vita *f* sociale.

social security *n* previdenza *f* sociale.

social worker *n* assistente *mf* sociale.

society [sə'saɪətɪ] *n* società *f inv*; (*organization, club*) associazione *f*, società.

sociology [ˌsəʊsɪ'ɒlədʒɪ] *n* sociologia *f.*

sock [sɒk] *n* calzino *m.*

socket ['sɒkɪt] *n* (*for plug*) presa *f*; (*for light bulb*) portalampada *m inv.*

sod [sɒd] *n* (Br: *vulg*: *nasty person*) stronzo *m* (-a *f*).

soda ['səʊdə] *n* (*soda water*) seltz *m inv*; (Am: *fizzy drink*) spuma *f.*

soda water *n* acqua *f* di seltz.

sofa ['səʊfə] *n* divano *m*, sofà *m inv.*

sofa bed *n* divano *m* letto.

soft [sɒft] *adj* (*bed, ground, skin*) soffice, morbido(-a); (*breeze, tap, sound*) leggero(-a).

soft cheese *n* formaggio *m* molle.

soft drink *n* analcolico *m*.

software ['sɒftweəʳ] *n* software *m inv*.

soil [sɔil] *n* (*earth*) suolo *m*.

solarium [səˈleərɪəm] *n* solarium *m inv*.

solar panel ['səʊlə-] *n* pannello *m* solare.

sold [səʊld] *pt & pp* → **sell**.

soldier ['səʊldʒəʳ] *n* soldato *m*, militare *m*.

sold out *adj* esaurito(-a).

sole [səʊl] ♦ *adj* (*only*) solo(-a), unico(-a); (*exclusive*) esclusivo(-a) ♦ *n* (*of shoe*) suola *f*; (*of foot*) pianta *f*; (*fish: pl inv*) sogliola *f*.

solemn ['sɒləm] *adj* (*person*) serio(-a); (*occasion*) solenne.

solicitor [səˈlɪsɪtəʳ] *n* (*Br*) = notaio *m*.

solid ['sɒlɪd] *adj* solido(-a); (*not hollow*) pieno(-a); (*gold, silver, oak*) massiccio(-a); (*uninterrupted*) ininterrotto(-a); **three hours ~** tre ore intere.

solo ['səʊləʊ] (*pl* **-s**) *n* assolo *m*; '~ **m/cs'** (*traffic sign*) 'riservato ai motocicli'.

soluble ['sɒljʊbl] *adj* solubile.

solution [səˈluːʃn] *n* soluzione *f*.

solve [sɒlv] *vt* risolvere.

some [sʌm] *adj* **1.** (*certain amount of*): **~ meat** della carne; **~ money** del denaro; **I had ~ difficulty getting here** ho avuto qualche difficoltà ad arrivare qui.
2. (*certain number of*): **~ sweets** delle caramelle; **~ boys** dei ragazzi; **~ people** della gente; **I've known him for ~ years** lo conosco da anni.
3. (*not all*) certi(-e); **~ jobs are better paid than others** certi lavori sono pagati meglio di altri.
4. (*in imprecise statements*): **she married ~ writer (or other)** ha sposato un certo scrittore; **they're staying in ~ posh hotel** stanno in un albergo di lusso.
♦ *pron* **1.** (*certain amount*) un po'; **can I have ~?** me ne dai un po'?; **~ of the money** una parte dei soldi.
2. (*certain number*) alcuni(-e), certi(-e); **can I have ~?** me ne dai qualcuno?; **~ (of them) left early** alcuni (di loro) sono andati via presto.
♦ *adv* (*approximately*) circa; **there were ~ 7,000 people there** c'erano circa 7 000 persone.

somebody ['sʌmbədɪ] = **someone**.

somehow ['sʌmhaʊ] *adv* (*some way or other*) in qualche modo, in un modo o nell'altro; (*for some reason*) per qualche motivo.

someone ['sʌmwʌn] *pron* qualcuno.

someplace ['sʌmpleɪs] (*Am*) = **somewhere**.

somersault ['sʌməsɔːlt] *n* capriola *f*, salto *m* mortale.

something ['sʌmθɪŋ] *pron* qualcosa; **it's really ~** è veramente eccezionale; **or ~** (*inf*) o qualcosa del genere; **~ like** all'incirca, pressappoco.

sometime ['sʌmtaɪm] *adv*: **~ in May** in maggio.

sometimes ['sʌmtaɪmz] *adv* a volte.

somewhere ['sʌmweəʳ] *adv* (*in or to unspecified place*) da qualche parte, in qualche posto; (*approximately*) all'incirca.

son [sʌn] *n* figlio *m*.

song [sɒŋ] *n* canzone *f*.

son-in-law *n* genero *m*.

sonnet ['sɒnɪt] *n* sonetto *m*.

soon [suːn] *adv* presto; **how ~ can you do it?** fra quanto può farlo?; **~ as (non) appena; as ~ as possible** al più presto possibile; **~ after** poco dopo; **~er or later** prima o poi.

soot [sʊt] *n* fuliggine *f*.

soothe [suːð] *vt* calmare; (*pain*) alleviare.

sophisticated [səˈfɪstɪkeɪtɪd] adj (refined, chic) sofisticato(-a), raffinato(-a); (complex) sofisticato, complesso(-a).

sorbet [ˈsɔːbeɪ] n sorbetto m.

sore [sɔːʳ] ♦ adj (painful) dolorante; (Am: inf: angry) incavolato(-a) ♦ n piaga f; **to have a ~ throat** avere mal di gola.

sorry [ˈsɒrɪ] adj: **I'm ~!** scusa!; **I'm ~ I'm late** scusa il ritardo; **~?** (asking for repetition) scusa?; **to feel ~ for sb** dispiacersi per qn; **I'm ~ you can't come** mi dispiace che tu non venga; **I'm ~ about the mess** scusa il disordine.

sort [sɔːt] ♦ n tipo m ♦ vt ordinare; **~ of** (more or less) più o meno; **it's ~ of difficult** è piuttosto difficile.

▶ **sort out** vt sep (classify) ordinare; (resolve) chiarire.

so-so adj & adv (inf) così così.

soufflé [ˈsuːfleɪ] n soufflé m inv.

sought [sɔːt] pt & pp → **seek**.

soul [səʊl] n (spirit) anima f; (soul music) musica f soul.

sound [saʊnd] ♦ n suono m; (noise) rumore m; (volume) volume m ♦ vt (horn, bell) suonare ♦ vi (alarm, bell, voice) suonare; (seem to be) sembrare ♦ adj (building, structure) solido(-a); (heart) sano(-a); (advice, idea) valido(-a); **to ~ like** sembrare; (seem to be) sembrare, avere l'aria di.

soundproof [ˈsaʊndpruːf] adj insonorizzato(-a).

soup [suːp] n zuppa f, minestra f.

soup spoon n cucchiaio m da minestra.

sour [ˈsaʊəʳ] adj (taste) aspro(-a); (milk) acido(-a); **to go ~** inacidire.

source [sɔːs] n (supply, origin) fonte f; (cause) causa f; (of river) sorgente f.

sour cream n panna f acida.

south [saʊθ] ♦ n sud m, meridione m ♦ adj del sud ♦ adv (fly, walk) verso sud; (be situated) a sud; **in the ~ of England** a sud dell'Inghilterra.

South Africa n il Sudafrica.

South America n l'America f del sud, il Sudamerica.

southbound [ˈsaʊθbaʊnd] adj diretto(-a) a sud.

southeast [ˌsaʊθˈiːst] n sud-est m.

southern [ˈsʌðən] adj meridionale, del sud.

South Pole n Polo m Sud.

southwards [ˈsaʊθwədz] adv verso sud.

southwest [ˌsaʊθˈwest] n sudovest m.

souvenir [ˌsuːvəˈnɪəʳ] n souvenir m inv, ricordo m.

Soviet Union [ˌsəʊvɪət-] n: **the ~** l'Unione f Sovietica.

sow¹ [səʊ] (pp **sown** [səʊn]) vt (seeds) seminare.

sow² [saʊ] n (pig) scrofa f.

soya [ˈsɔɪə] n soia f.

soya bean n seme m di soia.

soy sauce [ˌsɔɪ-] n salsa f di soia.

spa [spɑː] n terme fpl.

space [speɪs] ♦ n spazio m; (empty place) posto m; (room) spazio, posto; (period) periodo m ♦ vt distanziare.

spaceship [ˈspeɪsʃɪp] n astronave f.

space shuttle n shuttle m inv.

spacious [ˈspeɪʃəs] adj spazioso(-a).

spade [speɪd] n (tool) vanga f, badile m.

▶ **spades** npl (in cards) picche fpl.

spaghetti [spəˈgetɪ] n spaghetti mpl.

Spain [speɪn] n la Spagna.

span [spæn] ♦ pt → **spin** ♦ n (of time) periodo m, arco m di tempo.

Spaniard [ˈspænjəd] n spagnolo m (-a f).

spaniel [ˈspænjəl] n spaniel m inv.

Spanish [ˈspænɪʃ] adj spagnolo(-a); (language) spagnolo m.

spank [spæŋk] vt sculacciare.

spanner [ˈspænəʳ] n chiave f (arnese).

spare [speəʳ] ♦ adj (kept in reserve) di riserva; (not in use) in più ♦ n (spare part) ricambio m; (spare wheel) ruota f di scorta ♦ vt: **to ~ sb sthg** (money) dare qc a qn; **can you ~ me ten minutes?** hai dieci minuti?; **with ten minutes to ~** con dieci minuti di anticipo.

spare part n pezzo m di ricambio.

spare ribs npl costine fpl di maiale.

spare room n camera f degli ospiti.

spare time n tempo m libero.

spare wheel n ruota f di scorta.

spark [spɑːk] n scintilla f.

sparkling ['spɑːklɪŋ-] adj (mineral water, soft drink) frizzante.

sparkling wine n vino m frizzante.

spark plug n candela f.

sparrow ['spærəʊ] n passero m.

spat [spæt] pt & pp → **spit**.

speak [spiːk] (pt **spoke**, pp **spoken**) ♦ vt (language) parlare; (say) dire ♦ vi parlare; **who's ~ing?** (on phone) chi parla?; **can I ~ to Sarah? – ~ing!** (on phone) posso parlare con Sarah? – sono io!; **to ~ to sb about sthg** parlare a qn di qc.

▶ **speak up** vi (more loudly) parlare più forte.

speaker ['spiːkər] n (at conference) oratore m (-trice f); (loudspeaker, of stereo) altoparlante m; **an English ~** una persona che parla inglese.

spear [spɪər] n lancia f.

special ['speʃl] ♦ adj speciale ♦ n: **'today's ~'** 'piatto del giorno'.

special delivery n (Br) ≃ espresso m.

special effects npl effetti mpl speciali.

specialist ['speʃəlɪst] n (doctor) specialista mf.

speciality [,speʃɪ'ælətɪ] n specialità f inv.

specialize ['speʃəlaɪz] vi: **to ~ (in)** specializzarsi (in).

specially ['speʃəlɪ] adv (specifically) specialmente; (on purpose) appositamente; (particularly) particolarmente.

special offer n offerta f speciale.

special school n (Br) ≃ scuola f speciale.

specialty ['speʃltɪ] (Am) = **speciality**.

species ['spiːʃiːz] n specie f inv.

specific [spə'sɪfɪk] adj (particular) specifico(-a).

specification [,spesɪfɪ'keɪʃn] n (of machine, car) caratteristiche fpl tecniche.

specimen ['spesɪmən] n (MED) campione m; (example) esemplare m.

specs [speks] npl (inf) occhiali mpl.

spectacle ['spektəkl] n (sight) scena f.

spectacles ['spektəklz] npl occhiali mpl.

spectacular [spek'tækjʊlər] adj spettacolare.

spectator [spek'teɪtər] n spettatore m (-trice f).

sped [sped] pt & pp → **speed**.

speech [spiːtʃ] n (ability to speak) parola f; (manner of speaking) modo m di parlare; (talk) discorso m.

speech impediment [-ɪm,pedɪmənt] n difetto m di pronuncia.

speed [spiːd] (pt & pp **-ed** OR **sped**) ♦ n velocità f inv; (fast rate) alta velocità; (of film) sensibilità f inv; (bicycle gear) marcia f ♦ vi (move quickly) andare velocemente; (drive too fast) andare a velocità eccessiva; **'reduce ~ now'** 'rallentare'.

▶ **speed up** vi accelerare.

speedboat ['spiːdbəʊt] n fuoribordo m inv.

speeding ['spiːdɪŋ] n eccesso m di velocità.

speed limit n limite m di velocità.

speedometer [spɪ'dɒmɪtər] n tachimetro m.

spell [spel] (Br pt & pp **-ed** OR **spelt**, Am pt & pp **-ed**) ♦ vt (word, name) scrivere; (subj: letters) formare la parola ◆ n (period) periodo m; (magic) incantesimo m.

spelling ['spelɪŋ] n (correct order) ortografia f.

spelt [spelt] pt & pp (Br) → **spell**.

spend [spend] (pt & pp **spent** [spent]) vt (money) spendere; (time) passare.

sphere [sfɪəʳ] n sfera f.

spherical ['sferɪkl] adj sferico(-a).

spice [spaɪs] ◆ n spezia f ◆ vt condire con delle spezie.

spicy ['spaɪsɪ] adj piccante.

spider ['spaɪdəʳ] n ragno m.

spider's web n ragnatela f.

spike [spaɪk] n (metal) punta f.

spill [spɪl] (Br pt & pp **-ed** OR **spilt**, Am pt & pp **-ed**) ◆ vt versare ◆ vi versarsi.

spin [spɪn] (pt **span** OR **spun**, pp **spun**) ◆ vt (wheel) far girare; (washing) centrifugare ◆ n (on ball) effetto m; **to go for a ~** (inf) andare a fare un giro in macchina.

spinach ['spɪnɪdʒ] n spinaci mpl.

spine [spaɪn] n spina f dorsale; (of book) costa f.

spinster ['spɪnstəʳ] n zitella f.

spiral ['spaɪərəl] n spirale f.

spiral staircase n scala f a chiocciola.

spire ['spaɪəʳ] n guglia f.

spirit ['spɪrɪt] n spirito m; (mood) umore m.

▶ **spirits** npl (Br: alcohol) superalcolici mpl.

spit [spɪt] (Br pt & pp **spat**, Am pt & pp **spit**) ◆ vi (person) sputare; (fire, food) scoppiettare ◆ n (saliva) saliva f; (for cooking) spiedo m ◆ v impers: **it's spitting** pioviggina.

spite [spaɪt] : **in spite of** prep nonostante.

spiteful ['spaɪtfʊl] adj malevolo(-a).

splash [splæʃ] ◆ n (sound) tonfo m ◆ vt schizzare.

splendid ['splendɪd] adj splendido(-a).

splint [splɪnt] n stecca f.

splinter ['splɪntəʳ] n scheggia f.

split [splɪt] (pt & pp **split**) ◆ n (tear) strappo m; (crack, in skirt) spacco m ◆ vt (wood, stone) spaccare; (tear) strappare; (bill, cost, profits, work) dividere ◆ vi (wood, stone) spaccarsi; (tear) strapparsi.

▶ **split up** vi (couple) lasciarsi; (group) dividersi.

spoil [spɔɪl] (pt & pp **-ed** OR **spoilt**) vt (ruin) rovinare; (child) viziare.

spoke [spəʊk] ◆ pt → **speak** ◆ n raggio m.

spoken ['spəʊkn] pp → **speak**.

spokesman ['spəʊksmən] (pl **-men** [-mən]) n portavoce m inv.

spokeswoman ['spəʊks,wʊmən] (pl **-women** [-,wɪmɪn]) n portavoce f inv.

sponge [spʌndʒ] n (for cleaning, washing) spugna f.

sponge bag n (Br) nécessaire m inv (da viaggio).

sponge cake n pan m di Spagna.

sponsor ['spɒnsəʳ] n (of event, TV programme) sponsor m inv.

sponsored walk [,spɒnsəd-] n marcia f di beneficenza.

spontaneous [spɒn'teɪnjəs] adj spontaneo(-a).

spoon [spuːn] n cucchiaio m.

spoonful ['spuːnfʊl] n cucchiaiata f.

sport [spɔːt] n sport m inv.

sports car [spɔːts-] n automobile f sportiva.

sports centre [spɔːts-] n centro m sportivo.

sports jacket [spɔːts-] n giacca f sportiva.

sportsman ['spɔːtsmən] (pl **-men** [-mən]) n sportivo m.

sports shop [spɔːts-] n negozio m di articoli sportivi.

sportswoman ['spɔːts,wʊmən] (pl **-women** [-,wɪmɪn]) n sportiva f.

spot [spɒt] ◆ n (of paint, rain) goccia

f; (*on clothes*) macchia *f*; (*on skin*) brufolo *m*; (*place*) posto *m* ◆ *vt* notare; **on the ~** (*at once*) immediatamente; (*at the scene*) sul posto.

spotless ['spɒtlɪs] *adj* pulitissimo(-a).

spotlight ['spɒtlaɪt] *n* riflettore *m*.

spotty ['spɒtɪ] *adj* brufoloso(-a).

spouse [spaʊs] *n* (*fml*) coniuge *mf*.

spout [spaʊt] *n* beccuccio *m*.

sprain [spreɪn] *vt* (*ankle, wrist*) slogarsi.

sprang [spræŋ] *pt* → **spring**.

spray [spreɪ] ◆ *n* (*aerosol*) spray *m* *inv*; (*for perfume*) vaporizzatore *m*; (*droplets*) spruzzi *mpl* ◆ *vt* spruzzare.

spread [spred] (*pt & pp* **spread**) ◆ *vt* (*butter, jam, glue*) spalmare; (*map, tablecloth, blanket*) stendere; (*legs, fingers, arms*) distendere; (*disease, news, rumour*) diffondere ◆ *vi* diffondersi ◆ *n* (*food*) crema *f* da spalmare.

▶ **spread out** *vi* (*disperse*) dispersdersi.

spring [sprɪŋ] (*pt* **sprang**, *pp* **sprung**) ◆ *n* (*season*) primavera *f*; (*coil*) molla *f*; (*in ground*) sorgente *f* ◆ *vi* (*leap*) balzare; **in (the) ~** in primavera.

springboard ['sprɪŋbɔːd] *n* trampolino *m*.

spring-cleaning [-'kliːnɪŋ] *n* pulizie *fpl* di Pasqua.

spring onion *n* cipollina *f*.

spring roll *n* involtino *m* primavera.

sprinkle ['sprɪŋkl] *vt*: **to ~ sthg with sugar** spolverizzare qc di zucchero; **to ~ sthg with water** spruzzare dell'acqua su qc.

sprinkler ['sprɪŋklər] *n* (*for fire*) sprinkler *m inv*; (*for grass*) irrigatore *m*.

sprint [sprɪnt] ◆ *vi* (*run fast*) scattare ◆ *n* (*race*): **the 100-metres ~** i 100 metri piani.

Sprinter® ['sprɪntər] *n* (Br: *train*) treno usato su brevi distanze.

sprout [spraʊt] *n* (*vegetable*) cavo-

letto *m* di Bruxelles.

spruce [spruːs] *n* abete *m*.

sprung [sprʌŋ] ◆ *pp* → **spring** ◆ *adj* (*mattress*) a molle.

spud [spʌd] *n* (*inf*) patata *f*.

spun [spʌn] *pt & pp* → **spin**.

spur [spɜːr] *n* (*for horse rider*) sperone *m*; **on the ~ of the moment** d'impulso.

spurt [spɜːt] *vi* sprizzare.

spy [spaɪ] *n* spia *f*.

squall [skwɔːl] *n* burrasca *f*.

squalor ['skwɒlər] *n* squallore *m*.

square [skweər] ◆ *adj* (*in shape*) quadrato(-a) ◆ *n* (*shape*) quadrato *m*; (*in town*) piazza *f*; (*on chessboard*) scacco *m*; **2 ~ metres** 2 metri quadrati; **it's 2 metres ~** misura 2 metri per 2; **we're (all) ~ now** (*not owing money*) adesso siamo pari.

squash [skwɒʃ] ◆ *n* (*game*) squash *m*; (Am: *vegetable*) zucca *f*; (Br: *drink*): **orange/lemon ~** sciroppo *m* di arancia/limone ◆ *vt* schiacciare.

squat [skwɒt] ◆ *adj* tozzo(-a) ◆ *vi* (*crouch*) accovacciarsi.

squeak [skwiːk] *vi* (*door, wheel*) cigolare; (*mouse*) squittire.

squeeze [skwiːz] ◆ *vt* (*tube, orange*) spremere; (*hand*) stringere ◆ *vi*: **to ~ in** infilarsi.

squid [skwɪd] *n* calamaro *m*.

squint [skwɪnt] ◆ *n* strabismo *m* ◆ *vi*: **to ~ at** guardare con gli occhi socchiusi.

squirrel [Br 'skwɪrəl, Am 'skwɜːrəl] *n* scoiattolo *m*.

squirt [skwɜːt] *vi* schizzare.

St (*abbr of Street*) V.; (*abbr of Saint*) S.

stab [stæb] *vt* (*with knife*) pugnalare.

stable ['steɪbl] ◆ *adj* stabile ◆ *n* stalla *f*.

stack [stæk] *n* (*pile*) pila *f*; **~s of** (*inf*: *lots*) un mucchio di.

stadium ['steɪdjəm] *n* stadio *m*.

staff [stɑːf] *n* (*workers*) personale *m*.

stag [stæg] *n* cervo *m*.

stage [steɪdʒ] *n* (*phase*) stadio *m*; (*in theatre*) palcoscenico *m*.

stagger ['stægər] ♦ vt (arrange in stages) scaglionare ♦ vi barcollare.

stagnant ['stægnənt] adj stagnante.

stain [steɪn] ♦ n macchia f ♦ vt macchiare.

stained glass [,steɪnd-] n vetro m colorato.

stainless steel ['steɪnlɪs-] n acciaio m inossidabile.

staircase ['steəkeɪs] n scala f.

stairs [steəz] npl scale fpl.

stairwell ['steəwel] n tromba f delle scale.

stake [steɪk] n (share) quota f; (in gambling) posta f; (post) palo m; **at ~** in gioco.

stale [steɪl] adj (food) stantio(-a).

stalk [stɔːk] n gambo m.

stall [stɔːl] ♦ n (in market, at exhibition) banco m ♦ vi (car, engine) spegnersi.

▶ **stalls** npl (Br: in theatre) platea f.

stamina ['stæmɪnə] n resistenza f.

stammer ['stæmər] vi balbettare.

stamp [stæmp] ♦ n (for letter) francobollo m; (in passport, on document) timbro m ♦ vt (passport, document) timbrare ♦ vi: **to ~ on sthg** pestare qc.

stamp-collecting [-kə,lektɪŋ] n filatelia f.

stamp machine n distributore m di francobolli.

stand [stænd] (pt & pp **stood**) ♦ vi (be on feet) stare in piedi; (be situated) trovarsi; (get to one's feet) alzarsi ♦ vt (place) mettere; (bear) sopportare; (withstand) tollerare ♦ n (stall) banco m; (for umbrellas) portaombrelli m inv; (for coats) attaccapanni m inv; (on bike, motorbike) cavalletto m; (at sports stadium) tribuna f; **newspaper ~** edicola f; **to be ~ing** stare in piedi; **to ~ sb a drink** offrire da bere a qn; **'no ~ing'** (Am: AUT) 'divieto di sosta'.

▶ **stand back** vi tirarsi indietro.

▶ **stand for** vt fus (mean) stare per; (tolerate) tollerare.

▶ **stand in** vi: **to ~ in for sb** sostituire qn.

▶ **stand out** vi spiccare.

▶ **stand up** ♦ vi (be on feet) stare in piedi; (get to one's feet) alzarsi ♦ vt sep (inf: boyfriend, girlfriend etc) tirare un bidone a.

▶ **stand up for** vt fus difendere.

standard ['stændəd] ♦ adj (normal) standard (inv) ♦ n (level) livello m; (norm) standard m inv; **up to ~** (di livello) soddisfacente.

▶ **standards** npl (principles) principi mpl.

standard-class adj (Br: on train) di seconda classe.

standby ['stændbaɪ] adj (ticket) stand-by (inv).

stank [stæŋk] pt → **stink**.

staple ['steɪpl] n (for paper) punto m metallico.

stapler ['steɪplər] n cucitrice f.

star [stɑːr] ♦ n stella f ♦ vt (subj: film, play etc) avere come protagonista.

▶ **stars** npl (horoscope) oroscopo m.

starboard ['stɑːbəd] adj di tribordo.

starch [stɑːtʃ] n amido m.

stare [steər] vi: **to ~ at** fissare.

starfish ['stɑːfɪʃ] (pl inv) n stella f marina.

starling ['stɑːlɪŋ] n storno m.

Stars and Stripes n: **the ~** la bandiera a stelle e strisce.

start [stɑːt] ♦ n (beginning) inizio m; (starting place) partenza f ♦ vt cominciare, iniziare; (car, engine) mettere in moto; (company, club) fondare ♦ vi cominciare; (car, engine, on journey) partire; **prices ~ at** OR **from £5** i prezzi partono da 5 sterline; **to ~ doing sthg** OR **to do sthg** cominciare a fare qc; **to ~ with ...** per cominciare ....

▶ **start out** vi (on journey) partire; (be originally) cominciare.

▶ **start up** vt sep (car, engine) mettere in moto; (business) intraprendere; (*shop*) aprire.

starter ['stɑːtəʳ] *n* (Br: *of meal*) antipasto *m*; (*of car*) starter *m inv*; **for ~s** (*in meal*) per antipasto.

starter motor *n* motorino *m* di avviamento.

starting point ['stɑːtɪŋ-] *n* punto *m* di partenza.

startle ['stɑːtl] *vt* far trasalire.

starvation [stɑː'veɪʃn] *n* fame *f*.

starve [stɑːv] *vi* (*have no food*) morire di fame; **I'm starving!** muoio di fame!

state [steɪt] ◆ *n* stato *m* ◆ *vt* (*declare*) dichiarare; (*specify*) specificare; **the State** lo Stato; **the States** gli Stati Uniti.

statement ['steɪtmənt] *n* (*declaration*) dichiarazione *f*; (*from bank*) estratto *m* conto.

state school *n* scuola *f* statale.

statesman ['steɪtsmən] (*pl* **-men** [-mən]) *n* statista *m*.

static ['stætɪk] *n* (*on radio*, TV) scarica *f* (elettrostatica).

station ['steɪʃn] *n* stazione *f*.

stationary ['steɪʃnərɪ] *adj* stazionario(-a).

stationer's ['steɪʃnəz] *n* (*shop*) cartoleria *f*.

stationery ['steɪʃnərɪ] *n* cancelleria *f*.

station wagon *n* (Am) station wagon *f inv*.

statistics [stə'tɪstɪks] *npl* (*facts*) statistiche *fpl*.

statue ['stætʃuː] *n* statua *f*.

Statue of Liberty *n*: **the ~** la Statua della Libertà.

status ['steɪtəs] *n* (*legal position*) stato *m*; (*social position*) condizione *f* sociale; (*prestige*) prestigio *m*.

stay [steɪ] ◆ *n* (*time spent*) soggiorno *m* ◆ *vi* (*remain*) rimanere; (*as guest*) alloggiare; (*Scot: reside*) abitare; **to ~ the night** passare la notte.

▶ **stay away** *vi*: **to ~ away (from)** (*not attend*) non andare (a); (*not go near*) stare lontano (da).

▶ **stay in** *vi* rimanere a casa.

▶ **stay out** *vi* (*from home*) rimanere fuori.

▶ **stay up** *vi* rimanere alzato.

STD code *n* prefisso *m*.

steady ['stedɪ] ◆ *adj* (*not shaking, firm*) stabile; (*gradual, stable*) costante; (*job*) fisso(-a) ◆ *vt* (*stop from shaking*) tenere fermo.

steak [steɪk] *n* (*type of meat*) carne *f* di manzo; (*piece of meat*) bistecca *f*; (*piece of fish*) trancia *f*.

steak and kidney pie *n* pasticcio di carne di manzo e rognone.

steakhouse ['steɪkhaʊs, *pl* -haʊzɪz] *n* ristorante *m* specializzato in bistecche.

steal [stiːl] (*pt* **stole**, *pp* **stolen**) *vt* rubare; **to ~ sthg from sb** rubare qc a qn.

steam [stiːm] ◆ *n* vapore *m* ◆ *vt* (*food*) cuocere a vapore.

steamboat ['stiːmbəʊt] *n* battello *m* a vapore.

steam engine *n* locomotiva *f* a vapore.

steam iron *n* ferro *m* a vapore.

steel [stiːl] ◆ *n* acciaio *m* ◆ *adj* di acciaio.

steep [stiːp] *adj* (*hill, path*) ripido(-a); (*increase, drop*) notevole.

steeple ['stiːpl] *n* campanile *m*.

steer ['stɪəʳ] *vt* (*car, boat, plane*) condurre.

steering ['stɪərɪŋ] *n* sterzo *m*.

steering wheel *n* volante *m*.

stem [stem] *n* stelo *m*.

step [step] ◆ *n* (*stair*) gradino *m*; (*rung*) piolo *m*; (*pace*) passo *m*; (*measure*) misura *f*; (*stage*) mossa *f* ◆ *vi*: **to ~ on sthg** calpestare qc; **'mind the ~'** 'attenti al gradino'.

▶ **steps** *npl* (*stairs*) scala *f*.

▶ **step aside** *vi* (*move aside*) farsi da parte.

▶ **step back** *vi* (*move back*) tirarsi indietro.

step aerobics *n* step *m*.

stepbrother ['step,brʌðər] n fratellastro m.

stepdaughter ['step,dɔːtər] n figliastra f.

stepfather ['step,fɑːðər] n patrigno m.

stepladder ['step,lædər] n scala f (a pioli).

stepmother ['step,mʌðər] n matrigna f.

stepsister ['step,sɪstər] n sorellastra f.

stepson ['stepsʌn] n figliastro m.

stereo ['sterɪəʊ] (pl -s) ♦ adj stereofonico(-a) ♦ n (hi-fi) stereo m inv; (stereo sound) stereofonia f.

sterile ['sterail] adj sterile.

sterilize ['sterəlaɪz] vt sterilizzare.

sterling ['stɜːlɪŋ] ♦ adj (pound) sterlina ♦ n sterlina f.

sterling silver n argento m di buona lega.

stern [stɜːn] ♦ adj severo(-a) ♦ n poppa f.

stew [stjuː] n stufato m.

steward ['stjʊəd] n (on plane, ship) steward m inv; (at public event) membro m del servizio d'ordine.

stewardess ['stjʊədɪs] n hostess f inv.

stewed [stjuːd] adj (fruit) cotto(-a).

stick [stɪk] (pt & pp stuck) n (of wood) bastone m; (of chalk) pezzetto m; (of celery) costa f ♦ vt (glue) attaccare; (push, insert) ficcare; (inf: put) ficcare ♦ vi (become attached) attaccarsi; (jam) incastrarsi.

▶ **stick out** vi (protrude) sporgere; (be noticeable) saltare agli occhi.

▶ **stick to** vt fus (decision, promise) mantenere; (principles) tener fede a.

▶ **stick up** ♦ vt sep (poster, notice) attaccare ♦ vi sporgere.

▶ **stick up for** vt fus difendere.

sticker ['stɪkər] n adesivo m.

sticking plaster ['stɪkɪŋ-] n cerotto m.

stick shift n (Am: car) auto f con cambio manuale.

sticky ['stɪkɪ] adj (substance, hands, weather) appiccicoso(-a); (label, tape) adesivo(-a).

stiff [stɪf] ♦ adj duro(-a); (back, neck, person) rigido(-a) ♦ adv: **to be bored ~** (inf) essere annoiato a morte.

stile [staɪl] n gradini per scavalcare un recinto.

stiletto heels [stɪ'letəʊ-] npl tacchi mpl a spillo.

still [stɪl] ♦ adv ancora; (despite that) comunque ♦ adj (motionless) immobile; (quiet, calm) calmo(-a); (not fizzy) non gassato(-a); **we've ~ got ten minutes** abbiamo ancora dieci minuti; **~ more** ancora di più; **to stand ~** stare fermo.

Stilton ['stɪltn] n stilton m (formaggio simile al gorgonzola).

stimulate ['stɪmjʊleɪt] vt (encourage) stimolare.

sting [stɪŋ] (pt & pp stung) ♦ vt pungere ♦ vi (skin, eyes) pizzicare.

stingy ['stɪndʒɪ] adj (inf) tirchio(-a).

stink [stɪŋk] (pt stank OR stunk, pp stunk) vi (smell bad) puzzare.

stipulate ['stɪpjʊleɪt] vt stipulare.

stir [stɜːr] vt mescolare.

stir-fry ♦ n piatto m saltato ♦ vt saltare (in padella).

stirrup ['stɪrəp] n staffa f.

stitch [stɪtʃ] n (in sewing, knitting) punto m; **to have a ~** (stomach pain) avere una fitta.

▶ **stitches** npl (for wound) punti mpl.

stock [stɒk] ♦ n (of shop, business) stock m inv; (supply) scorta f; (FIN) azioni fpl; (in cooking) brodo m ♦ vt (have in stock) avere in magazzino; **in ~** in magazzino; **out of ~** esaurito.

stock cube n dado m (per il brodo).

Stock Exchange n Borsa f valori.

stocking ['stɒkɪŋ] n calza f.

stock market n borsa f valori.

stodgy ['stɒdʒɪ] adj (food) pesante.

stole [stəʊl] pt → steal.

stolen ['stəʊln] pp → steal.

stomach ['stʌmək] n (organ) stomaco m; (belly) pancia f.

stomachache ['stʌməkeɪk] n mal m di stomaco.

stomach upset [-'ʌpset] n disturbo m di stomaco.

stone [stəun] ◆ n (substance) pietra f; (in fruit) nocciolo m; (measurement: pl inv) = 6,35 kg; (gem) pietra preziosa ◆ adj di pietra.

stonewashed ['stəunwɒʃt] adj délavé (inv).

stood [stud] pt & pp → **stand**.

stool [stu:l] n (for sitting on) sgabello m.

stop [stɒp] ◆ n (for bus, train) fermata f; (in journey) tappa f ◆ vt (cause to cease) porre fine a; (car, machine) fermare; (prevent) impedire ◆ vi fermarsi; **to ~ sb/sthg from doing sthg** impedire a qn/qc di fare qc; **to ~ doing sthg** smettere di fare qc; **to put a ~ to sthg** porre fine a qc; **'stop'** (road sign) 'stop'; **'stopping at ...'** (train, bus) 'ferma a ...'.

▶ **stop off** vi fare una sosta.

stopover ['stɒp,əuvər] n sosta f.

stopper ['stɒpər] n tappo m.

stopwatch ['stɒpwɒtʃ] n cronografo m.

storage ['stɔ:rɪdʒ] n immagazzinaggio m.

store [stɔ:r] ◆ n (shop) negozio m; (supply) scorta f ◆ vt immagazzinare.

storehouse ['stɔ:haus, pl -hauzɪz] n magazzino m.

storeroom ['stɔ:rum] n stanzino m.

storey ['stɔ:rɪ] (pl -s) n (Br) piano m.

stork [stɔ:k] n cicogna f.

storm [stɔ:m] n tempesta f.

stormy ['stɔ:mɪ] adj (weather) burrascoso(-a).

story ['stɔ:rɪ] n (account, tale) storia f; (news item) notizia f; (Am) = **storey**.

stout [staut] ◆ adj (fat) corpulento(-a) ◆ n (drink) birra f scura.

stove [stəuv] n (for cooking) cucina f; (for heating) stufa f.

straight [streɪt] ◆ adj (not curved) diritto(-a); (hair, drink) liscio(-a); (consecutive) di seguito ◆ adv (in a straight line) dritto; (upright) in posizione eretta; (directly, without delay) direttamente; **~ ahead** sempre diritto; **~ away** subito.

straightforward [,streɪt'fɔ:wəd] adj (easy) semplice.

strain [streɪn] ◆ n (force) sforzo m; (tension, nervous stress) tensione f; (injury) distorsione f ◆ vt (muscle, eyes) sforzare; (food) scolare; (tea) filtrare.

strainer ['streɪnər] n colino m.

strait [streɪt] n stretto m.

strange [streɪndʒ] adj (unusual) strano(-a); (unfamiliar) sconosciuto(-a).

stranger ['streɪndʒər] n (unfamiliar person) sconosciuto m (-a f); (person from different place) forestiero m (-a f).

strangle ['stræŋgl] vt strangolare.

strap [stræp] n (of bag, camera) tracolla f; (of watch, shoe) cinturino m; (of dress) bretella f.

strapless ['stræplɪs] adj senza spalline.

strategy ['strætɪdʒɪ] n (plan) strategia f.

Stratford-upon-Avon [,strætfədəpɒn'eɪvn] n Stratford-upon-Avon.

straw [strɔ:] n paglia f; (for drinking) cannuccia f.

strawberry ['strɔ:bərɪ] n fragola f.

stray [streɪ] ◆ adj (animal) randagio(-a) ◆ vi vagare.

streak [stri:k] n (stripe, mark) striscia f; (period) periodo m.

stream [stri:m] n (river) ruscello m; (of traffic, people, blood) flusso m.

street [stri:t] n via f, strada f.

streetcar ['stri:tkɑ:r] n (Am) tram m inv.

street light n lampione m.

street plan n piantina f.

strength [strɛŋθ] n forza f; (of structure) robustezza f; (influence) potere m; (strong point) punto m di forza; (of feeling, smell) intensità f; (of drink) gradazione f alcolica.

strengthen ['strɛŋθn] vt (structure) rafforzare.

stress [strɛs] ♦ n (tension) stress m inv; (on word, syllable) accento m ♦ vt (emphasize) sottolineare; (word, syllable) accentare.

stretch [strɛtʃ] ♦ n (of land, water) distesa f; (of time) periodo m ♦ vt tendere; (body) stirare ♦ vi (land, sea) estendersi; (person, animal) stirarsi; **to ~ one's legs** (fig) sgranchirsi le gambe.

▶ **stretch out** ♦ vt sep (hand) tendere ♦ vi (lie down) distendersi.

stretcher ['strɛtʃər] n barella f.

strict [strɪkt] adj (person) severo(-a); (rule, instructions) rigido(-a); (exact) stretto(-a).

strictly ['strɪktlɪ] adv strettamente; **~ speaking** per essere precisi.

stride [straɪd] n falcata f.

strike [straɪk] (pt & pp **struck**) ♦ n (of employees) sciopero m ♦ vt (fml: hit) colpire; (fml: collide with) urtare; (a match) accendere ♦ vi (refuse to work) scioperare; (happen suddenly) colpire; **the clock struck eight** l'orologio ha battuto le otto.

striking ['straɪkɪŋ] adj (noticeable) impressionante; (attractive) appariscente.

string [strɪŋ] n spago m; (of pearls, beads) filo m; (of musical instrument, tennis racket) corda f; (series) serie f inv; **a piece of ~** un pezzo di spago.

strip [strɪp] ♦ n striscia f ♦ vt (paint, wallpaper) togliere ♦ vi (undress) spogliarsi.

stripe [straɪp] n striscia f.

striped [straɪpt] adj a strisce.

strip-search vt perquisire (facendo spogliare).

strip show n spogliarello m.

stroke [strəʊk] ♦ n (MED) colpo m; (in tennis) battuta f; (in golf) tiro m; (swimming style) stile m ♦ vt accarezzare; **a ~ of luck** un colpo di fortuna.

stroll [strəʊl] n passeggiata f.

stroller ['strəʊlər] n (Am: pushchair) passeggino m.

strong [strɒŋ] adj forte; (structure, bridge, chair) robusto(-a); (feeling, smell) intenso(-a).

struck [strʌk] pt & pp → **strike**.

structure ['strʌktʃər] n struttura f.

struggle ['strʌgl] ♦ n (great effort) sforzo m ♦ vi (fight) lottare; (in order to get free) divincolarsi; **to ~ to do sthg** sforzarsi di fare qc.

stub [stʌb] n (of cigarette) mozzicone m; (of cheque, ticket) matrice f.

stubble ['stʌbl] n (on face) barba f ispida.

stubborn ['stʌbən] adj (person) ostinato(-a).

stuck [stʌk] ♦ pt & pp → **stick** ♦ adj (jammed) incastrato(-a); (unable to continue, stranded) bloccato(-a).

stud [stʌd] n (on boots) borchia f; (fastener) bottone m automatico; (earring) miniorecchino m.

student ['stjuːdnt] n studente m (-essa f).

student card n carta f dello studente.

students' union [,stjuːdnts-] n (place) circolo m studentesco.

studio ['stjuːdɪəʊ] (pl -s) n studio m.

studio apartment (Am) = **studio flat**.

studio flat n (Br) monolocale m.

study ['stʌdɪ] ♦ n (learning) studio m ♦ vt & vi studiare.

stuff [stʌf] ♦ n (inf) roba f ♦ vt (put roughly) ficcare; (fill) riempire.

stuffed [stʌft] adj (food) ripieno(-a); (inf: full up) pieno(-a); (dead animal) imbalsamato(-a).

stuffing ['stʌfɪŋ] n (food) ripieno m; (of pillow, cushion) imbottitura f.

stuffy ['stʌfɪ] adj (room, atmosphere)

che sa di chiuso.

stumble ['stʌmbl] vi (when walking) inciampare.

stump [stʌmp] n (of tree) ceppo m.

stun [stʌn] vt (shock) sbalordire.

stung [stʌŋ] pt & pp → **sting**.

stunk [stʌŋk] pt & pp → **stink**.

stunning ['stʌnɪŋ] adj (very beautiful) favoloso(-a); (very surprising) sbalorditivo(-a).

stupid ['stjuːpɪd] adj stupido(-a).

sturdy ['stɜːdɪ] adj robusto(-a).

stutter ['stʌtər] vi balbettare.

sty [staɪ] n (pigsty) porcile m; (on eye) orzaiolo m.

style [staɪl] ◆ n stile m ◆ vt (hair) acconciare.

stylish ['staɪlɪʃ] adj elegante.

stylist ['staɪlɪst] n (hairdresser) acconciatore m (-trice f).

sub [sʌb] n (inf) (substitute) riserva f; (Br: subscription) quota f (d'iscrizione).

subdued [səb'djuːd] adj (person) abbacchiato(-a); (lighting, colour) smorzato(-a).

subject [n 'sʌbdʒekt, vb səb'dʒekt] ◆ n (topic) argomento m; (at school, university) materia f; (GRAMM) soggetto m; (fml: of country) cittadino m (-a f) ◆ vt: **to ~ sb to sthg** sottoporre qn a qc; '**~ to availability**' 'fino ad esaurimento'; **they are ~ to an additional charge** sono suscettibili di soprapprezzo.

subjunctive [səb'dʒʌŋktɪv] n congiuntivo m.

submarine [,sʌbmə'riːn] n sottomarino m.

submit [səb'mɪt] ◆ vt presentare ◆ vi sottomettersi.

subordinate [sə'bɔːdɪnət] adj subordinato(-a).

subscribe [səb'skraɪb] vi (to magazine, newspaper) abbonarsi.

subscription [səb'skrɪpʃn] n abbonamento m.

subsequent ['sʌbsɪkwənt] adj successivo(-a).

subside [səb'saɪd] vi (ground) cedere; (noise, feeling) smorzarsi.

substance ['sʌbstəns] n sostanza f.

substantial [səb'stænʃl] adj (large) sostanziale.

substitute ['sʌbstɪtjuːt] n (person) sostituto m (-a f); (thing) surrogato m; (SPORT) riserva f.

subtitles ['sʌb,taɪtlz] npl sottotitoli mpl.

subtle ['sʌtl] adj (difference, change) sottile; (person, plan) astuto(-a).

subtract [səb'trækt] vt sottrarre.

subtraction [səb'trækʃn] n sottrazione f.

suburb ['sʌbɜːb] n sobborgo m; **the ~s** la periferia.

subway ['sʌbweɪ] n (Br: for pedestrians) sottopassaggio m; (Am: underground railway) metropolitana f.

succeed [sək'siːd] ◆ vi (be successful) avere successo ◆ vt (fml: follow) succedere a; **to ~ in doing sthg** riuscire a fare qc.

success [sək'ses] n successo m.

successful [sək'sesfʊl] adj (plan, attempt) riuscito(-a); (film, book, politician) di successo; **to be ~** (person) riuscire.

succulent ['sʌkjʊlənt] adj succulento(-a).

such [sʌtʃ] ◆ adj tale ◆ adv: **~ a lot** così tanto; **it's ~ a lovely day** è una giornata così bella; **~ good luck** una tale fortuna; **~ a thing should never have happened** una cosa simile non sarebbe mai dovuta accadere; **~ as** come.

suck [sʌk] vt succhiare.

sudden ['sʌdn] adj improvviso(-a); **all of a ~** all'improvviso.

suddenly ['sʌdnlɪ] adv improvvisamente.

sue [suː] vt citare in giudizio.

suede [sweɪd] n pelle f scamosciata.

suffer ['sʌfər] ◆ vt (defeat, injury) subire ◆ vi soffrire; **to ~ from** (ill-

ness) soffrire di.

suffering ['sʌfrɪŋ] *n* sofferenza *f.*

sufficient [sə'fɪʃnt] *adj* (*fml*) sufficiente.

sufficiently [sə'fɪʃntlɪ] *adv* (*fml*) sufficientemente.

suffix ['sʌfɪks] *n* suffisso *m.*

suffocate ['sʌfəkeɪt] *vi* soffocare.

sugar ['ʃʊgər] *n* zucchero *m.*

suggest [sə'dʒest] *vt* suggerire; **to ~ doing sthg** suggerire di fare qc.

suggestion [sə'dʒestʃn] *n* (*proposal*) suggerimento *m*; (*hint*) accenno *m.*

suicide ['suɪsaɪd] *n* suicidio *m*; **to commit ~** suicidarsi.

suit [suːt] ◆ *n* (*for man*) vestito *m*; (*for woman*) tailleur *m inv*; (*in cards*) seme *m*; (JUR) causa *f* ◆ *vt* (*subj: clothes, colour, shoes*) star bene a; (*be convenient for*) andare bene a; (*be appropriate for*) addirsi a; **to be ~ed to** essere adatto a.

suitable ['suːtəbl] *adj* adatto(-a); **to be ~ for** essere adatto a.

suitcase ['suːtkeɪs] *n* valigia *f.*

suite [swiːt] *n* (*set of rooms*) suite *f inv*; (*furniture*): **a three-piece ~** un divano e due poltrone (coordinati).

sulk [sʌlk] *vi* mettere il broncio.

sultana [səl'tɑːnə] *n* (Br) uva *f* sultanina.

sultry ['sʌltrɪ] *adj* (*weather, climate*) caldo umido (caldo umida).

sum [sʌm] *n* somma *f.*

▶ **sum up** *vt sep* riassumere.

summarize ['sʌməraɪz] *vt* riassumere.

summary ['sʌmərɪ] *n* riassunto *m.*

summer ['sʌmər] *n* estate *f*; **in (the) ~** d'estate; **~ holidays** vacanze *fpl* estive.

summertime ['sʌmətaɪm] *n* estate *f.*

summit ['sʌmɪt] *n* (*of mountain*) cima *f*; (*meeting*) summit *m inv.*

summon ['sʌmən] *vt* (*send for*) convocare; (JUR) citare.

sumptuous ['sʌmptʃʊəs] *adj* sontuoso(-a).

sun [sʌn] ◆ *n* sole *m* ◆ *vt*: **to ~ o.s.** prendere il sole; **to catch the ~** prendere il sole; **in the ~** al sole; **out of the ~** al riparo dal sole.

Sun. (*abbr of* Sunday) dom.

sunbathe ['sʌnbeɪð] *vi* prendere il sole.

sunbed ['sʌnbed] *n* lettino *m.*

sun block *n* crema *f* solare a protezione totale.

sunburn ['sʌnbɜːn] *n* scottatura *f.*

sunburnt ['sʌnbɜːnt] *adj* scottato(-a).

sundae ['sʌndeɪ] *n* gelato guarnito con frutta o cioccolato, nocciole e panna montata.

Sunday ['sʌndɪ] *n* domenica *f*, → **Saturday.**

Sunday school *n* ≃ scuola *f* di catechismo.

sundress ['sʌndres] *n* prendisole *m inv.*

sundries ['sʌndrɪz] *npl* (*on bill*) varie *fpl.*

sunflower ['sʌn,flaʊər] *n* girasole *m.*

sunflower oil *n* olio *m* di semi di girasole.

sung [sʌŋ] *pt* → **sing.**

sunglasses ['sʌn,glɑːsɪz] *npl* occhiali *mpl* da sole.

sunhat ['sʌnhæt] *n* cappello *m* (*per il sole*).

sunk [sʌŋk] *pp* → **sink.**

sunlight ['sʌnlaɪt] *n* luce *f* del sole.

sun lounger [-,laʊndʒər] *n* (*chair*) lettino *m.*

sunny ['sʌnɪ] *adj* (*day*) di sole; (*weather*) bello(-a); (*room, place*) soleggiato(-a); **it's ~** c'è il sole.

sunrise ['sʌnraɪz] *n* alba *f.*

sunroof ['sʌnruːf] *n* tettuccio *m* apribile.

sunset ['sʌnset] *n* tramonto *m.*

sunshine ['sʌnʃaɪn] *n* luce *f* del sole; **in the ~** al sole.

sunstroke ['sʌnstrəʊk] *n* insolazione *f.*

suntan ['sʌntæn] *n* abbronzatura *f.*

suntan cream n crema f abbronzante.

suntan lotion n lozione f abbronzante.

super ['su:pər] ♦ adj fantastico(-a) ♦ n (petrol) super f inv.

superb [su:'pɜ:b] adj splendido(-a).

superficial [ˌsu:pə'fɪʃl] adj superficiale.

superfluous [su:'pɜ:fluəs] adj superfluo(-a).

Superglue® ['su:pəglu:] n colla f a presa rapida.

superior [su:'pɪərɪər] ♦ adj superiore ♦ n superiore mf.

supermarket ['su:pəˌmɑːkɪt] n supermercato m.

supernatural [ˌsu:pə'nætʃrəl] adj soprannaturale.

Super Saver® n (Br: rail ticket) biglietto ferroviario a tariffa ridotta, con condizioni particolari.

superstitious [ˌsu:pə'stɪʃəs] adj superstizioso(-a).

superstore ['su:pəstɔ:r] n grande supermercato m.

supervise ['su:pəvaɪz] vt sorvegliare.

supervisor ['su:pəvaɪzər] n (of workers) sovrintendente mf.

supper ['sʌpər] n (evening meal) cena f; (before bed) spuntino m.

supple ['sʌpl] adj agile.

supplement [n 'sʌplɪmənt, vb 'sʌplɪment] ♦ n supplemento m; (of diet) integratore m alimentare ♦ vt integrare.

supplementary [ˌsʌplɪ'mentərɪ] adj supplementare.

supply [sə'plaɪ] ♦ n (store) scorta f; (providing) approvvigionamento m; (of electricity, gas etc) erogazione f ♦ vt fornire; **to ~ sb with sthg** fornire qc a qn.

▶ **supplies** npl scorte fpl.

support [sə'pɔ:t] ♦ n (for cause, candidate) appoggio m; (object, encouragement) sostegno m ♦ vt (cause, cam-

paign, person) appoggiare; (SPORT) tifare per; (hold up) sostenere; (financially) mantenere.

supporter [sə'pɔ:tər] n (SPORT) tifoso m (-a f); (of cause, political party) sostenitore m (-trice f).

suppose [sə'pəʊz] ♦ vt (assume) immaginare; (think) credere ♦ conj = **supposing**; **I ~ so** penso di sì; **you were ~d to be home at six o'clock** dovevate essere a casa alle sei; **it's ~d to be the best** è ritenuto il migliore.

supposing [sə'pəʊzɪŋ] conj supponendo che.

supreme [sʊ'pri:m] adj eccezionale.

surcharge ['sɜ:tʃɑ:dʒ] n sovrapprezzo m.

sure [ʃʊər] ♦ adj sicuro(-a) ♦ adv (inf: yes) certo!; (Am: inf: certainly) certamente; **to be ~ of o.s.** essere sicuro di sé; **to make ~ that ...** assicurarsi che ...; **for ~** di sicuro.

surely ['ʃʊəlɪ] adv sicuramente.

surf [sɜ:f] ♦ n (foam) spuma f ♦ vi fare surf.

surface ['sɜ:fɪs] n superficie f.

surface area n superficie f (esterna).

surface mail n posta f ordinaria.

surfboard ['sɜ:fbɔ:d] n tavola f da surf.

surfing ['sɜ:fɪŋ] n surf m; **to go ~** andare a fare surf.

surgeon ['sɜ:dʒən] n chirurgo m.

surgery ['sɜ:dʒərɪ] n (treatment) chirurgia f; (Br: building) ambulatorio m; (Br: period) orario m d'ambulatorio.

surname ['sɜ:neɪm] n cognome m.

surplus ['sɜ:pləs] n eccedenza f.

surprise [sə'praɪz] ♦ n sorpresa f ♦ vt sorprendere.

surprised [sə'praɪzd] adj sorpreso(-a).

surprising [sə'praɪzɪŋ] adj sorprendente.

surrender [sə'rendər] ♦ vi arrendersi ◆ vt (fml: hand over) consegnare.

surround [sə'raʊnd] vt circondare.

surrounding [sə'raʊndɪŋ] adj circostante.

▶ **surroundings** npl dintorni mpl.

survey ['sɜːveɪ] n (investigation) studio m, indagine f; (poll) sondaggio m; (of land) rilevamento m (topografico); (Br: of house) sopralluogo m.

surveyor [sə'veɪəʳ] n (Br: of houses) perito m; (of land) agrimensore m.

survival [sə'vaɪvl] n sopravvivenza f.

survive [sə'vaɪv] ◆ vi sopravvivere ◆ vt sopravvivere a.

survivor [sə'vaɪvəʳ] n sopravvissuto m (-a f).

suspect [vb sə'spekt, n & adj 'sʌspekt] ◆ vt sospettare ◆ n sospetto m ◆ adj sospetto(-a); **to ~ sb of sthg** sospettare qn di qc.

suspend [sə'spend] vt sospendere.

suspender belt [sə'spendə-] n reggicalze m inv.

suspenders [sə'spendəz] npl (Br: for stockings) giarrettiere fpl; (Am: for trousers) bretelle fpl.

suspense [sə'spens] n suspense f.

suspension [sə'spenʃn] n sospensione f.

suspicion [sə'spɪʃn] n (mistrust, idea) sospetto m; (trace) accenno m.

suspicious [sə'spɪʃəs] adj (behaviour, situation) sospetto(-a); **to be ~ of** (distrustful) sospettare di.

swallow ['swɒləʊ] ◆ n (bird) rondine f ◆ vt & vi ingoiare.

swam [swæm] pt → **swim**.

swamp [swɒmp] n palude f.

swan [swɒn] n cigno m.

swap [swɒp] vt (possessions, places) scambiare; (ideas, stories) scambiarsi; **to ~ sthg for sthg** scambiare qc con qc.

swarm [swɔːm] n (of bees) sciame m.

swear [sweəʳ] (pt **swore**, pp **sworn**) ◆ vi (use rude language) imprecare; (promise) giurare ◆ vt: **to ~ to do sthg**

promettere di fare qc.

swearword ['sweəwɜːd] n parolaccia f.

sweat [swet] ◆ n sudore m ◆ vi sudare.

sweater ['swetəʳ] n maglione m.

sweatshirt ['swetʃɜːt] n felpa f.

swede [swiːd] n (Br) rapa f svedese.

Swede [swiːd] n svedese mf.

Sweden ['swiːdn] n la Svezia.

Swedish ['swiːdɪʃ] ◆ adj svedese ◆ n (language) svedese m ◆ npl: **the ~** gli svedesi.

sweep [swiːp] (pt & pp **swept**) vt (with brush, broom) scopare.

sweet [swiːt] ◆ adj dolce; (kind) gentile, carino(-a) ◆ n (Br) (candy) caramella f; (dessert) dolce m.

sweet-and-sour adj (pork) in agrodolce; (sauce) agrodolce.

sweet corn n granturco m.

sweetener ['swiːtnəʳ] n (for drink) dolcificante m.

sweet potato n patata f americana.

sweet shop n (Br) negozio m di dolciumi.

swell [swel] (pp **swollen**) vi (ankle, arm etc) gonfiarsi.

swelling ['swelɪŋ] n gonfiore m.

swept [swept] pt & pp → **sweep**.

swerve [swɜːv] vi (vehicle) sterzare.

swig [swɪg] n (inf) sorsata f.

swim [swɪm] (pt **swam**, pp **swum**) ◆ n nuotata f, bagno m ◆ vi (in water) nuotare; **to go for a ~** andare a fare il bagno.

swimmer ['swɪməʳ] n nuotatore m (-trice f).

swimming ['swɪmɪŋ] n nuoto m; **to go ~** andare in piscina.

swimming baths npl (Br) piscina f coperta.

swimming cap n cuffia f.

swimming costume n (Br) costume m da bagno.

swimming pool n piscina f.

swimming trunks npl costume

m da bagno (*da uomo*).

swimsuit ['swɪmsuːt] *n* costume *m* da bagno.

swindle ['swɪndl] *n* truffa *f*.

swing [swɪŋ] (*pt & pp* **swung**) ◆ *n* (*for children*) altalena *f* ◆ *vt & vi* (*from side to side*) dondolare.

swipe [swaɪp] *vt* (*credit card etc*) far passare nel lettore magnetico.

Swiss [swɪs] ◆ *adj* svizzero(-a) ◆ *n* (*person*) svizzero *m* (-a *f*) ◆ *npl*: **the ~** gli svizzeri.

Swiss cheese *n* formaggio *m* svizzero.

swiss roll *n* rotolo di pan di Spagna farcito di marmellata.

switch [swɪtʃ] ◆ *n* (*for light, power, television set*) interruttore *m* ◆ *vt* (*change*) cambiare; (*exchange*) scambiare ◆ *vi* cambiare.

▸ **switch off** *vt sep* spegnere;
switch on *vt sep* accendere.

switchboard ['swɪtʃbɔːd] *n* centralino *m*.

Switzerland ['swɪtsələnd] *n* la Svizzera.

swivel ['swɪvl] *vi* girarsi.

swollen ['swəʊlən] ◆ *pp* → **swell** ◆ *adj* (*ankle, arm etc*) gonfio(-a).

swop [swɒp] = **swap**.

sword [sɔːd] *n* spada *f*.

swordfish ['sɔːdfɪʃ] (*pl inv*) *n* pesce *m* spada.

swore [swɔːr] *pt* → **swear**.

sworn [swɔːn] *pp* → **swear**.

swum [swʌm] *pp* → **swim**.

swung [swʌŋ] *pt & pp* → **swing**.

syllable ['sɪləbl] *n* sillaba *f*.

syllabus ['sɪləbəs] *n* programma *m*.

symbol ['sɪmbl] *n* simbolo *m*.

sympathetic [ˌsɪmpə'θetɪk] *adj* (*understanding*) comprensivo(-a).

sympathize ['sɪmpəθaɪz] *vi*: **to ~ (with)** (*feel sorry*) provare compassione (per); (*understand*) capire.

sympathy ['sɪmpəθɪ] *n* (*understanding*) comprensione *f*.

symphony ['sɪmfənɪ] *n* sinfonia *f*.

symptom ['sɪmptəm] *n* sintomo *m*.

synagogue ['sɪnəgɒg] *n* sinagoga *f*.

synthesizer ['sɪnθəsaɪzər] *n* sintetizzatore *m*.

synthetic [sɪn'θetɪk] *adj* sintetico(-a).

syringe [sɪ'rɪndʒ] *n* siringa *f*.

syrup ['sɪrəp] *n* (*for fruit etc*) sciroppo *m*.

system ['sɪstəm] *n* sistema *m*; (*hi-fi, computer, for heating etc*) impianto *m*.

T

ta [tɑː] *excl* (Br: *inf*) grazie!

tab [tæb] *n* (*of cloth, paper etc*) etichetta *f*; (*bill*) conto *m*; **put it on my ~** lo metta sul mio conto.

table ['teɪbl] *n* (*piece of furniture*) tavolo *m*; (*of figures etc*) tavola *f*.

tablecloth ['teɪblklɒθ] *n* tovaglia *f*.

tablemat ['teɪblmæt] *n* sottopiatto *m*.

tablespoon ['teɪblspuːn] *n* cucchiaio *m* da tavola.

tablet ['tæblɪt] *n* (*pill*) compressa *f*; (*of chocolate*) tavoletta *f*; **~ of soap** saponetta *f*.

table tennis *n* ping-pong® *m*.

table wine *n* vino *m* da tavola.

tabloid ['tæblɔɪd] *n* tabloid *m inv*.

tack [tæk] *n* (*nail*) puntina *f*.

tackle ['tækl] ◆ *n* (*in football*) tackle *m*; (*in rugby*) placcaggio *m*; (*for fishing*) attrezzatura *f* ◆ *vt* (*in football*) contrastare; (*in rugby*) placcare; (*deal with*) affrontare.

tacky ['tækɪ] *adj* (*inf: jewellery, design etc*) pacchiano(-a).

taco ['tækəʊ] (*pl* **-s**) *n* taco *m* (*schiacciatina a base di farina di granturco farcita di carne o fagioli, tipica della cucina messicana*).

tact [tækt] *n* tatto *m*.

tactful ['tæktfʊl] *adj* discreto(-a).

tactics ['tæktɪks] *npl* tattica *f*.

tag [tæg] *n* (*label*) etichetta *f*.

tagliatelle [ˌtæɡljə'telɪ] *n* tagliatelle *fpl*.

tail [teɪl] *n* coda *f*.

▶ **tails** ◆ *n* (*of coin*) croce *f* ◆ *npl* (*formal dress*) frac *m inv*.

tailgate ['teɪlɡeɪt] *n* (*of car*) portellone *m*.

tailor ['teɪlər] *n* sarto *m*.

Taiwan [ˌtaɪ'wɑːn] *n* Taiwan *f*.

take [teɪk] (*pt* **took**, *pp* **taken**) *vt* 1. (*gen*) prendere.

2. (*carry, drive*) portare.

3. (*do, make*) fare; **to ~ a bath/shower** fare un bagno/una doccia; **to ~ an exam** fare OR dare un esame; **to ~ a decision** prendere una decisione.

4. (*time, effort*) volerci, richiedere; **how long will it ~?** quanto ci vorrà?; **it won't ~ long** non ci vorrà molto tempo.

5. (*size in clothes, shoes*) portare, avere; **what size do you ~?** (*clothes*) che taglia porta?; (*shoes*) che misura porta?

6. (*subtract*) sottrarre, togliere.

7. (*accept*) accettare; **do you ~ traveller's cheques?** accettate traveller's cheques?; **to ~ sb's advice** seguire il consiglio di qn.

8. (*contain*) contenere.

9. (*control, power*) assumere; **to ~ charge of** assumere la direzione di.

10. (*tolerate*) sopportare.

11. (*assume*): **I ~ it that ...** suppongo che ...

12. (*rent*) prendere in affitto.

▶ **take apart** *vt sep* (*dismantle*) smontare.

▶ **take away** *vt sep* (*remove*) portare via; (*subtract*) togliere.

▶ **take back** *vt sep* (*return*) riportare; (*statement*) ritrattare.

▶ **take down** *vt sep* (*picture, decorations*) togliere.

▶ **take in** *vt sep* (*include*) includere; (*understand*) capire; (*deceive*) abbindolare; (*clothes*) restringere.

▶ **take off** ◆ *vi* (*plane*) decollare ◆ *vt sep* (*remove*) togliere; (*as holiday*): **to ~ a week off** prendere una settimana di ferie.

▶ **take out** *vt sep* (*from container, pocket*) tirare fuori; (*loan, insurance policy*) ottenere; (*go out with*) portare fuori.

▶ **take over** *vi* assumere il comando; **to ~ over from sb** prendere le consegne da qn.

▶ **take up** *vt sep* (*begin*) dedicarsi a; (*use up*) prendere; (*trousers, dress*) accorciare.

takeaway ['teɪkəˌweɪ] *n* (Br) (*shop*) locale che prepara piatti pronti da asporto; (*food*) cibo *m* da asporto.

taken ['teɪkn] *pp* → **take**.

takeoff ['teɪkɒf] *n* (*of plane*) decollo *m*.

takeout ['teɪkaʊt] (Am) = **takeaway**.

takings ['teɪkɪŋz] *npl* incasso *m*.

talcum powder ['tælkəm-] *n* borotalco® *m*.

tale [teɪl] *n* (*story*) storia *f*; (*account*) racconto *m*.

talent ['tælənt] *n* talento *m*.

talk [tɔːk] ◆ *n* (*conversation*) conversazione *f*; (*speech*) discorso *m* ◆ *vi* parlare; **to ~ to sb (about sthg)** parlare con qn (di qc); **to ~ with sb** parlare con qn.

▶ **talks** *npl* negoziati *mpl*.

talkative ['tɔːkətɪv] *adj* loquace.

tall [tɔːl] *adj* alto(-a); **how ~ are you?** quanto sei alto?; **I'm five and a half feet ~** sono alto un metro e 65.

tame [teɪm] *adj* (*animal*) addomesticato(-a).

tampon ['tæmpɒn] *n* tampone *m*.

tan [tæn] ◆ *n* (*suntan*) abbronzatura *f* ◆ *vi* abbronzarsi ◆ *adj* (*colour*) marrone chiaro (*inv*).

tangerine [ˌtændʒə'riːn] *n* (*fruit*)

mandarino *m*.

tank [tæŋk] *n* (*container*) serbatoio *m*; (*vehicle*) carro *m* armato.

tanker ['tæŋkər] *n* (*truck*) autocisterna *f*.

tanned [tænd] *adj* (*suntanned*) abbronzato(-a).

tap [tæp] ◆ *n* (*for water*) rubinetto *m* ◆ *vt* (*hit*) dare un colpetto a.

tape [teɪp] ◆ *n* (*cassette, video*) cassetta *f*; (*in cassette*) nastro *m*; (*adhesive material*) nastro *m* adesivo; (*strip of material*) fettuccia *f* ◆ *vt* (*record*) registrare; (*stick*) attaccare con nastro adesivo.

tape measure *n* metro *m*.

tape recorder *n* registratore *m*.

tapestry ['tæpɪstrɪ] *n* arazzo *m*.

tap water *n* acqua *f* di rubinetto.

tar [taːr] *n* (*for roads*) catrame *m*; (*in cigarettes*) condensato *m*.

target ['taːgɪt] *n* bersaglio *m*.

tariff ['tærɪf] *n* (*price list*) tariffario *m*; (Br: *menu*) listino *m* prezzi; (*at customs*) tariffa *f* doganale.

tarmac ['taːmæk] *n* (*at airport*) pista *f*.

▶ **Tarmac®** *n* (*on road*) asfalto *m*.

tarpaulin [taːˈpɔːlɪn] *n* telone *m*.

tart [taːt] *n* (*sweet*) crostata *f*.

tartan ['taːtn] *n* (*design*) scozzese *m*; (*cloth*) tartan *m*.

tartare sauce [ˌtaːtə-] *n* salsa *f* tartara.

task [taːsk] *n* compito *m*.

taste [teɪst] ◆ *n* gusto *m*; (*flavour*) gusto, sapore *m* ◆ *vt* (*sample*) assaggiare; (*detect*) sentire il gusto di ◆ *vi*: **to ~ of sthg** sapere di qc; **it ~s bad** ha un cattivo sapore; **it ~s good** ha un buon sapore; **to have a ~ of sthg** (*food, drink*) assaggiare qc; (*fig: experience*) provare qc; **bad ~** cattivo gusto; **good ~** buon gusto.

tasteful ['teɪstfʊl] *adj* di buon gusto.

tasteless ['teɪstlɪs] *adj* (*food*) insipido(-a); (*comment, decoration*) di cattivo gusto.

tasty ['teɪstɪ] *adj* gustoso(-a).

tattoo [təˈtuː] (*pl* **-s**) *n* (*on skin*) tatuaggio *m*; (*military display*) parata *f*.

taught [tɔːt] *pt & pp* → **teach**.

Taurus ['tɔːrəs] *n* Toro *m*.

taut [tɔːt] *adj* teso(-a).

tax [tæks] ◆ *n* (*on income*) imposta *f*, tasse *fpl*; (*on import, goods*) tassa *f* ◆ *vt* (*goods, person*) tassare.

tax disc *n* (Br) ≃ bollo *m*.

tax-free *adj* esentasse (*inv*).

taxi ['tæksɪ] ◆ *n* taxi *m inv* ◆ *vi* (*plane*) rullare.

taxi driver *n* tassista *mf*.

taxi rank *n* (Br) posteggio *m* dei taxi.

taxi stand (Am) = **taxi rank**.

T-bone steak *n* costata *f* alla fiorentina.

tea [tiː] *n* tè *m inv*; (*evening meal*) cena *f*.

tea bag *n* bustina *f* di tè.

teacake ['tiːkeɪk] *n* panino dolce all'uvetta.

teach [tiːtʃ] (*pt & pp* **taught**) ◆ *vt* (*subject*) insegnare; (*person*) insegnare a ◆ *vi* insegnare; **to ~ sb sthg**, **to ~ sthg to sb** insegnare qc a qn; **to ~ sb (how) to do sthg** insegnare a qn a fare qc.

teacher ['tiːtʃər] *n* insegnante *mf*; (*in primary school*) maestro *m* (-a *f*); (*in secondary school*) professore *m* (-essa *f*).

teaching ['tiːtʃɪŋ] *n* insegnamento *m*.

tea cloth = **tea towel**.

teacup ['tiːkʌp] *n* tazza *f* da tè.

team [tiːm] *n* squadra *f*.

teapot ['tiːpɒt] *n* teiera *f*.

tear¹ [teər] (*pt* **tore**, *pp* **torn**) ◆ *vt* (*rip*) strappare ◆ *vi* (*rip*) strapparsi; (*move quickly*) precipitarsi ◆ *n* (*rip*) strappo *m*.

▶ **tear up** *vt sep* strappare.

tear² [tɪər] *n* lacrima *f*.

tearoom ['tiːrʊm] *n* sala *f* da tè.

tease [tiːz] *vt* prendere in giro.

tea set *n* servizio *m* da tè.

teaspoon ['ti:spu:n] *n* cucchiaino *m*.

teaspoonful ['ti:spu:n,fʊl] *n* cucchiaino *m*.

teat [ti:t] *n* (*of animal*) capezzolo *m*; (Br: *of bottle*) tettarella *f*.

teatime ['ti:taɪm] *n* ora *f* del tè.

tea towel *n* strofinaccio *m*.

technical ['teknɪkl] *adj* tecnico(-a).

technical drawing *n* disegno *m* tecnico.

technicality [,teknɪ'kælətɪ] *n* (*detail*) dettaglio *m* tecnico.

technician [tek'nɪʃn] *n* tecnico *m* (-a *f*).

technique [tek'ni:k] *n* tecnica *f*.

technological [,teknə'lɒdʒɪkl] *adj* tecnologico(-a).

technology [tek'nɒlədʒɪ] *n* tecnologia *f*.

teddy (bear) ['tedɪ-] *n* orsacchiotto *m*.

tedious ['ti:djəs] *adj* noioso(-a).

tee [ti:] *n* tee *m inv*.

teenager ['ti:n,eɪdʒər] *n* adolescente *mf*.

teeth [ti:θ] *pl* → **tooth**.

teethe [ti:ð] *vi*: **to be teething** mettere i denti.

teetotal [ti:'təʊtl] *adj* astemio(-a).

telegram ['telɪgræm] *n* telegramma *m*.

telegraph ['telɪgrɑ:f] ◆ *n* telegrafo *m* ◆ *vt* telegrafare.

telegraph pole *n* palo *m* del telegrafo.

telephone ['telɪfəʊn] ◆ *n* telefono *m* ◆ *vt* (*person*) telefonare a ◆ *vi* telefonare; **to be on the ~** (*talking*) essere al telefono; (*connected*) avere il telefono.

telephone booth *n* cabina *f* telefonica.

telephone box *n* cabina *f* telefonica.

telephone call *n* telefonata *f*.

telephone directory *n* elenco *m* telefonico.

telephone number *n* numero *m* di telefono.

telephonist [tɪ'lefənɪst] *n* (Br) centralinista *mf*.

telephoto lens [,telɪ'fəʊtəʊ-] *n* teleobiettivo *m*.

telescope ['telɪskəʊp] *n* telescopio *m*.

television ['telɪ,vɪʒn] *n* televisione *f*; (*set*) televisore *m*; **on (the) ~** (*broadcast*) alla televisione.

telex ['teleks] *n* telex *m inv*.

tell [tel] (*pt & pp* **told**) ◆ *vt* dire; (*story, joke*) raccontare; (*distinguish*) distinguere ◆ *vi*: **I can ~** si vede; **can you ~ me the time?** sa dirmi l'ora?; **to ~ sb sthg** dire qc a qn; **to ~ sb about sthg** raccontare qc a qn; **to ~ sb how to do sthg** dire a qn come fare qc; **to ~ sb to do sthg** dire a qn di fare qc.

▶ **tell off** *vt sep* rimproverare.

teller ['telər] *n* (*in bank*) cassiere *m* (-a *f*).

telly ['telɪ] *n* (Br: *inf*) tele *f*.

temp [temp] ◆ *n* impiegato *m* straordinario (impiegata *f* straordinaria) ◆ *vi* avere un impiego temporaneo.

temper ['tempər] *n* (*character*) carattere *m*; **to be in a ~** essere in collera; **to lose one's ~** andare in collera.

temperature ['temprətʃər] *n* temperatura *f*; **to have a ~** avere la febbre.

temple ['templ] *n* (*building*) tempio *m*; (*of forehead*) tempia *f*.

temporary ['tempərərɪ] *adj* temporaneo(-a).

tempt [tempt] *vt* tentare; **to be ~ed to do sthg** essere tentato di fare qc.

temptation [temp'teɪʃn] *n* tentazione *f*.

tempting ['temptɪŋ] *adj* allettante.

ten [ten] *num* dieci, → **six**.

tenant ['tenənt] *n* inquilino *m* (-a *f*).

tend [tend] *vi*: **to ~ to do sthg** tendere a fare qc.

tendency ['tendənsɪ] *n* tendenza *f*.

tender ['tendər] ◆ *adj* tenero(-a); (*sore*) dolorante ◆ *vt* (*fml: pay*) presentare.

tendon ['tendən] *n* tendine *m*.

tenement [:tenəmənt] *n* caseggiato *m*.

tennis ['tenɪs] *n* tennis *m*.

tennis ball *n* palla *f* da tennis.

tennis court *n* campo *m* da tennis.

tennis racket *n* racchetta *f* da tennis.

tenpin bowling ['tenpɪn-] *n* (Br) bowling *m*.

tenpins ['tenpɪnz] (Am) = **tenpin bowling**.

tense [tens] ◆ *adj* teso(-a) ◆ *n* (GRAMM) tempo *m*.

tension ['tenʃn] *n* tensione *f*.

tent [tent] *n* tenda *f*.

tenth [tenθ] *num* decimo(-a), → **sixth**.

tent peg *n* picchetto *m* da tenda.

tepid ['tepɪd] *adj* (*water*) tiepido(-a).

tequila [tɪ'kiːlə] *n* tequila *f*.

term [tɜːm] *n* (*word, expression*) termine *m*; (*at school, university*) trimestre *m*; **in the long ~** a lungo andare; **in the short ~** a breve scadenza; **in ~s of** per quanto riguarda; **in business ~s** dal punto di vista commerciale.

▶ **terms** *npl* (*price, of contract*) condizioni *fpl*.

terminal ['tɜːmɪnl] ◆ *adj* (*illness*) terminale ◆ *n* (*for buses*) capolinea *m*; (*at airport*) terminal *m inv*; (COMPUT) terminale *m*.

terminate ['tɜːmɪneɪt] *vi* (*train, bus*) fare capolinea.

terminus ['tɜːmɪnəs] *n* (*of buses*) capolinea *m*; (*of trains*) stazione *f* terminale.

terrace ['terəs] *n* (*patio*) terrazza *f*; **the ~s** (*at football ground*) le gradinate.

terraced house ['terəst-] *n* (Br) casa *f* a schiera.

terrible ['terəbl] *adj* terribile; (*very ill*): **to feel ~** stare malissimo.

terribly ['terəblɪ] *adv* (*extremely*) terribilmente; (*very badly*) malissimo.

terrier ['terɪər] *n* terrier *m inv*.

terrific [tə'rɪfɪk] *adj* (*inf*) (*very good*) fantastico(-a); (*very great*) grande.

terrified ['terɪfaɪd] *adj* terrorizzato(-a).

territory ['terətrɪ] *n* (*political area*) territorio *m*; (*terrain*) terreno *m*.

terror ['terər] *n* terrore *m*.

terrorism ['terərɪzm] *n* terrorismo *m*.

terrorist ['terərɪst] *n* terrorista *mf*.

terrorize ['terəraɪz] *vt* terrorizzare.

test [test] ◆ *n* (*at school*) prova *f*; (*check*) controllo *m*; (MED) esame *m* ◆ *vt* (*check*) controllare; (*give exam to*) esaminare; (*try*) provare; **driving ~** esame di guida.

testicles ['testɪklz] *npl* testicoli *mpl*.

tetanus ['tetənəs] *n* tetano *m*.

text [tekst] *n* testo *m*.

textbook ['tekstbʊk] *n* libro *m* di testo.

textile ['tekstaɪl] *n* tessuto *m*.

texture ['tekstʃər] *n* consistenza *f*; (*of fabric*) trama *f*.

Thai [taɪ] *adj* tailandese.

Thailand ['taɪlænd] *n* la Tailandia.

Thames [temz] *n*: **the ~** il Tamigi.

than [*weak form* ðən, *strong form* ðæn] ◆ *prep* di ◆ *conj* che; **you're better ~ me** sei più bravo di me; **I'd rather stay in ~ go out** preferisco restare a casa piuttosto che uscire; **more ~ six** più di sei.

thank [θæŋk] *vt*: **to ~ sb (for sthg)** ringraziare qn (per qc).

▶ **thanks** ◆ *npl* ringraziamenti *mpl* ◆ *excl* grazie!; **~s to** grazie a; **many ~s** grazie infinite.

Thanksgiving [θæŋks,gɪvɪŋ] *n* festa *f* del Ringraziamento (*festa nazionale americana*).

thank you *excl* grazie!; **~ very much!** tante or mille grazie!; **no ~!** no, grazie!

that [ðæt, *weak form of pron senses 3, 4 & conj* ðət] (*pl* **those**) *adj* **1.** (*referring to thing, person mentioned*) quel/quello (quella/quell'), quegli/quei (quelle) (*pl*); ~ **book** quel libro; **who's ~ man?** chi è quell'uomo?; **those chocolates are delicious** quei cioccolatini sono buonissimi.

2. (*referring to thing, person further away*) quello(-a) là; **I prefer ~ book** preferisco quel libro; **I'll have ~ one** prendo quello là.

♦ *pron* **1.** (*referring to thing mentioned*) ciò; **what's ~?** che cos'è (quello)?; **I can't do ~** non posso farlo; **who's ~?** chi è quello?; **is Lucy?** è Lucy?

2. (*referring to thing, person further away*) quello(-a), quelli(-e) (*pl*).

3. (*introducing relative clause*) che; **a shop ~ sells antiques** un negozio che vende oggetti d'antiquariato; **the film ~ I saw** il film che ho visto.

4. (*introducing relative clause: after prep*) cui; **the person ~ I was telling you about** la persona di cui ti stavo parlando; **the place ~ I'm looking for** il posto che sto cercando.

♦ *adv* tanto, così; **it wasn't ~ bad/good** non era così cattivo/buono.

♦ *conj* che; **tell him ~ I'm going to be late** digli che farò tardi.

thatched [ðætʃt] *adj* (*roof*) di paglia.

that's [ðæts] = **that is**.

thaw [θɔː] ♦ *vi* (*snow, ice*) sciogliersi ♦ *vt* (*frozen food*) scongelare.

the [*weak form* ðə, *before vowel* ði, *strong form* ðiː] *definite article* **1.** (*gen*) il/lo (la), i/gli (le); ~ **book** il libro; ~ **man** l'uomo; ~ **mirror** lo specchio; ~ **woman** la donna; ~ **island** l'isola; ~ **men** gli uomini; ~ **girls** le ragazze; ~ **Wilsons** i Wilsons.

2. (*with an adjective to form a noun*): ~ **British** i britannici; ~ **young** i giovani.

3. (*in dates*): **Friday ~ nineteenth of May** venerdì diciannove maggio; ~

twelfth il dodici; ~ **forties** gli anni quaranta.

4. (*in titles*): **Elizabeth ~ Second** Elisabetta Seconda.

theater ['θɪətər] *n* (*Am*) (*for plays, drama*) = **theatre**; (*for films*) cinema *m inv*.

theatre ['θɪətər] *n* (*Br*) (*for plays*) teatro *m*.

theft [θeft] *n* furto *m*.

their [ðeər] *adj* il loro (la loro), i loro (le loro) (*pl*); **their brother** loro fratello.

theirs [ðeəz] *pron* il loro (la loro), i loro (le loro) (*pl*); **a friend of ~** un loro amico.

them [*weak form* ðəm, *strong form* ðem] *pron* (*direct*) li (le); (*indirect*) gli; (*after prep with people*) loro; (*after prep with things*) essi(-e); **I know ~** li conosco; **it's ~** sono loro; **send it to ~** mandaglielo; **tell ~** diglielo; **he's worse than ~** è peggio di loro.

theme [θiːm] *n* tema *m*.

theme park *n* parco *m* di divertimenti.

themselves [ðəm'selvz] *pron* (*reflexive*) si; (*after prep*) se stessi (se stesse), sé; **they did it ~** l'hanno fatto da soli.

then [ðen] *adv* allora; (*next, afterwards*) dopo, poi; **from ~ on** da allora in poi; **until ~** fino ad allora.

theory ['θɪərɪ] *n* teoria *f*; **in ~** in teoria.

therapist ['θerəpɪst] *n* terapeuta *mf*.

therapy ['θerəpɪ] *n* terapia *f*.

there [ðeər] ♦ *adv* (*at, in, to that place*) lì, là ♦ *pron*: ~ **is** c'è; ~ **are** ci sono; **is anyone ~?** c'è nessuno?; **is Bob ~, please?** (*on phone*) c'è Bob, per cortesia?; **we're going ~ tomorrow** ci andiamo domani; **over ~** laggiù; ~ **you are** (*when giving*) ecco a lei.

thereabouts [ðeərə'bauts] *adv*: **or ~** o giù di lì.

therefore ['ðeəfɔːr] *adv* perciò.

there's [ðeəz] = **there is**.

thermal underwear [ˌθɜːml-] n biancheria f termica.

thermometer [θəˈmɒmɪtəʳ] n termometro m.

Thermos (flask)® [ˈθɜːməs-] n thermos® m inv.

thermostat [ˈθɜːməstæt] n termostato m.

these [ðiːz] pl → **this**.

they [ðeɪ] pron essi (esse); (referring to people) loro; ~'re tall sono alti.

thick [θɪk] adj (in size) spesso(-a); (hair) folto(-a); (sauce, smoke) denso(-a); (fog) fitto(-a); (inf: stupid) tonto(-a); it's one metre ~ ha uno spessore di un metro.

thicken [ˈθɪkn] ◆ vt (sauce, soup) rendere più denso ◆ vi (mist, fog) infittirsi.

thickness [ˈθɪknɪs] n spessore m.

thief [θiːf] (pl **thieves** [θiːvz]) n ladro m (-a f).

thigh [θaɪ] n coscia f.

thimble [ˈθɪmbl] n ditale m.

thin [θɪn] adj sottile; (person, animal) magro(-a); (soup, sauce) liquido(-a).

thing [θɪŋ] n cosa f; the ~ is il fatto è.

▶ **things** npl (clothes, possessions) cose fpl; how are ~s? (inf) come vanno le cose?

thingummyjig [ˈθɪŋəmɪdʒɪg] n (inf) coso m.

think [θɪŋk] (pt & pp **thought**) ◆ vt pensare ◆ vi pensare; to ~ that pensare che; to ~ about pensare a; to ~ of pensare a; to ~ of doing sthg pensare di fare qc; I ~ so penso di sì; I don't ~ so penso di no; do you ~ you could ...? potrebbe ...?; I'll think about it ci penserò; I can't ~ of his address non mi viene in mente il suo indirizzo; to ~ highly of sb avere una buona opinione di qn.

▶ **think over** vt sep riflettere su.

▶ **think up** vt sep escogitare.

third [θɜːd] num terzo(-a), → **sixth**.

third party insurance n assicu-

razione f contro terzi.

Third World n: the ~ il Terzo Mondo.

thirst [θɜːst] n sete f.

thirsty [ˈθɜːstɪ] adj: to be ~ avere sete.

thirteen [ˌθɜːˈtiːn] num tredici, → **six**.

thirteenth [ˌθɜːˈtiːnθ] num tredicesimo(-a), → **sixth**.

thirtieth [ˈθɜːtɪəθ] num trentesimo(-a), → **sixth**.

thirty [ˈθɜːtɪ] num trenta, → **six**.

this [ðɪs] (pl **these**) adj 1. (referring to thing, person mentioned) questo(-a); these chocolates are delicious questi cioccolatini sono buonissimi; ~ morning stamattina; ~ week questa settimana.

2. (referring to thing, person nearer) questo(-a); I prefer ~ book preferisco questo libro; I'll have ~ one prendo questo.

3. (inf: when telling a story): there was ~ man ... c'era un tizio ...

◆ pron 1. (referring to thing, person mentioned) questo(-a); ~ is for you questo è per te; what are these? che cosa sono questi?; ~ is David Gregory (introducing someone) questo è David Gregory; (on telephone) sono David Gregory.

2. (referring to thing, person nearer) questo(-a).

◆ adv: it was ~ big era grande così.

thistle [ˈθɪsl] n cardo m.

thorn [θɔːn] n spina f.

thorough [ˈθʌrə] adj (check, search) accurato(-a); (person) preciso(-a).

thoroughly [ˈθʌrəlɪ] adv (completely) a fondo.

those [ðəʊz] pl → **that**.

though [ðəʊ] ◆ conj benché, sebbene ◆ adv tuttavia; even ~ anche se.

thought [θɔːt] ◆ pt & pp → **think** ◆ n pensiero m; (idea) idea f.

thoughtful [ˈθɔːtfʊl] adj (quiet and serious) pensieroso(-a); (considerate) premuroso(-a).

thoughtless [ˈθɔːtlɪs] adj sconsiderato(-a).

thousand [ˈθaʊznd] num mille; a OR one ~ mille; ~s of migliaia di, → **six**.

thrash [θræʃ] vt (inf: defeat heavily) battere.

thread [θred] ♦ n (of cotton etc) filo m ♦ vt (needle) infilare.

threadbare [ˈθredbeər] adj logoro(-a).

threat [θret] n minaccia f.

threaten [ˈθretn] vt minacciare; to ~ to do sthg minacciare di fare qc.

threatening [ˈθretnɪŋ] adj minaccioso(-a).

three [θriː] num tre, → **six**.

three-D n: in ~ tridimensionale.

three-piece suite n divano m e due poltrone coordinati.

three-quarters [ˈ-kwɔːtəz] n tre quarti mpl; ~ of an hour tre quarti d'ora.

threshold [ˈθreʃhəʊld] n (fml) soglia f.

threw [θruː] pt → **throw**.

thrifty [ˈθrɪftɪ] adj parsimonioso(-a).

thrilled [θrɪld] adj contentissimo(-a).

thriller [ˈθrɪlər] n thriller m inv.

thrive [θraɪv] vi (plant, animal, person) crescere bene; (business, tourism, place) prosperare.

throat [θrəʊt] n gola f.

throb [θrɒb] vi (noise, engine) vibrare; my head is throbbing ho un mal di testa lancinante.

throne [θrəʊn] n trono m.

throttle [ˈθrɒtl] n (of motorbike) valvola f a farfalla.

through [θruː] ♦ prep attraverso; (because of) grazie a; (from beginning to end of) per tutta la durata di; (across all of) per tutto(-a) ♦ adv (to other side) attraverso; (from beginning to end) dall'inizio alla fine ♦ adj: to be ~ (with sthg) (finished) avere finito (con qc); you're ~ (on phone) è in linea; Monday ~ Thursday (Am) dal lunedì al giovedì; to go ~ (to somewhere else) passare; to let sb ~ far passare qn; I slept ~ the entire film ho dormito per tutto il film; ~ traffic traffico m di attraversamento; a ~ train un treno diretto; 'no ~ road' (Br) 'strada senza uscita'.

throughout [θruːˈaʊt] ♦ prep (day, morning, year) per tutto(-a); (place, country, building) in tutto(-a) ♦ adv (all the time) per tutto il tempo; (everywhere) dappertutto.

throw [θrəʊ] (pt threw, pp thrown [θrəʊn]) vt gettare; (ball, javelin) lanciare; (dice) tirare; to ~ sthg in the bin gettare qc nel cestino.

▶ **throw away** vt sep (get rid of) buttare OR gettare via.

▶ **throw out** vt sep (get rid of) buttare OR gettare via; (person) buttare fuori.

▶ **throw up** vi (inf: vomit) rimettere.

thru [θruː] (Am) = **through**.

thrush [θrʌʃ] n (bird) tordo m.

thud [θʌd] n tonfo m.

thug [θʌg] n delinquente mf.

thumb [θʌm] ♦ n pollice m ♦ vt: to ~ a lift fare l'autostop.

thumbtack [ˈθʌmtæk] n (Am) puntina f da disegno.

thump [θʌmp] ♦ n (punch) pugno m; (sound) tonfo m ♦ vt picchiare.

thunder [ˈθʌndər] n tuono m.

thunderstorm [ˈθʌndəstɔːm] n temporale m.

Thurs. (abbr of Thursday) gio.

Thursday [ˈθɜːzdɪ] n giovedì m inv, → **Saturday**.

thyme [taɪm] n timo m.

Tiber [ˈtaɪbər] n: the ~ il Tevere.

tick [tɪk] ♦ n (written mark) segno m; (insect) zecca f ♦ vt spuntare ♦ vi (clock, watch) fare tic tac.

▶ **tick off** vt sep (mark off) spuntare.

ticket [ˈtɪkɪt] n (for travel, cinema, theatre, match) biglietto m; (label) etichetta f; (speeding ticket, parking ticket) multa f.

ticket collector n controllore m.

ticket inspector n controllore m.

ticket machine n distributore m automatico di biglietti.

ticket office n biglietteria f.

tickle ['tɪkl] vt fare il solletico a.

ticklish ['tɪklɪʃ] adj: **to be ~** soffrire il solletico.

tick-tack-toe n (Am) tris m (gioco).

tide [taɪd] n (of sea) marea f.

tidy ['taɪdɪ] adj (room, desk, person) ordinato(-a); (hair, clothes) in ordine.

▶ **tidy up** vt sep riordinare, mettere in ordine.

tie [taɪ] (pt & pp **tied**, cont **tying**) ◆ n (around neck) cravatta f; (draw) pareggio m; (Am: on railway track) traversa f ◆ vt (fasten) legare; (laces) allacciare; (knot) fare ◆ vi (draw) pareggiare.

▶ **tie up** vt sep (fasten) legare; (laces) annodare.

tied up ['taɪd-] adj occupato(-a).

tiepin ['taɪpɪn] n fermacravatta m inv.

tier [tɪər] n (of seats) fila f.

tiger ['taɪgər] n tigre f.

tight [taɪt] ◆ adj stretto(-a); (rope) teso(-a); (chest) chiuso(-a); (schedule) serrato(-a); (inf: drunk) sbronzo(-a) ◆ adv (hold) stretto(-a).

tighten ['taɪtn] vt stringere.

tightrope ['taɪtrəup] n corda f (sulla quale si esibiscono i funamboli).

tights [taɪts] npl collant m inv; **a pair of ~** un paio di collant.

tile [taɪl] n (for roof) tegola f; (for floor, wall) mattonella f, piastrella f.

till [tɪl] ◆ n (for money) cassa f ◆ prep fino a ◆ conj finché non.

tiller ['tɪlər] n barra f del timone.

tilt [tɪlt] ◆ vt inclinare ◆ vi inclinarsi.

timber ['tɪmbər] n (wood) legname m; (of roof) trave f.

time [taɪm] ◆ n tempo m; (measured by clock) ora f; (of train, flight, bus) ora-

rio m; (moment) momento m; (occasion) volta f ◆ vt (measure) cronometrare; (arrange) programmare; **to ~ sthg well** fare qc al momento giusto; **I haven't got the ~** non ho tempo; **it's ~ to go** è ora di andare; **what's the ~?** che ore sono?; **two ~s two** due per due; **two at a ~** due per volta; **five ~s as much** cinque volte tanto; **in a month's ~** fra un mese; **to have a good ~** divertirsi; **all the ~** sempre; **every ~** ogni volta; **from ~ to ~** di tanto in tanto; **for the ~ being** per il momento; **in ~** (arrive) in tempo; **in good ~** per tempo; **last ~** l'ultima volta; **most of the ~** la maggior parte del tempo; **on ~** puntuale; **some of the ~** parte del tempo; **this ~** questa volta.

time difference n differenza f di fuso orario.

time limit n termine m massimo.

timer ['taɪmər] n timer m inv.

time share n multiproprietà f inv.

timetable ['taɪmˌteɪbl] n orario m; (of events) calendario m.

time zone n fuso m orario.

timid ['tɪmɪd] adj (shy) timido(-a); (easily frightened) pauroso(-a).

tin [tɪn] ◆ n (metal) stagno m; (container) scatola f ◆ adj di latta.

tinfoil ['tɪnfɔɪl] n stagnola f.

tinned food [tɪnd-] n (Br) cibo m in scatola.

tin opener [-ˌəupnər] n (Br) apriscatole m inv.

tinsel ['tɪnsl] n fili mpl argentati (per decorare l'albero di Natale).

tint [tɪnt] n tinta f.

tinted glass [ˌtɪntɪd-] n vetro m colorato.

tiny ['taɪnɪ] adj molto piccolo(-a).

tip [tɪp] ◆ n (point, end) punta f; (to waiter, taxi driver etc) mancia f; (piece of advice) suggerimento m; (rubbish dump) discarica f ◆ vt (waiter, taxi driver etc) dare la mancia a; (tilt) inclinare; (pour) versare.

▶ **tip over** ◆ vt sep rovesciare ◆ vi rovesciarsi.

tire ['taɪə'] ◆ vi stancarsi ◆ n (Am) = **tyre**.

tired ['taɪəd] adj stanco(-a); **to be ~ of** (fed up with) essere stanco di.

tired out adj esausto(-a).

tiring ['taɪərɪŋ] adj faticoso(-a).

tissue ['tɪʃuː] n (handkerchief) fazzolettino m di carta.

tissue paper n carta f velina.

tit [tɪt] n (vulg: breast) tetta f.

title ['taɪtl] n titolo m.

T-junction n incrocio m a T.

to [unstressed before consonant tə, unstressed before vowel tu, stressed tuː] prep **1.** (indicating direction) a; **to go ~ Milan** andare a Milano; **to go ~ France** andare in Francia; **to go ~ school** andare a scuola; **to go ~ the office** andare in ufficio.

2. (indicating position) a; **~ the left/right** a sinistra/destra.

3. (expressing indirect object) a; **to give sthg ~ sb** dare qc a qn; **to listen ~ the radio** ascoltare la radio.

4. (indicating reaction, effect) a; **to be favourable ~ sthg** essere favorevole a qc; **~ my surprise** con mia grande sorpresa.

5. (until) fino a; **to count ~ ten** contare fino a dieci; **we work from nine ~ five** lavoriamo dalle nove alle cinque.

6. (indicating change of state): **to turn ~ sthg** trasformarsi in qc; **it could lead ~ trouble** potrebbe causare problemi.

7. (Br: in expressions of time): **it's ten ~ three** sono le tre meno dieci; **at quarter ~ seven** alle sette meno un quarto.

8. (in ratios, rates): **40 miles ~ the gallon** = 100 chilometri con 7 litri; **there are sixteen ounces ~ the pound** sedici once fanno una libbra.

9. (of, for): **the keys ~ the car** le chiavi dell'automobile; **a letter ~ my daughter** una lettera a mia figlia.

10. (indicating attitude) con, verso; **to be rude ~ sb** essere scortese con qn.

◆ with infinitive **1.** (forming simple infinitive): **~ walk** camminare; **~ laugh** ridere.

2. (following another verb): **to begin ~ do sthg** cominciare a fare qc; **to try ~ do sthg** cercare di fare qc.

3. (following an adjective): **difficult ~ do** difficile da fare; **ready ~ go** pronto a partire.

4. (indicating purpose) per; **we came here ~ look at the castle** siamo venuti qui per visitare il castello.

toad [təʊd] n rospo m.

toadstool ['təʊdstuːl] n fungo m velenoso.

toast [təʊst] ◆ n (bread) pane m tostato; (when drinking) brindisi m inv ◆ vt (bread) tostare; **a piece OR slice of ~** una fetta di pane tostato.

toasted sandwich ['təʊstɪd-] n toast m inv.

toaster ['təʊstə'] n tostapane m inv.

toastie ['təʊstɪ] = **toasted sandwich**.

tobacco [tə'bækəʊ] n tabacco m.

tobacconist's [tə'bækənɪsts] n (shop) tabaccaio m.

toboggan [tə'bɒgən] n toboga m inv.

today [tə'deɪ] ◆ n oggi m ◆ adv oggi.

toddler ['tɒdlə'] n bambino m (-a f) (che muove i primi passi).

toe [təʊ] n (of person) dito m del piede.

toe clip n puntapiedi m inv.

toenail ['təʊneɪl] n unghia f del piede.

toffee ['tɒfɪ] n (sweet) caramella f mou (inv).

together [tə'geðə'] adv insieme; **~ with** insieme a.

toilet ['tɔɪlɪt] n (room) gabinetto m; (bowl) water m inv; **to go to the ~** andare al gabinetto; **where's the ~?** dov'è il gabinetto?

toilet bag n nécessaire m inv da toilette.

toilet paper n carta f igienica.

toiletries ['tɔɪlɪtrɪz] npl prodotti mpl cosmetici.

toilet roll n rotolo m di carta igienica.

toilet water n acqua f di colonia.

token ['təʊkn] n (metal disc) gettone m.

told [təʊld] pt & pp → tell.

tolerable ['tɒlərəbl] adj (fairly good) passabile; (bearable) sopportabile.

tolerant ['tɒlərənt] adj tollerante.

tolerate ['tɒləreɪt] vt tollerare.

toll [təʊl] n (for road, bridge) pedaggio m.

tollbooth ['təʊlbu:θ] n casello m.

toll-free adj (Am): ~ number ≃ numero m verde.

tomato [Br təˈmɑːtəʊ, Am təˈmeɪtəʊ] (pl -es) n pomodoro m.

tomato juice n succo m di pomodoro.

tomato ketchup n ketchup m.

tomato puree n conserva f di pomodoro.

tomato sauce n sugo m di pomodoro.

tomb [tu:m] n tomba f.

tomorrow [təˈmɒrəʊ] ♦ n domani m ♦ adv domani; **the day after ~** dopodomani; **~ afternoon** domani pomeriggio; **~ morning** domani mattina; **~ night** domani sera.

ton [tʌn] n (in Britain) = 1016 kg; (in U.S.) = 907 kg; (metric tonne) tonnellata f; **~s of** (inf) un sacco di.

tone [təʊn] n (of voice) tono m; (on phone) segnale m; (of colour) tonalità f inv.

tongs [tɒŋz] npl (for hair) arricciacapelli m inv; (for sugar) mollette fpl.

tongue [tʌŋ] n lingua f.

tonic ['tɒnɪk] n (tonic water) acqua f tonica; (medicine) ricostituente m.

tonic water n acqua f tonica.

tonight [təˈnaɪt] ♦ n (night) questa notte f; (evening) questa sera f ♦ adv (night) stanotte, questa notte; (evening) stasera, questa sera.

tonne [tʌn] n tonnellata f.

tonsillitis [ˌtɒnsɪˈlaɪtɪs] n tonsillite f.

too [tu:] adv (excessively) troppo; (also) anche; **it's ~ late to go out** è troppo tardi per uscire; **~ many** troppi(-e); **~ much** troppo(-a).

took [tʊk] pt → take.

tool [tu:l] n attrezzo m.

tool kit n attrezzi mpl.

tooth [tu:θ] (pl teeth) n dente m.

toothache ['tu:θeɪk] n mal m di denti.

toothbrush ['tu:θbrʌʃ] n spazzolino m da denti.

toothpaste ['tu:θpeɪst] n dentifricio m.

toothpick ['tu:θpɪk] n stuzzicadenti m.

top [tɒp] ♦ adj (highest) più alto(-a); (step, stair) ultimo(-a); (best) migliore; (most important) più importante ♦ n (of stairs, hill, page) cima f; (of table) piano m; (of class, league) primo m (-a f); (for bottle, tube, pen) tappo m; (for jar, box) coperchio m; (of pyjamas, bikini) sopra m inv; (blouse) camicetta f; (T-shirt) maglietta f; **at the ~ (of)** (stairs, list, mountain) in cima (a); **on ~ of** (table etc) sopra, su; (in addition to) oltre a; **at ~ speed** a tutta velocità; **~ gear** ≃ quinta f.

▶ **top up** ♦ vt sep (glass, drink) riempire ♦ vi (with petrol) fare il pieno.

top floor n ultimo piano m.

topic ['tɒpɪk] n argomento m.

topical ['tɒpɪkl] adj d'attualità.

topless ['tɒplɪs] adj: **to go ~** mettersi in topless.

topped [tɒpt] adj: **~ with** (cream etc) ricoperto(-a) di.

topping ['tɒpɪŋ] n guarnizione f (su pizza ecc.).

torch [tɔːtʃ] n (Br: electric light) torcia f elettrica.

tore [tɔːr] pt → tear¹.

torment [tɔːˈment] vt (annoy) tormentare.

torn [tɔːn] ♦ pp → tear¹ ♦ adj

(*ripped*) strappato(-a).

tornado [tɔːˈneɪdəʊ] (*pl* **-es** OR **-s**) *n* tornado *m*.

torrential rain [təˌrenʃl-] *n* pioggia *f* torrenziale.

tortoise [ˈtɔːtəs] *n* tartaruga *f*.

tortoiseshell [ˈtɔːtəʃel] *n* tartaruga *f*.

torture [ˈtɔːtʃə*r*] ◆ *n* tortura *f* ◆ *vt* torturare.

Tory [ˈtɔːrɪ] *n* membro del partito conservatore britannico.

toss [tɒs] *vt* (*throw*) lanciare; (*salad, vegetables*) mescolare; **to ~ a coin** fare testa o croce.

total [ˈtəʊtl] ◆ *adj* totale ◆ *n* totale *m*; **in ~** in totale.

touch [tʌtʃ] ◆ *n* (*sense*) tatto *m*; (*small amount*) tantino *m*; (*detail*) tocco *m* ◆ *vt* toccare ◆ *vi* toccarsi; **to get in ~ (with sb)** mettersi in contatto (con qn); **to keep in ~ (with sb)** tenersi in contatto (con qn).

▸ **touch down** *vi* (*plane*) atterrare.

touching [ˈtʌtʃɪŋ] *adj* toccante.

tough [tʌf] *adj* duro(-a); (*resilient*) tenace; (*hard, strong*) resistente.

tour [tʊə*r*] ◆ *n* (*journey*) viaggio *m*; (*of city, castle etc*) visita *f*; (*of pop group, theatre company*) tournée *f inv* ◆ *vt* visitare; **on ~** in tournée.

tourism [ˈtʊərɪzm] *n* turismo *m*.

tourist [ˈtʊərɪst] *n* turista *mf*.

tourist class *n* classe *f* turistica.

tourist information office *n* ufficio *m* d'informazione turistica.

tournament [ˈtɔːnəmənt] *n* torneo *m*.

tour operator *n* operatore *m* turistico (operatrice turistica *f*).

tout [taʊt] *n* bagarino *m*.

tow [təʊ] *vt* rimorchiare.

toward [təˈwɔːd] (Am) = **towards**.

towards [təˈwɔːdz] *prep* (Br) verso; (*with regard to*) nei confronti di; (*to help pay for*) per.

towaway zone [ˈtəʊəweɪ-] *n* (Am) zona *f* rimozione forzata.

towel [ˈtaʊəl] *n* asciugamano *m*.

toweling [ˈtaʊəlɪŋ] (Am) = **towelling**.

towelling [ˈtaʊəlɪŋ] *n* (Br) spugna *f*.

towel rail *n* portasciugamano *m*.

tower [ˈtaʊə*r*] *n* torre *f*.

tower block *n* (Br) grattacielo *m*.

Tower Bridge *n* Tower Bridge (*famoso ponte levatoio di Londra*).

Tower of London *n*: **the ~** la Torre di Londra.

town [taʊn] *n* città *f*; (*town centre*) centro *m* (città).

town centre *n* centro *m* (città).

town hall *n* comune *m*.

towpath [ˈtəʊpɑːθ, *pl* -pɑːðz] *n* alzaia *f*.

towrope [ˈtəʊrəʊp] *n* cavo *m* di rimorchio.

tow truck *n* (Am) carro *m* attrezzi.

toxic [ˈtɒksɪk] *adj* tossico(-a).

toy [tɔɪ] *n* giocattolo *m*.

toy shop *n* negozio *m* di giocattoli.

trace [treɪs] ◆ *n* traccia *f* ◆ *vt* (*find*) rintracciare.

tracing paper [ˈtreɪsɪŋ-] *n* carta *f* da ricalco.

track [træk] *n* (*path*) sentiero *m*; (*of railway*) binario *m*, rotaie *fpl*; (SPORT) pista *f*; (*song*) pezzo *m*.

▸ **track down** *vt sep* trovare.

tracksuit [ˈtræksuːt] *n* tuta *f* da ginnastica.

tractor [ˈtræktə*r*] *n* trattore *m*.

trade [treɪd] ◆ *n* (COMM) commercio *m*; (*job*) mestiere *m* ◆ *vt* scambiare ◆ *vi* commerciare.

trade-in *n* permuta *f*.

trademark [ˈtreɪdmɑːk] *n* marchio *m* di fabbrica.

trader [ˈtreɪdə*r*] *n* commerciante *mf*.

tradesman [ˈtreɪdzmən] (*pl* **-men** [-mən]) *n* (*deliveryman*) addetto *m* alle consegne; (*shopkeeper*) commerciante *mf*.

trade union n sindacato m.

tradition [trə'dɪʃn] n tradizione f.

traditional [trə'dɪʃənl] adj tradizionale.

traffic ['træfɪk] (pt & pp -ked) ◆ n (cars etc) traffico m ◆ vi: **to ~ in** trafficare in.

traffic circle n (Am) rotatoria f.

traffic island n salvagente m.

traffic jam n ingorgo m.

traffic lights npl semaforo m.

traffic warden n (Br) ≃ vigile m urbano (addetto al controllo dei divieti e limiti di sosta).

tragedy ['trædʒədɪ] n tragedia f.

tragic ['trædʒɪk] adj tragico(-a).

trail [treɪl] ◆ n (path) sentiero m; (marks) tracce fpl ◆ vi (be losing) essere in svantaggio.

trailer ['treɪlər] n (for boat, luggage) rimorchio m; (Am: caravan) roulotte f inv; (for film, programme) trailer m inv.

train [treɪn] ◆ n (on railway) treno m ◆ vt (teach) formare; (animal) addestrare ◆ vi (SPORT) allenarsi; **by ~** in treno.

train driver n macchinista m.

trainee [treɪ'niː] n (for profession) tirocinante mf; (for trade) apprendista mf.

trainer ['treɪnər] n (of athlete etc) allenatore m (-trice f).

▶ **trainers** npl (Br: shoes) scarpe fpl da ginnastica.

training ['treɪnɪŋ] n (instruction) formazione f, addestramento m; (exercises) allenamento m.

training shoes npl (Br) scarpe fpl da ginnastica.

tram [træm] n (Br) tram m inv.

tramp [træmp] n vagabondo m (-a f).

trampoline ['træmpəliːn] n trampolino m.

trance [trɑːns] n trance f.

tranquilizer ['træŋkwɪlaɪzər] (Am) = tranquillizer.

tranquillizer ['træŋkwɪlaɪzər] n

(Br) tranquillante m.

transaction [træn'zækʃn] n transazione f.

transatlantic [ˌtrænzət'læntɪk] adj transatlantico(-a).

transfer [n 'trænsfɜːr, vb træns'fɜːr] ◆ n trasferimento m; (of power, property) passaggio m; (picture) decalcomania f; (Am: ticket) biglietto che dà la possibilità di cambiare autobus, treno ecc. senza pagare alcun supplemento ◆ vt trasferire ◆ vi (change bus, plane etc) cambiare; **'~s'** (in airport) 'transiti'.

transfer desk n banco m transiti.

transform [træns'fɔːm] vt trasformare.

transfusion [træns'fjuːʒn] n trasfusione f.

transistor radio [træn'zɪstər-] n transistor m inv.

transit ['trænzɪt] : **in transit** adv in transito.

transitive ['trænzɪtɪv] adj transitivo(-a).

transit lounge n sala f transiti.

translate [træns'leɪt] vt tradurre.

translation [træns'leɪʃn] n traduzione f.

translator [træns'leɪtər] n traduttore m (-trice f).

transmission [trænz'mɪʃn] n trasmissione f.

transmit [trænz'mɪt] vt trasmettere.

transparent [træns'pærənt] adj trasparente.

transplant ['trænsplɑːnt] n trapianto m.

transport [n 'trænspɔːt, vb træn'spɔːt] ◆ n (cars, trains, planes etc) trasporti mpl; (moving) trasporto m ◆ vt trasportare.

transportation [ˌtrænspɔː'teɪʃn] n (Am) (cars, trains, planes etc) trasporti mpl; (moving) trasporto m.

trap [træp] ◆ n trappola f ◆ vt: **to be trapped** (stuck) essere intrappolato.

trapdoor [ˌtræp'dɔːr] n botola f.

trash [træʃ] n (Am: waste material) spazzatura f.

trashcan [ˈtræʃkæn] n (Am) pattumiera f.

trauma [ˈtrɔːmə] n (bad experience) trauma m.

traumatic [trɔːˈmætɪk] adj traumatico(-a).

travel [ˈtrævl] ♦ n viaggi mpl ♦ vt (distance) percorrere ♦ vi viaggiare.

travel agency n agenzia f di viaggi.

travel agent n agente mf di viaggi; ~'s (shop) agenzia f di viaggi.

Travelcard [ˈtrævlkɑːd] n biglietto che dà accesso ai mezzi pubblici di Londra per un'intera giornata.

travel centre n (in railway, bus station) ufficio informazioni e biglietteria.

traveler [ˈtrævlər] (Am) = **traveller**.

travel insurance n assicurazione f viaggio.

traveller [ˈtrævlər] n (Br) viaggiatore m (-trice f).

traveller's cheque n traveller's cheque m inv.

travelsick [ˈtrævəlsɪk] adj: **to be ~** (in car) soffrire il mal d'auto; (on boat) soffrire il mal di mare; (on plane) soffrire il mal d'aria.

trawler [ˈtrɔːlər] n peschereccio m.

tray [treɪ] n vassoio m.

treacherous [ˈtretʃərəs] adj (person) infido(-a); (roads, conditions) insidioso(-a).

treacle [ˈtriːkl] n (Br) melassa f.

tread [tred] (pt **trod**, pp **trodden**) ♦ n (of tyre) battistrada m inv ♦ vi: **to ~ on sthg** calpestare qc.

treasure [ˈtreʒər] n tesoro m.

treat [triːt] ♦ vt trattare; (patient, illness) curare ♦ n regalo m; **to ~ sb to sthg** offrire qc a qn.

treatment [ˈtriːtmənt] n (MED) cure fpl; (of person) trattamento m; (of subject) trattazione f.

treble [ˈtrebl] adj triplo(-a).

tree [triː] n albero m.

trek [trek] n escursione f.

tremble [ˈtrembl] vi tremare.

tremendous [trɪˈmendəs] adj (very large) enorme; (inf: very good) formidabile.

trench [trentʃ] n fosso m.

trend [trend] n (tendency) tendenza f; (fashion) moda f.

trendy [ˈtrendɪ] adj (inf) alla moda.

trespasser [ˈtrespəsər] n: '~s will be prosecuted' 'vietato l'accesso; i trasgressori saranno puniti ai termini di legge'.

trial [ˈtraɪəl] n (JUR) processo m; (test) prova f; **a ~ period** un periodo di prova.

triangle [ˈtraɪæŋgl] n triangolo m.

triangular [traɪˈæŋgjʊlər] adj triangolare.

tribe [traɪb] n tribù f inv.

tributary [ˈtrɪbjʊtrɪ] n tributario m, affluente m.

trick [trɪk] ♦ n trucco m; (conjuring trick) gioco m di prestigio ♦ vt imbrogliare, ingannare; **to play a ~ on sb** giocare un brutto tiro a qn.

trickle [ˈtrɪkl] vi (liquid) gocciolare, colare.

tricky [ˈtrɪkɪ] adj difficile.

tricycle [ˈtraɪsɪkl] n triciclo m.

trifle [ˈtraɪfl] n (dessert) zuppa f inglese.

trigger [ˈtrɪgər] n grilletto m.

trim [trɪm] ♦ n (haircut) spuntata f ♦ vt (hair, beard) spuntare; (hedge) regolare.

trinket [ˈtrɪŋkɪt] n ciondolo m, gingillo m.

trio [ˈtriːəʊ] (pl **-s**) n trio m.

trip [trɪp] ♦ n (journey) viaggio m; (short) gita f, escursione f ♦ vi inciampare.

▶ **trip up** vi inciampare.

triple [ˈtrɪpl] adj triplo(-a).

tripod [ˈtraɪpɒd] n treppiedi m inv.

triumph [ˈtraɪəmf] n trionfo m.

trivial [ˈtrɪvɪəl] adj (pej) insignificante, banale.

trod [trɒd] *pt* → **tread**.

trodden ['trɒdn] *pp* → **tread**.

trolley ['trɒlɪ] (*pl* **-s**) *n* (Br: *in super-market, at airport, for food etc*) carrello *m*; (Am: *tram*) tram *m inv*.

trombone [trɒm'bəʊn] *n* trombone *m*.

troops [truːps] *npl* truppe *fpl*.

trophy ['trəʊfɪ] *n* trofeo *m*.

tropical ['trɒpɪkl] *adj* tropicale.

trot [trɒt] ♦ *vi* (*horse*) trottare ♦ *n*: **on the ~** (*inf*) di fila.

trouble ['trʌbl] ♦ *n* problemi *mpl* ♦ *vt* (*worry*) preoccupare; (*bother*) disturbare; **to be in ~** essere nei guai; **to get into ~** mettersi nei guai; **to take the ~ to do sthg** darsi la pena di fare qc; **it's no ~** non si preoccupi; (*in reply to thanks*) di niente.

trough [trɒf] *n* (*for drinking*) abbeveratoio *m*.

trouser press ['trauzə'-] *n* stiracalzoni *m inv*.

trousers ['trauzəz] *npl* pantaloni *mpl*; **a pair of ~** un paio di pantaloni.

trout [traut] (*pl inv*) *n* trota *f*.

trowel ['trauəl] *n* (*for gardening*) paletta *f*.

truant ['truːənt] *n*: **to play ~** marinare la scuola.

truce [truːs] *n* tregua *f*.

truck [trʌk] *n* (*lorry*) camion *m inv*, autocarro *m*.

true [truː] *adj* vero(-a).

truly ['truːlɪ] *adv*: **yours ~** distinti saluti.

trumpet ['trʌmpɪt] *n* tromba *f*.

trumps [trʌmps] *npl* atout *m inv*.

truncheon ['trʌntʃən] *n* sfollagente *m inv*.

trunk [trʌŋk] *n* (*of tree*) tronco *m*; (Am: *of car*) bagagliaio *m*; (*case, box*) baule *m*; (*of elephant*) proboscide *f*.

trunk call *n* (Br) interurbana *f*.

trunk road *n* (Br) strada *f* statale.

trunks [trʌŋks] *npl* costume *m* da bagno da uomo.

trust [trʌst] ♦ *n* (*confidence*) fiducia *f* ♦ *vt* (*believe, have confidence in*) fidarsi di, aver fiducia in; (*fml: hope*) sperare.

trustworthy ['trʌst,wɜːðɪ] *adj* degno(-a) di fiducia.

truth [truːθ] *n* (*true facts*) verità *f*; (*quality of being true*) veridicità *f*.

truthful ['truːθfʊl] *adj* (*statement, account*) veritiero(-a); (*person*) sincero(-a).

try [traɪ] ♦ *n* (*attempt*) tentativo *m*, prova *f* ♦ *vt* provare; (JUR) giudicare ♦ *vi* provare; **to ~ to do sthg** provare a fare qc.

▶ **try on** *vt sep* (*clothes*) provare, provarsi.

▶ **try out** *vt sep* provare.

T-shirt *n* maglietta *f*.

tub [tʌb] *n* (*of margarine etc*) vaschetta *f*; (*inf: bath*) vasca *f* (da bagno).

tube [tjuːb] *n* (*container*) tubetto *m*; (Br: *inf: underground*) metropolitana *f*; (*pipe*) tubo *m*; **by ~** in metropolitana.

tube station *n* (Br: *inf*) stazione *f* della metropolitana.

tuck [tʌk] : **tuck in** ♦ *vt sep* (*shirt*) mettersi dentro; (*child, person*) rimboccare le coperte a ♦ *vi* (*inf*) mangiare di buon appetito.

tuck shop *n* (Br) *piccolo negozio di merendine, caramelle ecc., presso una scuola*.

Tudor ['tjuːdə'] *adj* Tudor (*inv*) (*sedicesimo secolo*).

Tues. (*abbr of* Tuesday) mar.

Tuesday ['tjuːzdɪ] *n* martedì *m inv*, → **Saturday**.

tuft [tʌft] *n* ciuffo *m*.

tug [tʌg] ♦ *vt* tirare ♦ *n* (*boat*) rimorchiatore *m*.

tuition [tjuː'ɪʃn] *n* lezioni *fpl*.

tulip ['tjuːlɪp] *n* tulipano *m*.

tumble-dryer ['tʌmbldraɪə'] *n* asciugabiancheria *m inv*.

tumbler ['tʌmblə'] *n* (*glass*) bicchiere *m* (*senza stelo*).

tummy ['tʌmɪ] n (inf) pancia f.

tummy upset n (inf) disturbi mpl di pancia.

tumor ['tu:mər] (Am) = **tumour**.

tumour ['tju:mər] n (Br) tumore m.

tuna (fish) [Br 'tju:nə, Am 'tu:nə] n (food) tonno m.

tuna melt n (Am) crostino di tonno e formaggio fuso.

tune [tju:n] ◆ n (melody) melodia f ◆ vt (radio, TV) sintonizzare; (engine) mettere a punto; (instrument) accordare; **in ~** (person) intonato; (instrument) accordato; **out of ~** (person) stonato; (instrument) scordato.

tunic ['tju:nɪk] n tunica f.

Tunisia [tju:'nɪzɪə] n la Tunisia.

tunnel ['tʌnl] n tunnel m inv, galleria f.

turban ['tɜ:bən] n turbante m.

turbo ['tɜ:bəʊ] (pl -s) n (car) turbo m inv.

turbulence ['tɜ:bjʊləns] n (when flying) turbolenza f.

turf [tɜ:f] n (grass) tappeto m erboso.

Turin [tjʊ'rɪn] n Torino f.

Turk [tɜ:k] n turco m (-a f).

turkey ['tɜ:kɪ] (pl -s) n tacchino m.

Turkey n la Turchia.

Turkish ['tɜ:kɪʃ] ◆ adj turco(-a) ◆ n (language) turco m ◆ npl: **the ~ i** turchi.

Turkish delight n dolciume fatto di gelatina e ricoperto di zucchero a velo.

turn [tɜ:n] ◆ n (in road) curva f; (of knob, key, switch) giro m; (go, chance) turno m ◆ vt girare; (a bend) prendere; (become) diventare; (cause to become) far diventare ◆ vi girare; (person) girarsi; (milk) andare a male; **to ~ into sthg** (become) diventare qc; **to ~ sthg into sthg** trasformare qc in qc; **to ~ left/right** girare a sinistra/a destra; **it's your ~** tocca a te; **at the ~ of the century** all'inizio del secolo; **to take it in ~s to do sthg** fare qc a turno; **to ~ sthg inside out** rigirare qc.

▶ **turn back** ◆ vt sep (person, car) mandare indietro ◆ vi tornare indietro.

▶ **turn down** vt sep (radio, volume, heating) abbassare; (offer, request) rifiutare.

▶ **turn off** ◆ vt sep (light, TV, engine) spegnere; (water, gas, tap) chiudere ◆ vi (leave road) girare, svoltare.

▶ **turn on** vt sep (light, TV, engine) accendere; (water, gas, tap) aprire.

▶ **turn out** ◆ vt fus (be in the end) rivelarsi ◆ vt sep (light, fire) spegnere ◆ vi (come, attend) affluire; **to ~ out to be sthg** risultare essere qc.

▶ **turn over** ◆ vi (in bed) girarsi, rigirarsi; (Br: change channels) cambiare canale ◆ vt sep girare.

▶ **turn round** ◆ vt sep (car, table etc) girare ◆ vi (person) girarsi, voltarsi.

▶ **turn up** ◆ vt sep (radio, volume, heating) alzare ◆ vi (come) venire.

turning ['tɜ:nɪŋ] n (off road) svolta f.

turnip ['tɜ:nɪp] n rapa f.

turn-up n (Br: on trousers) risvolto m.

turps [tɜ:ps] n (Br: inf) trementina f.

turquoise ['tɜ:kwɔɪz] adj turchese.

turtle ['tɜ:tl] n tartaruga f (acquatica).

turtleneck ['tɜ:tlnek] n maglia f a lupetto.

Tuscany ['tʌskənɪ] n la Toscana.

tutor ['tju:tər] n (private teacher) insegnante m privato (insegnante f privata).

tuxedo [tʌk'si:dəʊ] (pl -s) n (Am) smoking m inv.

TV n tivù f inv, TV f inv; **on ~** alla tivù.

tweed [twi:d] n tweed m.

tweezers ['twi:zəz] npl pinzette fpl.

twelfth [twelfθ] num dodicesimo(-a), → **sixth**.

twelve [twelv] num dodici, → **six**.

twentieth ['twentɪəθ] num ventesimo(-a); **the ~ century** il ventesimo secolo, → **sixth**.

twenty ['twentɪ] num venti, → **six**.

twice [twaɪs] adv due volte; **it's ~ as good** è due volte meglio; **~ as much** il doppio.

twig [twɪg] n ramoscello m.

twilight ['twaɪlaɪt] n crepuscolo m.

twin [twɪn] n gemello m (-a f).

twin beds npl letti mpl gemelli.

twine [twaɪn] n spago m.

twin room n stanza f a due letti.

twist [twɪst] vt (wire) torcere, piegare; (rope, hair) attorcigliare; (bottle top, lid, knob) girare; **to ~ one's ankle** slogarsi la caviglia.

twisting ['twɪstɪŋ] adj (road, river) tortuoso(-a).

two [tuː] num due, → **six**.

two-piece adj (swimsuit, suit) a due pezzi (inv).

type [taɪp] ♦ n (kind) tipo m ♦ vt & vi battere a macchina.

typewriter ['taɪpˌraɪtər] n macchina f da scrivere.

typhoid ['taɪfɔɪd] n tifoidea f.

typical ['tɪpɪkl] adj tipico(-a).

typist ['taɪpɪst] n dattilografo m (-a f).

tyre ['taɪər] n (Br) gomma f, pneumatico m.

U

U adj (Br: film) per tutti.

UFO n (abbr of unidentified flying object) UFO m inv.

ugly ['ʌglɪ] adj brutto(-a).

UHT adj (abbr of ultra heat treated) UHT.

UK n: **the ~** il Regno Unito.

ulcer ['ʌlsər] n ulcera f.

Ulster ['ʌlstər] n l'Ulster m.

ultimate ['ʌltɪmət] adj (final) finale; (best, greatest) ideale.

ultraviolet [ˌʌltrə'vaɪələt] adj ultravioletto(-a).

umbrella [ʌm'brelə] n ombrello m.

umpire ['ʌmpaɪər] n arbitro m.

UN n (abbr of United Nations): **the ~** l'ONU f.

unable [ʌn'eɪbl] adj: **to be ~ to do sthg** non poter fare qc.

unacceptable [ˌʌnək'septəbl] adj inaccettabile.

unaccustomed [ˌʌnə'kʌstəmd] adj: **to be ~ to sthg** non essere abituato(-a) a qc.

unanimous [juː'nænɪməs] adj unanime.

unattended [ˌʌnə'tendɪd] adj (baggage) incustodito(-a).

unattractive [ˌʌnə'træktɪv] adj (person, idea) poco attraente; (place) privo(-a) di attrattiva.

unauthorized [ʌn'ɔːθəraɪzd] adj non autorizzato(-a).

unavailable [ˌʌnə'veɪləbl] adj non disponibile.

unavoidable [ˌʌnə'vɔɪdəbl] adj inevitabile.

unaware [ˌʌnə'weər] adj: **to be ~ of sthg/that** ignorare qc/che.

unbearable [ʌn'beərəbl] adj insopportabile.

unbelievable [ˌʌnbɪ'liːvəbl] adj incredibile.

unbutton [ʌn'bʌtn] vt sbottonare.

uncertain [ʌn'sɜːtn] adj incerto(-a).

uncertainty [ʌn'sɜːtntɪ] n incertezza f.

uncle ['ʌŋkl] n zio m.

unclean [ʌn'kliːn] adj sporco(-a).

unclear [ʌn'klɪər] adj non chiaro(-a).

uncomfortable [ʌn'kʌmftəbl] adj (person, chair) scomodo(-a); (fig: awkward) a disagio.

uncommon [ʌn'kɒmən] adj (rare) raro(-a).

unconscious [ʌn'kɒnʃəs] adj (after accident) privo(-a) di sensi; (un-

aware) inconsapevole.

unconvincing [ˌʌnkən'vɪnsɪŋ] *adj* poco convincente.

uncooperative [ˌʌnkəʊ'ɒpərətɪv] *adj* poco disposto(-a) a collaborare.

uncork [ʌn'kɔːk] *vt* stappare.

uncouth [ʌn'kuːθ] *adj* villano(-a), grossolano(-a).

uncover [ʌn'kʌvəʳ] *vt* scoprire.

under ['ʌndəʳ] *prep* sotto; (*less than*) meno di, al di sotto di; (*according to*) secondo; **children ~ ten** bambini sotto i dieci anni; **~ the circumstances** date le circostanze; **to be ~ pressure** essere sotto pressione.

underage [ʌndər'eɪdʒ] *adj* minorenne.

undercarriage ['ʌndəˌkærɪdʒ] *n* carrello *m*.

underdone [ʌndə'dʌn] *adj* poco cotto(-a).

underestimate [ʌndər'estɪmeɪt] *vt* sottovalutare.

underexposed [ʌndərɪk'spəʊzd] *adj* (*photograph*) sottoesposto(-a).

undergo [ʌndə'gəʊ] (*pt* -went, *pp* -gone) *vt* subire.

undergraduate [ʌndə'grædjʊət] *n* studente *m* universitario (studentessa *f* universitaria).

underground ['ʌndəgraʊnd] ♦ *adj* (*below earth's surface*) sotterraneo(-a); (*secret*) clandestino(-a) ♦ *n* (Br: *railway*) metropolitana *f*.

undergrowth ['ʌndəgrəʊθ] *n* sottobosco *m*.

underline [ʌndə'laɪn] *vt* sottolineare.

underneath [ʌndə'niːθ] ♦ *prep* & *adv* sotto ♦ *n* sotto *m*.

underpants ['ʌndəpænts] *npl* mutande *fpl*, slip *m inv*.

underpass ['ʌndəpɑːs] *n* sottopassaggio *m*.

undershirt ['ʌndəʃɜːt] *n* (A*m*) maglietta *f*.

underskirt ['ʌndəskɜːt] *n* sottoveste *f*.

understand [ʌndə'stænd] (*pt* & *pp* -stood) ♦ *vt* capire; (*believe*) credere ♦ *vi* capire; **I don't ~** non capisco; **to make o.s. understood** farsi capire.

understanding [ʌndə'stændɪŋ] ♦ *adj* comprensivo(-a) ♦ *n* (*agreement*) accordo *m*; (*knowledge*) conoscenza *f*; (*interpretation*) interpretazione *f*; (*sympathy*) comprensione *f*.

understatement [ʌndə'steɪtmənt] *n*: **that's an ~!** a dir poco!

understood [ʌndə'stʊd] *pt* & *pp* → **understand**.

undertake [ʌndə'teɪk] (*pt* -took, *pp* -taken) *vt* intraprendere; **to ~ to do sthg** impegnarsi a fare qc.

undertaker ['ʌndəˌteɪkəʳ] *n* impresario di pompe funebri.

undertaking [ʌndə'teɪkɪŋ] *n* (*promise*) promessa *f*; (*task*) impresa *f*.

undertook [ʌndə'tʊk] *pt* → **undertake**.

underwater [ʌndə'wɔːtəʳ] ♦ *adj* subacqueo(-a) ♦ *adv* sott'acqua.

underwear ['ʌndəweəʳ] *n* biancheria *f* intima.

underwent [ʌndə'went] *pt* → **undergo**.

undesirable [ʌndɪ'zaɪərəbl] *adj* indesiderato(-a).

undo [ʌn'duː] (*pt* -did, *pp* -done) *vt* (*coat, shirt*) sbottonare; (*shoelaces*) slacciare; (*tie*) sciogliere il nodo di; (*parcel*) sfare.

undone [ʌn'dʌn] *adj* (*coat, shirt*) sbottonato(-a); (*shoelaces*) slacciato(-a).

undress [ʌn'dres] ♦ *vi* spogliarsi ♦ *vt* spogliare.

undressed [ʌn'drest] *adj* spogliato(-a); **to get ~** spogliarsi.

uneasy [ʌn'iːzɪ] *adj* a disagio.

uneducated [ʌn'edjʊkeɪtɪd] *adj* non istruito(-a).

unemployed [ʌnɪm'plɔɪd] ♦ *adj* disoccupato(-a) ♦ *npl*: **the ~** i disoccupati.

unemployment [ʌnɪm'plɔɪmənt]

n disoccupazione *f*.

unemployment benefit *n* sussidio *m* di disoccupazione.

unequal [ʌnˈiːkwəl] *adj* (*not the same*) disuguale; (*not fair*) iniquo(-a).

uneven [ʌnˈiːvn] *adj* (*surface, speed, beat*) irregolare; (*share, distribution*) ineguale.

uneventful [ʌnɪˈventfʊl] *adj* tranquillo(-a).

unexpected [ˌʌnɪkˈspektɪd] *adj* inaspettato(-a).

unexpectedly [ˌʌnɪkˈspektɪdlɪ] *adv* inaspettatamente.

unfair [ʌnˈfeər] *adj* ingiusto(-a).

unfairly [ʌnˈfeəlɪ] *adv* ingiustamente.

unfaithful [ʌnˈfeɪθfʊl] *adj* infedele.

unfamiliar [ˌʌnfəˈmɪljər] *adj* sconosciuto(-a); **to be ~ with** non conoscere bene.

unfashionable [ʌnˈfæʃnəbl] *adj* fuori moda.

unfasten [ʌnˈfɑːsn] *vt* (*seatbelt, belt, laces*) slacciare; (*knot*) sfare, sciogliere.

unfavourable [ʌnˈfeɪvrəbl] *adj* sfavorevole.

unfinished [ʌnˈfɪnɪʃt] *adj* incompiuto(-a).

unfit [ʌnˈfɪt] *adj* (*not healthy*) non in forma; **to be ~ for sthg** (*not suitable*) essere inadatto(-a) a qc.

unfold [ʌnˈfəʊld] *vt* spiegare (*tovaglia, cartina*).

unforgettable [ˌʌnfəˈgetəbl] *adj* indimenticabile.

unforgivable [ˌʌnfəˈgɪvəbl] *adj* imperdonabile.

unfortunate [ʌnˈfɔːtʃnət] *adj* (*unlucky*) sfortunato(-a); (*regrettable*) infelice; **it is ~ that** è un peccato che.

unfortunately [ʌnˈfɔːtʃnətlɪ] *adv* sfortunatamente.

unfriendly [ʌnˈfrendlɪ] *adj* poco amichevole.

unfurnished [ʌnˈfɜːnɪʃt] *adj* non ammobiliato(-a).

ungrateful [ʌnˈgreɪtfʊl] *adj* ingrato(-a).

unhappy [ʌnˈhæpɪ] *adj* (*sad*) infelice; (*not pleased*) insoddisfatto(-a); **to be ~ about sthg** essere insoddisfatto di qc.

unharmed [ʌnˈhɑːmd] *adj* indenne.

unhealthy [ʌnˈhelθɪ] *adj* (*person*) malaticcio(-a); (*food, smoking*) dannoso(-a) per la salute; (*place*) malsano(-a).

unhelpful [ʌnˈhelpfʊl] *adj* (*person*) poco disponibile; (*advice, instructions*) inutile.

unhurt [ʌnˈhɜːt] *adj* indenne.

unhygienic [ʌnhaɪˈdʒiːnɪk] *adj* non igienico(-a).

unification [juːnɪfɪˈkeɪʃn] *n* unificazione *f*.

uniform [ˈjuːnɪfɔːm] *n* uniforme *f*.

unimportant [ˌʌnɪmˈpɔːtənt] *adj* senza importanza.

unintelligent [ˌʌnɪnˈtelɪdʒənt] *adj* poco intelligente.

unintentional [ˌʌnɪnˈtenʃənl] *adj* involontario(-a).

uninterested [ʌnˈɪntrəstɪd] *adj* indifferente.

uninteresting [ʌnˈɪntrestɪŋ] *adj* poco interessante, noioso(-a).

union [ˈjuːnjən] *n* (*of workers*) sindacato *m*.

Union Jack *n*: **the ~** la bandiera nazionale del Regno Unito.

unique [juːˈniːk] *adj* unico(-a); **to be ~ to** essere proprio(-a) di.

unisex [ˈjuːnɪseks] *adj* unisex (*inv*).

unit [ˈjuːnɪt] *n* unità *f inv*; (*department, building*) reparto *m*; (*piece of furniture*) elemento *m*; (*machine*) apparecchio *m*.

unite [juːˈnaɪt] ♦ *vt* unire ♦ *vi* unirsi.

United Kingdom [juːˈnaɪtɪd-] *n*: **the ~** il Regno Unito.

United Nations [juːˈnaɪtɪd-] *npl*:

the ~ le Nazioni Unite.

United States (of America)
[juː'naɪtɪd-] *npl*: **the ~** gli Stati Uniti
(d'America).

unity ['juːnətɪ] *n* unità *f*.

universal [ˌjuːnɪ'vɜːsl] *adj* universale.

universe ['juːnɪvɜːs] *n* universo *m*.

university [ˌjuːnɪ'vɜːsətɪ] *n* università *f inv*.

unjust [ˌʌn'dʒʌst] *adj* ingiusto(-a).

unkind [ʌn'kaɪnd] *adj* scortese.

unknown [ˌʌn'nəʊn] *adj* scono-
sciuto(-a).

unleaded (petrol) [ˌʌn'ledɪd-] *n*
benzina *f* senza piombo.

unless [ən'les] *conj* a meno che
non; **~ it rains** a meno che non
piova.

unlike [ˌʌn'laɪk] *prep* a differenza
di; **that's ~ her** non è da lei.

unlikely [ʌn'laɪklɪ] *adj* improbabile; **he is ~ to arrive before six** è
improbabile che arrivi prima delle
sei.

unlimited [ʌn'lɪmɪtɪd] *adj* illimita-
to(-a); **~ mileage** = chilometraggio
illimitato.

unlisted [ʌn'lɪstɪd] *adj* (*Am: phone
number*): **to be ~** non essere
sull'elenco telefonico.

unload [ʌn'ləʊd] *vt* scaricare.

unlock [ʌn'lɒk] *vt* aprire.

unlucky [ʌn'lʌkɪ] *adj* (*unfortunate*)
sfortunato(-a); (*bringing bad luck*)
che porta sfortuna.

unmarried [ˌʌn'mærɪd] *adj* non
sposato(-a).

unnatural [ʌn'nætʃrəl] *adj* (*unusual*) inconsueto(-a); (*behaviour,
person*) poco naturale.

unnecessary [ʌn'nesəsərɪ] *adj*
inutile.

unobtainable [ˌʌnəb'teɪnəbl] *adj*
(*product*) non disponibile; (*phone
number*) non ottenibile.

unoccupied [ʌn'ɒkjʊpaɪd] *adj*
(*place, seat*) libero(-a).

unofficial [ˌʌnə'fɪʃl] *adj* non ufficia-

le; (*strike*) non autorizzato(-a).

unpack [ʌn'pæk] ♦ *vt* (*bags, suitcase*) disfare ♦ *vi* disfare le valigie.

unpleasant [ʌn'pleznt] *adj* (*smell,
weather, etc*) sgradevole; (*person*)
spiacevole, antipatico(-a).

unplug [ʌn'plʌg] *vt* staccare.

unpopular [ʌn'pɒpjʊlər] *adj* impopolare.

unpredictable [ʌnprɪ'dɪktəbl] *adj*
imprevedibile.

unprepared [ʌnprɪ'peəd] *adj*
impreparato(-a).

unprotected [ʌnprə'tektɪd] *adj*
senza protezione.

unqualified [ʌn'kwɒlɪfaɪd] *adj*
(*person*) non qualificato(-a).

unreal [ʌn'rɪəl] *adj* irreale.

unreasonable [ʌn'riːznəbl] *adj*
irragionevole.

unrecognizable [ʌnrekəg-
'naɪzəbl] *adj* irriconoscibile.

unreliable [ʌnrɪ'laɪəbl] *adj* inaffi-
dabile.

unrest [ʌn'rest] *n* agitazione *f*.

unroll [ʌn'rəʊl] *vt* srotolare.

unsafe [ʌn'seɪf] *adj* (*dangerous*)
pericoloso(-a); (*in danger*) in pericolo.

unsatisfactory [ʌnsætɪs'fæktərɪ]
adj insoddisfacente.

unscrew [ʌn'skruː] *vt* (*lid, top*) svitare.

unsightly [ʌn'saɪtlɪ] *adj* brutto(-a).

unskilled [ʌn'skɪld] *adj* (*worker*)
non qualificato(-a).

unsociable [ʌn'səʊʃəbl] *adj* poco
socievole.

unsound [ʌn'saʊnd] *adj* (*building,
structure*) poco saldo(-a); (*argument*)
che non regge.

unspoiled [ʌn'spɔɪlt] *adj* (*place,
beach*) incontaminato(-a).

unsteady [ʌn'stedɪ] *adj* instabile;
(*hand*) malfermo(-a).

unstuck [ʌn'stʌk] *adj*: **to come ~**
(*label, poster etc*) staccarsi.

unsuccessful [ʌnsək'sesful] *adj*
che non ha successo.

unsuitable [ˌʌn'suːtəbl] *adj* inadatto(-a), inadeguato(-a); (*moment*) inopportuno(-a).

unsure [ˌʌn'ʃɔːʳ] *adj*: **to be ~ (about)** non essere sicuro(-a) (di).

unsweetened [ˌʌn'swiːtnd] *adj* senza zucchero.

untidy [ʌn'taɪdɪ] *adj* (*person*) disordinato(-a); (*room, desk*) in disordine.

untie [ʌn'taɪ] (*cont* **untying** [ʌn'taɪɪŋ]) *vt* (*person*) slegare; (*knot*) sciogliere, sfare.

until [ən'tɪl] ♦ *prep* fino a ♦ *conj* finché; (*after negative, in past*) prima che, prima di; **it won't be ready ~ Thursday** non sarà pronto prima di giovedì.

untrue [ˌʌn'truː] *adj* falso(-a).

untrustworthy [ˌʌn'trʌst,wɜːðɪ] *adj* che non è degno di fiducia.

untying *cont* → **untie**.

unusual [ʌn'juːʒl] *adj* insolito(-a).

unusually [ʌn'juːʒəlɪ] *adv* (*more than usual*) insolitamente.

unwell [ʌn'wel] *adj* indisposto(-a); **to feel ~** non sentirsi bene.

unwilling [ʌn'wɪlɪŋ] *adj*: **to be ~ to do sthg** non voler fare qc.

unwind [ʌn'waɪnd] (*pt & pp* **unwound** [ʌn'waʊnd]) ♦ *vt* svolgere ♦ *vi* (*relax*) rilassarsi, distendersi.

unwrap [ˌʌn'ræp] *vt* aprire.

unzip [ˌʌn'zɪp] *vt* aprire (la cerniera di).

up [ʌp] *adv* 1. (*towards higher position*) su, in alto; **to go ~** salire; **we walked ~ to the top** siamo saliti fino in cima; **to pick sthg ~** raccogliere qc.
2. (*in higher position*) su, in alto; **she's ~ in her bedroom** è su nella sua stanza; **~ there** lassù.
3. (*into upright position*): **to stand ~** alzarsi; **to sit ~** (*from lying position*) tirarsi su a sedere; (*sit straight*) stare seduto diritto.
4. (*to increased level*): **prices are going ~** i prezzi stanno salendo.
5. (*northwards*): **~ in Scotland** in Scozia.

6. (*in phrases*): **to walk ~ and down** andare su e giù; **~ to ten people** fino a dieci persone; **are you ~ to travelling?** te la senti di viaggiare?; **what are you ~ to?** cosa stai combinando?; **it's ~ to you** sta a te decidere; **~ until ten o'clock** fino alle dieci.
♦ *prep* 1. (*towards higher position*): **to walk ~ a hill** salire su per una collina; **I went ~ the stairs** sono salito per le scale.
2. (*in higher position*) in cima a; **~ a hill** in cima ad una collina; **~ a ladder** in cima ad una scala.
3. (*at end of*): **they live ~ the road from us** abitano un po' più su di noi.
♦ *adj* 1. (*out of bed*) alzato(-a); **I was ~ at six today** mi sono alzato alle sei oggi.
2. (*at an end*): **time's ~** tempo scaduto.
3. (*rising*): **the ~ escalator** la scala mobile per salire.
♦ *n*: **~s and downs** alti e bassi *mpl*.

update [ˌʌp'deɪt] *vt* aggiornare.

uphill [ˌʌp'hɪl] *adv* in salita.

upholstery [ʌp'həʊlstərɪ] *n* tappezzeria *f*.

upkeep ['ʌpkiːp] *n* manutenzione *f*.

up-market *adj* rivolto(-a) alla fascia alta del mercato.

upon [ə'pɒn] *prep* (*fml: on*) su; **~ hearing the news ...** dopo aver appreso la notizia ...

upper ['ʌpəʳ] ♦ *adj* superiore ♦ *n* (*of shoe*) tomaia *f*.

upper class *n*: **the ~** i ceti alti.

uppermost ['ʌpəməʊst] *adj* (*highest*) il più alto (la più alta).

upper sixth *n* (*Br: SCH*) secondo anno del corso biennale che prepara agli 'A levels'.

upright ['ʌpraɪt] ♦ *adj* (*person*) diritto(-a); (*object*) verticale ♦ *adv* diritto.

upset [ʌp'set] (*pt & pp* **upset**) ♦ *adj* (*distressed*) addolorato(-a) ♦ *vt* (*dis-*

tress) addolorare, sconvolgere; (*cause to go wrong*) scombussolare; (*knock over*) rovesciare; **to have an ~ stomach** avere disturbi intestinali.

upside down [ˌʌpsaɪd-] ◆ *adj* capovolto(-a); (*person*) a testa in giù ◆ *adv* sottosopra.

upstairs [ˌʌpˈsteəz] ◆ *adj* di sopra ◆ *adv* (*on a higher floor*) di sopra, al piano superiore; **to go ~** andare di sopra.

up-to-date *adj* (*modern*) moderno(-a); (*well-informed*) aggiornato(-a).

upwards [ˈʌpwədz] *adv* (*to a higher place*) verso l'alto, in su; (*to a higher level*) verso l'alto; **~ of 100 people** più di 100 persone.

urban [ˈɜːbən] *adj* urbano(-a).

urban clearway [-ˈklɪəweɪ] *n* (*Br*) strada con divieto di sosta.

Urdu [ˈʊədɑː] *n* urdu *m*.

urge [ɜːdʒ] *vt*: **to ~ sb to do sthg** esortare qn a fare qc.

urgent [ˈɜːdʒənt] *adj* urgente.

urgently [ˈɜːdʒəntlɪ] *adv* (*immediately*) d'urgenza, urgentemente.

urinal [jʊəˈraɪnl] *n* (*fml*) (*bowl*) orinale *m*; (*place*) vespasiano *m*.

urinate [ˈjʊərɪneɪt] *vi* (*fml*) urinare.

urine [ˈjʊərɪn] *n* urina *f*.

us [ʌs] *pron* ci; (*after prep*) noi; **they know ~** ci conoscono; **it's ~** siamo noi; **send it to ~** mandacelo; **tell ~** dicci; **they're worse than ~** sono peggio di noi.

US *n* (*abbr of United States*): **the ~** gli USA.

USA *n* (*abbr of United States of America*): **the ~** gli USA.

usable [ˈjuːzəbl] *adj* utilizzabile.

use [*n* juːs, *vb* juːz] ◆ *n* uso *m* ◆ *vt* usare; (*run on*) andare a; **to be of ~** essere utile, servire; **to have the ~ of sthg** avere accesso a qc; **to make ~ of sthg** sfruttare qc; **'out of ~'** 'guasto'; **to be in ~** essere in uso; **it's no ~** non serve a niente; **what's the ~?** a che scopo?; **to ~ sthg as sthg** usare qc come qc; **'~ before ...'**

(*food, drink*) 'da consumarsi preferibilmente entro ...'.

▶ **use up** *vt sep* consumare.

used [*adj* juːzd, *aux vb* juːst] ◆ *adj* (*towel, glass etc*) sporco(-a); (*car*) usato(-a) ◆ *aux vb*: **I ~ to live near here** una volta abitavo qui vicino; **I ~ to go there every day** una volta ci andavo tutti i giorni; **to be ~ to sthg** essere abituato(-a) a qc; **to get ~ to sthg** abituarsi a qc.

useful [ˈjuːsfʊl] *adj* utile.

useless [ˈjuːslɪs] *adj* inutile; (*inf: very bad*): **he's ~** non è buono a nulla.

user [ˈjuːzəʳ] *n* utente *mf*.

usher [ˈʌʃəʳ] *n* (*at cinema, theatre*) maschera *f*.

usherette [ˌʌʃəˈret] *n* maschera *f*.

USSR *n*: **the (former) ~** l'(ex) URSS *f*.

usual [ˈjuːʒəl] *adj* solito(-a); **as ~** (*in the normal way*) come al solito.

usually [ˈjuːʒəlɪ] *adv* di solito.

utensil [juːˈtensl] *n* utensile *m*.

utilize [ˈjuːtəlaɪz] *vt* (*fml*) utilizzare.

utmost [ˈʌtməʊst] ◆ *adj* estremo(-a) ◆ *n*: **to do one's ~** fare tutto il possibile.

utopia [juːˈtəʊpjə] *n* utopia *f*.

utter [ˈʌtəʳ] ◆ *adj* totale ◆ *vt* (*word*) proferire, pronunciare; (*cry*) emettere.

utterly [ˈʌtəlɪ] *adv* completamente, del tutto.

U-turn *n* (*in vehicle*) inversione *f* a U.

V

vacancy [ˈveɪkənsɪ] *n* (*job*) posto *m* vacante; **'vacancies'** 'si affittano camere'; **'no vacancies'** 'completo'.

vacant [ˈveɪkənt] *adj* libero(-a).

vacate [vəˈkeɪt] *vt* (*fml: room, house*) lasciare libero.

vacation [vəˈkeɪʃn] ◆ n (Am) (period of time) vacanze fpl; (time off work) ferie fpl ◆ vi (Am) passare le vacanze; **to go on ~** andare in vacanza.

vacationer [vəˈkeɪʃənər] n (Am) villeggiante mf.

vaccination [ˌvæksɪˈneɪʃn] n vaccinazione f.

vaccine [Br ˈvæksiːn, Am vækˈsiːn] n vaccino m.

vacuum [ˈvækjʊəm] vt pulire con l'aspirapolvere.

vacuum cleaner n aspirapolvere m inv.

vague [veɪg] adj vago(-a); (shape, outline) indistinto(-a).

vain [veɪn] adj (pej: conceited) vanitoso(-a); **in ~** invano.

Valentine card [ˈvæləntaɪn-] n biglietto che si manda per San Valentino alla persona che si ama o di cui si è innamorati.

Valentine's Day [ˈvæləntaɪnz-] n San Valentino.

valet [ˈvæleɪ, ˈvælɪt] n (in hotel) chi si occupa del servizio lavanderia e stiratura.

valet service n (in hotel) servizio m di lavanderia; (for car) servizio di lavaggio.

valid [ˈvælɪd] adj (ticket, passport) valido(-a).

validate [ˈvælɪdeɪt] vt (ticket) convalidare.

Valium® [ˈvæliəm] n valium® m.

valley [ˈvælɪ] n valle f.

valuable [ˈvæljʊəbl] adj (jewellery, object) di valore; (advice, help) prezioso(-a).

▶ **valuables** npl oggetti mpl di valore.

value [ˈvæljuː] n (financial) valore m; (usefulness) utilità f; **a ~ pack** una confezione formato famiglia; **to be good ~ (for money)** essere conveniente.

▶ **values** npl (principles) valori mpl.

valve [vælv] n valvola f.

van [væn] n furgone m.

vandal [ˈvændl] n vandalo m (-a f).

vandalize [ˈvændəlaɪz] vt vandalizzare.

vanilla [vəˈnɪlə] n vaniglia f.

vanish [ˈvænɪʃ] vi svanire, scomparire.

vapor [ˈveɪpər] (Am) = **vapour**.

vapour [ˈveɪpər] n (Br) vapore m.

variable [ˈveərɪəbl] adj variabile.

varicose veins [ˈværɪkəʊs-] npl vene fpl varicose.

varied [ˈveərɪd] adj vario(-a).

variety [vəˈraɪətɪ] n varietà f inv.

various [ˈveərɪəs] adj vari(-e).

varnish [ˈvɑːnɪʃ] ◆ n vernice f ◆ vt verniciare.

vary [ˈveərɪ] vi & vt variare.

vase [Br vɑːz, Am veɪz] n vaso m.

Vaseline® [ˈvæsəliːn] n vaselina f.

vast [vɑːst] adj vasto(-a).

vat [væt] n tino m.

VAT [væt, viːˌɛrˈtiː] n (abbr of value added tax) IVA f.

vault [vɔːlt] n (in bank) camera f blindata; (in church) cripta f.

VCR n (abbr of video cassette recorder) videoregistratore m.

VDU n (abbr of visual display unit) monitor m inv.

veal [viːl] n vitello m.

veg [vedʒ] abbr = **vegetable**.

vegan [ˈviːgən] ◆ adj vegetaliano(-a) ◆ n vegetaliano m (-a f).

vegetable [ˈvedʒtəbl] n verdura f.

vegetable oil n olio m vegetale.

vegetarian [ˌvedʒɪˈteərɪən] ◆ adj vegetariano(-a) ◆ n vegetariano m (-a f).

vegetation [ˌvedʒɪˈteɪʃn] n vegetazione f.

vehicle [ˈviːəkl] n veicolo m.

veil [veɪl] n velo m.

vein [veɪn] n vena f.

Velcro® [ˈvelkrəʊ] n velcro® m.

velvet [ˈvelvɪt] n velluto m.

vending machine [ˈvendɪŋ-] n distributore m automatico.

venetian blind [vɪˌniːʃn-] n veneziana f.

Venice ['venɪs] n Venezia f.

venison ['venɪzn] n carne m di cervo.

vent [vent] n (for air, smoke etc) presa f d'aria.

ventilation [,ventɪ'leɪʃn] n ventilazione f.

ventilator ['ventɪleɪtər] n ventilatore m.

venture ['ventʃər] ◆ n impresa f ◆ vi (go) avventurarsi.

venue ['venjuː] n luogo m (di partita, concerto ecc.).

veranda [və'rændə] n veranda f.

verb [vɜːb] n verbo m.

verdict ['vɜːdɪkt] n verdetto m.

verge [vɜːdʒ] n (of road, lawn, path) bordo m; 'soft ~s' 'banchina non transitabile'.

verify ['verɪfaɪ] vt verificare.

vermin ['vɜːmɪn] n roditori che portano malattie e distruggono raccolti.

vermouth ['vɜːməθ] n vermut m inv.

versa → vice versa.

versatile ['vɜːsətaɪl] adj versatile.

verse [vɜːs] n (of song, poem) strofa f; (poetry) versi mpl.

version ['vɜːʃn] n versione f.

versus ['vɜːsəs] prep contro.

vertical ['vɜːtɪkl] adj verticale.

vertigo ['vɜːtɪgəʊ] n: **to suffer from ~** soffrire di vertigini.

very ['verɪ] ◆ adv molto ◆ adj: **at the ~ bottom** proprio in fondo; **~ much** molto; **not ~ big** non molto grande; **my ~ own room** una stanza tutta per me; **~ rich** ricchissimo, molto ricco; **it's the ~ thing I need** è proprio quello di cui avevo bisogno.

vessel ['vesl] n (fml: ship) vascello m.

vest [vest] n (Br: underwear) maglietta f; (sleeveless) canottiera f; (Am: waistcoat) gilè m inv.

Vesuvius [vɪ'suːvjəs] n Vesuvio m.

vet [vet] n (Br) veterinario m (-a f).

veteran ['vetrən] n (of war) vecchio

combattente m.

veterinarian [,vetərɪ'neərɪən] (Am) = **vet**.

veterinary surgeon ['vetərɪnrɪ-] (Br: fml) = **vet**.

VHF n (abbr of very high frequency) VHF f.

VHS n (abbr of video home system) VHS m.

via ['vaɪə] prep (place) via; (by means of) tramite.

viaduct ['vaɪədʌkt] n viadotto m.

vibrate [vaɪ'breɪt] vi vibrare.

vibration [vaɪ'breɪʃn] n vibrazione f.

vicar ['vɪkər] n pastore m.

vicarage ['vɪkərɪdʒ] n presbiterio m.

vice [vaɪs] n (moral fault) vizio m; (crime) crimine m; (Br: tool) morsa f.

vice-president n vice-presidente mf.

vice versa [,vaɪsɪ'vɜːsə] adv vice-versa.

vicinity [vɪ'sɪnətɪ] n: **in the ~** nelle vicinanze.

vicious ['vɪʃəs] adj (attack) violento(-a); (animal) feroce; (comment) cattivo(-a), maligno(-a).

victim ['vɪktɪm] n vittima f.

Victorian [vɪk'tɔːrɪən] adj vittoriano(-a).

victory ['vɪktərɪ] n vittoria f.

video ['vɪdɪəʊ] (pl -s) ◆ n (video recording) video m inv; (videotape) videocassetta f; (video recorder) videoregistratore m ◆ vt (using video recorder) videoregistrare; (using camera) filmare; **on ~** su videocassetta.

video camera n videocamera f.

video game n videogioco m.

video recorder n videoregistratore m.

video shop n videoteca f.

videotape ['vɪdɪəʊteɪp] n videocassetta f.

Vietnam [Br ,vjet'næm, Am ,vjet'nɑːm] n il Vietnam.

view [vjuː] ◆ n vista f; (opinion) opinione f ◆ vt (house) vedere; (situation) considerare; **in my ~** secondo me; **in ~ of** (considering) considerato; **to come into ~** apparire.

viewer ['vjuːəʳ] n (of TV) telespettatore m (-trice f).

viewfinder ['vjuːˌfaɪndəʳ] n mirino m.

viewpoint ['vjuːpɔɪnt] n (opinion) punto m di vista; (place) punto d'osservazione.

vigilant ['vɪdʒɪlənt] adj (fml) vigile.

villa ['vɪlə] n villa f.

village ['vɪlɪdʒ] n paese m.

villager ['vɪlɪdʒəʳ] n abitante mf di paese.

villain ['vɪlən] n (of book, film) cattivo m; (criminal) malvivente mf.

vinaigrette [ˌvɪnɪ'gret] n condimento per insalata a base di olio, aceto, sale, pepe ed erbe aromatiche.

vine [vaɪn] n (grapevine) vite f; (climbing plant) rampicante m.

vinegar ['vɪnɪgəʳ] n aceto m.

vineyard ['vɪnjəd] n vigna f.

vintage ['vɪntɪdʒ] ◆ adj (wine) d'annata ◆ n (year) annata f.

vinyl ['vaɪnɪl] n vinile m.

viola [vɪ'əʊlə] n viola f.

violence ['vaɪələns] n violenza f.

violent ['vaɪələnt] adj violento(-a).

violet ['vaɪələt] ◆ adj viola (inv) ◆ n (flower) viola f.

violin [ˌvaɪə'lɪn] n violino m.

violinist [ˌvaɪə'lɪnɪst] n violinista mf.

VIP n (abbr of very important person) vip mf inv.

virgin ['vɜːdʒɪn] n vergine f.

Virgo ['vɜːgəʊ] (pl -s) n Vergine f.

virtually ['vɜːtʃʊəlɪ] adv praticamente.

virtual reality ['vɜːtʃʊəl-] n realtà f virtuale.

virus ['vaɪrəs] n virus m inv.

visa ['viːzə] n visto m.

viscose ['vɪskəʊs] n viscosa f.

visibility [ˌvɪzɪ'bɪlətɪ] n visibilità f.

visible ['vɪzəbl] adj visibile.

visit ['vɪzɪt] ◆ vt (person) andare a trovare; (place) visitare ◆ n visita f.

visiting hours ['vɪzɪtɪŋ-] npl orario m delle visite.

visitor ['vɪzɪtəʳ] n (to person) visita f; (to place) visitatore m (-trice f).

visitor centre n (at tourist attraction) punto accoglienza per i visitatori di musei ecc.

visitors' book n registro m dei visitatori.

visitor's passport n (Br) passaporto m provvisorio.

visor ['vaɪzəʳ] n visiera f.

vital ['vaɪtl] adj vitale.

vitamin [Br 'vɪtəmɪn, Am 'vaɪtəmɪn] n vitamina f.

vivid ['vɪvɪd] adj vivido(-a).

V-neck n (design) scollo m a V.

vocabulary [və'kæbjʊlərɪ] n vocabolario m.

vodka ['vɒdkə] n vodka f.

voice [vɔɪs] n voce f.

voice mail n (COMPUT) messaggeria f vocale; **to send/receive ~** mandare/ricevere un messaggio vocale.

volcano [vɒl'keɪnəʊ] (pl -es OR -s) n vulcano m.

volleyball ['vɒlɪbɔːl] n pallavolo f.

volt [vəʊlt] n volt m inv.

voltage ['vəʊltɪdʒ] n voltaggio m.

volume ['vɒljuːm] n volume m.

voluntary ['vɒləntrɪ] adj volontario(-a).

volunteer [ˌvɒlən'tɪəʳ] ◆ n volontario m (-a f) ◆ vt: **to ~ to do sthg** offrirsi di fare qc.

vomit ['vɒmɪt] ◆ n vomito m ◆ vi vomitare.

vote [vəʊt] ◆ n voto m; (number of votes) voti mpl ◆ vi: **to ~ (for)** votare (per).

voter ['vəʊtəʳ] n elettore m (-trice f).

voucher ['vaʊtʃəʳ] n buono m.

vowel ['vaʊəl] n vocale f.

voyage ['vɔɪɪdʒ] n viaggio m (per mare).

vulgar ['vʌlgər] adj volgare.

vulture ['vʌltʃər] n avvoltoio m.

W (abbr of west) O.

wad [wɒd] n (of paper, banknotes) fascio m; (of cotton) batuffolo m.

waddle ['wɒdl] vi camminare come una papera.

wade [weɪd] vi camminare (a fatica).

wading pool ['weɪdɪŋ-] n (Am) piscina f per bambini.

wafer ['weɪfər] n (biscuit) cialda f.

waffle ['wɒfl] ◆ n (pancake) cialda dalla caratteristica superficie a quadretti che si mangia con sciroppo d'acero, panna o frutta ◆ vi (inf) parlare molto e dire poco.

wag [wæg] vt agitare.

wage [weɪdʒ] n salario m.
► **wages** npl salario m.

wagon ['wægən] n (vehicle) carro m; (Br: of train) vagone m.

waist [weɪst] n vita f.

waistcoat ['weɪskəʊt] n gilè m inv.

wait [weɪt] ◆ n attesa f ◆ vi aspettare; **to ~ for sb to do sthg** aspettare che qn faccia qc; **I can't ~!** non vedo l'ora!
► **wait for** vt fus aspettare.

waiter ['weɪtər] n cameriere m.

waiting room ['weɪtɪŋ-] n sala f d'attesa OR d'aspetto.

waitress ['weɪtrɪs] n cameriera f.

wake [weɪk] (pt **woke**, pp **woken**) ◆ vt svegliare ◆ vi svegliarsi.
► **wake up** ◆ vt sep svegliare ◆ vi svegliarsi.

Waldorf salad ['wɔːldɔːf-] n insalata a base di mele, sedano e noci, condita con maionese.

Wales [weɪlz] n il Galles.

walk [wɔːk] ◆ n (journey, path) passeggiata f ◆ vi camminare ◆ vt (distance) percorrere a piedi; (dog) portare a spasso; **to go for a ~** andare a fare una passeggiata; **it's a short ~** a piedi è vicino; **to take the dog for a ~** portare a spasso il cane; **'walk'** (Am) 'avanti'; **'don't ~'** (Am) 'alt'.
► **walk away** vi andarsene.
► **walk in** vi entrare.
► **walk out** vi (leave angrily) andarsene.

walker ['wɔːkər] n camminatore m (-trice f).

walking boots ['wɔːkɪŋ-] npl scarponcini mpl.

walking stick ['wɔːkɪŋ-] n bastone m.

Walkman® ['wɔːkmən] n walkman® m.

wall [wɔːl] n muro m; (internal) parete f, muro.

wallet ['wɒlɪt] n (for money) portafoglio m.

wallpaper ['wɔːlˌpeɪpər] n carta f da parati.

wally ['wɒlɪ] n (Br: inf) cretino m (-a f).

walnut ['wɔːlnʌt] n (nut) noce f.

waltz [wɔːls] n valzer m inv.

wander ['wɒndər] vi vagare.

want [wɒnt] vt volere; (need) aver bisogno di; **to ~ to do sthg** voler fare qc; **to ~ sb to do sthg** volere che qn faccia qc.

war [wɔːr] n guerra f.

ward [wɔːd] n (in hospital) reparto m.

warden ['wɔːdn] n (of park) guardiano m; (of youth hostel) custode mf.

wardrobe ['wɔːdrəʊb] n (cupboard) armadio m; (clothes) guardaroba m inv.

warehouse ['weəhaʊs, pl -haʊzɪz] n magazzino m.

warm [wɔːm] ◆ adj caldo(-a); (per-

son, smile) cordiale; *(welcome)* caloroso(-a) ♦ *vt* scaldare, riscaldare; **to be ~** *(person)* avere caldo; **it's ~** *(weather)* è OR fa caldo.

▶ **warm up** ♦ *vt sep* scaldare, riscaldare ♦ *vi (get warmer)* scaldarsi, riscaldarsi; *(do exercises)* riscaldarsi; *(machine, engine)* scaldare.

war memorial *n* monumento *m* ai caduti.

warmth [wɔːmθ] *n* calore *m*.

warn [wɔːn] *vt* avvertire, avvisare; **to ~ sb about sthg** avvisare qn di qc; **to ~ sb not to do sthg** avvertire qn di non fare qc.

warning ['wɔːnɪŋ] *n (of danger)* avvertimento *m*; *(advance notice)* preavviso *m*.

warranty ['wɒrəntɪ] *n (fml)* garanzia *f*.

warship ['wɔːʃɪp] *n* nave *f* da guerra.

wart [wɔːt] *n* verruca *f*.

was [wɒz] *pt* → **be**.

wash [wɒʃ] ♦ *vt* lavare ♦ *vi* lavarsi ♦ *n*: **to give sthg a ~** dare una lavata a qc; **to have a ~** lavarsi; **to ~ one's hands/face** lavarsi le mani/il viso.

▶ **wash up** *vi (Br: do washing-up)* lavare i piatti; *(Am: clean o.s.)* lavarsi.

washable ['wɒʃəbl] *adj* lavabile.

washbasin ['wɒʃˌbeɪsn] *n* lavabo *m*.

washbowl ['wɒʃbəʊl] *n (Am)* lavabo *m*.

washer ['wɒʃəʳ] *n (ring)* rondella *f*.

washing ['wɒʃɪŋ] *n* bucato *m*.

washing line *n* corda *f* del bucato.

washing machine *n* lavatrice *f*.

washing powder *n* detersivo *m* in polvere.

washing-up *n (Br)*: **to do the ~** fare i piatti.

washing-up bowl *n (Br)* bacinella *f*.

washing-up liquid *n (Br)* deter-sivo *m* liquido per piatti.

washroom ['wɒʃrum] *n (Am)* bagno *m*, gabinetto *m*.

wasn't [wɒznt] = **was not**.

wasp [wɒsp] *n* vespa *f*.

waste [weɪst] ♦ *n (rubbish)* rifiuti *mpl* ♦ *vt* sprecare; **a ~ of money** uno spreco di denaro; **a ~ of time** una perdita di tempo.

wastebin ['weɪstbɪn] *n* cestino *m* (dei rifiuti).

waste ground *n* terreno *m* abbandonato.

wastepaper basket [ˌweɪst-'peɪpəʳ-] *n* cestino *m* (per la carta straccia).

watch [wɒtʃ] ♦ *n (wristwatch)* orologio *m* ♦ *vt (observe)* guardare; *(spy on)* sorvegliare; *(be careful with)* fare attenzione a.

▶ **watch out** *vi (be careful)* stare attento, fare attenzione; **to ~ out for** *(look for)* cercare.

watchstrap ['wɒtʃstræp] *n* cinturino *m* dell'orologio.

water ['wɔːtəʳ] ♦ *n* acqua *f* ♦ *vt (plants, garden)* annaffiare ♦ *vi (eyes)* lacrimare; **it makes my mouth ~** mi fa venire l'acquolina in bocca.

water bottle *n* borraccia *f*.

watercolour ['wɔːtəˌkʌləʳ] *n* acquerello *m*.

watercress ['wɔːtəkres] *n* crescione *m*.

waterfall ['wɔːtəfɔːl] *n* cascata *f*.

watering can ['wɔːtərɪŋ-] *n* annaffiatoio *m*.

watermelon ['wɔːtəmelən] *n* cocomero *m*, anguria *f*.

waterproof ['wɔːtəpruːf] *adj* impermeabile.

water purification tablets [-pjʊərɪfɪ'keɪʃn-] *npl* compresse *fpl* per la disinfezione dell'acqua.

water skiing *n* sci *m* nautico.

watersports ['wɔːtəspɔːts] *npl* sport *mpl* acquatici.

water tank *n* cisterna *f*.

watertight ['wɔːtətaɪt] *adj* stagno(-a).

watt [wɒt] *n* watt *m inv*; **a 60-~ bulb** una lampadina da 60 watt.

wave [weɪv] ♦ *n* onda *f*; (*of crime, violence*) ondata *f* ♦ *vt* (*hand*) agitare; (*flag*) sventolare ♦ *vi* (*to attract attention*) fare un cenno (con la mano); (*when greeting, saying goodbye*) salutare con la mano.

wavelength ['weɪvleŋθ] *n* lunghezza *f* d'onda.

wavy ['weɪvɪ] *adj* (*hair*) ondulato(-a).

wax [wæks] *n* (*for candles*) cera *f*; (*in ears*) cerume *m*.

way [weɪ] *n* (*manner, means*) modo *m*; (*route*) strada *f*; (*direction*) parte *f*, direzione *f*; (*distance travelled*) tragitto *m*; **which ~ is the station?** da che parte è la stazione?; **the town is out of our ~** la città non è sulla nostra strada; **to be in the ~** essere d'intralcio; **to be on the ~** (*person*) stare arrivando; (*meal*) essere in arrivo; **to get out of sb's ~** lasciar passare qn; **to get under ~** cominciare; **a long ~ away** lontano; **to lose one's ~** smarrirsi; **on the ~ back** al ritorno; **on the ~ there** all'andata; **that ~** (*like that*) in quel modo; (*in that direction*) da quella parte; **this ~** (*like this*) in questo modo; (*in this direction*) da questa parte; **'give ~'** 'dare la precedenza'; **'~ in'** 'entrata'; **'~ out'** 'uscita'; **no ~!** (*inf*) neanche per sogno!

WC *n* (*abbr of water closet*) W.C. *m inv*.

we [wiː] *pron* noi; **~'re fine** stiamo bene.

weak [wiːk] *adj* debole; (*drink*) leggero(-a); (*soup*) liquido(-a).

weaken ['wiːkn] *vt* indebolire.

weakness ['wiːknɪs] *n* debolezza *f*.

wealth [welθ] *n* ricchezza *f*.

wealthy ['welθɪ] *adj* ricco(-a).

weapon ['wepən] *n* arma *f*.

wear [weəʳ] (*pt* **wore**, *pp* **worn**) ♦ *vt* portare, indossare ♦ *n* (*clothes*) abbigliamento *m*; **~ and tear** usura *f*.

▶ **wear off** *vi* passare.

▶ **wear out** *vi* consumarsi.

weary ['wɪərɪ] *adj* stanco(-a).

weasel ['wiːzl] *n* donnola *f*.

weather ['weðəʳ] *n* tempo *m*; **what's the ~ like?** che tempo fa?; **to be under the ~** (*inf*) sentirsi poco bene.

weather forecast *n* previsioni *fpl* del tempo.

weather forecaster [-fɔːkɑːstəʳ] *n* meteorologo *m* (-a *f*).

weather report *n* bollettino *m* meteorologico.

weather vane [-veɪn] *n* banderuola *f*.

weave [wiːv] (*pt* **wove**, *pp* **woven**) *vt* tessere.

web [web] *n* (*of spider*) ragnatela *f*.

Web site *n* (*COMPUT*) sito *m* Web.

Wed. (*abbr of Wednesday*) mer.

wedding ['wedɪŋ] *n* matrimonio *m*.

wedding anniversary *n* anniversario *m* di matrimonio.

wedding dress *n* abito *m* da sposa.

wedding ring *n* fede *f*.

wedge [wedʒ] *n* (*of cake*) fetta *f*; (*of wood etc*) cuneo *m*.

Wednesday ['wenzdɪ] *n* mercoledì *m inv*, → **Saturday**.

wee [wiː] ♦ *adj* (*Scot*) piccolo(-a) ♦ *n* (*inf*) pipì *f*.

weed [wiːd] *n* erbaccia *f*.

week [wiːk] *n* settimana *f*; **a ~ today** oggi a otto; **in a ~'s time** fra una settimana.

weekday ['wiːkdeɪ] *n* giorno *m* feriale.

weekend [ˌwiːk'end] *n* fine settimana *m inv*.

weekly ['wiːklɪ] ♦ *adj* settimanale ♦ *adv* ogni settimana ♦ *n* settimanale *m*.

weep [wiːp] (*pt & pp* **wept**) *vi* piangere.

weigh [weɪ] vt pesare; **how much does it ~?** quanto pesa?

weight [weɪt] n peso m; **to lose ~** dimagrire; **to put on ~** ingrassare.

▶ **weights** npl (for weight training) pesi mpl.

weightlifting ['weɪt,lɪftɪŋ] n sollevamento m pesi.

weight training n allenamento m ai pesi.

weir [wɪər] n chiusa f.

weird [wɪəd] adj strano(-a).

welcome ['welkəm] ◆ adj (guest) benvenuto(-a); (appreciated) gradito(-a) ◆ n accoglienza f ◆ vt (greet) dare il benvenuto a; (be grateful for) gradire ◆ excl benvenuto!; **you're ~ to help yourself** si serva pure; **to make sb feel ~** far sentire qn benaccetto; **you're ~!** prego!

weld [weld] vt saldare.

welfare ['welfeər] n (happiness, comfort) benessere m; (Am: money) sussidio m.

well [wel] (compar **better**, superl **best**) ◆ adj bene ◆ adv bene; (a lot) molto ◆ n pozzo m; **to get ~** guarire; **to go ~** andar bene; **~ done!** bravo!; **it may ~ happen** è assai probabile che accada; **it's ~ worth it** ne vale ben la pena; **as ~** (in addition) anche; **as ~ as** (in addition to) oltre a.

we'll [wiːl] = **we shall, we will**.

well-behaved [-bɪ'heɪvd] adj educato(-a).

well-built adj aitante.

well-done adj (meat) ben cotto (-a).

well-dressed [-'drest] adj vestito(-a) bene.

wellington (boot) ['welɪŋtən-] n stivale m di gomma.

well-known adj noto(-a).

well-off adj (rich) ricco(-a).

well-paid adj ben pagato(-a).

welly ['welɪ] n (Br: inf) stivale m di gomma.

Welsh [welʃ] ◆ adj gallese ◆ n (language) gallese m ◆ npl: **the ~** i gallesi.

Welshman ['welʃmən] (pl **-men** [-mən]) n gallese m.

Welsh rarebit [-'reəbɪt] n crostino di formaggio fuso.

Welshwoman ['welʃ,wumən] (pl **-women** [-,wɪmɪn]) n gallese f.

went [went] pt → **go**.

wept [wept] pt & pp → **weep**.

were [wɜːr] pt → **be**.

we're [wɪər] = **we are**.

weren't [wɜːnt] = **were not**.

west [west] ◆ n ovest m, occidente m ◆ adj dell'ovest ◆ adv (fly, walk) verso ovest; (be situated) a ovest; **in the ~ of England** nell'Inghilterra occidentale.

westbound ['westbaund] adj diretto(-a) a ovest.

West Country n: **the ~** l'Inghilterra f sud-occidentale.

West End n: **the ~** (of London) zona occidentale del centro di Londra, celebre per i suoi negozi, cinema e teatri.

western ['westən] ◆ adj occidentale ◆ n (film) western m inv.

West Indies [-'ɪndiːz] npl le Indie Occidentali.

Westminster ['westmɪnstər] n quartiere nel centro di Londra.

Westminster Abbey n l'abbazia f di Westminster.

westwards ['westwədz] adv verso ovest.

wet [wet] (pt & pp **wet** OR **-ted**) ◆ adj (soaked, damp) bagnato(-a); (rainy) piovoso(-a) ◆ vt bagnare; **to get ~** bagnarsi; **'~ paint'** 'vernice fresca'.

wet suit n muta f.

we've [wiːv] = **we have**.

whale [weɪl] n balena f.

wharf [wɔːf] (pl **-s** OR **wharves** [wɔːvz]) n banchina f.

what [wɒt] adj **1.** (in questions) che, quale; **~ colour is it?** di che colore è?; **he asked me ~ colour it was** mi ha chiesto di che colore era.

2. (in exclamations): **~ a surprise!** che sorpresa!; **~ a beautiful day!** che bella giornata!

♦ *pron* **1.** (*in direct questions*) (che) cosa; **~ is going on?** (che) cosa succede?; **~ are they doing?** (che) cosa fanno?; **~ is that?** (che) cos'è?; **~ is it called?** come si chiama?; **~ are they talking about?** di (che) cosa parlano?; **~ is it for?** a (che) cosa serve?

2. (*in indirect questions, relative clauses*) cosa; **she asked me ~ had happened** m'ha chiesto cos'era successo; **she asked me ~ I had seen** mi ha chiesto cosa avevo visto; **she asked me ~ I was thinking about** m'ha chiesto a cosa pensavo; **~ worries me is ...** ciò che OR quello che mi preoccupa ...; **I didn't see ~ happened** non ho visto cos'è successo; **you can't have ~ you want** non puoi avere quello che vuoi.

3. (*in phrases*): **~ for?** a che scopo?, perché?; **~ about going out for a meal?** cosa ne diresti di mangiare fuori?

♦ *excl* come?

whatever [wɒt'evər] *pron*: **take ~ you want** prendi quello che vuoi; **~ I do, I'll lose** qualsiasi cosa faccia, perderò; **~ that may be** quale che sia.

wheat [wiːt] *n* grano *m*, frumento *m*.

wheel [wiːl] *n* ruota *f*; (*steering wheel*) volante *m*.

wheelbarrow ['wiːlˌbærəʊ] *n* carriola *f*.

wheelchair ['wiːltʃeər] *n* sedia *f* a rotelle.

wheelclamp [ˌwiːl'klæmp] *n* bloccaruota *m inv*.

wheezy ['wiːzɪ] *adj* ansante.

when [wen] ♦ *adv* quando ♦ *conj* quando; (*although, seeing as*) sebbene, mentre; **~ it's ready** quando è pronto; **~ I've finished** quando avrò finito.

whenever [wen'evər] *conj* ogni volta che; **~ you like** quando vuoi.

where [weər] *adv & conj* dove; **this is ~ you'll be sleeping** è qui che dormirà.

whereabouts ['weərəbaʊts] ♦ *adv* dove ♦ *npl*: **his ~ are unknown** nessuno sa dove si trovi.

whereas [weər'æz] *conj* mentre.

wherever [weər'evər] *conj* dovunque; **~ you like** dove vuoi; **~ that may be** dove che sia.

whether ['weðər] *conj* se; **~ you like it or not** ti piaccia o no.

which [wɪtʃ] *adj* (*in questions*) quale; **~ room do you want?** quale stanza vuole?; **~ one?** quale?; **she asked me ~ room I wanted** mi ha chiesto quale stanza volevo.

♦ *pron* **1.** (*in questions*) quale; **~ is the cheapest?** qual è il più economico?; **~ do you prefer?** quale preferisci?; **he asked me ~ was the best** mi ha chiesto quale era il migliore; **he asked me ~ I preferred** mi ha chiesto quale preferivo.

2. (*introducing relative clause*) che; **the house ~ is on the corner** la casa che è all'angolo; **the television ~ I bought** il televisore che ho comprato.

3. (*introducing relative clause: after prep*) il quale (la quale); **the settee on ~ I'm sitting** il divano su cui siedo; **the book about ~ we were talking** il libro di cui stavamo parlando.

4. (*referring back*) il che, cosa che; **he's late, ~ annoys me** è in ritardo, il che mi secca molto.

whichever [wɪtʃ'evər] ♦ *pron* quello(-a), quelli(-e) (*pl*) che ♦ *adj*: **take ~ chocolate you like best** prendi il cioccolatino che preferisci; **~ chocolate you take** qualsiasi cioccolatino tu prenda.

while [waɪl] ♦ *conj* mentre; (*although*) sebbene ♦ *n*: **a ~** un po' (di tempo); **for a ~** per un po'; **in a ~** fra un po'.

whim [wɪm] *n* capriccio *m*.

whine [waɪn] *vi* gemere; (*complain*) frignare.

whip [wɪp] ♦ *n* frusta *f* ♦ *vt* (*with whip*) frustare.

whipped cream [wɪpt-] *n* panna *f* montata.

whirlpool ['wɜ:lpu:l] n (Jacuzzi)
vasca f per idromassaggi.

whisk [wɪsk] ♦ n (utensil) frusta f,
frullino m ♦ vt (eggs, cream) sbattere.

whiskers ['wɪskəz] npl (of person)
favoriti m; (of animal) baffi m.

whiskey ['wɪskɪ] (pl -s) n whisky m
inv (irlandese o americano).

whisky ['wɪskɪ] n whisky m inv
(scozzese).

whisper ['wɪspər] vt & vi sussurrare.

whistle ['wɪsl] ♦ n (instrument) fi-
schietto m; (sound) fischio m ♦ vi
fischiare.

white [waɪt] ♦ adj bianco(-a); (tea)
con latte ♦ n bianco m; (person)
bianco m (-a f); ~ **coffee** caffè m inv
con latte.

white bread n pane m bianco.

White House n: **the** ~ la Casa
Bianca.

white sauce n besciamella f.

white spirit n acquaragia f.

whitewash ['waɪtwɒʃ] vt imbiancare.

white wine n vino m bianco.

whiting ['waɪtɪŋ] (pl inv) n merlan-
go m.

Whitsun ['wɪtsn] n Pentecoste f.

who [hu:] pron (in questions) chi; (in
relative clauses) che.

whoever [hu:'evər] pron chiunque;
~ **it is** chiunque sia.

whole [həʊl] ♦ adj intero(-a) ♦ n:
the ~ **of the journey** tutto il viaggio;
on the ~ nel complesso; **the** ~ **time**
tutto il tempo.

wholefoods ['həʊlfu:dz] npl prodotti mpl integrali.

wholemeal bread ['həʊlmi:l-] n
(Br) pane m integrale.

wholesale ['həʊlseɪl] adv (COMM)
all'ingrosso.

wholewheat bread ['həʊl,wi:t-]
n (Am) = **wholemeal bread**.

whom [hu:m] pron (fml: in questions)
chi; (in relative clauses) che; **to** ~? a
chi?; **the person to** ~ **I wrote** la persona alla quale ho scritto.

whooping cough ['hu:pɪŋ-] n
pertosse f.

whose [hu:z] adj & pron: ~ **jumper is
this?** di chi è questo maglione?; **she
asked** ~ **jumper it was** ha chiesto di
chi era il maglione; **this is the
woman** ~ **son is a priest** questa è la
donna il cui figlio è un prete; ~ **is
this?** di chi è questo?

why [waɪ] adv & conj perché; ~ **not?**
perché no?; ~ **not do it tomorrow?**
perché non farlo domani?

wick [wɪk] n (of candle, lighter) stop-
pino m.

wicked ['wɪkɪd] adj (evil) malva-
gio(-a); (mischievous) malizioso(-a).

wicker ['wɪkər] adj di vimini.

wide [waɪd] ♦ adj largo(-a); (opening) ampio(-a); (range, variety)
vasto(-a); (difference, gap) grande
♦ adv: **to open sthg** ~ spalancare qc;
how ~ **is the road?** quanto è larga la
strada?; **it's 12 metres** ~ è largo 12
metri; ~ **open** spalancato.

widely ['waɪdlɪ] adv (known)
generalmente; (travel) molto.

widen ['waɪdn] ♦ vt (make broader)
allargare ♦ vi (gap, difference)
aumentare.

widespread ['waɪdspred] adj
molto diffuso(-a).

widow ['wɪdəʊ] n vedova f.

widower ['wɪdəʊər] n vedovo m.

width [wɪdθ] n larghezza f.

wife [waɪf] (pl **wives**) n moglie f.

wig [wɪg] n parrucca f.

wild [waɪld] adj (animal, plant) sel-
vatico(-a); (land, area) selvaggio(-a);
(uncontrolled) sfrenato(-a); (crazy)
folle; **to be** ~ **about** (inf) andare
pazzo(-a) per.

wild flower n fiore m di campo.

wildlife ['waɪldlaɪf] n flora e fauna
f.

will¹ [wɪl] aux vb 1. (expressing future
tense): **I** ~ **see you next week** ci
vediamo la settimana prossima; ~
you be here next Friday? sarai qui

wil

venerdì prossimo?; **yes I ~** sì; **no I won't** no.

2. (*expressing willingness*): **I won't do it** mi rifiuto di farlo.

3. (*expressing polite question*): **~ you have some more tea?** vuole ancora un po' di tè?

4. (*in commands, requests*): **~ you please be quiet!** volete tacere!; **close that window, ~ you?** chiudi la finestra, per favore.

will² [wɪl] *n* (*document*) testamento *m*; **against one's ~** contro la propria volontà.

willing ['wɪlɪŋ] *adj*: **to be ~ to do sthg** essere disposto(-a) a fare qc.

willingly ['wɪlɪŋlɪ] *adv* volentieri.

willow ['wɪləu] *n* salice *m*.

win [wɪn] (*pt & pp* **won**) ◆ *vt* vittoria *f*; ◆ *vt* vincere; (*support, approval, friends*) guadagnarsi ◆ *vi* vincere.

wind¹ [wɪnd] *n* vento *m*; (*in stomach*) flatulenza *f*.

wind² [waɪnd] (*pt & pp* **wound**) *vi* (*road, river*) snodarsi ◆ *vt*: **to ~ sthg round sthg** avvolgere qc intorno a qc.

▶ **wind up** *vt sep* (*Br: inf: annoy*) dare sui nervi a; (*car window*) tirare su, chiudere; (*clock, watch*) caricare.

windbreak ['wɪndbreɪk] *n* frangivento *m*.

windmill ['wɪndmɪl] *n* mulino *m* a vento.

window ['wɪndəu] *n* (*of house*) finestra *f*; (*of shop*) vetrina *f*; (*of car*) finestrino *m*.

window box *n* cassetta *f* per fiori.

window cleaner *n* lavavetri *mf*.

windowpane ['wɪndəu,peɪn] *n* vetro *m*.

window seat *n* (*on plane*) posto *m* finestrino.

window-shopping *n*: **to go ~** andare a guardare le vetrine.

windowsill ['wɪndəusɪl] *n* davanzale *m*.

windscreen ['wɪndskriːn] *n* (*Br*) parabrezza *m inv*.

windscreen wipers *npl* (*Br*) gicristalli *mpl*.

windshield ['wɪndʃiːld] *n* (*Am*) parabrezza *m inv*.

Windsor Castle ['wɪnzə-] *n* il castello di Windsor.

windsurfing ['wɪnd,sɜːfɪŋ] *n* windsurf *m*; **to go ~** fare del windsurf.

windy ['wɪndɪ] *adj* ventoso(-a); **it's ~** c'è vento.

wine [waɪn] *n* vino *m*.

wine bar *n* (*Br*) ≃ enoteca *f*.

wineglass ['waɪnglɑːs] *n* bicchiere *m* da vino.

wine list *n* lista *f* dei vini.

wine tasting [-,teɪstɪŋ] *n* degustazione *f* dei vini.

wine waiter *n* sommelier *mf inv*.

wing [wɪŋ] *n* ala *f*; (*Br: of car*) fiancata *f*.

▶ **wings** *npl*: **the ~s** (*in theatre*) le quinte.

wink [wɪŋk] *vi* strizzare l'occhio.

winner ['wɪnə'] *n* vincitore *m* (-trice *f*).

winning ['wɪnɪŋ] *adj* vincente.

winter ['wɪntə'] *n* inverno *m*; **in (the) ~** d'inverno.

wintertime ['wɪntətaɪm] *n* inverno *m*.

wipe [waɪp] *vt* pulire; **to ~ one's hands/feet** pulirsi le mani/le scarpe.

▶ **wipe up** ◆ *vt sep* (*liquid*) asciugare; (*dirt*) pulire ◆ *vi* (*dry the dishes*) asciugare i piatti.

wiper ['waɪpə'] *n* (*windscreen wiper*) tergicristallo *m*.

wire ['waɪə'] ◆ *n* filo *m* di ferro; (*electrical*) filo (elettrico) ◆ *vt* (*plug*) collegare.

wireless ['waɪəlɪs] *n* radio *f inv*.

wiring ['waɪərɪŋ] *n* impianto *m* elettrico.

wisdom ['wɪzdəm] *n* saggezza *f*, sapienza *f*.

wisdom tooth ['wɪzdəm-] *n* dente *m* del giudizio.

dom tooth

...ter-

...gio(-a).

...sire) desiderio m ...rare; **best ~es** (for ...iguri; (at end of let- **I ~ you'd told me** ...on me l'hai detto ...s younger vorrei tanto ... giovane; **to ~ for** sthg desiderare qc; **to ~ to do sthg** (fml) desiderare fare qc; **to ~ sb luck/happy birthday** augurare buona fortuna/buon compleanno a qn; **if you ~** (fml) se vuole.

witch [wɪtʃ] n strega f.

with [wɪð] prep **1.** (gen) con; **come ~ me** vieni con me; **a man ~ a beard** un uomo con la barba; **a room ~ a bathroom** una camera con bagno. **2.** (at house of) da, a casa di; **we stayed ~ friends** siamo stati da amici. **3.** (indicating emotion) di, per; **to tremble ~ fear** tremare di paura. **4.** (indicating opposition): **to argue ~ sb** litigare con qn; **to fight ~ sb** combattere contro qn. **5.** (indicating covering, contents) di; **to fill sthg ~ sthg** riempire qc di qc; **topped ~ cream** ricoperto di panna.

withdraw [wɪð'drɔː] (pt -drew, pp -drawn) ◆ vt (take out) ritirare; (money) prelevare ◆ vi (from race, contest) ritirarsi.

withdrawal [wɪð'drɔːəl] n (from bank account) prelievo m.

withdrawn [wɪð'drɔːn] pp → **withdraw**.

withdrew [wɪð'druː] pt → **withdraw**.

wither ['wɪðər] vi appassire.

within [wɪ'ðɪn] ◆ prep (inside) all'interno di; (not exceeding) entro ◆ adv all'interno, dentro; **~ walking distance** raggiungibile a piedi; **~ 10 miles of ...** a non più di 10 miglia da ...; **it arrived ~ a week** è arrivato nel giro di una settimana; **~ the next week** entro la prossima settimana.

without [wɪð'aʊt] prep senza; **~** doing sthg senza fare qc.

withstand [wɪð'stænd] (pt & pp -stood) vt resistere a.

witness ['wɪtnɪs] ◆ n testimone mf ◆ vt (see) assistere a.

witty ['wɪtɪ] adj arguto(-a).

wives [waɪvz] pl → **wife**.

wobbly ['wɒblɪ] adj (table, chair) traballante.

wok [wɒk] n padella larga e profonda usata nella cucina cinese.

woke [wəʊk] pt → **wake**.

woken ['wəʊkn] pp → **wake**.

wolf [wʊlf] (pl **wolves** ['wʊlvz]) n lupo m.

woman ['wʊmən] (pl **women**) n donna f.

womb [wuːm] n utero m.

women ['wɪmɪn] pl → **woman**.

won [wʌn] pt & pp → **win**.

wonder ['wʌndər] ◆ vi (ask o.s.) chiedersi, domandarsi ◆ n (amazement) meraviglia f; **to ~ if** domandarsi se; **I ~ if I could ask you a favour?** potrei chiederle un favore?

wonderful ['wʌndəfʊl] adj meraviglioso(-a).

won't [wəʊnt] = **will not**.

wood [wʊd] n (substance) legno m; (small forest) bosco m; (golf club) mazza f di legno.

wooden ['wʊdn] adj di legno.

woodland ['wʊdlənd] n terreno m boschivo.

woodpecker ['wʊd,pekər] n picchio m.

woodwork ['wʊdwɜːk] n (SCH) falegnameria f.

wool [wʊl] n lana f.

woolen ['wʊlən] (Am) = **woollen**.

woollen ['wʊlən] adj (Br) di lana.

woolly ['wʊlɪ] adj di lana.

wooly ['wʊlɪ] (Am) = **woolly**.

Worcester sauce ['wʊstər-] n salsa f Worcester.

word [wɜːd] n parola f; **in other ~s** in altre parole; **to have a ~ with sb** parlare con qn.

wording ['wɜːdɪŋ] n formulazione f.

word processing [-'prəʊsesɪŋ] n videoscrittura f.

word processor [-'prəʊsesəʳ] n sistema m di videoscrittura.

wore [wɔːʳ] pt → **wear**.

work [wɜːk] ♦ n lavoro m; (painting, novel etc) opera f ♦ vi lavorare; (operate, have desired effect) funzionare; (take effect) fare effetto ♦ vt (machine, controls) far funzionare; **out of ~** senza lavoro; **to be at ~** (at workplace) essere al lavoro; (working) lavorare; **to be off ~** (on holiday) essere in ferie; (ill) essere in malattia; **the ~s** (inf: everything) tutto quanto; **how does it ~?** come funziona?; **it's not ~ing** non funziona.

▶ **work out** ♦ vt sep (price, total) calcolare; (understand) capire; (solution) trovare; (method, plan) mettere a punto ♦ vi (result, be successful) funzionare; (do exercise) fare ginnastica; **it ~s out at £20 each** (bill, total) fa 20 sterline a testa.

worker ['wɜːkəʳ] n lavoratore m (-trice f).

working class ['wɜːkɪŋ-] n: **the ~** la classe operaia.

working hours ['wɜːkɪŋ-] npl orario m di lavoro.

workman ['wɜːkmən] (pl **-men** [-mən]) n operaio m.

work of art n opera f d'arte.

workout ['wɜːkaʊt] n allenamento m.

work permit n permesso m di lavoro.

workplace ['wɜːkpleɪs] n posto m di lavoro.

workshop ['wɜːkʃɒp] n (for repairs) officina f.

work surface n piano m di lavoro.

world [wɜːld] ♦ n mondo m ♦ adj mondiale; **the best in the ~** il migliore del mondo.

worldwide [,wɜːld'waɪd] adv in tutto il mondo.

World Wide Web n: **the ~** il World Wide Web.

worm [wɜːm] n verme m.

worn [wɔːn] ♦ pp → **wear** ♦ adj (clothes, carpet) consumato(-a).

worn-out adj (clothes, shoes etc) consumato(-a); (tired) esausto(-a).

worried ['wʌrɪd] adj preoccupato(-a).

worry ['wʌrɪ] ♦ n preoccupazione f ♦ vt preoccupare ♦ vi: **to ~ (about)** preoccuparsi (per).

worrying ['wʌrɪɪŋ] adj preoccupante.

worse [wɜːs] ♦ adj peggiore ♦ adv peggio; **to get ~** peggiorare; **~ off** (in worse position) in una situazione peggiore; (poorer) più povero.

worsen ['wɜːsn] vi peggiorare.

worship ['wɜːʃɪp] ♦ n culto m ♦ vt adorare.

worst [wɜːst] ♦ adj peggiore ♦ adv peggio ♦ n: **the ~** il peggiore (la peggiore).

worth [wɜːθ] prep: **how much is it ~?** quanto vale?; **it's ~ £50** vale 50 sterline; **it's ~ seeing** vale la pena vederlo; **it's not ~ it** non ne vale la pena; **£50 ~ of traveller's cheques** traveller's cheques per un valore di 50 sterline.

worthless ['wɜːθlɪs] adj di nessun valore.

worthwhile [,wɜːθ'waɪl] adj: **to be ~** valere la pena.

worthy ['wɜːðɪ] adj (winner, cause) degno(-a); **to be ~ of sthg** essere degno di qc.

would [wʊd] aux vb **1.** (in reported speech): **she said she ~ come** ha detto che sarebbe venuta.

2. (indicating condition): **what ~ you do?** tu cosa faresti?; **what ~ you have done?** tu cosa avresti fatto?; **I ~ be most grateful** le sarei molto grato.

3. (indicating willingness): **she ~n't go** non ci è voluta andare; **he ~ do anything for her** farebbe qualsiasi cosa per lei.

4. (*in polite questions*): ~ **you like a drink?** vuole qualcosa da bere?; ~ **you mind closing the window?** le spiacerebbe chiudere la finestra?
5. (*indicating inevitability*): **he ~ say that** era ovvio che dicesse così.
6. (*giving advice*): **I ~ report it if I were you** se fossi in voi lo riferirei.
7. (*expressing opinions*): **I ~ prefer ...** preferirei ...; **I ~ have thought (that) ...** avrei pensato che ...

wound¹ [wuːnd] ◆ *n* ferita *f* ◆ *vt* ferire.

wound² [waund] *pt & pp* → **wind²**.

wove [wəuv] *pt* → **weave**.

woven ['wəuvn] *pp* → **weave**.

wrap [ræp] *vt* (*package*) incartare; **to ~ sthg round sthg** avvolgere qc intorno a qc.

▶ **wrap up** ◆ *vt sep* (*package*) incartare ◆ *vi* (*dress warmly*) coprirsi bene.

wrapper ['ræpəʳ] *n* (*for sweets*) carta *f*.

wrapping ['ræpɪŋ] *n* involucro *m*.

wrapping paper *n* (*for present*) carta *f* da regalo; (*for parcel*) carta da pacchi.

wreath [riːθ] *n* corona *f*.

wreck [rek] ◆ *n* (*of plane, car*) rottame *m*; (*of ship*) relitto *m* ◆ *vt* (*destroy*) distruggere; (*spoil*) rovinare; **to be ~ed** (*ship*) fare naufragio.

wreckage ['rekɪdʒ] *n* (*of plane, car*) rottami *mpl*; (*of building*) macerie *fpl*.

wrench [rentʃ] *n* (Br: *monkey wrench*) chiave *f* inglese; (Am: *spanner*) chiave.

wrestler ['resləʳ] *n* lottatore *m* (-trice *f*).

wrestling ['reslɪŋ] *n* lotta *f* libera.

wretched ['retʃɪd] *adj* (*miserable*) infelice; (*very bad*) orribile.

wring [rɪŋ] (*pt & pp* **wrung**) *vt* (*clothes, cloth*) strizzare.

wrinkle ['rɪŋkl] *n* ruga *f*.

wrist [rɪst] *n* polso *m*.

wristwatch ['rɪstwɒtʃ] *n* orologio *m* da polso.

write [raɪt] (*pt* **wrote**, *pp* **written**) ◆ *vt* scrivere; (*cheque, prescription*) fare; (Am: *send letter to*) scrivere a ◆ *vi* scrivere; **to ~ to sb** (Br) scrivere a qn.

▶ **write back** *vi* rispondere.

▶ **write down** *vt sep* scrivere.

▶ **write off** ◆ *vt sep* (Br: *inf: car*) distruggere ◆ *vi*: **to ~ off for sthg** richiedere qc per posta.

▶ **write out** *vt sep* (*list, essay*) scrivere; (*cheque, receipt*) fare.

write-off *n* (*vehicle*) rottame *m*.

writer ['raɪtəʳ] *n* (*author*) scrittore *m* (-trice *f*).

writing ['raɪtɪŋ] *n* (*handwriting*) scrittura *f*; (*written words*) scritto *m*; (*activity*) scrivere *m*.

writing desk *n* scrivania *f*.

writing pad *n* blocchetto *m* per appunti.

writing paper *n* carta *f* da lettere.

written ['rɪtn] ◆ *pp* → **write** ◆ *adj* (*exam, notice, confirmation*) scritto(-a).

wrong [rɒŋ] ◆ *adv* male ◆ *adj* (*incorrect, unsuitable*) sbagliato(-a); (*bad, immoral*): **it's ~ to steal** non si deve rubare; **what's ~?** cosa c'è che non va?; **what's ~ with her?** cos'ha?; **something's ~ with the car** la macchina ha qualcosa che non va; **to be ~** (*person*) sbagliarsi; **to be in the ~** essere in torto; **to get sthg ~** sbagliare qc; **to go ~** (*machine*) non funzionare più; **'~ way'** (Am) cartello che segnala agli automobilisti il senso vietato.

wrongly ['rɒŋlɪ] *adv* (*accused*) ingiustamente; (*informed*) male.

wrong number *n*: **to get the ~** sbagliare numero.

wrote [rəut] *pt* → **write**.

wrought iron [rɔːt] *n* ferro *m* battuto.

wrung [rʌŋ] *pt & pp* → **wring**.

XYZ

xing (Am: *abbr of crossing*): **'ped ~'** 'passaggio pedonale'.

XL (*abbr of extra-large*) XL.

Xmas ['eksməs] *n* (*inf*) Natale *m*.

X-ray ◆ *n* (*picture*) radiografia *f* ◆ *vt* fare una radiografia a; **to have an ~** farsi una radiografia.

yacht [jɒt] *n* yacht *m inv*.

yard [jɑːd] *n* (*unit of measurement*) = 91,44 cm, iarda *f*; (*enclosed area*) cortile *m*; (Am: *behind house*) giardino *m*.

yard sale *n* (Am) vendita di oggetti di seconda mano organizzata da un privato nel giardino di casa.

yarn [jɑːn] *n* (*thread*) filato *m*.

yawn [jɔːn] *vi* (*person*) sbadigliare.

yd *abbr* = **yard**.

yeah [jeə] *adv* (*inf*) sì.

year [jɪər] *n* anno *m*; **next ~** l'anno prossimo; **this ~** quest'anno; **I'm 15 ~s old** ho 15 anni; **I haven't seen her for ~s** (*inf*) sono anni che non la vedo.

yearly ['jɪəlɪ] *adj* annuale, annuo(-a).

yeast [jiːst] *n* lievito *m*.

yell [jel] *vi* urlare.

yellow ['jeləʊ] ◆ *adj* giallo(-a) ◆ *n* giallo *m*.

yellow lines *npl* strisce *fpl* gialle (*che regolano la sosta dei veicoli*).

Yellow Pages® *n*: **the ~** le Pagine gialle.

yes [jes] *adv* sì; **to say ~** dire di sì.

yesterday ['jestədɪ] ◆ *n* ieri *m* ◆ *adv* ieri; **the day before ~** l'altro ieri; **~ afternoon** ieri pomeriggio; **~ morning** ieri mattina.

yet [jet] ◆ *adv* ancora ◆ *conj* ma; **have they arrived ~?** sono già arrivati?; **the best one ~** il migliore fino

a questo momento; **not ~** non ancora; **I've ~ to do it** devo ancora farlo; **~ again** ancora una volta; **~ another delay** ancora un altro ritardo.

yew [juː] *n* tasso *m* (*pianta*).

yield [jiːld] ◆ *vt* dare, rendere ◆ *vi* (*break, give way*) cedere; **'yield'** (Am: AUT) 'dare la precedenza'.

YMCA *n* associazione cristiana dei giovani che offre alloggi a buon prezzo.

yob [jɒb] *n* (Br: *inf*) teppista *mf*.

yoga ['jəʊgə] *n* yoga *m*.

yoghurt ['jɒgət] *n* yogurt *m inv*.

yolk [jəʊk] *n* tuorlo *m*, rosso *m* d'uovo.

York Minster [jɔːˈmɪnstər] *n* la cattedrale di York.

Yorkshire pudding ['jɔːkʃə-] *n* focaccina soffice servita tradizionalmente con arrosti di manzo.

you [juː] *pron* **1.** (*subject: singular*) tu; (*subject: polite form*) lei; (*subject: plural*) voi; **~ Italians** voi italiani.

2. (*direct object: singular*) ti; (*direct object: polite form*) la; (*direct object: plural*) vi; **I called ~, not him** ho chiamato te, non lui.

3. (*indirect object: singular*) ti; (*indirect object: polite form*) le; (*indirect object: plural*) vi.

4. (*after prep: singular*) te; (*after prep: polite form*) lei; (*after prep: plural*) voi; **I'm shorter than ~** sono più basso di te/lei/voi.

5. (*indefinite use*) si; **~ never know** non si sa mai; **swimming is good for ~** nuotare fa bene.

young [jʌŋ] ◆ *adj* giovane ◆ *npl*: **the ~** i giovani.

younger ['jʌŋgər] *adj* (*brother, sister*) minore, più giovane.

youngest ['jʌŋgəst] *adj* (*brother, sister*) minore, più giovane.

youngster ['jʌŋstər] *n* giovane *mf*.

your [jɔːr] *adj* **1.** (*singular subject*) il tuo (la tua), i tuoi (le tue) (*pl*); (*singular subject: polite form*) il suo (la sua), i suoi (le sue) (*pl*); (*plural sub-*

ject) il vostro (la vostra), i vostri (le vostre) *(pl)*; **~ dog** il tuo/suo/vostro cane; **~ house** la tua/sua/vostra casa; **~ children** i tuoi/suoi/vostri bambini; **~ mother** tua/sua/vostra madre.
2. *(indefinite subject)*: **it's good for ~ health** fa bene alla salute.

yours [jɔːz] *pron (referring to singular subject)* il tuo (la tua), i tuoi (le tue) *(pl)*; *(polite form)* il suo (la sua), i suoi (le sue) *(pl)*; *(referring to plural subject)* il vostro (la vostra), i vostri (le vostre) *(pl)*; **a friend of ~** un tuo/suo/vostro amico; **are these shoes ~?** queste scarpe sono tue/sue/vostre?

yourself [jɔː'self] *(pl -selves) pron*
1. *(reflexive: singular)* ti; *(reflexive: polite form)* si; *(reflexive: plural)* vi.
2. *(after prep: singular)* te; *(after prep: polite form)* sé; *(after prep: plural)* voi.
3. *(emphatic use: singular)* tu stesso(-a); *(emphatic use: polite form)* lei stesso(-a); *(emphatic use: plural)* voi stessi(-e); **did you do it ~?** *(singular)* l'hai fatto da solo?

youth [juːθ] *n (period of life)* gioventù *f; (quality)* giovinezza *f; (young man)* giovane *m*.

youth club *n* circolo *m* giovanile.
youth hostel *n* ostello *m* della gioventù.

Yugoslavia [ˌjuːgə'slɑːvɪə] *n* la Jugoslavia.

yuppie ['jʌpɪ] *n* yuppie *mf inv*.

YWCA *n associazione cristiana delle giovani che offre alloggi a buon prezzo*.

zebra [Br 'zebrə, Am 'ziːbrə] *n* zebra *f*.

zebra crossing *n (Br)* strisce *fpl* pedonali.

zero ['zɪərəʊ] *(pl -es) n* zero *m;* **five degrees below ~** cinque gradi sotto zero.

zest [zest] *n (of lemon, orange)* scorza *f*.

zigzag ['zɪɡzæɡ] *vi* procedere a zigzag.

zinc [zɪŋk] *n* zinco *m*.

zip [zɪp] ◆ *n (Br)* cerniera *f* OR chiusura *f* lampo *(inv)* ◆ *vt* chiudere la cerniera di.
▶ **zip up** *vt sep* chiudere la cerniera di.

zip code *n (Am)* codice *m* di avviamento postale.

zipper ['zɪpər] *n (Am)* cerniera *f* OR chiusura *f* lampo *(inv)*.

zit [zɪt] *n (inf)* brufolo *m*.

zodiac ['zəʊdɪæk] *n* zodiaco *m*.

zone [zəʊn] *n* zona *f*.

zoo [zuː] *(pl -s) n* zoo *m inv*.

zoom (lens) [zuːm-] *n* zoom *m inv*.

zucchini [zuːˈkiːnɪ] *(pl inv) n (Am)* zucchine *fpl*.